When the rules change, tax professionals turn to RIA for help...

S0-DSZ-141

RIA Federal Tax Handbook

RESEARCH INSTITUTE OF AMERICA

*For fast, accurate answers to your client's personal or business tax questions, or how the **Revenue Reconciliation Act of 1993** will affect them, you can rely on RIA for the most up-to-date information.*

RIA's 1994 Federal Tax Handbook

The most authoritative paperback reference for day-to-day tax questions. Over 1,500 numbered paragraphs provide answers to questions on individual and corporate taxation, pension plans, employee benefits, deductions, passive losses, estate and gift taxes, and much more. The Revenue Reconciliation Act of 1993 is fully integrated. Includes the latest tax rate tables for income, estate and gift, excise, and Social Security. Comprehensive topic index. Fully cross-referenced to RIA's **Federal Tax Coordinator 2d, Analysis of Federal Taxes: Income,** and **United States Tax Reporter**.

1-4 Copies	Each $24.00
5-24	21.00
25-49	19.00
50-74	15.00
75-99	12.00
100-249	10.00
250+	Call for quote

Product Code: FTHB. 756 pages. 7" x 9 1/4". Available November 1993.

Fill out and return the order form today or for faster service, call your RIA representative, or toll free 1-800-431-9025, ext. 4.

MULTIPLE COPY ▼ ORDER FORM

☐ **YES!** I want to order **RIA'S 1994 FEDERAL TAX HANDBOOK.** Please send me _____ copies at the discounted price of $ _____ per book. I understand that shipping and postage will be added.

☐ **YES!** I want to order **RIA'S COMPLETE ANALYSIS.** Please send me _____ copies at the discounted price of $ _____ per book. I understand that shipping and postage will be added.

NAME _____

SIGNATURE _____

COMPANY _____

ADDRESS _____

CITY _____ STATE ____ ZIP ____

TELEPHONE _____

OCCUPATION _____

☐ **Charge my credit card**
  ☐ VISA ☐ MasterCard ☐ Amex

ACCT NO. _____

EXP. DATE _____

SIGNATURE _____

☐ **Bill me**
(Shipping and postage charges will be added to your invoice)

☐ **Check here** if you would like to receive the 1995 edition of RIA'S FEDERAL TAX HANDBOOK sent on approval.

Note: If paying by credit card, please enclose this filled-out form in an envelope addressed to RIA, 117 East Stevens Ave., Valhalla, NY 10595-1264, Attn: Order Processing.

J6100-001

When you need a complete analysis of the new tax law, there's only one professional reference that has it all...

Get the full story on the 1993 tax package from...

The RIA Complete Analysis of the Revenue Reconciliation Act of 1993 with Code Sections as Amended and Committee Reports

1-4 Copies	Each $34.95
5-9	32.95
10-24	29.95
25-49	27.95
50-99	24.95
100-249	22.95
250+	Call for quote

RIA's editorial explanation of the new legislation with RIA's observations, illustrations, and recommendations that clarify points of law and their effect. Code Sections as Amended and arranged in Code Section order showing how the Code reads after the law changes are reflected. Congressional explanation of the new law (Committee Reports). Cross reference at the end of each Code Section showing where the Committee Report explanation can be found.

Product Code: CATL. 768 pages. 6 1/2" x 9 1/2"

For faster service, call your RIA representative, or toll free 1-800-431-9025, ext. 4.

RESEARCH INSTITUTE OF AMERICA, 117 EAST STEVENS AVE., VALHALLA, NY 10595-1264

NO POSTAGE
NECESSARY
IF MAILED
IN THE
UNITED STATES

BUSINESS REPLY MAIL
FIRST CLASS MAIL   PERMIT NO. 50   VALHALLA, NY

POSTAGE WILL BE PAID BY ADDRESSEE

RESEARCH INSTITUTE OF AMERICA
ATT: ORDER PROCESSING
117 EAST STEVENS AVENUE
VALHALLA NY 10595-1264

RIA Federal Tax Handbook

Prepared by **Research Institute of America**

James E. Cheeks (J.D., NY, IL Bar) *Senior Vice President and Publisher*
Thomas E. Delleart (M.B.A.) *Vice President and Publisher*
Robert Rywick (J.D. NY Bar) *Vice President, Editorial*

Professional Staff, New York City

I. Harvey Grosberg
(J.D., NY Bar)
Managing Editor, New York

Raymond W. Hadrick
(J.D., C.P.A., MA, FL, NY Bar)
Managing Editor, NY

Joseph Trapani
(J.D., NY Bar)
Managing Editor, New York

Thomas H. Brantley
(J.D., C.P.A., MA Bar)
Managing Editor, New York

Steven A. Zelman
(LL.M., NY, NJ Bar)
Administrative Editor, New York

Stanley Gladstone
(LL.M., C.P.A., NY, MD Bar)
Senior Editor

Sidney Weinman
(J.D., NY, NJ Bar)
Senior Editor

Andrew Katz
(LL.M., C.P.A., NY, NJ Bar)
Senior Editor

Eric Brandeis
(LL.M., C.P.A., NY Bar)

Louis A. Viola
(J.D., NY Bar)

Michael E. Overton
(LL.M., NY, VA Bar)

Richard S. Nadler
(LL.M., NY Bar)

Frank B. Laub
(C.P.A.)

Sarah Phelan
(J.D., NY Bar)

Jeffrey N. Pretsfelder
(C.P.A.)

Dennis P. McMahon
(LL.M., NY, MA Bar)

Frederic S. Kramer
(J.D., NY, RI Bar)

Frederick M. Stein
(LL.M., PA Bar)

Stanley V. Baginski
(LL.M., NY Bar)

Thomas Long
(LL.M., NY, NJ Bar)

Laurie Asch
(LL.M., NY Bar)

Burton J. DeFren
(J.D., NY Bar)

Scott E. Weiner
(J.D., NY Bar)

David Freid
(J.D., NY Bar)

Betsy McKenny
(J.D., NY, NJ Bar)

Linda Scheffel
(LL.M., NY Bar)

Cornell R. Fuerst
(J.D., NY, PA Bar)

Joseph N. Guterl
(LL.M., NY, NJ Bar)

Rachel Glatt
(J.D., NY Bar)

Carla M. Martin
(LL.M., AL, FL Bar)

Rosemary Saldan
(J.D., NY, KS Bar)

Janice C. McCoy
(LL.M., C.P.A., TX, MA Bar)

E.H. Rubinsky
(LL.M., NY Bar)

Peter A. Lakritz
(LL.M., OH, FL Bar)

Peter D. Ogrodnik
(LL.M., NJ Bar)

Isaac Godinger
(LL.M., NY Bar)

Simon Schneebalg
(LL.M., NY, DC Bar)

Marilyn K. Freedman
(LL.M., NY, CT, DC Bar)

James Quaglietta
(J.D., M.B.A., C.P.A., NJ Bar)

Robert P. Rothman
(J.D., NY Bar)

Suzanne B. Schmitt
(LL.M., NY Bar)

Carla J. Cole
(J.D., NY Bar)

Stuart M. Schwartz
(LL.M., NY, NJ Bar)

Consulting Editors
Leon Gold
(J.D., NY Bar)

Avi O. Liveson
(LL.M., NY, PA Bar)
Assoc. Prof., Hunter College
Dept. of Economics

Marcia K. Marshall
(J.D. NY Bar)

Benjamin R. Sears
(LL.M., TN Bar)

Director, Washington Tax Bureau
Peter M. Berkery, Jr.
(LL.M., DC, MD, HI Bar)

Administrative Staff, New York City

Frances Hutton
Denise Donahue
Hazel Brutsche
Terri Brady
Christine Haakonsen
Melanie Thomas
Mark Carway
Supervisors Editorial Services

JoAnn Mitchell
Bernadette Stanton
Veronica Wilson
Lourdes Leon
Jessye Mee
Sandra Fullwood
June Babb

Mae Jamison
Marie Landers
Sharon Edmond
Fred Fey
Frances Horiuchi
Julie Lynch
Claudie Hatem
Jonathan Thayer
Terri Ganssley
Pam Hammond
Dianne Ross
David Levine
Matthew Freeman
Suzanne McKeown
Edward Mack
Brooke Novick
Andrew Glicklin
Alicia Shaw

Megan Hartl
Kerry Ryan
Lawrence Hayden
Kevin Schaefer
Lawrence Berger
Taji Mabra
Rosa DeLara
Gregory Papadatos

Product Systems

Michael Kazazis
Michael Peterfreund
Managers
Jose Almeda
Joan Baselice
Andrew Battiste
Resa Cirrincione

Arendrell Cooper
Valencia Evans
Yonah Hirschman
Natalie Lee
Steven McGill
Pamela Otruba
Paul Schaffer
Jill Sherman

Editorial Questions Department

James M. Ozello
(J.D., NJ, NY, OH Bar)
Theresa Stawarz
Paralegal
Jean Marie Tracy
Paralegal

Simone M. Stephens

Indexing Deparment

Janet Mazefsky (MLS)
Indexing Editor
Urmila Mohamed (MLS)
Wei-Hong Lao (MLS)
James E. Starkey
Andrea Leal (MLS)

Office Supervisor, Washington Tax Bureau

Velma Goodwine-McDermon

Copyright 1993

By

Research Institute of America

90 Fifth Avenue

New York, N.Y. 10011

1994 RIA FEDERAL TAX HANDBOOK

CONTENTS

RESEARCH INSTITUTE OF AMERICA INC., 90 FIFTH AVENUE, NEW YORK, N.Y.

1

1994 Research Institute of America Federal Tax Handbook

The 1994 edition of the RIA Federal Tax Handbook is designed to answer the tax questions and resolve the tax problems that arise in everyday business and personal transactions. The Handbook helps in preparing 1993 federal income tax returns, and provides specific guidance to tax consequences of transactions occurring in 1994. It is prepared by the same professional staff that prepares the comprehensive federal tax service, RIA's Federal Tax Coordinator 2d, and the complete income tax service, RIA's Analysis of Federal Taxes: Income, and is derived from these tax services and RIA's Tax Guide.

The Handbook discusses and explains the common tax problems in clear, concise, nontechnical language. And, where appropriate, the Handbook includes:

illustration: To clarify the tax rules and problems discussed, with simple easy-to-follow illustrations.

caution: To warn of dangers that arise in particular tax situations and, where appropriate, to indicate what should be done.

recommendation: To provide specific, carefully studied guides to action which will keep taxes at a legal minimum.

observation: For professional analysis or commentary that is not part of cited authorities.

Forms to use:

The Handbook explains which IRS forms to use to report transactions, pay taxes, make elections, etc. For a complete list of all official forms discussed, with references to the paragraph where they are discussed, see the "Forms" entry in the Topic Index.

References:

"Code Sec." references are to sections of the Internal Revenue Code.

"Reg § " references are to sections of the federal tax regulations. "Prop Reg § " references are to proposed regulations, which are only cited in the text where IRS has indicated that "Taxpayers may rely" on them.

Footnote references beginning with letters are to paragraphs in RIA's Federal Tax Coordinator 2d and RIA's Analysis of Federal Taxes: Income. However, RIA's Analysis of Federal Taxes: Income does not include coverage of estate, gift and excise taxes. Accordingly, references to ¶ Q-1000 *et seq.* (gift tax), ¶ R-1000 *et seq.* (estate tax), and ¶ W-1000 *et seq.* (excise taxes) are only to paragraphs in RIA's Federal Tax Coordinator 2d. Footnote references beginning with numbers are to paragraphs in RIA's United States Tax Reporter.

¶ 101. Highlights of the 1994 Edition.

The 1994 RIA Federal Tax Handbook covers the following important new tax developments, including changes made by the Revenue Reconciliation Act of 1993 (Chapter 1 of Title XIII of the Omnibus Budget Reconciliation Act of 1993, P.L. 103-66, 8/10/93):

- '94 tax calendar for filing returns and paying tax (¶ 1000).
- '94 and '93 income tax rates for individuals and estates and trusts, reflecting new 36% and 39.6% rates (¶ 1100 *et seq.*).
- '94 and '93 wage bases and rates for social security and Medicare taxes, for employers, employees and self-employed taxpayers (¶ 1107 *et seq.*). The limit on the amount of an employee's wage and self-employment income subject to Health Insurance employment tax is eliminated for '94 and later years.
- '93 tax table for computing an individual's tax (¶ 1110).
- Corporate income tax rate increased to 35% (¶ 1111).
- Top estate and gift tax rate reinstated at 55% (¶ 1112).
- Applicable Federal Rates (¶ 1116), long-term tax-exempt rates (¶ 3567), low-income housing credit percentages (¶ 2320), and rates for underpayments (¶ 4862) and overpayments (¶ 4851).
- Depreciation ceilings for luxury autos placed in service in '93 (¶ 1960) and inclusion amount table for leased automobiles, including those first leased in '93 (¶ 1120).
- Employer-provided educational assistance exclusion extended (¶ 1258).
- Up to 85% of social security benefits may be taxable after '93 (¶ 1283).
- '93 AGI threshold amounts for savings bond interest exclusion (¶ 1339).
- Election to exclude income from discharge of "qualified real property business indebtedness" (¶ 1389).
- Deduction disallowed for certain compensation in excess of $1 million (¶ 1515).
- Self-employed's limited health insurance deduction is extended through '93 (¶ 1528).
- Travel expense deduction denied for spouse accompanying taxpayer after '93 (¶ 1545).
- '93 optional standard business mileage rate (¶ 1552), and the rate for charitable contribution (¶ 2120) and medical expense (¶ 2144) deductions.
- Deduction for club dues is barred after '93 (¶ 1561).
- Meal and entertainment expense deduction reduced from 80% to 50% of cost after '93 (¶ 1562).
- '93 high-low per diem amounts and high-cost key cities (¶ 1569).
- Deduction for certain lobbying expenses is not available after '93 (¶ 1620 *et seq.*).
- Supreme Court decision provides test for home office deduction (¶ 1632).
- Moving expenses are deducted "above the line" after '93 (¶ 1648).
- Increase in recovery period for nonresidential real property to 39 years (¶ 1919).
- Increased Section 179 expense election amount, with additional increase for enterprise zone property (¶ 1956 *et seq.*).
- 15-year amortization for goodwill and certain other business intangibles (¶ 1989 *et seq.*).
- '93 guidelines on "insubstantial benefits" received for payments to charities for fundraising and entertainment (¶ 2104).
- Substantiation requirements for charitable contributions of $250 or more after '93 (¶ 2134).
- Several new credits: the empowerment zone employment credit (¶ 2329), the Indian employment credit (¶ 2330), the employer Social Security credit (¶ 2331), and the credit for contributions to selected Community Development Corporations (¶ 2332). Several other credits extended: the low-income housing credit (¶ 2320), the incremental research credit (¶ 2323), the targeted jobs credit (¶ 2324) and orphan drugs credit (¶ 2334).
- Earned income credit is expanded and increased for '94 and later years (¶ 2338).
- Gain on publicly-traded securities can be rolled over tax-free into "specialized small business

investment companies" (¶ 2424).

- Involuntary conversion relief is extended where principal residence is damaged in Presidentially-declared disaster (¶ 2430).
- 50% of gain from qualified small business stock is excludable (¶ 2640 *et seq.*).
- New Code Sec. 481(a) adjustment rules for accounting method changes (¶ 2844 *et seq.*).
- Securities dealers must use mark-to-market rules for certain securities (¶ 2883).
- Increased withholding for supplemental wage payments (¶ 3013).
- '94 and '93 standard deduction (¶ 3109) and personal exemption amounts (¶ 3113).
- '94 and '93 threshold amounts for phase-out of personal exemptions (¶ 3114), and AGI threshold amounts at which reductions in itemized deductions begin (¶ 3112).
- Individual estimated tax safe harbors simplified for '94 and later years (¶ 3148 *et seq.*).
- Estimated tax penalty waived for underpayments resulting from '93 Revenue Reconciliation Act, for any period before Apr. 16, '94 for individuals (¶ 3157), or before Mar. 16, '94 for corporations (¶ 3357).
- Noncorporate taxpayers' alternative minimum tax and exemption increased. (¶ 3201 *et seq.*).
- Alternative minimum tax preference for appreciated charitable contribution property is repealed (¶ 3207).
- Accumulated earnings tax (¶ 3323) and personal holding company tax increased to 39.6% (¶ 3331).
- Corporate estimated tax rules revised (¶ 3351 *et seq.*).
- IRS says when it won't consider the receipt of a profits interest in a partnership in exchange for services to be taxable (¶ 3711).
- Payments to partners in liquidation of interest for goodwill or unrealized receivables treated as in exchange for interest in partnership property (¶ 3771).
- Disclosure requirement for quid pro quo charitable contributions after '93 (¶ 4113).
- Salary cap on contributions to retirement plans reduced to $150,000 in '94 (¶ 4320).
- Regs on eligible rollover distributions (¶ 4360) and trustee-trustee transfers ¶ 4320).
- Employee plan benefit and contribution ceilings for '93 as adjusted for inflation, including the maximum compensation taken into account (¶ 4320), defined benefit plan benefits (¶ 4328), CODA deferrals (¶ 4318), amounts with respect to highly compensated employees (¶ 4326), SEP contributions (¶ 4366), and the 15% excess distribution penalty (¶ 4346).
- '93 foreign housing cost exclusion amounts (¶ 4616).
- '94 and '93 threshold amounts at which income tax returns must be filed (¶ 4701).
- Election to pay additional '93 tax attributable to '93 Revenue Reconciliation Act increases in installments (¶ 4720).
- New information returns required for discharges of indebtedness after '93 (¶ 4745).
- IRS's Market Segment Specialization (MSSP) audit guidelines (¶ 4806).
- Procedures for getting refunds arising from retroactive changes made by '93 Revenue Reconciliation Act (¶ 4849).
- Accuracy-related penalty for substantial valuation misstatements revised for tax years beginning after '93 (¶ 4871).

¶ 1000. Tax Calendar—1994 Due Dates.

Here are the principal '94 tax due dates. The effect of Saturdays, Sundays, and federal (but not state) holidays has been taken into account.

January 18

Individuals. Make a payment of your estimated tax for '93, if you did not pay your income tax for the year through withholding (or did not pay in enough tax that way). Use Form 1040-ES. This is the final installment date for '93 estimated tax. However, you do not have to make this payment if you file your '93 return (Form 1040) and pay any tax due by Jan. 31, '94.

Farmers and fishermen. Pay your estimated tax for '93 using Form 1040-ES. You can then file your '93 income tax return (Form 1040) by Apr. 15. If you do not pay at this time, your '93 return will be due Mar. 1, '94.

January 31

All employers. Give your employees their copies of Form W-2 for '93. Retired employees should be given their copies of Form 1099-R.

All businesses. Give an annual information statement to recipients of certain payments you made during '93. (You can use a copy of the appropriate Form 1099.)

Real estate brokers. Give a copy of Form 1099-S to each seller involved in reportable real estate transactions.

Brokers (other than real estate brokers) and barter exchanges. Give a statement containing the same information required to be reported to IRS to all customers for whom you made dispositions in '93. A copy of Form 1099-B may be used for this purpose.

Receivers of mortgage interest. Give a statement containing the same information required to be reported to IRS to each individual from whom you received, in connection with a trade or business, interest of $600 or more on a mortgage during the year. You may use as the statement a copy of the Form 1098 that you file with IRS.

Lenders of money secured by property. Give a statement containing the same information required to be reported to IRS to each borrower from whom you acquired, in connection with a trade or business, an interest in property that is security for a debt, or who you had reason to know had abandoned such property. You may use as the statement a copy of the Form 1099-A that you file with IRS.

Receivers of cash payments over $10,000. Give to each person who paid you over $10,000 in cash, in connection with a trade or business, a statement that shows the name and address of your business and the total amount of cash you received from the payer during the year. If you had a single transaction with a payor during the year, you may use Form 8300. File Form 8300 with IRS by the 15th day after the date of the transaction.

Individuals. File your income tax return (Form 1040) for '93 if you did not pay your last installment of estimated tax by Jan. 18. Filing your return now prevents any penalty for late payment of the last installment.

February 15

Individuals. If you claimed exemption from income tax withholding for '93 on the Form W-4 you gave your employer, you must file a new Form W-4 by this date to continue your exemption for another year.

February 28

All businesses. File an information return (Form 1099) with IRS for certain payments you made during '93. There are different versions of Form 1099 for different types of payments. Use a separate Form 1096 to summarize and transmit each separate version. For a 30-day extension of time to file, use Form 8809.

Real estate brokers. File Form 1099-S for specified real estate transactions.

Brokers (other than real estate brokers) and barter exchanges. File Form 1099-B for each customer for whom you made dispositions in '93.

Receivers of mortgage interest. File Form 1098 for each individual from whom, in connection with a trade or business, you received interest of $600 or more on a mortgage during '93.

Lenders of money secured by property. File Form 1099-A for each borrower from whom, in connection with a trade or business, you acquired an interest in property that is security for a debt, or who you had reason to know abandoned such property, in '93.

All employers. File Form W-3 along with Copy A of all the Forms W-2 and W-2P you issued for '93.

Large food and beverage establishment employers. File Form 8027 to report tip income and allocated tips. Use Form 8027-T to summarize and transmit Forms 8027 if you have

more than one establishment.

March 1
Farmers and fishermen. File your '93 income tax return (Form 1040) and pay any tax due. However, you have until Apr. 15, if you paid your '93 estimated tax by Jan. 18, '94.

March 15
C corporations and S corporations. File a '93 calendar year income tax return (Form 1120, 1120-A or 1120S) and pay any tax still due. If you want an automatic six-month extension, file Form 7004 and deposit what you estimate you owe.

Corporations. File Form 2553 to choose to be treated as an S corporation, beginning with calendar year '94. If Form 2553 is filed late, S treatment will begin with calendar year '95.

April 15
Individuals. File an income tax return for '93 (Form 1040, 1040A, or 1040EZ), and pay any tax due. However, taxpayers who can't make payments should request an agreement to pay in installments on Form 9465. Taxpayers electing the three-installment option for additional taxes due to the '93 Act should file Form 8841. If you want an automatic four-month extension to file, file Form 4868 and pay any tax you estimate will be due. Then file Form 1040 or Form 1040A by Aug. 15. If you want an additional two-month extension, file Form 2688 as soon as possible, so that your application can be acted on before Aug. 15.

Individuals. If you are not paying your '94 income tax through withholding (or will not pay in enough tax during the year that way), pay the first installment of your '94 estimated tax by this date. Use Form 1040-ES.

Partnerships. File a '93 calendar year return (Form 1065). For an automatic three-month extension, file Form 8736.

Corporations. Deposit the first installment of estimated income tax for '94.

May 16
Partnerships and S corporations. If you selected a different tax year under Code Sec. 444 in the prior calendar year, file Form 8752 and pay the resulting required payment.

June 15
Individuals. Make the second installment pay-ment of your '94 estimated tax, if you are not paying your income tax for the year through withholding (or will not pay in enough tax that way). Use Form 1040-ES.

Corporations. Deposit the second installment of estimated income tax for '94.

August 1
All employers. If you maintain an employee benefit plan, such as a pension, profit-sharing, or stock bonus plan, file Form 5500, 5500-EZ, 5500-C/R for calendar year '93. If you use a fiscal year as your plan year, file the form by the last day of the seventh month after the plan year ends.

August 15
Individuals. If you were given an automatic four-month extension to file your income tax return for '93, file Form 1040 and pay any tax, interest, and penalties due. Otherwise, see Apr. 15.

September 15
Individuals. Make the third installment payment of your '94 estimated tax, if you are not paying your income tax for the year through withholding (or will not pay in enough tax that way). Use Form 1040-ES.

C corporations and S corporations. File a '93 calendar year income tax return (Form 1120 or 1120-A, or 1120S) and pay any tax due. This due date applies only if you were given an automatic six-month extension. Otherwise, see Mar. 15.

Corporations. Deposit the third installment of estimated income tax for '94.

During November
Income tax withholding. Request employees whose withholding exemptions will be different in '95 to fill out a new Form W-4.

Earned income credit. Request each eligible employee who wants to receive advance payments of the earned income credit during '95 to fill out a new Form W-5.

December 15
Corporations. Deposit the fourth installment of estimated income tax for '94.

Chapter 1   Tax Rates and Tables

¶ 1100 Tax Rates, Tax Tables ▰▰▰▰▰▰▰▰▰▰▰▰▰

Federal tax rates for income, gift, estate, excise and other taxes are set forth in this Chapter. Also included are current income tax tables.

¶ 1101 Income tax rates for individuals.

Different rates apply to:

■ single taxpayers (¶ 1102);

■ married persons filing joint returns and qualified widows and widowers (¶ 1103);

■ married persons filing separate returns (¶ 1104);

■ heads of households (¶ 1105).

Individuals with taxable income under a ceiling amount ($100,000 for '93) compute their tax under the tax tables. (Code Sec. 3) These tax tables are reproduced at ¶ 1110.

Individual income tax rates are indexed each year for inflation. (Code Sec. 1(f)) The rates below reflect that indexing.

Net capital gains are taxed at a maximum rate of 28%, see ¶ 2600 *et seq.*

The alternative minimum tax may also apply, see Chapter 14.

¶ 1102 Single individuals.

Taxpayers who are not married *at year's end* and who do not qualify as surviving spouses or heads of household, and certain married taxpayers living apart compute their tax under the following tax rates for single persons if they can't use the tax tables.

The rates for '93 are:

If taxable income is:	The tax is:
Not over $22,100 . . .	15% of taxable income.
Over $22,100 but not over $53,500	$3,315 plus 28% of the amount over $22,100.
Over $53,500 but not over $115,000	$12,107, plus 31% of the amount over $53,500.
Over $115,000 but not over $250,000	$31,172, plus 36% of the amount over $115,000.
Over $250,000	$79,772, plus 39.6% of the amount over $250,000.

The rates for '94 are:

If taxable income is:	The tax is:
Not over $22,750 . . .	15% of taxable income.
Over $22,750 but not over $55,100	$3,412.50 plus 28% of the amount over $22,750.
Over $55,100 but not over $115,000	$12,470.50, plus 31% of the amount over $55,100.
Over $115,000 but not over $250,000	$31,039.50, plus 36% of the amount over $115,000.
Over $250,000	$79,639.50, plus 39.6% of the amount over $250,000.

¶ 1103 Married filing joint returns.

Married taxpayers filing joint returns and surviving spouses who can't use the tax tables compute their tax on the basis of the rates indicated below.

The rates for '93 are:

If taxable income is:	The tax is:
Not over $36,900 . . .	15% of taxable income.
Over $36,900 but not over $89,150	$5,535, plus 28% of the amount over $36,900.
Over $89,150 but not over $140,000	$20,165, plus 31% of the amount over $89,150.
Over $140,000 but not over $250,000	$35,928.50, plus 36% of the amount over $140,000.
Over $250,000	$75,528.50, plus 39.6% of the amount over $250,000.

The rates for '94 are:

If taxable income is:	The tax is:
Not over $38,000 . . .	15% of taxable income.
Over $38,000 but not over $91,850	$5,700, plus 28% of the amount over $38,000.
Over $91,850 but not over $140,000	$20,778, plus 31% of the amount over $91,850.
Over $140,000 but not over $250,000	$35,704.50, plus 36% of the amount over $140,000.
Over $250,000	$75,304.50, plus 39.6% of the amount over $250,000.

¶ 1104 Married filing separate returns.

Married taxpayers filing separate returns who can't use the tax tables compute their tax on the basis of the rates indicated below.

The rates for '93 are:

If taxable income is:	The tax is:
Not over $18,450 . . .	15% of taxable income.
Over $18,450 but not over $44,575	$2,767.50, plus 28% of the amount over $18,450.
Over $44,575 but not over $70,000	$10,082.50, plus 31% of the amount over $44,575.
Over $70,000 but not over $125,000	$17,964.50, plus 36% of the amount over $70,000.
Over $125,000	$37,764.25, plus 39.6% of the amount over $125,000.

The rates for '94 are:

If taxable income is:	The tax is:
Not over $19,000 . . .	15% of taxable income.
Over $19,000 but not over $45,925	$2,850, plus 28% of the amount over $19,000.
Over $45,925 but not over $70,000	$10,389, plus 31% of the amount over $45,925.
Over $70,000 but not over $125,000	$17,852.25, plus 36% of the amount over $70,000.
Over $125,000	$37,652.25, plus 39.6% of the amount over $125,000.

¶ 1105 Head of household.

Unmarried persons maintaining households who can't use the tax tables compute their tax on the basis of the rates indicated below.

The rates for '93 are:

If taxable income is:	The tax is:
Not over $29,600 . . .	15% of taxable income.
Over $29,600 but not over $76,400	$4,440, plus 28% of the amount over $29,600.
Over $76,400 but not over $127,500	$17,544, plus 31% of the amount over $76,400.
Over $127,500 but not over $250,000	$33,385, plus 36% of the amount over $127,500.
Over $250,000	$77,485, plus 39.6% of the amount over $250,000.

The rates for '94 are:

If taxable income is:	The tax is:
Not over $30,500 . . .	15% of taxable income.
Over $30,500 but not over $78,700	$4,575, plus 28% of the amount over $30,500.
Over $78,700 but not over $127,500	$18,071, plus 31% of the amount over $78,700.
Over $127,500 but not over $250,000	$33,199, plus 36% of the amount over $127,500.
Over $250,000	$77,299, plus 39.6% of the amount over $250,000.

¶ 1106 Income tax rates for trusts and estates.

The income tax on trusts and decedent's estates is imposed at graduated rates on their taxable income. (Code Sec. 1(e)) Net capital gains are taxed at a maximum rate of 28%, see ¶ 2600 *et seq.*

The rates for '93 are:

If taxable income is:	The tax is:
Not over $1,500	15% of taxable income
Over $1,500 but not over $3,500	$225, plus 28% of the amount over $1,500
Over $3,500 but not over $5,500	$785, plus 31% of the amount over $3,500
Over $5,500 but not over $7,500	$1,405 plus 36% of the amount over $5,500
Over $7,500	$2,125 plus 39.6% of the amount over $7,500

The rates for '94 are:

If taxable income is:	The tax is:
Not over $1,500	15% of taxable income
Over $1,500 but not over $3,600	$225, plus 28% of the amount over $1,500

Over $3,600 but not over $5,500	$813, plus 31% of the amount over $3,600
Over $5,500 but not over $7,500	$1,402 plus 36% of the amount over $5,500
Over $7,500	$2,122 plus 39.6% of the amount over $7,500

Tax rates for bankruptcy estates. Bankruptcy estates compute their tax using the same rate schedule as married individuals filing separate tax returns. The alternative minimum tax may also apply, see Chapter 14.

¶ 1107 FICA (Social Security and Medicare) tax.

A FICA tax for employers and employees is imposed at a rate of 7.65%. This 7.65% rate is a combination of a 6.20% Social Security tax and a 1.45% Medicare tax. The employer and the employee are both liable for FICA taxes at the above rates. (Code Sec. 3101(a), (b); Code Sec. 3111(a), (b))

For '94, the 6.20% Social Security tax is computed on the first $60,600 of the employee's wages. Thus, the maximum Social Security tax for '94 is $3,757.20 (6.20%×$60,600). The 1.45% Medicare tax is computed on the total of the employee's wages (no ceiling).

For '93, the 6.20% Social Security tax was computed on the first $57,600 of the employee's wages, and the 1.45% Medicare tax was computed on the first $135,000 of wages. Thus, the maximum Social Security tax was $3,571.20 (6.20% of $57,600) and the maximum Medicare tax was $1,957.50 (1.45% of $135,000). The maximum FICA tax for '93 was $5,528.70, i.e., Social Security tax of $3,571.20 plus Medicare tax of $1,957.50.

¶ 1108 Self-employment tax.

A self-employment tax is imposed on self-employed people at a rate of 15.30%. This 15.30% rate is a combination of a 12.40% OASDI tax (i.e., an Old Age, Survivors, and Disability Insurance tax which is the equivalent of the Social Security tax imposed on employers and employees, see ¶ 1107), and a 2.90% Medicare tax. (Code Sec. 1401(a), (b))

For '94, the 12.40% OASDI tax is computed on the first $60,600 of self-employment income. Thus, the maximum OASDI tax for '94 is $7,514.40 (12.40% of $60,600). The 2.90% Medicare tax is computed on the entire amount of wages (no ceiling).

For '93, the 12.40% OASDI tax was computed on the first $57,600 of self-employment income, and the 2.90% Medicare tax was computed on the first $135,000 of self-employment income. Thus, the maximum OASDI tax was $7,142.40 (12.40% of $57,600) and the maximum Medicare tax was $3,915.00 (2.90% of $135,000). The maximum self-employment tax for '93 was $11,057.40, i.e., OASDI tax of $7,142.40 plus a Medicare tax of $3,915.00.

For the deduction of half of the self-employment tax, see ¶ 1743, and for the deduction for purposes of computing net earnings from self-employment to get the self-employment tax itself, see ¶ 3139.

¶ 1109 Federal unemployment tax (FUTA).

The tax is 6.2% through '98, and 6.0% for '99 and after, (Code Sec. 3301) of the first $7,000 paid each employee as wages during the calendar year. (Code Sec. 3306(b))

Generally, the employer can take a credit against FUTA tax for contributions paid into State unemployment funds. This credit can't exceed 5.4% of the first $7,000 of wages. (Code Sec. 3302)

¶ 1110 Tax Table for Individuals

The following table is taken from the official instructions to Form 1040.

1993 Tax Table

Use if your taxable income is less than $100,000. If $100,000 or more, use the Tax Rate Schedules.

Example. Mr. and Mrs. Brown are filing a joint return. Their taxable income on line 37 of Form 1040 is $25,300. First, they find the $25,300–25,350 income line. Next, they find the column for married filing jointly and read down the column. The amount shown where the income line and filing status column meet is $3,799. This is the tax amount they must enter on line 38 of their Form 1040.

Sample Table

At least	But less than	Single	Married filing jointly *	Married filing separately	Head of a household
			Your tax is—		
25,200	25,250	4,190	3,784	4,665	3,784
25,250	25,300	4,204	3,791	4,679	3,791
25,300	25,350	4,218	3,799	4,693	3,799
25,350	25,400	4,232	3,806	4,707	3,806

If line 37 (taxable income) is—		And you are—			
At least	But less than	Single	Married filing jointly *	Married filing separately	Head of a household
			Your tax is—		
0	5	0	0	0	0
5	15	2	2	2	2
15	25	3	3	3	3
25	50	6	6	6	6
50	75	9	9	9	9
75	100	13	13	13	13
100	125	17	17	17	17
125	150	21	21	21	21
150	175	24	24	24	24
175	200	28	28	28	28
200	225	32	32	32	32
225	250	36	36	36	36
250	275	39	39	39	39
275	300	43	43	43	43
300	325	47	47	47	47
325	350	51	51	51	51
350	375	54	54	54	54
375	400	58	58	58	58
400	425	62	62	62	62
425	450	66	66	66	66
450	475	69	69	69	69
475	500	73	73	73	73
500	525	77	77	77	77
525	550	81	81	81	81
550	575	84	84	84	84
575	600	88	88	88	88
600	625	92	92	92	92
625	650	96	96	96	96
650	675	99	99	99	99
675	700	103	103	103	103
700	725	107	107	107	107
725	750	111	111	111	111
750	775	114	114	114	114
775	800	118	118	118	118
800	825	122	122	122	122
825	850	126	126	126	126
850	875	129	129	129	129
875	900	133	133	133	133
900	925	137	137	137	137
925	950	141	141	141	141
950	975	144	144	144	144
975	1,000	148	148	148	148

1,000

At least	But less than	Single	Married filing jointly *	Married filing separately	Head of a household
1,000	1,025	152	152	152	152
1,025	1,050	156	156	156	156
1,050	1,075	159	159	159	159
1,075	1,100	163	163	163	163
1,100	1,125	167	167	167	167
1,125	1,150	171	171	171	171
1,150	1,175	174	174	174	174
1,175	1,200	178	178	178	178
1,200	1,225	182	182	182	182
1,225	1,250	186	186	186	186
1,250	1,275	189	189	189	189
1,275	1,300	193	193	193	193

If line 37 (taxable income) is—		And you are—			
At least	But less than	Single	Married filing jointly *	Married filing separately	Head of a household
			Your tax is—		
1,300	1,325	197	197	197	197
1,325	1,350	201	201	201	201
1,350	1,375	204	204	204	204
1,375	1,400	208	208	208	208
1,400	1,425	212	212	212	212
1,425	1,450	216	216	216	216
1,450	1,475	219	219	219	219
1,475	1,500	223	223	223	223
1,500	1,525	227	227	227	227
1,525	1,550	231	231	231	231
1,550	1,575	234	234	234	234
1,575	1,600	238	238	238	238
1,600	1,625	242	242	242	242
1,625	1,650	246	246	246	246
1,650	1,675	249	249	249	249
1,675	1,700	253	253	253	253
1,700	1,725	257	257	257	257
1,725	1,750	261	261	261	261
1,750	1,775	264	264	264	264
1,775	1,800	268	268	268	268
1,800	1,825	272	272	272	272
1,825	1,850	276	276	276	276
1,850	1,875	279	279	279	279
1,875	1,900	283	283	283	283
1,900	1,925	287	287	287	287
1,925	1,950	291	291	291	291
1,950	1,975	294	294	294	294
1,975	2,000	298	298	298	298

2,000

At least	But less than	Single	Married filing jointly *	Married filing separately	Head of a household
2,000	2,025	302	302	302	302
2,025	2,050	306	306	306	306
2,050	2,075	309	309	309	309
2,075	2,100	313	313	313	313
2,100	2,125	317	317	317	317
2,125	2,150	321	321	321	321
2,150	2,175	324	324	324	324
2,175	2,200	328	328	328	328
2,200	2,225	332	332	332	332
2,225	2,250	336	336	336	336
2,250	2,275	339	339	339	339
2,275	2,300	343	343	343	343
2,300	2,325	347	347	347	347
2,325	2,350	351	351	351	351
2,350	2,375	354	354	354	354
2,375	2,400	358	358	358	358
2,400	2,425	362	362	362	362
2,425	2,450	366	366	366	366
2,450	2,475	369	369	369	369
2,475	2,500	373	373	373	373
2,500	2,525	377	377	377	377
2,525	2,550	381	381	381	381
2,550	2,575	384	384	384	384
2,575	2,600	388	388	388	388
2,600	2,625	392	392	392	392
2,625	2,650	396	396	396	396
2,650	2,675	399	399	399	399
2,675	2,700	403	403	403	403

If line 37 (taxable income) is—		And you are—			
At least	But less than	Single	Married filing jointly *	Married filing separately	Head of a household
			Your tax is—		
2,700	2,725	407	407	407	407
2,725	2,750	411	411	411	411
2,750	2,775	414	414	414	414
2,775	2,800	418	418	418	418
2,800	2,825	422	422	422	422
2,825	2,850	426	426	426	426
2,850	2,875	429	429	429	429
2,875	2,900	433	433	433	433
2,900	2,925	437	437	437	437
2,925	2,950	441	441	441	441
2,950	2,975	444	444	444	444
2,975	3,000	448	448	448	448

3,000

At least	But less than	Single	Married filing jointly *	Married filing separately	Head of a household
3,000	3,050	454	454	454	454
3,050	3,100	461	461	461	461
3,100	3,150	469	469	469	469
3,150	3,200	476	476	476	476
3,200	3,250	484	484	484	484
3,250	3,300	491	491	491	491
3,300	3,350	499	499	499	499
3,350	3,400	506	506	506	506
3,400	3,450	514	514	514	514
3,450	3,500	521	521	521	521
3,500	3,550	529	529	529	529
3,550	3,600	536	536	536	536
3,600	3,650	544	544	544	544
3,650	3,700	551	551	551	551
3,700	3,750	559	559	559	559
3,750	3,800	566	566	566	566
3,800	3,850	574	574	574	574
3,850	3,900	581	581	581	581
3,900	3,950	589	589	589	589
3,950	4,000	596	596	596	596

4,000

At least	But less than	Single	Married filing jointly *	Married filing separately	Head of a household
4,000	4,050	604	604	604	604
4,050	4,100	611	611	611	611
4,100	4,150	619	619	619	619
4,150	4,200	626	626	626	626
4,200	4,250	634	634	634	634
4,250	4,300	641	641	641	641
4,300	4,350	649	649	649	649
4,350	4,400	656	656	656	656
4,400	4,450	664	664	664	664
4,450	4,500	671	671	671	671
4,500	4,550	679	679	679	679
4,550	4,600	686	686	686	686
4,600	4,650	694	694	694	694
4,650	4,700	701	701	701	701
4,700	4,750	709	709	709	709
4,750	4,800	716	716	716	716
4,800	4,850	724	724	724	724
4,850	4,900	731	731	731	731
4,900	4,950	739	739	739	739
4,950	5,000	746	746	746	746

Continued on next page

* This column must also be used by a qualifying widow(er).

1993 Tax Table—*Continued*

If line 37 (taxable income) is— At least	But less than	And you are— Single	Married filing jointly *	Married filing sepa-rately	Head of a house-hold
		Your tax is—			
5,000					
5,000	5,050	754	754	754	754
5,050	5,100	761	761	761	761
5,100	5,150	769	769	769	769
5,150	5,200	776	776	776	776
5,200	5,250	784	784	784	784
5,250	5,300	791	791	791	791
5,300	5,350	799	799	799	799
5,350	5,400	806	806	806	806
5,400	5,450	814	814	814	814
5,450	5,500	821	821	821	821
5,500	5,550	829	829	829	829
5,550	5,600	836	836	836	836
5,600	5,650	844	844	844	844
5,650	5,700	851	851	851	851
5,700	5,750	859	859	859	859
5,750	5,800	866	866	866	866
5,800	5,850	874	874	874	874
5,850	5,900	881	881	881	881
5,900	5,950	889	889	889	889
5,950	6,000	896	896	896	896
6,000					
6,000	6,050	904	904	904	904
6,050	6,100	911	911	911	911
6,100	6,150	919	919	919	919
6,150	6,200	926	926	926	926
6,200	6,250	934	934	934	934
6,250	6,300	941	941	941	941
6,300	6,350	949	949	949	949
6,350	6,400	956	956	956	956
6,400	6,450	964	964	964	964
6,450	6,500	971	971	971	971
6,500	6,550	979	979	979	979
6,550	6,600	986	986	986	986
6,600	6,650	994	994	994	994
6,650	6,700	1,001	1,001	1,001	1,001
6,700	6,750	1,009	1,009	1,009	1,009
6,750	6,800	1,016	1,016	1,016	1,016
6,800	6,850	1,024	1,024	1,024	1,024
6,850	6,900	1,031	1,031	1,031	1,031
6,900	6,950	1,039	1,039	1,039	1,039
6,950	7,000	1,046	1,046	1,046	1,046
7,000					
7,000	7,050	1,054	1,054	1,054	1,054
7,050	7,100	1,061	1,061	1,061	1,061
7,100	7,150	1,069	1,069	1,069	1,069
7,150	7,200	1,076	1,076	1,076	1,076
7,200	7,250	1,084	1,084	1,084	1,084
7,250	7,300	1,091	1,091	1,091	1,091
7,300	7,350	1,099	1,099	1,099	1,099
7,350	7,400	1,106	1,106	1,106	1,106
7,400	7,450	1,114	1,114	1,114	1,114
7,450	7,500	1,121	1,121	1,121	1,121
7,500	7,550	1,129	1,129	1,129	1,129
7,550	7,600	1,136	1,136	1,136	1,136
7,600	7,650	1,144	1,144	1,144	1,144
7,650	7,700	1,151	1,151	1,151	1,151
7,700	7,750	1,159	1,159	1,159	1,159
7,750	7,800	1,166	1,166	1,166	1,166
7,800	7,850	1,174	1,174	1,174	1,174
7,850	7,900	1,181	1,181	1,181	1,181
7,900	7,950	1,189	1,189	1,189	1,189
7,950	8,000	1,196	1,196	1,196	1,196
8,000					
8,000	8,050	1,204	1,204	1,204	1,204
8,050	8,100	1,211	1,211	1,211	1,211
8,100	8,150	1,219	1,219	1,219	1,219
8,150	8,200	1,226	1,226	1,226	1,226
8,200	8,250	1,234	1,234	1,234	1,234
8,250	8,300	1,241	1,241	1,241	1,241
8,300	8,350	1,249	1,249	1,249	1,249
8,350	8,400	1,256	1,256	1,256	1,256
8,400	8,450	1,264	1,264	1,264	1,264
8,450	8,500	1,271	1,271	1,271	1,271
8,500	8,550	1,279	1,279	1,279	1,279
8,550	8,600	1,286	1,286	1,286	1,286
8,600	8,650	1,294	1,294	1,294	1,294
8,650	8,700	1,301	1,301	1,301	1,301
8,700	8,750	1,309	1,309	1,309	1,309
8,750	8,800	1,316	1,316	1,316	1,316
8,800	8,850	1,324	1,324	1,324	1,324
8,850	8,900	1,331	1,331	1,331	1,331
8,900	8,950	1,339	1,339	1,339	1,339
8,950	9,000	1,346	1,346	1,346	1,346
9,000					
9,000	9,050	1,354	1,354	1,354	1,354
9,050	9,100	1,361	1,361	1,361	1,361
9,100	9,150	1,369	1,369	1,369	1,369
9,150	9,200	1,376	1,376	1,376	1,376
9,200	9,250	1,384	1,384	1,384	1,384
9,250	9,300	1,391	1,391	1,391	1,391
9,300	9,350	1,399	1,399	1,399	1,399
9,350	9,400	1,406	1,406	1,406	1,406
9,400	9,450	1,414	1,414	1,414	1,414
9,450	9,500	1,421	1,421	1,421	1,421
9,500	9,550	1,429	1,429	1,429	1,429
9,550	9,600	1,436	1,436	1,436	1,436
9,600	9,650	1,444	1,444	1,444	1,444
9,650	9,700	1,451	1,451	1,451	1,451
9,700	9,750	1,459	1,459	1,459	1,459
9,750	9,800	1,466	1,466	1,466	1,466
9,800	9,850	1,474	1,474	1,474	1,474
9,850	9,900	1,481	1,481	1,481	1,481
9,900	9,950	1,489	1,489	1,489	1,489
9,950	10,000	1,496	1,496	1,496	1,496
10,000					
10,000	10,050	1,504	1,504	1,504	1,504
10,050	10,100	1,511	1,511	1,511	1,511
10,100	10,150	1,519	1,519	1,519	1,519
10,150	10,200	1,526	1,526	1,526	1,526
10,200	10,250	1,534	1,534	1,534	1,534
10,250	10,300	1,541	1,541	1,541	1,541
10,300	10,350	1,549	1,549	1,549	1,549
10,350	10,400	1,556	1,556	1,556	1,556
10,400	10,450	1,564	1,564	1,564	1,564
10,450	10,500	1,571	1,571	1,571	1,571
10,500	10,550	1,579	1,579	1,579	1,579
10,550	10,600	1,586	1,586	1,586	1,586
10,600	10,650	1,594	1,594	1,594	1,594
10,650	10,700	1,601	1,601	1,601	1,601
10,700	10,750	1,609	1,609	1,609	1,609
10,750	10,800	1,616	1,616	1,616	1,616
10,800	10,850	1,624	1,624	1,624	1,624
10,850	10,900	1,631	1,631	1,631	1,631
10,900	10,950	1,639	1,639	1,639	1,639
10,950	11,000	1,646	1,646	1,646	1,646
11,000					
11,000	11,050	1,654	1,654	1,654	1,654
11,050	11,100	1,661	1,661	1,661	1,661
11,100	11,150	1,669	1,669	1,669	1,669
11,150	11,200	1,676	1,676	1,676	1,676
11,200	11,250	1,684	1,684	1,684	1,684
11,250	11,300	1,691	1,691	1,691	1,691
11,300	11,350	1,699	1,699	1,699	1,699
11,350	11,400	1,706	1,706	1,706	1,706
11,400	11,450	1,714	1,714	1,714	1,714
11,450	11,500	1,721	1,721	1,721	1,721
11,500	11,550	1,729	1,729	1,729	1,729
11,550	11,600	1,736	1,736	1,736	1,736
11,600	11,650	1,744	1,744	1,744	1,744
11,650	11,700	1,751	1,751	1,751	1,751
11,700	11,750	1,759	1,759	1,759	1,759
11,750	11,800	1,766	1,766	1,766	1,766
11,800	11,850	1,774	1,774	1,774	1,774
11,850	11,900	1,781	1,781	1,781	1,781
11,900	11,950	1,789	1,789	1,789	1,789
11,950	12,000	1,796	1,796	1,796	1,796
12,000					
12,000	12,050	1,804	1,804	1,804	1,804
12,050	12,100	1,811	1,811	1,811	1,811
12,100	12,150	1,819	1,819	1,819	1,819
12,150	12,200	1,826	1,826	1,826	1,826
12,200	12,250	1,834	1,834	1,834	1,834
12,250	12,300	1,841	1,841	1,841	1,841
12,300	12,350	1,849	1,849	1,849	1,849
12,350	12,400	1,856	1,856	1,856	1,856
12,400	12,450	1,864	1,864	1,864	1,864
12,450	12,500	1,871	1,871	1,871	1,871
12,500	12,550	1,879	1,879	1,879	1,879
12,550	12,600	1,886	1,886	1,886	1,886
12,600	12,650	1,894	1,894	1,894	1,894
12,650	12,700	1,901	1,901	1,901	1,901
12,700	12,750	1,909	1,909	1,909	1,909
12,750	12,800	1,916	1,916	1,916	1,916
12,800	12,850	1,924	1,924	1,924	1,924
12,850	12,900	1,931	1,931	1,931	1,931
12,900	12,950	1,939	1,939	1,939	1,939
12,950	13,000	1,946	1,946	1,946	1,946
13,000					
13,000	13,050	1,954	1,954	1,954	1,954
13,050	13,100	1,961	1,961	1,961	1,961
13,100	13,150	1,969	1,969	1,969	1,969
13,150	13,200	1,976	1,976	1,976	1,976
13,200	13,250	1,984	1,984	1,984	1,984
13,250	13,300	1,991	1,991	1,991	1,991
13,300	13,350	1,999	1,999	1,999	1,999
13,350	13,400	2,006	2,006	2,006	2,006
13,400	13,450	2,014	2,014	2,014	2,014
13,450	13,500	2,021	2,021	2,021	2,021
13,500	13,550	2,029	2,029	2,029	2,029
13,550	13,600	2,036	2,036	2,036	2,036
13,600	13,650	2,044	2,044	2,044	2,044
13,650	13,700	2,051	2,051	2,051	2,051
13,700	13,750	2,059	2,059	2,059	2,059
13,750	13,800	2,066	2,066	2,066	2,066
13,800	13,850	2,074	2,074	2,074	2,074
13,850	13,900	2,081	2,081	2,081	2,081
13,900	13,950	2,089	2,089	2,089	2,089
13,950	14,000	2,096	2,096	2,096	2,096

* This column must also be used by a qualifying widow(er).

Continued on next page

1993 Tax Table—Continued

If line 37 (taxable income) is— At least	But less than	Single	Married filing jointly*	Married filing separately	Head of a household
14,000					
14,000	14,050	2,104	2,104	2,104	2,104
14,050	14,100	2,111	2,111	2,111	2,111
14,100	14,150	2,119	2,119	2,119	2,119
14,150	14,200	2,126	2,126	2,126	2,126
14,200	14,250	2,134	2,134	2,134	2,134
14,250	14,300	2,141	2,141	2,141	2,141
14,300	14,350	2,149	2,149	2,149	2,149
14,350	14,400	2,156	2,156	2,156	2,156
14,400	14,450	2,164	2,164	2,164	2,164
14,450	14,500	2,171	2,171	2,171	2,171
14,500	14,550	2,179	2,179	2,179	2,170
14,550	14,600	2,186	2,186	2,186	2,186
14,600	14,650	2,194	2,194	2,194	2,194
14,650	14,700	2,201	2,201	2,201	2,201
14,700	14,750	2,209	2,209	2,209	2,209
14,750	14,800	2,216	2,216	2,216	2,216
14,800	14,850	2,224	2,224	2,224	2,224
14,850	14,900	2,231	2,231	2,231	2,231
14,900	14,950	2,239	2,239	2,239	2,239
14,950	15,000	2,246	2,246	2,246	2,246
15,000					
15,000	15,050	2,254	2,254	2,254	2,254
15,050	15,100	2,261	2,261	2,261	2,261
15,100	15,150	2,269	2,269	2,269	2,269
15,150	15,200	2,276	2,276	2,276	2,276
15,200	15,250	2,284	2,284	2,284	2,284
15,250	15,300	2,291	2,291	2,291	2,291
15,300	15,350	2,299	2,299	2,299	2,299
15,350	15,400	2,306	2,306	2,306	2,306
15,400	15,450	2,314	2,314	2,314	2,314
15,450	15,500	2,321	2,321	2,321	2,321
15,500	15,550	2,329	2,329	2,329	2,329
15,550	15,600	2,336	2,336	2,336	2,336
15,600	15,650	2,344	2,344	2,344	2,344
15,650	15,700	2,351	2,351	2,351	2,351
15,700	15,750	2,359	2,359	2,359	2,359
15,750	15,800	2,366	2,366	2,366	2,366
15,800	15,850	2,374	2,374	2,374	2,374
15,850	15,900	2,381	2,381	2,381	2,381
15,900	15,950	2,389	2,389	2,389	2,389
15,950	16,000	2,396	2,396	2,396	2,396
16,000					
16,000	16,050	2,404	2,404	2,404	2,404
16,050	16,100	2,411	2,411	2,411	2,411
16,100	16,150	2,419	2,419	2,419	2,419
16,150	16,200	2,426	2,426	2,426	2,426
16,200	16,250	2,434	2,434	2,434	2,434
16,250	16,300	2,441	2,441	2,441	2,441
16,300	16,350	2,449	2,449	2,449	2,449
16,350	16,400	2,456	2,456	2,456	2,456
16,400	16,450	2,464	2,464	2,464	2,464
16,450	16,500	2,471	2,471	2,471	2,471
16,500	16,550	2,479	2,479	2,479	2,479
16,550	16,600	2,486	2,486	2,486	2,486
16,600	16,650	2,494	2,494	2,494	2,494
16,650	16,700	2,501	2,501	2,501	2,501
16,700	16,750	2,509	2,509	2,509	2,509
16,750	16,800	2,516	2,516	2,516	2,516
16,800	16,850	2,524	2,524	2,524	2,524
16,850	16,900	2,531	2,531	2,531	2,531
16,900	16,950	2,539	2,539	2,539	2,539
16,950	17,000	2,546	2,546	2,546	2,546

If line 37 (taxable income) is— At least	But less than	Single	Married filing jointly*	Married filing separately	Head of a household
17,000					
17,000	17,050	2,554	2,554	2,554	2,554
17,050	17,100	2,561	2,561	2,561	2,561
17,100	17,150	2,569	2,569	2,569	2,569
17,150	17,200	2,576	2,576	2,576	2,576
17,200	17,250	2,584	2,584	2,584	2,584
17,250	17,300	2,591	2,591	2,591	2,591
17,300	17,350	2,599	2,599	2,599	2,599
17,350	17,400	2,606	2,606	2,606	2,606
17,400	17,450	2,614	2,614	2,614	2,614
17,450	17,500	2,621	2,621	2,621	2,621
17,500	17,550	2,629	2,629	2,629	2,629
17,550	17,600	2,636	2,636	2,636	2,636
17,600	17,650	2,644	2,644	2,644	2,644
17,650	17,700	2,651	2,651	2,651	2,651
17,700	17,750	2,659	2,659	2,659	2,659
17,750	17,800	2,666	2,666	2,666	2,666
17,800	17,850	2,674	2,674	2,674	2,674
17,850	17,900	2,681	2,681	2,681	2,681
17,900	17,950	2,689	2,689	2,689	2,689
17,950	18,000	2,696	2,696	2,696	2,696
18,000					
18,000	18,050	2,704	2,704	2,704	2,704
18,050	18,100	2,711	2,711	2,711	2,711
18,100	18,150	2,719	2,719	2,719	2,719
18,150	18,200	2,726	2,726	2,726	2,726
18,200	18,250	2,734	2,734	2,734	2,734
18,250	18,300	2,741	2,741	2,741	2,741
18,300	18,350	2,749	2,749	2,749	2,749
18,350	18,400	2,756	2,756	2,756	2,756
18,400	18,450	2,764	2,764	2,764	2,764
18,450	18,500	2,771	2,771	2,775	2,771
18,500	18,550	2,779	2,779	2,789	2,779
18,550	18,600	2,786	2,786	2,803	2,786
18,600	18,650	2,794	2,794	2,817	2,794
18,650	18,700	2,801	2,801	2,831	2,801
18,700	18,750	2,809	2,809	2,845	2,809
18,750	18,800	2,816	2,816	2,859	2,816
18,800	18,850	2,824	2,824	2,873	2,824
18,850	18,900	2,831	2,831	2,887	2,831
18,900	18,950	2,839	2,839	2,901	2,839
18,950	19,000	2,846	2,846	2,915	2,846
19,000					
19,000	19,050	2,854	2,854	2,929	2,854
19,050	19,100	2,861	2,861	2,943	2,861
19,100	19,150	2,869	2,869	2,957	2,869
19,150	19,200	2,876	2,876	2,971	2,876
19,200	19,250	2,884	2,884	2,985	2,884
19,250	19,300	2,891	2,891	2,999	2,891
19,300	19,350	2,899	2,899	3,013	2,899
19,350	19,400	2,906	2,906	3,027	2,906
19,400	19,450	2,914	2,914	3,041	2,914
19,450	19,500	2,921	2,921	3,055	2,921
19,500	19,550	2,929	2,929	3,069	2,929
19,550	19,600	2,936	2,936	3,083	2,936
19,600	19,650	2,944	2,944	3,097	2,944
19,650	19,700	2,951	2,951	3,111	2,951
19,700	19,750	2,959	2,959	3,125	2,959
19,750	19,800	2,966	2,966	3,139	2,966
19,800	19,850	2,974	2,974	3,153	2,974
19,850	19,900	2,981	2,981	3,167	2,981
19,900	19,950	2,989	2,989	3,181	2,989
19,950	20,000	2,996	2,996	3,195	2,996

If line 37 (taxable income) is— At least	But less than	Single	Married filing jointly*	Married filing separately	Head of a household
20,000					
20,000	20,050	3,004	3,004	3,209	3,004
20,050	20,100	3,011	3,011	3,223	3,011
20,100	20,150	3,019	3,019	3,237	3,019
20,150	20,200	3,026	3,026	3,251	3,026
20,200	20,250	3,034	3,034	3,265	3,034
20,250	20,300	3,041	3,041	3,279	3,041
20,300	20,350	3,049	3,049	3,293	3,049
20,350	20,400	3,056	3,056	3,307	3,056
20,400	20,450	3,064	3,064	3,321	3,064
20,450	20,500	3,071	3,071	3,335	3,071
20,500	20,550	3,079	3,079	3,349	3,079
20,550	20,600	3,086	3,086	3,363	3,086
20,600	20,650	3,094	3,094	3,377	3,094
20,650	20,700	3,101	3,101	3,391	3,101
20,700	20,750	3,109	3,109	3,405	3,109
20,750	20,800	3,116	3,116	3,419	3,116
20,800	20,850	3,124	3,124	3,433	3,124
20,850	20,900	3,131	3,131	3,447	3,131
20,900	20,950	3,139	3,139	3,461	3,139
20,950	21,000	3,146	3,146	3,475	3,146
21,000					
21,000	21,050	3,154	3,154	3,489	3,154
21,050	21,100	3,161	3,161	3,503	3,161
21,100	21,150	3,169	3,169	3,517	3,169
21,150	21,200	3,176	3,176	3,531	3,176
21,200	21,250	3,184	3,184	3,545	3,184
21,250	21,300	3,191	3,191	3,559	3,191
21,300	21,350	3,199	3,199	3,573	3,199
21,350	21,400	3,206	3,206	3,587	3,206
21,400	21,450	3,214	3,214	3,601	3,214
21,450	21,500	3,221	3,221	3,615	3,221
21,500	21,550	3,229	3,229	3,629	3,229
21,550	21,600	3,236	3,236	3,643	3,236
21,600	21,650	3,244	3,244	3,657	3,244
21,650	21,700	3,251	3,251	3,671	3,251
21,700	21,750	3,259	3,259	3,685	3,259
21,750	21,800	3,266	3,266	3,699	3,266
21,800	21,850	3,274	3,274	3,713	3,274
21,850	21,900	3,281	3,281	3,727	3,281
21,900	21,950	3,289	3,289	3,741	3,289
21,950	22,000	3,296	3,296	3,755	3,296
22,000					
22,000	22,050	3,304	3,304	3,769	3,304
22,050	22,100	3,311	3,311	3,783	3,311
22,100	22,150	3,322	3,319	3,797	3,319
22,150	22,200	3,336	3,326	3,811	3,326
22,200	22,250	3,350	3,334	3,825	3,334
22,250	22,300	3,364	3,341	3,839	3,341
22,300	22,350	3,378	3,349	3,853	3,349
22,350	22,400	3,392	3,356	3,867	3,356
22,400	22,450	3,406	3,364	3,881	3,364
22,450	22,500	3,420	3,371	3,895	3,371
22,500	22,550	3,434	3,379	3,909	3,379
22,550	22,600	3,448	3,386	3,923	3,386
22,600	22,650	3,462	3,394	3,937	3,394
22,650	22,700	3,476	3,401	3,951	3,401
22,700	22,750	3,490	3,409	3,965	3,409
22,750	22,800	3,504	3,416	3,979	3,416
22,800	22,850	3,518	3,424	3,993	3,424
22,850	22,900	3,532	3,431	4,007	3,431
22,900	22,950	3,546	3,439	4,021	3,439
22,950	23,000	3,560	3,446	4,035	3,446

* This column must also be used by a qualifying widow(er).

Continued on next page

1993 Tax Table—*Continued*

If line 37 (taxable income) is—		And you are—				If line 37 (taxable income) is—		And you are—				If line 37 (taxable income) is—		And you are—			
At least	But less than	Single	Married filing jointly *	Married filing separately	Head of a household	At least	But less than	Single	Married filing jointly *	Married filing separately	Head of a household	At least	But less than	Single	Married filing jointly *	Married filing separately	Head of a household
		Your tax is—						Your tax is—						Your tax is—			
23,000						**26,000**						**29,000**					
23,000	23,050	3,574	3,454	4,049	3,454	26,000	26,050	4,414	3,904	4,889	3,904	29,000	29,050	5,254	4,354	5,729	4,354
23,050	23,100	3,588	3,461	4,063	3,461	26,050	26,100	4,428	3,911	4,903	3,911	29,050	29,100	5,268	4,361	5,743	4,361
23,100	23,150	3,602	3,469	4,077	3,469	26,100	26,150	4,442	3,919	4,917	3,919	29,100	29,150	5,282	4,369	5,757	4,369
23,150	23,200	3,616	3,476	4,091	3,476	26,150	26,200	4,456	3,926	4,931	3,926	29,150	29,200	5,296	4,376	5,771	4,376
23,200	23,250	3,630	3,484	4,105	3,484	26,200	26,250	4,470	3,934	4,945	3,934	29,200	29,250	5,310	4,384	5,785	4,384
23,250	23,300	3,644	3,491	4,119	3,491	26,250	26,300	4,484	3,941	4,959	3,941	29,250	29,300	5,324	4,391	5,799	4,391
23,300	23,350	3,658	3,499	4,133	3,499	26,300	26,350	4,498	3,949	4,973	3,949	29,300	29,350	5,338	4,399	5,813	4,399
23,350	23,400	3,672	3,506	4,147	3,506	26,350	26,400	4,512	3,956	4,987	3,956	29,350	29,400	5,352	4,406	5,827	4,406
23,400	23,450	3,686	3,514	4,161	3,514	26,400	26,450	4,526	3,964	5,001	3,964	29,400	29,450	5,366	4,414	5,841	4,414
23,450	23,500	3,700	3,521	4,175	3,521	26,450	26,500	4,540	3,971	5,015	3,971	29,450	29,500	5,380	4,421	5,855	4,421
23,500	23,550	3,714	3,529	4,189	3,529	26,500	26,550	4,554	3,979	5,029	3,979	29,500	29,550	5,394	4,429	5,869	4,429
23,550	23,600	3,728	3,536	4,203	3,536	26,550	26,600	4,568	3,986	5,043	3,986	29,550	29,600	5,408	4,436	5,883	4,436
23,600	23,650	3,742	3,544	4,217	3,544	26,600	26,650	4,582	3,994	5,057	3,994	29,600	29,650	5,422	4,444	5,897	4,447
23,650	23,700	3,756	3,551	4,231	3,551	26,650	26,700	4,596	4,001	5,071	4,001	29,650	29,700	5,436	4,451	5,911	4,461
23,700	23,750	3,770	3,559	4,245	3,559	26,700	26,750	4,610	4,009	5,085	4,009	29,700	29,750	5,450	4,459	5,925	4,475
23,750	23,800	3,784	3,566	4,259	3,566	26,750	26,800	4,624	4,016	5,099	4,016	29,750	29,800	5,464	4,466	5,939	4,489
23,800	23,850	3,798	3,574	4,273	3,574	26,800	26,850	4,638	4,024	5,113	4,024	29,800	29,850	5,478	4,474	5,953	4,503
23,850	23,900	3,812	3,581	4,287	3,581	26,850	26,900	4,652	4,031	5,127	4,031	29,850	29,900	5,492	4,481	5,967	4,517
23,900	23,950	3,826	3,589	4,301	3,589	26,900	26,950	4,666	4,039	5,141	4,039	29,900	29,950	5,506	4,489	5,981	4,531
23,950	24,000	3,840	3,596	4,315	3,596	26,950	27,000	4,680	4,046	5,155	4,046	29,950	30,000	5,520	4,496	5,995	4,545
24,000						**27,000**						**30,000**					
24,000	24,050	3,854	3,604	4,329	3,604	27,000	27,050	4,694	4,054	5,169	4,054	30,000	30,050	5,534	4,504	6,009	4,559
24,050	24,100	3,868	3,611	4,343	3,611	27,050	27,100	4,708	4,061	5,183	4,061	30,050	30,100	5,548	4,511	6,023	4,573
24,100	24,150	3,882	3,619	4,357	3,619	27,100	27,150	4,722	4,069	5,197	4,069	30,100	30,150	5,562	4,519	6,037	4,587
24,150	24,200	3,896	3,626	4,371	3,626	27,150	27,200	4,736	4,076	5,211	4,076	30,150	30,200	5,576	4,526	6,051	4,601
24,200	24,250	3,910	3,634	4,385	3,634	27,200	27,250	4,750	4,084	5,225	4,084	30,200	30,250	5,590	4,534	6,065	4,615
24,250	24,300	3,924	3,641	4,399	3,641	27,250	27,300	4,764	4,091	5,239	4,091	30,250	30,300	5,604	4,541	6,079	4,629
24,300	24,350	3,938	3,649	4,413	3,649	27,300	27,350	4,778	4,099	5,253	4,099	30,300	30,350	5,618	4,549	6,093	4,643
24,350	24,400	3,952	3,656	4,427	3,656	27,350	27,400	4,792	4,106	5,267	4,106	30,350	30,400	5,632	4,556	6,107	4,657
24,400	24,450	3,966	3,664	4,441	3,664	27,400	27,450	4,806	4,114	5,281	4,114	30,400	30,450	5,646	4,564	6,121	4,671
24,450	24,500	3,980	3,671	4,455	3,671	27,450	27,500	4,820	4,121	5,295	4,121	30,450	30,500	5,660	4,571	6,135	4,685
24,500	24,550	3,994	3,679	4,469	3,679	27,500	27,550	4,834	4,129	5,309	4,129	30,500	30,550	5,674	4,579	6,149	4,699
24,550	24,600	4,008	3,686	4,483	3,686	27,550	27,600	4,848	4,136	5,323	4,136	30,550	30,600	5,688	4,586	6,163	4,713
24,600	24,650	4,022	3,694	4,497	3,694	27,600	27,650	4,862	4,144	5,337	4,144	30,600	30,650	5,702	4,594	6,177	4,727
24,650	24,700	4,036	3,701	4,511	3,701	27,650	27,700	4,876	4,151	5,351	4,151	30,650	30,700	5,716	4,601	6,191	4,741
24,700	24,750	4,050	3,709	4,525	3,709	27,700	27,750	4,890	4,159	5,365	4,159	30,700	30,750	5,730	4,609	6,205	4,755
24,750	24,800	4,064	3,716	4,539	3,716	27,750	27,800	4,904	4,166	5,379	4,166	30,750	30,800	5,744	4,616	6,219	4,769
24,800	24,850	4,078	3,724	4,553	3,724	27,800	27,850	4,918	4,174	5,393	4,174	30,800	30,850	5,758	4,624	6,233	4,783
24,850	24,900	4,092	3,731	4,567	3,731	27,850	27,900	4,932	4,181	5,407	4,181	30,850	30,900	5,772	4,631	6,247	4,797
24,900	24,950	4,106	3,739	4,581	3,739	27,900	27,950	4,946	4,189	5,421	4,189	30,900	30,950	5,786	4,639	6,261	4,811
24,950	25,000	4,120	3,746	4,595	3,746	27,950	28,000	4,960	4,196	5,435	4,196	30,950	31,000	5,800	4,646	6,275	4,825
25,000						**28,000**						**31,000**					
25,000	25,050	4,134	3,754	4,609	3,754	28,000	28,050	4,974	4,204	5,449	4,204	31,000	31,050	5,814	4,654	6,289	4,839
25,050	25,100	4,148	3,761	4,623	3,761	28,050	28,100	4,988	4,211	5,463	4,211	31,050	31,100	5,828	4,661	6,303	4,853
25,100	25,150	4,162	3,769	4,637	3,769	28,100	28,150	5,002	4,219	5,477	4,219	31,100	31,150	5,842	4,669	6,317	4,867
25,150	25,200	4,176	3,776	4,651	3,776	28,150	28,200	5,016	4,226	5,491	4,226	31,150	31,200	5,856	4,676	6,331	4,881
25,200	25,250	4,190	3,784	4,665	3,784	28,200	28,250	5,030	4,234	5,505	4,234	31,200	31,250	5,870	4,684	6,345	4,895
25,250	25,300	4,204	3,791	4,679	3,791	28,250	28,300	5,044	4,241	5,519	4,241	31,250	31,300	5,884	4,691	6,359	4,909
25,300	25,350	4,218	3,799	4,693	3,799	28,300	28,350	5,058	4,249	5,533	4,249	31,300	31,350	5,898	4,699	6,373	4,923
25,350	25,400	4,232	3,806	4,707	3,806	28,350	28,400	5,072	4,256	5,547	4,256	31,350	31,400	5,912	4,706	6,387	4,937
25,400	25,450	4,246	3,814	4,721	3,814	28,400	28,450	5,086	4,264	5,561	4,264	31,400	31,450	5,926	4,714	6,401	4,951
25,450	25,500	4,260	3,821	4,735	3,821	28,450	28,500	5,100	4,271	5,575	4,271	31,450	31,500	5,940	4,721	6,415	4,965
25,500	25,550	4,274	3,829	4,749	3,829	28,500	28,550	5,114	4,279	5,589	4,279	31,500	31,550	5,954	4,729	6,429	4,979
25,550	25,600	4,288	3,836	4,763	3,836	28,550	28,600	5,128	4,286	5,603	4,286	31,550	31,600	5,968	4,736	6,443	4,993
25,600	25,650	4,302	3,844	4,777	3,844	28,600	28,650	5,142	4,294	5,617	4,294	31,600	31,650	5,982	4,744	6,457	5,007
25,650	25,700	4,316	3,851	4,791	3,851	28,650	28,700	5,156	4,301	5,631	4,301	31,650	31,700	5,996	4,751	6,471	5,021
25,700	25,750	4,330	3,859	4,805	3,859	28,700	28,750	5,170	4,309	5,645	4,309	31,700	31,750	6,010	4,759	6,485	5,035
25,750	25,800	4,344	3,866	4,819	3,866	28,750	28,800	5,184	4,316	5,659	4,316	31,750	31,800	6,024	4,766	6,499	5,049
25,800	25,850	4,358	3,874	4,833	3,874	28,800	28,850	5,198	4,324	5,673	4,324	31,800	31,850	6,038	4,774	6,513	5,063
25,850	25,900	4,372	3,881	4,847	3,881	28,850	28,900	5,212	4,331	5,687	4,331	31,850	31,900	6,052	4,781	6,527	5,077
25,900	25,950	4,386	3,889	4,861	3,889	28,900	28,950	5,226	4,339	5,701	4,339	31,900	31,950	6,066	4,789	6,541	5,091
25,950	26,000	4,400	3,896	4,875	3,896	28,950	29,000	5,240	4,346	5,715	4,346	31,950	32,000	6,080	4,796	6,555	5,105

* This column must also be used by a qualifying widow(er).

Continued on next page

1993 Tax Table—*Continued*

Left column group:

If line 37 (taxable income) is— At least	But less than	Single	Married filing jointly *	Married filing separately	Head of a household
32,000					
32,000	32,050	6,094	4,804	6,569	5,119
32,050	32,100	6,108	4,811	6,583	5,133
32,100	32,150	6,122	4,819	6,597	5,147
32,150	32,200	6,136	4,826	6,611	5,161
32,200	32,250	6,150	4,834	6,625	5,175
32,250	32,300	6,164	4,841	6,639	5,189
32,300	32,350	6,178	4,849	6,653	5,203
32,350	32,400	6,192	4,856	6,667	5,217
32,400	32,450	6,206	4,864	6,681	5,231
32,450	32,500	6,220	4,871	6,695	5,245
32,500	32,550	6,234	4,879	6,709	5,259
32,550	32,600	6,248	4,886	6,723	5,273
32,600	32,650	6,262	4,894	6,737	5,287
32,650	32,700	6,276	4,901	6,751	5,301
32,700	32,750	6,290	4,909	6,765	5,315
32,750	32,800	6,304	4,916	6,779	5,329
32,800	32,850	6,318	4,924	6,793	5,343
32,850	32,900	6,332	4,931	6,807	5,357
32,900	32,950	6,346	4,939	6,821	5,371
32,950	33,000	6,360	4,946	6,835	5,385
33,000					
33,000	33,050	6,374	4,954	6,849	5,399
33,050	33,100	6,388	4,961	6,863	5,413
33,100	33,150	6,402	4,969	6,877	5,427
33,150	33,200	6,416	4,976	6,891	5,441
33,200	33,250	6,430	4,984	6,905	5,455
33,250	33,300	6,444	4,991	6,919	5,469
33,300	33,350	6,458	4,999	6,933	5,483
33,350	33,400	6,472	5,006	6,947	5,497
33,400	33,450	6,486	5,014	6,961	5,511
33,450	33,500	6,500	5,021	6,975	5,525
33,500	33,550	6,514	5,029	6,989	5,539
33,550	33,600	6,528	5,036	7,003	5,553
33,600	33,650	6,542	5,044	7,017	5,567
33,650	33,700	6,556	5,051	7,031	5,581
33,700	33,750	6,570	5,059	7,045	5,595
33,750	33,800	6,584	5,066	7,059	5,609
33,800	33,850	6,598	5,074	7,073	5,623
33,850	33,900	6,612	5,081	7,087	5,637
33,900	33,950	6,626	5,089	7,101	5,651
33,950	34,000	6,640	5,096	7,115	5,665
34,000					
34,000	34,050	6,654	5,104	7,129	5,679
34,050	34,100	6,668	5,111	7,143	5,693
34,100	34,150	6,682	5,119	7,157	5,707
34,150	34,200	6,696	5,126	7,171	5,721
34,200	34,250	6,710	5,134	7,185	5,735
34,250	34,300	6,724	5,141	7,199	5,749
34,300	34,350	6,738	5,149	7,213	5,763
34,350	34,400	6,752	5,156	7,227	5,777
34,400	34,450	6,766	5,164	7,241	5,791
34,450	34,500	6,780	5,171	7,255	5,805
34,500	34,550	6,794	5,179	7,269	5,819
34,550	34,600	6,808	5,186	7,283	5,833
34,600	34,650	6,822	5,194	7,297	5,847
34,650	34,700	6,836	5,201	7,311	5,861
34,700	34,750	6,850	5,209	7,325	5,875
34,750	34,800	6,864	5,216	7,339	5,889
34,800	34,850	6,878	5,224	7,353	5,903
34,850	34,900	6,892	5,231	7,367	5,917
34,900	34,950	6,906	5,239	7,381	5,931
34,950	35,000	6,920	5,246	7,395	5,945

Middle column group:

If line 37 (taxable income) is— At least	But less than	Single	Married filing jointly *	Married filing separately	Head of a household
35,000					
35,000	35,050	6,934	5,254	7,409	5,959
35,050	35,100	6,948	5,261	7,423	5,973
35,100	35,150	6,962	5,269	7,437	5,987
35,150	35,200	6,976	5,276	7,451	6,001
35,200	35,250	6,990	5,284	7,465	6,015
35,250	35,300	7,004	5,291	7,479	6,029
35,300	35,350	7,018	5,299	7,493	6,043
35,350	35,400	7,032	5,306	7,507	6,057
35,400	35,450	7,046	5,314	7,521	6,071
35,450	35,500	7,060	5,321	7,535	6,085
35,500	35,550	7,074	5,329	7,549	6,099
35,550	35,600	7,088	5,336	7,563	6,113
35,600	35,650	7,102	5,344	7,577	6,127
35,650	35,700	7,116	5,351	7,591	6,141
35,700	35,750	7,130	5,359	7,605	6,155
35,750	35,800	7,144	5,366	7,619	6,169
35,800	35,850	7,158	5,374	7,633	6,183
35,850	35,900	7,172	5,381	7,647	6,197
35,900	35,950	7,186	5,389	7,661	6,211
35,950	36,000	7,200	5,396	7,675	6,225
36,000					
36,000	36,050	7,214	5,404	7,689	6,239
36,050	36,100	7,228	5,411	7,703	6,253
36,100	36,150	7,242	5,419	7,717	6,267
36,150	36,200	7,256	5,426	7,731	6,281
36,200	36,250	7,270	5,434	7,745	6,295
36,250	36,300	7,284	5,441	7,759	6,309
36,300	36,350	7,298	5,449	7,773	6,323
36,350	36,400	7,312	5,456	7,787	6,337
36,400	36,450	7,326	5,464	7,801	6,351
36,450	36,500	7,340	5,471	7,815	6,365
36,500	36,550	7,354	5,479	7,829	6,379
36,550	36,600	7,368	5,486	7,843	6,393
36,600	36,650	7,382	5,494	7,857	6,407
36,650	36,700	7,396	5,501	7,871	6,421
36,700	36,750	7,410	5,509	7,885	6,435
36,750	36,800	7,424	5,516	7,899	6,449
36,800	36,850	7,438	5,524	7,913	6,463
36,850	36,900	7,452	5,531	7,927	6,477
36,900	36,950	7,466	5,542	7,941	6,491
36,950	37,000	7,480	5,556	7,955	6,505
37,000					
37,000	37,050	7,494	5,570	7,969	6,519
37,050	37,100	7,508	5,584	7,983	6,533
37,100	37,150	7,522	5,598	7,997	6,547
37,150	37,200	7,536	5,612	8,011	6,561
37,200	37,250	7,550	5,626	8,025	6,575
37,250	37,300	7,564	5,640	8,039	6,589
37,300	37,350	7,578	5,654	8,053	6,603
37,350	37,400	7,592	5,668	8,067	6,617
37,400	37,450	7,606	5,682	8,081	6,631
37,450	37,500	7,620	5,696	8,095	6,645
37,500	37,550	7,634	5,710	8,109	6,659
37,550	37,600	7,648	5,724	8,123	6,673
37,600	37,650	7,662	5,738	8,137	6,687
37,650	37,700	7,676	5,752	8,151	6,701
37,700	37,750	7,690	5,766	8,165	6,715
37,750	37,800	7,704	5,780	8,179	6,729
37,800	37,850	7,718	5,794	8,193	6,743
37,850	37,900	7,732	5,808	8,207	6,757
37,900	37,950	7,746	5,822	8,221	6,771
37,950	38,000	7,760	5,836	8,235	6,785

Right column group:

If line 37 (taxable income) is— At least	But less than	Single	Married filing jointly *	Married filing separately	Head of a household
38,000					
38,000	38,050	7,774	5,850	8,249	6,799
38,050	38,100	7,788	5,864	8,263	6,813
38,100	38,150	7,802	5,878	8,277	6,827
38,150	38,200	7,816	5,892	8,291	6,841
38,200	38,250	7,830	5,906	8,305	6,855
38,250	38,300	7,844	5,920	8,319	6,869
38,300	38,350	7,858	5,934	8,333	6,883
38,350	38,400	7,872	5,948	8,347	6,897
38,400	38,450	7,886	5,962	8,361	6,911
38,450	38,500	7,900	5,976	8,375	6,925
38,500	38,550	7,914	5,990	8,389	6,939
38,550	38,600	7,928	6,004	8,403	6,953
38,600	38,650	7,942	6,018	8,417	6,967
38,650	38,700	7,956	6,032	8,431	6,981
38,700	38,750	7,970	6,046	8,445	6,995
38,750	38,800	7,984	6,060	8,459	7,009
38,800	38,850	7,998	6,074	8,473	7,023
38,850	38,900	8,012	6,088	8,487	7,037
38,900	38,950	8,026	6,102	8,501	7,051
38,950	39,000	8,040	6,116	8,515	7,065
39,000					
39,000	39,050	8,054	6,130	8,529	7,079
39,050	39,100	8,068	6,144	8,543	7,093
39,100	39,150	8,082	6,158	8,557	7,107
39,150	39,200	8,096	6,172	8,571	7,121
39,200	39,250	8,110	6,186	8,585	7,135
39,250	39,300	8,124	6,200	8,599	7,149
39,300	39,350	8,138	6,214	8,613	7,163
39,350	39,400	8,152	6,228	8,627	7,177
39,400	39,450	8,166	6,242	8,641	7,191
39,450	39,500	8,180	6,256	8,655	7,205
39,500	39,550	8,194	6,270	8,669	7,219
39,550	39,600	8,208	6,284	8,683	7,233
39,600	39,650	8,222	6,298	8,697	7,247
39,650	39,700	8,236	6,312	8,711	7,261
39,700	39,750	8,250	6,326	8,725	7,275
39,750	39,800	8,264	6,340	8,739	7,289
39,800	39,850	8,278	6,354	8,753	7,303
39,850	39,900	8,292	6,368	8,767	7,317
39,900	39,950	8,306	6,382	8,781	7,331
39,950	40,000	8,320	6,396	8,795	7,345
40,000					
40,000	40,050	8,334	6,410	8,809	7,359
40,050	40,100	8,348	6,424	8,823	7,373
40,100	40,150	8,362	6,438	8,837	7,387
40,150	40,200	8,376	6,452	8,851	7,401
40,200	40,250	8,390	6,466	8,865	7,415
40,250	40,300	8,404	6,480	8,879	7,429
40,300	40,350	8,418	6,494	8,893	7,443
40,350	40,400	8,432	6,508	8,907	7,457
40,400	40,450	8,446	6,522	8,921	7,471
40,450	40,500	8,460	6,536	8,935	7,485
40,500	40,550	8,474	6,550	8,949	7,499
40,550	40,600	8,488	6,564	8,963	7,513
40,600	40,650	8,502	6,578	8,977	7,527
40,650	40,700	8,516	6,592	8,991	7,541
40,700	40,750	8,530	6,606	9,005	7,555
40,750	40,800	8,544	6,620	9,019	7,569
40,800	40,850	8,558	6,634	9,033	7,583
40,850	40,900	8,572	6,648	9,047	7,597
40,900	40,950	8,586	6,662	9,061	7,611
40,950	41,000	8,600	6,676	9,075	7,625

* This column must also be used by a qualifying widow(er).

Continued on next page

1993 Tax Table—*Continued*

If line 37 (taxable income) is— At least	But less than	Single	Married filing jointly *	Married filing separately	Head of a household
41,000					
41,000	41,050	8,614	6,690	9,089	7,639
41,050	41,100	8,628	6,704	9,103	7,653
41,100	41,150	8,642	6,718	9,117	7,667
41,150	41,200	8,656	6,732	9,131	7,681
41,200	41,250	8,670	6,746	9,145	7,695
41,250	41,300	8,684	6,760	9,159	7,709
41,300	41,350	8,698	6,774	9,173	7,723
41,350	41,400	8,712	6,788	9,187	7,737
41,400	41,450	8,726	6,802	9,201	7,751
41,450	41,500	8,740	6,816	9,215	7,765
41,500	41,550	8,754	6,830	9,229	7,779
41,550	41,600	8,768	6,844	9,243	7,793
41,600	41,650	8,782	6,858	9,257	7,807
41,650	41,700	8,796	6,872	9,271	7,821
41,700	41,750	8,810	6,886	9,285	7,835
41,750	41,800	8,824	6,900	9,299	7,849
41,800	41,850	8,838	6,914	9,313	7,863
41,850	41,900	8,852	6,928	9,327	7,877
41,900	41,950	8,866	6,942	9,341	7,891
41,950	42,000	8,880	6,956	9,355	7,905
42,000					
42,000	42,050	8,894	6,970	9,369	7,919
42,050	42,100	8,908	6,984	9,383	7,933
42,100	42,150	8,922	6,998	9,397	7,947
42,150	42,200	8,936	7,012	9,411	7,961
42,200	42,250	8,950	7,026	9,425	7,975
42,250	42,300	8,964	7,040	9,439	7,989
42,300	42,350	8,978	7,054	9,453	8,003
42,350	42,400	8,992	7,068	9,467	8,017
42,400	42,450	9,006	7,082	9,481	8,031
42,450	42,500	9,020	7,096	9,495	8,045
42,500	42,550	9,034	7,110	9,509	8,059
42,550	42,600	9,048	7,124	9,523	8,073
42,600	42,650	9,062	7,138	9,537	8,087
42,650	42,700	9,076	7,152	9,551	8,101
42,700	42,750	9,090	7,166	9,565	8,115
42,750	42,800	9,104	7,180	9,579	8,129
42,800	42,850	9,118	7,194	9,593	8,143
42,850	42,900	9,132	7,208	9,607	8,157
42,900	42,950	9,146	7,222	9,621	8,171
42,950	43,000	9,160	7,236	9,635	8,185
43,000					
43,000	43,050	9,174	7,250	9,649	8,199
43,050	43,100	9,188	7,264	9,663	8,213
43,100	43,150	9,202	7,278	9,677	8,227
43,150	43,200	9,216	7,292	9,691	8,241
43,200	43,250	9,230	7,306	9,705	8,255
43,250	43,300	9,244	7,320	9,719	8,269
43,300	43,350	9,258	7,334	9,733	8,283
43,350	43,400	9,272	7,348	9,747	8,297
43,400	43,450	9,286	7,362	9,761	8,311
43,450	43,500	9,300	7,376	9,775	8,325
43,500	43,550	9,314	7,390	9,789	8,339
43,550	43,600	9,328	7,404	9,803	8,353
43,600	43,650	9,342	7,418	9,817	8,367
43,650	43,700	9,356	7,432	9,831	8,381
43,700	43,750	9,370	7,446	9,845	8,395
43,750	43,800	9,384	7,460	9,859	8,409
43,800	43,850	9,398	7,474	9,873	8,423
43,850	43,900	9,412	7,488	9,887	8,437
43,900	43,950	9,426	7,502	9,901	8,451
43,950	44,000	9,440	7,516	9,915	8,465

If line 37 (taxable income) is— At least	But less than	Single	Married filing jointly *	Married filing separately	Head of a household
44,000					
44,000	44,050	9,454	7,530	9,929	8,479
44,050	44,100	9,468	7,544	9,943	8,493
44,100	44,150	9,482	7,558	9,957	8,507
44,150	44,200	9,496	7,572	9,971	8,521
44,200	44,250	9,510	7,586	9,985	8,535
44,250	44,300	9,524	7,600	9,999	8,549
44,300	44,350	9,538	7,614	10,013	8,563
44,350	44,400	9,552	7,628	10,027	8,577
44,400	44,450	9,566	7,642	10,041	8,591
44,450	44,500	9,580	7,656	10,055	8,605
44,500	44,550	9,594	7,670	10,069	8,619
44,550	44,600	9,608	7,684	10,083	8,633
44,600	44,650	9,622	7,698	10,098	8,647
44,650	44,700	9,636	7,712	10,114	8,661
44,700	44,750	9,650	7,726	10,129	8,675
44,750	44,800	9,664	7,740	10,145	8,689
44,800	44,850	9,678	7,754	10,160	8,703
44,850	44,900	9,692	7,768	10,176	8,717
44,900	44,950	9,706	7,782	10,191	8,731
44,950	45,000	9,720	7,796	10,207	8,745
45,000					
45,000	45,050	9,734	7,810	10,222	8,759
45,050	45,100	9,748	7,824	10,238	8,773
45,100	45,150	9,762	7,838	10,253	8,787
45,150	45,200	9,776	7,852	10,269	8,801
45,200	45,250	9,790	7,866	10,284	8,815
45,250	45,300	9,804	7,880	10,300	8,829
45,300	45,350	9,818	7,894	10,315	8,843
45,350	45,400	9,832	7,908	10,331	8,857
45,400	45,450	9,846	7,922	10,346	8,871
45,450	45,500	9,860	7,936	10,362	8,885
45,500	45,550	9,874	7,950	10,377	8,899
45,550	45,600	9,888	7,964	10,393	8,913
45,600	45,650	9,902	7,978	10,408	8,927
45,650	45,700	9,916	7,992	10,424	8,941
45,700	45,750	9,930	8,006	10,439	8,955
45,750	45,800	9,944	8,020	10,455	8,969
45,800	45,850	9,958	8,034	10,470	8,983
45,850	45,900	9,972	8,048	10,486	8,997
45,900	45,950	9,986	8,062	10,501	9,011
45,950	46,000	10,000	8,076	10,517	9,025
46,000					
46,000	46,050	10,014	8,090	10,532	9,039
46,050	46,100	10,028	8,104	10,548	9,053
46,100	46,150	10,042	8,118	10,563	9,067
46,150	46,200	10,056	8,132	10,579	9,081
46,200	46,250	10,070	8,146	10,594	9,095
46,250	46,300	10,084	8,160	10,610	9,109
46,300	46,350	10,098	8,174	10,625	9,123
46,350	46,400	10,112	8,188	10,641	9,137
46,400	46,450	10,126	8,202	10,656	9,151
46,450	46,500	10,140	8,216	10,672	9,165
46,500	46,550	10,154	8,230	10,687	9,179
46,550	46,600	10,168	8,244	10,703	9,193
46,600	46,650	10,182	8,258	10,718	9,207
46,650	46,700	10,196	8,272	10,734	9,221
46,700	46,750	10,210	8,286	10,749	9,235
46,750	46,800	10,224	8,300	10,765	9,249
46,800	46,850	10,238	8,314	10,780	9,263
46,850	46,900	10,252	8,328	10,796	9,277
46,900	46,950	10,266	8,342	10,811	9,291
46,950	47,000	10,280	8,356	10,827	9,305

If line 37 (taxable income) is— At least	But less than	Single	Married filing jointly *	Married filing separately	Head of a household
47,000					
47,000	47,050	10,294	8,370	10,842	9,319
47,050	47,100	10,308	8,384	10,858	9,333
47,100	47,150	10,322	8,398	10,873	9,347
47,150	47,200	10,336	8,412	10,889	9,361
47,200	47,250	10,350	8,426	10,904	9,375
47,250	47,300	10,364	8,440	10,920	9,389
47,300	47,350	10,378	8,454	10,935	9,403
47,350	47,400	10,392	8,468	10,951	9,417
47,400	47,450	10,406	8,482	10,966	9,431
47,450	47,500	10,420	8,496	10,982	9,445
47,500	47,550	10,434	8,510	10,997	9,459
47,550	47,600	10,448	8,524	11,013	9,473
47,600	47,650	10,462	8,538	11,028	9,487
47,650	47,700	10,476	8,552	11,044	9,501
47,700	47,750	10,490	8,566	11,059	9,515
47,750	47,800	10,504	8,580	11,075	9,529
47,800	47,850	10,518	8,594	11,090	9,543
47,850	47,900	10,532	8,608	11,106	9,557
47,900	47,950	10,546	8,622	11,121	9,571
47,950	48,000	10,560	8,636	11,137	9,585
48,000					
48,000	48,050	10,574	8,650	11,152	9,599
48,050	48,100	10,588	8,664	11,168	9,613
48,100	48,150	10,602	8,678	11,183	9,627
48,150	48,200	10,616	8,692	11,199	9,641
48,200	48,250	10,630	8,706	11,214	9,655
48,250	48,300	10,644	8,720	11,230	9,669
48,300	48,350	10,658	8,734	11,245	9,683
48,350	48,400	10,672	8,748	11,261	9,697
48,400	48,450	10,686	8,762	11,276	9,711
48,450	48,500	10,700	8,776	11,292	9,725
48,500	48,550	10,714	8,790	11,307	9,739
48,550	48,600	10,728	8,804	11,323	9,753
48,600	48,650	10,742	8,818	11,338	9,767
48,650	48,700	10,756	8,832	11,354	9,781
48,700	48,750	10,770	8,846	11,369	9,795
48,750	48,800	10,784	8,860	11,385	9,809
48,800	48,850	10,798	8,874	11,400	9,823
48,850	48,900	10,812	8,888	11,416	9,837
48,900	48,950	10,826	8,902	11,431	9,851
48,950	49,000	10,840	8,916	11,447	9,865
49,000					
49,000	49,050	10,854	8,930	11,462	9,879
49,050	49,100	10,868	8,944	11,478	9,893
49,100	49,150	10,882	8,958	11,493	9,907
49,150	49,200	10,896	8,972	11,509	9,921
49,200	49,250	10,910	8,986	11,524	9,935
49,250	49,300	10,924	9,000	11,540	9,949
49,300	49,350	10,938	9,014	11,555	9,963
49,350	49,400	10,952	9,028	11,571	9,977
49,400	49,450	10,966	9,042	11,586	9,991
49,450	49,500	10,980	9,056	11,602	10,005
49,500	49,550	10,994	9,070	11,617	10,019
49,550	49,600	11,008	9,084	11,633	10,033
49,600	49,650	11,022	9,098	11,648	10,047
49,650	49,700	11,036	9,112	11,664	10,061
49,700	49,750	11,050	9,126	11,679	10,075
49,750	49,800	11,064	9,140	11,695	10,089
49,800	49,850	11,078	9,154	11,710	10,103
49,850	49,900	11,092	9,168	11,726	10,117
49,900	49,950	11,106	9,182	11,741	10,131
49,950	50,000	11,120	9,196	11,757	10,145

* This column must also be used by a qualifying widow(er).

Continued on next page

1993 Tax Table—Continued

If line 37 (taxable income) is— At least	But less than	Single	Married filing jointly *	Married filing separately	Head of a house-hold
50,000					
50,000	50,050	11,134	9,210	11,772	10,159
50,050	50,100	11,148	9,224	11,788	10,173
50,100	50,150	11,162	9,238	11,803	10,187
50,150	50,200	11,176	9,252	11,819	10,201
50,200	50,250	11,190	9,266	11,834	10,215
50,250	50,300	11,204	9,280	11,850	10,229
50,300	50,350	11,218	9,294	11,865	10,243
50,350	50,400	11,232	9,308	11,881	10,257
50,400	50,450	11,246	9,322	11,896	10,271
50,450	50,500	11,260	9,336	11,912	10,285
50,500	50,550	11,274	9,350	11,927	10,299
50,550	50,600	11,288	9,364	11,943	10,313
50,600	50,650	11,302	9,378	11,958	10,327
50,650	50,700	11,316	9,392	11,974	10,341
50,700	50,750	11,330	9,406	11,989	10,355
50,750	50,800	11,344	9,420	12,005	10,369
50,800	50,850	11,358	9,434	12,020	10,383
50,850	50,900	11,372	9,448	12,036	10,397
50,900	50,950	11,386	9,462	12,051	10,411
50,950	51,000	11,400	9,476	12,067	10,425
51,000					
51,000	51,050	11,414	9,490	12,082	10,439
51,050	51,100	11,428	9,504	12,098	10,453
51,100	51,150	11,442	9,518	12,113	10,467
51,150	51,200	11,456	9,532	12,129	10,481
51,200	51,250	11,470	9,546	12,144	10,495
51,250	51,300	11,484	9,560	12,160	10,509
51,300	51,350	11,498	9,574	12,175	10,523
51,350	51,400	11,512	9,588	12,191	10,537
51,400	51,450	11,526	9,602	12,206	10,551
51,450	51,500	11,540	9,616	12,222	10,565
51,500	51,550	11,554	9,630	12,237	10,579
51,550	51,600	11,568	9,644	12,253	10,593
51,600	51,650	11,582	9,658	12,268	10,607
51,650	51,700	11,596	9,672	12,284	10,621
51,700	51,750	11,610	9,686	12,299	10,635
51,750	51,800	11,624	9,700	12,315	10,649
51,800	51,850	11,638	9,714	12,330	10,663
51,850	51,900	11,652	9,728	12,346	10,677
51,900	51,950	11,666	9,742	12,361	10,691
51,950	52,000	11,680	9,756	12,377	10,705
52,000					
52,000	52,050	11,694	9,770	12,392	10,719
52,050	52,100	11,708	9,784	12,408	10,733
52,100	52,150	11,722	9,798	12,423	10,747
52,150	52,200	11,736	9,812	12,439	10,761
52,200	52,250	11,750	9,826	12,454	10,775
52,250	52,300	11,764	9,840	12,470	10,789
52,300	52,350	11,778	9,854	12,485	10,803
52,350	52,400	11,792	9,868	12,501	10,817
52,400	52,450	11,806	9,882	12,516	10,831
52,450	52,500	11,820	9,896	12,532	10,845
52,500	52,550	11,834	9,910	12,547	10,859
52,550	52,600	11,848	9,924	12,563	10,873
52,600	52,650	11,862	9,938	12,578	10,887
52,650	52,700	11,876	9,952	12,594	10,901
52,700	52,750	11,890	9,966	12,609	10,915
52,750	52,800	11,904	9,980	12,625	10,929
52,800	52,850	11,918	9,994	12,640	10,943
52,850	52,900	11,932	10,008	12,656	10,957
52,900	52,950	11,946	10,022	12,671	10,971
52,950	53,000	11,960	10,036	12,687	10,985

If line 37 (taxable income) is— At least	But less than	Single	Married filing jointly *	Married filing separately	Head of a house-hold
53,000					
53,000	53,050	11,974	10,050	12,702	10,999
53,050	53,100	11,988	10,064	12,718	11,013
53,100	53,150	12,002	10,078	12,733	11,027
53,150	53,200	12,016	10,092	12,749	11,041
53,200	53,250	12,030	10,106	12,764	11,055
53,250	53,300	12,044	10,120	12,780	11,069
53,300	53,350	12,058	10,134	12,795	11,083
53,350	53,400	12,072	10,148	12,811	11,097
53,400	53,450	12,086	10,162	12,826	11,111
53,450	53,500	12,100	10,176	12,842	11,125
53,500	53,550	12,115	10,190	12,857	11,139
53,550	53,600	12,130	10,204	12,873	11,153
53,600	53,650	12,146	10,218	12,888	11,167
53,650	53,700	12,161	10,232	12,904	11,181
53,700	53,750	12,177	10,246	12,919	11,195
53,750	53,800	12,192	10,260	12,935	11,209
53,800	53,850	12,208	10,274	12,950	11,223
53,850	53,900	12,223	10,288	12,966	11,237
53,900	53,950	12,239	10,302	12,981	11,251
53,950	54,000	12,254	10,316	12,997	11,265
54,000					
54,000	54,050	12,270	10,330	13,012	11,279
54,050	54,100	12,285	10,344	13,028	11,293
54,100	54,150	12,301	10,358	13,043	11,307
54,150	54,200	12,316	10,372	13,059	11,321
54,200	54,250	12,332	10,386	13,074	11,335
54,250	54,300	12,347	10,400	13,090	11,349
54,300	54,350	12,363	10,414	13,105	11,363
54,350	54,400	12,378	10,428	13,121	11,377
54,400	54,450	12,394	10,442	13,136	11,391
54,450	54,500	12,409	10,456	13,152	11,405
54,500	54,550	12,425	10,470	13,167	11,419
54,550	54,600	12,440	10,484	13,183	11,433
54,600	54,650	12,456	10,498	13,198	11,447
54,650	54,700	12,471	10,512	13,214	11,461
54,700	54,750	12,487	10,526	13,229	11,475
54,750	54,800	12,502	10,540	13,245	11,489
54,800	54,850	12,518	10,554	13,260	11,503
54,850	54,900	12,533	10,568	13,276	11,517
54,900	54,950	12,549	10,582	13,291	11,531
54,950	55,000	12,564	10,596	13,307	11,545
55,000					
55,000	55,050	12,580	10,610	13,322	11,559
55,050	55,100	12,595	10,624	13,338	11,573
55,100	55,150	12,611	10,638	13,353	11,587
55,150	55,200	12,626	10,652	13,369	11,601
55,200	55,250	12,642	10,666	13,384	11,615
55,250	55,300	12,657	10,680	13,400	11,629
55,300	55,350	12,673	10,694	13,415	11,643
55,350	55,400	12,688	10,708	13,431	11,657
55,400	55,450	12,704	10,722	13,446	11,671
55,450	55,500	12,719	10,736	13,462	11,685
55,500	55,550	12,735	10,750	13,477	11,699
55,550	55,600	12,750	10,764	13,493	11,713
55,600	55,650	12,766	10,778	13,508	11,727
55,650	55,700	12,781	10,792	13,524	11,741
55,700	55,750	12,797	10,806	13,539	11,755
55,750	55,800	12,812	10,820	13,555	11,769
55,800	55,850	12,828	10,834	13,570	11,783
55,850	55,900	12,843	10,848	13,586	11,797
55,900	55,950	12,859	10,862	13,601	11,811
55,950	56,000	12,874	10,876	13,617	11,825

If line 37 (taxable income) is— At least	But less than	Single	Married filing jointly *	Married filing separately	Head of a house-hold
56,000					
56,000	56,050	12,890	10,890	13,632	11,839
56,050	56,100	12,905	10,904	13,648	11,853
56,100	56,150	12,921	10,918	13,663	11,867
56,150	56,200	12,936	10,932	13,679	11,881
56,200	56,250	12,952	10,946	13,694	11,895
56,250	56,300	12,967	10,960	13,710	11,909
56,300	56,350	12,983	10,974	13,725	11,923
56,350	56,400	12,998	10,988	13,741	11,937
56,400	56,450	13,014	11,002	13,756	11,951
56,450	56,500	13,029	11,016	13,772	11,965
56,500	56,550	13,045	11,030	13,787	11,979
56,550	56,600	13,060	11,044	13,803	11,993
56,600	56,650	13,076	11,058	13,818	12,007
56,650	56,700	13,091	11,072	13,834	12,021
56,700	56,750	13,107	11,086	13,849	12,035
56,750	56,800	13,122	11,100	13,865	12,049
56,800	56,850	13,138	11,114	13,880	12,063
56,850	56,900	13,153	11,128	13,896	12,077
56,900	56,950	13,169	11,142	13,911	12,091
56,950	57,000	13,184	11,156	13,927	12,105
57,000					
57,000	57,050	13,200	11,170	13,942	12,119
57,050	57,100	13,215	11,184	13,958	12,133
57,100	57,150	13,231	11,198	13,973	12,147
57,150	57,200	13,246	11,212	13,989	12,161
57,200	57,250	13,262	11,226	14,004	12,175
57,250	57,300	13,277	11,240	14,020	12,189
57,300	57,350	13,293	11,254	14,035	12,203
57,350	57,400	13,308	11,268	14,051	12,217
57,400	57,450	13,324	11,282	14,066	12,231
57,450	57,500	13,339	11,296	14,082	12,245
57,500	57,550	13,355	11,310	14,097	12,259
57,550	57,600	13,370	11,324	14,113	12,273
57,600	57,650	13,386	11,338	14,128	12,287
57,650	57,700	13,401	11,352	14,144	12,301
57,700	57,750	13,417	11,366	14,159	12,315
57,750	57,800	13,432	11,380	14,175	12,329
57,800	57,850	13,448	11,394	14,190	12,343
57,850	57,900	13,463	11,408	14,206	12,357
57,900	57,950	13,479	11,422	14,221	12,371
57,950	58,000	13,494	11,436	14,237	12,385
58,000					
58,000	58,050	13,510	11,450	14,252	12,399
58,050	58,100	13,525	11,464	14,268	12,413
58,100	58,150	13,541	11,478	14,283	12,427
58,150	58,200	13,556	11,492	14,299	12,441
58,200	58,250	13,572	11,506	14,314	12,455
58,250	58,300	13,587	11,520	14,330	12,469
58,300	58,350	13,603	11,534	14,345	12,483
58,350	58,400	13,618	11,548	14,361	12,497
58,400	58,450	13,634	11,562	14,376	12,511
58,450	58,500	13,649	11,576	14,392	12,525
58,500	58,550	13,665	11,590	14,407	12,539
58,550	58,600	13,680	11,604	14,423	12,553
58,600	58,650	13,696	11,618	14,438	12,567
58,650	58,700	13,711	11,632	14,454	12,581
58,700	58,750	13,727	11,646	14,469	12,595
58,750	58,800	13,742	11,660	14,485	12,609
58,800	58,850	13,758	11,674	14,500	12,623
58,850	58,900	13,773	11,688	14,516	12,637
58,900	58,950	13,789	11,702	14,531	12,651
58,950	59,000	13,804	11,716	14,547	12,665

* This column must also be used by a qualifying widow(er).

Continued on next page

1993 Tax Table—*Continued*

If line 37 (taxable income) is— At least	But less than	Single	Married filing jointly *	Married filing separately	Head of a household
			Your tax is—		
59,000					
59,000	59,050	13,820	11,730	14,562	12,679
59,050	59,100	13,835	11,744	14,578	12,693
59,100	59,150	13,851	11,758	14,593	12,707
59,150	59,200	13,866	11,772	14,609	12,721
59,200	59,250	13,882	11,786	14,624	12,735
59,250	59,300	13,897	11,800	14,640	12,749
59,300	59,350	13,913	11,814	14,655	12,763
59,350	59,400	13,928	11,828	14,671	12,777
59,400	59,450	13,944	11,842	14,686	12,791
59,450	59,500	13,959	11,856	14,702	12,805
59,500	59,550	13,975	11,870	14,717	12,819
59,550	59,600	13,990	11,884	14,733	12,833
59,600	59,650	14,006	11,898	14,748	12,847
59,650	59,700	14,021	11,912	14,764	12,861
59,700	59,750	14,037	11,926	14,779	12,875
59,750	59,800	14,052	11,940	14,795	12,889
59,800	59,850	14,068	11,954	14,810	12,903
59,850	59,900	14,083	11,968	14,826	12,917
59,900	59,950	14,099	11,982	14,841	12,931
59,950	60,000	14,114	11,996	14,857	12,945
60,000					
60,000	60,050	14,130	12,010	14,872	12,959
60,050	60,100	14,145	12,024	14,888	12,973
60,100	60,150	14,161	12,038	14,903	12,987
60,150	60,200	14,176	12,052	14,919	13,001
60,200	60,250	14,192	12,066	14,934	13,015
60,250	60,300	14,207	12,080	14,950	13,029
60,300	60,350	14,223	12,094	14,965	13,043
60,350	60,400	14,238	12,108	14,981	13,057
60,400	60,450	14,254	12,122	14,996	13,071
60,450	60,500	14,269	12,136	15,012	13,085
60,500	60,550	14,285	12,150	15,027	13,099
60,550	60,600	14,300	12,164	15,043	13,113
60,600	60,650	14,316	12,178	15,058	13,127
60,650	60,700	14,331	12,192	15,074	13,141
60,700	60,750	14,347	12,206	15,089	13,155
60,750	60,800	14,362	12,220	15,105	13,169
60,800	60,850	14,378	12,234	15,120	13,183
60,850	60,900	14,393	12,248	15,136	13,197
60,900	60,950	14,409	12,262	15,151	13,211
60,950	61,000	14,424	12,276	15,167	13,225
61,000					
61,000	61,050	14,440	12,290	15,182	13,239
61,050	61,100	14,455	12,304	15,198	13,253
61,100	61,150	14,471	12,318	15,213	13,267
61,150	61,200	14,486	12,332	15,229	13,281
61,200	61,250	14,502	12,346	15,244	13,295
61,250	61,300	14,517	12,360	15,260	13,309
61,300	61,350	14,533	12,374	15,275	13,323
61,350	61,400	14,548	12,388	15,291	13,337
61,400	61,450	14,564	12,402	15,306	13,351
61,450	61,500	14,579	12,416	15,322	13,365
61,500	61,550	14,595	12,430	15,337	13,379
61,550	61,600	14,610	12,444	15,353	13,393
61,600	61,650	14,626	12,458	15,368	13,407
61,650	61,700	14,641	12,472	15,384	13,421
61,700	61,750	14,657	12,486	15,399	13,435
61,750	61,800	14,672	12,500	15,415	13,449
61,800	61,850	14,688	12,514	15,430	13,463
61,850	61,900	14,703	12,528	15,446	13,477
61,900	61,950	14,719	12,542	15,461	13,491
61,950	62,000	14,734	12,556	15,477	13,505

If line 37 (taxable income) is— At least	But less than	Single	Married filing jointly *	Married filing separately	Head of a household
			Your tax is—		
62,000					
62,000	62,050	14,750	12,570	15,492	13,519
62,050	62,100	14,765	12,584	15,508	13,533
62,100	62,150	14,781	12,598	15,523	13,547
62,150	62,200	14,796	12,612	15,539	13,561
62,200	62,250	14,812	12,626	15,554	13,575
62,250	62,300	14,827	12,640	15,570	13,589
62,300	62,350	14,843	12,654	15,585	13,603
62,350	62,400	14,858	12,668	15,601	13,617
62,400	62,450	14,874	12,682	15,616	13,631
62,450	62,500	14,889	12,696	15,632	13,645
62,500	62,550	14,905	12,710	15,647	13,659
62,550	62,600	14,920	12,724	15,663	13,673
62,600	62,650	14,936	12,738	15,678	13,687
62,650	62,700	14,951	12,752	15,694	13,701
62,700	62,750	14,967	12,766	15,709	13,715
62,750	62,800	14,982	12,780	15,725	13,729
62,800	62,850	14,998	12,794	15,740	13,743
62,850	62,900	15,013	12,808	15,756	13,757
62,900	62,950	15,029	12,822	15,771	13,771
62,950	63,000	15,044	12,836	15,787	13,785
63,000					
63,000	63,050	15,060	12,850	15,802	13,799
63,050	63,100	15,075	12,864	15,818	13,813
63,100	63,150	15,091	12,878	15,833	13,827
63,150	63,200	15,106	12,892	15,849	13,841
63,200	63,250	15,122	12,906	15,864	13,855
63,250	63,300	15,137	12,920	15,880	13,869
63,300	63,350	15,153	12,934	15,895	13,883
63,350	63,400	15,168	12,948	15,911	13,897
63,400	63,450	15,184	12,962	15,926	13,911
63,450	63,500	15,199	12,976	15,942	13,925
63,500	63,550	15,215	12,990	15,957	13,939
63,550	63,600	15,230	13,004	15,973	13,953
63,600	63,650	15,246	13,018	15,988	13,967
63,650	63,700	15,261	13,032	16,004	13,981
63,700	63,750	15,277	13,046	16,019	13,995
63,750	63,800	15,292	13,060	16,035	14,009
63,800	63,850	15,308	13,074	16,050	14,023
63,850	63,900	15,323	13,088	16,066	14,037
63,900	63,950	15,339	13,102	16,081	14,051
63,950	64,000	15,354	13,116	16,097	14,065
64,000					
64,000	64,050	15,370	13,130	16,112	14,079
64,050	64,100	15,385	13,144	16,128	14,093
64,100	64,150	15,401	13,158	16,143	14,107
64,150	64,200	15,416	13,172	16,159	14,121
64,200	64,250	15,432	13,186	16,174	14,135
64,250	64,300	15,447	13,200	16,190	14,149
64,300	64,350	15,463	13,214	16,205	14,163
64,350	64,400	15,478	13,228	16,221	14,177
64,400	64,450	15,494	13,242	16,236	14,191
64,450	64,500	15,509	13,256	16,252	14,205
64,500	64,550	15,525	13,270	16,267	14,219
64,550	64,600	15,540	13,284	16,283	14,233
64,600	64,650	15,556	13,298	16,298	14,247
64,650	64,700	15,571	13,312	16,314	14,261
64,700	64,750	15,587	13,326	16,329	14,275
64,750	64,800	15,602	13,340	16,345	14,289
64,800	64,850	15,618	13,354	16,360	14,303
64,850	64,900	15,633	13,368	16,376	14,317
64,900	64,950	15,649	13,382	16,391	14,331
64,950	65,000	15,664	13,396	16,407	14,345

If line 37 (taxable income) is— At least	But less than	Single	Married filing jointly *	Married filing separately	Head of a household
			Your tax is—		
65,000					
65,000	65,050	15,680	13,410	16,422	14,359
65,050	65,100	15,695	13,424	16,438	14,373
65,100	65,150	15,711	13,438	16,453	14,387
65,150	65,200	15,726	13,452	16,469	14,401
65,200	65,250	15,742	13,466	16,484	14,415
65,250	65,300	15,757	13,480	16,500	14,429
65,300	65,350	15,773	13,494	16,515	14,443
65,350	65,400	15,788	13,508	16,531	14,457
65,400	65,450	15,804	13,522	16,546	14,471
65,450	65,500	15,819	13,536	16,562	14,485
65,500	65,550	15,835	13,550	16,577	14,499
65,550	65,600	15,850	13,564	16,593	14,513
65,600	65,650	15,866	13,578	16,608	14,527
65,650	65,700	15,881	13,592	16,624	14,541
65,700	65,750	15,897	13,606	16,639	14,555
65,750	65,800	15,912	13,620	16,655	14,569
65,800	65,850	15,928	13,634	16,670	14,583
65,850	65,900	15,943	13,648	16,686	14,597
65,900	65,950	15,959	13,662	16,701	14,611
65,950	66,000	15,974	13,676	16,717	14,625
66,000					
66,000	66,050	15,990	13,690	16,732	14,639
66,050	66,100	16,005	13,704	16,748	14,653
66,100	66,150	16,021	13,718	16,763	14,667
66,150	66,200	16,036	13,732	16,779	14,681
66,200	66,250	16,052	13,746	16,794	14,695
66,250	66,300	16,067	13,760	16,810	14,709
66,300	66,350	16,083	13,774	16,825	14,723
66,350	66,400	16,098	13,788	16,841	14,737
66,400	66,450	16,114	13,802	16,856	14,751
66,450	66,500	16,129	13,816	16,872	14,765
66,500	66,550	16,145	13,830	16,887	14,779
66,550	66,600	16,160	13,844	16,903	14,793
66,600	66,650	16,176	13,858	16,918	14,807
66,650	66,700	16,191	13,872	16,934	14,821
66,700	66,750	16,207	13,886	16,949	14,835
66,750	66,800	16,222	13,900	16,965	14,849
66,800	66,850	16,238	13,914	16,980	14,863
66,850	66,900	16,253	13,928	16,996	14,877
66,900	66,950	16,269	13,942	17,011	14,891
66,950	67,000	16,284	13,956	17,027	14,905
67,000					
67,000	67,050	16,300	13,970	17,042	14,919
67,050	67,100	16,315	13,984	17,058	14,933
67,100	67,150	16,331	13,998	17,073	14,947
67,150	67,200	16,346	14,012	17,089	14,961
67,200	67,250	16,362	14,026	17,104	14,975
67,250	67,300	16,377	14,040	17,120	14,989
67,300	67,350	16,393	14,054	17,135	15,003
67,350	67,400	16,408	14,068	17,151	15,017
67,400	67,450	16,424	14,082	17,166	15,031
67,450	67,500	16,439	14,096	17,182	15,045
67,500	67,550	16,455	14,110	17,197	15,059
67,550	67,600	16,470	14,124	17,213	15,073
67,600	67,650	16,486	14,138	17,228	15,087
67,650	67,700	16,501	14,152	17,244	15,101
67,700	67,750	16,517	14,166	17,259	15,115
67,750	67,800	16,532	14,180	17,275	15,129
67,800	67,850	16,548	14,194	17,290	15,143
67,850	67,900	16,563	14,208	17,306	15,157
67,900	67,950	16,579	14,222	17,321	15,171
67,950	68,000	16,594	14,236	17,337	15,185

* This column must also be used by a qualifying widow(er).

Continued on next page

1993 Tax Table—*Continued*

If line 37 (taxable income) is— At least	But less than	Single	Married filing jointly*	Married filing separately	Head of a household
68,000					
68,000	68,050	16,610	14,250	17,352	15,199
68,050	68,100	16,625	14,264	17,368	15,213
68,100	68,150	16,641	14,278	17,383	15,227
68,150	68,200	16,656	14,292	17,399	15,241
68,200	68,250	16,672	14,306	17,414	15,255
68,250	68,300	16,687	14,320	17,430	15,269
68,300	68,350	16,703	14,334	17,445	15,283
68,350	68,400	16,718	14,348	17,461	15,297
68,400	68,450	16,734	14,362	17,476	15,311
68,450	68,500	16,749	14,376	17,492	15,325
68,500	68,550	16,765	14,390	17,507	15,339
68,550	68,600	16,780	14,404	17,523	15,353
68,600	68,650	16,796	14,418	17,538	15,367
68,650	68,700	16,811	14,432	17,554	15,381
68,700	68,750	16,827	14,446	17,569	15,395
68,750	68,800	16,842	14,460	17,585	15,409
68,800	68,850	16,858	14,474	17,600	15,423
68,850	68,900	16,873	14,488	17,616	15,437
68,900	68,950	16,889	14,502	17,631	15,451
68,950	69,000	16,904	14,516	17,647	15,465
69,000					
69,000	69,050	16,920	14,530	17,662	15,479
69,050	69,100	16,935	14,544	17,678	15,493
69,100	69,150	16,951	14,558	17,693	15,507
69,150	69,200	16,966	14,572	17,709	15,521
69,200	69,250	16,982	14,586	17,724	15,535
69,250	69,300	16,997	14,600	17,740	15,549
69,300	69,350	17,013	14,614	17,755	15,563
69,350	69,400	17,028	14,628	17,771	15,577
69,400	69,450	17,044	14,642	17,786	15,591
69,450	69,500	17,059	14,656	17,802	15,605
69,500	69,550	17,075	14,670	17,817	15,619
69,550	69,600	17,090	14,684	17,833	15,633
69,600	69,650	17,106	14,698	17,848	15,647
69,650	69,700	17,121	14,712	17,864	15,661
69,700	69,750	17,137	14,726	17,879	15,675
69,750	69,800	17,152	14,740	17,895	15,689
69,800	69,850	17,168	14,754	17,910	15,703
69,850	69,900	17,183	14,768	17,926	15,717
69,900	69,950	17,199	14,782	17,941	15,731
69,950	70,000	17,214	14,796	17,957	15,745
70,000					
70,000	70,050	17,230	14,810	17,973	15,759
70,050	70,100	17,245	14,824	17,991	15,773
70,100	70,150	17,261	14,838	18,009	15,787
70,150	70,200	17,276	14,852	18,027	15,801
70,200	70,250	17,292	14,866	18,045	15,815
70,250	70,300	17,307	14,880	18,063	15,829
70,300	70,350	17,323	14,894	18,081	15,843
70,350	70,400	17,338	14,908	18,099	15,857
70,400	70,450	17,354	14,922	18,117	15,871
70,450	70,500	17,369	14,936	18,135	15,885
70,500	70,550	17,385	14,950	18,153	15,899
70,550	70,600	17,400	14,964	18,171	15,913
70,600	70,650	17,416	14,978	18,189	15,927
70,650	70,700	17,431	14,992	18,207	15,941
70,700	70,750	17,447	15,006	18,225	15,955
70,750	70,800	17,462	15,020	18,243	15,969
70,800	70,850	17,478	15,034	18,261	15,983
70,850	70,900	17,493	15,048	18,279	15,997
70,900	70,950	17,509	15,062	18,297	16,011
70,950	71,000	17,524	15,076	18,315	16,025

If line 37 (taxable income) is— At least	But less than	Single	Married filing jointly*	Married filing separately	Head of a household
71,000					
71,000	71,050	17,540	15,090	18,333	16,039
71,050	71,100	17,555	15,104	18,351	16,053
71,100	71,150	17,571	15,118	18,369	16,067
71,150	71,200	17,586	15,132	18,387	16,081
71,200	71,250	17,602	15,146	18,405	16,095
71,250	71,300	17,617	15,160	18,423	16,109
71,300	71,350	17,633	15,174	18,441	16,123
71,350	71,400	17,648	15,188	18,459	16,137
71,400	71,450	17,664	15,202	18,477	16,151
71,450	71,500	17,679	15,216	18,495	16,165
71,500	71,550	17,695	15,230	18,513	16,179
71,550	71,600	17,710	15,244	18,531	16,193
71,600	71,650	17,726	15,258	18,549	16,207
71,650	71,700	17,741	15,272	18,567	16,221
71,700	71,750	17,757	15,286	18,585	16,235
71,750	71,800	17,772	15,300	18,603	16,249
71,800	71,850	17,788	15,314	18,621	16,263
71,850	71,900	17,803	15,328	18,639	16,277
71,900	71,950	17,819	15,342	18,657	16,291
71,950	72,000	17,834	15,356	18,675	16,305
72,000					
72,000	72,050	17,850	15,370	18,693	16,319
72,050	72,100	17,865	15,384	18,711	16,333
72,100	72,150	17,881	15,398	18,729	16,347
72,150	72,200	17,896	15,412	18,747	16,361
72,200	72,250	17,912	15,426	18,765	16,375
72,250	72,300	17,927	15,440	18,783	16,389
72,300	72,350	17,943	15,454	18,801	16,403
72,350	72,400	17,958	15,468	18,819	16,417
72,400	72,450	17,974	15,482	18,837	16,431
72,450	72,500	17,989	15,496	18,855	16,445
72,500	72,550	18,005	15,510	18,873	16,459
72,550	72,600	18,020	15,524	18,891	16,473
72,600	72,650	18,036	15,538	18,909	16,487
72,650	72,700	18,051	15,552	18,927	16,501
72,700	72,750	18,067	15,566	18,945	16,515
72,750	72,800	18,082	15,580	18,963	16,529
72,800	72,850	18,098	15,594	18,981	16,543
72,850	72,900	18,113	15,608	18,999	16,557
72,900	72,950	18,129	15,622	19,017	16,571
72,950	73,000	18,144	15,636	19,035	16,585
73,000					
73,000	73,050	18,160	15,650	19,053	16,599
73,050	73,100	18,175	15,664	19,071	16,613
73,100	73,150	18,191	15,678	19,089	16,627
73,150	73,200	18,206	15,692	19,107	16,641
73,200	73,250	18,222	15,706	19,125	16,655
73,250	73,300	18,237	15,720	19,143	16,669
73,300	73,350	18,253	15,734	19,161	16,683
73,350	73,400	18,268	15,748	19,179	16,697
73,400	73,450	18,284	15,762	19,197	16,711
73,450	73,500	18,299	15,776	19,215	16,725
73,500	73,550	18,315	15,790	19,233	16,739
73,550	73,600	18,330	15,804	19,251	16,753
73,600	73,650	18,346	15,818	19,269	16,767
73,650	73,700	18,361	15,832	19,287	16,781
73,700	73,750	18,377	15,846	19,305	16,795
73,750	73,800	18,392	15,860	19,323	16,809
73,800	73,850	18,408	15,874	19,341	16,823
73,850	73,900	18,423	15,888	19,359	16,837
73,900	73,950	18,439	15,902	19,377	16,851
73,950	74,000	18,454	15,916	19,395	16,865

If line 37 (taxable income) is— At least	But less than	Single	Married filing jointly*	Married filing separately	Head of a household
74,000					
74,000	74,050	18,470	15,930	19,413	16,879
74,050	74,100	18,485	15,944	19,431	16,893
74,100	74,150	18,501	15,958	19,449	16,907
74,150	74,200	18,516	15,972	19,467	16,921
74,200	74,250	18,532	15,986	19,485	16,935
74,250	74,300	18,547	16,000	19,503	16,949
74,300	74,350	18,563	16,014	19,521	16,963
74,350	74,400	18,578	16,028	19,539	16,977
74,400	74,450	18,594	16,042	19,557	16,991
74,450	74,500	18,609	16,056	19,575	17,005
74,500	74,550	18,625	16,070	19,593	17,019
74,550	74,600	18,640	16,084	19,611	17,033
74,600	74,650	18,656	16,098	19,629	17,047
74,650	74,700	18,671	16,112	19,647	17,061
74,700	74,750	18,687	16,126	19,665	17,075
74,750	74,800	18,702	16,140	19,683	17,089
74,800	74,850	18,718	16,154	19,701	17,103
74,850	74,900	18,733	16,168	19,719	17,117
74,900	74,950	18,749	16,182	19,737	17,131
74,950	75,000	18,764	16,196	19,755	17,145
75,000					
75,000	75,050	18,780	16,210	19,773	17,159
75,050	75,100	18,795	16,224	19,791	17,173
75,100	75,150	18,811	16,238	19,809	17,187
75,150	75,200	18,826	16,252	19,827	17,201
75,200	75,250	18,842	16,266	19,845	17,215
75,250	75,300	18,857	16,280	19,863	17,229
75,300	75,350	18,873	16,294	19,881	17,243
75,350	75,400	18,888	16,308	19,899	17,257
75,400	75,450	18,904	16,322	19,917	17,271
75,450	75,500	18,919	16,336	19,935	17,285
75,500	75,550	18,935	16,350	19,953	17,299
75,550	75,600	18,950	16,364	19,971	17,313
75,600	75,650	18,966	16,378	19,989	17,327
75,650	75,700	18,981	16,392	20,007	17,341
75,700	75,750	18,997	16,406	20,025	17,355
75,750	75,800	19,012	16,420	20,043	17,369
75,800	75,850	19,028	16,434	20,061	17,383
75,850	75,900	19,043	16,448	20,079	17,397
75,900	75,950	19,059	16,462	20,097	17,411
75,950	76,000	19,074	16,476	20,115	17,425
76,000					
76,000	76,050	19,090	16,490	20,133	17,439
76,050	76,100	19,105	16,504	20,151	17,453
76,100	76,150	19,121	16,518	20,169	17,467
76,150	76,200	19,136	16,532	20,187	17,481
76,200	76,250	19,152	16,546	20,205	17,495
76,250	76,300	19,167	16,560	20,223	17,509
76,300	76,350	19,183	16,574	20,241	17,523
76,350	76,400	19,198	16,588	20,259	17,537
76,400	76,450	19,214	16,602	20,277	17,552
76,450	76,500	19,229	16,616	20,295	17,567
76,500	76,550	19,245	16,630	20,313	17,583
76,550	76,600	19,260	16,644	20,331	17,598
76,600	76,650	19,276	16,658	20,349	17,614
76,650	76,700	19,291	16,672	20,367	17,629
76,700	76,750	19,307	16,686	20,385	17,645
76,750	76,800	19,322	16,700	20,403	17,660
76,800	76,850	19,338	16,714	20,421	17,676
76,850	76,900	19,353	16,728	20,439	17,691
76,900	76,950	19,369	16,742	20,457	17,707
76,950	77,000	19,384	16,756	20,475	17,722

* This column must also be used by a qualifying widow(er).

Continued on next page

1993 Tax Table—*Continued*

If line 37 (taxable income) is—		And you are—			
At least	But less than	Single	Married filing jointly *	Married filing separately	Head of a household
		Your tax is—			
77,000					
77,000	77,050	19,400	16,770	20,493	17,738
77,050	77,100	19,415	16,784	20,511	17,753
77,100	77,150	19,431	16,798	20,529	17,769
77,150	77,200	19,446	16,812	20,547	17,784
77,200	77,250	19,462	16,826	20,565	17,800
77,250	77,300	19,477	16,840	20,583	17,815
77,300	77,350	19,493	16,854	20,601	17,831
77,350	77,400	19,508	16,868	20,619	17,846
77,400	77,450	19,524	16,882	20,637	17,862
77,450	77,500	19,539	16,896	20,655	17,877
77,500	77,550	19,555	16,910	20,673	17,893
77,550	77,600	19,570	16,924	20,691	17,908
77,600	77,650	19,586	16,938	20,709	17,924
77,650	77,700	19,601	16,952	20,727	17,939
77,700	77,750	19,617	16,966	20,745	17,955
77,750	77,800	19,632	16,980	20,763	17,970
77,800	77,850	19,648	16,994	20,781	17,986
77,850	77,900	19,663	17,008	20,799	18,001
77,900	77,950	19,679	17,022	20,817	18,017
77,950	78,000	19,694	17,036	20,835	18,032
78,000					
78,000	78,050	19,710	17,050	20,853	18,048
78,050	78,100	19,725	17,064	20,871	18,063
78,100	78,150	19,741	17,078	20,889	18,079
78,150	78,200	19,756	17,092	20,907	18,094
78,200	78,250	19,772	17,106	20,925	18,110
78,250	78,300	19,787	17,120	20,943	18,125
78,300	78,350	19,803	17,134	20,961	18,141
78,350	78,400	19,818	17,148	20,979	18,156
78,400	78,450	19,834	17,162	20,997	18,172
78,450	78,500	19,849	17,176	21,015	18,187
78,500	78,550	19,865	17,190	21,033	18,203
78,550	78,600	19,880	17,204	21,051	18,218
78,600	78,650	19,896	17,218	21,069	18,234
78,650	78,700	19,911	17,232	21,087	18,249
78,700	78,750	19,927	17,246	21,105	18,265
78,750	78,800	19,942	17,260	21,123	18,280
78,800	78,850	19,958	17,274	21,141	18,296
78,850	78,900	19,973	17,288	21,159	18,311
78,900	78,950	19,989	17,302	21,177	18,327
78,950	79,000	20,004	17,316	21,195	18,342
79,000					
79,000	79,050	20,020	17,330	21,213	18,358
79,050	79,100	20,035	17,344	21,231	18,373
79,100	79,150	20,051	17,358	21,249	18,389
79,150	79,200	20,066	17,372	21,267	18,404
79,200	79,250	20,082	17,386	21,285	18,420
79,250	79,300	20,097	17,400	21,303	18,435
79,300	79,350	20,113	17,414	21,321	18,451
79,350	79,400	20,128	17,428	21,339	18,466
79,400	79,450	20,144	17,442	21,357	18,482
79,450	79,500	20,159	17,456	21,375	18,497
79,500	79,550	20,175	17,470	21,393	18,513
79,550	79,600	20,190	17,484	21,411	18,528
79,600	79,650	20,206	17,498	21,429	18,544
79,650	79,700	20,221	17,512	21,447	18,559
79,700	79,750	20,237	17,526	21,465	18,575
79,750	79,800	20,252	17,540	21,483	18,590
79,800	79,850	20,268	17,554	21,501	18,606
79,850	79,900	20,283	17,568	21,519	18,621
79,900	79,950	20,299	17,582	21,537	18,637
79,950	80,000	20,314	17,596	21,555	18,652

If line 37 (taxable income) is—		And you are—			
At least	But less than	Single	Married filing jointly *	Married filing separately	Head of a household
		Your tax is—			
80,000					
80,000	80,050	20,330	17,610	21,573	18,668
80,050	80,100	20,345	17,624	21,591	18,683
80,100	80,150	20,361	17,638	21,609	18,699
80,150	80,200	20,376	17,652	21,627	18,714
80,200	80,250	20,392	17,666	21,645	18,730
80,250	80,300	20,407	17,680	21,663	18,745
80,300	80,350	20,423	17,694	21,681	18,761
80,350	80,400	20,438	17,708	21,699	18,776
80,400	80,450	20,454	17,722	21,717	18,792
80,450	80,500	20,469	17,736	21,735	18,807
80,500	80,550	20,485	17,750	21,753	18,823
80,550	80,600	20,500	17,764	21,771	18,838
80,600	80,650	20,516	17,778	21,789	18,854
80,650	80,700	20,531	17,792	21,807	18,869
80,700	80,750	20,547	17,806	21,825	18,885
80,750	80,800	20,562	17,820	21,843	18,900
80,800	80,850	20,578	17,834	21,861	18,916
80,850	80,900	20,593	17,848	21,879	18,931
80,900	80,950	20,609	17,862	21,897	18,947
80,950	81,000	20,624	17,876	21,915	18,962
81,000					
81,000	81,050	20,640	17,890	21,933	18,978
81,050	81,100	20,655	17,904	21,951	18,993
81,100	81,150	20,671	17,918	21,969	19,009
81,150	81,200	20,686	17,932	21,987	19,024
81,200	81,250	20,702	17,946	22,005	19,040
81,250	81,300	20,717	17,960	22,023	19,055
81,300	81,350	20,733	17,974	22,041	19,071
81,350	81,400	20,748	17,988	22,059	19,086
81,400	81,450	20,764	18,002	22,077	19,102
81,450	81,500	20,779	18,016	22,095	19,117
81,500	81,550	20,795	18,030	22,113	19,133
81,550	81,600	20,810	18,044	22,131	19,148
81,600	81,650	20,826	18,058	22,149	19,164
81,650	81,700	20,841	18,072	22,167	19,179
81,700	81,750	20,857	18,086	22,185	19,195
81,750	81,800	20,872	18,100	22,203	19,210
81,800	81,850	20,888	18,114	22,221	19,226
81,850	81,900	20,903	18,128	22,239	19,241
81,900	81,950	20,919	18,142	22,257	19,257
81,950	82,000	20,934	18,156	22,275	19,272
82,000					
82,000	82,050	20,950	18,170	22,293	19,288
82,050	82,100	20,965	18,184	22,311	19,303
82,100	82,150	20,981	18,198	22,329	19,319
82,150	82,200	20,996	18,212	22,347	19,334
82,200	82,250	21,012	18,226	22,365	19,350
82,250	82,300	21,027	18,240	22,383	19,365
82,300	82,350	21,043	18,254	22,401	19,381
82,350	82,400	21,058	18,268	22,419	19,396
82,400	82,450	21,074	18,282	22,437	19,412
82,450	82,500	21,089	18,296	22,455	19,427
82,500	82,550	21,105	18,310	22,473	19,443
82,550	82,600	21,120	18,324	22,491	19,458
82,600	82,650	21,136	18,338	22,509	19,474
82,650	82,700	21,151	18,352	22,527	19,489
82,700	82,750	21,167	18,366	22,545	19,505
82,750	82,800	21,182	18,380	22,563	19,520
82,800	82,850	21,198	18,394	22,581	19,536
82,850	82,900	21,213	18,408	22,599	19,551
82,900	82,950	21,229	18,422	22,617	19,567
82,950	83,000	21,244	18,436	22,635	19,582

If line 37 (taxable income) is—		And you are—			
At least	But less than	Single	Married filing jointly *	Married filing separately	Head of a household
		Your tax is—			
83,000					
83,000	83,050	21,260	18,450	22,653	19,598
83,050	83,100	21,275	18,464	22,671	19,613
83,100	83,150	21,291	18,478	22,689	19,629
83,150	83,200	21,306	18,492	22,707	19,644
83,200	83,250	21,322	18,506	22,725	19,660
83,250	83,300	21,337	18,520	22,743	19,675
83,300	83,350	21,353	18,534	22,761	19,691
83,350	83,400	21,368	18,548	22,779	19,706
83,400	83,450	21,384	18,562	22,797	19,722
83,450	83,500	21,399	18,576	22,815	19,737
83,500	83,550	21,415	18,590	22,833	19,753
83,550	83,600	21,430	18,604	22,851	19,768
83,600	83,650	21,446	18,618	22,869	19,784
83,650	83,700	21,461	18,632	22,887	19,799
83,700	83,750	21,477	18,646	22,905	19,815
83,750	83,800	21,492	18,660	22,923	19,830
83,800	83,850	21,508	18,674	22,941	19,846
83,850	83,900	21,523	18,688	22,959	19,861
83,900	83,950	21,539	18,702	22,977	19,877
83,950	84,000	21,554	18,716	22,995	19,892
84,000					
84,000	84,050	21,570	18,730	23,013	19,908
84,050	84,100	21,585	18,744	23,031	19,923
84,100	84,150	21,601	18,758	23,049	19,939
84,150	84,200	21,616	18,772	23,067	19,954
84,200	84,250	21,632	18,786	23,085	19,970
84,250	84,300	21,647	18,800	23,103	19,985
84,300	84,350	21,663	18,814	23,121	20,001
84,350	84,400	21,678	18,828	23,139	20,016
84,400	84,450	21,694	18,842	23,157	20,032
84,450	84,500	21,709	18,856	23,175	20,047
84,500	84,550	21,725	18,870	23,193	20,063
84,550	84,600	21,740	18,884	23,211	20,078
84,600	84,650	21,756	18,898	23,229	20,094
84,650	84,700	21,771	18,912	23,247	20,109
84,700	84,750	21,787	18,926	23,265	20,125
84,750	84,800	21,802	18,940	23,283	20,140
84,800	84,850	21,818	18,954	23,301	20,156
84,850	84,900	21,833	18,968	23,319	20,171
84,900	84,950	21,849	18,982	23,337	20,187
84,950	85,000	21,864	18,996	23,355	20,202
85,000					
85,000	85,050	21,880	19,010	23,373	20,218
85,050	85,100	21,895	19,024	23,391	20,233
85,100	85,150	21,911	19,038	23,409	20,249
85,150	85,200	21,926	19,052	23,427	20,264
85,200	85,250	21,942	19,066	23,445	20,280
85,250	85,300	21,957	19,080	23,463	20,295
85,300	85,350	21,973	19,094	23,481	20,311
85,350	85,400	21,988	19,108	23,499	20,326
85,400	85,450	22,004	19,122	23,517	20,342
85,450	85,500	22,019	19,136	23,535	20,357
85,500	85,550	22,035	19,150	23,553	20,373
85,550	85,600	22,050	19,164	23,571	20,388
85,600	85,650	22,066	19,178	23,589	20,404
85,650	85,700	22,081	19,192	23,607	20,419
85,700	85,750	22,097	19,206	23,625	20,435
85,750	85,800	22,112	19,220	23,643	20,450
85,800	85,850	22,128	19,234	23,661	20,466
85,850	85,900	22,143	19,248	23,679	20,481
85,900	85,950	22,159	19,262	23,697	20,497
85,950	86,000	22,174	19,276	23,715	20,512

* This column must also be used by a qualifying widow(er).

Continued on next page

1993 Tax Table—*Continued*

If line 37 (taxable income) is— At least	But less than	And you are— Single	Married filing jointly *	Married filing separately	Head of a household
86,000				Your tax is—	
86,000	86,050	22,190	19,290	23,733	20,528
86,050	86,100	22,205	19,304	23,751	20,543
86,100	86,150	22,221	19,318	23,769	20,559
86,150	86,200	22,236	19,332	23,787	20,574
86,200	86,250	22,252	19,346	23,805	20,590
86,250	86,300	22,267	19,360	23,823	20,605
86,300	86,350	22,283	19,374	23,841	20,621
86,350	86,400	22,298	19,388	23,859	20,636
86,400	86,450	22,314	19,402	23,877	20,652
86,450	86,500	22,329	19,416	23,895	20,667
86,500	86,550	22,345	19,430	23,913	20,683
86,550	86,600	22,060	19,444	23,931	20,698
86,600	86,650	22,376	19,458	23,949	20,714
86,650	86,700	22,391	19,472	23,967	20,729
86,700	86,750	22,407	19,486	23,985	20,745
86,750	86,800	22,422	19,500	24,003	20,760
86,800	86,850	22,438	19,514	24,021	20,776
86,850	86,900	22,453	19,528	24,039	20,791
86,900	86,950	22,469	19,542	24,057	20,807
86,950	87,000	22,484	19,556	24,075	20,822
87,000					
87,000	87,050	22,500	19,570	24,093	20,838
87,050	87,100	22,515	19,584	24,111	20,853
87,100	87,150	22,531	19,598	24,129	20,869
87,150	87,200	22,546	19,612	24,147	20,884
87,200	87,250	22,562	19,626	24,165	20,900
87,250	87,300	22,577	19,640	24,183	20,915
87,300	87,350	22,593	19,654	24,201	20,931
87,350	87,400	22,608	19,668	24,219	20,946
87,400	87,450	22,624	19,682	24,237	20,962
87,450	87,500	22,639	19,696	24,255	20,977
87,500	87,550	22,655	19,710	24,273	20,993
87,550	87,600	22,670	19,724	24,291	21,008
87,600	87,650	22,686	19,738	24,309	21,024
87,650	87,700	22,701	19,752	24,327	21,039
87,700	87,750	22,717	19,766	24,345	21,055
87,750	87,800	22,732	19,780	24,363	21,070
87,800	87,850	22,748	19,794	24,381	21,086
87,850	87,900	22,763	19,808	24,399	21,101
87,900	87,950	22,779	19,822	24,417	21,117
87,950	88,000	22,794	19,836	24,435	21,132
88,000					
88,000	88,050	22,810	19,850	24,453	21,148
88,050	88,100	22,825	19,864	24,471	21,163
88,100	88,150	22,841	19,878	24,489	21,179
88,150	88,200	22,856	19,892	24,507	21,194
88,200	88,250	22,872	19,906	24,525	21,210
88,250	88,300	22,887	19,920	24,543	21,225
88,300	88,350	22,903	19,934	24,561	21,241
88,350	88,400	22,918	19,948	24,579	21,256
88,400	88,450	22,934	19,962	24,597	21,272
88,450	88,500	22,949	19,976	24,615	21,287
88,500	88,550	22,965	19,990	24,633	21,303
88,550	88,600	22,980	20,004	24,651	21,318
88,600	88,650	22,996	20,018	24,669	21,334
88,650	88,700	23,011	20,032	24,687	21,349
88,700	88,750	23,027	20,046	24,705	21,365
88,750	88,800	23,042	20,060	24,723	21,380
88,800	88,850	23,058	20,074	24,741	21,396
88,850	88,900	23,073	20,088	24,759	21,411
88,900	88,950	23,089	20,102	24,777	21,427
88,950	89,000	23,104	20,116	24,795	21,442

If line 37 (taxable income) is— At least	But less than	And you are— Single	Married filing jointly *	Married filing separately	Head of a household
89,000				Your tax is—	
89,000	89,050	23,120	20,130	24,813	21,458
89,050	89,100	23,135	20,144	24,831	21,473
89,100	89,150	23,151	20,158	24,849	21,489
89,150	89,200	23,166	20,173	24,867	21,504
89,200	89,250	23,182	20,188	24,885	21,520
89,250	89,300	23,197	20,204	24,903	21,535
89,300	89,350	23,213	20,219	24,921	21,551
89,350	89,400	23,228	20,235	24,939	21,566
89,400	89,450	23,244	20,250	24,957	21,582
89,450	89,500	23,259	20,266	24,975	21,597
89,500	89,550	23,275	20,281	24,993	21,613
89,550	89,600	23,290	20,297	25,011	21,628
89,600	89,650	23,306	20,312	25,029	21,644
89,650	89,700	23,321	20,328	25,047	21,659
89,700	89,750	23,337	20,343	25,065	21,675
89,750	89,800	23,352	20,359	25,083	21,690
89,800	89,850	23,368	20,374	25,101	21,706
89,850	89,900	23,383	20,390	25,119	21,721
89,900	89,950	23,399	20,405	25,137	21,737
89,950	90,000	23,414	20,421	25,155	21,752
90,000					
90,000	90,050	23,430	20,436	25,173	21,768
90,050	90,100	23,445	20,452	25,191	21,783
90,100	90,150	23,461	20,467	25,209	21,799
90,150	90,200	23,476	20,483	25,227	21,814
90,200	90,250	23,492	20,498	25,245	21,830
90,250	90,300	23,507	20,514	25,263	21,845
90,300	90,350	23,523	20,529	25,281	21,861
90,350	90,400	23,538	20,545	25,299	21,876
90,400	90,450	23,554	20,560	25,317	21,892
90,450	90,500	23,569	20,576	25,335	21,907
90,500	90,550	23,585	20,591	25,353	21,923
90,550	90,600	23,600	20,607	25,371	21,938
90,600	90,650	23,616	20,622	25,389	21,954
90,650	90,700	23,631	20,638	25,407	21,969
90,700	90,750	23,647	20,653	25,425	21,985
90,750	90,800	23,662	20,669	25,443	22,000
90,800	90,850	23,678	20,684	25,461	22,016
90,850	90,900	23,693	20,700	25,479	22,031
90,900	90,950	23,709	20,715	25,497	22,047
90,950	91,000	23,724	20,731	25,515	22,062
91,000					
91,000	91,050	23,740	20,746	25,533	22,078
91,050	91,100	23,755	20,762	25,551	22,093
91,100	91,150	23,771	20,777	25,569	22,109
91,150	91,200	23,786	20,793	25,587	22,124
91,200	91,250	23,802	20,808	25,605	22,140
91,250	91,300	23,817	20,824	25,623	22,155
91,300	91,350	23,833	20,839	25,641	22,171
91,350	91,400	23,848	20,855	25,659	22,186
91,400	91,450	23,864	20,870	25,677	22,202
91,450	91,500	23,879	20,886	25,695	22,217
91,500	91,550	23,895	20,901	25,713	22,233
91,550	91,600	23,910	20,917	25,731	22,248
91,600	91,650	23,926	20,932	25,749	22,264
91,650	91,700	23,941	20,948	25,767	22,279
91,700	91,750	23,957	20,963	25,785	22,295
91,750	91,800	23,972	20,979	25,803	22,310
91,800	91,850	23,988	20,994	25,821	22,326
91,850	91,900	24,003	21,010	25,839	22,341
91,900	91,950	24,019	21,025	25,857	22,357
91,950	92,000	24,034	21,041	25,875	22,372

If line 37 (taxable income) is— At least	But less than	And you are— Single	Married filing jointly *	Married filing separately	Head of a household
92,000				Your tax is—	
92,000	92,050	24,050	21,056	25,893	22,388
92,050	92,100	24,065	21,072	25,911	22,403
92,100	92,150	24,081	21,087	25,929	22,419
92,150	92,200	24,096	21,103	25,947	22,434
92,200	92,250	24,112	21,118	25,965	22,450
92,250	92,300	24,127	21,134	25,983	22,465
92,300	92,350	24,143	21,149	26,001	22,481
92,350	92,400	24,158	21,165	26,019	22,496
92,400	92,450	24,174	21,180	26,037	22,512
92,450	92,500	24,189	21,196	26,055	22,527
92,500	92,550	24,205	21,211	26,073	22,543
92,550	92,600	24,220	21,227	26,091	22,558
92,600	92,650	24,236	21,242	26,109	22,574
92,650	92,700	24,251	21,258	26,127	22,589
92,700	92,750	24,267	21,273	26,145	22,605
92,750	92,800	24,282	21,289	26,163	22,620
92,800	92,850	24,298	21,304	26,181	22,636
92,850	92,900	24,313	21,320	26,199	22,651
92,900	92,950	24,329	21,335	26,217	22,667
92,950	93,000	24,344	21,351	26,235	22,682
93,000					
93,000	93,050	24,360	21,366	26,253	22,698
93,050	93,100	24,375	21,382	26,271	22,713
93,100	93,150	24,391	21,397	26,289	22,729
93,150	93,200	24,406	21,413	26,307	22,744
93,200	93,250	24,422	21,428	26,325	22,760
93,250	93,300	24,437	21,444	26,343	22,775
93,300	93,350	24,453	21,459	26,361	22,791
93,350	93,400	24,468	21,475	26,379	22,806
93,400	93,450	24,484	21,490	26,397	22,822
93,450	93,500	24,499	21,506	26,415	22,837
93,500	93,550	24,515	21,521	26,433	22,853
93,550	93,600	24,530	21,537	26,451	22,868
93,600	93,650	24,546	21,552	26,469	22,884
93,650	93,700	24,561	21,568	26,487	22,899
93,700	93,750	24,577	21,583	26,505	22,915
93,750	93,800	24,592	21,599	26,523	22,930
93,800	93,850	24,608	21,614	26,541	22,946
93,850	93,900	24,623	21,630	26,559	22,961
93,900	93,950	24,639	21,645	26,577	22,977
93,950	94,000	24,654	21,661	26,595	22,992
94,000					
94,000	94,050	24,670	21,676	26,613	23,008
94,050	94,100	24,685	21,692	26,631	23,023
94,100	94,150	24,701	21,707	26,649	23,039
94,150	94,200	24,716	21,723	26,667	23,054
94,200	94,250	24,732	21,738	26,685	23,070
94,250	94,300	24,747	21,754	26,703	23,085
94,300	94,350	24,763	21,769	26,721	23,101
94,350	94,400	24,778	21,785	26,739	23,116
94,400	94,450	24,794	21,800	26,757	23,132
94,450	94,500	24,809	21,816	26,775	23,147
94,500	94,550	24,825	21,831	26,793	23,163
94,550	94,600	24,840	21,847	26,811	23,178
94,600	94,650	24,856	21,862	26,829	23,194
94,650	94,700	24,871	21,878	26,847	23,209
94,700	94,750	24,887	21,893	26,865	23,225
94,750	94,800	24,902	21,909	26,883	23,240
94,800	94,850	24,918	21,924	26,901	23,256
94,850	94,900	24,933	21,940	26,919	23,271
94,900	94,950	24,949	21,955	26,937	23,287
94,950	95,000	24,964	21,971	26,955	23,302

* This column must also be used by a qualifying widow(er).

Continued on next page

1993 Tax Table—*Continued*

If line 37 (taxable income) is—		And you are—				If line 37 (taxable income) is—		And you are—			
At least	But less than	Single	Married filing jointly *	Married filing separately	Head of a household	At least	But less than	Single	Married filing jointly *	Married filing separately	Head of a household
			Your tax is—						Your tax is—		
95,000						**98,000**					
95,000	95,050	24,980	21,986	26,973	23,318	98,000	98,050	25,910	22,916	28,053	24,248
95,050	95,100	24,995	22,002	26,991	23,333	98,050	98,100	25,925	22,932	28,071	24,263
95,100	95,150	25,011	22,017	27,009	23,349	98,100	98,150	25,941	22,947	28,089	24,279
95,150	95,200	25,026	22,033	27,027	23,364	98,150	98,200	25,956	22,963	28,107	24,294
95,200	95,250	25,042	22,048	27,045	23,380	98,200	98,250	25,972	22,978	28,125	24,310
95,250	95,300	25,057	22,064	27,063	23,395	98,250	98,300	25,987	22,994	28,143	24,325
95,300	95,350	25,073	22,079	27,081	23,411	98,300	98,350	26,003	23,009	28,161	24,341
95,350	95,400	25,088	22,095	27,099	23,426	98,350	98,400	26,018	23,025	28,179	24,356
95,400	95,450	25,104	22,110	27,117	23,442	98,400	98,450	26,034	23,040	28,197	24,372
95,450	95,500	25,119	22,126	27,135	23,457	98,450	98,500	26,049	23,056	28,215	24,387
95,500	95,550	25,135	22,141	27,153	23,473	98,500	98,550	26,065	23,071	28,233	24,403
95,550	95,600	25,150	22,157	27,171	23,488	98,550	98,600	26,080	23,087	28,251	24,418
95,600	95,650	25,166	22,172	27,189	23,504	98,600	98,650	26,096	23,102	28,269	24,434
95,650	95,700	25,181	22,188	27,207	23,519	98,650	98,700	26,111	23,118	28,287	24,449
95,700	95,750	25,197	22,203	27,225	23,535	98,700	98,750	26,127	23,133	28,305	24,465
95,750	95,800	25,212	22,219	27,243	23,550	98,750	98,800	26,142	23,149	28,323	24,480
95,800	95,850	25,228	22,234	27,261	23,566	98,800	98,850	26,158	23,164	28,341	24,496
95,850	95,900	25,243	22,250	27,279	23,581	98,850	98,900	26,173	23,180	28,359	24,511
95,900	95,950	25,259	22,265	27,297	23,597	98,900	98,950	26,189	23,195	28,377	24,527
95,950	96,000	25,274	22,281	27,315	23,612	98,950	99,000	26,204	23,211	28,395	24,542
96,000						**99,000**					
96,000	96,050	25,290	22,296	27,333	23,628	99,000	99,050	26,220	23,226	28,413	24,558
96,050	96,100	25,305	22,312	27,351	23,643	99,050	99,100	26,235	23,242	28,431	24,573
96,100	96,150	25,321	22,327	27,369	23,659	99,100	99,150	26,251	23,257	28,449	24,589
96,150	96,200	25,336	22,343	27,387	23,674	99,150	99,200	26,266	23,273	28,467	24,604
96,200	96,250	25,352	22,358	27,405	23,690	99,200	99,250	26,282	23,288	28,485	24,620
96,250	96,300	25,367	22,374	27,423	23,705	99,250	99,300	26,297	23,304	28,503	24,635
96,300	96,350	25,383	22,389	27,441	23,721	99,300	99,350	26,313	23,319	28,521	24,651
96,350	96,400	25,398	22,405	27,459	23,736	99,350	99,400	26,328	23,335	28,539	24,666
96,400	96,450	25,414	22,420	27,477	23,752	99,400	99,450	26,344	23,350	28,557	24,682
96,450	96,500	25,429	22,436	27,495	23,767	99,450	99,500	26,359	23,366	28,575	24,697
96,500	96,550	25,445	22,451	27,513	23,783	99,500	99,550	26,375	23,381	28,593	24,713
96,550	96,600	25,460	22,467	27,531	23,798	99,550	99,600	26,390	23,397	28,611	24,728
96,600	96,650	25,476	22,482	27,549	23,814	99,600	99,650	26,406	23,412	28,629	24,744
96,650	96,700	25,491	22,498	27,567	23,829	99,650	99,700	26,421	23,428	28,647	24,759
96,700	96,750	25,507	22,513	27,585	23,845	99,700	99,750	26,437	23,443	28,665	24,775
96,750	96,800	25,522	22,529	27,603	23,860	99,750	99,800	26,452	23,459	28,683	24,790
96,800	96,850	25,538	22,544	27,621	23,876	99,800	99,850	26,468	23,474	28,701	24,806
96,850	96,900	25,553	22,560	27,639	23,891	99,850	99,900	26,483	23,490	28,719	24,821
96,900	96,950	25,569	22,575	27,657	23,907	99,900	99,950	26,499	23,505	28,737	24,837
96,950	97,000	25,584	22,591	27,675	23,922	99,950	100,000	26,514	23,521	28,755	24,852
97,000											
97,000	97,050	25,600	22,606	27,693	23,938						
97,050	97,100	25,615	22,622	27,711	23,953						
97,100	97,150	25,631	22,637	27,729	23,969						
97,150	97,200	25,646	22,653	27,747	23,984						
97,200	97,250	25,662	22,668	27,765	24,000						
97,250	97,300	25,677	22,684	27,783	24,015						
97,300	97,350	25,693	22,699	27,801	24,031						
97,350	97,400	25,708	22,715	27,819	24,046						
97,400	97,450	25,724	22,730	27,837	24,062						
97,450	97,500	25,739	22,746	27,855	24,077						
97,500	97,550	25,755	22,761	27,873	24,093						
97,550	97,600	25,770	22,777	27,891	24,108						
97,600	97,650	25,786	22,792	27,909	24,124						
97,650	97,700	25,801	22,808	27,927	24,139						
97,700	97,750	25,817	22,823	27,945	24,155						
97,750	97,800	25,832	22,839	27,963	24,170						
97,800	97,850	25,848	22,854	27,981	24,186						
97,850	97,900	25,863	22,870	27,999	24,201						
97,900	97,950	25,879	22,885	28,017	24,217						
97,950	98,000	25,894	22,901	28,035	24,232						

$100,000 or over — use Tax Rate Schedules

* This column must also be used by a qualifying widow(er).

¶ 1111 Corporate income tax rates.

The rates for domestic corporations (other than qualified personal corporations) are: (Code Sec. 11(b))[1]

Tax Years Beginning After Dec. 31, '92

Taxable income over—	But not over—	The tax is:	Of the amount over—
0	$ 50,000	15%	0
$ 50,000	75,000	$ 7,500 + 25%	$ 50,000
75,000	100,000	13,750 + 34%	75,000
100,000	335,000	22,250 + 39%	100,000
335,000	10,000,000	113,900 + 34%	335,000
10,000,000	15,000,000	3,400,000 + 35%	10,000,000
15,000,000	18,333,333	5,150,000 + 38%	15,000,000
18,333,333	—	35%	0

Fiscal year corporations with tax years that began in '92 and ended in '93 must use a blended rate (straddle computation) to figure their tax: (Code Sec. 15(a))[2]

(1) Figure the tax on taxable income using the rate in effect for '92 (see table below) and multiply the tax by the following fraction:

$$\frac{\text{Number of days in the tax year before Jan. 1, '93}}{\text{Total number of days in the tax year}}$$

Rates in effect for '92

Taxable income over—	But not over—	The tax is:	Of the amount over—
0	$ 50,000	15%	0
$ 50,000	75,000	$ 7,500 + 25%	$ 50,000
75,000	100,000	13,750 + 34%	75,000
100,000	335,000	22,250 + 39%	100,000
335,000	—	34%	0

(2) Figure the tax on taxable income using the rate in effect for '93 (see table above) and multiply the tax by the following fraction:

$$\frac{\text{Number of days in the tax year after Dec. 31, '92}}{\text{Total number of days in the tax year}}$$

(Note that a fiscal year beginning Feb. 1, '92 has 366 days. Use the actual number of days in a short tax year of less than 12 months.)

(3) Add the tax amounts in (1) and (2). This is the blended rate tax.

Fiscal year corporations using the blended rate tax computation, should write "Section 15" at the top of their return. Amended returns must be filed if necessary to reflect this computation.[3]

A qualified personal service corporation (as defined in ¶ 2812) is taxed at a flat 35% of its taxable income. (Code Sec. 11(b)(2))[4]

Foreign corporations are taxed at a flat 30% (or lower treaty rate) on their investment income from U.S. sources and at regular corporate rates on their income from U.S. sources (and in very rare cases from foreign sources) which is effectively connected with the conduct of a U.S. trade or business. A 4% tax is imposed on transportation income from U.S. sources.[5]

Special taxes or rates on corporations are:

---

1. ¶ D-1003; ¶ 114.01.
2. ¶ D-1007 et seq.; ¶ 154.
3. ¶ D-1007 et seq.; ¶ 154.
4. ¶ D-1005; ¶ 114.02.
5. ¶ O-10300 et seq.; ¶s 8814.02, 8824, 8874.

- the alternative minimum tax, Chapter 14;
- the environmental tax, ¶ 3358;
- the accumulated earnings tax, ¶ 3320;
- the personal holding company tax, ¶ 3330.

¶ 1112 Gift and estate tax rates (unified rate schedule).

The estate tax on estates of decedents is imposed on the decedent's taxable estate (gross estate less deductions). A unified credit against the estate tax is allowed as well as certain other credits, including a credit for state death taxes (table at ¶ 1114), see ¶ 5030. A gift tax is imposed on transfers of property by gift. The tax is based on the cumulative value of current and prior gifts (after a specified exclusion) and a marital deduction is allowed for gifts between spouses, see ¶ 5039 *et seq.* The graduated rates and the unified credit for estate and gift taxes are phased out (see below) for certain large gifts and large estates of decedents. (Code Sec. 2001, Code Sec. 2501)[6]

Unified Rate Schedule

(A)		(B)	(C) Tax on amount in Column A*	(D) Tax rate on excess over amounts in Column A*
Amount subject to tentative tax				
exceeding		but not exceeding		Percent
$ —		$ 10,000	$ —	18
10,000		20,000	1,800	20
20,000		40,000	3,800	22
40,000		60,000	8,200	24
60,000		80,000	13,000	26
80,000		100,000	18,200	28
100,000		150,000	23,800	30
150,000		250,000	38,800	32
250,000		500,000	70,800	34
500,000		750,000	155,800	37
750,000		1,000,000	248,300	39
1,000,000		1,250,000	345,800	41
1,250,000		1,500,000	448,300	43
1,500,000		2,000,000	555,800	45
2,000,000		2,500,000	780,800	49
2,500,000		3,000,000	1,025,800	53
3,000,000		—	1,290,800	55

* Before credits and phase-out of graduated rates.

Additional calculation to phase out graduated rates: The tentative tax computed with the applicable Unified Rate Table, above, is increased by an amount equal to 5% of so much of the taxable amount that's over $10,000,000 but not more than $21,040,000. (Code Sec. 2001(c)(2))[7]

For the additional estate tax on excess retirement accumulations, and the estate tax on nonincome distributions from a qualified domestic trust for a surviving spouse who isn't a U.S. citizen, see ¶s 5002, 5025.

---

6. ¶s Q-8028 *et seq.*, R-7000 *et seq.*; ¶s 20,009 *et seq.*, 25,009 *et seq.* (Estate & Gift).

7. ¶ R-7009; ¶ 20,014 (Estate & Gift).

¶ 1113 Unified credit against gift and estate taxes.

The unified credit, described in more detail in ¶s 5029, 5053, is $192,800 against the gift and estate taxes imposed on U.S. citizens and U.S. residents. (Code Sec. 2010(a), Code Sec. 2505(a))[8]

There is a $13,000 credit against the estate tax imposed on estates of nonresident aliens (reduced dollar for dollar for any unified gift tax credit allowed with respect to any gift made by the decedent). (Code Sec. 2102(c)(1), (3)(B))[9] Special credit amounts apply for certain residents of U.S. possessions (Code Sec. 2102(c)(2)) and for decedents to the extent required under any treaty obligation of the U.S. (Code Sec. 2102(c)(3)(A))[10]

¶ 1114 Maximum state death tax credit.

The credit may not exceed the amount determined under the following table. "Adjusted taxable estate" is the taxable estate (gross estate minus allowable deductions) reduced by $60,000. (Code Sec. 2011(b))[11]

Adjusted taxable estate	Amount of credit	Rate on excess
$ 40,000	$ 0	0.8%
90,000	400	1.6
140,000	1,200	2.4
240,000	3,600	3.2
440,000	10,000	4.0
640,000	18,000	4.8
840,000	27,600	5.6
1,040,000	38,800	6.4
1,540,000	70,800	7.2
2,040,000	106,800	8.0
2,540,000	146,800	8.8
3,040,000	190,800	9.6
3,540,000	238,800	10.4
4,040,000	290,800	11.2
5,040,000	402,800	12.0
6,040,000	522,800	12.8
7,040,000	650,800	13.6
8,040,000	786,800	14.4
9,040,000	930,800	15.2
10,040,000	1,082,800	16.0

¶ 1115 Excise tax rates (nonpenalty).

Here are "nonpenalty" excise tax rates. For penalty-type excise taxes, see the entries under "Excise taxes" in the Topic Index.[12]

Retail excise taxes

Aircraft, boats, furs, jewelry   Luxury taxes on these repealed retroactive to 1/1/93.

---

8. ¶s Q-8005, R-7100 *et seq.*; ¶s 20,104, 25,054 (Estate & Gift).

9. ¶ R-8028; ¶ 21,014.02 (Estate & Gift).

10. ¶s R-8029, R-8030; ¶ 21,014.02 (Estate & Gift).

11. ¶ R-7202; ¶ 20,114 (Estate & Gift).

12. ¶s W-3100 *et seq.*, W-2000 *et seq.*; ¶s 40,009.05 *et seq.*, 40,609 *et seq.* (Excise).

Passenger vehicles (weighing 6,000 lbs or less) and accessories sold with or installed within 6 months after vehicle placed in service	10% of the first retail sale amount that exceeds $30,000 (adjusted for inflation); exemptions provided.

Trucks, trailers, etc.

* auto truck chassis and bodies (for vehicles weighing more than 33,000 lbs),

* truck trailer and semi-trailer chassis and bodies (for vehicles weighing more than 26,000 lbs)

* tractors used chiefly for highway transportation

* accessories sold with one of the above or installed within 6 months after one of the above is placed in service	12% of first retail sale amount

Transportation fuel taxes

Gasoline	For 10/1/93-12/31/95: 18.4¢ per gal. For 1/1/96-9/30/99: 18.3¢ per gal. After 9/30/99: 4.3¢ per gal.
Gasoline used to produce gasohol	For 10/1/93-12/31/95: 14.44¢ per gal for gasoline used to produce 10% ethanol gasohol; 13.78¢ per gal for gasoline used to produce 10% non-ethanol gasohol; 15.43¢ per gal for gasoline used to produce 7.7% ethanol gasohol; 14.93¢ per gal for gasoline used to produce 7.7% non-ethanol gasohol; 16.25¢ per gal for gasoline used to produce 5.7% ethanol gasohol; 15.89¢ per gal for gasoline used to produce 5.7% non-ethanol gasohol. For 1/1/96-9/30/99: 14.33¢ per gal for gasoline used to produce 10% ethanol gasohol; 13.67¢ per gal for gasoline used to produce 10% non-ethanol gasohol; 15.32¢ per gal for gasoline used to produce 7.7% ethanol gasohol; 14.82¢ per gal for gasoline used to produce 7.7% non-ethanol gasohol; 16.14¢ per gal for gasoline used to produce 5.7% ethanol gasohol; 15.78¢ per gal for gasoline used to produce 5.7% non-ethanol gasohol. After 9/30/99: alcohol mixture rates may not be less than 4.3¢ per gallon.
Gasohol	For 10/1/93-12/31/95: 13¢ per gal for 10% ethanol gasohol; 12.4¢ per gal for 10% non-ethanol gasohol; 14.242¢ per gal for 7.7% ethanol gasohol; 13.78¢ per gal for 7.7% non-ethanol gasohol; 15.322¢ per gal for 5.7% ethanol gasohol; 14.98¢ per gal for 5.7% non-ethanol gasohol.

	For 1/1/96-9/30/99: 12.9¢ per gal for 10% ethanol gasohol; 12.3¢ per gal for 10% non-ethanol gasohol; 14.142¢ per gal for 7.7% ethanol gasohol; 13.68¢ per gal for 7.7% non-ethanol gasohol; 15.222¢ per gal for 5.7% ethanol gasohol; 14.88¢ per gal for 5.7% non-ethanol gasohol. After 9/30/99: 4.3¢ per gal.
Diesel fuel[13]	For 10/1/93-12/31/95: 24.4¢ per gal. For 1/1/96-9/30/99: 24.3¢ per gal. After 9/30/99: 4.3¢ per gal.
Diesel fuel (used in noncommercial boats)	Through 12/31/93: no tax. For 1/1/94 through 12/31/95 on removal at terminal of diesel fuel used in noncommercial boats: 24.4¢ per gal. For 1/1/96 through 9/30/99: 24.3¢ per gal. After 9/30/99: 4.3¢ per gal. For 1/1/94 through 12/31/99 where removal tax is not imposed, a tax is imposed on retail sale of diesel fuel used in noncommercial boats of: 24.4¢ per gal. After 12/31/99, the tax is 4.3¢ per gal.
Diesel fuel used to produce diesohol	For 10/1/93-12/31/95: 21.11¢ per gal for diesel fuel used to produce 10% ethanol diesohol; 20.44¢ per gal for diesel fuel used to produce 10% non-ethanol diesohol. For 1/1/96-9/30/99: 21¢ per gal for diesel fuel used to produce 10% ethanol diesohol; 20.33¢ per gal for diesel fuel used to produce 10% non-ethanol diesohol. After 9/30/99: alcohol mixture rates may not be less than 4.3¢ per gal.
Diesohol (diesel fuel/10% alcohol mixture)	For 10/1/93-12/31/95: 19¢ per gal for ethanol diesohol; 18.4¢ per gal for non-ethanol diesohol. For 1/1/96-9/30/99: 18.9¢ per gal for ethanol diesohol; 18.3¢ per gal for non-ethanol diesohol. After 9/30/99: 4.3¢ per gal for all diesohol.

13. Special rates apply to diesel fuel used in certain buses and trains. For special rates for diesel fuel used in noncommercial boats, see below.

| Special motor fuels—motor vehicle or motorboat use | For 10/1/93-12/31/95: 18.4¢ per gal; 12.95¢ per gal for qualified methanol or ethanol fuels; 12.35¢ per gal for qualified alcohol blend with no ethanol; 11.4¢ per gal for partially exempt methanol or ethanol fuels; 13¢ per gal for special motor fuel/10% ethanol blend; 12.4¢ per gal for special motor fuel/10% non-ethanol blend; 14.44¢ per gal used to produce special motor fuel/10% ethanol blend; 13.78¢ per gal used to produce special fuel/10% non-ethanol blend. |

For 1/1/96-9/30/99: 18.3¢ per gal; 12.85¢ per gal for qualified methanol or ethanol fuels; 11.3¢ per gal for partially exempt methanol or ethanol fuels; 12.9¢ per gal for special motor fuel/10% ethanol blend; 12.3¢ per gal for special motor fuel/10% non-ethanol blend; 14.33¢ per gal used to produce special motor fuel/10% ethanol blend; 13.67¢ per gal for gasoline used to produce special motor fuel/10% non-ethanol blend.

After 9/30/99: 4.3¢ per gal; not less than 4.3¢ per gal for all alcohol mixtures.

Compressed natural gas

Through 9/30/93: no tax.

After 9/30/93: on sale for use or use in a motor vehicle or motorboat (with certain exceptions), 48.54¢ per thousand cubic feet.

Fuel used in noncommercial aviation[14]

Gasoline: 1¢ per gal plus any excise tax imposed at removal from terminal or refinery, or on entry into U.S. (see "Gasoline" rates above).

Non-gasoline (jet) fuel —10/1/93-12/31/95: 21.9¢ per gal; 8.5¢ per gal for sale of 10% ethanol alcohol blend; 7.9¢ per gal for sale of 10% non-ethanol alcohol blend; 9.44¢ per gal used to produce a 10% ethanol alcohol blend; 8.78¢ per gal used to produce a 10% non-ethanol alcohol blend.

After 12/31/95: 4.3¢ per gal; not less than 4.3¢ per gal for all alcohol mixtures.

Partially exempt methanol or ethanol fuel: the comparable producers/importers tax on nongasoline aviation fuel/10% ethanol and nonethanol blends.

Fuel used in commercial transportation on inland waterways

For 10/1/93 through 12/31/93: 21.4¢ per gal.

For 1/1/94 through 12/31/94: 23.4¢ per gal.
For 1/1/95 through 12/31/95: 24.4¢ per gal.
After 12/31/95: 24.3¢ per gal.

14. Special rates apply to aviation fuel used in commercial aviation.

Manufacturers excise tax

Coal (except lignite)

- From underground mines

Lower of $1.10 per ton or 4.4% of selling price

- From surface mines

Lower of 55¢ per ton or 4.4% of selling price

Tires (of the type used on highway vehicles that are wholly or in part made of rubber.)

If the tire weighs:	The rate of tax is:
• Not more than 40 lbs.	No tax
• More than 40 lbs., but not more than 70 lbs.	15¢ per lb. in excess of 40 lbs.
• More than 70 lbs. but not more than 90 lbs.	$4.50 plus 30¢ per lb. in excess of 70 lbs.
• More than 90 lbs.	$10.50 plus 50¢ per lb. in excess of 90 lbs.

Fishing equipment

10% of mfrs. price of specified items; 3% for electric outboard motor and sonar devices; tax on sonar device limited to $30.

Bows and arrows   11% of mfrs. price

Pistols and revolvers   10% of mfrs. price

Other firearms, shells and cartridges   11% of mfrs. price

Gas guzzling passenger autos, as follows:

If the fuel economy of the model type in which the automobile falls is:	The tax is:
At least 22.5	0
At least 21.5 but less than 22.5	$1,000
At least 20.5 but less than 21.5	1,300
At least 19.5 but less than 20.5	1,700
At least 18.5 but less than 19.5	2,100
At least 17.5 but less than 18.5	2,600
At least 16.5 but less than 17.5	3,000
At least 15.5 but less than 16.5	3,700
At least 14.5 but less than 15.5	4,500
At least 13.5 but less than 14.5	5,400
At least 12.5 but less than 13.5	6,400
Less than 12.5	7,700

Communications and transportation taxes

Local and toll telephone service and teletypewriter service

3% of amount paid.

Transportation of persons by air

10% of amount paid for domestic transportation before '96; $6 departure tax per person for international flights before '96. Exemptions allowed.

Transportation of persons by ship

$3 international departure tax per person on a "covered voyage" by ship.

Transportation of property by air

6.25% of amount paid for domestic transportation before '96.

Use taxes

Harbor maintenance tax

- port use

.125% of the value of commercial cargo loaded or unloaded at U.S. ports; exceptions for cargo donated for overseas use and for cargo (other than cargo destined for a foreign country) shipped between U.S. mainland and Alaska (except for crude oil), Hawaii, and/or U.S. possessions, as well as cargo shipped between Alaska, Hawaii, and/or U.S. possessions.

Highway motor vehicles

- weighing at least 55,000 lbs but not over 75,000 lbs

$100 per year plus $22 for each 1,000 lbs (or fraction thereof) over 55,000 lbs. Special rate for small owner-operators.

- weighing over 75,000 lbs

$550. Special rate for small owner-operators.

Foreign insurance

- casualty and indemnity

4¢ per $1 of premium

- life, sickness and accident

1¢ per $1 of premium

- reinsurance

1¢ per $1 of premium

Other excise taxes

Wagering

- wagers

1/4% of amount of state authorized wagers; 2% of amount of other wagers.

- occupation of accepting wagers

$500 per year ($50 per year for persons accepting only state authorized wagers).

Environmental taxes

- crude oil received at U.S. refinery and imported petroleum

9.7¢ per barrel

- crude oil spill tax

5¢ per barrel.

- chemicals sold by producers, manufacturers, importers

various rates, based on type of chemical. Certain imported substances various rates, based on rates for chemicals

- ozone depleting chemicals

various rates, based on base rate and ozone depletion factor.

¶ 1116 Applicable Federal Rates

The IRS tables below show the Applicable one-month Federal Rates (AFRs). The tables provide short-term (obligations not exceeding three years), mid-term (over three years but not over nine years) and long-term (over nine years) rates (in percentages) based on annual, semiannual, quarterly and monthly compounding assumptions.[15]

Applicable Federal Rate	Annual	Semiannual	Quarterly	Monthly
November '93				
Short-Term				
AFR	3.68	3.65	3.63	3.62
110%	4.06	4.02	4.00	3.99
120%	4.43	4.38	4.36	4.34
Mid-Term				
AFR	4.92	4.86	4.83	4.81
110%	5.42	5.35	5.31	5.29
120%	5.91	5.83	5.79	5.76
150%	7.42	7.29	7.22	7.18
175%	8.69	8.51	8.42	8.36
Long-Term				
AFR	5.84	5.76	5.72	5.69
110%	6.44	6.34	6.29	6.26
120%	7.03	6.91	6.85	6.81
October '93				
Short-Term				
AFR	3.69	3.66	3.64	3.63
110%	4.07	4.03	4.01	4.00
120%	4.44	4.39	4.37	4.35
Mid-Term				
AFR	5.00	4.94	4.91	4.89
110%	5.50	5.43	5.39	5.37
120%	6.02	5.93	5.89	5.86
150%	7.55	7.41	7.34	7.30
175%	8.84	8.65	8.56	8.50
Long-Term				
AFR	5.84	5.76	5.72	5.69
110%	6.44	6.34	6.29	6.26
120%	7.03	6.91	6.85	6.81
September '93				
Short-Term				
AFR	3.91	3.87	3.85	3.84
110%	4.31	4.26	4.24	4.22
120%	4.69	4.64	4.61	4.60
Mid-Term				
AFR	5.35	5.28	5.25	5.22
110%	5.89	5.81	5.77	5.74
120%	6.44	6.34	6.29	6.26
150%	8.08	7.92	7.84	7.79
175%	9.45	9.24	9.14	9.07
Long-Term				
AFR	6.28	6.18	6.13	6.10
110%	6.92	6.80	6.74	6.71
120%	7.56	7.42	7.35	7.31
August '93				
Short-Term				
AFR	3.85	3.81	3.79	3.78
110%	4.23	4.19	4.17	4.15

Applicable Federal Rate	Annual	Semiannual	Quarterly	Monthly
120%	4.62	4.57	4.54	4.53
Mid-Term				
AFR	5.32	5.25	5.22	5.19
110%	5.86	5.78	5.74	5.71
120%	6.40	6.30	6.25	6.22
150%	8.04	7.88	7.80	7.75
175%	9.40	9.19	9.09	9.02
Long-Term				
AFR	6.36	6.26	6.21	6.18
110%	7.01	6.89	6.83	6.79
120%	7.65	7.51	7.44	7.40
July '93				
Short-Term				
AFR	3.95	3.91	3.89	3.88
110%	4.35	4.30	4.28	4.26
120%	4.74	4.69	4.66	4.64
Mid-Term				
AFR	5.54	5.47	5.43	5.41
110%	6.11	6.02	5.98	5.95
120%	6.67	6.56	6.51	6.47
150%	8.38	8.21	8.13	8.07
175%	9.80	9.57	9.46	9.38
Long-Term				
AFR	6.61	6.50	6.45	6.41
110%	7.28	7.15	7.09	7.05
120%	7.95	7.80	7.73	7.68
June '93				
Short-Term				
AFR	3.62	3.59	3.57	3.56
110%	3.99	3.95	3.93	3.92
120%	4.36	4.31	4.29	4.27
Mid-Term				
AFR	5.33	5.26	5.23	5.20
110%	5.87	5.79	5.75	5.72
120%	6.41	6.31	6.26	6.23
150%	8.05	7.89	7.81	7.76
175%	9.42	9.21	9.11	9.04
Long-Term				
AFR	6.47	6.37	6.32	6.29
110%	7.13	7.01	6.95	6.91
120%	7.79	7.64	7.57	7.52
May '93				
Short-Term				
AFR	3.72	3.69	3.67	3.66
110%	4.10	4.06	4.04	4.03
120%	4.48	4.43	4.41	4.39
Mid-Term				
AFR	5.46	5.39	5.35	5.33
110%	6.02	5.93	5.89	5.86
120%	6.57	6.47	6.42	6.38

15. ¶ J-3746; ¶s 12,714.01, 90,900.

Applicable Federal Rate	Annual	Semiannual	Quarterly	Monthly
150%	8.25	8.09	8.01	7.96
175%	9.65	9.43	9.32	9.25
Long-Term				
AFR	6.53	6.43	6.38	6.35
110%	7.19	7.07	7.01	6.97
120%	7.87	7.72	7.65	7.60
April '93				
Short-Term				
AFR	3.75	3.72	3.70	3.69
110%	4.13	4.09	4.07	4.06
120%	4.51	4.46	4.44	4.42
Mid-Term				
AFR	5.45	5.38	5.34	5.32
110%	6.01	5.92	5.88	5.85
120%	6.56	6.46	6.41	6.37
150%	8.23	8.07	7.99	7.94
175%	9.64	9.42	9.31	9.24
Long-Term				
AFR	6.52	6.42	6.37	6.34
110%	7.18	7.06	7.00	6.96
120%	7.85	7.70	7.63	7.58
March '93				
Short-Term				
AFR	3.96	3.92	3.90	3.89
110%	4.36	4.31	4.29	4.27
120%	4.76	4.70	4.67	4.65
Mid-Term				
AFR	5.88	5.80	5.76	5.73
110%	6.48	6.38	6.33	6.30
120%	7.08	6.96	6.90	6.86
150%	8.89	8.70	8.61	8.55
175%	10.41	10.15	10.02	9.94
Long-Term				
AFR	6.95	6.83	6.77	6.73
110%	7.65	7.51	7.44	7.40
120%	8.37	8.20	8.12	8.06
February '93				
Short-Term				
AFR	4.23	4.19	4.17	4.15
110%	4.66	4.61	4.58	4.57
120%	5.09	5.03	5.00	4.98
Mid-Term				
AFR	6.22	6.13	6.08	6.05
110%	6.85	6.74	6.68	6.65
120%	7.50	7.36	7.29	7.25
150%	9.41	9.20	9.10	9.03
175%	11.02	10.73	10.59	10.50
Long-Term				
AFR	7.16	7.04	6.98	6.94
110%	7.89	7.74	7.67	7.62

Applicable Federal Rate	Annual	Semiannual	Quarterly	Monthly
120%	8.63	8.45	8.36	8.30
January '93				
Short-Term				
AFR	4.37	4.32	4.30	4.28
110%	4.81	4.75	4.72	4.70
120%	5.25	5.18	5.15	5.12
Mid-Term				
AFR	6.34	6.24	6.19	6.16
110%	6.98	6.86	6.80	6.76
120%	7.63	7.49	7.42	7.38
150%	9.58	9.36	9.25	9.18
175%	11.22	10.92	10.77	10.68
Long-Term				
AFR	7.30	7.17	7.11	7.07
110%	8.05	7.89	7.81	7.76
120%	8.78	8.60	8.51	8.45
December '92				
Short-Term				
AFR	4.07	4.03	4.01	4.00
110%	4.48	4.43	4.41	4.39
120%	4.90	4.84	4.81	4.79
Mid-Term				
AFR	6.15	6.06	6.01	5.98
110%	6.78	6.67	6.62	6.58
120%	7.40	7.27	7.21	7.16
150%	9.30	9.09	8.99	8.92
175%	10.89	10.61	10.47	10.38
Long-Term				
AFR	7.34	7.21	7.15	7.10
110%	8.09	7.93	7.85	7.80
120%	8.84	8.65	8.56	8.50
November '92				
Short-Term				
AFR	3.61	3.58	3.56	3.55
110%	3.98	3.94	3.92	3.91
120%	4.35	4.30	4.28	4.26
Mid-Term				
AFR	5.68	5.60	5.56	5.54
110%	6.25	6.16	6.11	6.08
120%	6.83	6.72	6.66	6.63
150%	8.58	8.40	8.31	8.26
175%	10.04	9.80	9.68	9.61
Long-Term				
AFR	7.00	6.88	6.82	6.78
110%	7.71	7.57	7.50	7.45
120%	8.43	8.26	8.18	8.12

¶ 1117 Addresses of IRS Offices

The addresses of Internal Revenue Service Centers, District Offices and Problem Resolution Offices are listed below:

Service Centers

Alabama—Memphis, TN 37501
Alaska—Ogden, UT 84201
Arizona—Ogden, UT 84201
Arkansas—Memphis, TN 37501
California
  Counties of Alpine, Amador, Butte, Calaveras, Colusa, Contra Costa, Del Norte, El Dorado, Glenn, Humboldt, Lake, Lassen, Marin, Mendocino, Modoc, Napa, Nevada, Placer, Plumas, Sacramento, San Joaquin, Shasta, Sierra, Siskiyou, Solano, Sonoma, Sutter, Tehama, Trinity, Yolo, and Yuba—Ogden, UT 84201
  All Other Counties—Fresno, CA 93888
Colorado—Ogden, UT 84201
Connecticut—Andover, MA 05501
Delaware—Philadelphia, PA 19255
District of Columbia—Philadelphia, PA 19255
Florida—Atlanta, GA 39901
Georgia—Atlanta, GA 39901
Hawaii—Fresno, CA 93888
Idaho—Ogden, UT 84201
Illinois—Kansas City, MO 64999
Indiana—Cincinnati, OH 45999
Iowa—Kansas City, MO 64999
Kansas—Austin, TX 73301
Kentucky—Cincinnati, OH 45999
Louisiana—Memphis, TN 37501
Maine—Andover, MA 05501
Maryland—Philadelphia, PA 19255
Massachusetts—Andover, MA 05501
Michigan—Cincinnati, OH 45999
Minnesota—Kansas City, MO 64999
Mississippi—Memphis, TN 37501
Missouri—Kansas City, MO 64999
Montana—Ogden, UT 84201
Nebraska—Ogden, UT 84201
Nevada—Ogden, UT 84201
New Hampshire—Andover, MA 05501
New Jersey—Holtsville, NY 00501
New Mexico—Austin, TX 73301
New York
  New York City and Counties of Nassau, Rockland, Suffolk and Westchester—Holtsville, NY 00501
  All Other Counties—Andover, MA 05501
North Carolina—Memphis, TN 37501
North Dakota—Ogden, UT 84201
Ohio—Cincinnati, OH 45999
Oklahoma—Austin, TX 73301

Oregon—Ogden, UT 84201
Pennsylvania—Philadelphia, PA 19255
Rhode Island—Andover, MA 05501
South Carolina—Atlanta, GA 39901
South Dakota—Ogden, UT 84201
Tennessee—Memphis, TN 37501
Texas—Austin, TX 73301
Utah—Ogden, UT 84201
Vermont—Andover, MA 05501
Virginia—Philadelphia, PA 19255
Washington—Ogden, UT 84201
West Virginia—Cincinnati, OH 45999
Wisconsin—Kansas City, MO 64999
Wyoming—Ogden, UT 84201
  American Samoa—Philadelphia, PA 19255
  Guam: Permanent residents—Commissioner of Revenue and Taxation, 855 West Marine Dr., Agana, GU 96910
  Guam: Nonpermanent residents—Philadelphia, PA 19255
  Puerto Rico—Philadelphia, PA 19255
  Virgin Islands: Nonpermanent residents—Philadelphia, PA 19255
  Virgin Islands: Permanent residents—V.I. Bureau of Internal Revenue, Lockhart Garden No. 1A, Charlotte Amalie, St. Thomas, VI 00802
  Foreign country: *U.S. citizens and those filing Form 2555, Form 2555-EZ, or Form 4563* —Philadelphia, PA 19255
  All A.P.O. or F.P.O. addresses—Philadelphia, PA 19255

District Offices

Alabama—500 22nd St. S., Birmingham 35233
Alaska—949 E. 36th Ave., Anchorage 99508
Arizona—210 E. Earll Dr., Phoenix 85012
Arkansas—700 W. Capital Ave., Room 1002, Little Rock 72201
California:
  Laguna Niguel—24000 Avila Rd. 92656
  Los Angeles—300 N.Los Angeles St. 90012-3363
  Sacramento—2345 Fair Oaks Blvd. 95825
  San Francisco—450 Golden Gate Ave. 94102
  San Jose—55 S. Market St. 95113
Colorado—600 17th St., Denver 80202
Connecticut—135 High St., Hartford 06103
Delaware—844 King St., Wilmington 19801
District of Columbia (part of Baltimore District)
Florida:

Fort Lauderdale—3rd Fl., Bldg. B, 1 University Dr. 33324

Jacksonville—400 W. Bay St. 33202

Georgia—401 W. Peachtree St., Atlanta 30365

Hawaii—300 Ala Moana Blvd., Honolulu 96850

Idaho—550 W. Fort St., Boise 83724

Illinois:

Chicago—230 S. Dearborn St. 60604

Springfield—320 W. Washington St. 62701

Indiana—575 N. Pennsylvania, Indianapolis 46204

Iowa—210 Walnut St., Des Moines 50309

Kansas—412 S. Main, Wichita 67202

Kentucky—601 W. Broadway, Louisville 40202

Louisiana—600 S. Maestri Place, New Orleans 70130

Maine—68 Sewall St., Augusta 04330

Maryland—31 Hopkins Plaza, Baltimore 21201

Massachusetts—John F. Kennedy Federal Bldg., Boston 02203

Michigan—477 Michigan Ave., Detroit 48226

Minnesota—316 N. Robert St., St Paul 55101

Mississippi—100 W. Capital St., Jackson 39269

Missouri—1222 Spruce St., St. Louis 63103

Montana—301 S. Park Ave., Helena 59626

Nebraska—106 S. 15th St., Omaha 68102

Nevada—4750 W. Oakey Blvd., Las Vegas 89102

New Hampshire—80 Daniel St., Portsmouth 03801

New Jersey—970 Broad St., Newark 07102

New Mexico—517 Gold Ave. S.W., Albuquerque 87102

New York:

Albany—Clinton Ave. and N. Pearl St. 12207

Brooklyn—35 Tillary St. 11201

Buffalo—111 W. Huron St. 14202

Manhattan—120 Church St. 10007

North Carolina—320 Federal Pl., Greensboro 27401

North Dakota—657 2nd Ave. N., Fargo 58102

Ohio:

Cincinnati—550 Main St. 45202

Cleveland—1240 E. 9th St. 44199

Oklahoma—200 NW 4th St., Oklahoma City 73102

Oregon—1220 SW 3rd Ave., Portland 97209

Pennsylvania:

Philadelphia—600 Arch St. 19106

Pittsburgh—1000 Liberty Ave. 15222

Puerto Rico—Carlos E. Chardon St., Hato Rey

Rhode Island—380 Westminster Mall, Providence 02903

South Carolina—1835 Assembly St., Columbia 29201

South Dakota—115 4th Ave. SE, Aberdeen 57401

Tennessee—801 Broadway, Nashville 37203

Texas:

Austin—300 E. 8th St. 78701

Dallas—1100 Commerce St. 75242

Houston—1919 Smith St. 77002

Utah—465 S. 400 East, Salt Lake City 84111

Vermont—199 Main St., Burlington 05401

Virgin Islands—22 Crystal Glade, Charlotte Amalie, St. Thomas

Virginia—400 N. 8th St., Richmond 23240

Washington—915 2nd Ave., Seattle 98174

West Virginia—425 Juliana St., Parkersburg 26102

Wisconsin—310 W. Wisconsin Ave., Room 1230, Milwaukee 53203-2221

Wyoming—308 W. 21st St., Cheyenne 82001

*Service Center
Problem Resolution Offices*

(Address correspondence to: Problem Resolution Office, Internal Revenue Service, with the appropriate address from the following list)

Andover Service Center, 310 Lowell St. (Stop 120), Andover, MA 05501

Atlanta Service Center, P.O. Box 48-549 (Stop 29A), Doraville, GA 30362

Austin Service Center, P.O. Box 934 (Stop 1005 AUSC), Austin, TX 78767

Austin Compliance Center, P.O. Box 2986 (Stop 1005 AUCC), Austin, TX 78768

Brookhaven Service Center, P.O. Box 960 (Stop 102), Holtsville, NY 11742

Cincinnati Service Center, P.O. Box 267 (Stop 11), Covington, KY 41019

Fresno Service Center, P.O. Box 12161, Fresno, CA 93776

Kansas City Service Center, P.O. Box 24551 (Stop 2), Kansas City, MO 64131

Memphis Service Center, P.O. Box 30309 AMF (Stop 77), Memphis, TN 38130

Ogden Service Center, P.O. Box 9941 (Stop 1005 OSC), Ogden, UT 84409

Philadelphia Service Center, P.O. Box 16053 DP:111, Philadelphia, PA 19114

*District Problem
Resolution Offices*

(Address correspondence to: Problem Resolution Office, Internal Revenue Service, with the appropriate address from the following list)

Aberdeen District, 115 4th Ave. S.E., Aberdeen, SD 57401
(604)226-7278

Albany District, Leo O'Brien Federal Building, Clinton Ave. & N. Pearl St., Albany, NY 12207
(518)472-4482

35

Albuquerque District, P.O. Box 1040 (Stop 1005 ALB), Albuquerque, NM 87103
(505)766-3760

Anchorage District, P.O. Box 101500, Anchorage, AK 99510
(907)271-6877

Atlanta District, P.O. Box 1065, Room 1520 (Stop 202-D), Atlanta, GA 30370
(404)331-5232

Augusta District, 220 Main Mall Road, South Portland, ME 04106
(207)780-3309

Austin District, P.O. Box 1863 (Stop 1005 AUS), Austin, TX 78767
(512)499-5875

Baltimore District, P.O. Box 1553, Room 620A, Baltimore, MD 21203
(301)962-3324

Birmingham District, 500 22nd St. S. (Stop 316), Birmingham, AL 35233
(205)731-1177

Boise District, 550 W. Fort St., Box 041, Boise, ID 83724-0041
(208)334-1324

Boston District, P.O. Box 9103 JFK Bldg., Boston, MA 02203
(617)565-1857

Brooklyn District, G.P.O. Box R, Brooklyn, NY 11202
(718)488-2080

Buffalo District, P.O. Box 500, Niagara Square Station, Buffalo, NY 14201
(716)846-4574

Burlington District, Courthouse Plaza, 199 Main St., Burlington, VT 05401
(802)860-2008

Cheyenne District, 308 W. 21st St. (Stop 1005 CHE), Cheyenne, WY 82001
(307)772-2489

Chicago District, 230 S. Dearborn St., Room 3214, Chicago, IL 60604
(312)886-9183

Cincinnati District, P.O. Box 1818, Cincinnati, OH 45201
(513)684-3094

Cleveland District, P.O. Box 99709, Cleveland, OH 44199
(216)522-7134

Columbia District, P.O. Box 386, MDP-03, Columbia, SC 29202-0386
(803)765-5939

Dallas District, P.O. Box 50008 (Stop 1005 DAL), Dallas, TX 75250
(214)767-1289

Denver District, P.O. Box 1302 (Stop 1005 DEN), Denver, CO 80201
(303)446-1012

Des Moines District, P.O. Box 1337, Room 359, Des Moines, IA 50305
(515)284-6669

Detroit District, P.O. Box 330500 (Stop 7), Detroit, MI 48232
(313)226-4086

Fargo District, P.O. Box 8, Fargo, ND 58107
(701)239-5141

Ft. Lauderdale District, P.O. Box 17167, Plantation, FL 33318
(305)424-2385

Greensboro District, 320 Federal Place, Room 125, Greensboro, NC 27401
(919)378-2180

Hartford District, 135 High St. (Stop 219), Hartford, CT 06103
(203)240-4023

Helena District, Federal Building, 301 S. Park St., Helena, MT 59626-0016
(406)449-5244

Honolulu District, P.O. Box 50089, Honolulu, HI 96850-4992
(808)541-3300

Houston District, 1919 Smith St. (Stop 1005-HOU), Houston, TX 77002
(713)653-3660

Indianapolis District, P.O. Box 44687 (Stop 11), Indianapolis, IN 46244
(317)226-6332

Assistant Commissioner (International), P.O. Box 44817, L'Enfant Plaza Station, Washington, D.C. 20026-4817
(202)874-1930

Jackson District, 100 W. Capitol St., Suite 504 (Stop 31), Jackson, MS 39269
(601)965-4800

Jacksonville District, P.O. Box 35045 (Stop D:PRO), Jacksonville, FL 32202
(904)232-3440

Laguna Niguel District, P.O. Box 30207, Laguna Niguel, CA 92607-0207
(714)643-4182

Las Vegas District, 4750 W. Oakey Blvd, Room 303, Las Vegas, NV 89102
(702)455-1096

Little Rock District, 700 West Capital Ave., Little Rock, AR 72201
(501)324-6260

Los Angeles District, P.O. Box 1791, Los Angeles, CA 90053
(213)894-6111

Louisville District, P.O. Box 1735, Louisville, KY 40201
(502)582-6030

Manhattan District, P.O. Box 408, Church St. Station, New York, NY 10008
(212)264-2850

Milwaukee District, 310 W Wisconsin Ave, Room M-28, Milwaukee, WI 53203
(414)297-3046

Nashville District, P.O. Box 1107 (Stop 22), Nashville, TN 37202
(615)736-5219

New Orleans District, 600 S. Maestri Place (Stop 12), New Orleans, LA 70130
(504)589-3001

Newark District, P.O. Box 1143, Newark, NJ 07102
(201)645-6698

Oklahoma City District, P.O. Box 1040 (Stop 1005 OKC), Oklahoma City, OK 73101
(405)297-4064

Omaha District, 106 S. 15th St. (Stop 2), Omaha, NE 68102
(402)221-4181

Parkersburg District, P.O. Box 1388, Parkersburg, WV 26102
(304)420-6616

Philadelphia District, P.O. Box 12010, Philadelphia, PA 19106
(215)597-3377

Phoenix District, 210 E. Earll Dr. (Stop 1005 PX), Phoenix, AZ 85012-2623
(602)207-8240

Pittsburgh District, P.O. Box 705, Pittsburgh, PA 15230
(412)644-5987

Portland District, P.O. Box 3341, Portland, OR 97208
(503)326-2333

Portsmouth District, P.O. Box 720, Portsmouth, NH 03802
(603)433-0571

Providence District, 380 Westminster St., Providence, RI 02903
(401)528-4492

Richmond District, P.O. Box 10113, Room 5502, Richmond, VA 23240
(804)771-2643

Sacramento District, P.O. Box 2900 (Stop SA 5043), Sacramento, CA 95812
(916)978-4079

Salt Lake City District, P.O. Box 2069 (Stop 1005 SLC), Salt Lake City, UT 84110
(801)524-6287

San Francisco District, P.O. Box 36136 (Stop 4-0-0-4), 450 Golden Gate Ave., San Francisco, CA 94102
(415)556-5046

San Jose District, P.O. Box 100 (Stop HQ0004), San Jose, CA 95103
(408)291-7132

Seattle District, P.O. Box 2207 (Stop 405), Seattle, WA 98111
(206)553-7439

Springfield District, P.O. Box 19201 (Stop 22), Springfield, IL 62794-9201
(217)492-4517

St. Louis District, P.O. Box 66776 (Stop 002), St. Louis, MO 63166
(314)539-6770

St. Paul District, P.O. Box 64599, St. Paul, MN 55164
(612)290-3077

Wichita District, P.O. Box 2907 (Stop 1005-WIC), Wichita, KS 67201
(316)291-6506

Wilmington District, 409 Silverside Rd., Room 152, Wilmington, DE 19809
(302)791-4502

National Office

National Office, 1111 Constitution Ave., N.W., Room 3003 C:PRP, Washington, D.C. 20224
(202)622-6100

¶ 1118 List of IRS Publications

Here is a numerical list of popular IRS publications.

To order most publications, call IRS at 1-800-829-3676.

caution: IRS adds (drops) publications on a continuing basis.

No.	Title	No.	Title
1	Your Rights as a Taxpayer	516	Tax Information for U.S. Government Civilian Employees Stationed Abroad
3	Tax Information for Military Personnel (Including Reservists Called to Active Duty)	517	Social Security and other Information for Members of the Clergy and Religious Workers
4	Student's Guide to Federal Income Tax	519	U.S. Tax Guide for Aliens
5	Appeal Rights and Preparation of Protests for Unagreed Cases	520	Scholarships and Fellowships
15	Circular E, Employer's Tax Guide	521	Moving Expenses
17	Your Federal Income Tax	523	Selling Your Home
51	Circular A, Agricultural Employer's Tax Guide	524	Credit for the Elderly or the Disabled
54	Tax Guide for U.S. Citizens and Resident Aliens Abroad	525	Taxable and Nontaxable income
78	Cumulative List of Organizations	526	Charitable Contributions
80	Circular SS, Federal Tax Guide for Employers in the Virgin Islands, Guam, American Samoa, and the Commonwealth of the Northern Mariana Islands	527	Residential Rental Property (Including Rental of Vacation Homes)
		529	Miscellaneous Deductions
		530	Tax Information for First-Time Homeowners
225	Farmer's Tax Guide	531	Reporting Income From Tips
334	Tax Guide for Small Business	533	Self-Employment Tax
349	Federal Highway Use Tax on Heavy Vehicles	534	Depreciation
		535	Business Expenses
378	Fuel Tax Credits and Refunds	536	Net Operating Losses
448	Federal Estate and Gift Taxes	537	Installment Sales
463	Travel, Entertainment, and Gift Expenses	538	Accounting Periods and Methods
		541	Tax Information on Partnerships
493	Alternative Tax Withholding Methods and Tables	542	Tax Information on Corporations
		544	Sales and Other Dispositions of Assets
501	Exemptions, Standard Deduction, and Filing Information	547	Nonbusiness Disasters, Casualties, and Thefts
502	Medical and Dental Expenses	550	Investment Income and Expenses
503	Child and Dependent Care Expenses	551	Basis of Assets
		552	Recordkeeping for Individuals
504	Divorced or Separated Individuals	553	Highlights of 1993 Tax Changes
505	Tax Withholding and Estimated Tax	554	Tax Information for Older Americans
508	Educational Expenses	555	Federal Tax Information on Community Property
509	Tax Calendar for 1994		
510	Excise Taxes for 1994	556	Examination of Returns, Appeal Rights, and Claims for Refund
513	Tax Information for Visitors to the United States	557	Tax-Exempt Status For Your Organization
514	Foreign Tax Credit for Individuals		
515	Withholding of Tax on Nonresident Aliens and Foreign Corporations	559	Survivors, Executors, and Administrators

No.	Title	No.	Title
560	Retirement Plans for the Self-Employed	723D	Actuarial Values 1—Valuation of Last Survivor Charitable Remainders—Part D
561	Determining the Value of Donated Property	723E	Actuarial Values II—Factors at 10 Percent Involving One and Two Lives
564	Mutual Fund Distributions		
570	Tax Guide for Individuals With Income From U.S. Possessions	733	Rewards for Information Provided by Individuals to the IRS
571	Tax-Sheltered Annuity Programs for Employees of Public Schools and Certain Tax-Exempt Organizations	783	Certificate of Discharge of Property from Federal Tax Lien
575	Pension and Annuity Income (Including Simplified General Rule)	784	Application for Certificate of Subordination of Federal Tax Lien
		794	Favorable Determination Letter
578	Tax Information for Private Foundations and Foundation Managers	892	Exempt Organization Appeal Procedures for Unagreed Issues
583	Taxpayers Starting a Business	901	U.S. Tax Treaties
584	Nonbusiness Disaster, Casualty, and Theft Loss Workbook	904	Interrelated Computations for Estate and Gift Taxes
587	Business Use of Your Home	907	Information for Persons with Handicaps Disabilities
589	Tax Information on S Corporations		
590	Individual Retirement Arrangements (IRAs)	908	Bankruptcy and Other Debt Cancellation
593	Tax Highlights for U.S. Citizens and Residents Going Abroad	909	Alternative Minimum Tax for Individuals
594	Understanding the Collection Process	910	Guide to Free Tax Services
		911	Tax Information for Direct Sellers
595	Tax Guide for Commercial Fishermen	915	Social Security Benefits and Equivalent Railroad Retirement Benefits
596	Earned Income Credit	917	Business Use of Car
597	Information on the United States-Canada Income Tax Treaty	919	Is My Withholding Correct for 1994?
598	Tax on Unrelated Business Income of Exempt Organizations	924	Reporting of Real Estate Transactions to IRS
641	Bulletin Index-Digest System—Service No. 1, Income Tax	925	Passive Activity and At-Risk Rules
642	Bulletin Index-Digest System—Service No. 2, Estate and Gift Taxes	926	Employment Taxes for Household Employers
		929	Tax Rules for Children and Dependents
643	Bulletin Index-Digest System—Service No. 3, Employment Taxes	936	Home Mortgage Interest Deduction
		937	Employment Taxes and Information Returns
644	Bulletin Index-Digest System—Service No. 4, Excise Taxes	938	Real Estate Mortgage (REMICs) Reporting Information
676	Catalog of Federal Tax Forms, Form Letters, and Notices	939	Pension General Rule (Nonsimplified Method)
686	Certification for Reduced Tax Rates in Tax Treaty Countries	945	Tax Information for Those Affected by Operation Desert Storm
721	Tax Guide to U.S. Civil Service Retirement Benefits	946	How To Begin Depreciating Your Property
723C	Actuarial Values 1—Valuation of Last Survivor Charitable Remainders—Part C	947	Practice Before the IRS and Power of Attorney
		952	Sick Pay Reporting

No.	Title	No.	Title
953	International Tax Information for Business	1457	Actuarial Values Alpha Volume
1004	Identification Numbers Under ERISA	1458	Actuarial Values Beta Volume
		1459	Actuarial Values Gamma Volume
1035	Extending the Tax Assessment Period	1470	Package for the Special Enrollment Examination
1045	Information for Tax Practitioners	1507	Procedures for Electronic/Magnetic Media Filing of Employee Benefit Plan Returns Forms 5500, 5500-C/R and 5500EZ
1066	Small Business Tax Workshop		
1105	Child Support Enforcement Handbook	1514	IRS Deskguide for Tax Professionals, Return Preparers and Advisors
1194	Taxpayer Information Publications		
1200	Reference Listing of Federal Tax Forms and Publications	1524	Procedures for Electronic and Magnetic Media Filing of Form 1065, U.S. Partnership Return of Income
1212	List of Original Issue Discount Instruments		
1281	Backup Withholding on Missing and Incorrect TINs	1542	Per Diem Rates
		1544	Reporting Cash Payments of Over $10,000
1320	Problem Resolution Offices Function and Phone Numbers (Operation LINK)	1565	A Married Couple's Guide to Understanding Your Benefit Choices at Retirement from a Defined Contribution Plan
1383	The Correspondence Process (Income Tax Accounts)		
1388	Should You Be Filing Information Returns	1566	A Married Couple's Guide to Understanding Your Benefit Coices at Retirement from a Defined Benefit Plan
1391	Deductibility of Payments Made to Charities Conducting Fund-Raising Events		
		1600	Disaster Losses
1437	Procedures for Electronic and Magnetic Media Filing of U.S. Fiduciary Income Tax Returns, Form 1041	1678	Handbook for 1040PC Format Preparers
		1679	A Guide to Backup Withholding

¶ 1119 "PS-58" Rate Table

This table is used to determine the cost of current life insurance protection includible in an employee's income with respect to certain split dollar life insurance arrangements, see ¶ 1269, and life insurance provided under a qualified pension or profit sharing plan, see ¶ 4343.

Age	Premium	Age	Premium	Age	Premium	Age	Premium
15	$ 1.27	28	2.20	41	4.73	52	10.79
16	1.38	29	2.31	42	5.07	53	11.69
17	1.48	30	2.43	43	5.44	54	12.67
18	1.52	31	2.57	43	5.44	55	13.74
19	1.56	32	2.70	44	5.85	56	14.91
20	1.61	33	$2.86	45	6.30	57	16.18
21	1.67	34	3.02	45	6.30	58	17.56
22	1.73	35	3.21	46	6.78	59	19.08
23	1.79	36	3.41	47	7.32	60	20.73
24	1.86	37	3.63	48	$7.89	61	22.53
25	1.93	38	3.87	49	8.53	62	24.50
26	2.02	39	4.14	50	9.22	63	26.63
27	2.11	40	4.42	51	9.97	64	28.98

Age	Premium	Age	Premium	Age	Premium	Age	Premium
65	$31.51	70	48.06	74	67.33	78	94.09
66	34.28	71	52.29	75	73.23	79	102.23
67	37.31	72	56.89	76	79.63	80	111.04
68	40.59	73	61.89	77	86.57	81	120.57
69	44.17						

¶ 1120 MACRS, ACRS and Leased Auto Tables

Here are MACRS and ACRS depreciation (cost recovery) tables, and the cost recovery tables and income-inclusion-amount tables under the luxury auto rules.

The tables reproduced are the MACRS—general depreciation as well as alternative depreciation system (ADS) tables—and ACRS tables, and the cost recovery tables under the luxury auto and other listed property rules (used to determine income inclusion amounts by lessees of automobiles and other listed property). Under the general depreciation system (GDS) of MACRS, the table rates are based on: (1) the 200% declining balance method for 3-, 5-, 7-, and 10-year personal property; (2) the 150% declining balance method for 15-, and 20-year personal property; and (3) the straight-line method for residential and nonresidential realty. Under the alternative depreciation system (ADS) of MACRS, the table rates for personal and real property are based on the straight-line method. The use of the tables is discussed in Chapter 5. (IRS alternative minimum tax tables are not reproduced in this Handbook. For those tables, see the Appendix to Federal Tax Coordinator 2d Chapter L-7400.)

Table 1
General Depreciation System
Applicable Depreciation Method: 200 or 150 Percent
Declining Balance Switching to Straight Line
Applicable Recovery Periods: 3, 5, 7, 10, 15, 20 years
Applicable Convention: Half-year

If the Recovery Year is:	and the Recovery Period is:					
	3-year	5-year	7-year	10-year	15-year	20-year
			the Depreciation Rate is:			
1	33.33	20.00	14.29	10.00	5.00	3.750
2	44.45	32.00	24.49	18.00	9.50	7.219
3	14.81	19.20	17.49	14.40	8.55	6.677
4	7.41	11.52	12.49	11.52	7.70	6.177
5		11.52	8.93	9.22	6.93	5.713
6		5.76	8.92	7.37	6.23	5.285
7			8.93	6.55	5.90	4.888
8			4.46	6.55	5.90	4.522
9				6.56	5.91	4.462
10				6.55	5.90	4.461
11				3.28	5.91	4.462
12					5.90	4.461
13					5.91	4.462
14					5.90	4.461
15					5.91	4.462
16					2.95	4.461
17						4.462
18						4.461
19						4.462
20						4.461
21						2.231

Table 2
General Depreciation System
Applicable Depreciation Method: 200 or 150 Percent
Declining Balance Switching to Straight Line
Applicable Recovery Periods: 3, 5, 7, 10, 15, 20 years
Applicable Convention: Mid-quarter
(property placed in service in first quarter)

If the Recovery Year is:	and the Recovery Period is:					
	3-year	5-year	7-year	10-year	15-year	20-year
			the Depreciation Rate is:			
1	58.33	35.00	25.00	17.50	8.75	6.563
2	27.78	26.00	21.43	16.50	9.13	7.000
3	12.35	15.60	15.31	13.20	8.21	6.482
4	1.54	11.01	10.93	10.56	7.39	5.996
5		11.01	8.75	8.45	6.65	5.546
6		1.38	8.74	6.76	5.99	5.130
7			8.75	6.55	5.90	4.746
8			1.09	6.55	5.91	4.459
9				6.56	5.90	4.459
10				6.55	5.91	4.459
11				0.82	5.90	4.459
12					5.91	4.460
13					5.90	4.459
14					5.91	4.460
15					5.90	4.459
16					0.74	4.460
17						4.459
18						4.460
19						4.459
20						4.460
21						0.557

Table 3
General Depreciation System
Applicable Depreciation Method: 200 or 150 Percent
Declining Balance Switching to Straight Line
Applicable Recovery Periods: 3, 5, 7, 10, 15, 20 years
Applicable Convention: Mid-quarter
(property placed in service in second quarter)

If the Recovery Year is:	and the Recovery Period is:					
	3-year	5-year	7-year	10-year	15-year	20-year
			the Depreciation Rate is:			
1	41.67	25.00	17.85	12.50	6.25	4.688
2	38.89	30.00	23.47	17.50	9.38	7.148
3	14.14	18.00	16.76	14.00	8.44	6.612
4	5.30	11.37	11.97	11.20	7.59	6.116
5		11.37	8.87	8.96	6.83	5.658
6		4.26	8.87	7.17	6.15	5.233
7			8.87	6.55	5.91	4.841
8			3.33	6.55	5.90	4.478
9				6.56	5.91	4.463
10				6.55	5.90	4.463
11				2.46	5.91	4.463
12					5.90	4.463
13					5.91	4.463
14					5.90	4.463
15					5.91	4.462
16					2.21	4.463
17						4.462
18						4.463
19						4.462
20						4.463
21						1.673

Table 4
General Depreciation System
Applicable Depreciation Method: 200 or 150 Percent
Declining Balance Switching to Straight Line
Applicable Recovery Periods: 3, 5, 7, 10, 15, 20 years
Applicable Convention: Mid-quarter
(property placed in service in third quarter)

If the Recovery Year is:	and the Recovery Period is:					
	3-year	5-year	7-year	10-year	15-year	20-year
			the Depreciation Rate is:			
1	25.00	15.00	10.71	7.50	3.75	2.813
2	50.00	34.00	25.51	18.50	9.63	7.289
3	16.67	20.40	18.22	14.80	8.66	6.742
4	8.33	12.24	13.02	11.84	7.80	6.237
5		11.30	9.30	9.47	7.02	5.769
6		7.06	8.85	7.58	6.31	5.336
7			8.86	6.55	5.90	4.936
8			5.53	6.55	5.90	4.566
9				6.56	5.91	4.460
10				6.55	5.90	4.460
11				4.10	5.91	4.460
12					5.90	4.460
13					5.91	4.461
14					5.90	4.460
15					5.91	4.461
16					3.69	4.460
17						4.461
18						4.460
19						4.461
20						4.460
21						2.788

Table 5
General Depreciation System
Applicable Depreciation Method: 200 or 150 Percent
Declining Balance Switching to Straight Line
Applicable Recovery Periods: 3, 5, 7, 10, 15, 20 years
Applicable Convention: Mid-quarter
(property placed in service in fourth quarter)

If the Recovery Year is:	and the Recovery Period is:					
	3-year	5-year	7-year	10-year	15-year	20-year
			the Depreciation Rate is:			
1	8.33	5.00	3.57	2.50	1.25	0.938
2	61.11	38.00	27.55	19.50	9.88	7.430
3	20.37	22.80	19.68	15.60	8.89	6.872
4	10.19	13.68	14.06	12.48	8.00	6.357
5		10.94	10.04	9.98	7.20	5.880
6		9.58	8.73	7.99	6.48	5.439
7			8.73	6.55	5.90	5.031
8			7.64	6.55	5.90	4.654
9				6.56	5.90	4.458
10				6.55	5.91	4.458
11				5.74	5.90	4.458
12					5.91	4.458
13					5.90	4.458
14					5.91	4.458
15					5.90	4.458
16					5.17	4.458
17						4.458
18						4.459
19						4.458
20						4.459
21						3.901

¶ 1120   Chapter 1 / 1994 RIA FEDERAL TAX HANDBOOK

Table 6
General Depreciation System
Applicable Depreciation Method: Straight Line
Applicable Recovery Period: 27.5 years
Applicable Convention: Mid-month

If the Recovery Year is:	And the Month in the First Recovery Year the Property is Placed in Service is:											
	1	2	3	4	5	6	7	8	9	10	11	12
	the Depreciation Rate is:											
1	3.485	3.182	2.879	2.576	2.273	1.970	1.667	1.364	1.061	0.758	0.455	0.152
2	3.636	3.636	3.636	3.636	3.636	3.636	3.636	3.636	3.636	3.636	3.636	3.636
3	3.636	3.636	3.636	3.636	3.636	3.636	3.636	3.636	3.636	3.636	3.636	3.636
4	3.636	3.636	3.636	3.636	3.636	3.636	3.636	3.636	3.636	3.636	3.636	3.636
5	3.636	3.636	3.636	3.636	3.636	3.636	3.636	3.636	3.636	3.636	3.636	3.636
6	3.636	3.636	3.636	3.636	3.636	3.636	3.636	3.636	3.636	3.636	3.636	3.636
7	3.636	3.636	3.636	3.636	3.636	3.636	3.636	3.636	3.636	3.636	3.636	3.636
8	3.636	3.636	3.636	3.636	3.636	3.636	3.636	3.636	3.636	3.636	3.636	3.636
9	3.636	3.636	3.636	3.636	3.636	3.636	3.636	3.636	3.636	3.636	3.636	3.636
10	3.637	3.637	3.637	3.637	3.637	3.637	3.636	3.636	3.636	3.636	3.636	3.636
11	3.636	3.636	3.636	3.636	3.636	3.636	3.637	3.637	3.637	3.637	3.637	3.637
12	3.637	3.637	3.637	3.637	3.637	3.637	3.636	3.636	3.636	3.636	3.636	3.636
13	3.636	3.636	3.636	3.636	3.636	3.636	3.637	3.637	3.637	3.637	3.637	3.637
14	3.637	3.637	3.637	3.637	3.637	3.637	3.636	3.636	3.636	3.636	3.636	3.636
15	3.636	3.636	3.636	3.636	3.636	3.636	3.637	3.637	3.637	3.637	3.637	3.637
16	3.637	3.637	3.637	3.637	3.637	3.637	3.636	3.636	3.636	3.636	3.636	3.636
17	3.636	3.636	3.636	3.636	3.636	3.636	3.637	3.637	3.637	3.637	3.637	3.637
18	3.637	3.637	3.637	3.637	3.637	3.637	3.636	3.636	3.636	3.636	3.636	3.636
19	3.636	3.636	3.636	3.636	3.636	3.636	3.637	3.637	3.637	3.637	3.637	3.637
20	3.637	3.637	3.637	3.637	3.637	3.637	3.636	3.636	3.636	3.636	3.636	3.636
21	3.636	3.636	3.636	3.636	3.636	3.636	3.637	3.637	3.637	3.637	3.637	3.637
22	3.637	3.637	3.637	3.637	3.637	3.637	3.636	3.636	3.636	3.636	3.636	3.636
23	3.636	3.636	3.636	3.636	3.636	3.636	3.637	3.637	3.637	3.637	3.637	3.637
24	3.637	3.637	3.637	3.637	3.637	3.637	3.636	3.636	3.636	3.636	3.636	3.636
25	3.636	3.636	3.636	3.636	3.636	3.636	3.637	3.637	3.637	3.637	3.637	3.637
26	3.637	3.637	3.637	3.637	3.637	3.637	3.636	3.636	3.636	3.636	3.636	3.636
27	3.636	3.636	3.636	3.636	3.636	3.636	3.637	3.637	3.637	3.637	3.637	3.637
28	1.970	2.273	2.576	2.879	3.182	3.485	3.636	3.636	3.636	3.636	3.636	3.636
29	0.000	0.000	0.000	0.000	0.000	0.000	0.152	0.455	0.758	1.061	1.364	1.667

44

Table 7

General Depreciation System
Applicable Depreciation Method: Straight Line
Applicable Recovery Period: 31.5 years
Applicable Convention: Mid-month

If the Recovery Year is:	And the Month in the First Recovery Year the Property is Placed in Service is:											
	1	2	3	4	5	6	7	8	9	10	11	12
	the Depreciation Rate is:											
1	3.042	2.778	2.513	2.249	1.984	1.720	1.455	1.190	0.926	0.661	0.397	0.132
2	3.175	3.175	3.175	3.175	3.175	3.175	3.175	3.175	3.175	3.715	3.175	3.175
3	3.175	3.175	3.175	3.175	3.175	3.175	3.175	3.175	3.175	3.175	3.175	3.175
4	3.175	3.175	3.175	3.175	3.175	3.175	3.175	3.175	3.175	3.175	3.175	3.175
5	3.175	3.175	3.175	3.175	3.175	3.175	3.175	3.175	3.175	3.175	3.175	3.175
6	3.175	3.175	3.175	3.175	3.175	3.175	3.175	3.175	3.175	3.175	3.175	3.175
7	3.175	3.175	3.175	3.175	3.175	3.175	3.175	3.175	3.175	3.175	3.175	3.175
8	3.175	3.174	3.175	3.174	3.175	3.174	3.175	3.175	3.175	3.175	3.175	3.175
9	3.174	3.175	3.174	3.175	3.174	3.175	3.174	3.175	3.174	3.175	3.174	3.175
10	3.175	3.174	3.175	3.174	3.175	3.174	3.175	3.174	3.175	3.174	3.175	3.174
11	3.174	3.175	3.174	3.175	3.174	3.175	3.174	3.175	3.174	3.175	3.174	3.175
12	3.175	3.174	3.175	3.174	3.175	3.174	3.175	3.174	3.175	3.174	3.175	3.174
13	3.174	3.175	3.174	3.175	3.174	3.175	3.174	3.175	3.174	3.175	3.174	3.175
14	3.175	3.174	3.175	3.174	3.175	3.174	3.175	3.174	3.175	3.174	3.175	3.174
15	3.174	3.175	3.174	3.175	3.174	3.175	3.174	3.175	3.174	3.175	3.174	3.175
16	3.175	3.174	3.175	3.174	3.175	3.174	3.175	3.174	3.175	3.174	3.175	3.174
17	3.174	3.175	3.174	3.175	3.174	3.175	3.174	3.175	3.174	3.175	3.174	3.175
18	3.175	3.174	3.175	3.174	3.175	3.174	3.175	3.174	3.175	3.174	3.175	3.174
19	3.174	3.175	3.174	3.175	3.174	3.175	3.174	3.175	3.174	3.175	3.174	3.175
20	3.175	3.174	3.175	3.174	3.175	3.174	3.175	3.174	3.175	3.174	3.175	3.174
21	3.174	3.175	3.174	3.175	3.174	3.175	3.174	3.175	3.174	3.175	3.174	3.175
22	3.175	3.174	3.175	3.174	3.175	3.174	3.175	3.174	3.175	3.174	3.175	3.174
23	3.174	3.175	3.174	3.175	3.174	3.175	3.174	3.175	3.174	3.175	3.174	3.175
24	3.175	3.174	3.175	3.174	3.175	3.174	3.175	3.174	3.175	3.174	3.175	3.174
25	3.174	3.175	3.174	3.175	3.174	3.175	3.174	3.175	3.174	3.175	3.174	3.175
26	3.175	3.174	3.175	3.174	3.175	3.174	3.175	3.174	3.175	3.174	3.175	3.174
27	3.174	3.175	3.174	3.175	3.174	3.175	3.174	3.175	3.174	3.175	3.174	3.175
28	3.175	3.174	3.175	3.174	3.175	3.174	3.175	3.174	3.175	3.174	3.175	3.174
29	3.174	3.175	3.174	3.175	3.174	3.175	3.174	3.175	3.174	3.175	3.174	3.175
30	3.175	3.174	3.175	3.174	3.175	3.174	3.175	3.174	3.175	3.174	3.175	3.174
31	3.174	3.175	3.174	3.175	3.174	3.175	3.174	3.175	3.174	3.175	3.174	3.175
32	1.720	1.984	2.249	2.513	2.778	3.042	3.175	3.174	3.175	3.174	3.175	3.174
33	0.000	0.000	0.000	0.000	0.000	0.000	0.132	0.397	0.661	0.926	1.190	1.455

Table 8
General and Alternative Depreciation Systems
Applicable Depreciation Method: Straight Line
Applicable Recovery Periods: 2.5-50 years
Applicable Convention: Half-year

If the Recovery Year is:	and the Recovery Period is: the Depreciation Rate is:															
	2.5	3.0	3.5	4.0	4.5	5.0	5.5	6.0	6.5	7.0	7.5	8.0	8.5	9.0	9.5	10.0
1	20.00	16.67	14.29	12.50	11.11	10.00	9.09	8.33	7.69	7.14	6.67	6.25	5.88	5.56	5.26	5.00
2	40.00	33.33	28.57	25.00	22.22	20.00	18.18	16.67	15.39	14.29	13.33	12.50	11.77	11.11	10.53	10.00
3	40.00	33.33	28.57	25.00	22.22	20.00	18.18	16.67	15.38	14.29	13.33	12.50	11.76	11.11	10.53	10.00
4		16.67	28.57	25.00	22.23	20.00	18.18	16.67	15.39	14.28	13.33	12.50	11.77	11.11	10.53	10.00
5				12.50	22.22	20.00	18.19	16.66	15.38	14.29	13.34	12.50	11.76	11.11	10.52	10.00
6						10.00	18.18	16.67	15.39	14.28	13.33	12.50	11.77	11.11	10.53	10.00
7								8.33	15.38	14.29	13.34	12.50	11.76	11.11	10.52	10.00
8										7.14	13.33	12.50	11.77	11.11	10.53	10.00
9												6.25	11.76	11.11	10.52	10.00
10														5.56	10.53	10.00
11																5.00

If the Recovery Year is:	and the Recovery Period is: the Depreciation Rate is:															
	10.5	11.0	11.5	12.0	12.5	13.0	13.5	14.0	14.5	15.0	15.5	16.0	16.5	17.0	17.5	18.0
1	4.76	4.55	4.35	4.17	4.00	3.85	3.70	3.57	3.45	3.33	3.23	3.13	3.03	2.94	2.86	2.78
2	9.52	9.09	8.70	8.33	8.00	7.69	7.41	7.14	6.90	6.67	6.45	6.25	6.06	5.88	5.71	5.56
3	9.52	9.09	8.70	8.33	8.00	7.69	7.41	7.14	6.90	6.67	6.45	6.25	6.06	5.88	5.71	5.56
4	9.53	9.09	8.69	8.33	8.00	7.69	7.41	7.14	6.90	6.67	6.45	6.25	6.06	5.88	5.71	5.55
5	9.52	9.09	8.70	8.33	8.00	7.69	7.41	7.14	6.90	6.67	6.45	6.25	6.06	5.88	5.72	5.56
6	9.53	9.09	8.69	8.33	8.00	7.69	7.41	7.14	6.89	6.67	6.45	6.25	6.06	5.88	5.71	5.55
7	9.52	9.09	8.70	8.34	8.00	7.69	7.41	7.14	6.90	6.67	6.45	6.25	6.06	5.88	5.72	5.56
8	9.53	9.09	8.69	8.33	8.00	7.69	7.41	7.15	6.89	6.66	6.45	6.25	6.06	5.88	5.71	5.55
9	9.52	9.09	8.70	8.34	8.00	7.69	7.41	7.14	6.90	6.67	6.45	6.25	6.06	5.88	5.72	5.56
10	9.53	9.09	8.69	8.33	8.00	7.70	7.40	7.15	6.89	6.66	6.45	6.25	6.06	5.88	5.71	5.55
11	9.52	9.09	8.70	8.34	8.00	7.69	7.41	7.14	6.90	6.67	6.45	6.25	6.06	5.89	5.72	5.56
12		4.55	8.69	8.33	8.00	7.70	7.40	7.15	6.89	6.66	6.45	6.25	6.06	5.88	5.71	5.55
13				4.17	8.00	7.69	7.41	7.14	6.90	6.67	6.45	6.25	6.06	5.89	5.72	5.56
14						3.85	7.40	7.15	6.89	6.66	6.46	6.25	6.06	5.88	5.71	5.55
15								3.57	6.90	6.67	6.45	6.25	6.06	5.89	5.72	5.56
16										3.33	6.46	6.25	6.06	5.88	5.71	5.55
17												3.12	6.07	5.89	5.72	5.56
18														2.94	5.71	5.55
19																2.78

If the Recovery Year is:	and the Recovery Period is: the Depreciation Rate is:															
	18.5	19.0	19.5	20.0	20.5	21.0	21.5	22.0	22.5	23.0	23.5	24.0	24.5	25.0	25.5	26.0
1	2.70	2.63	2.56	2.500	2.439	2.381	2.326	2.273	2.222	2.174	2.128	2.083	2.041	2.000	1.961	1.923
2	5.41	5.26	5.13	5.000	4.878	4.762	4.651	4.545	4.444	4.348	4.255	4.167	4.082	4.000	3.922	3.846
3	5.41	5.26	5.13	5.000	4.878	4.762	4.651	4.545	4.444	4.348	4.255	4.167	4.082	4.000	3.922	3.846
4	5.41	5.26	5.13	5.000	4.878	4.762	4.651	4.545	4.445	4.348	4.255	4.167	4.082	4.000	3.922	3.846
5	5.40	5.26	5.13	5.000	4.878	4.762	4.651	4.546	4.444	4.348	4.255	4.167	4.082	4.000	3.922	3.846
6	5.41	5.26	5.13	5.000	4.878	4.762	4.651	4.545	4.445	4.348	4.255	4.167	4.082	4.000	3.921	3.846
7	5.40	5.26	5.13	5.000	4.878	4.762	4.651	4.546	4.444	4.348	4.255	4.167	4.082	4.000	3.922	3.846
8	5.41	5.26	5.13	5.000	4.878	4.762	4.651	4.545	4.445	4.348	4.255	4.167	4.082	4.000	3.921	3.846
9	5.40	5.27	5.13	5.000	4.878	4.762	4.651	4.546	4.444	4.348	4.255	4.167	4.081	4.000	3.922	3.846
10	5.41	5.26	5.13	5.000	4.878	4.762	4.651	4.545	4.445	4.348	4.255	4.167	4.082	4.000	3.921	3.846
11	5.40	5.27	5.13	5.000	4.878	4.762	4.651	4.546	4.444	4.348	4.256	4.166	4.081	4.000	3.922	3.846
12	5.41	5.26	5.13	5.000	4.878	4.762	4.651	4.545	4.445	4.348	4.255	4.167	4.082	4.000	3.921	3.846
13	5.40	5.27	5.13	5.000	4.878	4.762	4.651	4.546	4.444	4.348	4.256	4.166	4.081	4.000	3.922	3.846
14	5.41	5.26	5.13	5.000	4.878	4.762	4.651	4.545	4.445	4.348	4.255	4.167	4.082	4.000	3.921	3.846
15	5.40	5.27	5.13	5.000	4.878	4.762	4.651	4.546	4.444	4.348	4.256	4.166	4.081	4.000	3.922	3.846
16	5.41	5.26	5.12	5.000	4.878	4.762	4.651	4.545	4.445	4.348	4.255	4.167	4.082	4.000	3.921	3.846
17	5.40	5.27	5.13	5.000	4.878	4.762	4.652	4.546	4.444	4.347	4.256	4.166	4.081	4.000	3.922	3.846
18	5.41	5.26	5.12	5.000	4.878	4.762	4.651	4.545	4.445	4.348	4.255	4.167	4.082	4.000	3.921	3.846
19	5.40	5.27	5.13	5.000	4.878	4.761	4.652	4.546	4.444	4.347	4.256	4.166	4.081	4.000	3.922	3.846
20		2.63	5.12	5.000	4.879	4.762	4.651	4.545	4.445	4.348	4.255	4.167	4.082	4.000	3.921	3.847
21				2.500	4.878	4.761	4.652	4.546	4.444	4.347	4.256	4.166	4.081	4.000	3.922	3.846
22					2.381	4.651	4.545	4.445	4.348	4.255	4.167	4.082	4.000	3.921	3.847	
23							2.273	4.444	4.347	4.256	4.166	4.081	4.000	3.922	3.846	
24									2.174	4.255	4.167	4.082	4.000	3.921	3.847	
25											2.083	4.081	4.000	3.922	3.846	
26												2.000	3.921	3.847	3.846	
27																1.923

If the Recovery Year is:	and the Recovery Period is: the Depreciation Rate is:															
	26.5	27.0	27.5	28.0	28.5	29.0	29.5	30.0	30.5	31.0	31.5	32.0	32.5	33.0	33.5	34.0
1	1.887	1.852	1.818	1.786	1.754	1.724	1.695	1.667	1.639	1.613	1.587	1.563	1.538	1.515	1.493	1.471
2	3.774	3.704	3.636	3.571	3.509	3.448	3.390	3.333	3.279	3.226	3.175	3.125	3.077	3.030	2.985	2.941
3	3.774	3.704	3.636	3.571	3.509	3.448	3.390	3.333	3.279	3.226	3.175	3.125	3.077	3.030	2.985	2.941
4	3.774	3.704	3.636	3.571	3.509	3.448	3.390	3.333	3.279	3.226	3.175	3.125	3.077	3.030	2.985	2.941
5	3.774	3.704	3.636	3.571	3.509	3.448	3.390	3.333	3.279	3.226	3.175	3.125	3.077	3.030	2.985	2.941
6	3.774	3.704	3.636	3.571	3.509	3.448	3.390	3.333	3.279	3.226	3.175	3.125	3.077	3.030	2.985	2.941
7	3.773	3.704	3.636	3.572	3.509	3.448	3.390	3.333	3.279	3.226	3.175	3.125	3.077	3.030	2.985	2.941
8	3.774	3.704	3.636	3.571	3.509	3.448	3.390	3.333	3.279	3.226	3.175	3.125	3.077	3.030	2.985	2.941
9	3.773	3.704	3.637	3.572	3.509	3.448	3.390	3.333	3.279	3.226	3.175	3.125	3.077	3.030	2.985	2.941
10	3.774	3.704	3.636	3.571	3.509	3.448	3.390	3.333	3.279	3.226	3.174	3.125	3.077	3.030	2.985	2.941
11	3.773	3.704	3.637	3.572	3.509	3.448	3.390	3.333	3.279	3.226	3.175	3.125	3.077	3.030	2.985	2.941
12	3.774	3.704	3.636	3.571	3.509	3.448	3.390	3.333	3.279	3.226	3.174	3.125	3.077	3.030	2.985	2.941
13	3.773	3.703	3.637	3.572	3.509	3.448	3.390	3.334	3.279	3.226	3.175	3.125	3.077	3.030	2.985	2.941
14	3.773	3.704	3.636	3.571	3.509	3.448	3.390	3.333	3.279	3.226	3.174	3.125	3.077	3.030	2.985	2.941
15	3.774	3.703	3.637	3.572	3.509	3.449	3.390	3.334	3.278	3.226	3.175	3.125	3.077	3.031	2.985	2.941
16	3.773	3.704	3.636	3.571	3.509	3.448	3.390	3.333	3.279	3.226	3.174	3.125	3.077	3.030	2.985	2.941
17	3.774	3.703	3.637	3.572	3.509	3.449	3.390	3.334	3.278	3.226	3.175	3.125	3.077	3.031	2.985	2.941
18	3.773	3.704	3.636	3.571	3.508	3.448	3.390	3.333	3.279	3.226	3.174	3.125	3.077	3.030	2.985	2.941
19	3.774	3.703	3.637	3.572	3.509	3.449	3.390	3.334	3.278	3.226	3.175	3.125	3.077	3.031	2.985	2.941
20	3.773	3.704	3.636	3.571	3.508	3.448	3.390	3.333	3.279	3.226	3.174	3.125	3.077	3.030	2.985	2.941
21	3.774	3.703	3.637	3.572	3.509	3.449	3.389	3.334	3.278	3.225	3.175	3.125	3.077	3.031	2.985	2.941
22	3.773	3.704	3.636	3.571	3.508	3.448	3.390	3.333	3.279	3.226	3.174	3.125	3.077	3.030	2.985	2.941
23	3.774	3.703	3.637	3.572	3.509	3.449	3.389	3.334	3.278	3.225	3.175	3.125	3.077	3.031	2.985	2.941
24	3.773	3.704	3.636	3.571	3.508	3.448	3.390	3.333	3.279	3.226	3.174	3.125	3.077	3.030	2.985	2.941
25	3.774	3.703	3.637	3.572	3.509	3.449	3.389	3.334	3.278	3.225	3.175	3.125	3.077	3.031	2.985	2.942
26	3.773	3.704	3.636	3.571	3.508	3.448	3.390	3.333	3.279	3.226	3.174	3.125	3.077	3.030	2.985	2.941
27	3.774	3.703	3.637	3.572	3.509	3.449	3.389	3.334	3.278	3.225	3.175	3.125	3.077	3.031	2.985	2.942
28		1.852	3.636	3.571	3.508	3.448	3.390	3.333	3.279	3.226	3.174	3.125	3.077	3.030	2.985	2.941
29				1.786	3.509	3.449	3.389	3.334	3.278	3.225	3.175	3.125	3.077	3.031	2.985	2.942
30						1.724	3.390	3.333	3.279	3.226	3.174	3.125	3.077	3.030	2.985	2.941
31								1.667	3.278	3.225	3.175	3.125	3.076	3.031	2.986	2.942
32										1.613	3.174	3.125	3.077	3.030	2.985	2.941
33												1.562	3.076	3.031	2.986	2.942
34														1.515	2.985	2.941
36																1.471

If the Recovery Year is:	34.5	35.0	35.5	36.0	36.5	37.0	37.5	38.0	38.5	39.0	39.5	40.0	40.5	41.0	41.5	42.0
							and the Recovery Period is: the Depreciation Rate is:									
1	1.449	1.429	1.408	1.389	1.370	1.351	1.333	1.316	1.299	1.282	1.266	1.250	1.235	1.220	1.205	1.190
2	2.899	2.857	2.817	2.740	2.740	2.703	2.667	2.632	2.597	2.564	2.532	2.500	2.469	2.439	2.410	2.381
3	2.899	2.857	2.817	2.778	2.740	2.703	2.667	2.632	2.597	2.564	2.532	2.500	2.469	2.439	2.410	2.381
4	2.899	2.857	2.817	2.778	2.740	2.703	2.667	2.632	2.597	2.564	2.532	2.500	2.469	2.439	2.410	2.381
5	2.899	2.857	2.817	2.778	2.740	2.703	2.667	2.632	2.597	2.564	2.532	2.500	2.469	2.439	2.410	2.381
6	2.899	2.857	2.817	2.778	2.740	2.703	2.667	2.632	2.597	2.564	2.532	2.500	2.469	2.439	2.410	2.381
7	2.898	2.857	2.817	2.778	2.740	2.703	2.667	2.632	2.597	2.564	2.532	2.500	2.469	2.439	2.410	2.381
8	2.899	2.857	2.817	2.778	2.740	2.703	2.667	2.631	2.597	2.564	2.532	2.500	2.469	2.439	2.410	2.381
9	2.898	2.857	2.817	2.778	2.740	2.703	2.667	2.632	2.597	2.564	2.532	2.500	2.469	2.439	2.410	2.381
10	2.899	2.857	2.817	2.778	2.740	2.703	2.667	2.631	2.598	2.564	2.532	2.500	2.469	2.439	2.410	2.381
11	2.898	2.857	2.817	2.778	2.740	2.703	2.667	2.632	2.597	2.564	2.532	2.500	2.469	2.439	2.410	2.381
12	2.899	2.857	2.817	2.778	2.740	2.703	2.667	2.631	2.598	2.564	2.532	2.500	2.469	2.439	2.410	2.381
13	2.898	2.857	2.817	2.778	2.740	2.703	2.667	2.632	2.597	2.564	2.532	2.500	2.469	2.439	2.410	2.381
14	2.899	2.857	2.817	2.778	2.740	2.703	2.667	2.631	2.598	2.564	2.531	2.500	2.469	2.439	2.409	2.381
15	2.898	2.857	2.817	2.778	2.740	2.703	2.666	2.632	2.597	2.564	2.532	2.500	2.469	2.439	2.410	2.381
16	2.899	2.857	2.817	2.778	2.740	2.703	2.667	2.631	2.598	2.564	2.531	2.500	2.469	2.439	2.409	2.381
17	2.898	2.857	2.817	2.778	2.740	2.703	2.666	2.632	2.597	2.564	2.532	2.500	2.469	2.439	2.410	2.381
18	2.899	2.857	2.817	2.778	2.740	2.702	2.667	2.631	2.598	2.564	2.531	2.500	2.469	2.439	2.409	2.381
19	2.898	2.857	2.817	2.778	2.739	2.703	2.666	2.632	2.597	2.564	2.532	2.500	2.469	2.439	2.410	2.381
20	2.898	2.857	2.817	2.778	2.740	2.702	2.667	2.631	2.598	2.564	2.531	2.500	2.469	2.439	2.409	2.381
21	2.899	2.857	2.817	2.778	2.739	2.703	2.666	2.632	2.597	2.564	2.532	2.500	2.469	2.439	2.410	2.381
22	2.898	2.857	2.817	2.777	2.740	2.702	2.667	2.631	2.598	2.564	2.531	2.500	2.469	2.439	2.409	2.381
23	2.899	2.857	2.817	2.778	2.739	2.703	2.666	2.632	2.597	2.564	2.532	2.500	2.469	2.439	2.410	2.381
24	2.898	2.857	2.817	2.777	2.740	2.702	2.667	2.631	2.598	2.564	2.531	2.500	2.469	2.439	2.409	2.381
25	2.899	2.857	2.817	2.778	2.739	2.703	2.666	2.632	2.597	2.564	2.532	2.500	2.469	2.439	2.410	2.381
26	2.898	2.857	2.817	2.777	2.740	2.702	2.667	2.631	2.598	2.564	2.531	2.500	2.469	2.439	2.409	2.381
27	2.899	2.857	2.817	2.778	2.739	2.703	2.666	2.632	2.597	2.564	2.532	2.500	2.469	2.439	2.410	2.381
28	2.898	2.858	2.817	2.777	2.740	2.702	2.667	2.631	2.598	2.564	2.531	2.500	2.469	2.439	2.409	2.381
29	2.899	2.857	2.817	2.778	2.739	2.703	2.666	2.632	2.597	2.564	2.532	2.500	2.469	2.439	2.410	2.381
30	2.898	2.858	2.817	2.777	2.740	2.702	2.667	2.631	2.598	2.564	2.531	2.500	2.469	2.439	2.409	2.381
31	2.899	2.857	2.817	2.778	2.739	2.703	2.666	2.632	2.597	2.564	2.532	2.500	2.469	2.439	2.410	2.381
32	2.898	2.858	2.816	2.777	2.740	2.702	2.667	2.631	2.598	2.564	2.531	2.500	2.470	2.439	2.409	2.381
33	2.899	2.857	2.817	2.778	2.739	2.703	2.666	2.632	2.597	2.565	2.532	2.500	2.469	2.439	2.410	2.381
34	2.898	2.858	2.816	2.777	2.740	2.702	2.667	2.631	2.598	2.564	2.531	2.500	2.470	2.439	2.409	2.381
35	2.899	2.857	2.817	2.778	2.739	2.703	2.666	2.632	2.597	2.565	2.532	2.500	2.469	2.439	2.410	2.381
36		1.429	2.816	2.777	2.740	2.702	2.667	2.631	2.598	2.564	2.531	2.500	2.470	2.439	2.409	2.381
37				1.389	2.739	2.703	2.666	2.632	2.597	2.565	2.532	2.500	2.469	2.439	2.410	2.381
38						1.351	2.667	2.631	2.598	2.564	2.531	2.500	2.469	2.439	2.410	2.381
39								1.316	2.597	2.565	2.532	2.500	2.469	2.439	2.410	2.381
40										1.282	2.531	2.500	2.470	2.439	2.409	2.381
41												1.250	2.469	2.439	2.410	2.380
42														1.220	2.409	2.381
43																1.190

If the Recovery Year is:	42.5	43.0	43.5	44.0	44.5	45.0	45.5	46.0	46.5	47.0	47.5	48.0	48.5	49.0	49.5	50.0
	— the Depreciation Rate is:															
1	1.176	1.163	1.149	1.136	1.124	1.111	1.099	1.087	1.075	1.064	1.053	1.042	1.031	1.020	1.010	1.000
2	2.353	2.326	2.299	2.273	2.247	2.222	2.198	2.174	2.151	2.128	2.105	2.083	2.062	2.041	2.020	2.000
3	2.353	2.326	2.299	2.273	2.247	2.222	2.198	2.174	2.151	2.128	2.105	2.083	2.062	2.041	2.020	2.000
4	2.353	2.326	2.299	2.273	2.247	2.222	2.198	2.174	2.151	2.128	2.105	2.083	2.062	2.041	2.020	2.000
5	2.353	2.326	2.299	2.273	2.247	2.222	2.198	2.174	2.151	2.128	2.105	2.083	2.062	2.041	2.020	2.000
6	2.353	2.326	2.299	2.273	2.247	2.222	2.198	2.174	2.151	2.128	2.105	2.083	2.062	2.041	2.020	2.000
7	2.353	2.326	2.299	2.273	2.247	2.222	2.198	2.174	2.150	2.128	2.105	2.083	2.062	2.041	2.020	2.000
8	2.353	2.326	2.299	2.273	2.247	2.222	2.198	2.174	2.151	2.128	2.105	2.083	2.062	2.041	2.020	2.000
9	2.353	2.325	2.299	2.273	2.247	2.222	2.198	2.174	2.150	2.128	2.105	2.083	2.062	2.041	2.020	2.000
10	2.353	2.326	2.299	2.273	2.247	2.222	2.198	2.174	2.151	2.128	2.105	2.083	2.062	2.041	2.020	2.000
11	2.353	2.325	2.299	2.273	2.247	2.222	2.198	2.174	2.150	2.128	2.105	2.083	2.062	2.041	2.020	2.000
12	2.353	2.326	2.299	2.273	2.247	2.222	2.198	2.174	2.151	2.128	2.105	2.083	2.062	2.041	2.020	2.000
13	2.353	2.325	2.299	2.273	2.247	2.222	2.198	2.174	2.150	2.128	2.105	2.083	2.062	2.041	2.020	2.000
14	2.353	2.326	2.299	2.273	2.247	2.222	2.198	2.174	2.151	2.128	2.105	2.083	2.062	2.041	2.020	2.000
15	2.353	2.325	2.299	2.273	2.247	2.222	2.198	2.174	2.150	2.128	2.105	2.083	2.062	2.041	2.020	2.000
16	2.353	2.326	2.299	2.273	2.247	2.222	2.198	2.174	2.151	2.128	2.105	2.083	2.062	2.041	2.020	2.000
17	2.353	2.325	2.299	2.273	2.247	2.222	2.198	2.174	2.150	2.127	2.105	2.083	2.062	2.041	2.020	2.000
18	2.353	2.326	2.299	2.273	2.247	2.222	2.198	2.174	2.151	2.128	2.105	2.083	2.062	2.041	2.020	2.000
19	2.353	2.325	2.299	2.273	2.247	2.222	2.198	2.174	2.150	2.127	2.105	2.084	2.062	2.041	2.020	2.000
20	2.353	2.326	2.299	2.273	2.247	2.222	2.198	2.174	2.151	2.128	2.105	2.083	2.062	2.041	2.020	2.000
21	2.353	2.325	2.299	2.273	2.247	2.222	2.198	2.174	2.150	2.127	2.105	2.084	2.062	2.041	2.020	2.000
22	2.353	2.326	2.299	2.273	2.247	2.222	2.198	2.174	2.151	2.128	2.105	2.083	2.062	2.041	2.020	2.000
23	2.353	2.325	2.299	2.272	2.247	2.222	2.198	2.174	2.150	2.127	2.105	2.084	2.062	2.041	2.020	2.000
24	2.353	2.326	2.299	2.273	2.247	2.222	2.198	2.174	2.151	2.128	2.105	2.083	2.062	2.041	2.020	2.000
25	2.353	2.325	2.299	2.272	2.247	2.222	2.198	2.174	2.150	2.127	2.105	2.084	2.062	2.041	2.020	2.000
26	2.353	2.326	2.299	2.273	2.247	2.222	2.198	2.174	2.151	2.128	2.106	2.083	2.062	2.041	2.020	2.000
27	2.353	2.325	2.299	2.272	2.247	2.223	2.198	2.174	2.150	2.127	2.105	2.084	2.062	2.041	2.020	2.000
28	2.353	2.326	2.299	2.273	2.247	2.222	2.198	2.174	2.151	2.128	2.106	2.083	2.062	2.041	2.020	2.000
29	2.353	2.325	2.299	2.272	2.247	2.223	2.198	2.174	2.150	2.127	2.105	2.084	2.062	2.041	2.020	2.000
30	2.353	2.326	2.299	2.273	2.248	2.222	2.197	2.174	2.151	2.128	2.106	2.083	2.062	2.041	2.020	2.000
31	2.353	2.325	2.299	2.272	2.247	2.223	2.198	2.174	2.150	2.127	2.105	2.084	2.062	2.041	2.021	2.000
32	2.353	2.326	2.299	2.273	2.248	2.222	2.197	2.174	2.151	2.128	2.106	2.083	2.062	2.041	2.020	2.000
33	2.353	2.325	2.298	2.272	2.247	2.223	2.198	2.174	2.150	2.127	2.105	2.084	2.062	2.041	2.021	2.000
34	2.353	2.326	2.299	2.273	2.248	2.222	2.197	2.174	2.151	2.128	2.106	2.083	2.062	2.040	2.020	2.000
35	2.353	2.325	2.298	2.272	2.247	2.223	2.198	2.174	2.150	2.127	2.105	2.084	2.062	2.041	2.021	2.000
36	2.353	2.326	2.299	2.273	2.248	2.222	2.197	2.174	2.151	2.128	2.106	2.083	2.062	2.040	2.020	2.000
37	2.353	2.325	2.298	2.272	2.247	2.223	2.198	2.174	2.150	2.127	2.105	2.084	2.061	2.041	2.021	2.000
38	2.353	2.326	2.299	2.273	2.248	2.222	2.197	2.174	2.151	2.128	2.106	2.083	2.062	2.040	2.020	2.000
39	2.353	2.325	2.298	2.272	2.247	2.223	2.198	2.174	2.150	2.127	2.105	2.084	2.061	2.041	2.021	2.000
40	2.353	2.326	2.299	2.273	2.248	2.222	2.197	2.173	2.151	2.128	2.106	2.083	2.062	2.040	2.020	2.000
41	2.352	2.325	2.298	2.272	2.247	2.223	2.198	2.174	2.150	2.127	2.105	2.084	2.061	2.041	2.021	2.000
42	2.353	2.326	2.299	2.273	2.248	2.222	2.197	2.173	2.151	2.128	2.106	2.083	2.062	2.040	2.020	2.000
43	2.352	2.325	2.298	2.272	2.247	2.223	2.198	2.174	2.150	2.127	2.105	2.084	2.061	2.041	2.021	2.000
44		1.163	2.299	2.273	2.248	2.222	2.197	2.173	2.151	2.128	2.106	2.083	2.062	2.040	2.020	2.000
45				1.136	2.247	2.223	2.198	2.174	2.150	2.127	2.105	2.084	2.061	2.041	2.021	2.000
46						1.111	2.197	2.173	2.151	2.128	2.106	2.083	2.062	2.040	2.020	2.000
47								1.087	2.150	2.127	2.105	2.084	2.061	2.041	2.021	2.000
48										1.064	2.106	2.083	2.062	2.040	2.020	2.000
49												1.042	2.061	2.041	2.021	2.000
50														1.020	2.020	2.000
51																1.000

Table 9
General and Alternative Depreciation Systems
Applicable Depreciation Method: Straight Line
Applicable Recovery Periods: 2.5 - 50 years
Applicable Convention: Mid-quarter
(property placed in service in first quarter)

If the Recovery Year is:	and the Recovery Period is: the Depreciation Rate is:														
	2.5	3.0	3.5	4.0	4.5	5.0	5.5	6.0	6.5	7.0	7.5	8.0	8.5	9.0	9.5
1	35.00	29.17	25.00	21.88	19.44	17.50	15.91	14.58	13.46	12.50	11.67	10.94	10.29	9.72	9.21
2	40.00	33.33	28.57	25.00	22.22	20.00	18.18	16.67	15.38	14.29	13.33	12.50	11.77	11.11	10.53
3	25.00	33.33	28.57	25.00	22.22	20.00	18.18	16.67	15.39	14.28	13.33	12.50	11.76	11.11	10.53
4		4.17	17.86	25.00	22.23	20.00	18.18	16.67	15.38	14.29	13.33	12.50	11.77	11.11	10.53
5				3.12	13.89	20.00	18.18	16.66	15.39	14.28	13.34	12.50	11.76	11.11	10.52
6						2.50	11.37	16.67	15.38	14.29	13.33	12.50	11.77	11.11	10.53
7							2.08	9.62	14.28	13.34	12.50	11.76	11.11	10.52
8									1.79	8.33	12.50	11.77	11.12	10.53
9											1.56	7.35	11.11	10.52
10													1.39	6.58

If the Recovery Year is:	and the Recovery Period is: the Depreciation Rate is:														
	10.0	10.5	11.0	11.5	12.0	12.5	13.0	13.5	14.0	14.5	15.0	15.5	16.0	16.5	17.0
1	8.75	8.33	7.95	7.61	7.29	7.00	6.73	6.48	6.25	6.03	5.83	5.65	5.47	5.30	5.15
2	10.00	9.52	9.09	8.70	8.33	8.00	7.69	7.41	7.14	6.90	6.67	6.45	6.25	6.06	5.88
3	10.00	9.52	9.09	8.70	8.33	8.00	7.69	7.41	7.14	6.90	6.67	6.45	6.25	6.06	5.88
4	10.00	9.53	9.09	8.69	8.33	8.00	7.69	7.41	7.14	6.90	6.67	6.45	6.25	6.06	5.88
5	10.00	9.52	9.09	8.70	8.33	8.00	7.69	7.41	7.14	6.90	6.67	6.45	6.25	6.06	5.88
6	10.00	9.53	9.09	8.69	8.34	8.00	7.69	7.41	7.14	6.90	6.67	6.45	6.25	6.06	5.88
7	10.00	9.52	9.09	8.70	8.33	8.00	7.69	7.41	7.14	6.90	6.67	6.45	6.25	6.06	5.88
8	10.00	9.53	9.09	8.69	8.34	8.00	7.69	7.41	7.15	6.89	6.66	6.45	6.25	6.06	5.88
9	10.00	9.52	9.09	8.70	8.33	8.00	7.70	7.40	7.14	6.90	6.67	6.45	6.25	6.06	5.88
10	10.00	9.53	9.10	8.69	8.34	8.00	7.69	7.41	7.15	6.89	6.66	6.45	6.25	6.06	5.88
11	1.25	5.95	9.09	8.70	8.33	8.00	7.70	7.40	7.14	6.90	6.67	6.45	6.25	6.06	5.88
12			1.14	5.43	8.34	8.00	7.69	7.41	7.15	6.89	6.66	6.45	6.25	6.06	5.89
13					1.04	5.00	7.70	7.40	7.14	6.90	6.67	6.46	6.25	6.06	5.88
14							0.96	4.63	7.15	6.89	6.66	6.45	6.25	6.06	5.89
15									0.89	4.31	6.67	6.46	6.25	6.06	5.88
16											0.83	4.03	6.25	6.07	5.89
17													0.78	3.79	5.88
18															0.74

If the Recovery Year is:	17.5	18.0	18.5	19.0	19.5	20.0	20.5	21.0	21.5	22.0	22.5	23.0	23.5	24.0	24.5
								the Depreciation Rate is:							
1	5.00	4.86	4.73	4.61	4.49	4.375	4.268	4.167	4.070	3.977	3.889	3.804	3.723	3.646	3.571
2	5.71	5.56	5.41	5.26	5.13	5.000	4.878	4.762	4.651	4.545	4.444	4.348	4.255	4.167	4.082
3	5.71	5.56	5.41	5.26	5.13	5.000	4.878	4.762	4.651	4.545	4.444	4.348	4.255	4.167	4.082
4	5.71	5.56	5.40	5.26	5.13	5.000	4.878	4.762	4.651	4.546	4.444	4.348	4.255	4.167	4.082
5	5.72	5.55	5.41	5.26	5.13	5.000	4.878	4.762	4.651	4.545	4.445	4.348	4.255	4.167	4.082
6	5.71	5.56	5.40	5.26	5.13	5.000	4.878	4.762	4.651	4.546	4.444	4.348	4.255	4.167	4.082
7	5.72	5.55	5.41	5.26	5.13	5.000	4.878	4.762	4.651	4.545	4.445	4.348	4.255	4.167	4.082
8	5.71	5.56	5.40	5.26	5.13	5.000	4.878	4.762	4.651	4.546	4.444	4.348	4.255	4.167	4.082
9	5.72	5.55	5.41	5.26	5.13	5.000	4.878	4.762	4.651	4.545	4.445	4.348	4.255	4.167	4.082
10	5.71	5.56	5.40	5.27	5.13	5.000	4.878	4.762	4.651	4.546	4.444	4.348	4.256	4.166	4.081
11	5.72	5.55	5.41	5.26	5.13	5.000	4.878	4.762	4.651	4.545	4.445	4.348	4.255	4.167	4.082
12	5.71	5.56	5.40	5.27	5.13	5.000	4.878	4.762	4.651	4.546	4.444	4.348	4.256	4.166	4.081
13	5.72	5.55	5.41	5.26	5.13	5.000	4.878	4.762	4.651	4.545	4.445	4.348	4.255	4.167	4.082
14	5.71	5.56	5.40	5.27	5.12	5.000	4.878	4.762	4.651	4.546	4.444	4.348	4.256	4.166	4.081
15	5.72	5.55	5.41	5.26	5.13	5.000	4.878	4.762	4.651	4.545	4.445	4.348	4.255	4.167	4.082
16	5.71	5.56	5.40	5.27	5.12	5.000	4.878	4.762	4.651	4.546	4.444	4.348	4.256	4.166	4.081
17	5.72	5.55	5.41	5.26	5.13	5.000	4.878	4.762	4.652	4.545	4.445	4.348	4.255	4.167	4.082
18	3.57	5.56	5.40	5.27	5.12	5.000	4.878	4.761	4.651	4.546	4.444	4.347	4.256	4.166	4.081
19		0.69	3.38	5.26	5.13	5.000	4.878	4.762	4.652	4.545	4.445	4.348	4.255	4.167	4.082
20				0.66	3.20	5.000	4.879	4.761	4.651	4.546	4.444	4.347	4.256	4.166	4.081
21						0.625	3.049	4.762	4.652	4.545	4.445	4.348	4.255	4.167	4.082
22								0.595	2.907	4.546	4.444	4.347	4.256	4.166	4.081
23										0.568	2.778	4.348	4.255	4.167	4.082
24												0.543	2.660	4.166	4.081
25														0.521	2.551

If the Recovery Year is:	25.0	25.5	26.0	26.5	27.0	27.5	28.0	28.5	29.0	29.5	30.0	30.5	31.0	31.5	32.0
								the Depreciation Rate is:							
1	3.500	3.431	3.365	3.302	3.241	3.182	3.125	3.070	3.017	2.966	2.917	2.869	2.823	2.778	2.734
2	4.000	3.922	3.846	3.774	3.704	3.636	3.571	3.509	3.448	3.390	3.333	3.279	3.226	3.175	3.125
3	4.000	3.922	3.846	3.774	3.704	3.636	3.571	3.509	3.448	3.390	3.333	3.279	3.226	3.175	3.125
4	4.000	3.922	3.846	3.774	3.704	3.636	3.571	3.509	3.448	3.390	3.333	3.279	3.226	3.175	3.125
5	4.000	3.922	3.846	3.774	3.704	3.636	3.571	3.509	3.448	3.390	3.333	3.279	3.226	3.175	3.125
6	4.000	3.922	3.846	3.774	3.704	3.636	3.572	3.509	3.448	3.390	3.333	3.279	3.226	3.175	3.125
7	4.000	3.921	3.846	3.773	3.704	3.636	3.571	3.509	3.448	3.390	3.333	3.279	3.226	3.175	3.125
8	4.000	3.922	3.846	3.774	3.704	3.636	3.572	3.509	3.448	3.390	3.333	3.279	3.226	3.174	3.125
9	4.000	3.921	3.846	3.773	3.704	3.636	3.571	3.509	3.448	3.390	3.333	3.279	3.226	3.175	3.125
10	4.000	3.922	3.846	3.774	3.704	3.637	3.572	3.509	3.448	3.390	3.333	3.279	3.226	3.174	3.125
11	4.000	3.921	3.846	3.773	3.704	3.636	3.571	3.509	3.448	3.390	3.333	3.279	3.226	3.175	3.125
12	4.000	3.922	3.846	3.774	3.704	3.637	3.572	3.509	3.448	3.390	3.333	3.279	3.226	3.174	3.125
13	4.000	3.921	3.846	3.773	3.703	3.636	3.571	3.509	3.448	3.390	3.334	3.278	3.226	3.175	3.125
14	4.000	3.922	3.846	3.774	3.704	3.637	3.572	3.509	3.448	3.390	3.333	3.279	3.226	3.174	3.125
15	4.000	3.921	3.846	3.773	3.703	3.636	3.571	3.509	3.449	3.390	3.334	3.278	3.226	3.175	3.125
16	4.000	3.922	3.846	3.774	3.704	3.637	3.572	3.509	3.448	3.390	3.333	3.279	3.226	3.174	3.125
17	4.000	3.921	3.846	3.773	3.703	3.636	3.571	3.509	3.449	3.390	3.334	3.278	3.226	3.175	3.125
18	4.000	3.922	3.846	3.774	3.704	3.637	3.572	3.508	3.448	3.390	3.333	3.279	3.226	3.174	3.125
19	4.000	3.921	3.847	3.773	3.703	3.636	3.571	3.509	3.449	3.390	3.334	3.278	3.225	3.175	3.125
20	4.000	3.922	3.846	3.774	3.704	3.637	3.572	3.509	3.448	3.390	3.333	3.279	3.225	3.174	3.125
21	4.000	3.921	3.847	3.773	3.703	3.636	3.571	3.509	3.449	3.390	3.334	3.278	3.226	3.175	3.125
22	4.000	3.922	3.846	3.774	3.704	3.637	3.572	3.508	3.448	3.389	3.333	3.279	3.225	3.174	3.125
23	4.000	3.921	3.847	3.773	3.703	3.636	3.571	3.509	3.449	3.390	3.334	3.278	3.226	3.175	3.125
24	4.000	3.922	3.846	3.774	3.704	3.637	3.572	3.508	3.448	3.389	3.333	3.279	3.225	3.174	3.125
25	4.000	3.921	3.847	3.773	3.703	3.636	3.571	3.509	3.449	3.390	3.334	3.278	3.226	3.175	3.125
26	0.500	2.451	3.846	3.774	3.704	3.637	3.572	3.508	3.448	3.389	3.333	3.279	3.225	3.174	3.125
27			0.481	2.358	3.703	3.636	3.571	3.509	3.449	3.390	3.334	3.278	3.226	3.175	3.125
28					0.463	2.273	3.572	3.508	3.448	3.389	3.333	3.279	3.225	3.174	3.125
29							0.446	2.193	3.449	3.390	3.334	3.278	3.226	3.175	3.125
30									0.431	2.118	3.333	3.279	3.225	3.174	3.125
31											0.417	2.049	3.226	3.175	3.125
32													0.403	1.984	3.125
33															0.391

If the Recovery Year is:	and the Recovery Period is:														
	32.5	33.0	33.5	34.0	34.5	35.0	35.5	36.0	36.5	37.0	37.5	38.0	38.5	39.0	39.5
	the Depreciation Rate is:														
1	2.692	2.652	2.612	2.574	2.536	2.500	2.465	2.431	2.397	2.365	2.333	2.303	2.273	2.244	2.215
2	3.077	3.030	2.985	2.941	2.899	2.857	2.817	2.778	2.740	2.703	2.667	2.632	2.597	2.564	2.532
3	3.077	3.030	2.985	2.941	2.899	2.857	2.817	2.778	2.740	2.703	2.667	2.632	2.597	2.564	2.532
4	3.077	3.030	2.985	2.941	2.899	2.857	2.817	2.778	2.740	2.703	2.667	2.632	2.597	2.564	2.532
5	3.077	3.030	2.985	2.941	2.899	2.857	2.817	2.778	2.740	2.703	2.667	2.632	2.597	2.564	2.532
6	3.077	3.030	2.985	2.941	2.898	2.857	2.817	2.778	2.740	2.703	2.667	2.632	2.597	2.564	2.532
7	3.077	3.030	2.985	2.941	2.899	2.857	2.817	2.778	2.740	2.703	2.667	2.632	2.597	2.564	2.532
8	3.077	3.030	2.985	2.941	2.898	2.857	2.817	2.778	2.740	2.703	2.667	2.631	2.597	2.564	2.532
9	3.077	3.030	2.985	2.941	2.899	2.857	2.817	2.778	2.740	2.703	2.667	2.632	2.597	2.564	2.532
10	3.077	3.030	2.985	2.941	2.898	2.857	2.817	2.778	2.740	2.703	2.667	2.631	2.598	2.564	2.532
11	3.077	3.030	2.985	2.941	2.899	2.857	2.817	2.778	2.740	2.703	2.667	2.632	2.597	2.564	2.532
12	3.077	3.030	2.985	2.941	2.898	2.857	2.817	2.778	2.740	2.703	2.667	2.631	2.598	2.564	2.532
13	3.077	3.030	2.985	2.941	2.899	2.857	2.817	2.778	2.740	2.703	2.667	2.632	2.597	2.564	2.532
14	3.077	3.030	2.985	2.941	2.898	2.857	2.817	2.778	2.740	2.703	2.667	2.631	2.598	2.564	2.531
15	3.077	3.030	2.985	2.941	2.899	2.857	2.817	2.778	2.740	2.703	2.666	2.632	2.597	2.564	2.532
16	3.077	3.031	2.985	2.941	2.898	2.857	2.817	2.778	2.740	2.703	2.667	2.631	2.598	2.564	2.531
17	3.077	3.030	2.985	2.941	2.899	2.857	2.817	2.778	2.740	2.702	2.666	2.632	2.597	2.564	2.532
18	3.077	3.031	2.985	2.941	2.898	2.857	2.817	2.778	2.740	2.703	2.667	2.631	2.598	2.564	2.531
19	3.077	3.030	2.985	2.941	2.899	2.857	2.817	2.778	2.739	2.702	2.666	2.632	2.597	2.564	2.532
20	3.077	3.031	2.985	2.941	2.898	2.857	2.817	2.778	2.740	2.703	2.667	2.631	2.598	2.564	2.531
21	3.077	3.030	2.985	2.941	2.899	2.857	2.817	2.777	2.739	2.702	2.666	2.632	2.597	2.564	2.532
22	3.077	3.031	2.985	2.941	2.898	2.857	2.817	2.778	2.740	2.703	2.667	2.631	2.598	2.564	2.531
23	3.077	3.030	2.985	2.941	2.899	2.857	2.817	2.777	2.739	2.702	2.666	2.632	2.597	2.564	2.532
24	3.077	3.031	2.985	2.941	2.898	2.857	2.817	2.778	2.740	2.703	2.667	2.631	2.598	2.564	2.531
25	3.077	3.030	2.985	2.942	2.899	2.857	2.817	2.777	2.739	2.702	2.666	2.632	2.597	2.564	2.532
26	3.077	3.031	2.985	2.941	2.898	2.857	2.817	2.778	2.740	2.703	2.667	2.631	2.598	2.564	2.531
27	3.077	3.030	2.985	2.942	2.899	2.858	2.817	2.777	2.739	2.702	2.666	2.632	2.597	2.564	2.532
28	3.077	3.031	2.985	2.941	2.898	2.857	2.817	2.778	2.740	2.703	2.667	2.631	2.598	2.564	2.531
29	3.077	3.030	2.985	2.942	2.899	2.858	2.817	2.777	2.739	2.702	2.666	2.632	2.597	2.564	2.532
30	3.076	3.031	2.986	2.941	2.898	2.857	2.816	2.778	2.740	2.703	2.667	2.631	2.598	2.564	2.531
31	3.077	3.030	2.985	2.942	2.899	2.858	2.817	2.777	2.739	2.702	2.666	2.632	2.597	2.564	2.532
32	3.076	3.031	2.986	2.941	2.898	2.857	2.816	2.778	2.740	2.703	2.667	2.631	2.598	2.564	2.531
33	1.923	3.030	2.985	2.942	2.899	2.858	2.817	2.777	2.739	2.702	2.666	2.632	2.597	2.564	2.532
34		0.379	1.866	2.941	2.898	2.857	2.817	2.778	2.740	2.703	2.667	2.631	2.598	2.565	2.531
35				0.368	1.812	2.858	2.817	2.777	2.739	2.702	2.666	2.632	2.597	2.564	2.532
36						0.357	1.760	2.778	2.740	2.703	2.667	2.631	2.598	2.565	2.531
37							0.347	1.712	2.702	2.666	2.632	2.597	2.564	2.532
38								0.338	1.667	2.631	2.598	2.565	2.531
39									0.329	1.623	2.564	2.532
40										0.321	1.582

If the Recovery Year is:	and the Recovery Period is:														
	40.0	40.5	41.0	41.5	42.0	42.5	43.0	43.5	44.0	44.5	45.0	45.5	46.0	46.5	47.0
	the Depreciation Rate is:														
1	2.188	2.160	2.134	2.108	2.083	2.059	2.035	2.011	1.989	1.966	1.944	1.923	1.902	1.882	1.862
2	2.500	2.469	2.439	2.410	2.381	2.353	2.326	2.299	2.273	2.247	2.222	2.198	2.174	2.151	2.128
3	2.500	2.469	2.439	2.410	2.381	2.353	2.326	2.299	2.273	2.247	2.222	2.198	2.174	2.151	2.128
4	2.500	2.469	2.439	2.410	2.381	2.353	2.326	2.299	2.273	2.247	2.222	2.198	2.174	2.151	2.128
5	2.500	2.469	2.439	2.410	2.381	2.353	2.326	2.299	2.273	2.247	2.222	2.198	2.174	2.150	2.128
6	2.500	2.469	2.439	2.410	2.381	2.353	2.326	2.299	2.273	2.247	2.222	2.198	2.174	2.151	2.128
7	2.500	2.469	2.439	2.410	2.381	2.353	2.326	2.299	2.273	2.247	2.222	2.198	2.174	2.150	2.128
8	2.500	2.469	2.439	2.410	2.381	2.353	2.326	2.299	2.273	2.247	2.222	2.198	2.174	2.151	2.128
9	2.500	2.469	2.439	2.410	2.381	2.353	2.325	2.299	2.273	2.247	2.222	2.198	2.174	2.150	2.128
10	2.500	2.469	2.439	2.410	2.381	2.353	2.326	2.299	2.273	2.247	2.222	2.198	2.174	2.151	2.128
11	2.500	2.469	2.439	2.410	2.381	2.353	2.325	2.299	2.273	2.247	2.222	2.198	2.174	2.150	2.128
12	2.500	2.469	2.439	2.410	2.381	2.353	2.326	2.299	2.273	2.247	2.222	2.198	2.174	2.151	2.128
13	2.500	2.469	2.439	2.410	2.381	2.353	2.325	2.299	2.273	2.247	2.222	2.198	2.174	2.150	2.128
14	2.500	2.469	2.439	2.410	2.381	2.353	2.326	2.299	2.273	2.247	2.222	2.198	2.174	2.151	2.128
15	2.500	2.469	2.439	2.409	2.381	2.353	2.325	2.299	2.273	2.247	2.222	2.198	2.174	2.150	2.128
16	2.500	2.469	2.439	2.410	2.381	2.353	2.326	2.299	2.273	2.247	2.222	2.198	2.174	2.151	2.128
17	2.500	2.469	2.439	2.409	2.381	2.353	2.325	2.299	2.273	2.247	2.222	2.198	2.174	2.150	2.127
18	2.500	2.469	2.439	2.410	2.381	2.353	2.326	2.299	2.273	2.247	2.222	2.198	2.174	2.151	2.128
19	2.500	2.469	2.439	2.409	2.381	2.353	2.325	2.299	2.273	2.247	2.222	2.198	2.174	2.150	2.127
20	2.500	2.469	2.439	2.410	2.381	2.353	2.326	2.299	2.273	2.247	2.222	2.198	2.174	2.151	2.128
21	2.500	2.469	2.439	2.409	2.381	2.353	2.325	2.299	2.272	2.247	2.222	2.198	2.174	2.150	2.127
22	2.500	2.469	2.439	2.410	2.381	2.353	2.326	2.299	2.273	2.247	2.222	2.198	2.174	2.151	2.128
23	2.500	2.469	2.439	2.409	2.381	2.353	2.325	2.299	2.272	2.247	2.222	2.198	2.174	2.150	2.127
24	2.500	2.469	2.439	2.410	2.381	2.353	2.326	2.299	2.273	2.247	2.222	2.198	2.174	2.151	2.128
25	2.500	2.469	2.439	2.409	2.381	2.353	2.325	2.299	2.272	2.247	2.222	2.198	2.174	2.150	2.127
26	2.500	2.469	2.439	2.410	2.381	2.353	2.326	2.299	2.273	2.247	2.223	2.198	2.174	2.151	2.128
27	2.500	2.469	2.439	2.409	2.381	2.353	2.325	2.299	2.272	2.247	2.222	2.198	2.174	2.150	2.127
28	2.500	2.469	2.439	2.410	2.381	2.353	2.326	2.299	2.273	2.247	2.223	2.198	2.174	2.151	2.128
29	2.500	2.469	2.439	2.409	2.381	2.353	2.325	2.299	2.272	2.248	2.222	2.198	2.174	2.150	2.127
30	2.500	2.470	2.439	2.410	2.381	2.353	2.326	2.299	2.273	2.247	2.223	2.197	2.174	2.151	2.128
31	2.500	2.469	2.439	2.409	2.381	2.353	2.325	2.299	2.272	2.248	2.222	2.198	2.174	2.150	2.127
32	2.500	2.470	2.439	2.410	2.381	2.353	2.326	2.299	2.273	2.247	2.223	2.197	2.174	2.151	2.128
33	2.500	2.469	2.439	2.409	2.381	2.353	2.325	2.298	2.272	2.248	2.222	2.198	2.174	2.150	2.127
34	2.500	2.470	2.439	2.410	2.381	2.353	2.326	2.299	2.273	2.247	2.223	2.197	2.174	2.151	2.128
35	2.500	2.469	2.439	2.409	2.381	2.353	2.325	2.298	2.272	2.248	2.222	2.198	2.174	2.150	2.127
36	2.500	2.470	2.439	2.410	2.381	2.353	2.326	2.299	2.273	2.247	2.223	2.197	2.174	2.151	2.128
37	2.500	2.469	2.439	2.409	2.381	2.353	2.325	2.298	2.272	2.248	2.222	2.198	2.174	2.150	2.127
38	2.500	2.470	2.439	2.410	2.381	2.353	2.326	2.299	2.273	2.247	2.223	2.197	2.174	2.151	2.128
39	2.500	2.469	2.439	2.409	2.381	2.352	2.325	2.298	2.272	2.248	2.222	2.198	2.174	2.150	2.127
40	2.500	2.470	2.440	2.410	2.380	2.353	2.326	2.299	2.273	2.247	2.223	2.197	2.173	2.151	2.128
41	0.312	1.543	2.439	2.409	2.381	2.352	2.325	2.298	2.272	2.248	2.222	2.198	2.174	2.150	2.127
42			0.305	1.506	2.380	2.353	2.326	2.299	2.273	2.247	2.223	2.197	2.173	2.151	2.128
43					0.298	1.470	2.325	2.298	2.272	2.248	2.222	2.198	2.174	2.150	2.127
44							0.291	1.437	2.273	2.247	2.223	2.197	2.173	2.151	2.128
45									0.284	1.405	2.222	2.198	2.174	2.150	2.127
46											0.278	1.373	2.173	2.151	2.128
47													0.272	1.344	2.127
48															0.266

If the Recovery Year is:	and the Recovery Period is:					
	47.5	48.0	48.5	49.0	49.5	50.0
	the Depreciation Rate is:					
1	1.842	1.823	1.804	1.786	1.768	1.750
2	2.105	2.083	2.062	2.041	2.020	2.000
3	2.105	2.083	2.062	2.041	2.020	2.000
4	2.105	2.083	2.062	2.041	2.020	2.000
5	2.105	2.083	2.062	2.041	2.020	2.000
6	2.105	2.083	2.062	2.041	2.020	2.000
7	2.105	2.083	2.062	2.041	2.020	2.000
8	2.105	2.083	2.062	2.041	2.020	2.000
9	2.105	2.083	2.062	2.041	2.020	2.000
10	2.105	2.083	2.062	2.041	2.020	2.000
11	2.105	2.083	2.062	2.041	2.020	2.000
12	2.105	2.083	2.062	2.041	2.020	2.000
13	2.105	2.083	2.062	2.041	2.020	2.000
14	2.105	2.083	2.062	2.041	2.020	2.000
15	2.105	2.083	2.062	2.041	2.020	2.000
16	2.105	2.083	2.062	2.041	2.020	2.000
17	2.105	2.083	2.062	2.041	2.020	2.000
18	2.105	2.084	2.062	2.041	2.020	2.000
19	2.105	2.083	2.062	2.041	2.020	2.000
20	2.105	2.084	2.062	2.041	2.020	2.000
21	2.105	2.083	2.062	2.041	2.020	2.000
22	2.105	2.084	2.062	2.041	2.020	2.000
23	2.105	2.083	2.062	2.041	2.020	2.000
24	2.106	2.084	2.062	2.041	2.020	2.000
25	2.105	2.083	2.062	2.041	2.020	2.000
26	2.106	2.084	2.062	2.041	2.020	2.000
27	2.105	2.083	2.062	2.041	2.020	2.000
28	2.106	2.084	2.062	2.041	2.020	2.000
29	2.105	2.083	2.062	2.041	2.020	2.000
30	2.106	2.084	2.062	2.041	2.020	2.000
31	2.105	2.083	2.062	2.041	2.020	2.000
32	2.106	2.084	2.062	2.040	2.021	2.000
33	2.105	2.083	2.062	2.041	2.020	2.000
34	2.106	2.084	2.062	2.040	2.021	2.000
35	2.105	2.083	2.062	2.041	2.020	2.000
36	2.106	2.084	2.062	2.040	2.021	2.000
37	2.105	2.083	2.061	2.041	2.020	2.000
38	2.106	2.084	2.062	2.040	2.021	2.000
39	2.105	2.083	2.061	2.041	2.020	2.000
40	2.106	2.084	2.062	2.040	2.021	2.000
41	2.105	2.083	2.061	2.041	2.020	2.000
42	2.106	2.084	2.062	2.040	2.021	2.000
43	2.105	2.083	2.061	2.041	2.020	2.000
44	2.106	2.084	2.062	2.040	2.021	2.000
45	2.105	2.083	2.061	2.041	2.020	2.000
46	2.106	2.084	2.062	2.040	2.021	2.000
47	2.105	2.083	2.061	2.041	2.020	2.000
48	1.316	2.084	2.062	2.040	2.021	2.000
49		0.260	1.288	2.041	2.020	2.000
50				0.255	1.263	2.000
51						0.250

Table 10
General and Alternative Depreciation Systems
Applicable Depreciation Method: Straight Line
Applicable Recovery Periods: 2.5-50 years
Applicable Convention: Mid quarter (property placed
in service in second quarter)

If the Recovery Year is:	and the Recovery Period is: the Depreciation Rate is:														
	2.5	3.0	3.5	4.0	4.5	5.0	5.5	6.0	6.5	7.0	7.5	8.0	8.5	9.0	9.5
1	25.00	20.83	17.86	15.63	13.89	12.50	11.36	10.42	9.62	8.93	8.33	7.81	7.35	6.94	6.58
2	40.00	33.33	28.57	25.00	22.22	20.00	18.18	16.67	15.38	14.29	13.33	12.50	11.77	11.11	10.53
3	35.00	33.34	28.57	25.00	22.22	20.00	18.18	16.67	15.38	14.28	13.33	12.50	11.76	11.11	10.53
4		12.50	25.00	25.00	22.22	20.00	18.18	16.66	15.39	14.29	13.34	12.50	11.77	11.11	10.53
5				9.37	19.45	20.00	18.19	16.67	15.38	14.28	13.33	12.50	11.76	11.11	10.52
6						7.50	15.91	16.66	15.39	14.29	13.34	12.50	11.77	11.11	10.53
7							6.25	13.46	14.28	13.33	12.50	11.76	11.11	10.52
8									5.36	11.67	12.50	11.77	11.12	10.53
9											4.69	10.29	11.11	10.52
10													4.17	9.21

If the Recovery Year is:	and the Recovery Period is: the Depreciation Rate is:														
	10.0	10.5	11.0	11.5	12.0	12.5	13.0	13.5	14.0	14.5	15.0	15.5	16.0	16.5	17.0
1	6.25	5.95	5.68	5.43	5.21	5.00	4.81	4.63	4.46	4.31	4.17	4.03	3.91	3.79	3.68
2	10.00	9.52	9.09	8.70	8.33	8.00	7.69	7.41	7.14	6.90	6.67	6.45	6.25	6.06	5.88
3	10.00	9.52	9.09	8.70	8.33	8.00	7.69	7.41	7.14	6.90	6.67	6.45	6.25	6.06	5.88
4	10.00	9.53	9.09	8.70	8.33	8.00	7.69	7.41	7.14	6.90	6.67	6.45	6.25	6.06	5.88
5	10.00	9.52	9.09	8.69	8.33	8.00	7.69	7.41	7.14	6.90	6.67	6.45	6.25	6.06	5.88
6	10.00	9.53	9.09	8.70	8.33	8.00	7.69	7.41	7.14	6.90	6.67	6.45	6.25	6.06	5.88
7	10.00	9.52	9.09	8.69	8.34	8.00	7.69	7.41	7.15	6.89	6.66	6.45	6.25	6.06	5.88
8	10.00	9.53	9.09	8.70	8.33	8.00	7.69	7.41	7.14	6.90	6.67	6.45	6.25	6.06	5.88
9	10.00	9.52	9.09	8.69	8.34	8.00	7.69	7.40	7.15	6.89	6.66	6.45	6.25	6.06	5.88
10	10.00	9.53	9.09	8.70	8.33	8.00	7.70	7.41	7.14	6.90	6.67	6.45	6.25	6.06	5.88
11	3.75	8.33	9.10	8.69	8.34	8.00	7.69	7.40	7.15	6.89	6.66	6.45	6.25	6.06	5.88
12			3.41	7.61	8.33	8.00	7.70	7.41	7.14	6.90	6.67	6.46	6.25	6.06	5.89
13					3.13	7.00	7.69	7.40	7.15	6.89	6.66	6.45	6.25	6.06	5.88
14							2.89	6.48	7.14	6.90	6.67	6.46	6.25	6.06	5.89
15									2.68	6.03	6.66	6.45	6.25	6.06	5.88
16											2.50	5.65	6.25	6.06	5.89
17													2.34	5.31	5.88
18															2.21

If the Recovery Year is:	and the Recovery Period is:														
	17.5	18.0	18.5	19.0	19.5	20.0	20.5	21.0	21.5	22.0	22.5	23.0	23.5	24.0	24.5
	the Depreciation Rate is:														
1	3.57	3.47	3.38	3.29	3.21	3.125	3.049	2.976	2.907	2.841	2.778	2.717	2.660	2.604	2.551
2	5.71	5.56	5.41	5.26	5.13	5.000	4.878	4.762	4.651	4.545	4.444	4.348	4.255	4.167	4.082
3	5.71	5.56	5.41	5.26	5.13	5.000	4.878	4.762	4.651	4.545	4.444	4.348	4.255	4.167	4.082
4	5.71	5.56	5.40	5.26	5.13	5.000	4.878	4.762	4.651	4.545	4.444	4.348	4.255	4.167	4.082
5	5.72	5.55	5.41	5.26	5.13	5.000	4.878	4.762	4.651	4.546	4.445	4.348	4.255	4.167	4.082
6	5.71	5.56	5.40	5.26	5.13	5.000	4.878	4.762	4.651	4.545	4.444	4.348	4.255	4.167	4.082
7	5.72	5.55	5.41	5.26	5.13	5.000	4.878	4.762	4.651	4.546	4.445	4.348	4.255	4.167	4.082
8	5.71	5.56	5.40	5.26	5.13	5.000	4.878	4.762	4.651	4.545	4.444	4.348	4.255	4.167	4.082
9	5.72	5.55	5.41	5.27	5.13	5.000	4.878	4.762	4.651	4.546	4.445	4.348	4.255	4.167	4.081
10	5.71	5.56	5.40	5.26	5.13	5.000	4.878	4.762	4.651	4.545	4.444	4.348	4.255	4.167	4.082
11	5.72	5.55	5.41	5.27	5.13	5.000	4.878	4.762	4.651	4.546	4.445	4.348	4.255	4.166	4.081
12	5.71	5.56	5.40	5.26	5.13	5.000	4.878	4.762	4.651	4.545	4.444	4.348	4.256	4.167	4.082
13	5.72	5.55	5.41	5.27	5.13	5.000	4.878	4.762	4.651	4.546	4.445	4.348	4.255	4.166	4.081
14	5.71	5.56	5.40	5.26	5.12	5.000	4.878	4.762	4.651	4.545	4.444	4.348	4.256	4.167	4.082
15	5.72	5.55	5.41	5.27	5.13	5.000	4.878	4.762	4.651	4.546	4.445	4.348	4.255	4.166	4.081
16	5.71	5.56	5.40	5.26	5.12	5.000	4.878	4.762	4.651	4.545	4.444	4.348	4.256	4.167	4.082
17	5.72	5.55	5.41	5.27	5.13	5.000	4.878	4.762	4.652	4.546	4.445	4.348	4.255	4.166	4.081
18	5.00	5.56	5.40	5.26	5.12	5.000	4.878	4.762	4.651	4.545	4.444	4.347	4.256	4.167	4.082
19		2.08	4.73	5.27	5.13	5.000	4.878	4.761	4.652	4.546	4.445	4.348	4.255	4.166	4.081
20				1.97	4.48	5.000	4.878	4.762	4.651	4.545	4.444	4.347	4.256	4.167	4.082
21						1.875	4.269	4.761	4.652	4.546	4.445	4.348	4.255	4.166	4.081
22							1.786	4.070	4.545	4.444	4.347	4.256	4.167	4.082
23								1.705	3.889	4.348	4.255	4.166	4.081
24										1.630	3.724	4.167	4.062
25											1.562	3.571

If the Recovery Year is:	and the Recovery Period is:														
	25.0	25.5	26.0	26.5	27.0	27.5	28.0	28.5	29.0	29.5	30.0	30.5	31.0	31.5	32.0
	the Depreciation Rate is:														
1	2.500	2.451	2.404	2.358	2.315	2.273	2.232	2.193	2.155	2.119	2.083	2.049	2.016	1.984	1.953
2	4.000	3.922	3.846	3.774	3.704	3.636	3.571	3.509	3.448	3.390	3.333	3.279	3.226	3.175	3.125
3	4.000	3.922	3.846	3.774	3.704	3.636	3.571	3.509	3.448	3.390	3.333	3.279	3.226	3.175	3.125
4	4.000	3.922	3.846	3.774	3.704	3.636	3.571	3.509	3.448	3.390	3.333	3.279	3.226	3.175	3.125
5	4.000	3.922	3.846	3.774	3.704	3.636	3.571	3.509	3.448	3.390	3.333	3.279	3.226	3.175	3.125
6	4.000	3.921	3.846	3.774	3.704	3.636	3.572	3.509	3.448	3.390	3.333	3.279	3.226	3.175	3.125
7	4.000	3.922	3.846	3.774	3.704	3.636	3.571	3.509	3.448	3.390	3.333	3.279	3.226	3.175	3.125
8	4.000	3.921	3.846	3.773	3.704	3.636	3.572	3.509	3.448	3.390	3.333	3.279	3.226	3.175	3.125
9	4.000	3.922	3.846	3.774	3.704	3.636	3.571	3.509	3.448	3.390	3.333	3.279	3.226	3.174	3.125
10	4.000	3.921	3.846	3.773	3.704	3.637	3.572	3.509	3.448	3.390	3.333	3.279	3.226	3.175	3.125
11	4.000	3.922	3.846	3.774	3.704	3.636	3.571	3.509	3.448	3.390	3.333	3.279	3.226	3.174	3.125
12	4.000	3.921	3.846	3.773	3.704	3.637	3.572	3.509	3.448	3.390	3.334	3.279	3.226	3.175	3.125
13	4.000	3.922	3.846	3.774	3.703	3.636	3.571	3.509	3.448	3.390	3.333	3.279	3.226	3.174	3.125
14	4.000	3.921	3.846	3.773	3.704	3.637	3.572	3.509	3.448	3.390	3.334	3.278	3.226	3.175	3.125
15	4.000	3.922	3.846	3.774	3.703	3.636	3.571	3.509	3.449	3.390	3.333	3.279	3.226	3.174	3.125
16	4.000	3.921	3.846	3.773	3.704	3.637	3.572	3.509	3.448	3.390	3.334	3.278	3.226	3.175	3.125
17	4.000	3.922	3.846	3.774	3.703	3.636	3.571	3.509	3.449	3.390	3.333	3.279	3.226	3.174	3.125
18	4.000	3.921	3.846	3.773	3.704	3.637	3.572	3.508	3.448	3.390	3.334	3.278	3.226	3.175	3.125
19	4.000	3.922	3.846	3.774	3.703	3.636	3.571	3.509	3.449	3.390	3.333	3.279	3.226	3.174	3.125
20	4.000	3.921	3.847	3.773	3.704	3.637	3.572	3.508	3.448	3.390	3.334	3.278	3.226	3.175	3.125
21	4.000	3.922	3.846	3.774	3.703	3.636	3.571	3.509	3.449	3.389	3.333	3.279	3.225	3.174	3.125
22	4.000	3.921	3.847	3.773	3.704	3.637	3.572	3.508	3.448	3.390	3.334	3.278	3.226	3.175	3.125
23	4.000	3.922	3.846	3.774	3.703	3.636	3.571	3.509	3.449	3.389	3.333	3.279	3.225	3.174	3.125
24	4.000	3.921	3.847	3.773	3.704	3.637	3.572	3.508	3.448	3.390	3.334	3.278	3.226	3.175	3.125
25	4.000	3.922	3.846	3.774	3.703	3.636	3.571	3.509	3.449	3.389	3.333	3.279	3.225	3.174	3.125
26	1.500	3.431	3.847	3.773	3.704	3.637	3.572	3.508	3.448	3.390	3.334	3.278	3.226	3.175	3.125
27			1.442	3.302	3.703	3.636	3.571	3.509	3.449	3.389	3.333	3.279	3.225	3.174	3.125
28					1.389	3.182	3.572	3.508	3.448	3.390	3.334	3.278	3.226	3.175	3.125
29							1.339	3.070	3.449	3.389	3.333	3.279	3.225	3.174	3.125
30									1.293	2.966	3.334	3.278	3.226	3.175	3.125
31											1.250	2.869	3.225	3.174	3.125
32													1.210	2.778	3.125
33															1.172

If the Recovery Year is:	and the Recovery Period is:														
	32.5	33.0	33.5	34.0	34.5	35.0	35.5	36.0	36.5	37.0	37.5	38.0	38.5	39.0	39.5
	the Depreciation Rate is:														
1	1.923	1.894	1.866	1.838	1.812	1.786	1.761	1.736	1.712	1.689	1.667	1.645	1.623	1.603	1.582
2	3.077	3.030	2.985	2.941	2.899	2.857	2.817	2.778	2.740	2.703	2.667	2.632	2.597	2.564	2.532
3	3.077	3.030	2.985	2.941	2.899	2.857	2.817	2.778	2.740	2.703	2.667	2.632	2.597	2.564	2.532
4	3.077	3.030	2.985	2.941	2.899	2.857	2.817	2.778	2.740	2.703	2.667	2.632	2.597	2.564	2.532
5	3.077	3.030	2.985	2.941	2.898	2.857	2.817	2.778	2.740	2.703	2.667	2.632	2.597	2.564	2.532
6	3.077	3.030	2.985	2.941	2.899	2.857	2.817	2.778	2.740	2.703	2.667	2.632	2.597	2.564	2.532
7	3.077	3.030	2.985	2.941	2.898	2.857	2.817	2.778	2.740	2.703	2.667	2.632	2.597	2.564	2.532
8	3.077	3.030	2.985	2.941	2.899	2.857	2.817	2.778	2.740	2.703	2.667	2.631	2.597	2.564	2.532
9	3.077	3.030	2.985	2.941	2.898	2.857	2.817	2.778	2.740	2.703	2.667	2.632	2.598	2.564	2.532
10	3.077	3.030	2.985	2.941	2.899	2.857	2.817	2.778	2.740	2.703	2.667	2.631	2.597	2.564	2.532
11	3.077	3.030	2.985	2.941	2.898	2.857	2.817	2.778	2.740	2.703	2.667	2.632	2.598	2.564	2.532
12	3.077	3.030	2.985	2.941	2.899	2.857	2.817	2.778	2.740	2.703	2.667	2.631	2.597	2.564	2.532
13	3.077	3.030	2.985	2.941	2.898	2.857	2.817	2.778	2.740	2.703	2.667	2.632	2.598	2.564	2.532
14	3.077	3.030	2.985	2.941	2.899	2.857	2.817	2.778	2.740	2.703	2.666	2.631	2.597	2.564	2.531
15	3.077	3.031	2.985	2.941	2.898	2.857	2.817	2.778	2.740	2.703	2.667	2.632	2.598	2.564	2.532
16	3.077	3.030	2.985	2.941	2.899	2.857	2.817	2.778	2.740	2.703	2.666	2.631	2.597	2.564	2.531
17	3.077	3.031	2.985	2.941	2.898	2.857	2.817	2.778	2.740	2.703	2.667	2.632	2.598	2.564	2.532
18	3.077	3.030	2.985	2.941	2.899	2.857	2.817	2.778	2.740	2.702	2.666	2.631	2.597	2.564	2.531
19	3.077	3.031	2.985	2.941	2.898	2.857	2.817	2.778	2.739	2.703	2.667	2.632	2.598	2.564	2.532
20	3.077	3.030	2.985	2.941	2.899	2.857	2.817	2.778	2.740	2.702	2.666	2.631	2.597	2.564	2.531
21	3.077	3.031	2.985	2.941	2.898	2.857	2.817	2.778	2.739	2.703	2.667	2.632	2.598	2.564	2.532
22	3.077	3.030	2.985	2.941	2.899	2.857	2.817	2.777	2.740	2.702	2.666	2.631	2.597	2.564	2.531
23	3.077	3.031	2.985	2.941	2.898	2.857	2.817	2.778	2.739	2.703	2.667	2.632	2.598	2.564	2.532
24	3.077	3.030	2.985	2.942	2.899	2.857	2.817	2.777	2.740	2.702	2.666	2.631	2.597	2.564	2.531
25	3.077	3.031	2.985	2.941	2.898	2.857	2.817	2.778	2.739	2.703	2.667	2.632	2.598	2.564	2.532
26	3.077	3.030	2.985	2.942	2.899	2.857	2.817	2.777	2.740	2.702	2.666	2.631	2.597	2.564	2.531
27	3.077	3.031	2.985	2.941	2.898	2.857	2.817	2.778	2.739	2.703	2.667	2.632	2.598	2.564	2.532
28	3.077	3.030	2.985	2.942	2.899	2.858	2.817	2.777	2.740	2.702	2.666	2.631	2.597	2.564	2.531
29	3.077	3.031	2.985	2.941	2.898	2.857	2.817	2.778	2.739	2.703	2.667	2.632	2.598	2.564	2.532
30	3.076	3.030	2.985	2.942	2.899	2.858	2.816	2.777	2.740	2.702	2.666	2.631	2.597	2.564	2.531
31	3.077	3.031	2.986	2.941	2.898	2.857	2.817	2.778	2.739	2.703	2.667	2.632	2.598	2.564	2.532
32	3.076	3.030	2.985	2.942	2.899	2.858	2.816	2.777	2.740	2.702	2.666	2.631	2.597	2.564	2.531
33	2.692	3.031	2.986	2.941	2.898	2.857	2.817	2.778	2.739	2.703	2.667	2.632	2.598	2.564	2.532
34		1.136	2.612	2.942	2.899	2.858	2.816	2.777	2.740	2.702	2.666	2.631	2.597	2.565	2.531
35				1.103	2.536	2.857	2.817	2.778	2.739	2.703	2.667	2.632	2.598	2.564	2.532
36						1.072	2.464	2.777	2.740	2.702	2.666	2.631	2.597	2.565	2.531
37								1.042	2.397	2.703	2.667	2.632	2.598	2.564	2.532
38										1.013	2.333	2.631	2.597	2.565	2.531
39												0.987	2.273	2.564	2.532
40														0.962	2.215

If the Recovery Year is:	and the Recovery Period is:														
	40.0	40.5	41.0	41.5	42.0	42.5	43.0	43.5	44.0	44.5	45.0	45.5	46.0	46.5	47.0
	the Depreciation Rate is:														
1	1.563	1.543	1.524	1.506	1.488	1.471	1.453	1.437	1.420	1.404	1.389	1.374	1.359	1.344	1.330
2	2.500	2.469	2.439	2.410	2.381	2.353	2.326	2.299	2.273	2.247	2.222	2.198	2.174	2.151	2.128
3	2.500	2.469	2.439	2.410	2.381	2.353	2.326	2.299	2.273	2.247	2.222	2.198	2.174	2.151	2.128
4	2.500	2.469	2.439	2.410	2.381	2.353	2.326	2.299	2.273	2.247	2.222	2.198	2.174	2.151	2.128
5	2.500	2.469	2.439	2.410	2.381	2.353	2.326	2.299	2.273	2.247	2.222	2.198	2.174	2.151	2.128
6	2.500	2.469	2.439	2.410	2.381	2.353	2.326	2.299	2.273	2.247	2.222	2.198	2.174	2.150	2.128
7	2.500	2.469	2.439	2.410	2.381	2.353	2.326	2.299	2.273	2.247	2.222	2.198	2.174	2.151	2.128
8	2.500	2.469	2.439	2.410	2.381	2.353	2.326	2.299	2.273	2.247	2.222	2.198	2.174	2.150	2.128
9	2.500	2.469	2.439	2.410	2.381	2.353	2.326	2.299	2.273	2.247	2.222	2.198	2.174	2.151	2.128
10	2.500	2.469	2.439	2.410	2.381	2.353	2.325	2.299	2.273	2.247	2.222	2.198	2.174	2.150	2.128
11	2.500	2.469	2.439	2.410	2.381	2.353	2.326	2.299	2.273	2.247	2.222	2.198	2.174	2.151	2.128
12	2.500	2.469	2.439	2.410	2.381	2.353	2.325	2.299	2.273	2.247	2.222	2.198	2.174	2.150	2.128
13	2.500	2.469	2.439	2.410	2.381	2.353	2.326	2.299	2.273	2.247	2.222	2.198	2.174	2.151	2.128
14	2.500	2.469	2.439	2.409	2.381	2.353	2.325	2.299	2.273	2.247	2.222	2.198	2.174	2.150	2.128
15	2.500	2.469	2.439	2.410	2.381	2.353	2.326	2.299	2.273	2.247	2.222	2.198	2.174	2.151	2.128
16	2.500	2.469	2.439	2.409	2.381	2.353	2.325	2.299	2.273	2.247	2.222	2.198	2.174	2.150	2.128
17	2.500	2.469	2.439	2.410	2.381	2.353	2.326	2.299	2.273	2.247	2.222	2.198	2.174	2.151	2.127
18	2.500	2.469	2.439	2.409	2.381	2.353	2.325	2.299	2.273	2.247	2.222	2.198	2.174	2.150	2.128
19	2.500	2.469	2.439	2.410	2.381	2.353	2.326	2.299	2.273	2.247	2.222	2.198	2.174	2.151	2.127
20	2.500	2.469	2.439	2.409	2.381	2.353	2.325	2.299	2.273	2.247	2.222	2.198	2.174	2.150	2.128
21	2.500	2.469	2.439	2.410	2.381	2.353	2.326	2.299	2.273	2.247	2.222	2.198	2.174	2.151	2.127
22	2.500	2.469	2.439	2.409	2.381	2.353	2.325	2.299	2.273	2.247	2.222	2.198	2.174	2.150	2.128
23	2.500	2.469	2.439	2.410	2.381	2.353	2.326	2.299	2.272	2.247	2.222	2.198	2.174	2.151	2.127
24	2.500	2.469	2.439	2.409	2.381	2.353	2.325	2.299	2.273	2.247	2.222	2.198	2.174	2.150	2.128
25	2.500	2.469	2.439	2.410	2.381	2.353	2.326	2.299	2.272	2.247	2.222	2.198	2.174	2.151	2.127
26	2.500	2.469	2.439	2.409	2.381	2.353	2.325	2.299	2.273	2.247	2.222	2.198	2.174	2.150	2.128
27	2.500	2.469	2.439	2.410	2.381	2.353	2.326	2.299	2.272	2.247	2.223	2.198	2.174	2.151	2.127
28	2.500	2.469	2.439	2.409	2.381	2.353	2.325	2.299	2.273	2.247	2.222	2.198	2.174	2.150	2.128
29	2.500	2.469	2.439	2.410	2.381	2.353	2.326	2.299	2.272	2.248	2.223	2.197	2.174	2.151	2.127
30	2.500	2.469	2.439	2.409	2.381	2.353	2.325	2.299	2.273	2.247	2.222	2.198	2.174	2.150	2.128
31	2.500	2.470	2.439	2.410	2.381	2.353	2.326	2.299	2.272	2.248	2.223	2.197	2.174	2.151	2.127
32	2.500	2.469	2.439	2.409	2.381	2.353	2.325	2.298	2.273	2.247	2.222	2.198	2.174	2.150	2.128
33	2.500	2.470	2.439	2.410	2.381	2.353	2.326	2.299	2.272	2.248	2.223	2.197	2.174	2.151	2.127
34	2.500	2.469	2.439	2.409	2.381	2.353	2.325	2.298	2.273	2.247	2.222	2.198	2.174	2.150	2.128
35	2.500	2.470	2.439	2.410	2.381	2.353	2.326	2.299	2.272	2.248	2.223	2.197	2.174	2.151	2.127
36	2.500	2.469	2.439	2.409	2.381	2.353	2.325	2.298	2.273	2.247	2.222	2.198	2.174	2.150	2.128
37	2.500	2.470	2.439	2.410	2.381	2.353	2.326	2.299	2.272	2.248	2.223	2.197	2.174	2.151	2.127
38	2.500	2.469	2.439	2.409	2.381	2.353	2.325	2.298	2.273	2.247	2.222	2.198	2.174	2.150	2.128
39	2.500	2.470	2.439	2.410	2.381	2.352	2.326	2.299	2.272	2.248	2.223	2.197	2.173	2.151	2.127
40	2.500	2.469	2.440	2.409	2.380	2.353	2.325	2.298	2.273	2.247	2.222	2.198	2.174	2.150	2.128
41	0.937	2.161	2.439	2.410	2.381	2.352	2.326	2.299	2.272	2.248	2.223	2.197	2.173	2.151	2.127
42			0.915	2.108	2.380	2.353	2.325	2.298	2.273	2.247	2.222	2.198	2.174	2.150	2.128
43					0.893	2.058	2.326	2.299	2.272	2.248	2.223	2.197	2.173	2.151	2.127
44							0.872	2.011	2.273	2.247	2.222	2.198	2.174	2.150	2.128
45									0.852	1.967	2.223	2.197	2.173	2.151	2.127
46											0.833	1.923	2.174	2.150	2.128
47													0.815	1.882	2.127
48															0.798

If the Recovery Year is:	and the Recovery Period is:					
	47.5	48.0	48.5	49.0	49.5	50.0
	the Depreciation Rate is:					
1	1.316	1.302	1.289	1.276	1.263	1.250
2	2.105	2.083	2.062	2.041	2.020	2.000
3	2.105	2.083	2.062	2.041	2.020	2.000
4	2.105	2.083	2.062	2.041	2.020	2.000
5	2.105	2.083	2.062	2.041	2.020	2.000
6	2.105	2.083	2.062	2.041	2.020	2.000
7	2.105	2.083	2.062	2.041	2.020	2.000
8	2.105	2.083	2.062	2.041	2.020	2.000
9	2.105	2.083	2.062	2.041	2.020	2.000
10	2.105	2.083	2.062	2.041	2.020	2.000
11	2.105	2.083	2.062	2.041	2.020	2.000
12	2.105	2.083	2.062	2.041	2.020	2.000
13	2.105	2.083	2.062	2.041	2.020	2.000
14	2.105	2.083	2.062	2.041	2.020	2.000
15	2.105	2.083	2.062	2.041	2.020	2.000
16	2.105	2.083	2.062	2.041	2.020	2.000
17	2.105	2.083	2.062	2.041	2.020	2.000
18	2.105	2.084	2.062	2.041	2.020	2.000
19	2.105	2.083	2.062	2.041	2.020	2.000
20	2.105	2.084	2.062	2.041	2.020	2.000
21	2.105	2.083	2.062	2.041	2.020	2.000
22	2.105	2.084	2.062	2.041	2.020	2.000
23	2.105	2.083	2.062	2.041	2.020	2.000
24	2.105	2.084	2.062	2.041	2.020	2.000
25	2.106	2.083	2.062	2.041	2.020	2.000
26	2.105	2.084	2.062	2.041	2.020	2.000
27	2.106	2.083	2.062	2.041	2.020	2.000
28	2.105	2.084	2.062	2.041	2.020	2.000
29	2.106	2.083	2.062	2.041	2.020	2.000
30	2.105	2.084	2.062	2.041	2.020	2.000
31	2.106	2.083	2.062	2.041	2.020	2.000
32	2.105	2.084	2.062	2.040	2.021	2.000
33	2.106	2.083	2.062	2.041	2.020	2.000
34	2.105	2.084	2.062	2.040	2.021	2.000
35	2.106	2.083	2.062	2.041	2.020	2.000
36	2.105	2.084	2.061	2.040	2.021	2.000
37	2.106	2.083	2.062	2.041	2.020	2.000
38	2.105	2.084	2.061	2.040	2.021	2.000
39	2.106	2.083	2.062	2.041	2.020	2.000
40	2.105	2.084	2.061	2.040	2.021	2.000
41	2.106	2.083	2.062	2.041	2.020	2.000
42	2.105	2.084	2.061	2.040	2.021	2.000
43	2.106	2.083	2.062	2.041	2.020	2.000
44	2.105	2.084	2.061	2.040	2.021	2.000
45	2.106	2.083	2.062	2.041	2.020	2.000
46	2.105	2.084	2.061	2.040	2.021	2.000
47	2.106	2.083	2.062	2.041	2.020	2.000
48	1.842	2.084	2.061	2.040	2.021	2.000
49		0.781	1.804	2.041	2.020	2.000
50				0.765	1.768	2.000
51						0.750

Table 11
General and Alternative Depreciation Systems
Applicable Depreciation Method: Straight Line
Applicable Recovery Periods: 2.5 - 50 years
Applicable Convention: Mid-quarter (property placed in
service in third quarter)

If the Recovery Year is:	and the Recovery Period is:														
	2.5	3.0	3.5	4.0	4.5	5.0	5.5	6.0	6.5	7.0	7.5	8.0	8.5	9.0	9.5
	the Depreciation Rate is:														
1	15.00	12.50	10.71	9.38	8.33	7.50	6.82	6.25	5.77	5.36	5.00	4.69	4.41	4.17	3.95
2	40.00	33.33	28.57	25.00	22.22	20.00	18.18	16.67	15.38	14.29	13.33	12.50	11.76	11.11	10.53
3	40.00	33.34	28.57	25.00	22.22	20.00	18.18	16.67	15.39	14.28	13.33	12.50	11.77	11.11	10.53
4	5.00	20.83	28.58	25.00	22.23	20.00	18.18	16.66	15.38	14.29	13.33	12.50	11.76	11.11	10.52
5			3.57	15.62	22.22	20.00	18.18	16.67	15.39	14.28	13.34	12.50	11.77	11.11	10.53
6					2.78	12.50	18.19	16.66	15.38	14.29	13.33	12.50	11.76	11.11	10.52
7							2.27	10.42	15.39	14.28	13.34	12.50	11.77	11.11	10.53
8									1.92	8.93	13.33	12.50	11.76	11.11	10.52
9											1.67	7.81	11.77	11.11	10.53
10													1.47	6.95	10.52
11															1.32

If the Recovery Year is:	And the Recovery Period is:														
	10.0	10.5	11.0	11.5	12.0	12.5	13.0	13.5	14.0	14.5	15.0	15.5	16.0	16.5	17.0
	the Depreciation Rate is:														
1	3.75	3.57	3.41	3.26	3.13	3.00	2.88	2.78	2.68	2.59	2.50	2.42	2.34	2.27	2.21
2	10.00	9.52	9.09	8.70	8.33	8.00	7.69	7.41	7.14	6.90	6.67	6.45	6.25	6.06	5.88
3	10.00	9.52	9.09	8.70	8.33	8.00	7.69	7.41	7.14	6.90	6.67	6.45	6.25	6.06	5.88
4	10.00	9.52	9.09	8.69	8.33	8.00	7.69	7.41	7.14	6.90	6.67	6.45	6.25	6.06	5.88
5	10.00	9.53	9.09	8.70	8.33	8.00	7.69	7.41	7.14	6.90	6.67	6.45	6.25	6.06	5.88
6	10.00	9.52	9.09	8.69	8.33	8.00	7.69	7.41	7.14	6.89	6.67	6.45	6.25	6.06	5.88
7	10.00	9.53	9.09	8.70	8.34	8.00	7.69	7.41	7.14	6.90	6.66	6.45	6.25	6.06	5.88
8	10.00	9.52	9.09	8.69	8.33	8.00	7.70	7.40	7.14	6.89	6.67	6.45	6.25	6.06	5.88
9	10.00	9.53	9.09	8.70	8.34	8.00	7.69	7.41	7.15	6.90	6.66	6.45	6.25	6.06	5.88
10	10.00	9.52	9.09	8.69	8.33	8.00	7.70	7.40	7.14	6.89	6.67	6.45	6.25	6.06	5.88
11	6.25	9.53	9.10	8.70	8.34	8.00	7.69	7.41	7.15	6.90	6.66	6.45	6.25	6.06	5.88
12		1.19	5.68	8.69	8.33	8.00	7.70	7.40	7.14	6.89	6.67	6.45	6.25	6.06	5.89
13				1.09	5.21	8.00	7.69	7.41	7.15	6.90	6.66	6.46	6.25	6.06	5.88
14						1.00	4.81	7.40	7.14	6.89	6.67	6.45	6.25	6.06	5.89
15							0.93	4.47	6.90	6.66	6.46	6.25	6.06	5.88	
16									0.86	4.17	6.45	6.25	6.07	5.89	
17											0.81	3.91	6.06	5.88	
18													0.76	3.68	

And the Recovery Period is: the Depreciation Rate is:

If the Recovery Year is:	17.5	18.0	18.5	19.0	19.5	20.0	20.5	21.0	21.5	22.0	22.5	23.0	23.5	24.0	24.5
1	2.14	2.08	2.03	1.97	1.92	1.875	1.829	1.786	1.744	1.705	1.667	1.630	1.596	1.563	1.531
2	5.71	5.56	5.40	5.26	5.13	5.000	4.878	4.762	4.651	4.545	4.444	4.348	4.255	4.167	4.082
3	5.71	5.56	5.40	5.26	5.13	5.000	4.878	4.762	4.651	4.545	4.444	4.348	4.255	4.167	4.082
4	5.72	5.56	5.41	5.26	5.13	5.000	4.878	4.762	4.651	4.545	4.444	4.348	4.255	4.167	4.082
5	5.71	5.55	5.40	5.26	5.13	5.000	4.878	4.762	4.651	4.546	4.444	4.348	4.255	4.167	4.082
6	5.72	5.56	5.41	5.26	5.13	5.000	4.878	4.762	4.651	4.545	4.445	4.348	4.255	4.167	4.082
7	5.71	5.55	5.40	5.26	5.13	5.000	4.878	4.762	4.651	4.546	4.444	4.348	4.255	4.167	4.082
8	5.72	5.56	5.41	5.26	5.13	5.000	4.878	4.762	4.651	4.545	4.445	4.348	4.255	4.167	4.081
9	5.71	5.55	5.40	5.27	5.13	5.000	4.878	4.762	4.651	4.546	4.444	4.348	4.255	4.166	4.082
10	5.72	5.56	5.41	5.26	5.13	5.000	4.878	4.762	4.651	4.545	4.444	4.348	4.255	4.167	4.081
11	5.71	5.55	5.40	5.27	5.13	5.000	4.878	4.762	4.651	4.546	4.444	4.348	4.256	4.166	4.082
12	5.72	5.56	5.41	5.26	5.13	5.000	4.878	4.762	4.651	4.545	4.445	4.348	4.255	4.167	4.081
13	5.71	5.55	5.40	5.27	5.13	5.000	4.878	4.762	4.651	4.546	4.444	4.348	4.256	4.166	4.082
14	5.72	5.56	5.41	5.26	5.13	5.000	4.878	4.762	4.651	4.545	4.445	4.348	4.255	4.167	4.081
15	5.71	5.55	5.40	5.27	5.12	5.000	4.878	4.762	4.651	4.546	4.444	4.348	4.256	4.166	4.082
16	5.72	5.56	5.41	5.26	5.13	5.000	4.878	4.762	4.652	4.545	4.445	4.348	4.255	4.167	4.081
17	5.71	5.55	5.40	5.27	5.12	5.000	4.878	4.762	4.651	4.546	4.444	4.348	4.256	4.166	4.082
18	5.72	5.56	5.41	5.26	5.13	5.000	4.878	4.762	4.652	4.545	4.445	4.347	4.255	4.167	4.081
19	0.71	3.47	5.40	5.27	5.12	5.000	4.878	4.761	4.651	4.546	4.444	4.348	4.256	4.166	4.082
20			0.68	3.29	5.13	5.000	4.879	4.762	4.652	4.545	4.445	4.347	4.255	4.167	4.081
21					0.64	3.125	4.878	4.761	4.651	4.546	4.444	4.348	4.256	4.166	4.082
22							0.610	2.976	4.652	4.545	4.445	4.347	4.255	4.167	4.081
23									0.581	2.841	4.444	4.348	4.256	4.166	4.082
24											0.556	2.717	4.255	4.167	4.081
25													0.532	2.604	4.082
26															0.510

and the Recovery Period is: the Depreciation Rate is:

If the Recovery Year is:	25.0	25.5	26.0	26.5	27.0	27.5	28.0	28.5	29.0	29.5	30.0	30.5	31.0	31.5	32.0
1	1.500	1.471	1.442	1.415	1.389	1.364	1.339	1.316	1.293	1.271	1.250	1.230	1.210	1.190	1.172
2	4.000	3.922	3.846	3.774	3.704	3.636	3.571	3.509	3.448	3.390	3.333	3.279	3.226	3.175	3.125
3	4.000	3.922	3.846	3.774	3.704	3.636	3.571	3.509	3.448	3.390	3.333	3.279	3.226	3.175	3.125
4	4.000	3.922	3.846	3.774	3.704	3.636	3.571	3.509	3.448	3.390	3.333	3.279	3.226	3.175	3.125
5	4.000	3.921	3.846	3.774	3.704	3.636	3.571	3.509	3.448	3.390	3.333	3.279	3.226	3.175	3.125
6	4.000	3.922	3.846	3.774	3.704	3.636	3.572	3.509	3.448	3.390	3.333	3.279	3.226	3.175	3.125
7	4.000	3.921	3.846	3.774	3.704	3.636	3.571	3.509	3.448	3.390	3.333	3.279	3.226	3.175	3.125
8	4.000	3.922	3.846	3.774	3.704	3.636	3.572	3.509	3.448	3.390	3.333	3.279	3.226	3.175	3.125
9	4.000	3.921	3.846	3.773	3.704	3.636	3.571	3.509	3.448	3.390	3.333	3.279	3.226	3.175	3.125
10	4.000	3.922	3.846	3.774	3.704	3.636	3.572	3.509	3.448	3.390	3.333	3.279	3.226	3.174	3.125
11	4.000	3.921	3.846	3.773	3.704	3.637	3.571	3.509	3.448	3.390	3.333	3.279	3.226	3.175	3.125
12	4.000	3.922	3.846	3.774	3.704	3.636	3.572	3.509	3.448	3.390	3.334	3.279	3.226	3.174	3.125
13	4.000	3.921	3.846	3.773	3.703	3.637	3.571	3.509	3.448	3.390	3.333	3.278	3.226	3.175	3.125
14	4.000	3.922	3.846	3.774	3.704	3.636	3.572	3.509	3.448	3.390	3.334	3.279	3.226	3.174	3.125
15	4.000	3.921	3.846	3.773	3.703	3.637	3.571	3.509	3.449	3.390	3.333	3.278	3.226	3.175	3.125
16	4.000	3.922	3.846	3.774	3.704	3.636	3.572	3.509	3.448	3.390	3.334	3.279	3.226	3.174	3.125
17	4.000	3.921	3.846	3.773	3.703	3.637	3.571	3.508	3.449	3.390	3.333	3.278	3.226	3.175	3.125
18	4.000	3.922	3.846	3.774	3.704	3.636	3.572	3.509	3.448	3.390	3.334	3.279	3.226	3.175	3.125
19	4.000	3.921	3.846	3.773	3.703	3.637	3.571	3.508	3.449	3.390	3.333	3.278	3.226	3.175	3.125
20	4.000	3.922	3.847	3.774	3.704	3.636	3.572	3.509	3.448	3.390	3.334	3.279	3.226	3.174	3.125
21	4.000	3.921	3.846	3.773	3.703	3.637	3.571	3.508	3.449	3.390	3.333	3.278	3.225	3.175	3.125
22	4.000	3.922	3.847	3.774	3.704	3.636	3.572	3.509	3.448	3.389	3.334	3.279	3.226	3.174	3.125
23	4.000	3.921	3.846	3.773	3.703	3.637	3.571	3.508	3.449	3.390	3.333	3.278	3.225	3.175	3.125
24	4.000	3.922	3.847	3.774	3.704	3.636	3.572	3.509	3.448	3.389	3.334	3.279	3.226	3.174	3.125
25	4.000	3.921	3.846	3.773	3.703	3.637	3.571	3.508	3.449	3.390	3.333	3.278	3.225	3.175	3.125
26	2.500	3.922	3.847	3.774	3.704	3.636	3.572	3.509	3.448	3.389	3.334	3.279	3.226	3.174	3.125
27		0.490	2.404	3.773	3.703	3.637	3.571	3.508	3.449	3.390	3.333	3.278	3.225	3.175	3.125
28				0.472	2.315	3.636	3.572	3.509	3.448	3.389	3.334	3.279	3.226	3.174	3.125
29						0.455	2.232	3.508	3.449	3.390	3.333	3.278	3.225	3.175	3.125
30								0.439	2.155	3.389	3.334	3.279	3.226	3.174	3.125
31										0.424	2.083	3.278	3.225	3.175	3.125
32												0.410	2.016	3.174	3.125
33														0.397	1.953

If the Recovery Year is:	And the Recovery Period is: the Depreciation Rate is:														
	32.5	33.0	33.5	34.0	34.5	35.0	35.5	36.0	36.5	37.0	37.5	38.0	38.5	39.0	39.5
1	1.154	1.136	1.119	1.103	1.087	1.071	1.056	1.042	1.027	1.014	1.000	0.987	0.974	0.962	0.949
2	3.077	3.030	2.985	2.941	2.899	2.857	2.817	2.778	2.740	2.703	2.667	2.632	2.597	2.564	2.532
3	3.077	3.030	2.985	2.941	2.899	2.857	2.817	2.778	2.740	2.703	2.667	2.632	2.597	2.564	2.532
4	3.077	3.030	2.985	2.941	2.899	2.857	2.817	2.778	2.740	2.703	2.667	2.632	2.597	2.564	2.532
5	3.077	3.030	2.985	2.941	2.899	2.857	2.817	2.778	2.740	2.703	2.667	2.632	2.597	2.564	2.532
6	3.077	3.030	2.985	2.941	2.898	2.857	2.817	2.778	2.740	2.703	2.667	2.632	2.597	2.564	2.532
7	3.077	3.030	2.985	2.941	2.899	2.857	2.817	2.778	2.740	2.703	2.667	2.632	2.597	2.564	2.532
8	3.077	3.030	2.985	2.941	2.898	2.857	2.817	2.778	2.740	2.703	2.667	2.631	2.597	2.564	2.532
9	3.077	3.030	2.985	2.941	2.899	2.857	2.817	2.778	2.740	2.703	2.667	2.632	2.597	2.564	2.532
10	3.077	3.030	2.985	2.941	2.898	2.857	2.817	2.778	2.740	2.703	2.667	2.631	2.598	2.564	2.532
11	3.077	3.030	2.985	2.941	2.899	2.857	2.817	2.778	2.740	2.703	2.667	2.632	2.597	2.564	2.532
12	3.077	3.030	2.985	2.941	2.898	2.857	2.817	2.778	2.740	2.703	2.667	2.631	2.598	2.564	2.532
13	3.077	3.030	2.985	2.941	2.899	2.857	2.817	2.778	2.740	2.703	2.667	2.632	2.597	2.564	2.532
14	3.077	3.030	2.985	2.941	2.898	2.857	2.817	2.778	2.740	2.703	2.667	2.631	2.598	2.564	2.532
15	3.077	3.031	2.985	2.941	2.899	2.857	2.817	2.778	2.740	2.703	2.666	2.632	2.597	2.564	2.531
16	3.077	3.030	2.985	2.941	2.898	2.857	2.817	2.778	2.740	2.702	2.667	2.631	2.598	2.564	2.532
17	3.077	3.031	2.985	2.941	2.899	2.857	2.817	2.778	2.740	2.703	2.666	2.632	2.597	2.564	2.531
18	3.077	3.030	2.985	2.941	2.898	2.857	2.817	2.778	2.740	2.702	2.667	2.631	2.598	2.564	2.532
19	3.077	3.031	2.985	2.941	2.899	2.857	2.817	2.778	2.740	2.703	2.666	2.632	2.597	2.564	2.531
20	3.077	3.030	2.985	2.941	2.898	2.857	2.817	2.778	2.739	2.702	2.667	2.631	2.598	2.564	2.532
21	3.077	3.031	2.985	2.941	2.899	2.857	2.817	2.778	2.740	2.703	2.666	2.632	2.597	2.564	2.531
22	3.077	3.030	2.985	2.941	2.898	2.857	2.817	2.777	2.739	2.702	2.667	2.631	2.598	2.564	2.532
23	3.077	3.031	2.985	2.941	2.899	2.857	2.817	2.778	2.740	2.703	2.666	2.632	2.597	2.564	2.531
24	3.077	3.030	2.985	2.942	2.898	2.857	2.817	2.777	2.739	2.702	2.667	2.631	2.598	2.564	2.532
25	3.077	3.031	2.985	2.941	2.899	2.857	2.817	2.778	2.740	2.703	2.666	2.632	2.597	2.564	2.531
26	3.077	3.030	2.985	2.942	2.898	2.858	2.817	2.777	2.739	2.702	2.667	2.631	2.598	2.564	2.532
27	3.077	3.031	2.985	2.941	2.899	2.857	2.817	2.778	2.740	2.703	2.666	2.632	2.597	2.564	2.531
28	3.077	3.030	2.985	2.942	2.898	2.858	2.817	2.777	2.739	2.702	2.667	2.631	2.598	2.564	2.532
29	3.076	3.031	2.985	2.941	2.899	2.857	2.817	2.778	2.740	2.703	2.666	2.632	2.597	2.564	2.531
30	3.077	3.030	2.986	2.942	2.898	2.858	2.817	2.777	2.739	2.702	2.667	2.631	2.598	2.564	2.532
31	3.076	3.031	2.985	2.941	2.899	2.857	2.816	2.778	2.740	2.703	2.666	2.632	2.597	2.564	2.531
32	3.077	3.030	2.986	2.942	2.898	2.858	2.817	2.777	2.739	2.702	2.667	2.631	2.598	2.564	2.532
33	3.076	3.031	2.985	2.941	2.899	2.857	2.816	2.778	2.740	2.703	2.666	2.632	2.597	2.564	2.531
34	0.385	1.894	2.986	2.942	2.898	2.858	2.817	2.777	2.739	2.702	2.667	2.631	2.598	2.565	2.532
35			0.373	1.838	2.899	2.857	2.816	2.778	2.740	2.703	2.666	2.632	2.597	2.564	2.531
36					0.362	1.786	2.817	2.777	2.739	2.702	2.667	2.631	2.598	2.565	2.532
37							0.352	1.736	2.740	2.703	2.666	2.632	2.597	2.564	2.531
38									0.342	1.689	2.667	2.631	2.598	2.565	2.532
39											0.333	1.645	2.597	2.564	2.531
40													0.325	1.603	2.532
41															0.316

If the Recovery Year is:	And the Recovery Period is: the Depreciation Rate is:														
	40.0	40.5	41.0	41.5	42.0	42.5	43.0	43.5	44.0	44.5	45.0	45.5	46.0	46.5	47.0
1	0.938	0.926	0.915	0.904	0.893	0.882	0.872	0.862	0.852	0.843	0.833	0.824	0.815	0.806	0.798
2	2.500	2.469	2.439	2.410	2.381	2.353	2.326	2.299	2.273	2.247	2.222	2.198	2.174	2.151	2.128
3	2.500	2.469	2.439	2.410	2.381	2.353	2.326	2.299	2.273	2.247	2.222	2.198	2.174	2.151	2.128
4	2.500	2.469	2.439	2.410	2.381	2.353	2.326	2.299	2.273	2.247	2.222	2.198	2.174	2.151	2.128
5	2.500	2.469	2.439	2.410	2.381	2.353	2.326	2.299	2.273	2.247	2.222	2.198	2.174	2.151	2.128
6	2.500	2.469	2.439	2.410	2.381	2.353	2.326	2.299	2.273	2.247	2.222	2.198	2.174	2.150	2.128
7	2.500	2.469	2.439	2.410	2.381	2.353	2.326	2.299	2.273	2.247	2.222	2.198	2.174	2.151	2.128
8	2.500	2.469	2.439	2.410	2.381	2.353	2.326	2.299	2.273	2.247	2.222	2.198	2.174	2.150	2.128
9	2.500	2.469	2.439	2.410	2.381	2.353	2.326	2.299	2.273	2.247	2.222	2.198	2.174	2.151	2.128
10	2.500	2.469	2.439	2.410	2.381	2.353	2.325	2.299	2.273	2.247	2.222	2.198	2.174	2.150	2.128
11	2.500	2.469	2.439	2.410	2.381	2.353	2.326	2.299	2.273	2.247	2.222	2.198	2.174	2.151	2.128
12	2.500	2.469	2.439	2.410	2.381	2.353	2.325	2.299	2.273	2.247	2.222	2.198	2.174	2.150	2.128
13	2.500	2.469	2.439	2.409	2.381	2.353	2.326	2.299	2.273	2.247	2.222	2.198	2.174	2.151	2.128
14	2.500	2.469	2.439	2.410	2.381	2.353	2.325	2.299	2.273	2.247	2.222	2.198	2.174	2.150	2.128
15	2.500	2.469	2.439	2.409	2.381	2.353	2.326	2.299	2.273	2.247	2.222	2.198	2.174	2.151	2.128
16	2.500	2.469	2.439	2.410	2.381	2.353	2.325	2.299	2.273	2.247	2.222	2.198	2.174	2.150	2.128
17	2.500	2.469	2.439	2.409	2.381	2.353	2.326	2.299	2.273	2.247	2.222	2.198	2.174	2.151	2.127
18	2.500	2.469	2.439	2.410	2.381	2.353	2.325	2.299	2.273	2.247	2.222	2.198	2.174	2.151	2.128
19	2.500	2.469	2.439	2.409	2.381	2.353	2.326	2.299	2.273	2.247	2.222	2.198	2.174	2.150	2.127
20	2.500	2.469	2.439	2.409	2.381	2.353	2.325	2.299	2.273	2.247	2.222	2.198	2.174	2.150	2.127
21	2.500	2.469	2.439	2.409	2.381	2.353	2.326	2.299	2.273	2.247	2.222	2.198	2.174	2.151	2.128
22	2.500	2.469	2.439	2.410	2.381	2.353	2.325	2.299	2.273	2.247	2.222	2.198	2.174	2.150	2.127
23	2.500	2.469	2.439	2.409	2.381	2.353	2.326	2.299	2.272	2.247	2.222	2.198	2.174	2.151	2.128
24	2.500	2.469	2.439	2.410	2.381	2.353	2.325	2.299	2.273	2.247	2.222	2.198	2.174	2.150	2.127
25	2.500	2.469	2.439	2.409	2.381	2.353	2.326	2.299	2.272	2.247	2.222	2.198	2.174	2.151	2.128
26	2.500	2.469	2.439	2.410	2.381	2.353	2.325	2.299	2.273	2.247	2.222	2.198	2.174	2.150	2.127
27	2.500	2.469	2.439	2.409	2.381	2.353	2.326	2.299	2.272	2.247	2.223	2.198	2.174	2.151	2.128
28	2.500	2.469	2.439	2.410	2.381	2.353	2.325	2.299	2.273	2.247	2.222	2.198	2.174	2.150	2.127
29	2.500	2.469	2.439	2.409	2.381	2.353	2.326	2.299	2.272	2.247	2.223	2.198	2.174	2.151	2.128
30	2.500	2.469	2.439	2.410	2.381	2.353	2.325	2.299	2.273	2.248	2.222	2.197	2.174	2.151	2.128
31	2.500	2.469	2.439	2.409	2.381	2.353	2.326	2.299	2.273	2.247	2.248	2.198	2.174	2.150	2.127
32	2.500	2.470	2.439	2.410	2.381	2.353	2.325	2.299	2.273	2.247	2.223	2.198	2.174	2.151	2.128
33	2.500	2.469	2.439	2.409	2.381	2.353	2.326	2.298	2.272	2.247	2.223	2.198	2.174	2.150	2.127
34	2.500	2.470	2.439	2.410	2.381	2.353	2.325	2.299	2.273	2.248	2.222	2.197	2.174	2.151	2.128
35	2.500	2.469	2.439	2.409	2.381	2.353	2.326	2.298	2.272	2.247	2.223	2.198	2.174	2.150	2.127
36	2.500	2.470	2.439	2.410	2.381	2.353	2.325	2.299	2.273	2.248	2.222	2.197	2.174	2.151	2.128
37	2.500	2.469	2.439	2.409	2.381	2.353	2.326	2.298	2.272	2.247	2.223	2.198	2.174	2.150	2.127
38	2.500	2.470	2.439	2.410	2.381	2.353	2.325	2.299	2.273	2.248	2.222	2.197	2.174	2.151	2.128
39	2.500	2.469	2.439	2.409	2.381	2.353	2.326	2.298	2.272	2.247	2.223	2.198	2.174	2.150	2.127
40	2.500	2.470	2.439	2.410	2.380	2.352	2.325	2.299	2.273	2.248	2.222	2.197	2.173	2.150	2.127
41	1.562	2.469	2.439	2.409	2.381	2.353	2.326	2.298	2.272	2.247	2.223	2.198	2.174	2.151	2.128
42		0.309	1.525	2.410	2.380	2.352	2.325	2.299	2.273	2.248	2.222	2.197	2.173	2.150	2.127
43				0.301	1.488	2.353	2.326	2.298	2.272	2.247	2.223	2.198	2.173	2.151	2.128
44					0.294	1.453	2.299	2.273	2.248	2.247	2.222	2.198	2.173	2.150	2.127
45							0.287	1.420	2.247	2.223	2.198	2.173	2.151	2.128
46									0.281	1.389	2.197	2.174	2.151	2.128
47											0.275	1.358	2.150	2.127
48														0.269	1.330

If the Recovery Year is:	And the Recovery Period is:					
	47.5	48.0	48.5	49.0	49.5	50.0
	the Depreciation Rate is:					
1	0.789	0.781	0.773	0.765	0.758	0.750
2	2.105	2.083	2.062	2.041	2.020	2.000
3	2.105	2.083	2.062	2.041	2.020	2.000
4	2.105	2.083	2.062	2.041	2.020	2.000
5	2.105	2.083	2.062	2.041	2.020	2.000
6	2.105	2.083	2.062	2.041	2.020	2.000
7	2.105	2.083	2.062	2.041	2.020	2.000
8	2.105	2.083	2.062	2.041	2.020	2.000
9	2.105	2.083	2.062	2.041	2.020	2.000
10	2.105	2.083	2.062	2.041	2.020	2.000
11	2.105	2.083	2.062	2.041	2.020	2.000
12	2.105	2.083	2.062	2.041	2.020	2.000
13	2.105	2.083	2.062	2.041	2.020	2.000
14	2.105	2.083	2.062	2.041	2.020	2.000
15	2.105	2.083	2.062	2.041	2.020	2.000
16	2.105	2.083	2.062	2.041	2.020	2.000
17	2.105	2.083	2.062	2.041	2.020	2.000
18	2.105	2.084	2.062	2.041	2.020	2.000
19	2.105	2.083	2.062	2.041	2.020	2.000
20	2.105	2.084	2.062	2.041	2.020	2.000
21	2.105	2.083	2.062	2.041	2.020	2.000
22	2.105	2.084	2.062	2.041	2.020	2.000
23	2.105	2.083	2.062	2.041	2.020	2.000
24	2.106	2.084	2.062	2.041	2.020	2.000
25	2.105	2.083	2.062	2.041	2.020	2.000
26	2.106	2.084	2.062	2.041	2.020	2.000
27	2.105	2.083	2.062	2.041	2.020	2.000
28	2.106	2.084	2.062	2.041	2.020	2.000
29	2.105	2.083	2.062	2.041	2.020	2.000
30	2.106	2.084	2.062	2.041	2.020	2.000
31	2.105	2.083	2.062	2.041	2.020	2.000
32	2.106	2.084	2.062	2.041	2.020	2.000
33	2.105	2.083	2.062	2.041	2.021	2.000
34	2.106	2.084	2.062	2.040	2.020	2.000
35	2.105	2.083	2.062	2.041	2.021	2.000
36	2.106	2.084	2.062	2.040	2.020	2.000
37	2.105	2.083	2.061	2.041	2.021	2.000
38	2.106	2.084	2.062	2.040	2.020	2.000
39	2.105	2.083	2.061	2.041	2.021	2.000
40	2.106	2.084	2.062	2.040	2.020	2.000
41	2.105	2.083	2.061	2.041	2.021	2.000
42	2.106	2.084	2.062	2.040	2.020	2.000
43	2.105	2.083	2.061	2.041	2.021	2.000
44	2.106	2.084	2.062	2.040	2.020	2.000
45	2.105	2.083	2.061	2.041	2.021	2.000
46	2.106	2.084	2.062	2.040	2.020	2.000
47	2.105	2.083	2.061	2.041	2.021	2.000
48	2.106	2.084	2.062	2.040	2.020	2.000
49	0.263	1.302	2.061	2.041	2.021	2.000
50			0.258	1.275	2.020	2.000
51					0.253	1.250

Table 12
General and Alternative Depreciation Systems
Applicable Depreciation Method: Straight Line
Applicable Recovery Periods: 2.5 - 50 years
Applicable Convention: Mid-quarter (property placed
in service in fourth quarter)

and the Recovery Period is:

If the Recovery Year is:	2.5	3.0	3.5	4.0	4.5	5.0	5.5	6.0	6.5	7.0	7.5	8.0	8.5	9.0	9.5
							the Depreciation Rate is:								
1	5.00	4.17	3.57	3.13	2.78	2.50	2.27	2.08	1.92	1.79	1.67	1.56	1.47	1.39	1.32
2	40.00	33.33	28.57	25.00	22.22	20.00	18.18	16.67	15.39	14.29	13.33	12.50	11.76	11.11	10.53
3	40.00	33.33	28.57	25.00	22.22	20.00	18.18	16.67	15.38	14.28	13.33	12.50	11.77	11.11	10.53
4	15.00	29.17	28.57	25.00	22.22	20.00	18.18	16.67	15.39	14.29	13.33	12.50	11.76	11.11	10.52
5			10.72	21.87	22.23	20.00	18.19	16.66	15.38	14.28	13.33	12.50	11.77	11.11	10.53
6					8.33	17.50	18.18	16.67	15.39	14.29	13.34	12.50	11.76	11.11	10.52
7							6.82	14.58	15.38	14.28	13.33	12.50	11.77	11.11	10.53
8									5.77	12.50	13.34	12.50	11.76	11.11	10.52
9											5.00	10.94	11.77	11.11	10.53
10													4.41	9.73	10.52

and the Recovery Period is:

If the Recovery Year is:	10.0	10.5	11.0	11.5	12.0	12.5	13.0	13.5	14.0	14.5	15.0	15.5	16.0	16.5	17.0
							the Depreciation Rate is:								
1	1.25	1.19	1.14	1.09	1.04	1.00	0.96	0.93	0.89	0.86	0.83	0.81	0.78	0.76	0.74
2	10.00	9.52	9.09	8.70	8.33	8.00	7.69	7.41	7.14	6.90	6.67	6.45	6.25	6.06	5.88
3	10.00	9.52	9.09	8.69	8.33	8.00	7.69	7.41	7.14	6.90	6.67	6.45	6.25	6.06	5.88
4	10.00	9.52	9.09	8.70	8.33	8.00	7.69	7.41	7.14	6.90	6.67	6.45	6.25	6.06	5.88
5	10.00	9.53	9.09	8.69	8.33	8.00	7.69	7.41	7.14	6.90	6.67	6.45	6.25	6.06	5.88
6	10.00	9.52	9.09	8.70	8.34	8.00	7.69	7.41	7.14	6.90	6.67	6.45	6.25	6.06	5.88
7	10.00	9.53	9.09	8.69	8.33	8.00	7.69	7.41	7.14	6.89	6.67	6.45	6.25	6.06	5.88
8	10.00	9.52	9.09	8.70	8.34	8.00	7.69	7.40	7.15	6.90	6.66	6.45	6.25	6.06	5.88
9	10.00	9.53	9.09	8.69	8.33	8.00	7.70	7.41	7.14	6.89	6.67	6.45	6.25	6.06	5.88
10	10.00	9.52	9.09	8.70	8.34	8.00	7.69	7.40	7.15	6.90	6.66	6.45	6.25	6.06	5.88
11	8.75	9.53	9.09	8.69	8.33	8.00	7.70	7.41	7.14	6.89	6.67	6.45	6.25	6.06	5.89
12		3.57	7.96	8.70	8.34	8.00	7.69	7.40	7.15	6.90	6.66	6.45	6.25	6.06	5.88
13				3.26	7.29	8.00	7.70	7.41	7.14	6.89	6.67	6.45	6.25	6.06	5.89
14						3.00	6.73	7.40	7.15	6.90	6.66	6.46	6.25	6.06	5.88
15								2.78	6.25	6.89	6.67	6.45	6.25	6.06	5.89
16										2.59	5.83	6.46	6.25	6.06	5.89
17												2.42	5.47	6.07	5.88
18														2.27	5.15

If the Recovery Year is:	and the Recovery Period is:														
	17.5	18.0	18.5	19.0	19.5	20.0	20.5	21.0	21.5	22.0	22.5	23.0	23.5	24.0	24.5
	the Depreciation Rate is:														
1	0.71	0.69	0.68	0.66	0.64	0.625	0.610	0.595	0.581	0.568	0.556	0.543	0.532	0.521	0.510
2	5.71	5.56	5.41	5.26	5.13	5.000	4.878	4.762	4.651	4.545	4.444	4.348	4.255	4.167	4.082
3	5.71	5.56	5.40	5.26	5.13	5.000	4.878	4.762	4.651	4.545	4.444	4.348	4.255	4.167	4.082
4	5.72	5.56	5.41	5.26	5.13	5.000	4.878	4.762	4.651	4.546	4.444	4.348	4.255	4.167	4.082
5	5.71	5.55	5.40	5.26	5.13	5.000	4.878	4.762	4.651	4.545	4.444	4.348	4.255	4.167	4.082
6	5.72	5.56	5.41	5.26	5.13	5.000	4.878	4.762	4.651	4.546	4.445	4.348	4.255	4.167	4.082
7	5.71	5.55	5.40	5.26	5.13	5.000	4.878	4.762	4.651	4.545	4.444	4.348	4.255	4.167	4.082
8	5.72	5.56	5.41	5.26	5.13	5.000	4.878	4.762	4.651	4.546	4.445	4.348	4.255	4.167	4.082
9	5.71	5.55	5.40	5.26	5.13	5.000	4.878	4.762	4.651	4.545	4.444	4.348	4.255	4.167	4.081
10	5.72	5.56	5.41	5.27	5.13	5.000	4.878	4.762	4.651	4.546	4.445	4.348	4.255	4.166	4.082
11	5.71	5.55	5.40	5.26	5.13	5.000	4.878	4.762	4.651	4.545	4.444	4.348	4.256	4.167	4.081
12	5.72	5.56	5.41	5.27	5.13	5.000	4.878	4.762	4.651	4.546	4.445	4.348	4.255	4.166	4.082
13	5.71	5.55	5.40	5.26	5.13	5.000	4.878	4.762	4.651	4.545	4.444	4.348	4.256	4.167	4.081
14	5.72	5.56	5.41	5.27	5.13	5.000	4.878	4.762	4.651	4.546	4.445	4.348	4.255	4.166	4.082
15	5.71	5.55	5.40	5.26	5.12	5.000	4.878	4.762	4.651	4.545	4.444	4.348	4.256	4.167	4.081
16	5.72	5.56	5.41	5.27	5.13	5.000	4.878	4.762	4.652	4.546	4.445	4.348	4.255	4.166	4.082
17	5.71	5.55	5.40	5.26	5.12	5.000	4.878	4.762	4.651	4.545	4.444	4.348	4.256	4.167	4.081
18	5.72	5.56	5.41	5.27	5.13	5.000	4.878	4.762	4.652	4.546	4.445	4.347	4.255	4.166	4.082
19	2.14	4.86	5.40	5.26	5.12	5.000	4.878	4.762	4.651	4.545	4.444	4.348	4.256	4.167	4.081
20			2.03	4.61	5.13	5.000	4.878	4.761	4.652	4.546	4.445	4.347	4.255	4.166	4.082
21					1.92	4.375	4.879	4.762	4.651	4.545	4.444	4.348	4.256	4.167	4.081
22							1.829	4.166	4.652	4.546	4.445	4.347	4.255	4.166	4.082
23									1.744	3.977	4.444	4.348	4.256	4.167	4.081
24											1.667	3.804	4.255	4.166	4.082
25													1.596	3.646	4.081
26															1.531

If the Recovery Year is:	and the Recovery Period is:														
	25.0	25.5	26.0	26.5	27.0	27.5	28.0	28.5	29.0	29.5	30.0	30.5	31.0	31.5	32.0
	the Depreciation Rate is:														
1	0.500	0.490	0.481	0.472	0.463	0.455	0.446	0.439	0.431	0.424	0.417	0.410	0.403	0.397	0.391
2	4.000	3.922	3.846	3.774	3.704	3.636	3.571	3.509	3.448	3.390	3.333	3.279	3.226	3.175	3.125
3	4.000	3.922	3.846	3.774	3.704	3.636	3.571	3.509	3.448	3.390	3.333	3.279	3.226	3.175	3.125
4	4.000	3.922	3.846	3.774	3.704	3.636	3.571	3.509	3.448	3.390	3.333	3.279	3.226	3.175	3.125
5	4.000	3.922	3.846	3.774	3.704	3.636	3.571	3.509	3.448	3.390	3.333	3.279	3.226	3.175	3.125
6	4.000	3.921	3.846	3.773	3.704	3.636	3.572	3.509	3.448	3.390	3.333	3.279	3.226	3.175	3.125
7	4.000	3.922	3.846	3.774	3.704	3.636	3.571	3.509	3.448	3.390	3.333	3.279	3.226	3.175	3.125
8	4.000	3.921	3.846	3.773	3.704	3.636	3.572	3.509	3.448	3.390	3.333	3.279	3.226	3.175	3.125
9	4.000	3.922	3.846	3.774	3.704	3.636	3.571	3.509	3.448	3.390	3.333	3.279	3.226	3.174	3.125
10	4.000	3.921	3.846	3.773	3.704	3.636	3.572	3.509	3.448	3.390	3.333	3.279	3.226	3.175	3.125
11	4.000	3.922	3.846	3.774	3.704	3.637	3.571	3.509	3.448	3.390	3.333	3.279	3.226	3.174	3.125
12	4.000	3.921	3.846	3.773	3.704	3.636	3.572	3.509	3.448	3.390	3.333	3.279	3.226	3.175	3.125
13	4.000	3.922	3.846	3.774	3.703	3.637	3.571	3.509	3.448	3.390	3.334	3.279	3.226	3.174	3.125
14	4.000	3.921	3.846	3.773	3.704	3.636	3.572	3.509	3.448	3.390	3.333	3.278	3.226	3.175	3.125
15	4.000	3.922	3.846	3.774	3.703	3.637	3.571	3.509	3.449	3.390	3.334	3.279	3.226	3.174	3.125
16	4.000	3.921	3.846	3.773	3.704	3.636	3.572	3.509	3.448	3.390	3.333	3.278	3.226	3.175	3.125
17	4.000	3.922	3.846	3.774	3.703	3.637	3.571	3.508	3.449	3.390	3.334	3.279	3.226	3.174	3.125
18	4.000	3.921	3.846	3.773	3.704	3.636	3.572	3.509	3.448	3.390	3.333	3.278	3.226	3.175	3.125
19	4.000	3.922	3.846	3.774	3.703	3.637	3.571	3.508	3.449	3.390	3.334	3.279	3.226	3.174	3.125
20	4.000	3.921	3.846	3.773	3.704	3.636	3.572	3.509	3.448	3.390	3.333	3.278	3.226	3.175	3.125
21	4.000	3.922	3.847	3.774	3.703	3.637	3.571	3.508	3.449	3.389	3.334	3.279	3.226	3.174	3.125
22	4.000	3.921	3.846	3.773	3.704	3.636	3.572	3.509	3.448	3.390	3.333	3.278	3.225	3.175	3.125
23	4.000	3.922	3.847	3.774	3.703	3.637	3.571	3.508	3.449	3.389	3.334	3.279	3.226	3.174	3.125
24	4.000	3.921	3.846	3.773	3.704	3.636	3.572	3.509	3.448	3.390	3.333	3.278	3.225	3.175	3.125
25	4.000	3.922	3.847	3.774	3.703	3.637	3.571	3.508	3.449	3.389	3.334	3.279	3.226	3.174	3.125
26	3.500	3.921	3.846	3.773	3.704	3.636	3.572	3.509	3.448	3.390	3.333	3.278	3.225	3.175	3.125
27		1.471	3.366	3.774	3.703	3.637	3.571	3.508	3.449	3.389	3.334	3.279	3.226	3.174	3.125
28				1.415	3.241	3.636	3.572	3.509	3.448	3.390	3.333	3.278	3.225	3.175	3.125
29						1.364	3.125	3.508	3.449	3.389	3.334	3.279	3.226	3.174	3.125
30								1.316	3.017	3.390	3.333	3.278	3.225	3.175	3.125
31										1.271	2.917	3.279	3.226	3.174	3.125
32												1.229	2.822	3.175	3.125
33													1.190	2.734	

If the Recovery Year is:	and the Recovery Period is: the Depreciation Rate is:														
	32.5	33.0	33.5	34.0	34.5	35.0	35.5	36.0	36.5	37.0	37.5	38.0	38.5	39.0	39.5
1	0.385	0.379	0.373	0.368	0.362	0.357	0.352	0.347	0.342	0.338	0.333	0.329	0.325	0.321	0.316
2	3.077	3.030	2.985	2.941	2.899	2.857	2.817	2.778	2.740	2.703	2.667	2.632	2.597	2.564	2.532
3	3.077	3.030	2.985	2.941	2.899	2.857	2.817	2.778	2.740	2.703	2.667	2.632	2.597	2.564	2.532
4	3.077	3.030	2.985	2.941	2.899	2.857	2.817	2.778	2.740	2.703	2.667	2.632	2.597	2.564	2.532
5	3.077	3.030	2.985	2.941	2.899	2.857	2.817	2.778	2.740	2.703	2.667	2.632	2.597	2.564	2.532
6	3.077	3.030	2.985	2.941	2.899	2.857	2.817	2.778	2.740	2.703	2.667	2.632	2.597	2.564	2.532
7	3.077	3.030	2.985	2.941	2.898	2.857	2.817	2.778	2.740	2.703	2.667	2.632	2.597	2.564	2.532
8	3.077	3.030	2.985	2.941	2.899	2.857	2.817	2.778	2.740	2.703	2.667	2.631	2.597	2.564	2.532
9	3.077	3.030	2.985	2.941	2.898	2.857	2.817	2.778	2.740	2.703	2.667	2.632	2.597	2.564	2.532
10	3.077	3.030	2.985	2.941	2.899	2.857	2.817	2.778	2.740	2.703	2.667	2.631	2.597	2.564	2.532
11	3.077	3.030	2.985	2.941	2.898	2.857	2.817	2.778	2.740	2.703	2.667	2.632	2.598	2.564	2.532
12	3.077	3.030	2.985	2.941	2.899	2.857	2.817	2.778	2.740	2.703	2.667	2.631	2.597	2.564	2.532
13	3.077	3.030	2.985	2.941	2.898	2.857	2.817	2.778	2.740	2.703	2.667	2.632	2.598	2.564	2.532
14	3.077	3.030	2.985	2.941	2.899	2.857	2.817	2.778	2.740	2.703	2.667	2.631	2.597	2.564	2.532
15	3.077	3.030	2.985	2.941	2.898	2.857	2.817	2.778	2.740	2.703	2.667	2.632	2.598	2.564	2.531
16	3.077	3.031	2.985	2.941	2.899	2.857	2.817	2.778	2.740	2.703	2.666	2.631	2.597	2.564	2.531
17	3.077	3.030	2.985	2.941	2.898	2.857	2.817	2.778	2.740	2.702	2.667	2.632	2.598	2.564	2.532
18	3.077	3.031	2.985	2.941	2.899	2.857	2.817	2.778	2.740	2.703	2.666	2.631	2.597	2.564	2.531
19	3.077	3.030	2.985	2.941	2.898	2.857	2.817	2.778	2.740	2.702	2.667	2.632	2.598	2.564	2.532
20	3.077	3.031	2.985	2.941	2.899	2.857	2.817	2.778	2.739	2.703	2.666	2.631	2.597	2.564	2.531
21	3.077	3.030	2.985	2.941	2.898	2.857	2.817	2.778	2.740	2.702	2.667	2.632	2.598	2.564	2.532
22	3.077	3.031	2.985	2.941	2.899	2.857	2.817	2.778	2.739	2.703	2.666	2.631	2.597	2.564	2.531
23	3.077	3.030	2.985	2.941	2.898	2.857	2.817	2.777	2.740	2.702	2.667	2.632	2.598	2.564	2.532
24	3.077	3.031	2.985	2.941	2.899	2.857	2.817	2.778	2.739	2.703	2.666	2.631	2.597	2.564	2.531
25	3.077	3.030	2.985	2.942	2.898	2.857	2.817	2.777	2.740	2.702	2.667	2.632	2.598	2.564	2.531
26	3.077	3.031	2.985	2.941	2.899	2.857	2.817	2.778	2.739	2.703	2.666	2.631	2.597	2.564	2.532
27	3.077	3.030	2.985	2.942	2.898	2.858	2.817	2.777	2.740	2.702	2.667	2.632	2.598	2.564	2.531
28	3.077	3.031	2.985	2.941	2.899	2.857	2.817	2.778	2.739	2.703	2.666	2.631	2.597	2.564	2.532
29	3.076	3.030	2.985	2.942	2.898	2.858	2.817	2.777	2.740	2.703	2.666	2.631	2.597	2.564	2.531
30	3.077	3.031	2.985	2.941	2.899	2.857	2.817	2.778	2.739	2.703	2.666	2.631	2.597	2.564	2.532
31	3.076	3.030	2.986	2.942	2.898	2.858	2.816	2.777	2.740	2.702	2.667	2.632	2.598	2.564	2.531
32	3.077	3.031	2.985	2.941	2.899	2.857	2.817	2.778	2.739	2.703	2.666	2.631	2.597	2.564	2.532
33	3.076	3.030	2.986	2.942	2.898	2.858	2.816	2.777	2.740	2.702	2.667	2.632	2.598	2.564	2.531
34	1.154	2.652	2.985	2.941	2.899	2.857	2.817	2.778	2.739	2.703	2.666	2.631	2.597	2.565	2.532
35			1.120	2.574	2.898	2.858	2.816	2.777	2.740	2.702	2.667	2.632	2.598	2.564	2.531
36					1.087	2.500	2.817	2.778	2.739	2.703	2.666	2.631	2.597	2.565	2.532
37							1.056	2.430	2.740	2.702	2.667	2.632	2.598	2.564	2.531
38									1.027	2.365	2.666	2.631	2.597	2.565	2.532
39											1.000	2.303	2.598	2.564	2.531
40													0.974	2.244	2.532
41															0.949

If the Recovery Year is:	and the Recovery Period is: the Depreciation Rate is:													
	40.0	40.5	41.0	41.5	42.0	42.5	43.0	43.5	44.0	44.5	45.0	45.5	46.0	46.5	47.0
1	0.313	0.309	0.305	0.301	0.298	0.294	0.291	0.287	0.284	0.281	0.278	0.275	0.272	0.269	0.266
2	2.500	2.469	2.439	2.410	2.381	2.353	2.326	2.299	2.273	2.247	2.222	2.198	2.174	2.151	2.128
3	2.500	2.469	2.439	2.410	2.381	2.353	2.326	2.299	2.273	2.247	2.222	2.198	2.174	2.151	2.128
4	2.500	2.469	2.439	2.410	2.381	2.353	2.326	2.299	2.273	2.247	2.222	2.198	2.174	2.151	2.128
5	2.500	2.469	2.439	2.410	2.381	2.353	2.326	2.299	2.273	2.247	2.222	2.198	2.174	2.151	2.128
6	2.500	2.469	2.439	2.410	2.381	2.353	2.326	2.299	2.273	2.247	2.222	2.198	2.174	2.150	2.128
7	2.500	2.469	2.439	2.410	2.381	2.353	2.326	2.299	2.273	2.247	2.222	2.198	2.174	2.151	2.128
8	2.500	2.469	2.439	2.410	2.381	2.353	2.326	2.299	2.273	2.247	2.222	2.198	2.174	2.150	2.128
9	2.500	2.469	2.439	2.410	2.381	2.353	2.325	2.299	2.273	2.247	2.222	2.198	2.174	2.151	2.128
10	2.500	2.469	2.439	2.410	2.381	2.353	2.326	2.299	2.273	2.247	2.222	2.198	2.174	2.150	2.128
11	2.500	2.469	2.439	2.410	2.381	2.353	2.325	2.299	2.273	2.247	2.222	2.198	2.174	2.151	2.128
12	2.500	2.469	2.439	2.410	2.381	2.353	2.326	2.299	2.273	2.247	2.222	2.198	2.174	2.150	2.128
13	2.500	2.469	2.439	2.410	2.381	2.353	2.325	2.299	2.273	2.247	2.222	2.198	2.174	2.151	2.128
14	2.500	2.469	2.439	2.409	2.381	2.353	2.326	2.299	2.273	2.247	2.222	2.198	2.174	2.150	2.128
15	2.500	2.469	2.439	2.410	2.381	2.353	2.325	2.299	2.273	2.247	2.222	2.198	2.174	2.151	2.128
16	2.500	2.469	2.439	2.409	2.381	2.353	2.326	2.299	2.273	2.247	2.222	2.198	2.174	2.150	2.128
17	2.500	2.469	2.439	2.410	2.381	2.353	2.325	2.299	2.273	2.247	2.222	2.198	2.174	2.151	2.127
18	2.500	2.469	2.439	2.409	2.381	2.353	2.326	2.299	2.273	2.247	2.222	2.198	2.174	2.150	2.128
19	2.500	2.469	2.439	2.410	2.381	2.353	2.325	2.299	2.273	2.247	2.222	2.198	2.174	2.151	2.127
20	2.500	2.469	2.439	2.409	2.381	2.353	2.326	2.299	2.273	2.247	2.222	2.198	2.174	2.150	2.128
21	2.500	2.469	2.439	2.410	2.381	2.353	2.325	2.299	2.273	2.247	2.222	2.198	2.174	2.151	2.127
22	2.500	2.469	2.439	2.409	2.381	2.353	2.326	2.299	2.273	2.247	2.222	2.198	2.174	2.150	2.128
23	2.500	2.469	2.439	2.410	2.381	2.353	2.325	2.299	2.272	2.247	2.222	2.198	2.174	2.151	2.127
24	2.500	2.469	2.439	2.409	2.381	2.353	2.326	2.299	2.273	2.247	2.222	2.198	2.174	2.150	2.128
25	2.500	2.469	2.439	2.410	2.381	2.353	2.325	2.299	2.272	2.247	2.222	2.198	2.174	2.151	2.127
26	2.500	2.469	2.439	2.409	2.381	2.353	2.326	2.299	2.273	2.247	2.222	2.198	2.174	2.150	2.128
27	2.500	2.469	2.439	2.410	2.381	2.353	2.325	2.299	2.272	2.247	2.222	2.198	2.174	2.151	2.127
28	2.500	2.469	2.439	2.409	2.381	2.353	2.326	2.299	2.273	2.247	2.223	2.198	2.174	2.150	2.128
29	2.500	2.469	2.439	2.410	2.381	2.353	2.325	2.299	2.272	2.247	2.222	2.197	2.174	2.151	2.127
30	2.500	2.469	2.439	2.409	2.381	2.353	2.326	2.299	2.273	2.248	2.223	2.198	2.174	2.150	2.128
31	2.500	2.469	2.439	2.410	2.381	2.353	2.325	2.299	2.272	2.247	2.222	2.197	2.174	2.151	2.127
32	2.500	2.469	2.439	2.409	2.381	2.353	2.326	2.299	2.273	2.248	2.223	2.198	2.174	2.150	2.128
33	2.500	2.470	2.439	2.410	2.381	2.353	2.325	2.299	2.272	2.247	2.222	2.197	2.174	2.151	2.127
34	2.500	2.469	2.439	2.409	2.381	2.353	2.326	2.298	2.273	2.248	2.223	2.198	2.174	2.150	2.128
35	2.500	2.470	2.439	2.410	2.381	2.353	2.325	2.299	2.272	2.247	2.222	2.197	2.174	2.151	2.127
36	2.500	2.469	2.439	2.409	2.381	2.353	2.326	2.298	2.273	2.248	2.223	2.198	2.174	2.150	2.128
37	2.500	2.470	2.439	2.410	2.381	2.353	2.325	2.299	2.272	2.247	2.222	2.197	2.174	2.151	2.127
38	2.500	2.469	2.439	2.409	2.381	2.353	2.326	2.298	2.273	2.248	2.223	2.198	2.174	2.150	2.128
39	2.500	2.470	2.439	2.410	2.381	2.353	2.325	2.299	2.272	2.247	2.222	2.197	2.174	2.151	2.127
40	2.500	2.469	2.439	2.409	2.380	2.352	2.326	2.298	2.273	2.248	2.223	2.198	2.173	2.150	2.128
41	2.187	2.470	2.439	2.410	2.381	2.353	2.325	2.299	2.272	2.247	2.222	2.197	2.174	2.151	2.127
42		0.926	2.135	2.409	2.380	2.352	2.326	2.298	2.273	2.248	2.223	2.198	2.173	2.150	2.128
43			0.904	2.083	2.353	2.325	2.299	2.272	2.247	2.222	2.197	2.174	2.151	2.127
44					0.882	2.035	2.298	2.273	2.248	2.223	2.198	2.173	2.150	2.128
45						0.862	1.988	2.247	2.222	2.197	2.174	2.151	2.127
46							0.843	1.945	2.198	2.173	2.150	2.128
47								0.824	1.902	2.151	2.127
48									0.806	1.862

If the Recovery Year is:	and the Recovery Period is:					
	47.5	48.0	48.5	49.0	49.5	50.0
	the Depreciation Rate is:					
1	0.263	0.260	0.258	0.255	0.253	0.250
2	2.105	2.083	2.062	2.041	2.020	2.000
3	2.105	2.083	2.062	2.041	2.020	2.000
4	2.105	2.083	2.062	2.041	2.020	2.000
5	2.105	2.083	2.062	2.041	2.020	2.000
6	2.105	2.083	2.062	2.041	2.020	2.000
7	2.105	2.083	2.062	2.041	2.020	2.000
8	2.105	2.083	2.062	2.041	2.020	2.000
9	2.105	2.083	2.062	2.041	2.020	2.000
10	2.105	2.083	2.062	2.041	2.020	2.000
11	2.105	2.083	2.062	2.041	2.020	2.000
12	2.105	2.083	2.062	2.041	2.020	2.000
13	2.105	2.083	2.062	2.041	2.020	2.000
14	2.105	2.083	2.062	2.041	2.020	2.000
15	2.105	2.083	2.062	2.041	2.020	2.000
16	2.105	2.083	2.062	2.041	2.020	2.000
17	2.105	2.083	2.062	2.041	2.020	2.000
18	2.105	2.084	2.062	2.041	2.020	2.000
19	2.105	2.083	2.062	2.041	2.020	2.000
20	2.105	2.084	2.062	2.041	2.020	2.000
21	2.105	2.083	2.062	2.041	2.020	2.000
22	2.105	2.084	2.062	2.041	2.020	2.000
23	2.105	2.083	2.062	2.041	2.020	2.000
24	2.105	2.084	2.062	2.041	2.020	2.000
25	2.106	2.083	2.062	2.041	2.020	2.000
26	2.105	2.084	2.062	2.041	2.020	2.000
27	2.106	2.083	2.062	2.041	2.020	2.000
28	2.105	2.084	2.062	2.041	2.020	2.000
29	2.106	2.083	2.062	2.041	2.020	2.000
30	2.105	2.084	2.062	2.041	2.020	2.000
31	2.106	2.083	2.062	2.041	2.020	2.000
32	2.105	2.084	2.062	2.041	2.020	2.000
33	2.106	2.083	2.062	2.041	2.021	2.000
34	2.105	2.084	2.062	2.040	2.020	2.000
35	2.106	2.083	2.062	2.041	2.021	2.000
36	2.105	2.084	2.061	2.040	2.020	2.000
37	2.106	2.083	2.062	2.041	2.021	2.000
38	2.105	2.084	2.061	2.040	2.020	2.000
39	2.106	2.083	2.062	2.041	2.021	2.000
40	2.105	2.084	2.061	2.040	2.020	2.000
41	2.106	2.083	2.062	2.041	2.021	2.000
42	2.105	2.084	2.061	2.040	2.020	2.000
43	2.106	2.083	2.062	2.041	2.021	2.000
44	2.105	2.084	2.061	2.040	2.020	2.000
45	2.106	2.083	2.062	2.041	2.021	2.000
46	2.105	2.084	2.061	2.040	2.020	2.000
47	2.106	2.083	2.062	2.041	2.021	2.000
48	2.105	2.084	2.061	2.040	2.020	2.000
49	0.790	1.823	2.062	2.041	2.021	2.000
50			0.773	1.785	2.020	2.000
51					0.758	1.750

Table 13

Alternative Depreciation System
Applicable Depreciation Method: Straight Line
Applicable Recovery Period: 40 years
Applicable Convention: Mid-month

If the Recovery Year is:	And the Month in the First Recovery Year the Property is Placed in Service is:											
	1	2	3	4	5	6	7	8	9	10	11	12
	the Depreciation Rate is:											
1	2.396	2.188	1.979	1.771	1.563	1.354	1.146	0.938	0.729	0.521	0.313	0.104
2 to 40	2.500	2.500	2.500	2.500	2.500	2.500	2.500	2.500	2.500	2.500	2.500	2.500
41	0.104	0.312	0.521	0.729	0.937	1.146	1.354	1.562	1.771	1.979	2.187	2.396

Table 14
Business Auto Tables

Accelerated MACRS Depreciation Rates for Business
"Luxury" Automobiles Used 100% for Business
(IRS Pub No. 917 (1992) p.9.) [This table is discussed at ¶ 1960]

MACRS Depreciation Table for a Car

Column 1	Column 2	Column 3	Column 4	Column 5	Column 6	Column 7	Column 8	Column 9	Column 10	Column 11
		Mid-Quarter Convention								
Recovery Year	Half-Year Conversion	Car placed in service 1st Quarter	Car placed in service 2nd Quarter	Car placed in service 3rd Quarter	Car placed in service 4th Quarter	Maximum Depreciation Limit — Placed in service in '87 or '88	Maximum Depreciation Limit — Placed in service in '89 or '90	Maximum Depreciation Limit — Placed in service in '91	Maximum Depreciation Limit — Placed in service in '92	Maximum Depreciation Limit — Placed in service in '93
1	20.00%	35.00%	25.00%	15.00%	5.00%	$2,560	$2,660	$2,660	$2,760	$2,860
2	32.00%	26.00	30.00	34.00	38.00	$4,100	$4,200	$4,300	$4,400	$4,600
3	19.20%	15.60	18.00	20.40	22.80	$2,450	$2,550	$2,550	$2,650	$2,750
4	11.52%	11.01	11.37	12.24	13.68	$1,475	$1,475	$1,575	$1,575	$1,675
5	11.52%	11.01	11.37	11.30	10.94	$1,475	$1,475	$1,575	$1,575	$1,675
6	5.76%	1.38	4.26	7.06	9.58	$1,475	$1,475	$1,575	$1,575	$1,675

Table 15

Straight-Line MACRS Depreciation Rates for Business
"Luxury" Automobiles Used 100% for Business
(IRS Pub No. 917 (1992) p.9.) [This table is discussed at ¶ 1960]

Alternative MACRS Depreciation Table for a Car

Column 1	Column 2	Column 3	Column 4	Column 5	Column 6	Column 7	Column 8	Column 9	Column 10	Column 11
		Mid-Quarter Convention								
Recovery Year	Half-Year Conversion	Car placed in service 1st Quarter	Car placed in service 2nd Quarter	Car placed in service 3rd Quarter	Car placed in service 4th Quarter	Maximum Depreciation Limit — Placed in service in '87 or '88	Maximum Depreciation Limit — Placed in service in '89 or '90	Maximum Depreciation Limit — Placed in service in '91	Maximum Depreciation Limit — Placed in service in '92	Maximum Depreciation Limit — Placed in service in '93
1	10.00%	17.50%	12.50%	7.50%	2.50%	$2,560	$2,660	$2,660	$2,760	$2,860
2	20.00%	20.00	20.00	20.00	20.00	$4,100	$4,200	$4,300	$4,400	$4,600
3	20.00%	20.00	20.00	20.00	20.00	$2,450	$2,550	$2,550	$2,650	$2,750
4	20.00%	20.00	20.00	20.00	20.00	$1,475	$1,475	$1,575	$1,575	$1,675
5	20.00%	20.00	20.00	20.00	20.00	$1,475	$1,475	$1,575	$1,575	$1,675
6	10.00%	2.50	7.50	12.50	17.50	$1,475	$1,475	$1,575	$1,575	$1,675

Table I
15-year Real Property Except Low-Income Housing
(15-Year 175% Declining Balance Full Month Convention)

If the Recovery Year is:	(Month Placed in Service)											
	1	2	3	4	5	6	7	8	9	10	11	12
1	12	11	10	9	8	7	6	5	4	3	2	1
2	10	10	11	11	11	11	11	11	11	11	11	12
3	9	9	9	9	10	10	10	10	10	10	10	10
4	8	8	8	8	8	8	9	9	9	9	9	9
5	7	7	7	7	7	7	8	8	8	8	8	8
6	6	6	6	6	7	7	7	7	7	7	7	7
7	6	6	6	6	6	6	6	6	6	6	6	6
8	6	6	6	6	6	6	5	6	6	6	6	6
9	6	6	6	6	5	6	5	5	5	6	6	6
10	5	6	5	6	5	5	5	5	5	5	6	5
11	5	5	5	5	5	5	5	5	5	5	5	5
12	5	5	5	5	5	5	5	5	5	5	5	5
13	5	5	5	5	5	5	5	5	5	5	5	5
14	5	5	5	5	5	5	5	5	5	5	5	5
15	5	5	5	5	5	5	5	5	5	5	5	5
16	-	-	1	1	2	2	3	3	4	4	4	5

Table II
Low-Income Housing
(15-Year 200% Declining Balance Full Month Convention)

If the Recovery Year is:	(Month Placed in Service)											
	1	2	3	4	5	6	7	8	9	10	11	12
1	13	12	11	10	9	8	7	6	4	3	2	1
2	12	12	12	12	12	12	12	13	13	13	13	13
3	10	10	10	10	11	11	11	11	11	11	11	11
4	9	9	9	9	9	9	9	9	10	10	10	10
5	8	8	8	8	8	8	8	8	8	8	8	9
6	7	7	7	7	7	7	7	7	7	7	7	7
7	6	6	6	6	6	6	6	6	6	6	6	6
8	5	5	5	5	5	5	5	5	5	5	6	6
9	5	5	5	5	5	5	5	5	5	5	5	5
10	5	5	5	5	5	5	5	5	5	5	5	5
11	4	5	5	5	5	5	5	5	5	5	5	5
12	4	4	4	5	4	5	5	5	5	5	5	5
13	4	4	4	4	4	4	5	4	5	5	5	5
14	4	4	4	4	4	4	4	4	4	5	4	4
15	4	4	4	4	4	4	4	4	4	4	4	4
16	-	-	1	1	2	2	2	3	3	3	4	4

Table III
Low-income Housing
(15-Year 200% Declining Balance)
(Assuming No Mid-Month Convention)

If the Recovery Year is:	(Month Placed in Service)											
	1	2	3	4	5	6	7	8	9	10	11	12
1	13.3	12.1	11.1	10.0	8.9	7.8	6.6	5.6	4.4	3.3	2.2	1.1
2	11.6	11.7	11.9	12.0	12.1	12.3	12.5	12.6	12.7	12.9	13.0	13.2
3	10.0	10.1	10.2	10.4	10.5	10.7	10.8	10.9	11.1	11.2	11.3	11.4
4	8.7	8.8	8.9	9.0	9.1	9.2	9.3	9.5	9.6	9.7	9.8	9.9
5	7.5	7.6	7.7	7.8	7.9	8.0	8.1	8.2	8.3	8.4	8.5	8.6
6	6.5	6.6	6.7	6.8	6.9	6.9	7.0	7.1	7.2	7.3	7.4	7.4
7	5.7	5.7	5.8	5.9	5.9	6.0	6.1	6.1	6.2	6.3	6.4	6.5
8	4.9	5.0	5.0	5.1	5.2	5.2	5.3	5.3	5.4	5.5	5.5	5.6
9	4.6	4.6	4.6	4.6	4.6	4.6	4.6	4.6	4.6	4.7	4.8	4.8
10	4.6	4.6	4.6	4.6	4.6	4.6	4.6	4.6	4.6	4.6	4.6	4.6
11	4.6	4.6	4.6	4.6	4.6	4.6	4.6	4.6	4.6	4.6	4.6	4.6
12	4.5	4.6	4.6	4.6	4.6	4.6	4.6	4.6	4.6	4.6	4.6	4.6
13	4.5	4.5	4.6	4.5	4.6	4.6	4.6	4.6	4.6	4.5	4.6	4.6
14	4.5	4.5	4.5	4.5	4.5	4.5	4.5	4.6	4.6	4.5	4.5	4.5
15	4.5	4.5	4.5	4.5	4.5	4.5	4.5	4.5	4.5	4.5	4.5	4.5
16	0.0	0.4	0.7	1.1	1.5	1.9	2.3	2.6	3.0	3.4	3.7	4.1

Table IV
18-year Real Property
(18-year 175% Declining Balance, Assuming Mid-Month Convention)
(placed in service after June 22, 1984)

Year	Month Placed in Service											
	1	2	3	4	5	6	7	8	9	10	11	12
1st	9%	9%	8%	7%	6%	5%	4%	4%	3%	2%	1%	0.4%
2nd	9%	9%	9%	9%	9%	9%	9%	9%	9%	10%	10%	10%
3rd	8%	8%	8%	8%	8%	8%	8%	8%	9%	9%	9%	9%
4th	7%	7%	7%	7%	7%	8%	8%	8%	8%	8%	8%	8%
5th	7%	7%	7%	7%	7%	7%	7%	7%	7%	7%	7%	7%
6th	6%	6%	6%	6%	6%	6%	6%	6%	6%	6%	6%	6%
7th	5%	5%	5%	5%	6%	6%	6%	6%	6%	6%	6%	6%
8-12th	5%	5%	5%	5%	5%	5%	5%	5%	5%	5%	5%	5%
13th	4%	4%	4%	5%	4%	4%	5%	4%	4%	4%	5%	5%
14-17th	4%	4%	4%	4%	4%	4%	4%	4%	4%	4%	4%	4%
18th	4%	3%	4%	4%	4%	4%	4%	4%	4%	4%	4%	4%
19th		1%	1%	1%	2%	2%	2%	3%	3%	3%	3%	3.6%

Table V
18-year Real Property
(18-Year-175% Declining Balance, Assuming No Mid-Month Convention)
(placed in service after March 15 and before June 23, 1984)

Year	Month Placed in Service										
	1	2	3	4	5	6	7	8	9	10-11	12
1st	10%	9%	8%	7%	6%	6%	5%	4%	3%	2%	1%
2nd	9%	9%	9%	9%	9%	9%	9%	9%	9%	10%	10%
3rd	8%	8%	8%	8%	8%	8%	8%	8%	9%	9%	9%
4th	7%	7%	7%	7%	7%	7%	8%	8%	8%	8%	8%
5th	6%	7%	7%	7%	7%	7%	7%	7%	7%	7%	7%
6th	6%	6%	6%	6%	6%	6%	6%	6%	6%	6%	6%
7th	5%	5%	5%	5%	6%	6%	6%	6%	6%	6%	6%
8-12th	5%	5%	5%	5%	5%	5%	5%	5%	5%	5%	5%
13th	4%	4%	4%	5%	5%	4%	4%	5%	4%	4%	4%
14-18th	4%	4%	4%	4%	4%	4%	4%	4%	4%	4%	4%
19th		1%	1%	1%	2%	2%	2%	3%	3%	4%	

Table VI
19-year Real Property
(19-Year 175% Declining Balance, Assuming Mid-Month Convention)

Year	Month Placed in Service											
	1	2	3	4	5	6	7	8	9	10	11	12
1st	8.8%	8.1%	7.3%	6.5%	5.8%	5.0%	4.2%	3.5%	2.7%	1.9%	1.1%	0.4%
2nd	8.4%	8.5%	8.5%	8.6%	8.7%	8.8%	8.8%	8.9%	9.0%	9.0%	9.1%	9.2%
3rd	7.6%	7.7%	7.7%	7.8%	7.9%	7.9%	8.0%	8.1%	8.1%	8.3%	8.3%	8.3%
4th	6.9%	7.0%	7.0%	7.1%	7.1%	7.2%	7.3%	7.3%	7.4%	7.4%	7.5%	7.6%
5th	6.3%	6.3%	6.4%	6.4%	6.5%	6.5%	6.6%	6.6%	6.7%	6.8%	6.8%	6.9%
6th	5.7%	5.7%	5.8%	5.9%	5.9%	5.9%	6.0%	6.0%	6.1%	6.1%	6.2%	6.2%
7th	5.2%	5.2%	5.3%	5.3%	5.3%	5.4%	5.4%	5.5%	5.5%	5.6%	5.6%	5.6%
8th	4.7%	4.7%	4.8%	4.8%	4.8%	4.9%	4.9%	5.0%	5.0%	5.1%	5.1%	5.1%
9th	4.2%	4.3%	4.3%	4.4%	4.4%	4.5%	4.5%	4.5%	4.5%	4.6%	4.6%	4.7%
10-19th	4.2%	4.2%	4.2%	4.2%	4.2%	4.2%	4.2%	4.2%	4.2%	4.2%	4.2%	4.2%
20th	0.2%	0.5%	0.9%	1.2%	1.6%	1.9%	2.3%	2.6%	3.0%	3.3%	3.7%	4.0%

Table VII
18-year Real Property
(placed in service after June 22, 1984)
For Which Alternate ACRS Method
(Assuming Mid-Month Convention)
Over an 18-Year Periods is Elected

Year	Month Placed in Service					
	1-2	3-4	5-7	8-9	10-11	12
1st	5%	4%	3%	2%	1%	0.2%
2-10th	6%	6%	6%	6%	6%	6%
11th	5%	5%	5%	5%	5%	5.8%
12-18th	5%	5%	5%	5%	5%	5%
19th	1%	2%	3%	4%	5%	5%

Table VIII
18-year Real Property
(placed in service after March 15 and before June 23, 1984)
For Which Alternate ACRS Method (Assuming No Mid-Month Convention)
Over an 18-year Period is Elected

Year	Month Placed in Service						
	1	2-3	4-5	6-7	8-9	10-11	12
1st	6%	5%	4%	3%	2%	1%	0.5%
2-10th	6%	6%	6%	6%	6%	6%	6%
11th	5%	5%	5%	5%	5%	5%	5.5%
12-18th	5%	5%	5%	5%	5%	5%	5%
19th		1%	2%	3%	4%	5%	5%

Table IX
19-year Real Property For Which Alternate ACRS Method
(Assuming Mid-Month Convention)
Over a 19-Year Period is Elected

Year	Month Placed in Service											
	1	2	3	4	5	6	7	8	9	10	11	12
1st	5.0%	4.6%	4.2%	3.7%	3.3%	2.9%	2.4%	2.0%	1.5%	1.1%	0.7%	0.2%
2-13th	5.3%	5.3%	5.3%	5.3%	5.3%	5.3%	5.3%	5.3%	5.3%	5.3%	5.3%	5.3%
14-19th	5.2%	5.2%	5.2%	5.2%	5.2%	5.2%	5.2%	5.2%	5.2%	5.2%	5.2%	5.2%
20th	0.2%	0.6%	1.0%	1.5%	1.9%	2.3%	2.8%	3.2%	3.7%	4.1%	4.5%	5.0%

Table X
18-year Real Property
(placed in service after June 22, 1984)
For Which Alternate ACRS Method
(Assuming Mid-Month Convention)
Over a 35-Year Periods is Elected

Year	Month Placed in Service				
	1-2	3-6	7-10	11	12
1st	3%	2%	1%	0.4%	0.1%
2-30th	3%	3%	3%	3%	3%
31st	2%	2%	2%	2.6%	2.9%
32-35th	2%	2%	2%	2%	2%
36th		1%	2%	2%	2%

Table XI
18-year Real Property
(placed in service after March 15 and before June 23, 1984)
15-year Real Property and Low-income housing
placed in service before May 9, 1985
For Which Alternate ACRS Method Over a
35-Year Periods is Elected

Year	Month Placed in Service		
	1-2	3-6	7-12
1st	3%	2%	1%
2-30th	3%	3%	3%
31-35th	2%	2%	2%
36th		1%	2%

Table XII
Low-Income Housing (placed in service after May 8, 1985)
For Which Alternate ACRS Method (Assuming no Mid-Month Convention)
Over a 35-Year Period is Elected

Year	Month Placed in Service											
	1	2	3	4	5	6	7	8	9	10	11	12
1st	2.9%	2.6%	2.4%	2.1%	1.9%	1.7%	1.4%	1.2%	1.0%	0.7%	0.5%	0.2%
2-20th	2.9%	2.9%	2.9%	2.9%	2.9%	2.9%	2.9%	2.9%	2.9%	2.9%	2.9%	2.9%
21-35th	2.8%	2.8%	2.8%	2.8%	2.8%	2.8%	2.8%	2.8%	2.8%	2.8%	2.8%	28%
36th		0.3%	0.5%	0.8%	1.0%	1.2%	1.5%	1.7%	1.9%	2.2%	2.4%	2.7%

Table XIII
19-year Real Property For Which Alternate ACRS Method
(Assuming Mid-Month Convention)
Over a 35-Year Period is Elected

Year	Month Placed in Service											
	1	2	3	4	5	6	7	8	9	10	11	12
1st	2.7%	2.5%	2.3%	2.0%	1.8%	1.5%	1.3%	1.1%	0.8%	0.6%	0.4%	0.1%
2-20th	2.9%	2.9%	2.9%	2.9%	2.9%	2.9%	2.9%	2.9%	2.9%	2.9%	2.9%	2.9%
21-35th	2.8%	2.8%	2.8%	2.8%	2.8%	2.8%	2.8%	2.8%	2.8%	2.8%	2.8%	2.8%
36th	0.2%	0.4%	0.6%	0.9%	1.1%	1.4%	1.6%	1.8%	2.1%	2.3%	2.5%	2.8%

Table XIV
18-year Real Property
(placed in service after June 22, 1984)
19-year Real Property
For Which Alternate ACRS Method
(Assuming Mid-Month Convention)
Over a 45-year Period is Elected

Year	Month Placed in Service											
	1	2	3	4	5	6	7	8	9	10	11	12
1st	2.1%	1.9%	1.8%	1.6%	1.4%	1.2%	1%	0.8%	0.6%	0.5%	0.3%	0.1%
2-11th	2.3%	2.3%	2.3%	2.3%	2.3%	2.3%	2.3%	2.3%	2.3%	2.3%	2.3%	2.3%
12-45th	2.2%	2.2%	2.2%	2.2%	2.2%	2.2%	2.2%	2.2%	2.2%	2.2%	2.2%	2.2%
46th	0.1%	0.3%	0.4%	0.6%	0.8%	1%	1.2%	1.4%	1.6%	1.7%	1.9%	2.1%

Table XV
18-year Real Property
(placed in service after March 15 and before June 23, 1984)
15-year Real Property and Low-income housing
placed in service after December 31, 1980
For Which Alternate ACRS Method Over a
45-Year Period is Elected

Year	Month Placed in Service											
	1	2	3	4	5	6	7	8	9	10	11	12
1st	2.3%	2%	1.9%	1.7%	1.5%	1.3%	1.2%	0.9%	0.7%	0.6%	0.4%	0.2%
2-10th	2.3%	2.3%	2.3%	2.3%	2.3%	2.3%	2.3%	2.3%	2.3%	2.3%	2.3%	2.3%
11-45th	2.2%	2.2%	2.2%	2.2%	2.2%	2.2%	2.2%	2.2%	2.2%	2.2%	2.2%	2.2%
46th		0.3%	0.4%	0.6%	0.8%	1%	1.1%	1.4%	1.6%	1.7%	1.9%	2.1%

Table XVI
Straight-Line ACRS Depreciation Rates for ACRS Listed
Property Except Autos (Reg § 1.280F-3T(e)(2)(i))

Applicable Straight-line Recovery Percentages
for 5-year, 12-year, and 25-year Listed Property

Year	Recovery Period		
	5	12	25
1st	10%	4%	2%
2nd through 5th	20	9	4
6th	10	8	4
7th through 12th		8	4
13th		4	4
14th through 25th			4
26th			2

Table XVII
Straight-Line ACRS Depreciation Rates for ACRS Listed
Real Property (IRS Pub No. 534 (11/88) p. 98)

40-Year Straight-Line Recovery Period
for 18-year or 19-year Listed Property

Year	Month Placed in Service											
	1	2	3	4	5	6	7	8	9	10	11	12
1st	2.4	2.2	2.0	1.8	1.6	1.4	1.1	0.9	0.7	0.5	0.3	0.1
2-40th	2.5	2.5	2.5	2.5	2.5	2.5	2.5	2.5	2.5	2.5	2.5	2.5
41st	0.1	0.3	0.5	0.7	0.9	1.1	1.4	1.6	1.8	2.0	2.2	2.4

Table XVIII
Leased MACRS Business Listed Property

Income Inclusion Amounts — Step (1) Computation Rates — for
Business Listed Property (Except Autos) Leased After '86
(Reg §1.280F-7T(b)(2)(i)(C)) [This table is discussed in Chapter 5 INVALID]

Type of Property	First Taxable Year During Lease in Which Business Use Percentage is 50% or Less											
	1	2	3	4	5	6	7	8	9	10	11	12 & Later
Property with a Recovery Period of Less Than 7 Years under the Alternative Depreciation System (Such as Computers, Trucks and Airplanes)	0.0%	10.0%	22.0%	21.2%	12.7%	12.7%	12.7%	12.7%	12.7%	12.7%	12.7%	12.7%
Property with a 7- to 10-Year Recovery Period under the Alternative Depreciation System (Such as Recreation Property)	0.0%	9.3%	23.8%	31.3%	33.8%	32.7%	31.6%	30.5%	25.0%	15.0%	15.0%	15.0%
Property with Recovery Period of more Than 10 Years under the Alternative Depreciation System (Such as Certain Property with No Class Life)	0.0%	10.1%	26.3%	35.4%	39.6%	40.2%	40.8%	41.4%	37.5%	29.2%	20.8%	12.5%

Table XIX
Leased MACRS Business Listed Property

Income Inclusion Amounts — Step (2) Computation Rates — for
Business Listed Property (Except Autos) Leased After '86
(Reg §1.280F-7T(b)(2)(i)(C)) [This table is discussed in Chapter 5 INVALID]

Type of Property	First Taxable Year During Lease in Which Business Use Percentage is 50% or Less											
	1	2	3	4	5	6	7	8	9	10	11	12 & Later
Property with a Recovery Period of Less Than 7 Years under Alternative Depreciation System (Such as Computers, Trucks and Airplanes)	2.1%	−7.2%	−19.8%	−20.1%	−12.4%	−12.4%	−12.4%	−12.4%	−12.4%	−12.4%	−12.4%	−12.4%
Property with a 7- to 10-Year Recovery Period under the Alternative Depreciation System (Such as Recreation Property)	3.9%	−3.8%	−17.7%	−25.1%	−27.8%	−27.2%	−27.1%	−27.6%	−23.7%	−14.7%	−14.7%	−14.7%
Property with a Recovery Period of More Than 10 Years under the Alternative Depreciation System (Such as Certain Property with No Class Life)	6.6%	−1.6%	−16.9%	−25.6%	−29.9%	−31.1%	−32.8%	−35.1%	−33.3%	−26.7%	−19.7%	−12.2%

Table XX

Income Inclusion Amounts for Business "Luxury"
Automobiles With Lease Terms Beginning in Calendar Year '90 or '89

Fair Market Value of Automobile		Tax Year During Lease				
Over	Not Over	1st Year	2nd Year	3rd Year	4th Year	5th or Later Year
$ 12,800	$13,100	$ 0	$ 0	$ 0	$ 1	$ 2
13,100	13,400	0	2	3	5	9
13,400	13,700	3	11	15	21	26
13,700	14,000	8	19	29	37	45
14,000	14,300	12	29	42	53	64
14,300	14,600	16	38	55	70	83
14,600	14,900	20	47	69	86	101
14,900	15,200	24	56	83	102	120
15,200	15,500	28	65	97	118	139
15,500	15,800	33	74	110	134	158
15,800	16,100	37	83	123	151	176
16,100	16,400	41	93	136	167	195
16,400	16,700	45	102	150	183	213
16,700	17,000	49	111	164	199	232
17,000	17,500	55	123	182	220	258
17,500	18,000	62	138	204	248	289
18,000	18,500	69	153	227	275	319
18,500	19,000	76	168	250	301	351
19,000	19,500	83	184	271	329	382
19,500	20,000	90	199	294	356	413
20,000	20,500	97	214	317	382	445
20,500	21,000	104	229	339	410	476
21,000	21,500	111	244	362	437	507
21,500	22,000	117	260	384	464	538
22,000	23,000	128	282	419	504	585
23,000	24,000	142	313	463	558	647
24,000	25,000	156	343	508	613	709
25,000	26,000	170	373	554	666	772
26,000	27,000	183	404	599	720	834
27,000	28,000	197	435	643	774	897
28,000	29,000	211	465	688	829	959
29,000	30,000	225	495	734	882	1,021
30,000	31,000	239	526	778	936	1,084
31,000	32,000	253	556	824	990	1,146
32,000	33,000	267	586	869	1,044	1,209
33,000	34,000	281	617	913	1,099	1,270
34,000	35,000	295	647	959	1,152	1,333
35,000	36,000	309	677	1,004	1,206	1,396
36,000	37,000	322	708	1,049	1,260	1,458
37,000	38,000	336	738	1,094	1,315	1,520
38,000	39,000	350	769	1,139	1,368	1,583
39,000	40,000	364	799	1,184	1,423	1,664
40,000	41,000	378	829	1,230	1,476	1,707
41,000	42,000	392	860	1,274	1,530	1,770
42,000	43,000	406	890	1,319	1,585	1,832

Fair Market Value of Automobile		Tax Year During Lease				
Over	Not Over	1st Year	2nd Year	3rd Year	4th Year	5th or Later Year
43,000	44,000	420	920	1,365	1,638	1,894
44,000	45,000	434	951	1,409	1,693	1,956
45,000	46,000	448	981	1,454	1,747	2,019
46,000	47,000	461	1,012	1,499	1,801	2,081
47,000	48,000	475	1,042	1,545	1,854	2,144
48,000	49,000	489	1,073	1,589	1,909	2,205
49,000	50,000	503	1,103	1,634	1,963	2,268
50,000	51,000	517	1,133	1,680	2,016	2,331
51,000	52,000	531	1,164	1,724	2,071	2,393
52,000	53,000	545	1,194	1,770	2,124	2,455
53,000	54,000	559	1,224	1,815	2,179	2,517
54,000	55,000	573	1,255	1,859	2,233	2,580
55,000	56,000	587	1,285	1,905	2,286	2,643
56,000	57,000	600	1,316	1,950	2,340	2,705
57,000	58,000	614	1,346	1,995	2,395	2,767
58,000	59,000	628	1,376	2,041	2,448	2,829
59,000	60,000	642	1,407	2,085	2,502	2,892
60,000	62,000	663	1,452	2,153	2,584	2,985
62,000	64,000	691	1,513	2,243	2,691	3,110
64,000	66,000	719	1,574	2,332	2,800	3,235
66,000	68,000	746	1,635	2,423	2,907	3,360
68,000	70,000	774	1,695	2,514	3,015	3,484
70,000	72,000	802	1,756	2,603	3,124	3,609
72,000	74,000	830	1,817	2,693	3,232	3,733
74,000	76,000	858	1,877	2,784	3,340	3,858
76,000	78,000	885	1,939	2,873	3,448	3,983
78,000	80,000	913	1,999	2,964	3,556	4,107
80,000	85,000	962	2,106	3,121	3,745	4,325
85,000	90,000	1,031	2,258	3,346	4,015	4,638
90,000	95,000	1,101	2,409	3,572	4,285	4,949
95,000	100,000	1,170	2,562	3,796	4,556	5,261
100,000	110,000	1,275	2,789	4,135	4,960	5,729
110,000	120,000	1,414	3,093	4,585	5,501	6,352
120,000	130,000	1,553	3,397	5,036	6,040	6,976
130,000	140,000	1,692	3,701	5,486	6,580	7,600
140,000	150,000	1,831	4,004	5,937	7,121	8,223
150,000	160,000	1,970	4,308	6,388	7,660	8,847
160,000	170,000	2,109	4,612	6,838	8,201	9,469
170,000	180,000	2,248	4,916	7,288	8,741	10,093
180,000	190,000	2,387	5,220	7,739	9,281	10,716
190,000	200,000	2,526	5,524	8,189	9,821	11,340
200,000	210,000	2,665	5,828	8,639	10,362	11,963
210,000	220,000	2,804	6,131	9,091	10,901	12,587
220,000	230,000	2,943	6,435	9,541	11,442	13,210
230,000	240,000	3,082	6,739	9,992	11,981	13,834
240,000	250,000	3,221	7,043	10,442	12,522	14,457

Table XXI

Income Inclusion Amounts for Business "Luxury"
Automobiles With Lease Terms Beginning in Calendar Year 1991

Fair Market Value of Automobile		Tax Year During Lease				
Over	Not Over	1st	2nd	3rd	4th	5th and Later
$ 13,400	$13,700	$2	$4	$6	$6	$6
13,700	14,000	5	10	16	18	18
14,000	14,300	8	17	25	29	32
14,300	14,600	11	23	35	41	45
14,600	14,900	14	30	44	52	58
14,900	15,200	17	36	54	64	71
15,200	15,500	20	43	63	75	85
15,500	15,800	23	49	73	87	98
15,800	16,100	26	55	83	98	112
16,100	16,400	29	62	92	110	124
16,400	16,700	32	68	102	121	138
16,700	17,000	35	75	111	133	151
17,000	17,500	39	83	125	147	169
17,500	18,000	44	94	140	167	191
18,000	18,500	49	105	156	186	213
18,500	19,000	54	116	172	205	235
19,000	19,500	59	126	189	224	257
19,500	20,000	63	138	204	243	279
20,000	20,500	68	148	220	263	301
20,500	21,000	73	159	236	282	323
21,000	21,500	78	170	252	301	345
21,500	22,000	83	180	269	319	368
22,000	23,000	90	197	292	348	401
23,000	24,000	100	218	324	387	445
24,000	25,000	110	240	356	425	489
25,000	26,000	120	261	388	463	534
26,000	27,000	130	283	419	502	578
27,000	28,000	140	304	452	540	622
28,000	29,000	149	326	484	578	666
29,000	30,000	159	347	516	617	710
30,000	31,000	169	369	547	655	755
31,000	32,000	179	390	580	693	799
32,000	33,000	189	412	611	732	843
33,000	34,000	199	433	644	769	888
34,000	35,000	208	455	676	808	931
35,000	36,000	218	477	707	846	976
36,000	37,000	228	498	739	885	1,020
37,000	38,000	238	519	772	923	1,064
38,000	39,000	248	541	803	961	1,109
39,000	40,000	258	562	835	1,000	1,153
40,000	41,000	267	584	867	1,038	1,197
41,000	42,000	277	606	899	1,076	1,241
42,000	43,000	287	627	931	1,115	1,285
43,000	44,000	297	649	962	1,153	1,330
44,000	45,000	307	670	995	1,191	1,374
45,000	46,000	317	692	1,026	1,230	1,418

Fair Market Value of Automobile		Tax Year During Lease				
Over	Not Over	1st	2nd	3rd	4th	5th and Later
46,000	47,000	326	714	1,058	1,268	1,462
47,000	48,000	336	735	1,091	1,306	1,506
48,000	49,000	346	756	1,123	1,344	1,551
49,000	50,000	356	778	1,154	1,383	1,595
50,000	51,000	366	799	1,187	1,421	1,639
51,000	52,000	376	821	1,218	1,459	1,684
52,000	53,000	385	843	1,250	1,498	1,727
53,000	54,000	395	864	1,282	1,536	1,772
54,000	55,000	405	886	1,314	1,574	1,816
55,000	56,000	415	907	1,346	1,613	1,860
56,000	57,000	425	929	1,378	1,650	1,905
57,000	58,000	435	950	1,410	1,689	1,949
58,000	59,000	444	972	1,442	1,727	1,993
59,000	60,000	454	993	1,474	1,766	2,037
60,000	62,000	469	1,026	1,521	1,824	2,103
62,000	64,000	489	1,068	1,586	1,900	2,192
64,000	66,000	508	1,112	1,649	1,977	2,280
66,000	68,000	528	1,155	1,713	2,053	2,369
68,000	70,000	548	1,198	1,777	2,130	2,457
70,000	72,000	567	1,241	1,841	2,206	2,546
72,000	74,000	587	1,284	1,905	2,283	2,634
74,000	76,000	607	1,327	1,969	2,359	2,723
76,000	78,000	626	1,370	2,033	2,436	2,811
78,000	80,000	646	1,413	2,097	2,512	2,900
80,000	85,000	680	1,489	2,208	2,647	3,054
85,000	90,000	730	1,596	2,368	2,838	3,276
90,000	95,000	779	1,704	2,528	3,029	3,497
95,000	100,000	828	1,812	2,687	3,221	3,718
100,000	110,000	902	1,973	2,927	3,508	4,049
110,000	120,000	1,000	2,188	3,247	3,891	4,492
120,000	130,000	1,098	2,404	3,566	4,274	4,934
130,000	140,000	1,197	2,619	3,885	4,658	5,375
140,000	150,000	1,295	2,834	4,205	5,041	5,817
150,000	160,000	1,393	3,050	4,524	5,424	6,259
160,000	170,000	1,492	3,265	4,844	5,806	6,702
170,000	180,000	1,590	3,480	5,164	6,189	7,144
180,000	190,000	1,688	3,696	5,483	6,572	7,586
190,000	200,000	1,787	3,911	5,802	6,955	8,029
200,000	210,000	1,885	4,126	6,122	7,338	8,471
210,000	220,000	1,983	4,342	6,441	7,721	8,913
220,000	230,000	2,081	4,557	6,761	8,104	9,355
230,000	240,000	2,180	4,772	7,080	8,487	9,798
240,000	250,000	2,278	4,988	7,399	8,870	10,240

Table XXII

Income Inclusion Amounts for Business "Luxury"
Automobiles with Lease Terms Beginning in Calendar Year '92

Fair Market Value of Automobile		Tax Year During Lease				
Over	Not Over	1st	2nd	3rd	4th	5th and Later
$ 13,700	$14,000	0	2	2	2	4
14,000	14,300	3	7	10	13	15
14,300	14,600	5	13	18	23	26
14,600	14,900	8	18	27	32	38
14,900	15,200	11	23	35	43	49
15,200	15,500	13	29	44	52	61
15,500	15,800	16	35	51	62	72
15,800	16,100	18	40	60	72	84
16,100	16,400	21	46	68	82	95
16,400	16,700	23	52	76	92	106
16,700	17,000	26	57	84	102	118
17,000	17,500	29	65	95	115	133
17,500	18,000	33	74	109	132	152
18,000	18,500	38	83	123	148	171
18,500	19,000	42	92	137	164	190
19,000	19,500	46	102	150	181	209
19,500	20,000	50	111	164	198	228
20,000	20,500	55	120	178	214	247
20,000	21,000	59	129	192	230	267
21,000	21,500	63	139	205	247	285
21,500	22,000	67	148	219	263	305
22,000	23,000	74	162	239	288	333
23,000	24,000	82	180	268	321	371
24,000	25,000	90	199	295	354	409
25,000	26,000	99	217	323	387	447
26,000	27,000	107	236	350	420	485
27,000	28,000	116	254	378	453	523
28,000	29,000	124	273	405	486	561
29,000	30,000	133	291	433	518	600
30,000	31,000	141	310	469	552	637
31,000	32,000	150	328	488	584	676
32,000	33,000	158	347	515	618	713
33,000	34,000	167	365	543	650	752
34,000	35,000	175	384	570	684	789
35,000	36,000	184	402	598	716	828
36,000	37,000	192	421	625	750	865
37,000	38,000	200	440	652	783	904
38,000	39,000	209	458	680	816	942
39,000	40,000	217	477	707	849	980
40,000	41,000	226	495	735	882	1,018
41,000	42,000	234	514	762	915	1,056
42,000	43,000	243	532	790	948	1,094
43,000	44,000	251	551	817	981	1,132
44,000	45,000	260	569	845	1,013	1,171
45,000	46,000	268	588	872	1,047	1,208
46,000	47,000	277	606	900	1,079	1,247

Fair Market Value of Automobile		Tax Year During Lease				
Over	Not Over	1st	2nd	3rd	4th	5th and Later
47,000	48,000	285	625	927	1,113	1,284
48,000	49,000	293	644	955	1,145	1,323
49,000	50,000	302	662	982	1,179	1,360
50,000	51,000	310	681	1,010	1,211	1,399
51,000	52,000	319	699	1,037	1,245	1,436
52,000	53,000	327	718	1,065	1,277	1,475
53,000	54,000	336	736	1,092	1,311	1,513
54,000	55,000	334	755	1,120	1,343	1,551
55,000	56,000	353	773	1,147	1,377	1,589
56,000	57,000	361	792	1,175	1,409	1,627
57,000	58,000	370	810	1,202	1,442	1,666
58,000	59,000	378	829	1,230	1,475	1,703
59,000	60,000	386	848	1,257	1,508	1,741
60,000	62,000	399	875	1,299	1,557	1,799
62,000	64,000	416	912	1,354	1,623	1,875
64,000	66,000	433	949	1,409	1,689	1,951
66,000	68,000	450	987	1,463	1,755	2,027
68,000	70,000	467	1,024	1,518	1,821	2,103
70,000	72,000	484	1,061	1,573	1,887	2,179
72,000	74,000	501	1,098	1,628	1,953	2,255
74,000	76,000	518	1,135	1,683	2,019	2,331
76,000	78,000	535	1,172	1,738	2,085	2,407
78,000	80,000	551	1,209	1,794	2,150	2,484
80,000	85,000	581	1,274	1,889	2,267	2,617
85,000	90,000	623	1,367	2,027	2,431	2,807
90,000	95,000	666	1,459	2,165	2,595	2,998
95,000	100,000	708	1,552	2,302	2,761	3,188
100,000	110,000	771	1,691	2,508	3,008	3,474
110,000	120,000	856	1,876	2,783	3,338	3,854
120,000	130,000	940	2,062	3,058	3,668	4,234
130,000	140,000	1,025	2,247	3,333	3,997	4,616
140,000	150,000	1,110	2,432	3,608	4,327	4,996
150,000	160,000	1,194	2,618	3,883	4,656	5,377
160,000	170,000	1,279	2,803	4,158	4,986	5,758
170,000	180,000	1,363	2,988	4,434	5,316	6,138
180,000	190,000	1,448	3,174	4,708	5,645	6,519
190,000	200,000	1,532	3,359	4,983	5,976	6,899
200,000	210,000	1,617	3,544	5,258	6,305	7,280
210,000	220,000	1,702	3,729	5,533	6,635	7,661
220,000	230,000	1,786	3,915	5,808	6,965	8,041
230,000	240,000	1,871	4,100	6,083	7,294	8,422
240,000	250,000	1,955	4,286	6,358	7,624	8,802

Table XXIII

*Income Inclusion Amounts for Business "Luxury"
Automobiles with Lease Terms Beginning in Calendar Year '93*

Fair Market Value of Automobile		Tax Year During Lease				
Over	Not Over	1st	2nd	3rd	4th	5th and Later
$ 14,300	$14,600	1	1	2	2	3
14,600	14,900	3	5	7	9	9
14,900	15,200	4	9	13	15	17
15,200	15,500	6	13	18	22	25
15,500	15,800	8	16	24	29	32
15,800	16,100	9	20	30	35	40
16,100	16,400	11	24	35	42	48
16,400	16,700	13	27	41	49	55
16,700	17,000	14	32	46	55	63
17,000	17,500	17	36	54	64	73
17,500	18,000	20	42	63	75	87
18,000	18,500	22	49	72	86	99
18,500	19,000	25	55	82	97	112
19,000	19,500	28	61	91	108	125
19,500	20,000	31	67	100	120	137
20,000	20,500	34	74	109	130	150
20,500	21,000	37	80	118	142	163
21,000	21,500	39	86	128	153	175
21,500	22,000	42	92	138	163	189
22,000	23,000	47	101	151	181	207
23,000	24,000	52	114	170	202	233
24,000	25,000	58	127	187	225	259
25,000	26,000	64	139	206	247	285
26,000	27,000	69	152	224	270	310
27,000	28,000	75	164	243	292	335
28,000	29,000	81	176	262	313	362
29,000	30,000	86	189	280	336	387
30,000	31,000	92	201	299	358	412
31,000	32,000	98	214	317	380	438
32,000	33,000	103	226	336	402	464
33,000	34,000	109	239	354	424	490
34,000	35,000	115	251	373	446	515
35,000	36,000	120	264	391	469	540
36,000	37,000	126	276	410	491	566
37,000	38,000	132	288	429	513	591
38,000	39,000	137	301	447	535	617
39,000	40,000	143	314	465	557	643
40,000	41,000	149	326	484	579	669
41,000	42,000	154	339	502	601	695
42,000	43,000	160	351	521	623	720
43,000	44,000	166	363	539	646	746
44,000	45,000	171	376	558	668	771
45,000	46,000	177	388	577	690	796
46,000	47,000	183	401	594	713	822
47,000	48,000	189	413	613	735	847
48,000	49,000	194	426	631	757	874

Fair Market Value of Automobile		Tax Year During Lease				
Over	Not Over	1st	2nd	3rd	4th	5th and Later
49,000	50,000	200	438	650	779	899
50,000	51,000	206	450	669	801	925
51,000	52,000	211	463	687	824	950
52,000	53,000	217	475	706	846	975
53,000	54,000	223	488	724	867	1,002
54,000	55,000	228	501	742	890	1,027
55,000	56,000	234	513	761	912	1,052
56,000	57,000	240	525	780	934	1,078
57,000	58,000	245	538	798	956	1,104
58,000	59,000	251	550	817	978	1,130
59,000	60,000	257	563	835	1,000	1,155
60,000	62,000	265	581	863	1,034	1,191
62,000	64,000	277	606	900	1,078	1,245
64,000	66,000	288	631	937	1,123	1,295
66,000	68,000	299	656	974	1,167	1,347
68,000	70,000	311	681	1,011	1,211	1,398
70,000	72,000	322	706	1,048	1,255	1,450
72,000	74,000	333	731	1,085	1,300	1,500
74,000	76,000	345	756	1,121	1,345	1,551
76,000	78,000	356	781	1,158	1,389	1,603
78,000	80,000	367	806	1,195	1,434	1,654
80,000	85,000	387	849	1,261	1,510	1,744
85,000	90,000	416	911	1,353	1,622	1,871
90,000	95,000	444	974	1,445	1,733	1,999
95,000	100,000	472	1,036	1,538	1,843	2,128
100,000	110,000	515	1,130	1,676	2,010	2,319
110,000	120,000	572	1,254	1,861	2,232	2,575
120,000	130,000	629	1,379	2,046	2,453	2,831
130,000	140,000	685	1,504	2,231	2,674	3,088
140,000	150,000	742	1,628	2,416	2,896	3,344
150,000	160,000	799	1,753	2,600	3,119	3,599
160,000	170,000	856	1,877	2,786	3,340	3,855
170,000	180,000	912	2,002	2,971	3,561	4,112
180,000	190,000	969	2,127	3,155	3,783	4,368
190,000	200,000	1,026	2,251	3,340	4,006	4,623
200,000	210,000	1,083	2,376	3,525	4,227	4,879
210,000	220,000	1,140	2,500	3,710	4,449	5,135
220,000	230,000	1,196	2,625	3,895	4,670	5,392
230,000	240,000	1,253	2,749	4,081	4,892	5,647
240,000	250,000	1,310	2,874	4,265	5,114	5,903

Chapter 2   Income—Taxable and Exempt

¶ 1200 Gross Income ▰▰▰▰▰▰▰▰▰

Gross income consists of all income, from all sources, such as compensation for services, business income, interest, rents, dividends and gains from the sale of property. Only items specifically exempt may be excluded.

Gross income is the starting point in determining tax liability and is broadly defined. (Code Sec. 61)[1]

¶ 1201 Assignment of income.

The person who earns income and is entitled to receive it is taxed on it. He cannot avoid tax on it by assigning it to another.[2] But if taxpayer assigns or transfers the income-producing *property* before the income is earned, the assignee will be taxed on the income.[3]

¶ 1202 Income from co-owned property—joint tenancies, etc.

In a tenancy in common (co-owners without survivorship), each co-owner is taxable on that part of the income attributable to his share.[4] Co-owners who are joint tenants (with survivorship) split income from their property according to their ownership interests.[5]

Similarly, any gain (or loss) from sale of jointly-owned property is divided among the co-owners unless the joint ownership was created to save taxes on the sale, in which case the original owner is taxed on the full amount of the gain.[6]

Co-owners who are husband and wife and file joint returns report their combined income and gains and losses from the jointly-owned property. If the spouses file separately, the income, etc., from the property is split equally if they so share it under state law.[7]

¶ 1203 Community property and income.

Federal tax law recognizes the principle of community income in community property states (AZ, CA, ID, LA, NV, NM, TX, WA and WI) or countries, which treats half of community income and expenses as belonging to each spouse.[8] Community income is all the income from community property (including business property) and salaries, etc., for the services of either or both spouses. Income from separate property during marriage is community income only in ID, LA, TX and WI.[9]

If one spouse acts as if he is solely entitled to the community income and fails to notify his spouse of the nature and amount of the income before the return due date (with extensions), IRS may deny him any community property benefit. (Code Sec. 66(b))[10]

Community property income for a calendar year is taxed to the spouse who earned it if in that year the couple lived apart, filed separate returns, *and* one or both spouses had earned income no part of which was transferred between them. (Code Sec. 66(a), (d)(1))[11]

¶ 1204 Claim of right.

Income received without restriction—income the taxpayer has dominion and control over—must be reported in the year received, even if there is a possibility it may have to be repaid in a later year.[12] For deduction in the repayment year, see ¶ 2863 *et seq.*

¶ 1205 Recoveries attributable to an earlier year's deduction or credit—tax benefit rule.

The recovery of an amount deducted or credited in an earlier tax year is included in taxpayer's income in the current (recovery) year, except to the extent the deduction or

1. ¶ J-1000 *et seq.*; ¶ 614.
2. ¶ J-8151 *et seq.*; ¶ 614.192.
3. ¶ J-8172 *et seq.*; ¶ 1024.
4. ¶ J-8103; ¶ 614.202.
5. ¶s J-8101, J-8102; ¶ 614.202.
6. ¶ J-8107; ¶ 614.202.
7. ¶ J-8100 *et seq.*; ¶ 614.202.
8. ¶ A-5001; ¶ 79,006.51.
9. ¶ A-5008.
10. ¶ A-5013; ¶ 664.
11. ¶ A-5016; ¶ 664.
12. ¶ J-8001 *et seq.*; ¶ 4514.069 *et seq.*

Footnote references beginning with letters are to paragraphs in RIA's Federal Tax Coordinator 2d and RIA's Analysis of Federal Taxes: Income. Footnote references beginning with numbers are to paragraphs in RIA's United States Tax Reporter.

credit did *not* reduce federal income tax imposed in the earlier year. (Code Sec. 111(a))[13]

This "tax benefit rule" also applies to the recovery of taxes, e.g., state income taxes deducted in an earlier year, where there is a refund or credit of taxes paid or the cancellation of taxes accrued.[14] (Individuals whose total itemized deductions were reduced under the 3%/80% rule (for taxpayers whose AGI exceeds specified dollar limits, see ¶ 3112) must use a worksheet (in IRS Pub No. 525) to compute the amount of state and local tax refund includible in income.)[15]

recommendation: State tax refunds are reported by the state to IRS on an information return (¶ 4745). If a taxpayer's earlier deduction of the refunded tax didn't result in a tax benefit, he should report the refund on his income tax return (to match the information return) and then reverse it (and explain that no benefit was received). Otherwise, IRS will send a notice to taxpayer asking why the refund wasn't reported.

Similarly, if there is a downward price adjustment (e.g., price reduction) during the tax year that affects an amount paid or incurred on which a credit was allowed in an earlier year, taxpayer's tax for the adjustment year is increased by the amount of credit attributable to the adjustment, to the extent it reduced his tax in the earlier year. This doesn't apply to the foreign tax credit or the investment tax credit. (Code Sec. 111(b))[16]

The increase of a carryover that hasn't expired as of the beginning of the tax year of the recovery (of a deduction) or adjustment (to a credit item) is treated as a reduction of tax imposed. (Code Sec. 111(c))[17]

The tax rates for the recovery (or adjustment) year are used to compute the tax on the portion that is not excludable.[18]

¶ 1206 Miscellaneous taxable and exempt income.

Here is the taxable or exempt status of items not covered elsewhere in this Handbook:

■ Alcohol fuel credit. Gross income includes the credit allowable for the year. (Code Sec. 87)[19]

■ Barter, or the swapping of goods and services, is taxable to each party to the swap to the extent of the fair market value of the goods or services received. The dollar value of barter "credits" received by members of barter clubs for goods or services rendered to other members is taxable.[20] For information returns of barter exchanges, see ¶ 4745.

■ Car pool expenses reimbursed by fellow members. Nontaxable unless received as part of a trade or business.[21]

■ Energy conservation subsidies provided (directly or indirectly) by a public utility to customers for purchasing or installing any "energy conservation measure." Not taxable. (Code Sec. 136)[22]

■ Escrow funds or property, and the income from them. Not taxable to the stakeholder but may be taxable to the ultimate recipient when paid to him.[23]

■ Executor's or administrator's fees or commissions that are waived. Not taxed to executor, etc., who files a formal waiver within six months after appointment, or whose conduct amounts to an implied waiver.[24]

■ Foster care payments by agencies to foster care provider for caring for qualified foster individual (child or adult) in the care provider's home, and "difficulty-of-care" payments. Not income, subject to conditions and limits. (Code Sec. 131)[25]

■ Illegal income. Taxable whether from an illegal business, an actual crime, or immoral or unethical practices, e.g., embezzlement. (Repayment is an itemized deduction.)[26]

---

13. ¶ J-5500 *et seq.*; ¶ 1114 *et seq.*   17. ¶ J-5519; ¶ 1114.   21. ¶ J-1386.   24. ¶ J-1397; ¶ 4514.042.
14. ¶ J-5701; ¶ 1114.   18. ¶ J-5524; ¶ 1114.09.   22. ¶ J-1408 *et seq.*   25. ¶ J-1475 *et seq.*; ¶ 1314.
15. ¶ J-5701.1.   19. ¶ L-17505; ¶ 874.   23. ¶ J-1361; ¶ 4514.087.   26. ¶ J-1600 *et seq.*; ¶ 614.176.
16. ¶ J-5510; ¶ 1114.   20. ¶s J-1010, J-1012.

Footnote references beginning with letters are to paragraphs in RIA's Federal Tax Coordinator 2d and RIA's Analysis of Federal Taxes: Income. Footnote references beginning with numbers are to paragraphs in RIA's United States Tax Reporter.

■ "Insider's" short-term stock sale profits which SEC requires be turned over to corporation. Taxable to corporation on receipt.[27]

■ Insurance reimbursement for living expenses incurred due to the loss of use of taxpayer's residence (owned or rented) resulting from a casualty. Taxable, to extent it covers taxpayer's normal living expenses. Nontaxable, to extent it covers additional living expenses.[28] Use and occupancy insurance reimbursements for loss of profits if business is suspended are taxable.[29]

■ Interest earned on life insurance or annuity contracts applied to prepay premiums. Taxable to the insured whether prepayment is made by "advance premiums," "premium deposit funds," etc.[30]

■ Juror's commuting allowance. Not taxable.[31]

■ Leaves under employer-sponsored leave-sharing plan (e.g., the federal government's leave-sharing plan) which permits employees with a medical emergency to receive leave that other employees surrender or deposit into a leave bank. Taxable to recipient-employee as compensation.[32]

■ Medicare (Part A and Part B). Not taxable (except for Part B amounts attributable to medical deductions taken in an earlier year).[33]

■ Mortgage assistance payments by a federal agency to a mortgagee on mortgagor's behalf. Not taxable to the mortgagor. But payments not made for the general welfare (e.g., interest reduction payments to mortgagee) are taxable to the mortgagor.[34]

■ Rate reduction or nonrefundable credit provided by utility to customer for participation in energy conservation program. Not taxable.[35]

■ Rebates of part of purchase price by auto companies to retail customers. Not taxable.[36]

■ Relocation payments and similar government subsidies for moving expenses and for actual direct losses of property because of displacement from personal residences, as a result of urban renewal projects. Not taxable, to extent payments are made by government to compensate for (and are actually so used for) these expenses.[37] Taxable, to extent payments are made by nongovernmental landlords as part of co-op or condo conversion.[38]

■ Security deposits or payments. If purpose is to guarantee performance of an obligation, not taxable where repayment is required if the obligation is performed. When the recipient becomes entitled to retain the payments because of a default, they are income.[39] If purpose of deposit is to protect taxpayer's interest in its property and not to secure payment of amounts due, it is not taxable.[40]

¶ 1207 Compensation Income

All forms of compensation received for personal services must be included in gross income.

¶ 1208 Gross income.

Gross income includes compensation for services including: wages, salaries, fees, salesmen's commissions (including commissions on the salesman's sales to himself or his family), percentage of profits paid as compensation, commissions on insurance premiums, bonuses (including Christmas bonuses), termination pay, severance pay, golden parachute payments (with excess golden parachute payments subject to a 20% excise tax imposed on the recipient), (Code Sec. 4999(a))[41] rewards, jury duty fees (Code

27. ¶ J-1396.	31. ¶ J-1386.	35. ¶ J-1407.	39. ¶ J-1361; ¶ 4514.166.
28. ¶ J-1311 et seq.; ¶ 1234.	32. ¶ J-1406.	36. ¶ J-1388; ¶ 10,124.20.	40. ¶ G-2470; ¶ 4514.166.
29. ¶ J-5828; ¶ 614.167.	33. ¶ J-1305.	37. ¶ J-1467; ¶ 614.006.	41. ¶ H-3003; ¶ 49,994.
30. ¶ J-4017; ¶ 1014.03.	34. ¶ J-1464.	38. ¶ J-1407; ¶ 614.006.	

Footnote references beginning with letters are to paragraphs in RIA's Federal Tax Coordinator 2d and RIA's Analysis of Federal Taxes: Income. Footnote references beginning with numbers are to paragraphs in RIA's United States Tax Reporter.

Sec. 61(a)(1); Reg § 1.61-2(a)(1))[42] and fringe benefits not covered by any statutory exclusion. (Code Sec. 61(a)(1)) Vacation pay also is taxable.[43]

Pension or retirement allowances to employees (reported to recipients on Form 1099-R) are (with some exceptions, see ¶ 1226, ¶ 1287) taxable to the recipient, see ¶ 4338 *et seq.*(Reg § 1.61-11(a))[44]

Amounts withheld from an employee's pay by his employer for income and social security taxes, savings bonds, union dues, etc., represent compensation constructively received by the employee and must be included in his income for the year in which withheld.[45]

The employee is taxed even if the employer can't deduct part or all of the compensation because it's "unreasonable." (Reg § 1.162-8)[46]

¶ 1209 Tips and similar payments.

Tips and similar payments for special services are income. (Reg § 1.61-2(a)(1)) But a waiter may deduct the portion of tips that he turns over to assistants.[47] A tipped employee must maintain sufficient evidence (such as on daily record Form 4070A) to establish the amount of tip income he receives in a tax year. (Reg § 31.6053-4(a))[48]

¶ 1210 Compensation distinguished from gift.

Gifts are excluded from the gross income of the recipient. (Code Sec. 102(a)) However, unless a transfer by or for an employer to or for the benefit of an employee qualifies as a holiday gift of nominal value (see ¶ 1211) or as a de minimis fringe benefit (¶ 1249), the transfer is not excludable as a gift. (Code Sec. 102(c))[49]

¶ 1211 Holiday "gifts."

If, as a means of promoting goodwill, an employer makes a general distribution to employees of hams, turkeys and other merchandise of nominal value at Christmas or a comparable holiday, the value of the gifts is not included in the employees' income. But if an employer distributes cash, gift certificates or similar items of readily convertible cash value, the value of the gifts is additional wages or salary, *regardless* of the value.[50]

¶ 1212 Noncash compensation.

If services rendered by the taxpayer are paid for in property or services rather than money, the fair market value of the property or services must be included in income. For example, a vacation trip awarded as a prize is income at its fair market value. Where a price has been specified for the services being rendered, that price is considered the fair market value of the property or services received if there is no evidence showing a different value. (Code Sec. 83; Reg § 1.61-2(d))[1]

¶ 1213 Notes receivable as compensation.

Notes and other evidences of indebtedness received in payment for services or in settlement of a claim for compensation are taxable as compensation in the amount of their fair market value at the time they are received. (Reg § 1.61-2(d)(4))[2]

¶ 1214 Bargain purchase from employer.

If property, including stock, is transferred by an employer to an employee for less than its fair market value, the difference is compensation. (Code Sec. 83(a); Reg § 1.83-1(a))[3]

42. ¶ H-1001 *et seq.*; ¶ 614.007.
43. ¶s H-1001, H-1011; ¶ 1624.218.
44. ¶ H-5000; ¶ 4014.
45. ¶ H-2152; ¶ 614.007.
46. ¶ H-1019; ¶ 614.014.
47. ¶s H-1008, H-4417.
48. ¶ H-4418; ¶ 60,534.
49. ¶ H-1024 *et seq.*; ¶ 1024.
50. ¶ H-1029; ¶ 1324.06.
1. ¶ H-2500 *et seq.*; ¶s 614.007, 614.032.
2. ¶ H-2511; ¶ 614.034.
3. ¶ H-2504; ¶ 614.030.

Footnote references beginning with letters are to paragraphs in RIA's Federal Tax Coordinator 2d and RIA's Analysis of Federal Taxes: Income. Footnote references beginning with numbers are to paragraphs in RIA's United States Tax Reporter.

¶ 1215   Below-market interest rate loans from employer.

An employee or independent contractor who receives a below-market compensation-related loan (except for certain de minimis loans), recognizes compensation income equal to:

■ on a demand compensation-related loan, the foregone interest (interest at the applicable federal rate over actual interest payable), and

■ on any other compensation-related loan, the excess of the amount borrowed over the present value of all payments required to be made under the terms of the loan. (Code Sec. 7872(a)(1), (b)(1))[4]

Certain employee-relocation loans are exempt from these rules. (Reg § 1.7872-5T(b)(6))[5]

¶ 1216   Restricted stock or other property.

A person receiving a beneficial interest in stock or other property for his services has compensation income equal to the value of that property at the time of receipt. But if his interest in the property is subject to substantial risk of forfeiture (is "restricted") and cannot be transferred free of that risk, then income generally is deferred until the interest in the property either: (1) is no longer subject to that risk, *or* (2) becomes transferable free of the risk, whichever occurs earlier. (Code Sec. 83)[6]

But the employee (or other owner of the property) has income if he sells or disposes of the property before (1) or (2), above. (Code Sec. 83(a))[7]

A person's rights in property are subject to a substantial risk of forfeiture if his rights to full enjoyment of the property are conditioned, directly or indirectly, upon the future performance (or refraining from performance) of substantial services by any individual. (Code Sec. 83(c)(1); Reg § 1.83-3(c)(1)) Examples of substantial risks of forfeiture include a requirement that the property be returned to the employer if total earnings don't increase, (Reg § 1.83-3(c)(2))[8] and SEC restrictions on stock, such as the "short swing" rule (insider must pay over profits if the stock is sold within six months of receipt). (Code Sec. 83(c)(3))[9]

¶ 1217   Election not to defer income from restricted stock or other property.

An employee who receives restricted stock or other property may elect to recognize the income immediately instead of deferring it. (Code Sec. 83(b)(1))[10]

recommendation: Elect if the income that would be recognized at grant (and therefore the tax on that income) would be negligible; for example, where the employee pays fair market value for the restricted property. This defers tax on any post-grant appreciation until sale, and may eliminate any income tax completely if the property (minus its restrictions) is held until death.

If the stock or other property is forfeited after the election is made, the employee can't get a deduction or refund of tax previously paid on income reported. (Code Sec. 83(b)(1))[11] But the employee will have capital gain or loss at the time of forfeiture. (Reg § 1.83-2(a))[12]

The election must be made within 30 days after the property is transferred to the employee. (Code Sec. 83(b)(2)) To elect, file a written statement (specified in the regs) with the Internal Revenue office where the person who performs the services files his return. A copy of the statement must be attached to the income tax return for the tax year the property was transferred. (Reg § 1.83-2(c))[13]

4. ¶s H-2001, H-2002; ¶ 78,724.01.
5. ¶ H-2006; ¶ 78,724.02.
6. ¶s H-2500, H-2515 *et seq.*; ¶ 834.01.
7. ¶ H-2539 *et seq.*; ¶ 834.01.
8. ¶ H-2518; ¶ 834.02.
9. ¶s H-2522, H-2523; ¶ 834.02.
10. ¶ H-2531; ¶ 834.03.
11. ¶ M-3503; ¶ 834.03.
12. ¶ I-1020; ¶ 834.03.
13. ¶ H-2533 *et seq.*; ¶ 834.03.

Footnote references beginning with letters are to paragraphs in RIA's Federal Tax Coordinator 2d and RIA's Analysis of Federal Taxes: Income. Footnote references beginning with numbers are to paragraphs in RIA's United States Tax Reporter.

¶ 1218 Income from restricted stock.

Where an amount is includible for a year (after receipt) in which the interest in the property first becomes not subject to a substantial risk of forfeiture or is transferable free of that risk, the amount of income is the excess of: (1) the fair market value (FMV) of the property in that year (figured without regard to restrictions other than one that by its terms will never lapse), over (2) the amount, if any, paid for the property. (Code Sec. 83(a))[14]

The compensation income that is includible in the year of receipt of the stock or other property under the special election (¶ 1217) is the excess of: (1) the FMV of the property at the time of receipt, over (2) the amount, if any, paid for the property. FMV is determined without regard to any restrictions on the property, except a restriction that by its terms will never lapse. (Code Sec. 83(b)(1))[15]

¶ 1219 Nonstatutory stock options.

An option other than an option under an employee stock purchase plan, see ¶ 1220, or an incentive stock option, see ¶ 1221, that is granted in connection with the performance of services, to buy stock at a bargain results in compensation income to the employee (or independent contractor) grantee. (Code Sec. 83) If the option has a readily ascertainable fair market value (FMV) when it is granted, the employee (or independent contractor) realizes compensation income when the option is granted, not at exercise or transfer of the option (or at any later time). Compensation is the option's FMV minus any amount paid for the option. (Code Sec. 83; Reg § 1.83-7(a))[16]

An option "ordinarily" has a readily ascertainable FMV only if it (or a substantially identical option) is actively traded on an established market. If not so traded, it has value only if certain conditions specified in the regs exist. (Reg § 1.83-7(b))[17]

If the option doesn't have a readily ascertainable FMV when granted, the employee does not realize compensation until the optioned property is transferred at exercise of the option. The amount of compensation is the FMV of the property at the time of transfer less any amount paid for the property. (Reg § 1.83-7(a))[18]

¶ 1220 Employee stock purchase plan options.

These are options issued to employees under an employer plan to buy stock in the employer. The employee pays no tax on the option or the stock until he disposes of the stock. If the option price at least equals the stock's fair market value (FMV) at grant, gain is long-term capital gain, but is ordinary compensation income if the stock is sold within two years after the option was granted or within one year after he receives it. The difference between the FMV of the stock at exercise and the price paid is also ordinary compensation income. (Code Sec. 423(a), (c))[19]

If the option price is less than 100% but at least 85% of the stock's FMV at grant, the optionee includes in income as ordinary income on a disposition after the holding period is met, the lesser of the FMV of the stock when the option was granted, minus the option price, or the excess of the FMV at the time of disposition or optionee's death over the amount paid for the share under the option. (Code Sec. 423(c); Reg § 1.423-2(k))[20]

The plan itself must be nondiscriminatory, i.e., available to all employees (with certain exceptions). (Code Sec. 423(b)(4))[21]

---

14. ¶ H-2524 *et seq.*; ¶ 834.01.
15. ¶ H-2532; ¶ 834.01.
16. ¶s H-2853, H-2858; ¶ 834.07.
17. ¶ H-2874; ¶ 834.07.
18. ¶ H-2863; ¶ 834.07.
19. ¶ H-2952 *et seq.*; ¶ 4234.01.
20. ¶ H-2953; ¶ 4234.01.
21. ¶ H-2970; ¶ 4234.02.

Footnote references beginning with letters are to paragraphs in RIA's Federal Tax Coordinator 2d and RIA's Analysis of Federal Taxes: Income. Footnote references beginning with numbers are to paragraphs in RIA's United States Tax Reporter.

¶ 1221 **Incentive stock options (ISO).**

An ISO is an option granted to an employee by an employer corporation (or its parent or sub) to buy stock in one of those corporations. There are no regular income tax consequences when an ISO is granted or exercised; the employee has capital gain when the stock is sold at a gain. (Code Sec. 421(a)) (For alternative minimum tax aspects, see ¶ 3208.)[22] To qualify for this tax treatment, an ISO must meet various requirements: (Code Sec. 422(b))[23] stock acquired through the exercise of an ISO cannot be disposed of within two years after the option is granted or one year after the stock is transferred to the employee. (Code Sec. 422(a)(1)) Also, for the entire time from the date that an ISO is granted until three months (one year in case of total and permanent disability) before its exercise, the option holder must be an employee of the option grantor (or its parent or sub). (Code Sec. 422(a)(2), (c)(6))[24]

Where there is a disposition before these holding periods are satisfied, income is includible in the employee's tax year in which the disposition takes place. (Code Sec. 421(b)) Gain on the disposition is realized as ordinary income to the extent of the lesser of the FMV of the option stock on the date of exercise, minus the option price, or the amount realized on the disposition of the stock, minus the option price. (Reg § 14a.422A-1)[25]

¶ 1222 **Sale or cancellation of employment contract.**

Proceeds from an employee's sale of rights under an employment contract to be performed are ordinary income. The same is true of amounts received from an employer in cancellation of an employment contract.[26]

¶ 1223 **Members of Armed Forces.**

Gross income does not include any exclusion authorized by the Internal Revenue Code (below), or any "qualified military benefit." (Code Sec. 134(a)) A "qualified military benefit" is any allowance or in-kind benefit (other than personal use of an automobile) received by a member or former member of the uniformed services of the U.S., or his dependent, and which was excludable from gross income on Sept. 9, '86, under any provision of law, reg or administrative practice (other than the Code) in effect on that date. (Code Sec. 134(b)(1)) The following are among excludable allowances: veteran's benefits, medical benefits, disability benefits, professional education, moving and storage, group-term life insurance, survivor and retirement protection plan premiums, subsistence, uniform, housing, overseas cost-of-living, evacuation, family separation allowances, death gratuities, interment allowance, various travel allowances and dependent benefits.[27]

The Code also excludes combat pay (limited to $500 a month for commissioned officers), (Code Sec. 112; Reg § 1.112-1)[28] and certain retirement pay, as explained at ¶ 1287. (Code Sec. 104(a)(4); Reg § 1.104-1(c))[29]

¶ 1224 **VA and state benefits to veterans.**

Benefits under any law administered by the Veterans' Administration are excludable from the recipient's gross income. (Code Sec. 134(a)(3)) This includes interest earned on dividends left on deposit with the Dept of Veterans Affairs.[30] State bonuses to veterans for service rendered to the U.S. are also exempt.[31]

¶ 1225 **Government employees' compensation.**

Federal, state and municipal government employees, including federal judges, are taxable on their salary, wages and other compensation the same as other employees.[32]

---

22. ¶ H-2750; ¶ 4214.01.
23. ¶ H-2763; ¶ 422A4.02.
24. ¶ H-2796 et seq.; ¶ 422A4.01.
25. ¶ H-2800; ¶ 4224.01.
26. ¶ H-1038 et seq.
27. ¶ H-3102; ¶ 1344.01.
28. ¶ H-3106 et seq.; ¶ 1124.01.
29. ¶ H-3120; ¶ 1044.04.
30. ¶ H-3129.
31. ¶ H-3130.
32. ¶ H-3131; ¶ 614.036.

Footnote references beginning with letters are to paragraphs in RIA's Federal Tax Coordinator 2d and RIA's Analysis of Federal Taxes: Income. Footnote references beginning with numbers are to paragraphs in RIA's United States Tax Reporter.

¶ 1226 Members of clergy.

In addition to the taxable salaries and fees they receive, members of the clergy are also taxable on offerings from marriages, funerals, masses, etc., but not on offerings to the church. (Reg § 1.61-2(a))[33]

The rental value of a home furnished to a member of the clergy, and the cost of utilities paid for that member as part of the compensation for carrying out duties as a member are not taxable as income if the member is duly ordained, licensed or commissioned. (Code Sec. 107(1); Reg § 1.107-1(a))

A member of the clergy who receives a rental allowance as part of his compensation is not taxed on the allowance to the extent it is used in the year received to rent or provide a home (Code Sec. 107(2)) or pay expenses directly related to providing a home, (Reg § 1.107-1(c)) but only if the employer church or organization designates the payment as a rental allowance before the payment is made. (Reg § 1.107-1(b))[34]

¶ 1227 Compensation of minors.

The income of a minor from compensation earned by him or received in respect of his services is income to him, even if received by the parent. (Code Sec. 73(a))[35] However, if the child is under age 14, the rate of tax imposed on his unearned income may depend on the parent's tax rate, see ¶ 3133.

¶ 1228 Fringe Benefits

Fringe benefits received by an employee in addition to cash compensation are generally taxable.

¶ 1229 Taxation of fringe benefits.

A fringe benefit provided to any person in connection with the performance of services by that person is treated as compensation for those services. (Reg § 1.61-21(a)(3))[36] Unless a fringe benefit is specifically excluded (see ¶ 1243 *et seq.*), it is includible in the gross income of the recipient (Code Sec. 61(a)(1))[37] (i.e., the person performing the services, even though that person didn't actually receive the benefit). (Reg § 1.61-21(a)(4))[38]

¶ 1230 Valuation of taxable fringe benefits—general rule.

An employee who receives a taxable fringe benefit must include in gross income the fair market value (FMV) of the benefit minus: (1) any payment for the benefit, and (2) any amount specifically excluded by some Code provision. (Reg § 1.61-21(b)(1))[39] The FMV of a fringe benefit is the amount that an individual would have to pay for the particular fringe benefit in an arm's-length transaction. (Reg § 1.61-21(b)(2))[40]

Unless a special valuation rule (¶ 1231 *et seq.*) applies, an employer-provided vehicle is valued at the comparable lease cost, and (Reg § 1.61-21(b)(4))[41] flights on an employer-provided aircraft are valued at comparable charter or lease cost. (Reg § 1.61-21(b)(6), (7))[42]

Chauffeur services are valued separately from vehicle availability. Chauffeur services are valued at comparable arm's-length transaction costs or by reference to the chauffeur's compensation (including any nontaxable lodging, see ¶ 1270). (Reg § 1.61-21(b)(5))[43]

¶ 1231 Special valuation rules for autos, other vehicles and airflights.

Special valuation rules may be used under certain circumstances for certain commonly provided fringe benefits (e.g., automobiles, noncommercial flights, commuting).

---

33. ¶ H-3151; ¶ 614.007.
34. ¶ H-3153 *et seq.*
35. ¶ H-3180.
36. ¶ H-1051; ¶ 614.027.
37. ¶ H-1051; ¶ 614.027.
38. ¶ H-1053 *et seq.*; ¶ 614.027.
39. ¶ H-1055; ¶ 614.027.
40. ¶ H-1056; ¶ 614.027.
41. ¶ H-2212; ¶ 614.027(a).
42. ¶ H-2302 *et seq.*; ¶ 614.027(b).
43. ¶ H-2269 *et seq.*; ¶ 614.027(a)(4).

Footnote references beginning with letters are to paragraphs in RIA's Federal Tax Coordinator 2d and RIA's Analysis of Federal Taxes: Income. Footnote references beginning with numbers are to paragraphs in RIA's United States Tax Reporter.

(Reg § 1.61-21(b), (c)(1),(3))[44] Where the special rules are not used either by choice, or where they are not permitted, the value of the fringe benefit in question must be determined under the general valuation principles at ¶ 1230. (Reg § 1.61-21(c)(5))[45]

An employee may not use a special valuation rule to value a fringe benefit provided by an employer, unless the employer uses the same rule to value the benefit. (Reg § 1.61-21(c)(2))[46]

¶ 1232   Annual lease value method for automobiles—use of IRS table.

To compute the annual lease value, first determine fair market value (FMV) as of the first date an auto is made available to any employee for personal use. Under safe harbor rules, where the auto is bought in an arm's length purchase by the employer, the FMV is the cost, including sales tax, title fees and other purchase expenses. Where leased, it is the suggested retail price less 8%, the retail value as reported in a nationally recognized publication that regularly reports such values, (Reg § 1.61-21(d)(5)) or the manufacturer's invoice price plus 4%.[47] Then, find the dollar range in column (1) of the table below which corresponds to the FMV of the automobile. The corresponding amount in column (2) is the auto's annual lease value. (Reg § 1.61-21(d)(2)(iii))

Automobile fair market value (1)	Annual lease value (2)	Automobile fair market value (1)	Annual lease value (2)
$0 to 999	$600	22,000 to 22,999	6,100
1,000 to 1,999	850	23,000 to 23,999	6,350
2,000 to 2,999	1,100	24,000 to 24,999	6,600
3,000 to 3,999	1,350	25,000 to 25,999	6,850
4,000 to 4,999	1,600	26,000 to 27,999	7,250
5,000 to 5,999	1,850	28,000 to 29,999	7,750
6,000 to 6,999	2,100	30,000 to 31,999	8,250
7,000 to 7,999	2,350	32,000 to 33,999	8,750
8,000 to 8,999	2,600	34,000 to 35,999	9,250
9,000 to 9,999	2,850	36,000 to 37,999	9,750
10,000 to 10,999	3,100	38,000 to 39,999	10,250
11,000 to 11,999	3,350	40,000 to 41,999	10,750
12,000 to 12,999	3,600	42,000 to 43,999	11,250
13,000 to 13,999	3,850	44,000 to 45,999	11,750
14,000 to 14,999	4,100	46,000 to 47,999	12,250
15,000 to 15,999	4,350	48,000 to 49,999	12,750
16,000 to 16,999	4,600	50,000 to 51,999	13,250
17,000 to 17,999	4,850	52,000 to 53,999	13,750
18,000 to 18,999	5,100	54,000 to 55,999	14,250
19,000 to 19,999	5,350	56,000 to 57,999	14,750
20,000 to 20,999	5,600	58,000 to 59,999	15,250
21,000 to 21,999	5,850		

For automobiles with a FMV in excess of $59,999 the annual lease value equals: $(.25 \times$ automobile FMV$) + \$500$.[48]

  illustration: On Jan. 1, of Year 1, X Co. provides a car worth $10,000 free to its employee E. None of the fringe benefits exclusions from income apply. The annual lease value (see chart above) is $3,100, and this is the value of E's benefit for Year 1. E must include $3,100 (minus 0, the amount he paid for the car) in income.

---

44. ¶s H-1056 *et seq.*, H-2300   45. ¶ H-1057; ¶ 614.027.   47. ¶ H-2220.   48. ¶s H-2218, H-2219.
   et seq.; ¶ 614.027.   46. ¶ H-1059; ¶ 614.027.

Footnote references beginning with letters are to paragraphs in RIA's Federal Tax Coordinator 2d and RIA's Analysis of Federal Taxes: Income. Footnote references beginning with numbers are to paragraphs in RIA's United States Tax Reporter.

This method takes into account the value of insuring and maintaining the auto, but not the value of fuel, which can be valued based on all facts and circumstances, or alternatively at 5½¢ per mile for all miles driven by the employee. (Reg § 1.61-21(d)(3))[49]

The annual lease values computed above are determined on the basis of an assumed four-year lease term (beginning on the first date this method is used and ending on Dec. 31, of the following fourth full calendar year). The annual lease value for each following four-year period is determined on the basis of the FMV on the Jan. 1, following the preceding period using the lease valuation table. (Reg § 1.61-21(d)(2)(iv))[50]

Subject to certain restrictions, an employer with a fleet of 20 or more autos may determine the annual lease value of each auto in the fleet as if its FMV were equal to the "fleet-average value." (Reg § 1.61-21(d)(5))[1]

¶ 1233 Prorated annual lease value.

Where an employer-provided automobile is continuously available to the employee for periods of 30 or more days, but less than an entire calendar year, the value of the availability of the automobile is the prorated annual lease value, computed by multiplying the annual lease value by a fraction, the numerator of which is the number of days of availability, and the denominator of which is 365. (Reg § 1.61-21(d)(4))[2]

¶ 1234 Daily lease value.

Where an employer-provided auto is continuously available to the employee for at least one but less than 30 days, the value of the use of the auto is its daily lease value. This value is calculated by multiplying the auto's annual lease value by a fraction, the numerator of which is four times the number of days of the automobile's availability, and the denominator of which is 365. A 30-day period may be used even if availability is less than 30 days if this produces a lower valuation. (Reg § 1.61-21(d)(4))[3]

¶ 1235 Cents-per-mile valuation method.

Under this method, the value of the benefit equals the total number of miles the employee drove the vehicle for personal purposes in the tax year times the optional standard mileage rate, see ¶ 1552. The cents-per-mile rate is applied prospectively from the first day of the tax year following publication of the rate by IRS. The mileage rate must be applied to personal mileage independent of business mileage.[4]

This method takes into account the value of insuring and maintaining the vehicle, and the value of fuel provided by the employer. If fuel is not provided, the cents-per-mile rate may be reduced by no more than 5.5¢ per mile, or the amount specified in an applicable Revenue Ruling or Procedure. (Reg § 1.61-21(e)(3))[5]

The cents-per-mile method may not be used to value employee use of an employer-provided automobile if the automobile's fair market value, as of the date it is first made available to any employee for personal use, exceeds the maximum recovery deductions (as adjusted for inflation) allowable under Code Sec. 280F for the first five tax years the auto is in service, see ¶ 1960.[6] This maximum refers only to the employer's cost. If the employee contributes to the purchase price or lease cost, a car whose value is greater than the maximum may be eligible for the cents-per-mile method. (Reg § 1.61-21(e)(1))[7]

49. ¶ H-2215; ¶ 614.027(a)(1).
50. ¶ H-2226; ¶ 614.027(a)(1).
1. ¶ H-2238 *et seq.*; ¶ 614.027(a)(1).

2. ¶ H-2223; ¶ 614.027(a)(1).
3. ¶ H-2225.
4. ¶ H-2248; ¶ 614.027(a)(2).

5. ¶ H-2257 *et seq.*; ¶ 614.027(a)(2).

6. ¶ H-2252; ¶ 614.027(a)(2).
7. ¶ H-2253.

Footnote references beginning with letters are to paragraphs in RIA's Federal Tax Coordinator 2d and RIA's Analysis of Federal Taxes: Income. Footnote references beginning with numbers are to paragraphs in RIA's United States Tax Reporter.

¶ 1236   Commuting value method—$1.50 per one-way commute.

Under this method, the value of the employee's use of a vehicle, including an automobile, for commuting purposes only is computed as $1.50 per one-way commute (for example, from home to work, or work to home). If there is more than one employee who commutes in a single vehicle, the commuting benefit is still valued at $1.50 per one way commute for each employee. (Reg § 1.61-21(f)(3))[8] Various requirements must be satisfied. (Reg § 1.61-21(f)(1))

This method may not be used to value the commuting use of any chauffeur-driven vehicle, except for the commuting use of the vehicle by the chauffeur. (Reg § 1.61-21(f)(2))[9]

¶ 1237   Employer-provided airflights.

Airflights provided by an employer for an employee's personal purposes are fringe benefits includible in the employee's gross income. (Reg § 1.61-21(a)(1))[10]

Special valuation methods are available to value noncommercial flights on employer-provided aircraft (¶ 1240), and "space available" flights on commercial aircraft (¶ 1241). Use of a special method is optional. If an employer uses either of the special rules, however, he must generally use it to value all flights taken by employees in a calendar year. (Reg § 1.61-21(g)(14)(i), (h)(5)(i))[11]

¶ 1238   SIFL formula for noncommercial flights.

Value is determined by multiplying the "base aircraft valuation formula"—also known as the Standard Industry Fair Level Formula (SIFL formula)—in effect at the time of the flight by the appropriate "aircraft multiple," and then adding the applicable "terminal charge." (Reg § 1.61-21(g)(5))[12]

¶ 1239   Trip including both personal and business flights.

If an employee takes a trip on an employer-provided aircraft primarily for his employer's business which includes both personal flights and business flights, the value of the personal flights is a taxable fringe benefit. The value of the benefit is equal to the excess of the value of all the flights comprising the trip, over the value of the flights the employee would have taken had he travelled only for business purposes. If the employee combines personal and business flights on a trip which is primarily for personal purposes, the amount includible is the value of the personal flights that would have been taken had there been only personal flights. The value of all these flights may be computed under the special valuation rules, above. (Reg § 1.61-21(g)(4))[13]

¶ 1240   "Seating capacity" rule for noncommercial flights.

A special valuation method—the "seating capacity" rule—is available for noncommercial flights on employer-provided aircraft where at least half of the aircraft's passenger seating capacity is occupied by employees whose flights are primarily for the employer's business (and whose flights are excludable from their income as a working condition fringe, see ¶ 1248). In this situation, the includible value of the flight taken by the employee for personal purposes is zero. (Reg § 1.61-21(g)(12))[14]

¶ 1241   "Space-available" rule for commercial flights.

If an employer provides an employee with a flight on a commercial aircraft for the employee's personal purposes, the flight is a taxable fringe benefit whose value must be

---

8. ¶ H-2262; ¶ 614.027(a)(3).
9. ¶ H-2263; ¶ 614.027(a)(3).
10. ¶ H-2301; ¶ 614.027(b).
11. ¶ H-2301 *et seq.*; ¶ 614.027(b)(1).
12. ¶s H-2304, H-2307 *et seq.*; ¶ 614.027(b)(1).
13. ¶s H-2314, H-2315; ¶ 614.027(b)(1).
14. ¶ H-2319; ¶ 614.027(b)(1).

Footnote references beginning with letters are to paragraphs in RIA's Federal Tax Coordinator 2d and RIA's Analysis of Federal Taxes: Income. Footnote references beginning with numbers are to paragraphs in RIA's United States Tax Reporter.

included in the employee's gross income (¶ 1237). If the flight is a "space-available flight," its value may be computed under a special rule: 25% of the actual carrier's highest unrestricted coach fare for the flight taken. (Reg § 1.61-21(h)(1))[15]

¶ 1242 Frequent flyer bonus program.

To encourage passengers to fly on their planes, some airlines offer free flights (and in some cases free car rental and hotel accommodations) to passengers who have flown a specific number of miles with them. Employees who travel frequently for their employer are often free to use the benefits of the frequent flyer bonus program for their own personal travel. IRS has not addressed the issue concerning the tax treatment of these and similar programs. IRS says that these issues are still under consideration.[16]

¶ 1243 Excludable fringe benefits.

Fringe benefits are not included in gross income, if: (1) the fringe benefit is excluded under a specific Code Section (¶ 1244), (Code Sec. 61(a)) or (2) the fringe benefit qualifies as one of the following: (Code Sec. 132(a))[17]

- no additional cost service (¶ 1245);
- qualified employee discount (¶ 1246);
- working condition fringe (¶ 1248);
- de minimis fringe (¶ 1249);
- qualified transportation fringe (¶ 1251);
- qualified moving expense reimbursement after '93 (¶ 1252).

A fringe benefit that is expressly provided for in any other Code Section can't be excluded from gross income under these Code Sec. 132 rules, except as a de minimis fringe or as a qualified moving expense reimbursement. (Code Sec. 132(l))[18]

¶ 1244 Fringe benefits excluded under a specific Code Section.

Fringe benefits excluded under a specific Code Section include:[19]

- holiday and other gifts of nominal value, see ¶ 1211;
- stock options, see ¶ 1219;
- clergy member's home, see ¶ 1226;
- employee achievement awards, see ¶ 1253;
- moving expenses, see ¶ 1256;
- educational assistance, see ¶ 1258;
- medical care coverage, including accident and health insurance, see ¶ 1259 *et seq.*;
- group-term life insurance, see ¶ 1265;
- meals and lodging, see ¶ 1270;
- supper money, see ¶ 1270;
- qualified campus lodging, see ¶ 1273;
- cafeteria (flexible benefit) plans, see ¶ 1274;
- dependent care assistance programs, see ¶ 1276;
- scholarships, see ¶ 1377;
- cost of living allowances to certain U.S. government employees, see ¶ 4626;
- on-premises athletic facilities, see ¶ 1254.

---

15. ¶ H-2337; ¶ 614.027(b)(2).   17. ¶ H-1051; ¶ 1324.   18. ¶ H-1052; ¶ 1324.   19. ¶ H-1052; ¶ 614.027.
16. ¶ H-2204.

Footnote references beginning with letters are to paragraphs in RIA's Federal Tax Coordinator 2d and RIA's Analysis of Federal Taxes: Income. Footnote references beginning with numbers are to paragraphs in RIA's United States Tax Reporter.

¶ 1245 No-additional-cost services.

No-additional-cost services are excluded from an employee's gross income. (Code Sec. 132(a)(1))[20] These are services provided by an employer to an employee for personal use by the employee, his spouse or dependent children, if:

(1) the services are ordinarily offered for sale to nonemployee customers in the ordinary course of the line of business in which the employee works,

(2) the employer incurs no substantial additional cost (including foregone revenue) in providing the services to the employee—this is computed without regard to any amounts paid by the employee for the services, (Code Sec. 132(b)) and[21]

(3) special nondiscrimination rules are satisfied. (Code Sec. 132(j)(1))[22]

No-additional-cost services include services that would remain unused if the employee customers did not use them, e.g., hotel accommodations, transportation by air, train, bus, subway or cruise line, and telephone services. (Reg § 1.132-2(a)(2))[23]

¶ 1246 Qualified employee discounts.

Qualified employee discounts are excluded from an employee's gross income. (Code Sec. 132(a)(2))[24] A "qualified employee discount" is an "employee discount" allowed with respect to "qualified property or services" provided by an employer to an employee, the employee's spouse or dependent children to the extent the discount doesn't exceed the limitations at ¶ 1247. (Code Sec. 132(c)(1))[25]

An "employee discount" is the excess of:

(1) the price at which property or services are offered by an employer for sale to nonemployee customers, over

(2) the price at which the employer offers the same property or services to employees for use by those employees. (Code Sec. 132(c)(3))[26]

"Qualified property or services" means any property (other than real property and other than personal property of a kind held for investment) or services that are offered for sale to nonemployee customers in the ordinary course of the employer's line of business in which the employee works. (Code Sec. 132(c)(4), (k))[27]

¶ 1247 Limitations on "qualified employee discounts."

The excludable amount of a "qualified employee discount" with respect to property is limited to the gross profit percentage of the price at which that property is offered by the employer to customers. (Code Sec. 132(c)(1)(A)) Gross profit percentage equals the aggregate sales price of the property sold by the employer to all customers, whether employees or nonemployees, (Reg § 1.132-3(c)(1)(i)) over the aggregate cost of the property, (Code Sec. 132(c)(2)(A)(i)) divided by the aggregate sales price. (Code Sec. 132(c)(2)(A)(ii))[28]

The excludable amount with respect to services is limited to 20% of the price at which the employer offers the service to nonemployee customers. (Code Sec. 132(c)(1)(B), (k))[29]

¶ 1248 Working condition fringes.

Working condition fringes are excluded from the employee's gross income. (Code Sec. 132(a)(3))[30] A "working condition fringe" is any property or services provided to an employee by the employer to the extent the cost of the property or services would have been deductible by the employee either under Code Sec. 162 (as trade or business expenses) or under Code Sec. 167 (as depreciation expenses) if the employee had paid for

20. ¶ H-1871; ¶ 1324.03.   23. ¶ H-1872; ¶ 1324.03.   26. ¶ H-1904; ¶ 1324.04.   29. ¶ H-1914; ¶ 1324.04.
21. ¶ H-1871; ¶ 1324.03.   24. ¶ H-1901; ¶ 1324.04.   27. ¶ H-1903; ¶ 1324.04.   30. ¶ H-1701; ¶ 1324.05.
22. ¶ H-1930 *et seq.*   25. ¶ H-1902; ¶ 1324.04.   28. ¶ H-1909; ¶ 1324.04.

Footnote references beginning with letters are to paragraphs in RIA's Federal Tax Coordinator 2d and RIA's Analysis of Federal Taxes: Income. Footnote references beginning with numbers are to paragraphs in RIA's United States Tax Reporter.

104

the property or services himself. (Code Sec. 132(d))[31] Examples are: employer-paid subscriptions to business periodicals; employer expenditures for on-the-job training or business travel; and the use of employer-provided vehicles for business purposes.[32]

Certain benefits qualify as working condition fringes only if special requirements are satisfied. These benefits include: the use of consumer goods manufactured for sale to nonemployee customers and provided to employees for product testing and evaluation outside the employer's work place; (Reg § 1.132-5(n)(1))[33] the personal use of vehicles otherwise used in connection with the business of farming; (Reg § 1.132-5(g))[34] job placement assistance;[35] "qualified automobile demonstration use" by automobile salesmen; (Code Sec. 132(j)(3))[36] the use of employer-owned aircraft for business travel; (Reg § 1.132-5(k))[37] certain forms of transportation and other employer-provided security measures provided because of bona fide business-oriented security concerns; (Reg § 1.132-5(m))[38] and the use of "qualified nonpersonal use vehicles." (Reg § 1.132-5(h))[39]

If an employer provides the use of a vehicle and includes the entire amount in the employee's income (without excluding any working condition fringe benefit amount), the employee can deduct the value multiplied by the percentage of business use as a miscellaneous itemized deduction (subject to the 2% floor). This deduction can't be computed under the cents-per-mile (¶ 1235) method. (Reg § 1.162-25(b))[40]

No qualified transportation fringe benefit (including amounts in excess of the dollar limit) may be excluded as a working condition fringe benefit. (Code Sec. 132(f)(7))[41]

¶ 1249 De minimis fringe benefits.

De minimis fringe benefits are excluded from the recipient's gross income. (Code Sec. 132(a)(4)) A "de minimis fringe" is any property or service whose value is so small that accounting for it is unreasonable or administratively impracticable, taking into account the frequency with which similar fringe benefits are provided by the employer to its employees. (Code Sec. 132(e)(1))[42]

Examples of de minimis fringes include:

- transportation (e.g., taxi fare) where other available means of transportation are unsafe, in excess of value over $1.50 per each one-way commute; (Reg § 1.132-6(d))
- occasional typing of personal letters by a company secretary;
- occasional cocktail parties or picnics for employees and their guests;
- traditional holiday gifts of property (not cash) with a low fair market value;
- occasional theater or sporting event tickets;
- coffee and donuts, soft drinks;
- occasional personal use of copying machine (85% of use must be for business purpose);
- local phone calls;
- flowers, fruit, books or similar items provided to employees under special circumstances, such as sickness or outstanding performance. (Reg § 1.132-6(e)(1))

No qualified transportation fringe benefit (including amounts in excess of the dollar limit) may be excluded as a de minimis fringe benefit. (Code Sec. 132(f)(7))[43]

¶ 1250 Meals at employer-operated eating facilities.

Meals at employer-operated eating facilities are de minimis fringes (¶ 1249) if the facility's annual revenues exceed its direct operating costs and certain nondiscrimination rules are satisfied. (Code Sec. 132(e)(2); Reg § 1.132-7(c))[44]

---

31. ¶ H-1701; ¶ 1324.05.
32. ¶ H-1701; ¶ 1324.05.
33. ¶ H-1709; ¶ 1324.05.
34. ¶ H-2370; ¶ 1324.05.

35. ¶ H-1701.
36. ¶ H-2364; ¶ 1324.05.
37. ¶ H-2351; ¶ 1324.05.
38. ¶ H-2373 *et seq.*; ¶ 1324.05.

39. ¶ H-2354; ¶ 1324.05.
40. ¶s H-2363, L-1914.
41. ¶ H-2201.1.

42. ¶ H-1802 *et seq.*; ¶ 1324.06.
43. ¶ H-2201.1.
44. ¶ H-1821; ¶ 1324.06.

Footnote references beginning with letters are to paragraphs in RIA's Federal Tax Coordinator 2d and RIA's Analysis of Federal Taxes: Income. Footnote references beginning with numbers are to paragraphs in RIA's United States Tax Reporter.

"Direct operating costs" are the costs of the food and beverages served and the cost of labor for services relating to the facility performed primarily on the facility's premises. (Reg § 1.132-7(b)(1))[45]

¶ 1251 Qualified transportation fringe benefits.

An employee (other than a self-employed person) may exclude from income qualified transportation fringe benefits up to specified dollar amounts (see below). (Code Sec. 132(a)(5), (f)(5)) These benefits include: (Code Sec. 132(f)(1), (5))[46]

(1) Transportation in a commuter highway vehicle (specially defined), if in connection with travel between the employee's residence and place of employment.

(2) Transit passes for use on a mass transit facility (e.g., rail, bus or ferry) or a commuter highway vehicle.

(3) Qualified parking at or near the employer's business premises or a location from which the employee commutes to work by mass transit or hired commuter vehicle. Any parking at or near the employee's residence is not qualified parking.

Up to $155 a month of qualified parking and up to $60 a month of the combined value of transit passes and transportation by commuter highway vehicle may be excluded in '93 and '94. (Code Sec. 132(f)(2))[47] These amounts are adjusted for inflation. (Code Sec. 132(f)(6))[48]

Cash reimbursements by the employer are excludable. In the case of transit passes, however, reimbursements are excludable only where vouchers, tokens, etc., aren't readily available for direct distribution by the employer to the employee. (Code Sec. 132(f)(3))[49]

¶ 1252 Qualified moving expense reimbursement after '93.

For expenses incurred after '93, a taxpayer may exclude from gross income any fringe benefit that qualifies as a qualified moving expense reimbursement. (Code Sec. 132(a)(6))[50] A qualified moving expense reimbursement is any amount received (directly or indirectly) by the taxpayer from an employer as a payment of (or reimbursement for) moving expenses that would have been deductible had the taxpayer paid them directly. But the expenses are not excludable if the taxpayer actually deducted them in an earlier year. (Code Sec. 132(g))[1]

¶ 1253 Employee achievement awards.

Employee achievement awards are excludable from the employee's gross income only to the extent the employer can deduct the cost of the award—generally limited to $400 for any one employee, or $1,600 for a "qualified plan award," see ¶ 1584. (Code Sec. 74(c)(2))[2]

¶ 1254 On-premises athletic facilities.

The value of an "on-premises athletic facility" provided by an employer is excluded from an employee's gross income. (Code Sec. 132(j)(4)(A))[3]

¶ 1255 Employer payment of employee's personal expenses.

Where an employer pays the debts or personal expenses of an employee, or reimburses the employee's payment, the employee must include the employer's payment or reimbursement in his (employee's) income.[4]

Company payments to financial counseling firms for advice to executives on handling personal financial affairs, including investments, insurance, real estate, tax planning and

45. ¶ H-1823; ¶ 1324.06.   48. ¶ H-2203.2.   1. ¶ H-1971; ¶ 1324.09.   3. ¶ H-1951; ¶ 1324.07.
46. ¶ H-2201.1.   49. ¶ H-2022.4.   2. ¶ J-1219; ¶ 744.03.   4. ¶ H-2151; ¶ 624.
47. ¶ H-2203.1.   50. ¶ H-1971; ¶ 1324.09.

Footnote references beginning with letters are to paragraphs in RIA's Federal Tax Coordinator 2d and RIA's Analysis of Federal Taxes: Income. Footnote references beginning with numbers are to paragraphs in RIA's United States Tax Reporter.

return preparation, retirement benefits and estate planning, are taxable to the executives.[5]

An employer's payment of an employee's income taxes (federal or state) or other taxes is income to the employee. Pyramiding of income, and of tax, results where the employer agrees to pay all the employee's tax. (Reg § 1.61-14)[6]

¶ 1256 Moving expense reimbursement.

Unless the post-'93 Code Sec. 132(a)(6) exclusion rules apply, (see ¶ 1252) an employer's payment or reimbursement of the expenses of moving an employee, his family, household goods, etc., to the area of a new or other place of employment is income to the employee. (Code Sec. 82)[7] This includes amounts furnished by an employer to assist a relocated employee to buy a home at his new post.[8] The employer must give the employee Form 4782 describing the reimbursements. For deduction of moving expenses by the employee, see ¶ 1645.

¶ 1257 Reimbursement by employer in connection with employee's sale of his home.

An employer's reimbursement for an employee's loss on sale of the employee's home is income to the employee whether the reimbursement is to cover a sale at an actual loss (selling price less than basis) or only a sale for less than an estimated market value.[9]

However, if the employer buys the employee's home at its fair market value, the employee has no income other than gain on the sale.

Where, as an alternative to reimbursing an employee for a loss on the sale of his home, the employer buys the home for more than its fair market value, that *excess* is taxable to the employee and is ineligible for any rollover of gain (see ¶ 2437).[10]

If the employer purchases the home (i.e., for sale to a third party), expenses incurred by the employer in connection with that later sale aren't taxed to the employee if these costs wouldn't be imposed on the seller under local law or custom. This applies to employer payments for broker commissions, FHA appraisal fees, taxes and insurance.[11]

If the employer doesn't buy the home but only sells it for the employee as his agent, any selling expenses borne by the employer are includible in the employee's income.[12]

¶ 1258 Educational assistance programs before '95.

For tax years beginning before '95, (Code Sec. 127(d)) employers can set up educational assistance programs under which employees can receive up to $5,250 per year of "educational assistance" tax-free, whether or not job-related. (Code Sec. 127(a)) Expenses paid by an employer for education or training provided to the employee which are not excludible under this provision can only be excluded from income if they qualify as a working condition fringe benefit (¶ 1248). (Code Sec. 132(j)(8))

No deduction or credit can be taken by the employee for any amount excluded from income. (Code Sec. 127(c)(7))[13]

The term "educational assistance" means the employer's payment for or provision of tuition, fees, books, supplies and equipment under an educational assistance program (Code Sec. 127(c)(1)) including graduate-level courses.[14]

Eligibility requirements can't discriminate in favor of employees who are "highly compensated employees" (see ¶ 4326). (Code Sec. 127(b)(2); Reg § 1.127-2(e)(1))[15]

The above exclusion was retroactively extended from July 1, '92, after most '92 returns were filed. For how to get a refund of taxes paid on post-June 30, '92 amounts, see ¶ 4849.

---

5. ¶ H-2510.
6. ¶ H-2157; ¶ 614.147.
7. ¶ H-4516; ¶ 824.01.

8. ¶ H-2160; ¶ 824.01.
9. ¶s H-2161, H-2162; ¶ 824.01.
10. ¶ H-2162; ¶ 824.01.

11. ¶ H-2165.
12. ¶s H-2163, H-2165.
13. ¶ H-2064; ¶ 1274.

14. ¶ H-2065; ¶ 1274.
15. ¶ H-2069; ¶ 1274.01.

Footnote references beginning with letters are to paragraphs in RIA's Federal Tax Coordinator 2d and RIA's Analysis of Federal Taxes: Income. Footnote references beginning with numbers are to paragraphs in RIA's United States Tax Reporter.

¶ 1259 Employee's medical expenses reimbursed or insured by employer.

An employee can exclude from gross income amounts received from his employer, directly or indirectly, as reimbursement for expenses for the medical care of himself, his spouse, and his dependents. However, reimbursement is includible in the employee's income to the extent it exceeds medical expenses or it is attributable to medical expense deductions he took in a previous year. (Code Sec. 105(b); Reg § 1.105-2)[16]

An employee also excludes from gross income the cost of employer-provided *coverage* under an accident or health plan. (Code Sec. 106)[17] However, if the employer-provided policy, trust, etc., provides other benefits, only the portion of the employer contributions for the accident and health coverage is excludable. (Reg § 1.106-1)[18]

Insurance premiums paid for partners and more-than-2% S corporation shareholders (who are treated as partners) are not excludable.[19]

Highly compensated individuals who benefit from an employer's "self-insured" medical reimbursement plan that discriminates in favor of employees who are "highly compensated employees" (defined in ¶ 4326) must include "excess reimbursements" in income. (Code Sec. 105(h))[20]

¶ 1260 Employer's payments for employee's loss of limb, disfigurement, etc.

Lump sum or installment amounts received under an employer's plan as payment for permanent loss or loss of use of a member or function of the body, or permanent disfigurement, of the employee, his spouse or his dependent are tax-free, but only if the payment is based on the nature of the injury without regard to the period the employee is absent from work. (Code Sec. 105(c))[21]

¶ 1261 Worker's compensation.

Amounts received under worker's compensation laws for personal injuries or sickness are excludable from the employee's income. But worker's compensation is includible in income to the extent it's attributable to medical expense deductions taken in an earlier year. (Code Sec. 104(a)(1); Reg § 1.104-1(b))[22]

¶ 1262 Death benefits.

An exclusion from income is allowed for amounts received by an employee's beneficiaries or estate, that are paid, in a single sum or otherwise, by or on behalf of an employer by reason of an employee's death. (Code Sec. 101(b)(1)) The total exclusion can't exceed $5,000 with respect to any deceased employee, regardless of the number of employers, beneficiaries or years in which payments are received. (Reg § 1.101-2(a)(3))[23] Where benefits of more than $5,000 are paid to more than one beneficiary, the exclusion is apportioned among them, according to their respective shares of the payments. (Reg § 1.101-2(c)(1))[24]

✏ *illustration:* Employer pays $6,000 to employee's Widow, $3,000 to his Daughter, and $1,000 to his Son. Widow excludes $3,000 ($5,000 × $6,000/$10,000). Daughter excludes $1,500 ($5,000 × $3,000/$10,000). Son excludes $500 ($5,000 × $1,000/$10,000).

The exclusion also applies to a distribution received by a beneficiary or estate of a self-employed individual, if the distribution is made from: a qualified employee trust or a Code Sec. 403(a) annuity plan. (Code Sec. 101(b)(3)(B))[25]

---

16. ¶ H-1108 *et seq.*; ¶ 1054.01.   19. ¶ H-1102; ¶ 1065.01(40).   22. ¶ H-1351; ¶ 1044.01.   24. ¶ H-1621; ¶ 1014.06.
17. ¶ H-1102; ¶ 1064.   20. ¶ H-1140; ¶ 1054.05.   23. ¶ H-1601; ¶ 1014.06.   25. ¶ H-1603; ¶ 1041.06.
18. ¶ H-1105; ¶ 1062.   21. ¶ H-1201; ¶ 1054.02.

Footnote references beginning with letters are to paragraphs in RIA's Federal Tax Coordinator 2d and RIA's Analysis of Federal Taxes: Income. Footnote references beginning with numbers are to paragraphs in RIA's United States Tax Reporter.

¶ 1263 Employee death benefits paid as annuities.

If employee death benefits are paid in the form of an annuity, the amount otherwise excludable as a "death benefit" under ¶ 1262 is treated as part of the employee's cost of the annuity (investment in the contract) and so becomes excludable from the beneficiary's income over the years he receives annuity payments through the normal operation of the annuity rules. (Code Sec. 101(b)(2)(D))[26]

¶ 1264 Employer-paid individual life insurance policies.

Premiums paid by an employer for policies on the life of an employee are taxable to the employee if the proceeds are payable to the employee's beneficiary (except for group-term insurance, see ¶ 1265) but not where the employer is the beneficiary. (Reg § 1.61-2(d)(2))[27]

¶ 1265 Group-term life insurance premiums.

An employee isn't taxed on premiums paid by the employer on insurance covering the employee's life under a group-term life insurance policy, if his total coverage under all such plans of all his employers doesn't exceed $50,000.[28] If his total coverage exceeds $50,000, he is taxed on the "cost" (¶ 1266) of coverage over $50,000 minus the amount he paid. (Code Sec. 79(a))[29]

Illustration: J has two jobs. He is employed by A Co and B Co. Each company has a noncontributory group life insurance plan. J is covered for $35,000 by A and for $45,000 by B. He is taxed on the cost of $30,000 of insurance ($35,000 + $45,000 – $50,000).

An employee whose total coverage exceeds $50,000 for only part of the year includes the employer's payments for that part of the year coverage, even if his average coverage for the year is under this ceiling. (Code Sec. 79(a))[30]

A disabled terminated employee isn't taxable on group term coverage even if it exceeds $50,000. (Code Sec. 79(b)(1))[31]

A retired employee is treated the same as any other employee except that the $50,000 cap generally does *not* apply to certain employees who reached age 55 or retired on or before Jan. 1, '84.[32]

The exclusion doesn't apply to any insurance protection in excess of the maximum allowed by state law for employee group insurance. (Reg § 1.79-1(e))[33]

The exclusion and use of the table-cost method (¶ 1266) is available to a key employee only if the plan does not discriminate in favor of key employees (at any time during the key employee's tax year) (Reg § 1.79-4T, Q&A-11) as to eligibility to participate and in the type and amount of the benefits that are available under the plan. (Code Sec. 79(d))[34] If the plan is discriminatory each of the key employees must include the *greater of* the actual cost of the insurance *or* the cost determined from IRS's uniform premium table. (Code Sec. 79(d)(1)(B))[35]

The actual cost for a key employee in a discriminatory plan is determined by apportioning the net premium allocable to the group-term coverage during the key employee's tax year among the covered employees. (Reg § 1.79-4T, Q&A-6(b))[36]

¶ 1266 "Cost" of taxable group-term insurance—IRS uniform premium table.

The employer must compute the "cost" of taxable group term insurance coverage and notify the employee on Form W-2 of the amount included in his income. The employee computes the cost only where he has two or more employers who provide him with coverage.

26. ¶ H-1622; ¶ 1014.08.   29. ¶ H-1518; ¶ 794.01.   32. ¶s H-1553, H-1554; ¶ 794.06.   35. ¶ H-1564; ¶ 794.05.
27. ¶ H-1502 *et seq.*; ¶ 614.031.   30. ¶ H-1521; ¶ 794.01.   33. ¶ H-1548.   36. ¶ H-1564; ¶ 794.05.
28. ¶ H-1518; ¶ 794.   31. ¶ H-1550; ¶ 794.03.   34. ¶ H-1563; ¶ 794.05.

Footnote references beginning with letters are to paragraphs in RIA's Federal Tax Coordinator 2d and RIA's Analysis of Federal Taxes: Income. Footnote references beginning with numbers are to paragraphs in RIA's United States Tax Reporter.

The cost for each month of coverage is the number of thousands of dollars of coverage over $50,000 (to the nearest tenth) times the amount in the IRS uniform premium table below for the employee's attained age on the last day of the employee's tax year. (Reg § 1.79-3(d)(2))[37]

Cost per $1,000 of Protection per Month

Age	Cost
Under 30	8¢
30 through 34	9¢
35 through 39	11¢
40 through 44	17¢
45 through 49	29¢
50 through 54	48¢
55 through 59	75¢
60 through 64	$ 1.17
65 through 69	$ 2.10
70 and older	$ 3.76

If the employee contributes to the plan, all his contributions for the tax year are considered made for that part of his coverage over $50,000. (Code Sec. 79(a)(2))[38]

illustration: J is 51 and is employed by both A and B. J's group-term coverage with A is $35,000 and with B is $45,000, for the entire year. J pays premiums of $50 during the year under the B plan. The amount included in J's income is computed as follows:

Employer A coverage (in thousands)	$ 35
Employer B coverage (in thousands)	45
Total coverage (in thousands)	$ 80
Less: Exclusion (in thousands)	50
Excess amount (in thousands)	$ 30
Multiply by cost per $1,000 per month, age 51 (from IRS table above)	0.48
Cost of excess insurance for one month	$ 14.40
Multiply by number of full months coverage at above cost	12
Cost of excess insurance for tax year	$172.80
Less: Premium paid by employee	50.00
Taxable income	$122.80

¶ 1267 Group-term coverage of nonemployees.

The cost (as determined at ¶ 1266) of group-term life insurance on the life of an individual other than an employee (such as the employee's spouse or dependent) provided in connection with the performance of services by the employee is includible in the gross income of the employee. (Reg § 1.61-2(d)(2)(ii)(b)) If, however, the face amount of employer-provided group-term insurance payable on the death of an employee's spouse or dependent doesn't exceed $2,000, it is an excludable de minimis fringe (¶ 1249), until IRS's notice that a contrary rule applies.[39]

¶ 1268 Group-permanent insurance premiums.

Group-permanent insurance premiums that an employer pays on an employee's life are included in the employee's income. Where a group term policy provides permanent benefits, the amount included in income for the permanent benefits is computed under a complex formula. (Reg § 1.79-1(d))[40]

---

37. ¶ H-1521; ¶ 794.01.   39. ¶ H-1558; ¶s 614.031,   40. ¶ H-1542; ¶ 794.01.
38. ¶ H-1522.   1324.06.

Footnote references beginning with letters are to paragraphs in RIA's Federal Tax Coordinator 2d and RIA's Analysis of Federal Taxes: Income. Footnote references beginning with numbers are to paragraphs in RIA's United States Tax Reporter.

¶ 1269 Split-dollar life insurance.

Under a "split-dollar" insurance arrangement, the employer pays part of the premium (to the extent of the annual increase in cash surrender value) and the employee pays the rest. Out of the insurance proceeds the employer gets either the cash surrender value or the amount it paid; the employee can designate the beneficiary of the balance.[41]

The employee is taxed annually on the total amount of his benefits under the insurance arrangement. This taxable amount is generally determined under IRS's PS-58 table (reproduced in ¶ 1119, *not* the group term table at ¶ 1266), plus cash dividends or other benefits received, reduced by any part of the premiums he pays. Insurance proceeds received by the employer and the employee's beneficiaries are tax-free.[42]

¶ 1270 Meals and lodging furnished by or on behalf of employer.

Meals or lodging (including utilities) furnished to an employee and his family (spouse and dependents) is nontaxable to the employee if these tests (Code Sec. 119)[43] are met:

(1) the meals and lodging are furnished by or on behalf of the employer for the convenience of the employer (such as where there aren't enough eating places near work), (Reg § 1.119-1(a)(2))[44] and

(2) (a) in the case of meals, they are furnished on the employer's business premises, or (b) in the case of lodging, the employee is required to accept the lodging as a condition of his employment.

For meals and lodging furnished at a "camp" in a foreign country, see ¶ 4622.

Except for the value of certain meals served at "employer-operated eating facilities," see ¶ 1250, and "qualified campus lodging," see ¶ 1273, the value (not the cost) of meals or lodging that fails to meet these tests is income to the employee. (Reg § 1.61-2(d)(3), Reg § 1.119-1(a)(1))[45]

Cash allowances for meals are taxable.[46] However, occasional "supper money" paid to overtime employees is excludable as a de minimis fringe benefit, see ¶ 1249.[47]

¶ 1271 Whether lodging is a condition of employment.

Exclusion for lodging applies only if the employee is required to accept it to enable him to properly perform his duties. (Reg § 1.119-1(b)) The employee's presence must be required from a business standpoint—e.g., ranches, hotels, motels and resorts.[48]

¶ 1272 Employee's option to take cash or meals or lodging.

If the employee has the option to take either cash, or meals or lodging furnished in kind, the value of meals or lodging furnished is income to the employee. But the mere fact that the employee has a right to decline to accept meals doesn't require including their value in his income. (Reg § 1.119-1(a)(3))[49]

¶ 1273 Qualified campus lodging.

The value of qualified campus lodging furnished to an employee of an educational institution is excludable from his gross income. (Code Sec. 119(d))[50]

Qualified campus lodging is lodging that is not eligible for the exclusion at ¶ 1270, that is located on or near a campus of a tax-exempt educational institution, and that is furnished by the institution to an employee, his spouse, and his dependents for use as a residence. (Code Sec. 119(d)(3), (4))[1]

The exclusion does not apply if rent is inadequate. Specifically, the employee must

---

41. ¶ H-1508; ¶ 1014.02.
42. ¶ H-1509 *et seq.*; ¶ 1014.02.
43. ¶ H-1751; ¶ 1194.01.
44. ¶ H-1764 *et seq.*; ¶ 1194.02.
45. ¶s H-1751, H-1784; ¶s 614.027, 1194 *et seq.*
46. ¶ H-1789; ¶ 1194.03.
47. ¶ H-1790.
48. ¶ H-1775; ¶ 1194.02.
49. ¶ H-1764; ¶ 1194.02.
50. ¶ H-1794; ¶ 1194.06.
1. ¶ H-1796; ¶ 1194.06.

Footnote references beginning with letters are to paragraphs in RIA's Federal Tax Coordinator 2d and RIA's Analysis of Federal Taxes: Income. Footnote references beginning with numbers are to paragraphs in RIA's United States Tax Reporter.

include in income the excess of: (1) the lesser of (a) 5% of the appraised value (as of the close of the tax year) of the qualified campus lodging, or (b) the average of the rentals paid by individuals other than employees or students for comparable lodging provided by the institution; over (2) the rent paid by the employee. (Code Sec. 119(d)(2))[2]

¶ 1274 Cafeteria plans (including flexible spending accounts).

No amount is included in the gross income of the participant in a cafeteria plan solely because, under the plan, the participant may choose among the benefits of the plan. (Code Sec. 125(a))[3] A "cafeteria plan" (also referred to as a flexible benefit plan) is a written plan under which participants (all of whom are employees) may choose their own "menu" of benefits consisting of cash and "qualified benefits" (¶ 1275). (Code Sec. 125(d))[4] In general, a cafeteria plan cannot include any plan which provides for deferred compensation, except for certain 401(k) plans and certain post-retirement insurance maintained by educational institutions (Code Sec. 125(d)) and matching contribution plans under Code Sec. 401(m) and certain premium rebates and policy dividend payments. (Prop Reg § 1.125-2, Q&A-4(c), -5(b), on which "Taxpayers may rely")[5]

Employer contributions to a cafeteria plan can be made under a salary reduction agreement with the participant, provided that it relates to compensation that has not been received (actually or constructively) by and does not become currently available to the participant. (Prop Reg § 1.125-1, Q&A-6, on which "Taxpayers may rely")[6]

The cafeteria plan also can include one or more "flexible spending accounts" (FSAs), which are funded by employee contributions on a pre-tax salary reduction basis to provide coverage for specified expenses (e.g., qualified medical expenses or dependent care assistance costs) that are incurred during the coverage period may be reimbursed. This reimbursement must be subject to reasonable conditions, including a maximum amount that can't substantially exceed the total premium (including employer- and employee-paid portions) for the participant's coverage. However, the participant must use the FSA amounts for the specified expenses, or else forfeit any amounts remaining in his FSA at the end of the plan year. (Prop Reg § 1.125-1, Q&A-7, on which "Taxpayers may rely")[7]

A cafeteria plan may also offer participants the opportunity to buy certain benefits with after-tax contributions. (Prop Reg § 1.125-2, Q&A-4(b), on which "Taxpayers may rely")[8]

In the case of a "highly compensated participant," the exclusion from gross income under Code Sec. 125(a) will not apply to any benefit attributable to a plan year for which the plan discriminates in favor of highly compensated participants as to contributions or benefits or in eligibility to participate. (Code Sec. 125(b)(1)) An individual is a "highly compensated participant" if he is an officer or more-than-5% shareholder of the employer, a highly compensated employee or a spouse or dependent of such a person. (Code Sec. 125(e)(1))[9]

In the case of a key employee (as defined in Code Sec. 416(i)(1)), the gross income exclusion provided by Code Sec. 125(a) will not apply to any plan year if the qualified benefits provided to key employees under the plan exceed 25% of the aggregate of such benefits provided for all employees under the plan. (Code Sec. 125(b)(2))[10]

¶ 1275 Qualified benefits of cafeteria plans.

A "qualified benefit" is any benefit that is excluded from income by a specific provision of the Code. Qualified benefits that may be offered include: (1) group-term life insurance (including amounts that aren't excludable because the dollar coverage limit is exceeded); (2) coverage under an accident or health plan under Code Sec. 105 and Code Sec. 106; (3) dependent care assistance programs under Code Sec. 129; or (4) vacation days if the plan

---

2. ¶ H-1794; ¶ 1194.06.   5. ¶ H-2417 *et seq.*; ¶ 1254.04.   7. ¶ H-2464 *et seq.*; ¶ 1254.05.   9. ¶ H-2457; ¶ 1254.06.
3. ¶ H-2401; ¶ 1254.   6. ¶ H-2420.   8. ¶ H-2415.   10. ¶ H-2452; ¶ 1254.06.
4. ¶ H-2405; ¶ 1254.01.

Footnote references beginning with letters are to paragraphs in RIA's Federal Tax Coordinator 2d and RIA's Analysis of Federal Taxes: Income. Footnote references beginning with numbers are to paragraphs in RIA's United States Tax Reporter.

precludes any participant from using, or receiving cash for, in a later plan year, any vacation days remaining unused at the end of the plan year. (Code Sec. 125(f); Prop Reg § 1.125-2, Q&A-4(a), -5(c), on which "Taxpayers may rely")[11]

The following benefits are not qualified benefits for purposes of the cafeteria plan rules:

(1) scholarships or fellowships under Code Sec. 117, see ¶ 1377;

(2) educational assistance programs under Code Sec. 127, see ¶ 1258;

(3) employer-provided fringe benefits under Code Sec. 132, see ¶ 1245 *et seq.*; (Code Sec. 125(f))

(4) meals and lodgings furnished for the employer's convenience under Code Sec. 119, see ¶ 1270. (Reg § 1.125-2T(1)(a))[12]

¶ 1276 Dependent care assistance payments.

Payments incurred by an employer for dependent care assistance under a written plan are excluded from an employee's gross income. (Code Sec. 129(a)(1))[13]

The amount an employee can exclude (computed on Form 2441 with Form 1040 or Schedule 2 with Form 1040A) can't exceed the employee's earned income, but excluding employer dependent care assistance payments) or in case of a married employee, the earned income of the lower earning spouse. (Code Sec. 129(b))[14] The aggregate exclusion is further limited to $5,000 ($2,500 for a married individual filing separately). (Code Sec. 129(a)(2)(A)) Any excess is includible in the tax year the dependent care services were provided. (Code Sec. 129(a)(2)(B))[15]

Dependent care assistance is the payment of, or provision of, those services that if paid for by the employee would be considered employment-related expenses under the child care credit rules (see ¶ 2349). (Code Sec. 129(e)(1))[16] An employee includes a self-employed individual who can be covered under a self-employed retirement plan. If the individual owns the entire interest in an unincorporated trade or business he is treated as his own employer. A partnership is treated as the employer of each partner who is eligible to be included in a self-employed retirement plan. (Code Sec. 129(e)(3), (4))[17]

The plan must satisfy specific nondiscrimination rules and certain other requirements. (Code Sec. 129(d))[18] If an otherwise qualified program fails to meet these requirements, the program will be a dependent care assistance program under which expenses are still excludable for nonhighly compensated employees. (Code Sec. 129(d)(1))[19]

¶ 1277 Time for Reporting Compensation

Compensation income is reported according to the recipient's accounting method, subject to constructive receipt, repaid income and deferred income rules.

¶ 1278 Cash basis taxpayers.

Cash basis taxpayers report compensation for the tax year they actually receive it.[20]

Compensation paid by check is reported for the year the check is received, even if the check covers past or future services, or is not cashed until the following year.[21]

Compensation income must be reported for the year it is constructively received, even though it is not actually received until a later year. Income is constructively received for the year it is credited to the taxpayer's account, set apart for him, or otherwise made available so he can draw upon it at any time, or could have drawn upon it during the tax year if he had given notice of intention to withdraw. (Reg § 1.451-2(a))[22]

11. ¶ H-2413; ¶ 1254.01.	14. ¶ H-1402; ¶ 1294.	17. ¶ H-1413 *et seq.*; ¶ 1294.02.	20. ¶ H-3503; ¶ 4514.003.
12. ¶ H-2416; ¶ 1254.02.	15. ¶ H-1402 *et seq.*; ¶ 1294.	18. ¶ H-1426 *et seq.*; ¶ 1294.01.	21. ¶ H-3506; ¶ 4514.004.
13. ¶ H-1401; ¶ 1294.	16. ¶ H-1418; ¶ 1294.02.	19. ¶ H-1417; ¶ 1294.01.	22. ¶ H-3507; ¶ 4514.036.

Footnote references beginning with letters are to paragraphs in RIA's Federal Tax Coordinator 2d and RIA's Analysis of Federal Taxes: Income. Footnote references beginning with numbers are to paragraphs in RIA's United States Tax Reporter.

¶ 1279 Accrual basis taxpayers.

Accrual basis taxpayers report compensation for the tax year in which it accrues. Compensation accrues when all events have occurred that fix the right to receive the income and its amount can be determined with reasonable accuracy. (Reg § 1.451-1(a))[23]

If the right to compensation for services or its amount cannot be determined until the services are completed, the amount of compensation is ordinarily not reported until the tax year the services are completed and the determination can be made. (Reg § 1.451-1(a))[24]

¶ 1280 Advances and drawing accounts.

A cash basis taxpayer who receives advances against commissions that have not been earned reports the advances as income for the year they are received, if he is not required to repay the amounts received in excess of commissions. If he must repay the excess drawings, those amounts are not income until offset by a credit for commissions earned.[25]

¶ 1281 Deferred compensation plans.

Deferred compensation plans are arrangements designed to save taxes by postponing receipt of some of a high-salaried employee's compensation from the high-bracket year he earns it to a later year when he is expected to be in a lower bracket.[26] Deferral arrangements also include "excess benefit plans," "top-hat plans" and "supplemental executive retirement plans" (SERPs) which provide highly compensated employees with retirement benefits that would otherwise be limited in amount, or subject to additional taxation, if provided through the qualified pension or profit-sharing plans described in ¶ 4310 et seq..

Funded deferred compensation is taxed to the employee the first year his rights aren't subject to a substantial risk of forfeiture or are transferable. (Reg § 1.83-3(e))[27] Deferred compensation placed in a "rabbi trust" whose assets are subject to the claims of the employer's creditors is not includible in the employee's income until paid or made available to the employee (even where the employee insures payment by the employer).[28] IRS has issued model rabbi trust provisions.[29]

Unfunded deferred compensation is not taxed until actually received if: (1) the deferral is agreed to before the compensation is earned, (2) the deferred amount is not unconditionally placed in trust or in escrow for the benefit of the employee or independent contractor, and (3) the promise to pay is merely a contractual obligation not evidenced by notes or secured in any way.[30]

¶ 1282 Social Security, Unemployment and Certain Disability Payments ▬▬▬

Social security benefits may be partly taxable. Unemployment benefits are fully taxable. Payments under military and government disability pensions may be excludible from income.

¶ 1283 Social security payments.

A taxpayer whose "provisional income" (i.e., modified adjusted gross income (AGI) plus one half of the social security benefits (including Tier 1 Railroad Retirement benefits) received) for a tax year exceeds a threshold amount is taxed on a portion of social security benefits received that year, as follows:

If provisional income exceeds a "base amount," taxpayer must include in gross income the lesser of:

---

23. ¶ G-2467; ¶ 4514.021.   25. ¶ H-3512; ¶ 614.023.   27. ¶ H-3205 et seq.; ¶ 834.01.   29. ¶ T-9963.
24. ¶ H-3526; ¶ 4514.011.   26. ¶ H-3200 et seq.; ¶ 4104.   28. ¶ H-3223; ¶ 4514.046.   30. ¶ H-3231.

Footnote references beginning with letters are to paragraphs in RIA's Federal Tax Coordinator 2d and RIA's Analysis of Federal Taxes: Income. Footnote references beginning with numbers are to paragraphs in RIA's United States Tax Reporter.

- 50% of the social security benefits received that year; (Code Sec. 86(a)(1)(A)) or

- 50% of the excess of provisional income over the "base amount." (Code Sec. 86(a)(1)(B))[31]

"Modified AGI" means AGI: (1) determined without regard to the social security benefits, or the exclusions for foreign earned income and housing costs (¶ 4614 *et seq.*), savings bond proceeds for education expenses (¶ 1338), and income from sources within U.S. possessions and Puerto Rico, and (2) increased by the amount of tax-exempt interest received or accrued by taxpayer during the tax year. (Code Sec. 86(b))[32]

The "base amount" is $32,000 for married individuals filing a joint return; zero for a married individual filing a separate return who does not live apart from his spouse for the entire tax year; and $25,000 for all other individuals, (Code Sec. 86(c)(1)) such as those filing as single, head of household or qualifying widow(er).[33]

illustration: G's modified AGI for the tax year consists of pension income of $15,000. His social security benefit is $12,000. He is married and files a joint return. His wife has no income. The sum of their modified AGI ($15,000) plus one-half of his social security benefit ($6,000) is $21,000. This is less than their base amount ($32,000) so no part of his social security benefit is included in their gross income.

Benefits a taxpayer repays during a tax year reduce the benefits taxed that year, whether the repayment is for overpayments received during the repayment year or any earlier year. (Code Sec. 86(d)(2)(A))[34]

If any portion of a lump-sum social security benefit received during a tax year is attributable to an earlier (post-'83) tax year(s), the taxpayer can elect to include in gross income with respect to that portion, the sum of the increases in gross income that would have resulted had the portion been paid in the earlier year(s) to which it is attributable. (Code Sec. 86(e)(1))[35]

For tax years beginning after '93, a second tier calculation must be made to determine the includible amount. If provisional income exceeds an "adjusted base amount," taxpayer must include in gross income the lesser of:

- 85% of the social security benefits received that year; or

- the sum of: (a) the amount included under the above 50% rule or, if less, one-half of the difference between his "adjusted base amount" and "base amount," plus (b) 85% of the excess of provisional income over the "adjusted base amount." (Code Sec. 86(a)(2))

The "adjusted base amount" is $44,000 for married individuals filing jointly; zero for a married individual filing separately who does not live apart from his spouse for the entire tax year); and $34,000 for all other individuals. (Code Sec. 86(c)(2))

¶ 1284 Railroad Retirement Act benefits other than Tier 1 benefits.

Railroad Retirement Act benefits other than Tier 1 benefits subject to the rules at ¶ 1283 are treated as benefits provided under an employer plan that meets the requirements of Code Sec. 401(a), see ¶ 4320. (Code Sec. 72(r)(1), (3)) Lump-sum termination (early retirement) payments have been held to be taxable under these rules, not tax-free under other language in the Railroad Retirement Act.[36]

¶ 1285 Unemployment compensation.

Unemployment compensation is fully taxable. (Code Sec. 85(a)) "Unemployment compensation" means any amount received under a law of the U.S. or of a state which is in the nature of unemployment compensation. (Code Sec. 85(b)) It includes disability benefits paid under federal or state law as a substitute for unemployment benefits to individuals who are ineligible for unemployment benefits because they are disabled.[37]

---

31. ¶ J-1431; ¶ 864.04.   33. ¶ J-1432; ¶ 864.03.   35. ¶ J-1439; ¶ 864.08.   37. ¶ H-3007 *et seq.*; ¶ 854.01.
32. ¶ J-1433; ¶ 864.02.   34. ¶ J-1437.   36. ¶ J-1443.

Footnote references beginning with letters are to paragraphs in RIA's Federal Tax Coordinator 2d and RIA's Analysis of Federal Taxes: Income. Footnote references beginning with numbers are to paragraphs in RIA's United States Tax Reporter.

¶ 1286 Strike and lockout benefits.

Strike and lockout benefits paid to an employee by a union, from union dues, including both cash and the fair market value of goods received, are included in the employee's income unless the facts clearly show that the benefits are intended as a gift.[38]

¶ 1287 Certain military and government disability pensions.

Members of the armed forces of any country, or the National Oceanic and Atmospheric Administration, or the Public Health Service may be eligible to exclude from their gross income amounts received as pension, annuity or similar allowance for personal injuries or sickness resulting from active service. (Code Sec. 104(a)(4))[39]

¶ 1288 Dividends

A distribution of property by a corporation to its shareholders is taxed as ordinary income to the shareholders if it is a dividend. Not all corporate distributions are dividends. On the other hand, some transactions that don't appear to be dividends (e.g., a transaction structured as a loan by a corporation to its shareholder) may be taxed as a constructive dividend.

For other corporate distributions, e.g., liquidating distributions, see Chapter 16.

¶ 1289 How dividends are taxed to shareholders.

Dividends are taxed to the shareholders as ordinary income, to the extent the distributing corporation has earnings and profits (E&P). (Code Sec. 301(c)(1)) The part of a distribution in excess of E&P is treated as a tax-free return of capital and is applied against (reduces) the shareholder's basis in the stock. (Code Sec. 301(c)(2)) Any remaining excess (once basis is reduced to zero) is treated as payment for the stock, i.e., as capital gain if the stock is a capital asset in the shareholder's hands. (Code Sec. 301(c)(3))[40]

¶ 1290 Who is taxed on dividends?

Dividends are taxable to the person who has the present, enforceable right to receive them, whether or not he is the owner of the underlying stock.[41] Dividends received by an agent are taxable to his principal.[42]

If the stock is sold before a dividend is declared and paid, or between the declaration and record dates, the dividends are taxed to the buyer. Dividends on stock sold on or after the record date are taxed to the seller. (Reg § 1.61-9(c))[43]

¶ 1291 When dividends become taxable.

Dividends are taxable in the year received or unqualifiedly made subject to the shareholder's demand. This applies to both cash and accrual shareholders. Thus, if a corporation pays a dividend on Dec. 30 last year, and the shareholder receives the check on Jan. 2 this year, the shareholder reports it on this year's return. (Reg § 1.301-1(b))[44]

¶ 1292 Dividend defined.

A dividend is a distribution of property by a corporation to its shareholders with respect to its stock, out of accumulated or current earnings and profits. (Code Sec. 316(a)) The distribution must be made in the ordinary course of the corporation's business, but it may be extraordinary in amount. (Reg § 1.316-1(a)(1))[45]

---

38. ¶ H-3009.
39. ¶ H-3120; ¶ 1044.04.
40. ¶ J-2620 *et seq.*; ¶ 3014.06.
41. ¶ J-2701; ¶ 3014.04.
42. ¶ J-2705; ¶ 3014.04.
43. ¶ J-2706; ¶ 3014.04.
44. ¶ J-2751; ¶ 3014.07.
45. ¶ J-2626; ¶ 3164.

Footnote references beginning with letters are to paragraphs in RIA's Federal Tax Coordinator 2d and RIA's Analysis of Federal Taxes: Income. Footnote references beginning with numbers are to paragraphs in RIA's United States Tax Reporter.

"Property" includes money, securities and any other property except stock in the distributor corporation or rights to acquire that stock. (Code Sec. 317(a)) Property also includes any economic benefit the corporation gives its shareholders, in whatever form, (Reg § 1.317-1) e.g., paying their debts (see ¶ 1293).[46]

¶ 1293 Constructive or disguised dividends.

A dividend may result without a direct payment to the shareholder (assuming sufficient earnings and profits), if the corporation makes a payment to a third party that is for the shareholder's benefit and made with respect to his stock.[47]

It doesn't matter if dividends are prohibited or limited by state law, the corporate charter or agreements with creditors.[48] Nor does the fact that the other shareholders get nothing; a dividend needn't be proportionate and needn't be formally declared.[49] But proportionate advances tend to indicate dividends (see ¶ 1294).[50]

¶ 1294 Loan v. dividend.

A shareholder may borrow money from the corporation with or without interest, and with or without security. If the agreement and the genuine intent (at withdrawal) is that the amount be repaid to the corporation, and there is persuasive evidence of both that intent *and* the shareholder's ability to carry it out, the amount received is treated as a loan, and not as a dividend.[1] (But part of it still may be treated as a dividend if a below-market interest rate is involved, see ¶ 1296.)

¶ 1295 Excessive compensation or rent and other constructive dividend situations.

When excessive or unreasonably large amounts are paid to a shareholder or a member of his family as salary (Reg § 1.162-(7)(b)(1)) or rent, the excess is treated as a constructive dividend (assuming sufficient earnings and profits).[2] Other constructive dividend situations include:

■ bargain sales or rentals *to* shareholders or their families—dividends to the extent of the bargain;[3]

■ sales by a shareholder to the corporation at an inflated price—dividends to the extent of the excess;[4]

■ corporation's payments of a shareholder's debts[5] or personal expenses;[6]

■ using corporate funds to buy out other shareholders;[7]

■ diverting corporate income directly to the shareholders;[8]

■ shifting income between brother corporations; (Code Sec. 304)[9]

■ payment of corporation's debts by brother corporation—dividend by brother corporation to common shareholder. (Code Sec. 304)[10]

¶ 1296 Dividends from below-market interest rate loans between corporation and shareholder.

For any below-market interest rate loan (¶ 1310) made (directly or indirectly) between a corporation and a shareholder, the corporation/lender is treated as having paid a dividend, equal to the amount of the foregone interest, that is includible in the shareholder/borrower's income. Certain de minimis ($10,000 or less) loans are excepted. (Code Sec. 7872(a))[11]

---

46. ¶s J-2627, J-2635; ¶ 3174.
47. ¶ J-2900 *et seq.*; ¶ 3014.14.
48. ¶ J-2634.
49. ¶s J-2630, J-2900 *et seq.*; ¶ 3014.01.
50. ¶ J-2909; ¶ 3014.14.
1. ¶ J-2906 *et seq.*; ¶ 3014.14.
2. ¶ J-2921 *et seq.*; ¶ 3014.09.
3. ¶ J-2928 *et seq.*; ¶ 3014.11.
4. ¶ J-2923; ¶ 3014.11.
5. ¶ J-2938; ¶ 3014.14.
6. ¶ J-2946; ¶ 3014.13.
7. ¶ J-2964; ¶ 3014.11.
8. ¶ J-2960; ¶ 3014.14.
9. ¶ J-2965.
10. ¶ J-2968.
11. ¶ J-2920; ¶ 78,724 *et seq.*

Footnote references beginning with letters are to paragraphs in RIA's Federal Tax Coordinator 2d and RIA's Analysis of Federal Taxes: Income. Footnote references beginning with numbers are to paragraphs in RIA's United States Tax Reporter.

¶ 1297 Determining the amount of a dividend (cash and in-kind).

The amount of a dividend is the sum of the cash plus the fair market value (FMV) of any other property received, (Code Sec. 301(b)(1)) reduced (but not below zero) by the amount of any liability: (1) of the corporation that the shareholder assumes in connection with the distribution, or (2) to which the property is subject. (Code Sec. 301(b)(2)) FMV is determined as of the date of distribution. (Code Sec. 301(b)(3))[12]

A dividend consisting of the corporation's obligations equals the FMV of the notes. (Reg § 1.301-1(d)) For amount of stock dividends, see ¶ 1302.

The above rules apply to both corporate (whether U.S. or foreign) and noncorporate shareholders,[13] as well as to dividends from a foreign corporation to its domestic corporate shareholder. (Code Sec. 245, Code Sec. 301(b)(1))[14] But a corporate shareholder may get a dividends-received deduction (see ¶ 3311 *et seq.*). (Code Sec. 301(c)(1), (e))[15]

¶ 1298 Basis for property received in distribution.

The basis to the shareholder (whether a corporation or individual) for property received as a dividend is the property's fair market value at distribution, (Code Sec. 301(d)) i.e., the amount treated as a dividend (see ¶ 1297) but without the reduction for liabilities.[16]

¶ 1299 Holding period for property received.

The shareholder's holding period for property received as a taxable dividend begins on the date of receipt (actual or constructive). (Code Sec. 1223(2))[17]

¶ 1300 Receipt of stock or rights to stock.

With certain exceptions (see ¶ 1301), a "stock dividend," i.e., a corporation's distribution of its own stock, or rights (e.g., options or warrants) to buy its stock, that is made with respect to the shareholder's stock (i.e., not as compensation) is not taxable to the shareholder. (Code Sec. 305) But a corporation's distribution of stock, or rights to buy stock, in *another* corporation (even if affiliated) is a "regular" dividend in kind, taxed under the rules at ¶ 1297.[18]

Stock splits are treated as stock dividends if identical stock is distributed on the stock held.[19]

For special rules for stock (rights) received in connection with corporate organizations, reorganizations or divisions, see Chapter 16.

¶ 1301 Taxable stock dividends (or rights).

All stock dividends (or rights) are tax-free *except*:

(1) a distribution in which *any* shareholder has the option to take cash or other property instead of the stock (or rights); (Code Sec. 305(b)(1); Reg § 1.305-2)[20]

(2) a "disproportionate" distribution that results in the receipt of property by some shareholders and, for others, an increase in their proportionate interests in the corporation's assets or earnings and profits; (Code Sec. 305(b)(2); Reg § 1.305-3)[21]

(3) a distribution that results in the receipt of preferred stock by some common shareholders and the receipt of common stock by others; (Code Sec. 305(b)(3); Reg § 1.305-4)[22]

(4) any distributions in respect of preferred stock, including a redemption premium treated as a distribution (for preferred stock issued after Oct. 9, '90, the premium is included as OID, see ¶ 1319 *et seq.*), *other than* an increase in the conversion ratio of convertible preferred made solely to take into account a stock dividend or stock split with

---

12. ¶s J-2776, J-2777; ¶ 3014.02.   15. ¶s J-2777, J-2781, J-2806;   17. ¶s I-8903, I-8918.   20. ¶s J-2808 *et seq.*, J-2801.
13. ¶ J-2777; ¶ 3014.02.   ¶ 2434 *et seq.*   18. ¶ J-2773; ¶ 3054.01.   21. ¶s J-2827 *et seq.*, J-2801.
14. ¶ J-2782; ¶ 3014.02(1).   16. ¶ J-2779; ¶ 3014.02(2).   19. ¶ J-2801.   22. ¶s J-2801, J-2832.

Footnote references beginning with letters are to paragraphs in RIA's Federal Tax Coordinator 2d and RIA's Analysis of Federal Taxes: Income. Footnote references beginning with numbers are to paragraphs in RIA's United States Tax Reporter.

respect to the stock into which the preferred is convertible; (Code Sec. 305(b)(4); Reg § 1.305-5)[23]

(5) any distribution of convertible preferred stock unless IRS is satisfied it won't have the result in (2), above; (Code Sec. 305(b)(5); Reg § 1.305-6)[24]

(6) constructive stock distributions, e.g., a change in conversion ratio or redemption price. (Code Sec. 305(c); Reg § 1.305-7)[25]

¶ 1302 Amount of taxable stock (or rights) dividend.

Where a stock (or rights) dividend is taxable, the dividend amount is the fair market value (FMV) at distribution, of the stock (rights), under the "regular" dividend-in-kind rules (¶ 1297).[26] Where the dividend is taxable because of a cash election, the "dividend" equals: (1) the cash received, for shareholders electing cash, and (2) the FMV at distribution, of the stock (rights), for those receiving stock (rights). (Reg § 1.305-1(b))[27]

A stock (or rights) dividend on preferred stock is taxable only to the extent of the preference dividends discharged. (Reg § 1.305-5(d))[28]

¶ 1303 Cash for fractional shares.

Where a corporation's purpose in distributing cash (instead of scrip or fractional shares) in a distribution that otherwise qualifies as a nontaxable stock dividend is to save trouble, expense and inconvenience, and not to give any shareholder(s) an increased interest, the distribution is a nontaxable stock dividend. (Reg § 1.305-3(c)) The cash received is treated as an amount realized on the sale of a fractional share. The gain or loss is the cash received minus the basis of the share sold. (Reg § 1.305-3(c)(2))[29]

¶ 1304 Dividends from regulated investment companies.

Ordinary dividends a regulated investment company (RIC, see ¶ 4201) distributes to its shareholders are taxed to them just like other corporate dividends (¶ 1297). (Code Sec. 852; Reg § 1.852-4(a))[30] But capital gain dividends, which the RIC need not actually distribute, result in capital gain income for them, (Code Sec. 852(b)(3)(D))[31] and exempt-interest dividends are treated as tax-exempt interest (¶ 1335). (Code Sec. 852(b)(5)(B))[32]

For year-end dividends, and dividends paid after the RIC's tax year ends, see ¶ 4203.

¶ 1305 Dividends from real estate investment trusts.

Real estate investment trusts (REITs, see ¶ 4202) distribute ordinary dividends and capital gain dividends which (as with RICs, see ¶ 1304) the beneficiaries or shareholders (investors) treat, respectively, as ordinary income (except there's no dividends-received deduction) (Code Sec. 857(c)) and capital gain. (Code Sec. 857(b)(3)(B))[33]

For year-end dividends, and dividends paid after the REIT's tax year ends, see ¶ 4203.

¶ 1306 Dividends to co-op patrons.

Distributions made by a co-op on its stock or other proprietary interests are taxed under the "regular" dividend rules (¶ 1297). But the dividends-received deduction doesn't apply if the co-op is exempt. (Code Sec. 246(a)(1))[34]

Patronage dividends and per-unit retain allocations received in money are included in income by the patron in the year received. Qualified written notices of allocation and qualified per-unit retain certificates are included in income at their stated dollar amount when received. Other property (but not nonqualified allocations or nonqualified per-unit

23. ¶s J-2801, J-2833 *et seq.*
24. ¶s J-2801, J-2843 *et seq.*
25. ¶s J-2801, J-2844 *et seq.*; ¶ 3054.02.
26. ¶s J-2806, J-2824; ¶ 3054.02.
27. ¶ J-2809; ¶ 3054.03.
28. ¶ J-2833.
29. ¶ J-2816; ¶ 3054.01.
30. ¶ E-6159; ¶ 8524.02.
31. ¶ E-6152; ¶ 8524.02.
32. ¶ E-6160; ¶ 8524.02.
33. ¶ E-6616; ¶ 8574.02.
34. ¶ J-2867.

Footnote references beginning with letters are to paragraphs in RIA's Federal Tax Coordinator 2d and RIA's Analysis of Federal Taxes: Income. Footnote references beginning with numbers are to paragraphs in RIA's United States Tax Reporter.

retain certificates) is included at its fair market value when received. (Code Sec. 1385)[35]

But the amount of any patronage dividend isn't included in income to the extent it is: (1) properly taken into account as an adjustment to basis of property, or (2) attributable to personal, living or family items. (Code Sec. 1385(b))[36]

For discussion of co-ops, patronage dividends, and related terms, see ¶ 4206 *et seq.*

¶ *1307* Interest Income ▬▬▬▬▬▬▬▬▬▬▬▬▬▬▬▬▬▬▬▬▬▬▬▬▬▬▬▬▬▬▬▬▬▬▬

Regardless of the name given to payments or the form of the transaction, interest received is generally fully taxable as ordinary income, unless specifically exempt.

¶ *1308* Taxation of interest.

Unless specifically exempt, interest is included in gross income. Any interest received by or credited to taxpayer is fully taxable as ordinary income. (Code Sec. 61(a)(4); Reg § 1.61-7(a))[37]

The interest is taxable even if it is usurious (unless applicable state law automatically converts the illegal portion into a payment of principal). (Reg § 1.61-7(a))[38]

¶ *1309* What is interest?

Interest is the price paid for the use of another's money or for the right to defer payment of money owed to another, regardless of the form of the transaction.[39]

Although to be interest, generally a payment must be made with respect to a bona fide debt,[40] other "interest" payments imposed by law, e.g., on judgments, tax refunds, installment sales, etc., are also interest.[41]

¶ *1310* Below-market interest-rate loans.

The foregone interest on a "below-market" loan is taxed to the lender as interest income. (Code Sec. 7872) A "below-market" loan means:

■ a demand loan where interest is payable on the loan at a rate less than the applicable federal rate (AFR, see ¶ 1314), (Code Sec. 7872(e)(1)(A)) or

■ a term loan where the amount loaned exceeds the present value of all payments due under the loan. (Code Sec. 7872(e)(1)(B))[42]

For a below-market demand loan, the "interest" for any period is the excess of: (1) the interest that would have been payable on the loan if it accrued annually at the AFR, over (2) any interest payable on the loan and properly allocable to the period. (Code Sec. 7872(e)(2)) For below-market term loans, the "interest" (treated as original issue discount, see ¶ 1318 *et seq.*) is the excess of: (1) the amount loaned, over (2) the present value of all payments required to be made under the loan. (Code Sec. 7872(b)(2)(B))[43]

¶ *1311* Unstated (imputed) interest on deferred payment sales.

For certain deferred payment or installment sales (¶ 1312) where the sales contract fails to provide for interest at a minimum rate specified by the Code or by IRS, part of the payments received is treated as interest ("unstated interest") that is taxable to the seller despite any contrary intention of the parties. (Code Sec. 483)[44]

A cash method seller includes unstated interest allocated to a payment as interest income in the tax year the payment is received. An accrual method seller includes the unstated interest in the tax year the payment is due. (Reg § 1.483-2(a)(1)(ii))[45]

---

35. ¶ J-2868 *et seq.*; ¶ 13,814.13.
36. ¶ J-2871; ¶ 13,814.13.
37. ¶ J-2976.
38. ¶ J-2989; ¶ 614.068.
39. ¶ J-2977 *et seq.*; ¶ 614.067.
40. ¶ J-2978; ¶ 614.068.
41. ¶ J-3008 *et seq.*.
42. ¶ J-3033 *et seq.*
43. ¶s J-3035, J-3037.
44. ¶ J-3450 *et seq.*; ¶ 4834.
45. ¶ J-3454; ¶ 4834.01.

Footnote references beginning with letters are to paragraphs in RIA's Federal Tax Coordinator 2d and RIA's Analysis of Federal Taxes: Income. Footnote references beginning with numbers are to paragraphs in RIA's United States Tax Reporter.

¶ 1312 Payments subject to unstated interest rules.

With certain exceptions (¶ 1317), the unstated interest rules apply to any payment where *all* the following requirements are met:

(1) The payment must be made on account of the sale or exchange of property.

(2) The payment must be part of the sales price under the contract.

(3) The "sales price" (determined at the time of sale) must be more than $3,000. "Sales price" includes the amount of any down payment, any liability encumbering the property, and any amount treated as unstated interest under these rules, but not any *stated* interest payments.

(4) The payment must be due (under the contract) more than six months after the date of the sale or exchange.

(5) At least one payment under the contract must be due more than one year after the date of the sale or exchange.

(6) There must be total unstated interest (¶ 1313) under the contract. (Code Sec. 483(c)(1); Reg § 1.483-1(b)(1), Reg § 1.483-2(b)(1)(i))[46]

A debt instrument of the buyer given in exchange for property is not itself treated as a payment. Rather, any payment due under the instrument is treated as due under the sales contract. (Code Sec. 483(c)(2))[47]

¶ 1313 What is "total unstated interest"?

There is "total unstated interest" under the contract if the sum of all payments (other than *stated* interest payments) due under it more than six months after the date of the sale or exchange exceeds the sum of: (1) the present value of all those payments, plus (2) the present value of all interest payments due under the contract (regardless of when due). The total unstated interest equals the excess, if any. (Code Sec. 483(b))[48]

The present value of a payment is determined as of the date of the sale, etc., using a "test" rate prescribed by IRS. This test rate, which depends on the type of property sold, is a discount rate equal to the then applicable federal rate (¶ 1314) compounded semi-annually. (Code Sec. 483(b), Code Sec. 1274(b)(2))[49]

¶ 1314 Applicable federal rate (AFR).

IRS issues tables (reproduced at ¶ 1116) showing the AFRs to be used in determining whether there is unstated interest (or OID in some cases, see ¶ 1322) on a sale or exchange of property, and if there is, the amount of that unstated interest. The tables show short-term, mid-term and long-term rates.[50]

The rate to use on a particular sale or exchange depends on the term over which the payments are to be made. If the term is three years or less, use the short-term rate. If the term is more than three years but not more than nine years, use the mid-term rate. If the term is more than nine years, use the long-term rate. (Code Sec. 1274(d)(1)(A))[1]

The rate to use also depends on when the contract for the sale, etc., was made. (Code Sec. 1274(d)(2))[2]

¶ 1315 Determining amount of total unstated interest.

The amount of total unstated interest the seller must report as interest income on a deferred payment sale is determined in the same manner used to determine whether there is total unstated interest under the contract (¶ 1313). (Code Sec. 483(b))[3]

The following discount rates are used:

---

46. ¶ J-3500 *et seq.*; ¶ 4834.01.
47. ¶ J-3505; ¶ 4834.01.
48. ¶ J-3511; ¶ 4834.01.
49. ¶ J-3511 *et seq.*; ¶ 4834.01.
50. ¶ J-3742 *et seq.*
1. ¶ J-3742.; ¶ 12,714.01.
2. ¶ J-3744 *et seq.*
3. ¶ J-3512 *et seq.*; ¶ 4834.01.

Footnote references beginning with letters are to paragraphs in RIA's Federal Tax Coordinator 2d and RIA's Analysis of Federal Taxes: Income. Footnote references beginning with numbers are to paragraphs in RIA's United States Tax Reporter.

(1) For sales or exchanges of property (except those described below), the discount rate may not exceed 9% compounded semiannually if the stated principal amount of the debt instrument is not over a specified amount, as adjusted for inflation. The specified amount is $3,332,400 for sales and exchanges in '93. If the stated principal amount is over the specified amount, the discount rate is 100% of the AFR (¶ 1314), compounded semiannually. (Code Sec. 483(b), Code Sec. 1274A(a))[4]

(2) For sales or exchanges of new investment credit property, the discount rate is 100% of the AFR, compounded semiannually. (Code Sec. 483(b))[5]

(3) For sales or exchanges where part of the sold property is leased back to the seller, the discount rate is 110% of the AFR, compounded semiannually. (Code Sec. 1274(e))[6]

(4) For sales or exchanges of land between family members where the aggregate sales price for all land sales between those individuals in that calendar year is not over $500,000, the discount rate can't exceed 6% compounded semiannually. (Code Sec. 483(e))[7]

¶ 1316 Allocating total unstated interest.

For any deferred payment to which the unstated interest rules apply, that part of the total unstated interest under the contract (¶ 1315) which is properly allocable to that payment is treated as interest. This "interest" amount is determined in a manner consistent with the method used to compute the amount of currently includible OID (¶ 1325). (Code Sec. 483(a)) This means that unstated interest income must be reported on an economic accrual basis.[8]

¶ 1317 Exceptions to unstated interest rules.

Even if all the requirements listed at ¶ 1312 are met, there's no unstated interest on:

(1) sales or exchanges where the sales price (¶ 1312) is $3,000 or less; (Code Sec. 483(d)(2))[9]

(2) any debt instrument given in connection with a sale or exchange of property if the instrument's issue price is figured under the OID rules (¶ 1319 et seq.); (Code Sec. 483(d)(1))[10]

(3) any amount received on the sale of patent rights described in Code Sec. 1235(a) that is contingent on the productivity, use or disposition of those rights; (Code Sec. 483(d)(4))[11]

(4) payments made under a tax-exempt obligation issued by a buyer such as a state or municipal government; (Reg § 1.483-1(d)(3)(i))[12]

(5) amounts received under certain annuity contracts;[13]

(6) lump-sum divorce payments and property settlements payable in installments;[14]

(7) distributions in complete liquidation of a corporation (even if made in a series of distributions over more than one year); (Reg § 1.483-1(b)(1))[15]

(8) sales or exchanges made under a binding written contract entered into before July, '63, unless the contract was substantially changed after June, '63. (Reg § 1.483-1(b)(4))[16]

¶ 1318 Current inclusion of original issue discount (OID) as interest income.

If a debt instrument is acquired from an issuer for an amount that is less than the amount the issuer will have to pay the holder when the instrument matures, the difference is original issue discount (OID). No matter which method of accounting the holder uses, he must report a part of the OID as interest income in each tax year the debt

---

4. ¶ J-3513 et seq.; ¶ 4834.01.   8. ¶ J-3581.   11. ¶ J-3568; ¶ 4834.01.   14. ¶ J-3570.
5. ¶ J-3515; ¶ 12,714.01(c).   9. ¶ J-3566; ¶ 4834.01.   12. ¶ J-3572.   15. ¶ J-3571.
6. ¶ J-3516; ¶ 12,714.01(c).   10. ¶ J-3567; ¶ 4834.01.   13. ¶ J-3569; ¶ 4834.01.   16. ¶ J-3574.
7. ¶ J-3517; ¶ 4834.01.

Footnote references beginning with letters are to paragraphs in RIA's Federal Tax Coordinator 2d and RIA's Analysis of Federal Taxes: Income. Footnote references beginning with numbers are to paragraphs in RIA's United States Tax Reporter.

instrument is held, even though the OID won't be paid until maturity (¶ 1325). (Code Sec. 1272)[17]

The current inclusion rule does not apply to a holder who purchases a debt instrument at a premium. (Code Sec. 1275(a)(1))[18]

Debt instruments subject to the OID current inclusion rules are bonds, debentures, notes, certificates or other evidences of indebtedness (e.g., face amount certificates, certificates of deposit). (Code Sec. 1275(a)(1); Reg § 1.1232-1(c)(1))[19]

These rules also apply to bonds, and preferred stock purchased after Apr. 30, '93, if purchased after being stripped. (Code Sec. 305(e); Code Sec. 1286(a))[20]

But these rules *don't apply* to:

(1) Tax-exempt obligations (unless stripped). (Code Sec. 1272(a)(2)(A), Code Sec. 1286(d))

(2) U.S. savings bonds. (Code Sec. 1272(a)(2)(B))

(3) Short-term obligations (i.e., with a fixed maturity date not more than one year from the date of issue). (Code Sec. 1272(a)(2)(C))

(4) Debt instruments issued by natural persons before Mar. 2, '84. (Code Sec. 1272(a)(2)(D))

(5) Certain nonbusiness loans of $10,000 or less between natural persons. (Code Sec. 1272(a)(2)(E))

(6) Debt instruments (other than corporate debt instruments) issued before July 2, '82. (Code Sec. 1272(a), (b))

(7) Face amount certificates issued before '76. (Reg § 1.1232-1(c)(3))

(8) Corporate debt instruments issued before May 28, '69. (Code Sec. 1272(b))[21]

¶ 1319 OID defined.

The OID on a debt instrument is the excess (if any) of: (1) the instrument's stated redemption price at maturity (¶ 1320), over (2) its issue price (¶ 1321). (Code Sec. 1273(a)(1))[22]

The OID is treated as zero, however, if that excess is less than: 0.25% of the stated redemption price at maturity, multiplied by the number of years to maturity. (Code Sec. 1273(a)(3))[23]

¶ 1320 Stated redemption price at maturity.

For OID purposes, an instrument's *stated redemption price at maturity* is usually its face value. It includes interest payable at maturity *but not* interest payable at a fixed rate at periodic intervals of a year or less during the entire term of the instrument. (Code Sec. 1273(a)(2))[24]

¶ 1321 Issue price.

The issue price of a debt instrument depends on whether it is issued for cash or property, and if issued for property, whether the instrument or property is publicly traded:

■ For a *publicly offered debt instrument issued for money,* the issue price is the initial offering price to the public at which a substantial amount of the instruments is sold. (Code Sec. 1273(b)(1))[25]

■ For a *privately offered debt instrument issued for money,* the issue price is the price

---

17. ¶ J-3600 *et seq.*; ¶ 12,714.01(a).
18. ¶ J-3603; ¶ 12,714.
19. ¶s J-3653, J-3654; ¶ 12,714.
20. ¶ J-3900 *et seq.*
21. ¶ J-3657 *et seq.*; ¶ 12,714.
22. ¶ J-3700 *et seq.*; ¶ 12,714.
23. ¶ J-3702; ¶ 12,714.
24. ¶ J-3704.
25. ¶ J-3717.

Footnote references beginning with letters are to paragraphs in RIA's Federal Tax Coordinator 2d and RIA's Analysis of Federal Taxes: Income. Footnote references beginning with numbers are to paragraphs in RIA's United States Tax Reporter.

paid by the first buyer of that instrument. (Code Sec. 1273(b)(2))[26]

■ For a *debt instrument issued for property where there is public trading,* the issue price is the instrument's fair market value (FMV), if it's publicly traded. If the instrument itself is not publicly traded but is issued for property (i.e., stock or securities) that is publicly traded, its issue price is the FMV of that property. (Code Sec. 1273(b)(3); Reg § 1.1232-3(b)(2)(iii))[27]

■ For a *nonpublicly traded debt instrument issued for nonpublicly traded property,* the issue price is its stated principal amount, if the instrument pays adequate stated interest (¶ 1322), or its imputed principal amount (¶ 1323), if it does not. (Code Sec. 1274(a))[28] For exceptions, see ¶ 1324.

¶ 1322 Adequate stated interest.

There is adequate stated interest for a debt instrument if the sum of the present values of all payments of principal and interest due under it equals or exceeds its stated principal amount. The present values are determined using the same discount rate used to determine the imputed principal amount (¶ 1323). (Code Sec. 1274(c)(2))[29]

¶ 1323 Imputed principal amount.

The imputed principal amount of a debt instrument is the sum of the present values of all payments of principal and interest due under it, computed as of the date of the sale or exchange by using the discount rates at ¶ 1315 (Code Sec. 1274(b)(2)).[30]

In a "potentially abusive situation" (e.g., a tax shelter), the imputed principal amount of a debt instrument received in exchange for property is the fair market value of that property, adjusted to account for other considerations involved in the transaction. (Code Sec. 1274(b)(3)(A))[31]

¶ 1324 Exceptions to imputed OID rules for nonpublicly traded debt instruments.

The issue price of a nonpublicly traded debt instrument issued for nonpublicly traded property is its stated redemption price at maturity (so that there is no OID), instead of the amount determined under the rules at ¶ 1321, in these transactions: (Code Sec. 1273(b)(4))[32]

(1) sales involving total payments of $250,000 or less; (Code Sec. 1274(e)(3)(C))

(2) sales or exchanges by an individual of his principal residence; (Code Sec. 1274(c)(3)(B))

(3) sales or exchanges of certain farms where the sales price cannot exceed $1,000,000; (Code Sec. 1274(c)(3)(A))

(4) certain sales of patents; (Code Sec. 1274(c)(3)(E))

(5) certain transfers of land between related taxpayers where the total price for all land sales between them for the year is not more than $500,000; (Code Sec. 1274(c)(3)(F))

(6) sales or exchanges (after June 30, '85) where, in exchange for property, a nonaccrual method buyer (other than a dealer) issues a debt instrument whose principal amount doesn't exceed a specified amount ($2,380,300 for sales and exchanges in '93), if the "regular" issue price rules otherwise would apply *and* buyer and seller jointly elect cash method treatment for the instrument; (Code Sec. 1274A(c))

(7) sales or exchanges before July 1, '85 (and after '84), of certain farm property.[33]

observation: Even if there is no OID because the rules described at ¶ 1321 don't

---

26. ¶ J-3720.

27. ¶ J-3722.

28. ¶ J-3724; ¶ 12,714.01(c).

29. ¶ J-3725 *et seq.*; ¶ 12,714.01(c).

30. ¶ J-3726 *et seq.*; ¶ 12,714.01(c).

31. ¶ J-3738 *et seq.*; ¶ 12,714.01(c).

32. ¶s J-3701, J-3766.

33. ¶ J-3750 *et seq.*; ¶ 12,714.01(c).

Footnote references beginning with letters are to paragraphs in RIA's Federal Tax Coordinator 2d and RIA's Analysis of Federal Taxes: Income. Footnote references beginning with numbers are to paragraphs in RIA's United States Tax Reporter.

apply, there may still be unstated interest under the rules at ¶ 1311.

¶ 1325 Determining amount of currently includible OID.

A holder of a debt instrument issued (after '84) with OID who is required to include part of the OID in gross income currently must include in gross income for his tax year, an amount equal to the sum of the daily portions of the OID for each day that he held the debt instrument during that year. (Code Sec. 1272(a)(1))[34]

To determine the daily OID portion, allocate to each day in any "accrual period" (below) that day's ratable portion of the increase (during that period) in the instrument's adjusted issue price (below). This increase equals the excess of: (1) the adjusted issue price at the beginning of the accrual period multiplied by the yield to maturity (based on compounding at the end of each accrual period), over (2) the sum of the amounts payable as interest on the instrument during that accrual period. (Code Sec. 1272(a)(3))[35]

The adjusted issue price of a debt instrument at the beginning of any accrual period equals the sum of its issue price, plus all adjustments (i.e., OID inclusions) in that issue price for all earlier accrual periods. (Code Sec. 1272(a)(4))[36]

Accrual period generally means a six-month period (or shorter period from date of issuance) ending on a day in the calendar year corresponding to the debt instrument's maturity date, or a date six months before that date. (Code Sec. 1272(a)(5))[37]

illustration: On July 16, Year 1, S Corporation issues a debt instrument with a face value of $100,000 (its stated redemption price at maturity) to L, a calendar year taxpayer, for an issue price of $79,215. The debt instrument matures on July 15, Year 3, and pays no interest currently. The yield to maturity is 12%. The total amount of OID is $20,785 ($100,000 − $79,215). L computes the amount of OID he includes in gross income in Year 1 as follows:

(1) Multiply the issue price of $79,215 by .12. The result is $9,505.

(2) Divide $9,505 by 2. The result is $4,753.

(3) Divide $4,753 by 184 (the number of days in the first accrual period which begins on July 16, Year 1, and ends on Jan. 15, Year 3, the date that corresponds to the date that is six months before the maturity date). The result is $25.83.

(4) Multiply $25.83 by 169 (the number of days in the first accrual period that fall within L's Year 1 tax year). The result is $4,365.27. This is the part of the OID that L includes in gross income as interest income in Year 1. The balance of the OID for the first accrual period is included in L's taxable income in Year 2.

¶ 1326 OID inclusion where holder paid acquisition premium.

If the holder of a debt instrument bought it from someone other than the original issuer, paying an acquisition premium (i.e., an amount in excess of the original issue price plus all OID required to be included in the gross income of earlier holders), then the holder's current OID inclusion (¶ 1325) is reduced. This is done by reducing each daily includible OID portion by this constant fraction: the numerator is the acquisition premium, and the denominator is the total OID (before reduction) allocable to the days after the purchase date and ending on the date of maturity. However, the reduction applies only to the OID inclusion and isn't taken into account in computing the instrument's adjusted issue price at the beginning of an accrual period.(Code Sec. 1272(a)(7))[38]

---

34. ¶ J-3801; ¶ 12,714.01(a). 36. ¶ J-3802; ¶ 12,714.01(a). 37. ¶ J-3801; ¶ 12,714.01(a). 38. ¶ J-3810; ¶ 12,714.01(a).
35. ¶ J-3801; ¶ 12,714.01(a).

Footnote references beginning with letters are to paragraphs in RIA's Federal Tax Coordinator 2d and RIA's Analysis of Federal Taxes: Income. Footnote references beginning with numbers are to paragraphs in RIA's United States Tax Reporter.

¶ 1327 Accrued market discount on disposition of "market discount bonds."

Gain on the disposition of any "market discount bond" (¶ 1329) is treated as ordinary income to the extent of the "accrued market discount" (¶ 1330) on the bond (Code Sec. 1276(a)(1), (e)) (unless the holder elects to include the market discount currently, see ¶ 1331). These ordinary income amounts are treated as interest income, with certain exceptions. (Code Sec. 1276(a)(4))[39]

The accrued market discount "interest" is computed under a "ratable accrual" method or, at taxpayer's election, a "constant interest rate" method. (Code Sec. 1276(b))[40]

Dispositions by gift and transfers to controlled corporations also can result in interest income under this rule. (Code Sec. 1276(d)(1)(A))[41] If the disposition is other than by sale, exchange or involuntary conversion, the amount realized is equal to the bond's fair market value. (Code Sec. 1276(a)(2))[42]

This interest treatment applies even if the gain wouldn't otherwise be recognized, but regs may provide for nonrecognition in certain nontaxable transactions. (Code Sec. 1276(a)(1), (d)(1))[43]

¶ 1328 Accrued market discount when partial principal payment made.

If the principal on a market discount bond (acquired after Oct. 22, '86) is paid in more than one installment, then any partial principal payment is included as ordinary income to the extent of the accrued market discount on the bond. (Code Sec. 1276(a)(3)(A))[44]

Any amount that has been included in gross income under this rule reduces the amount of any accrued market discount that is included on any later disposition of, or further partial principal payments on, the bond. (Code Sec. 1276(a)(3)(B))[45]

If bond principal can be paid in two or more payments, the accrued market discount is to be determined under regs. (Code Sec. 1276(b)(3))[46]

¶ 1329 Market discount bonds.

Market discount bonds are any "bonds" having a "market discount" (¶ 1330), except for short-term obligations (one year or less), bonds issued before July 19, '84 if bought before May 1, '93, tax-exempt obligations bought before May, 1, '93, U.S. savings bonds and certain installment obligations. (Code Sec. 1278(a)(1)(A), (B))[47]

¶ 1330 "Market discount" defined.

The market discount on a bond is the excess (if any) of its stated redemption price at maturity (¶ 1320) over taxpayer's basis for the bond immediately after acquiring it. (Code Sec. 1278(a)(2))[48] The market discount is zero if it is less than a specified de minimis amount. (Code Sec. 1278(a)(2)(C))[49]

Special rules determine the stated redemption price at maturity for this purpose if the bond was issued with OID. (Code Sec. 1278(a)(4))[50]

¶ 1331 Election to include accrued market discount in income currently.

Instead of including a bond's accrued market discount as interest income on disposition (¶ 1327), taxpayer may elect to include the discount in gross income for the tax years to which it is attributable, i.e., currently. Taxpayer may use either the ratable accrual method or the constant interest rate method. (Code Sec. 1278(b)(1)(B))[1]

---

39. ¶ J-3951; ¶ 12,764.   43. ¶s J-3951, J-3965;   46. ¶ J-3964.   49. ¶ J-3954; ¶ 12,764.01.
40. ¶ J-3959; ¶ 12,764.01.   ¶ 12,764.01.   47. ¶s J-3952, J-3956;   50. ¶ J-3953; ¶ 12,764.01.
41. ¶ J-3966; ¶ 12,764.01.   44. ¶ J-3962; ¶ 12,764.01.   ¶ 12,764.01.   1. ¶ J-3969; ¶ 12,764.01.
42. ¶ J-3951; ¶ 12,764.01.   45. ¶ J-3963; ¶ 12,764.01.   48. ¶ J-3953; ¶ 12,764.01.

Footnote references beginning with letters are to paragraphs in RIA's Federal Tax Coordinator 2d and RIA's Analysis of Federal Taxes: Income. Footnote references beginning with numbers are to paragraphs in RIA's United States Tax Reporter.

Elect by attaching to a timely filed income tax return, a statement that market discount has been included in gross income under Code Sec. 1278(b), describing the method used to determine the amount attributable to that tax year.[2]

¶ 1332 Acquisition discount on certain short-term obligations.

Certain holders (below) of short-term obligations are currently taxed on their daily portions of the "acquisition discount" (for government obligations, or nongovernment obligations if the holder so elects) or OID (for nongovernment obligations), for each day during the year that they hold the obligation. Any other interest payable on the obligation also must be taken into account as it accrues. (Code Sec. 1281(a), Code Sec. 1283(c))[3]

This mandatory accrual of market discount applies to any obligation having a term of not more than one year that is:

(1) held by an accrual basis taxpayer;

(2) held primarily for sale to customers in the ordinary course of taxpayer's trade or business;

(3) held by a bank, regulated investment company, or common trust fund (Chapter 20);

(4) a stripped bond or stripped coupon which taxpayer stripped and retains; or

(5) identified by taxpayer as being part of a hedging transaction. (Code Sec. 1281(b)(1))[4]

An obligation's "acquisition discount" is the excess of its stated redemption price at maturity (¶ 1320) over taxpayer's basis in it. (Code Sec. 1283(a)(2))[5]

The daily portion of the acquisition discount may be computed by the ratable accrual method or, if taxpayer so elects, the constant interest method. (Code Sec. 1283(b))[6]

The mandatory accrual rule does not apply to short-term loans a commercial bank makes to its customers in the ordinary course of its business.[7]

Special rules apply to obligations held by pass-through entities. (Code Sec. 1281(b)(2))[8]

¶ 1333 Computing interest when marketable bonds are sold.

When fixed-interest bonds (not in default) are sold between interest dates, the amount paid by the buyer which represents the interest accrued as of the sale date is taxable interest to the seller. (Reg § 1.61-7(d)) Interest accrued after the sale date is taxable to the buyer on receipt.[9]

Bonds in default are usually traded "flat" (no part of the selling price is allocated between interest and principal). If there is accrued interest, the part of the selling price that represents interest accrued before the sale is taxable interest to the seller.[10]

¶ 1334 Interest credited to frozen deposits.

Interest credited to a frozen deposit (i.e., in a bankrupt or insolvent (actual or threatened) financial institution) during a calendar year, that is includible in the depositor's income for the year, can't exceed the sum of the net withdrawals during the year plus the amount withdrawable at the end of the year. (Code Sec. 451(g)(1))[11]

¶ 1335 Tax-exempt interest.

Interest on all state and local bonds (i.e., obligations of a state, the District of Columbia, a U.S. possession, certain Indian tribal governments or any political subdivision of the foregoing) is exempt from federal income tax. (Code Sec. 103(a), (c); Code Sec. 7871(a)(4))[12] For special "educational expense" exclusion for certain U.S. savings bonds, see ¶ 1338 *et seq.*

---

2. ¶ J-3969.1.

3. ¶s J-3931, J-3936; ¶ 12,814.

4. ¶ J-3932; ¶ 12,814.

5. ¶ J-3931; ¶ 12,814.01.

6. ¶ J-3930; ¶ 12,814.01.

7. ¶ J-3931.

8. ¶ J-3932; ¶ 12,814.

9. ¶ J-3002.

10. ¶ J-3003 *et seq.*

11. ¶ J-3410; ¶ 4514.185.

12. ¶ J-3060; ¶ 1034.

Footnote references beginning with letters are to paragraphs in RIA's Federal Tax Coordinator 2d and RIA's Analysis of Federal Taxes: Income. Footnote references beginning with numbers are to paragraphs in RIA's United States Tax Reporter.

✪observation: Even if interest isn't subject to federal income tax, it may have to be taken into account, e.g., in calculating the taxable portion of social security benefits (¶ 1283), for alternative minimum tax purposes for certain bonds (¶ 3207), and in calculating earnings and profits (¶ 3522). There is also a bar against deducting interest on debt incurred or continued to buy or carry tax-exempt bonds (¶ 1719).

Every person required to file a return must report on it all eax-exempt interest received or accrued during the tax year. (Code Sec. 6012(d))[13]

The interest exemption *does not apply* to arbitrage bonds, (Code Sec. 103(a), (b)(2))[14] hedge bonds, (Code Sec. 149(g))[15] private activity bonds that aren't "qualified," (Code Sec. 103(b)(1))[16] or to pre-Aug. 16, '86 industrial development bonds.[17]

¶ 1336   50% exclusion for interest on certain ESOP loans.

Banks, insurance companies, regulated investment companies and corporations actively engaged in the business of lending money can exclude 50% of the interest they earn on "securities acquisition loans," i.e., certain loans to ESOPs (¶ 4315), or to companies with ESOPs, where the loan proceeds are used to buy employer securities. (Code Sec. 133)[18]

¶ 1337   Interest on U.S. savings bonds.

Interest on U.S. savings bonds now being issued is earned in two ways: On Series HH "face amount" bonds, it is paid semiannually by check. On Series EE "discount" bonds, it is reflected as an increase in the bond's value over stated periods. The interest on these bonds (and on any unmatured or extended Series E and Series H bonds now outstanding) is fully taxable unless the exclusion at ¶ 1338 applies.[19]

Cash basis taxpayers must report the interest on Series HH (or H) bonds in the year received. (Reg § 352.2)[20]

A cash basis owner of Series EE bonds (and outstanding Series E bonds) may either: (1) defer reporting any interest (i.e., the bond's increase in value) until the year of final maturity, redemption, or other disposition, whichever is earlier, or (2) elect to report the annual increase in value in each year's return. (The owner may also exchange the bonds for Series HH bonds to continue the above tax-deferral.) (Reg § 351.8(b), (c))[21]

Some Series E bonds can, at the owner's option, be held up to 30 years beyond their original maturity ("final maturity"). A cash basis owner who hasn't elected to report the interest on a Series E bond annually (under (2), above) must report all of the interest on the bond in the year in which the bond is redeemed or disposed of or, if earlier, the year in which it reaches "final maturity." (Code Sec. 454(a); Reg § 1.454-1(a)(1))[22]

✪observation: Series E bonds issued before Dec., '65 reach final maturity 40 years after their issue date. Series E bonds issued after Nov., '65, and all Series EE bonds, reach final maturity 30 years after their issue dates. This means that any accrued interest on Series E bonds issued in '53 is taxable in '93 (except for E bonds that are exchanged for HH bonds).

Accrual basis taxpayers include the interest on the above bonds as it accrues.[23]

¶ 1338   Exclusion of U.S. savings bond redemption income by individual who pays higher education expenses.

An individual who pays qualified higher education expenses (¶ 1340) during a tax year

---

13. ¶ J-3060.1.
14. ¶ J-3270 *et seq.*; ¶ 1484 *et seq.*
15. ¶ J-3312.4 *et seq.*; ¶ 1496.06.
16. ¶s J-3060 *et seq.*, J-3100, J-3231 *et seq.*, J-3270; ¶ 1414.01.
17. ¶s J-3152 *et seq.*, J-3208 *et seq.*, J-3230; ¶ 1034.01.
18. ¶ J-3016 *et seq.*; ¶ 1334 *et seq.*
19. ¶s J-3073, J-3418 *et seq.*; ¶ 4544.01.
20. ¶s J-3419, J-3420; ¶ 90,850.
21. ¶ J-3418; ¶ 4544.03.
22. ¶s J-3420, J-3421.
23. ¶ J-3418 *et seq.*; ¶ 90,850.

Footnote references beginning with letters are to paragraphs in RIA's Federal Tax Coordinator 2d and RIA's Analysis of Federal Taxes: Income. Footnote references beginning with numbers are to paragraphs in RIA's United States Tax Reporter.

excludes from that year's gross income any amount (subject to limits, see ¶ 1339) of income from the redemption, during that year, of any "qualified U.S. savings bond" (Series EE bond issued after '89). (Code Sec. 135(a), (c)(1))[24] Use Form 8815 to compute the excludable amount. Use Form 8818 to keep a record of the redemption of the bonds.[25]

A married individual must file a joint return to get the exclusion. (Code Sec. 135(d)(2))[26]

The individual must have purchased the bond(s) after having reached age 24 (Code Sec. 135(c)(1)(B)) and must be the sole owner (or joint owner with his spouse). The exclusion isn't available to the owner of a bond that was bought by another individual (other than a spouse). Nor is it available to a parent who buys the bonds and puts them in the name of a child or other dependent. But the owner may designate an individual (including a child) as the beneficiary for amounts payable at death without losing the exclusion.[27]

The exclusion applies only if the owner redeems the bonds, i.e., not if he transfers them to the educational institution.[28]

¶ 1339 Limit on exclusion of savings bond redemption income.

If taxpayer's aggregate redemption proceeds (principal plus interest) for a tax year exceed the qualified higher education expenses paid in that year, the amount of interest that's excludable under the rules at ¶ 1338 is limited to this fraction of the otherwise excludable amount: the numerator is the qualified higher education expenses paid during the year and the denominator is the aggregate proceeds redeemed during the year. (Code Sec. 135(b)(1))[29]

Illustration: Taxpayer redeems $8,000 ($4,000 interest, $4000 principal) and pays qualified higher education expenses of $6,000. The ratio of expenses to redemption amount is 75% ($6,000 ÷ $8,000) so that $3,000 of the interest (75% × $4,000) (and the $4,000 principal) is excludable.[30]

The exclusion is phased out for a taxpayer whose modified adjusted gross income (AGI) for the year exceeds $40,000 ($60,000 for a joint return), as adjusted for inflation ('93 amounts are $45,500/$68,250; '94 amounts are reduced to $41,200/$61,850 under '93 legislation). The amount of the reduction (not below zero) equals the amount otherwise excludable (*but for* this phaseout) multiplied by this fraction: the excess of modified AGI over the ($40,000/$60,000) phaseout amount, divided by $15,000 ($30,000 for a joint return) (Code Sec. 135(b)(2)) ($15,000/$30,000 amounts are *not* adjusted for inflation). Thus, for '93, the exclusion is completely lost when AGI reaches $60,500, or $98,250 for a joint return ('94 amounts are reduced to $56,200 and $91,850).[31]

Modified AGI is AGI determined without this savings bond interest exclusion or the Code Secs. 911, 931 and 933 exclusions for income earned abroad, and after application of Code Sec. 86 (taxing certain social security payments), Code Sec. 469 (limiting passive activity losses) and Code Sec. 219 (deduction of IRA contributions). (Code Sec. 135(c)(4))[32]

¶ 1340 Qualified higher education expenses.

Qualified higher education expenses are tuition and fees required for the enrollment or attendance of taxpayer, taxpayer's spouse or any dependent for whom taxpayer is allowed a dependency exemption, at an eligible educational institution, (Code Sec. 135(c)(2)(A)) e.g., most colleges, junior colleges, nursing schools and area vocational schools, but not any proprietary institution. (Code Sec. 135(c)(3)) Expenses with respect to any course or other education involving sports, games or hobbies, other than as part of a degree program, don't count. (Code Sec. 135(c)(2)(B))[33]

The expenses otherwise taken into account must be reduced by the total amounts

24. ¶s J-3073.1, J-3073.2.
25. ¶ J-3073.1; ¶ 1354.02.
26. ¶ J-3073.1; ¶ 1354.
27. ¶ J-3073.2; ¶ 1354.01.
28. ¶ J-3073.1; ¶ 1354.02.
29. ¶ J-3073.5; ¶ 1354.02.
30. ¶ J-3073.5; ¶ 1354.02.
31. ¶ J-3073.6; ¶ 1354.03.
32. ¶ J-3073.6; ¶ 1354.03.
33. ¶s J-3073.3, J-3073.4; ¶ 1354.02.

Footnote references beginning with letters are to paragraphs in RIA's Federal Tax Coordinator 2d and RIA's Analysis of Federal Taxes: Income. Footnote references beginning with numbers are to paragraphs in RIA's United States Tax Reporter.

received for excludable qualified scholarships (¶ 1377), certain educational assistance allowances and other tax-exempt payments (other than gifts, bequests, devises or inheritances). (Code Sec. 135(d)(1))[34]

¶ 1341 When to report interest income.

Cash basis taxpayers must report interest in the tax year it is actually or constructively received, regardless of when the interest is accrued on the debtor's books.[35] Interest isn't constructively received if taxpayer's control of its receipt is subject to substantial limits or restrictions. (Reg § 1.451-2(a))[36]

Savings institution interest, or interest on life insurance dividends left to accumulate, is considered received when credited to the depositor's (policyholder's) account and subject to his withdrawal.[37]

illustration: A bank credits a certificate holder with quarterly interest on its books, on Dec. 31, Year 1. On Jan. 15, Year 2, the certificate holder seeks to withdraw the interest. He is taxable on the interest in Year 1, when the bank credited it to his account on *its* books, even if the bank may require 30 days notice before withdrawal.

Where a bank charges a penalty for premature withdrawals from a time savings account, the gross amount of interest paid or credited during the withdrawal year must be reported as interest that year, even if the penalty partially or completely offsets the interest.[38] For deduction of forfeited interest, see ¶ 2167.

Interest on coupon bonds is taxable in the year the coupon becomes due and payable. It doesn't matter when the bond-owner presents the coupon for payment.[39]

Accrual basis taxpayers report interest in the tax year in which the right to receive the interest becomes fixed, regardless of when it is received.[40] But if it appears reasonably certain the interest won't be paid because the debtor is insolvent, the creditor can delay reporting the interest until its collection appears reasonably certain.[41]

For cash and accrual taxpayers, there are special rules on when to include interest with respect to below-market rate loans (¶ 1310). (Code Sec. 7872)[42]

observation: Where interest is not paid at periodic intervals of one year or less, the OID rules require it to be currently included (¶ 1318).

¶ 1342 Rents and Royalties

Rent is the payment for the use of real or tangible personal property. Royalties are payments for the use of certain rights, e.g., intangible rights such as patents. Both are includible in gross income.

¶ 1343 Rents.

Rents are includible in gross income, whether paid in cash or property. If paid in property, the property's fair market value (at receipt) is the amount taxed as rent.[43]

Rents are reported by cash basis taxpayers when received, and by accrual basis taxpayers when due unless they're considered uncollectible.[44]

¶ 1344 Bonuses; cancellation payments.

A bonus or extra payment by the tenant to the lessor or sublessor on the execution of the lease is taxable as rent to the lessor or sublessor.[45]

---

34. ¶ J-3073.3; ¶ 1354.02.
35. ¶ J-3403.
36. ¶ J-3405; ¶ 4514.053.
37. ¶s J-3408, J-3416;
    ¶ 4514.053.

38. ¶ J-2996.
39. ¶ J-3414.
40. ¶ J-3401; ¶ 4514.011.

41. ¶ J-3402; ¶ 4514.023.
42. ¶ J-3407; ¶ 78,724.
43. ¶ J-2200 *et seq.*; ¶ 614.084.

44. ¶ J-2551; ¶s 4514.001,
    4514.023.
45. ¶ J-2553.

Footnote references beginning with letters are to paragraphs in RIA's Federal Tax Coordinator 2d and RIA's Analysis of Federal Taxes: Income. Footnote references beginning with numbers are to paragraphs in RIA's United States Tax Reporter.

If the tenant pays the landlord for permission to cancel the lease, the payments are rent to the landlord (whether cash or accrual basis) in the year received. Payments to the landlord for modifying a lease or consenting to a sublease are also considered rent.[46] For where the lesser pays the tenant to cancel the lease, see ¶ 1591.

¶ 1345 Advance rentals and security deposits.

An advance rental is currently taxable, even if it is refundable or can be applied against the property's purchase price. (Reg § 1.61-8(b))[47] But a security deposit (¶ 1206) is not taxable rent.[48]

¶ 1346 Deferred rentals.

Where the special rules on deferred payment leases over $250,000 apply (see ¶ 1593), the lessor has a "constant accrual" of rental income in the same way that rental expenses are deductible by the lessee (Code Sec. 467).[49]

¶ 1347 Tenant's payment of landlord's expenses.

Where a tenant is required under the lease to pay interest, property taxes, mortgage principal, etc., thus satisfying the *landlord's* own payment obligation, the payments are treated as rent paid by the tenant to the landlord. (Reg § 1.61-8(c))[50]

¶ 1348 Tenant's improvements to the leased property.

Where a tenant erects a building or makes other improvements to leased property, the resulting increase in the property's value is not income to the landlord either at the time the improvements are made or at the end of the lease term. (Code Sec. 109) But the landlord does have rental income if the improvements are made as rent substitutes.[1]

¶ 1349 Royalties.

Royalties are payments for the use of copyrights, patents, trademarks, secret processes and similar intangibles, as well as payments for the right to exploit mineral or other natural resources. Royalties are taxable as ordinary income, (Code Sec. 61(a)(6)) regardless of the name given to them by the parties or the form of payment (e.g., lump sum or property such as stock).[2]

Royalties are included by cash basis taxpayers on receipt (actual or constructive), and by accrual basis taxpayers when their rights to them are fixed.[3]

¶ 1350 Life Insurance Proceeds

Life insurance proceeds payable by reason of the insured's death are fully excludable or, if paid later than death under an interest option or in installments, partially excludable. The exclusion may be lost if the contract is transferred during the insured's life.

¶ 1351 How lump-sum life insurance proceeds are taxed.

If the proceeds of a qualified "life insurance contract" ((¶ 1352) that are payable by reason of the insured's death are received (by the beneficiary) in a lump sum, they are fully excludable from the recipient's income (Code Sec. 101(a))[4] unless the policy has been transferred for value (¶ 1356). For dividends and other lifetime payments, see ¶ 1355.

For life insurance contracts that don't qualify, only the excess of the death benefit proceeds over the contract's net surrender value (i.e., value on surrender) is excludable.

---

46. ¶ J-2214 *et seq.*; ¶ 4514.022. 49. ¶ L-6800 *et seq.*; ¶ 4674.   1. ¶ J-2500 *et seq.*; ¶ 1094.01.   3. ¶ J-2604.
47. ¶ J-2217; ¶ 4514.193.   50. ¶ J-2211; ¶ 614.094.   2. ¶ J-2600 *et seq.*; ¶ 614.084.   4. ¶ J-4000 *et seq.*; ¶ 4514.001.
48. ¶ J-2552; ¶ 4514.194.

Footnote references beginning with letters are to paragraphs in RIA's Federal Tax Coordinator 2d and RIA's Analysis of Federal Taxes: Income. Footnote references beginning with numbers are to paragraphs in RIA's United States Tax Reporter.

The net surrender value is treated as a payment received under an annuity contract (¶ 1357 *et seq.*). (Code Sec. 7702(g)(2)) Also, the owner of the contract is taxed (in the year it fails to qualify) on the income earned on it during the insured's lifetime. This income equals the excess of: (1) the sum of the net surrender value increase plus the cost of life insurance protection provided, over (2) premiums paid for the year. (Code Sec. 7702(g)(1)(B))[5]

¶ 1352 Life insurance contract defined.

To qualify as a life insurance contract, a contract must: (1) be a life insurance (or endowment) contract under local law; *and* (2) satisfy either (a) a cash value accumulation test, or (b) a combined guideline premium requirement/cash value corridor test. (Code Sec. 101(f), Code Sec. 7702(a), (h))[6] Pre-'85 contracts must entail risk shifting and risk distribution.[7]

¶ 1353 Proceeds paid in installments.

If the life insurance proceeds payable on the insured's death are paid in installments or for life, only a portion (below) of each payment is excluded. Any part of a payment that exceeds the excluded portion is taxable when received. But if the amount of the total anticipated payments can't exceed the total amount payable at the insured's death, then each payment is fully excludable, whenever it's made. (Code Sec. 101(d)(1); Reg § 1.101-4(a)(1)(i))[8]

The excludable portion of each payment is: (1) the excludable amount held by the insurer with respect to the particular beneficiary, divided by (2) the number of payments to be made or, if payments are for life, the number of payments anticipated over the life expectancy of the beneficiary. This same prorated amount of each payment is excludable, regardless of how many payments are made (Reg § 1.101-4) (i.e., even if the beneficiary exceeds his anticipated life expectancy).[9]

A beneficiary who is the spouse of an insured who died before Oct. 23, '86, may exclude an *additional* $1,000 each year of amounts received by reason of the insured's death.[10]

¶ 1354 Proceeds left at interest.

Where excludable life insurance proceeds are held by the insurer under an agreement to pay interest, the interest is taxable to the recipient whether the interest option was chosen by the insured or by his beneficiaries or estate. No part of this interest may be excluded under the proration rules (¶ 1353). (Code Sec. 101(c); Reg § 1.101-3(a))[11]

¶ 1355 Proceeds paid before death of insured.

Payments made under life insurance or endowment contracts before the death of the insured (e.g., loans, refunds, dividends) are treated as made under an annuity contract (¶ 1357 *et seq.*). (Code Sec. 72(a))[12]

¶ 1356 Death benefits exclusion where contract was transferred for consideration.

If a life insurance contract is transferred for valuable consideration, e.g., by sale, the transferee's exclusion for the life insurance proceeds he receives under the contract by reason of the insured's death is limited to the value of the consideration he paid for the contract, plus the net premiums and other amounts he paid after the transfer. (Code Sec. 101(a)(2))[13] Where only an interest in the contract is transferred, the limitation applies only to the portion of the proceeds that is attributable to the transferred interest.[14]

---

5. ¶ J-4100 *et seq.*; ¶ 77,024.07.   8. ¶ J-4018; ¶ 1014.04.   11. ¶ J-4017; ¶ 1014.03.   13. ¶ J-4029; ¶ 1014.02.
6. ¶ J-4050 *et seq.*; ¶ 77,024.   9. ¶ J-4020; ¶ 1014.04.   12. ¶ J-4419 *et seq.*; ¶ 724.   14. ¶ J-4031; ¶ 1014.02.
7. ¶ J-4150 *et seq.*; ¶ 1014.   10. ¶ J-4014; ¶ 1014.05.

Footnote references beginning with letters are to paragraphs in RIA's Federal Tax Coordinator 2d and RIA's Analysis of Federal Taxes: Income. Footnote references beginning with numbers are to paragraphs in RIA's United States Tax Reporter.

This limitation doesn't apply if:

- the transfer is to the insured, his partner, his partnership or a corporation in which he is a shareholder or officer; (Code Sec. 101(a)(2)(B)) or

- the transferee's basis for the policy (or interest) is determined in whole or in part by reference to the transferor's basis, (Code Sec. 101(a)(2)(A))[15] as in a tax-free reorganization. (Reg § 1.101-1(b)(5), Ex 2)[16]

Where the transfer is gratuitous, i.e., a gift, the above limitation doesn't apply and the full death benefits exclusion is preserved. (Reg § 1.101-1(b)(2))[17]

¶ 1357 Taxation of Annuity Payments

Annuity payments consist generally of two parts: nontaxable return of capital (based on a special exclusion ratio), and taxable interest.

Annuity payments, which are lifetime payments under life insurance, endowment and annuity contracts, are includible in gross income. (Code Sec. 72(a))[18] For exclusion under the "annuity rule," see ¶ 1358. For other payments under the contract (e.g., cash withdrawals, loans, dividends), see ¶ 1368.

¶ 1358 The annuity rule (and "exclusion ratio").

If an annuity payment is received "as an annuity" (i.e., it is a sum of money (or property) payable at regular intervals over a period of more than one full year from the starting date (¶ 1366)), then all or part of it may be excludable. (Reg § 1.72-1(b), Reg § 1.72-2(b)) The part of each "annuity" payment that represents return of investment (e.g., premiums paid) is excludable from the recipient's income until the entire investment is recovered. Excess receipts are fully taxable. (Code Sec. 72(b)(1); Reg § 1.72-4(a))[19]

The excludable portion is computed by multiplying each payment received by an "exclusion ratio," determined by dividing the investment in the contract (¶ 1364) by the contract's expected return (¶ 1365), as of the annuity starting date, and rounding to the nearest tenth. The exclusion ratio must be redetermined if the contract is transferred for valuable consideration, matures, is surrendered, or is exchanged. (Reg § 1.72-4(a)(4)) (For the "safe harbor" exclusion ratio for distributions from qualified plans, see ¶ 1367 *et seq.*)[20]

Once computed, this exclusion ratio is applied to each "annuity" payment received under the contract. (Code Sec. 72(b); Reg § 1.72-4(a)) However, the excludable portion of any payment can't exceed the amount of investment in the contract that is unrecovered immediately before the payment is received. (Code Sec. 72(b)(2))[21]

If there was no investment in the contract, all payments are taxable in full. If the investment exceeds the total expected return, all payments are tax-free. (Reg § 1.72-4(d))[22]

For annuities that started before '87, the exclusion ratio, once determined, applies to all future payments (unless there is a later modification or exchange of the contract) regardless of how long the annuitant lives. (Reg § 1.72-4(a))[23]

¶ 1359 Natural person not holder of annuity contract.

If an annuity contract is held by a person who is not a natural person, the annuity rule doesn't apply. The income on the contract (for the holder's tax year) must be treated as ordinary income received or accrued by the holder during that year. (Code Sec. 72(u)(1))[24]

A natural person doesn't include a trust or corporation. But holding by a trust, etc., *as agent* for a natural person is disregarded. (Code Sec. 72(u)(1))[25]

---

15. ¶ J-4030; ¶ 1014.02.	18. ¶ J-4401; ¶ 724.	21. ¶ J-4503; ¶ 724.	24. ¶ J-4402; ¶ 724.25.
16. ¶ J-4042.	19. ¶ J-4500 *et seq.*; ¶ 724.	22. ¶ J-4503.	25. ¶ J-4402; ¶ 724.25.
17. ¶ J-4032; ¶ 1014.02.	20. ¶ J-4503; ¶ 724.	23. ¶ J-4503; ¶ 724.06.	

Footnote references beginning with letters are to paragraphs in RIA's Federal Tax Coordinator 2d and RIA's Analysis of Federal Taxes: Income. Footnote references beginning with numbers are to paragraphs in RIA's United States Tax Reporter.

However, an *employer* that is the nominal owner (agent) of an annuity contract whose beneficial owners are (the employer's) employees is considered to hold the contract.[26]

The natural person rule does not apply to contracts: acquired by an estate by reason of the decedent's death; held by a qualified plan or IRA; that are "qualified funding assets" (¶ 1382); purchased by an employer on termination of a qualified plan and held until all amounts under the contract are distributed to the employee (or employee's beneficiary) for whom the contract was purchased; or that are immediate annuities. (Code Sec. 72(u)(3))[27]

¶ 1360 After-death distribution requirements for annuity contracts.

Unless the contract requires certain distributions if the holder (or "primary annuitant" for contracts not held by an individual) dies before his entire interest is distributed, the contract payments won't be entitled to the partial exclusion under the "annuity rule." The contract must provide that: (1) if any holder dies on or after the annuity starting date (¶ 1366) (and before the entire interest in the contract has been distributed), the balance will be distributed at least as rapidly as it was at the date of death, and (2) if any holder dies before the starting date, the entire interest must be distributed within five years of his death. (Code Sec. 72(s)(1))[28]

However, distributions that are payable to (or for) a designated beneficiary can be made for the beneficiary's life or a period not ending past his life expectancy. As long as the payments begin within one year of the holder's death, they'll be considered distributed on that starting date. (Code Sec. 72(s)(2)) A beneficiary who is the holder's surviving spouse will be considered the holder for this purpose. (Code Sec. 72(s)(3))[29]

The after-death distribution requirements don't apply to: contracts provided under qualified pension, profit-sharing, stock bonus or annuity plans; tax-sheltered annuities; individual retirement annuities (or contracts provided under IRAs); qualified funding assets (¶ 1382), regardless of any qualified assignment; (Code Sec. 72(s)(5))[30] or contracts issued before Jan. 19, '85.[31]

¶ 1361 Variable annuities.

A variable annuity contract is one where the amount paid varies depending on investment experience, cost of living indexes, market fluctuations, etc. The excludable portion of each payment is computed by dividing the investment in the contract (¶ 1364) by the total number of anticipated payments. (Reg § 1.72-2(b)(3), Reg § 1.72-4(d)(3))[32]

The excludable amount stays the same regardless of changes in the amount received. (Reg § 1.72-2(b)(3))[33] However, if in a tax year the amount of variable annuity payments received is *less* than the excludable amount, taxpayer may elect (by attaching a specified statement to the return) to recompute the exclusion formula for later years' payments. (Reg § 1.72-4(d)(3)(ii), (iv))[34]

¶ 1362 Joint and survivor annuity contracts.

Under a joint and survivor annuity contract, payments are made during the lives of two annuitants and, after the death of one, during the life of the survivor. A single exclusion ratio, computed based on the aggregate expected return to both annuitants, is applied to the payments received by both annuitants. (Reg § 1.72-2(a)(2))[35]

¶ 1363 Payments under employee annuities that started before July 2, '86 are fully taxable.

In certain cases an employee who contributed to the cost of his pension or annuity is taxed on the full amount of annuity payments received under the contract. This applies to

---

26. ¶ J-4402; ¶ 724.25.   29. ¶ J-4440; ¶ 724.01.   32. ¶ J-4550; ¶ 724.08.   34. ¶ J-4551; ¶ 724.08.
27. ¶ J-4403; ¶ 724.25.   30. ¶ J-4442; ¶ 724.01.   33. ¶ J-4550; ¶ 724.08.   35. ¶ J-4539 *et seq.*; ¶ 724.15.
28. ¶s J-4440, J-4441; ¶ 724.01.   31. ¶ J-4440; ¶ 724.01.

Footnote references beginning with letters are to paragraphs in RIA's Federal Tax Coordinator 2d and RIA's Analysis of Federal Taxes: Income. Footnote references beginning with numbers are to paragraphs in RIA's United States Tax Reporter.

contracts that started before July 2, '86, where the employee's investment in the contract was less than the contract payments to be received within three years after the date of the first payment. (The annuity payments were fully excludable by the employee until— in that three-year period—his entire cost was recovered.) (Reg § 1.72-13) For employee annuities starting after July 1, '86, the regular annuity rules apply (¶ 1357 *et seq.*).[36]

¶ 1364 Investment in the contract.

The "investment in the contract" is, in general, the net cost of the contract as of the annuity starting date (¶ 1366) or, if later, the date of the first contract payment. It equals the aggregate amount of premiums and other consideration paid (as of that date) for the contract, minus the aggregate amount previously received under the contract that was excluded from income. (Code Sec. 72(c)(1))[37] It must also be reduced to account for any refund feature. (Code Sec. 72(c)(2))[38] Separate computations may be required for pre-July '86 and post-June '86 investments. (Reg § 1.72-6(d))[39]

For an employee annuity , investment in the contract includes certain employer contributions that were taxable to the owner (employee). (Reg § 1.72-8(a))[40] Where the safe-harbor method is elected (¶ 1367), no refund feature adjustment is required.[41]

For a survivor-annuitant under an employee pension, the investment also includes the $5,000 death benefit exclusion (¶ 1262), if applicable. (Reg § 1.72-8(b))[42]

¶ 1365 Expected return from the contract.

The "expected return from the contract" is the total amount to be received (or estimated to be received) under the contract. It is computed as of the annuity starting date (¶ 1366) (Code Sec. 72(b)(1)) and does not take into account any amount for dividends or other payments *not* received as an annuity. (Code Sec. 72(c)(3); Reg § 1.72-7(a))[43]

If the annuity is for a fixed term and does not depend on any life expectancy, the expected return is the amount of the payment specified for each period multiplied by the number of periods. (Reg § 1.72-5(c))[44]

If the annuity is payable for life or joint lives, the expected return is the amount of the *annual* payment multiplied by the number of years of life expectancy using IRS actuarial tables. (Code Sec. 72(c)(3)(A); Reg § 1.72-5(a))[45]

If the annuity is for an amount certain payable in periodic installments, the expected return is the total amount guaranteed. (Reg § 1.72-5(d))[46]

¶ 1366 Annuity starting date.

The "annuity starting date" is the first day of the first period for which an amount is received *as an annuity* under the contract. This is the date when the contractual obligation becomes fixed or, if later, the first day of the period that ends on the date of the first annuity payment. (Code Sec. 72(c)(4); Reg § 1.72-4(b)(1))[47]

Special rules apply if the contract is transferred or exchanged. (Code Sec. 72(g)(3))[48]

¶ 1367 Safe-harbor exclusion ratio (simplified general rule) for certain employee annuities.

A distributee who either: (1) is less than 75 when the payments start, or (2) is 75 or older and has less than five years of guaranteed payments,[49] may elect a simplified safe harbor method to determine the tax-free and taxable portion of annuity payments that:

(a) depend on the life of the distributee or the joint lives of the distributee and beneficiary, *and*

---

36. ¶ H-11040 *et seq.*; ¶ 724.07.

37. ¶ J-4511; ¶ 724.10.

38. ¶ J-4520; ¶ 724.12.

39. ¶ J-4515 *et seq.*; ¶ 724.10.

40. ¶ J-4522; ¶ 724.11.

41. ¶ H-11022.

42. ¶ H-11037; ¶ 724.11.

43. ¶ J-4511 *et seq.*; ¶ 724.14.

44. ¶ J-4537; ¶ 724.14.

45. ¶ J-4533 *et seq.*; ¶ 724.14.

46. ¶ J-4538; ¶ 724.14.

47. ¶ J-4508; ¶ 724.09.

48. ¶ J-4510; ¶ 724.09.

49. ¶s H-11016, H-11017; ¶ 4024.02.

Footnote references beginning with letters are to paragraphs in RIA's Federal Tax Coordinator 2d and RIA's Analysis of Federal Taxes: Income. Footnote references beginning with numbers are to paragraphs in RIA's United States Tax Reporter.

(b) are made from a Code Sec. 401(a) qualified employee plan, a Code Sec. 403(a) qualified employee annuity, or a Code Sec. 403(b) tax-sheltered annuity.[50]

The portion of each monthly payment that is excluded from the electing distributee's income is a level dollar amount, determined by dividing the investment in the contract (¶ 1364) by the number of expected annuity payments (see table below). This same amount will be excluded from each monthly payment, even if the amount of the payments changes (e.g., for cost of living increases or a reduced survivor annuity).[1]

If annuity payments are to be made to multiple beneficiaries, the total amount to be excluded from all monthly payments is determined by reference to the age of the oldest beneficiary. Each beneficiary will exclude a portion of this total excludable amount from each annuity payment received, based on the ratio his monthly annuity bears to the total amount of the monthly annuity payments to all beneficiaries.[2]

The total number of monthly payments expected to be received (whether under a single life annuity or a joint and survivor one) is based on the distributee's age as of the birthday preceding the annuity starting date, as follows:[3]

Age of Distributee	Number of Payments
55 and under	300
56-60	260
61-65	240
66-70	170
71 and over	120

A distributee elects to use the safe-harbor method by using it to report the taxable portion of the annuity payments received in a year, on his income tax return[4] (attaching a signed statement if he's entitled to the $5,000 employee death benefit exclusion, see ¶ 1262).[5]

¶ 1368 Amounts "not" received as an annuity—cash withdrawals, dividends, etc.

Payments under life insurance, endowment and annuity contracts (other than modified endowment contracts, see ¶ 1370) that are not "annuities" (e.g., cash withdrawals, loans, dividends, etc.) are fully taxable if received on or after the annuity starting date (¶ 1366). (Code Sec. 72(e)(2)(A), (3)(A))[6]

"Nonannuity" amounts received before the annuity starting date are *not taxable* to the extent that, as of the date of distribution, they don't exceed the cost of the policy (i.e., accumulated net premiums paid), and *taxable* to the extent allocable to income (i.e., the excess of the contract's cash value over the owner's investment) at that time. (Code Sec. 72(e)(2)(B), (3)(B))[7] (Veteran's insurance dividends are tax-free, regardless of cost.)[8]

Receipts less than the contract's cost don't give rise to a deductible loss.[9]

The contract's cost is reduced by the nontaxable amount of the dividend, etc., for purposes of computing the taxable portion of later payments. (Code Sec. 72(e)(6)(B))[10]

For these purposes, all contracts (other than immediate annuities or qualified plan annuities) issued by the same company (or its affiliates) to the same policyholder during any one calendar year are treated as a single contract. (Code Sec. 72(e)(11))[11]

For contracts entered into before Aug. 14, '82, and amounts allocable to investment made in contracts before that date, different rules apply.[12]

---

50. ¶ H-11018; ¶ 4024.02.
1. ¶ H-11019; ¶ 4024.02.
2. ¶ H-11021; ¶ 4024.02.
3. ¶ H-11023; ¶ 4024.02.

4. ¶ H-11024.
5. ¶ H-11022; ¶ 4024.02.
6. ¶ J-4414; ¶ 724.17.

7. ¶ J-4414 *et seq.*; ¶ 724.17.
8. ¶ J-4419.
9. ¶ J-4907.

10. ¶ J-4511.
11. ¶ J-4424; ¶ 724.17.
12. ¶ J-4416; ¶ 724.17.

Footnote references beginning with letters are to paragraphs in RIA's Federal Tax Coordinator 2d and RIA's Analysis of Federal Taxes: Income. Footnote references beginning with numbers are to paragraphs in RIA's United States Tax Reporter.

¶ 1369 10% penalty on premature distributions from annuity contracts.

A penalty is imposed (except as noted below) on a person who receives any nonannuity distribution (¶ 1368) before the annuity starting date (¶ 1366). The penalty, which is imposed in the tax year the distribution is received, equals 10% of the taxable portion of the distribution. (Code Sec. 72(q)(1))[13] Calculate and pay the penalty on Form 5329.

The 10% penalty *does not apply* to any distribution:

(1) made on or after the date taxpayer (recipient) reaches age 59½;

(2) made on or after the death of the holder (or the primary annuitant, where the holder isn't an individual);

(3) attributable to taxpayer's total and indefinite disability;

(4) that is part of a series of substantially equal periodic payments (not less frequently than annually) made for the life (or life expectancy) of taxpayer or the joint lives (or joint life expectancies) of taxpayer and his designated beneficiary;

(5) made from a Code Sec. 401(a) qualified employee plan, a Code Sec. 403(a) qualified annuity plan, a Code Sec. 403(b) tax-sheltered annuity plan or a Code Sec. 818(a)(3) retirement plan provided for employees of a life insurance company (but for the separate penalty on premature distributions from these plans, see ¶ 4345);

(6) made from an individual retirement account or annuity (but for the separate penalty on premature distributions from these plans, see ¶ 4345);

(7) made under an annuity contract which is purchased by an employer on termination of a qualified plan (bonus, pension, profit-sharing or annuity) and which is held by the employer until the employee separates from service;

(8) under an immediate annuity;

(9) under a "qualified funding asset" (¶ 1382) but without regard to any qualified assignment;

(10) to which the Code Sec. 72(t) tax on premature distributions from qualified plans applies (without regard to the Code Sec. 72(t)(2) exceptions), see ¶ 4345;

(11) allocable to pre-Aug. 14, '82 investment in the contract. (Code Sec. 72(q)(2))[14]

¶ 1370 Modified endowment contracts.

A modified endowment contract is a life insurance contract (entered into after June 20, '88) which fails to meet a "7-pay test" (or that is exchanged for such a contract). The test is failed if the accumulated amount paid under the contract during the first seven years exceeds the net level premiums that would have been paid as paid-up future benefits. (Code Sec. 7702A(a), (b))[15]

Payments under a modified endowment contract that are received before the annuity starting date (¶ 1366) are includible in gross income to the extent allocable to income on the contract, as described at ¶ 1368. (Code Sec. 72(e)(10)(A)(i))[16] This applies to any amount received as a loan, or assigned or pledged on the value of the contract, unless the assignment, etc., is made solely to cover the payment of burial expenses or prearranged funeral expenses where the maximum death benefit under the contract doesn't exceed $25,000. (Code Sec. 72(e)(10)(B)) However, taxpayer's investment in the contract (¶ 1364) is increased by the amount taxed to him (as a loan or assignment). (Code Sec. 72(e)(4)(A))[17]

Certain amounts received under a modified endowment contract which are includible in gross income are subject to a 10% penalty tax (Code Sec. 72(v)(1), (2))[18] (use Form 5329).

---

13. ¶ J-4438.
14. ¶ J-4439; ¶ 724.21.
15. ¶ J-4426 *et seq.*; ¶ 724.17.
16. ¶ J-4425; ¶ 724.17.
17. ¶ J-4435; ¶ 724.17.
18. ¶ J-4436; ¶ 724.17.

Footnote references beginning with letters are to paragraphs in RIA's Federal Tax Coordinator 2d and RIA's Analysis of Federal Taxes: Income. Footnote references beginning with numbers are to paragraphs in RIA's United States Tax Reporter.

¶ 1371   Private annuities.

A private annuity generally involves the transfer of money or property to an individual or organization in exchange for the transferee's promise to make lifetime payments to the transferor. These transfers typically are made:

- to family members, controlled entities, or unrelated purchasers;
- to charitable organizations;
- in settlement of a will contest.[19]

    RIA *observation:* Most private annuity transactions have estate planning objectives. Typically, a parent with a substantial estate will transfer depreciable, income-producing, or personal property to a child in exchange for the child's promise to pay the parent a fixed, periodic income for a set period of time. If properly structured, no gift tax will be due and the transferred assets will pass on to the next generation free of estate tax.

An "unsecured" private annuity arrangement is taxed as follows: The transfer doesn't result in immediate taxable gain (or loss). Instead, any gain is reportable ratably over the lifetime of the transferor (i.e., annuitant). The amount of gain is equal to the excess of the present value of the annuity (determined under regs) over the transferor's adjusted basis in the transferred property. Any loss may be disallowed if the arrangement is between related parties (¶ 2448 *et seq.*).[20]

If the arrangement is "secured" (i.e., the property transferred also is collateral for the payments), it is taxed (except for gift tax aspects) under the rules for commercial annuities (¶ 1357 *et seq.*).[21] In applying those rules, the annuitant's basis in the property he transferred for the annuity is used as his investment in the contract.[22]

The value of annuities issued by charitable organizations is determined under special IRS tables.[23]

¶ 1372   Gifts and Inheritances

Property received as a gift, bequest, devise or inheritance is exempt from income tax.

¶ 1373   Gifts.

A recipient of a gift is not taxed on the receipt of the gift. However, the recipient is taxed on income (unless it's tax-exempt) from the gifted property. (Code Sec. 102; Reg § 1.102-1)[24]

For employee awards, see ¶ 1584.

For gift tax, see ¶ 5039 *et seq.*

¶ 1374   Inheritances.

Tax-free bequests, devises and inheritances are money and any property that pass on the death of a person by his will or under intestacy, including amounts received in settlement of a will contest.[25]

For estate tax, see ¶ 5000 *et seq.*.

¶ 1375   Prizes, Scholarships, Etc

Prizes and awards are taxable except for certain prizes transferred to a charity or a government unit, and qualified scholarship grants.

---

19. ¶ J-4802; ¶ 724.01.   21. ¶s J-4802, J-4811.   23. ¶ P-6600 *et seq.*; ¶ 724.01.   25. ¶ J-6014 *et seq.*; ¶ 1024.01.
20. ¶ J-4805 *et seq.*; ¶ 724.01.   22. ¶ J-4804; ¶ 724.01.   24. ¶ J-6000 *et seq.*

Footnote references beginning with letters are to paragraphs in RIA's Federal Tax Coordinator 2d and RIA's Analysis of Federal Taxes: Income. Footnote references beginning with numbers are to paragraphs in RIA's United States Tax Reporter.

¶ 1376 Prizes and awards.

All prizes and awards (with certain exceptions, see ¶s 1377 and 1253) are includible in gross income (Code Sec. 74(a); Reg § 1.74-1(b)) *unless*: the prize is primarily for religious, charitable, scientific, educational, artistic, literary, etc., achievement; the recipient was selected without any action on his part, and isn't thus required to render substantial future services; *and* it is transferred by the payor to a governmental unit or charity the recipient designated (Code Sec. 74(b))[26] before getting any benefit from it.[27] IRS specifies the requirements of the designation (including model language).[28]

For a prize paid in property or services, the amount includible in the recipient's income is the prize's current fair market value (resale value, not sponsor's cost). (Reg § 1.74-1(a)(2))[29]

¶ 1377 Scholarships and fellowships.

A scholarship or fellowship is not taxable, to the extent it is a "qualified scholarship" granted to a degree candidate at an "educational organization" and is not a stipend (¶ 1379). (Code Sec. 117(a), (c))[30]

A "qualified scholarship" means any amount received as a scholarship and used for qualified tuition and related expenses. (Code Sec. 117(b)(1)) Qualified tuition, etc., expenses are tuition and fees required for enrollment at an educational organization, and fees, books, supplies and equipment required for the course of instruction there. (Code Sec. 117(b)(2))[31] An "educational organization" is one that normally maintains a regular faculty, curriculum and regularly enrolled student body in attendance. (Code Sec. 117(b)(2)(A))[32]

¶ 1378 Qualified tuition reductions for employees of educational institutions.

Qualified tuition reductions for employees of educational institutions are excluded from the recipient's gross income. (Code Sec. 117(d)) A "qualified tuition reduction" is the amount of tuition reduction provided to an employee of an educational organization (¶ 1377) for below-graduate level education (and not services, see ¶ 1379) at that or a similar institution, for the employee (whether active, retired, or disabled), the employee's spouse or dependent children. (Code Sec. 117(d)(2)) But a tuition reduction for a graduate student engaged in teaching or research can be tax-free. (Code Sec. 117(d)(5))[33]

A qualified tuition reduction provided with respect to a "highly compensated employee" (¶ 4326) is excludable only if it is available to all employees on a nondiscriminatory basis. (Code Sec. 117(d)(3))[34]

¶ 1379 Payments for teaching or research.

The exclusions described at ¶s 1377 and 1378 don't apply to the portion of any amount received that represents payment for teaching, research or other services performed by the student as a condition for receiving the qualified benefit. (Code Sec. 117(c))[35]

¶ 1380 Damages ▬▬▬▬▬▬▬

Compensation for personal injuries (including punitive damages received in connection with a physical injury) is generally tax-free. Damages for injury to business are ordinary income or a return of capital depending on whether they are for lost profits or injuries to capital.

---

26. ¶ J-1201 *et seq.*; ¶ 744.01.
27. ¶ J-1208; ¶ 744.01.
28. ¶ J-1206 *et seq.*
29. ¶ J-1213.
30. ¶ J-1230; ¶ 1174.01.
31. ¶ J-1238; ¶ 1174.01.
32. ¶ J-1240; ¶ 1174.01.
33. ¶ J-1262 *et seq.*; ¶ 1174.02.
34. ¶ J-1268; ¶ 1174.02.
35. ¶ J-1245; ¶ 1174.01.

Footnote references beginning with letters are to paragraphs in RIA's Federal Tax Coordinator 2d and RIA's Analysis of Federal Taxes: Income. Footnote references beginning with numbers are to paragraphs in RIA's United States Tax Reporter.

¶ 1381   Nonbusiness damages.

Any damages received (whether by suit or agreement and whether as lump-sum or as periodic payments) as compensation for personal injuries or sickness are tax-free. This exclusion applies only to *compensatory* amounts, (Code Sec. 104(a)(2)) including payments for income lost while taxpayer was disabled by the injury.[36] It doesn't apply to any interest payable on the tax-free damages.[37]

Personal injuries include mental pain and suffering, injury to reputation or to other personal or family rights, as well as physical injury or sickness. Thus, compensatory damages for *nonbusiness* libel and slander are tax-free (as are Agent Orange Settlement Fund payments to Vietnam veterans).[38]

An amount received on account of a job discrimination or wrongful discharge dispute with an employer is considered received for a personal injury (i.e., tax-free) if the relevant cause of action reflects a tort-like remedy, regardless of how the injury is measured (e.g., by back pay).[39]

Punitive damages are not tax-free unless received in connection with a physical injury or sickness. (Code Sec. 104(a))[40]

Where a lump-sum award is specifically allocated by the parties between compensatory and punitive damages, or between personal and business injury, that allocation controls whether any of the award is tax-free. But if no allocation is made, the courts look to the nature of the claims (e.g., primary nature of the harm inflicted) and the payor's intent.[41]

¶ 1382   Amounts received for accepting assignment of personal injury liability.

Amounts received by an assignee (e.g., an insurance company) for accepting certain assignments of a liability to make periodic payments as damages for personal injury or sickness (in a case involving *physical* injury or sickness) are excludable from the assignee's gross income, up to the aggregate cost of any "qualified funding asset" used to satisfy the liability. A "qualified funding asset" means a commercial annuity contract, or a U.S. obligation, having payment periods corresponding to those of the liability, which the assignee: (1) purchased within 60 days from the date of the assignment, and (2) uses to satisfy that liability. (Code Sec. 130(a), (c), (d))[42]

¶ 1383   Business damages.

Damages received for injury to business that represent compensation for lost profits (including business interruption insurance proceeds) are taxable as ordinary income. This applies to awards for breach of a contract of sale and for business slander. Amounts received for injury to capital (e.g., injury to good will, fraudulent stock sale) are tax-free to the extent of basis; any excess is ordinary income.[43] Punitive damages (e.g., insiders' profits, treble damages under antitrust laws) are taxable. (Reg § 1.61-14(a))[44]

There is a special deduction for certain expired net operating losses that resulted from the injury. (Code Sec. 186)[45]

¶ 1384   Income Realized on Discharge or Cancellation of Indebtedness ▬▬▬▬

Gross income includes income from discharge of indebtedness.

Reduction or cancellation of debt (recourse or nonrecourse) is income to the debtor, (Code Sec. 61(a)(12)) because it makes available assets previously offset by obligations.[46]

Cancellation of debt (COD) income thus can result where a creditor accepts less than

---

36. ¶ J-5801; ¶ 1044.02.
37. ¶ J-5815.
38. ¶ J-5801 *et seq.*; ¶ 1044.02.
39. ¶ J-5803 *et seq.*

40. ¶s J-5813, J-5814; ¶ 1044.02.
41. ¶ J-5809 *et seq.*; ¶ 1044.02.
42. ¶ J-5831 *et seq.*; ¶s 1304, 1304.01.

43. ¶s J-5817 *et seq.*, J-5828; ¶ 614.167.
44. ¶ J-5827; ¶ 614.168.

45. ¶ K-8501 *et seq.*; ¶ 1864.
46. ¶ J-7001; ¶ 1084.

Footnote references beginning with letters are to paragraphs in RIA's Federal Tax Coordinator 2d and RIA's Analysis of Federal Taxes: Income. Footnote references beginning with numbers are to paragraphs in RIA's United States Tax Reporter.

full payment as a complete discharge of the debt, or where events or circumstances make its collection unlikely.[47]

But if the debtor's payment of the liability would have given rise to a deduction, the debtor won't have income from the discharge. (Code Sec. 108(e)(2))[48]

There is no income from the cancellation of all or part of the debt from certain government student loans, if the debtor is required to work for a period of time in certain professions as consideration for the discharge. (Code Sec. 108(f)(1))[49]

For the information return by banks, etc., that discharge indebtedness, see ¶ 4745.

¶ 1385 Discharge of indebtedness of solvent debtors outside bankruptcy.

Any discharge of indebtedness, other than in a bankruptcy case (¶ 1387), of a solvent debtor results in the current (i.e., year of discharge) recognition of income in the amount of the discharge (Reg § 1.61-12(a))[50] (except for certain farm (¶ 1388) or real property (¶ 1389) indebtedness).

¶ 1386 Discharge of indebtedness of insolvent debtor outside bankruptcy.

If the indebtedness is discharged when the debtor is insolvent (but not in a bankruptcy case), the discharge is excluded from the debtor's gross income up to the amount of the insolvency. (Code Sec. 108(a)(1)(B), (2)(A), (3))[1]

The amount excluded under this "insolvency exclusion" must be applied to reduce the debtor's tax attributes, such as loss or credit carryovers or basis in assets. (Use Form 982 to report the reduction of tax attributes.) Or the debtor can elect (on Form 982) to apply any or all of the excluded amount *first* to reduce his basis in *depreciable* assets (or real property held as inventory). (Code Sec. 108(b)(5)(A), Code Sec. 1017(b)(3))[2]

Any balance of the discharged debt (excess over the amount by which the debtor is insolvent) is treated as COD income, as in the case of a wholly solvent debtor (¶ 1385). (Code Sec. 108(a)(2)(B), (3))[3]

A debtor is insolvent for this purpose if, immediately before the debt is discharged, his liabilities exceed the fair market value of his assets. (Code Sec. 108(d)(3))[4]

¶ 1387 Discharge of indebtedness of bankrupt debtor.

No amount is included in a debtor's gross income by reason of a discharge of indebtedness in a bankruptcy case, (Code Sec. 108(a)(1)(A)) even if the debtor is solvent after the discharge. (Code Sec. 108(a)(2))[5]

The amount of discharged debt that is excluded under this rule must be applied to reduce certain of the debtor's tax attributes (Code Sec. 108(b)(1)) (use Form 982) unless the debtor elects (on Form 982) to apply any or all of the excluded amount *first* to reduce his basis in depreciable assets (or real property held as inventory). (Code Sec. 108(b)(5)(A), Code Sec. 1017(b)(3))[6]

¶ 1388 Discharge of indebtedness of solvent farmers.

A solvent taxpayer whose "qualified farm indebtedness" is discharged (outside bankruptcy) by certain unrelated lenders does not have COD income, to the extent the discharge doesn't exceed the sum of his adjusted tax attributes plus the aggregate adjusted bases (as of the start of the year after discharge) of his business or income-producing property. (Code Sec. 108(a)(1)(C), (g)(3)) Any excess is COD income. (But the insolvency (¶ 1386) or bankruptcy (¶ 1387) rules have precedence.) (Code Sec. 108(a)(2))[7]

"Qualified farm indebtedness" is debt incurred directly in connection with taxpayer's

---

47. ¶ J-7001 *et seq.*; ¶ 614.114.
48. ¶ J-7504; ¶ 1084.04.
49. ¶ J-7508; ¶ 1084.04.

50. ¶s J-7001, J-7200 *et seq.*; ¶ 1084.01.
1. ¶ J-7401; ¶ 1084.01.

2. ¶ J-7404; ¶ 1084.02.
3. ¶ J-7401; ¶ 1084.01.
4. ¶ J-7403; ¶ 1084.01.

5. ¶ J-7401; ¶ 1084.01.
6. ¶ J-7404; ¶ 1084.02.
7. ¶ J-7405 *et seq.*; ¶ 1084.01.

Footnote references beginning with letters are to paragraphs in RIA's Federal Tax Coordinator 2d and RIA's Analysis of Federal Taxes: Income. Footnote references beginning with numbers are to paragraphs in RIA's United States Tax Reporter.

farm business if at least 50% of taxpayer's total gross receipts for the three tax years preceding the tax year of the discharge is attributable to farming. (Code Sec. 108(g)(2))[8]

¶ 1389 Election to exclude income from discharge of qualified real property business indebtedness.

A solvent taxpayer other than a C corporation whose "qualified real property business indebtedness" (QRPBI) is discharged (outside bankruptcy) can elect to exclude the discharged amount from income, to the extent of the excess (if any) of (1) the outstanding amount of the QRPBI immediately before the discharge over (2) the fair market value (at discharge) of the property securing the QRPBI less the outstanding principal amount of any other QRPBI secured by the property at that time. (Code Sec. 108(a)(1)(D), (c)(2)(A), (c)(3)(C))[9] The excluded amount must be applied to reduce the basis of taxpayer's depreciable real property. (Code Sec. 108(c)(1)(A))[10]

Elect on taxpayer's return for the tax year of discharge. (Code Sec. 108(c)(2)(B))[11]

The amount excluded under this rule can't exceed the total adjusted bases of depreciable real property held by taxpayer immediately before the discharge, after any basis reductions under the insolvency (¶ 1386) or bankruptcy (¶ 1387) rules (which take precedence). (Code Sec. 108(a)(2)(B), (c)(2)(A)).[12]

QRPBI is indebtedness (other than qualified farm indebtedness) incurred or assumed by taxpayer in connection with real property used in a trade or business and secured by the real property (Code Sec. 108(c)(3)(A)) if:

(1) the debt was incurred or assumed before '93, (Code Sec. 108(c)(3)(B)) or

(2) the debt was incurred after '92, but then only if the debt:

(a) is qualified acquisition indebtedness, (Code Sec. 108(c)(3)(B)) i.e., indebtedness incurred or assumed to acquire, construct, reconstruct, or substantially improve the property, (Code Sec. 108(c)(4)) or

(b) was incurred to refinance debt in (1) or (2), but only to the extent it doesn't exceed the amount of the indebtedness being refinanced. (Code Sec. 108(c)(3))[13]

¶ 1390 Discounted purchase of debtor's own obligations.

When a debtor buys or otherwise acquires his own obligations for less than face value (i.e., at a discount), he usually realizes taxable income to the extent of the discount (face value less purchase price). (Reg § 1.61-12(a))[14] This also applies if a party related to the debtor acquires the debtor's indebtedness from an unrelated party. (Code Sec. 108(e)(4)(A); Reg § 1.108-2)[15]

If a corporate debtor buys its own bonds (directly or indirectly) for a price less than their issue price plus any amount of OID (¶ 1319) already deducted, the corporation has taxable income equal to the excess of: (1) issue price plus OID already deducted (or face less discount not yet discounted), over (2) purchase price. (Reg § 1.61-12(c)(3))[16]

For the debtor to be taxed, the obligation must require the unconditional payment of a fixed amount. If the obligation really represents an equity interest, a corporate debtor will be, in effect, acquiring its own stock and thus won't be taxed on the "discount."[17]

¶ 1391 Satisfaction of debt with property or services (including "stock for debt").

If a debtor transfers property (other than debt) to, or performs services for, a creditor in full satisfaction of the debt, and the property or services are worth the amount owed, there is no *cancellation* of the debt since it is actually being paid. But a debtor who performs services in payment of his debt is considered to have taxable *compensation* in

8. ¶ J-7406; ¶ 1084.01.   11. ¶ J-7408.4.   14. ¶ J-7010; ¶ 614.136.   16. ¶ J-7203; ¶ 614.136.
9. ¶ J-7408.1.   12. ¶ J-7408.1.   15. ¶ J-7015 *et seq.*.   17. ¶ J-7006.
10. ¶ J-7408.3.   13. ¶ J-7408.2.

Footnote references beginning with letters are to paragraphs in RIA's Federal Tax Coordinator 2d and RIA's Analysis of Federal Taxes: Income. Footnote references beginning with numbers are to paragraphs in RIA's United States Tax Reporter.

the amount of the debt. (Reg § 1.61-12(a))[18]

On the other hand, a debtor who transfers property in satisfaction of the debt has gain (or loss) to the extent the face amount of the debt exceeds (or is less than) his basis in the transferred property. The type of gain (or loss), or whether any loss is deductible, is determined under the regular sale or exchange rules (¶ 2400 *et seq.*).[19] For "debt-for-debt" exchanges, see ¶ 1392.

Debtor corporations that transfer stock to a creditor in satisfaction of their indebtedness are treated as having satisfied it with an amount of money equal to the fair market value of the stock. That is, the debtor corporation has taxable income to the extent the principal of the debt exceeds the value of the stock. However, this "stock-for-debt" income inclusion does not apply—that is, the income is *not* recognized—for stock transferred before '95 (except for stock transferred in a Title 11 (bankruptcy) or similar case filed before '94) by a corporate debtor that is insolvent (to the extent insolvent) or in a Title 11 case, unless the debt (issued after Oct. 9, '90) is exchanged for certain preferred stock.[20]

¶ 1392 Debt-for-debt exchanges.

A debtor may satisfy an outstanding "old" debt by issuing a "new" debt. The old debt is treated as having been satisfied with an amount of money equal to the issue price of the new debt. (Code Sec. 108(e)(11)(A)) Thus, the excess (if any) of the "old" adjusted issue price over the "new" issue price is COD income to the debtor.[21]

For this purpose, "issue price" is determined under the OID rules (¶ 1321 *et seq.*). If, however, the OID rules do not apply but the Code Sec. 483 unstated interest rules (¶ 1311 *et seq.*) *do* apply, then the new debt's issue price is its stated redemption price at maturity (¶ 1320) less the amount of unstated interest. (Code Sec. 108(e)(11)(B))[22]

---

18. ¶ J-7031. 20. ¶s J-7014, J-7307; ¶ 1084.04. 21. ¶ J-7205; ¶ 1084.04. 22. ¶ J-7205; ¶ 1084.04.
19. ¶ J-7206; ¶ 614.114.

Footnote references beginning with letters are to paragraphs in RIA's Federal Tax Coordinator 2d and RIA's Analysis of Federal Taxes: Income. Footnote references beginning with numbers are to paragraphs in RIA's United States Tax Reporter.

Chapter 3   Deductions—Expenses of a Business

¶ 1500 Start-Up Expenditures

Start-up expenditures must be capitalized, unless a taxpayer elects to amortize them over an at-least-60-month period.

¶ 1501 Election to amortize start-up expenditures.

Start-up expenditures (below) must be capitalized and can't be deducted (Code Sec. 195(a)) unless the taxpayer elects (use Form 4562) to amortize those expenditures over a period of at least 60 months. (Code Sec. 195(b)(1))[1]

Start-up expenditures are amounts paid or incurred in connection with:

■ investigating the creation of or acquisition or establishment of an active trade or business; (Code Sec. 195(c)(1)(A)(i))

■ creating an active trade or business; (Code Sec. 195(c)(1)(A)(ii)) or

■ any activity engaged in for profit and for the production of income before the day the active trade or business begins, in anticipation of that activity becoming an active trade or business. (Code Sec. 195(c)(1)(A)(iii))

The expenditure must be one that, if paid or incurred in connection with the operation of an existing active trade or business (in the same field as the taxpayer's new business), would be deductible for the year in which paid or incurred. (Code Sec. 195(c)(1)(B))[2]

An acquired active trade or business begins when the taxpayer acquires the business. (Code Sec. 195(c)(2)(B))[3] Regs are to determine when an active trade or business that is not acquired begins. (Code Sec. 195(c)(2)(A))[4]

Start-up expenses do not include any amounts deductible:

■ under Code Sec. 163(a) (i.e., as interest expenses);

■ under Code Sec. 164 (i.e., as taxes); or

■ under Code Sec. 174 (i.e., as research and experimental expenses). (Code Sec. 195(c)(1))[5]

¶ 1502 Treatment of deferred start-up expenses on disposition of business.

If the trade or business is disposed of before the end of the amortization period, any deferred expenses not yet deducted may be deducted to the extent that the disposition results in a loss under Code Sec. 165. (Code Sec. 195(b)(2))[6]

¶ 1503 Fruitless searches.

A corporation that makes expenditures in fruitlessly searching for or investigating a new venture may deduct them as a loss when it abandons the effort.[7]

A noncorporate taxpayer not engaged in the business of locating or promoting new ventures may not deduct expenditures made in fruitlessly searching for or investigating a new venture. However, once a taxpayer has focused on the acquisition of a specific business or investment, unsuccessful start-up expenses that are related to an attempt to acquire that business or investment are deductible as business or investment losses under Code Sec. 165.[8]

¶ 1504 Expanding an existing business.

A taxpayer can deduct expenditures made to expand an existing business. The taxpayer must show:

■ that the business contemplated and the one already conducted are closely related or "intramural," *and*

---

1. ¶ L-5001; ¶ 1954.   3. ¶ L-5005.   5. ¶ L-5009; ¶ 1954.01.   7. ¶ L-5017.
2. ¶ L-5009; ¶ 1954.   4. ¶ L-5003; ¶ 1954.01.   6. ¶ L-5021; ¶ 1954.04.   8. ¶ L-5018.

Footnote references beginning with letters are to paragraphs in RIA's Federal Tax Coordinator 2d and RIA's Analysis of Federal Taxes: Income. Footnote references beginning with numbers are to paragraphs in RIA's United States Tax Reporter.

■ that the expenditures are ordinary and necessary expenses of the business conducted when the expenses were incurred, and not capital expenditures.[9]

¶ 1505 Ordinary and Necessary Business Expenses

Individuals, corporations and other taxpayers can deduct ordinary and necessary expenses paid or incurred during the tax year in carrying on any trade or business.

For the percentage limit on meal and entertainment deductions, see ¶ 1562.

For capital expenditures, see ¶ 1655 *et seq.*

For the "at-risk" limits on certain losses, see ¶ 1791 *et seq.*, and for the rules limiting the deduction of losses generated by "passive" activities, see ¶ 1798 *et seq.*

For the time for claiming deductions, see ¶ 2826 and ¶ 2835 *et seq.*

¶ 1506 "Ordinary and necessary" requirement.

A deductible business expense must be both ordinary and necessary in relation to the taxpayer's industry. (Code Sec. 162(a))[10]

An expense is *ordinary* if it's customary or usual in the taxpayer's business.[11] But an unusual expense may be ordinary if it is reasonably related to the taxpayer's trade or business.[12]

A *necessary* expense is one that is appropriate and helpful in developing and maintaining the taxpayer's business. It need not be essential or indispensable. Usually the taxpayer's judgment as to what is necessary will be accepted.[13]

Expenditures are deductible as ordinary and necessary even though they turn out to have been unwise.[14]

¶ 1507 Connection to taxpayer's trade or business.

To be deductible as a business expense, an item must be incurred in connection with a trade or business. (Code Sec. 162(a)) The item must be directly connected with or pertaining to a trade or business carried on by the taxpayer. (Reg § 1.162-1(a))[15]

Serving as an employee is a business.[16] A trade or business need not be the taxpayer's principal occupation; a sideline can qualify.[17]

¶ 1508 Expense must benefit person claiming deduction.

A deductible expense must be an expense of *the taxpayer's* business. Expenses incurred on another's behalf are not deductible.[18]

A corporation's payment of the personal expenses of its stockholders is not deductible.[19]

Payment by a corporation of the personal expenses of its officers and employees is not deductible, except to the extent the payment represents reasonable compensation (see ¶ 1513) or is made for business reasons to provide benefits to employees in general.[20]

An expenditure by a corporate officer isn't deductible by the officer if it is made to pay an expense of the corporation.[21]

If a taxpayer pays the debts or other obligations of someone else, the payment may or may not qualify as a business expense.[22] Deductions have been allowed where the payment of another's obligation is made for a good business reason, e.g., to preserve sales-force morale and customer goodwill; to reestablish or protect credit standing; to avoid loss

---

9. ¶ L-5101.
10. ¶ L-1200 *et seq.*; ¶ 1624.012.
11. ¶ L-1201; ¶ 1624.
12. ¶s L-1201, L-1209; ¶ 1624.012.
13. ¶ L-1201; ¶ 1824.012.
14. ¶ L-1210.
15. ¶ L-1002; ¶ 1624.
16. ¶s L-1106, L-3900; ¶ 1624.
17. ¶ L-1100 *et seq.*; ¶ 1624.002.
18. ¶ L-4400; ¶ 1624.104.
19. ¶ L-1214; ¶ 1624.104.
20. ¶ L-4414.
21. ¶ L-4405; ¶ 1624.009.
22. ¶ L-1214; ¶ 1624.104.

Footnote references beginning with letters are to paragraphs in RIA's Federal Tax Coordinator 2d and RIA's Analysis of Federal Taxes: Income. Footnote references beginning with numbers are to paragraphs in RIA's United States Tax Reporter.

of business patronage, etc.[23]

¶ 1509 Right to deduction—*Cohan* rule.

Deductions are allowed as a matter of "legislative grace." Consequently when IRS wholly or partly disallows a deduction, the taxpayer has the burden of proving he is entitled to deduct the claimed amount.[24]

Where his records or other proof are not adequate to substantiate expense deductions, the taxpayer may be allowed to deduct an estimated amount under the *Cohan* rule. But the deduction may be for much less than he spent, since the court in making an estimate may bear heavily upon a taxpayer whose inexactitude is of his own making.[25]

The *Cohan* rule does not apply to travel or entertainment expenses, listed property, or business gifts, see ¶ 1573 *et seq.*

¶ 1510 Expenses of taxable social clubs and other membership organizations.

Organizations that are not exempt from tax under the rules discussed in ¶ 4100 *et seq.*, which are operated primarily to furnish services or goods to members, can deduct expenses of furnishing services, insurance, goods, or other items to members only to the extent of income derived during the year from members or transactions with members. (Code Sec. 277(a))[26] Any excess of expenses over income is not deductible, but may be carried over to the following taxable year. (Code Sec. 277(a))[27]

¶ 1511 Compensation Deduction

Reasonable amounts that are paid or incurred in connection with a trade or business as compensation for personal services actually rendered are deductible. Payments for fringe benefits such as life insurance and medical benefits are deductible as compensation, subject to some limits.

¶ 1512 Compensation paid for personal services.

To be deductible as a trade or business expense, compensation must be paid or incurred for personal services rendered. (Code Sec. 162(a)(1)) This rule applies to compensation paid for personal services of professionals and other independent contractors, as well as employees.[28]

A parent can deduct reasonable wages he pays his unemancipated minor child for personal services actually rendered as a bona fide employee in the business.[29]

For deductibility of amounts paid for fringe benefits, see ¶ 1523 *et seq.* For when compensation can be deducted, see ¶ 1531 *et seq.*

¶ 1513 Reasonableness of compensation.

Compensation is deductible only to the extent it is *reasonable.* (Code Sec. 162(a)(1))[30]

The question of reasonableness rarely arises unless the payments are to a person "related" to the taxpayer—that is, to the members of an employer's family, or to stockholders of the employer, or to members of a stockholder's family.[31]

The unreasonable portion of compensation is nondeductible. If the recipient is a stockholder, the unreasonable portion may be treated as a dividend. (Reg § 1.162-7(b)(1))[32]

---

23. ¶ L-1214 *et seq.*; ¶ 1624.026.
24. ¶ L-4501; ¶ 1624.017.
25. ¶ L-4507 *et seq.*; ¶ 1624.014.
26. ¶ L-4305; ¶ 2774.

27. ¶ L-4306; ¶ 2774.
28. ¶ H-3600 *et seq.*; ¶ 1624.205.
29. ¶ H-3741; ¶ 1624.212.

30. ¶ H-3700 *et seq.*; ¶ 1624.205.
31. ¶s H-3702 *et seq.*, H-3738 *et seq.*; ¶ 1624.229.

32. ¶ H-3607; ¶ 1624.229.

Footnote references beginning with letters are to paragraphs in RIA's Federal Tax Coordinator 2d and RIA's Analysis of Federal Taxes: Income. Footnote references beginning with numbers are to paragraphs in RIA's United States Tax Reporter.

¶ 1514 Factors determining reasonableness.

Reasonable compensation is the amount that would ordinarily be paid for like services by like enterprises under like circumstances. (Reg § 1.162-7(b)(3))[33] Other factors determining reasonableness include:

- duties performed by the employee;
- character and amount of responsibility;
- amount of time required;
- ability and achievements of the employee;
- volume of business handled by the employee;
- complexities of the business;
- relationship of compensation to gross and net income of the business;
- living conditions in locality;
- compensation history of the employee;
- salary policy as to all employees.[34]

The test of whether compensation is reasonable is normally applied to the compensation paid to the particular individual and not to the total compensation paid to a group of employees.[35] Services rendered in earlier years can be taken into account in determining the reasonableness of compensation paid during the current year.[36]

Reasonableness of compensation for part-time services is determined under the usual reasonableness rules. Generally, salaries that are reasonable for an employee's full-time services are not reasonable for his part-time services.[37]

¶ 1515 Deduction limit after '93 for compensation over $1,000,000 paid to top five officers.

No deduction is allowed for tax years beginning after '93 to a publicly held corporation for applicable employee remuneration (below) in excess of $1,000,000 per year paid to a covered employee (Code Sec. 162(m)(1))[38] —the CEO and the four highest paid officers other than the CEO. (Code Sec. 162(m)(3))[39]

The $1 million limit is reduced (but not below zero) by the amount, if any, paid to the executive but not deductible under the golden parachute rules. (Code Sec. 162(m)(4)(F))[40]

Applicable employee remuneration means a covered employee's aggregate remuneration for services performed (either during the deduction year or during another tax year) which would be deductible in its entirety for the tax year if the $1 million limitation did not apply. (Code Sec. 162(m)(4)(A)) But it does not include commissions generated directly by the executive's performance, (Code Sec. 162(m)(4)(B)), certain other performance-based compensation, (Code Sec. 162(m)(4)(C)) qualified plan contributions for employees and certain excludable employee fringe benefits, (Code Sec. 162(m)(4)(E)) and remuneration paid under a written binding contract that was in effect on Feb. 17, '93, (Code Sec. 162(m)(4)(D))[41]

¶ 1516 Payment in property other than cash.

The deduction for compensation paid in property, including a bargain sale and including restricted property, is the amount that is compensation income to the person who performed the services, to the extent the compensation is reasonable. (Code Sec. 83(h)) This is normally the fair market value of the property less the amount paid for the property by the employee, if any.[42] (For special rules on restricted property, see ¶ 1216; for

33. ¶ H-3701; ¶ 1624.229.
34. ¶ H-3706; ¶ 1624.229.
35. ¶ H-3703; ¶ 1624.229.

36. ¶ H-3730; ¶ 1624.229.
37. ¶ H-3734; ¶ 1624.229.
38. ¶ H-3761; ¶ 1624.009.

39. ¶ H-3763; ¶ 1624.009.
40. ¶ H-3777; ¶ 1624.009.

41. ¶ H-3764 *et seq.*; ¶ 1624.009.
42. ¶ H-3926; ¶ 1624.273.

Footnote references beginning with letters are to paragraphs in RIA's Federal Tax Coordinator 2d and RIA's Analysis of Federal Taxes: Income. Footnote references beginning with numbers are to paragraphs in RIA's United States Tax Reporter.

special rules where compensation is in the form of noncash fringe benefits, see ¶ 1523.)

The deduction is allowed for the tax year of the employer in which, or with which, the employee's tax year ends. (Code Sec. 83(h))[43]

Illustration: X Corporation, which is on a fiscal year that ends on Sept. 30, pays employee J in stock on July 1, Year 1. J, who is on a calendar year, reports the income on his return for Year 1. X deducts the payment on its return for the year ending Sept. 30, Year 2, because that is X's tax year in which the tax year of J, in which the amounts are included in income, ends.

If payment is made in property other than the employer's stock, and the value of the property exceeds the employer's basis for the property, the excess is income to the employer (capital gain or ordinary income, depending on the character of the property used). (Reg § 1.83-6(b)) The employer has a loss deduction where the basis of the property exceeds its fair market value[44] (subject to related-taxpayer restrictions on losses).[45]

Illustration: L Corp pays employee R General Motors stock with a value of $2,500 and a basis to L of $1,000. L has a compensation deduction of $2,500 and a $1,500 gain.

If payment is in stock of the employer, no gain or loss results. (Code Sec. 1032)[46]

¶ 1517 Contingent compensation.

Contingent compensation paid under a free bargain between the employer and the individual made before services are rendered, not influenced by any consideration on the part of the employer other than that of securing on fair and advantageous terms the services of the individual, is deductible. This is true even though the arrangement results in higher compensation than would otherwise be allowed as a deduction. The circumstances to be considered in determining reasonableness of the amount are those existing at the date when the contract for services is made, not when the contract is questioned. (Reg § 1.162-7(b)(2), (3))[47]

¶ 1518 Stock options.

The employer is not allowed a compensation deduction with respect to options that qualified as statutory stock options or that are granted under an employee stock purchase plan, unless the employee has income by reason of a disqualified (premature) distribution of his plan stock (see ¶ 1220 *et seq.*). (Code Sec. 421(a), (b))[48]

¶ 1519 Payment of employee debts or expenses.

An employer's payment of an employee's debts or personal expenses is compensation to the employee and deductible as compensation by the employer, just as if the employee had been paid directly and he had used the money to pay his debts or expenses.[49]

Furnishing property to an employee for his personal use is additional compensation to him and gives rise to a compensation deduction by the employer. For example, the employer can deduct depreciation and maintenance expenses it pays on a car, house, etc., furnished for an employee's personal use and treated by the employer as compensation. (Code Sec. 274(e)(3))[50]

¶ 1520 Services rendered to another.

No deduction is allowed for payments by the taxpayer for services rendered to someone other than the taxpayer—for example, payments by a stockholder to employees of the corporation for services to the corporation, or by a corporation to its officers for services to subsidiaries and related corporations, or by a corporation to employees of a sub. But

43. ¶ H-3653; ¶ 834.04.
44. ¶ H-3658.
45. ¶ I-3500 *et seq.*
46. ¶ H-3658; ¶ 10,324.
47. ¶ H-3714; ¶ 1624.229.
48. ¶ H-2958; ¶ 4214.01.
49. ¶ H-4010; ¶ 1624.273.
50. ¶s H-2150 *et seq.*, H-2160; ¶ 1624.205.

Footnote references beginning with letters are to paragraphs in RIA's Federal Tax Coordinator 2d and RIA's Analysis of Federal Taxes: Income. Footnote references beginning with numbers are to paragraphs in RIA's United States Tax Reporter.

salary paid by a parent corporation to its own executives for supervising the operations of a sub is deductible by the parent as an expense of the parent's business.[1]

¶ 1521 "Golden parachute" payments.

No deduction is allowed for an "excess parachute payment." (Code Sec. 280G)[2]

"Excess parachute payment" is the amount by which a parachute payment exceeds the base amount (below) allocated to it. (Code Sec. 280G(b)(1)) If there is only one parachute payment the entire base amount is allocated to it.[3]

A "parachute payment" is any payment in the nature of compensation to (or for the benefit of) a "disqualified individual" (described below) *if*:

(1) the payment is contingent on a change (a) in the ownership or effective control of the corporation, *or* (b) in the ownership of a substantial portion of the assets of the corporation, *and*

(2) the aggregate present value of all such contingent compensation payments equals, or exceeds, three times the base amount. (Code Sec. 280G(b))[4] This base amount is the average annualized compensation income includible in a disqualified individual's gross income in the five-tax-year period preceding the tax year in which the change of ownership or control of the corporation occurs. (Code Sec. 280G(b), (d))[5]

A "disqualified individual" is any individual who is:

(1) an employee, independent contractor, or other person specified in regs to be issued who performs personal services for a corporation, *and*

(2) is an officer, shareholder or highly compensated individual. (Code Sec. 280G(c))[6]

"Highly compensated individual" means anyone who is a member of the highest paid 1% of employees or, if less, the highest paid 250 employees. (Code Sec. 280G(c))[7]

However, the amount of an "excess parachute payment" can be reduced to the extent that the taxpayer can establish by "clear and convincing evidence" that the payment is reasonable compensation for personal services actually rendered, before or after the date of change of ownership or control. (Code Sec. 280G(b)(4))[8]

The parachute payment rules do not apply to any corporation eligible to be an S corporation. Nor do they apply to a corporation whose stock is not readily tradeable if shareholder approval has been obtained. (Code Sec. 280G(b)(5))[9]

Payments to or from a qualified pension or profit-sharing plan are not parachute payments. (Code Sec. 280G(b)(6))[10]

¶ 1522 Contributions to funded welfare benefit plans.

An employer's contribution to a "welfare benefit fund" is deductible only for the tax year paid, and only to the extent the contribution does not exceed the "qualified cost" of the welfare benefit plan for its tax year that relates to (ends with or within) the employer's tax year. (Code Sec. 419(a), (b))[11] Contributions by independent contractors are also subject to this rule. (Code Sec. 419(g))[12] The rule, however, does not apply to a ten-or-more employer plan if no employer (or related employer) normally contributes more than 10% of total contributions, unless the plan uses experience ratings to determine each employer's contribution. (Code Sec. 419A(f)(6))[13]

A welfare benefit fund is a fund that is part of an employer's plan through which the employer provides welfare benefits to employees or their beneficiaries, but does not include amounts held under certain kinds of insurance contracts. (Code Sec. 419(e))[14]

---

1. ¶ H-3612; ¶s 1624.104, 1624.206.
2. ¶ H-3801; ¶ 280G4.
3. ¶ H-3847.2; ¶ 280G4.
4. ¶ H-3805; ¶ 280G4.

5. ¶ H-3839; ¶ 280G4.
6. ¶ H-3815; ¶ 280G4.
7. ¶ H-3815; ¶ 280G4.
8. ¶ H-3847.4; ¶ 280G4.

9. ¶ H-3810; ¶ 280G4.
10. ¶ H-3814; ¶ 280G4.
11. ¶s H-4101, H-4113 *et seq.*; ¶ 4194.

12. ¶ H-4112; ¶ 4194.01.
13. ¶ H-4155; ¶ 4194.02.
14. ¶ H-4103 *et seq.*; ¶ 4194.02.

Footnote references beginning with letters are to paragraphs in RIA's Federal Tax Coordinator 2d and RIA's Analysis of Federal Taxes: Income. Footnote references beginning with numbers are to paragraphs in RIA's United States Tax Reporter.

¶ 1523   Compensation paid as noncash fringe benefits.

Where the employer furnishes a noncash fringe benefit to an employee as compensation, the employer may deduct as compensation only the costs it incurs in providing the property to its employees, not the property's value. Where the property is depreciable, the employer is entitled to a depreciation deduction. Where the property is leased by the employer, the employer is entitled to a deduction for the leasing costs as an ordinary and necessary business expense. (Reg § 1.162-25T(a))[15]

¶ 1524   Employee's life insurance.

An employer can't deduct premiums if the employer is directly or indirectly a beneficiary of any part of the policy. (Code Sec. 264(a)(1)) However, the premiums are deductible where only the insured employee or his beneficiaries will get the proceeds.[16]

Premiums on group term insurance are deductible even though the employee is not taxed on group term coverage of $50,000 or less.[17]

¶ 1525   Medical benefits.

The employer's payment of health and accident insurance premiums for employees and their families, or the employer's direct payment or reimbursement of actual expenses if under a plan, is deductible. (Reg § 1.162-10(a))[18] IRS treats these amounts as additional compensation deductible by the employer to the extent that it, when added to other compensation, is reasonable.[19]

¶ 1526   Continuation coverage (COBRA).

A group health plan (of or contributed to by an employer) must provide that each qualified beneficiary who would lose coverage under the plan as a result of a qualifying event is entitled to elect continuation coverage under the plan within a specified at-least-60-day election period. (Code Sec. 4980B(f)(1))[20]

The "qualified beneficiaries" are the spouse or dependent child of a covered employee as well as the employee himself and a deceased employee's surviving spouse in certain cases. (Code Sec. 4980B(g)(1))[21]

The "qualifying events" that entitle an employee to continuation coverage include: death of the covered employee; termination or reduction of hours of the covered employee's employment; divorce or legal separation from the covered employee; cessation of a child's dependency; and the employee's entitlement to certain Medicare benefits. (Code Sec. 4980(f)(3))[22]

The continuation coverage must be identical to coverage provided under the plan to similarly situated beneficiaries who have not had a qualifying event. (Code Sec. 4980B(f)(2)(A))[23] Coverage for a qualified beneficiary must begin on the date of the qualifying event and end not earlier than: a statutory maximum period, the end of the plan, the failure to pay a premium, or the eligibility for group health plan coverage or Medicare.[24]

For plan years beginning after Aug. 10, '93, the coverage of the cost of pediatric vaccines must not be reduced below the coverage provided by the plan as of May 1, '93. (Code Sec. 4980B(f)(1))[25]

---

15. ¶ H-4002; ¶ 1624.283.
16. ¶ H-4031; ¶ 2644.
17. ¶ H-4037; ¶ 794.07.

18. ¶s H-4071, G-4073; ¶ 1624.277.
19. ¶ H-4072; ¶ 1624.229.

20. ¶ H-1250 *et seq.*; ¶ 49,80B4.
21. ¶ H-1267; ¶ 49,80B4.
22. ¶ H-1303; ¶ 49,80B4.

23. ¶ H-1273; ¶ 49,80B4.
24. ¶ H-1295; ¶ 49,80B4.
25. ¶ H-1250 *et seq.*; ¶ 49,80B4.

Footnote references beginning with letters are to paragraphs in RIA's Federal Tax Coordinator 2d and RIA's Analysis of Federal Taxes: Income. Footnote references beginning with numbers are to paragraphs in RIA's United States Tax Reporter.

¶ 1527   Excise tax for failure to provide continuation coverage.

An employer (or in the case of a multiemployer plan, the plan) and certain responsible (nonemployee) persons are liable for an excise tax (Code Sec. 4980B(e))[26] if, with certain exceptions, a group health plan fails to provide the continuation coverage or the coverage of the cost of pediatric vaccines described at ¶ 1526. (Code Sec. 4980B(a))[27]

¶ 1528   Self-employed individual's health insurance deduction before '94.

A self-employed individual (or a more-than-2%-shareholder of an S corporation, see below) can deduct as a business expense 25% of the amount paid for medical insurance on himself, his spouse and his dependents. (Code Sec. 162(l)(1)) The amount paid for insurance must be reduced by the amount of the pre-'94 health insurance credit allowed under the rules at ¶ 2337.

The deduction doesn't apply to any tax year beginning after '93. (Code Sec. 162(l)(6))[28]

No deduction is allowed to the extent the deduction exceeds the individual's earned income as defined in Code Sec. 401(c) (net earnings from self-employment) derived from the trade or business with respect to which the plan providing the coverage is established. (Code Sec. 162(l)(2)(A))[29] For purposes of applying the earned income limit to the deduction of a more-than-2% S corporation shareholder, that shareholder's wages from the S corporation are treated as his earned income. (Code Sec. 162(l)(5)(A))[30]

No individual who is eligible to participate in any subsidized health plan maintained by any employer of the individual or of the individual's spouse is entitled to the deduction. This test for eligibility is made for each calendar month. (Code Sec. 162(l)(2))(B)[31]

The above deduction was retroactively extended from June 30, '92, after most '92 returns were filed. For how to get a refund of taxes paid on post-June 30, '92 amounts, see ¶ 4849.

¶ 1529   Death benefits to employee's beneficiaries.

Payments to the widow or other beneficiaries of a deceased employee, as by continuing his salary for a reasonable period, (including amounts excludable as death benefits, see ¶ 1262) are deductible by the employer to the extent they qualify as a business expense. A benefit paid as a gift based on the beneficiary's may not qualify as a business expense. (Reg § 1.404(a)-12)[32]

¶ 1530   Compensation payments as capital outlays.

Compensation payments that result in the acquisition of property or rights that have value or are useful to the business must be capitalized, i.e., added to the basis of property. Thus, capitalization has been required for payments for services in organizing and incorporating a company; in acquiring valuable property, or in negotiating its sale.[33]

Payments that are purportedly compensation may in reality be the purchase price of property. If so, no expense deduction is allowed. This may arise when a business or other property is purchased and the former owner agrees to continue to perform services. If the payments for services are reasonable in relation to the services rendered, they are deductible. But if the payments for services are excessive, a part may be considered payment for the purchase price of the property. (Reg § 1.162-7(b)(1))[34]

¶ 1531   Year for deducting compensation.

The employer deducts compensation in the year deduction is allowed under his cash or accrual accounting method (¶ 2817 et seq.) with special rules for compensation in property

---

26. ¶ H-1316; ¶ 49,80B4.   29. ¶ L-3510; ¶ 1624.403.   31. ¶ L-3510; ¶ 1624.403.   33. ¶ H-3603; ¶ 1624.081.
27. ¶ H-1315; ¶ 49,80B4.   30. ¶ L-3510; ¶ 1624.403.   32. ¶ H-4051; ¶ 1624.277.   34. ¶ H-3604.
28. ¶ L-3510; ¶ 1624.403.

Footnote references beginning with letters are to paragraphs in RIA's Federal Tax Coordinator 2d and RIA's Analysis of Federal Taxes: Income. Footnote references beginning with numbers are to paragraphs in RIA's United States Tax Reporter.

and bargain sales (¶ 1212 *et seq.*) and contributions to employee benefit plans (¶ 4333).

If salary is paid or accrued in one year for services to be rendered in a later year, the deduction is allowed only over the period during which the services are rendered. This applies to both cash and accrual-basis employers.[35]

An employer's contributions to a nonqualified deferred compensation plan are deductible in the tax year in which an amount attributable to the contribution is includible in the gross income of employees participating in the plan, (Code Sec. 404(a)(5)) even if the employer is an accrual basis taxpayer.[36] Benefits provided under a welfare benefit fund, (Code Sec. 404(b)(2)(B)) and payments of bonuses or other amounts within 2½ months after the close of the tax year in which significant services required for payment have been performed (Reg § 1.404(b)-1T, Q&A-2(c)) aren't treated as deferred compensation.[37]

For limitations on accrual-basis taxpayers' deductions for compensation paid to related cash-basis taxpayers, see ¶ 2839.

¶ 1532 Bonuses paid to employees.

A cash basis employer deducts bonuses only for the year in which the bonuses are actually paid. But an accrual basis taxpayer deducts bonuses for the year in which the liability to pay the bonus becomes fixed.[38]

Bonuses by an accrual basis taxpayer are deductible in the tax year when all the events have occurred that establish the fact of liability to pay the bonus, the amount can be determined with reasonable accuracy, and economic performance has occurred with respect to the liability (see ¶ 2836). (Reg § 1.461-1(a)(2)(i))[39]

In order to deduct a year-end bonus in the year of accrual rather that the year of actual payment an employer must pay the bonus within a brief period of time after the close of the employer's tax year. Under a rebuttable presumption, if an employer pays bonuses within 2 ½ months after the close of the tax year, then a deduction for the bonuses won't be subject to the deferred compensation rules (¶ 1531) which would act to bar the deduction until the bonus is included in the employee's income. (Reg § 1.404(b)-1T)[40]

The presumption that payment after 2 ½ months is deferred compensation can only be rebutted by showing that: (1) it was either administratively or economically impossible to avoid a later payment, and (2) as of the end of the employer's tax year, the impracticability was unforeseeable. (Reg § 1.404(b)-1T)[41]

¶ 1533 Vacation pay.

Cash basis employers take a deduction when the vacation pay is paid in accordance with the general rules for cash basis employers.[42]

For an accrual basis employer, vacation pay earned during any tax year but not paid on or before 2½ months after the end of the tax year is deductible for the tax year of the employer in which it is paid. (Code Sec. 404(a)(5))[43]

¶ 1534 Travel Expenses

The costs of travel away from home can qualify as deductible expenses.

¶ 1535 Deduction for travel costs.

Ordinary and necessary expenses incurred while traveling "away from home" in pursuit of a trade or business are deductible. Those expenses include amounts (other than amounts that are lavish or extravagant) paid for meals (subject to a percentage limit, see ¶ 1562) and lodging. (Code Sec. 162(a)(2))[44]

---

35. ¶ H-3932.
36. ¶ H-3673.
37. ¶ H-3671.

38. ¶s H-3901, H-3916;
     ¶ 1624.218.
39. ¶ H-3916.

40. ¶ H-3919.
41. ¶ H-3919.
42. ¶ H-3922.

43. ¶ H-3922.
44. ¶ L-1701; ¶ 1624.114.

Footnote references beginning with letters are to paragraphs in RIA's Federal Tax Coordinator 2d and RIA's Analysis of Federal Taxes: Income. Footnote references beginning with numbers are to paragraphs in RIA's United States Tax Reporter.

Deductible travel expenses undertaken for business include baggage charges, air, rail and bus fares, cost of transporting sample cases or display materials, expenses for sample rooms, cost of maintaining or operating a car, house trailer or airplane, telephone and telegraph expenses, laundry and dry cleaning costs, taxi fares, etc., from the airport or station to the hotel and back, from one customer to another, transportation from where meals and lodging are obtained to the temporary work assignment, and reasonable tips incident to any of the above expenses. Reg § 1.162-2(a)))[45]

Travel expenses don't include expenses of the taxpayer's own entertainment.[46]

¶ 1536 Home defined for travel expense purposes.

A taxpayer's home for travel expense purposes is his "tax home"—his principal place of business, employment station, or post of duty, regardless of where his family lives.[47]

Where an individual has no principal place of business or employment but continually changes work locations (e.g., a traveling salesmen), his regular residence is his tax "home."[48] If such a taxpayer has no regular place of abode in a real and substantial sense, he has no "home" and can't deduct travel expenses.[49]

If a taxpayer regularly works at two or more separate locations, his tax home is the general area where his *principal* employment or business is located. The principal place is determined on the facts of the particular case. Important factors are: (1) time spent, (2) business activity, and (3) financial return. Income is the most significant factor.[50] In rare circumstances, a taxpayer may have two tax homes.[1]

Costs of traveling to and from the minor place of employment, 80% (50% after '93) of the cost of meals, and lodging at the minor post are deductible travel expenses.[2]

Certain state legislators may elect to treat their residence in their legislative district (instead of the state capitol) as their tax home. (Code Sec. 162(h))[3]

¶ 1537 Temporary assignment away from home.

A temporary assignment away from home—an assignment whose termination can be foreseen within a fixed and reasonably short period—doesn't shift the "tax home." Therefore, a taxpayer may deduct the necessary traveling expenses in getting to his temporary assignment and also for the return trip to his tax home after the temporary assignment is completed, and his expenses for lodging and 80% (50% after '93) of the cost of meals while he is in the place to which he is temporarily assigned, even for his days off.[4] If he returns home on his nonworking days, he may deduct his travel expenses to his home, but his travel expenses deduction is limited to the amount he would have spent to stay at his temporary location.[5]

A taxpayer is not treated as being temporarily away from home if his period of employment exceeds one year.[6] In the case of employment away from home at a single location for less than one year, the facts and circumstances determine whether employment is temporary.[7]

¶ 1538 Indefinite assignment away from home.

An indefinite assignment away from home shifts the "tax home" and taxpayer can't deduct the expenses of travel, meals and lodging while in the location of the "indefinite" assignment.[8] Employment is indefinite if it lasts for one year or more.[9] In the case of employment away from home at a single location for less than one year, the facts and circumstances determine whether employment is indefinite.[10]

45. ¶ L-1705; ¶ 1624.114.
46. ¶ L-1713.
47. ¶ L-1801; ¶ 1624.125.
48. ¶ L-1802; ¶ 1624.125.
49. ¶ L-2024; ¶ 1624.125.
50. ¶ L-1807; ¶ 1624.141.
1. ¶ L-1808.
2. ¶ L-1805; ¶ 1624.141.
3. ¶ L-2025.
4. ¶ L-1810; ¶ 1624.130.
5. ¶ L-1813.
6. ¶ L-1815.
7. ¶ L-1811.
8. ¶ L-1814; ¶ 1624.130.
9. ¶ L-1816.
10. ¶ L-1811.

Footnote references beginning with letters are to paragraphs in RIA's Federal Tax Coordinator 2d and RIA's Analysis of Federal Taxes: Income. Footnote references beginning with numbers are to paragraphs in RIA's United States Tax Reporter.

¶ 1539 Overnight trip.

Travel expense deduction for meals and lodging isn't allowed unless the trip takes the taxpayer away from home *overnight*, or at least long enough to require rest or sleep.[11] The individual need not be away from his tax home for an entire 24-hour day or throughout the hours from dusk to dawn if his relief from duty is long enough to get necessary sleep. Layover sufficient only for a short rest and to get a meal isn't "overnight."[12] Although they were not traveling, state troopers who were required to eat exclusively in roadside restaurants were allowed by the Eighth Circuit to deduct the cost as an ordinary and necessary business expense, but IRS disagrees with this result.[13]

¶ 1540 U.S. travel for business and pleasure.

Transportation costs to and from the destination are deductible only if the trip is related primarily to the taxpayer's business. Expenses at the destination that are allocable to the taxpayer's business are deductible even if the expenses of getting to and from the destination are disallowed because the trip was primarily a pleasure trip.[14] If the trip is primarily for business, but the taxpayer extends his stay for personal reasons, makes side trips, or engages in other nonbusiness activities, he may deduct only the expenses, such as lodging and 80% (50% after '93) of the cost of meals, that he would have incurred if the trip had been totally for business. But no allocation is required for transportation costs to and from the business destination. (Reg § 1.162-2(b)(1))[15]

¶ 1541 Foreign travel for business and pleasure.

If travel is primarily for pleasure, the rules at ¶ 1540 apply, so that only the amount directly allocable to business is deductible. But under special rules for foreign travel, even where travel is primarily for business, a portion of transportation, meals and lodgings, etc., expenses of the business part (as well as all the pleasure part) is nondeductible. The nondeductible part is computed on a time ratio, usually in the proportion of nonbusiness days to all travel days.

This allocation and denial of deduction is not made if: (1) travel is for one week or less; or (2) less than 25% of the time is spent in nonbusiness activity; or (3) the individual traveling had no substantial control over the arranging of the trip; or (4) a personal vacation was not a major consideration in making the trip. (Code Sec. 274(c); Reg § 1.162-2(b), Reg § 1.274-4(f)(5))[16] For foreign conventions, see ¶ 1543.

¶ 1542 Convention expenses.

Travel expenses incurred in attending a convention are deductible if attendance will benefit or advance the taxpayer's business or the employee's responsibilities as distinguished from serving some social, political, or other nonbusiness function. The fact that attendance is voluntary doesn't prevent deduction. (Reg § 1.162-2(d))[17]

¶ 1543 Foreign conventions.

No business expense deduction is allowed for expenses allocable to a convention, seminar, or similar meeting held outside the North American area (defined below) unless the taxpayer establishes that the meeting is directly related to the active conduct of his trade or business, or to an activity relating to the production of income and that, after taking specified factors into account, it is as reasonable for the meeting to be held outside the North American area as within it. (Code Sec. 274(h)(1))

North American area means the U.S., its possessions, the Trust Territory of the Pacific Islands, Canada and Mexico. (Code Sec. 274(h)(3)(A)) U.S. possessions include Puerto

---

11. ¶ L-1710; ¶ 1624.147.
12. ¶ L-1710; ¶ 1624.147.
13. ¶s L-1009, L-1709; ¶ 1624.147.
14. ¶ L-1702; ¶ 1624.119.
15. ¶ L-1702; ¶ 1624.119.
16. ¶ L-1727 *et seq.*; ¶ 2744.04.
17. ¶ L-1716; ¶ 1624.119.

Footnote references beginning with letters are to paragraphs in RIA's Federal Tax Coordinator 2d and RIA's Analysis of Federal Taxes: Income. Footnote references beginning with numbers are to paragraphs in RIA's United States Tax Reporter.

Rico and the U.S. Virgin Islands.[18] "North American" also includes Bermuda and certain Caribbean countries under certain conditions, (Code Sec. 274(h)(6)(A))[19] including Barbados, Costa Rica, the Dominican Republic, Grenada, Guyana, Honduras, Jamaica, St. Lucia, and Trinidad and Tobago.

¶ 1544 Cruise ship convention.

A deduction of up to $2,000 per individual per year is allowed for attending business conventions, etc., held aboard a cruise ship, but only if the ship is registered in the U.S. and all ports of call of the cruise ship are located in the U.S. or its possessions. (Code Sec. 274(h)(2)) A married couple filing a joint return could deduct $4,000 if each spent at least $2,000 for attending a business-related cruise ship convention.[20]

A taxpayer claiming the deduction must attach to his return two specified written substantiation statements (including one signed by the sponsor). (Code Sec. 274(h)(5))[21]

¶ 1545 Travel expense deduction for a companion.

An individual taxpayer's travel expense deduction for a family member who accompanied the taxpayer on a business trip or convention is denied *unless* the taxpayer can establish that the other's presence serves a bona fide business purpose. Incidental services such as typing notes, assisting in entertaining customers, etc., are not enough to permit the deduction of the family member's travel expenses. But a deduction was allowed for a wife's expenses where her presence was considered important for the company's public image, and she attended dinners, social functions, etc.[22]

For amounts paid or incurred after '93, no deduction is allowed (other than a deduction under Code Sec. 217 (concerning moving expenses)) for travel expenses paid or incurred with respect to a spouse, dependent, or other individual accompanying the taxpayer (or an officer or employee of the taxpayer) unless(Code Sec. 274(m)(3)):

- the individual is an employee of the taxpayer,
- the travel of the individual is for a bona fide business purpose, and
- the expenses would otherwise be deductible by the individual.[23]

If a wife accompanies her husband on a business trip and her expenses aren't deductible, the deductible expense for transportation and lodging is the single rate cost of similar accommodations for the husband. But the full rental for a car in which both spouses travel is deductible, since no part of the expense is attributable to the "extra" spouse.[24]

¶ 1546 Luxury water travel.

The deduction allowed for travel by ocean liner, cruise ship, or other form of "luxury" water transportation is limited to twice the highest domestic per diem allowance of executive branch U.S. government employees (other than high-ranking executive personnel) multiplied by the number of days of luxury water travel. (Code Sec. 274(m)(1)(A)) If the cost includes separately stated amounts for meals and entertainment, these amounts must be reduced by 20% (50% after '93) (see ¶ 1562). The per diem rule does not apply to cruise ship, convention, or seminar expenses to which the rules at ¶ 1544 apply, (Code Sec. 274(m)(l)(B)(i)) or to:

- expenses treated as compensation paid to an employee or otherwise included in the gross income of the recipient;
- reimbursed expenses where the services are performed for an employer and the employer hasn't treated the reimbursement as compensation;
- expenses for recreational or social activities primarily for the benefit of employees;

---

18. ¶s L-1743, L-1744; ¶ 2744.04.   20. ¶ L-1721; ¶ 2744.04.   22. ¶ L-1739 *et seq.*; ¶ 1624.119.   24. ¶ L-1739 *et seq.*; ¶ 1624.119.
19. ¶ L-1745; ¶ 2744.04.   21. ¶ L-1722; ¶ 2740.   23. ¶ Z-9999.

Footnote references beginning with letters are to paragraphs in RIA's Federal Tax Coordinator 2d and RIA's Analysis of Federal Taxes: Income. Footnote references beginning with numbers are to paragraphs in RIA's United States Tax Reporter.

- services and facilities made available by the taxpayer to the general public;

- services and facilities sold to customers. (Code Sec. 274(m)(1)(B)(ii))[25]

¶ 1547 Transportation Expenses

Costs of local transportation (including the cost of operating and maintaining a car directly attributable to the conduct of a trade or business) can qualify as deductible expenses.

¶ 1548 Transportation expenses other than commuting expenses.

Transportation expenses (but not commuting expenses, see ¶ 1549) directly attributable to the conduct of the taxpayer's business are deductible even though he is not away from home overnight. (Reg § 1.162-1(a)) These expenses (sometimes called local travel expenses though they can involve long trips) include air, train, bus and cab fares and costs of operating automobiles, but don't include meals and lodging.[26]

¶ 1549 Expenses of commuting.

Expenses of commuting between a taxpayer's residence and his regular business location wherever situated, aren't deductible, (Reg § 1.162-2(e), (f)) even to a remote area where there is no residential area nearby and no public transportation.[27] A taxpayer who goes to a "temporary" or minor work assignment beyond the "general area of his tax home" and returns home each evening may deduct the expenses of the daily round trip transportation.[28] If he works at two or more places each day, he can deduct the cost of getting from one to the other. A taxpayer may deduct expenses of traveling between his home and other business locations only if his home is his principal place of business.[29]

¶ 1550 Automobile expenses.

The expenses of operating and maintaining a car used for business purposes, such as gasoline, oil, repairs, insurance, depreciation, interest to purchase the car, taxes, licenses, garage rent, parking, fees, tolls, etc., are deductible.[30] If a taxpayer makes both personal and business use of his car, he must apportion his expenses between business (deductible) and personal (nondeductible) transportation.[31]

🅡🄸🄰 *caution:* An employee who uses a car for his job is subject to the 2%-of-AGI floor on deducting the *un*reimbursed auto expenses he incurs, see ¶ 3103.

¶ 1551 Transporting tools to work.

A taxpayer may deduct only *additional* expenses incurred because of the need to transport tools, etc., to work *and* only if the additional expenses can be determined accurately. The deduction is only for that portion of the cost of transporting the tools, etc., that exceeds the cost of commuting *by the same mode of transportation* without the tools, etc.[32]

¶ 1552 Business standard mileage rate.

Employees or self-employed individuals can use the optional business standard mileage rate in computing the deductible costs of operating passenger automobiles owned by them (including vans and pickup or panel trucks) for business purposes.

A taxpayer who chooses to deduct an amount equal to the business standard mileage rate times the number of business miles traveled uses a rate of 28¢ per mile for all business miles traveled in '93.[33]

---

25. ¶ L-1708; ¶ 2744.05.
26. ¶ L-1601; ¶ 1624.150.
27. ¶ L-1608 *et seq.*; ¶ 1624.151.
28. ¶ L-1605; ¶ 1624.141.
29. ¶ L-1604 *et seq.*; ¶ 1624.153.
30. ¶ L-1902; ¶ 1624.150.
31. ¶ L-1909; ¶ 1624.157.
32. ¶ L-1611; ¶ 1624.151.
33. ¶ L-1903; ¶ 1624.157(b).

Footnote references beginning with letters are to paragraphs in RIA's Federal Tax Coordinator 2d and RIA's Analysis of Federal Taxes: Income. Footnote references beginning with numbers are to paragraphs in RIA's United States Tax Reporter.

A deduction using the standard mileage rate is in lieu of deducting operating and fixed costs. Thus, a taxpayer who uses the standard mileage rate forgoes deductions for depreciation, maintenance and repairs, tires, gasoline (including all taxes thereon), oil, insurance, and registration fees. But deductions for parking fees and tolls are still available.[34]

Use of the standard mileage rate is not available where taxpayer's car is used for hire (e.g., as a taxi) or in fleet operations, nor is it available if the car has previously been depreciated using any method other than the straight-line method, or if Code Sec. 179 additional first-year depreciation has been claimed, or if ACRS has been used.[35]

A rural mail carrier taking deductions for using his car on his mail route uses 150% of the optional business standard mileage rate (42¢ in '93) for all miles driven. But a mail carrier who has claimed depreciation deductions on his car may not use this method.[36]

A taxpayer may use the optional business standard mileage rate in substantiating reimbursed expenses paid by another.[37] For consequences if the reimbursement is made under an accountable plan, or under a nonaccountable plan, see ¶ 3103.

¶ 1553 Form 2106.

Form 2106 includes schedules for the computation of auto expenses and depreciation, for using the optional business standard mileage rate, and for making the allocation between business and nonbusiness use.[38]

¶ 1554 Entertainment Expenses

Costs incurred for entertainment must meet strict tests in order to be deductible. An 80% rule (50% after '93) limits otherwise-allowable deductions for meals and entertainment.

Entertainment expenses, except as limited by the rules in ¶ 1562 (percentage limit) and ¶ 1564, are deductible if they are ordinary and necessary expenses of carrying on a trade or business. (Code Sec. 274(a), (e); Reg § 1.162-1(a)) Strict substantiation requirements must be met (¶ 1573). But no deduction is allowed unless the taxpayer can show that the entertainment expenses are: (1) "directly related" to the active conduct of a trade or business (¶ 1557), or (2) "associated" with the active conduct of a trade or business (¶ 1558), or (3) covered by one of the exceptions at ¶ 1559. (Code Sec. 274(a))[39]

"Entertainment" includes any activity generally considered to be entertainment, amusement or recreation. This covers entertaining guests at night clubs, theaters, sporting events, and at entertainment facilities such as yachts, country clubs, hunting lodges, etc. If the expense involves the use of an entertainment facility, special rules apply, see ¶ 1560. (Reg § 1.274-2(b)(1))

Expenses of entertaining customers or clients at the taxpayer's home may be ordinary and necessary. But only the *extra* expense incurred because they are present is deductible. Failure to show a business purpose for entertaining bars a deduction.[40]

¶ 1555 Who may be entertained?

IRS says that a "business associate" who may be entertained is a person with whom the taxpayer could reasonably expect to engage or deal in the active conduct of his trade or business. Examples are customers, suppliers, clients, employees, agents, partners, or professional advisors, *whether established or prospective*. (Reg § 1.274-2(b)(2)(iii))[41]

¶ 1556 Entertainment expenses of spouse.

A taxpayer can deduct the cost of entertainment allocable to his spouse or to the spouse of a business customer if he can show he had a clear business purpose rather than a

---

34. ¶ L-1905; ¶ 1624.157(b).   36. ¶ L-1913; ¶ 2744.17.   38. ¶ L-1901; ¶ 1624.157(c).   40. ¶ L-2109 *et seq.*; ¶ 2744.01.
35. ¶ L-1903; ¶ 1624.157(b).   37. ¶ L-4715; ¶ 2744.17.   39. ¶s L-2101, L-2119; ¶ 2744.01.   41. ¶ L-2103.

Footnote references beginning with letters are to paragraphs in RIA's Federal Tax Coordinator 2d and RIA's Analysis of Federal Taxes: Income. Footnote references beginning with numbers are to paragraphs in RIA's United States Tax Reporter.

personal or social purpose for incurring the expenses. For example, a customer's spouse may join the party for the entertainment because it is impracticable, under the circumstances, to entertain the customer without the spouse. The cost of entertaining the customer's spouse is deductible. Further, if the taxpayer's spouse joins the party because the customer's spouse is present, the cost of the entertainment allocable to the taxpayer's spouse is also deductible. (Reg § 1.274-2(d)(2), (4))[42]

¶ 1557 "Directly related" entertainment.

Entertainment expenses are deductible if they are directly related to the active conduct of the taxpayer's trade or business. This test is met if the entertainment:

■ involved an active discussion aimed at getting immediate revenue;

■ occurred in a clear business setting such as a hospitality room; or

■ the expenditure must be reported as compensation for services performed by an individual other than an employee. (Reg § 1.274-2(c)(1))[43]

Expenditures are not generally considered directly related where entertainment occurs in circumstances where there is little or no possibility of engaging in the active conduct of business, such as night clubs, theaters, or sporting events, but they may be deductible under the "associated with" rule, below. (Reg § 1.274-2(c)(7))[44]

¶ 1558 "Associated with" entertainment.

Entertainment expenses that do not meet the "directly related" test but that are "associated" with the active conduct of the taxpayer's business are deductible if the entertainment directly "precedes or follows" a substantial and bona fide business discussion. (Reg § 1.274-2(d)(1))[45]

An entertainment expense is generally associated with the active conduct of a taxpayer's business if the taxpayer can show a clear business purpose in incurring the expenditure. (Reg § 1.274-2(d)(2))[46]

The portion of an otherwise deductible expense allocable to the wife of a person who engaged in the discussion is ordinarily considered associated with the active conduct of the business, see ¶ 1556. (Reg § 1.274-2(d)(4))[47]

Whether a business discussion is substantial depends on all the facts of each case. The taxpayer must show that he or his representative actively engaged in a discussion, meeting, negotiation, or other bona fide business transaction (other than entertainment) in order to get income or some other specific business benefit.

The meeting does not have to be for any specific length of time, but the business discussion must be substantial in relation to the entertainment. It is not necessary that more time be devoted to business than entertainment. (Reg § 1.274-2(d)(3)(i))[48]

¶ 1559 Exceptions to entertainment expense rules.

Certain ordinary and necessary entertainment expenses are deductible even if they are not "directly related" to or "associated" with the active conduct of the taxpayer's trade or business. But they are subject to the strict substantiation requirements (¶ 1573) that apply to other entertainment expenses. The exceptions are:

(1) Food and beverages furnished on the taxpayer's business premises primarily for the taxpayer's employees.[49]

(2) The expense of providing recreational, social, or similar activities primarily for the benefit of the taxpayer's employees. The expenses paid must be primarily for the benefit

---

42. ¶ L-2104 et seq.; ¶ 2744.01.
43. ¶ L-2113; ¶ 2744.01.
44. ¶ L-2117; ¶ 2744.01.
45. ¶ L-2119; ¶ 2744.01.
46. ¶ L-2119; ¶ 2744.01.
47. ¶ L-2104; ¶ 2744.01.
48. ¶ L-2120; ¶ 2744.01.
49. ¶ L-2123; ¶ 2744.01.

Footnote references beginning with letters are to paragraphs in RIA's Federal Tax Coordinator 2d and RIA's Analysis of Federal Taxes: Income. Footnote references beginning with numbers are to paragraphs in RIA's United States Tax Reporter.

of employees other than "highly-compensated employees" (defined at ¶ 4326).[50]

(3) Goods, services, and the use of a facility, if treated as compensation and as wages by the employer for withholding tax purposes. For example, an employer rewards an employee and his wife with an expense-paid vacation trip. The employer can deduct the cost if he treats the expenses as compensation and wages subject to withholding.[1]

(4) Expenses connected with directors, stockholder, employee or trade association meetings.[2]

(5) Cost of providing entertainment or recreational facilities to the general public as a means of advertising or promoting good will in the community.[3]

(6) Expense of providing entertainment, goods, and services, or use of facilities, that are sold to the public in a bona fide transaction for adequate and full consideration.[4]

(7) Reimbursed expenses or allowances of employees where the employer has not treated the expenses as wages subject to withholding, and reimbursed entertainment expenses of self-employed individuals reimbursed or covered with an allowance by the client or customer. (Code Sec. 274(e); Reg § 1.274-2(f)(1))[5]

¶ 1560 Entertainment facilities.

No deduction is allowed for any expense paid or incurred for "an entertainment facility" used in conjunction with any activity that is generally considered to be entertainment, amusement or recreation. (Code Sec. 274(a)(1)(B)) But a deduction is specifically allowed in the case of social, athletic, sporting and other clubs where the taxpayer establishes that the facility was used primarily to further the taxpayer's business and that the item was directly related to the active conduct of that business. (Code Sec. 274(a)(2))[6]

Entertainment facilities include yachts, hunting lodges, fishing camps, swimming pools, tennis courts, and bowling alleys. Facilities also may include airplanes, automobiles, hotel suites, apartments, and houses located in recreational areas (e.g., beach cottages and ski lodges). However, a facility is not treated as an entertainment facility unless it's actually used at least in part for entertainment. Expenses of an automobile or an airplane used on business trips are allowed. (Reg § 1.274-2(e)(2))[7]

The following expenditures not subject to the entertainment facility rules:

■ Interest, taxes, and casualty losses on entertainment facilities—these are deductible as ordinary interest, taxes, or casualty losses.

■ Out-of-pocket expenses for such items as food and beverages, or expenses for catering furnished during entertainment at a facility, are subject to the general entertainment deduction rules.

■ Actual business use of a facility, such as using a plane or car for business transportation or chartering a yacht to an unrelated person. (Reg § 1.274-2(e)(3)(iii), Reg § 1.274-6)[8]

¶ 1561 Club dues.

Fees paid to any social, athletic, or sporting club or organization before '94 are treated as an expenditure for an entertainment facility and subject to the rules at ¶ 1560.

If a taxpayer uses the club for business purposes more than 50% of calendar days the facility is used, he can, before '94, deduct that portion of the dues allocable to entertainment that is "directly related" to the active conduct of the taxpayer's business. If the club was used to furnish business meals under the exception discussed at ¶ 1559, the portion of the dues or fees allocable to that use is directly related entertainment. (Reg § 1.274-2(c)(6))

50. ¶ L-2126; ¶ 2744.01.   3. ¶ L-2132; ¶ 2744.01.   5. ¶ L-2125; ¶ 2744.01.   7. ¶ L-2150; ¶ 2744.02.
1. ¶ L-2124; ¶ 2744.01.   4. ¶ L-2133; ¶ 2744.01.   6. ¶ L-2149; ¶ 2744.02.   8. ¶ L-2152 et seq.; ¶ 2744.02.
2. ¶ L-2130; ¶ 2744.01.

Footnote references beginning with letters are to paragraphs in RIA's Federal Tax Coordinator 2d and RIA's Analysis of Federal Taxes: Income. Footnote references beginning with numbers are to paragraphs in RIA's United States Tax Reporter.

For tax years beginning after '93, no deduction is allowed for amounts paid or incurred for membership in any club organized for business, pleasure, recreation or other social purpose. (Code Sec. 274(a)(3))[9]

¶ 1562 Meal and entertainment deduction limits—the 80% rule (50% after '93).

The amount of an otherwise allowable deduction for meal or entertainment expenses is reduced by 80% (50% for tax years beginning after '93). Specifically, this reduction applies to any expense for food or beverages, and any item with respect to entertainment, amusement, or recreation, or for a facility used for such activity. (Code Sec. 274(n)(1))

The 80% (50%) limit does not apply to:

■ Expenses treated as compensation paid to an employee or otherwise included in the gross income of the recipient of the meal or entertainment. (Code Sec. 274(n)(2)(A))

■ Meals and entertainment expenses that are reimbursed. (Code Sec. 274(n)(2)(A)) Instead, the percentage limit applies to the person making the reimbursement. But where an employer pays or reimburses moving expenses that are included in the employee's income (see ¶ 1256), the percentage limit applies to the employee and not the employer. (Code Sec. 274(n)(2)(D))

■ Traditional recreational expenses for employees. (Code Sec. 274(n)(2)(A))

■ Services and facilities made available by the taxpayer to the general public. (Code Sec. 274(n)(2)(A))

■ Expenses of goods, services, or use of facilities, sold by the taxpayer in a bona fide transaction (entertainment sold to customers). (Code Sec. 274(n)(2)(A))

■ Food or beverage expenses that are excludable from the gross income of the recipient under the de minimis fringe benefit rules. (Code Sec. 274(n)(2)(B))

■ An expense that is part of a package that includes a ticket to attend certain charitable sporting events. (Code Sec. 274(n)(2)(C)) The event must: (1) be organized for the primary purpose of benefiting a tax-exempt charitable organization, (2) contribute 100% of the net proceeds to the charity, and (3) use volunteers for substantially all work performed in carrying out the event. (Code Sec. 274(l)(1)(B))

■ Food or beverage expenses of crews of certain drilling rigs and crews of certain commercial vessels. (Code Sec. 274(n)(2)(E))[10]

¶ 1563 Limits on deductions for skyboxes.

A limit is placed on the amount deductible for luxury "skyboxes" at sporting events. Where a skybox or other private luxury box is leased for more than one event, the amount allowable as a deduction is limited to the face value of nonluxury box seat tickets for the seats in the box covered by the lease. (Code Sec. 274(l)(2)) This amount is reduced by 20% (50% after '93) to determine the deduction. (Code Sec. 274(n))[11]

¶ 1564 Other restrictions on meal and entertainment deductions.

No deduction is allowed for any food or beverage expense unless—

(1) the expense is not lavish or extravagant under the circumstances, and

(2) the taxpayer (or one of taxpayer's employees) is present when the food or beverages are furnished, (Code Sec. 274(k)(1)) and

(3) the taxpayer establishes that the expenditure was directly related (¶ 1557) to the active conduct of taxpayer's business or, for an expenditure directly preceding or following a substantial and bona fide business discussion, was associated with the active conduct of

---

9. ¶ L-2155 *et seq.*; ¶ 2744.03.   10. ¶ L-2138 *et seq.*; ¶ 2744.01.   11. ¶ L-2146; ¶ 2744.01.

Footnote references beginning with letters are to paragraphs in RIA's Federal Tax Coordinator 2d and RIA's Analysis of Federal Taxes: Income. Footnote references beginning with numbers are to paragraphs in RIA's United States Tax Reporter.

the taxpayer's business (¶ 1558). (Code Sec. 274(a), (k))[12]

Neither the lavish or extravagant limit nor the presence test applies to any expense that is excepted from the percentage limit under ¶ 1562, above. (Code Sec. 274(k)(2))[13]

In determining the deduction for the cost of a ticket to an entertainment or recreation activity, the amount taken into account can't exceed the face value of the ticket. But the face value limit does not apply to a ticket to a charitable sporting event that is excepted from the percentage limit (see ¶ 1562). (Code Sec. 274(l)(1)(A))[14]

¶ 1565   Expense Allowances and Reimbursement Arrangements

An employee or independent contractor who operates under an expense account or other arrangement for reimbursement of expenses is subject to certain rules for reporting reimbursements and deductions.

Expense allowances and reimbursements received by an employee for expenses he pays or incurs, solely for the benefit of his employer, for travel, transportation, entertainment, gifts, and other business expenses, and for expenses he pays or incurs with respect to listed property, must be reported as income unless the employee: (1) is required to and does make an accounting for his business expenses to his employer (see ¶ 1566), (2) the amount of the expenses at least equals the total of the allowances and reimbursements, (3) the expenses are incurred solely for the benefit of the employer, and (4) the employee is paid for the expenses through advances, reimbursements or otherwise, or he charges them to the employer directly or indirectly. (Reg § 1.162-17(b)(1), Reg § 1.274-5(e)(2)(i))[15]

An employee who wants to deduct the excess of deductible expenses incurred over reimbursements received from his employer must maintain his own records substantiating all of the expenditures and all of the reimbursements. (Reg § 1.274-5T(f)(2)(iii)) The employee must also submit a statement as part of his tax return showing: (1) the total amount of reimbursements he received; (2) the nature of his occupation; and (3) (where applicable) the number of days away from home on business, and the total of expenses broken down into such categories as transportation, meals and lodging while away from home overnight, entertainment, gifts, etc. (Reg § 1.162-17(b)(3))[16]

An employee must include in his income reimbursements or allowances received from his employer to the extent they exceed deductible business expenses actually incurred, even though the employee accounts to his employer. (Reg § 1.162-17(b)(2), Reg § 1.274-5(e)(2)(ii), Reg § 1.274-5T(f)(2)(ii))[17] For rules that apply where the employee has not adequately accounted to his employer, see ¶ 1571.

¶ 1566   Accounting to employer for expenses.

An employee accounts to his employer for reimbursed business expenses by submitting to him an account book, diary, log, statement of expenses, trip sheet, or similar record maintained by the employee, along with supporting documentary evidence. The submitted material must be recorded at or near the time the expenses were incurred, and must be an "adequate record" of those expenses as explained at ¶ 1578. (Reg § 1.274-5(e)(4), Reg § 1.274-5T(f)(4))[18]

The employee must account for all amounts received from the employer during the tax year (for travel, entertainment, gifts and the use of listed property) as advances, reimbursements or allowances, or as direct or indirect charges to the employer through credit cards or otherwise. (Reg § 1.274-5(e)(4), Reg § 1.274-5T(f)(4))[19]

If an employer fails to maintain adequate accounting procedures, the employee must substantiate his expense account information separately. (Reg § 1.274-5(e)(5)(iii),

---

12. ¶s L-2134 *et seq.*, L-2113, L-2119; ¶ 2744.01.
13. ¶ L-2135.
14. ¶ L-2145; ¶ 2744.01.
15. ¶ L-4700 *et seq.*; ¶ 2744.16.
16. ¶ L-4750; ¶ 2744.16.
17. ¶ L-4745; ¶ 2744.16.
18. ¶ L-4707; ¶ 2744.16.
19. ¶ L-4707.

Footnote references beginning with letters are to paragraphs in RIA's Federal Tax Coordinator 2d and RIA's Analysis of Federal Taxes: Income. Footnote references beginning with numbers are to paragraphs in RIA's United States Tax Reporter.

166

Reg § 1.274-5T(f)(3))[20]

An employee who is "related" to his employer (certain close relatives of an individual employer, or a more than 10% stockholder of a corporate employer) may be asked by IRS to substantiate his expense accounts even though he has accounted to his employer. (Reg § 1.274-5(e)(5)(ii), Reg § 1.274-5T(f)(5)(ii))[21]

¶ 1567 Employees' mileage allowance.

An employee who receives a fixed mileage allowance of not more than the optional business standard mileage rate (¶ 1552) to cover transportation expenses while traveling away from home or for transportation expenses, is deemed to have made an adequate accounting to his employer if the elements of time, place, and business purpose of the travel are substantiated. (Reg § 1.274-5(f))[22]

¶ 1568 Employees' per diem allowance.

If a payor (i.e., the employer, its agent, or a third party) pays a per diem allowance in lieu of reimbursing actual expenses for lodging, meal and incidental expenses incurred or to be incurred by an employee for travel away from home, the amount of the expenses that is treated as substantiated for each calendar day (or part of that day) is the lesser of the per diem allowance or the amount computed at the federal per diem rate for the locality of travel for that day (or part of that day).[23]

An employee who is "related" to his employer (see ¶ 1566) *is not* considered to have accounted to his employer for per diem allowances and must substantiate any deductions he claims, but he may use the fixed mileage allowance rule.[24]

¶ 1569 Simplified (high-low) method for substantiating per diem allowances.

A simplified method can be used for per diem amounts paid for travel within the continental U.S. (but not where the per diem covers only meals and incidental expenses). An employer can reimburse up to $150 a day ($147 before Mar. 12, '93) for any area on the IRS list of high-cost areas, and up to $94 ($93 before Mar. 12, '93) for other areas.

For purposes of applying the high-low substantiation method, the meals and incidentals (M&IE) rate is $36 ($34 before Mar. 12, '93) for a high-cost locality and $28 ($26 before Mar. 12, '93) for other localities.

observation: IRS doesn't specify lodging expense rates for localities in the continental U.S. However, given the $150/$94 (per-day) and $35/$28 (M&IE) rates, the lodging rate would presumably be treated as $114 ($150 minus $36) for high-cost areas and as $66 ($94 minus $28) for other areas.

For allowances paid for expenses paid or incurred for travel away from home before Mar. 12, '93 the lodging expense rate is $113 for a high-cost locality and $67 for any other locality in the continental U.S.

For travel outside the continental U.S., a separately identified lodging expense rate and M&IE rate is available for each locality outside the continental U.S.[25]

¶ 1570 Fixed and variable rate (FAVR) allowances for employee automobile expenses.

Where an employer provides a mileage allowance under a reimbursement or other expense allowance arrangement in regard to an employee-owned car, the substantiation requirement (¶ 1565 *et seq.*) is satisfied as to the amount if the employer reimburses in accordance with a "fixed and variable rate" (FAVR) allowance.

A FAVR allowance is periodic fixed payments to cover fixed costs such as depreciation, coupled with periodic variable payments to cover operating costs such as gasoline.

---

20. ¶ L-4710; ¶ 2744.16. 22. ¶ L-4715. 24. ¶ L-4713; ¶ 2744.16. 25. ¶ L-4718; ¶ 2744.18.
21. ¶ L-4713; ¶ 2744.16. 23. ¶ 4717; ¶ 2744.18.

Footnote references beginning with letters are to paragraphs in RIA's Federal Tax Coordinator 2d and RIA's Analysis of Federal Taxes: Income. Footnote references beginning with numbers are to paragraphs in RIA's United States Tax Reporter.

Among other things, a FAVR allowance may be paid only to an employee who substantiates at least 5,000 miles driven in connection with the performance of services as an employee, and at least ten employees must be covered by the FAVR allowance.[26]

¶ 1571 Employee who does not account to his employer.

An employee who is not required to or fails to make an adequate accounting is required to submit Form 2106 to claim deductions for employee business expenses. In addition, the employee must provide the information required for listed property as discussed at ¶ 1577. The employee must also be able to substantiate each element of his business expenditures. (Reg § 1.274-5T(f)(3))[27]

¶ 1572 Reimbursed expenses of a self-employed person.

Expenses of a self-employed person incurred on behalf of and reimbursed by a client or customer are not included in the self-employed's gross income if the self-employed substantiates the expenses under the rules at ¶ 1573. But if he doesn't substantiate those reimbursed expenses, he must include the reimbursements in gross income and he loses any deduction for the expenses. (Reg § 1.274-5(g)(1), (2), Reg § 1.274-5T(h)(1), (2))[28]

The client or customer doesn't have to substantiate the reimbursements it pays to a self-employed person for the expenses of business travel or business gifts. The client or customer must substantiate its reimbursements to a self-employed person for entertainment expenses, but only if the self-employed person has accounted for those expenses to the client or customer. Thus, in the case of reimbursed entertainment expenses for which the self-employed person has accounted to his client or customer, both the self-employed person and the client or customer must substantiate the expenses. (Reg § 1.274-5(g)(2), (4), Reg § 1.274-5T(h)(2), (4))[29]

¶ 1573 Substantiating T&E and "Listed Property" Expenses ▬▬▬▬

In order to deduct travel and entertainment expenses, each expense must be substantiated. With respect to listed property, certain elements of each expenditure or business use must be proved.

Taxpayers must substantiate each element of every T&E expense for which a deduction is claimed. (Code Sec. 274(d)(1), (2), (3)) The elements of away from home travel expenses are explained at ¶ 1574; entertainment expenses, at ¶ 1576; and business gifts, at ¶ 1585.

Taxpayers may not claim deductions or credits with respect to "listed property" unless they substantiate every element of each expenditure with respect to the listed property and every element of each use of the listed property for business or investment purposes. (Code Sec. 274(d)(4)) The elements of listed property expenditures and uses are explained at ¶ 1577. "Listed property" is passenger automobiles and other property used as a means of transportation—for example, taxicabs, airplanes, trucks, boats, etc.—certain computers, and property used for entertainment, recreation or amusement. For a full discussion of "listed property," see ¶ 1959 *et seq.*

Generally, proper substantiation is accomplished with "adequate records," see ¶ 1578 *et seq.*, or by a taxpayer statement supported by sufficient corroborating evidence, see ¶ 1580. (Code Sec. 274(d))[30] Approximations or estimates are no good. (Reg § 1.274-5(a), Reg § 1.274-5T(a))[31]

All elements of an expenditure or use must be proved. Failure to prove any one will bar the deduction. (Reg § 1.274-5(c)(1), Reg § 1.274-5T(c)(1))[32]

---

26. ¶ L-4737 *et seq.*; ¶ 2744.18.   28. ¶ L-4757; ¶ 2744.16.   30. ¶ L-4600 *et seq.*; ¶ 2744.10.   32. ¶s L-4644, L-4608; ¶ 2744.10.
27. ¶ L-4710.   29. ¶ L-4758; ¶ 2744.16.   31. ¶ L-4601; ¶ 2744.10.

Footnote references beginning with letters are to paragraphs in RIA's Federal Tax Coordinator 2d and RIA's Analysis of Federal Taxes: Income. Footnote references beginning with numbers are to paragraphs in RIA's United States Tax Reporter.

¶ 1574 Proving travel and transportation expenses.

As to expenses of away-from-home travel (including costs of meals and lodgings), the taxpayer must prove all of the following elements by adequate records or by a sufficiently corroborated statement:

(1) The amount of each separate expenditure for traveling away from home, such as the cost of transportation or lodging. The daily cost of breakfast, lunch, and dinner and other incidental travel elements may be aggregated if they are set forth in reasonable categories, such as for meals, oil and gas, taxi fares, etc.

(2) The dates of the departure and return home for each trip, and the number of days spent on business away from home.

(3) The destinations or locality of the travel.

(4) The business reason for the travel or the nature of the business benefit derived or expected to be derived as a result of the travel. (Reg § 1.274-5(b)(2), Reg § 1.274-5T(b)(2))[33]

Incidental transportation expenses, e.g., tips, aren't subject to these rules. Where records are incomplete and documentary proof is unavailable, the taxpayer may establish the amount of incidental transportation expenses by reasonable approximations. (Reg § 1.162-17(d)(3))[34]

¶ 1575 Optional meal allowance.

Employees and self-employed individuals who are away from home on business travel may use standard per diem amounts to compute meal expense deductions instead of keeping records to substantiate the actual amount of the expense.[35]

If a payor (i.e., employer, its agent, or third party) pays a per diem allowance only for meals and incidental expenses in lieu of reimbursing these actual expenses incurred for travel away from home, the amount of the expenses that is deemed substantiated is the lesser of the per diem allowance or the amount computed at the federal meal and incidental expense (M&IE) rate for the locality of travel for the period the employee is away from home.[36] For federal M&IE rates, see ¶ 1569.

Using standard per diem amounts only releases the taxpayer from the duty of substantiating the actual amount. Time, place and business purpose must still be substantiated.

An employee may deduct an amount computed under this method only as an itemized deduction. This itemized deduction is subject to the percentage limit on meal and entertainment expenses (¶ 1562) and the 2% floor on miscellaneous itemized deductions (see ¶ 3107).

A self-employed individual deducts the amount in determining adjusted gross income. This deduction is subject to the percentage limit on meal and entertainment expenses.[37]

¶ 1576 Proving entertainment expenses.

For entertainment expenses, all these elements must be proved:

(1) The amount of each separate expenditure, except that incidental items like cab fares and telephone calls may be aggregated on a separate basis.

(2) The date the entertainment took place.

(3) The name (if any), address or location, and the type of entertainment, such as dinner or theater, if that information is not clear from the designation of the place.

---

33. ¶ L-4630; ¶ 2744.10.   35. ¶ L-4632; ¶ 2744.10.   36. ¶s L-4632, L-4717; ¶ 2744.10.   37. ¶ L-4632; ¶ 2744.18.
34. ¶ L-4633.

Footnote references beginning with letters are to paragraphs in RIA's Federal Tax Coordinator 2d and RIA's Analysis of Federal Taxes: Income. Footnote references beginning with numbers are to paragraphs in RIA's United States Tax Reporter.

(4) The reason for entertaining, or the nature of the business benefit derived or expected to be derived as a result of entertaining, and the nature of any business discussion or activity that took place.

(5) The occupation or other information relative to the person or persons entertained, including name, title or other designation, sufficient to establish his business relationship to the taxpayer. (Reg § 1.274-5(b)(3), Reg § 1.274-5T(b)(3))[38]

Instead of proving (4), above, a taxpayer deducting an expense for entertaining before or after a substantial and bona fide business discussion on the ground that the entertaining was "associated" with the active conduct of his business must prove the date and duration of the business discussion, where the discussion took place, the nature of the discussion, and the business reason for the entertainment or the nature of business benefit derived or expected to be derived as the result of entertaining. The persons entertained who participated in the business discussion must be identified. (Reg § 1.274-5(b)(4), Reg § 1.274-5T(b)(4))[39]

¶ 1577 Listed property.

In the case of listed property (including listed property used for local transportation), all the relevant elements from the following list must be proved for each expenditure or business use of the property:

(1) The amount and date of each separate expenditure with respect to the item of listed property (for example, the cost and date of acquisition or leasing, the cost and date of maintenance and repairs, etc.).

(2) The amount and date of each use of the item of listed property for business or investment, based on an appropriate measure (mileage for automobiles and other property used for transportation, time for other types of property, unless IRS approves an alternative method), and the total use of the item of listed property for the taxable period.

(3) The business purpose for each expenditure or use with respect to the item of listed property. (Reg § 1.274-5T(b)(6))[40]

In addition, tax returns require certain information with respect to the use of listed property. (Reg § 1.274-5T(d))[41]

¶ 1578 Adequate records.

Adequate records of T&E expenses and of listed property expenditures and uses consist of a currently maintained account book, diary, log, statement of expenses, trip sheet, or similar record and, where necessary (see ¶ 1579), documentary evidence such as receipts and paid bills, which together are sufficient to establish each element of every expenditure or use that must be substantiated. Information reflected on a receipt need not be duplicated in an account book or other record so long as the account book or other record and the receipt complement each other in an orderly fashion. (Reg § 1.274-5(c)(2)(i), Reg § 1.274-5T(c)(2)(i))[42]

Generally, adequate records must be written. But computer records are also adequate records. (Reg § 1.274-5T(c)(2)(ii)(C)(2))[43]

Where the business purpose of an expenditure is evident from the surrounding facts and circumstances, a written explanation of the business purpose isn't required. (Reg § 1.274-5(c)(2)(ii)(B), Reg § 1.274-5T(c)(2)(ii)(B))[44]

---

38. ¶ L-4635; ¶ 2744.10.   40. ¶ L-4644; ¶ 2744.10.   42. ¶ L-4616 *et seq.*; ¶ 2744.13.   44. ¶ L-4609; ¶ 2744.13.
39. ¶ L-4638; ¶ 2744.10.   41. ¶s L-4467, L-4468.   43. ¶ L-4616.

Footnote references beginning with letters are to paragraphs in RIA's Federal Tax Coordinator 2d and RIA's Analysis of Federal Taxes: Income. Footnote references beginning with numbers are to paragraphs in RIA's United States Tax Reporter.

¶ 1579 Adequate documentary evidence.

Documentary evidence, such as receipted bills and cancelled checks, is required to support all expenditures for lodging while away from home and for any other expenditures of $25 or more. (Reg § 1.274-5(c)(2)(iii), Reg § 1.274-5T(c)(2)(iii))[45]

Documentary evidence is ordinarily considered adequate to support an expenditure if it discloses the amount, date, place, and essential character of the expenditure. For example, a hotel receipt is sufficient to support expenditures for business travel if it contains the name and location of the hotel, the date or dates taxpayer stayed there, and separate amounts for charges such as for lodging, meals, and telephone. A restaurant receipt is sufficient to support an expenditure for a business meal if it contains the name and location of the restaurant, the date and amount of the expenditure, and an indication that a charge (if any) is made for an item other than meals and beverages. A canceled check, together with a bill from the payee, ordinarily will establish the cost but may not alone show business purpose. (Reg § 1.274-5(c)(2)(iii), Reg § 1.274-5T(c)(2)(iii))[46]

¶ 1580 Sufficiently corroborated statements.

Taxpayers may substantiate the elements of their expenditures and uses not only by adequate records, but also by their own statements, written or oral, if those statements are supported by sufficient corroborating evidence. (Code Sec. 274(d))[47]

Corroborating evidence may be oral, but if so, should be from a disinterested, unrelated party who has knowledge of the expenditure or use in question. Written evidence has greater probative value, and its probative value increases if set down close to the time of the expenditure or use in question. (Reg § 1.274-5T(c)(1))

A taxpayer's statement, whether written or oral, must contain specific, detailed information about the element being substantiated, and the taxpayer must present other corroborative evidence sufficient to establish that element. (Reg § 1.274-5(c)(3), Reg § 1.274-5T(c)(3)(i))[48]

¶ 1581 Inadequate substantiation—remedies.

Where a taxpayer has not fully substantiated a particular element of an expenditure or use, but he does establish to the satisfaction of IRS that he has substantially complied with the adequate records requirements, IRS may permit the taxpayer to establish the missing element by other evidence that it considers adequate. (Reg § 1.274-5(c)(2)(v), Reg § 1.274-5T(c)(2)(v))

Where a taxpayer establishes that, by reason of "the inherent nature of the situation," he was unable to get either fully adequate records, or fully sufficient corroborating evidence in support of his own statement, he will be treated as satisfying the substantiation requirements if he presents other evidence that possesses the highest degree of probative value under the circumstances. (Reg § 1.274-5(c)(4), Reg § 1.274-5T(c)(4))[49]

Where a taxpayer establishes that he has maintained adequate records of an expenditure or use, but is unable to produce the records because they have been lost through circumstances beyond his control (e.g., damage by fire, flood, earthquake or other casualty), the taxpayer has a right to prove his entitlement to a deduction or credit by a reasonable reconstruction of the expenditure or use in question. (Reg § 1.274-5(c)(5), Reg § 1.274-5T(c)(5))[50]

¶ 1582 Business Gifts and Employee Awards

The costs of ordinary and necessary business gifts to individuals other than

---

45. ¶ L-4619; ¶ 2744.13. 47. ¶ L-4626 *et seq.*; ¶ 2744.14. 49. ¶ L-4628; ¶ 2744.15. 50. ¶ L-4623; ¶ 2744.15.
46. ¶ L-4619. 48. ¶ L-4626.

Footnote references beginning with letters are to paragraphs in RIA's Federal Tax Coordinator 2d and RIA's Analysis of Federal Taxes: Income. Footnote references beginning with numbers are to paragraphs in RIA's United States Tax Reporter.

employees are deductible, subject to a $25 per-year per-person limit. Gifts to employees aren't deductible as gifts, but may be deductible as compensation. Certain noncash awards to employees are deductible.

¶ 1583 Business gifts.

The cost of ordinary and necessary business gifts may be deducted up to $25 a year to any one individual. Gift means any item excludable from gross income under Code Sec. 102 (see ¶ 1210), but not excludable under any other Code income tax provision. (Code Sec. 274(b))[1] However, any item for general distribution having a cost of not more than $4 and on which the giver's name is clearly and permanently imprinted, and signs, display racks, or other promotional material donated to a retailer to be used on his business premises, are not classified as gifts. (Code Sec. 274(b)(1); Reg § 1.274-3(b)(2))[2]

Since no amount transferred by or for an employer to or for the benefit of an employee is excludable as a gift (under Code Sec. 102) no such amount is deductible as a gift, though it may be deductible under other rules (e.g., as compensation).[3]

¶ 1584 Employee achievement awards.

An employer can deduct the cost of "employee achievement awards." (Code Sec. 274(j)) The maximum deduction for awards made to one employee is $400 per year unless the award is a qualified plan award; then the maximum deduction for any one employee is $1,600, including the cost of awards that aren't qualified plan awards. (Code Sec. 274(j)(2)) The award must be given as part of a meaningful presentation under conditions and circumstances that don't create a likelihood that the payment is disguised compensation. (Code Sec. 274(j)(3))

An employee achievement award is an item of tangible personal property awarded to an employee because of length of service, achievement, or safety achievement. (Code Sec. 274(j)(3))[4] Tangible personal property doesn't include cash or any gift certificate other than a nonnegotiable gift certificate conferring only the right to receive tangible personal property. (Reg § 1.274-3(b)(2)(iv))

A qualified plan award is an item awarded as part of a permanent, written, nondiscriminatory plan of the employer. (Code Sec. 274(j)(3)(B); Reg § 1.274-3(d))

A length-of-service award will not qualify for deduction under these rules if given during an employee's first five years of employment, or if a length-of-service award was given to the same employee during the same year or any of the earlier four years. (Code Sec. 274(j)(4)(A))

Safety achievement awards do not qualify if given to managerial, administrative, professional or clerical employees, or if such awards previously have been given to more than 10% of other employees during the year. (Code Sec. 274(j)(4)(C))[5]

No deduction is allowed for an employee achievement award (under the normal Code Sec. 162 ordinary and necessary rules or the Code Sec. 212 production of income rules) except under the above rules. (Code Sec. 274(j)(1))[6]

¶ 1585 Business gift expenses.

All these elements must be proved by adequate records or a sufficiently corroborated statement:

(1) description of the gift,

(2) taxpayer's cost,

(3) when the gift was made,

---

1. ¶ L-2306; ¶ 2744.08.   3. ¶ H-4009; ¶ 1624.363.   5. ¶ L-2315; ¶ 2744.09.   6. ¶ 2313 *et seq.*.
2. ¶ L-2312; ¶ 2744.08.   4. ¶ L-2312; ¶ 2744.09.

Footnote references beginning with letters are to paragraphs in RIA's Federal Tax Coordinator 2d and RIA's Analysis of Federal Taxes: Income. Footnote references beginning with numbers are to paragraphs in RIA's United States Tax Reporter.

(4) occupation or other information about the person receiving the gift, including his name, title, or other designation sufficient to establish his business relationship to the taxpayer,

(5) the reason for making the gift or the nature of business benefit derived or expected. (Reg § 1.274-5(b)(5), Reg § 1.274-5T(b)(5))[7]

¶ 1586 Rent Expense

Rent paid for the use of property used in whole or in part in the taxpayer's trade, business, or profession, or for the production of income, is deductible. But rent paid for personal-use property is not.

Rent for the use of real or personal property in the taxpayer's trade, business, or profession, is deductible. (Code Sec. 162(a)(3)) But rent for personal-use property is not. (Code Sec. 262(a); Reg § 1.262-1(b)(3))[8]

Besides normal cash rent payable periodically, rent includes a lump sum paid as advance rental, bonus, etc.; a percentage of the tenant's receipts or profits; the tenant's payment of the expenses of maintaining the rented property, such as taxes, insurance, etc.; and payment in property other than money (deductible to the extent of the property's fair market value).[9]

¶ 1587 Rent to related lessor.

Rentals paid between parties who are related either as members of a family or by stock ownership may not be deductible to the extent that they exceed the rent that would have been paid in an arm's-length transaction.

A corporation may deduct fair and reasonable rentals paid to corporate stockholders or their relatives. But excessive rentals can be treated as nondeductible dividends.[10] Reasonable rental payments by a stockholder for use of corporate property are deductible.[11]

¶ 1588 Rent under leaseback arrangements.

A transfer by sale or gift coupled with a leaseback may be more advantageous than a mortgage loan and can create tax benefits for the transferor. The seller may be able to raise more cash from selling than by mortgaging the property. He also may be able to claim a rent deduction substantially higher than the depreciation and interest he could have claimed had he retained title and mortgaged the property. Tax advantages (including rent deduction) of a sale and leaseback arrangement may be lost if IRS treats it as a mortgage loan, a tax-free exchange or a sham transaction.[12]

A gift and leaseback is sometimes made to shift tax from high-bracket taxpayer to low-bracket family member, or to a trust for family members—for example, a physician's gift of medical equipment or a building to a trust for his children, leased back from the trust. (Or this might be a *sale* to the trust, with leaseback.)

A gift in trust with a leaseback of the property to the grantor will generally be upheld as a valid rental or royalty arrangement by the courts if: (1) the transfer is complete and irrevocable, (2) the trustee is independent, and (3) the rental is reasonable. Reasonableness of rent and the independence of the trustee are questions of fact.[13]

¶ 1589 Rent or purchase; lease with purchase options.

A payment is deductible as rent only if the taxpayer has not taken or is not taking title to the property and has no equity interest in it. (Code Sec. 162(a)(3)) Thus, payments made under conditional sales contracts are not deductible as rent.[14]

---

7. ¶ L-4643; ¶ 2744.10.
8. ¶ L-6604; ¶ 1624.285.

9. ¶ L-6605 *et seq.*; ¶ 1624.285.
10. ¶ L-6702; ¶ 1624.299.

11. ¶ L-6710; ¶ 1624.299.
12. ¶ L-6300 *et seq.*; ¶ 1624.299.

13. ¶ L-6317; ¶ 1624.299.
14. ¶ L-6209; ¶ 1624.284.

Footnote references beginning with letters are to paragraphs in RIA's Federal Tax Coordinator 2d and RIA's Analysis of Federal Taxes: Income. Footnote references beginning with numbers are to paragraphs in RIA's United States Tax Reporter.

A lease that contains an option permitting the lessee to buy the property may be construed as a sale so that none of the payments is deductible as rent. Whether the lease is considered to be a sale depends essentially upon the intent of the parties, as shown in the agreement, read in light of the facts and circumstances existing at the time the agreement was made.[15] Important factors indicating sale instead of lease include nominal option price, excessive rent, designating part of the payment as interest, rental plus option price equal to the property's value plus interest, and application of rent payments to the lessee's equity in the property.[16]

¶ 1590 Lease acquisition costs.

Payments made by a lessee to get a business lease are not currently deductible but must be amortized over the unexpired period of the lease. (Reg § 1.162-11(a)) This rule applies whether the tenant is on the cash or accrual basis and even though he has an option to buy the property.[17]

If the lease is not renewable, lease acquisition costs are to be amortized over the unexpired term of the lease.[18]

If the lease is renewable any renewal period must be taken into account in determining the amortization period, if less than 75% of the lease cost is attributable to the portion of the term of the lease (exclusive of the renewal period) remaining on the date of acquisition of the lease.[19]

¶ 1591 Lessor's costs.

Costs incurred by a lessor in leasing his property, or by a lessee in subletting, are not currently deductible but must be amortized ratably over the term of the lease.[20]

A lessor who makes capital improvements to property he has leased can deduct depreciation over the useful life of the improvements, without regard to the duration of the lease. (Reg § 1.167(a)-4)[21]

A lessor's payments for cancellation of a lease must be amortized and deducted over the remaining term of the *cancelled* lease,[22] except that if the payment is made in order to enter into a lease with a new tenant, the payment must be amortized over the term of the *new* lease.[23]

¶ 1592 Year of deduction for rent.

The taxable year in which the rent is paid by a cash basis taxpayer or incurred by an accrual basis taxpayer is generally the proper year for deduction.[24] But advance rentals must be apportioned and deducted over the term of the lease or other rental period.[25]

¶ 1593 Deferred payments for the use of property or services.

Rent and interest attributable to a deferred rental agreement must be both reported and deducted as if both parties are accrual basis taxpayers. This rule applies to leases of over $250,000 that require either: (1) at least one payment for the use of property to be paid after the close of the calendar year following the calendar year of the use of the property, or (2) increases (or decreases) in the amounts to be paid as rent. (Code Sec. 467)[26]

For lessees, the deductible rental amount for the tax year is the sum of:

(1) rent deemed accrued by (a) allocating rents in accordance with the rental agreement, and (b) taking into account the present value of rent to be paid after the close of the period, and

15. ¶ L-6222 *et seq.*; ¶ 1624.305.	18. ¶ L-6501; ¶ 1624.323.	21. ¶ L-6404.	24. ¶ L-6616; ¶ 1624.285.
16. ¶ L-6200 *et seq.*; ¶ 1624.305.	19. ¶ L-6504 *et seq.*; ¶ 1624.323.	22. ¶ L-6405; ¶ 1624.081.	25. ¶ L-6617; ¶ 1624.081.
17. ¶ L-6501; ¶ 1624.323.	20. ¶ L-6401; ¶ 1624.081.	23. ¶ L-6407.	26. ¶ L-6801; ¶ 4674.

Footnote references beginning with letters are to paragraphs in RIA's Federal Tax Coordinator 2d and RIA's Analysis of Federal Taxes: Income. Footnote references beginning with numbers are to paragraphs in RIA's United States Tax Reporter.

(2) interest for the year on amounts taken into account for earlier tax years (under (1), above), but which are as yet unpaid. (Code Sec. 467(b)(1))[27]

Present value and interest are computed using a rate equal to 110% of the applicable federal rate, see ¶ 1116.

If the agreement is silent as to rent allocation or the agreement is a disqualified leaseback or long-term agreement, then constant rental accrual applies. (Code Sec. 467(b)(2), (3)) The constant rental amount is an amount paid as of the close of each lease period which would result in a total present value equal to the present value of the total payments required under the lease. (Code Sec. 467(e)(1))[28]

A rental agreement is a disqualified leaseback or long-term agreement (with certain safe-harbor exceptions) if:

(1) it is part of a leaseback transaction to any person who had an interest in the leased property within two years before the leaseback, (Code Sec. 467(e)(2)) or the term of the agreement exceeds 75% of a prescribed recovery period, (Code Sec. 467(b)(4)) *and*

(2) a principal purpose of the increased rents provided in the agreement is tax avoidance. (Code Sec. 467(b)(4))[29]

Under regs to be issued, similar rules will apply to certain deferred payments for services. (Code Sec. 467(g))[30]

¶ 1594 Research and Experimental Expenditures

Taxpayers have to choose whether to immediately deduct or to capitalize research and experimental (R&E) expenditures. In some cases, they also have the option of writing off the expenditures over several years.

R&E expenses are deductible if made in connection with a trade or business. Deductions are not limited to expenses incurred in carrying on a trade or business but can include start-up expenses. But where the R&E activity doesn't involve a trade or business (e.g., when it is only an investment), no deduction is allowed. (Code Sec. 174(a); Reg § 1.174-3(a))[31]

The taxpayer can adopt the current expense method without IRS consent only for the first tax year he has qualifying expenditures. Consent is required after that first year.[32]

If the taxpayer adopts current expense treatment, he must use that treatment for all qualifying expenses for the year he adopts it and for all later years, unless he gets IRS permission to switch. (Code Sec. 174(a)(3))[33]

For research and experimental expenditures that are not chargeable to depreciable or depletable property, instead of current deduction or capitalizing the taxpayer can elect (use Form 4502) to deduct the expenditures ratably over a period of 60 months or longer as deferred expenses, beginning with the month the taxpayer first realized benefits from the expenditures. (Code Sec. 174(b)(1); Reg § 1.174-4(b)(1))[34]

All taxpayers, including partners and S corporation shareholders, may elect to deduct all or any portion of these costs ratably over ten years. (Code Sec. 59(e)(1))[35]

For limitations on deductions for research and experimental expenses that also qualify for the research credit or the orphan drug credit, see ¶ 2323 and ¶ 2334.

For alternative minimum tax treatment of research and experimental expenditures, see ¶ 3208.

---

27. ¶ L-6803; ¶ 4674.
28. ¶ L-6805; ¶ 4674.
29. ¶ L-6808; ¶ 4674.
30. ¶ L-6800 *et seq.*; ¶ 4674.
31. ¶ L-3101 *et seq.*; ¶ 1744.02.
32. ¶ L-3119.
33. ¶ L-3117.
34. ¶ L-3121 *et seq.*; ¶ 1744.01.
35. ¶ A-8121; ¶ 594.

Footnote references beginning with letters are to paragraphs in RIA's Federal Tax Coordinator 2d and RIA's Analysis of Federal Taxes: Income. Footnote references beginning with numbers are to paragraphs in RIA's United States Tax Reporter.

¶ 1595 Legal and Accounting Expenses

Legal expenses and accounting and related expenses may be deductible.

For expenses of determining or contesting tax liability, see ¶ 1610.

¶ 1596 Legal expenses.

Attorney's fees, court costs and other legal expenses can qualify as deductible business expenses. Legal expenses are not deductible if they are either capital expenditures or a personal expense of the taxpayer. (Code Sec. 162, Code Sec. 262(a), Code Sec. 263)[36]

Qualified legal expenses can include expenses incurred in litigation, for legal advice, and for the drafting of instruments.[37] Deduction is barred for expenditures incurred to acquire, perfect or defend title to property.[38]

¶ 1597 Accounting and related expenses.

Accounting and related expenses incurred in operating the taxpayer's business are deductible.[39] The cost of installing a new up-to-date accounting system is not a capital expenditure.[40]

¶ 1598 Insurance Premiums

Certain premiums that qualify as trade or business expenses, or as investment expenses, are deductible.

¶ 1599 Insurance premiums on nonlife policies.

Premiums for insurance against various types of risks, such as property damage, are generally deductible as business expenses, (Code Sec. 162; Reg § 1.162-1(a)) but premiums on policies on taxpayer's residence, or for other personal use, are not. (Code Sec. 262(a); Reg § 1.262-1(b))[41]

Self-insurance reserve funds are not deductible even if taxpayer can't get business insurance coverage for certain business risks.[42] Neither are payments to "captive" insurance subsidiaries or other similar arrangements where there is no true risk-shifting.[43] A limited deduction is allowed, however, for certain payments made to a medical malpractice self-insurance pool.[44]

Premiums are nondeductible capital expenditures where paid for property insurance during construction. So are premiums for title insurance and for public liability and worker's compensation insurance paid in connection with the construction of a building.[45]

¶ 1600 Life insurance premiums.

Life insurance premiums aren't deductible if the taxpayer is directly or indirectly a beneficiary. (Code Sec. 264(a)(1); Reg § 1.264-1) For example, the cost of a corporation's key man insurance isn't deductible.[46] Premiums paid by an individual for personal life insurance aren't deductible. (Reg § 1.262-1(b)(1))[47]

For deductibility of group-term life insurance premiums, see ¶ 1524.

¶ 1601 Time for deducting insurance premiums.

If a taxpayer pays a premium for one year's coverage which applies in part to the following taxable year, the entire premium is deductible in the year paid by a cash basis taxpayer and in the year accrued by an accrual basis taxpayer.[48]

---

36. ¶s L-2901, L-2967;   39. ¶ L-2957.   43. ¶ L-3520.   46. ¶ L-3407; ¶ 2644.
      ¶ 1624.040.   40. ¶ L-2958.   44. ¶ L-3515.   47. ¶ L-3401; ¶ 2644.
37. ¶ L-2902; ¶ 1624.040.   41. ¶ L-3500 *et seq.*; ¶ 1624.032.   45. ¶ L-3530.   48. ¶ L-3526; ¶ 1624.081.
38. ¶ L-2908; ¶ 2634.01.   42. ¶ L-3518; ¶ 1624.032.

Footnote references beginning with letters are to paragraphs in RIA's Federal Tax Coordinator 2d and RIA's Analysis of Federal Taxes: Income. Footnote references beginning with numbers are to paragraphs in RIA's United States Tax Reporter.

But if premiums for several years are paid in advance, IRS and most courts require the premium to be amortized and deducted over the life of the policy, though one court has allowed a full deduction to a cash basis taxpayer in the year of payment where the taxpayer had consistently deducted premiums in the year of payment.[49]

¶ 1602 Bribes, Kickbacks, Fines and Penalties

No deduction is allowed for certain illegal bribes, kickbacks, rebates and other payments. And fines and penalties for violation of a law, including tax penalties, are not deductible.

No deduction is allowed for any illegal bribe, kickback or other illegal payment under any law of the U.S., or under any law of a state (if the state law is generally enforced), that subjects the payor to a criminal penalty or the loss of license or privilege to engage in business, whether or not that penalty or loss of license actually occurs. A kickback includes a payment in consideration of the referral of a client, patient, or customer. (Code Sec. 162(c)(2))[50]

Business kickbacks, fee-splitting, etc., that aren't specifically disallowed are deductible if they qualify as ordinary and necessary.[1]

¶ 1603 Kickbacks, rebates, and bribes under Medicare and Medicaid.

No deduction is allowed for any payments consisting of any kickback, rebate, or bribe made by any provider of services, supplier, physician, or other person who furnishes Medicare or Medicaid items or services, if made in connection with the furnishing of such items or services or the making or receiving of such payments. A kickback includes a payment for the referral of a client, patient, or customer. For these payments, deduction is denied regardless of legality. (Code Sec. 162(c)(3))[2]

¶ 1604 Illegal business.

The ordinary and necessary expenses incurred in operating an illegal business are deductible, even though payment of the expense and the acts performed by the employees of the business are illegal (e.g., a bookmaker's expenses).[3]

There's no deduction or credit for amounts paid or incurred in connection with illegal drug traffic, (Code Sec. 280E) although gross receipts may be adjusted for costs of goods sold.[4]

¶ 1605 Unlawful payments to government officials or employees.

No business expense deduction is allowed for any payment made directly or indirectly to any federal, state, or local public official or employee if the payment is an illegal bribe or kickback. If the payment is to an official or an employee of a foreign government, no deduction is allowed if the payment violates the U.S. Foreign Corrupt Practices Act. (Code Sec. 162(c)(1))[5]

¶ 1606 Fines and penalties.

No business expense deduction is allowed for fines or similar penalties paid to a government for the violation of any law. (Code Sec. 162(f))[6] For example, state law penalties on public school teachers for striking are not deductible. Similarly, penalties paid for violating federal environmental protection laws are not deductible.[7]

Also, penalties paid in connection with federal, state, and local taxes are generally not

---

49. ¶ L-3526; ¶ 1624.081.
50. ¶ L-2605; ¶ 1624.384.
1. ¶ L-2605; ¶ 1624.384.

2. ¶ L-2610; ¶ 1624.384.
3. ¶ L-2616; ¶ 1624.382.

4. ¶ L-2617; ¶ 280E4.
5. ¶ L-2601; ¶ 1624.384.

6. ¶ L-2701 *et seq.*; ¶ 1624.388.
7. ¶ L-2701.

Footnote references beginning with letters are to paragraphs in RIA's Federal Tax Coordinator 2d and RIA's Analysis of Federal Taxes: Income. Footnote references beginning with numbers are to paragraphs in RIA's United States Tax Reporter.

deductible—for example, penalties for negligence, delinquency, or fraud relating to federal taxes, (Reg § 1.162-21(b)) and for failure to withhold federal payroll taxes.[8]

¶ 1607 Public policy.

Public policy is not a ground for denying deduction. Unless a payment is nondeductible by law, it is deductible if ordinary and necessary. (Reg § 1.162-1)[9]

¶ 1608 Miscellaneous Business Expenses

Advertising expenses, tax determination expenses, royalty payments, circulation costs, trademark and trade name expenditures, mine exploration and development costs, and other miscellaneous costs of carrying on a business are deductible subject to certain conditions and limits.

¶ 1609 Advertising and business promotion costs.

Advertising and business promotion costs relating to an existing business can be deducted currently, even though the business benefit they generate may extend over a period beyond the year they are incurred or paid.[10]

Production costs of a business catalog that will remain unchanged for several years must be capitalized according to IRS, but some courts disagree.[11] Display equipment (cabinets, signs, etc.) must be capitalized if it has a useful life beyond the tax year.[12]

¶ 1610 Determining or contesting tax liability.

Costs relating to tax matters that are ordinary and necessary in the course of the conduct of taxpayer's trade or business, including costs of tax advice, are deductible. The deduction applies to expenses incurred in: (1) preparing tax returns, (2) determining tax liability, (3) contesting tax liability, (4) securing tax counsel. (Reg § 1.212-1(l))[13] This includes expenses incurred by an individual taxpayer in:[14]

■ preparing that portion of the individual's tax return that relates to the taxpayer's business as sole proprietor,

■ preparing schedules relating to income or loss from rentals or royalties, or farm income and expenses, and

■ resolving asserted tax deficiencies relating to a business, to rental or royalty income, or to a farm.

For deduction of tax determination costs as nonbusiness expenses, (i.e., as miscellaneous itemized deductions subject to the 2% (¶ 3107) floor), see ¶ 2164.

For alternative minimum tax treatment of nonbusiness expenses by an individual, see ¶ 3208.

¶ 1611 Royalty payments.

Royalty payments made for the right to use patents, copyrights and similar rights are deductible.[15] Payments to acquire the property itself are capital expenditures.[16]

¶ 1612 Circulation costs.

Publishers of periodicals can deduct currently their expenditures to establish, maintain and increase circulation. (Code Sec. 173)[17] Or, instead, they may elect to capitalize those costs. (Reg § 1.173-1(c))[18] A taxpayer may elect to amortize circulation costs over three years beginning with the year in which the expenditure is made. (Code Sec. 59(e)(1)) For

---

8. ¶ L-2709; ¶ 1624.388.   11. ¶ L-2205; ¶ 1624.355.   14. ¶ L-3000.   17. ¶ L-2213; ¶ 1734.01.
9. ¶ L-2609; ¶ 1624.377.   12. ¶ L-2206; ¶ 1624.355.   15. ¶ L-3201; ¶ 1624.284.   18. ¶ L-2215 *et seq.*; ¶ 1734.
10. ¶ L-2204; ¶ 1624.355.   13. ¶ L-3000 *et seq.*; ¶ 2124.14.   16. ¶ L-3203; ¶ 1624.284.

Footnote references beginning with letters are to paragraphs in RIA's Federal Tax Coordinator 2d and RIA's Analysis of Federal Taxes: Income. Footnote references beginning with numbers are to paragraphs in RIA's United States Tax Reporter.

alternative minimum tax treatment of circulation costs, see ¶ 3209.

¶ 1613 Trademark and trade name expenditures.

For property acquired before Aug. 11, '93, these expenditures are not deductible.[19]

For 15-year amortization of trademarks and trade names acquired after Aug. 10, '93, see ¶ 1991.

¶ 1614 Transfers of franchises, trademarks and trade names.

In the case of a transfer of a franchise, trademark or trade name, a deduction is allowed to the transferee for payments contingent on the productivity, use, or disposition of the franchise, trademark or trade name transferred. (Code Sec. 1253(d)(1))[20] Any other amount paid or incurred is treated as chargeable to capital account (Code Sec. 1253(d)(2)) and must be amortized under the rules for intangibles at ¶ 1989.

For property acquired before Aug. 11, '93 (or electively, before July 26, '91), a deduction was allowed to the transferee for other payments but only if the transferor retained any significant power, right, or continuing interest in the franchise, trademark or trade name transferred and the payment was made in discharge of a principal sum of no more than $100,000 agreed upon in the transfer agreement.[21]

¶ 1615 Stock redemption expenses.

Stock redemption expenses that are reimbursements or direct assumption of costs incurred by a selling stockholder, and are incurred in connection with an actual redemption of stock, are not deductible by the corporation. This is so without regard to the reason (e.g., greenmail) for the corporation's repurchase. (Code Sec. 162(k))[22]

¶ 1616 Cooperative housing maintenance and lease expenses.

Cooperative housing maintenance and lease expenses are deductible if the cooperative unit is used in a trade or business or for the production of income. However, no deduction is allowed to a cooperative housing stockholder for any payment to the cooperative (in excess of the stockholder's share of taxes and interest) to the extent the payment is properly allocable to amounts chargeable to the cooperative's capital account. The basis of the stockholder's stock is increased by the amount of any deduction disallowed under this rule. (Code Sec. 216(d))[23]

¶ 1617 Mine exploration costs.

Domestic mine exploration costs incurred before a mine has reached the development stage are nondeductible capital expenditures. However, taxpayers may elect to deduct mining exploration expenditures for minerals (other than oil and gas) that qualify for percentage depletion. (Code Sec. 617)[24]

Exploration costs deducted under the election are subject to recapture when the mine reaches the producing stage, when taxpayer receives a bonus or royalty, or when he disposes of all or part of the property, whichever happens first (except where the IRS allows recapture to be postponed on disposition of a *part* interest). (Code Sec. 617(b)(1))[25]

All taxpayers, including partners and S corporation shareholders, may elect to deduct all or any portion of their deductible mine exploration costs ratably over ten years. (Code Sec. 59(e))[26]

Corporations' deductions for exploration costs are cut back 30% if they elect to write off the costs in the year they are incurred. (Code Sec. 291(b)(1)) The amount cut back must be amortized over 60 months. (Code Sec. 291(b))[27]

---

19. ¶ L-3300 *et seq.*; ¶ 1778.41.
20. ¶ I-8415 *et seq.*; ¶ 12534.01.
21. ¶ I-8400 *et seq.*; ¶ 12,534.01.
22. ¶s L-5305, L-5410; ¶ 1624.402.
23. ¶ K-5900 *et seq.*; ¶ 2164.01.
24. ¶ N-3103; ¶ 6174.
25. ¶ N-3601 *et seq.*; ¶ 6174.01.
26. ¶ N-3116; ¶ 594.
27. ¶ N-3111; ¶ 2914.

Footnote references beginning with letters are to paragraphs in RIA's Federal Tax Coordinator 2d and RIA's Analysis of Federal Taxes: Income. Footnote references beginning with numbers are to paragraphs in RIA's United States Tax Reporter.

¶ 1618 Mine development costs.

A taxpayer who incurs expenditures for the development of minerals other than oil or gas may:

■ deduct such expenditures in the year they were paid or incurred; (Code Sec. 616(a))[28]

■ elect to treat them as deferred expenses and deduct them ratably as the units of produced minerals benefited by such expenditures are sold; (Code Sec. 616(b); Reg § 1.616-2(a))[29] or

■ treat them as deferred expenses and elect to amortize them ratably over ten years. (Code Sec. 59(e))[30]

Corporations' deductions for mine development costs are cut back 30% if the corporation elects to write off the costs in the year incurred. (Code Sec. 291(b)(1)(B)) The amount cut back must be amortized over 60 months. (Code Sec. 291(b))[31]

¶ 1619 Intangible oil and gas and geothermal well drilling and development costs.

Geological and geophysical costs incurred in exploring for oil and gas are capital expenditures.[32] Taxpayers, however, may capitalize, amortize or expense the so-called intangible drilling and development costs (IDCs) of oil, gas and geothermal wells. (Code Sec. 59(e), Code Sec. 263(c); Reg § 1.612-4, Reg § 1.612-5)[33]

In general, such intangible costs include only those costs that in themselves don't have a salvage value, such as labor and fuel.[34]

Deducted IDCs are recaptured as ordinary income on disposition of the oil or gas wells. (Code Sec. 1254(a)(1)(A))[35]

For alternative minimum tax treatment of IDCs, see ¶ 3207.

¶ 1620 Lobbying costs, influencing public on legislation.

Deductible business expenses include lobbying expenses paid or incurred before '94 in carrying on taxpayer's business and directly connected with:

■ appearances before or sending communications to Congress or of any legislative body of a state or political subdivision;

■ communication between the taxpayer and an organization of which he is a member with respect to legislation or proposed legislation of direct interest to the taxpayer and the organization.[36]

Deductible lobbying expenses don't include any contributions, gifts, or other payments for participation, or intervention in any political campaign on behalf of or in opposition to any candidate for public office.[37]

Deduction is denied for a contribution, gift or other payment made in connection with any attempt to influence the general public or part of the public with respect to legislative matters, elections, or referendums.[38]

For amounts paid or incurred after '93, deductible business expenses do not include:

■ any amount paid or incurred in influencing legislation, (Code Sec. 162(e)(1)(A))

■ any amount paid or incurred in connection with participation in or intervention in any political campaign or any attempt to influence the general public with respect to elections, legislative matters, or referendums, (Code Sec. 162(e)(2)(C))

■ any amount paid or incurred in communicating directly with a covered executive branch official on official matters, (Code Sec. 162(e)(1)(D)

---

28. ¶ N-3118; ¶ 6164.   31. ¶ N-3126.   34. ¶ N-3206; ¶ 6124.009.   37. ¶s L-2416, L-2422;
29. ¶ N-3128; ¶ 6164.   32. ¶ N-3201; ¶ 6124.001.   35. ¶ N-3411; ¶ 12,544 et seq.   ¶ 1624.395.
30. ¶ N-3139; ¶ 6164.04.   33. ¶ N-3202 et seq.; ¶ 6124.008. 36. ¶ L-2402; ¶ 1624.395.   38. ¶ L-2410; ¶ 1624.395.

Footnote references beginning with letters are to paragraphs in RIA's Federal Tax Coordinator 2d and RIA's Analysis of Federal Taxes: Income. Footnote references beginning with numbers are to paragraphs in RIA's United States Tax Reporter.

■ the portion of dues paid to a tax-exempt organization allocable to lobbying by the organization for which no deduction is allowed, if the organization informs taxpayer of the nondeductible portion. (Code Sec. 162(e)(3))

In-house expenditures of $2,000 or less per year aren't subject to these post-'93 rules. (Code Sec. 162(e)(5)(B)(i))

The disallowance concerning legislation, above, doesn't apply to legislation of a local government. (Code Sec. 162(e)(2)(A)) In effect, costs of influencing this legislation are deductible under pre-'94 rules, above.[39]

¶ 1621 Civil damages.

Civil damages paid under judgments and out-of-court settlements arising out of normal business operations are deductible as business expenses,[40] if the litigation is directly connected with the taxpayer's business.[41]

Treble damage payments under federal antitrust law to private parties are deductible in full except where the taxpayer (payor) in a criminal proceeding for violation of federal anti-trust law is convicted or pleads not guilty or no contest, in which case the deduction is limited to one-third of the treble damage payment. (Code Sec. 162(g); Reg § 1.162-22)[42]

¶ 1622 Other deductible costs of carrying on a trade or business.

These include:[43]

■ cost of materials and supplies not consumed in the process of manufacturing;[44]

■ annual license and regulatory fees;[45]

■ amounts paid to cancel burdensome contracts;[46]

■ cost of moving business equipment and machinery;[47]

■ current membership fees, dues and assessments paid for business association, etc. (but not admission fees).[48]

¶ 1623 Employee Business Expenses

Employees are engaged in the trade or business of being an employee and thus are entitled to deduct certain expenses as ordinary and necessary business expenses, within limits.

Employees may deduct their employment-connected business expenses such as travel expenses, union dues, work clothes, etc., as described in the following paragraphs.

However, unreimbursed employee business expenses are generally deductible only to the extent that when aggregated with other miscellaneous itemized deductions they exceed 2% of adjusted gross income, see ¶ 3107. (Reg § 1.67-1T(a)(1)(i))[49] For employees' unreimbursed moving expenses, see ¶ 1645 *et seq.*; for alternative minimum tax treatment of an individual's nonbusiness expenses, see ¶ 3208.

¶ 1624 Cost of seeking and securing employment.

An employee can deduct the expenses of seeking new employment in his same trade or business, whether or not he gets the new job. Any local transportation expenses and any travel expenses away from home and costs such as typing, printing and postage are deductible.

An employee can't deduct the cost of seeking employment in a different trade or business even if he gets the job. If an unemployed person is seeking a job and no substantial

---

39. ¶ L-2400.1 *et seq.*.   42. ¶ L-2714; ¶ 1624.391.   45. ¶ L-4217 *et seq.*   48. ¶ L-4233; ¶ 1624.061.
40. ¶ L-2500 *et seq.*; ¶ 1624.040.   43. ¶ L-4200 *et seq.*; ¶ 1624.404.   46. ¶ L-4214 *et seq.*   49. ¶ L-3900 *et seq.*; ¶ 1624.067.
41. ¶ L-2502; ¶ 1624.040.   44. ¶ L-4207 *et seq.*   47. ¶ L-4210 *et seq.*; ¶ 1624.052.

Footnote references beginning with letters are to paragraphs in RIA's Federal Tax Coordinator 2d and RIA's Analysis of Federal Taxes: Income. Footnote references beginning with numbers are to paragraphs in RIA's United States Tax Reporter.

lack of continuity occurred between the time of the past employment and the seeking of the new employment, his trade or business is the services performed for his past employer. Where there is no continuity, or where a person looks for a job for the first time, the expenses aren't deductible, even if a job results.

If an individual travels to a destination where he both seeks new employment in his present trade or business and engages in personal activities, his travel expenses to and from the destination are deductible only if the trip is primarily related to seeking the new employment. Expenses allocable to seeking the job at the destination are deductible even if the travel expenses are not.[50]

¶ 1625 Labor union dues, fees, and assessments.

Deduction has been permitted for dues, fines paid to remain in the union, strike funds, compulsory payments for unemployment benefits, and a mandatory service charge paid to a union by a nonmember. Deductions were denied for noncompulsory unemployment benefit fund payments, assessments for sick, accident, or death benefits, and other payments that were in exchange for valuable benefits.[1]

¶ 1626 Uniforms and special work clothes.

Deduction for the cost and maintenance of clothing is allowed if:

■ the employee's occupation is one that specifically requires special apparel or equipment as a condition of employment, and

■ the special apparel or equipment isn't adaptable to general or continued usage so as to take the place of ordinary clothing.

Thus, protective clothing, such as safety shoes, helmets, fishermen's boots, work gloves, oil clothes, etc., are deductible if required for the job. But work clothing and standard work shoes aren't deductible even if the worker's union requires them.[2] Clothes ruined on the job aren't deductible unless the above tests are met.[3]

¶ 1627 Other deductible employee expenses.

These include:

■ membership dues in professional or business societies,[4]

■ small tools and supplies,[5]

■ salesman's briefcase used in business,[6]

■ salesman's commissions paid to a third party who made the sales,[7]

■ expenses incurred by a securities analyst for a stock brokerage firm in seeking to get new business for the employer and by so doing increase his own salary,[8]

■ payments by a blind employee for readers' services,[9]

■ expenses of business use of home, see ¶ 1630 *et seq.*

¶ 1628 Deductions from individual's business or profession.

Individuals can deduct the expenses of their business or profession, such as supplies, rent, transportation, business, travel, telephone, etc., if they are self-employed. But a professional who is an employee deducts expenses allowed to employees.

Professionals, whether or not employees, can also deduct expenses peculiar to their professions such as dues to professional organizations, subscriptions to professional journals, malpractice insurance and payments to assistants. The cost of professional books, furniture, instruments and equipment are deductible if their useful lives are short.

50. ¶ L-3902; ¶ 1624.067.   3. ¶ L-3805; ¶ 1624.067.   6. ¶ L-3917.   8. ¶ L-4416.
1. ¶s L-3908, L-3910; ¶ 1624.067. 4. ¶s L-3917, L-4100; ¶ 1624.195. 7. ¶ L-4238; ¶ 1624.104.   9. ¶ L-3907.
2. ¶ L-3801; ¶ 1624.067.   5. ¶ L-3917; ¶ 1624.152.

Footnote references beginning with letters are to paragraphs in RIA's Federal Tax Coordinator 2d and RIA's Analysis of Federal Taxes: Income. Footnote references beginning with numbers are to paragraphs in RIA's United States Tax Reporter.

(Reg § 1.162-6) But expenses incurred by business or professional people to build up their reputations are capital expenditures to develop or enhance goodwill, unless the expenses can be tied directly to the production of added income.[10]

Costs of entering a profession or securing the right to practice are nondeductible. (Reg § 1.212-1(f))[11] The following material highlights the rules on deduction for professionals, etc.:

Accountants can't deduct costs of a CPA review course or the CPA exam.[12]

Lawyers have been allowed to deduct bar association dues, but not costs of securing admission to practice (including bar examination fees, expenses to be admitted to second state bar, travel) (Reg § 1.162-5, Reg § 1.212-1(f)) which must be amortized over taxpayer's remaining life expectancy. The cost of bar review courses can't be amortized.[13]

Doctors and dentists can't deduct costs of securing the right to practice, fees on their initial licensing, etc. (Reg § 1.212-1(f))[14] Fees paid to a hospital for staff privileges are amortizable over taxpayer's useful life, or the useful life of the hospital privilege if shorter.[15] Compensation paid for services rendered by assistants is deductible. (Reg § 1.162-6)[16]

Teachers can deduct the cost of membership in professional societies, educational journals, and travel to teachers' conventions and similar events. Professors in a college or university may deduct the costs of research, writing, or lecturing that the college expects of its professors, even though they receive no payment or extra compensation. Deductible costs may include travel, research costs, and stenographic services.[17]

¶ 1629 Impairment-related work expenses.

Impairment-related work expenses are deductible (on Form 2106). They are ordinary and necessary expenses, including attendant care services at the place of employment, to enable an individual who has a handicap to work. (Code Sec. 67(d)) Impairment-related work expenses are not subject to the 2%-of-adjusted-gross-income floor. (Code Sec. 67(b)(7))[18]

¶ 1630 Residence Used in Part for Business—Home Office Deduction ▰▰▰▰

Employees, self-employed individuals, and investors may take office-at-home deductions if tough tests are met.

With limited exceptions discussed at ¶ 1632 *et seq.*, no deduction is allowed with respect to the business use of a dwelling unit that's also used by the taxpayer as a residence during the tax year. (Code Sec. 280A(a)) This rule applies to individuals, trusts, estates, partnerships, and S corporations. However, this disallowance doesn't apply to any deduction allowable without regard to its connection with either a business or income-producing activity. (Code Sec. 280A(b)) For example, the deductions allowed for interest, (Code Sec. 163) certain taxes, (Code Sec. 164) and casualty losses (Code Sec. 165) may be deducted without regard to their connection with the taxpayer's trade or business or income-producing activities. In effect, this means that the disallowance applies only to otherwise deductible business expenses (Code Sec. 162) and depreciation.[19]

The home office deduction is not allowed for expenses of an income-producing activity, unless the activity is a trade or business.[20]

---

10. ¶ L-4100 *et seq.*; ¶ 1624.191.   14. ¶s L-4100, L-4101;   16. ¶ L-4101; ¶ 1624.191.   18. ¶ L-3906 *et seq.*; ¶ 674.
11. ¶ L-4100; ¶ 1624.193.   ¶ 1624.193.   17. ¶ L-4108; ¶s 1624.191,   19. ¶ L-1300 *et seq.*; ¶ 280A4.
12. ¶ L-3719; ¶ 1624.193.   15. ¶ L-4107.   1624.195.   20. ¶ L-1302; ¶ 280A4.
13. ¶ L-4102; ¶ 1624.195.

Footnote references beginning with letters are to paragraphs in RIA's Federal Tax Coordinator 2d and RIA's Analysis of Federal Taxes: Income. Footnote references beginning with numbers are to paragraphs in RIA's United States Tax Reporter.

¶ 1631 These residence expenses may be deductible.

In situations in the following paragraphs, otherwise allowable business expenses (but not investment expenses) are deductible (subject to the limits discussed at ¶s 1637 and 1638) even though they are incurred with respect to the business use of a portion of a taxpayer's residence. In addition, the cost of capital improvements made with respect to the entire residence may be recovered through depreciation to the extent the improvements are allocable to the portion of the residence used for the taxpayer's business.[21]

An employee gets a deduction (subject to the 2% floor on miscellaneous itemized deductions, see ¶ 3107) only if the exclusive business use of a portion of his residence is for the convenience of his employer. (Code Sec. 280A(c)(1))[22]

Any charge (including taxes) for basic local telephone services with respect to the first telephone line for any residence is treated as a personal expense. (Code Sec. 262(b))

¶ 1632 Residence used as principal place of business.

Deduction is allowed to the extent allocable to a portion of a residence *used exclusively* and *on a regular basis* (¶ 1637) as the taxpayer's principal place of business for *any* trade or business of the taxpayer. (Code Sec. 280A(c)(1)(A))[23] The determination of a taxpayer's *principal* place of business requires a comparative analysis of: (1) the relative importance of the activities performed at each business location, and (2) the time spent at each place, i.e., the amount of time spent at the home compared with the amount of time spent in each of the other places where business activities occur. If the nature of the trade or profession requires the taxpayer to meet or confer with clients or patients or to deliver goods or services to a customer, the place where that contact occurs, particularly where that place is a facility with unique or special characteristics, is often important. Thus an anesthesiologist was denied a deduction since the most important part of his job (medical treatment) was performed at hospitals and not at his home office.[24]

The fact that functions performed at home are essential to the business is relevant in determining principal place of business, but it's not controlling. The availability of alternative office space is not relevant.

There may be cases where there is no principal place of business. A home office or place of business does not qualify the taxpayer for the deduction simply because no other location seems to be the principal place.[25]

¶ 1633 Residence used to meet clients.

Deduction is allowed to the extent allocable to a portion of a residence that is *used exclusively* and *on a regular basis* (¶ 1637) as a place of business that is used by patients, clients, or customers in meeting or dealing with the taxpayer in the normal course of his trade or business. (Code Sec. 280A(c)(1)(B)) This permits a doctor, lawyer, sales rep, insurance agent, claims adjuster, etc., to deduct office-at-home expenses even though he operates his business or profession from an office away from his residence.[26]

¶ 1634 Separate structure not attached to residence.

A deduction is allowed for costs allocable to a portion of a separate structure not attached to the residence if it is used *exclusively* and *on a regular basis* (¶ 1637) in connection with the taxpayer's business. (Code Sec. 280A(c)(1)(C)) For example, an artist's studio in a structure next to but not attached to his residence qualified under this rule.[27]

---

21. ¶ L-1324 *et seq.*   23. ¶ L-1309; ¶ 280A4.   25. ¶ L-1310   27. ¶ L-1315; ¶ 280A4.
22. ¶ L-1316; ¶ 280A4.   24. ¶ L-1310   26. ¶ L-1314; ¶ 280A4.

Footnote references beginning with letters are to paragraphs in RIA's Federal Tax Coordinator 2d and RIA's Analysis of Federal Taxes: Income. Footnote references beginning with numbers are to paragraphs in RIA's United States Tax Reporter.

¶ 1635 Residence used by wholesaler or retailer for storage of inventory.

Deduction is allowed to the extent allocable to space within the residence the taxpayer uses *on a regular basis* to store inventory in his business of selling products at retail or wholesale, if the residence is the sole fixed location of the trade or business. (Code Sec. 280A(c)(2)) The space in the residence doesn't have to be used *exclusively* to store inventory, but must be so used on a regular basis and must be a separately identifiable space suitable for storage.[28]

¶ 1636 Nonexclusive use of home as day-care facility.

Deduction is allowed if a residence is used to provide day-care services for compensation on a regular basis to children, physically or mentally handicapped individuals, or persons 65 or over. If there is only part-time use of a portion of the residence, allocation must be made first on the basis of the proportion of total space used to furnish services and then on the basis of the amount of time that space is used for those services compared to the total time the space is available for all uses. The deduction is allowed only if the day-care services are not primarily educational and comply with any applicable state licensing, certification, or approval requirements. (Code Sec. 280A(c)(4))[29]

¶ 1637 "Exclusive" use on a "regular" basis.

For purposes of ¶s 1632 through 1636, the taxpayer is required to use the property or portion of the property for business on a regular basis; ¶s 1632 through 1634 require a taxpayer to use the property or portion of the property exclusively as a place of business.

Exclusive use of a portion of the taxpayer's residence or a detached structure (such as a detached garage) means that the taxpayer must use a specific portion of a residence or detached structure for carrying on his business. For example, a taxpayer who uses a den in his residence to write legal briefs and prepare tax returns as well as for personal purposes doesn't meet the exclusive use test.[30] However, the Tax Court says that a portion of a room used exclusively for business can qualify for the deduction, even though the room is not divided.[31]

Expenses attributable to the exclusive but incidental or occasional trade or business use of a portion of a dwelling unit are not deductible because the space is not used on a regular basis.[32]

¶ 1638 Gross income limit on home office deduction.

The deduction is limited to the gross income derived from the activity reduced by all other deductible expenses that are allowable regardless of qualified use and by the business deductions which are not allocable to the use of the home itself. (Code Sec. 280A(c)(5)(A), (B)) Expenses disallowed solely because they exceed business income can be carried forward (Code Sec. 280A(c)(5)) subject to the gross income limitation in the later year.[33]

¶ 1639 Allocation of home office expenses.

Allocation of expenses and depreciation or cost recovery on a house is generally based on a comparison of space used for business and personal purposes.[34]

¶ 1640 Rental by employer of space in employee's home.

No deduction is allowed for expenses attributable to the rental by an employee of all or part of his home to his employer if the employee uses the rented portion to perform services as an employee of the employer. (Code Sec. 280A(c)(6))[35]

---

28. ¶ L-1318.
29. ¶ L-1319 *et seq.*; ¶ 280A4.
30. ¶ L-1305 *et seq.*; ¶ 280A4.
31. ¶ L-1307.
32. ¶ L-1308.
33. ¶ L-1323 *et seq.*; ¶ 280A4.
34. ¶ L-1327.
35. ¶ L-1303; ¶ 280A4.

Footnote references beginning with letters are to paragraphs in RIA's Federal Tax Coordinator 2d and RIA's Analysis of Federal Taxes: Income. Footnote references beginning with numbers are to paragraphs in RIA's United States Tax Reporter.

¶ 1641 Education Expenses

A taxpayer can deduct costs incurred to maintain or improve skills required in his business or employment, but not costs incurred to meet minimum requirements for a trade or profession or to qualify for a new trade or profession.

¶ 1642 Education expenses.

Education expenses are deductible if made by a taxpayer either to maintain or improve skills required in his business or employment or to meet the express requirements of his employer, or the requirements of law or regs, imposed as a condition to retaining his salary, status or employment. (Reg § 1.162-5)[36]

A lawyer who has actually practiced law may generally deduct the expenses of any further legal education on the grounds that it maintains or improves required skills even though the education qualifies him to practice as a specialist.[37]

If the taxpayer is not a lawyer but is employed in allied fields where a legal education is helpful or customary, deduction for costs of a legal education is denied. (Reg § 1.162-5(b)(3))[38]

Deductions aren't allowed if the education:

■ is needed to meet the minimum requirements for taxpayer's present or intended employment, trade, business or profession, (Reg § 1.162-5(b)(2))[39] or

■ is undertaken to fulfill general education aspirations or for other personal reasons,[40] or

■ is part of a program of study that will lead to qualifying the individual in a new trade or business. (Reg § 1.162-5(b)(3)(i))[41]

Expenses that are otherwise deductible won't be disallowed because the course of studies leads to a degree. (Reg § 1.162-5(a))[42]

For education expenses paid for by the employer (including those of a self-employed individual), see ¶ 1258.

¶ 1643 Travel and transportation expenses of education.

The expenses of travel as a form of education are not deductible. (Code Sec. 274(m)(2))[43] This does not preclude deduction of travel expenses that are a necessary adjunct to other deductible education expenses.[44]

Local transportation expenses for qualified educational activities are deductible only if taxpayer is employed, and they are limited to the expenses in going between: (1) the general area of his principal business location and a school beyond that general area, or (2) his place of employment and a school within the same general area.[45]

Costs of seminar cruises or tours are disallowed where primarily for personal purposes even though part of the time is devoted to qualifying professional education.[46] Even if not for personal purposes, deduction is limited under the rules at ¶s 1543 and 1544.

¶ 1644 Teachers' education expenses.

If the minimum teaching requirements have *already* been met, a teacher may deduct the expense of any education required to retain his or her position, salary or status, even if the education will qualify the teacher to teach a new or different subject. (Reg § 1.162-5) Costs of courses to renew a provisional teaching certificate, or that lead to a *permanent* certificate are deductible if necessary to continue teaching.[47]

Cost of education to maintain or improve skills is deductible even though it leads to an

---

36. ¶ L-3701; ¶ 1624.185.   39. ¶ L-3713; ¶ 1624.185.   42. ¶ L-3702; ¶ 1624.185.   45. ¶ L-3732; ¶ 1624.185.
37. ¶s L-3723, L-3721.   40. ¶ L-3701; ¶ 1624.193.   43. ¶ L-3736; ¶ 1624.185.   46. ¶ L-3735.
38. ¶ L-3716 *et seq.*   41. ¶ L-3716; ¶ 1624.185.   44. ¶ L-3736; ¶ 1624.185.   47. ¶ L-3703; ¶ 1624.185.

Footnote references beginning with letters are to paragraphs in RIA's Federal Tax Coordinator 2d and RIA's Analysis of Federal Taxes: Income. Footnote references beginning with numbers are to paragraphs in RIA's United States Tax Reporter.

advanced degree (Reg § 1.162-5(c)) or qualifies the teacher for a change of duties. (Reg § 1.162-5(b))[48] Education to meet minimum requirements isn't deductible. (Reg § 1.162-5(b)(2))[49]

¶ 1645 Moving Expenses

An employee or self-employed individual may deduct certain expenses of moving to a new home if the move results from a change in the individual's principal place of work and if distance and time (working at the new location) tests are met. The specific rules differ depending on whether the expenses were incurred before '94 or after '93. Exceptions apply to members of the armed forces.

Report moving expenses on Form 3903.

¶ 1646 Deductible itemized direct and indirect expenses moving expenses before '94.

For expenses incurred before '94, an employee or self-employed individual who moves his residence because of a change in his principal place of work can deduct as itemized deductions the reasonable direct expenses of moving himself, his family and his household and can also deduct a limited amount of indirect moving expenses. To qualify, he must meet the pre-'94 distance test (¶ 1649) and either the 39- or 78-week employment test (¶ 1650).[50]

Deductible *direct* expenses include:

■ the reasonable expenses of moving personal effects and household goods, including automobile shipping charges, but not the cost of shipping furniture bought en route, and

■ costs of travel (including transportation, the pre-'94 limit of 80% of the costs of meals, and lodging in transit) of the taxpayer and his family (but not servants).[1]

Deductible *indirect* expenses are:

■ Pre-move house-hunting costs. Costs of round trips, lodging and 80% of the cost of meals for the employee and members of his household if the employee has already gotten employment at the new job site and the principal purpose for the round trips was to search for a new residence.

■ Temporary living expenses at new principal job location. Costs of lodging and 80% of the costs of meals incurred by the employee and members of his household during any period of 30 consecutive days after getting employment and while occupying temporary quarters are deductible.[2]

■ Costs of selling old residence, buying or leasing new residence, and terminating old lease. These include attorney's fees, escrow fees, appraisal fees, real estate agent's commissions, title costs, and "points" paid for services rather than for interest, state transfer taxes and advertising expenses.[3]

These sales or purchase expenses cannot be used again either to reduce the amount realized on the sale of the old residence or to increase the basis of the new residence.[4]

The pre-'94 80% limit on the cost of meals applies even if the employee is reimbursed for the moving expenses by his or her employer or if the employer paid the expenses, where the reimbursement or payment is includible in the income of the employee under the Code Sec. 82 reimbursement-of-moving-expense rules (see ¶ 1256).[5]

¶ 1647 Dollar limits on indirect expenses before '94.

For expenses incurred before '94, an employee can deduct all the reasonable direct moving expenses without dollar limitation. But indirect moving expenses (except for

---

48. ¶ L-3718; ¶ 1624.185.

49. ¶ L-3714; ¶ 1624.185.

50. ¶ L-3600 *et seq.*; ¶ 2174.01.

1. ¶ L-3623; ¶ 2174.01.

2. ¶s L-3632, L-3633; ¶ 2174.01.

3. ¶ L-3634; ¶ 2174.01.

4. ¶ L-3635; ¶ 2174.01.

5. ¶ L-2139.

Footnote references beginning with letters are to paragraphs in RIA's Federal Tax Coordinator 2d and RIA's Analysis of Federal Taxes: Income. Footnote references beginning with numbers are to paragraphs in RIA's United States Tax Reporter.

foreign moves as explained at ¶ 1651) are limited to:

■ $1,500 for pre-move house-hunting trips and temporary living expenses at the new location, and

■ $3,000 for expenses of qualified residence sale, purchase or lease, less any amount allowable for house-hunting and temporary living expenses.

If husband and wife both work at the new location but file separate returns, the $1,500 and $3,000 limits are $750 and $1,500 per spouse. If only one spouse works at the new location and separate returns are filed, the spouse with the deduction can deduct up to $1,500 and $3,000. Where *both* spouses, filing separate returns, started work at new principal places of work that met the distance tests and did not reside together during the tax year *each* can deduct up to $1,500 and $3,000. If both spouses started work at new locations at least 35 miles apart and did not reside together, the limits on a joint return are $3,000 and $6,000.[6]

If the taxpayer's car is used he may deduct actual out-of-pocket expenses (not depreciation) or 9¢ per mile in lieu of actual costs.[7]

The pre-'94 moving expense deduction isn't subject to the 2%-of-AGI floor on miscellaneous itemized deductions.[8]

¶ 1648 Deductible above-the-line expenses after '93.

For expenses incurred after '93, an employee or self-employed individual who moves his residence because of a change in his principal place of work may deduct the reasonable expenses of (Code Sec. 217(b)(1)):

■ moving household goods and personal effects from the old residence to the new place of residence, and

■ traveling (including lodging) from the old residence to the new place of residence.[9]

Deductible moving expenses do not include meals.[10]

In the case of any individual other than the taxpayer, the expenses above are deductible only if the individual has both the former residence and the new residence as his principal place of abode and is a member of the taxpayer's household. (Code Sec. 217(b)(2))[11]

observation: There are no dollar limits on the amount of post-'93 moving expenses that are deductible.

¶ 1649 35-mile (50-mile after '93) distance test.

The new job site must be at least 35 miles (50 miles after '93) farther from the taxpayer's old principal residence than was the old principal job site. If he didn't have a full-time job before the move, the new job site must be at least 35 miles (50 miles after '93) from his old residence. (Code Sec. 217(c)(1))[12]

¶ 1650 39-week/78-week time tests.

A "39-week test" or a "78-week test" must be met: (Code Sec. 217(c)(2))

■ 39-week test. An employee must be employed full-time in the general location of his new principal place of work for at least 39 weeks during the 12-month period immediately following his arrival in the new area. (Code Sec. 217(c)(2)(A))

■ 78-week test. The taxpayer must be a "full time employee" or must "perform services as a self-employed individual on a full time basis" in the general location of his new principal place of work for at least 78 weeks during the 24-month period immediately following his

---

6. ¶ L-3628; ¶ 2174.01.   8. ¶ L-3619; ¶ 674(a).   10. ¶ L-3623; ¶ 2174.01.   12. ¶ L-3616; ¶ 2174.01.
7. ¶ L-3626; ¶ 2174.01.   9. ¶ L-3623et seq.; ¶ 2174.01.   11. ¶ L-3622.

Footnote references beginning with letters are to paragraphs in RIA's Federal Tax Coordinator 2d and RIA's Analysis of Federal Taxes: Income. Footnote references beginning with numbers are to paragraphs in RIA's United States Tax Reporter.

arrival there. Thirty-nine of the 78 weeks must be during the 12-month period above.(Code Sec. 217(c)(2)(B))

Joint filers qualify for the deduction if either spouse satisfies the 39-week or 78-week test. But weeks worked by one spouse can't be added to weeks worked by the other. (Reg § 1.217-2(c)(4)(v), Reg § 1.217-1(c)(4))

Failure to meet the 39- or 78-week test doesn't bar deduction if the failure was caused by: (1) death or disability, or (2) involuntary separation from employment (other than for willful misconduct), or re-transfer for the benefit of the employer (*not* initiated by the employee), after getting full-time employment in which the taxpayer could reasonably have been expected to meet the test. (Code Sec. 217(d)(1))[13]

¶ 1651 Foreign moves (from the U.S.).

Expenses of moving from the U.S. or its possessions to a new principal place of work outside the U.S. or its possessions include the reasonable expenses (no dollar ceiling) of moving household goods and personal effects to and from storage, and of storing these items while the new place of work is the taxpayer's principal place of work. (Code Sec. 217(h)) For moving expenses incurred before '94, "temporary living expenses" for 90 consecutive days in connection with foreign moves are deductible.[14] For indirect moving expenses incurred before '94, ceilings are:

■ $4,500 ($2,250 on separate returns of married persons) for pre-move house-hunting trips and temporary living expenses at the new location, and

■ $6,000 ($3,000 on separate returns) for expenses of qualified residence sale, purchase or lease, less any amount allowable for house-hunting and temporary living expenses.[15]

Report expenses of foreign moves on Form 3903F.

Moving expenses aren't deductible to the extent they are allocable to exempt foreign-source earned income. In the absence of evidence to the contrary, reimbursement of moving expenses to move to a foreign country is attributed to future services to be performed at the new place of work. (Reg § 1.911-3(e)(5)(i))[16]

¶ 1652 Moving to U.S. not connected with employment.

Moving expense deductions under special rules are allowed for persons who worked abroad and move to the U.S. (or its possessions) on retirement, and for the spouse or dependent who moves to the U.S. following the death of a person who worked abroad. (Code Sec. 217(i))[17]

¶ 1653 When to deduct moving expenses.

A taxpayer may: (1) deduct in the year the expenses were paid or incurred even though the 39- or 78-week condition isn't satisfied before the due date for filing (including extensions), (Code Sec. 217(d)(2); Reg § 1.217-2(a)(2)) or (2) wait until the applicable condition is satisfied and then file an amended return claiming the deduction for the tax year the moving expense was paid or incurred. (Reg § 1.217-2(d))[18]

¶ 1654 Moving expenses of members of the armed forces.

A move by an active duty member of the armed forces pursuant to a military order and incident to a permanent change of station can qualify for deduction regardless of the distance moved or the length of time worked at the new station. Cash reimbursements or allowances are excludable from income to the extent of moving and storage expenses actually paid or incurred, as are all in-kind moving and storage services provided by the military. This exclusion also applies to the spouse and dependents of an armed services

---

13. ¶ L-3603 *et seq.*
14. ¶ L-3643; ¶ 2174.03.

15. ¶s L-3627, L-3628; ¶ 2174.03.
16. ¶ L-3644; ¶ 9114.11.

17. ¶ L-3647; ¶ 2174.03.

18. ¶ L-3602; ¶ 2174.01.

Footnote references beginning with letters are to paragraphs in RIA's Federal Tax Coordinator 2d and RIA's Analysis of Federal Taxes: Income. Footnote references beginning with numbers are to paragraphs in RIA's United States Tax Reporter.

member when they don't accompany the member and move to a location different from that *to* which he moves or different from that *from* which he moves. Where the military moves the member and the member's family to or from separate locations and they incur unreimbursed expenses, their moves are treated as a single move to the member's new principal place of work. (Code Sec. 217(g))[19]

¶ 1655 Capital Expenditures

Capital expenditures generally may not be deducted except through depreciation, depletion, or amortization deductions.

These rules apply only to the extent they don't conflict with the uniform capitalization rules (¶ 1661 *et seq.*).

A capital expenditure differs from a deductible expense because the anticipated benefit of the capital expenditure extends beyond the tax year.

Capital expenditures include amounts paid or incurred to add to the value, or to substantially extend the useful life, of property owned by the taxpayer. (Code Sec. 263; Reg § 1.263(a)-1)[20] (For repairs and maintenance of property, see ¶ 1668.)

Examples of capital expenditures include:

■ Original cost of getting a business license that is good or renewable for an indefinite period.[21]

■ Initiation fees or initial admission fees paid for business association, etc., memberships.[22]

■ Costs incurred by a corporation related to the issuance, redemption and sale of its stock.[23]

■ Installation costs of purchased machinery, equipment, etc., including labor, material and freight charges to the extent that these expenses do not conflict with the uniform capitalization rules (see ¶ 1661).[24]

■ Costs other than interest incurred to borrow funds and other finance costs are capital expenditures to be amortized over the life of the loan. (For capitalization of interest on produced property, see ¶ 1663.) This applies to commissions and other fees paid to get a loan, cost of issuing bonds, including legal fees and printing costs and finder's fees and commissions paid by a lender to get borrowers.[25]

■ Payments made to get the goodwill of a business, including payments for the use of an individual's name in a business bought from him; the cost of acquiring a dealer's franchise;[26] cost of acquiring customer lists.[27]

For amortization of "Code Sec. 197" intangibles, see ¶ 1989.

¶ 1656 Costs of acquisition, construction or erection of property.

Costs of acquisition, construction or erection of property are included in inventory if the costs are allocable to property which is inventory, and the costs are capitalized if allocable to other property. (Code Sec. 263A(a))[28] These rules apply to real or tangible personal property that taxpayers produce and inventory that taxpayers acquire for resale. (Code Sec. 263A(b)(2)(A))[29] See ¶ 1661 *et seq.*

¶ 1657 Taxes, interest, and carrying charges—election to capitalize.

Some taxes and carrying charges that would normally be deducted currently or amortized may be capitalized if the taxpayer so elects.[30]

---

19. ¶ L-3641; ¶ 2174.02.
20. ¶ L-5601; ¶ 2634.
21. ¶ L-4217.
22. ¶ L-4232.
23. ¶ L-5305; ¶ 1624.402.
24. ¶ L-5811; ¶ 2634.16.
25. ¶ L-6601 *et seq.*; ¶ 1624.081.
26. ¶ L-5711; ¶ 2634.10.
27. ¶ L-5713; ¶ 2634.10.
28. ¶ G-5152; ¶ 263A4.
29. ¶s G-5158, G-5167; ¶ 263A4.
30. ¶ L-5901; ¶ 2664.

Footnote references beginning with letters are to paragraphs in RIA's Federal Tax Coordinator 2d and RIA's Analysis of Federal Taxes: Income. Footnote references beginning with numbers are to paragraphs in RIA's United States Tax Reporter.

For depreciable property this has the effect of deferring the deduction to later years as depreciation. For nondepreciable property, such as unimproved real estate, the capitalized expenses increase basis and serve to reduce gain (or increase loss) on a later sale of the property. (Code Sec. 266; Reg § 1.212-1(n), Reg § 1.266-1)[31]

¶ 1658 Annual election for unimproved and unproductive real estate.

A taxpayer can elect to capitalize taxes, mortgage interest and deductible carrying charges on unimproved and unproductive real property. (Reg § 1.266-1(b))[32]

¶ 1659 Election for expenditures on real estate improvement project.

A taxpayer engaged in the development of real estate or the construction of an improvement to real estate can elect to capitalize the following items relating to the project:

■ interest on loans,

■ taxes measured by compensation paid to employees and taxes imposed on the purchase of materials, or on the storage, use, or other consumption of materials,

■ other necessary charges, including fire insurance premiums. (Reg § 1.266-1(b)(1))[33]

¶ 1660 Capitalizing taxes, interest, etc., before installing or using personal property.

The election to capitalize deductible items also applies to interest on a loan to finance the purchase, transportation and installation of machinery and other assets, state and local taxes imposed on the taxpayer, transportation, storage, use or other consumption of the property, and state and local taxes, including sales and use taxes, and state and federal unemployment taxes and the taxpayer's share of federal social security taxes on the wages of employees engaged in transportation and installation of the assets. (Reg § 1.266-1)[34]

¶ 1661 Uniform capitalization rules.

A taxpayer must:

(1) include in inventory costs the "allocable costs" (defined below) of "property" (also defined below) that is inventory; (Code Sec. 263A(a)(1)(A))

(2) capitalize the allocable costs of any other property. (Code Sec. 263A(a)(2)(B))

The *allocable costs* are:

■ the direct costs of the property; (Code Sec. 263A(a)(2)(A))

■ the indirect costs, to the extent of the property's proper share of that part (or all) of the costs allocable to that property. (Code Sec. 263A(a)(2)(B))

Allocable costs include all depreciation deductions with respect to the taxpayer's assets.

Interest is an allocable cost, but only where the underlying debt was incurred or continued to finance certain produced property, see ¶ 1663.

Taxes are allocable indirect costs. (Code Sec. 263A(a)(2)(B))

Allocable costs don't include:

■ selling, marketing, advertising and distribution expenses; (Reg § 1.263A-1(e)(3)(iii)(A))

■ any amounts allowable as a deduction under Code Sec. 174 for research and experimental expenditures; (Code Sec. 263A(c)(2))

■ any cost to the extent allowable as a deduction under Code Sec. 263(c) (intangible drilling and development costs), Code Sec. 616(a) (mining development expenses) or Code Sec. 617(a) (mining exploration expenses); (Code Sec. 263A(c)(3))

■ any qualified creative expense incurred by a "writer," "photographer" or "artist" which

---

31. ¶ L-1154; ¶ 2634.   32. ¶ L-5911; ¶ 2664.   33. ¶ L-5904.   34. ¶s L-5901, L-5905.

Footnote references beginning with letters are to paragraphs in RIA's Federal Tax Coordinator 2d and RIA's Analysis of Federal Taxes: Income. Footnote references beginning with numbers are to paragraphs in RIA's United States Tax Reporter.

would otherwise be deductible. Expenses related to printing photographic plates, motion picture films, video tapes or similar items are not qualified creative expenses; (Code Sec. 263A(h))

■ "deductible service costs." (Reg § 1.263A-1(e)(3)(iii)(K))

What is property? A taxpayer must include in inventory or capitalize the allocable costs with respect to:

■ real or tangible personal property (defined below) that the taxpayer *produced* (defined below); (Code Sec. 263A(b)(1))

■ real or personal Code Sec. 1221(1) property—inventory and property held primarily for sale to customers in the ordinary course of the taxpayer's trade or business—that the taxpayer acquired for resale. (Code Sec. 263A(b)(2)(A))

Tangible personal property ((1), above) includes a film, sound recording, video tape, book or similar property. (Code Sec. 263A(b))

A taxpayer "produces" tangible property if he constructs, builds, installs, manufactures, develops or improves it. (Code Sec. 263A(g)(1))

Where a taxpayer makes progress or advance payments to a contractor, the taxpayer is treated as producing any property the contractor produces for the taxpayer under the contract, to the extent of those payments (whether paid or incurred by the taxpayer under the contract or otherwise). (Code Sec. 263A(g)(2))

Property acquired for resale ((2), above) includes intangible as well as tangible property.

"Property" doesn't include (and therefore allocable costs don't have to be capitalized with respect to):

■ Any property produced by the taxpayer for use by the taxpayer other than in a trade or business or an activity conducted for profit. (Code Sec. 263A(c)(1))

■ Any property produced by the taxpayer under a long-term contract (Code Sec. 263A(c)(4)) except for certain home construction contracts. (Code Sec. 460(e)(1)) But long-term contracts not subject to the post-Feb 28, '86 accounting rules for long-term contracts (see ¶ 2850 *et seq.*) are subject to the capitalization rules.

■ Timber and certain ornamental trees. (Code Sec. 263A(c)(5)(A))

■ Personal property acquired for resale by certain taxpayers with average annual gross receipts of $10,000,000 or less. (Code Sec. 263A(b)(2)(B))[35]

Taxpayers who acquire and hold property for resale (such as retailers and wholesalers) may elect a simplified resale method to determine the additional costs properly allocable to the resale property. (Reg § 1.263A-3(d))[36]

¶ 1662 How to allocate costs to property.

Allocable costs (see ¶ 1661) must be allocated to inventory or capitalized according to the following rules:

■ Direct labor costs should generally be allocated by means of a specific identification ("tracing") method. (Reg § 1.263A-1T(b)(3)(ii))

■ Indirect costs should be allocated to particular production, resale, etc., activities using either a specific identification ("tracing") method, the standard cost method, or a method using burden rates, such as ratios based on direct costs, hours, or other items, or similar formulas, so long as the method employed reasonably allocates indirect costs among production, resale, etc., activities. (Reg § 1.263A-1T(b)(3)(iii)(A)(1)) Indirect costs, however, may not be allocated to inventory under the "practical capacity concept."

---

35. ¶s G-5151 *et seq.*, L-1650;   36. ¶s G-5151 *et seq.*, L-1650;
   ¶ 263A4.   ¶ 263A4.

Footnote references beginning with letters are to paragraphs in RIA's Federal Tax Coordinator 2d and RIA's Analysis of Federal Taxes: Income. Footnote references beginning with numbers are to paragraphs in RIA's United States Tax Reporter.

(Reg § 1.263A-1T(b)(2)(vii))[37]

¶ 1663 Interest capitalization rules.

A taxpayer must capitalize interest he pays or incurs during a production period (defined below) (Code Sec. 263A(f)(1)(A)) that is allocable (also explained below) to property he produces (Code Sec. 263A(f)(1)(B)) if that property:

(1) has a long useful life (defined below); (Code Sec. 263A(f)(1)(B)(i))

(2) has an estimated production period exceeding two years; (Code Sec. 263A(f)(1)(B)(ii)) or

(3) has an estimated production period exceeding one year and a cost exceeding $1,000,000. (Code Sec. 263A(f)(1)(B)(iii))

The taxpayer must also capitalize any interest on debt allocable to an asset needed to produce the above property. (Code Sec. 263A(f)(3))

A taxpayer must capitalize interest whether he produces the property for his own use or for sale.

The "production period" with respect to any property begins on the date production of the property begins. (Code Sec. 263A(f)(4)(B)(i)) The production period ends the date the property is ready to be placed in service or is ready to be held for sale. (Code Sec. 263A(f)(4)(B)(ii))

Property has a "long useful life" ((1), above) if it is real property or property with a class life of 20 years or more. (Code Sec. 263A(f)(4)(A)(ii))

Taxpayer doesn't capitalize interest with respect to real or personal property acquired solely for resale.

A taxpayer doesn't capitalize interest allocable to property that's not subject to the capitalization rules, such as property produced under a long-term contract (see the discussion of this and other exceptions at ¶ 1661). Thus, a taxpayer who produces property under a long term contract capitalizes interest only to the extent he doesn't report income under the percentage of completion method.[38]

Allocating interest to produced property. Interest is allocable to property a taxpayer produces if the taxpayer incurred or continued the underlying debt to finance the construction or production of the property.

A taxpayer is treated as having incurred or continued debt to finance the production of income: (1) where the debt can be specifically traced to production expenditures, and (2) where the debt can't be so traced, but where production or construction expenditures exceed the debt that is directly traceable.

The interest on the debt incurred or continued to finance production is allocated to the property produced as follows:[39]

(1) interest (other than qualified residence interest) on a debt that is directly attributable to production expenditures with respect to the produced property is assigned to that property; (Code Sec. 263A(f)(2)(A)(i)) and

(2) interest on any other debt is assigned to the produced property to the extent that the taxpayer's interest costs could have been reduced if production expenditures (not attributable to the debt in (1), above) had not been incurred (Code Sec. 263A(f)(2)(A)(ii)) (that is, had the expenditures that were incurred for construction been used instead to repay the debt).

---

37. ¶s G-5175, G-5157; ¶ 263A4.   38. ¶ L-5915 *et seq.*; ¶ 263A4.   39. ¶ L-5926 *et seq.*; ¶ 263A4.

Footnote references beginning with letters are to paragraphs in RIA's Federal Tax Coordinator 2d and RIA's Analysis of Federal Taxes: Income. Footnote references beginning with numbers are to paragraphs in RIA's United States Tax Reporter.

¶ 1664 Computer software costs.

Where the taxpayer *develops* the software program, it can either consistently expense the costs currently or consistently capitalize the costs and amortize them over five years (or any shorter life that can be clearly established).

For computer software (as defined in ¶ 1991) *acquired* after Aug. 10, '93 (or electively, after July 25, '91), either 15-year amortization (¶ 1991 *et seq.*) or 36-month straight-line depreciation (¶ 1971) applies.

Rental payments for leased software can be deducted just like any other rentals.[40]

For property acquired before Aug. 11, '93, (or electively before July 26, '91), the purchaser of a computer software program treated it in one of two ways depending on how it was billed by the seller:

■ If the charge for the computer software was included in the price of the hardware without a separate identification of the charge for software, then the buyer had to consistently treat the entire amount the same as the cost of the hardware.

■ If the charge for the software was separately stated, it could be consistently amortized over five years (or any shorter useful life the taxpayer established).

¶ 1665 Commissions paid upon transfer of property.

Commissions paid for the *purchase* of real estate or other property are not deductible as expenses but must be capitalized and added to the cost of the property, whether or not the taxpayer is engaged in the real estate business.[41]

A partnership or S corporation producing property to which the interest capitalization rules apply must first capitalize interest as described above. The remaining production expenditures must be allocated to the partners or shareholders based on respective shares. The owners are then subject to the interest capitalization rules.[42]

Commissions paid for the *sale* of real estate or other property by a taxpayer who is not engaged in the real estate business must be offset against the selling price to determine the gain or loss realized on the sale. If the seller is engaged in the real estate business, the commissions on property sales are deductible business expenses.[43]

¶ 1666 Interest and carrying charges relating to straddles.

The interest and carrying charges properly allocable to personal property that is part of a straddle (¶ 2642) aren't deductible, but must be charged to the capital account of the property for which they were paid or incurred. (Code Sec. 263(g)(1)) However this requirement doesn't apply to any identified hedging transactions (¶ 2649). (Code Sec. 263(g)(3))[44]

"Interest and carrying charges" means the excess of:

■ the sum of interest on indebtedness incurred or continued to buy or carry personal property that is part of a straddle, and amounts paid or incurred to insure, store, or transport that personal property, *over*

■ the sum of: (1) the amount of interest income, including original issue discount, from the property includible in gross income for the taxable year, (2) any amount treated as ordinary income under Code Secs. 1271(a)(3)(A), 1281(a) (dealing with acquisition discount on short-term government and nongovernment obligations), or Code Sec. 1278 (dealing with market discount bonds), (3) the excess of any dividends includible in income over the dividends received deductions allowable with respect to those dividends under Code Secs. 243, 244 or 245, and (4) any payment with respect to a security loan that's included in gross income for the tax year. (Code Sec. 263(g)(2)) Also, the term "interest"

---

40. ¶ L-5613 *et seq.*; ¶ 1674.033.   42. ¶ L-5963 *et seq.*   43. ¶ I-2537; ¶ 2634.05.   44. ¶ L-5985; ¶ 2634.
41. ¶ I-2536.

Footnote references beginning with letters are to paragraphs in RIA's Federal Tax Coordinator 2d and RIA's Analysis of Federal
Taxes: Income. Footnote references beginning with numbers are to paragraphs in RIA's United States Tax Reporter.

includes amounts paid or incurred in connection with personal property used in a short sale.[45]

¶ 1667 Architectural and transportation barrier removal expenses.

A taxpayer can elect to treat up to $15,000 of qualified architectural and transportation barrier removal expenses as a deduction rather than as a charge to capital account. (Code Sec. 190(a), (c)) To elect, claim the deduction as a separate item identified as such on the timely filed (including extension) return for the tax year for which the election is to apply. (Reg § 1.190-3(a))[46] For the credit for eligible access expenditures, see ¶ 2327.

¶ 1668 Repairs.

The cost of repairing business property of the taxpayer is deductible currently as a business expense, while an improvement that materially adds to the value or utility of the property or appreciably prolongs its useful life must be capitalized. (Reg § 1.162-4)[47]

Expenditures as part of a general plan of reconditioning, renovating, improving or altering property must be capitalized even though certain portions of the work standing alone might properly be classifiable as repairs.[48]

---

45. ¶ L-5985 *et seq.*; ¶ 2634.   46. ¶s L-5806, L-5807; ¶ 1904.02.   47. ¶ L-6101; ¶ 1624.171.   48. ¶ L-6108; ¶ 1624.183.

Footnote references beginning with letters are to paragraphs in RIA's Federal Tax Coordinator 2d and RIA's Analysis of Federal Taxes: Income. Footnote references beginning with numbers are to paragraphs in RIA's United States Tax Reporter.

Chapter 4 Interest Expense—Taxes—Losses—Bad Debts

¶ 1700 Deduction for Interest

Interest is deductible, as long as it is incurred with respect to a valid debt and is actually paid or accrued during the tax year. But special rules bar or limit the deduction for interest incurred in personal transactions and on certain kinds of debt.

To be deductible, the charge for interest need not be reasonable,[1] and may even be usurious.[2] But it must be definitely ascertainable,[3] and be with respect to a valid debt.[4]

The deduction for interest incurred in connection with certain types of indebtedness is subject to various limitations (¶ 1722 et seq.), and some interest may not be deducted at all (¶ 1712 et seq.). For limits on the deduction of interest incurred in a passive activity, see ¶ 1798 et seq. For interest expenses that must be included in inventory or capitalized, see ¶ 1655 et seq.

For individuals, interest is deductible only as an itemized deduction.[5]

caution: The deduction of interest is subject to the reduction that applies to certain other itemized deductions if adjusted gross income exceeds specified amounts (¶ 3112).

¶ 1701 Interest is payment for the use or forbearance of money.

Interest can include the amount paid: (1) for the borrower's *use* of money during the term of a loan, and (2) for his *detention* of money after the due date for repayment. Merely designating a payment as "interest" won't necessarily make it deductible.[6] Nor does the fact that the payment is taxable interest to the lender make it deductible by the payor-borrower.[7]

The following forms of "interest" are true interest for federal tax purposes:

■ Interest and finance charges paid to lenders[8] (including "points," see ¶ 1703).

■ Premiums the borrower is required to pay the lender to get the loan.[9]

■ Discounts (including original issue discount, see ¶ 1742)—i.e., where the borrower receives less than the face amount of the loan but is required to repay the full face amount, the difference is interest.[10]

■ Foregone interest on below-market loans that the borrower is "deemed" to have paid to the lender (¶ 1310).[11]

■ Interest paid by banks or other financial institutions on deposits, certificates or other evidences of indebtedness.[12]

■ Payments of redeemable ground rents.[13]

■ Installment sale interest that is separately stated or definitely determinable and provable (¶ 1710), subject to the rules for credit cards (¶ 1709).[14] For "unstated interest," see ¶ 1741.

■ Interest on deposits, down payments, etc., where the seller defers delivery of a purchased item.[15]

■ Interest on certain delinquent tax payments, whether or not the tax itself is deductible.[16]

■ Interest on judgment debts.[17]

■ Interest on declared but unpaid dividends.[18]

1. ¶ K-5001; ¶ 1634(e).
2. ¶ K-5002; ¶ 1634.021.
3. ¶ K-5024; ¶ 1634.025.
4. ¶ K-5060 et seq.
5. ¶ K-5000; ¶ 1634(f).

6. ¶s K-5020, K-5021; ¶ 1634(a).
7. ¶ K-5020; ¶ 1634.
8. ¶ K-5031; ¶ 1634(g).
9. ¶ K-5028; ¶s 1634.001, 1634.051.

10. ¶ K-5028; ¶s 1634.001, 1634.051.
11. ¶ K-5039; ¶ 78,724 et seq.
12. ¶ K-5042.
13. ¶ K-5044; ¶ 1634(h).

14. ¶ K-5029 et seq.; ¶ 1634.050.
15. ¶ K-5045.
16. ¶ K-5048; ¶ 1634.013.
17. ¶ K-5050; ¶ 1635.014(35).
18. ¶ K-5051; ¶ 1635.014(75).

Footnote references beginning with letters are to paragraphs in RIA's Federal Tax Coordinator 2d and RIA's Analysis of Federal Taxes: Income. Footnote references beginning with numbers are to paragraphs in RIA's United States Tax Reporter.

■ Interest on deferred payments of legacies.[19]

For deducting amounts forfeited on premature withdrawal of a bank deposit, see ¶ 2167.

¶ 1702 Mortgage interest.

Interest on a mortgage on real estate (including a condominium), is deductible, as are penalties for prepaying the mortgage or for paying it late. The deduction may be subject to the limits on deducting personal interest (¶ 1712) unless the interest is "qualified residence interest" (¶ 1726 *et seq.*).[20] For "points," see ¶ 1703.

For who deducts mortgage interest, see ¶ 1707.

¶ 1703 "Points."

"Points" (loan origination fees, loan processing fees, loan discount fees, etc., which are a specified percentage of the amount borrowed) that a borrower pays, out of his own funds, to a lender in order to get a mortgage loan are deductible as interest only if they are *solely* for the use or forbearance of money and not a charge for services. On the other hand, points paid for services of the lender *in lieu of* specific service charges (e.g., a one-point charge for appraisal, etc.) are not deductible as interest. Nor is a "commitment fee" charged for the lender's agreement to make a future loan.[21]

Where the *seller* (lender) pays the points, the payments are not deductible as interest. Rather, they are included in the seller's selling expenses, reducing the amount realized on sale. A seller in the business of building and selling houses has been allowed to deduct these "points" payments, but as a *business* expense.[22]

For when points, including points paid in connection with a personal residence, are deducted, see ¶ 1739.

¶ 1704 Corporate debt or equity; "thin " capitalization.

Corporations may favor heavy debt capitalization because interest paid on debt is deductible, while dividends paid on stock are not. But a corporation's debt obligations may be treated as equity (stock) so that "interest" paid on them would be a nondeductible dividend. Also, repayment of a debt is not taxable to the lender (corporation), while a stock redemption may be taxable, as a dividend, to the corporation's shareholders (¶ 3525 *et seq.*).

The corporate issuer's characterization (at issuance) of a corporate instrument (issued after 10/24/92) as stock or debt is binding on the issuer and all holders (unless the holder's inconsistent treatment is disclosed on his return), but not on IRS. (Code Sec. 385(c))[23]

Key factors that are relevant in determinations by IRS, or with respect to instruments not described above, as to whether purported corporate debt will be treated as debt for federal tax purposes include:

(1) the names given to the certificates evidencing the "debt;"

(2) the presence or absence of a fixed maturity date;

(3) the source of payments;

(4) the right to enforce payment of principal and interest;

(5) any resulting participation in management;

(6) whether the "debt" is subordinate to the corporation's other debt;

(7) whether the "debt" is convertible into stock;

19. ¶ K-5052.   21. ¶ K-5026; ¶ 1634.005.   22. ¶ K-5027.   23. ¶ K-5790 *et seq.*
20. ¶s K-5043, K-5034;
     ¶s 1634.001, 1634.050.

Footnote references beginning with letters are to paragraphs in RIA's Federal Tax Coordinator 2d and RIA's Analysis of Federal Taxes: Income. Footnote references beginning with numbers are to paragraphs in RIA's United States Tax Reporter.

(8) the intent of the parties;

(9) whether there is a high ratio of debt to equity;

(10) identity of interest between creditor and shareholder;

(11) the corporation's ability to get loans from outside lenders;

(12) the extent to which the advance was used to acquire capital assets;

(13) the "debtor's" failure to repay on time or to seek a postponement;

(14) the economic realities of the transaction;

(15) the business purpose of the transaction.[24]

¶ 1705 Who may deduct interest?

With limited exceptions (¶s 1706, 1707), a taxpayer's interest deduction is limited to interest that taxpayer pays or accrues on taxpayer's *own* indebtedness, and not for interest on debts of other persons.[25]

However, in the case of joint obligors—that is, persons who are jointly and severally liable for a debt (e.g., co-signers on a note)—each obligor may deduct the amount of interest that he actually pays on that debt.[26]

A person who is only secondarily liable for the debt, e.g., as endorser or guarantor, generally may not deduct interest on the debt. But if the guarantor, etc., actually pays all or part of the debt, he may be allowed to deduct the interest (or take a bad debt deduction, see ¶ 1837 *et seq.*).[27]

¶ 1706 Interest paid by another.

In certain cases where a person other than taxpayer pays or accrues the interest on taxpayer's debt, the payments are treated as made by taxpayer so as to allow a deduction for the interest. This occurs when the interest payor is acting (or is treated as acting) merely as taxpayer's agent (e.g., where a tenant pays the interest on his landlord's mortgage), or where taxpayer has parted with some consideration for the payor's payment.[28]

¶ 1707 Who deducts mortgage interest.

A taxpayer who is personally liable for a mortgage debt is entitled to deduct the mortgage interest he actually pays out of his own funds even if, when he makes the payments, he no longer owns the property subject to the mortgage. However, where a conveyance of mortgaged property would, under state law, automatically relieve the transferor of personal liability on the mortgage, the transferor isn't entitled to deduct the payments he makes after the transfer.[29]

A taxpayer who is *not* personally liable for a mortgage debt may deduct the mortgage interest that he actually pays *only* if he is the legal or equitable owner (solely or jointly with others) of the mortgaged property. This applies even where another person *is* personally liable for the mortgage.[30]

¶ 1708 Shareholders' share of cooperative housing corporation's mortgage payments.

Tenant-stockholders of cooperative housing corporations (co-ops) may deduct their share of the co-op's mortgage interest payments (subject to the "qualified residence interest" limits, see ¶ 1726 *et seq.*). (Code Sec. 216)[31]

---

24. ¶ K-5800 *et seq.*; ¶ 1634.057.   27. ¶ K-5134; ¶ 1664.450.   29. ¶ K-5136.   31. ¶s K-5141, K-5900 *et seq.*;
25. ¶ K-5120 *et seq.*; ¶ 1634.015.   28. ¶ K-5130; ¶ 1634.018.   30. ¶ K-5136; ¶ 1634.015.   ¶ 2164.01.
26. ¶ K-5131; ¶ 1634.015.

Footnote references beginning with letters are to paragraphs in RIA's Federal Tax Coordinator 2d and RIA's Analysis of Federal Taxes: Income. Footnote references beginning with numbers are to paragraphs in RIA's United States Tax Reporter.

¶ 1709 Finance charges.

The amount of "finance charges" imposed on the unpaid balances of "revolving charge accounts" or "budget charge accounts" of retail stores, or on the unpaid balances of bank and oil company credit card accounts, is deductible as interest (subject to the bar on personal interest deductions, see ¶ 1712), but only to the extent the payment is real "interest," i.e., not a service charge, etc.[32]

¶ 1710 6% rule on installment purchases.

If carrying charges (including finance charges, service charges, etc.) on an installment purchase of personal property or educational services are *separately stated*, but the amount of *interest* included in those charges cannot be ascertained, the installment payments are considered to include a 6% interest charge based on the average unpaid balance under the contract during the year. (Code Sec. 163(b))[33]

¶ 1711 Rule of 78s method.

A Rule of 78s method may not be used to the compute interest, except for certain consumer loan transactions with repayment terms not exceeding five years. Interest computed under this method must be recomputed under an economic accrual method for federal income tax purposes.[34]

¶ 1712 No deduction for personal interest.

Noncorporate taxpayers may not deduct "personal interest." (Code Sec. 163(h)(1), (5))[35] Personal interest is all interest *other than*:

■ Interest properly allocable to trade or business debt (other than the trade or business of being an employee).

■ Qualified residence interest (¶ 1726 *et seq.*).

■ Investment interest (¶ 1724).

■ Interest considered in computing income or loss from a passive activity (¶ 1798 *et seq.*).

■ Interest on estate tax payments deferred because a future interest or closely held business interest is included in the estate (¶ 5036). (Code Sec. 163(h)(2))[36]

¶ 1713 Net direct interest expense—market discount bonds.

A taxpayer's "net direct interest expense" on debt incurred or continued to purchase or carry a taxable market discount bond (¶ 1329) is deductible in a tax year only to the extent the expense exceeds the portion of the market discount allocable to the days during the year the bond was held by taxpayer. (Code Sec. 1277(a); Code Sec. 1278(a)(1)(C))[37] (For tax-exempt bonds, see ¶ 1719.)

"Net direct interest expense" is any excess of: (1) the interest paid or accrued on debt incurred or continued to buy or carry a market discount bond, over (2) the amount of interest (including OID) includible in income for the tax year with respect to the bond. (Code Sec. 1277(c))[38]

The disallowed interest expenses are generally deductible in the year taxpayer disposes of the bond. (Code Sec. 1277(b)(2)(A)) But taxpayer may elect, on a bond-by-bond basis, to deduct an earlier year's disallowed "net direct interest expenses" in a year in which (but only to the extent that) taxpayer has net interest income. (Code Sec. 1277(b)(1))[39]

---

32. ¶ K-5029.
33. ¶ K-5151; ¶ 1634.050.
34. ¶ K-5153 *et seq.*; ¶ 1634.030.
35. ¶ K-5510 *et seq.*; ¶ 1634.054.
36. ¶ K-5511; ¶ 1634.054.
37. ¶ K-5341; ¶ 12,764.02.
38. ¶ K-5342; ¶ 12,764.02.
39. ¶ K-5343; ¶ 12,764.02.

Footnote references beginning with letters are to paragraphs in RIA's Federal Tax Coordinator 2d and RIA's Analysis of Federal Taxes: Income. Footnote references beginning with numbers are to paragraphs in RIA's United States Tax Reporter.

¶ 1714   Net direct interest expense—short-term government obligations.

The "net direct interest expense" (¶ 1713) with respect to any short-term government obligation is deductible in a tax year only to the extent the expense exceeds the total of:

■ the sum of the daily portions of the acquisition discount for each day during the year that taxpayer held the obligation, (Code Sec. 1282(a)(1)) plus

■ the amount of any other (stated) interest payable on the obligation that accrues during the tax year while taxpayer held the obligation and that, because of taxpayer's accounting method, wasn't included in taxpayer's gross income. (Code Sec. 1282(a)(2))[40]

Deduction of disallowed interest expense generally is deferred until (as with market discount bonds, see ¶ 1713) taxpayer disposes of the obligation or makes the special election. (Code Sec. 1282(c))[41]

These rules also apply to any short-term nongovernmental obligation except that, unless taxpayer elects otherwise, original issue discount (OID, see ¶ 1318 *et seq.*) instead of acquisition discount is taken into account. (Code Sec. 1283(c))[42]

However, there is no deferral for *any* of these short-term obligations if taxpayer elects to include acquisition discount (or OID) in gross income currently. (Code Sec. 1282(b))[43]

¶ 1715   Interest on business life insurance loans.

No deduction is allowed for any interest paid or accrued on any indebtedness with respect to one or more life insurance policies owned by taxpayer, covering the life of any officer or employee or individual financially interested in any trade or business carried on by taxpayer, to the extent the aggregate indebtedness with respect to policies covering any one officer, etc., exceeds $50,000. (Code Sec. 264(a)(4)) This disallowance, which applies even if the loan proceeds are used for good business purposes, applies to policies purchased (or received in an exchange) after June 20, '86.[44]

¶ 1716   Single premium life insurance, endowment and annuity contracts.

No deduction is allowed for interest on debt incurred or continued to buy or carry single premium life insurance, endowment or annuity contracts. (Code Sec. 264(a)(2); Reg § 1.264-2) A contract is "single premium" if "substantially all" the premiums are paid within four years from the purchase date, or if an amount is deposited with the insurer for payment of a "substantial" number of future premiums on the contract. (Code Sec. 264(b); Reg § 1.264-3)[45]

¶ 1717   Planned "systematic borrowing" against life insurance contracts.

No deduction is allowed for interest on debt incurred or continued to buy or carry a life insurance, endowment or annuity contract under a "plan of purchase"—i.e., a plan that contemplates the systematic direct or indirect borrowing of part or all of the increases in the contract's cash value. (Code Sec. 264(a)(3)) The deduction is barred regardless of who lends the money (the insurer, a bank, etc.). (Code Sec. 264(a)(3)) And it may be barred even if taxpayer gives collateral for the loan.[46]

But even if the borrowing is under a "systematic plan," the interest is deductible (subject to the other bars and limits on interest deductions), if:

(1) the total interest paid or accrued that year with respect to a "systematic plan" is not over $100 (otherwise entire interest deduction is disallowed); or

(2) the borrowing was on an unforeseen loss of income or substantial increase in financial obligations; or

---

40. ¶ K-5344; ¶ 12,814.02.   42. ¶ K-5344; ¶ 12,814.03.   44. ¶ K-5350; ¶ 2644.   46. ¶ K-5580 *et seq.*; ¶ 2644.

41. ¶ K-5343; ¶ 12,814.02.   43. ¶ K-5345; ¶ 12,814.02.   45. ¶ K-5570 *et seq.*; ¶ 2644.

Footnote references beginning with letters are to paragraphs in RIA's Federal Tax Coordinator 2d and RIA's Analysis of Federal Taxes: Income. Footnote references beginning with numbers are to paragraphs in RIA's United States Tax Reporter.

(3) the borrowing was incurred in connection with taxpayer's business; or

(4) at least four of the first seven annual premiums are paid without *any* borrowing. (Code Sec. 264(c))[47]

¶ 1718 Loans from qualified employer plans.

No deduction is allowed for interest on any loan from a qualified employer plan that is not treated as a distribution, but is treated as a loan, for the period: (1) on or after the first day the individual to whom the loan is made is a key employee, or (2) during which the loan is secured by amounts attributable to elective deferrals under a Code Sec. 401(k) plan (¶ 4318) or a Code Sec. 403(b) annuity (¶ 4370 *et seq.*). (Code Sec. 72(p)(3))[48]

¶ 1719 Tax-exempt securities.

No deduction is allowed for interest on debt incurred or continued to buy or carry tax-exempt securities (e.g., state or local bonds, see ¶ 1335), (Code Sec. 265(a)(2)) or stock of a mutual fund (¶ 4201) distributing exempt interest. (Code Sec. 265(a)(4))[49]

¶ 1720 Registration-required obligations.

No deduction is allowed for interest on "registration-required obligations" that are not in registered form. (Code Sec. 163(f)(1))[50]

¶ 1721 Interest on corporate acquisition indebtedness.

The deduction allowed to a corporation for the interest it pays or accrues during a tax year on certain "corporate acquisition indebtedness" may not exceed $5,000,000. But all or part of the excess may not be subject to disallowance if specified tests (acquisition purpose, subordination, convertibility, and debt-equity) are met (Code Sec. 279).[1]

¶ 1722 Investment Interest Deduction Limitations ▰▰▰▰▰▰▰▰▰▰▰▰▰

Noncorporate taxpayers can deduct investment interest only to the extent of net investment income.

For where interest deduction is *barred*, see ¶ 1712 *et seq.*

¶ 1723 Investment interest deductions of noncorporate taxpayers.

The amount of investment interest (¶ 1724) that may be deducted in any tax year by a noncorporate taxpayer (i.e., individual, estate or trust) is generally limited to taxpayer's "net investment income" (¶ 1725) for the year. (Code Sec. 163(d)(1), (4)(A)) Use Form 4952 to compute the limitation.[2]

Interest that is disallowed because of this limit can be carried over and deducted in later years, subject to the later year's limits. (Code Sec. 163(d)(2))[3]

Special rules apply to partnerships[4] and S corporations.[5]

¶ 1724 "Investment interest."

Investment interest is interest paid or accrued on indebtedness properly allocable to property held for investment. (Code Sec. 163(d)(3)(A))[6] But the deduction limit doesn't apply to interest expense which must be capitalized (e.g., construction interest), or which is disallowed under Code Sec. 265 (¶ 1719).[7]

Property held for investment is: (1) any property which produces income (e.g., interest,

---

47. ¶ K-5580 *et seq.*; ¶ 2644.
48. ¶s K-5501, H-11065 *et seq.*;
    ¶ 724.23.
49. ¶s K-5520 *et seq.*, K-5547;
    ¶ 2654.

50. ¶ K-5550 *et seq.*;
    ¶ 1635.010(20)
1. ¶ K-5400 *et seq.*; ¶ 2794.

2. ¶ K-5310 *et seq.*; ¶ 1634.053.
3. ¶ K-5318; ¶ 1634.053.
4. ¶ K-5321; ¶ 7024.01.

5. ¶ K-5322.
6. ¶ K-5312; ¶ 1634.053.
7. ¶ K-5311.

Footnote references beginning with letters are to paragraphs in RIA's Federal Tax Coordinator 2d and RIA's Analysis of Federal Taxes: Income. Footnote references beginning with numbers are to paragraphs in RIA's United States Tax Reporter.

dividends, annuities or royalties) properly allocable to portfolio income under the passive loss rules (¶ 1808) (e.g., *not* property subject to a net lease), and (2) any interest in an activity involving a trade or business in which taxpayer does not materially participate, if that activity isn't "passive" under the passive loss rules (¶ 1813). (Code Sec. 163(d)(5)(A)) Investment interest also includes any amount allowable as a deduction in connection with personal property used in a short sale. (Code Sec. 163(d)(3)(C))[8]

But investment interest doesn't include any interest that is: (1) taken into account in determining taxpayer's income or loss from a passive activity, (2) qualified residence interest (¶ 1727), (Code Sec. 163(d)(3)(B)) or (3) properly allocable to a rental real estate activity in which, under the passive loss rules (¶ 1823), taxpayer actively participates.[9]

✔️ *observation:* Investment interest is not personal interest, and is thus not subject to the deduction bar described at ¶ 1712.

¶ 1725 Investment interest definitions.

Taxpayer's "net investment income" for a tax year is the excess of "investment income" over "investment expenses" for the year. (Code Sec. 163(d)(4)(A))[10] (For the definition of net investment interest for alternative minimum tax purposes, see ¶ 3208.)

"Investment income" is (1) gross income from property held for investment (as described at ¶ 1724), (2) any excess of *net gain* attributable to the disposition of investment property over *net capital gain* determined by only taking into account gains and losses from these dispositions, plus (3) so much of the *net capital gain* (or *net gain,* if less) described in (2), as he elects to include in investment income. (Code Sec. 163(d)(4)(B))[11] (For the effect of such an election on gain qualifying for the maximum 28% capital gains rate, see ¶ 2603.)

"Investment expenses" are deductible expenses *other than interest* which are directly connected with the production of investment income, (Code Sec. 163(d)(4)(C)) but limited to the amount allowed after applying the "2%-of-adjusted-gross-income-floor" (¶ 3107). Nonbusiness bad debts (¶ 1842) are taken into account only to the extent they are currently deductible.[12]

Investment income and expenses do not include any income or expenses taken into account in computing income or loss from a passive activity (¶ 1798 *et seq.*). (Code Sec. 163(d)(4)(D))[13]

¶ 1726 Qualified Residence Interest ■■■■■■■■■■■■■■■

Certain rules that otherwise bar or limit the deductibility of interest don't apply to "qualified residence interest"—i.e., up to $1,000,000 of debt incurred in connection with and secured by taxpayer's "qualified residence."

Qualified residence interest (¶ 1727) is exempt from the deduction bars or limit on:

■ personal interest (¶ 1712); (Code Sec. 163(h)(2)(D); Reg § 1.163-10T(b))

■ investment interest (¶ 1724); (Code Sec. 163(d)(3)(B)(i); Reg § 1.163-10T(b)) or

■ passive activity interest (¶ 1803). (Code Sec. 469(j)(7); Reg § 1.163-10T(b))[14]

Nor is it subject to the uniform capitalization rules (¶ 1661). (Reg § 1.163-10T(b))[15]

But qualified residence interest *is* subject to the "general" bars and limits for:

■ interest in connection with single premium insurance (¶ 1716);

■ interest relating to tax-exempt income (¶ 1719);

■ interest on related-party transactions (¶ 2839);

---

8. ¶ K-5312; ¶ 1634.053.
9. ¶ K-5312 *et seq.*; ¶ 1634.053.
10. ¶ K-5314; ¶ 1634.053.

11. ¶ K-5315.
12. ¶ K-5317; ¶ 1634.053.

13. ¶s K-5315, K-5317; ¶ 1634.053.

14. ¶ K-5472; ¶ 1634.052.
15. ¶ K-5472; ¶ 1634.052.

Footnote references beginning with letters are to paragraphs in RIA's Federal Tax Coordinator 2d and RIA's Analysis of Federal Taxes: Income. Footnote references beginning with numbers are to paragraphs in RIA's United States Tax Reporter.

- interest under the "at-risk" rules (¶ 1791 *et seq.*);
- accrued discount (¶ 1713); and
- certain straddle interest (¶ 2642 *et seq.*). (Reg § 1.163-10T(b))[16]

For the treatment of "qualified residence interest" for alternative minimum tax purposes, see ¶ 3208.

¶ 1727 What is "qualified residence interest"?

"Qualified residence interest" is any interest paid or accrued during the tax year on acquisition indebtedness (¶ 1728) or home equity indebtedness (¶ 1729) with respect to any property that, at the time the interest is accrued, is taxpayer's qualified residence (¶ 1730). (Code Sec. 163(h)(3)(A))[17]

A single debt may be part acquisition indebtedness and part home equity indebtedness.[18]

¶ 1728 Acquisition indebtedness.

Acquisition indebtedness is debt that is incurred in acquiring, constructing or substantially improving taxpayer's "qualified residence" (or adjoining land) (¶ 1730) *and* that is secured by the residence. Any new debt taxpayer incurs to refinance his acquisition indebtedness also qualifies, but only up to the balance of that "old" debt. (Code Sec. 163(h)(3)(B)(i))[19] Under regs to be issued, debt will be treated as incurred in acquiring, etc., a residence if the debt proceeds can be traced to payment of the costs of the acquisition, etc.[20]

Illustration: Taxpayer acquires a qualified residence for $250,000 giving a $200,000 mortgage. The $200,000 debt is acquisition indebtedness. Later, after he has paid the mortgage down to $49,000 and the house is worth $400,000, he refinances with a new $200,000 mortgage. Only $49,000 of this "new" debt is acquisition indebtedness (but an additional $100,000 may qualify as home equity indebtedness, see ¶ 1729).

Interest accruing on acquisition indebtedness (but not debt incurred to pay that interest) is also treated as acquisition indebtedness until it is paid. (Reg § 1.163-11T(a), (c))[21]

The aggregate amount treated as acquisition indebtedness (i.e., deductible as "qualified residence interest," see ¶ 1726) for any period may not exceed $1,000,000 ($500,000 for a married individual filing a separate return). (Code Sec. 163(h)(3)(B)(ii)) However, these dollar amounts are reduced (not below zero) by the aggregate amount of outstanding "pre-Oct. 13, '87 indebtedness." Regs prescribe how to allocate the interest where the debt exceeds these limits. (Reg § 1.163-10T(e))[22]

"Pre-Oct. 13, '87 indebtedness" (which is treated as acquisition indebtedness without regard to the above dollar limits) is indebtedness incurred: (1) on or before Oct. 13, '87, that, at all times from that date until the interest is paid or accrued, was secured by a qualified residence; or (2) *after* Oct. 13, '87, to refinance indebtedness described in (1) and secured by the qualified residence, but only to the extent of the balance of the refinanced indebtedness (and subject to special limits on the refinancing period). (Code Sec. 163(h)(3)(D))[23]

¶ 1729 Home equity indebtedness.

Home equity indebtedness is any debt (other than acquisition indebtedness, see ¶ 1728) that is secured by taxpayer's qualified residence (¶ 1730), to the extent the aggregate amount of the indebtedness doesn't exceed the fair market value of the residence (as

16. ¶ K-5472 *et seq.*; ¶ 1634.052.   19. ¶ K-5483; ¶ 1634.052.   22. ¶s K-5484, K-5488;   23. ¶ K-5488; ¶ 1634.052.
17. ¶ K-5471; ¶ 1634.052.   20. ¶ K-5486.   ¶ 1634.052.
18. ¶s K-5483, K-5489;   21. ¶ K-5492; ¶ 1634.052.
¶ 1634.052.

Footnote references beginning with letters are to paragraphs in RIA's Federal Tax Coordinator 2d and RIA's Analysis of Federal Taxes: Income. Footnote references beginning with numbers are to paragraphs in RIA's United States Tax Reporter.

reduced by the amount of acquisition indebtedness on it). The aggregate amount treated as home equity indebtedness (i.e., deductible as "qualified residence interest," see ¶ 1726) for any period may not exceed $100,000 ($50,000 for a married individual filing a separate return). (Code Sec. 163(h)(3)(C))[24]

⊘observation: In other words, home equity indebtedness is limited to the taxpayer's net equity in the residence, with a $100,000 ($50,000) ceiling.

Interest accruing on home equity indebtedness is treated as home equity indebtedness until it is paid. (Reg § 1.163-11T(a))[25]

¶ 1730 Qualified residence.

A qualified residence is: (1) taxpayer's principal residence (i.e., one that would qualify for nonrecognition of gain on a rollover sale, see ¶ 2437 *et seq.*), (Code Sec. 163(h)(4)(A)(i)(I)) and/or (2) any other residence ("second residence") taxpayer properly elects to treat as "qualified" for the tax year. A second residence rented out to others during the year can't "qualify" unless taxpayer also uses it as a residence during that year, for more than the greater of 14 days or 10% of the number of days that it is rented out for a fair rental. (Code Sec. 163(h)(4)(A)(i)(II)) But a second residence that isn't rented out at any time during the year may "qualify" even if taxpayer hasn't used it as a dwelling unit in that year. (Code Sec. 163(h)(4)(A)(iii)) A taxpayer who has more than one residence that meets these tests may choose each year which to treat as the second (qualified) residence. (Code Sec. 163(h)(4)(A)(i))[26]

A residence for this purpose includes a condominium or cooperative housing corporation (co-op). Any indebtedness secured by stock in a co-op is treated as secured by the house or apartment taxpayer is entitled to occupy. Even if local restrictions prohibit using the stock as security for the debt, the stock will be treated as securing the debt if taxpayer can show that it was incurred to acquire the stock. (Code Sec. 163(h)(4)(B))[27] A time-share can also qualify if it satisfies the above tests for rental property. (Reg § 1.163-10T(p)(6))[28]

A residence under construction may be treated as a qualified residence for a period of up to 24 months, but only if it qualifies (without regard to this provision) as of the time it is ready for occupancy. (Reg § 1.163-10T(p)(5))[29]

For married taxpayers filing jointly, the second residence may be owned and/or used by either spouse. If the spouses file separately, each spouse may have only one principal residence (unless the other spouse gives written consent otherwise). (Code Sec. 163(h)(4)(A))[30]

¶ 1731 Allocation Rules for Interest and Debt ▬▬▬▬▬▬▬▬▬▬▬

The proceeds of a debt may be used in ways which trigger more than one of the limitations on the deductibility of interest on the debt. In order to determine which limit to apply, the interest and underlying debt must be properly allocated, generally by tracing the use of the borrowed money.

The limitations on the deduction of personal interest (¶ 1712), investment interest (¶ 1723) and passive activity interest (¶ 1803) are all triggered by how the proceeds of the underlying debt are used. Thus, where the proceeds of a single debt are used for multiple purposes—e.g., to make investments *and* to buy "personal" items—more than one of these limitations may apply to interest on that debt, so that the debt must be allocated among the various expenditures (¶ 1732). (Code Sec. 469(l)(4); Reg § 1.163-8T)[31]

The interest expense allocation rules do not control the allocation of interest for any

---

24. ¶ K-5489; ¶ 1634.052.	26. ¶ K-5473 *et seq.*; ¶ 1634.052.	28. ¶ K-5481.	30. ¶ K-5480; ¶ 1634.052.
25. ¶ K-5489.	27. ¶ K-5480; ¶ 1634.052.	29. ¶ K-5482.	31. ¶ K-5232; ¶ 1634.055.

Footnote references beginning with letters are to paragraphs in RIA's Federal Tax Coordinator 2d and RIA's Analysis of Federal Taxes: Income. Footnote references beginning with numbers are to paragraphs in RIA's United States Tax Reporter.

purpose other than those listed above.[32]

¶ 1732 How interest is allocated.

Interest expense is allocated in the same manner as the debt with respect to which the interest accrues. Debt is allocated by tracing disbursements of the debt proceeds to specific expenditures. (Reg § 1.163-8T(a)(3), (c)(1)) Except for qualified residence interest (¶ 1727), debt proceeds and related interest expense are allocated solely by reference to how the proceeds are used, without regard to the nature of any property securing the debt. (Reg § 1.163-8T(c)(1))[33]

The interest, as allocated, is then subject to the appropriate limitation on deductibility, as follows:

■ Interest allocated to a passive activity expenditure (current or former) is subject to the passive activity interest limitations. (Reg § 1.163-8T(a)(4)(i)(B))

■ Interest allocated to an investment expenditure is subject to the investment interest limitations. (Reg § 1.163-8T(a)(4)(i)(C))

■ Interest allocated to a personal expenditure is subject to the personal interest limitations. (Reg § 1.163-8T(a)(4)(i)(D))

■ Interest allocated to a trade or business expenditure is treated as trade or business interest (i.e., it's not subject to the personal interest limits). (Reg § 1.163-8T(a)(4)(i)(A))[34]

¶ 1733 Taxpayers who must allocate interest.

The interest expense allocation rules apply to all taxpayers *other than* widely-held C corporations. Thus, these rules apply to a pass-through entity (e.g., partnership or S corporation) that borrows money to make distributions to its owners (partners or shareholders), or whose debt is allocated to those distributions. Repayments of a pass-through entity's debt that is allocated partly to a distribution to its owners and partly to other expenditures are treated first as a repayment of the portion of the debt allocated to the distribution. IRS will issue regs on how to allocate the interest expense on debt a pass-through entity incurs from its owners, as well as any entity debt that the owners repay.[35]

¶ 1734 Time for allocation.

Debt is allocated to an expenditure for the period: (1) beginning on the date the proceeds of the debt are used or treated as used to make the expenditure, and (2) ending on the date the debt is repaid or reallocated under the rules described at ¶ 1736, whichever is earlier. (Reg § 1.163-8T(c)(2)(i))[36]

Generally, interest expense that accrues on a debt is allocated in the same manner as the debt is allocated from time to time, regardless of when the interest is actually paid. (Reg § 1.163-8T(c)(2)(ii)(A))[37]

¶ 1735 Qualified residence interest not subject to allocation rules.

Qualified residence interest (¶ 1726 *et seq.*) is allowable as a deduction without regard to the manner in which that interest expense (or the underlying debt) is allocated. (Reg § 1.163-8T(m)(3))[38]

illustration: E takes out a loan for $20,000. The loan is secured by a residence. E uses the loan proceeds to buy a car strictly for personal use. The debt and the interest are allocable to personal expenditures, so that the interest would normally be subject to the personal interest limitations (¶ 1712). If, however, the interest is qualified residence interest, it is not personal interest and would be fully deductible.

---

32. ¶ K-5234.
33. ¶ K-5231; ¶ 1634.055(a).
34. ¶ K-5232.
35. ¶ K-5259 *et seq.*; ¶ 1634.056.
36. ¶ K-5233; ¶ 1634.055(a).
37. ¶ K-5233; ¶ 1634.055(a).
38. ¶ K-5238; ¶ 1634.055.

Footnote references beginning with letters are to paragraphs in RIA's Federal Tax Coordinator 2d and RIA's Analysis of Federal Taxes: Income. Footnote references beginning with numbers are to paragraphs in RIA's United States Tax Reporter.

¶ 1736 Reallocation.

Where the use of debt proceeds, or of assets bought with debt proceeds, changes, the interest on the debt must be reallocated to the new use. The interest, as so reallocated, will be subject to any appropriate limitations. (Reg § 1.163-8T(j)(1))[39]

¶ 1737 When Interest May Be Deducted

The proper time for deducting interest is generally determined by the taxpayer's method of accounting. Special rules govern when mortgage "points," unstated interest and original issue discount must be deducted.

¶ 1738 Cash method taxpayers.

Cash method taxpayers deduct interest generally only if it is actually *paid* during the tax year. (Code Sec. 163(a)) The interest can be paid with funds borrowed from another creditor. But paying with funds borrowed from the same creditor, or giving a note for the interest or adding the unpaid interest to principal, isn't payment.[40]

Interest that is prepaid, including "points" (¶ 1703) paid or "discount" (i.e., some of the principal is withheld) is deductible in the tax year to which, and to the extent that, the interest is allocable—i.e., as it "accrues." Cash method taxpayers thus deduct points and discount ratably over the term of the loan. (Code Sec. 461(g))[41] For deduction of "points" on a home mortgage, see ¶ 1739.

A taxpayer who "pays" the points by receiving discounted loan proceeds gets no current deduction. Instead, this creates original issue discount (OID) income (¶ 1318 *et seq.*) for taxpayer, and an OID deduction for the *lender* (¶ 1742). But in certain cases, for administrative convenience, IRS will allow a taxpayer to allocate these points ratably over the period of the debt.[42]

¶ 1739 "Points" on a home mortgage.

"Points" paid by a cash method taxpayer on indebtedness incurred in connection with the purchase or improvement of (and secured by) his principal residence are deductible in the tax year of actual payment, i.e., in advance. The charging of points must reflect an established business practice in the geographical area where the loan is made, and the deduction allowed may not exceed the number of points generally charged in that area. (Code Sec. 461(g)(2)) In addition, the amounts must also be clearly designated as points incurred in connection with the indebtedness (e.g., as "loan origination fees"), be computed as a percentage of the stated principal amount of the indebtedness, *and* be paid directly by taxpayer (withholding from loan proceeds isn't "payment") to the lender (or mortgage broker). This is satisfied where taxpayer provides, from funds that haven't been borrowed for this purpose as part of the overall transaction, an amount that is at least equal to the amount required to be applied as points at the closing. If the loan was used to improve taxpayer's principal residence, the points must be paid with funds other than those borrowed from the lender.[43]

Points paid to *refinance* an existing mortgage generally are deductible only ratably over the loan term. However, where the refinancing is incurred for home improvements, points paid from separate funds may be deducted currently.[44]

---

39. ¶ K-5254 *et seq.*;   41. ¶ K-5207; ¶s 1634.005,   43. ¶ K-5208 *et seq.*; ¶s 1634.005,   44. ¶ K-5209.3; ¶s 1634.005,
   ¶ 1634.055(b).   1634.032, 4614.75.   4614.75.   4614.75.
40. ¶ K-5200 *et seq.*; ¶s 1634.030,   42. ¶ K-5206; ¶ 1634.032.
   1634.031.

Footnote references beginning with letters are to paragraphs in RIA's Federal Tax Coordinator 2d and RIA's Analysis of Federal Taxes: Income. Footnote references beginning with numbers are to paragraphs in RIA's United States Tax Reporter.

¶ 1740 Accrual method taxpayers.

Accrual method taxpayers deduct interest when:

- all the events have occurred which fix the fact of the liability;
- the amount of the liability can be determined with reasonable accuracy; and
- economic performance has occurred.[45]

The interest is deductible only in the year it accrues, without regard to when the (accrual basis) taxpayer pays it. For these purposes, interest accrues ratably over the life of a loan. However, interest that is contingent on events other than the creditor's demand for payment does not accrue until the contingency happens.[46]

Contested interest (where the debtor claims he doesn't owe it) is not accruable or deductible. But if the accrual basis taxpayer *pays* the contested interest, it is deductible in the year of payment. (Code Sec. 461(f))[47]

¶ 1741 Unstated interest.

On certain deferred payment or installment sales, part of each payment is treated as interest ("unstated interest") that is deductible by the buyer as interest expense. The amount of this "unstated interest" attributed to the buyer is determined under the rules governing how much unstated interest the seller must include in gross income (¶ 1311 *et seq.*). (Code Sec. 483(a))[48]

The unstated interest allocated to a payment is deducted by cash method buyers in the year the payment is made, and by accrual method buyers in the year the payment is due. (Reg § 1.483-2(a)(1)(ii))[49]

The unstated interest rules *do not apply* to:

- buyers of personal use property; (Code Sec. 1275(b)(1))
- buyers of personal property on installment where payments include separately stated carrying charges, and part of the payments is otherwise treated as interest. (Code Sec. 483(d)(3))[50]

¶ 1742 Original issue discount (OID).

The issuer of a debt instrument issued with OID (discussed at ¶ 1318 *et seq.*) is allowed (with some exceptions) to deduct part of the OID (¶ 1743) in each tax year the underlying debt instrument is outstanding, even though the OID is not paid until maturity. (Code Sec. 163(e)(1); Reg § 1.163-3(a)(1), Reg § 1.163-4(a)(1)) This current deduction rule applies regardless of the method of accounting used by the issuer.[1] However, a cash basis obligor of a short-term obligation can only deduct OID (and other interest) when it is paid. (Code Sec. 163(e)(2)(C))[2]

OID for this purpose has the same meaning as for purposes of requiring the holder to include OID in gross income currently *except*:

- The de minimis exception does not apply. (Code Sec. 163(e)(2)(B))[3]
- A nonpublicly traded debt instrument issued by a buyer to the seller in exchange for personal use property is not treated as issued with OID that the seller can deduct currently. (Code Sec. 1275(b)(1))[4]

For certain high yield OID obligations (at least five percentage points over applicable federal rate for month of issue) issued after July 10, '89, a C corporation can't deduct (or otherwise take into account) any part of the OID until actually paid. In some cases, the

---

45. ¶ K-5210 *et seq.*; ¶ 1634.035 *et seq.*
46. ¶s K-5210, K-5211; ¶ 1634.035(10).
47. ¶s G-2568, G-2570; ¶ 4614.56 *et seq.*
48. ¶ K-5280 *et seq.*; ¶ 4834.
49. ¶ K-5283; ¶ 4834.01.
50. ¶s K-5281, K-5282; ¶ 4834.01.
1. ¶ K-5700 *et seq.*; ¶ 1634.051.
2. ¶ K-5710; ¶ 1634.051.
3. ¶ K-5722.
4. ¶ K-5719.

Footnote references beginning with letters are to paragraphs in RIA's Federal Tax Coordinator 2d and RIA's Analysis of Federal Taxes: Income. Footnote references beginning with numbers are to paragraphs in RIA's United States Tax Reporter.

deduction may be barred for all or part of the OID, depending on the obligation's yield, maturity date and amount of OID. (Code Sec. 163(e)(5))[5]

¶ 1743 Amount of OID deductible currently.

The amount of OID that the issuer of a debt instrument deducts currently is determined in the same manner as the amount of OID the holder must include in gross income currently (¶ 1325), but without the reduction for any acquisition premium paid by the holder. (Code Sec. 163(e)(2)(B))[6]

¶ 1744 Deduction for Taxes

The Code allows deductions for some state, local, U.S. possessions and foreign taxes, whether or not they are connected with a trade or business, and some federal taxes (but not income tax).

observation: The deduction for taxes allocable to a passive interest is subject to the passive loss rules (¶ 1798 *et seq.*).

Only payments that are really taxes (regardless of what they are called) are deductible as taxes. Taxes are charges imposed on persons or property by governmental authority to raise funds for the support of government or for public purposes. The mere fact that a levy is called a "tax" isn't conclusive.[7]

Fees imposed primarily as charges for government services, e.g., fees for a driver's license or car inspection, or passport fees, aren't deductible as taxes.[8]

Penalties paid to a government for violation of a law are not taxes. (Code Sec. 162(f))[9]

¶ 1745 Which taxes are deductible?

Deductible *state, local and foreign taxes* are:

■ state, local and foreign income, war profits and excess profits taxes;

■ state, local and foreign real property taxes;

■ state and local personal property taxes;

■ other state, local and foreign taxes (e.g., occupational taxes) paid or accrued in business or for the production of income unless incurred in connection with an acquisition or disposition of property. (Code Sec. 164(a)(1), (3))

State or local sales or use taxes paid or incurred in connection with the acquisition or disposition of property are not deductible (buyer treats them as part of the cost, seller treats them as a reduction in the amount realized). Other sales taxes are deductible only if paid or incurred in carrying on a trade or business or for the production of income. (Code Sec. 164(a))[10]

For state unemployment and disability taxes, see ¶ 1746.

These *federal taxes* are deductible as taxes:

■ environmental tax (¶ 3358); (Code Sec. 164(a)(4))

■ federal (and state) generation-skipping tax imposed on income distributions (¶ 5057 *et seq.*); (Code Sec. 164(a)(5), (b)(4))[11]

■ estate tax attributable to income in respect of a decedent (¶ 3971);

■ self-employment taxes (¶ 3137 *et seq.*) are one-half deductible. (Code Sec. 164(f))[12]

Taxes not included in these lists (such as gasoline, diesel and other motor fuel taxes, transfer taxes on securities and real estate, and motor vehicle registration fees) are not

5. ¶ K-5747 *et seq.*; ¶ 1634.051.   7. ¶ K-4003; ¶ 1644.   9. ¶ K-4009; ¶ 1644.002.   11. ¶ K-4000 *et seq.*; ¶ 1644.
6. ¶ K-5741 *et seq.*; ¶ 1634.051   8. ¶ K-4003 *et seq.*; ¶ 1644.001.   10. ¶ L-2351; ¶ 1644.   12. ¶ K-4401; ¶ 1644.

Footnote references beginning with letters are to paragraphs in RIA's Federal Tax Coordinator 2d and RIA's Analysis of Federal Taxes: Income. Footnote references beginning with numbers are to paragraphs in RIA's United States Tax Reporter.

deductible as *taxes* (although some motor vehicle fees may qualify as personal property taxes), but may be deductible as *business expenses* or *expenses for the production of income* (¶ 1505 *et seq.*). (Reg § 1.164-2(f))[13]

These taxes are not deductible as taxes, expenses or otherwise:

(1) Federal income taxes, including amounts withheld from wages, interest, etc.

(2) Alternative minimum tax.

(3) Social security (FICA) tax on employees, and Railroad Retirement tax on employees and employee representatives. (Code Sec. 275(a)(1); Reg § 1.164-2(a))

(4) Federal war profits and excess profits taxes. (Code Sec. 275(a)(2))

(5) Estate, inheritance, legacy, succession and gift taxes, (Code Sec. 275(a)(3); Reg § 1.164-2(c)) except as noted above, whether state, federal or foreign.

(6) Income, war profits and excess profits taxes of any foreign country or U.S. possession if taxpayer takes the foreign tax credit for them (¶ 2357 *et seq.*) or if the taxes are paid or accrued with respect to foreign trade income of an FSC (¶ 4629 *et seq.*). (Code Sec. 275(a)(4); Reg § 1.164-2(d)) However, a deduction is allowed for any tax that isn't allowable as a foreign tax credit because of Code Sec. 901(j) (which denies the credit for taxes paid to foreign countries with which the U.S. has severed diplomatic relations, etc.). (Code Sec. 901(j)(3))

(7) Excise taxes imposed on: charities' excess expenditures to influence legislation; private foundations; qualified pension, etc., plans; qualified investment entities (REITs and RICs); excess golden parachute payments and greenmail. (Code Sec. 275(a)(6))[14]

For the deductibility of taxes for alternative minimum tax purposes, see ¶ 3208.

¶ 1746 State unemployment and disability taxes.

Employers' contributions to state unemployment insurance funds are deductible as taxes if the state so classifies them. Whether an employee's contributions to a state unemployment insurance fund or disability plan are deductible as taxes similarly is determined on a state-by-state basis.[15]

¶ 1747 Local benefit assessments.

Assessments that tend to increase the value of the assessed property (whether or not the value does increase) aren't deductible as taxes (but may be capitalized). However, deduction *is* allowed, to the extent taxpayer shows that the assessment is properly allocable to maintenance or interest charges. (Code Sec. 164(c)(1); Reg § 1.164-4(b)(1))[16]

¶ 1748 Limitations on deduction for taxes if individual doesn't itemize.

In general, an individual may deduct taxes only if he itemizes his deductions. (Code Sec. 63, Code Sec. 161) For an individual who doesn't itemize, the deduction for taxes is limited to the following taxes that are deductible from gross income in arriving at adjusted gross income (AGI): taxes attributable to a trade or business (including taxes on real property), taxes attributable to property held for the production of rents or royalties, and one-half of any self-employment taxes imposed on him. (Code Sec. 62; Code Sec. 164(f))[17]

observation: There is a reduction in the amount that may be deducted for itemized deductions if taxpayer's AGI exceeds specified amounts (¶ 3112).

---

13. ¶s K-4000, L-2350 *et seq.*; ¶ 1644
14. ¶ L-2358; ¶ 1644.
15. ¶s K-4003 *et seq.*, L-2353 *et seq.*; ¶ 1644.024.
16. ¶ K-4600 *et seq.*; ¶ 1644.015.
17. ¶ L-2351.

Footnote references beginning with letters are to paragraphs in RIA's Federal Tax Coordinator 2d and RIA's Analysis of Federal Taxes: Income. Footnote references beginning with numbers are to paragraphs in RIA's United States Tax Reporter.

¶ 1749 Who deducts the tax?

Taxes generally are deductible only by the person on whom they are imposed. (Reg § 1.164-1(a))[18]

One who voluntarily pays a tax imposed on another isn't entitled to a deduction. Thus, a shareholder can't deduct his payment of the corporation's taxes, or vice versa.[19]

Property taxes are ordinarily imposed on, and therefore are deductible by, the property owner. (For who deducts for the year of sale, see ¶ 1758.) A person who owns a beneficial interest in property may deduct property taxes he pays in order to protect that interest.[20]

Taxes imposed on property that is leased are deductible by the landlord, even if it is the tenant who makes the tax payment. A tenant who pays the taxes on the leased premises treats the payment as additional rent. (Reg § 1.162-11(a)) But a tenant may deduct, *as taxes,* taxes paid on improvements he makes where the useful life of the improvements will terminate before the end of the lease.[21]

¶ 1750 Married couple's state income taxes.

Spouses filing joint federal returns may deduct on that return all deductible taxes paid by either spouse, whether or not they file joint *state* returns.[22]

If the spouses file separate federal and separate state returns, then each spouse may deduct only the state income taxes imposed on and actually paid by that spouse. If a joint state return was filed, then for federal tax purposes, that joint state tax is prorated according to each spouse's gross income, but not to exceed the amount actually paid by the spouse.[23]

¶ 1751 Taxes on co-owned property.

An individual's deduction for taxes on property he owns with other persons as tenants-in-common may be limited to his pro rata part of the taxes, i.e., the amount attributable to his interest, even if he pays *all* of the taxes on the property. The tenant's deduction thus is limited to his pro rata share where he is only assessed for his share, where he has a right to contribution from the other tenants, or where his share won't be subject to sale on their default.[24]

Tenants by the entirety (i.e., spouses) and joint tenants with right of survivorship are entitled to deduct in full the taxes they pay on the jointly-owned property.[25]

¶ 1752 Cooperative and condominium housing realty taxes.

Tenant-stockholders of cooperative housing corporations (co-ops) deduct their share of the co-op's real estate taxes. (Code Sec. 216)[26] Condominium owners deduct the real estate taxes on their individual interests.[27]

¶ 1753 When cash basis taxpayers deduct taxes.

A cash basis taxpayer's taxes are deductible on his return for the tax year he pays them. Payroll taxes are deductible by the taxpayer when they are withheld from his wages.[28]

The tax is deductible in the year of payment even if taxpayer contests the liability and seeks to recover the payment.[29] For special rule for contested tax, see ¶ 1756.

For prepaid taxes, see ¶ 1754.

18. ¶ K-4101 *et seq.*; ¶ 1644.011.
19. ¶ K-4102; ¶ 1644.011.
20. ¶ K-4103; ¶ 1644.01.
21. ¶ K-4104; ¶ 1624.285.

22. ¶ K-4105; ¶ 1644.01.
23. ¶ K-4105; ¶ 1644.020.
24. ¶ K-4109; ¶ 1645.011(6).

25. ¶ K-4109; ¶ 1645.011(6).
26. ¶ K-5900 *et seq.*; ¶ 2164.01.
27. ¶ K-4103; ¶ 1645.011(45).

28. ¶ K-4201 *et seq.*; ¶ 1644.006.
29. ¶ K-4201; ¶s 1644.007, 4614.56.

Footnote references beginning with letters are to paragraphs in RIA's Federal Tax Coordinator 2d and RIA's Analysis of Federal Taxes: Income. Footnote references beginning with numbers are to paragraphs in RIA's United States Tax Reporter.

¶ 1754 Prepaid taxes.

A cash basis taxpayer may deduct an advance payment of tax in the year of payment as long as it's an actual good faith payment and not a mere deposit. But the advance payment of state taxes that are later refunded won't be deductible unless the taxpayer had a reasonable basis, at the time of payment, for believing he owed the taxes.[30]

Deduction in the year of payment also is allowed for advance estimated tax payments made under a pay-as-you-go tax collection system.[31]

¶ 1755 When accrual basis taxpayers deduct taxes.

An accrual basis taxpayer deducts a tax liability in his tax year in which all events have occurred which determine the fact that he is liable for the tax, and which fix the amount of that liability. It doesn't matter that the payment isn't due until a later year.[32] For ratable accrual of real estate taxes, see ¶ 1757. For construction period taxes, see ¶ 1657.

An accrual basis taxpayer who pays an additional tax without protest or appeal deducts that additional tax in the year in which the tax was originally due, and not when it is later assessed or paid.[33] For contested tax, see ¶ 1756.

¶ 1756 Contested tax.

An accrual basis taxpayer who contests an assessment may not deduct the contested portion of the tax until the contest is ended and the amount determined. A contest exists where there is an overt act of protest or suit.[34]

A taxpayer (cash or accrual) who, by transferring sufficient cash or property, pays the contested liability without giving up the contest may deduct the tax in the year of payment, if otherwise deductible in that (or an earlier) year. But the contest must have existed at the time of transfer. (Code Sec. 461(f))[35] This doesn't apply to foreign or U.S. possession income, war profits and excess profits tax, (Code Sec. 461(f)) i.e., these taxes may not be deducted until the contest is finally determined.[36]

¶ 1757 Election by accrual method taxpayers to accrue realty taxes ratably.

An accrual basis taxpayer may elect to accrue real property taxes which relate to a definite period of time ratably over that period. (Code Sec. 461(c)(1); Reg § 1.461-1(c)(1))[37]

IRS consent is not required for an election made for the first tax year in which taxpayer incurs real estate taxes. The election must be made by the return due date (with extensions) for that first tax year. In all other cases, the election may be made at any time, but only if IRS consents.(Code Sec. 461(c)(2); Reg § 1.461-3(c)) To get IRS's consent, apply in writing (on Form 3115) to IRS within 90 days (or within 180 days, if taxpayer applies for an automatic extension) after the beginning of the first tax year to which the election applies.[38]

The election is binding unless IRS consents to revocation. (Reg § 1.461-1(c)(4))[39]

¶ 1758 Apportionment of real property taxes between seller and buyer.

For both cash and accrual taxpayers, the real property tax on property that is sold during the tax year is considered to be imposed:

■ *on the seller* to the extent properly allocable to that part of the "real property tax year" (period to which the tax relates) ending on the day before the date of sale; and

---

30. ¶ K-4203; ¶s 1644.02, 1645.021(5).
31. ¶ K-4204; ¶s 1644.02, 1645.006(30).
32. ¶ K-4300 *et seq.*; ¶ 1644.007.
33. ¶ K-4312.
34. ¶ K-4311 *et seq.*; ¶s 1644.007, 1644.008.
35. ¶s G-2385, G-2570; ¶s 1644.007, 4614.56.
36. ¶ K-4314.
37. ¶ K-4319 *et seq.*; ¶s 1644.012, 4614.45.
38. ¶s K-4321, K-4322.
39. ¶ K-4326; ¶ 4614.45.

Footnote references beginning with letters are to paragraphs in RIA's Federal Tax Coordinator 2d and RIA's Analysis of Federal Taxes: Income. Footnote references beginning with numbers are to paragraphs in RIA's United States Tax Reporter.

■ *on the buyer* to the extent properly allocable to that part of the real property tax year beginning on the date of sale. (Code Sec. 164(d)(1))[40]

For when the seller or buyer deducts the sale year realty tax, see ¶ 1759.

¶ 1759   When seller or buyer deducts real property tax.

An *accrual basis* seller or buyer deducts his share of the sale year realty tax (as apportioned, see ¶ 1758) in his income tax year in which the accrual date falls. If an election to accrue realty taxes ratably (¶ 1757) is in effect for that year, his share of the tax is deductible in the year it accrues under the election. (Code Sec. 164(a), (d)(2)(B); Reg § 1.164-6(d)(6))[41]

A *cash basis* seller or buyer deducts his portion of the sale year realty tax in the income tax year he pays it. But where the tax isn't payable until after the sale date, or where the buyer is liable for the tax under local law, the *seller* may, at his option, deduct the tax either in the year of sale (whether or not he actually paid it) or in the year of payment, if later. Thus, the seller can deduct a tax paid by the buyer. (Reg § 1.164-6(d)(1)(ii))[42]

¶ 1760   Excessive deduction of real property tax before sale.

If the seller (cash or accrual) deducted more than his share of realty taxes on property he sold in a later year, and that "excess" tax payment is allocable to and deductible by the buyer, as described at ¶ 1758, the seller is treated as receiving a recovery in the sale year. The seller must include this "recovery" in gross income for the sale year, to the extent he got a tax benefit (i.e., his "excess" deduction) in that earlier year. (Reg § 1.164-6(d)(6))[43]

¶ 1761   Personal property taxes.

Personal property taxes imposed by a state or local government are deductible. (Code Sec. 164(a)(2)) A deductible personal property tax is a tax that is imposed annually on personal property, on an ad valorem basis (i.e., based on the value of the personal property). (Code Sec. 164(b)(1))[44]

¶ 1762   Deduction for Losses

Taxpayers may sustain a loss when their property is transferred, stolen, destroyed, confiscated, abandoned, taken by foreclosure or becomes worthless, and they receive less than adequate compensation for it. This loss may be deductible.

Subject to the limits discussed in the following paragraphs and the passive loss rules (¶ 1798 *et seq.*), taxpayers may deduct losses they sustain that are not compensated for by insurance or otherwise. (Code Sec. 165(a))[45]

For losses from a sale or exchange, see ¶ 2400 *et seq.*

¶ 1763   What is a deductible loss?

A deductible loss arises when a taxpayer loses or gives up money, property or rights, or when these items lose value as a result of an identifiable event. It must be shown that taxpayer sustained a loss of a type that is deductible, that the loss was sustained in the tax year, and the amount of the loss.[46]

To be deductible, a loss must be evidenced by a closed and completed transaction fixed by identifiable events, (Reg § 1.165-1(b)) such as a sale, exchange, foreclosure, stock redemption, casualty, theft, abandonment, governmental condemnation or seizure. Mere fluctuations in an asset's value don't result in deductible losses.[47]

---

40. ¶ K-4114; ¶ 1644.016.
41. ¶s K-4125, K-4126; ¶ 1644.01.
42. ¶ K-4121 *et seq.*; ¶ 1644.016.
43. ¶ K-4127; ¶ 1644.016(d).
44. ¶ K-4502; ¶ 1644.010.
45. ¶ M-1000; ¶ 1654.
46. ¶ M-1000 *et seq.*; ¶ 1654.020 *et seq.*
47. ¶ M-1101; ¶ M-1305 *et seq.*; ¶ 1654.020 *et seq.*

Footnote references beginning with letters are to paragraphs in RIA's Federal Tax Coordinator 2d and P.IA's Analysis of Federal Taxes: Income. Footnote references beginning with numbers are to paragraphs in RIA's United States Tax Reporter.

¶ 1764 Limits on losses of individuals.

Individuals may deduct losses only if they're from a trade or business, (Code Sec. 165(c)(1))[48] a transaction entered into for profit, (Code Sec. 165(c)(2))[49] or a casualty (¶ 1780) or theft (¶ 1788). (Code Sec. 165(c)(3))[50]

An individual's losses on transactions entered into for personal purposes are deductible only if they qualify as casualty or theft losses. (Code Sec. 165(c)(3))[1] Thus, no loss deduction is allowed for a loss on taxpayer's residence or car (if used only for personal purposes) unless the loss is from casualty or theft. These rules also apply to losses of estates and trusts.[2]

Property that taxpayer holds partly for personal use and partly for business or income-producing use is treated as two properties: one personal, one business (or income-producing). Loss on the personal part (except by casualty or theft) is nondeductible.[3]

¶ 1765 What is a trade or business?

A trade or business ("business") is a pursuit or occupation carried on for profit (¶ 1766), whether or not profit actually results. An isolated transaction isn't a business. Taxpayer may engage in one business, in more than one business, or in no business.[4] Merely investing in corporations, however actively, isn't a business.[5]

¶ 1766 Transactions for profit.

A transaction is entered into for profit if taxpayer intends to receive income from it overall. For a transaction involving property, taxpayer must intend to receive income from it or to profit from disposing of it.[6]

Profit must be the primary motive, and not merely incidental. Where a profit motive predominates, a secondary nonprofit motive won't preclude a loss deduction.[7]

An activity is presumed to be engaged in for profit for a tax year if it shows a profit for any three or more out of five consecutive years ending in that tax year (or two out of seven years, for breeding, showing or racing of horses). (Code Sec. 183(d))[8] A taxpayer who has not engaged in an activity for more than five years (seven, for horse breeding, etc.) can elect (on Form 5213) to postpone the determination as to whether these presumptions apply until the close of the fourth tax year (sixth, for horse breeding, etc.) after the tax year taxpayer first engages in the activity. (Code Sec. 183(e); Reg § 12.9)[9]

Whether the activities of an S corporation are "engaged in for profit" is determined at the entity level, (Reg § 1.183-1(f)) as it is for partnerships.[10]

¶ 1767 Hobby (not-for-profit) losses.

For individuals, partnerships, estates, trusts and S corporations, deductions attributable to an activity "not engaged in for profit" (Code Sec. 183(a))[11] are allowed only as follows:

(1) The full amount of deductions for interest, state and local property taxes, and any other deductions allowable for the tax year without regard to whether the activity is engaged in for profit. (Code Sec. 183(b)(1); Reg § 1.183-1(b)(1)(i))

(2) Amounts allowable as deductions only if the activity were engaged in for profit, but only if the allowance *doesn't* result in a basis adjustment, *and only* to the extent the gross

---

48. ¶ M-1501; ¶s 1654, 1654.060 *et seq.*
49. ¶ M-1510; ¶s 1654, 1654.060 *et seq.*
50. ¶s M-1600, M-2100; ¶s 1654.300 *et seq.*, 1654.350 *et seq.*

1. ¶ M-1500; ¶ 1654.
2. ¶s C-2215, C-7214.
3. ¶ M-1420; ¶s 1654.061, 1654.430.
4. ¶ L-1100 *et seq.*; ¶ 1654.060 *et seq.*

5. ¶ M-2904.
6. ¶ M-1510; ¶ 1654.060 *et seq.*
7. ¶ M-1512.
8. ¶ M-5818; ¶ 1834.02.

9. ¶s M-5821, M-5848; ¶ 1834.02.
10. ¶ M-5802; ¶ 1834.
11. ¶s M-5800, M-5802; ¶ 1834 *et seq.*

Footnote references beginning with letters are to paragraphs in RIA's Federal Tax Coordinator 2d and RIA's Analysis of Federal Taxes: Income. Footnote references beginning with numbers are to paragraphs in RIA's United States Tax Reporter.

income from the activity exceeds the deductions in (1), above. (Code Sec. 183(b)(2); Reg § 1.183-1(b)(1)(ii))

(3) Amounts allowable as deductions only if the activity were engaged in for profit, that if allowed *would* result in a basis adjustment (e.g., depreciation), *but only* to the extent the gross income from the activity exceeds deductions allowed or allowable under (1) and (2), above. (Code Sec. 183(b)(2); Reg § 1.183-1(b)(1)(iii), (b)(3))[12]

In other words, deduction for items attributable to the "not for profit" activity is allowed to the extent of income from it, or for the full amount of related deductions allowable regardless of profit-seeking, *whichever is larger.*[13]

However, the deductions allowable under these rules are subject to the 2% floor (¶ 3107) on miscellaneous itemized deductions. (Reg § 1.67-1T(a)(1)(iv))[14]

¶ 1768   Owner's expenses of vacation home.

Where an individual, trust, estate, partnership or S corporation owns a vacation home or a dwelling unit (below) and uses it for both personal and rental purposes, deduction of expenses is limited. (Code Sec. 280A(a))[15] The owner's personal use of the home (or portion of it) for even one day in the tax year triggers these limits. (Code Sec. 280A(e)(1))[16]

On the other hand, certain deductions, e.g., mortgage interest, property taxes and casualty losses, are allowed in full (to the extent otherwise allowed) without regard to business use of the property. (Code Sec. 280A(b))[17]

For any tax year in which the owner uses the (rented) vacation home or other dwelling unit for personal purposes, the owner's deduction for maintenance, utilities, depreciation, etc., can't exceed the percentage of those total expenses for the year "attributable" to the rental period. (Code Sec. 280A(e)(1))[18] The deductions attributable to rental use are *further* limited to no more than: (1) the gross income derived from rental use for that year, *minus* the sum of (2) the deductions allocable to rental use that are allowable whether or not the unit (or portion of it) was used for rental (e.g., interest and taxes), and (3) deductions allocable to the business or rental activity but which are not allocable to the use of the home itself. (Code Sec. 280A(c)(5))[19]

The proper ratio for allocating interest and taxes to the rental period is: (1) number of days for which the property is rented, to (2) number of days of total use (according to IRS but not some courts which would use "number of days in the year").[20]

A home is used as a residence in any tax year in which the owner's use of the unit (or a portion of it) for personal purposes exceeds the longer of: (1) 14 days, or (2) 10% of the period of rental use. (Code Sec. 280A(d)(1))[21]

These limits do not apply to a dwelling unit that has been rented out for a consecutive period of: (1) 12 months or more that begins or ends in the tax year, *or* (2) less than 12 months that begins in the tax year and at the end of which the unit is sold or exchanged. During this "qualified rental period," the unit must be rented, or held for rental, at a fair rent. (Code Sec. 280A(d)(3))[22]

If a home is rented for less than 15 days a year, the owner may not deduct *any* of the rental expenses, but isn't taxed on any of the rental income. (Code Sec. 280A(g))[23]

¶ 1769   Worthless stock or securities.

A taxpayer may deduct a loss from worthlessness of stock or other securities (i.e., a bond, debenture, note, certificate or other evidence of indebtedness issued by a corporation or by a government (or its political subdivision) with interest coupons or in registered form). (Code Sec. 165(a), (g)(1))[24]

---

12. ¶ M-5804; ¶ 1834.	16. ¶ M-6016; ¶ 280A4.	19. ¶ M-6018; ¶ 280A4.	22. ¶ M-6022; ¶ 280A4.
13. ¶ M-5804; ¶ 1834.	17. ¶ M-6000; ¶ 280A4.	20. ¶ M-6020; ¶ 280A4.	23. ¶ M-6015; ¶ 280A4.
14. ¶ A-2709; ¶ 674.	18. ¶ M-6016; ¶ 280A4.	21. ¶ M-6005; ¶ 280A4.	24. ¶ M-3301; ¶ 1654.200 *et seq.*
15. ¶ M-6001; ¶ 280A4.			

Footnote references beginning with letters are to paragraphs in RIA's Federal Tax Coordinator 2d and RIA's Analysis of Federal Taxes: Income. Footnote references beginning with numbers are to paragraphs in RIA's United States Tax Reporter.

Taxpayer must be able to show that the security had value at the end of the year preceding the deduction year and that an identifiable event caused a loss in the deduction year.[25]

The amount of the loss is, to the extent not compensated for (e.g., by insurance), the security's adjusted basis for determining loss on sale (¶ 2470). (Code Sec. 165(b))[26]

The deduction is a capital loss if the security is a capital asset to taxpayer. (Code Sec. 165(g)(1)) An ordinary loss deduction is allowed if the security is:

■ not a capital asset; (Reg § 1.165-5(b))

■ Code Sec. 1244 stock of a "small business corporation" (¶ 2636 *et seq.*);

■ (for corporate taxpayers), stock in an "affiliated" corporation (at least 80%-owned by taxpayer), where more than 90% of the affiliate's gross receipts has been from sources other than passive income (royalties, dividends, etc.). (Code Sec. 165(g)(3))[27]

Certain losses by, or on stock of, small business investment companies also are ordinary losses. (Code Sec. 1242, Code Sec. 1243)[28]

Total worthlessness of the security is required for the loss deduction. No loss deduction is allowed for partial worthlessness or for mere decline in value. (But dealers who inventory securities are, in effect, allowed a loss deduction for mere decline in value.) (Reg § 1.165-4, Reg § 1.165-5)[29]

No loss deduction is allowed on a shareholder's surrender of stock to the corporation, whether or not the surrender is pro rata. Instead, the shareholder's basis for stock surrendered is added to his basis for stock retained.[30]

¶ 1770 Demolition losses.

No deduction is allowed to the owner or lessee of a building for any loss on demolition of the building, or for any of the demolition expenses. (Code Sec. 280B(1)) The loss or expenses must be capitalized and added to the basis of the land. (Code Sec. 280B(2))[31]

¶ 1771 Abandonment loss.

A loss deduction is allowed for loss of usefulness or for obsolescence of nondepreciable property, both tangible and intangible (e.g., land, good will), *if*:

■ the loss is incurred in business or a transaction entered into for profit, and it arises from the sudden termination of usefulness in the business or transaction; *and*

■ the property is permanently discarded from use, or the business or transaction is discontinued. (Reg § 1.165-2)[32]

The amount of the loss cannot exceed the adjusted basis of the property for determining loss on a sale or other disposition (¶ 2470). (Reg § 1.165-1(c))[33]

The loss is an ordinary loss. (Reg § 1.165-2)[34]

For losses on mortgaged property, see ¶s 1777 and 1778.

¶ 1772 Costs of investigating proposed venture.

A corporation that pays or incurs expenses in *unsuccessfully* searching for or investigating a new venture may deduct those costs as a business loss, when it abandons the search or investigation. But for a noncorporate taxpayer, these expenses are personal and nondeductible.[35] For *successful* investigation expenses, see ¶ 1500 *et seq.*

---

25. ¶ M-3304; ¶ 1654.210.
26. ¶ M-3305; ¶ 1654.205.
27. ¶s M-3312; M-3313; ¶ 1654.203.
28. ¶ M-3308; ¶ 1654.203.
29. ¶s G-5021, M-3304; ¶ 1654.200 *et seq.*
30. ¶ M-3501.
31. ¶ M-2200; ¶s 1654.180, 280B4.
32. ¶ M-2301; ¶ 1654.150 *et seq.*
33. ¶ M-2351.
34. ¶ M-2353.
35. ¶ L-5016 *et seq.*

Footnote references beginning with letters are to paragraphs in RIA's Federal Tax Coordinator 2d and RIA's Analysis of Federal Taxes: Income. Footnote references beginning with numbers are to paragraphs in RIA's United States Tax Reporter.

¶ 1773 Gambling losses.

Taxpayer may deduct gambling losses suffered in the tax year, but only to the extent of that year's gambling gains. (Code Sec. 165(d)) Losses from one kind of gambling (e.g., horse bets) are deductible against gains from another kind (e.g., newspaper pool).[36] Individuals not engaged in the gambling business deduct them (to the extent of gambling gains) only as itemized deductions, subject to the 2% floor.[37]

¶ 1774 When to deduct loss.

A loss is deductible only for the tax year in which it is sustained. (Code Sec. 165(a)) This is the year the loss occurs, as evidenced by closed and completed transactions and as fixed by identifiable events occurring in that year. (Reg § 1.165-1(d))[38]

For special rules for casualty or theft losses, see ¶s 1785 and 1790.

¶ 1775 Deducting reimbursable losses.

If taxpayer has a claim for reimbursement on which there's a reasonable (at least 40%) prospect of recovery, that "reimbursable" loss may not be deducted until it's reasonably certain that the reimbursement will or won't be made. This may be ascertained by, among other things, settlement, adjudication or abandonment of the claim. (Code Sec. 165(a); Reg § 1.165-1(d))[39]

¶ 1776 How much loss is deductible?

The amount of a loss sustained on disposition of property is the adjusted basis of the property, minus the amount of any money and the fair market value of any property received in exchange. (Code Sec. 165(b); Reg § 1.165-1(c))[40]

No loss is deductible to the extent taxpayer was reimbursed or compensated for it (¶ 1784). (Code Sec. 165(a))[41] Deduction isn't allowed to the extent that property has salvage value. (Reg § 1.165-1(c))[42]

For casualty and theft losses, see ¶ 1780 *et seq.* and ¶ 1788 *et seq.*

¶ 1777 Mortgagee's loss (or gain) on mortgaged property.

The mortgagee (mortgage creditor) treats a loss on mortgaged property as follows:

A loss on *compromise or settlement* of the debt of an insolvent debtor is treated as a bad debt (¶ 1837 *et seq.*).[43]

A loss on *surrender of mortgaged property* is treated as a bad debt loss, equal to the sum of: the excess of the debt's basis over the fair market value (FMV) of the property surrendered; plus legal and other expenses connected with surrender; plus accrued interest previously reported as income. (Reg § 1.166-1(c)) (The mortgagee has a gain if the debt's basis is *less* than the FMV of the surrendered property.)[44] For where the surrender is a repossession by the seller, see ¶ 2463.

A loss on a *mortgage foreclosure* is treated as a bad debt loss equal to the sum of: the excess of the debt's basis over the property's net proceeds from the foreclosure; plus accrued interest previously reported as income; plus legal and other expenses. This is true whether the price is paid by the mortgagee (by applying the debt to the price) or someone else. (Reg § 1.166-6)[45]

A mortgagee that bids on the property at the foreclosure sale *also* realizes a loss to the extent the debt applied to the bid exceeds the property's FMV. He realizes a taxable gain to the extent FMV exceeds the amount of the debt so applied. FMV is assumed to equal

---

36. ¶ M-6101; ¶s 1654.500, 1654.501.
37. ¶ M-6105.
38. ¶ M-1301; ¶s 1654.090, 1654.111.
39. ¶ M-2136; ¶ 1654.130.
40. ¶ M-1401.
41. ¶ M-1408; ¶ 1654.090.
42. ¶ M-1401.
43. ¶ M-3709; ¶ 1664.350 *et seq.*
44. ¶ M-3710; ¶ 1664.353.
45. ¶ M-3701; ¶ 1664.350 *et seq.*

Footnote references beginning with letters are to paragraphs in RIA's Federal Tax Coordinator 2d and RIA's Analysis of Federal Taxes: Income. Footnote references beginning with numbers are to paragraphs in RIA's United States Tax Reporter.

the bid price, absent convincing proof to the contrary. (Reg § 1.166-6(b))[46]

¶ 1778 Owner's loss on foreclosure, surrender or abandonment of mortgaged property.

The owner of mortgaged property, whether or not he is the mortgagor and whether or not he is personally liable for the mortgage debt, realizes a loss (occasionally a gain) on foreclosure of the mortgage or surrender of the property. The foreclosure (or surrender) is considered a sale or exchange.[47] The amount of gain or loss is the owner's basis, minus the mortgage debt discharged or satisfied, plus any excess of proceeds over debt.[48]

The owner of property who is not liable on the mortgage debt realizes a loss on abandoning it to the mortgagee. Abandonment is generally treated as a sale or exchange.[49]

¶ 1779 Loss on tax sale.

The tax treatment of an owner whose property is sold for delinquent taxes is similar to that for foreclosure (¶ 1778). The tax sale is a sale or exchange.[50]

¶ 1780 Casualty losses.

A deduction is allowed for losses arising from a casualty (¶ 1781) where taxpayer actually sustains a loss *and* the loss is on *property*. (Code Sec. 165(c)(3)) The property must suffer physical damage and not just a decline in value, even if that decline results from being in or near an area where casualties have occurred and might occur again.[1]

Casualty losses are reported on Form 4684.[2]

¶ 1781 "Casualty" defined.

A casualty is the complete or partial destruction of property resulting from an identifiable event of a sudden, unexpected or unusual nature such as a fire or storm. Progressive deterioration from a steadily operating cause isn't a casualty.[3]

¶ 1782 Amount of casualty loss.

The amount of a casualty loss depends on whether taxpayer held the property for personal or for business purposes, as follows (for amount of *deduction*, see ¶ 1783):

For property held for personal use, the amount of the casualty loss is the *lesser* of: (1) the property's adjusted basis (i.e., its basis for determining loss on disposition, see ¶ 2470), or (2) its decline in value (i.e., its fair market value (FMV) immediately before the casualty *minus* its FMV immediately afterward). This applies whether the property is totally destroyed or merely damaged. (Reg § 1.165-7(b)) Also, the amount is reduced for any salvage value, insurance or other compensation received (¶ 1784). (Reg § 1.165-1(c)(4))[4]

For property used in business or held for the production of income, the amount of the casualty loss is determined under the same rules as for personal-use property (above), except that if the property is *totally* destroyed, the amount of the loss is the property's adjusted basis in all cases. (Reg § 1.165-7(b)(1))[5]

The decline in a property's value should be ascertained by competent appraisal where possible.[6]

Costs of repairing, replacing, or cleaning up property after a casualty can be used to measure the amount of the loss (decline in value) if: the repair, etc., is necessary to restore the property to its pre-casualty condition; the amount spent isn't excessive; the repairs do no more than take care of the damage suffered; and the post-repair value is no greater than the pre-casualty value. (Reg § 1.165-7(a)(2))[7]

---

46. ¶ M-3704; ¶ 1664.352.
47. ¶ M-3801; ¶ 1654.451.
48. ¶ M-3803.
49. ¶ M-3808; ¶ 1654.155.

50. ¶ M-3806; ¶s 1654.155, 1654.451.
1. ¶ M-1601; ¶ 1654.300 *et seq.*
2. ¶ M-1600.

3. ¶ M-1701; ¶ 1654.301.
4. ¶s M-1801, M-1807; ¶ 1654.304.

5. ¶ M-1802; ¶ 1654.304.
6. ¶ M-1809; ¶ 1654.304.
7. ¶ M-1815; ¶ 1654.304.

Footnote references beginning with letters are to paragraphs in RIA's Federal Tax Coordinator 2d and RIA's Analysis of Federal Taxes: Income. Footnote references beginning with numbers are to paragraphs in RIA's United States Tax Reporter.

¶ 1783 Limits on casualty loss deduction for personal-use property—$100/10%-of-AGI floors.

A taxpayer may deduct a casualty loss on property not used in business or held for production of income only to the extent that: (1) the casualty loss exceeds $100 ("$100 floor"), and (2) all of taxpayer's casualty losses for the tax year exceed 10% of adjusted gross income for the year ("percentage of income limit"). (Code Sec. 165(h))[8]

$100 floor. Each personal-use property casualty is subject to a separate $100 floor to determine the extent it is deductible. But events closely related in origin give rise to a single casualty. Thus, a single storm's damage to taxpayer's house and car is one casualty, so that only the total damage has to exceed $100 to be deductible.[9]

Also, a single $100 floor applies where the same casualty causes loss to a husband and wife if they file a joint return, whether the loss is to property jointly or separately owned. But separate $100 floors apply to each spouse if they file separately, whether the property is separately or jointly owned. (Reg § 1.165-7(b)(4))[10]

Where property is held for both business (or profit) and personal purposes, the $100 floor applies only to the personal part of the loss. (Reg § 1.165-7(b)(4)(iv))[11]

Percentage of income limitation. In addition to the $100 per casualty "floor" (above), personal-use property casualties are subject to this other limit: If personal casualty losses (defined below) for a tax year exceed personal casualty gains for that tax year, taxpayer may deduct those losses for that year, but only to the extent of the sum of:

(1) the amount of the personal casualty gains for the year, plus

(2) the amount by which (a) the excess of personal casualty losses over gains ((1) above), exceeds (b) 10% of taxpayer's adjusted gross income (AGI) (computed without regard to casualty gains). (Code Sec. 165(h)(2)(A))[12]

In determining a taxpayer's personal casualty gains and losses, the amount of any recognized loss is subject to the $100 floor before netting. (Code Sec. 165(h)(3)(B))[13]

If the personal casualty gains for any tax year exceed the personal casualty losses for that year, all these gains and losses will be treated as capital gains and losses. (Code Sec. 165(h)(2)(B))[14]

¶ 1784 Insurance or other compensation.

The casualty loss deduction isn't allowed to the extent the loss is compensated by insurance or otherwise. (Code Sec. 165(a)) However, costs incurred in collecting the compensation reduce the recovery so as to increase the loss deduction.[15] For "gain" when compensation exceeds loss, see ¶ 2430.

Where an individual's casualty and theft losses are not attributable to a business or a for-profit transaction, a loss covered by insurance is taken into account only if taxpayer files a timely insurance claim. (Code Sec. 165(h)(4)(E)) However, this limitation applies only to the extent the insurance policy would have provided reimbursement had the claim been filed.[16]

Compensation includes property insurance, damage recoveries, debt forgiveness, cash or property received from taxpayer's employer or from disaster relief agencies to rehabilitate the property, and condemnation awards. Compensation doesn't include personal items, e.g., food, medical supplies and other forms of subsistence (including insurance) paying taxpayer for family living expenses (limited to the amounts paid over and above normal living expenses) due to loss of use of their home. (Code Sec. 123) Nor does it include use and occupancy insurance reimbursements for lost business profits.[17]

Deduction is not allowed for a loss made good by *deducted* repairs.[18]

8. ¶ M-1900 *et seq.*; ¶ 1654.304.   10. ¶ M-1904 *et seq.*; ¶ 1654.304.   13. ¶ M-1908; ¶ 1654.304.   16. ¶ M-1914; ¶ 1654.304.
9. ¶s M-1901; M-1902;   11. ¶ M-1906; ¶ 1654.304.   14. ¶ 1910; ¶ 1654.304.   17. ¶ M-1411 *et seq.*
   ¶ 1654.304.   12. ¶ M-1907; ¶ 1654.304.   15. ¶ M-1408; ¶ 1654.304.   18. ¶ M-1815.

Footnote references beginning with letters are to paragraphs in RIA's Federal Tax Coordinator 2d and RIA's Analysis of Federal Taxes: Income. Footnote references beginning with numbers are to paragraphs in RIA's United States Tax Reporter.

A casualty loss to inventory is automatically reflected in cost of goods sold (¶ 2871). It is not separately deducted as a loss unless adjustments are made to inventory.[19]

¶ 1785 When to deduct casualty losses.

A casualty loss (like other losses, see ¶ 1769) is considered "sustained" (and deductible) only during the tax year the loss occurs, as fixed by identifiable events occurring in that year. (Code Sec. 165(a); Reg § 1.165-1(d)(1)) A loss may be sustained in the tax year even though repairs or replacements aren't made until a later year. And a loss may be sustained in a year *after* the casualty occurs, as when trees died a year after the year a blizzard damaged them.[20] For early deduction of disaster losses, see ¶ 1786.

¶ 1786 Early deduction for disaster losses.

A taxpayer may *elect* to deduct a disaster loss (defined below) on the return for the tax year *before* the year the loss occurred. (Code Sec. 165(i))[21]

observation: Claiming a disaster loss on the earlier year's return saves taxes immediately, without waiting until the end of the year the loss was sustained. In some cases, it may result in a net operating loss, which will bring a refund through a carryback to an earlier year. On the other hand, deduction for the later loss year may save taxes where taxpayer expects to be in a higher bracket that year.

Individuals who incur a disaster loss with respect to nonbusiness property are subject to the regular $100/10%-of-AGI floors (¶ 1783). (Code Sec. 165(i))[22]

A disaster loss is a loss that's attributable to a disaster occurring in an area the President later says is entitled to federal assistance. (Code Sec. 165(i)(1))[23] Also, the loss must be *otherwise* deductible as a loss. (Reg § 1.165-11(b)(3))For example, a drought disaster loss (ordinarily not a deductible casualty loss) would be deductible where incurred in the course of a trade or business or profit-seeking transaction.[24]

The election is made on the return (original or amended) for the previous year. It should be made by the later of: (1) the due date for the disaster year return (without regard to extensions), or (2) the due date for the previous year return *with* permitted extensions. (Reg § 1.165-11(e))[25]

¶ 1787 Elections to treat frozen bank deposits as losses from casualty or from transaction entered into for profit.

If a "qualified individual" (anyone other than the institution's officers, 1% owners and persons related to either) has a loss on a deposit in a bankrupt or insolvent qualified financial institution, and that loss may be reasonably estimated, the loss may be treated, at taxpayer's election:

(1) as a casualty or theft loss instead of as a nonbusiness bad debt (¶ 1843), (Code Sec. 165(l)(1), (2))[26] or

(2) as a loss incurred in a transaction entered into for profit. The individual may make this election only if no part of his deposits in the financial institution is federally insured, and only for up to $20,000 ($10,000 for married individuals filing a separate return) of the loss. (Code Sec. 165(l)(5))[27]

The election applies to all losses for the year that taxpayer incurs on deposits with a financial institution, and may not be revoked without IRS's consent. (Code Sec. 165(l)(6))[28]

The elections are made by claiming the loss (casualty or ordinary) on the income tax return for the tax year in which a reasonable estimate of the loss can be made. (If no election was made for a year that's still open, an amended return (Form 1040X) is used.)[29]

---

19. ¶ M-1808; ¶s 1654.302, 4714.21.
20. ¶ M-1610; ¶ 1654.305.
21. ¶ M-2001; ¶ 1654.520.
22. ¶ M-2009.
23. ¶ M-2002; ¶ 1654.520.
24. ¶ M-2004.
25. ¶ M-2011 *et seq.*; ¶ 1654.520.
26. ¶ M-1761; ¶ 1654.530.
27. ¶ M-1765; ¶ 1654.530.
28. ¶ M-1773; ¶ 1654.530.
29. ¶ M-1771; ¶ 1654.530.

Footnote references beginning with letters are to paragraphs in RIA's Federal Tax Coordinator 2d and RIA's Analysis of Federal Taxes: Income. Footnote references beginning with numbers are to paragraphs in RIA's United States Tax Reporter.

¶ 1788   Theft losses.

Theft losses are deductible under rules that closely follow those for casualty losses, including the $100/10%-of-AGI floors (¶ 1780 et seq.). (Code Sec. 165(a), (h)(1), (2)) A theft is the unlawful taking and removing of money or property with the intent to deprive the owner of it, and includes larceny, robbery, embezzlement, (Reg § 1.165-8(d)) burglary, extortion, kidnapping for ransom, blackmail and false representation.[30]

A taking by a person known to have a claim to the property (e.g., spouse, joint owner) isn't a theft unless there's evidence of criminal intent.[31]

¶ 1789   Amount of theft loss.

For theft of business or investment property, the *deductible loss* is the adjusted basis of the property minus insurance or other compensation received or recoverable. (Reg § 1.165-8(c))[32]

For theft of personal-use property, the *loss* is: (1) the lesser of the property's fair market value (FMV) immediately before theft or its adjusted basis, reduced by (2) insurance or other compensation received or recoverable. (Reg § 1.165-8(c)) The $100/10%-of-AGI floors (¶ 1783) are then applied to determine the amount of the loss that is *deductible*. (Code Sec. 165(c)(3))[33]

If stolen personal-use property is recovered in the deduction year, the loss is the lesser of: (1) the property's adjusted basis, or (2) the decline in its FMV between theft and recovery. If it is recovered in a year after deduction has been taken, the excess of the earlier deduction over the loss determined as above is included in income (under the tax benefit rule, see ¶ 1205), to the extent the earlier loss deduction decreased taxpayer's tax.[34]

¶ 1790   When to deduct theft loss.

A theft loss is deductible (on Form 4684) in the year the theft loss is *discovered* , regardless of when the theft actually occurred. But the deduction is postponed to the extent taxpayer, in the year of discovery, had a reimbursement claim on which there was a reasonable prospect of recovery. (Reg § 1.165-8(a))[35]

¶ 1791   At-Risk Limitations

Deductions from certain leveraged investment activities are limited to the aggregate amount the taxpayer-investor has "at risk."

¶ 1792   Taxpayers subject to "at risk" rules.

The at-risk rules apply to: (1) individuals, and (2) C corporations but only if more than 50% in value of the corporation's stock is owned by not more than five individuals at any time during the last half of its tax year. (Code Sec. 465(a)(1))[36] But even if this stock ownership is met, the at-risk rules *do not apply* to:

■ certain active businesses ("qualifying businesses") carried on by a qualified C corporation (i.e., *not* a personal holding company, foreign personal holding company or personal service corporation determined by substituting 5% for 10% in Code Sec. 269A(b)(2)), (Code Sec. 465(c)(7))[37] or

■ the activity of equipment leasing. (Code Sec. 465(c)(4))[38]

🅡*observation:* Even though the at-risk rules do not apply to pass-through entities

---

30. ¶ M-2100 et seq.; ¶ 1654.350   32. ¶ M-2125; ¶ 1654.370.   35. ¶ M-2132; ¶ 1654.380.   37. ¶ M-4527 et seq.; ¶ 4654(e).
     et seq.   33. ¶ M-2126; ¶ 1654.370.   36. ¶s M-4522, M-4526.   38. ¶ M-4509; ¶ 4654(c).
31. ¶ M-2104.   34. ¶ M-2129.

Footnote references beginning with letters are to paragraphs in RIA's Federal Tax Coordinator 2d and RIA's Analysis of Federal Taxes: Income. Footnote references beginning with numbers are to paragraphs in RIA's United States Tax Reporter.

such as estates, trusts, S corporations, and partnerships, they *do* apply to determine whether a person with an interest in any of those entities may deduct items of loss, etc., that are passed through.

¶ 1793 "At risk" activities.

The at-risk rules apply to:

■ certain specified activities: (1) holding, producing or distributing motion pictures or video tapes, (2) farming, (3) equipment leasing, (4) exploring for, or exploiting, oil and gas resources, (5) exploring for, or exploiting, geothermal resources; (Code Sec. 465(c)(1)) and

■ a "catch-all" group of activities that taxpayer engages in, in carrying on a trade or business or in the production of income, other than those above. (Code Sec. 465(c)(3))[39]

In applying the at-risk rules to the specified activities, taxpayer's activity with respect to each property (e.g., each film in (1), above) is treated as a separate activity. (Code Sec. 465(c)(2)(A)) Activities in the "catch-all" group are treated as one activity ("aggregated") if either: (1) taxpayer actively participates in the management of the trade or business, or (2) the trade or business is carried on by a partnership or S corporation *and* 65% or more of the losses for the tax year is allocable to persons who actively participate in its management. (Code Sec. 465(c)(3)(B))[40]

For the at-risk rules otherwise applicable to real property, see ¶ 1797.

¶ 1794 How the at-risk rules work.

For a taxpayer engaged in an at-risk activity (¶ 1793), any loss from the activity for the tax year is deductible in that year only to the extent that taxpayer is at risk (¶ 1795) with respect to the activity at the end of the year. (Code Sec. 465(a)) The losses so limited are the excess of the deductions allocable to the activity that otherwise would be allowed for the year, over the income (other than recapture, see ¶ 1796) received or accrued by taxpayer during the year from that same activity. (Code Sec. 465(d))[41]

Any loss thus disallowed in the current year is treated as allocable to the same activity in the next tax year, and may be deducted in the later year subject to that year's at-risk limit for the activity. (Code Sec. 465(a)(2)) Thus, a current year's "loss" may include "suspended" loss accounts from earlier years. (Code Sec. 465(d))[42]

Form 6198 is used to compute the deductible loss from an at-risk activity.[43]

¶ 1795 Amounts considered "at risk."

A taxpayer is considered at risk for an activity to the extent of:

(1) the amount of money and the adjusted basis of other property taxpayer contributed to the activity, (Code Sec. 465(b)(1)) plus

(2) amounts borrowed with respect to the activity to the extent taxpayer is personally liable for the repayment or has pledged property, other than property used in the activity, as security for the borrowed amount. The borrowings can't exceed the fair market value of taxpayer's interest in the pledged property. No property is treated as security if it is directly or indirectly financed by indebtedness secured by property in (1), above. (Code Sec. 465(b)(1), (2))[44]

Amounts borrowed "at risk" ((2) above) do not include borrowings from any person who has an interest in the activity other than as a creditor, or from a related person as specially defined. A corporation is at risk with respect to amounts it borrowed from a shareholder. (Code Sec. 465(b)(3))[45]

Any amounts, even equity capital contributed by taxpayer, are not treated as at risk if

39. ¶ M-4501; ¶ 4654.
40. ¶ M-4517 *et seq.*; ¶ 4654(b).
41. ¶ M-4587; ¶ 4654.
42. ¶ M-4590; ¶ 4564.
43. ¶ M-4500; ¶ 4654.
44. ¶ M-4533 *et seq.*; ¶ 4654(a).
45. ¶ M-4545 *et seq.*; ¶ 4654(a).

Footnote references beginning with letters are to paragraphs in RIA's Federal Tax Coordinator 2d and RIA's Analysis of Federal Taxes: Income. Footnote references beginning with numbers are to paragraphs in RIA's United States Tax Reporter.

the amounts are protected against loss through nonrecourse financing, guarantees, stop loss agreements or similar arrangements. (Code Sec. 465(b)(4))[46]

In determining the amount at risk for any tax year, the amount for that year is reduced by any losses allowed under these limitations in an earlier year. (Code Sec. 465(b)(5))[47]

¶ 1796 Recapture of previously allowed losses.

If taxpayer's amount at risk is less than zero (e.g., by distributions to taxpayer or by debt changing from recourse to nonrecourse), taxpayer recognizes income to the extent of that negative amount. (Code Sec. 465(e)(1)(A)) However, the amount recaptured is limited to the excess of the losses previously allowed in that activity over any amounts previously recaptured. (Code Sec. 465(e)(2)) The amount added to income under this recapture is treated as a deduction allocable to the activity in the first succeeding year, and is allowed if and to the extent taxpayer's at-risk basis is increased. (Code Sec. 465(e)(1)(B))[48]

¶ 1797 At-risk rules for real property.

A taxpayer engaged in the activity of holding real property is subject to the at-risk rules, for losses on property placed in service after '86.[49]

In addition, taxpayer is considered at risk for his share of any "qualified nonrecourse financing" secured by the real property. (Code Sec. 465(b)(6)(A))

This means financing:

■ that is borrowed by taxpayer with respect to the activity of holding real property (as specially defined);

■ that is borrowed by taxpayer from a qualified person (as specially defined) or from any federal, state, or local government or instrumentality or is guaranteed by any federal, state or local government;

■ except as regs provide, on which no one is personally liable for repayment; and

■ that is not convertible debt. (Code Sec. 465(b)(6)(B))[50]

¶ 1798 "Passive Activity" Losses and Credits ▬▬▬▬▬▬▬▬▬▬

Passive activity losses may be used only to offset passive activity income. The excess is carried forward to the following year(s) until used, or until taxpayer disposes of the interest in the activity in a taxable transaction. Passive activity credits may be used only to offset tax on income from passive activities, with a carryover of any excess. Nonetheless, as to rental real estate activities, a natural person who actively participates may get a deduction allowance, and so may certain taxpayers materially participating in the real property business after '93.

¶ 1799 Disallowance of passive activity losses and credits.

A taxpayer specified at ¶ 1800 is not allowed to deduct a passive activity loss (¶ 1802) (Code Sec. 469(a)(1)(A)) or use a passive activity credit (¶ 1812) (Code Sec. 469(a)(1)(B)) except with respect to certain rental real estate activities (¶ 1821 *et seq.*). (Reg § 1.469-1T(a)(2))[1] For deduction of suspended losses on disposition of the activity, see ¶ 1826.

A passive activity deduction disallowed for a tax year under these rules is not taken into account as a deduction in computing taxable income. (Reg § 1.469-1T(d)(3))[2]

Whether a loss is disallowed under these rules is determined *after* the application of the at-risk rules (¶ 1791 *et seq.*), and the interest deduction limitations (¶ 1722 *et seq.*), as well

---

46. ¶ M-4555 *et seq.*; ¶ 4654(a).   48. ¶ M-4593; ¶ 4654(f).   50. ¶ M-4503 *et seq.*; ¶ 4654(d).   2. ¶ M-4603; ¶ 4694.47.
47. ¶ M-4591; ¶ 4654.   49. ¶ M-4502; ¶ 4654(d).   1. ¶ M-4600 *et seq.*; ¶ 4694 *et seq.*

Footnote references beginning with letters are to paragraphs in RIA's Federal Tax Coordinator 2d and RIA's Analysis of Federal Taxes: Income. Footnote references beginning with numbers are to paragraphs in RIA's United States Tax Reporter.

as other provisions measuring taxable income. (Reg § 1.469-1T(d))[3]

Where taxpayer's disallowed passive activity losses are derived from more than one activity, a ratable portion of the loss (if any) from each passive activity, in general, is disallowed. (Reg § 1.469-1T(f)(2)(i))[4] Any loss so disallowed is then generally allocated ratably among all passive activity deductions (¶ 1803) from the activity for the year. (Reg § 1.469-1T(f)(2)(ii))[5] If all or any portion of a passive activity credit is disallowed, a ratable portion of each credit from each passive activity, in general, is disallowed. (Reg § 1.469-1T(f)(3)(i))[6]

The passive activity limits are calculated on Form 8582 (individuals, estates, and trusts), Form 8582-CR (credits for individuals, estates, and trusts), or Form 8810 (closely held corporations and personal service corporations).[7]

¶ 1800 Who is subject to the passive activity rules?

The passive activity limits apply to any individual, estate, trust (Code Sec. 469(a)(2)(A)) (other than a trust, or portion of a trust, which is a grantor trust), (Reg § 1.469-1T(b)(2)) personal service corporation (PSC) as specially defined (Code Sec. 469(a)(2)(C)) and closely held C corporation as specially defined (except as described at ¶s 1802 and 1803). (Code Sec. 469(a)(2)(B))[8] For pass-through entities, see ¶ 1801.

Spouses filing a joint return are treated as one taxpayer, with certain exceptions. (Reg § 1.469-1T(j)(1))[9]

The passive activity rules don't apply, except as regs may provide, to any corporation that isn't a PSC or a closely held corporation for the tax year. (Reg § 1.469-1T(g)(1))[10] But the rules *do* apply to any of the corporation's losses or credits that arose during a tax year when it *was* a closely held C corporation or a PSC. (Code Sec. 469(f)(2))[11]

The passive activity rules apply to an affiliated group of corporations that files a consolidated return, but only if the consolidated group as a whole is properly treated as a closely held C corporation or as a PSC. (Reg § 1.469-1(h)(4)(ii))[12]

¶ 1801 Pass-through entities.

Partnerships (unless publicly traded, see below) and S corporations are not subject to the passive activity rules. (Code Sec. 469(a)(2)) However, the rules *do* apply to the losses and credits passed through to the partners and shareholders.[13]

The passive activity rules apply to publicly traded partnerships (PTPs) that are not treated as corporations. The rules are applied separately with respect to items attributable to each PTP (except in certain situations involving the low-income housing and rehabilitation credits). (Code Sec. 469(k)(1))[14]

A PTP is a partnership the interests of which are traded on an established securities market (national or local exchange, any over-the-counter market) or are readily tradable on a secondary market (or the substantial equivalent). (Code Sec. 469(k)(2))[15]

¶ 1802 Passive activity loss defined.

A passive activity loss for a tax year is the amount, if any, by which the aggregate losses from all passive activities for the tax year exceed the aggregate income from all passive activities for that year, i.e., the excess of "passive activity deductions" (¶ 1803) over "passive activity gross income" (¶ 1805) for the year. (Code Sec. 469(d)(1); Reg § 1.469-2T(b)(1))[16]

For a closely held C corporation, the passive activity loss is the excess of passive

---

3. ¶ M-4603 *et seq.*; ¶s 4694.30, 4694.47.
4. ¶ M-5501; ¶ 4694.40.
5. ¶ M-5502; ¶ 4694.42.
6. ¶ M-5604; ¶ 4694.44.

7. ¶ M-5200.
8. ¶ M-4701 *et seq.*; ¶ 4694.
9. ¶ M-4702; ¶ 4694.70.
10. ¶ M-4705; ¶ 4694.

11. ¶ M-4705.
12. ¶ M-4708; ¶ 4694.75.
13. ¶s M-4709, M-5302; ¶ 4694.80.

14. ¶ M-4710; ¶ 4694.85.
15. ¶ M-4710; ¶ 4694.85.
16. ¶ M-4601; ¶ 4694.20.

Footnote references beginning with letters are to paragraphs in RIA's Federal Tax Coordinator 2d and RIA's Analysis of Federal Taxes: Income. Footnote references beginning with numbers are to paragraphs in RIA's United States Tax Reporter.

227

activity deductions over the sum of passive activity gross income *plus* the corporation's net active (but not portfolio) income for the tax year. (Code Sec. 469(e)(2)(A); Reg § 1.469-1T(g)(4))[17]

For how passive loss characterization affects other Code provisions, see ¶ 1827.

¶ 1803   What is a passive activity deduction?

A deduction is a "passive activity deduction" for a tax year only if it: (1) arises in connection with the conduct of an activity that is a passive activity for that year (¶ 1813), or (2) is carried over as a passive activity deduction from an earlier tax year (¶ 1825). (Reg § 1.469-2T(d)(1)) A deduction "arises" in the tax year the item would be deductible under taxpayer's method of accounting if taxable income for all tax years were determined without regard to the passive loss rules, the Code Sec. 613A(d) rules denying percentage depletion for oil and gas wells or the Code Sec. 1211 capital loss limitation rules. (Reg § 1.469-2(d)(8))[18]

The character (as a passive activity deduction) of an item allocated to taxpayer by a partnership or S corporation is determined, in any case in which participation is relevant, by taxpayer's participation in the activity that generated the item for the entity's tax year. (Reg § 1.469-2T(e))[19]

For when loss on the sale or other disposition of an interest in property is a passive activity deduction, see ¶ 1804.

Passive activity deductions *do not include* (Code Sec. 469(e)(1)(A)(i)(III); Reg § 1.469-2T(d)(2)) (and thus the passive loss limits don't restrict the deductibility of):[20]

■ interest expense properly allocable to portfolio income; (Code Sec. 469(e)(1)(A)(i)(III))[21]

■ an expense (other than interest) clearly and directly allocable to portfolio income; (Code Sec. 469(e)(1)(A)(i)(II))

■ state, local, or foreign income, war profits, or excess profits tax expenses;

■ a deduction allowed for a charitable contribution;

■ miscellaneous itemized deductions subject to the 2% of AGI floor (without regard to any amount disallowed because of the floor);

■ a dividend-received deduction with respect to any dividend that's not included in passive activity gross income;

■ a net operating loss carryover, or a capital loss carryover (under the five-year carryover rules for corporations);

■ nonrecurring casualty and theft losses.[22]

■ a deduction or loss allocable to business or rental use of a a dwelling unit for any tax year to which the Code Sec. 280A(c)(5) limits apply.[23]

Deductions in excess of a partner's (or shareholder's) basis, or in excess of the at-risk limits, aren't passive activity deductions for the tax year. (Reg § 1.469-2T(d)(6))[24]

¶ 1804   Loss on sale, exchange or other disposition as passive activity deduction.

Passive activity deductions include any loss recognized on the sale, exchange or other disposition of an interest in property used in an activity at the time of disposition, and any deduction allowed on account of the abandonment or worthlessness of the interest, *if and only if* the activity was a passive activity (¶ 1813) of taxpayer for the tax year of disposition (or other event giving rise to the deduction). (Reg § 1.469-2T(d)(5)(i))[25]

If the interest in property disposed of was used in more than one activity during the 12-

---

17. ¶ M-5507 *et seq.*; ¶ 4694.36.   20. ¶ M-5401 *et seq.*; ¶ 4694.31.   22. ¶ M-5421; ¶ 4694.31.   24. ¶ M-4606.
18. ¶ M-5401; ¶ 4694.30.   21. ¶ M-5416 *et seq.*; ¶s 4694.23,   23. ¶ M-5109.   25. ¶ M-5406; ¶ 4694.32.
19. ¶ M-5402.   4694.31.

Footnote references beginning with letters are to paragraphs in RIA's Federal Tax Coordinator 2d and RIA's Analysis of Federal Taxes: Income. Footnote references beginning with numbers are to paragraphs in RIA's United States Tax Reporter.

month period ending on the date of disposition, the amount realized from the disposition (as well as the adjusted basis of the interest) must be allocated among the activities (with a de minimis exception) on a basis that reasonably reflects those uses. (Reg § 1.469-2(d)(5)(iii), Reg § 1.469-2T(d)(5)(i), (ii))[26]

Passive activity deductions don't include:

■ a loss from the disposition of property that produces portfolio income, (Reg § 1.469-2T(d)(2)(iv)) or

■ a deduction for a disposition of an entire interest in a passive activity if, under the rules for those dispositions (¶ 1826), the deduction is not treated as a passive activity deduction. (Reg § 1.469-2T(d)(2)(v))[27]

¶ 1805 Passive activity gross income.

Passive activity gross income is, in general, gross income from a passive activity (¶ 1813). (Reg § 1.469-2T(c)(1))[28] The character (as passive activity gross income) of a partner's or S corporation shareholder's allocable items of gross income is determined, in general, by reference to the partner's or shareholder's participation in the activity(ies) that generated the items for the entity's tax year. (Reg § 1.469-2T(e)(1))[29] For when gain on disposition of a property interest is passive activity gross income, see ¶ 1806.

Passive activity gross income does not include portfolio income (¶ 1808), (Code Sec. 469(e)(1)(A); Reg § 1.469-2T(c)(3)(i)) or compensation for personal services (as specially defined in the regs). (Code Sec. 469(e)(3); Reg § 1.469-2T(c)(4))[30]

Other items specifically excluded are:

■ gross income from intangible property (e.g., patent) if taxpayer's personal efforts contributed significantly to the creation of the property, or from a covenant not to compete;

■ gross income attributable to a tax refund;

■ gross income from a qualified low-income housing project; (Reg § 1.469-2T(c)(7))

■ gross income from an oil or gas property, if any loss from a working interest in the property for any earlier tax year was treated as a loss not from a passive activity. (Code Sec. 469(c)(3)(B); Reg § 1.469-2T(c)(6))[31]

■ gross income of an individual from a covenant not to compete;

■ gross income that is treated as not from a passive activity under the regs;

■ gross income attributable to the reimbursement of a casualty loss, if the reimbursement is included in gross income, if the loss had been deducted in an earlier year and the deduction for the loss wasn't a passive activity deduction. (Reg § 1.469-2(c)(7))[32]

¶ 1806 Gain on sale, exchange or other disposition of interest in passive activity.

Gain recognized on the sale, exchange or other disposition of an interest in property generally is treated as passive activity gross income for the year the gain is recognized, if the activity in which the property was used was a passive activity (¶ 1813) for the year of disposition. (Reg § 1.469-2T(c)(2)(i)(A))[33]

If the property disposed of was used in more than one activity in the 12-month period before disposition, the amount realized on disposition (as well as the adjusted basis of the interest in the property) must be allocated among those activities (with a de minimis exception) on a basis that reasonably reflects those uses. (Reg § 1.469-2T(c)(2)(ii)) But gain from the disposition of an interest in property that is substantially appreciated (fair market value exceeds 120% of adjusted basis) is treated as *not* from a passive activity unless the interest was used in a passive activity for either 20% of the period taxpayer

---

26. ¶ M-5406; ¶ 4694.32.   28. ¶ M-5301; ¶ 4694.21.   30. ¶ M-5325 *et seq.*; ¶ 4694.22.   32. ¶ M-5334.
27. ¶ M-5421; ¶ 4694.31.   29. ¶ M-5302; ¶ 4694.80.   31. ¶ M-5333 *et seq.*; ¶ 4694.22.   33. ¶ M-5304; ¶ 4694.28.

Footnote references beginning with letters are to paragraphs in RIA's Federal Tax Coordinator 2d and RIA's Analysis of Federal Taxes: Income. Footnote references beginning with numbers are to paragraphs in RIA's United States Tax Reporter.

held the interest or the entire 24-month period ending on the date of disposition. (Reg § 1.469-2(c)(2)(iii))[34]

If taxpayer acquires an interest in property in a transaction other than a nonrecognition transaction (as defined in Code Sec. 7701(a)(45)), the ownership and use of the interest before the transaction won't be taken into account for purposes of applying these rules to taxpayer's later disposition of the interest. (Reg § 1.469-2(c)(2)(iv)) In certain instances, property held in a "dealing activity" (i.e., for sale to customers in the ordinary course of business) is treated as being held in the last nondealing activity in which it was used before its sale. (Reg § 1.469-2(c)(2)(v)(A))[35]

For disposition of *entire* interest in a passive activity, see ¶ 1826.

¶ 1807 Disposition of interest in partnership or S corporation.

Where there is a disposition of a partnership interest or S corporation stock, a ratable portion of the net gain is treated as gain from the disposition of an interest in each trade or business, rental, or investment activity in which the entity owns an interest. (Reg § 1.469-2T(e)(3)(ii)(A))[36] However, gain attributable to certain substantially appreciated property (¶ 1806) is not passive activity gross income if the amount of that gain exceeds 10% of the gain allocated to the activity. (Reg § 1.469-2(e)(3)(iii); Reg § 1.469-2T(e)(3)(iii))[37]

Similarly, a ratable portion of the loss is treated as loss from the disposition of an interest in each trade or business, etc., in which the entity owns an interest. (Reg § 1.469-2T(e)(3)(ii)(A))[38]

¶ 1808 Portfolio income.

Portfolio income (treated as not passive activity gross income, see ¶ 1805) includes all gross income *other than* income derived in the ordinary course of a trade or business (¶ 1809) attributable to:

■ interest;

■ dividends from a C corporation or from an S corporation's accumulated earnings and profits;

■ annuities;

■ royalties;

■ net income from publicly traded partnerships (¶ 1801);

■ income (including dividends) from a RIC (¶ 4201), REIT (¶ 4202), REMIC (¶ 4204), Code Sec. 1381(a) cooperative (¶ 4206), common trust fund (¶ 4209), controlled foreign corporation (¶ 4636) or qualified electing fund (¶ 4643);

■ gain (loss) from the disposition of property that produces portfolio income;

■ gain (loss) from the disposition of property held for investment; (Code Sec. 469(e)(1)(A); Reg § 1.469-2T(c)(3)(ii))

■ income, gain or loss from investment of working capital (¶ 1809).[39]

To the extent taxpayer receives interest income on a loan to a pass-through entity in which he has an ownership interest ("self-charged" interest), the interest isn't treated as portfolio interest income and may be used to offset interest expense passed through to him.[40]

---

34. ¶ M-5305; ¶ 4694.28.   36. ¶ M-5708; ¶ 4694.82.   38. ¶ M-5708; ¶ 4694.82.   40. ¶ M-5312.
35. ¶ M-5307 *et seq.*; ¶ 4694.28.   37. ¶ M-5306.   39. ¶ M-5325 *et seq.*

Footnote references beginning with letters are to paragraphs in RIA's Federal Tax Coordinator 2d and RIA's Analysis of Federal Taxes: Income. Footnote references beginning with numbers are to paragraphs in RIA's United States Tax Reporter.

¶ 1809 When is income derived in the ordinary course of a trade or business?

Income that would otherwise be portfolio income (¶ 1808) is treated as derived in the ordinary course of a trade or business—i.e., *not* portfolio income—only if derived from the trade or business of lending money, from trade accounts receivable, and in certain other limited situations specified in the regs or by IRS. (Reg § 1.469-2T(c)(3)(ii), (iii))[41]

Any income, gain or loss attributable to an investment of working capital is treated as portfolio income, not as derived in the ordinary course of business. (Code Sec. 469(e)(1)(B))[42] "Working capital" is current assets minus current liabilities.[43]

A dealer's income or gain from property is not derived in the ordinary course of a trade or business if the dealer held the property for investment at any time before the income or gain is recognized. (Reg § 1.469-2T(e)(3)(iii)(A))[44]

¶ 1810 Recharacterization of passive income as nonpassive income.

The following income is treated as income that is *not* from a passive activity (Reg § 1.469-2T(f)(1)) (so it can't shelter passive losses from other activities):

(1) A ratable portion of taxpayer's net passive income from each significant participation passive activity (SPPA, see ¶ 1811), if taxpayer's passive activity gross income from all SPPAs exceeds his passive activity deductions from those SPPAs. (Reg § 1.469-2T(f)(2)(i))[45]

(2) Taxpayer's net passive income from a rental activity, if less than 30% of the unadjusted basis of the property used or held for use by customers, is subject to depreciation. (Reg § 1.469-2T(f)(3))[46]

(3) Taxpayer's net rental activity income from an item of property used in certain development activities. (Reg § 1.469-2(f)(5), Reg § 1.469-11(c)(2)(ii))[47]

(4) Taxpayer's net rental activity income from an item of property (not described in (3), above) rented for use in a trade or business in which taxpayer materially participates ("self-rented property"). (Reg § 1.469-2(f)(6))[48]

(5) The lesser of taxpayer's (a) equity-financed interest income from an equity-financed lending activity, or (b) net passive income from the activity. (Reg § 1.469-2T(f)(4))[49]

(6) Taxpayer's net royalty income from intangible property held by a partnership, S corporation, estate or trust if taxpayer acquired his interest in the entity *after* the entity had created the property or had performed substantial services or incurred substantial costs in its development or marketing, (Reg § 1.469-2T(f)(7)(i)) with certain exceptions. (Reg § 1.469-2T(f)(7)(iii))[50]

The amount treated as nonpassive under (1), (2) and (5), above, is limited to the greatest amount treated as nonpassive under *any one* of these rules. (Reg § 1.469-2T(f)(8))[1]

¶ 1811 What is a significant participation passive activity (SPPA)?

A significant participation passive activity (SPPA) is any trade or business in which taxpayer significantly participates (for more than 100 hours) for the tax year but doesn't materially participate (¶ 1814). (Reg § 1.469-2T(f)(2)(ii))[2]

¶ 1812 Passive activity credit defined.

A "passive activity credit" is the amount (if any) by which: (1) the sum of all credits from passive activities ("passive credits," see below) allowable for the tax year, exceeds (2)

---

41. ¶ M-5329 *et seq.*; ¶ 4694.23.
42. ¶ M-5329; ¶ 4694.23.
43. ¶ D-2842.
44. ¶ M-5329.
45. ¶ M-5336; ¶ 4694.25.
46. ¶ M-5338; ¶ 4694.25.
47. ¶ M-5340; ¶ 4694.25.
48. ¶ M-5340; ¶ 4694.25.
49. ¶ M-5339; ¶ 4694.26.
50. ¶ M-5341; ¶ 4694.26.
1. ¶ M-5338 *et seq.*; ¶ 4694.26.
2. ¶ M-5336; ¶ 4694.25.

Footnote references beginning with letters are to paragraphs in RIA's Federal Tax Coordinator 2d and RIA's Analysis of Federal Taxes: Income. Footnote references beginning with numbers are to paragraphs in RIA's United States Tax Reporter.

taxpayer's regular tax liability for the year allocable to all passive activities. (Code Sec. 469(d)(2)) This can be a credit attributable to the tax year arising in connection with the conduct of an activity that is "passive" (¶ 1813) for the year, as well as a credit carried over (¶ 1825) from an earlier tax year in which it was attributable but was disallowed under the passive activity rules. (Reg § 1.469-3T(b)(1))[3]

The regular tax liability allocable to all passive activities ((2) above) is the excess of taxpayer's regular tax liability for the tax year, over the amount of regular tax liability on taxpayer's income *as reduced* by the passive activity loss for the year. (Reg § 1.469-3T(d)(1))[4]

Where taxpayer is a closely held corporation, the passive activity credit for the tax year is reduced by its net active income tax liability. (Code Sec. 469(e)(2); Reg § 1.469-1T(g)(5))[5]

The "passive credits" are the general business credits, the Puerto Rico and possessions credit, the orphan drug clinical testing credit, the alcohol fuels credit, the low income housing credit, the research credit, the credit for fuel from nonconventional sources, (Code Sec. 469(d)(2)(A); Reg § 1.469-3T(b)(1)(i)(B)) and, under certain conditions, the credit attributable to an increase in qualified progress expenditures. (Reg § 1.469-3T(b)(2))[6] For discussion of credits, see ¶ 2300 *et seq.*

Where the activity that gives rise to taxpayer's credit is conducted by a partnership or S corporation, the determination of whether the credit is "passive" is based on taxpayer's participation in the activity (if participation is relevant) for the entity's tax year. (Reg § 1.469-3T(b)(3))[7]

¶ 1813 What is a passive activity?

A passive activity is any activity involving the conduct of any trade or business, in which taxpayer doesn't materially participate (¶ 1814). (Code Sec. 469(c)(1)) A trade or business includes any activity which involves the conduct of business or rental operations that aren't treated as incidental to an activity of holding property for investment, (Reg § 1.469-1(e)(2)) or any activity with respect to which expenses are allowable as a deduction under Code Sec. 212 (for the production, etc., of income). (Code Sec. 469(c)(6))[8] Trade or business also includes any activity involving research or experimentation (under the Code Sec. 174 rules for deducting business-related research or experimental expenditures, see ¶ 1594. (Code Sec. 469(c)(5))[9]

For rental activities, see ¶ 1820.

¶ 1814 What is "material participation"?

A taxpayer materially participates in an activity only if he is involved in the activity's operations on a regular, continuous and substantial basis (¶ 1815 *et seq.*). (Code Sec. 469(h)) A closely held C corporation or personal service corporation materially participates in an activity, in general, only if one or more of its shareholders who own more than 50% of its stock (by value) themselves materially participate. (Code Sec. 469(h)(4)(A))[10]

¶ 1815 Material participation by individuals.

An individual materially participates in an activity for a tax year *if and only if*:

(1) The individual participates (as defined at ¶ 1818) in it for more than 500 hours during the year. (Reg § 1.469-5T(a)(1))

(2) The individual's participation in the activity for the tax year is substantially all of the participation in it by all individuals (including nonowner individuals) for the year.

---

3. ¶ M-5601; ¶ 4694.35.   6. ¶ M-5601; ¶ 4694.35.   8. ¶ M-4800 *et seq.*; ¶s 4694.01,   9. ¶ M-4800 *et seq.*; ¶ 4694.02.
4. ¶ M-5603.   7. ¶ M-5602; ¶ 4694.35.   4694.02.   10. ¶ M-4902 *et seq.*; ¶ 4694.06.
5. ¶ M-5607; ¶ 4694.36.

Footnote references beginning with letters are to paragraphs in RIA's Federal Tax Coordinator 2d and RIA's Analysis of Federal Taxes: Income. Footnote references beginning with numbers are to paragraphs in RIA's United States Tax Reporter.

(Reg § 1.469-5T(a)(2))

(3) The individual participates in the activity for more than 100 hours during the tax year and that isn't less than that of any other individual (including nonowners) for that year. (Reg § 1.469-5T(a)(3))

(4) The activity is a "significant participation activity " for the tax year, and the individual's aggregate participation in all significant participation activities that year exceeds 500 hours. A "significant participation activity" is a trade or business in which the individual significantly participates (for more than 100 hours), but in which he doesn't otherwise materially participate. (Reg § 1.469-5T(a)(4), (c))

(5) The individual materially participated in the activity for any five tax years (consecutive or not) during the ten immediately preceding tax years (including years before the passive activity rules were in effect). (Reg § 1.469-5T(a)(5), Reg § 1.469-11T(a)(4))

(6) The individual materially participated in a personal service activity for any three tax years (consecutive or not) before the tax year, if the activity is a personal service activity. (Reg § 1.469-5T(a)(6))

(7) The individual meets a facts and circumstances test (¶ 1816). (Reg § 1.469-5T(a)(7))[11]

For purposes of (5) and (6), above, taxpayer materially participated in an activity for an earlier tax year if that activity included significant Code Sec. 469 activities that are substantially the same as significant Code Sec. 469 activities that were included in an activity in which taxpayer materially participated (without regard to (5)) for that preceding year. (Reg § 1.469-5(j)(1))[12]

In determining whether an individual materially participated for a pre-'87 tax year, only the more-than-500 hour test ((1), above) applies. (Reg § 1.469-5(j)(2))[13]

¶ 1816 Facts and circumstances test.

An individual materially participates in an activity if he participates on a regular, continuous and substantial basis during the year, based on all the facts and circumstances. (Reg § 1.469-5T(a)(7))[14] An individual who participates in the activity for 100 hours or less during the year doesn't meet this test. (Reg § 1.469-5T(b)(2)(iii))[15]

The fact that the individual (except for certain retirees and surviving spouses, in the case of farming activities) satisfies participation standards under other Code provisions isn't taken into account for this purpose. (Reg § 1.469-5T(b)(2)(i)) Nor is the individual's participation in the management of the activity, unless there's no other paid manager, and no other individual performs management services that exceed (by hours) those performed by the individual. (Reg § 1.469-5T(b)(2)(ii))[16]

¶ 1817 Limited partners.

An individual limited partner is not treated as materially participating in any activity of a limited partnership with respect to his interest in that partnership (or to any gain of loss from the activity recognized on a sale or exchange of that interest) *unless* the individual would be treated as materially participating under the 500-hour, five tax-years-out-of-ten, or three-year-personal-service-activity tests at ¶ 1815 (items (1), (5) or (6), respectively), if he weren't a limited partner. (Code Sec. 469(h)(2); Reg § 1.469-5T(e)(2))[17]

An individual's partnership interest is *not* treated as a limited partnership interest if the individual is a general partner in the partnership at all times during the partnership's tax year ending with or within the individual's tax year. (Reg § 1.469-5T(e)(3)(ii))[18]

---

11. ¶ M-4901 *et seq.*; ¶ 4694.06.   13. ¶ M-4909; ¶ 4694.06.   15. ¶ M-4912; ¶ 4694.06.   17. ¶ M-5003 *et seq.*; ¶ 4694.06.
12. ¶ M-4911; ¶ 4694.06.   14. ¶ M-4912 *et seq.*; ¶ 4694.06.   16. ¶ M-4917; ¶ 4694.06.   18. ¶ M-5004; ¶ 4694.06.

Footnote references beginning with letters are to paragraphs in RIA's Federal Tax Coordinator 2d and RIA's Analysis of Federal Taxes: Income. Footnote references beginning with numbers are to paragraphs in RIA's United States Tax Reporter.

¶ 1818 Participation defined.

Any work done by an individual (without regard to the capacity in which he does the work) in connection with the activity, where the individual owns (directly or indirectly) an interest in the activity at the time the work is done, is treated as participation by that individual in the activity, except as otherwise provided. (Reg § 1.469-5(f)(1))[19]

Work not of a type customarily done by an owner isn't treated as participation if one of its principal purposes is to avoid the passive loss rules. (Reg § 1.469-5T(f)(2)(i))[20]

An individual's work as an investor is not participation unless the individual is directly involved in day-to-day management or operations. (Reg § 1.469-5T(f)(2)(ii))[21]

¶ 1819 Spouse's participation.

In determining whether a married taxpayer materially participates in an activity, the participation of taxpayer's spouse is taken into account, (Code Sec. 469(h)(5)) without regard to whether the spouse owns an interest in the activity, or whether the spouses file a joint return for the year. (Reg § 1.469-5T(f)(3))[22]

¶ 1820 Rental activities.

Rental activities are passive activities (Code Sec. 469(c)(2)) without regard to material participation (Code Sec. 469(c)(4)) (except for the $25,000 allowance under the "active participation" test, see ¶ 1821, and post-'93 material participation by certain persons in the real property business, see ¶ 1824).[23]

A rental activity is any activity where payments are principally for the use of tangible property, (Code Sec. 469(j)(8)) without regard to whether a lease, service contract, or other arrangement is involved. (Reg § 1.469-1T(e)(3)(i)(B)) However, a rental activity doesn't include an activity involving the use of tangible property if:

(1) The average period the customer uses the property is—

... seven days or less, (Reg § 1.469-1T(e)(3)(ii)(A)) or

... 30 days or less, and the owner (or someone on the owner's behalf) provides significant personal services (as defined in the regs). (Reg § 1.469-1T(e)(3)(ii)(B))

(2) The owner (or someone on the owner's behalf) provides extraordinary personal services (as defined in the regs), without regard to the average period the customer uses the property. (Reg § 1.469-1T(e)(3)(ii)(C))

(3) The rental of the tangible property is incidental to a nonrental activity of taxpayer (Reg § 1.469-1T(e)(3)(ii)(D)) (as measured by certain percentage and other tests). (Reg § 1.469-1T(e)(3)(vi))

(4) Taxpayer customarily makes the property available during defined business hours for nonexclusive use by various customers (Reg § 1.469-1T(e)(3)(ii)(E)) (e.g., a golf course).

(5) The property is provided for use in a nonrental activity of a partnership, joint venture, or S corporation in which taxpayer owns an interest, where taxpayer provided the property in his capacity as owner of that interest (Reg § 1.469-1T(e)(3)(ii)(F)) (not as a renter of the property to the partnership, etc.).[24]

¶ 1821 The $25,000 allowance for 10%-or-more owner who actively participates in rental real estate activity.

A natural person who: (1) has at least a 10% interest in any rental real estate activity (¶ 1822), and (2) otherwise "actively participates" in that activity (¶ 1823), may offset up to $25,000 of nonpassive income with that portion of the passive activity loss, or of the

---

19. ¶ M-4902; ¶ 4694.06.   21. ¶ M-4903; ¶ 4694.06.   23. ¶ M-5000 et seq.; ¶s 4694.01,   24. ¶ M-5101 et seq.; ¶ 4694.03.
20. ¶ M-4903; ¶ 4694.06.   22. ¶ M-4902; ¶ 4694.06.   4694.60, 4694.63.

Footnote references beginning with letters are to paragraphs in RIA's Federal Tax Coordinator 2d and RIA's Analysis of Federal Taxes: Income. Footnote references beginning with numbers are to paragraphs in RIA's United States Tax Reporter.

deduction equivalent of the passive activity credit, attributable to that activity. (Code Sec. 469(i)(1), (2))[25]

The $25,000 allowance is $12,500 for a married person filing a separate return who lives apart from his spouse at all times during the tax year, (Code Sec. 469(i)(5)(A)(i)) and zero for a married person filing a separate return who does not live apart from his spouse at all times during the tax year. (Code Sec. 469(i)(5)(B))[26]

The $25,000 ($12,500) is reduced (but not below zero) by 50% of the amount by which taxpayer's adjusted gross income (AGI) exceeds $100,000 ($50,000 for married persons filing separately). (Code Sec. 469(i)(3)(A), (5))[27]

observation: Thus, the $25,000 is phased out completely for a taxpayer with AGI of $150,000 ($75,000 for married persons filing separately).

¶ 1822 Who is a 10%-or-more owner?

An individual is a 10%-or-more owner with respect to any interest in any rental real estate activity for any period only if *at all times* during that period (i.e., the tax year or shorter period the individual held the interest) his interest was at least 10% (by value) of all interests in that activity. (Code Sec. 469(i)(6)(A)) The individual's interest includes any interest of his spouse (Code Sec. 469(i)(6)(D)) even if they don't file a joint return.[28]

Separate buildings (and smaller units, also) are treated as separate activities if the degree of integration of the business and other relevant factors don't require treating them as parts of a larger activity (e.g., an integrated shopping center).[29]

¶ 1823 What is "active participation"?

Taxpayer must participate in an activity in a significant and bona fide sense to actively participate in it. Taxpayer participates if he makes management decisions, e.g., approves new tenants, decides on rental terms, approves capital or repair expenditures or arranges for others to provide services (such as repairs). He need not have regular, continuous and substantial involvement in operations. However, a merely formal and nominal participation in management, without a genuine exercise of independent discretion and judgment, is insufficient.[30] The active participation test is less stringent than the material participation requirement (¶ 1814).[31]

In determining whether taxpayer actively participates, the participation of taxpayer's spouse is taken into account. (Code Sec. 469(i)(6)(D))[32]

Taxpayer is not treated as actively participating (except as regs may provide) with respect to any interest as a limited partner. (Code Sec. 469(i)(6)(C))[33]

¶ 1824 Exception for post-'93 material participation in real property business.

For any tax year beginning after '93 in which a taxpayer qualifies, the rule that treats all rental activities as passive activities does not apply. (Code Sec. 469(c)(2))[34]

For a taxpayer to qualify for the tax break for a particular post-'93 tax year:

■ more than half of the personal services that the taxpayer performs during that year must be performed in real property trades or businesses in which the taxpayer materially participates, (Code Sec. 469(c)(7)(B)(i)) and

■ the taxpayer must perform more than 750 hours of services during the tax year in real property trades or businesses in which the taxpayer materially participates. (Code Sec. 469(c)(7)(B)(ii))[35]

If a joint return is filed, the above requirements are satisfied only if either spouse

---

25. ¶ M-5110; ¶ 4694.60. 28. ¶ M-5112 *et seq.*; ¶ 4694.60. 31. ¶ M-5111; ¶ 4694.60. 34. ; ¶ 4694.63.

26. ¶ M-5110; ¶ 4694.60. 29. ¶ M-5112. 32. ¶ M-5111; ¶ 4694.70. 35. ¶ M-5120.2; ¶ 4694.63.

27. ¶ M-5110; ¶ 4694.60. 30. ¶ M-5111. 33. ¶ M-5111; ¶ 4694.60.

Footnote references beginning with letters are to paragraphs in RIA's Federal Tax Coordinator 2d and RIA's Analysis of Federal Taxes: Income. Footnote references beginning with numbers are to paragraphs in RIA's United States Tax Reporter.

separately satisfies each requirement. (Code Sec. 469(c)(7)(B))[36]

A closely-held C corporation qualifies if more than 50% of its gross receipts for the tax year are derived from real property trades or businesses in which it materially participates. (Code Sec. 469(c)(7)(D)(i))[37]

⬥*observation:* In other words, a taxpayer who materially participates in a rental real estate activity avoids automatic passive activity characterization (and therefore may use any losses or credits generated by the activity to offset other, non-passive income).

The above rules are applied as if each interest of the taxpayer in rental real estate were a separate activity. (Code Sec. 469(c)(7)(A)(ii)) However, the taxpayer can elect to treat all interests in rental real estate as one activity. (Code Sec. 469(c)(7)(A))

A real property trade or business is any real property development, redevelopment, construction, reconstruction, acquisition, conversion, rental, operation, management, leasing or brokerage trade or business. (Code Sec. 469(c)(7)(C))[38]

Services performed as an employee are disregarded unless the employee is a more-than-5%-owner of the employer. (Code Sec. 469(c)(7)(D))[39]

¶ 1825 Carryover of disallowed deductions and credits.

Any deduction (or credit) from a passive activity that is disallowed under the passive loss rules for a tax year is allocated among taxpayer's activities for the next tax year in a manner that reasonably reflects the extent each activity continues the business and rental operations that made up the loss activity. As so allocated, it is treated as a deduction (or credit) from that activity for that next tax year. (Code Sec. 469(b); Reg § 1.469-1(f)(4)(i))

¶ 1826 Disposition of taxpayer's entire interest in passive activity.

If a taxpayer disposes of his entire interest in any passive activity (or former passive activity), and all gain or loss realized on the disposition is recognized, the excess of: (1) the sum of any loss from the activity for the year of disposition (including any carryover losses, see ¶ 1825), plus any loss realized on disposition, over (2) the net income or gain for that tax year from all passive activities (without regard to the losses in (1)), is treated as loss *not* from a passive activity. (Code Sec. 469(g)(1)(A))[40]

Where the disposition is by installment sale, the amount treated as a nonpassive loss is the portion of the losses from each tax year that bears the same ratio to all these losses as the gain recognized on the sale bears to the gross profit from the sale. (Code Sec. 469(g)(3))[41]

Special rules apply where a disposition is to a related party, (Code Sec. 469(g)(1)(B)) where the interest in the activity is transferred by death (Code Sec. 469(g)(2)) and where a disposition is by gift. (Code Sec. 469(j)(6))[42]

¶ 1827 Effect of passive loss rules on other Code Sections.

A passive activity deduction disallowed for a tax year under the passive activity rules is not taken into account as a deduction in computing taxable income. (Reg § 1.469-1T(d)(3)) But, a passive activity deduction that is allowed under the passive activity rules may still be disallowed under the Code Sec. 613A limit on percentage depletion of oil and gas wells, or under the Code Sec. 1211 limit on capital losses. (Reg § 1.469-1(d)(2))[43]

¶ 1828 Net Operating Losses (NOLs) ▰▰▰▰▰▰▰▰▰▰▰▰▰▰▰▰▰▰▰▰

An NOL sustained in one year may be used to reduce the taxable income for

---

36. ¶ M-5120.3; ¶ 4694.63.   38. ¶ M-5120.6; ¶ 4694.63.   40. ¶ M-5701; ¶ 4694.50.   42. ¶ M-5704 *et seq.*; ¶ 4694.50.
37. ¶ M-5120.4; ¶ 4694.63.   39. ¶ M-5120.5; ¶ 4694.63.   41. ¶ M-5701; ¶ 4694.50.   43. ¶ M-4603; ¶ 4694.47.

Footnote references beginning with letters are to paragraphs in RIA's Federal Tax Coordinator 2d and RIA's Analysis of Federal Taxes: Income. Footnote references beginning with numbers are to paragraphs in RIA's United States Tax Reporter.

another year's. It may be carried back to earlier years and yield tax refunds. If not exhausted in earlier years (or if taxpayer elects not to use the carryback) it may be carried forward to later years and reduce the tax for those years.

¶ 1829 NOL defined.

An NOL is the excess of business deductions (computed with certain modifications) over gross income in a particular tax year. A deduction is allowed for that loss, through an NOL carryback or carryover, in some other tax year(s) in which gross income exceeds business deductions. (Code Sec. 172)[44]

An NOL deduction is allowed to individuals, corporations, (Code Sec. 172) estates and trusts. (Code Sec. 642(d)) It isn't allowed to partnerships (Code Sec. 703(a)(2)(D)) or common trust funds (Code Sec. 584(g)) (but the deduction is allowed to the partners beneficiaries),[45] regulated investment companies, (Code Sec. 852(b)(2)(B)) or S corporations (losses are passed through to shareholders). (Code Sec. 1366(a))[46]

¶ 1830 NOL carryovers and carrybacks.

Ordinarily, an NOL may be carried back three years and forward 15 years. (Code Sec. 172(b)(1)(A))[47] A decedent's NOL can be carried back, but not forward.[48]

An NOL attributable to a product liability loss may be carried back for ten years. (Code Sec. 172(b)(1)(C)) The carry *forward* is the usual 15 years. (Code Sec. 172(b)(1)(A)(ii)) (The ten-year carryback is not precluded by making the election at ¶ 1831 to forgo the carryback.) (Reg § 1.172-13(c)(4)) To carry back the loss under the regular three-year/15-year rules, taxpayer must so elect. (Code Sec. 172(f)(6))[49]

Other carryback or carryover periods apply to banks, small business investment companies and REITs. (Code Sec. 172(b)(1))[50]

Special rules limit the carryback of losses attributable to interest allocable to a corporate equity reduction transaction (CERT). (Code Sec. 172(b)(1)(E), (h))[1]

¶ 1831 Election to forgo NOL carryback.

Any taxpayer may elect not to use the carryback period and instead only carry over the NOL for the allowed *carryover* period. Once the election is made for any tax year it is irrevocable for that year. (Code Sec. 172(b)(3))[2]

¶ 1832 How the NOL deduction works.

Assume an NOL sustained in '93:

STEP (1). Compute the NOL. Note some deductions aren't allowed for this purpose (¶ 1833 *et seq.*).

STEP (2). Find the earliest year to which this loss can be carried (here '90).

STEP (3). Add this loss to all other NOLs carried to the year ('90), and deduct the total as an *NOL deduction.* Note that the '93 loss is fully absorbed if '90 taxable income (before NOL deduction) exceeds the sum of '93 loss, plus pre-'93 losses, carried to '90. File for refund if applicable.

STEP (4). To the extent the '93 loss isn't deducted in '90, it's carried to the next earliest year to which it may be carried ('91). Note that the amount carried to '91 is reduced by "intervening years' modifications" (¶ 1836).

STEP (5). Repeat step (3)—that is, add the '93 loss that may be carried to the next year ('91) to all other NOLs carried to that year, and deduct the total as an NOL deduction.

---

44. ¶ M-4100 *et seq.*; ¶ 1724.　　47. ¶ M-4301; ¶ 1724.08.　　49. ¶ M-4322; ¶ 1724.08.　　1. ¶ M-4306 *et seq.*; ¶ 1724.08.
45. ¶ M-4003.　　48. ¶ M-4004.　　50. ¶ M-4326 *et seq.*; ¶ 1724.08.　　2. ¶ M-4303; ¶ 1724.08.
46. ¶ M-4003; ¶ 1724 *et seq.*

Footnote references beginning with letters are to paragraphs in RIA's Federal Tax Coordinator 2d and RIA's Analysis of Federal Taxes: Income. Footnote references beginning with numbers are to paragraphs in RIA's United States Tax Reporter.

LATER STEPS. Repeat steps (3) and (4) until the full amount of the NOL is deducted or the number of years to which it may be carried is exhausted, whichever happens first.[3]

¶ 1833 Computing the NOL for noncorporate taxpayers.

To compute one year's NOL (which may be carried to another year), start with the deficit in taxable income for the year, and then make these modifications:

■ NOL carryback or carryover deduction from other years. Not allowed.

■ Personal exemptions. Not allowed.

■ Capital losses. Deduction allowed to a limited extent.

■ Nonbusiness deductions. Deduction allowed to a limited extent. (Code Sec. 172(d)); Reg § 1.172-3(a))[4]

¶ 1834 Computing the NOL for corporate taxpayers.

A corporation's NOL is figured the same as its taxable income. But in computing the NOL for the year:

■ NOL carrybacks and carryovers from other years aren't deducted;

■ the deduction for dividends received is taken without limiting it by a percentage of the corporation's taxable income;

■ the deduction for dividends paid on certain preferred stock of public utilities is computed without limiting it to the taxable income for the year. (Code Sec. 172(d)); Reg § 1.172-2(a))[5]

¶ 1835 Amount of NOL deduction.

The NOL deduction in any year is the sum of all NOL carrybacks and carryovers to that year. (Code Sec. 172(a))[6]

Where a husband and wife who make a joint return for the deduction year made a joint return for all other tax years involved in computing the NOL deduction, that deduction is computed on the basis of their joint NOLs and combined taxable incomes. (Reg § 1.172-7(c)) Special rules apply if they didn't make joint returns for all applicable years. (Reg § 1.172-7)[7]

For refunds based on NOL carrybacks, see ¶ 4847. For limits on the NOL deduction for alternative minimum tax purpose, see ¶ 3211.

¶ 1836 Loss exceeds income in year to which carried; "intervening year."

If the NOL carried to an earlier tax year exceeds the taxable income for that year, modifications must be made in that year's taxable income, in computing the unused portion of the NOL that can be carried to the current year. These "intervening year modifications" apply only in computing NOL carryovers, and don't affect taxable income for other purposes. (Code Sec. 172(b)(2); Reg § 1.172-5)[8]

¶ 1837 Deduction for Bad Debts

Bad debts are deductible whether or not connected with taxpayer's business. Deduction is allowed for total worthlessness and, in some cases, for partial worthlessness, of a debt.

Business bad debts are deductible as ordinary deductions. They are deductible if partly worthless as well as when wholly worthless. Nonbusiness bad debts are deducted only as

---

3. ¶ M-4402; ¶ 1724.06.   6. ¶ M-4401; ¶ 1724.06.   8. ¶ M-4200 et seq.; ¶s 1724,
4. ¶ M-4109; ¶ 1724.09.   7. ¶ M-4407; ¶ 1724.03.   1724.06(b), 1724.10.
5. ¶ M-4105; ¶ 1724.09.

Footnote references beginning with letters are to paragraphs in RIA's Federal Tax Coordinator 2d and RIA's Analysis of Federal Taxes: Income. Footnote references beginning with numbers are to paragraphs in RIA's United States Tax Reporter.

short-term capital losses, and only when wholly worthless (¶ 1842).[9]

An item can't be deductible both as a bad debt and as a loss. If it could be treated as either, it must be treated as a bad debt.[10]

However, a worthless debt that is evidenced by a security, and is owed by a corporation or a government, is a loss, and not a bad debt, unless owed to a bank. (Code Sec. 165(g), Code Sec. 166(e), Code Sec. 582(a))[11]

¶ 1838 Bad debts of guarantors.

If taxpayer makes a guarantee agreement in the course of his trade or business, he's entitled to a business bad debt deduction for any payment he makes as guarantor, of principal or interest. (Reg § 1.166-9(a))[12]

If taxpayer makes a guarantee agreement in a transaction for profit (but not in the course of his business), and he makes a payment of principal or interest, he's entitled to a nonbusiness bad debt deduction in the year his right of subrogation becomes totally worthless. (Reg § 1.166-9(b))[13]

¶ 1839 When worthless debt is deductible.

Deduction is allowed for the tax year the debt becomes wholly worthless. (For *partial* worthlessness of *business* debts, see ¶ 1841.) Taxpayer must show the debt had value at the beginning of the year and no value at the end, and that the worthlessness occurred in the particular tax year claimed.[14]

Worthlessness is a question of fact requiring consideration of all pertinent evidence, including the debtor's financial condition and the value of any security. (Reg § 1.166-2(a))[15]

Ordinarily, there's some identifiable event that demonstrates a debt's worthlessness, such as the debtor's bankruptcy or death, though these events may not be conclusive.[16]

¶ 1840 Amount of bad debt deduction.

The amount deductible for a wholly worthless debt is its adjusted basis for determining loss on a sale or exchange (¶ 2400 *et seq.*), regardless of its face value. (Code Sec. 166(b); Reg § 1.166-1(d))[17] The adjustments used to figure adjusted basis are generally the debtor's payments on the debt. But a deduction allowed for a debt's partial worthlessness reduces the debt's basis to that extent, whether or not taxpayer got a tax benefit from his deduction.[18]

No deduction is allowed if the creditor (taxpayer) has no basis for the debt.[19] Thus, there's no deduction for wages, rents, alimony, etc., that were never received unless these items were included in income. (Reg § 1.166-1(e))[20] Where taxpayer reports receivables at fair market value (FMV) rather than face, the deduction can't exceed FMV. (Reg § 1.166-1(d)(2))[21]

Where taxpayer fails to prove a debt's exact basis, it may be estimated by the court if taxpayer proves his right to *some* deduction.[22]

If a debt is compromised because of inability to pay the full amount, taxpayer deducts the debt's adjusted basis minus any cash and the value of any property received. If the debt is compromised for some other reason, taxpayer does not have a bad debt (but may have a loss).[23]

---

9. ¶ M-2900 *et seq.*; ¶ 1664.
10. ¶ M-2503; ¶ 1654.040.
11. ¶s M-3301, M-3309;
    ¶ 1664.160.
12. ¶ M-3207; ¶ 1664.450.

13. ¶ M-3210; ¶ 1664.450.
14. ¶ M-2700; ¶ 1664.220.
15. ¶ M-2702; ¶ 1664.220.
16. ¶ M-2703; ¶ 1664.225.

17. ¶ M-2402; ¶ 1664.210.
18. ¶s M-2406; M-2407;
    ¶ 1664.270.
19. ¶ M-2404; ¶ 1664.210.

20. ¶ M-2506; ¶ 1664.210.
21. ¶ M-2402; ¶ 1664.210.
22. ¶ M-2405.
23. ¶ M-2408.

Footnote references beginning with letters are to paragraphs in RIA's Federal Tax Coordinator 2d and RIA's Analysis of Federal Taxes: Income. Footnote references beginning with numbers are to paragraphs in RIA's United States Tax Reporter.

¶ 1841   Deduction for partially worthless business debts.

A deduction is allowed for partially worthless debts *only if*:

- the debt is a business debt;
- IRS is satisfied that the specific debt is recoverable only in part;
- the amount deducted was *charged off* on the books during the tax year; *and*
- the debt is not evidenced by a security. (Code Sec. 162(a)(2), (d)(1), Code Sec. 166(e))[24]

For deductibility of "worthless securities" as a loss, see ¶ 1769.

Taxpayer may charge off and deduct a debt for partial worthlessness as it occurs. Or he can defer charge-off and deduction to a later year when partial worthlessness is greater, thus deducting several years' partial worthlessness in one year. Or he can defer deduction until total worthlessness.[25]

¶ 1842   Business v. nonbusiness bad debts.

The need to determine whether a debt is a business or nonbusiness debt (¶ 1843) arises only for noncorporate taxpayers, because a corporation's debts are always business debts. (Code Sec. 166(d))[26]

- Business bad debts are fully deductible against income, (Code Sec. 166(a)) while non-business bad debts are short-term capital losses of limited deductibility. (Code Sec. 166(d)(1)(B))[27]

- Business and nonbusiness debts are deductible when wholly worthless, but only business debts are deductible when partly worthless. (Code Sec. 166(a), (d)(1)(A))[28]

¶ 1843   When a debt is a business debt.

A *business debt* is either:

- a debt created or acquired in the course of taxpayer's trade or business (whether or not it was related to that business when it became worthless); or

- a debt the loss from whose worthlessness is incurred in taxpayer's trade or business. This applies if the loss is proximately related to taxpayer's business when the debt becomes worthless. A bad debt is proximately related to business if business is the dominant motivation for the debt. (Reg § 1.166-5(b))[29]

A *nonbusiness debt* is a debt other than a business debt. (Code Sec. 166(d)(2); Reg § 1.166-5(b), (d))[30]

¶ 1844   Shareholders' loans or guarantees for their corporations as business debts.

A shareholder in a corporation can't treat the corporation's business as his business even if he's the sole shareholder. Thus, an individual shareholder's loan to his corporation isn't a business debt unless he shows the debt is related to his own business.[31]

Devoting one's time and energies to the affairs of a corporation is not of itself a trade or business. But a shareholder's loan to his corporation can be a business debt if he's in the business of promoting, financing, and selling corporations. He must be seeking other than a mere investor's return, since investing isn't a business.[32]

If the shareholder is also an officer or other employee of the corporation, he may claim the loan, guarantee, or indemnity was made to protect his job (i.e., a business debt

---

24. ¶ M-2800 *et seq.*; ¶ 1664.270   27. ¶s M-2401; M-2901;   29. ¶ M-2902; ¶ 1664.301.
    et seq.   ¶s 1664.210, 1664.300.   30. ¶ M-2902; ¶ 1664.301.
25. ¶ M-2801; ¶ 1664.270 *et seq.*   28. ¶s M-2401; M-2800;   31. ¶ M-2904; ¶ 1664.303.
26. ¶ M-2800; ¶s 1664, 1664.300.   ¶s 1664.210, 1664.270,   32. ¶ M-2911; ¶ 1664.302.
                                    1664.300.

Footnote references beginning with letters are to paragraphs in RIA's Federal Tax Coordinator 2d and RIA's Analysis of Federal Taxes: Income. Footnote references beginning with numbers are to paragraphs in RIA's United States Tax Reporter.

because connected with his business of being an employee). Business debt status is allowed if his dominant motive (not just a significant motive) for the loan, etc., was to protect his job. Which motive is dominant is determined by several factors, especially the amount of salary as compared to the amount invested. These principles also apply to a shareholder-employee who claims that his loan or guarantee for another corporation (e.g., his corporation's customer) was to protect his job.[33]

---

33. ¶ M-2914 *et seq.*; ¶ 1664.309.

Footnote references beginning with letters are to paragraphs in RIA's Federal Tax Coordinator 2d and RIA's Analysis of Federal Taxes: Income. Footnote references beginning with numbers are to paragraphs in RIA's United States Tax Reporter.

Chapter 5 MACRS, ACRS, Depreciation, Amortization of Intangibles, Depletion

¶ 1900 The Depreciation Allowance ▬▬▬▬▬▬

The Code allows an annual deduction of a portion of the cost or other basis of capital assets used during the year in a trade or business or held for the production of income. This annual deduction may be depreciation under the Modified Accelerated Cost Recovery System (MACRS) or under pre-'87 ACRS, or "useful-life" depreciation, generally for pre-'81 depreciable property. Fifteen-year amortization applies for Section 197 intangibles. For certain "depreciable" property amortization or depletion is allowed instead of a depreciation deduction.

Except for the limited Section 179 expense deduction, discussed at ¶ 1956 *et seq.*, a taxpayer who buys business or income-producing property with a useful-life of more than one year cannot deduct its full cost as an expense for that year. (Code Sec. 263(a); Reg § 1.263(a)-2(a)) Instead, recovery of the cost of that property must be spread over more than one year.

The annual deduction is called a "Modified-ACRS" depreciation deduction or "MACRS" deduction (either under the speedy general depreciation system—"GDS"—or the straight-line alternative depreciation system—"ADS") if it applies to recovery property (defined at ¶ 1909) placed in service after '86 (and not excluded from MACRS). (Code Sec. 168)

The annual deduction is called an "ACRS deduction" (or "cost recovery deduction") if it applies to recovery property placed in service after '80 and subject to pre-'87 ACRS, see ¶ 1936 *et seq.*

The annual deduction is called a "depreciation deduction" if it applies to property placed in service before '81, or if it applies to property placed in service after '80 that doesn't qualify for MACRS or ACRS. (Code Sec. 167)[1]

The annual deduction is called "amortization," if it applies to any intangible property (e.g., lease acquisition costs, see ¶ 1921; or research and experimental expenditures, see ¶ 1594 and to certain tangible property discussed at ¶ 1986 *et seq.*[2] Fifteen-year amortization applies to Section 197 intangibles, see ¶ 1989 *et seq.*

The annual deduction is called "depletion" (¶ 1993 *et seq.*) if it applies to exhaustible natural deposits, i.e., oil and gas, or timber. (Code Sec. 611)[3]

Form 4562 is used to claim the deduction for depreciation. Individuals and other non-corporate taxpayers (including S corporations) don't have to complete or attach Form 4562 if the only depreciation claimed is for assets (other than listed property, see ¶ 1959) placed in service before the tax year.[4]

¶ 1901 What property is depreciable?

Real property (except land, as explained below), personal property and intangibles (as explained at (¶ 1902)) are depreciable if the property:

- is used in a trade or business, or held for the production of income; (Code Sec. 167(a))[5]

- has an exhaustible useful-life that can be determined with reasonable accuracy; (Reg § 1.167(a)-1(b))[6] and

- is not inventory, stock in trade (Reg § 1.167(a)-2) or property held as an investment.[7]

Property isn't depreciable if it isn't exhaustible or subject to wear and tear, such as land, (Reg § 1.167(a)-2) radium,[8] goodwill, (Reg § 1.167(a)-3)[9] natural resources such as

---

1. ¶ L-7502; ¶s 1674, 2634 *et seq.*
2. ¶ L-12501 *et seq.*
3. ¶ N-2250 *et seq.*; ¶s 6109, 6114 *et seq.*

4. ¶ L-7500; ¶ 1674.001.
5. ¶ L-7900 *et seq.*; ¶ 1674.006 *et seq.*

6. ¶ L-7903 *et seq.*; ¶ 1674.006 *et seq.*
7. ¶ L-7905; ¶ 1674.006 *et seq.*

8. ¶ L-7903.
9. ¶ L-8002; ¶s 1674.006(b), 1674.007, 1674.013.

Footnote references beginning with letters are to paragraphs in RIA's Federal Tax Coordinator 2d and RIA's Analysis of Federal Taxes: Income. Footnote references beginning with numbers are to paragraphs in RIA's United States Tax Reporter.

oil, gas or minerals in the ground (Reg § 1.167(a)-2) (which instead qualify for *depletion*).[10]

The mere fact that property diminishes in value doesn't mean that the property is depreciable. If the decrease in value isn't the result of exhaustion, wear and tear or obsolescence, it isn't depreciable. (Reg § 1.167(a)-1(a))[11]

Property used solely for personal purposes, isn't depreciable. (Reg § 1.167(a)-2) Where the same property is used both for personal and for business or income producing purposes, depreciation is deductible only to the extent of nonpersonal uses.[12] Property acquired for personal use but later converted to business or income-production is depreciable from the date of conversion.[13]

¶ 1902 Are intangible assets depreciable?

Patents and copyrights are depreciable. (Reg § 1.163(a)-3)[14] The Supreme Court has said that intangible assets, like a subscription list, are depreciable if they are used in a trade or business and have a limited, ascertainable useful life. Mass assets such as customers-list of accounts, supply or location contract rights, licenses or franchises, non-competition rights, insurance expirations, credit information files, etc., are depreciable.[15]

However, for property acquired after Aug. 10, '93 (or electively after July 25, '91), 15-year amortization applies to section 197 intangibles, see ¶ 1989 *et seq.* Certain property excluded from 15-year amortization is depreciated under specific useful-life rules, see ¶ 1971. Depreciation is to be computed under regs to be prescribed for certain rights to receive tangible property or services, interests in patents and copyrights and contract rights good for less than 15 years or fixed in amount. (Code Sec. 167(f)(2))[16]

¶ 1903 Who is entitled to depreciation deductions?

Ordinarily the owner of depreciable property is the person entitled to deduct depreciation.[17] This is the equitable owner, and not the owner of bare legal title.[18]

A *lessor* (landlord) deducts depreciation on property that is already on the leased premises when he leases out the property and on any improvements he constructs during the term of the lease. (Reg § 1.167(a)-4) But he can't deduct depreciation where the lease requires the lessee to replace property at the lessee's expense because the lessor suffers no "depreciable" loss, i.e., wear and tear, etc.[19]

A person who inherits property subject to a lease deducts depreciation only on the same improvements that the decedent lessor could depreciate.[20]

A *lessee* (tenant) may ordinarily deduct depreciation with respect to the cost of improvements he makes, see ¶ 1921. Costs of acquiring a lease are amortizable, not depreciable,[21] see ¶ 1921.

If a life tenancy is in depreciable property, the life tenant deducts depreciation as if he were the absolute owner of the property. (Code Sec. 167(d)) After the life tenant's death, the depreciation deduction, if any, is allowed to the remainderman. (Reg § 1.167(h)-1)[22]

A tenant-stockholder of a cooperative housing corporation who uses his proprietary lease in a trade or business or for the production of income, depreciates the portion of the cost of his stock allocable to depreciable property. (Code Sec. 216(c)(1)) The allowance for depreciation is limited to the adjusted basis of the stock. But depreciation in excess of adjusted basis may be carried over to later years. (Code Sec. 216(c)(2))[23]

---

10. ¶s L-7929, N-2250 *et seq.*; ¶ 6109 *et seq.*
11. ¶ L-7501.
12. ¶ L-7908; ¶ 1674.006.
13. ¶s L-7915, L-7933.
14. ¶ L-8025 *et seq.*; ¶ 1674.025.
15. ¶ L-8011 *et seq.*; ¶ 1674.013.
16. ¶ L-8030; ¶ 1674.013.
17. ¶ L-7802; ¶ 1674.002.
18. ¶ L-7803 *et seq.*; ¶ 1674.002.
19. ¶ L-7808; ¶ 1674.023.
20. ¶ L-7811; ¶ 1674.023.
21. ¶ L-7809; ¶s 1624.323, 1674.023.
22. ¶ L-7830; ¶ 1674.117.
23. ¶s K-5918 *et seq.*, L-7828; ¶ 2164.01.

Footnote references beginning with letters are to paragraphs in RIA's Federal Tax Coordinator 2d and RIA's Analysis of Federal Taxes: Income. Footnote references beginning with numbers are to paragraphs in RIA's United States Tax Reporter.

¶ 1904   When depreciation deduction is taken.

The deduction of the cost of depreciable property is spread out over its recovery period, see ¶ 1922, or its useful-life. (Reg § 1.263(a)-1, Reg § 1.263(a)-2)[24] For the limited Section 179 expense election, see ¶ 1956.

Failure to take a deduction in one year doesn't allow a taxpayer to take a larger deduction in a later year. (Reg § 1.167(a)-10(a)) But a taxpayer who failed to deduct allowable depreciation for a year can claim a refund for that year (if still open) where his failure to deduct resulted in an overpayment of tax.[25]

¶ 1905   When depreciation begins.

The depreciation period generally begins when the asset is placed in service. (Reg § 1.167(a)-10(b))

Once an asset is placed in service, depreciation conventions govern when depreciation begins, see ¶ 1907.

An asset is "placed in service" when it is in a condition or state of readiness and availability for a specifically defined function.[26] Once an asset is placed in service, neither insufficiency of earnings, nor temporary idleness of the asset (without its withdrawal from business purposes), prevents a deduction for depreciation or amortization.[27]

For when depreciation begins for additions or improvements to realty, see ¶ 1920.

¶ 1906   When depreciation ends.

The allowance of a deduction for depreciation ends when the asset is retired from service, or its cost or other basis is fully recovered, or it is sold or disposed of—whichever occurs first. (Code Sec. 167, Code Sec. 168(d); Reg § 1.167(a)-10(b), Reg § 1.167(b)-0(a))

For assets not retired, depreciation conventions govern when depreciation ends, see ¶ 1907.

¶ 1907   Depreciation conventions govern when depreciation begins or ends.

Depreciation conventions are prescribed for recovery property, (Code Sec. 168(a)(3), (d)) see ¶ 1925 *et seq.*, and are optional for nonrecovery (e.g., useful-life) property.[28]

The prescribed depreciation conventions for recovery property are the mid-month or full-month conventions for real property, (Code Sec. 168(d)(2))[29] see ¶s 1925 and 1946; and the half-year or mid-quarter conventions for depreciable personal property, (Code Sec. 168(d)(1), (d)(3))[30] see ¶ 1926.

The half-year convention treats all property placed in service during any tax year or disposed of during any tax year as placed in service or disposed of on the mid-point of such tax year. (Code Sec. 168(d)(4)(A)) The mid-quarter convention treats property as placed in service or disposed of on the mid-point of the applicable quarter. (Code Sec. 168(d)(4)(C))

illustration: A calendar year taxpayer actually placed in service a computer on Jan. 2 of the current year. If the half-year convention applies to this depreciable property (see ¶ 1926), the deemed placed in service date is July 1 of the current year—thus, only a half-year depreciation is allowed for the computer for the current year. If the first quarter's mid-quarter convention applies (see ¶ 1926), the deemed placed in service date for the computer is mid-Feb. of the current year—thus, only 10.5 months of depreciation is allowed for the current year.

---

24. ¶s L-5601 *et seq.*, L-5701; ¶ 2634 *et seq.*
25. ¶ L-7507; ¶ 1674.085(a).
26. ¶ L-7602; ¶ 1674.085.
27. ¶ L-7704.
28. ¶ L-7610 *et seq.*; ¶s 1674.056, 1674.085(c).
29. ¶s L-8713, L-11210 *et seq.*; ¶ 1684.01.
30. ¶ L-8703 *et seq.*; ¶ 1684.01.

Footnote references beginning with letters are to paragraphs in RIA's Federal Tax Coordinator 2d and RIA's Analysis of Federal Taxes: Income. Footnote references beginning with numbers are to paragraphs in RIA's United States Tax Reporter.

The mid-month convention for MACRS realty treats such property placed in service during any tax year or disposed of during any tax year as placed in service or disposed of on the mid-point of such month, see ¶ 1925. For the full-month convention for pre-'87 ACRS realty, see ¶ 1946.

Where no depreciation convention is adopted for useful-life depreciable property (¶ 1971 *et seq.*), a proportionate part of one year's depreciation is allowed for that part of the first year during which the asset was placed in service. (Reg § 1.167(a)-10(b))

¶ 1908 Depreciation deduction for year of sale or disposition.

Depreciation deductions under MACRS are allowed up to the day of sale or other disposition subject to the MACRS' half-year, or mid-quarter, or mid-month conventions. (Code Sec. 168(d)(4); Reg § 301.7429-2(a)) No MACRS depreciation deduction is allowed under either the half-year or mid-quarter convention for property placed in service and disposed of in the same year. (Reg § 1.168(d)-1(b)(3)(ii)) No ACRS deduction is allowed for ACRS personal property for the year of sale or other disposition. For ACRS real property, however, cost recovery is allowed up to the mid-month or full-month (see ¶ 1946) before the disposition.[31]

Depreciation on nonrecovery property is generally allowed up to the day of the sale or other disposition.[32] However, the deduction for the year of sale is disallowed if the gain or loss on the sale was due to an under estimation of salvage value.[33]

¶ 1909 The Modified Accelerated Cost Recovery System (MACRS) ▄▄▄▄▄

Under MACRS, recovery property is depreciated by applying to its depreciable basis a prescribed depreciation method for its prescribed recovery period. Alternatively, the straight-line method for the prescribed recovery period may be elected. A generally longer straight-line rate may be elected (required for certain recovery property) under ADS—the "Alternative Depreciation System." Real property is depreciable only under the straight-line method.

Recovery property is tangible property used in a trade or business or for the production of income and depreciable under Code Sec. 167(a) (discussed at ¶ 1901). (Code Sec. 168(a))[34]

Recovery property is depreciable under MACRS, as discussed below, or depreciable under pre-'87 ACRS, as discussed at ¶ 1936 *et seq.*

With certain exceptions (¶ 1910), MACRS is mandatory for recovery property placed in service during the tax year. (Code Sec. 168(a))

Under MACRS, elections (e.g., straight-line, 150% declining balance or unit-of-production method) are made on the taxpayer's return for the year the recovery property is placed in service; and, once made, they are irrevocable. (Code Sec. 168(b)(5))

Under MACRS, depreciation deductions are computed by using:

(1) a prescribed recovery period (¶ 1922),

(2) a prescribed depreciation method (¶ 1923), and

(3) a prescribed convention (¶ 1925 *et seq.*). (Code Sec. 168(a))[35]

Intangible property can't qualify as recovery property. (Code Sec. 168(a))[36] Fifteen-year amortization applies to Section 197 intangibles, see ¶ 1989 *et seq.* Capital outlays for intangible depreciable property may be recovered through depreciation deductions computed under the useful-life depreciation rules (¶ 1971 *et seq.*) or through amortization deductions, if any. (¶ 1986 *et seq.*)

---

31. ¶ L-7700 *et seq.*; ¶ 1688.402   32. ¶ L-7701; ¶ 1674.085(b).   34. ¶ L-8201 *et seq.*; ¶s 1674.006   35. ¶ L-8100 *et seq.*; ¶ 1684 *et seq.*
et seq.   33. ¶ L-11721; ¶ 1674.044.   *et seq.*, 1684.   36. ¶ L-8200 *et seq.*; ¶ 1674.013.

Footnote references beginning with letters are to paragraphs in RIA's Federal Tax Coordinator 2d and RIA's Analysis of Federal Taxes: Income. Footnote references beginning with numbers are to paragraphs in RIA's United States Tax Reporter.

¶ 1910 Property excluded from MACRS.

The following property is not depreciable under MACRS:

■ Acquisitions of pre-'87 property, "churned" (i.e., "acquired") from a related person for purpose of qualifying the property as MACRS property, see ¶ 1911.

■ Property the taxpayer properly elects to depreciate under a depreciation method not expressed in term of years; e.g., the unit-of-production, or income-forecast method. (Code Sec. 168(f)(1))

■ Public utility property for which the taxpayer doesn't use the MACRS normalization method of accounting. (Code Sec. 168(f)(2))

■ Any motion picture films or video tape. (Code Sec. 168(f)(3)) This includes videocassettes.[37]

■ Any master sound recordings. (Code Sec. 168(f)(4))

For 15-year amortization of films, sound recordings, video tapes, etc. acquired after Aug. 10, '93, see ¶ 1991.

¶ 1911 Acquisition of pre-'87 recovery or depreciable property not depreciable under MACRS because of the anti-churning rules.

Depreciable personal property placed in service before '87 cannot be brought within MACRS by the same taxpayer or a "related person." But this is true only where the otherwise "churning" transaction for the first year of the transfer results in more generous depreciation for the property under MACRS than under ACRS or under the useful-life depreciation system. However, residential and nonresidential ACRS real property placed in service before '87 (except for certain nonrecognition transactions) is brought within MACRS by a post-'86 transfer to the same taxpayer or a "related person." (Code Sec. 168(f)(5), (i)(7))

Depreciable personal or real property placed in service before '81 cannot be brought within MACRS by the same taxpayer or a "related person." (Code Sec. 168(f)(5)(A)(i))[38]

The anti-churning rules are imposed to prevent the use of asset transfers as a mechanism to change the recovery period or method for property acquired:

■ in an intercompany transfer from another member of an affiliated group, or

■ in certain other related party transfers.[39]

Thus, the effect of the anti-churning rule is to make the affected transferee "step into the shoes" of the transferor with respect to the recovery period and method of the transferred property to the extent the basis of such property in the transferee's hands equals the transferor's adjusted basis.[40]

The anti-churning rules don't apply to property transferred by reason of death of a taxpayer under Code Sec. 1014.[41] Also, they don't apply to property placed in service before '87 for personal use and converted to business use after '86.[42]

¶ 1912 Determining in which MACRS recovery class an asset belongs.

The assignment of MACRS property to a recovery class is made by reference to that property's class as of Jan. 1, '86. (Code Sec. 168(i)(1))[43] The assignment to a MACRS recovery class is determined as follows: (Code Sec. 168(e)(1))

---

37. ¶ L-8212; ¶ 1684.
38. ¶ L-8300 *et seq.*; ¶ 1684.04.
39. ¶ L-8309; ¶ 1684.04.
40. ¶ L-8308; ¶ 1684.04.
41. ¶ L-8400 *et seq.*.
42. ¶ L-8306; ¶ 1684.04.
43. ¶ L-8202 *et seq.*

Footnote references beginning with letters are to paragraphs in RIA's Federal Tax Coordinator 2d and RIA's Analysis of Federal Taxes: Income. Footnote references beginning with numbers are to paragraphs in RIA's United States Tax Reporter.

MACRS Recovery Class	Property With a Class Life (in Years) of:
3-Year	4 or less
5-Year	More than 4 but less than 10
7-Year	10 or more but less than 16
10-Year	16 or more but less than 20
15-Year	20 or more but less than 25
20-Year	25 or more

MACRS removes three classes of real property from the above classification and assigns them to the:

■ 27.5-year class if the property is residential rental property;

■ 31.5-year class if the property is nonresidential real property (placed in service before May 13, '93);

■ 39-year class if the property is nonresidential real property (placed in service after May 12, '93); and

■ 50-year class for any railroad grading and tunnel bore. (Code Sec. 168(c))

¶ 1913 The three-year MACRS class.

This class includes:

■ depreciable personal property with a class life of four years or less; (Code Sec. 168(e)(1))

■ race horses more than two years old when placed in service and other horses more than 12 when placed in service. (Code Sec. 168(e)(3)(A))[44]

observation: Automobiles and taxis have a class life of three years, and light-duty trucks have a class life of four years. Nevertheless, MACRS specifically assigns these vehicles to the five-year class, see ¶ 1914.

¶ 1914 The five-year MACRS class.

This class includes depreciable personal property with a class life of more than four years and less than ten years, (Code Sec. 168(e)(1)) and:[45]

■ automobiles or light-general purpose trucks; (Code Sec. 168(e)(3)(B)(i))

■ semiconductor manufacturing equipment (Code Sec. 168(e)(3)(B)(ii)) in ADR class 36.0;

■ computer-based telephone central office switching equipment; (Code Sec. 168(e)(3)(B)(iii))

■ qualified technological equipment; (Code Sec. 168(e)(3)(B)(iv))[46]

■ research and experimentation Code Sec. 1245 property; (Code Sec. 168(e)(3)(B)(v))

■ equipment used to produce, distribute, or use electrical energy derived from a geothermal deposit;[47] equipment that uses exclusively and directly solar or wind energy to generate electricity; and certain equipment that converts biomass into a useful form of energy; (Code Sec. 168(e)(3)(B)(vi))

■ cargo containers; and

■ breeding and dairy cattle.

For property placed in service before '91, the five-year class also included certain equipment that could convert ocean thermal energy into electrical or other form of useful energy.[48]

---

44. ¶ L-8204; ¶ 1684.01.   46. ¶ L-9619; ¶ 1684.01.   47. ¶ L-16426 *et seq.*; ¶ 1684.01.   48. ¶ L-8205; ¶ 1684.01.
45. ¶ L-8205; ¶ 1684.01.

Footnote references beginning with letters are to paragraphs in RIA's Federal Tax Coordinator 2d and RIA's Analysis of Federal Taxes: Income. Footnote references beginning with numbers are to paragraphs in RIA's United States Tax Reporter.

¶ 1915 The seven-year MACRS class.

This class includes property with a class life of ten years or more, but less than 16, (Code Sec. 168(e)(1)) and property that does not have a class life and is not specifically assigned to any other MACRS class. (Code Sec. 168(e)(3)(C)(ii)) Also included are:

■ breeding and work horses, 12 years or younger, and any horse not in any other category;

■ railroad tracks; (Code Sec. 168(e)(3)(C)(i))

■ pre-'89 (pre-'90 if transitional property) single-purpose agricultural and horticultural structures, such as pigpens, milk parlors, etc.[49]

¶ 1916 The ten-year MACRS class.

This class includes property with a class life of 16 years or more but less than 20. (Code Sec. 168(e)(1))[50] Also included are:

■ a single purpose agricultural or horticultural structure; (Code Sec. 168(e)(3)(D)(i)) placed in service after '88 (after '89, if transitional property);

■ any tree or vine bearing fruit or nuts (Code Sec. 168(e)(3)(D)(ii)) placed in service after '88.[1]

¶ 1917 The 15-year MACRS class.

This class includes property with a class life of 20 years or more but less than 25 years. (Code Sec. 168(e)(1)) It also includes:

■ municipal wastewater treatment plants; (Code Sec. 168(e)(3)(E)(i))

■ telephone distribution plants and comparable equipment used for two-way exchange of voice and data communications. (Code Sec. 168(e)(3)(E)(ii))[2]

¶ 1918 The 20-year MACRS class.

This class includes municipal sewers with a class life of 50 years, (Code Sec. 168(e)(3)(F)) and property with a class life of 25 years or more. (Code Sec. 168(e)(1))

¶ 1919 Residential and nonresidential buildings under MACRS.

A 27.5-year class life is specifically assigned to residential rental property, (Code Sec. 168(c)(1)) including manufactured homes that are residential rental property, and elevators and escalators in that type of property.

observation: There is no special class life for low-income housing. Thus, that type of property is 27.5-year class property under MACRS.

For property placed in service before May 13, '93, nonresidential real property has a 31.5-year class assigned it. The 31.5-year class also applies to property placed in service before '94 if a taxpayer entered into a binding written contract to buy or construct the property before May 13, '93 or if construction of the property was begun before May 13, '93.

For nonresidential real property placed in service after May 12, '93, a 39-year class life is specifically assigned to the property, (Code Sec. 168(c)) and to elevators and escalators in that type of property.[3]

---

49. ¶ L-8206; ¶ 1684.01. 1. ¶ L-8207; ¶ 1684.01. 2. ¶ L-8208; ¶ 1684.01. 3. ¶ L-8210; ¶ 1684.02.
50. ¶ L-8207; ¶ 1684.01.

Footnote references beginning with letters are to paragraphs in RIA's Federal Tax Coordinator 2d and RIA's Analysis of Federal Taxes: Income. Footnote references beginning with numbers are to paragraphs in RIA's United States Tax Reporter.

¶ 1920 Additions or improvements to real property.

The depreciation for any additions to, or improvement of, any real property (whether or not recovery property) is determined in the same manner as the depreciation deduction for the real property would be determined if the real property were placed in service at the same time as the addition or improvement. (Code Sec. 168(i)(6)(A))[4]

⚫ *illustration:* A calendar year taxpayer bought and placed in service a residential apartment complex in '80 and another one in '85. In the current year, taxpayer made additions and improvements to both properties. The additions and improvements are 27.5-year class property for purpose of MACRS depreciation. If the '80 and '85 properties were factories, then the additions and improvements would be 39-year class properties.

The applicable MACRS depreciation period for additions or improvements to real property begins on the later of: (Code Sec. 168(i)(6)(B))

(1) the date the addition or improvement is placed in service, or

(2) the date the property is placed in service.

¶ 1921 Depreciation of leasehold improvements and amortization of lease acquisition costs by lessees.

Lessees are treated as any other owner-taxpayer for purposes of determining MACRS deductions for lessees' improvements subject to MACRS rules. Thus, a lessee's MACRS deductions for the property are determined without regard to the lease term. (Code Sec. 168(i)(8))

⚫ *observation:* This means that the lessee depreciates the MACRS property over its class life even if the lease term is shorter or longer.

Where the lease ends or terminates before the end of the MACRS recovery period of the lessee's improvement, and the lessee doesn't retain the improvement, the lessee has a gain or loss for the remaining unrecovered basis of the property.[5]

⚫ *observation:* The remaining basis of unamortized leasehold improvements that are left behind when a lease terminates is deductible as a loss. A gain would arise where, for example, the tenant is paid an amount to terminate the lease which amount exceeds the basis of the leasehold improvements (and lease acquisition costs, if any).

For amortization of lease acquisition costs, see ¶ 1590.

¶ 1922 MACRS depreciation periods.

The MACRS depreciation period for each class is: (Code Sec. 168(c))[6]

MACRS Class	Depreciation Period
3-year property	3 years
5-year property	5 years
7-year property	7 years
10-year property	10 years
15-year property	15 years
20-year property	20 years
Residential rental property	27.5 years
Nonresidential real property (placed in service before May 13, '93)	31.5 years

---

4. ¶ L-9105.   5. ¶ L-9106; ¶ 1684.02.   6. ¶ L-8802; ¶s 1684.01, 1684.02.

Footnote references beginning with letters are to paragraphs in RIA's Federal Tax Coordinator 2d and RIA's Analysis of Federal Taxes: Income. Footnote references beginning with numbers are to paragraphs in RIA's United States Tax Reporter.

Nonresidential real property
(placed in service after May 12,
'93)   39 years
Railroad grading or tunnel bore   50 years

For the MACRS depreciation periods under the "alternative depreciation system" (ADS), see ¶ 1931.

Accelerated depreciation periods apply for "qualified Indian reservation property" placed in service after '93 and before 2004. (Code Sec. 168(j))[7]

¶ 1923 MACRS depreciation methods.

There are three depreciation methods used for MACRS property: the 200% and 150% declining balance methods with an appropriate switch to straight-line to maximize deductions, and the straight-line method. (Code Sec. 168(b))[8]

The 200% declining balance method can be used for MACRS property in the three-, five-, seven-, and ten-year recovery classes except for any tree or vine bearing fruit or nuts, in the ten-year class, see below. (Code Sec. 168(b)(1))

The 150% declining balance method must be used for MACRS property in the 15- and 20-year classes, (Code Sec. 168(b)(2)(A)) any property (placed in service after '88) used in a farming business, (Code Sec. 168(b)(2)(B)) and, if the taxpayer elects, any other property (other than that for which the straight-line must be used). (Code Sec. 168(b)(2)(C))

The straight-line method must be used for all residential rental property in the 27.5-year class; for all nonresidential real property in the 39-year class (31.5-year class before May 13, '93); for any railroad grading or tunnel bore; and for any tree or vine bearing fruit or nuts placed in service after '88. (Code Sec. 168(b)(3))[9]

For property not required to use the straight-line method, MACRS permits a taxpayer to elect straight-line depreciation only over the same recovery period listed at ¶ 1922 in which the property belongs. This election, if made, must be made for all property within a recovery class, but can be made for any or all classes. But once made, it is irrevocable for that year. (Code Sec. 168(b)(3), (5))[10]

observation: For most MACRS property, taxpayers generally may elect a longer straight-line recovery period under the "Alternative Depreciation System," see ¶ 1931 *et seq.*

MACRS (i.e., Code Sec. 168) doesn't provide statutory rate tables based on the above prescribed methods. IRS, however, has issued optional MACRS rate tables (reproduced in ¶ 1120) which may be used in computing MACRS depreciation deductions.[11]

The depreciation methods of MACRS personal property are subject to the half-year or mid-quarter depreciation conventions (see ¶ 1926 *et seq.*), and the straight-line depreciation method for MACRS realty is subject to the mid-month depreciation convention, as discussed at ¶ 1925.

For the depreciation methods that must be used for alternative minimum tax purposes, see ¶ 3205 *et seq.*.

¶ 1924 MACRS depreciation for personal property in short tax year.

The depreciation allowance for MACRS personal property placed in service or disposed of in a short year can't be determined by using the IRS optional MACRS rate tables. The depreciation allowance is instead determined by: (1) multiplying the property's depreciable basis by the applicable depreciation rate, and (2) multiplying the product obtained in

---

7. ¶ L-8806; ¶ 1684.01.   9. ¶ L-8917; ¶s 1684.01, 1684.02.   10. ¶ L-8920 *et seq.*; ¶ 1684.01.   11. ¶ L-8902; ¶ 1684.01.
8. ¶ L-8902; ¶s 1684.01, 1684.02.

Footnote references beginning with letters are to paragraphs in RIA's Federal Tax Coordinator 2d and RIA's Analysis of Federal Taxes: Income. Footnote references beginning with numbers are to paragraphs in RIA's United States Tax Reporter.

step (1) by a fraction, the numerator of which is the number of months (including fractions of months) the property is deemed in service during the short year under the applicable convention (¶ 1927 *et seq.*) and the denominator of which is 12.[12]

When a taxpayer has a short tax year other than the first tax year in the recovery period, the MACRS depreciation allowance for that short year must account for the difference between recovery years and tax years.[13]

¶ 1925 The mid-month depreciation convention of MACRS realty.

The mid-month depreciation convention applies in determining MACRS depreciation deductions for the year real property in the 27.5-year, the 39-year class (31.5-year class before May 13, '93) or the 50-year class is placed in service or is disposed of. Under this rule, all realty placed in service (or disposed of) during any month is treated as placed in service (or disposed of) on the mid-point of that month in computing MACRS depreciation deductions for the acquisition and disposition years. (Code Sec. 168(d)(4)(B))

¶ 1926 The half-year and mid-quarter depreciation conventions under MACRS.

In the case of "personal" property (that is, property other than residential rental or nonresidential real property and railroad gradings and tunnels, the half-year depreciation convention applies for the acquisition and disposition year of such property. Under this rule, with two exceptions discussed below, only a half-year of MACRS depreciation is allowed for "personal" property for the acquisition or disposition year. (Code Sec. 168(d)(1), (4)(A))

To prevent taxpayers from bunching the acquisition of "personal" property during the last three months of the tax year and claiming a depreciation deduction for such property for half year, MACRS substitutes a mid-quarter convention for the half-year convention. Thus, the mid-quarter—and not the half-year—convention applies to all "personal" property placed in service during a tax year if more than 40% of the total basis of all "personal" property placed in service during the year is placed in service during the last three months of that tax year. This rule doesn't apply to any property placed in service and disposed during the same year. (Code Sec. 168(d)(3))

The mid-quarter convention is the only applicable convention for MACRS personal property placed in service in a tax year of three months or less.[14]

The mid-quarter convention (as explained above) applies only to personal property depreciable under MACRS.[15]

¶ 1927 How the half-year depreciation convention applies in a short tax year.

IRS prescribes two general rules for determining the mid-point in a short tax year under the half year convention (¶ 1926). When a short year begins on the first day of a month or ends on the last day of a month, the short year consists of the number of months (including any part of a month) that it includes. The mid-point is then determined by dividing the number of months the short tax year includes by two. For example, a short tax year that begins on June 20 and ends on Dec. 31 consists of seven months and the mid-point is the middle of September.[16]

Illustration: A short tax year begins on Mar. 15 and ends on Dec. 31. It thus consists of ten months, and its mid-point is Aug. 1.

Where a second short tax year begins in the same month that the first short tax year ends, that month is excluded from the first short tax year and is included only in the second short tax year. This is because under the above rule, no month can be counted more than once.

---

12. ¶ L-9002 *et seq.*; ¶ 1684.01.   14. ¶ L-8706 *et seq.*; ¶ 1684.01.   15. ¶ L-8103; ¶ 1684.01.   16. ¶ L-8705; ¶ 1684.01.
13. ¶ L-9007; ¶ 1684.01.

Footnote references beginning with letters are to paragraphs in RIA's Federal Tax Coordinator 2d and RIA's Analysis of Federal Taxes: Income. Footnote references beginning with numbers are to paragraphs in RIA's United States Tax Reporter.

illustration: Where a short tax year neither begins on the first day of a month nor ends on the last day of a month, the tax year is measured by the number of days in the short tax year and its mid-point is determined by dividing the number of days in that year by two. If, under this computation, the mid-point doesn't fall on the first or the mid-point of a month, the property is treated as placed in service or disposed of on the nearest preceding first or mid-point of a month.

Regardless of which of the above two rules applies, property subject to the half-year convention is always treated as placed in service or disposed of either on the first day or on the mid-point of a month.[17]

¶ 1928 How the mid-quarter depreciation convention applies in a short tax year.

IRS prescribes two general rules for determining the mid-point in a short tax year under the mid-quarter convention (¶ 1926).

For a short tax year consisting of four or eight full calendar months, quarters are determined on the basis of whole months. Thus, the mid-point of each quarter is either the first or the mid-point of a month and property is treated as placed in service on the mid-point.

For a short taxable year consisting of anything other than four or eight full calendar months, the taxpayer determines the number of days in the tax year, divides by four to determine the length of each quarter, and determines the mid-point by dividing the number of days in each quarter by two. If the mid-point is a day other than the first or the mid-point of a month, property is treated as placed in service on the nearest preceding first or mid-point of the month.[18]

¶ 1929 Determining depreciation for MACRS personal property for tax years following a short year.

For MACRS personal property placed in service before a short tax year, the depreciation allowance for any tax year following the short tax year is determined by consistently using one of two methods:

(1) Under the "allocation method," the depreciation allowance for each tax year following the short tax year is calculated by allocating to that tax year the depreciation attributable to the portions of the "recovery years" that fall within that tax year. Then, for each recovery year included, the depreciation attributable to each recovery year is multiplied by a fraction. This fraction consists of the number of months (including fractions of months) of the recovery year that are included in the tax year, over 12.

(2) Under the "simplified method," a taxpayer calculates MACRS depreciation by multiplying the unrecovered basis of the property by the applicable depreciation rate. Where the tax year for which the MACRS depreciation deduction is being computed is itself a short tax year, the MACRS depreciation as computed above must also be multiplied by a fraction consisting of the number of months (including fractions of months) in the tax year, over 12.

This rule also applies to a tax year in which the property is disposed of.[19]

¶ 1930 MACRS deductions for real property in short tax years.

MACRS depreciation deductions for real property for the year it is placed in service, or disposed of, is based on the mid-month convention and on the number of months the property is in service (see ¶ 1925) regardless of the length of the taxpayer's tax year.[20]

---

17. ¶ L-8705; ¶ 1684.01.   18. ¶ L-8712; ¶ 1684.01.   19. ¶ L-9003 *et seq.*; ¶ 1684.01.   20. ¶ L-9104; ¶ 1684.01.

Footnote references beginning with letters are to paragraphs in RIA's Federal Tax Coordinator 2d and RIA's Analysis of Federal Taxes: Income. Footnote references beginning with numbers are to paragraphs in RIA's United States Tax Reporter.

¶ 1931 The straight-line "alternative depreciation system" (ADS) of MACRS.

The alternative depreciation system (ADS) generally is a straight-line depreciation system under which there is only one depreciation period for personal property and only one depreciation period for realty. (Code Sec. 168(g)(2)(C), (3)(B)) ADS uses the same depreciation conventions as MACRS, (Code Sec. 168(g)(2)(B)) see ¶s 1925 and 1926, and like MACRS, disregards salvage value. (Code Sec. 168(g)(2)(A))

Depreciation deductions must be computed under ADS only for certain specified properties, see ¶ 1932. However, ADS must be used for all properties including properties depreciated under MACRS for purpose of computing: (1) earnings and profits of corporations, (Code Sec. 312(k)(3)(A)) and (2) the depreciation tax preference under the alternative minimum tax. But in computing the depreciation tax preference, the 150% declining balance method is used except for real property and personal property depreciable only under straight-line. (Code Sec. 56(a)(1)(A))[21] ADS may be elected for all other properties— on a class by class basis for personal property and on an individual basis for residential rental and nonresidential real properties. (Code Sec. 168(g)(7)(A))

An ADS election is a year-by-year election; and, once made, it is irrevocable. (Code Sec. 168(g)(7)(B)) This election is in addition to the similar, year-by-year straight-line MACRS election, discussed at ¶ 1923.

Property excluded from MACRS because a depreciation method not measured in term of years is elected (¶ 1910) is also excluded from ADS. (Code Sec. 168(f)(1))

¶ 1932 MACRS property required to be depreciated under ADS.

The following MACRS property must be depreciated under ADS:

■ "Luxury" automobiles and other "listed" (i.e., mixed-use) property used 50% or more for personal purposes (see ¶ 1963). (Code Sec. 280F(b)(1))

■ Properties used predominantly outside the U.S.,[22] (Code Sec. 168(g)(1)(A)) except certain properties listed in the Code.[23] (Code Sec. 168(g)(4))

■ Tax-exempt use property,[24] see ¶ 1934. (Code Sec. 168(g)(1)(B))

■ With two exceptions, tax-exempt bond financed property (¶ 1935),[25] (Code Sec. 168(g)(1)(C)) part or all of which is directly or indirectly financed by tax-exempt bonds issued after Mar. 1, '86, which don't qualify under the refunding exception.[26] The two exceptions are—

(1) property that qualifies under a pre-Mar. 2, '86 "construction or binding agreement" rule;[27] and qualified waste disposal facilities;[28]

(2) low or moderate income housing meeting the requirements of a "qualified residential rental project" under Code Sec. 142(a)(7).[29] (Code Sec. 168(g)(5)(C))

■ Imported business equipment from countries that discriminate against U.S. goods from the date such equipment is placed on a restricted list by Presidential Executive Order. (Code Sec. 168(g)(6))[30]

■ Pre-production costs of farming property excluded from the inventory-capitalization rule of Code Sec. 263A (discussed in ¶ 1661 et seq.).[31]

■ Intermodal cargo containers not used predominantly in the direct transportation of property to or from the U.S.[32]

---

21. ¶s L-9402 et seq., A-8209; ¶s 564, 1684.03.
22. ¶ L-9406; ¶s 280F4, 1684.03.
23. ¶ L-9406; ¶ 1684.03.

24. ¶ L-9600 et seq.; ¶s 1684.03, 1684.06.
25. ¶ L-9500 et seq.; ¶ 1684.03.
26. ¶ L-9505; ¶ 1684.03.

27. ¶ L-9540; ¶ 1684.05.
28. ¶ L-8223.
29. ¶ J-3155; ¶ 1684.03.

30. ¶ L-9405; ¶ 1684.03.
31. ¶ L-9402; ¶s 263A4, 1684.03.
32. ¶s L-9402, L-9407.

Footnote references beginning with letters are to paragraphs in RIA's Federal Tax Coordinator 2d and RIA's Analysis of Federal Taxes: Income. Footnote references beginning with numbers are to paragraphs in RIA's United States Tax Reporter.

¶ 1933 ADS depreciation periods.

The prescribed ADS straight-line periods, except for certain MACRS class properties listed below, are:

■ five years—for automobiles, light-purpose trucks, (Code Sec. 168(g)(3)(D)) and qualified technological equipment;[33] (Code Sec. 168(g)(3)(C))

■ 12 years—for personal (Code Sec. 1245 class) property with no class life, (Code Sec. 168(g)(2)(C)(ii)) except for five-year and specifically assigned property described below;

■ 27.5 years—for low or moderate income housing property financed by tax-exempt bonds as described in Code Sec. 142(a)(7); (Code Sec. 168(g)(5)(C))

■ 40 years—for nonresidential real property and for residential rental property other than low or moderate income housing qualifying for the 27.5-year period; (Code Sec. 168(g)(2)(C)) and any Code Sec. 1245 real property with no ADR class life. (Code Sec. 168(g)(3)(E))

Specially assigned property. The straight-line ADS depreciation period for semiconductor manufacturing equipment is: five years; computer-based telephone central office switching equipment: 9.5 years; railroad tracks: 10 years; single-purpose agricultural or horticultural structure: 15 years; trees or vines bearing fruit or nuts placed in service after '88: 20 years; municipal wastewater treatment plant: 24 years; telephone distribution plan equipment: 24 years; property in the MACRS 20-year and 50-year classes: 50 years. (Code Sec. 168(g)(3)(B))

All other MACRS property. The straight-line depreciation period assigned by ADS.[34]

For tax-exempt use property subject to a lease (other than qualified technological equipment), the above depreciation periods can't be less than 125% of the lease term. (Code Sec. 168(g)(3)(A))[35]

¶ 1934 MACRS deductions for property used by or leased to tax-exempt entities.

MACRS depreciation deductions for most tax-exempt use property must be computed under the straight-line "Alternative Depreciation System" (ADS) over the longer of: (1) the applicable ADS depreciation period for the property, or (2) 125% of the lease term. (Code Sec. 168(g)(1)(B))[36]

¶ 1935 Straight-line depreciation deductions for MACRS property financed with tax-exempt bonds.

Depreciable assets except qualified residential rental projects (low or moderate income housing) directly or indirectly financed with tax-exempt obligations generally issued after Mar. 1, '86, are depreciable only under the straight-line "Alternative Depreciation System" of MACRS. The portion of the cost of property attributable to tax-exempt financing is depreciable under ADS, the rest is depreciable under the general depreciation rules of MACRS. (Code Sec. 168(g)(1)(C), (5)(A))[37]

Low or moderate income housing financed with tax-exempt bonds are depreciable on a straight-line basis over 27.5 years and not over 40 years as under ADS. To qualify for this shorter period, the property must be a qualified residential rental project within the meaning of Code Sec. 142(a)(7). (Code Sec. 168(g)(5)(C))[38]

---

33. ¶ L-9618 *et seq.*; ¶ 1684.03.   36. ¶ L-9602; ¶s 1684.03,   37. ¶ L-9500 *et seq.*.   38. ¶ L-9502.
34. ¶ L-9403; ¶ 1684.03.   1684.06.
35. ¶ L-9602; ¶ 1684.06.

Footnote references beginning with letters are to paragraphs in RIA's Federal Tax Coordinator 2d and RIA's Analysis of Federal Taxes: Income. Footnote references beginning with numbers are to paragraphs in RIA's United States Tax Reporter.

¶ *1936* The Pre-'87 Accelerated Cost Recovery System (ACRS) ▬▬▬▬▬▬

Under pre-'87 ACRS, virtually all recovery property placed in service before '87 (and post-'86 transitional property) is "depreciated" (its cost is recovered) by applying to its unadjusted basis a statutory set rate for its statutory-set recovery period. Alternatively, the straight-line rate could have been elected over certain specified "optional recovery periods."

With certain exceptions (¶ 1937), ACRS was mandatory for tangible depreciable property placed in service before '87 and after '80.[39] For certain qualifying transitional property placed in service after '86, ACRS continues to apply.[40]

Under pre-'87 ACRS, elections were made on the taxpayer's return for the year the recovery property was placed in service, and, once made, they were irrevocable.[41]

¶ *1937* Property excluded from pre-'87 ACRS.

The following property was not depreciable under pre-'87 ACRS:

■ Property placed in service before '81.

■ Pre-'87 acquisition of pre-'81 property "churned," i.e., "acquired" for the purpose of bringing such property within ACRS, e.g., acquired from a related person.

■ Property the taxpayer properly elected to depreciate under a depreciation method not expressed in terms of years, such as the unit-of-production or income-forecast method.

■ Public utility property for which the taxpayer didn't use the normalization method of accounting.

■ Certain foreign-held assets.[42]

■ Certain pre-'85 motion picture film or video tape.[43]

■ '87-'88 master sound recordings unless taxpayer elected to treat as three-year property.[44]

¶ *1938* ACRS recovery periods.

Pre-'87 ACRS placed recovery property (whether new or used) into seven recovery period classes or categories:[45]

■ 3-year Property;

■ 5-year Property;

■ 10-year Property;

■ 15-year Public Utility Property;

■ 15-year Real Property;

■ 18-year Real Property;

■ 19-year Real Property.

Taxpayers could have elected to deduct the cost of ACRS property on a straight-line basis over one of the following optional recovery periods:[46]

Recovery Period Class	Optional Recovery Periods
3-year Property	3, 5 or 12 years
5-year Property	5, 12 or 25 years
10-year Property	10, 25 or 35 years

---

39. ¶ L-10900 *et seq.*; ¶ 1688.400.   42. ¶ L-10901; ¶ 1688.408.   45. ¶ L-10902; ¶s 1688.401,   46. ¶ L-11216; ¶s 1688.401,
40. ¶ L-10912 *et seq.*   43. ¶ L-10901.   1688.403.   1688.403.
41. ¶ L-10900 *et seq.*; ¶ 1688.405.   44. ¶ L-10901.

Footnote references beginning with letters are to paragraphs in RIA's Federal Tax Coordinator 2d and RIA's Analysis of Federal Taxes: Income. Footnote references beginning with numbers are to paragraphs in RIA's United States Tax Reporter.

15-year Real Property, Public Utility Property and Low-Income Housing	15, 35 or 45 years
18-year Real Property	18, 35 or 45 years
19-year Real Property	19, 35 or 45 years

¶ 1939 Determining the ACRS recovery class for an asset.

Under pre-'87 ACRS, recovery property was assigned to one of the prescribed ACRS recovery class periods (¶ 1938). This was done by taking the ADR midpoint class-life as of Jan. 1, '81 (the then "present class life") and statutorily assigned that particular property to one of the ACRS recovery class-periods. For example, the Jan. 1, '81, ADR class life for office furniture, fixtures and equipment was ten years; therefore the "present class life" for this equipment was ten years.

Here's how recovery property was assigned to the three-, five-, 10-, 15-, 18-, and 19-year ACRS classes based on their respective ADR midpoint lives as of Jan. 1, '81.[47]

Property with ADR midpoint life as of 1-1-81 of:	ACRS Class was:
four years or less	3-year
More than four but not more than 18 years	5-year
More than 18 but less than 25 years (for public utility) and 12.5 years or less (for real property)	10-year
More than 25 years (for public utility) and more than 12.5 years (for low-income housing)	15-year
More than 12.5 years for real property (except low-income housing or public utility)	19-year

¶ 1940 The three-year ACRS class.

This class included tangible personal property (except elevators and escalators) with an ADR class life (¶ 1939) of four years or less, and such property used in connection with research and experimentation (as defined in Code Sec. 174). Automobiles, light-duty trucks, special tools and R&D machinery equipment were included. So were race horses over two years old when placed in service by the taxpayer and other horses over 12 years old when placed in service by the taxpayer.[48]

¶ 1941 The five-year ACRS class.

This class included Code Sec. 1245 class property not included in either the three-year or ten-year class or the 15-year public utility class. Included in the five-year class were:[49]

■ most depreciable equipment except long-lived public utility property;

■ single purpose agricultural and horticultural structures, such as pigpens, milk parlors, etc.;

■ storage facilities (not including buildings and their structural components) for petroleum and its primary products (as defined in Reg § 1.993-3(g)(3)(i)), except petrochemicals;

■ certain public utility property not included in the three-, ten-, or 15-year public utility classes;

■ telephone central office equipment;

■ breeding or work horses, 12 years or younger.

---

47. ¶ L-10903.   48. ¶ L-10904; ¶ 1688.401.   49. ¶ L-10905; ¶ 1688.401.

Footnote references beginning with letters are to paragraphs in RIA's Federal Tax Coordinator 2d and RIA's Analysis of Federal Taxes: Income. Footnote references beginning with numbers are to paragraphs in RIA's United States Tax Reporter.

¶ 1942 The ten-year ACRS class.

This class included:

■ certain public utility property and real property (including elevators and escalators) within the ADR midpoint life listed at ¶ 1939;

■ railroad tank cars;

■ manufactured (e.g., mobile) homes, as defined in Code Sec. 603(6) of the '74 Housing and Community Development Act;

■ theme park structures;

■ coal utilization property used in a public utility power plant.[50]

¶ 1943 The 15-year ACRS public utility class.

This class included property, other than "Code Sec. 1250 class property" or three-year class property, with an ADR life exceeding 25 years.[1]

¶ 1944 The 19-, 18-, or 15-year real property ACRS class.

All real property including elevators and escalators with an ADR class life of more than 12.5 years and placed in service by the taxpayer before '87 and after May 8, '85, was 19-year real property unless it was 15- or 18-year property:[2]

(1) 15-year real property was: low-income housing realty; real property placed in service before Mar. 16, '84 and after '80;[3] or real property placed in service after Mar. 15, '84 but qualified as "transitional 15-year class property,"[4]

(2) 18-year real property placed in service before May 9, '85 and after Mar. 15, '84 (or was transitional 18-year property) and was not low-income housing or 15-year class property.[5]

¶ 1945 Determining cost recovery deductions under pre-'87 ACRS.

Taxpayers could have chosen between one of two ACRS methods: (1) the accelerated statutory rates, or (2) a straight line rate using one of three elective recovery periods listed at ¶ 1938. Both methods applied the proper rate against the unadjusted basis of recovery property (¶ 2458 *et seq.*). Thus, salvage value was not considered.

These are the accelerated statutory rates (in percentages) applicable to pre-'87 ACRS personal property:[6]

If the recovery year is:	The applicable percentage for the class of property is:			
	3-year	5-year	10-year	15-year public utility
1	25	15	8	5
2	38	22	14	10
3	37	21	12	9
4		21	10	8
5		21	10	7
6			10	7
7-10			9	6
11-15				6

For the ACRS rate tables for 19-, 18-, and 15-year ACRS realty, see ¶ 1949 *et seq.*

50. ¶ L-10906; ¶ 1688.401.   2. ¶ L-10911; ¶ 1688.403.   4. ¶ L-10914 *et seq.*   6. ¶ L-11301; ¶s 1688.401,
1. ¶ L-10907; ¶ 1688.401.   3. ¶ L-10909; ¶ 1688.403.   5. ¶ L-10910 *et seq.*; ¶ 1688.403.   1688.402.

Footnote references beginning with letters are to paragraphs in RIA's Federal Tax Coordinator 2d and RIA's Analysis of Federal Taxes: Income. Footnote references beginning with numbers are to paragraphs in RIA's United States Tax Reporter.

A taxpayer electing the optional straight-line recovery method had to use the same recovery period for all property of that class placed in service in the election year.[7]

For the year personal property was placed in service and straight-line ACRS was elected, the taxpayer had to apply the "half-year convention" rule.[8]

Where pre-'87 ACRS property is disposed of before the end of that recovery period, no cost recovery deduction is available for the disposition (which includes retirement) year, see ¶ 1908.

Different, more restrictive, recovery periods or rates applied to certain ACRS property:[9]

■ leased to tax-exempt entities ("tax-exempt use property"), see ¶ 1954;

■ financed by tax-exempt industrial development bonds (IDBs), see ¶ 1955;

■ used predominantly outside the U.S.;[10]

■ subject to the "luxury" auto and "listed property" rules, see ¶ 1959 *et seq.*

For the tax preferences and adjustments from accelerated ACRS deductions that must be taken into account for alternative minimum tax purposes, see ¶ 3205 *et seq.*

¶ 1946 Cost recovery methods for pre-'87 ACRS real property.

Under pre-'87 ACRS, the accelerated cost recovery rates (see ¶ 1949 *et seq.*) were based on the number of months the property was in service for the acquisition or disposition year. Cost recovery began as of the middle of the month the building was placed in service (the beginning of the month for property placed in service before June 23, '84).

The accelerated statutory rate for real property in the 19-, 18- or 15-year class was 175% declining balance method. The 200% declining balance method was used in the rates for low-income housing property. IRS issued rate tables (reproduced in ¶ 1120) using the above declining balance methods with appropriately-timed switches to straight-line to maximize the ACRS deduction.[11]

Depreciation deductions for 19-, 18- or 15-year real property for the year the property is disposed of are based on the number of months the property is in service during the year regardless of the length of the taxpayer's tax year and regardless of the recovery period and method used by the taxpayer.[12]

The optional straight-line method could have been elected on a property-by-property basis, and could have been used over the regular 19-, 18- or 15-year recovery period or over the extended recovery periods of either 35-years or 45-years.[13]

For the tax preferences and adjustments under ACRS that must be taken into account for alternative minimum tax purposes, see ¶ 3205 *et seq.*

¶ 1947 ACRS treatment for pre-'87 substantial improvements to realty.

"Substantial improvements" were treated as separate depreciable buildings rather than as components of the building.[14]

A building's improvement qualified as a "substantial improvement" for ACRS purposes if both of these requirements were met:[15]

(1) Over a two-year period, the amounts added to the capital account for the building were at least 25% of the building's adjusted basis (disregarding adjustments for depreciation or amortization) as of the first day of that period.

(2) The improvement was made at least three years after the building was placed in service.

---

7. ¶ L-11302.
8. ¶ L-11300 *et seq.*; ¶s 1688.401, 1688.405.
9. ¶ L-11300; ¶ 1684.06.
10. ¶ L-11500 *et seq.*; ¶ 1688.407.
11. ¶ L-11307; ¶ 1688.403.
12. ¶ L-11317; ¶ 1688.403.
13. ¶ L-11216; ¶ 1688.403.
14. ¶ L-11316; ¶ 1688.404.
15. ¶ L-11316; ¶ 1688.404.

Footnote references beginning with letters are to paragraphs in RIA's Federal Tax Coordinator 2d and RIA's Analysis of Federal Taxes: Income. Footnote references beginning with numbers are to paragraphs in RIA's United States Tax Reporter.

¶ 1948 Component or composite depreciation for ACRS buildings.

The composite method had to be used for the entire structure except for:

(1) components the taxpayer properly elected to amortize, for example, low-income housing rehabilitation expenditures;

(2) substantial improvements (as defined at ¶ 1947), treated as separate buildings;

(3) the first post-'80 component of a pre-'81 building. The recovery deduction for this first post-'80 (but pre-'87) component of such pre-'81 building was computed as if it were a separate building and deduction for later pre-'87 components was computed in the same manner, whether or not it was a substantial improvement.[16]

¶ 1949 ACRS rate tables for 19-year real property.

Use the following rate tables (reproduced in ¶ 1120) to figure depreciation deductions for 19-year property (¶ 1944):[17]

Table VI provides the rates for 19-year real property (other than low-income housing) placed in service after May 8, '85. It is based on the use of the mid-month convention and the 19-year 175% declining balance method switching to the straight-line method at a time to maximize ACRS deductions.

Optional straight-line rate Tables IX, XIII and XIV are used when an optional 19-year, or 35-year, or 45-year straight-line ACRS deduction method (respectively) was elected for 19-year real property (other than low-income housing) placed in service after May 8, '85.

¶ 1950 ACRS rate tables for 18-year real property.

The following ACRS rates tables (reproduced in ¶ 1120) apply to 18-year real property (¶ 1944):[18]

Table IV provides the rates used for 18-year real property placed in service after June 22, '84.

Table V provides the rates used for 18-year real property placed in service after Mar. 15, '84, but before June 23, '84.

Optional straight-line rate tables. Tables VII, VIII, X and XIV are used when one of the optional straight-line ACRS deduction methods for 18-year real property was elected. These optional straight-line rate tables are used as follows:

Table VII is used when the 18-year straight-line method was elected for 18-year real property placed in service after June 22, '84. This table is based on the use of the mid-month convention.

Table VIII is used when the 18-year straight-line method was elected for 18-year real property placed in service after Mar. 15, '84, but before June 23, '84. This table is based on the use of a full-month convention.

Table X is used when the optional 35-year straight-line ACRS deduction method was elected for 18-year real property placed in service after June 22, '84.

Table XIV is used when the optional 45-year straight-line ACRS deduction method was elected for 18-year real property placed in service after June 22, '84. This table is also based on the use of the mid-month convention.

¶ 1951 Accelerated rates for 15-year ACRS real property.

Table I (reproduced in ¶ 1120) applies to all ACRS realty in the 15-year recovery class except low-income housing property.[19]

---

16. ¶ L-11315; ¶ 1688.404.   17. ¶ L-11311; ¶ 1688.403.   18. ¶ L-11312; ¶ 1688.403(a).   19. ¶ L-11313; ¶ 1688.403(b).

Footnote references beginning with letters are to paragraphs in RIA's Federal Tax Coordinator 2d and RIA's Analysis of Federal Taxes: Income. Footnote references beginning with numbers are to paragraphs in RIA's United States Tax Reporter.

¶ 1952 Rates for ACRS low-income housing property.

The tables referred to below (reproduced in ¶ 1120) present the rates to be used for low-income housing:[20]

Table III is used for low-income housing placed in service after May 8, '85.

Table II is used for low-income housing placed in service before May 9, '85.

Tables XII and XV , straight-line rates. The optional minimum straight-line ACRS recovery period for low-income housing placed in service after Mar. 15, '84, and before '87, is 15 years and the full-month convention applies. Use Tables XII and XV for low-income housing placed in service after May 8, '85 for which the taxpayer elected an optional straight-line recovery period (i.e., 35-year, or 45-year straight-line, respectively).

¶ 1953 ACRS deductions for short tax years.

The ACRS deduction for a short tax year is figured by multiplying the ACRS deduction determined for a full tax year by a fraction. The numerator is the number of months in the short tax year and the denominator is 12. Proposed regs prescribed rules for determining ACRS deductions for tax years after the short year.[21]

The above proration rule doesn't apply in the case of ACRS real property for the tax year the property was placed in service or is disposed of.[22]

The above proration rule does apply to ACRS real property for a short tax year if that short tax year isn't the year the property was placed in service or disposed of.[23]

¶ 1954 ACRS deductions for property used by or leased to exempt entities.

ACRS deductions for most tax exempt use personal property had to be computed by using the straight-line method over the longer of: (1) the property's Jan. 1, '81, class life (12 years if it had no Jan. 1, '81, class life), or (2) 125% of the lease term.[24]

ACRS deductions for tax-exempt use real property had to be computed by using the straight-line method over the longer of: (1) 40 years, or (2) 125% of the lease term.[25]

¶ 1955 Straight-line cost recovery deductions for ACRS property financed with tax-exempt bonds.

Depreciable assets placed in service before '87 (but after '82), except residential rental property, financed with tax-exempt industrial development bonds (IDBs) issued before Mar. 2, '86 (and after June '82) were restricted to straight-line ACRS deductions over the regular or optional ACRS recovery periods. Depreciation or amortization was barred. But certain facilities were exempt from this restriction.[26]

¶ 1956 Election to Expense Up to $17,500

Taxpayers, except trusts, estates and certain noncorporate lessors, can elect (on Form 4562) to expense up to $17,500 per year of the cost of certain eligible personal property used in the active conduct of a trade or business.

For the increased expense election for enterprise zone property, see 1958.

The maximum deduction amount of $17,500 is reduced dollar for dollar where the taxpayer places in service during the tax year qualified tangible personal property in excess of $200,000. (Code Sec. 179(b)(2)) In addition, the amount of deduction is further limited to the amount of taxable income from any of taxpayer's active trades or businesses. (Code Sec. 179(b)(3)) However, the amount that can't be deducted because of this "taxable income" limitation is carried over indefinitely to later years until it can be

---

20. ¶ L-11314; ¶ 1688.403.   22. ¶ L-11305; ¶ 1688.407.   24. ¶ L-9602; ¶ 1684.06.   26. ¶ L-9700 *et seq.*
21. ¶ L-11305 *et seq.*; ¶ 1688.407.   23. ¶ L-11305; ¶ 1688.407.   25. ¶ L-9602; ¶ 1684.06.

Footnote references beginning with letters are to paragraphs in RIA's Federal Tax Coordinator 2d and RIA's Analysis of Federal Taxes: Income. Footnote references beginning with numbers are to paragraphs in RIA's United States Tax Reporter.

deducted. (Code Sec. 179(b)(3)(B))[27]

Where an expense election deduction is allocated to a taxpayer from a partnership or an S corporation, the $17,500 deduction limitation, the $200,000 investment limitation and the "taxable income" limitation are applied at both the partnership (or S corporation) level and the taxpayer level. (Code Sec. 179(d)(8); Reg § 1.179-2(c))[28]

In determining the annual dollar limitation for the expense election, all members of a controlled group on a particular Dec. 31 are treated as one taxpayer, (Code Sec. 179(d)(7); Reg § 1.179-2(b)(7)(i))[29] and the up to $17,500 expense deduction may be taken by any single group member or may be allocated among the members but the allocation cannot exceed the cost of qualifying property placed in service by that member in the year. (Reg § 1.179-2(b)(1))

Married taxpayers filing separately may elect other than a 50-50 allocation of the expense deduction. Absent the election, the 50-50 allocation applies. (Code Sec. 179(b)(4); Reg § 1.179-2(e)(1))[30]

The recapture period of the expense election is the entire recovery period of the qualifying Section 179 property. (Code Sec. 179(d)(10)) The recapture amount (reported on Form 4797) equals the expense deduction taken minus the MACRS depreciation amount that would have been allowed on the expensed amount from the time the property was placed in service up to and including the year of recapture. (Reg § 1.179-1(e)(1))[31]

¶ 1957 Eligible property.

Property eligible for the expense election is recovery property that was "purchased" for use in the active trade or business of the taxpayer. Property used in the production of income (Code Sec. 212 property) is therefore not Section 179 property. The election is not available for the portion of the property's basis that is determined by reference to the basis of other property held at any time by the purchaser (e.g., trade-ins).[32]

Purchase is any acquisition of property *except*:

(1) property acquired from any person whose relationship to the purchaser would cause the disallowance of losses under Code Secs. 267 or 707(b)—this includes (a) family members (but *only* spouses, ancestors and lineal descendants), (b) 50%-owned corporations, (c) grantors, fiduciaries and beneficiaries of trusts, and (d) 50%-owned partnerships;

(2) property acquired by one member from another member of the same controlled group;

(3) property (a) whose basis is determined by reference to the adjusted basis of the person from whom acquired (e.g., gifts), or (b) which is acquired from a decedent. (Code Sec. 179(d)(2); Reg § 1.179-3(d))[33]

¶ 1958 Increased expense election for enterprise zone property.

After Aug. 9, '93, the $17,500 Section 179 expense election is increased by $20,000 (for a total of up to $37,500) for qualified zone property of an enterprise zone business. (Code Sec. 1397A(a)(1))[34] In addition, the amount taken into account under the $200,000 phaseout rule (¶ 1956) is 50% of the cost of such property. (Code Sec. 1397A(a)(2))[35]

Qualified zone property is depreciable tangible personal property (a) purchased by the taxpayer after the empowerment zone designation took affect, (b) the original use of which begins with the taxpayer, and (c) which is used substantially is a business in the zone. (Code Sec. 1397C(a)(1))[36]

The increased expensing allowance is not treated as an adjustment for purposes of the alternative minimum tax.[37]

27. ¶ L-9907 et seq.; ¶ 1794.01.   30. ¶ L-9907; ¶ 1794.01.   33. ¶ L-9925; ¶ 1794.02.   36. ¶ L-9953; ¶ 1397A4.
28. ¶ L-9909 et seq.; ¶ 1794.01.   31. ¶ L-9935; ¶ 1794.03.   34. ¶ L-9951; ¶ 1397A4.   37. ¶ L-9963; ¶ 1397A4.
29. ¶ L-9908; ¶ 1794.01.   32. ¶s L-9903, L-9922; ¶ 1794.02.   35. ¶ L-9952; ¶ 1397A4.

Recapture applies if the qualified zone property ceases to be used in an empowerment zone by an enterprise zone business. (Code Sec. 1397A(b))[38]

¶ 1959 "Luxury" Automobiles and "Listed Property"

The depreciation deductions under MACRS and the deduction under the Section 179 expense election are limited for business "luxury" automobiles and other "listed property." Lessees of such property are subject to special rules.

Code Sec. 280F limits the MACRS depreciation deductions and the Section 179 expense election deduction for certain depreciable assets referred to as "listed property," defined below. (Code Sec. 280F(b)(1), (d)(1), (d)(4)) For these limitations, see ¶ 1962 *et seq.*

Code Sec. 280F also provides more restrictive limits to the above two deductions for one item of "listed property"—the business "luxury" automobile. (Code Sec. 280F(a)(1), (d)(1)) For these limitations, see ¶ 1960. In the case of rented (i.e., leased) automobiles and other listed property, "income inclusion amounts," rather than deduction limitations, apply to such leases, see ¶ 1967 *et seq.*

The current depreciation deduction for business autos and listed property depreciable under pre-'87 ACRS is also limited.

"Listed property" consists of:

■ any passenger automobile (except for ambulances or hearses used directly in a trade or business, taxis and other vehicles used directly for transporting people or property for pay, and trucks or vans specified by IRS regs);

■ any other property used as a means of transportation (e.g., trucks, buses, trains, boats, airplanes), except for vehicles that, by reason of their nature, are not likely to be used more than a de minimis amount for personal purposes;

■ any property of a type generally used for entertainment, recreation or amusement, including photographic, phonographic, communication and video recording equipment, except if that property is used either exclusively at the taxpayer's regular business establishment, or in connection with the taxpayer's principal trade or business;

■ any computer or peripheral equipment except those owned or leased by the taxpayer, and used exclusively at the taxpayer's regular business establishment;

■ any cellular telephone or other similar telecommunications equipment;

■ any other property specified by IRS regs. (Code Sec. 280F(d)(4), (5); Reg § 1.280F-6T(b)(1))[39]

¶ 1960 MACRS and Section 179 expense election deductions for owned business automobiles.

The MACRS depreciation deduction (including the Section 179 expense deduction) for use of any passenger auto is limited to amounts specified in the Code (Code Sec. 280F(a)(1)(A)) with those amounts adjusted for inflation for autos placed in service after '88. (Code Sec. 280F(d)(7)) The maximum deduction allowances for any auto first placed in service in '93 and used 100% for business are as follows:[40]

■ $2,860 for the first year it is placed in service;

■ $4,600 for the second tax year;

■ $2,750 for the third tax year;

■ $1,675 for each succeeding tax year.

The limitation allowances for business autos first placed in service before '93 are in Tables 14 and 15 in ¶ 1120. Table 14 applies when the 200% declining balance method is

---

38. ¶ L-9964; ¶ 1397A4. 39. ¶s L-10002, L-10003; ¶s 1684.01, 1794.02, 280F4. 40. ¶ L-10004 *et seq.*; ¶ 280F4.

Footnote references beginning with letters are to paragraphs in RIA's Federal Tax Coordinator 2d and RIA's Analysis of Federal Taxes: Income. Footnote references beginning with numbers are to paragraphs in RIA's United States Tax Reporter.

used; Table 15 applies when the straight-line depreciation method (¶ 1963) is used.[41]

For purpose of the above limitations, the Section 179 expense election deduction is treated as depreciation. (Code Sec. 280F(d)(1); Reg § 1.280F-2T(b)(4))

caution: This means that no expense deduction greater than $2,860 is allowable for a car used 100% for business in the year it is placed in service.

illustration: In '93, a calendar year taxpayer buys and places in service a new $20,000 car. The car is used for business as follows: 100% for '93 and '94, and 80% for all later years. Here are the MACRS depreciation deductions for each tax year assuming no expense election, and no mid-quarter depreciation convention. (For this purpose, the accelerated rates under the "half-year convention" column of Table 14 in ¶ 1120 are used.)

Year	MACRS Deductions
'93 (20% of $20,000 is $4,000 but limited to $2,860. 100% of $2,860)	$ 2,860
'94 (32% of $20,000 is $6,400 but limited to $4,600. 100% of $4,600)	4,600
'95 (19.20% of $20,000 is $3,840 but limited to $2,750. 80% of $2,750)	2,200
'96 (11.52% of $20,000 is $2,304 but limited to $1,675. 80% of $1,675)	1,340
Total '93 through '96 MACRS deductions	$11,000

Self-employed and sole proprietors report their car and truck expenses on Schedule C (Schedule C-EZ for certain small businesses) or if they are farmers on Schedule F of Form 1040 with Form 4562 attached. Employees deduct employee business expenses on Form 2106. But if an employee is reimbursed for business related car expenses under an accountable plan and the expenses don't exceed the reimbursements, Form 2106 doesn't have to be filed.[42]

The "predominantly used in a qualified business use" requirement is the test for determining whether a business auto qualifies for accelerated depreciation and the Section 179 expense election. The "business-investment use percentage," however, determines the amount of the above deductions. These terms are explained at ¶ 1961.

Where the business-investment use percentage is less than 100%, the annual deduction limits are reduced proportionally to correspond to the taxpayer's business/investment use percentage. (Code Sec. 280F(a)(2))[43] Moreover, depreciation after the normal recovery period is based on unrecovered basis, i.e., adjusted basis determined as if the auto had been used 100% for business, so that the disallowed MACRS depreciation for the earlier years allocable to personal use is lost forever. (Code Sec. 280F(a)(1)(B), (d)(8))

Where the auto is not predominantly used in a qualified business use only straight-line depreciation (and no expense election) is available, as explained at ¶ 1963.

For the year an auto is first used for business,[44] the taxpayer may elect not to be subject to the above limitations by choosing to deduct only the amount determined under the IRS standard mileage allowance method, discussed in ¶ 1552.

¶ 1961 "Qualified business use" and "business-investment use" for listed property explained.

"Qualified business use," with exceptions explained below, is any use in a trade or business of the taxpayer. (Code Sec. 280F(d)(6)(B))[45] However, this term does not include production-of-income use for which a deduction is allowable under Code Sec. 212. (Reg § 1.280F-6T(d)(2)) Therefore, use of listed property for the production of income not in a trade or business does not count in determining whether such property is "predominantly used" (i.e., used more than 50% on an annual basis) in a qualified business use.

---

41. ¶ L-10011.
42. ¶ L-10004.
43. ¶ L-10004; ¶ 280F4.
44. ¶ L-10013 et seq.; ¶ 280F4.
45. ¶ L-10025 et seq.; ¶ 280F4.

Footnote references beginning with letters are to paragraphs in RIA's Federal Tax Coordinator 2d and RIA's Analysis of Federal Taxes: Income. Footnote references beginning with numbers are to paragraphs in RIA's United States Tax Reporter.

(Code Sec. 280F(b)(1), (3), (d)(1)) Thus, if an asset is used 49% in a trade or business and 51% for the production of income not in a trade or business, the asset is not "predominantly used" in a "qualified business use." (Reg § 1.280F-6T(d)(5), Ex (1))[46]

"Qualified business use" does not include:

(1) Leasing property to any 5% owner of the taxpayer or to any person related to the taxpayer. Leasing aircraft to such persons, however, is "qualified business use" if business use of the aircraft, without counting the lease use, is at least 25% of the aircraft's total use.

(2) The use of listed property as compensation for services by a 5% owner or a related person.

(3) The use of listed property as compensation for services by any person other than a 5% owner or a related person, unless the provider of the property includes the value of the compensation in the recipient's gross income, properly reports it and, where necessary, treats it as wages subject to withholding. (Code Sec. 280F(d)(6)(C))[47]

For "qualified business use" by an employee, see ¶ 1964.

The amount of the allowable depreciation and expense-election deduction (or the "equivalent inclusion amount" with respect to leased listed property, discussed at ¶ 1968) is computed by the use of the "business/investment use" percentage. (Reg § 1.280F-6T(d)(3)(i))[48]

The term "business/investment use" means the total of business use and investment use of any listed property for the taxable year. Whether a particular use is business or investment use (with one important exception applicable to automobiles, explained below) is determined under the normal rules of Code Secs. 162 and 212. (Reg § 1.280F-6T(d)(3)(i)) For example, if an item of listed property is used 70% in a trade or business and 20% for the production of income, the taxpayer may claim, if the property otherwise qualifies, speedy depreciation deductions (including the expense election deduction) based on 90% business/investment use. (Reg § 1.280F-6T(d)(5), Ex (2))[49]

In the case of a taxpayer's automobile used by another person (even if such other person is a 5% owner or a related person) use by such a person is treated as "business investment use" of the taxpayer if:

(1) its use is directly connected with the taxpayer's business,

(2) that use is properly reported by the taxpayer as income to the other person and, where required, tax is withheld on that income, or

(3) the use of the taxpayer's automobile by that other person results in payment of fair market rent. (Reg § 1.280F-6T(d)(3)(iv))

Illustration: Taxpayer is the sole proprietor of a plumbing contracting business. X, a brother of taxpayer, and Y, an unrelated individual, are employees of taxpayer's plumbing business. X and Y are allowed to use the business' automobiles for personal use and for commuting. However, the rental value of this personal and commuting use is included as part of their compensation and taxes withheld on these amounts. The personal and commuting use of the automobiles by X and Y is "business investment use" under rule (2) above. The personal and commuting use would also qualify as "business investment use" if, instead of reporting its value as compensation and withholding tax on it, X and Y paid taxpayer fair rental value for such personal and commuting use under rule (3) above. (Reg § 1.280F-6T(d)(5), Ex (4) & (5))

---

46. ¶ L-10024; ¶ 280F4. 48. ¶ L-10029; ¶ 280F4. 49. ¶ L-10029; ¶ 280F4.
47. ¶s L-10025, L-10027; ¶ 280F4.

Footnote references beginning with letters are to paragraphs in RIA's Federal Tax Coordinator 2d and RIA's Analysis of Federal Taxes: Income. Footnote references beginning with numbers are to paragraphs in RIA's United States Tax Reporter.

¶ 1962 MACRS and Section 179 expense election deductions for owned listed property other than automobiles.

All listed property used more than 50% on an annual basis in a qualified business use (defined at ¶ 1961) qualifies for: (1) the available speedy depreciation methods; and, if otherwise available, (2) the Section 179 expense election deduction. As in the case of business autos, only straight-line depreciation under ADS is allowed for listed property whose qualified business use is 50% or less. (Code Sec. 280F(b)(1); Reg § 1.280F-3T(c)(1))[50]

The actual deduction amount for any of the above available deductions, however, is computed by the use of the "business/investment use" percentage (defined at ¶ 1961) and not by the qualified business use percentage. (Reg § 1.280F-6T(d)(3)(i))[1]

The disallowed MACRS depreciation and expense-election deduction (if any) for the current and earlier years allocable to personal use is lost for all later years. (Code Sec. 280F(d)(2); Reg § 1.280F-4T(a)(1))[2]

¶ 1963 MACRS and Section 179 expense election deductions for owned listed property where qualified business use is 50% or less.

For the year listed property (including automobiles) is placed in service a speedy depreciation deduction (including the expense election deduction, if any) is allowed for the property only if the property is predominantly used in a qualified business use—as defined at ¶ 1961—for that year. If, for the acquisition year, the listed property is used 50% or less in a qualified business use (i.e., it is not used predominantly on an annual basis in a qualified business use), the property: (1) does not qualify for the expense election (Reg § 1.280F-3(c)(1)), and (2) is depreciable only under straight-line and the "ADS" recovery periods (Code Sec. 280F(b)(1))[3] listed at ¶ 1933.

observation: Under Code Sec. 280F(b)(1), if qualified business use for a listed property starts out by being 50% or less, the straight-line ADS deduction method is required for that property for that year and for all later years. A taxpayer can't switch to the regular, accelerated MACRS deduction method for the property for any later year that qualified business use or business/investment use rises to more-than-50%.

When the more-than-50% qualified business use requirement is not met in a post-acquisition year, (during its normal recovery period), the listed property becomes, retroactively to the year of acquisition, straight-line ADS property. (Reg § 1.280F-3T(c)(2))[4] Depreciation in excess of straight-line (including the expense election deduction) previously taken with respect to the property is recaptured. (Code Sec. 280F(b)(2)(A); Reg § 1.280F-3T(b)(2), (d)(2))[5]

¶ 1964 Requirements for "listed property" deductions by employees.

Listed property that an individual owns in connection with his employment is eligible for MACRS deductions only if the property is required for the convenience of the employer and as a condition of employment. The terms "convenience of the employer," and "condition of employment" have the same meaning as those terms are used in determining the exclusion from gross income for lodging furnished to an employee, as discussed in ¶ 1270 *et seq*.

In order to satisfy the condition of employment requirement, the property must be required in order for the employee to properly perform the duties of his or her employment. This requirement is not satisfied merely by an employer's statement that the property is required as a condition of employment. (Code Sec. 280F(d)(3))[6]

Illustration: B is an inspector for X Construction Co with many construction sites in the

---

50. ¶ L-10018; ¶ 280F4.   2. ¶ L-10019; ¶ 280F4.   4. ¶ L-10021; ¶ 280F4.   6. ¶ L-10022; ¶ 280F4.
1. ¶ L-10029; ¶ 280F4.   3. ¶ L-10018; ¶ 280F4.   5. ¶s L-10021, L-10032; ¶ 280F4.

Footnote references beginning with letters are to paragraphs in RIA's Federal Tax Coordinator 2d and RIA's Analysis of Federal Taxes: Income. Footnote references beginning with numbers are to paragraphs in RIA's United States Tax Reporter.

local area. B travels to the various construction sites on a regular basis and B uses her own car to make these trips. X neither explicitly requires B to use her own car nor does it provide a car for B. However, X reimburses B for any cost she incurs in traveling to the various job sites. Here, B's use of her car in her employment is for the convenience of her employer and is required as a condition of employment. But if X made a car available to B, who chose to use her own car instead, then the "convenience of her employer" and the "requirement as a condition of employment" tests would not be met. (Reg § 1.280F-6T(a)(4), Ex (2) & (3))

¶ 1965 Depreciation and Section 179 expense-election deduction for employees' home computers.

A computer at home, even if used exclusively for the employer's work, is listed property where the taxpayer-employee doesn't qualify under the "office-at-home" requirements of Code Sec. 280A(c)(1), discussed in ¶ 1630 *et seq*. Thus, a home computer used in a separate office-at-home and qualifying under those rules is not listed property.[7]

Where a home computer is listed property, the employee gets no depreciation or other deduction, as discussed at ¶ 1962, unless the employee proves that the computer is: (1) for the convenience of the employer, and (2) required as a condition of employment. (Reg § 1.280F-6T(a)) IRS states that to meet these tests there must be a clear showing that an employee can't perform his employee duties without the home computer. Thus, the tests aren't met where an office computer enables the employee to perform his duties.[8]

One way of proving that a home computer meets the "convenience of the employer test," discussed at ¶ 1964, is to show that employees who do not buy a home computer are professionally disadvantaged. But this test isn't met:

■ merely by showing that the employer encourages or subsidizes the acquisition of a home computer for those employees who wish to have one;[9]

■ where the employee buys a home computer because the office computer is often used by others during working hours. This is true even though the home computer is used exclusively for work and the employer provides the employee with a written statement indicating that the purchase of the home computer is a condition of employment.

¶ 1966 Lessors not affected.

Lessors of listed property who are regularly engaged in the business of leasing that property are not subject to the MACRS limitations applicable to owners for any listed property they lease or hold for leasing. (Code Sec. 280F(c)(1))[10]

¶ 1967 Lessees' limitations.

Lessees of business automobiles and other listed property under leases of 30 days or more are subject to the MACRS limitations discussed in the preceding paragraphs, although indirectly. (Code Sec. 280F(c)(2), (3))[11]

Deductions for rental payments are not limited. Instead, lessees must include in gross income amounts calculated to approximate the present value of the MACRS limitations (including the expense-election deduction limitation) to which the lessees would have been subject if they had purchased rather than leased the listed property. These "inclusion amounts" are figured from IRS's tables, as discussed at ¶ 1968 *et seq*.

The "inclusion amount" for business automobiles is based on the fair market value of the automobile and the lessee's business/investment use. An amount must be included in the lessee's gross income for each year the automobile is leased, whether or not it is used 100% for business/investment purposes. (Reg § 1.280F-5T(d), (e))[12]

---

7. ¶ L-10023.
8. ¶ L-10023; ¶ 280F4.
9. ¶ L-10023.
10. ¶ L-10201; ¶ 280F4.
11. ¶ L-10200 *et seq*.; ¶ 280F4.
12. ¶ L-10202; ¶ 280F4.

Footnote references beginning with letters are to paragraphs in RIA's Federal Tax Coordinator 2d and RIA's Analysis of Federal Taxes: Income. Footnote references beginning with numbers are to paragraphs in RIA's United States Tax Reporter.

For listed property other than business automobiles, there is no annual "inclusion amount." The lessee must, however, take an "inclusion amount" into income for the first year the property ceases to be used predominantly in a qualified business use, (Reg § 1.280F-5T(f)) as explained at ¶ 1969.[13]

The fair market value of the property is equal to its fair market value on the first day of the lease term. If, however, the capitalized cost of the leased property is specified in the lease, that amount is its "fair market value." (Reg § 1.280F-5T(h)(2))[14]

¶ 1968 "Inclusion amount" for leased MACRS business automobiles.

For leased autos with a fair market value of $250,000 or less, the inclusion amount (reported on Form 2106 or Form 4562, see ¶ 1960) for each tax year of the lease is computed as follows: (Reg § 1.280F-7(a)(2))[15]

(1) Find the line from the applicable "Leased Business Auto Table" reproduced in ¶ 1120 (e.g., Table XXIII for '93 leases, Table XXII for '92 leases, etc.) which includes the fair market value of the leased automobile.

(2) Prorate the dollar amount for the number of days in the lease term included in the taxable year at issue.

(3) Multiply the prorated dollar amount by the business/investment use percentage for the automobile for that taxable year. The resulting amount is the correct inclusion amount.

For the last tax year of the lease, the dollar amount for the preceding year must be used. For example, a two-year lease of a $25,100 car beginning on June 1, '91, uses the following table inclusion amounts under the above formulas: for '91—$120, for '92—$261, for '93—$261.[16]

¶ 1969 "Inclusion amount" for MACRS leased listed property other than automobiles.

A lessee of listed property other than automobiles must include in gross income an "inclusion amount" in the first tax year in which the leased property is not used "predominantly"—i.e., more than 50%—in a "qualified business use," see ¶ 1961. (Reg § 1.280F-5T(f)(1))

The "inclusion amount" for MACRS listed property other than automobiles is the sum of the amount computed under Step (1) and Step (2), below. (Reg § 1.280F-7(b)(2))

STEP (1) : Multiply the following three items: (a) the fair market value of the property, (b) the business/investment use of the property for the year that use is 50% or less, and (c) the applicable percentage from table XIX reproduced in ¶ 1120. (Reg § 1.280F-7(b)(2)(i))

STEP (2) : Multiply the following three items: (a) the fair market value of the property, (b) the average of the business/investment use for all tax years (in which the property is leased) that precede the year the business/investment use is 50% or less, and (c) the applicable percentage from Table XVIII reproduced in ¶ 1120. (Reg § 1.280F-7(b)(2)(ii))

Special computation rules apply when a lease term for listed property begins within nine months of the end of the lessee's tax year, or when the lease term is less than one year. (Reg § 1.280F-5T(g))[17]

¶ 1970 Special limitations for owners and lessees of business autos and listed property depreciable under pre-'87 ACRS.

The depreciation deduction for business "luxury" autos depreciable under pre-'87 ACRS are subject to certain prescribed limits depending on when the ACRS auto was placed in service. Special rules also apply to ACRS deductions for pre-'87 "listed property" and to

---

13. ¶ L-10205; ¶ 280F4.   15. ¶ L-10204; ¶ 280F4.   16. ¶ L-10204; ¶ 280F4.   17. ¶ L-10206 *et seq.*
14. ¶ L-10205; ¶ 280F4.

Footnote references beginning with letters are to paragraphs in RIA's Federal Tax Coordinator 2d and RIA's Analysis of Federal Taxes: Income. Footnote references beginning with numbers are to paragraphs in RIA's United States Tax Reporter.

lessees of business autos and other listed property subject to pre-'87 ACRS.[18]

¶ 1971 Depreciation Deduction Under the "Useful-Life" Rules ▬▬▬▬

Nonrecovery property, i.e., property placed in service before '81 and certain post-'80 property for which MACRS or ACRS deduction is not allowable, qualifies for depreciation allowances under the useful-life rules.

Under the useful-life rules, the available depreciation methods are prescribed (see ¶ 1974 *et seq.*) but the depreciation periods are determined either under: (1) the taxpayer's facts and circumstances, as discussed at ¶ 1973,[19] or (2) the class life ADR rules, discussed at ¶ 1985.[20] (A third method, the guideline system, was used only for assets placed in service before '71.)[21]

For property acquired after Aug. 10, '93 (or electively after July 25, '91), certain property excluded from 15-year amortization (¶ 1989 *et seq.*) is also depreciated under the useful-life rules. Computer software (as defined at ¶ 1991) is depreciated using the straight-line method with a useful life of 36 months. (Code Sec. 167(f)(1)) Rights to service debts secured by residential realty is depreciated using the straight-line method with a useful life of 108 months. (Code Sec. 167(f)(3)) Depreciation is to be computed under regs to be prescribed for certain rights to receive tangible property or services, interests in patents and copyrights and contract rights good for less than 15 years or fixed in amount. (Code Sec. 167(f)(2))[22]

¶ 1972 Basis for "useful-life" depreciation.

The basis on which depreciation is taken is the adjusted basis under Code Sec. 1011 for the purpose of gain or loss on a sale or other disposition. (Code Sec. 167(c)(1)) For property acquired after Aug. 10, '93 (or electively after July 25, '91), if property is acquired subject to a lease, no portion of the adjusted basis can be allocated to the leasehold interest, and the entire adjusted basis is taken into account in determining any depreciation for the property subject to the lease. (Code Sec. 167(c)(2))

¶ 1973 Depreciation periods under the "useful-life" rules.

Under the useful-life system, the depreciation period depends on the facts and circumstances of each case. It's the period during which a depreciable asset, or group of similar assets, may reasonably be expected to be useful to the taxpayer in his trade or business or in income production. It depends chiefly on the taxpayer's own experience with similar assets.[23] In the absence of such experience, the general experience in the industry may be used. In either event, the taxpayer has the burden of proving that the useful-life used is correct. (Reg § 1.167(a)-1(b))[24]

¶ 1974 Methods of "useful-life" depreciation.

In general, a taxpayer may use any method of depreciation for nonrecovery property as long as it results in a reasonable allowance. (Code Sec. 167(a); Reg § 1.167(b)-0) For depreciable property that isn't recovery property, see ¶s 1910 and 1937.

A taxpayer may use a different method of depreciation for each separate asset account. (Reg § 1.167(b)-0(c), Reg § 1.167(c)-1(c)) Alternatively, a taxpayer may use multiple asset accounts. (Reg § 1.167(a)-7, Reg § 1.167(a)-10(b), Reg § 1.167(b)-1(b))[25]

The taxpayer chooses the depreciation method. Ordinarily, the straight-line method is used where the taxpayer fails to make his own selection (Reg § 1.167(b)-1(a)) or selects an

---

18. ¶s L-10101 *et seq.*, L-10300 *et seq.*

19. ¶ L-11800 *et seq.*; ¶ 1674.040 *et seq.*

20. ¶ L-12300 *et seq.*; ¶ 1674.090 *et seq.*

21. ¶ L-12404 *et seq.*; ¶ 1674.098.

22. ¶ L-00000 *et seq.*; ¶ 00000.

23. ¶ L-11801; ¶ 1674.041.

24. ¶ L-11804; ¶ 1674.041.

25. ¶ L-11900 *et seq.*; ¶ 1674.001.

Footnote references beginning with letters are to paragraphs in RIA's Federal Tax Coordinator 2d and RIA's Analysis of Federal Taxes: Income. Footnote references beginning with numbers are to paragraphs in RIA's United States Tax Reporter.

improper method.[26]

¶ 1975 Depreciation methods for "useful-life" realty.

Useful-life real property qualified for the following useful-life depreciation methods:

■ 200% DB method—If the property was new residential rental property with a useful-life of three years or more when first placed in service by the taxpayer. This method also applied to (1) used residential property placed in service by the taxpayer before July 25, '69, (2) "substantially rehabilitated historic property," with respect to additions to capital account occurring before '82 and after June 30, '76. (Reg § 1.167(j)-1(a), Reg § 1.167(j)-2)[27]

■ 150% DB method—For new real property (other than residential rental) with a useful-life of three years or more when first placed in service by the taxpayer. (Reg § 1.167(j)-2)[28]

■ 125% DB method—For post-July 24, '69 used residential rental property with a 20-year or longer useful-life when first placed in service by the taxpayer. (Reg § 1.167(j)-6)[29]

■ Straight-line method—For all other used real property, including railroad grading and tunnel bores, and for all of the above realty if chosen by the taxpayer. (Reg § 1.167(j)-5)[30]

■ 60-month elective straight-line method—For pollution control facilities added to pre-'76 plants, (Code Sec. 169(a))[31] see ¶ 1987.

¶ 1976 Straight-line "useful-life" depreciation.

The straight-line depreciation deduction is computed by dividing the adjusted basis of the property at the beginning of the tax year, less the estimated salvage value, by the remaining depreciation period. (Reg § 1.167(b)-1(a))[32] A proration may be required for the first and last years, see ¶ 1905.

Intangible property is generally limited to the straight-line method.[33] For certain intangibles with set depreciation periods, see ¶ 1971

¶ 1977 Speedy "useful-life" depreciation.

For useful-life property, the 200% declining balance method, the sum-of-the-years digits method and any other consistent method that produces allowances for the first two-thirds of the property's depreciation period not exceeding those under the 200% declining balance method were allowed for certain tangible personal property and residential rental housing which were new when first placed in service by the taxpayer. (Reg § 1.167(c)-1, Reg § 1.167(j)-3)[34] These methods could not be used for motion picture film, video tape, videocassettes or sound recordings.[35]

¶ 1978 Declining balance—200%, 150% and 125% methods.

The 200% declining balance method is twice the straight-line rate, while the 150% method is one and a half times the straight-line rate.[36]

The depreciation allowance under the declining balance method is computed by applying a uniform rate (e.g., 200% or 150% of the straight-line rate) to the unrecovered basis of the property at the beginning of the year. While salvage isn't taken into account in this computation, the property may not be depreciated below its reasonable salvage value. (Reg § 1.167(b)-2(a))[37]

26. ¶ L-11922; ¶ 1674.112.
27. ¶s L-11901, L-11935 *et seq.*; ¶s 1674.100, 1674.110.
28. ¶ L-11931; ¶s 1674.100, 1674.110.
29. ¶ L-11935; ¶ 1674.110.
30. ¶s L-11932, L-12502; ¶ 1684.02.
31. ¶ L-12600 *et seq.*; ¶ 1694.
32. ¶ L-12001; ¶ 1674.100(a).
33. ¶s L-11901, L-11908; ¶ 1674.013.
34. ¶s L-11910, L-11935; ¶ 1674.100(b) *et seq.*
35. ¶ L-11916; ¶ 1674.001.
36. ¶ L-11907 *et seq.*; ¶ 1674.100(b).
37. ¶ L-12003 *et seq.*; ¶ 1674.100(b).

Footnote references beginning with letters are to paragraphs in RIA's Federal Tax Coordinator 2d and RIA's Analysis of Federal Taxes: Income. Footnote references beginning with numbers are to paragraphs in RIA's United States Tax Reporter.

¶ 1979 Sum-of-the-years-digits method.

The usual way of computing the sum-of-the-years digits depreciation allowance is to multiply the basis of the property reduced only by salvage value by a fraction consisting of the remaining years of the depreciation period at the beginning of the tax year over the sum of the digits for each of the years in the total depreciation period. (This denominator remains the same as long as the depreciation period isn't changed.) Thus, for an asset with a five-year depreciation period, the fraction is 5/15 for the first year, 4/15 for the second year, etc.

Another way of computing the sum-of-the-years-digits method is under the remaining life plan by applying the decimal equivalents in the table in the regs to the unrecovered basis of the property, less salvage, at the beginning of the year. (Reg § 1.167(b)-3(a)(2))[38]

¶ 1980 Other permitted "useful-life" depreciation methods.

These are:

■ sliding scale or declining rate method used for taxicabs;[39]

■ income forecast method used for T.V., videocassettes and motion picture films. (For 15-year amortization for film, sound recordings, video tapes, etc. acquired after Aug. 10, '93, see ¶ 1991);[40]

■ operating day method used for equipment affected chiefly by wear and tear rather than obsolescence, such as rotary oil drills;[41]

■ sinking fund method; (Reg § 1.167(b)-4(a))[42]

■ unit-of-production method used for property, the usefulness of which is closely related to its use in production or to a source of supply or similar factor. (Reg § 1.167(b)-0(b), Reg § 1.611-5(a), (b)(2))[43]

¶ 1981 Changing method of "useful-life" depreciation.

A change in method of depreciating any particular useful-life asset (on Form 3115) ordinarily requires IRS consent. But this IRS permission is granted *automatically* for most changes. (Reg § 1.167(e)-1(a), (b))[44]

¶ 1982 Salvage value.

This is the amount that will be realized on sale, on retirement or other disposition of depreciable property. It is an estimate based on the taxpayer's own experience. (Reg § 1.167(a)-1)[45]

With one exception discussed below, useful-life property can't be depreciated below salvage value. (Reg § 1.167(a)-1(c), Reg § 1.167(b)-2(a))[46] In the case of depreciable personal property only, taxpayers could elect (for the year it is placed in service) to reduce salvage value by up to 10% of adjusted basis. (Reg § 1.167(f)-1(a)) This applied to tangible and intangible personal property (except livestock) with a useful-life of three years or more when acquired. (Reg § 1.167(f)-1)[47]

¶ 1983 Depreciation based on useful-lives of separate components.

Owners of pre-'81 buildings subject to useful-life depreciation could have depreciated the building shell and all its components, such as heating equipment, plumbing, elevators, etc., at a single rate based on a composite useful-life. Alternatively, the building shell and each component could have been depreciated separately based on their separate

---

38. ¶ L-12011 *et seq.*;
   ¶ 1674.100(b).
39. ¶ L-10710.

40. ¶ L-10704; ¶ 1674.100.
41. ¶ L-10709; ¶ 1674.100(a).
42. ¶ L-10711; ¶ 1674.110(a).

43. ¶ L-10702; ¶ 1674.100(c).
44. ¶ L-11924 *et seq.*;
   ¶ 1674.112(c).

45. ¶ L-11707; ¶ 1674.044.
46. ¶ L-11711; ¶ 1674.044.
47. ¶ L-11715; ¶ 1674.115.

Footnote references beginning with letters are to paragraphs in RIA's Federal Tax Coordinator 2d and RIA's Analysis of Federal Taxes: Income. Footnote references beginning with numbers are to paragraphs in RIA's United States Tax Reporter.

useful-lives. (Reg § 1.167(a)-7)[48] For the rules required under cost recovery, see ¶s 1920 and 1948.

¶ 1984 Gain or loss on retirement of "useful-life" depreciable assets from non-ADR accounts.

An asset is retired for depreciation purposes when it is permanently withdrawn from use in the trade or business or in the production of income. A retirement occurs when depreciable property is sold or exchanged, placed in a supplies or scrap account, or abandoned. (Reg § 1.167(a)-8(a))[49]

■ *Item accounts.* Retirement (whether normal or abnormal) of a depreciable asset in a separate item account has the following tax effects: (1) if the asset is sold or exchanged at arm's length, or abandoned, gain or loss is recognized; (Reg § 1.167(a)-8(a), (c)) (2) if the asset isn't abandoned but is retired and transferred to a supplies or scrap account, gain isn't recognized, but loss is recognized. (Reg § 1.167(a)-8(a)(3))

■ *Multiple asset account.* If an asset is retired from a multiple asset account by an arm's length sale or exchange or by abandonment, gain or loss is recognized in the same manner as in the case of retirements from separate item accounts.

But if the asset is transferred to a supplies or scrap account (or otherwise retired without disposition or abandonment), the recognition of gain or loss depends on whether the retirement is abnormal or normal.

If abnormal, gain isn't recognized, but loss is recognized. If normal, gain isn't recognized. Loss is recognized only if the depreciation rate was based on the maximum expected life of the longest lived asset in the account. (Reg § 1.167(a)-8(a))

A retirement is abnormal if made for a reason not contemplated in setting the depreciation rate, e.g., a casualty loss. Retirement is normal in other cases. (Reg § 1.167(a)-8(b))[50]

¶ 1985 Class life ADR system.

Taxpayers may depreciate useful-life assets placed in service during the tax year under the class life ADR system, instead of the useful-life system. The class life ADR system can't be used for pre-'71 assets, for "recovery property" (Reg § 1.167(a)-11)[1] or for Code Sec. 1250 realty placed in service after '73. (Reg § 1.167(a)-11(b)(5)(vi)(1))[2]

A taxpayer under the ADR system:

■ cannot depreciate salvage value even though salvage value isn't reduced from basis in determining the depreciation deduction; (Reg § 1.167(a)-11(c)(1))[3]

■ must comply with the rules for recognizing gain or loss for "ordinary" or "extraordinary" retirements. (Reg § 1.167(a)-11(d)(3))[4]

¶ 1986 Special Amortization Provisions

The cost of a number of special facilities and expenditures may be amortized, usually over a period of 60 months at the taxpayer's election.

Expenditures made for the following properties may be amortized on Form 4562 over the period indicated instead of being depreciated under MACRS:

■ Costs of certified pollution control facilities for pre-'76 plants—60-month amortization election available, see ¶ 1987.

■ Costs of certain reforestation expenditures—84-month amortization election available, see ¶ 1988.

■ Research and experimental expenditures connected with a trade or business may be

48. ¶ L-12111; ¶ 1688.404.
49. ¶ L-12204; ¶ 1674.067.
50. ¶ L-12212; ¶ 1674.067.

1. ¶ L-12300 *et seq.*; ¶ 1674.090 *et seq.*
2. ¶ L-12322 *et seq.*; ¶ 1674.092.
3. ¶ L-12335 *et seq.*; ¶ 1674.093.
4. ¶ L-12340 *et seq.*; ¶ 1674.097.

amortized over a 60-month period, see ¶ 1594.

■ Organization costs may be amortized over a 60-month period, see ¶ 3518 (corporations) and ¶ 3707 (partnerships).

■ Bond premium or discount, see ¶ 2168 *et seq.*.

■ Lease acquisition costs and certain pre-'87 leasehold improvements, see ¶ 1590.

¶ 1987 Pollution control facilities for pre-'76 plants.

Instead of taking MACRS depreciation, a taxpayer may elect to amortize, over 60 months, part or all of the cost of certified pollution control facilities (Code Sec. 169(a))— new identifiable treatment facilities used in connection with a plant or other property in operation before '76. (Code Sec. 169(d)) The deduction for each month is the amortizable basis of the facility at the end of the month (computed without regard to the amortization deduction for that month) divided by the number of months (including the month for which the deduction is computed) remaining in the 60-month period. (Code Sec. 169(a))[5] Use Form 4562.

The amortizable basis is that portion of the facility's adjusted basis that qualifies for amortization, (Code Sec. 169(f))[6] reduced by 20%. (Code Sec. 291(a)(5)) (The 20% reduction applies to an S corporation only if it was formerly a C corporation and only for the first three tax years after a C tax year.) (Code Sec. 1363(b)(4))[7] MACRS depreciation may be taken on any portion that doesn't qualify. (Code Sec. 169(g))

¶ 1988 Amortization of reforestation expenditures.

A taxpayer may elect to amortize, over a seven-year period, up to $10,000 of reforestation expenditures in connection with qualified timber property. (Code Sec. 194) Use Form 4562. An individual need not itemize to deduct. (Code Sec. 62(a)(11))[8]

Trusts don't qualify for the deduction, (Code Sec. 194(b)(3)) but estates do. (Reg § 1.194-2(b)(7))[9]

Reforestation expenditures are subject to recapture as ordinary income (to the extent of gain) where there is a disposition of the timber property within ten years. (Code Sec. 1245(b)(8))[10]

¶ 1989 Amortization of Intangibles

For property acquired after Aug. 10, '93 (or, electively, after July 25, '91), the cost of most acquired intangible assets, including goodwill and going concern value, is amortized ratably over a 15-year period.

¶ 1990 Fifteen-year amortization of intangibles.

For property acquired after Aug. 10, 93, taxpayers can claim a deduction for "amortizable section 197 intangibles" by amortizing the adjusted basis (for purposes of determining gain) of that intangible ratably over a 15-year period beginning with the month in which the intangible is acquired. (Code Sec. 197(a)) No other depreciation or amortization deduction is permitted with respect to any amortizable section 197 intangible. (Code Sec. 197(b))[11]

For property acquired after Aug. 10, '93 under a binding written contract in effect on Aug. 10, '93 and all times afterwards before the acquisition, taxpayers may elect to not have the 15-year amortization provisions apply.[12]

Taxpayers may elect to have 15-year amortization apply to property acquired after July

---

5. ¶ L-12600 *et seq.*; ¶ 1694.   7. ¶ L-12605.   9. ¶ N-6302; ¶ 1944.02.   11. ¶ L-7951; ¶ 1974.
6. ¶ L-12604; ¶s 1694, 2914.   8. ¶ N-6301; ¶ 1944 *et seq.*   10. ¶ N-6316; ¶ 12,454.03.   12. ¶ L-7982.3; ¶ 1974.

Footnote references beginning with letters are to paragraphs in RIA's Federal Tax Coordinator 2d and RIA's Analysis of Federal Taxes: Income. Footnote references beginning with numbers are to paragraphs in RIA's United States Tax Reporter.

25, '91. If the election is made, it applies to *all* property acquired after that date.[13]

No loss deduction is permitted on the disposition of an amortizable section 197 intangible if the taxpayer retains one or more other intangibles acquired in the same transaction or series of related transactions along with the intangible disposed of. (Code Sec. 197(f)(1)(A)) On the disposition of the intangible, the bases of the other intangibles acquired in the same transaction or series of related transactions is increased by the amount of the loss barred. (Code Sec. 197(f)(1)(A)(ii)) The basis of each retained section 197 intangible is increased by the product of (1) the amount of the loss not recognized solely by reason of this rule, and (2) a fraction consisting of the basis of the intangible over the total bases of all such retained section 197 intangibles.[14]

Anti-churning rules are provided to keep taxpayers from converting existing goodwill, going concern value, or any other intangible for which a depreciation or amortization deduction isn't allowable under prior law into amortizable section 197 intangibles. (Code Sec. 197(f)(9))[15]

¶ 1991 Amortizable section 197 intangible.

An amortizable section 197 intangible is any section 197 intangible acquired after Aug. 10, '93 and held in connection with the conduct of a trade or business or a Code Sec. 212 activity for the production of income, etc. (Code Sec. 197(c)(1)) Amortizable section 197 intangibles include:[16]

■ goodwill, (Code Sec. 197(d)(1)(A))

■ going concern value, (Code Sec. 197(d)(1)(B))

■ workforce in place, (Code Sec. 197(d)(1)(C)(i))

■ business books and records, operating systems, or any other information base (including lists or other information with respect to current or prospective customers), (Code Sec. 197(d)(1)(C)(ii))

■ patents, copyrights, formula, process, design, pattern, know-how, format or similar item, (Code Sec. 197(d)(1)(C)(iii))

■ customer-based intangibles, (Code Sec. 197(d)(1)(C)(iv)) including the deposit base and any similar asset of a financial institution. (Code Sec. 197(d)(2)(B)) Customer based intangibles are the composition of market, market share, and any other value resulting from the future provision of goods or services out of relationships with customers (contractual or otherwise) in the ordinary course of business, (Code Sec. 197(d)(2)(A))

■ supplier-based intangibles. (Code Sec. 197(d)(1)(C)(v)) Supplier-based intangibles are the value resulting from the future acquisitions of goods or services out of relationships (contractual or otherwise) in the ordinary course of business with suppliers of goods or services to be used or sold by the taxpayer, (Code Sec. 197(d)(3))

■ government granted licenses, permits or other right, (Code Sec. 197(d)(1)(D)) and

■ franchises, trademarks and trade names. (Code Sec. 197(d)(1)(F))

caution: Certain patents, copyrights, and government granted rights (above) qualify only if acquired with the acquisition of a business, see below.

Section 197 intangibles also include any other item that is similar to workforce in place, information base, know-how, customer-based intangibles or supplier-based intangibles. (Code Sec. 197(d)(1)(C)(vi))[17]

The following intangibles are treated as section 197 intangibles only if acquired in connection with the acquisition of a business:[18]

■ covenant not to compete or similar arrangements, (Code Sec. 197(d)(1)(E))

---

13. ¶ L-7982.1; ¶ 1974.   15. ¶ L-7983 *et seq.*; ¶ 1974.   17. ¶ L-7952; ¶ 1974.   18. ¶ L-7952; ¶ 1974.
14. ¶ L-7977; ¶ 1974.   16. ¶ L-7952 *et seq.*; ¶ 1974.

Footnote references beginning with letters are to paragraphs in RIA's Federal Tax Coordinator 2d and RIA's Analysis of Federal Taxes: Income. Footnote references beginning with numbers are to paragraphs in RIA's United States Tax Reporter.

■ computer software. Computer software is any program that is designed to cause a computer to perform a desired function. (Code Sec. 197(e)(3)(B)) The term computer software does *not* include any data base or similar item unless the data base or item is in the public domain and is incidental to the operation of otherwise qualifying computer software. (Code Sec. 197(e)(3)(B)) This is true regardless of the form in which the data base or similar item is maintained or stored. A data base doesn't include a dictionary feature used to spell-check a word processing program. (For computer software excluded from 15-year amortization, see ¶ 1992. For software developed by the taxpayer and for treatment before Aug. 11, '93, see ¶ 1664),

■ films, sound recordings, video tapes and books, (Code Sec. 197(e)(4)(A))

■ copyrights and patents, (Code Sec. 197(e)(4)(C))

■ rights to receive tangible property or services under a contract granted by the government, (Code Sec. 197(e)(4)(B))

■ mortgage servicing rights secured by residential real property, Code Sec. 197(e)(7)) and

■ contract rights and government grants if the right has a fixed duration of less than 15 years, or fixed in amount and, without regard to Code Sec. 197 would be recoverable under a method similar to the unit of production method. (Code Sec. 197(e)(4)(D))

¶ 1992 Intangibles excluded from section 197 intangibles.

The following are never treated as section 197 intangibles regardless of how acquired:[19]

■ interests in corporations, partnerships, trusts and estates, (Code Sec. 197(e)(1)(A))

■ computer software (as defined at ¶ 1992) that is readily available for purchase by the general public, (Code Sec. 197(e)(3)(A)). For 36-month straight line depreciation see ¶ 1971. For pre-Aug. 11, '93 treatment see ¶ 1664.

■ futures, foreign currency contracts and notional principal contracts, (Code Sec. 197(e)(1)(B))

■ land, Code Sec. 197(e)(2))

■ leases of tangible property, (Code Sec. 197(e)(5)(A))

■ debt instruments, except for deposit bases and similar items, (Code Sec. 197(e)(5)(B))

■ sports franchises, (Code Sec. 197(e)(6))

■ any fees for professional services or transaction costs incurred by parties to a transaction with respect to which any part of the gain or loss isn't recognized under the rules in Code Secs. 351 through 368 that govern corporate organizations and reorganizations, (Code Sec. 197(e)(8)) and

■ accounts receivable.

In addition, self-created intangibles are not subject to 15-year amortization if they are (1) created by the taxpayer, (2) not an intangibles described in Code Sec. 197(d)(1)(D), (E) or (F), i.e.,not an intangible such as certain licenses and permits granted by a governmental unit covenants not to compete made in connection with the acquisition of an interest in a trade or business, and franchises, trademarks and trade names, and (3) not an intangible created in connection with a transaction (or a series of related transactions) that involves the acquisition of assets which constitute a trade or business or a substantial portion of one. (Code Sec. 197(c)(2))[20]

¶ 1993 Depletion Deduction ▰▰▰▰▰▰▰▰▰▰▰▰▰▰▰▰▰▰

All exhaustible natural deposits and timber qualify for deduction of a reasonable

---

19. ¶ L-7952.1; ¶ 1974.   20. ¶ L-7975; ¶ 1974.

Footnote references beginning with letters are to paragraphs in RIA's Federal Tax Coordinator 2d and RIA's Analysis of Federal Taxes: Income. Footnote references beginning with numbers are to paragraphs in RIA's United States Tax Reporter.

allowance for depletion based on the taxpayer's cost or other basis of the resources—cost depletion. For mines and certain interests in oil or gas wells, the depletion deductions may be computed as a specified percentage of gross income if that is greater than cost depletion.

A taxpayer can claim percentage depletion on one property and cost depletion on another. Or, he can claim, on the same property, cost depletion for one year and percentage for another.[21]

Where the property is entitled to either cost or percentage depletion, the allowable deduction is the greater of the two. (Code Sec. 613)[22] Percentage depletion for oil and gas wells (except for gas from certain domestic geothermal deposits or geopressured brine) is limited to "independent producers and royalty owners" (see ¶ 1999). The allowable deduction is never less than cost depletion. (Code Sec. 611 , Code Sec. 612, Code Sec. 613)

There is no official form for computing depletion, but Form T must be attached to the income tax return if a deduction for depletion of timber is taken.[23]

The basis of the property must be reduced by the depletion deduction allowed or allowable, whichever is larger.[24]

¶ 1994 Who can deduct depletion?

A taxpayer may take a depletion deduction only if he owns an "economic interest" in the mineral deposit or the timber. Owners of economic interest include:

■ Owner-operator.[25]

■ Lessors and lessees.[26] But IRS and some but not all courts deny that a lessee has an economic interest under a lease terminable without cause on short notice.[27]

■ Owner of a royalty interest, or retained net profits interest.[28]

■ Owner of a production payment to the extent it isn't treated as a mortgage loan. (Reg § 1.611-1(b))

¶ 1995 Cost depletion.

This deduction is based on the property's adjusted basis, the number of recoverable units of mineral at the beginning of the year and the number of units sold or for which payment is received during the year. (Reg § 1.611-2(a))

Taxpayer's total cost depletion deductions can't exceed his basis for the mineral property.[29]

¶ 1996 Basis for depletion.

Basis of property for cost depletion and gain or loss is its cost or other basis plus or minus basis adjustments. (Code Sec. 612) It doesn't include the basis of nonmineral property, such as amounts recoverable through depreciation, or the residual value of land and improvements at the end of operations. (Reg § 1.612-1(b)(1))[30] Besides basis adjustments applicable to property generally, a number of additional basis adjustments also apply to natural resources. (Code Sec. 1016(a))

¶ 1997 Percentage depletion.

This is a specified percentage of the "gross income from the property" for the tax year. It can never exceed 50% (100% for oil and gas properties) of the taxable income (see ¶ 1998) before deducting depletion. (Code Sec. 613(a))

21. ¶ N-2250 *et seq.*
22. ¶ N-2025.
23. ¶ N-3101 *et seq.*; ¶ 6114.027.
24. ¶ N-3007.

25. ¶ N-2056; ¶ 6109(b).
26. ¶ N-2058 *et seq.*; ¶ 6114.018.
27. ¶ N-2060; ¶ 6114.018.

28. ¶ N-2055; ¶ 6114.007.
29. ¶ N-2002 *et seq.*; ¶ 6114.020 *et seq.*

30. ¶ N-3000 *et seq.*; ¶s 6124, 6124.001.

Footnote references beginning with letters are to paragraphs in RIA's Federal Tax Coordinator 2d and RIA's Analysis of Federal Taxes: Income. Footnote references beginning with numbers are to paragraphs in RIA's United States Tax Reporter.

278

Percentage depletion, like cost depletion, reduces basis. But percentage depletion continues to be deductible as long as there is gross income from the property even after taxpayer's basis for the property has been reduced to zero. Cost depletion is to be used where higher than percentage depletion. (Code Sec. 613(a))[31]

A corporation's deductible depletion allowance for iron ore or coal (including lignite) is cut back by 20% of the otherwise allowable percentage depletion deduction in excess of the adjusted basis of the property at the close of the tax year (determined without regard to the depletion deduction for the tax year). (Code Sec. 291(a)(2)) For when the cutback applies to an S corporation, see ¶ 1987.

The minerals listed below qualify for percentage depletion at the rates shown. (Code Sec. 613(b); Reg § 1.613-2(b))[32]

	Rate (%)
Oil and gas	(See ¶ 1999)
Sulphur and uranium	22
U.S. deposits of: anorthosite, clay, laterite, and nephelite syenite (to the extent that alumina and aluminum compounds are extracted therefrom), asbestos, bauxite, celestite, chromite, corundum, fluorspar, graphite, ilmenite, kyanite, mica, olivine, quartz crystals (radio grade), rutile, block steatite talc and zircon	22
U.S. deposits of ores of antimony, beryllium, bismuth, cadmium, cobalt, columbium, lead, lithium, manganese, mercury, molybdenum, nickel, platinum and platinum group metals, tantalum, thorium, tin, titanium, tungsten, vanadium and zinc	22
U.S. deposits of: gold, silver, copper, and iron ore and oil shale	15
Geothermal deposits in U.S. or its possessions	15
Metal mines that don't qualify for 22% or 15% rate, above	14
Rock asphalt and vermiculite	14
Ball clay, bentonite, china clay, sagger clay, and refractory clay exclusive of clay entitled to the 22% rate, above, or to 7½% or 5% rates	14
Asbestos (not entitled to 22% rate above), brucite, coal, lignite, perlite, sodium chloride and wollastonite	10
Natural gas from geopressurized brine from U.S. wells drilled after Sept. '78 and before '84	10
Clay and shale used or sold for use in the manufacture of sewer pipe or brick, and clay, shale, and slate used or sold for use as sintered or burned lightweight aggregates	7½
Clay used or sold for use, in the manufacture of drainage and roofing tile, flower pots and kindred products	5
Gravel, peat, pumice, sand, scoria, shale (other than shale entitled to 15% or 7½% rates, above) and stone (other than dimension and ornamental stone)	5
Bromine, calcium chloride and magnesium chloride (if from brine wells)	5

Other minerals: 14%, except generally 5% if used or sold as rip rap, ballast, road material, rubble, concrete aggregates or for similar purposes.

Natural resources that don't qualify for percentage depletion include timber, (Reg § 1.611-1(a)) soil, sod, dirt, turf, water, mosses and minerals from sea water, the air or similar inexhaustible sources. (Code Sec. 613(b)(7)) Coal or iron ore disposed of with a

---

31. ¶ N-2300 *et seq.*; ¶ 6134 *et seq.*

32. ¶ N-2310; ¶s 2914, 6134 *et seq.*

Footnote references beginning with letters are to paragraphs in RIA's Federal Tax Coordinator 2d and RIA's Analysis of Federal Taxes: Income. Footnote references beginning with numbers are to paragraphs in RIA's United States Tax Reporter.

retained economic interest that qualifies for capital gain-ordinary loss treatment does not qualify for percentage depletion. (Code Sec. 613(b)(7), (c))[33]

For the treatment of percentage depletion in excess of cost depletion for alternative minimum tax purposes, see ¶ 3207.

¶ *1998* Taxable income from the property.

The taxable income from the property is the excess of the gross income from the property over the allowable deductions (exclusive of depletion) attributable to the mining processes (including mining transportation) on which depletion is claimed. (Reg § 1.613-5(a))[34]

¶ *1999* Oil, gas and geothermal deposits percentage depletion.

Percentage depletion applies to oil and gas only in the following cases:[35]

■ *Crude oil and natural gas production of independent producers and royalty owners.* 15% depletion is allowed a taxpayer who isn't a retailer or refiner for so much of his "average daily production" of domestic crude oil and domestic natural gas as does not exceed his "depletable oil quantity" or "depletable natural gas quantity." "Marginal production" may qualify for a higher percentage depletion rate (not to exceed 25%) if the price of domestic crude oil is reduced. (Code Sec. 613A(c))

The maximum depletable amount is 1,000 barrels of oil or 6,000,000 cubic feet of gas per day. A taxpayer who has both crude oil and natural gas production allocates the maximum depletable amount between oil and gas at the rate of 6,000 cubic feet of gas per barrel of oil. Over-ceiling production isn't entitled to any depletion. (Code Sec. 613(d), Code Sec. 613A)

The deduction may not exceed 65% of the taxpayer's net income from all sources. (Code Sec. 613A(d)) Also, the amount of the deduction for any costs for which taxpayer claims the 15% enhanced oil recovery credit must be reduced by that credit amount. (Code Sec. 43(d)(2))

■ *Production from pre-'86 geothermal deposits and natural gas production from geopressured brine* located in the U.S. or its possession. (Code Sec. 613(e), Code Sec. 613A(b)(3))[36]

■ *Percentage depletion.* Percentage depletion is not available with respect to any lease bonus, advance royalty or other amount payable without regard to production from any oil, gas or geothermal property. (Code Sec. 613(e)(3), Code Sec. 613A(d)(5))[37] The restriction on the use of percentage depletion applies only to oil and natural gas; other minerals from oil and gas wells can qualify for percentage depletion.[38]

¶ *2000* Related and commonly controlled producers.

The depletable ceiling amounts applicable to oil or gas production of independent producers or royalty owners who are related or are under common control is allocated among them. Allocation is required among corporations that are part of a controlled group; corporations, trusts and estates owned by the same or related persons; and an individual and his spouse and minor children. (Code Sec. 613A(c)(8))[39]

¶ *2001* Aggregation and division of depletable property.

Cost or percentage depletion must be computed separately for each "property." (Code Sec. 612, Code Sec. 613)[40]

A "property" is each separate interest owned by the taxpayer in each separate tract or parcel of land. (Code Sec. 614(a))

---

33. ¶ N-2313; ¶s 6114.023, 6314.04.
34. ¶ N-2702; ¶ 6134.009 *et seq.*

35. ¶ N-2400 *et seq.*; ¶ 613A4.
36. ¶ N-2411; ¶s 6134.001(e), 613A4.

37. ¶ N-2105; ¶ 613A4.02.
38. ¶ N-2400 *et seq.*
39. ¶ N-2433; ¶ 613A4.01.

40. ¶ N-2901; ¶s 6109(d), 6144 *et seq.*

Footnote references beginning with letters are to paragraphs in RIA's Federal Tax Coordinator 2d and RIA's Analysis of Federal Taxes: Income. Footnote references beginning with numbers are to paragraphs in RIA's United States Tax Reporter.

"Interest" means "economic interest." It includes working or operating interests, royalties, overriding royalties and net profits interests. It also includes production payments to the extent they aren't treated as loans. (Reg § 1.614-1(a)(2))

Two or more separate properties may be aggregated and treated as a single property. (Code Sec. 614(b), (c), (e))

A single interest in a "mine" may be treated as two or more separate properties, at the taxpayer's election. (Code Sec. 614(c)(2); Reg § 1.614-3(b))

Footnote references beginning with letters are to paragraphs in RIA's Federal Tax Coordinator 2d and RIA's Analysis of Federal Taxes: Income. Footnote references beginning with numbers are to paragraphs in RIA's United States Tax Reporter.

281

Chapter 6   Charitable Contributions—Medical Expenses—Alimony—Other Nonbusiness Deductions

¶ *2100* Charitable Contribution Deduction

An individual who itemizes can deduct charitable contributions up to 50%, 30% or 20% of his adjusted gross income, depending on the type of property contributed and the type of donee. A corporation can deduct charitable contributions up to 10% of its taxable income. Amounts that exceed the ceilings can be carried forward for five years. The amount of the deduction allowed for property contributions is usually the property's fair market value, but the deduction is reduced for gifts of certain types of property. A contribution of $250 or more isn't deductible unless taxpayer substantiates it.

A deductible charitable contribution is one that:

■ is to or for the use of a qualified charitable organization (¶ 2101); (Code Sec. 170(c))

■ is paid within the taxpayer's tax year, regardless of the taxpayer's accounting method (except for certain accrual basis corporations, see ¶ 2131); (Code Sec. 170(a))

■ is within the applicable statutory ceilings for individuals (¶ 2122 *et seq.*) and corporations (¶ 2130); (Code Sec. 170(b)) *and*

■ meets certain substantiation requirements (¶ 2133). (Reg § 1.170A-13)[1]

The costs of promoting or influencing legislation, e.g., lobbying expenditures, aren't deductible charitable contributions. (Reg § 170A-1(h)(6))[2]

¶ *2101* Qualified charitable organizations.

A qualified charitable organization is one which fits into one of the categories specified in the law, and which IRS has ruled (or the donor establishes) is eligible to receive deductible charitable contributions.[3] Qualified charitable organizations include:

■ a corporation, trust, community chest, fund or foundation (including private foundation), that is organized *and* operated exclusively for charitable, religious, educational, scientific or literary purposes, or for the prevention of cruelty to children or animals, or to foster and conduct national or international amateur sports competition (but only if no part of the organization's activities involves the provision of athletic facilities or equipment); and that is organized or created in the U.S. or its possessions, or under their laws; and no part of whose net earnings inures to the benefit of any private shareholder or individual; (Code Sec. 170(c)(2))[4]

■ a U.S. state or possession, a political subdivision of any of these, the U.S., the District of Columbia, but only if the gift is made exclusively for public purposes; (Code Sec. 170(c)(1))[5]

■ war veterans' organizations, their posts or auxiliaries, and trusts or foundations for the benefit of these organizations, organized in the U.S. or its possessions, if no part of their net earnings benefits any private shareholder or individual; (Code Sec. 170(c)(3))[6]

■ a domestic fraternal society, order or association operating under the lodge system, if the gift is for a charitable purpose; (Code Sec. 170(c)(4))[7]

■ a nonprofit cemetery company chartered solely for burial purposes. (Code Sec. 170(c)(5))[8]

IRS Pub. No. 78, "Cumulative List of Organizations described in Section 170(c)," lists qualified charitable organizations. The list, updated and revised annually, isn't exhaustive.[9]

A charity won't "qualify" if a substantial part of its activities is lobbying, or if it

---

1. ¶ K-2803; ¶ 1704 *et seq.*   4. ¶ K-2861; ¶ 1704.20 *et seq.*   6. ¶ K-2913; ¶ 1704.27.   8. ¶ K-2923; ¶ 1704.28.
2. ¶ K-2803; ¶ 1704.30.   5. ¶ K-2898; ¶ 1704.25.   7. ¶ K-2919; ¶ 1704.26.   9. ¶ K-2943; ¶ 1704.21.
3. ¶ K-2850 *et seq.*; ¶ 1704.20.

Footnote references beginning with letters are to paragraphs in RIA's Federal Tax Coordinator 2d and RIA's Analysis of Federal Taxes: Income. Footnote references beginning with numbers are to paragraphs in RIA's United States Tax Reporter.

participates in any political campaign. (Reg § 1.170A-1(h))[10]

Contributions made to a once-qualifying organization that has since been disqualified still can qualify if the donor wasn't aware of the change in status.[11]

For an organization's requirements to disclose the deductibility of contributions to it, see ¶ 4113.

¶ 2102 Contributions made to or for an individual.

Contributions made to or for an individual are not deductible unless made to the individual as an agent for a qualified organization.[12]

For costs of maintaining a student in taxpayer's home, see ¶ 2121.

¶ 2103 Contribution for taxpayer's economic benefit.

To the extent the donor derives an economic benefit from a transfer to charity, the transfer isn't a charitable contribution. Thus, no charitable deduction is allowed for:

■ tuition (including required "donation" of excess "tuition" payment) even for parochial school;[13]

■ payment in connection with aged person's admission to a home operated by a charity, to the extent allocable to care to be given (may be partly a *medical* expense, see ¶ 2142) or the privilege of being admitted.[14]

¶ 2104 Fund-raising events, entertainment, etc., for charity.

Where amounts are paid in connection with admission to fund-raising events for charity (e.g., shows, lotteries and athletic events), the receipt of admission tickets or other privileges raises a presumption that the payment is not a gift. Taxpayer must show that a clearly identifiable part of the payment is a gift. Only that part of the payment made with the intention of making a gift *and* for which taxpayer receives no consideration qualifies as a contribution.[15] The charity must show (in its solicitation, tickets, receipts or other related documents) the value (or reasonable estimate) of the event, and how much of the contribution is deductible.[16] For an organization's fundraising disclosure requirements, see ¶ 4113.

However, the donor may deduct a contribution in full if the benefit is inconsequential or insubstantial. This applies if the charity informs patrons how much is deductible *and* any of these tests is met: (1) the fair market value of all benefits received in connection with the payment is not more than 2% of the payment, or $62 (for '93), if less; or (2) for '93, the payment is at least $31 and in connection with it the donor receives only token benefits (bookmarks, calendars, mugs, posters, tee shirts, etc.) generally costing less than $6.20; or (3) the charity mails or otherwise distributes free, unordered items to patrons.[17]

Under a special rule, payment to a college or university where the donor receives a *right to buy* seating at an athletic event is 80% deductible as a contribution. No amount paid for the tickets themselves is deductible. (Code Sec. 170(l))[18]

Taxpayer's failure to use the ticket, etc., doesn't increase the amount of the deduction.[19]

Amounts paid for raffle tickets, to play bingo, etc., are not contributions. They are deductible only as gambling losses (¶ 1773).[20]

¶ 2105 Charitable contribution v. business expense.

Transfers to a charity that are directly related to taxpayer's business and are made with a "reasonable expectation of financial return commensurate with" the amount transferred may be deductible as business expenses, and not as charitable contributions. But

---

10. ¶ K-2869 *et seq.*; ¶ 1704.30.   13. ¶s K-3106, K-3107; ¶ 1704.38.   16. ¶ K-3100; ¶ 1704.38.   19. ¶ K-3093.
11. ¶ K-2949; ¶ 1704.21.   14. ¶ K-3045; ¶ 1704.38.   17. ¶ K-3101.   20. ¶ K-3089; ¶ 1704.38.
12. ¶ K-2951.   15. ¶ K-3088.   18. ¶ K-3088; ¶ 1704.38.

Footnote references beginning with letters are to paragraphs in RIA's Federal Tax Coordinator 2d and RIA's Analysis of Federal Taxes: Income. Footnote references beginning with numbers are to paragraphs in RIA's United States Tax Reporter.

no business expense deduction is allowed for the transfer if *any* part of it is deductible as a charitable contribution. (Reg § 1.162-15(a)(2))[21]

⊘*observation:* Business expense treatment may be preferable where the "contribution" exceeds the charitable deduction ceiling (¶ 2122 *et seq.*).

¶ 2106 Gift of property.

A gift of property to a qualified organization is a charitable contribution to the extent of the property's fair market value (FMV) at the time of the gift, whether or not it has appreciated, (Reg § 1.170A-1(c)) except for gifts of ordinary income-type property (¶ 2107) and certain gifts of tangible personal property or capital gain property (¶ 2110).[22]

No gain is realized on a charitable contribution of appreciated property (except for certain bargain sales, see ¶ 2112).[23]

⊘*observation:* This means taxpayer can deduct his basis in the property plus his paper profit, which he isn't taxable on.

If a taxpayer donates property with a basis in excess of FMV, the contribution deduction is limited to FMV, even if it is less than basis.[24] No loss deduction is allowed on the difference between the property's basis and FMV.[25]

For substantiation requirements, see ¶ 2133.

¶ 2107 Contribution of ordinary income-type appreciated property.

For a charitable gift of ordinary income-type property (below), the amount considered contributed (property's fair market value (FMV)) must be reduced by the amount of ordinary (recapture) income which would have been recognized if the property had been sold by the donor for its then FMV. (Code Sec. 170(e)(1))[26]

Ordinary income-type property is property which, if sold by taxpayer (donor) at its FMV on the date it was contributed, would have resulted in *some* amount of gain other than long-term capital gain. This includes: inventory or other property held for sale to customers; Code Sec. 306 stock (¶ 3534 *et seq.*); capital assets held for less than the long-term holding period; property subject to depreciation, etc., recapture; property used in taxpayer's trade or business; and art works, letters, memoranda and similar property created by or for taxpayer. (Code Sec. 170(e)(1); Reg § 1.170A-4(b))[27]

Special rules also apply to a corporation's "qualified research contribution," (Code Sec. 170(e)(4))[28] and to gifts of inventory, see ¶ 2108.

¶ 2108 C corporation's contribution of inventory-type property.

A C corporation that contributes inventory, property held primarily for sale to customers in the ordinary course of its trade or business, or depreciable or real property used in its trade or business, makes only half the normal reduction described at ¶ 2107, but the resulting charitable deduction can't exceed twice the basis of the contributed property. This applies *only* if the contribution is to an exempt Code Sec. 501(c)(3) organization (other than certain private foundations) that uses the property solely for the care of the ill, the needy or infants, and that meets other specified requirements. (Code Sec. 170(e)(3))[29]

¶ 2109 No reduction in charitable deduction where income realized on contribution.

The donor does not reduce the charitable contribution amount where his contribution of property causes him to realize income in the same tax year in which he made the gift.

---

21. ¶ K-3066 *et seq.*; ¶ 1624.363. 23. ¶ K-3150 *et seq.*; ¶ 1704.42. 26. ¶ K-3159 *et seq.*; ¶ 1704.42. 28. ¶ K-3198 *et seq.*; ¶ 1704.42.
22. ¶ K-3150 *et seq.*; ¶ 1704.40 24. ¶ K-3151; ¶ 1704.42. 27. ¶ K-3162; ¶ 1704.42. 29. ¶ K-3181 *et seq.*; ¶ 1704.42.
   et seq. 25. ¶ M-1015.

Footnote references beginning with letters are to paragraphs in RIA's Federal Tax Coordinator 2d and RIA's Analysis of Federal Taxes: Income. Footnote references beginning with numbers are to paragraphs in RIA's United States Tax Reporter.

Thus, he may deduct the full fair market value of donated installment obligations, obligations issued at a discount or other receivables. (Reg § 1.170A-4(a))[30]

¶ 2110 Tangible personal property and contributions to certain private foundations.

For the contributions listed below, the amount treated as contributed and deductible (subject to deduction ceilings, see ¶ 2122 *et seq.*) is the property's fair market value (FMV) reduced by the total amount of the gain that would have been long-term capital gain if the property were sold for its then FMV on the date it was contributed. (Code Sec. 170(e)(1)(B)) Thus, the contribution is limited to the donor's basis.[31]

This reduction applies to:

■ *contributions of tangible personal property* that is unrelated to the donee's exempt function (e.g., art to a church that then sells it); (Code Sec. 170(e)(1)(B)(i))

■ *any capital gain property* (except for publicly traded stock) given to a private foundation that is not an operating foundation or community foundation and that does not make timely qualifying distributions. (Code Sec. 170(e)(1)(B)(ii), (e)(5))[32]

¶ 2111 Liabilities transferred as part of contribution.

The donor's charitable contribution must be reduced by any liability that is assumed (e.g., by the donee) in connection with the gift. (Reg § 1.170A-3(d)) Where the donor transfers property subject to a liability, the amount of that debt is treated as an amount realized for purposes of the bargain sale rules, see ¶ 2112 (but not for the rule at ¶ 2109).[33]

A reduction also must be made for the amount of any interest on the liability attributable to any period after the contribution was made. (Code Sec. 170(f)(5))[34]

¶ 2112 Bargain sale to charity.

A taxpayer who sells property to (or exchanges it with) a charity and receives less than its fair market value (FMV) may treat the "bargain" element as a charitable contribution. (Code Sec. 1011(b); Reg § 1.170A-4(c)(2)) In computing the deduction, the amount considered contributed (excess of FMV over selling price) must be reduced by the amount of any required adjustment for ordinary income-type appreciated property (¶ 2107) for the contribution portion. (Reg § 1.170A-4(c), Reg § 1.1011-2(a))[35]

But the donor generally also realizes taxable gain on a bargain sale. His basis for measuring gain is only the portion of his total cost or other basis for the property that the bargain selling price (amount realized) bears to the property's FMV. (Code Sec. 1011(b); Reg § 1.1011-2) This is basis times selling price, divided by FMV. (Reg § 1.170A-4(c)(2)(i))[36]

Illustration: J owns long-term stock that cost $12,000 and is worth $20,000 when he sells it to charity for $12,000. A contribution deduction of $8,000 ($20,000 – $12,000) is allowable. J's basis for the stock is reduced to $7,200 ($12,000 cost × $12,000 selling price ÷ $20,000 FMV) against his $12,000 selling price, giving J a $4,800 taxable gain.[37]

If property is transferred subject to indebtedness, the amount realized includes the amount of the debt even if it's not assumed by the transferee. (Reg § 1.1011-2(a)(3))[38]

A charitable gift of a partnership interest (e.g., in a tax shelter limited partnership) that is subject to partnership liabilities is a bargain sale. The partner's share of the liabilities is considered his sales proceeds.[39]

---

30. ¶ K-3180 *et seq.*
31. ¶ K-3169 *et seq.*; ¶ 1704.42.
32. ¶ K-3169 *et seq.*; ¶ 1704.42.
33. ¶s K-3155, K-3228; ¶ 1704.44.
34. ¶ K-3157; ¶ 1704.44.
35. ¶ K-3221 *et seq.*; ¶ 1704.43.
36. ¶ K-3224.
37. ¶ K-3223; ¶ 1704.43.
38. ¶ K-3228; ¶ 1704.43.
39. ¶ K-3228.

Footnote references beginning with letters are to paragraphs in RIA's Federal Tax Coordinator 2d and RIA's Analysis of Federal Taxes: Income. Footnote references beginning with numbers are to paragraphs in RIA's United States Tax Reporter.

¶ 2113 Gift of stock to charity followed by redemption or repurchase ("charitable bail-out").

Owners of closely held corporations may in effect withdraw earnings from their firms tax-free by making a charitable contribution of their corporate stock, which the corporation then redeems. As long as the charity has no legal obligation to sell back the stock, the donor is allowed a charitable deduction even if it was preplanned that the stock would be redeemed shortly after contribution.[40]

¶ 2114 Contributions of partial interests in property not in trust.

No charitable deduction is allowed for a contribution, outside a trust, of less than the donor's entire interest in the donated property (e.g., where the donor transfers only his right to use the property (¶ 2118) or his income interest in it), except to the extent the deduction would have been allowed had the transfer been in trust. (Code Sec. 170(f)(3)(A))[41] But this bar doesn't apply to contributions of:

(1) A remainder interest, if made to a trust that satisfies the requirements of a charitable remainder trust (¶ 2115) or a pooled income fund (¶ 2116). (Code Sec. 170(f)(2)(A)) Otherwise, no deduction is allowed unless *all* interests in the property are contributed to charity (see (5), below) or the remainder interest is the donor's *entire* interest in the property (see (6), below).[42]

(2) An income interest, if made to a trust that satisfies the requirements of a charitable lead trust (¶ 2117). (Code Sec. 170(f)(2)(B)) Otherwise, no deduction is allowed unless *all* interests in the property are contributed to charity (see (5), below) or the income interest is the donor's *entire* interest in the property (see (6), below).[43]

(3) A charitable remainder in a personal residence or farm. (Code Sec. 170(f)(3)(B)(i))[44]

(4) Real property interests (including remainders and perpetual restrictions) to a charity exclusively for "conservation purposes." (Code Sec. 170(f)(3)(B)(iii), (h))[45]

(5) A partial interest in property, where *all* of the donor's interests in the property are given to one or more charities (e.g., income interest to one charity and remainder interest to another charity). (Reg § 1.170A-6(a))[46]

(6) An undivided portion of donor's entire interest (even if partial) in property, (Code Sec. 170(f)(3)(B)(ii)) e.g., a remainder or income interest.[47]

¶ 2115 Charitable remainder trusts.

A charitable remainder trust is a trust formed to make current distributions to one or more noncharitable income beneficiaries and to pay the entire remainder to charity or use it for a charitable purpose. It must be *either* a "charitable remainder annuity trust" or a "charitable remainder unitrust." (Code Sec. 170(f)(2)(A))

¶ 2116 Pooled income funds.

A pooled income fund is a trust formed to pay income to one or more noncharitable beneficiaries and the remainder to charity. The trust must be maintained by the donee charity (no donor or income beneficiary may be a trustee) and meet certain other requirements. (Code Sec. 642(c)(5); Reg § 1.642(c)-5)[48]

¶ 2117 Contribution of income interest in trust—charitable lead trusts.

A charitable deduction is allowed for a contribution of an income interest in trust (remainder to a noncharity) *only* if: (1) the donor is taxable on the trust income, and (2) the donated income interest is either a "guaranteed annuity" or a "unitrust interest."

---

40. ¶ K-3218.
41. ¶ K-3250 *et seq.*; ¶ 1704.45.
42. ¶ K-3251 *et seq.*.
43. ¶ K-3346 *et seq.*
44. ¶ K-3442 *et seq.*
45. ¶ K-3480 *et seq.*; ¶ 1704.45.
46. ¶ K-3475.
47. ¶ K-3453 *et seq.*; ¶ 1704.45.
48. ¶ K-3364 *et seq.*; ¶s 1704.46, 6424.03.

(Code Sec. 170(f)(2)(B); Reg § 1.170A-6) This type of trust is a "charitable lead trust."[49]

¶ 2118   Contributing use of property.

A taxpayer who gives a charity the *right to use* property, while retaining the property itself, can't take a charitable deduction for the rental or other value of this right. The gift is nondeductible under the gift-of-partial-interest rules (¶ 2114). (Code Sec. 170(f)(3)(A))[50]

¶ 2119   Performing services for charity.

No charitable deduction is allowed for the value of services taxpayer renders to charity. (Reg § 1.170A-1(g))[1] But taxpayer is allowed a charitable deduction for unreimbursed out-of-pocket expenditures—80% (50% after '93), for meal expenses—necessarily incurred in performing services (other than lobbying) free for a charity. (Code Sec. 170(f)(6), Code Sec. 274(n)(1); Reg § 1.170A-1(g))[2]

If taxpayer uses his car in performing these services, he may deduct a standard mileage rate of 12¢ per mile (for '93) as a contribution. Or he can deduct his actual (unreimbursed) expenses for gas and oil. Parking fees and tolls are deductible in either case, as are deductions otherwise allowable for interest or taxes connected with the car, but not depreciation, insurance and repairs.[3]

¶ 2120   Travel expenses.

No charitable deduction is allowed for taxpayer's travel expenses (including meals and lodging), whether or not reimbursed, while away from home unless there is no significant element of personal pleasure, recreation or vacation in the travel. (Code Sec. 170(j)) Even then, only 80% (50% after '93) of meal costs can be deducted (Code Sec. 274(n)(1)) and only amounts necessarily incurred for meals and lodging while away from home overnight in rendering these services.[4]

¶ 2121   Maintaining student in taxpayer's home.

A charitable deduction is allowed to a taxpayer who, under a written agreement with a charity and without compensation, maintains an elementary or high school student in his home. The student must not be taxpayer's dependent or relative. (Code Sec. 170(g); Reg § 1.170A-2(g))[5]

Taxpayer's charitable contribution in any year is the amount so contributed, but not more than $50 times the number of full calendar months (15 days or more is a "month") during the year for which the individual was a member of taxpayer's household and a full-time student. (Code Sec. 170(g); Reg § 1.170A-2(f), (g))[6]

¶ 2122   Charitable deduction ceilings for individuals.

There is a ceiling on the amount an individual may deduct each year as a charitable contribution, based both on the type of property contributed and the type of charity to which the contribution is made. The ceilings (below) for any tax year are a percentage of taxpayer's "contribution base" (below) for the year, subject to an overall 50% ceiling for all charitable gifts. (Code Sec. 170(b)(1))[7] For carryover of amounts not deductible because of these ceilings, see ¶ 2128.

If the contributions are all *to* "50% charities" (listed at ¶ 2123), the year's ceiling is 50% of taxpayer's contribution base for the year, except for contributions of appreciated capital gain property (¶ 2125). (Code Sec. 170(b)(1)(A))[8]

49. ¶ K-3346 *et seq.*; ¶ 1704.46.
50. ¶ K-3440; ¶ 1704.45.
1. ¶ K-3551; ¶ 1704.36.
2. ¶s K-3601, K-3626; ¶s 1704.37, 2744.01.

3. ¶ K-3627 *et seq.*; ¶ 1704.37.
4. ¶s K-3601 *et seq.*, K-3633 *et seq.*; ¶s 1704.37, 2744.01.
5. ¶ K-3650 *et seq.*; ¶ 1704.33.

6. ¶ K-3655; ¶ 1704.33.
7. ¶ K-3670 *et seq.*; ¶ 1704.05 *et seq.*

8. ¶ K-3671; ¶ 1704.05.

Footnote references beginning with letters are to paragraphs in RIA's Federal Tax Coordinator 2d and RIA's Analysis of Federal Taxes: Income. Footnote references beginning with numbers are to paragraphs in RIA's United States Tax Reporter.

If the contributions are all *to* "30% charities" (¶ 2124) or are "for the use of" *any* charities, the deduction ceiling is 30% of taxpayer's contribution base (except for contributions of appreciated capital gain property, see ¶ 2125) or, if less, 50% of his contribution base minus his contributions to 50% charities. (Code Sec. 170(b)(1)(B); Reg § 1.170A-8(c))[9]

An individual's "contribution base" for a year is his adjusted gross income (AGI) for the year, but without deducting any NOL carryback to that year. (Code Sec. 170(b)(1)(F))[10]

For spouses filing joint returns, these ceilings apply to the couple's combined contributions and their combined contribution base. (Reg § 1.170A-2(a)(1), Reg § 1.170A-8(a)(1))[11]

¶ 2123 50% charities.

For purposes of the deduction ceilings for individuals (¶ 2122), "50% charities" are:

(1) churches (or church conventions or associations);

(2) tax-exempt educational organizations;

(3) tax-exempt hospitals and certain medical research organizations;

(4) certain organizations holding property for state and local colleges and universities;

(5) a U.S. state or possession, or any political subdivision of any of these, or the U.S. or the District of Columbia, if the contribution is for exclusively public purposes;

(6) an organization organized and operated exclusively for charitable, religious, educational, scientific or literary purposes, or for the prevention of cruelty to children or animals, or to foster national or international amateur sports competition if it normally gets a substantial part of its support from the government or general public;

(7) certain private foundations;

(8) certain membership organizations more than one-third of whose support comes from the public. (Code Sec. 170(b)(1)(A))[12]

¶ 2124 30% charities.

For purposes of the ceilings on an individual's charitable deduction (¶ 2122), "30% charities" are qualifying charitable organizations (¶ 2101) that are not 50% charities (¶ 2123), e.g., war veterans' organizations, fraternal orders, cemetery companies, and certain private nonoperating foundations. (Code Sec. 170(b)(1)(B); Reg § 1.170A-8(c))[13]

¶ 2125 Gifts of appreciated capital gain property to 50% charities—30% ceiling.

An individual's deduction ceiling for gifts of appreciated long-term capital gain property to 50% charities is 30% of his contribution base (¶ 2122) unless he makes an election to reduce the amount of his contribution (in which case the 50% ceiling applies, see ¶ 2126). (Code Sec. 170(b)(1)(C))[14] For ceiling on gifts to 30% charities, see ¶ 2127.

¶ 2126 Individual's election of 50% ceiling for appreciated property contributions.

An individual donor whose gift of capital gain property to a 50% charity is otherwise subject to the 30% ceiling (¶ 2125) may elect the 50% ceiling for the gift, but only if he reduces the amount of his contribution. His contribution would then be limited to his basis in the property. (Code Sec. 170(b)(1)(C)(iii))[15]

observation: Elect where the appreciation is small (value of increased current deduction greater than loss of eventual deduction of appreciation) or where the 30% limit will prevent deduction of the appreciation even over the carryover period.

Once made, the election applies to all contributions of appreciated long-term capital

9. ¶s K-3671, K-3674, K-3684 *et seq.*; ¶s 1704.05, 1704.10 *et seq.*

10. ¶ K-3672; ¶ 1704.05.
11. ¶ K-3673; ¶ 1704.06.
12. ¶ K-3721; ¶ 1704.08.

13. ¶ K-3684 *et seq.*; ¶s 1704.05, 1704.10 *et seq.*

14. ¶ K-3696; ¶ 1704.11.
15. ¶ K-3704; ¶ 1704.11.

Footnote references beginning with letters are to paragraphs in RIA's Federal Tax Coordinator 2d and RIA's Analysis of Federal Taxes: Income. Footnote references beginning with numbers are to paragraphs in RIA's United States Tax Reporter.

gain property to 50% charities made by the donor in the tax year. In computing carry-overs to this year, contributions of long-term capital gain property in an earlier year for which the election was not made are reduced as if they were subject to the reduced contribution rule when made. (Code Sec. 170(b)(1)(C)(iii); Reg § 1.170A-8(d)(2))[16]

Elect by attaching to the income tax return for the election year a statement specified in the regs. (Reg § 1.170A-8(d)(2)(iii))[17]

¶ 2127   Gifts of appreciated capital gain property to 30% charities—20% ceiling.

An individual's deduction ceiling for gifts of appreciated long-term capital gain property to 30% charities is 20% of his contribution base (¶ 2122) (and there is no election like the one for gifts to 50% charities, see ¶ 2126). (Code Sec. 170(b)(1)(D))[18]

¶ 2128   Carryover of excess contributions by individuals.

If an individual's charitable gifts for a tax year exceed the percentage ceilings for the year, the excess may be carried forward and deducted for up to five years (subject to the later year's ceiling). (Code Sec. 170(d)(1)) A statement must be filed with the return for the year in which the carryover is deducted. The carryforward is available even if the individual didn't itemize in the contribution year. (Reg § 1.170A-10(a)(2))[19]

The five-year carryforward is allowed for contributions:

■ to 50% charities that exceed 50% of the individual's contribution base; (Code Sec. 170(d)(1)(A))

■ of appreciated long-term capital gain property to 50% charities that exceed 30% (50% if special election is made) of the individual's contribution base; (Code Sec. 170(b)(1)(C))

■ to 30% charities that exceed 30% of the individual's contribution base; (Code Sec. 170(b)(1)(B))

■ of appreciated long-term capital gain property to 30% charities that exceed 20% of the individual's contribution base. (Code Sec. 170(b)(1)(D))[20]

An individual's contributions and carryovers are taken into account in this order: (1) gifts for the year to 50% charities; (2) carryover of gifts to 50% charities from the preceding five years, from the earliest year first; (3) gifts for the year to 30% charities; (4) carryover of gifts to 30% charities from the preceding five years, from the earliest year first. (Code Sec. 170(b)(1)(B), (d)(1); Reg § 1.170A-10(b)(2))[21]

¶ 2129   Excess contributions on decedent's final return.

If an individual dies, any charitable contribution that can't be used on the decedent's final return (under the normal ceilings) is lost. (Reg § 1.170A-10(d)(4)(iii))[22]

¶ 2130   Corporation's charitable deduction ceiling and carryover.

A corporation's charitable deduction for a tax year can't exceed 10% of its taxable income for the year. Taxable income for this purpose is computed without deductions for charitable contributions or dividends received, or net operating loss or capital loss carrybacks to the year. (Code Sec. 170(b)(2); Reg § 1.170A-11(a))[23]

To the extent contributions in any year exceed this limit, the excess can be carried forward and deducted for five years. (Code Sec. 170(d)(2))[24]

¶ 2131   When to deduct charitable contributions.

A charitable contribution is deductible in the tax year it is paid (subject to the percentage ceilings), (Code Sec. 170(a)) regardless of the donor's accounting method (except for

---

16. ¶ K-3704 *et seq.*   19. ¶ K-3686; ¶ 1704.13.   21. ¶ K-3692; ¶ 1704.05.   23. ¶ K-3830 *et seq.*; ¶ 1704.14.
17. ¶s K-3705, K-3706.   20. ¶ K-3686 *et seq.*; ¶s 1704.05,   22. ¶ K-3691; ¶ 1704.13.   24. ¶ K-3830 *et seq.*; ¶ 1704.14.
18. ¶ K-3700; ¶ 1704.11.   1704.13.

Footnote references beginning with letters are to paragraphs in RIA's Federal Tax Coordinator 2d and RIA's Analysis of Federal
   Taxes: Income. Footnote references beginning with numbers are to paragraphs in RIA's United States Tax Reporter.

accrual method corporations, see ¶ 2132) or when the contribution was pledged. (Reg § 1.170A-1(a)(1))[25]

A contribution is "paid" when it is unconditionally delivered to the donee. A contribution by check that is delivered unconditionally is paid when delivered, if it clears in due course. If the check is mailed unconditionally and clears in due course, the contribution is paid when mailed. (Reg § 1.170A-1(b))[26]

A contribution charged on a credit card is deductible by a cash basis donor in the year the charge is made, *not* any later year the credit card company is paid.[27]

¶ 2132 Accrual method corporation's election to take deduction in year contribution is authorized.

An accrual method corporation whose board of directors has authorized a charitable contribution during the tax year may elect to deduct the contribution (or part of it) in that (authorization) year, if the contribution is paid by the fifteenth day of the third month following the close of the year. (Code Sec. 170(a)(2))[28]

The election must be made at the time the tax return is filed, by reporting the contribution in the return. A declaration signed by a principal officer together with a copy of the directors' resolution authorizing the contribution must accompany the return. (Code Sec. 170(a)(2); Reg § 1.170A-11(b))[29]

¶ 2133 Proof of charitable contribution.

A charitable deduction is not allowed unless the taxpayer can prove his right to it. (Code Sec. 170(a)(1)) For cash contributions, taxpayer must keep either a cancelled check, receipt or other reliable evidence. (Reg § 1.170A-13(a)(1))[30] For contributions of property (other than cash), taxpayer must have a receipt from the donee and keep records showing the donee's name and describing the gift. (Reg § 1.170A-13(b)(1))[31]

For additional substantiation required for contributions of $250 or more, see ¶ 2134, over $500 but not more than $5,000, see ¶ 2135, or over $5,000, see ¶ 2136.

For information return requirement imposed on the *donee*, see ¶ 4745.

¶ 2134 Substantiation requirement for contributions of $250 or more after '93.

No charitable deduction is allowed for any (cash or property) contribution of $250 or more (made after '93) unless taxpayer substantiates it by a contemporaneous written acknowledgement (a cancelled check won't do) from the donee organization, unless the donee files a substantiating return (under regs to be issued). (Code Sec. 170(f)(8))[32]

¶ 2135 Proving noncash property contributions exceeding $500—Form 8283.

A taxpayer who claims more than $500 (but not over $5,000, see ¶ 2136) as a deduction for a contribution of noncash property must, in addition to the substantiation described at ¶ 2134, attach Form 8283 to his tax return, showing certain required information. (Reg § 1.170A-13(b)(3)) IRS will disallow the deduction (for the property contribution) if the form isn't filed unless the failure was due to reasonable cause.[33]

¶ 2136 Proving noncash property contributions exceeding $5,000—appraisal requirement.

For contributions of property other than money with an aggregate claimed value *over $5,000* (over $10,000, for certain publicly traded securities), no charitable deduction is allowed to an individual, closely held corporation, personal service corporation, partnership or S corporation unless the donor gets a "qualified appraisal" for each item of property contributed, and attaches an appraisal summary (Form 8283) to the return.

25. ¶ K-3851 *et seq.*; ¶s 1704.02, 1704.03.
26. ¶ K-3858 *et seq.*; ¶ 1704.02.
27. ¶ K-3861; ¶ 1704.02.
28. ¶ K-3850 *et seq.*; ¶ 1704.03.
29. ¶ K-3850 *et seq.*; ¶ 1704.03.
30. ¶ K-3919; ¶ 1704.50.
31. ¶s K-3926, K-3927; ¶ 1704.50.
32. ¶ K-3932.1 *et seq.*
33. ¶ K-3933 *et seq.*; ¶ 1704.50.

Footnote references beginning with letters are to paragraphs in RIA's Federal Tax Coordinator 2d and RIA's Analysis of Federal Taxes: Income. Footnote references beginning with numbers are to paragraphs in RIA's United States Tax Reporter.

(Reg § 1.170A-13(c))[34]

✔observation: An appraisal summary, which must be attached to the donor's return, is not the same as a qualified appraisal, which calls for substantially different information and is retained by the donor.

C corporations that claim deductions over $5,000 for property contributed don't have to get qualified appraisals, but must file a partially completed Form 8283 with their returns. The same is true for donors of certain publicly traded securities, and of nonpublicly traded stock, where the deduction claimed is greater than $5,000 but not more than $10,000. (Reg § 1.170A-13(c))[35]

IRS will waive the qualified appraisal requirement in certain cases.[36]

¶ 2137 Medical Expenses

An individual who itemizes can deduct the amount by which certain unreimbursed medical and dental expenses paid during the year for himself, his spouse and his dependents exceed 7.5% of his adjusted gross income.

¶ 2138 How much is deductible—7.5%-of-adjusted-gross-income-floor.

The amount of medical expenses (¶ 2140) that an individual may deduct in a tax year is the amount by which his unreimbursed payments made in the year for those expenses exceed 7.5% of his adjusted gross income (AGI) for the year. There is no ceiling on the deduction. (Code Sec. 213(a))[37] But any expense allowed as a Code Sec. 21 dependent care credit (¶ 2347) can't be treated as a medical expense. (Code Sec. 213(e)) And the deduction for any pre-'94 tax year must be reduced by any amount allowable as a Code Sec. 32 health insurance credit for the year (¶ 2337). (Code Sec. 213(f))[38]

For the percentage floor on deductible medical expenses for purposes of the alternative minimum tax, see ¶ 3208.

¶ 2139 Whose medical expenses may taxpayer deduct?

A taxpayer may deduct his own medical expenses, and those of his spouse and dependents, if the status as spouse, etc., exists either when the medical care was rendered or when the expenses were paid. (Reg § 1.213-1(e)(3)) A child of divorced parents is, for this purpose, considered a dependent of both parents (so that each parent may deduct the medical expenses he pays for the child). (Code Sec. 213(d)(5))[39]

¶ 2140 Deductible medical expenses.

Deductible medical expenses are amounts paid for the diagnosis, mitigation, treatment, prevention of disease or for the purpose of affecting any structure or function of the body, as well as related payments for insurance (¶ 2141) and transportation (¶ 2144), (Code Sec. 213(d)(1))[40] and the costs of nursing services. (Reg § 1.213-1(e)(1)(ii))[41]

The cost of eyeglasses, artificial teeth or limbs, (Reg § 1.213-1(e)(1)(ii)) hearing aids and similar items also are deductible medical expenses.[42]

The cost of a procedure that affects the structure or function of the body is deductible, regardless of taxpayer's motive for undergoing it. Thus, legal abortions and other discretionary medical costs may be deductible.[43]

Expenses merely beneficial to the individual's general health aren't deductible as costs for medical care. (Reg § 1.213-1(e)(1)(ii))[44] Nor is a deduction allowed for costs of cosmetic

---

34. ¶ K-3940 *et seq.*; ¶s 1704.50, 1704.51.
35. ¶s K-3940, K-3950 *et seq.*; ¶ 1704.50.
36. ¶ K-3954.
37. ¶ K-2000 *et seq.*; ¶ 2134 *et seq.*
38. ¶ K-2002; ¶s 2134, 2134.04.
39. ¶ K-2301 *et seq.*; ¶s 2134.01, 2134.02.
40. ¶ K-2100; ¶s 2134.04, 2134.08.
41. ¶ K-2110.
42. ¶ K-2121.
43. ¶ K-2109; ¶ 2134.04.
44. ¶ K-2103; ¶ 2134.04.

Footnote references beginning with letters are to paragraphs in RIA's Federal Tax Coordinator 2d and RIA's Analysis of Federal Taxes: Income. Footnote references beginning with numbers are to paragraphs in RIA's United States Tax Reporter.

surgery or similar procedures unless the surgery, etc., is necessary to ameliorate a deformity arising from, or directly related to, a congenital abnormality, a personal injury resulting from an accident or trauma or a disfiguring disease. (Code Sec. 213(d)(9))[45]

The only drugs that count as medical expenses are prescribed drugs and insulin. (Code Sec. 213(b), (d)(3))[46]

Payments for illegal operations or treatments are not deductible medical expenses. (Reg § 1.213-1(e)(1)(ii))[47]

¶ 2141 Accident and health insurance.

The cost of insurance that is deductible as a medical expense is limited to amounts paid for insurance that covers *medical care* as defined at ¶ 2140. (Code Sec. 213(d)(1)(C))[48]

Amounts paid as *voluntary* premiums under Part B of Medicare for supplementary medical insurance are deductible as medical care, (Code Sec. 213(d)(1)(C)) but not the *mandatory* employment or self-employment taxes paid for basic coverage under Medicare A.[49]

For tax years beginning before '94, a self-employed individual's medical expense deduction doesn't include any amount paid for medical insurance to which the special 25% business expense deduction applies (¶ 1528). (Code Sec. 162(l)(3), (l)(6))[50]

¶ 2142 Care at hospitals and other institutions.

The cost of in-patient care, including a percentage of the cost of meals, and lodging (¶ 2145), furnished by a hospital is a deductible medical expense. (Reg § 1.213-1(e)(1)(v))[1]

The cost of in-patient care, including a percentage of the cost of meals, and lodging, at an institution that furnishes medical care but is *not* a hospital qualifies if the individual is there primarily for the availability of medical care, and the meals and lodging are furnished as a necessary incident to that care. If this test isn't met, only that part of the cost of his care attributable to medical care qualifies. The medical care status depends on the patient's condition and the nature of the services he receives and not on the nature of the institution, which may be federal, state, local or private. Thus, where this test is met, a medical deduction is allowed for:

■ costs (including tuition, a percentage of the cost of meals, and lodging) of a mentally or physically handicapped person at a special school. (Reg § 1.213-1(e)(1)(v)) Costs allocable to medical care at a regular school qualify if the school supplies a cost breakdown;[2]

■ costs of a nursing home or home for the aged. But if the person is there for personal or family reasons, only the cost of medical care qualifies. (Reg § 1.213-1(e)(1)(v))[3]

¶ 2143 Capital expenditures for equipment or improvements to taxpayer's property.

Amounts incurred for elevators, swimming pools and other permanent improvements to taxpayer's property (including capital expenditures to accommodate a residence to a physically handicapped individual) may qualify as a medical expense if the primary purpose is for the medical care of the taxpayer, his spouse or dependents. But the medical deduction is limited to that portion of the expenses that exceeds the amount by which the improvement increases the value of taxpayer's property. (Reg § 1.213-1(e)(1)(iii))[4]

Illustration: On his doctor's advice, J installs an elevator in his two-story, single family home to avoid climbing stairs and to alleviate his heart condition. The cost of installing it is $5,000 and it decreases the value of J's home by $3,000 (because buyers don't want a single family home with an elevator). The full $5,000 is a medical expense.

45. ¶ K-2109; ¶ 2134.04.
46. ¶ K-2124 *et seq.*; ¶ 2134.06.
47. ¶ K-2106; ¶ 2134.04.
48. ¶ K-2126 *et seq.*; ¶ 2134.08.
49. ¶ K-2126; ¶ 2134.08.
50. ¶ L-3510; ¶ 1624.403.
1. ¶ K-2128; ¶ 2134.04.
2. ¶ K-2133 *et seq.*; ¶s 2134.10, 2134.11.
3. ¶ K-2131; ¶ 2134.11.
4. ¶ K-2113 *et seq.*; ¶ 2134.13.

Footnote references beginning with letters are to paragraphs in RIA's Federal Tax Coordinator 2d and RIA's Analysis of Federal Taxes: Income. Footnote references beginning with numbers are to paragraphs in RIA's United States Tax Reporter.

Some expenses incurred by or for a physically handicapped individual to remove structural barriers in his residence to accommodate his physical condition, e.g., constructing access ramps, widening doorways and installing special support bars, are presumed not to increase the value of the residence and may be deductible in full. (Reg § 1.213-1(e)(1)(iii))[5]

Capital expenditures that are related only to the sick person and are detachable from the property are not permanent improvements, so their full cost can be a medical expense, e.g., detachable inclinators and air conditioners. (Reg § 1.213-1(e)(1)(iii))[6]

All the costs of operating or maintaining a medical capital asset are deductible, even if none or only a portion of the cost of the asset itself qualifies. (Reg § 1.213-1(e)(1)(iii))[7]

¶ 2144   Transportation expenses.

The costs of transportation primarily for and essential to medical care qualify as medical expenses. (Code Sec. 213(d)(1)(B)) This includes food and lodging expense (¶ 2145) while en route to the place of medical treatment, (Reg § 1.213-1(e)(1)(iv)) as well as taxi, train, plane and bus fares and the cost of ambulance services.[8]

Deductible medical expenses also include certain out-of-pocket car expenses, e.g., for gas, oil, parking fees and tolls, but not depreciation, repair, insurance or maintenance. Instead of claiming the actual costs of gas and oil, taxpayer may deduct a flat 9¢ in '93 for each mile he uses the car for qualified medical transportation.[9]

¶ 2145   Costs of meals and lodging.

Expenses for meals and lodging away from home aren't medical expenses unless they're part of the cost of care in a hospital or other institution, or part of travel expenses for medical care (¶s 2142, 2144). And then only 80% (50%, after '93) of the expenses for *meals* are deductible.[10]

Taxpayer may deduct as a medical expense amounts paid for lodging (excluding food) while away from home where the lodging is primarily for and essential to medical care in a hospital or equivalent. The deduction is limited to $50 per night for each individual. (Code Sec. 213(d)(2))[11]

No deduction is allowed for lavish or extravagant lodging or where there is any significant element of personal pleasure, recreation or vacation in the travel. (Code Sec. 213(d)(2)(B))[12]

¶ 2146   Decedent's medical expenses.

Expenses for a decedent's medical care that are paid out of his estate are treated as paid by him when the expenses were incurred (and deducted in that year) if: (1) they are paid within one year after his death, (2) they aren't deducted for federal estate tax purposes, and (3) a statement is filed with the income tax return (or amended return) showing that the expenses haven't been allowed for estate tax purposes and that an estate tax deduction for them is waived. (Code Sec. 213(c))[13]

observation: The choice of an income tax or estate tax deduction depends primarily on the extent to which the expense is deductible for income tax purposes, the decedent's top income tax rate, and the top effective estate tax rate.

¶ 2147   When to deduct medical expenses.

Only medical expenses actually paid during the tax year are deductible. Deduction is thus allowed for payments in the year even though the expenses were incurred in an earlier year. (Reg § 1.213-1(a)(1)) If the payment is made by credit card, the amount is

---

5. ¶ K-2117; ¶ 2134.13.
6. ¶ K-2121; ¶s 2134.04, 2134.12.
7. ¶ K-2120; ¶ 2134.13.

8. ¶ K-2200 *et seq.*; ¶s 2134.04, 2134.09.
9. ¶ K-2210; ¶s 2134.04, 2134.09.

10. ¶ K-2211 *et seq.*
11. ¶ K-2212; ¶s 2134.04, 2134.09.

12. ¶ K-2212; ¶s 2134.04, 2134.09.
13. ¶ K-2405; ¶ 2134.03.

Footnote references beginning with letters are to paragraphs in RIA's Federal Tax Coordinator 2d and RIA's Analysis of Federal Taxes: Income. Footnote references beginning with numbers are to paragraphs in RIA's United States Tax Reporter.

deductible in the year the charge is made regardless of when the credit card bill is paid.[14]

Advance payment of anticipated medical expenses doesn't qualify for a current deduction unless there is a contractual obligation to pay in the current year.[15]

Certain insurance premiums paid by a taxpayer who is under 65 during the payment year, for medical care for himself, his spouse and dependents for the period *after* he reaches 65 are deductible in the year paid. (Reg § 1.213-1(e)(4)(i)(b)[16]

¶ 2148 Medical expenses compensated for by insurance or otherwise.

Medical expenses are not deductible if they have been compensated for by insurance or otherwise. (Code Sec. 213(a)) Taxpayer must reduce his medical expenses by amounts so compensated before applying the 7.5%-of-AGI floor. But no reduction is required for amounts received as compensation for loss of earnings or damages for personal injuries.[17]

If reimbursements in a tax year exceed medical expenses in that year, no medical deduction is allowed.[18] Any part of the excess that is attributable to an employer's contribution is taxable; the rest is tax-free.[19]

¶ 2149 Reimbursement in year after medical expenses are paid.

If a taxpayer is reimbursed for medical expenses in a year after he paid (and deducted) them, the reimbursement must be reported as income to the extent attributable to the earlier deduction. (Reg § 1.213-1(g)) Reimbursement is not included in income to the extent the earlier medical deduction did not reduce taxpayer's tax, or where no medical expenses were deducted because taxpayer didn't itemize. (Reg § 1.213-1(g))[20]

¶ 2150 Alimony or Separate Maintenance ▃▃▃▃▃▃▃▃▃▃▃▃▃▃

Payments of alimony or separate maintenance made under a divorce or separation instrument are deductible by the payor spouse and taxable to the payee spouse. Alimony must be paid in cash and may not continue beyond the death of the payee spouse. A payment that is fixed as child support is not alimony.

For pre-'85 instruments, see ¶ 2156.

For deduction of related legal expenses, see ¶ 2165.

¶ 2151 Tax treatment of alimony or separate maintenance payments.

Payments of alimony or separate maintenance (¶ 2152) are taxable to the payee spouse and deductible by the payor spouse. (Code Sec. 71, Code Sec. 215)[21]

The payments are taxable to the payee spouse in the year received. (Reg § 1.71-1(b)(5)) They are deductible by the payor spouse (on Form 1040) in the year paid, as a deduction from gross income. (Code Sec. 62(a)(10), Code Sec. 215(a))[22]

✎ observation: The payor spouse doesn't have to itemize to be allowed the alimony deduction. But he can't use Form 1040A or Form 1040EZ.

The above rules don't apply if the spouses file a joint return. (Code Sec. 71(c))[23]

¶ 2152 Alimony requirements.

To qualify as alimony, a payment must be under a divorce or separation instrument (¶ 2153). And it must be made in cash. (Code Sec. 71(b)(1)) A transfer of property other than cash cannot be alimony.[24]

---

14. ¶ K-2401; ¶ 2134.03.
15. ¶ K-2403; ¶ 2134.03.
16. ¶ K-2404.
17. ¶ K-2601 *et seq.*; ¶s 2134.14, 2134.15.

18. ¶ K-2605.
19. ¶ H-1112.
20. ¶ K-2604; ¶ 2134.15.

21. ¶ K-6001 *et seq.*; ¶s 714 *et seq.*, 2154.
22. ¶ A-2621; ¶s 714 *et seq.*, 2154.

23. ¶ K-6007; ¶ 714.03.
24. ¶ K-6036; ¶ 714.01.

Footnote references beginning with letters are to paragraphs in RIA's Federal Tax Coordinator 2d and RIA's Analysis of Federal Taxes: Income. Footnote references beginning with numbers are to paragraphs in RIA's United States Tax Reporter.

A cash transfer that the parties do not want to treat as alimony can be treated otherwise (i.e., as a property settlement) if the parties so designate (¶ 2158).[25]

And there must be no requirement that the payments continue beyond the death of the payee spouse (e.g., to the spouse's estate) or that any substitute payment (in cash or property) be made after the death of the payee spouse—i.e., the payments must end at the payee spouse's death. (Code Sec. 71(b)(1)(D)) If this rule isn't satisfied, *none* of the payments (even those made during the life of the payee spouse) is alimony. (Reg § 1.71-1T(b), Q&A-10)[26]

The payments don't have to be periodic, or in discharge of a legal support obligation arising out of the marital or family relationship. (Reg § 1.71-1T(a), Q&A-3)[27]

¶ 2153 Payments must be under a divorce or separation instrument.

To qualify as alimony, a payment must be made under a divorce or separation instrument. (Code Sec. 71(b)(1)(A))[28] This means:

(1) a decree of divorce or separate maintenance or a written instrument issued incident to the decree,

(2) a written separation agreement, or

(3) a decree not described in (1) above, e.g., a temporary support order. (Code Sec. 71(b)(2))[29]

If made under a decree of divorce or separate maintenance (or a written instrument incident to the decree), the payment must be made after the decree. (Reg § 1.71-1(b)(1)(i))[30] If made under a separation agreement, the payment must be made after the execution of that agreement. (Reg § 1.71-1(b)(2))[31]

¶ 2154 Separate household requirement.

Spouses who are legally separated (but not divorced) under a divorce or separate maintenance decree must not live in the same household when the payment is made, or it won't be alimony. (Code Sec. 71(b)(1)(C)) But if the spouses are not legally separated, a payment under a written separation agreement or temporary support order may be alimony even if they are members of the same household. (Reg § 1.71-1T(b), Q&A-9)[32]

The spouses are not treated as members of the same household if one spouse is preparing to leave it, and does leave within one month after the payment.[33]

¶ 2155 Payments to a third party.

Payments made in cash by the payor spouse to a third party on behalf of the payee spouse under the terms of the divorce or separation instrument can be alimony. (Code Sec. 71(b)(1)(A)) Thus, cash payments of the payee spouse's rent, mortgage, tax or tuition liabilities that the payor spouse makes as required by the instrument can qualify as alimony, as can payments made to a third party at the payee spouse's written request.[34]

But payments made to maintain property *owned by the payor spouse* but used by the payee spouse (including mortgage payments, realty taxes, and insurance premiums) are *not* payments on behalf of the payee spouse (i.e., not alimony) even if made under the terms of the divorce or separation instrument. (Reg § 1.71-1T(b))[35]

¶ 2156 Annuities and life insurance contracts.

Where an annuity is transferred incident to a decree of divorce or separation, the transferee (payee spouse) is entitled to the usual annuity treatment (¶ 1357 *et seq.*) for amounts received under the contract. Thus, the portion of each contract payment that is

---

25. ¶ K-6009; ¶ 714.01.   28. ¶ K-6013; ¶ 714.   31. ¶ K-6030; ¶ 714.06.   34. ¶ K-6037; ¶ 714.01.
26. ¶ K-6011; ¶ 714.01.   29. ¶ K-6013; ¶ 714.01.   32. ¶ K-6010; ¶ 714.01.   35. ¶ K-6038.
27. ¶ K-6003; ¶ 714.   30. ¶ K-6020.   33. ¶ K-6010.

Footnote references beginning with letters are to paragraphs in RIA's Federal Tax Coordinator 2d and RIA's Analysis of Federal Taxes: Income. Footnote references beginning with numbers are to paragraphs in RIA's United States Tax Reporter.

taxable to the payee spouse is reduced by the payor spouse's (transferor's) investment in the contract.[36]

If the payor spouse pays premiums for insurance on his life as required by the divorce or separation instrument, the premiums are alimony if the other (payee) spouse owns the policy.[37]

The transfer of a life insurance contract to a spouse incident to divorce or separation does not result in the loss of the exclusion for the policy's death benefits (¶ 1350 *et seq.*).[38]

¶ 2157 Payments for the support of the payor's children.

A payment under a divorce or separation instrument that is "fixed" (or treated as fixed) as support for a child of the payor spouse is *not* alimony. (Code Sec. 71(c)(1))[39] This applies if the instrument designates a specified amount of money or a part of a payment to be child support. The actual amount may fluctuate. (Reg § 1.71-1T(c))[40]

A portion of a payment may be *treated* as fixed if the payment is to be reduced on the happening of a specified contingency relating to the child, (Code Sec. 71(c)(2)) e.g., on the child's eighteenth birthday, or when he dies, marries or leaves school.[41] A payment may also be treated as fixed if it ends or is reduced at a time that can clearly be associated with the contingency. (Reg § 1.71-1T(c))[42]

If a divorce or separation instrument provides a specified amount for alimony and a specified amount for child support, and the payor spouse pays less than the amount designated for child support, then the *entire* payment is treated as child support and no part is treated as alimony. (Code Sec. 71(c)(3))[43]

¶ 2158 Designating that payments are not to be treated as alimony.

If a divorce or separation instrument designates a payment that would otherwise qualify as alimony as *not* to be treated as alimony, then the payment will not qualify as alimony. (Code Sec. 71(b)(1)(B))[44]

¶ 2159 Alimony trusts.

Where the payor spouse transfers property into a trust with the payee spouse as a beneficiary, the trust's payments to the payee spouse are treated under the usual trust rules (¶ 3900 *et seq.*) and not as alimony even if they meet the alimony requirements. Thus, payments out of trust principal or tax-exempt income are not taxed to the payee spouse or deductible by the payor spouse. (Code Sec. 215(d))[45]

¶ 2160 Recapture rules—excess front-loading of alimony.

If there are "excess" alimony payments ("front-loading"), the payor spouse must "recapture" the "excess" by including it in his gross income for the third post-separation year (below). (Code Sec. 71(f)(1)(A))[46] The same amount is deducted by the payee spouse in computing adjusted gross income for *his* third post-separation year. (Code Sec. 71(f)(1)(B))[47]

✒️observation: The payee spouse doesn't have to itemize to be allowed the deduction.

The "recapture" amount is the sum of:

(1) the excess of (a) the alimony or separate maintenance payments in the second post-separation year, over (b) the sum of the payments in the third year plus $15,000; (Code Sec. 71(f)(2)(B)) *plus*

(2) the excess of (a) the payments in the first post-separation year, over (b) the sum of

---

36. ¶ J-4502; ¶s 714.04, 10,414.
37. ¶s K-6040, K-6045; ¶ 714.01.
38. ¶ J-4504; ¶s 714.04, 1014.02.
39. ¶ K-6064; ¶ 714.02.
40. ¶ K-6065.
41. ¶ K-6067; ¶ 714.02.
42. ¶ K-6068; ¶ 714.02.
43. ¶ K-6065; ¶ 714.02.
44. ¶ K-6009; ¶ 714.01.
45. ¶s K-6039 *et seq.*, C-5428 *et seq.*; ¶ 2154.02.
46. ¶ K-6047; ¶ 714.03.
47. ¶ K-6048; ¶ 714.03.

Footnote references beginning with letters are to paragraphs in RIA's Federal Tax Coordinator 2d and RIA's Analysis of Federal Taxes: Income. Footnote references beginning with numbers are to paragraphs in RIA's United States Tax Reporter.

the average of the payments in the second year (minus any excess payment in (1), above) and third year, plus $15,000. (Code Sec. 71(f)(2)(A))[48]

🖊️*Illustration:* H makes alimony payments of $50,000 in the first post-separation year, $20,000 in the second year, and nothing in the third year. H must recapture $32,500: $5,000 from the second year ($20,000 – ($0 + $15,000)) and $27,500 from the first year ($50,000 – ($7,500 + $15,000)), where the $7,500 equals $15,000 ($20,000 – $5,000) ÷ 2, i.e., the average of the second and third year payments after reduction of the second year payments by the $5,000 recaptured from Year Two.

🖊️*observation:* The payor spouse is in effect allowed to pay up to $15,000 of excess alimony in each of the first two post-separation years without having to recapture the excess.

The first post-separation year is the first calendar year in which the payor spouse paid alimony, etc., to the payee spouse. The second and third post-separation years are the succeeding calendar years. (Code Sec. 71(f)(6))[49]

There's no recapture where payments cease because either spouse dies or the payee spouse remarries before the close of the third post-separation year. (Code Sec. 71(f)(5)(A)) Nor does recapture apply to temporary support payments (Code Sec. 71(f)(5)(B)) or to payments that fluctuate as a result of a continuing liability to pay, for at least three years, a fixed portion of income from the earnings of a business, property or services. (Code Sec. 71(f)(5)(C))[50]

¶ 2161 Pre-'85 instruments.

The rules discussed at ¶ 2150 *et seq.*, do not apply to a pre-'85 instrument unless it is: (1) modified after '84 to expressly provide that those (post-'84) rules are to apply, or (2) incorporated by a post-'84 divorce decree that changes the terms of the payments.[1]

To be alimony under a pre-'85 instrument, payments must be "periodic." These payments are periodic:

■ A fixed amount each period (e.g., $100 a month) for an indefinite time.

■ An indefinite amount (e.g., 25% of the payor's income) for a fixed or indefinite period.

■ Installments of a stated (or determinable) lump-sum amount, if the period of payments specified is more than ten years (but the maximum amount deductible each year by the payor spouse is 10% of the principal sum, with no carryover of any excess).

■ Installments over a period of ten years or less, if the payments are subject to any of these contingencies: death of either spouse, remarriage of the payee spouse, or change in economic status of either spouse.

"Periodic" payments don't have to be made at regular intervals. (Reg § 1.71-1(d))[2]

If a spouse transferred property in trust, periodic payments by the trust to the payee spouse are taxable to the payee whether made from principal or income. Since the payments are not taxable income to the grantor (payor) spouse, that spouse can't deduct them as alimony. (Reg § 1.71-1(c)(3), Reg § 1.215-1)[3]

The portion of any periodic payment that the terms of the decree, instrument or agreement *specifically fixed* as payable for support of the payor spouse's minor children is not alimony, i.e., it's not deductible by the payor spouse or taxable to the payee spouse. (Reg § 1.71-1(c))[4]

---

48. ¶ K-6047 *et seq.*; ¶ 714.03.
49. ¶ K-6049; ¶ 714.03.
50. ¶ K-6051; ¶ 714.03.

1. ¶ K-6100 *et seq.*; ¶ 714.
2. ¶ K-6139 *et seq.*; ¶s 714.12, 714.13.

3. ¶ K-6177 *et seq.*; ¶s 714.15, 2154.02.

4. ¶ K-6191 *et seq.*; ¶ 714.16.

Footnote references beginning with letters are to paragraphs in RIA's Federal Tax Coordinator 2d and RIA's Analysis of Federal Taxes: Income. Footnote references beginning with numbers are to paragraphs in RIA's United States Tax Reporter.

¶ 2162 "Nonbusiness" Expenses ▰▰▰▰▰▰▰▰▰▰▰▰

Individuals may deduct most ordinary and necessary expenses that, though not connected with their trade or business, are paid or incurred during the tax year for the collection or production of income, the management, conservation or maintenance of property held for the production of income, or the determination, collection or refund of any tax.

However, a *personal expense* or a *capital expenditure* for which deductions are prohibited cannot be deducted as a nonbusiness expense. (Code Sec. 262(a), Code Sec. 263; Reg § 1.212-1(e))[5]

For 2%-of-adjusted gross income floor on nonbusiness expense deductions, see ¶ 3107. For treatment of nonbusiness expenses under the alternative minimum tax, see ¶ 3208.

¶ 2163 "Nonbusiness" (investment) expenses.

Taxpayer may deduct a wide variety of expenses related to his investments (not amounting to a business) if they are ordinary and necessary for the production or collection of income, or for the management, conservation or maintenance of property held for the production of income. (Code Sec. 212(1), (2))[6]

Office-at-home expenses allocable to "nonbusiness" investment activities aren't deductible. (This doesn't affect deductions for interest, taxes or casualty losses.) (Code Sec. 280A)[7]

Expenses of a convention, seminar, or similar meeting are not deductible as nonbusiness (investment) expenses. (Code Sec. 274(h)(7))[8]

For limitations on deducting nonbusiness expenses relating to an investment that is a "passive activity," see ¶ 1798 *et seq.*

For limitations on deducting expenses of vacation homes used partly by the owner and also rented out, see ¶ 1768.

¶ 2164 Tax determination costs.

Individuals may deduct as a "nonbusiness" expense all the ordinary and necessary expenses incurred in connection with the determination, collection, or refund of any tax. (Code Sec. 212(3)) This applies to income, estate, gift, property and any other tax imposed by federal, state, municipal or foreign authorities. Included are the costs of: preparing tax returns, determining the extent of liability, contesting tax liability, getting tax counsel, protesting assessments, prosecuting refunds, compromising liability, (Reg § 1.212-1(e)) a tax text used by an individual to help prepare his own tax return,[9] tax advice[10] (including estate planning),[11] an appraisal of property to substantiate a claimed deduction,[12] contesting taxes for which taxpayer could be liable as transferee[13] and contesting civil penalties, whether taxpayer is successful or not.[14]

¶ 2165 "Nonbusiness" legal expenses.

An individual may deduct nonbusiness legal fees such as attorney's fees, court costs, etc., if they're incurred to produce income, preserve income-producing property, etc. (Reg § 1.212-1(k))[15]

Nonbusiness legal expenses incurred to acquire, perfect, or defend title to property are *not* deductible. But any amount of those costs that is allocable to collecting accrued rents on the property may be deducted. (Reg § 1.212-1(k))[16]

---

5. ¶s L-1400, L-1415; ¶s 2124 *et seq.*, 2624, 2634.
6. ¶ L-1401 *et seq.*; ¶ 2124 *et seq.*
7. ¶ L-1300; ¶ 280A4.

8. ¶ L-1724; ¶s 2124.01, 2744.07.
9. ¶ L-3001; ¶ 2124.14.
10. ¶ L-3008; ¶ 2124.14.

11. ¶ L-3010; ¶ 2124.14.
12. ¶ L-3006.
13. ¶ L-3016.

14. ¶ L-3007; ¶ 2124.14.
15. ¶ L-2900 *et seq.*; ¶ 2124.12.
16. ¶ L-2908 *et seq.*; ¶ 2124.12.

Footnote references beginning with letters are to paragraphs in RIA's Federal Tax Coordinator 2d and RIA's Analysis of Federal Taxes: Income. Footnote references beginning with numbers are to paragraphs in RIA's United States Tax Reporter.

Legal expenses in connection with divorce, separation or a support decree are personal expenses which cannot be deducted by either spouse, (Reg § 1.262-1(b)(7))[17] *except that*:

■ the part of legal fees attributable to the production or collection of taxable alimony is deductible by the payee spouse, (Reg § 1.262-1)[18] and

■ taxpayer can deduct fees paid to his attorney for tax research and advice relating to a divorce and property settlement if the fee for the tax work is segregated, but not legal fees he pays to his spouse's attorney for tax advice given to the spouse.[19]

¶ 2166 Tax-exempt income expenses.

A taxpayer may not deduct costs incurred in the production of tax-exempt income. (Code Sec. 265(a)(1))[20] For bar on deduction of interest on indebtedness incurred or continued to buy or carry tax-exempt securities, see ¶ 1719.

If expenses are attributable to both taxable and tax-exempt income, and can't be specifically identified, they must be prorated. (Reg § 1.265-1(c))[21]

¶ 2167 Premature withdrawal penalties.

An individual may deduct any interest or principal he forfeits to a bank or other financial institution as a penalty for premature withdrawal from a time savings account, certificate of deposit or similar deposit. The penalty is deductible from gross income in computing adjusted gross income, (Code Sec. 62(a)(9))[22] rather than as an interest expense (so it can't be netted against interest income).[23]

> *observation:* The interest deduction limits (¶s 1712 *et seq.*,1722 *et seq.*) don't apply.

¶ 2168 Bond Premium Amortization

Bond premium (amount payable in excess of the bond's face amount) is amortizable in certain cases. The amortized amount reduces basis and, for taxable bonds, is treated as an offset to interest received.

Premium on tax-exempt bonds *must* be amortized by all owners. (Code Sec. 171(a)(2); Reg § 1.171-1(a)(1)) Premium on taxable bonds *may* be amortized, at taxpayer's election (¶ 2170). (Code Sec. 171(a)(1), (c); Reg § 1.171-1(a)(2))[24]

"Bonds" subject to these rules include a bond, debenture, note, certificate or other interest-bearing evidence of indebtedness issued by a corporation, a government or its political subdivision, or an individual. Obligations that are taxpayer's stock in trade or properly includible in inventory aren't "bonds" (except for dealers, see ¶ 2172). (Code Sec. 171(d); Reg § 1.171-4(c))[25]

¶ 2169 How amortization works.

For both taxable and tax-exempt bonds, amortization results in a reduction in basis. (Code Sec. 1016(a)(5))[26]

For *taxable* bonds (but not tax-exempts), amortization also results in a deduction in computing taxable income, for the amount of amortizable bond premium attributable to the tax year. (Code Sec. 171(a); Reg § 1.171-1(b)(2))[27] The deduction is used to offset the interest paid on the bond (for bonds acquired after '87). (Code Sec. 171(e); Reg § 1.171-1(b)(2))[28]

The amount of amortizable premium for any bond is the excess of the basis of the bond (for determining loss on sale) over the amount payable at maturity, (Code Sec. 171(b)(1);

17. ¶ L-2960; ¶s 2124.13, 2624.
18. ¶ L-2963; ¶s 2124.13, 2624.
19. ¶ L-3011; ¶ 2124.13.
20. ¶ K-9000 *et seq.*; ¶ 2654.

21. ¶ K-9002; ¶ 2654.
22. ¶ K-5880; ¶ 624.
23. ¶ K-5882.

24. ¶ K-5611 *et seq.*; ¶s 1714.01, 10,164.
25. ¶ K-5618; ¶s 1714, 1714.02.

26. ¶ K-5639; ¶ 1714.01.
27. ¶s K-5627, K-5628; ¶ 1714.01.
28. ¶ K-5629; ¶ 1714.01.

Footnote references beginning with letters are to paragraphs in RIA's Federal Tax Coordinator 2d and RIA's Analysis of Federal Taxes: Income. Footnote references beginning with numbers are to paragraphs in RIA's United States Tax Reporter.

Reg § 1.171-2)[29] based on taxpayer's yield to maturity (Code Sec. 171(b)(3)) (for obligations issued before Sept. 28, '85, any reasonable method may be used).[30] Amortizable bond premium may include capitalized expenses, e.g., buying commissions. (Reg § 1.171-2(d))[31]

¶ 2170 Election to amortize bond premium.

The taxpayer elects to amortize bond premium (on taxable bonds) by claiming a deduction for bond premium amortization (or interest offset) on his return for the first tax year for which the election is to apply, and attaching a statement showing the computation of the deduction. (Reg § 1.171-3(a), (c))[32]

¶ 2171 Convertible bonds and callable bonds.

For convertible bonds, if the option to convert on a specified date rests with the bondholder, then premium allocable to the interest feature is amortizable, but not premium attributable to the conversion privilege. (Code Sec. 171(b)(1); Reg § 1.171-2(c)(1))[33]

Premium on callable bonds is amortizable to maturity or to an earlier call date depending on the date the bond is acquired and whether the bond is taxable. (Code Sec. 171(b)(1)(B), (3)(B); Reg § 1.171-2(b))[34]

¶ 2172 Dealers in securities.

Dealers in securities (other than tax-exempts) aren't permitted or required to amortize bond premium. This doesn't apply to securities the dealer buys, sells and holds for his own account. (Reg § 1.171-4(c))[35]

For certain tax-exempt bonds, dealers must reduce either basis or cost of sales by the amount of annual amortization. (Code Sec. 75)[36]

¶ 2173 Qualified Clean Fuel Vehicles and Refueling Property ▬▬▬

A deduction is allowed for the cost of motor vehicles that are propelled by clean-burning fuel and for qualified refueling property used in the storage or delivery of clean-burning fuel.

¶ 2174 Qualified clean-fuel vehicles and refueling property deduction before '95.

For property placed in service after June 30, '93 (and before 2005), a limited deduction from gross income is available for the cost of any qualified clean-fuel vehicle (¶ 2175) or qualified clean-fuel vehicle refueling property (¶ 2176), in the tax year the property is placed in service. (Code Sec. 179A(a)(1))[37]

🖐*observation:* The deduction is not a miscellaneous itemized deduction and is not subject to the 2% floor for those deductions.

The portion of the cost of a qualified clean-fuel vehicle that may be deducted is limited to:

■ $5,000, for any truck or van with a gross vehicle weight rating of more than 10,000 pounds but not more than 26,000 pounds;

■ $50,000, for any truck or van with a gross vehicle weight rating of more than 26,000 pounds, or any bus which seats at least 20 adults (excluding the driver);

■ $2,000, for any other type of qualified clean-fuel vehicle. (Code Sec. 179A(b)(1)(A))[38]

If a vehicle may be propelled by both clean-burning and other fuels, the deductible portion of its cost is limited to the incremental cost of permitting the use of the clean-burning fuel. (Code Sec. 179A(a)(2))[39]

---

29. ¶ K-5615.
30. ¶ K-5660 *et seq.*; ¶ 1714.03.
31. ¶ K-5624; ¶ 1714.03.
32. ¶ K-5632.
33. ¶s K-5614, K-5623; ¶ 1714.06.
34. ¶s K-5622, K-5644 *et seq.*
35. ¶ K-5651; ¶ 1714.01.
36. ¶ K-5652 *et seq.*; ¶s 1714.01, 754 *et seq.*
37. ¶ K-7000.1.
38. ¶ K-7000.4.
39. ¶ K-7000.2.

Footnote references beginning with letters are to paragraphs in RIA's Federal Tax Coordinator 2d and RIA's Analysis of Federal Taxes: Income. Footnote references beginning with numbers are to paragraphs in RIA's United States Tax Reporter.

The portion of the cost of qualified clean-fuel vehicle refueling property that may be deducted can't exceed $100,000 in the aggregate, for property placed in service at a location. (Code Sec. 179A(b)(2))[40]

The deduction for any of these properties is the excess of: (1) $100,000, over (2) the aggregate amount of deductions taken by a taxpayer, or related person (under Code Secs. 267(b) or 707(b)(1)) or predecessor, for qualified clean-fuel vehicle refueling property at that location for all previous tax years. (Code Sec. 179A(b)(2))[41]

Recapture rules apply. (Code Sec. 179A(e))[42]

The deduction is reduced: by 25%, for property placed in service in 2002; by 50%, for property placed in service in 2003; and by 75%, for property placed in service in 2004. (Code Sec. 179A(b)(1)(B))[43] The deduction isn't available for property placed in service after 2004. (Code Sec. 179A(g))[44]

¶ 2175 Qualified clean-fuel vehicle.

A *qualified clean-fuel vehicle* is property:

(1) which is acquired for use (not resale) by taxpayer;

(2) whose original use begins with taxpayer;

(3) which either (a) is installed on a motor vehicle that has been altered to be propelled by a clean-burning fuel, or (b) is a motor vehicle produced by an original equipment manufacturer and designed so that it can be propelled by clean-burning fuel, with certain limitations; (Code Sec. 179A(c)(1)) *and*

(4) which complies with certain environmental standards. (Code Sec. 179A(c)(2))[45]

A qualified clean-fuel vehicle doesn't include any qualified electric vehicle. (Code Sec. 179A(c)(3))[46]

¶ 2176 Qualified clean-fuel vehicle refueling property.

Qualified clean-fuel vehicle refueling property is property:

(1) which is subject to depreciation;

(2) whose original use begins with taxpayer; *and*

(3) which is used either for the storage or dispensing of a clean-burning fuel, or the recharging of electric motor vehicles. (Code Sec. 179A(d))[47]

Clean burning fuels are natural gas, liquefied natural gas, liquefied petroleum gas, hydrogen, electricity or any other fuel if at least 85% of it is methanol, ethanol, or any other alcohol or ether. (Code Sec. 179A(e)(1))[48]

---

40. ¶ K-7000.6.   43. ¶ K-7005.   45. ¶ K-7000.12 *et seq.*   47. ¶ K-7000.17 *et seq.*
41. ¶ K-7000.6.   44. ¶ K-7001.   46. ¶ K-7000.12.   48. ¶ K-7000.20.
42. ¶ K-7000.8 *et seq.*

Footnote references beginning with letters are to paragraphs in RIA's Federal Tax Coordinator 2d and RIA's Analysis of Federal Taxes: Income. Footnote references beginning with numbers are to paragraphs in RIA's United States Tax Reporter.

Chapter 7   Tax Credits

¶ 2300 Tax Credits

Tax credits are either business credits intended to provide special incentives for the achievement of certain economic objectives, or personal credits, which provide a tax benefit to taxpayers falling into special categories (e.g., the elderly or disabled, etc.). The foreign tax credit, however, may apply to both business and nonbusiness taxpayers.

The three main categories of tax credits are:

(1) The business incentive credits, see ¶ 2301.

(2) The personal (refundable and nonrefundable) credits, see ¶ 2302.

(3) The foreign tax credit, see ¶ 2357 *et seq.*

For tax credits attributable to certain "passive" activities, see ¶ 1798 *et seq.*

¶ 2301 Business incentive credits.

The business incentive credits fall into one of two groups:

■ General business credits—

. . . the investment credit (¶ 2306 *et seq.*) (which includes the rehabilitation credit (¶ 2311), the energy credit (¶ 2314) and the reforestation credit (¶ 2315));

. . . alcohol fuel credit (¶ 2322);

. . . the low-income housing credit (¶ 2320 *et seq.*);

. . . the incremental research credit (¶ 2323);

. . . the targeted jobs credit (¶ 2324 *et seq.*);

. . . the enhanced oil recovery credit (¶ 2326);

. . . the disabled access credit (¶ 2327);

. . . the credit for producing electricity from certain renewable resources (¶ 2328).

. . . the empowerment zone employment credit (¶ 2329);

. . . the Indian employment credit (¶ 2330);

. . . the employer Social Security credit (¶ 2331); and

. . . the credit for contributions to selected community development corporations (¶ 2332).

■ Special business credits—

. . . the production credit for alternative (nonconventional source) energy (¶ 2333);

. . . the clinical testing expense credit for drugs for rare diseases or conditions (¶ 2334).

¶ 2302 Personal (refundable and nonrefundable) credits.

Taxpayers, whether or not in business, may qualify for one or more of the following:

■ Refundable credits—

. . . the earned income credit (¶ 2336 *et seq.*);

. . . the credit for tax withheld (¶ 2343);

. . . the credit for excess social security tax withheld (¶ 2344);

. . . the credit for excise tax for certain nontaxable uses of fuels; (Code Sec. 6420, Code Sec. 6421, Code Sec. 6427(l))

. . . the credit for light-weight diesel vehicle owners (¶ 2345).

Footnote references beginning with letters are to paragraphs in RIA's Federal Tax Coordinator 2d and RIA's Analysis of Federal Taxes: Income. Footnote references beginning with numbers are to paragraphs in RIA's United States Tax Reporter.

■ Nonrefundable credits—

. . . the credit for the elderly and the permanently and totally disabled (¶ 2346);

. . . the credit for household and dependent care expenses (¶ 2347 *et seq.*);

. . . the home mortgage credit (¶ 2353);

. . . the minimum tax credit (¶ 2356).

¶ *2303* Business Credits

Certain business incentive credits are combined into one "general business credit" for purposes of determining each credit's allowance limitation for the tax year. Other business credits have their own allowance limits.

¶ *2304* General business credit.

The investment tax credit (i.e., the rehabilitation, the energy and the reforestation credits), targeted jobs credit, alcohol fuel credit, research credit, low-income housing credit, enhanced oil recovery credit, disabled access credit, credit for producing electricity from certain renewable resources, empowerment zone employment credit, Indian employment credit, and employer Social Security credit comprise one general business credit. (Code Sec. 38(b)) The selected community development corporation credit is also included in the current year business credit. A credit is allowed against income tax for a particular tax year equal to the sum of:

(1) the business credit carry*forwards* carried to the tax year,

(2) the *current year* business credit, and

(3) the business credit carry*backs* carried to the tax year. (Code Sec. 38(a))[1]

The credit allowed for any tax year (except for the empowerment zone employment credit, see below) is limited to the excess of taxpayer's "net income tax" over the greater of: (1) the tentative minimum tax for the tax year, or (2) 25% of the amount of the taxpayer's "net regular tax" which exceeds $25,000. (Code Sec. 38(c)(1))[2] Husbands and wives who file separate returns are each limited to $12,500 instead of $25,000, but if either spouse has no carryforward, carryback or current year general business credit in the tax year that ends within or with the other spouse's tax year, the other spouse gets the full amount of $25,000. (Code Sec. 38(c)(2)(A))[3]

For estates and trusts, the $25,000 amount must be reduced to an amount equal to $25,000 multiplied by a fraction whose numerator is the total income of the estate or trust which is not allocated to beneficiaries, and whose denominator is the total income of the estate or trust. (Code Sec. 38(c)(2)(D))[4]

Net income tax is the sum of the regular tax liability and the alternative minimum tax, reduced by the credits listed below. Net regular tax is the regular tax liability reduced by the sum of the following credits: (Code Sec. 38(c)(1)) (1) household and dependent care credit; (Code Sec. 21) (2) credit for the elderly and the permanently and totally disabled; (Code Sec. 22) (3) mortgage credit; (Code Sec. 25) (4) foreign tax and possessions tax credits; (Code Sec. 27) (5) clinical testing expense credit; (Code Sec. 28) and (6) alternative fuel production credit. (Code Sec. 29)[5]

The empowerment zone employment credit is limited to the excess of the taxpayer's net income tax over the greater of (1) 75% of his tentative minimum tax , or (2) 25% of so much of his net regular tax liability as exceeds $25,000. This limitation is reduced by the general credits (not including the empowerment zone employment credit) allowed for the tax year. (Code Sec. 38(c)(2)) The effect is that the empowerment zone employment credit

---

1. ¶ L-15200; ¶ 384.04.   3. ¶ L-15204; ¶ 384.02.   4. ¶ L-15207; ¶ 384.02.   5. ¶ L-15202; ¶ 384.03.
2. ¶ L-15202; ¶ 384.02.

Footnote references beginning with letters are to paragraphs in RIA's Federal Tax Coordinator 2d and RIA's Analysis of Federal Taxes: Income. Footnote references beginning with numbers are to paragraphs in RIA's United States Tax Reporter.

may be used to offset up to 25% of a taxpayer's alternative minimum tax.[6]

The general business credits are claimed on Form 3800, but only when more than one of the component credits is claimed or there is a carryback or carryover of credits.[7]

¶ 2305 Carryback, carryforward and deduction of unused business credits.

There is a three-year carryback and 15-year carryforward (on Form 3800) for the unused business credit on an earliest-year-first (FIFO) basis. (Code Sec. 39(a))[8] There's no carryback of:

■ the enhanced oil recovery credit to a tax year beginning before '91, (Code Sec. 39(d)(1))

■ the disabled access credit to a tax year ending before Nov. 5, '90, (Code Sec. 39(d)(2))

■ the credit for producing electricity from certain renewable resources to a tax year ending before '93 (before '94 if the credit is attributable to wind as the qualified energy source). (Code Sec. 39(d)(3))

■ the empowerment zone employment credit to a tax year ending before '94, (Code Sec. 39(d)(4))

■ the Indian employment credit to a tax year ending before Aug. 10, '93, (Code Sec. 39(d)(5)) and

■ the employer Social Security credit to a tax year ending before Aug. 10, '93, (Code Sec. 39(d)(6))

Deduction for unused credits: If any portion of a qualified business credit (investment credit, targeted jobs credit, alcohol fuel credit, research credit, enhanced oil recovery credit, empowerment zone employment credit, and Indian employment credit) (Code Sec. 196(c)) has not been allowed after the carryover period expires, the taxpayer is allowed to deduct the unused portion in the first tax year after the last tax year of the carryover period (or in the tax year of death or cessation if earlier). (Code Sec. 196(a), (b)) However, for the research credit for a tax year beginning before '90 and for the investment tax credit (other than the rehabilitation credit), the deduction is 50% of the unused amount. (Code Sec. 196(d))[9]

¶ 2306 The investment tax credits.

The investment tax credit (claimed on Form 3468) consists of:

(1) the rehabilitation investment credit, (Code Sec. 47) see ¶ 2311 *et seq.*;

(2) the energy credit, (Code Sec. 48(a)) see ¶ 2314; and

(3) the reforestation credit, (Code Sec. 48(b) see ¶ 2315.[10]

¶ 2307 What is investment credit property?

Investment credit property is any depreciable or amortizable property eligible for the rehabilitation, the energy, or the reforestation credit. (Code Sec. 50(a)(5))

Not all depreciable or amortizable property qualifies for the investment credit. Certain otherwise qualified property is denied the applicable credit if it is:

■ Property used "predominantly" outside the U.S., except for property listed in Code Sec. 168(g)(4)—generally dealing with rolling stock, spacecraft, satellites, etc. (Code Sec. 50(b)(1))

■ Property used predominantly to furnish, or in connection with the furnishing of, permanent lodging, except for certain nonlodging commercial facilities, lodging facilities used by transients, certified historic structures and energy property. (Code Sec. 50(b)(2))

■ Property used by certain tax-exempt organizations. (Code Sec. 50(b)(3)) If property is

---

6. ¶ L-15202.1; ¶ 38B4.03.   8. ¶ L-15209; ¶ 394.01.   9. ¶ L-15212; ¶ 394.02.   10. ¶ L-16500 *et seq.*; ¶s 474, 484.
7. ¶ L-15200; ¶ 384.

Footnote references beginning with letters are to paragraphs in RIA's Federal Tax Coordinator 2d and RIA's Analysis of Federal Taxes: Income. Footnote references beginning with numbers are to paragraphs in RIA's United States Tax Reporter.

leased to a partnership or other pass-through entity, a proportionate share of the property is treated as leased to each tax-exempt entity partner (under the rules of Code Sec. 168(h)(5) and (6)) in determining whether any portion of the property is tax-exempt use property. (Code Sec. 50(b)(4))

■ Property used by the U.S. or other governmental units, except for short-lease property. (Code Sec. 50(b)(4))[11]

¶ 2308 Noncorporate lessor's entitlement to the investment credit.

Noncorporate lessors, including partnerships and S corporations, are entitled to the investment credit for property they lease out (with an exception for property used by the lessor in his trade or business, other than the leasing of property, for at least 24 months before it's leased out) only if:

(1) the property was manufactured or produced by the lessor in the ordinary course of his business, or

(2) the term of the lease (including renewal options) is for less than 50% of the class life of the property, and for the first 12 months after the property is transferred to the lessee, the Code Sec. 162 deductions allowed to the lessor with respect to the property (other than rental payments and reimbursed expenses) exceed 15% of the rental income from the property. (Reg § 1.46-4(d))[12]

¶ 2309 Election to pass the investment credit through to lessee.

A lessee of new investment credit property may be entitled to take the investment credit on the property if the lessor elects to pass it to him. (Code Sec. 50(d)); Reg § 1.48-4)) The election statement is described in the regs. (Reg § 1.48-4(f),(g)) The effect is to treat the lessee as having acquired the property for its fair market value, but the lessor's basis is used instead when lessor and lessee are members of the same controlled group. The lessee uses the same investment credit life for the property as the lessor.[13]

But a lessor's election to pass the investment credit, with respect to property with an over 14-year ADR depreciation "class life," to his lessee results in only a partial transfer of the credit, if the lease is for a period which is less than 80% of the property's "class life" and isn't a "net lease." (Reg § 1.48-4(a)(2))[14]

¶ 2310 Allowance of credit for later decreases in nonqualified nonrecourse financing for at-risk investment credit property.

If there is a net decrease in the amount of nonqualified nonrecourse financing (under the at-risk limitation rules, see ¶ 1791) as of the close of a tax year following the tax year in which property was placed in service, the net decrease will be treated as an increase in the credit base for the property. Thus, an increase in the amount that the taxpayer has at risk with respect to a particular investment credit property is additional qualified investment. (Code Sec. 49(a)(2))

The increase in credit base attributable to a decrease in nonrecourse financing is treated as having been invested in the tax year the property was first placed in service. However, the credit is allowed in the tax year the amount at-risk is increased. (Code Sec. 49(a)(2))

Nonqualified nonrecourse financing is not treated as decreased through the surrender or other use of the property. (Code Sec. 49(a)(2))[15]

---

11. ¶ L-16501; ¶ 504.02.   13. ¶s L-16506, L-17010 et seq.;   14. ¶ L-17015; ¶ 484.10.   15. ¶ L-16505; ¶ 498.40.
12. ¶ L-17024 et seq.; ¶ 484.10.   ¶ 484.10.

Footnote references beginning with letters are to paragraphs in RIA's Federal Tax Coordinator 2d and RIA's Analysis of Federal Taxes: Income. Footnote references beginning with numbers are to paragraphs in RIA's United States Tax Reporter.

¶ 2311 Rehabilitation investment credits.

The rehabilitation credit for a building is 10% (20% for a certified historic structure) of the qualified rehabilitation expenditure. (Code Sec. 47(a)) A rehabilitated building (other than a certified historic structure) is eligible for the credit only if the building was first placed in service before '36. (Code Sec. 47(c)(1)(B))[16]

A qualified rehabilitation expenditure is any amount charged to capital and incurred in connection with the rehabilitation (including reconstruction, or an addition or improvement) of a qualified rehabilitated building (¶ 2312) that's depreciable under Code Sec. 168, and which is nonresidential real property, residential rental property, or real property with a class life of more than 12.5 years. Qualified expenditures don't include expenditures with respect to which straight-line depreciation isn't used.[17] (Code Sec. 47(c)(2)) Nor do they include any expenditures in connection with the rehabilitation of a building that are allocable to that portion of the building that is (or that may reasonably be expected to be) tax exempt use property. (Code Sec. 47(c)(2)(B)(v))[18]

In addition to owner-taxpayers of qualified property, the rehabilitation credits are available to lessees for qualified expenditures incurred by them, but only if, on the rehabilitation's completion date, the remaining term of the lease (without regard to renewal) is at least the recovery period under Code Sec. 168(c). (Code Sec. 47(c)(2)(B)(vi))[19]

¶ 2312 Which buildings qualify for the rehabilitation credit?

The term "qualified rehabilitated building" means any building (and its structural components) that satisfies all of the following requirements: (Code Sec. 47(c)(1))

(1) Except for a certified historic structure, the building was first placed in service before '36, see ¶ 2311.

(2) The building has been substantially rehabilitated (see below). (Code Sec. 47(c)(1)(A))

(3) The building was placed in service before the beginning of the rehabilitation. (Code Sec. 47(c)(1)(A))

(4) For any building other than a certified historic structure, the building retains in place (a) at least 75% of the external walls (including at least 50% as external walls), and (b) at least 75% of its internal structural framework. (Code Sec. 47(c)(1)(A))

(5) The building must be depreciable or amortizable. (Code Sec. 47(c)(1)(A))[20]

A substantial rehabilitation ((2), above) is one in which the qualified rehabilitation expenditures during the 24-month period selected by the taxpayer (as prescribed in regs) and ending with or within the year exceed the greater of: (Code Sec. 47(c)(1)(C))

(1) $5,000; or

(2) the adjusted basis of the building and its structural components as of the first day of the 24-month period, or of the holding period (without regard to reconstruction), whichever is later.

In the case of any rehabilitation which may reasonably be expected to be completed in phases set forth in architectural plans and specifications completed before the rehabilitation begins, a 60-month (instead of 24-month) period applies. (Code Sec. 47(c)(1)(C))[21]

Rehabilitation includes reconstruction. (Code Sec. 47(c)(1)(D))[22]

¶ 2313 Progress expenditure rehabilitation credit.

If any building being rehabilitated by or for the taxpayer has a "normal rehabilitation period" of two years or more, and it's reasonable to expect the building to be a qualified

---

16. ¶ L-16103; ¶ 498.40.
17. ¶ L-16102; ¶ 474.
18. ¶ L-16115.
19. ¶ L-16102; ¶ 474.
20. ¶ L-16103; ¶ 474.
21. ¶ L-16113; ¶ 474.
22. ¶ L-16106; ¶ 474.

Footnote references beginning with letters are to paragraphs in RIA's Federal Tax Coordinator 2d and RIA's Analysis of Federal Taxes: Income. Footnote references beginning with numbers are to paragraphs in RIA's United States Tax Reporter.

rehabilitated building (¶2312) in the hands of the taxpayer when placed in service, (Code Sec. 47(d)(2)) the taxpayer may irrevocably elect (on Form 3468) to account for qualified rehabilitation expenditures made with respect to such property in the following manner: (Code Sec. 47(d)(1); Reg § 1.46-5(g)(1))

(1) with respect to a self-rehabilitated building (i.e., a building where it is reasonable to believe that more than half these expenditures will be made *directly* by the taxpayer), any qualified rehabilitation expenditure is taken into account for the tax year in which it is properly chargeable to capital account (that is, properly includible in computing the property's basis), and

(2) with respect to a nonself-rehabilitated building, (i.e., a building were it is reasonable to believe that no more than half the qualified expenditure will be made directly by the taxpayer), any qualified rehabilitation expenditure is taken into account in the tax year it is paid.[23]

¶2314 Energy credit for solar and geothermal property.

The energy credit (claimed on Form 3468) is 10% (Code Sec. 48(a)(2)) of the basis of each energy property placed in service during the tax year. (Code Sec. 48(a)(1))

"Energy property" for which the credit is allowed is: (Code Sec. 48(a)(3))

(1) equipment that uses solar energy to generate electricity, to heat or cool (or provide hot water for use in) a structure, or to provide solar process heat;

(2) equipment used to produce, distribute, or use energy from a geothermal deposit (within the meaning of Code Sec. 613(e)(2)), but only, in the case of electricity generated by geothermal power, up to but not including the electrical transmission stage.

No credit is allowed for property unless it is depreciable or amortizable; its construction, reconstruction or erection is completed by the taxpayer or, if acquired by the taxpayer, its original use begins with the taxpayer; and it meets the official quality and performance standards in effect at the time of acquisition. (Code Sec. 48(a)(3))

No credit is allowed for public utility property (Code Sec. 48(a)(3)) or for property which also qualifies for the rehabilitation credit. (Code Sec. 48(a)(2))[24] If property is financed in whole or in part by subsidized financing or tax-exempt private activity bonds, the amount taken into account as qualified investment is proportionately reduced. (Code Sec. 48(a)(4))[25]

¶2315 Reforestation credit for businesses.

The reforestation credit is 10% of the basis of qualified timber property amortizable under Code Sec. 194, i.e., that portion of the basis of the qualified timber property attributable to reforestation expenditures. (Code Sec. 48(b), Code Sec. 194(c)(2))

¶2316 Recapture of investment credits.

Where investment credit property is disposed of or ceases to be investment credit property with respect to the taxpayer before the end of the recapture period, the credit taken for all earlier years as to the property is recaptured on Form 4255 (i.e., added to the tax liability for the recapture year). (Code Sec. 50(a)(1)) The recapture percentage is 100% during the first full year after the property is placed in service. This percentage decreases by 20 percentage points every succeeding full year. No credit is recaptured after the fifth full year. (Code Sec. 50(a)(1))

Recapture applies only to credit used to reduce tax liability. If any part of it isn't used, carrybacks and carryovers of the credit must be appropriately adjusted. (Code Sec. 50(a)(3))

---

23. ¶L-16200; ¶474.   24. ¶L-16502; ¶484.   25. ¶L-16504; ¶484.

Footnote references beginning with letters are to paragraphs in RIA's Federal Tax Coordinator 2d and RIA's Analysis of Federal Taxes: Income. Footnote references beginning with numbers are to paragraphs in RIA's United States Tax Reporter.

No recapture applies to a transfer by reason of death, (Code Sec. 50(a)(2)(E)) or by reason of a mere change in form of doing business. (Code Sec. 50(a)(4)(B))

Transfers between spouses or transfers incident to divorce (under the rules of Code Sec. 1041(a)) won't result in recapture. (Code Sec. 50(a)(5)(B))[26]

¶ 2317 Determining the progress expenditure credits recapture for investment credit property.

Different recapture computation methods apply to progress expenditures credit depending on whether the recapture year occurs before or after the progress expenditure property is placed in service. (Code Sec. 50(a))[27]

¶ 2318 Recapture because of later increases in nonqualified nonrecourse financing for at-risk investment credit property.

If the amount of nonqualified nonrecourse financing (see ¶ 1797) with respect to at-risk property increases as of the close of the tax year, then the tax for the tax year is increased by the total decrease in credits allowed in earlier tax years which would result if the credit base for the earlier credits had been reduced by the amount of the increase in the nonqualified nonrecourse financing. For purposes of computing credit recapture, the increase in nonqualified nonrecourse financing is treated as reducing the credit base and correspondingly reducing the qualified investment in the year the property was first placed in service. (Code Sec. 49(b)(1))

The transfer of (or an agreement to transfer) any evidence of indebtedness will not be treated as an increase in nonqualified nonrecourse financing, if the transfer occurs (or the agreement is entered into) more than one year after the indebtedness was incurred. (Code Sec. 49(b)(2))[28]

¶ 2319 Energy credit recapture under the at-risk limitation rules.

If the taxpayer fails to pay the principal on a level payment nonqualified nonrecourse loan (¶ 1797) used for qualified energy property, the taxpayer is treated as increasing the amount of nonqualified nonrecourse financing to the extent of the credit recapture. (Code Sec. 49(b)(3))[29]

¶ 2320 Low-income housing credit for qualified buildings.

The low-income housing credit, part of the general business credit, (Code Sec. 38(b)(5)) is allowed annually over a ten-year "credit period" beginning with the tax year the qualified building is placed in service, or, under an irrevocable election (on Form 8609), the next tax year. (Code Sec. 42(f)(1)) The credit period for an existing building can't begin before the first tax year of the tax period for rehabilitation expenses for the building. (Code Sec. 42(f)(5)(A))[30]

The credit equals the qualified basis of the qualified building times the applicable percentage (Code Sec. 42(a)) prescribed by IRS for the month placed in service or elected in agreement with the housing credit agency. (Code Sec. 42(b)(2)(A)) The building owner can't claim a credit amount in excess of the allocation received from the state or housing credit agency for that year. (Reg § 1.42-1T(e)(1))[31]

IRS prescribes percentages that will yield, over a ten-year period, credit mounts that will have a present value equal to 70% of the qualified basis of new buildings (not federally subsidized) and 30% of the qualified basis of existing buildings and federally subsidized new buildings as follows:[32]

---

26. ¶ L-17301.
27. ¶ L-17314; ¶ 474.
28. ¶ L-17307; ¶ 494.
29. ¶ L-16419.
30. ¶ L-15700 *et seq.*; ¶ 424.02.
31. ¶ L-15702; ¶ 424.02.
32. ¶ L-15718; ¶ 424.01.

Footnote references beginning with letters are to paragraphs in RIA's Federal Tax Coordinator 2d and RIA's Analysis of Federal Taxes: Income. Footnote references beginning with numbers are to paragraphs in RIA's United States Tax Reporter.

Month	Year	70% present value credit	30% present value credit
Nov.	'93	8.26%	3.54%
Oct.	'93	8.27%	3.54%
Sept.	'93	8.36%	3.58%
Sept.	'93	8.36%	3.58%
Aug.	'93	8.37%	3.59%
July	'93	8.42%	3.61%
June	'93	8.38%	3.59%
May	'93	8.40%	3.60%
Apr.	'93	8.40%	3.60%
Mar.	'93	8.51%	3.65%
Feb.	'93	8.57%	3.67%
Jan.	'93	8.60%	3.69%
Dec.	'92	8.59%	3.68%

To claim the credit, taxpayers must file Form 8586 for each tax year in the ten-year credit period. (Code Sec. 42(g)(4))[33] Form 8609 must be filed with the taxpayer's income tax return for each of the 15 years in the compliance period to certify that the project continues to qualify. (Code Sec. 42(l))[34]

A qualified low-income building is a building that at all times during the "compliance period" of 15 tax years beginning with the first tax year of the credit period, is part of a qualified low-income housing project. (Code Sec. 42(c)(2), (i)(1), (g)) In addition, no credit is allowed unless an extended low income housing commitment (for a 15-year period) between the taxpayer and the housing credit agency is in effect at the end of the tax year. (Code Sec. 42(h)(6))[35]

¶ 2321 Recapture of low-income housing credit.

If, at the close of any year in the compliance period, the qualified basis of a building is less than it was at the close of the earlier tax year, the taxpayer's tax for the year is increased (Code Sec. 42(j)(1), (4)(B)) by the sum of:

(1) the total decrease in taxpayer's general business tax credits for all earlier tax years that would have resulted if the accelerated portion of the credit (see below) allowable for the earlier tax years were not allowed for all earlier tax years with respect to the decrease in qualified basis, plus

(2) an amount of nondeductible interest on (1), above, computed at the rate charged for overpayment of tax, see ¶ 4851. (Code Sec. 42(j)(2))

The accelerated portion of the credit for the earlier tax years is the excess of the total credit allowed for the earlier tax years over the total credit that would have been allowable for those years if the total credit that would have been allowable for the entire compliance period were allowable ratably over 15 years. (Code Sec. 42(j)(3))[36]

Recapture (reported on Form 8611) results from a disposition of a building or interest in one unless: (1) the taxpayer furnishes a bond of a term and in an amount satisfactory to IRS, and (2) it is reasonably expected that the building will continue to be operated as a qualified low-income building for the building's remaining compliance period. (Code Sec. 42(j)(6))[37]

¶ 2322 Alcohol fuel credit before 2001.

A credit (computed on Form 6478) is allowed as part of the general business credit (Code Sec. 38(b)(3)) for alcohol (other than that produced from petroleum, natural gas,

---

33. ¶ S-3456; ¶ 424.03.   35. ¶ L-15704 et seq.; ¶ 424.03.   36. ¶ L-16050 et seq.   37. ¶ L-16050 et seq.
34. ¶ S-3458; ¶ 424.03.

Footnote references beginning with letters are to paragraphs in RIA's Federal Tax Coordinator 2d and RIA's Analysis of Federal Taxes: Income. Footnote references beginning with numbers are to paragraphs in RIA's United States Tax Reporter.

coal or peat, or with a proof less than 150) (Code Sec. 40(d)(1)) used as a fuel. The credit equals the sum of: (1) the alcohol mixture credit, (2) the alcohol credit, and (3) the small ethanol producer credit. (Code Sec. 40(a))

The credit applies to sales or uses before Jan. 1, 2001, for periods during which the Highway Trust Fund financing rate is in effect. (Code Sec. 40(e)(1)) If the credit ceases to apply, the credit cannot be carried over to any tax year beginning after the three-tax year period beginning with the tax year in which the credit ceased to apply. (Code Sec. 40(e)(2))

The fuel credit will be reduced to take into account excise tax exemptions. (Code Sec. 40(c))

The alcohol mixture credit is 60¢ for each 190-or-greater-proof gallon of alcohol (54¢ for ethanol) used by the taxpayer in the production of a qualified mixture. A "qualified mixture" is a mixture of alcohol and gasoline or of alcohol and a special fuel that is either sold by the taxpayer producing the mixture to any person for use as a fuel or used as a fuel by the taxpayer producing the mixture. (Code Sec. 40(b)(1), (h)(1))

The alcohol credit is 60¢ per gallon (54¢ for ethanol) of 190-or-greater proof alcohol that during the tax year is either:

(1) used by the taxpayer as a fuel in a trade or business, or

(2) sold by the taxpayer at retail to a person and placed in the fuel tank of that person's vehicle. (Code Sec. 40(b)(2)(A), (h)(1))

A taxpayer gets no credit as a user (under (1) above) with respect to any alcohol that was sold in a retail sale described in (2), above. (Code Sec. 40(b)(2)(B))

If the alcohol has a proof of at least 150 but less than 190, the alcohol mixture credit and the alcohol credit is 45¢ per gallon (40¢ for ethanol). (Code Sec. 40(b)(3), (h)(2))

A tax of 60¢ per gallon (54¢ for ethanol) (reported on Form 720) applies if a credit was taken and the mixture or alcohol is used other than as a fuel, the mixture is separated, or the alcohol is mixed. For alcohol with a proof less than 190 the tax is 45¢ per gallon (40¢ for ethanol). (Code Sec. 40(d)(3), (h)(3))

A "small" ethanol producer is eligible for a credit of 10¢ per gallon of qualified ethanol fuel production. The credit is limited to 15 million gallons of production. (Code Sec. 40(b)(4))

A small producer is one whose productive capacity for alcohol does not exceed 30 million gallons at any time during the tax year. For this purpose, "alcohol" is defined as methanol or ethanol, without regard to proof or source restrictions. (Code Sec. 40(g))

A taxpayer can elect not to take the credit (Code Sec. 40(f)(1)) simply by not taking the credit. (Reg § 5h.4(f))[38]

¶ 2323 Incremental research expenses credit before July 1, '95.

The research expense credit is a component of the general business credit. (Code Sec. 38(b)(4)) The research credit (claimed on Form 6765) equals the sum of:

(1) Twenty percent of the excess (if any) of the qualified research expenses for the tax year over a base amount. (Code Sec. 41(a)(1)) The base amount is a fixed-base percentage of taxpayer's average annual gross receipts (from a U.S. trade or business, net of returns and allowances) for the four tax years before the credit year, and can't be less than 50% of the year's qualified research expenses. (Code Sec. 41(c)(1), (2)) The fixed base percentage, which can't exceed 16%, is the percentage (rounded to the nearest .01%) that taxpayer's total qualified research expenses is of total gross receipts for tax years beginning after '83 and before '89. A "start-up company," i.e., one that didn't have receipts and expenses during at least three tax years in that period, uses 3% (for tax years beginning before '94)

---

38. ¶ L-17500 *et seq.*; ¶ 404.04.

Footnote references beginning with letters are to paragraphs in RIA's Federal Tax Coordinator 2d and RIA's Analysis of Federal Taxes: Income. Footnote references beginning with numbers are to paragraphs in RIA's United States Tax Reporter.

or (for tax years beginning after '93) uses a 3% fixed base percentage for the first five tax years beginning after '93 for which the taxpayer has qualified research expenses (other percentages apply for later years). (Code Sec. 41(c)(3))[39]

(2) The "university basic research credit," i.e., 20% of the basic research payments determined under Code Sec. 41(e)(1)(A). (Code Sec. 41(a)(2))[40]

"Qualified research expenses" are amounts the taxpayer pays or incurs during the tax year "in carrying on any trade or business" (including certain "start-up" costs) of the taxpayer for: "in-house" research expenses, which consist of certain wages and supplies, and "contract" research expenses, which equal 65% of amounts paid to certain nonemployees. (Code Sec. 41(b); Reg § 1.41-2)[41]

The 20% university basic research credit component applies to 100% of cash expenditures by corporations (except S corporations, personal holding companies, or service organizations) for basic research over the sum of: (1) the minimum basic research amount, plus (2) the maintenance-of-effort amount. (Code Sec. 41(e); Reg § 1.41-7)[42]

The "minimum basic research amount" (Code Sec. 41(e)(4); Reg § 1.41-7) is the greatest of:

(1) 1% of the average amount paid for in-house and contract research expenses during the base period (the three tax years before the first tax year beginning after '83); (Code Sec. 41(e)(7)(B))

(2) the contract research expense for the base period; or

(3) 50% of the basic research payments if taxpayer wasn't in existence for a full year in the base period.[43]

The maintenance-of-effort amount is: (1) the average charitable contribution to all educational institutions during the base period (see above) multiplied by the cost-of-living adjustment, *minus* (2) the charitable contributions to educational institutions for the year. (Code Sec. 41(e)(5)(A))[44]

Any expense taken into account in computing the clinical testing expense credit (¶ 2334) for a tax year cannot be taken into account in computing the credit for incremental research expenses. (Code Sec. 28(c)(1)) However, any qualified clinical testing expenses for any tax year which are qualified research expenses are to be taken into account in determining "base period research expenses" in later tax years. (Code Sec. 28(c)(2))[45]

No deduction is allowed for that portion of the otherwise deductible qualified research expenses or basic research expenses that equals the research credit for the tax year. (Code Sec. 280C(c)(1)) If a taxpayer capitalizes rather than deducts expenses, the amount of such expenses capitalized during the year must be reduced by the excess of the credit over the amount allowable (without regard to the above disallowance) as a deduction for the tax year. (Code Sec. 280C(c)(2))[46] But a taxpayer may avoid this reduction for any tax year by claiming a reduced credit for the year. The election limits the taxpayer to a credit in the amount of the research credit before any reduction less the product of that credit amount times the maximum corporate tax rate. (Code Sec. 280C(c)(3))[47]

The credit terminates for amounts paid or incurred after June 30, '95. (Code Sec. 41(h)(1))

---

39. ¶ L-15309 *et seq.*; ¶ 414.01.   43. ¶s L-15508, L-15507;   44. ¶ L-15509; ¶ 414.02.   46. ¶ L-3131; ¶s 414.04, 280C4.
40. ¶ L-15300; ¶ 414.01.   ¶ 414.02.   45. ¶ L-15606; ¶ 414.04.   47. ¶ L-15308; ¶s 414.04, 280C4.
41. ¶ L-15401 *et seq.*; ¶ 414.01.
42. ¶ L-15501 *et seq.*; ¶s 414.01,
    414.02.

Footnote references beginning with letters are to paragraphs in RIA's Federal Tax Coordinator 2d and RIA's Analysis of Federal Taxes: Income. Footnote references beginning with numbers are to paragraphs in RIA's United States Tax Reporter.

¶ 2324 Employer's targeted jobs credit before '95.

The targeted jobs credit is a component of the general business credit. (Code Sec. 38(b)(2)) The targeted jobs credit allows employers who, before Jan. 1, '95, hire members of certain target groups (¶ 2325) to get a credit (use Form 5884) against income tax of 40% of first-year wages up to $6,000 of wages (i.e., $2,400 maximum) per employee. (Code Sec. 51(a), (b), (c)) (For qualified summer youth employees, the credit is 40% of the first $3,000 of qualified wages ($1,200 maximum per employee).) (Code Sec. 51(d)(12)(B)) The employee must be employed for at least 90 days or have completed at least 120 hours of work (Code Sec. 51(i)(3)) (except for summer youth employees, see ¶ 2325) and more than half of the employee's wages must be for services in the employer's trade or business. (Code Sec. 51(f)(1))[48]

The targeted job credit reduces the employer's wage deduction dollar for dollar. (Code Sec. 280C(a); Reg § 1.280C-1)[49] But the taxpayer can elect not to take the credit. (Code Sec. 51(j))[50]

The wages can't be used for a federally funded job, (Code Sec. 51(c)(2)(A))[1] and don't apply to any amount paid or incurred for an individual who performs the same or substantially similar services as those of employees participating in or affected by a strike or lockout at the employer's plant. (Code Sec. 51(c)(3))[2]

Creditable wages are reduced by the amount of supplementation payments made by a state to the employer under section 482(e) of the Social Security Act. (Code Sec. 51(c)(2))[3]

¶ 2325 Target groups.

The target groups are:[4]

(1) *Economically disadvantaged youths* at least 18 but not 23 on the date hired. (Code Sec. 51(d)(3))

(2) *Eligible work incentive employees.* (Code Sec. 51(d)(9))

(3) *Vocational rehabilitation individuals* who have a physical or mental disability that is a substantial handicap to employment and who have been referred to the employer while receiving, or after completing, certain vocational rehabilitation services. (Code Sec. 51(d)(2))

(4) *Economically disadvantaged ex-convicts* who are hired within five years of release from prison, or conviction, whichever is later. (Code Sec. 51(d)(7))

(5) *General assistance recipients.* (Code Sec. 51(d)(6))

(6) *Economically disadvantaged Vietnam veterans.* (Code Sec. 51(d)(4))

(7) *Economically disadvantaged youths* who are at least 16 but not 18 years old on the date they are hired, or by May 1 of the calendar year of hire (if May 1 is later than the hiring date). The credit applies only to wages paid for services performed during any 90-day period between May 1 and Sept. 15, and the employee may not have previously worked for the employer. The employee must be employed for at least 14 days or have completed 20 hours of work. (Code Sec. 51(i)(3), (d)(12))[5]

(8) *Economically disadvantaged cooperative education students* who have attained age 16 but not age 20, and who have not graduated from high school or vocational school (which has given Form 6199 to the employer). (Code Sec. 51(d)(8))

(9) *Supplemental security income recipients.* (Code Sec. 51(d)(5))

A new employee must be certified as a member of a target group. (Code Sec. 51(d)(16)(A))[6]

---

48. ¶ L-17800 *et seq.*; ¶ 514.
49. ¶ L-17806; ¶ 514.
50. ¶ L-17807; ¶ 514.

1. ¶ L-17810; ¶ 514.
2. ¶ L-17813; ¶ 514.

3. ¶ L-17810; ¶ 514.
4. ¶ L-17818 *et seq.*; ¶ 514.

5. ¶s L-17805, L-17827; ¶ 514.
6. ¶ L-17816; ¶ 514.

Footnote references beginning with letters are to paragraphs in RIA's Federal Tax Coordinator 2d and RIA's Analysis of Federal Taxes: Income. Footnote references beginning with numbers are to paragraphs in RIA's United States Tax Reporter.

No credit is allowed for employees who are related to the employer or to certain owners of the employer. (Code Sec. 51(i))[7]

¶ 2326 Enhanced oil recovery credit.

The enhanced oil recovery (EOR) credit for any tax year is 15% of the taxpayer's qualified enhanced oil recovery costs for the tax year. (Code Sec. 43(a)) These are amounts paid or incurred for: qualifying tangible property that is depreciable or amortizable; qualifying tertiary injectant costs that qualify for a deduction under Code Sec. 193; and qualifying intangible drilling and development costs (IDCs) that are eligible for the Code Sec. 263(c) expensing election. (Code Sec. 43(c)(1))

The credit is phased out as the average per barrel wellhead price of domestic crude oil ("reference price," see ¶ 2333) for the last calendar year that ended before the tax year in question exceeds $28 (adjusted for inflation after '91). The reduction is the result of multiplying: (1) (the reference price minus $28) divided by $6, times (2) the otherwise allowable credit. (Code Sec. 43(b))

The EOR credit (claimed on Form 8830) is only available for costs paid or incurred in tax years beginning after '90 and only for projects with respect to which the first injection of liquids, gas or other matter begins after '90. (Code Sec. 43(c)(2); Reg § 1.43-4(d)))[8]

¶ 2327 Disabled access credit.

An "eligible small business" may elect (on Form 8826) to apply a credit against income tax of 50% of the amount of "eligible access expenditures" for the tax year that is over $250 and not more than $10,250. (Code Sec. 44(a))

⦿observation: Thus, the maximum amount of the credit for any tax year is $5,000, 50% of ($10,250 – $250).

For partnerships and S corporations this limitation applies at both the entity and the individual partner or shareholder levels. (Code Sec. 44(d)(3))

An "eligible small business" for any tax year is any person who either:

(1) has gross receipts that don't exceed $1 million for the tax year *before* that in which the credit is elected, net of returns and allowances, or

(2) employed no more than 30 full-time employees during the tax year *before* the tax year in which the credit is elected. For purposes of this rule, an employee who is employed at least 30 hours a week for 20 or more calendar weeks in the tax year is considered to be full-time. (Code Sec. 44(b), (d)(5))

Eligible access expenditures are amounts paid or incurred to enable the business to comply with the Americans With Disabilities Act of '90 (as in effect on Nov. 5, '90). (Code Sec. 44(c)(1)) These expenses include *only* expenses which are necessary to comply with the Disabilities Act, that are paid or incurred:

■ for the purpose of removing architectural, communication, physical or transportation barriers in connection with any facility first placed in service before Nov. 6, '90, which prevent a business from being accessible to, or usable by, individuals with disabilities;

■ to provide qualified interpreters or other effective methods of making aurally delivered materials available to individuals with hearing impairments;

■ to provide qualified readers, taped texts and other effective methods of making visually delivered materials available to individuals with visual impairments;

■ to acquire or modify equipment or devices for individuals with disabilities; or

■ to provide other similar services, modifications, materials or equipment. (Code Sec. 44(c))

---

7. ¶ L-17816; ¶ 514.   8. ¶ L-17600 *et seq.*; ¶ 434.

Footnote references beginning with letters are to paragraphs in RIA's Federal Tax Coordinator 2d and RIA's Analysis of Federal Taxes: Income. Footnote references beginning with numbers are to paragraphs in RIA's United States Tax Reporter.

A taxpayer must be able to show that it meets the standards issued by IRS with the concurrence of the Architectural and Transportation Barriers Compliance Board and set forth in IRS regs. (Code Sec. 44(c))[9]

¶ 2328 Credit for producing electricity from certain renewable resources.

The renewable electricity production credit (claimed on Form 8835) is 1.5¢ per kilowatt hour of electricity produced by taxpayers from wind or "closed-loop biomass" (generally, organic plants, except timber, grown for the sole purpose of being used to generate electricity) at a "qualifying facility" during the ten-year period after the facility is placed in service. (Code Sec. 45(a), (c)(2))[10]

The credit is allowed for qualified electricity sold to an unrelated person (Code Sec. 45(a)(2)(B))[11] and produced from domestic or U.S. possession facilities originally placed in service by the taxpayer after '92 (for a "closed-loop biomass" facility) or after '93 (for a wind-energy facility) and before July 1, '99. (Code Sec. 45(c)(3))[12] Taxpayers are entitled to the credit in proportion to their ownership interest in the qualifying facility. (Code Sec. 45(d)(3))[13]

The credit for any particular facility is reduced proportionately (not dollar-for-dollar) to the extent the facility is financed with governmental grants, tax-exempt bonds, subsidized financing or other credits. (Code Sec. 45(b)(3))[14]

The credit is proportionately phased out when the national average price of electricity produced from the applicable renewable resource exceeds a threshold price of 8¢ per kilowatt hour. Under the phaseout rule, the amount of the credit is reduced by a certain percentage. This percentage is determined by dividing the excess of the "reference price" for the calendar year of sale over 8¢ per KWH by 3¢. (Code Sec. 45(b)(1)) The "reference price," with respect to a calendar year, is the annual average contract price per KWH of electricity generated from the same qualified energy resource and sold in the U.S. in the previous year. (Code Sec. 45(d)(2)(c))[15] Both the credit rate and the 8¢ phaseout rate are adjusted for post-'92 inflation—to the nearest multiple of 0.1¢—by the inflation adjustment factor for the calendar year of sale. (Code Sec. 45(b)(2))[16]

¶ 2329 Empowerment zone employment credit before 2005.

After Aug. 9, '93, employers are entitled to an empowerment zone employment credit (claimed on Form 8844), as part of the general business credit, for any tax year equal to 20% (phased out after 2001) of the qualified zone wages paid or incurred during the calendar year that ends with or within that tax year. (Code Sec. 1396(a))

The amount of qualified zones wages taken into account for each employee may not exceed $15,000 for a calendar year. (Code Sec. 1396(c)(2)) Thus, the maximum credit per qualified employee is $3,000 per year (i.e., 20% of $15,000 for calendar years '94 through 2001).[17]

The credit will not be available after 2004. (Code Sec. 1396(b))[18]

For limitations on the credit based on tax liability, see ¶ 2304.

The employer's deduction for wages paid must be reduced by the empowerment zone employment credit for the year. (Code Sec. 280C(a))[19]

¶ 2330 Indian employment credit before 2004.

For wages paid or incurred after '93, the Indian employment credit (claimed on Form 8845) is 20% of the excess, if any, of the sum of qualified wages and qualified employee health insurance costs (not in excess of $20,000 per employee) paid or incurred (other than paid under salary reduction arrangements) to qualified employees during the tax

9. ¶ L-17900 *et seq.*; ¶ 444.
10. ¶ L-17751 *et seq.*
11. ¶ L-17754; ¶ 454.
12. ¶ L-17772; ¶ 454.
13. ¶ L-17755; ¶ 454.
14. ¶ L-17764; ¶ 454.
15. ¶s L-17760, L-17763; ¶ 454.
16. ¶ L-17761 *et seq.*; ¶ 454
17. ¶ L-15630 *et seq.*; ¶ 13,964.
18. ¶ L-15632; ¶ 13,964.
19. ¶ L-15641; ¶ 13,964.

Footnote references beginning with letters are to paragraphs in RIA's Federal Tax Coordinator 2d and RIA's Analysis of Federal Taxes: Income. Footnote references beginning with numbers are to paragraphs in RIA's United States Tax Reporter.

year (Code Sec. 45A(a)(1),(b)(2)) over the sum of these same costs paid or incurred in calendar year '93—determined as if the Indian employment credit had been in effect in '93. (Code Sec. 45A(a)(2)) The credit is part of the general business credit. (Code Sec. 38(b)(10))

A qualified employee is an enrolled member of an Indian tribe (or the spouse of one) who meets specific residence, wage-rate, and other requirements. (Code Sec. 45A(c))

Credits previously claimed with respect to certain terminated employees are recaptured. (Code Sec. 45A(d))

Deductions for wages and health insurance costs must be reduced by the full amount of the credit. (Code Sec. 280C(a))

The credit is scheduled to end for tax years beginning after Dec. 31, 2003. (Code Sec. 45A(f))[20]

¶ 2331 Employer Social Security credit with respect to employee cash tips.

For taxes paid after '93, a food and beverage establishment is allowed a credit (on Form 8846) for the amount of the employer's FICA tax obligation (7.65%) attributable to employee-reported tips in excess of those treated as wages for purposes of satisfying minimum wage provisions applicable to an employee under section 6(a)(1) of the Fair Labor Standards Act of '38 (determined without regards to section 3(m) of the Act). (Code Sec. 45B(a); Code Sec. 45B(b)) The credit is part of the general business credit. (Code Sec. 38(b)(11))

No deduction is allowed for any amount taken into account in determining the employer Social Security credit. (Code Sec. 45B(c))

A taxpayer can elect to have the credit not apply for any tax year. (Code Sec. 45B(d))[21]

¶ 2332 Credit for contributions to community development corporations.

After Aug. 9, '93, a taxpayer can claim a credit (on Form 8847) for qualified contributions (including certain long-term loans and investments) to community development corporations (CDCs) selected by the Secretary of HUD. The amount of the credit is 5% of the "qualified contribution" for each tax year during the credit period, i.e., the 10-year period beginning with the tax year in which the contribution is made. Thus, the taxpayer may claim a total of 50% of the contribution during the 10-year credit period.[22]

Business Credits Not Included in General Business Credit

¶ 2333 Alternate (nonconventional source) fuel production credit.

A $3 per barrel of oil-equivalent (measured on a btu basis) tax credit (claimed by attaching a self-made schedule to the return) is allowed for the production of qualified fuels sold to an unrelated party. (Code Sec. 29(a), (d)(5), (d)(6))[23] The $3 amount, except in the case of gas from a tight formation, is adjusted for inflation (the adjustment factor for '92 is 1.8430—the '93 factor won't be released until '94). (Code Sec. 29(b)(2), (d)(2))[24]

Qualified fuels include oil produced from shale and tar sand; gas produced from geopressured brine, Devonian shale, coal seam or tight formations (with some restrictions); gas produced from biomass; and liquid, gaseous or solid synthetic fuels produced from coal. (Code Sec. 29(c))[25]

The credit is allowed for alternative energy which is: (1) *sold* before the year 2003, and (2) *produced* from a domestic well drilled or in a facility placed in service before '93 (and after '79). (Code Sec. 29(f))[26]

A facility that produces gas from biomass or produces liquid, gaseous or solid synthetic

---

20. ¶ L-15670 *et seq.*; ¶ 45A4.   22. ¶ L-15650 *et seq.*; ¶ 384.01.   24. ¶ L-17710 *et seq.*; ¶ 294.02.   26. ¶ L-17700; ¶ 294.04.
21. ¶ L-17860 *et seq.*; ¶ 45B4.   23. ¶ L-17700 *et seq.*; ¶ 294.   25. ¶ L-17703; ¶ 294.01.

Footnote references beginning with letters are to paragraphs in RIA's Federal Tax Coordinator 2d and RIA's Analysis of Federal
Taxes: Income. Footnote references beginning with numbers are to paragraphs in RIA's United States Tax Reporter.

fuels from coal (including lignite) will be treated as placed in service before '93 if the facility is placed in service before '97 under a written binding contract in effect before '96. If the facility is originally placed in service after '92, production from the facility will qualify for the credit if the specified fuels produced by the facility are sold before Jan. 1, 2008. (Code Sec. 29(g))[27]

The fuel production credit will phase out as the annual average wellhead price per barrel for all domestic crude oil not subject to U.S. regulation (called the "reference price") rises from $23.50 per barrel. The amount of the reduction is the result of multiplying: (1) (the reference price ($15.98 for '92) minus $23.50) divided by $6, times (2) the amount of credit allowed before the phaseout adjustment. (Code Sec. 29(b)(1))[28]

The credit for any particular facility is reduced proportionately (not dollar-for-dollar) to the extent the facility or equipment was financed with grants, subsidized energy loans or tax-exempt financing. (Code Sec. 29(b)(3))[29]

The credit otherwise allowable for any facility is reduced dollar-for-dollar (not proportionately) to the extent that the energy investment credit (discussed at ¶ 2314 *et seq.*) was allowed for that facility until the full business energy credit is recaptured. (Code Sec. 29(b)(4))[30]

The credit for a project is reduced by the excess of: (1) the aggregate amount of any enhanced oil recovery credit allowed currently or for a prior tax year with respect to that project, over (2) the aggregate amount recaptured with respect to amounts described in (1) for any prior tax year, i.e., amounts of enhanced oil recovery credit already used in prior years to offset the nonconventional fuel credit. (Code Sec. 29(b)(5))

The credit can't exceed the taxpayer's regular tax liability (see ¶ 2355) for the tax year, reduced by the sum of the tentative minimum tax (see ¶ 3201), and the household and dependent care credit, the credit for the elderly and disabled, the credit for home mortgages, the foreign tax and possession credits and the clinical testing expense credit. (Code Sec. 29(b)(6))[31]

¶ 2334 Qualified clinical testing expense ("orphan drug") credit before '95.

Any taxpayer that incurs qualified clinical testing expenses before Jan. 1, '95, may claim (on Form 6765) a credit equal to 50% of those expenses for the tax year. (Code Sec. 28(a), (e))[32] Qualified clinical testing expenses are amounts which, with certain modifications, would qualify as "qualified research expenses" for the qualified research credit. (Code Sec. 28(b)(1)(A), (D))

The 50% credit is otherwise limited to taxpayer's regular tax liability (see ¶ 2355) for the year reduced by the tentative minimum tax (see ¶ 3201), the credits allowable under Subpart A of the Code and the foreign tax and possession credits. (Code Sec. 28(d)(2))[33]

¶ 2335 Personal (Refundable and Nonrefundable) Credits ▄▄▄▄▄▄▄▄

Taxpayers, whether or not in business, may qualify for one or more refundable or non-refundable personal credits. The nonrefundable personal credits must be aggregated for purpose of computing their maximum allowance.

The *refundable* credits are the credits:

- for earned income by certain taxpayers, see ¶ 2336 *et seq.*;

- for tax withheld, see ¶ 2343;

- for excess social security tax withheld, see ¶ 2344;

- for excise tax for certain nontaxable uses of fuels; (Code Sec. 6420, Code Sec. 6421, Code Sec. 6427(l))

---

27. ¶ L-17705.1.
28. ¶ L-17710; ¶ 294.02.
29. ¶ L-17713; ¶ 294.02.
30. ¶ L-17714; ¶ 294.02.
31. ¶ L-17716; ¶ 294.02.
32. ¶ L-15600 *et seq.*; ¶ 284.
33. ¶ L-15602; ¶ 284.01.

Footnote references beginning with letters are to paragraphs in RIA's Federal Tax Coordinator 2d and RIA's Analysis of Federal Taxes: Income. Footnote references beginning with numbers are to paragraphs in RIA's United States Tax Reporter.

- for light weight diesel vehicles, see ¶ 2345.

The *non*refundable credits are:

- the credit for the elderly and the permanently and totally disabled, see ¶ 2346;
- the credit for household and dependent care expenses, see ¶ 2347 *et seq.*;
- the mortgage credit, see ¶ 2353;
- the credit for electric vehicles, see ¶ 2354;
- the minimum tax credit, see ¶ 2356.

For the limit on the combined amount of personal nonrefundable credits, see ¶ 2355.

¶ 2336 The earned income credit before '94 — the basic credit (including supplemental young child credit).

For tax years beginning before '94, an eligible individual (¶ 2340) is allowed a credit equal to the sum of the basic earned income credit (below) and the health insurance credit (¶ 2337). (For post-'93 years, see ¶ 2338.) Use Schedule EIC (Form 1040 or 1040A) to claim the credit.

The basic earned income credit equals the "credit percentage" (below) of so much of the taxpayer's earned income (¶ 2339) for the tax year as did not exceed $7,750 for '93, subject to a limit. Under the limit, the amount of the allowable credit can't exceed the excess (if any) of the credit percentage of $5,714 over the "phaseout percentage" of so much of the taxpayer's adjusted gross income (or, if greater, earned income) as exceeded $12,200 for '93.

For tax years beginning in '93, the percentages are:

Number of qualifying children:	The phaseout percentage is:	The credit percentage is:
1	13.21	18.5
2 or more	13.93	19.5

Supplemental young child credit. If a taxpayer had a "qualifying child" (see ¶ 2341) who had not reached the age of one as of the close of the calendar year (in which or with which the taxpayer's tax year ended) the above credit percentage is increased by five percentage points and the phaseout percentage is increased by 3.57 percentage points.[34]

¶ 2337 The health insurance credit before '94.

The pre-'94 health insurance credit is determined in the same way as the basic earned income credit (¶ 2336) except that the credit percentage is 6% and the phaseout percentage is 4.285%.

The health insurance credit can't exceed the amounts paid for insurance coverage which constitutes medical care and that insurance must include coverage for at least one "qualifying child" (¶ 2341).[35]

¶ 2338 Earned income credit after '93.

For tax years beginning after '93, an eligible individual (¶ 2340) is allowed a credit equal to to the credit percentage times so much of the individual's earned income for the tax year as does not exceed the earned income amount. (Code Sec. 32(a)(1)) However, the EIC for a tax year can't be more than the excess (if any) of (1) the credit percentage of the earned income amount, over (2) the phaseout percentage of so much of the adjusted gross income (or if greater, earned income) of the individual for the tax year as exceeds the phaseout amount. (Code Sec. 32(a)(2))These amounts are determined as follows:[36]

---

34. ¶ A-4212; ¶ 324.01.   35. ¶ A-4208 *et seq.*; ¶ 324.01.   36. ¶ A-4202; ¶ 324.01.

Footnote references beginning with letters are to paragraphs in RIA's Federal Tax Coordinator 2d and RIA's Analysis of Federal Taxes: Income. Footnote references beginning with numbers are to paragraphs in RIA's United States Tax Reporter.

In the case of eligible individual with:	The Credit % is:	The Earned Income Amount is:	The Phaseout % is:	The Phaseout Amount is:
		FOR '94		
No qualifying children	7.65%	$4,000	7.65%	$ 5,000
1 qualifying child	26.3%	$7,750	15.98%	$11,000
2 or more qualifying children	30%	$8,425	17.68%	$11,000
		FOR '95		
No qualifying children	7.65%	$4,000*	7.65%	$ 5,000*
1 qualifying child	34%	$6,000*	15.98%	$11,000*
2 or more qualifying children	36%	$8,425*	20.22%	$11,000*
		AFTER '95		
No qualifying children	7.65%	$4,000*	7.65%	$ 5,000*
1 qualifying child	34%	$6,000*	15.98%	$11,000*
2 or more qualifying children	40%	$8,424*	21.06%	$11,000*

* To be indexed for inflation

observation: The EIC for '94 is completely phased out at the following amounts of earned income (or AGI, whichever is greater):

■ $9,000 for an eligible individual with no qualifying children,

■ $23,753 for an eligible individual with one qualifying child,

■ $25,293 for an eligible individual with two qualifying children.

¶ 2339 Earned income defined.

Earned income includes wages, salaries, tips, other employee compensation and an individual's net earnings from self-employment less one-half of the self-employment tax under Code Sec. 164(f). (Code Sec. 32(c)(2)(A)) It also includes certain compensation that is excluded from gross income, such as disability income, the rental value of a parsonage, and the value of meals and lodging furnished for the convenience of the employer. Earned income also is reduced by any net loss in earnings from self-employment, (Reg § 1.43-2(c)(2)) and it does not include any amount received as a pension or an annuity, any amount subject to the 30% withholding tax on U.S. income (not connected with U.S. business) of nonresident alien individuals, (Code Sec. 32(c)(2)(B)) unemployment compensation or workmen's compensation. (Reg § 1.43-2(c)(2)) Also, earned income is determined without regard to any community property laws. (Code Sec. 32(c)(2))[37]

¶ 2340 Eligible individual.

Any individual who has a "qualifying child" (¶ 2341) for the tax year is an eligible individual. For tax years beginning after '93, an individual who does not have a qualifying child for the tax year is also an eligible individual *if:*

■ the individual's principal place of abode is in the U.S. for more than half the tax year, and

■ either the individual or the individual's spouse (if any) is older than 24 but younger than 65 before the end of the tax year, and

■ the individual can't be claimed as the dependent of another taxpayer for any tax year beginning in the same calendar year as the individual's tax year. (Code Sec. 32(c)(1))

If two or more individuals can be otherwise treated as eligible individuals with respect to the same qualifying child (for tax years beginning in the same calendar year), then only

37. ¶ A-4213 *et seq.* ¶ 324.05.

Footnote references beginning with letters are to paragraphs in RIA's Federal Tax Coordinator 2d and RIA's Analysis of Federal Taxes: Income. Footnote references beginning with numbers are to paragraphs in RIA's United States Tax Reporter.

the individual with the highest adjusted gross income (for those tax years) can be an eligible individual with respect to that qualifying child. (Code Sec. 32(c)(1)(C))

Someone who is a "qualifying child" cannot be treated as an eligible individual in the same year. Nor can any individual who elects to exclude foreign income for the tax year be an eligible individual for that tax year. (Code Sec. 32(c)(1))

Married individuals are eligible for only one credit on their combined earned income and must file a joint return to claim the credit. (Code Sec. 32(d))

Except where a short period return is filed due to an individual's death, only individuals filing a return for a full 12-month year can claim the credit. (Code Sec. 32(e))[38]

¶ 2341 Qualifying child.

A qualifying child is an individual who is one of the following:

■ The taxpayer's son or daughter, or a descendant of either. A married child may not be a qualifying child *unless* the taxpayer is entitled to a dependency deduction for the child (or would be except that the taxpayer is a custodial parent who has released the dependency deduction claim under Code Sec. 152(e)(2), or the noncustodial parent claims the exemption under a pre-'85 divorce or separation agreement). A child who is legally adopted, or who is placed with the taxpayer by an authorized placement agency for adoption by the taxpayer, is treated as a child by blood.

■ The taxpayer's stepson or stepdaughter.

■ The taxpayer's "eligible foster child," i.e., someone not described above for whom the taxpayer cares as his or her own child and who has the same principal place of abode as the taxpayer for the taxpayer's entire tax year. (Code Sec. 32(c)(3)(B))[39]

A qualifying child must have the same principal place of abode as the taxpayer for more than one-half of the taxpayer's tax year (unless the child is an eligible foster child, above). The abode must be in the U.S. (Code Sec. 32(c)(3)(A)(ii), (E))[40]

A qualifying child must meet one of the following criteria:

■ is permanently and totally disabled at any time during the tax year;

■ has not reached age 19 as of the close of the calendar year (in which the taxpayer's tax year begins); or

■ is a student who has not reached the age of 24 as of the close of the calendar year (in which the taxpayer's tax year begins). (Code Sec. 32(c)(3)(C))[41]

The following identification requirements must be met: (Code Sec. 32(c)(3)(D))

■ the taxpayer must include the name and age of each child on the taxpayer's tax return for the tax year;

■ where the child has reached age one before the close of the taxpayer's tax year, the taxpayer must include the child's taxpayer identification number (i.e., social security number) on the return;

■ where the taxpayer is claiming the health insurance credit, IRS may require the taxpayer to include an insurance policy number or other adequate evidence of insurance.[42]

¶ 2342 Advance payment of earned income credit—Form W-5.

An eligible individual may elect to receive advance payment of the earned income credit by providing his or her employer with a Form W-5. (Code Sec. 3507(b))[43] The amount advanced depends on the employee's earnings in the pay period, and is determined from IRS tables. (Code Sec. 3507(c)(1)) The portion of the credit attributable to the supplemental young child and health care credits was not available on an advance basis. (Code

---

38. ¶ A-4217; ¶ 324.02.   40. ¶ A-4221; ¶ 324.02.   42. ¶ A-4223; ¶ 324.02.   43. ¶ H-4802; ¶ 324.03.
39. ¶ A-4220; ¶ 324.02.   41. ¶ A-4222; ¶ 324.02.

Footnote references beginning with letters are to paragraphs in RIA's Federal Tax Coordinator 2d and RIA's Analysis of Federal Taxes: Income. Footnote references beginning with numbers are to paragraphs in RIA's United States Tax Reporter.

324

Sec. 3507(c)(2))[44] The employer adds the advance payment to the employee's paycheck. The advance payment is reflected in the employee's Form W-2 as a separate item. (Code Sec. 6051(a)(7)) Everyone who has received advanced payments of earned income during the year must file an income tax return. (Code Sec. 6012(a)(8)) Advance payments in excess of the employee's earned income credit are recaptured. (Code Sec. 32(g))[45]

¶ 2343 Credit for tax withheld.

The amount of income tax withheld from wages, pensions, annuities, gambling winnings, etc., in a calendar year is a credit for the last tax year beginning in that calendar year. (Code Sec. 31(a))[46] The credit for amounts withheld under the backup withholding rules is allowed for the tax year of the recipient of the income in which the income is received. (Code Sec. 31(c))[47]

If a husband and wife file separate returns, each must claim credit for the actual amount of tax withheld from his or her salary or wages. In a community property state, each spouse may claim a credit for half of the tax withheld on community wages. (Code Sec. 31(a); Reg § 1.31-1(a))[48]

¶ 2344 Credit for excess social security tax withheld.

Where more than the maximum social security tax (see ¶ 1107) is withheld from an employee's wages because he worked for two or more employers, the excess may be claimed as a credit against his income tax on his return. (Code Sec. 31(b)(1), Code Sec. 6413(c)(1); Reg § 1.31-2(a)(2), Reg § 31.6413(c)-1) If a husband and wife both work, the ceiling is applied separately to each.

If more than the maximum was withheld by one employer, the employee may not claim the excess against his income tax. His employer should repay him the over-collection.[49]

¶ 2345 Credit or refund for owners of light weight diesel vehicles.

A one-time payment (generally in the form of an income tax credit claimed on Form 4136) is available to the original purchaser of a "qualified diesel-powered highway vehicle" purchased before Jan. 1, '95. (Code Sec. 6427(g)(1), (5)) The payment amounts are $102 for a car and $198 for a truck. (Code Sec. 6427(g)(3))[50]

¶ 2346 Credit for the elderly and the permanently and totally disabled.

The credit is available to any individual who: (1) reaches 65 before the end of the tax year, or (2) is under 65 at the end of the tax year, is retired with a permanent and total disability, and receives disability income from a public or private employer. (Code Sec. 22(b))[1]

Permanently and totally disabled means that the individual is unable to engage in any substantial gainful activity because of a medically determinable physical or mental impairment which can be expected to result in death, or that has lasted or can be expected to last for a continuous period of at least 12 months. (Code Sec. 22(e)(3))[2]

Married individuals must file a joint return to claim the credit unless they qualify as married living apart (see ¶ 3131). (Code Sec. 22(e)(1)) A nonresident alien is not eligible for the credit (Code Sec. 22(f)), unless he is married to a U.S. spouse with whom he files jointly, and both elect to be taxed on worldwide income. (Reg § 1.37-1(d))[3]

The credit is 15% of the specified initial amount (Step 1 below), reduced by both an amount that is based on the taxpayer's adjusted gross income (Step 2) and the sum of the taxpayer's incomes from tax-free pensions and annuities (Step 3) (use Schedule R (Form 1040)):

44. ¶ H-4804; ¶ 324.03.	47. ¶ J-9007; ¶s 314.01, 34,064.	50. ¶ W-1744.	2. ¶ A-4102.
45. ¶s H-4802, H-4837; ¶ 324.03.	48. ¶ A-4006.	1. ¶ A-4101; ¶ 224.	3. ¶ A-4101.
46. ¶s A-4013, A-4005; ¶ 314.01.	49. ¶ A-4002; ¶ 314.02.		

Footnote references beginning with letters are to paragraphs in RIA's Federal Tax Coordinator 2d and RIA's Analysis of Federal Taxes: Income. Footnote references beginning with numbers are to paragraphs in RIA's United States Tax Reporter.

Step (1): The initial amount with respect to which the credit may be computed is—

■ $5,000 for a single person, 65 or over;

■ $5,000 for a married couple filing jointly if only one spouse is a qualified individual, 65 or over;

■ $7,500 for a married couple filing jointly and both spouses are qualified individuals and 65 or over;

■ $3,750 for a married individual, 65 or over, filing a separate return. (Code Sec. 22(c)(2)(A)) For individuals under age 65, see below.

Step (2): Where a taxpayer's adjusted gross income exceeds certain amounts, the applicable initial amount determined in Step (1) (above) must be reduced by one-half of the excess. The reduction is one-half of adjusted gross income in excess of $7,500 for a single person and $10,000 for a married person filing jointly ($5,000 if filing separately). (Code Sec. 22(d)) The reduction applies regardless of the taxpayer's age.

⚫️*observation:* Step (2) (above) eliminates the credit for a married couple filing jointly with adjusted gross income of at least $25,000 (if both are 65 or over) or of least $20,000 (if one is), and for a single person with adjusted gross income of at least $17,500.

Step (3) : The initial amount as adjusted under Step (2) (above) must be further reduced by the sum of the amounts received by the individual (or, in the case of a joint return, by either spouse) as a pension or annuity or as a disability benefit—

■ that is excluded from gross income and payable under title II of the Social Security Act, the Railroad Retirement Act of '74, or a law administered by the VA; or

■ that is excluded from gross income under any provision of law not in the Internal Revenue Code. (Code Sec. 22(c)(3)(A))

For purposes of the above rules, a social security benefit, as defined under the Code Sec. 86 rules, or workmen's compensation that reduces such a benefit, is treated as an amount received as a pension or annuity. (Code Sec. 86(f)(1))[4]

Taxpayers under age 65 compute the credit in the same way as above, except that the "initial amount" is limited to the lower of the initial amount shown in Step (1), above, or

■ for other than joint returns, the taxpayer's disability income for the year;

■ for a married couple filing jointly, neither of whom has reached age 65, the sum of the spouses' disability income;

■ for a married couple filing jointly, only one of whom has reached age 65, the sum of $5,000 plus the disability income of the spouse who has not reached age 65. (Code Sec. 22(c)(2)(B))[5]

¶ 2347 Credit for household and dependent care ("child-care") expenses.

The credit is 30% of employment-related expenses (see ¶ 2349) incurred by taxpayers with adjusted gross income of $10,000 or less. The percentage decreases by 1% for each $2,000 (or fraction of that amount) of adjusted gross income over $10,000, but not below 20%. Thus, for taxpayers with adjusted gross income over $28,000, the applicable percentage is 20%. (Code Sec. 21(a)(1), (2))[6]

The maximum amount of employment-related expenses that may be used to compute the credit is $2,400 if the expenses are incurred for one qualifying individual, and $4,800 if they are incurred for two or more qualifying individuals, at any time during the tax year. (Code Sec. 21(c); Reg § 1.44A-2(a)) However, the dollar amount of expenses eligible for the credit is reduced, dollar for dollar, by the aggregate amount excludable from gross income under the Code Sec. 129 (¶ 1276) dependent care assistance exclusion. (Code

---

4. ¶s A-4105, A-4107; ¶ 224.02.   5. ¶ A-4106; ¶ 224.02.   6. ¶ A-4302; ¶ 214.

Footnote references beginning with letters are to paragraphs in RIA's Federal Tax Coordinator 2d and RIA's Analysis of Federal Taxes: Income. Footnote references beginning with numbers are to paragraphs in RIA's United States Tax Reporter.

Sec. 21(c))[7]

To qualify for the credit, a taxpayer must (a) furnish more than half the cost of maintaining a household that includes as a member one or more qualifying individuals (¶ 2348), and (b) incur employment-related expenses (¶ 2349) that enable the taxpayer to be gainfully employed. (Code Sec. 21(a), (e)(1))[8]

For limits on the credit, see ¶ 2355.

¶ 2348 Qualifying individual defined.

The household must include one or more individuals who:

(1) is under age 13 and for whom the taxpayer is entitled to a dependency deduction (any agreement to let the noncustodial parent claim the child as an exemption is disregarded);

(2) is a dependent of the taxpayer (other than a dependent in (1), above) who is physically or mentally incapable of caring for himself regardless of age, even if the taxpayer can't claim the dependency exemption because the person has gross income in excess of the exemption amount;

(3) is the spouse of the taxpayer, if the spouse is physically or mentally incapable of caring for himself or herself; (Code Sec. 21(b)(1)) or

(4) is a child meeting the special dependency test of divorced parents, see ¶ 2352.[9]

¶ 2349 Employment-related expenses.

Employment-related expenses qualifying for the credit include expenses for household services and for the care of qualifying individuals. Thus, costs of a housekeeper, maid, babysitter or cook ordinarily qualify.

Payments for services provided outside the taxpayer's household are taken into account only if incurred for the care of:

■ a dependent who is under 13 years old, or

■ any other qualifying individual (¶ 2348) who regularly spends at least eight hours each day in the taxpayer's household. (Code Sec. 21(b)(2)(B))[10]

However, the expenses incurred for services that are performed by a *dependent care center* qualify for the credit only if the center complies with all applicable laws and regulations of a state or unit of local government, and the dependent in whose behalf the expenses are incurred spends at least eight hours each day in the taxpayer's household. (Code Sec. 21(b)(2)(B), (C))[11]

observation: Thus the credit is not available for expenses of full institutional care.

¶ 2350 Payments to relatives.

Payments to relatives of a taxpayer or to members of his household for services are counted in computing the credit only if the person to whom the payments are made isn't a dependent of the taxpayer or his spouse or a child of the taxpayer who is under age 19 at the close of the tax year. (Code Sec. 21(e)(6))[12]

¶ 2351 Earned income limit.

The amount of employment-related expenses that may be taken into account can't exceed, in the case of an individual who is not married at the close of the tax year, that individual's earned income, or, in the case of an individual who is married at the close of the tax year, the lesser of the individual's earned income or the earned income of the

---

7. ¶ A-4303; ¶ 214.04.   9. ¶ A-4312; ¶ 214.02.   11. ¶ A-4320 *et seq.*; ¶ 214.09.   12. ¶ A-4324; ¶ 214.01.
8. ¶s A-4301, A-4315 *et seq.*;   10. ¶ A-4320.
   ¶ 214.03.

Footnote references beginning with letters are to paragraphs in RIA's Federal Tax Coordinator 2d and RIA's Analysis of Federal Taxes: Income. Footnote references beginning with numbers are to paragraphs in RIA's United States Tax Reporter.

spouse for the year (even if only married for part of the year). (Code Sec. 21(d)(1))[13]

The income deemed to be earned by a spouse who is a full-time student or who is incapable of self-care is $200 per month if there is one qualifying individual in the household, and $400 a month if there are two or more qualifying individuals in the household. (Code Sec. 21(d)(2))[14]

¶ 2352 Claiming the child-care credit.

The credit (claimed on Form 2441 if Form 1040 is filed, or Schedule 2 if Form 1040A is filed) is available to married couples only if they file a joint return. An individual legally separated from his spouse under a decree of divorce or separate maintenance isn't considered married. (Code Sec. 21(e)(2), (3))[15]

A married individual living apart from his spouse may claim the credit on a separate return if he maintains a household and furnishes over one-half the cost of that household for the tax year, which is the principal place of abode of a qualifying individual for more than half of the tax year, and from which the other spouse is absent for the last six months of the tax year. (Code Sec. 21(e)(4))[16]

Divorced or legally separated parents who seek to claim the credit for an under-13-year-old child must meet the custody test. That is, where the child receives more than half of his support during the year from his parents, and is in the custody of one or both of the parents for more than half of the calendar year, he's a qualifying individual with respect to the parent who has the longer custody, i.e., that parent may claim him for purposes of the credit. The parent need *not* be able to claim the child as a dependent and may even have released the dependency exemption (¶ 3124) to the other parent. (Code Sec. 21(e)(5))[17]

No credit can be claimed unless the taxpayer reports on his or her Form 2441 (or Schedule 2, Form 1040A) the correct name, address and taxpayer identification number of the dependent care provider. A tax-exempt provider doesn't have to supply a TIN. (Code Sec. 21(e)(9)) The dependent care provider should provide this information and certify the TIN on Form W-10. If the care provider doesn't comply with a request, the taxpayer should furnish whatever information is available, and include a statement that the other required information was requested but wasn't given.[18]

¶ 2353 Mortgage credit.

Under a qualified mortgage credit certificate program established by a state or local government, a taxpayer can take a credit (on Form 8396). (Code Sec. 25(h)) The credit is equal to the mortgage credit certificate rate multiplied by the interest paid by the taxpayer on a mortgage. (Code Sec. 25(a))[19] If the credit rate exceeds 20%, the maximum amount of the credit is $2,000. (Code Sec. 25(a)(2)(A))[20]

¶ 2354 Credit for qualified electric vehicle before 2005—Form 8834.

A tax credit is available (use Form 8834) for the cost of a qualified electric vehicle placed in service after June 30, '93 and before 2005. The amount of the credit is 10% of the vehicle's cost, (Code Sec. 30(a)) limited to a maximum credit of $4,000 for any vehicle (phased out starting in 2001). The credit can't reduce tax below certain levels. (Code Sec. 30(b))

A qualified electric vehicle is one powered primarily by an electric motor drawing current from rechargeable batteries, fuel cells or other portable sources of electrical current. (Code Sec. 30(c)(1))[21]

---

13. ¶ A-4305; ¶ 214.05.   16. ¶ A-4311; ¶ 214.07.   18. ¶ A-4326; ¶ 214.08.   20. ¶ A-4009; ¶ 254.01.
14. ¶ A-4307; ¶ 214.06.   17. ¶ A-4314; ¶ 214.07.   19. ¶ A-4008; ¶ 254.01.   21. ¶ L-18010 et seq.
15. ¶s A-4300, A-4310; ¶ 214.07.

Footnote references beginning with letters are to paragraphs in RIA's Federal Tax Coordinator 2d and RIA's Analysis of Federal Taxes: Income. Footnote references beginning with numbers are to paragraphs in RIA's United States Tax Reporter.

ⓒ*observation:* A personal-use vehicle can qualify for the credit.

¶ 2355 Limit on combined amount of personal nonrefundable credits.

The combined amount of the otherwise allowable dependent care credit (¶ 2347 *et seq.*), credit for the elderly and permanently and totally disabled (¶ 2346), and the mortgage credit (¶ 2353) is allowed as a tax credit to the extent that this aggregate amount doesn't exceed the excess of taxpayer's regular tax liability over the tentative minimum tax (without regard to the alternative minimum tax foreign tax credit). (Code Sec. 26(a)) Regular tax liability does not include the following types of tax: (Code Sec. 26(b)(2))

(1) The alternative minimum tax. (Code Sec. 55)

(2) The environmental tax. (Code Sec. 59A)

(3) Penalty taxes on certain premature distributions. (Code Sec. 72(m)(5)(B), (q), (t), (v))

(4) Accumulated earnings tax. (Code Sec. 531)

(5) Personal holding company tax. (Code Sec. 541)

(6) Certain recoveries of foreign expropriation losses. (Code Sec. 1351(d)(1))

(7) Tax on certain built-in gains of S corporations. (Code Sec. 1374)

(8) Tax imposed when passive investment income of an S corporation having Subchapter C earnings and profits exceeds 25% of gross receipts. (Code Sec. 1375)

(9) The tax on nonqualified withdrawals from a Merchant Marine capital construction fund. (Code Sec. 7518(g)(6))

(10) The 30% tax on U.S. source income earned by nonresident aliens and foreign corporations. (Code Sec. 871(a), Code Sec. 881)

(11) The interest paid as additional income on tax deferred by installment sales of timeshares and residential lots. (Code Sec. 453(l)(3), Code Sec. 453A(c))

(12) Recapture of federal subsidy from use of mortgage bonds and mortgage credit certificates. (Code Sec. 143(m))

(13) Tax on transfers of residual interests in a REMIC to a disqualified organization. (Code Sec. 860E(e))

(14) The branch profits tax. (Code Sec. 884)[22]

¶ 2356 Minimum tax credit.

This is a credit (computed on Form 8801, Form 8827 for corporations) equal to the adjusted net minimum tax that a taxpayer paid in all previous (post-'86) years with respect to "deferral preferences" (and for a corporation also "exclusion preferences"), less any minimum tax credits taken in those years. (Code Sec. 53(a), (b)) The credit is limited to the excess of: (1) taxpayer's regular tax liability (¶ 2355) for the year to which the credit is being carried, *over* (2) the sum of the following for the year to which the credit is being carried: all nonrefundable tax credits, and the tentative minimum tax (¶ 3201). (Code Sec. 53(c), (d)(2))

A taxpayer's adjusted net minimum tax is:

(1) *for a noncorporate taxpayer,* the total alternative minimum tax for the year, less the amount of alternative minimum tax liability that would have arisen if the only applicable preferences and alternative minimum tax adjustments were "exclusion preferences" and if the 90% alternative minimum tax foreign tax credit didn't apply, or *for a corporation,* the net minimum tax (alternative minimum tax) for the year, *plus*

---

22. ¶ L-18100 *et seq.*; ¶ 264.

Footnote references beginning with letters are to paragraphs in RIA's Federal Tax Coordinator 2d and RIA's Analysis of Federal Taxes: Income. Footnote references beginning with numbers are to paragraphs in RIA's United States Tax Reporter.

(2) the amount of nonconventional fuels credit, orphan drug credit and electric vehicle credit not allowed solely by reason of the limitation on that credit that is a function of the taxpayer's tentative minimum tax. (Code Sec. 53(d)(1)(B))[23]

Deferral preferences are all of the alternative minimum tax preferences and adjustments except those for: (1) percentage depletion, (2) tax-exempt interest, (3) exclusion of a portion of the gain on qualified small business stock, (4) alternative tax itemized deductions of noncorporate taxpayers, (5) the standard deduction, and (6) personal exemptions.

The preferences/alternative minimum tax adjustments that aren't deferral preferences are "exclusion preferences."[24]

¶ 2357 Foreign Tax Credit

Most U.S. taxpayers who pay income taxes to foreign governments may deduct those taxes for U.S. tax purposes or may credit them dollar-for-dollar against their U.S. income tax liability.

The foreign tax credit is elective and is allowed against U.S. income tax for income tax paid to a foreign country (or province, state, city, etc., thereof) or U.S. possession. (Code Sec. 901; Reg § 1.901-1(a)) Taxpayers may choose each year between taking a credit or a deduction for foreign income taxes. (Code Sec. 27, Code Sec. 164) If credit is claimed for any foreign income taxes, no deductions may be claimed for other foreign income taxes, but other foreign taxes otherwise deductible (e.g., foreign real property taxes) may be deducted. (Reg § 1.901-1(c))[25]

Except for the "deemed" foreign tax paid, discussed at ¶ 2364, the credit is allowed only to the person on whom the tax was imposed, but a U.S. citizen or resident alien, who is a member of a partnership or a beneficiary of an estate or trust, or stockholder of a regulated investment company that made the necessary election, may claim (as a credit) his share of the foreign tax paid or accrued by the partnership, estate, trust or mutual fund. On a joint return, the credit is for the taxes of both spouses. (Code Sec. 853, Code Sec. 901)[26]

Credit is allowed to:

■ *U.S. citizens* (except to the extent they are entitled to U.S. tax exemption for earned income from U.S. possessions and foreign countries); (Code Sec. 901(b)(1), Code Sec. 911(a), Code Sec. 931(a), Code Sec. 932; Reg § 1.901-1(g)(3), (5), Reg § 1.911-6(a))

■ *domestic corporations*(Code Sec. 901(b)(1)) or electing possessions corporations, (Code Sec. 901(g)) see ¶ 2365;

■ *aliens* residing in the U.S., or residing during the entire tax year in Puerto Rico; (Code Sec. 901(b)(3))

■ *domestic or resident estates and trusts* (to the extent allocable to the estate or trust rather than the beneficiaries). (Code Sec. 642(a))

Nonresident aliens and foreign corporations can claim the credit *only* for foreign or possessions tax on certain income effectively connected with their U.S. business. (Code Sec. 906)[27]

For the limit on the foreign tax credit for alternative minimum tax purposes, see ¶ 3213.

¶ 2358 When and how to claim foreign tax credit.

The credit is claimed on Form 1116 by an individual, trust or estate and on Form 1118 by a corporation. (Reg § 1.905-2(a)(1))[28]

---

23. ¶ A-8132; ¶ 534.   25. ¶ O-4002 *et seq.*; ¶ 9014.02.   27. ¶ O-4108; ¶ 9014.01.   28. ¶ O-5501; ¶ 9014.
24. ¶ A-8134; ¶ 534.   26. ¶ O-4100 *et seq.*; ¶ 9014.01.

Footnote references beginning with letters are to paragraphs in RIA's Federal Tax Coordinator 2d and RIA's Analysis of Federal Taxes: Income. Footnote references beginning with numbers are to paragraphs in RIA's United States Tax Reporter.

An accrual basis taxpayer takes the tax as a credit in the tax year it accrues. A cash basis taxpayer takes the tax as a credit in the tax year it is paid. However, a cash basis taxpayer can make a binding election to take credit, for *all* qualified foreign taxes, in the year they accrue rather than in the year they are paid. (Code Sec. 905(a); Reg § 1.905-1(a))[29]

¶ 2359 What taxes qualify for foreign tax credit?

A foreign levy (i.e., a payment required from a person by a foreign country) qualifies as a creditable foreign tax only if: (1) it is a tax, and (2) its predominant character is that of an income tax in the U.S. sense. (Reg § 1.901-2(a)(1))

Income taxes, war profits taxes and excess profits taxes paid or accrued during the tax year to a foreign country or a U.S. possession qualify for the foreign tax credit. (Code Sec. 901(b)(1)) A tax "in lieu of" such a tax also qualifies. (Code Sec. 903)

Foreign taxes on wages, dividends, interest and royalties normally qualify for the credit. (Reg § 1.901-2(a))[30]

No credit is allowed for taxes paid or accrued with respect to income attributable to a period beginning six months after a country becomes a country that the U.S. doesn't recognize, that the U.S. has severed relations (or doesn't conduct relations) with, or that the Secretary of State has designated as a country that repeatedly provides support for acts of international terrorism. (Code Sec. 901(j)(1),(2))[31]

For denial of the credit to taxpayers participating in an international boycott, see ¶ 4647.

¶ 2360 Limitations on the foreign tax credit.

The foreign tax credit is computed separately for certain categories of income. The foreign tax credit for each category is the lesser of: (1) the amount of foreign taxes paid or accrued with respect to that category, or (2) the U.S. tax on the foreign income in that category. (Code Sec. 901(b), Code Sec. 904(a), (d)) The following formula is used to determine the foreign tax credit.[32]

$$\frac{\text{Total taxable income within the separate category from all foreign sources}}{\text{Total taxable income}} \times \text{U.S. income tax} = \begin{array}{c}\text{Maximum}\\ \text{credit for}\\ \text{that category}\end{array}$$

The taxpayer adds up its net income and net losses within each category from all sources outside the U.S. and calculates that category's separate foreign tax credit limitation. The separate categories are: passive income, high withholding tax interest, financial services income, certain dividends from a DISC, certain distributions from foreign sales corporations (FSC), dividends from 10% to 50% U.S.-owned foreign corporations, shipping income, taxable foreign trade income and income not described in the above categories (general overall category). (Code Sec. 904(d))[33]

Additional restrictions apply on foreign credits for foreign mineral income (Reg § 1.901-3(a))[34] and foreign oil and gas extraction income. (Reg § 1.907(a)-1, (b)-1, (c)-1, (d)-1, (e)-1, (f)-1)[35]

¶ 2361 Determining foreign taxable income.

The foreign tax credit can't exceed the foreign tax paid or accrued. If the taxpayer has no foreign source income that is taxable in the U.S., no credit is allowed.[36] In some situations, foreign source income may be recharacterized as domestic income, see ¶ 4660.

---

29. ¶ O-5504; ¶ 9014.02.
30. ¶ O-4200 *et seq.*; ¶ 9014.02.
31. ¶ O-4007 *et seq.*.

32. ¶ O-4401; ¶ 9044.01.
33. ¶ O-4300 *et seq.*; ¶ 9014.02.
34. ¶ O-5100 *et seq.*; ¶ 9014.02.

35. ¶ O-5200 *et seq.*; ¶s 9044.01, 9074.

36. ¶ O-4402 *et seq.*; ¶ 9044.01.

Footnote references beginning with letters are to paragraphs in RIA's Federal Tax Coordinator 2d and RIA's Analysis of Federal Taxes: Income. Footnote references beginning with numbers are to paragraphs in RIA's United States Tax Reporter.

(Code Sec. 904(a), (b), (f))

Capital gains are subject to special rules. Taxable income from foreign sources for purposes of the tax credit includes capital gain only up to the lesser of foreign capital gain or the excess of *all* capital gains over capital losses. Where there is a capital gain rate differential a special rule applies which limits the amount of the net foreign source capital gain or loss which is counted as foreign income in the numerator of the fraction set forth in ¶ 2360. (Code Sec. 904(b)(1), (2); Reg § 1.904(b)-1(b)(1), (2))[37]

¶ 2362 Carryover and carryback of excess foreign tax.

If foreign income taxes paid or accrued exceed the amount that may be credited for the tax year, the excess qualifies for a two-year carryback and a five-year carryover. (Code Sec. 904(c))[38]

¶ 2363 Determining amount of foreign tax payments.

Payments of foreign income taxes must be translated into dollars using the exchange rates in effect at the time of the payments. (Code Sec. 986(a)(1)(A); Reg § 1.905-3T(b))[39]

¶ 2364 Domestic corporation's credit for foreign tax on foreign affiliate; the deemed credit.

A domestic corporation is deemed to have paid, and may claim credit for, a portion of the foreign taxes paid or accrued by a foreign corporation in which it holds at least 10% of the voting stock (first tier corporation).

A domestic corporation is also deemed to have paid a portion of the taxes paid or accrued by a foreign second tier or third tier corporation in certain cases. (Code Sec. 902; Reg § 1.902-1)[40]

The domestic corporation claims the credit against dividend income from the foreign affiliate, and has to treat a portion of the foreign tax paid by that affiliate as additional taxable dividend income (called "gross up"). (Code Sec. 78, Code Sec. 902; Reg § 1.78-1(a))

¶ 2365 Possessions tax credit for U.S. corporations in Puerto Rico and the Virgin Islands.

If a domestic corporation has at least 80% of its gross income for the three-year period preceding the close of the tax year from sources within a U.S. possession (i.e., Puerto Rico or the U.S. Virgin Islands), and at least 75% of its gross income for that period is derived from the active conduct of a trade or business in a possession, it can elect (on Form 5712) a possessions tax credit. (Code Sec. 936(a)(2)) The corporation's allowable credit for any tax year is equal to the portion of its U.S. tax attributable to the sum of its:

(1) "active possession business income"—i.e., taxable income from sources outside the U.S. from the active conduct of a business within a U.S. possession, from the sale or exchange of substantially all of the assets used in that business; (Code Sec. 936(a)(1)(A)) and

(2) qualified investment income from sources within a possession in which it actively conducts business, including certain investments made in qualified Caribbean Basin countries. (Code Sec. 936(a)(1)(B), (d)(4))[41]

However, for tax years beginning after '93, the amount in (1), above, may not exceed an economic-activity limitation or, at taxpayer's election, a percentage (60%, for tax years beginning in '94) of the credit otherwise allowable on this income. (Code Sec. 936(a)(4))[42]

---

37. ¶ O-4404; ¶ 9044.01.   39. ¶ O-5300 *et seq.*   41. ¶ O-1500 *et seq.*; ¶ 9314.06.   42. ¶ O-1500 *et seq.*; ¶ 9314.06.
38. ¶ O-4601 *et seq.*; ¶ 9044.01.   40. ¶ O-4800 *et seq.*; ¶ 9024.

Footnote references beginning with letters are to paragraphs in RIA's Federal Tax Coordinator 2d and RIA's Analysis of Federal Taxes: Income. Footnote references beginning with numbers are to paragraphs in RIA's United States Tax Reporter.

Chapter 8   Sales and Exchanges—Tax Free Exchanges—Basis

¶ 2400 Gain or Loss on Sales or Exchanges ▐

When a taxpayer sells or exchanges property at a price higher than his cost or tax basis, he realizes a gain. If a taxpayer sells at less than his basis, he realizes a loss. A taxpayer does not realize gain or loss when property in his hands merely goes up or down in value.

¶ 2401 Computing gain or loss on a sale or exchange.

Taxpayers are taxed to the extent the amount realized from a sale or exchange exceeds their adjusted basis (usually cost, increased for improvements and decreased for depreciation). If the cost or adjusted basis of the property disposed of exceeds the amount realized, the difference is a loss. (Code Sec. 1001(a))[1]

illustration: In Year 1, S bought a machine for $10,000 and placed it in service. S used it solely in business. For Years 1 and 2, S claims total depreciation deductions of $6,300. S sells the machine for $2,700 in Year 3. S's loss is $1,000: $3,700 adjusted basis ($10,000 – $6,300) less $2,700 received on the sale.

¶ 2402 Amount realized.

The amount realized on a sale or other disposition of property is the amount of money plus the fair market value of any property received by the seller. (Code Sec. 1001(b))[2]

If a taxpayer sells a capital asset, his selling expenses (such as brokers' commissions) ordinarily reduce the amount realized, thus reducing the gain or increasing the loss realized on the sale.[3]

For whether unstated interest on a deferred sale of property is treated as part of the selling price of the property, see ¶ 1311.

¶ 2403 Seller's obligations assumed by buyer.

Where the buyer of property assumes a debt of the seller, or pays one, the amount of the debt is added to the amount realized by the seller. (Reg § 1.1001-2(a)) Thus, taxes and legal fees of the seller paid for by the buyer are part of the sales price.[4]

¶ 2404 Amount realized on sale of property subject to a debt.

If property is sold subject to a mortgage or other debt, the amount of the mortgage is included in the sales price whether or not the seller is personally liable on the mortgage debt. This is so whether or not the buyer assumes the mortgage.[5]

In determining the gain or loss on property, its fair market value is treated as being not less than the amount of the nonrecourse debt to which it is subject. (Code Sec. 7701(g))[6]

¶ 2405 Open sales.

When a seller receives payment in the form of a property right or obligation whose value depends on future events, if the seller can prove that the right or obligation has no ascertainable value, he reports gain only when the proceeds from the obligation exceed his basis, and loss is fixed only when further payments can't reasonably be expected.[7] For restrictions on "open" sales under the installment sale rules, see ¶ 2710.

---

1. ¶ I-2501; ¶ 10,014.   3. ¶ I-2033; ¶ 10,014.   5. ¶ I-2517.   7. ¶ G-6568; ¶ 4534.49.
2. ¶ I-2502; ¶ 10,014.   4. ¶ I-2517; ¶ 10,014.03.   6. ¶ I-2522.

Footnote references beginning with letters are to paragraphs in RIA's Federal Tax Coordinator 2d and RIA's Analysis of Federal Taxes: Income. Footnote references beginning with numbers are to paragraphs in RIA's United States Tax Reporter.

¶2406 Repossession of mortgaged real estate.

When real property is sold and the sale gives rise to a debt to the seller secured by the real property (a purchase-money mortgage or similar lien), and the seller later repossesses the property (through voluntary transfer or foreclosure) because of actual or imminent default by the buyer, then:

■ no loss results to the seller from the repossession or reacquisition, nor does the mortgage debt become worthless; and

■ the seller's gain on repossession is limited to the money and the value of other property (except the repossessed property) received by the seller with respect to the original sale to the extent these amounts haven't already been reported as income. The resulting gain can't exceed the gain on the original sale. (Code Sec. 1038)[8]

If taxpayer sold his residence and gain was not recognized (¶2438) or was excluded (¶2445) and he repossesses and then resells within one year after the date of the repossession, no gain or loss results to the seller from the repossession. (Code Sec. 1038(e))[9] In effect, the reacquisition is generally disregarded and the resale is considered to be a sale of the residence occurring on the date of the original sale. (Reg § 1.1038-2(a)(2)) This means the taxpayer must recalculate his original nonrecognition or exclusion amounts (with any adjustments reported in the year of resale). (Reg § 1.1038-2(c)(1))[10]

observation: If the resale isn't made within one year, the regular repossession rules above apply.

¶2407 Personal property repossessed.

Gain or loss to the seller on repossession of personal property sold in a deferred payment transaction not on the installment method is the difference between the fair market value of the property when repossessed and the basis of the defaulted obligation (decreased by amounts paid on the note and increased for costs incurred in connection with the repossession). Gain or loss is reported in the year of repossession.[11]

¶2408 When cash basis taxpayers report gain or loss.

A cash basis seller reports gain on a sale or exchange in the year the sales proceeds are received, actually or constructively. A loss is reported in the year the transaction is completed by a fixed, identifiable event.[12]

¶2409 When accrual basis taxpayers report gain or loss.

An accrual basis seller reports gain or loss in the year the sale is completed and an unqualified right to the purchase price arises—in most cases, when title passes to the buyer.[13]

Except as modified by the stock exchange rules (¶2411), gain or loss on the sale of securities arises when the seller has sold or committed himself to sell specific shares.[14] Gain or loss on the exchange of securities arises when the taxpayer acquires a right to specific securities.[15]

¶2410 Delivery of deed or title in escrow.

Where both the deed (or other evidence of title) and the purchase price are placed in escrow pending examination and approval of the title by the buyer, a sale isn't completed (and gain or loss isn't realized) until the buyer signifies approval. Until then, the seller doesn't have an unqualified right to payment. Once the buyer approves title, the seller

8. ¶ G-6851 *et seq.*; ¶ 10,384.
9. ¶ G-6877 *et seq.*; ¶ 10,384.
10. ¶ G-6877 *et seq.*; ¶ 10,384.
11. ¶ G-6801; ¶ 453B4.07.
12. ¶ I-2601; ¶ 4464.05.
13. ¶ I-2602; ¶ 4464.07.
14. ¶ I-2615; ¶s 12,234.07, 4514.112.
15. ¶ I-2616; ¶s 12,234.07, 4514.112.

Footnote references beginning with letters are to paragraphs in RIA's Federal Tax Coordinator 2d and RIA's Analysis of Federal Taxes: Income. Footnote references beginning with numbers are to paragraphs in RIA's United States Tax Reporter.

can't postpone reporting gain by directing the escrow agent to hold the payment until the next year.[16]

But if the deed is delivered in escrow as security for the performance of an unconditional obligation of the buyer (usually payment of the purchase price), the sale is completed when the deed is delivered in escrow and the buyer enters into possession of the property.[17]

¶ 2411 Stock exchange sales.

In stock exchange transactions, cash and accrual basis taxpayers realize gain or loss when the sale is entered into (trade date), and not on the later settlement date.[18]

¶ 2412 Sales of load mutual funds with reinvestment right.

A load charge incurred in buying mutual fund shares is disregarded (in whole or in part) in computing gain or loss on the disposition of those shares within 90 days, if the buyer was given a reinvestment right under which shares in the same (or another) mutual fund could be bought at less than the usual load charge. The load charge is disregarded to the extent of the reduction in the load charge on the later purchase. (Code Sec. 852(f))[19]

¶ 2413 Nontaxable Exchanges

A taxpayer doesn't recognize gain or loss on exchanges of common or preferred stock for other common or preferred stock of the same corporation. A corporation doesn't recognize gain or loss when it sells or exchanges its own stock for property or services. Certain U.S. obligations can be exchanged tax-free.

¶ 2414 Stock for stock of same corporation.

No gain or loss is recognized on the exchange of common stock for other common, or preferred stock for other preferred, of the same corporation. (Code Sec. 1036(a)) The exchange is tax-free whether it's between a shareholder and the corporation or between two shareholders.[20]

An exchange between individual shareholders of common stock for preferred stock in the same corporation is not tax-free,[21] but reorganization exchanges of stock for stock or stock and securities of the same or different corporations may be tax-free, see ¶ 3541 *et seq.*

¶ 2415 Corporation's sale or exchange of its own stock for property or services.

A corporation doesn't recognize gain or loss on the sale or exchange of its stock (including treasury stock) for money, other property or services. (Code Sec. 1032(a); Reg § 1.1032-1)[22]

¶ 2416 Tax-free exchanges of U.S. obligations.

IRS regs may provide for the tax-free exchange of one U.S. obligation (bond, note, certificate of indebtedness, etc.) for another. (Code Sec. 1037(a)) The Treasury designates the specific obligations it will exchange for the previously issued obligations without recognition of gain or loss.[23]

---

16. ¶s I-1112, I-1114;
    ¶s 12,234.08, 4514.087.
17. ¶ I-1124; ¶s 4514.087,
    4514.101.
18. ¶ I-2615; ¶ 4514.112.
19. ¶ P-5038 *et seq.*; ¶ 8524.02.
20. ¶ I-3301; ¶ 10,364.
21. ¶ I-3301; ¶ 10,014.
22. ¶s 3201; 3208; ¶ 10,324.
23. ¶ I-3400 *et seq.*; ¶ 10,374.

Footnote references beginning with letters are to paragraphs in RIA's Federal Tax Coordinator 2d and RIA's Analysis of Federal Taxes: Income. Footnote references beginning with numbers are to paragraphs in RIA's United States Tax Reporter.

¶ *2417* "Like-Kind" (Code Sec 1031) Exchanges

No gain or loss is recognized where business or investment property is exchanged solely for like-kind property. Multi-party exchanges may qualify. However, gain, but not loss, is recognized if boot is also received.

This nonrecognition provision doesn't apply to: stock in trade (inventory) and other property held primarily for sale; stocks, bonds, and notes; chooses in action; interests in a partnership; certificates of trust or beneficial interest; or other securities or evidences of indebtedness or interest. (Code Sec. 1031(a))[24]

Nonrecognition is not elected. It is mandatory if the conditions are met.[25]

"Like-kind" refers to the nature, character, or class of the property, not to its grade or quality. Thus, an exchange of real estate for real estate is an exchange of "like-kind" property. It doesn't matter where the real estate is located (but foreign and U.S. real property can't be like-kind) or whether it's improved or not. (Code Sec. 1031(h); Reg § 1.1031(a)-1(b))[26]

An exchange of real property for a 30-year leasehold on real property is a like-kind exchange. Trade-ins are a common type of nontaxable exchange. Whether the taxpayer pays money or not, the trade-in is still a nontaxable exchange. (Reg § 1-1031(a)-1(c))[27]

Report on Form 8824, in addition to Schedule D or Form 4797 (whichever applies).[28]

¶ *2418* Multi-party (including deferred) nontaxable exchanges.

If a taxpayer wants to (or will only) exchange his property for like-kind property, but the party who wants taxpayer's property doesn't own the like-kind property, the taxpayer can still get a nontaxable exchange if the other party acquires the like-kind property and taxpayer then exchanges his property for that like-kind property.

illustration: Taxpayer A holds Whiteacre for investment. He doesn't want to sell it if that would result in tax, but he would exchange it for Blackacre. B wants Whiteacre but doesn't own Blackacre. C owns Blackacre and is willing to sell, but doesn't want Whiteacre. B buys Blackacre from C for cash. A transfers Whiteacre to B for Blackacre. The exchange is nontaxable to A.

The exchange is nontaxable (if the time limits at ¶ 2421 are met) even where the taxpayer transfers property in exchange for a written promise by the transferee to deliver like-kind property to the taxpayer in the future, i.e., a deferred or nonsimultaneous exchange.[29]

¶ *2419* Taxing "boot" in otherwise nontaxable exchange.

If a taxpayer receives boot—money or any other property that doesn't qualify for nonrecognition of gain—in an otherwise nontaxable exchange of stock (¶ 2414), like-kind property (¶ 2417) or U.S. obligations (¶ 2416):

■ gain to the taxpayer is recognized (is taxable) in an amount not exceeding the value of the boot received, (Code Sec. 1031(b)) but

■ loss to the taxpayer isn't recognized (isn't deductible) to any extent. (Code Sec. 1031(c))[30]

illustration: Taxpayer exchanges business real estate worth $50,000 and having an adjusted basis of $30,000 for business real estate worth $40,000 plus $10,000 cash. His total gain is $20,000 ($40,000 + $10,000 – $30,000 basis), but the amount recognized is

24. ¶ I-3050 *et seq.*; ¶ 10,314.04.   26. ¶ I-3059.   28. ¶ I-3051.   30. ¶ I-3160; ¶ 10,314.13.
25. ¶ I-3052; ¶ 10,314.04.   27. ¶ I-3076.   29. ¶ I-3095 *et seq.*; ¶ 10,314.08.

Footnote references beginning with letters are to paragraphs in RIA's Federal Tax Coordinator 2d and RIA's Analysis of Federal Taxes: Income. Footnote references beginning with numbers are to paragraphs in RIA's United States Tax Reporter.

limited to the boot—$10,000. The tax on the remaining $10,000 gain is deferred because the transaction qualifies as a like-kind exchange.

Where the taxpayer gives money in the nontaxable exchange, no gain is recognized. But if the boot given is property other than money, gain or loss may be recognized. Thus, where stock that has depreciated in value is given in connection with a nontaxable exchange of real estate, loss on the stock is recognized to the extent the stock's adjusted basis exceeds its fair market value. (Reg § 1.1031(d)-1(e))[31]

¶ 2420 Assumption of liabilities.

Liabilities assumed or acquired are treated as a cash equivalent (boot). (Code Sec. 1031(d)) The taxpayer who assumes the liability or gets the property subject to a liability is the one giving the boot, while the taxpayer whose liability is assumed or who transfers property subject to a liability *receives* the boot.[32] If each party assumes a liability of the other (or acquires property subject to a liability), only the net liability is boot given or received. (Reg § 1.1031(b)-1(c))

illustration: Taxpayer's investment realty has an adjusted basis of $40,000, a value of $115,000, and a mortgage of $60,000. He exchanges his property for investment real estate which is worth $100,000 and is subject to a $50,000 mortgage, and he also gets $5,000 cash. His realized gain is $75,000, since he receives consideration of $115,000: (1) property worth $50,000 ($100,000 value − $50,000 mortgage), (2) $60,000 mortgage on the property *he* transfers, and (3) $5,000 cash, while his adjusted basis was $40,000. But the gain *recognized* is limited to the boot of $15,000, computed as follows:

Mortgage on property given up by taxpayer	$60,000
Mortgage on property received by taxpayer	50,000
Net reduction of taxpayer's indebtedness	$10,000
Cash paid to taxpayer	5,000
Maximum gain to be recognized	$15,000

Consideration received in the form of cash or other property is not offset by consideration given in the form of an assumption of liabilities or a receipt of property subject to a liability. But consideration given in the form of cash or other property is offset against consideration received in the form of an assumption of liabilities or a transfer of property subject to a liability. (Reg § 1.1031(d)-2, Ex (2))

¶ 2421 Time limits on like-kind exchanges.

Like-kind treatment is barred if the property to be received is not identified (e.g., by being specified in the contract) on or before 45 days after the transfer, or is not received within 180 days after the transfer or by the due date (with extensions) of the return for the year of transfer if earlier. (Code Sec. 1031(a)(3))[33]

¶ 2422 Related-party exchanges.

Where a taxpayer exchanges like-kind property with a related (under Code Sec. 267(b), see ¶ 2450, or Code Sec. 707(b)(1), see ¶ 3732) taxpayer and, within two years of the date of the last transfer that was part of the exchange, either party disposes of the property received in the exchange, then gain or loss not recognized in the exchange is recognized on the date the later disposition occurs. A disposition includes indirect transfers. Exceptions are made for death, certain involuntary conversions, and non-tax-avoidance transactions. (Code Sec. 1031(f))[34] Form 8824 must be filed for the year of the exchange *and also* for the two years following the exchange.[35]

---

31. ¶ I-3165.
32. ¶ I-3167; ¶ 10,314.12.
33. ¶ I-3099; ¶ 10,314.08.
34. ¶ 3132 *et seq.*; ¶ 10,314.07.
35. ¶ I-3132.

Footnote references beginning with letters are to paragraphs in RIA's Federal Tax Coordinator 2d and RIA's Analysis of Federal Taxes: Income. Footnote references beginning with numbers are to paragraphs in RIA's United States Tax Reporter.

¶ 2423 Exchanges of multiple properties.

These are exchanges in which more than one "exchange group" (see below) is created, or exchanges in which only one exchange group is created but there is more than one property being transferred or received within that exchange group. To compute gain in an exchange of multiple properties:

■ separate the properties transferred into "exchange groups;"

■ offset all liabilities assumed by the taxpayer as part of the exchange by all liabilities of which the taxpayer is relieved as part of the exchange, with the excess liabilities assumed or relieved allocated;

■ apply the rules of Code Sec. 1031 and the regs separately to each exchange group to determine the amount of gain recognized in the exchange;

■ apply the rules of Code Sec. 1031 and the regs separately to each exchange group to determine the basis of the properties received in the exchange. (Reg § 1.1031(j)-1(a)(2)(i))

Each "exchange group" consists of the properties transferred and received in the exchange, all of which are of a like kind or like class. (Reg § 1.1031(j)-1(b)(2)(i))[36]

¶ 2424 Rollover of Gain from Sale of Publicly Traded Securities into Specialized Small Business Investment Companies (SSBICs) ▬▬▬▬▬▬

C corporations and individuals can elect to roll over limited amounts of gain from the sale of publicly traded securities tax-free into an investment in a Specialized Small Business Investment Company (SSBIC) if certain conditions are met.

¶ 2425 Rollover of securities sale gain into specialized small business investment companies.

For sales made after Aug. 9, '93, taxpayers other than estates, trusts, partnerships, and S corporations may elect to limit the amount of gain they recognize on the sale of "publicly traded securities" to the excess of the amount realized on the sale, over: (Code Sec. 1044(a))

■ the cost of any common stock or partnership interest in a specialized small business investment company (SSBIC, see ¶ 2426) purchased by the taxpayer during the 60-day period beginning on the date of the sale, (Code Sec. 1044(a)(1)) reduced by

■ any part of that cost previously taken into account under this rule (other than gain treated as ordinary income). (Code Sec. 1044(a)(2))[37]

The amount of gain an individual may exclude (roll over) under the SSBIC rules for any tax year is limited to the lesser of: (1) $50,000, or (2) $500,000 reduced by gain excluded (rolled over) under this rule in all preceding years. (Code Sec. 1044(b)(1)) For married individuals filing jointly, the limits are $25,000 and $250,000, respectively. (Code Sec. 1044(b)(3)) The amount of gain qualifying for the rollover is allocated equally between spouses who file jointly, for purposes of applying this limit to later years. (Code Sec. 1044(b)(3)(B))[38]

A corporation's rollover for any tax year is limited to the lesser of (1) $250,000 or (2) $1,000,000 reduced by any gain excluded under this rule in all preceding years. (Code Sec. 1044(b)(2)) This includes exclusions by members of the corporation's controlled group, or by its predecessor. (Code Sec. 1044(b)(4))[39]

🅥*caution:* The above rule applies to *sales,* but not to *exchanges,* of publicly traded securities.

"Publicly traded securities" are securities traded on an open market. (Code

---

36. ¶ I-3182 *et seq.*; ¶ 10,314.07.　　37. ¶ I-3791; ¶ 10,444.　　　38. ¶ I-3792; ¶ 10,444.　　　39. ¶ I-3793; ¶ 10,444.

Footnote references beginning with letters are to paragraphs in RIA's Federal Tax Coordinator 2d and RIA's Analysis of Federal Taxes: Income. Footnote references beginning with numbers are to paragraphs in RIA's United States Tax Reporter.

Sec. 1044(c)(1))[40]

¶ 2426   Specialized small business investment company (SSBIC) defined.

An SSBIC is any partnership or corporation licensed by the Small Business Administration under Sec. 301(d) of the Small Business Investment Act of '58 as in effect on May 13, '93. (Code Sec. 1044(c)(3))[41]

¶ 2427   Involuntary Conversions

No gain is recognized when property is compulsorily or involuntarily converted into property similar or related in service or use. Where property is involuntarily converted into money or into property that isn't similar or related in service or use, a taxpayer can avoid tax on any gain, if he so elects and he buys property that is similar or related in service or use or if he acquires control of a corporation that owns such property (or acquires the property within a specified time). The cost of the replacement property must be equal to or more than the net proceeds from the converted property. And the replacement must generally be made within two years after the close of the first tax year in which any part of the gain is realized.

If the taxpayer suffers a loss on the involuntary conversion, there's no election. The loss is recognized or not recognized without regard to the involuntary conversion rules. (Reg § 1.1033(a)-1(a))[42]

Individuals use Form 1040, Schedule D, to report gain or loss from an involuntary conversion. Form 4797 is used to report an involuntary conversion of assets used in a trade or business.[43]

¶ 2428   Nonrecognition of gain on involuntary conversions.

Where property is converted into other property similar or related in service or use to the converted property, no gain is recognized. (Code Sec. 1033(a)(1)) However, where property is converted into dissimilar property or into money, the taxpayer must, within a specified time, purchase "replacement" property (see ¶ 2434),[44] or must purchase 80% control of a corporation owning or, within the specified time, acquiring replacement property.[45] Gain is recognized only to the extent the amount realized on the conversion exceeds the cost of the replacement property. (Code Sec. 1033(a)(2)(A))[46]

illustration: X's insured property having a basis of $10,000 is destroyed by fire. The insurance is $15,000, so X has a $5,000 gain. If X timely buys replacement property for $13,000, $2,000 of the gain is taxable ($15,000 – $13,000). If the new property costs $15,000, none of the gain is taxed.

¶ 2429   "Involuntary conversion" defined.

An involuntary conversion is the compulsory or involuntary conversion of taxpayer's property into similar property, dissimilar property or money as a result of the property's destruction, theft, seizure, requisition or condemnation (actual or threatened, see ¶ 2431). (Code Sec. 1033(a))

Involuntary conversion includes certain *sales*—sales in actual or threatened condemnation (¶ 2431), certain sales (or the destruction) of livestock due to disease, (Code Sec. 1033(d)) and the sale or exchange of livestock (in excess of the number taxpayer would sell if he followed his usual business practices) solely on account of drought. (Code Sec. 1033(e))[47]

---

40. ¶ I-3794; ¶ 10,440.   42. ¶ I-3700; ¶ 10,334.   44. ¶ I-3700; ¶ 10,334.22.   46. ¶ I-3700; ¶ 10,334.33.
41. ¶ I-3794; ¶ 10,444.   43. ¶ I-3773.   45. ¶ I-3743; ¶ 10,334.23.   47. ¶ N-1216 *et seq.*; ¶ 10,334.08.

Footnote references beginning with letters are to paragraphs in RIA's Federal Tax Coordinator 2d and RIA's Analysis of Federal Taxes: Income. Footnote references beginning with numbers are to paragraphs in RIA's United States Tax Reporter.

¶ 2430 Insurance proceeds.

Insurance proceeds that compensate for the loss of the right to use the property due to loss or destruction may qualify for nonrecognition as involuntary conversion proceeds. However, the proceeds of a use and occupancy insurance contract that expressly insures against actual lost profits are not proceeds of an involuntary conversion. Instead, these proceeds are treated as taxable income. (Reg § 1.1033(a)-2(c)(8))[48]

If a taxpayer's principal residence or its contents is compulsorily or involuntarily converted after Aug. 31, '91 as a result of a Presidentially-declared disaster: (a) no gain is recognized on the insurance proceeds on unscheduled property, and (b) the rest of the proceeds, if invested in property similar or related in use to the residence or its contents, is treated as a single unit for purposes of the replacement rules (except that a four-year instead of two-year replacement period applies). (Code Sec. 1033(h))[49]

¶ 2431 Condemnations—actual or threatened.

A disposition under the threat or imminence of condemnation is treated as an involuntary conversion. (Code Sec. 1033(a)(2)(E)(ii))

Threat or imminence of condemnation exists when taxpayer is informed, orally or in writing, by a representative of a governmental body or authorized public official, that the body or official has decided to acquire the property, and taxpayer has reasonable grounds to believe that condemnation proceedings will be initiated if he doesn't voluntarily sell. Threat or imminence of condemnation also exists where the taxpayer gets information as to a decision to acquire the property for public use through a report in the news media, if a representative of the governmental body or public official involved confirms the published report and taxpayer has reasonable grounds to believe that the necessary steps to condemn will be taken if he doesn't sell.[50]

Sales to third parties (as distinguished from the condemning agency) also qualify as involuntary conversions if made under the threat or imminence of condemnation.[1]

¶ 2432 Condemnation awards—amount realized.

The amount realized from a condemnation award is the difference between the award and the adjusted basis of the condemned property.[2] The taxpayer's legal fees, engineering costs and other expenses necessitated by a condemnation proceeding reduce the amount realized. But sums withheld from the award to pay liens on the property don't reduce the amount realized.[3]

¶ 2433 Severance damages.

Where only part of the property is condemned, the owner may be paid severance damages as compensation for a loss of value in the part of the property retained. Severance damages may be paid, for example, because of impairment of access to, or flooding or erosion of, the property retained.[4]

Payments are considered severance damages only if specifically agreed to in the condemnation proceeding; otherwise, the entire award is considered made for the condemned property.[5]

Where severance damage proceeds are used to acquire replacement property, the taxpayer may elect nonrecognition under the involuntary conversion rules with respect to any gain from receipt of the severance damages.[6]

---

48. ¶ I-3724; ¶ 10,334.11.
49. ¶ I-3772.1 *et seq.*; ¶ 10,334.40.
50. ¶ I-3703; ¶ 10,334.02.

1. ¶ I-3705.
2. ¶ I-3700; ¶ 10,334.11.

3. ¶ I-3764; ¶ 10,334.13.
4. ¶ I-3768; ¶ 10,334.14.

5. ¶ I-3770; ¶ 10,334.14.
6. ¶ I-3768; ¶ 10,334.14.

Footnote references beginning with letters are to paragraphs in RIA's Federal Tax Coordinator 2d and RIA's Analysis of Federal Taxes: Income. Footnote references beginning with numbers are to paragraphs in RIA's United States Tax Reporter.

¶ 2434 Replacement property.

The replacement property must be similar or related in service or use to the property replaced. (Code Sec. 1033(a)(1)) "Similar or related in service or use" means the use of the replacement property must be substantially similar to the use of the replaced property.[7]

This test as applied to an owner-lessor of property looks to the use of the replacement property from the lessor's viewpoint, not the lessee's. If the replacement property involves similar business risks, management and landlord services, etc., it will qualify even though the lessee's use of the new property differs from the lessee's use of the old.[8]

¶ 2435 Replacement of condemned real estate.

A replacement of condemned real estate held for productive business use or for rental or investment qualifies for nonrecognition treatment if the replacement property is property of a like-kind. (Code Sec. 1033(g)(1)) Determination of whether replacement property is of like-kind is made under the rules at ¶ 2417, a more liberal standard than the "similar use" rule. For example, improved realty isn't similar in use to unimproved realty, (Reg § 1.1033(a)-2(c)(9)(i)) but they are of like-kind.[9]

The like-kind rule doesn't apply to real estate held primarily for sale (Code Sec. 1033(g)(1)) or where control of a corporation owning replacement property is acquired. (Code Sec. 1033(g)(2))[10]

¶ 2436 Replacement period.

Except as provided in ¶ 2430, converted property must be replaced within a period:

(1) beginning with (a) the date the property was destroyed, stolen, condemned, etc., or (b) the date condemnation or requisition was first threatened or became imminent, whichever is earlier, (Code Sec. 1033(a)(2)(B)) and

(2) ending (a) two years after the close of the first tax year in which any part of the gain is realized (three years in the case of condemnation or threat of condemnation of real property described at ¶ 2435), or (b) at a later date allowed by IRS upon application by the taxpayer. (Code Sec. 1033(a)(2)(B), (g)(4))[11]

¶ 2437 Rollover or Exclusion of Gain on Sale of Residence ■■■■■■■■■■■

A taxpayer who realizes a gain on the sale of his old principal residence does not recognize the gain if he buys a new principal residence within a two-year period before or after the sale, except to the extent the adjusted sales price of the old residence exceeds the cost of the new residence. Under certain conditions, a 55 or older taxpayer who sells or exchanges his principal residence can make a one-time election to exclude up to $125,000 of any gain from gross income. (Code Sec. 1034)

¶ 2438 Nonrecognition of gain on sale of a residence.

If a taxpayer sells a principal residence, and buys and uses another principal residence within a period beginning two years before and ending two years after the date of the sale, gain on the sale will not be recognized where the cost of the new residence equals or exceeds the adjusted selling price of the old. (Extended periods apply for members of the armed forces and taxpayers with a tax home outside the U.S. after the sale of the old residence.)[12] If the cost of the new residence is less than the selling price of the old, gain is recognized to the extent of the difference. (Code Sec. 1034(a); Reg § 1.1034-1(a))

---

7. ¶ I-3725; ¶ 10,334.22.   9. ¶ I-3727; ¶ 10,334.02.   11. ¶ I-3734; ¶ 10,334.26.   12. ¶ I-4619; ¶ 10,334.03.
8. ¶ I-3730; ¶ 10,334.22.   10. ¶ I-3727; ¶ 10,334.22.

Footnote references beginning with letters are to paragraphs in RIA's Federal Tax Coordinator 2d and RIA's Analysis of Federal Taxes: Income. Footnote references beginning with numbers are to paragraphs in RIA's United States Tax Reporter.

The nonrecognition of gain is mandatory, not optional, if the sale and purchase come within the terms of the law. (Reg § 1.1034-1(a))[13]

The cost of the new residence includes cash paid and any mortgages to which the property is subject, costs of improvements made within the period allowed for purchasing and constructing a new residence that are capital expenditures, and commissions and other purchasing expenses. (Reg § 1.1034-1(c)(4))[14] But items deducted as moving expenses (¶ 1645 *et seq.*) are not part of the cost of the new residence. (Code Sec. 217(e))

The adjusted selling price is the amount realized on the sale less any expenses incurred by the taxpayer to make the property more saleable (fixing-up expenses) if they: (1) are for work performed during the 90-day period ending on the day the contract to sell was made, (2) are paid within 30 days after the date of the sale, (3) are otherwise nondeductible in computing taxable income, and (4) aren't capital expenditures or improvements. (Code Sec. 1034(b)) Capital expenditures are added to the cost of the old residence. (Reg § 1.1034-1(b)(6))[15]

¶ 2439 More than one replacement in two-year period.

If during the replacement period taxpayer acquired successively more than one principal residence, only the last one acquired in the period may be treated as the new residence (with one exception, see below) in determining the gain from the sale of the old residence on which tax is postponed. (Code Sec. 1034(c)(4)) Gain on the other temporary residences is taxed.[16]

The exception applies where the second (or later) sale within the two-year period was in connection with the start of work by the taxpayer as an employee or self-employed individual at a new principal place of work, the second (or later) residence sold qualifies as a former residence under the Code Sec. 217 deduction for moving expenses, and the taxpayer also satisfies the moving expense distance and time tests, explained in ¶ 1649 and ¶ 1650. (Code Sec. 1034(d)(2))[17]

¶ 2440 Principal residence defined.

If taxpayer owns more than one residence, only the sale of the principal residence qualifies for nonrecognition, ordinarily the place he occupies a majority of the time.[18]

The taxpayer must have an ownership (not a lease) interest in the property (i.e., legal title) for it to be considered his principal residence.[19]

A temporary rental of either the old or the new residence won't disqualify it as a principal residence. (Reg § 1.1034-1(c)(3)(i))[20]

¶ 2441 Reporting sale and purchase—Form 2119.

A taxpayer uses Form 2119 to show the details of the sale of the old residence and the purchase or expected purchase of the new one.[21]

¶ 2442 Condemnation of residence as a sale.

Taxpayer can elect to treat the condemnation of his or her residence or the sale or exchange of property under threat or imminence of condemnation as a sale. (Code Sec. 1034(i))[22]

¶ 2443 Residence used partly for business.

If property used for both personal and income-producing purposes is sold, gain or loss attributable to the income-producing part is recognized in full. The portion allocable to the residential use can qualify for nonrecognition of gain but loss isn't deductible. The

---

13. ¶ I-4619; ¶ 10,344.
14. ¶ I-4647; ¶ 10,344.01.
15. ¶ I-4645; ¶ 10,344.05.
16. ¶ I-4635; ¶ 10,344.03.
17. ¶ I-4636; ¶ 10,344.03.
18. ¶ I-4602; ¶ 10,344.01.
19. ¶ I-4602; ¶ 10,334.01.
20. ¶ I-4617.
21. ¶ I-4650; ¶ 10,344.07.
22. ¶ I-4641; ¶ 10,344.01.

Footnote references beginning with letters are to paragraphs in RIA's Federal Tax Coordinator 2d and RIA's Analysis of Federal Taxes: Income. Footnote references beginning with numbers are to paragraphs in RIA's United States Tax Reporter.

computation must be made as if there were two separate sales. The selling price, expenses and adjusted basis of the property are allocated between the residential part and the nonresidential part. (Reg § 1.1034-1(c)(3)(ii))[23]

¶ 2444 Husband and wife sale and purchase of residence.

If a husband and wife hold title to their residence jointly, sell the old residence, and jointly acquire a new residence within the statutory period, the transaction is as if one person were selling and buying the property and the nonrecognition provisions automatically apply to them jointly. Also, if they consent, they can be treated as one person where they don't own both old and new residence jointly. (Code Sec. 1034(g); Reg § 1.1034-1(f))[24]

Where the replacement rule is applied separately, the taxpayer's gain on sale of the old residence is recognized to the extent that his or her share of the adjusted sale price of old residence exceeds his or her contribution to the cost of the new residence. (Code Sec. 1034(g))[25]

Where newlyweds sell their individual principal residences and each invests in one new residence to which they take title jointly, the nonrecognition provisions apply to both former principal residences.[26] And where spouses separate and sell their jointly owned residence, each purchasing a new residence, the nonrecognition provisions apply to both new residences.[27]

¶ 2445 Principal residence sold by persons age 55 or over—$125,000 exclusion.

If a taxpayer 55 years or older (before the date of sale or exchange) who sells or exchanges property he owned and used as his principal residence for periods aggregating three years or more during the five-year period ending on the date of the sale or exchange, then he may elect (on Form 2119, see ¶ 2447) to exclude from his gross income up to $125,000 ($62,500 on a separate return by a married individual) of gain on the sale. (Code Sec. 121(a), (b)(1))[28] The three-out-of-five year test is considered met by a taxpayer who becomes physically or mentally incapable of self-care and resides in a licensed care facility where he owns and uses the property as his principal residence during the five years for periods totalling at least one year. (Code Sec. 121(d)(9))[29]

If on the date of the sale or exchange of the property only a portion of it was used as the taxpayer's principal residence for the period required to qualify for the exclusion, then the exclusion is available to only a portion of the taxpayer's total gain on the sale or exchange. (Code Sec. 121(d)(5))[30]

Once the taxpayer (or his spouse) has made an election with respect to a sale or exchange, he can't elect again for any later sale or exchange of a principal residence. (Code Sec. 121(b)(2))[31]

If the gain from the sale of a principal residence qualifies not only for this exclusion but also for nonrecognition as gain from an involuntary conversion or because the gain is rolled over by the purchase of another principal residence (¶ 2438), the amount realized on the sale or exchange without the exclusion is determined first and then reduced by the exclusion. (Code Sec. 121(d)(7)) Thus, the amount which must be invested in order to fully satisfy the nonrecognition provisions of Code Secs. 1033 or 1034 is reduced by the amount of gain not included in the taxpayer's gross income because of an election made under this exclusion rule. (Reg § 1.121-5(g)(1))[32]

Principal residence means the same as for purposes of the nonrecognition rules for gain on sale of a residence, (Reg § 1.121-3(a))[33] see ¶ 2440.

---

23. ¶ I-4618; ¶ 10,344.05.   26. ¶ I-4630; ¶ 10,344.05.   29. ¶ I-4719; ¶ 1214.02.   32. ¶ I-4730; ¶ 1214.
24. ¶ I-4630; ¶ 10,344.05.   27. ¶ I-4633; ¶ 10,344.05.   30. ¶ I-4724; ¶ 1214.02.   33. ¶ I-4717; ¶ 1214.
25. ¶ I-4629; ¶ 10,344.05.   28. ¶ I-4700 *et seq.*; ¶ 1214.   31. ¶ I-4725; ¶ 1214.03.

Footnote references beginning with letters are to paragraphs in RIA's Federal Tax Coordinator 2d and RIA's Analysis of Federal Taxes: Income. Footnote references beginning with numbers are to paragraphs in RIA's United States Tax Reporter.

¶ 2446 Husband and wife 55-or-over exclusion.

If the taxpayer is married and only one spouse is 55 or over, they can exclude gain if: (1) the residence is held by them as joint tenants, tenants by the entirety, or community property, (2) they file a joint return for the year of sale, and (3) both join in the election. (Code Sec. 121(d)(1))[34]

The ownership and occupancy test may be satisfied by either spouse. However, there is only one life-time election for a married couple; the election doesn't apply separately to each spouse. If a married couple is divorced after having made its one election, no further elections are available to either of them or to their new spouses if they marry again.[35]

A surviving spouse who sells property after the deceased spouse's death is considered to meet the holding and use test if the deceased spouse met it and if the surviving spouse hasn't remarried. However, the surviving spouse can't get the exclusion on the sale of the property if an earlier election made by either or both spouses is in effect. (Code Sec. 121(d)(2))[36]

Where a qualifying unmarried taxpayer sells his principal residence, then marries later in the same year, and elects on the return for that year, his spouse doesn't have to join in the election even if they file a joint return. In addition, if the nonelecting spouse sells her principal residence following the end of the marriage (e.g., after the electing spouse dies) she can still elect because she isn't married at the time she sells her residence and she hasn't previously made or joined in an election.[37]

¶ 2447 Election and revocation of 55-or-over election—Form 2119.

The election to exclude gain from a sale may be made or revoked on Form 2119 (see ¶ 2441) at any time before the expiration of the period for filing a claim for credit or refund of income tax.[38]

A taxpayer who is married at the time of the sale or exchange may not make or revoke an election unless his or her spouse joins the taxpayer. If the taxpayer's spouse dies after the sale, the decedent's representative must join in the election or revocation. (Reg § 1.121-4(a))[39]

¶ 2448 Sales and Exchanges Between Related Taxpayers ▪▪▪▪▪

No gain or loss is recognized on a transfer of property between spouses (or former spouses incident to divorce). No deduction is allowed for any loss from the sale or exchange of property between specified related taxpayers. A loss from a transfer between members of the same controlled group is generally deferred until the property is transferred outside the group. (Code Sec. 1041)

¶ 2449 Gain or loss on transfer to spouse.

No gain or loss is recognized on a transfer of property to (or in trust for the benefit of) the transferor's spouse, or to a former spouse incident to a divorce. (Code Sec. 1041(a))[40] Certain transfers to third parties on behalf of the spouse or former spouse are included. (Reg § 1.1041-1T(c))[41] However, the no-gain-or-loss rule doesn't apply to transfers in trust where liability exceeds basis, (Code Sec. 1041(e))[42] to transfers in trust of installment obligations, (Code Sec. 453B(g))[43] or where the transferee spouse is a nonresident alien. (Code Sec. 1041(d))[44]

A transfer of property is incident to divorce if it occurs within one year after the date the marriage ceases (Code Sec. 1041(c)(1)) or the transfer is related to the cessation of the

---

34. ¶ I-4713; ¶ 1214.01.
35. ¶ I-4725; ¶ 1214.02.
36. ¶ I-4714; ¶ 1214.04.

37. ¶ I-4725; ¶ 1214.04.
38. ¶ I-4732; ¶ 1214.05.
39. ¶ I-4734; ¶ 1214.05.

40. ¶s I-3609, I-3601; ¶ 10,414.
41. ¶ I-3604; ¶ 10,414.
42. ¶ I-3605.

43. ¶ I-3606.
44. ¶ I-3608

Footnote references beginning with letters are to paragraphs in RIA's Federal Tax Coordinator 2d and RIA's Analysis of Federal Taxes: Income. Footnote references beginning with numbers are to paragraphs in RIA's United States Tax Reporter.

marriage. (Code Sec. 1041(c)(2)) A transfer is related to the cessation if the transfer is under a divorce or separation instrument and the transfer occurs not more than six years after the date the marriage ceases. For later transfers, there is a presumption that the transfer is not related to the cessation. (Reg § 1041-1T(b), Q&A-7)[45]

¶ 2450 Losses from sales and exchanges between related taxpayers.

No deduction is allowed for losses from sales or exchanges between certain related taxpayers. The following are related taxpayers:

Members of the seller's family, but only brothers and sisters (whole or half blood), spouse, ancestors and lineal descendants. (Code Sec. 267(a), (b)(1), (c)(4))[46] In-laws are not members of the seller's family.[47]

Controlled corporations. A taxpayer and his controlled corporation, and a fiduciary and a corporation controlled by the trust or grantor. Control is direct or indirect ownership of more than 50% in value of the outstanding stock of the corporation. (Code Sec. 267(b)(2), (8))

Control group member. Corporations that are members of the same controlled group of corporations. (Code Sec. 267(b)(3))[48] Loss from a sale or exchange between members of a controlled group is deferred, as explained at ¶ 2452.

A corporation and a partnership if the same persons own more than 50% in value of the outstanding stock of the corporation, and more than 50% of the capital interest, or the profits interest, in the partnership. (Code Sec. 267(b)(10))[49]

An S corporation and another S corporation if the same persons own more than 50% in value of the outstanding stock of each corporation. (Code Sec. 267(b)(11))

An S corporation and a C corporation if the same persons own more than 50% in value of the outstanding stock of each corporation. (Code Sec. 267(b)(12))[50]

Trustees, grantors, and beneficiaries, that is, the grantor and the fiduciary of a trust; the fiduciary and the beneficiary of a trust; the fiduciaries of two different trusts with the same grantor; a fiduciary of one trust and the beneficiary of another trust with the same grantor; and a trust fiduciary and a corporation more than 50% in value of the outstanding stock of which is owned directly or indirectly by or for the trust or its grantor. (Code Sec. 267(b)(4), (5), (6), (7), (8))[1]

Exempt organizations. A person and an exempt organization controlled directly or indirectly, by that person or the members of his family. (Code Sec. 267(b)(9))[2]

In applying the related taxpayer rules, ownership of stock is attributed to the taxpayer as follows:

(1) A stockholder is considered to own a proportionate share of the stock owned by the corporation.

(2) A partner is considered to own a proportionate share of the stock owned by the partnership.

(3) If an individual owns some stock in a corporation, he is considered the owner of stock owned by his partner.

(4) A beneficiary is considered to own a proportionate share of the stock owned by the trust or estate.

(5) An individual is considered to own stock owned by members of his family, as defined above, whether or not he is the actual owner of stock in the same corporation. (Code Sec. 267(c); Reg § 1.267(c)-1)[3]

45. ¶ I-3610; ¶ 10,414.
46. ¶ I-3512; ¶ 2674.
47. ¶ I-3515; ¶ 2674.
48. ¶ I-3522; ¶ 2674.
49. ¶ I-3532; ¶ 2674.
50. ¶ I-3531; ¶ 2674.
1. ¶ I-3527; ¶ 2674.
2. ¶ I-3530; ¶ 2674.
3. ¶ I-3516; ¶ 2674.

Footnote references beginning with letters are to paragraphs in RIA's Federal Tax Coordinator 2d and RIA's Analysis of Federal Taxes: Income. Footnote references beginning with numbers are to paragraphs in RIA's United States Tax Reporter.

¶ 2451 Later sale by related buyer.

A related buyer is allowed to reduce his gain on property he resells at a gain by the loss disallowed to his seller if these conditions are met: (1) a loss deduction was barred under the rules on related taxpayers (¶ 2450), (2) the resale or exchange is at a gain, and the property is either the property on which the loss was disallowed or property the basis of which is determined by reference to the basis of that property (e.g., a replacement due to an involuntary conversion of the property purchased from the related taxpayer), and (3) the loss deduction on the original sale to the taxpayer was not barred under the wash sale rules (¶ 2455). (Code Sec. 267(d); Reg § 1.267(d)-1)[4]

¶ 2452 Loss between members of controlled group.

With some exceptions, a loss from a transfer between members of the same controlled group is deferred (rather than denied). The loss is recognized when the property is transferred outside the group if the loss would be recognized under consolidated return principles. (Code Sec. 267(f)(2))[5]

Deferred gain or loss on depreciable property is annually recognized to the extent of the lesser of: (1) the seller's deferred loss, or (2) the total depreciation the seller could have claimed had the seller not sold it. (Reg § 1.267(f)-1T(d))[6]

¶ 2453 Gain on sale of employer stock to ESOP or EWOC.

A taxpayer (but not a C corporation) or executor who sells qualified securities to an employee stock ownership plan (ESOP) or eligible worker-owned cooperative (EWOC) that holds specified percentages of the securities, may elect nonrecognition of gain if the seller buys "qualified replacement property" (securities of another corporation that doesn't exceed certain passive income limits) within a specified period of time. The seller's gain is recognized only to the extent the proceeds of sale exceed his cost for the replacement property. Nonrecognition treatment applies only if the gain on the sale of the stock would otherwise have been long-term capital gain. (Code Sec. 1042)[7]

¶ 2454 Wash Sales

No loss deduction is allowed for any loss from any sale or other disposition of stock or securities (including contracts or options to acquire or sell stock or securities) if within a period beginning 30 days before and ending 30 days after the sale the taxpayer acquires, or has entered into a contract or option to acquire, substantially identical stock or securities.[8]

¶ 2455 Losses on wash sales.

Losses on the sale of stock or securities (or contract or option to acquire or sell such) are not deductible if, within a period beginning 30 days before the date of the sale and ending 30 days after the date of the sale, the taxpayer acquires or has entered into a contract or option to acquire stock or securities that are substantially identical. (Code Sec. 1091(a); Reg § 1.1091-1(a))[9]

Illustration: June 1: Taxpayer buys 100 shares of Corp A stock for $15 per share. Dec. 2: Taxpayer buys 100 shares of Corp A stock for $10 per share. Dec. 30: Taxpayer sells the 100 shares of Corp A stock bought on June 1 for $10 per share realizing a $500 loss. Result: no loss deduction allowed because substantially identical stock was purchased less than 30 days before the sale. The same result would occur if the second

---

4. ¶ I-3541; ¶ 2674.   6. ¶ I-3524; ¶ 2674.   8. ¶ I-3908.   9. ¶ I-3901; ¶ 10,914.
5. ¶s E-8250, I-3524 *et seq.*;   7. ¶ H-12103 *et seq.*; ¶ 10,424.
   ¶ 2674.

Footnote references beginning with letters are to paragraphs in RIA's Federal Tax Coordinator 2d and RIA's Analysis of Federal Taxes: Income. Footnote references beginning with numbers are to paragraphs in RIA's United States Tax Reporter.

purchase (Dec. 2) had been made on the following Jan. 29.

Special wash sale rules apply to residual interests in REMICs, (Code Sec. 860F(d))[10] and to tax straddles. (Reg § 1.1092(b)-1T, Reg § 1.1092(b)-5T)[11]

For basis of the acquired stock, see ¶ 2494. For holding period, see ¶ 2651 *et seq.*

¶ 2456 Substantially identical securities.

"Substantially identical securities" requires something less than precise correspondence. Stock or securities of different issuers or obligors are not substantially identical. Stock or securities of the same issuer are substantially identical if they are substantially the same in all important particulars.[12]

¶ 2457 Dealers.

The wash sale rule doesn't apply to a dealer in stocks or securities if the loss is sustained in a transaction made in the ordinary course of that business. (Code Sec. 1091(a))[13]

¶ 2458 Basis of Property

A taxpayer's basis for property acquired in a taxable exchange is usually its cost, subject to certain adjustments.

In general, basis for computing loss and gain is the same, whatever the transaction may be. But in some cases the basis for computing loss differs from the basis for computing gain. These cases are:

■ property converted from personal use to business or income-producing use, see ¶ 2469;

■ property acquired by gift, see ¶ 2502.

For determining basis in corporate transactions and in nontaxable exchanges, see ¶ 2478 *et seq.*

For basis of property acquired by gift, from a decedent or from a spouse, see ¶ 2501 *et seq.*

¶ 2459 Cost as basis.

The original basis for property is its cost to the taxpayer, except where otherwise specifically provided (Code Sec. 1012) or where the transaction is not made at arm's length (see below). Cost is the amount paid in cash, liabilities incurred (¶ 2461) or other property. (Reg § 1.1012-1(a))[14] Payments made in connection with the acquisition of property, e.g., commissions and legal fees, are included in basis as part of the property's cost.[15]

When property is not bought in an arms-length deal, its basis is its fair market value.[16] This can occur in sham transactions, or where the buyer, for personal reasons, pays more than what the property is worth (e.g., to help out a friend).[17]

¶ 2460 Determining cost.

IRS and most courts say that the cost basis of property received in an arm's length taxable exchange is the fair market value of the property *received* in the exchange, at the time of the exchange. However, where the fair market value of the property received cannot be determined with a fair degree of certainty the fair market value of the property given up will be used as a way of valuing the property received.[18]

But a substantial minority of courts say the cost basis of property received in an arm's length taxable exchange is the fair market value (on the date of the exchange) of the

---

10. ¶ I-3916; ¶ 860A4.   13. ¶ I-3917; ¶ 10,914.   15. ¶ P-1102; ¶ 10,124.   17. ¶ P-1108; ¶ 10,124.22.
11. ¶ I-7528; ¶ 10,924.   14. ¶ P-1119; ¶ 10,124.   16. ¶ P-1107; ¶ 10,124.04. 17. ¶ P-1113 1; ¶ 10,124.03.
12. ¶ I-3914 *et seq.*

Footnote references beginning with letters are to paragraphs in RIA's Federal Tax Coordinator 2d and RIA's Analysis of Federal Taxes: Income. Footnote references beginning with numbers are to paragraphs in RIA's United States Tax Reporter.

property given up.[19]

¶ 2461 Mortgages and other liabilities as part of basis.

Taxpayer's cost of property includes the amount of a mortgage or other liability that he assumes in connection with the purchase, plus the amount of any liabilities that the purchased property is subject to (whether or not the taxpayer assumes the liabilities).[20] Redeemable ground rents are treated as mortgages. (Code Sec. 1055)[21]

illustration: J buys a building by paying $20,000 cash and giving an $80,000 mortgage. J's basis is $100,000. It would also be $100,000 if instead J assumed an existing $80,000 mortgage. And it would be $100,000 if, in addition to paying $20,000 cash, J acquired the building subject to the mortgage without assuming it, or if J agreed to pay $80,000 but no mortgage was involved, or if J agreed to pay his seller's debt of $80,000.

Mortgages or other liabilities aren't part of taxpayer's cost if they are contingent *and* there's a clear indication they might never have to be paid or that taxpayer doesn't intend to pay.[22]

¶ 2462 Amount of debt included in basis.

If the OID rules (see ¶ 1742 *et seq.*) or the unstated interest rules (¶ 1741) apply so that a part of a debt included in the buyer's cost for the property is treated as OID or unstated interest, the buyer's basis does not include the OID or interest portion.[23] However, to the extent that OID or unstated interest is capitalized rather than deducted it is included in basis. (Reg § 1.483-2(a)(1)(i))[24]

For adjustments to the basis of OID instruments, see ¶ 2466.

¶ 2463 Basis of repossessed mortgaged real estate.

A seller's basis in repossessed property is equal to the adjusted basis of the mortgage debt (determined under Code Secs. 453 and 1011) to the seller (as of the date of repossession), *plus* the sum of: (1) the repossession gain, and (2) the amount of money and the fair market value of other property (other than the buyer's obligations) which the seller transfers in connection with the repossession.[25]

If the mortgage debt is not discharged on repossession, the seller's basis in the mortgage debt is zero. (Code Sec. 1038(c))

¶ 2464 Satisfaction of debt or claim with property.

The cost basis of property received in whole or partial satisfaction of a debt or claim is the amount of the debt or claim satisfied but not more than the fair market value of the property.[26]

¶ 2465 Property acquired through exercise of options.

The basis of property acquired by exercising of an option or warrant other than an option granted for services is (a) the basis of the option plus (b) the option price.[27]

¶ 2466 Holder's basis in certain debt instruments acquired at a discount.

The holder's basis in a debt instrument issued with original issue discount (OID) is increased by the OID currently included in gross income under the rules discussed in ¶ 1318 *et seq.* (Code Sec. 1272(d)(2))[28]

Short-term debt instruments. If the holder includes the daily portions of acquisition discount (or OID) in gross income, that holder increases his basis in the debt instrument

---

19. ¶ P-1113 1.
20. ¶ P-1133 *et seq.*; ¶ 10,124.04.
21. ¶ P-1175; ¶ 10,554.

22. ¶ P-1134; ¶ 10,124.04.
23. ¶s P-1138, P-1139.
24. ¶ P-1815.

25. ¶ G-6872; ¶ 10,384.
26. ¶ P-1116; ¶ 10,384.

27. ¶ P-1165 *et seq.*; ¶ 10,124.13.
28. ¶ P-5044.

Footnote references beginning with letters are to paragraphs in RIA's Federal Tax Coordinator 2d and RIA's Analysis of Federal Taxes: Income. Footnote references beginning with numbers are to paragraphs in RIA's United States Tax Reporter.

by the amount so included. (Code Sec. 1283(d)(1))[29]

Tax-exempt obligations issued with OID. A holder's basis is increased by the amount of OID that the holder would have had to include in gross income currently if the obligation had not been tax-exempt. (Code Sec. 1288(a)(2), (b)(3))[30]

Market-discount bonds. Under regs to be issued, adjustments are made to bonds to reflect gain recognized under the market-discount bond rules discussed in ¶ 1329 *et seq.* (Code Sec. 1276(d)(2))[31] Where the election is made to include accrued market discount in income currently, the basis of the bond is increased by the amount of income so included. (Code Sec. 1278(b)(4))[32]

For determining cost of, and original basis in, property received in exchange for an OID debt instrument, see ¶ 2462.

¶ 2467 Cost of intangible assets.

The basis of goodwill, a patent, a copyright, or a covenant not to compete is the amount taxpayer paid for it.[33]

Where a patent is obtained from the government, the basis is the cost of development, such as research and experimental expenditures (but not if deducted currently), drawings, attorneys' and governmental fees, etc. The value of any time spent on an invention is not part of an inventor's basis. The basis of a copyright acquired from the government is the cost of securing the copyright from the government, including the cost of producing the work covered by the copyright, but not including the value of the author's time.[34]

Accounts receivable in the hands of a cash basis taxpayer have a zero basis.[35]

¶ 2468 Basis allocation, including acquisition of businesses which are "applicable asset acquisitions."

If a single transaction involves a number of separate properties, the total cost is allocated to establish the cost of the individual properties. The total basis is allocated to each item in proportion to the fair market value of each item at time of acquisition.[36]

However, for an "applicable asset acquisition," the residual method must be used to allocate the purchase price. Under the residual method, the purchase price is allocated first to cash (Class I assets), then to readily marketable stock and securities (Class II assets), then to other tangible and intangible assets such as land, buildings, equipment, accounts receivable, covenants not to compete, etc., but only up to the fair market value of these assets (Class III assets), and the remainder to goodwill or going concern value (Class IV assets). The parties to an applicable asset acquisition may agree in writing to an allocation of consideration for, or a determination of the fair market value of, any asset (including covenants not to compete) in the acquisition. The parties are bound by the allocation or valuation unless IRS determines that it is not appropriate. (Code Sec. 1060(a); Reg § 1.1060-1T(d), (e))[37]

An applicable asset acquisition is any direct or indirect transfer of a group of assets that is a trade or business in the hands of either the seller or buyer and (except for certain like-kind exchanges) the buyer's basis in the transferred assets is determined wholly by reference to the buyer's consideration. (Code Sec. 1060(c); Reg § 1.1060-1T(b)(1))[38]

⊘*observation:* The use of the residual method prevents a taxpayer who bought a business and paid a premium over the value of the business from allocating the premium to depreciable or amortizable assets which would result in increased tax deductions for the buyer. Instead, the premium is allocated to goodwill or going concern value

---

29. ¶ P-5047.	32. ¶ J-3969; ¶ 12,764.	35. ¶ P-1121; ¶ 10,124.38.	37. ¶ P-1400 *et seq.*; ¶ 10,604.
30. ¶ P-5048.	33. ¶ P-1422; ¶ 10,124.38.	36. ¶ P-1300 *et seq.*; ¶ 10,604.	38. ¶ P-1401 1 *et seq.*; ¶ 10,604.
31. ¶ J-3950 *et seq.*; ¶ 12,764.	34. ¶ P-1178.		

Footnote references beginning with letters are to paragraphs in RIA's Federal Tax Coordinator 2d and RIA's Analysis of Federal Taxes: Income. Footnote references beginning with numbers are to paragraphs in RIA's United States Tax Reporter.

352

which is nondeductible.

The buyer and seller have to provide IRS with specified information about the assets (use Form 8594). (Code Sec. 1060(b); Reg § 1.1060-1T(h)(2)(i))[39]

¶2469 Personal use property converted to business use.

When a residence or other nonbusiness property is converted from personal use to business or income-producing use, for purposes of calculating losses or depreciation (but not for purposes of calculating gain) the basis for the property on the date of its conversion is the lower of its adjusted basis or fair market value on that date. This basis must thereafter be adjusted for depreciation, etc., after conversion. (Reg § 1.167(g)-1)[40]

¶2470 Adjusted basis.

Basis must be increased or decreased to reflect certain events, such as capital improvements or depreciation, whether the original basis was cost or something else.[41]

The basis of property is adjusted (increased) to include the amount of the capital expenditures with respect to the property. (Code Sec. 1016(a)(1))[42] A lessee's basis for his leasehold is increased by his capital expenditures.[43] However, a lessee's capital improvements do not increase or diminish the lessor's basis of the leased property unless they are includible in the lessor's gross income as rent. (Code Sec. 1019)[44]

Basis can't be increased for items that are deductible as expenses, except for items the taxpayer has capitalized, such as carrying charges, see ¶1666.

Basis must be reduced by the deduction under Code Sec. 179A(a)(1) (discussed in ¶2173 *et seq.*) for a portion of the cost of any qualified clean-fuel vehicle and any qualified clean-fuel vehicle refueling property. (Code Sec. 179A(e)(6))[45]

For adjusted basis for alternative minimum tax purposes, see ¶3212.

¶2471 Contributions and returns of capital.

A stockholder's contribution of property to his corporation will increase his basis for his corporate stock.[46] A partner's contribution of cash to his partnership increases his basis in his partnership interest. See ¶3716 *et seq.*.

Basis must be reduced for receipts representing return of capital, (Code Sec. 1016(a)(1); Reg § 1.1016-2(a)) such as damages taxpayer received for injury to his property.[47]

illustration: In Year 1, P, on the calendar-year basis, bought for $80,000 real property to be used as a factory. P also paid commissions of $2,000 and title search and legal fees of $600. The total cost of $82,600 was allocated $10,325 to the land and $72,275 to the building. P immediately spent $20,000 in remodeling the building. P was allowed depreciation deductions of $27,600 for Years 1 through 4. In Year 4 the building suffered an uninsured deductible $5,000 casualty loss from fire. This loss was deducted. The adjusted basis of the property as of Jan. 1, Year 5, is:

	Land	Building
Original cost, including fees and commissions	$10,325	$72,275
Adjustment to basis:		
Add: Improvement		20,000
		$92,275
Subtract:		
Depreciation	$27,600	

39. ¶ S-4301.
40. ¶ P-1908.
41. ¶ P-1700 *et seq.*; ¶s 10,114.01, 10,164.01.
42. ¶ P-1801; ¶ 10,164.01.
43. ¶ L-6510; ¶ 10,164.
44. ¶ P-1809; ¶ 10,194.
45. ¶ K-7000 *et seq.*
46. ¶ F-1916; ¶ 10,164.02.
47. ¶ P-1821; ¶ 10,164.03.

Footnote references beginning with letters are to paragraphs in RIA's Federal Tax Coordinator 2d and RIA's Analysis of Federal Taxes: Income. Footnote references beginning with numbers are to paragraphs in RIA's United States Tax Reporter.

Casualty loss	5,000	32,600
Adjusted basis Jan. 1, Year 5	$10,325	$59,675

¶ 2472 Depreciation or amortization.

Basis must be reduced for depreciation, cost recovery, or amortization deductions with respect to the property. The amount of the reduction is the larger of:

■ the amount of the depreciation, cost recovery, amortization, or depletion deductions *allowable* under the law, or

■ the amount that was actually *allowed* and resulted in a reduction of tax. (Code Sec. 1016(a)(2))

Allowable depreciation (or cost recovery) is the amount the taxpayer was entitled to deduct under the law, whether or not he actually took more or less and whether or not a tax benefit results. Where a taxpayer has no depreciation method, the amount allowable is the amount allowable under the straight-line method.[48]

The depreciation (or cost recovery) *allowed* is the amount claimed on a tax return and allowed by IRS.[49]

In the case of business autos for which the optional business standard mileage rate (see ¶ 1552) is used, depreciation is considered to have been allowed at the rate of 7.5¢ per mile for '82, 8¢ for '83 through '85, 9¢ for '86, 10¢ for '87, 10.5¢ for '88, 11¢ for '89, '90 and '91, and 11.5¢ for '92 and '93. For expenses paid or incurred before '90, an auto is considered to be driven no more than 15,000 business miles a year, or 60,000 total miles.[50]

¶ 2473 Partial losses due to casualty or theft.

If property is partly lost or destroyed through casualty or theft, the basis is reduced by:

■ the amount of insurance or other reimbursement received, and

■ the amount of deductible loss. No reduction is required for the amount of a loss which is not deductible under the rule (discussed in ¶ 1780 *et seq.*) barring deduction for the first $100 of casualty or theft loss or for the amount of loss below the 10%-of-AGI floor.

Expenditures with respect to such property, for example to remove debris and to restore the property to pre-casualty condition, increase the basis, except where they are deducted as repairs.[1]

¶ 2474 Basis of credit property reduced by certain credits earned.

The basis of investment credit ("Section 38") property, for purposes of computing depreciation or cost recovery deductions and gain or loss, must be reduced by 100% of the amount of the rehabilitation credit for which the property qualifies. (Code Sec. 50(c))[2] The cost or other basis of energy credit property and reforestation credit property must be reduced by 50% of the allowed credit. (Code Sec. 50(c)(3)(A))[3] Special rules apply for assets placed in service before '86 and for qualified progress expenditures.[4]

If a credit is taken for the cost of a qualified electric vehicle (see ¶ 2354), the basis of the property is reduced by the amount of the credit. (Code Sec. 30(d)(1))[5]

¶ 2475 Recaptured tax credits.

Where certain tax credits are recaptured, a percentage (¶ 2474) of the recapture amount is added back to basis immediately before the event causing the recapture. The term "recapture amount" means any increase in tax (or adjustment in carrybacks or carryovers) due to the credit recapture provision. (Code Sec. 50(c)(2), (3))[6]

48. ¶ P-1902; ¶ 1674.
49. ¶ P-1903; ¶s 1674, 1684.
50. ¶ P-1909; ¶ 1624.157.
1. ¶ P-1811; ¶ 1654.304.
2. ¶ P-2002; ¶ 504.03.
3. ¶ P-2000; ¶ 504.03.
4. ¶s P-2002, P-2003.
5. ¶ L-18015
6. ¶ P-2007.

Footnote references beginning with letters are to paragraphs in RIA's Federal Tax Coordinator 2d and RIA's Analysis of Federal Taxes: Income. Footnote references beginning with numbers are to paragraphs in RIA's United States Tax Reporter.

¶ 2476 Special lessor-lessee rule doesn't require basis-reduction adjustment.

A lessor of certain credit property may elect to pass the credit for the leased property to the lessee. In such a case, the lessor is not required to make the basis-reduction adjustment (¶ 2474). (Code Sec. 50(d)(5))[7]

¶ 2477 Partnership or S corporation.

The basis of a partner's interest in a partnership or of a shareholder's stock in an S corporation is adjusted to reflect a partner's or shareholder's share of the required adjustments to the basis of partnership or S corporation property when credits are either allowed or recaptured. (Code Sec. 50(c)(5))[8]

¶ 2478 Property Acquired in Nontaxable Exchanges ▬▬▬▬▬▬

The basis of property received in a nontaxable exchange, depending on the type of transaction, generally will be the same as its basis in the hands of the transferor or will be the same as the basis of the property transferred by the recipient in the exchange. If gain is recognized in part on the transaction, the basis of the property received may have to be adjusted.

¶ 2479 Basis of property received by corporation in tax-free transfer or as a contribution to capital.

The basis of property received by a controlled corporation in a tax-free transfer, whether upon the incorporation of the corporation or otherwise (see ¶ 3510 *et seq.*), is equal to the basis of the property in the transferor's hands increased by any gain recognized by the transferor on the transfer. (Code Sec. 362(a)(1))[9]

The basis to a corporation of property acquired from a shareholder as a contribution to capital equals the basis of that property in the hands of the shareholder increased by the gain (if any) recognized by the shareholder on the transfer. (Code Sec. 362(a)(2))[10]

¶ 2480 Acquirer's basis in property received in reorganization.

The basis of property received by the acquiring corporation in a tax-free reorganization (¶ 3541 *et seq.*) is the transferor's (target's) basis increased by any gain recognized to the target. However, if the property consists of stock or securities of the target, this rule applies only if the property was acquired in exchange for stock or securities of the acquirer or the acquirer's parent corporation. (Code Sec. 362(b))[11]

¶ 2481 Target's basis in property received in reorganization.

The basis of property (other than stock and securities of another corporation that is a party to the reorganization, see ¶ 3552 *et seq.*) that is received under a plan of reorganization by the acquired corporation (target) equals the fair market value of the property. (Code Sec. 358(a)(2), (f))[12]

¶ 2482 Acquisition of property by corporation for its stocks or bonds in taxable exchanges.

In cases other than tax-free contributions or reorganizations, the basis of property a corporation acquires in exchange for its stock is the fair market value of the stock at the time of the exchange.[13] The cost to a corporation of property it acquires in exchange for its bonds is the face amount of the bonds.[14] For the rules regarding bonds with OID or unstated interest, see ¶ 2462.

---

7. ¶ P-2008.   9. ¶ F-1808; ¶ 3624.01.   11. ¶ F-4305; ¶ 3624.02.   13. ¶ P-1158; ¶ 10,124.47.
8. ¶ P-2009.   10. ¶ F-1808; ¶ 3624.03.   12. ¶ F-4304; ¶ 3584.02.   14. ¶ P-1160; ¶ 10,124.46.

Footnote references beginning with letters are to paragraphs in RIA's Federal Tax Coordinator 2d and RIA's Analysis of Federal Taxes: Income. Footnote references beginning with numbers are to paragraphs in RIA's United States Tax Reporter.

¶ 2483   Basis of property to distributee shareholders or security holders.

For purposes of determining basis, property received by a distributee in connection with a transfer to a controlled corporation, a reorganization, or a corporate division (¶ 3510 *et seq.*) is classified as either nonrecognition property or other property. "Nonrecognition property" is property received without recognition of gain or loss to the recipient (stock in the transferee corporation in the case of a transfer to a controlled corporation, and stock or securities in the distributing corporation in tax-free reorganizations and corporate divisions). (Code Sec. 358(a)(1)) "Other property" is anything except "nonrecognition property" and money.

The basis of "nonrecognition property" is the same as the basis of the property given up in the exchange, but this amount is:

■ decreased by any money received, by the fair market value of any "other property" received, and by the loss, if any, recognized by the distributee on the exchange; and

■ increased by any part of distribution that is treated as a dividend, and by any other gain recognized by the distributee on the exchange. (Code Sec. 358(a)(1))

The basis must be allocated among the nonrecognition property received in the transaction without recognition of gain or loss. (Reg § 1.358-2(a)(2))

Where liabilities of the distributee are assumed as part of the deal, or where the distributee transfers property subject to liabilities, the amount of the liabilities assumed or acquired is treated as money received by the distributee (for basis purposes only) and would thus decrease the basis of the stock or securities received by the transferor. (Code Sec. 358(d)(1))

¶ 2484   Basis of other property received in tax-free transfer to corporation and corporate reorganization or division.

The basis of property, other than stock or securities which may be received without the recognition of gain, received by a shareholder upon a tax-free transfer to a controlled corporation, a reorganization, or a corporate division (¶ 3510 *et seq.*), is its fair market value. (Code Sec. 358(a)(2))[15]

¶ 2485   Basis of corporation in property and former partners in stock after partnership incorporates.

If a partnership incorporates, the basis of the corporation in the partnership's property and the basis of the former partners in their stock in the corporation depends on the method used to incorporate.

If the partnership transfers all of its assets subject to its liabilities to a newly formed corporation in return for all its stock, then distributes the stock to the partners, the corporation's basis in the partnership's assets is equal to the partnership's basis in the assets before the transaction and each partner's basis in the stock of the corporation is equal to the adjusted basis of that partner's interest in the partnership.

If the partnership distributes all of its assets subject to liabilities to the partners, who in turn transfer them to the new corporation for its stock, the corporation's basis in its assets is the same as the partners' basis in the assets prior to their contribution to the corporation and partners' basis in the stock of the corporation is the same as their basis in the assets distributed in liquidation reduced by liabilities assumed by the corporation.

If the partners transfer their interests in the partnership to the new corporation in exchange for its stock and the corporation then liquidates the partnership, the corporation's basis in its assets is equal to the partners' basis in their partnership interests

15. ¶s F-1804, 4034, 4304, 5014;
    ¶ 3584.02.

Footnote references beginning with letters are to paragraphs in RIA's Federal Tax Coordinator 2d and RIA's Analysis of Federal Taxes: Income. Footnote references beginning with numbers are to paragraphs in RIA's United States Tax Reporter.

before the transaction and the partners' basis in their stock is equal to their basis in their partnership interests reduced by the liabilities assumed by the corporation.[16]

¶ 2486 Property received as a dividend.

The basis for property received as a dividend, including stock or stock rights received as a taxable stock dividend, is its fair market value on the date of distribution. (Code Sec. 301(d))[17]

¶ 2487 Basis allocation for nontaxable stock dividend.

If a shareholder gets a nontaxable dividend of stock or stock rights, the (adjusted) basis of the old stock (that is, of the stock on which the dividend was distributed) is allocated between the old and new stock (or rights) in proportion to the fair market value of each on the date of distribution. (Code Sec. 307(a)) Where only part of the stock dividend is nontaxable, the basis of the old stock is allocated between the old stock and that part of the new stock (or rights) which is not taxable, in proportion to the fair market value of each on the date of distribution. The date of distribution is, in both cases, the date on which the new stock (or the stock rights) was distributed, not the record date.[18]

✓ Illustration: S bought one share of voting common for $45. The corporation distributed two new shares of voting common for each share held. This gave S three shares of voting common with a basis of $15 each. If he had owned two shares before the distribution, one purchased for $30 and the other for $45, he would have six shares: three with a basis of $10 each, and three with a basis of $15 each.

However, upon a distribution of stock rights whose fair market value at the time of their distribution is less than 15% of the fair market value of the stock on which they were distributed at that time, the taxpayer's basis for the stock is allocated to the stock and the basis for the rights received is zero, unless the taxpayer elects to allocate basis to the rights. (Code Sec. 307(b)(1))[19]

¶ 2488 Stock purchased through a bank under an automatic investment service.

A participating stockholder's basis per share of stock is the price paid by the bank for the stockholder's allocable portion of the same stock purchased for all participants on the same date plus a proportionate share of the brokerage commission.[20]

¶ 2489 Stock acquired through dividend reinvestment plans.

Where a shareholder can choose between cash dividends or additional stock, and where the stock is available to those who choose it at a bargain price, the basis of the stock equals the amount of the distribution measured by the fair market value of the stock as of the date of the distribution.[21]

¶ 2490 Corporate shareholders that get certain extraordinary dividends.

These shareholders may have to reduce their basis in that stock by the nontaxed portion of the dividend. (Code Sec. 1059)[22]

¶ 2491 Identifying shares transferred.

Where taxpayer can adequately identify which shares of stock, or which bonds, are transferred, the basis used is the basis of that stock or those bonds.

Shares of stock or bonds are adequately identified where it can be shown that the shares or bonds that were delivered to the transferee are from a lot acquired on a certain

---

16. ¶ F-1813; ¶ 10,124.46.
17. ¶s P-5300 et seq., P-5400 et seq.; ¶ 3014.03.
18. ¶s P-5305, P-5405; ¶ 3074.01.
19. ¶ P-5401; ¶ 3074.03.
20. ¶ P-1164.
21. ¶ P-5303.
22. ¶ P-5100 et seq.; ¶ 10,594.

Footnote references beginning with letters are to paragraphs in RIA's Federal Tax Coordinator 2d and RIA's Analysis of Federal Taxes: Income. Footnote references beginning with numbers are to paragraphs in RIA's United States Tax Reporter.

date or for a certain price. (Reg § 1.1012-1(c)(1))[23]

If a number of lots were acquired and the ones sold can't be adequately identified, a first-in, first-out (FIFO) rule applies. (Reg § 1.1012-1(c)(1)) But it applies only to the particular account from which the stock or bonds were transferred, so that stock or bonds in another account, even though acquired earlier, are disregarded.[24]

¶ 2492 Adequate identification v. wrong delivery.

In the cases below, where the taxpayer specifically identifies certain shares or bonds as the ones to be transferred, these will be treated as the ones transferred even though some other lot is actually delivered.

(1) *Sale of stock or bonds held by broker or agent.* If at the time of the sale the taxpayer specifies to his broker or agent the particular shares or bonds to be transferred, and within a reasonable time the taxpayer receives a written confirmation of the transfer instruction, the stock or bonds so specified are treated as the ones transferred. (Reg § 1.1012-1(c)(3)(i))

(2) *Single certificate represents different lots of stock.* The rule in (1), above, also applies where taxpayer himself holds a stock certificate which represents lots of stock acquired at different times or prices and he directs sale of a specific part of the stock when he delivers the certificate to the broker or agent. (Reg § 1.1012-1(c)(3)(ii))

(3) *If a trustee, executor or administrator* at the time of transfer (including a distribution), specifies in writing on the trust's or estate's books the particular stock or bonds to be transferred and, in the case of a distribution, gives the distributee a written document specifying the stock transferred to him, the stock or bonds so specified are treated as the ones transferred. (Reg § 1.1012-1(c)(4))[25]

¶ 2493 Mutual fund shares.

A taxpayer who sells mutual fund shares held by a custodian or agent may elect to determine the basis of the shares sold by determining the average basis of the shares on either a "single-category method" or a "double-category method."[26] Generally, the single-category method groups in one category all shares regardless of holding period; the double-category method divides all shares by their holding period. The basis is then averaged over all the shares in their respective category. (Reg § 1.1012-1(e)) A shareholder who doesn't elect either of the above methods uses the normal first-in, first-out (FIFO) method for determining which shares were sold, see ¶ 2491.

¶ 2494 Stock acquired in wash sale.

Where a loss is disallowed under the wash sale rule (¶ 2454), the basis of the acquired stock takes account of the unrecognized loss in the following manner: (Code Sec. 1091(d))

(1) If the sales price is less than the repurchase price, the basis of the new stock is the basis of the stock sold plus the difference between the repurchase and the sales prices.

Illustration: T owns 100 shares of X company common which cost $100 per share. On May 1, T sells the 100 shares at $80 per share. On May 20, T buys 100 shares of X common at $90 per share. No loss is allowed on the May 1 sale. The basis of each share acquired May 20 is $110: the basis of the shares sold ($100) plus the $10 difference between the repurchase and sale prices ($90 – $80). (Reg § 1.1091-2(a))

(2) If the sales price is more than the repurchase price, the basis of the new stock is the basis of the stock sold minus the difference between the sale and the repurchase prices.[27]

Illustration: If, in the above illustration, the May 1 sale price had been $90 per share

---

23. ¶ P-5202; ¶ 10,124.78.   25. ¶ P-5205.   26. ¶ P-5214; ¶ 10,124.78.   27. ¶ P-5019; ¶ 10,914.
24. ¶ P-5212 *et seq.*; ¶ 10,124.83.

Footnote references beginning with letters are to paragraphs in RIA's Federal Tax Coordinator 2d and RIA's Analysis of Federal Taxes: Income. Footnote references beginning with numbers are to paragraphs in RIA's United States Tax Reporter.

and the May 20 repurchase price was $80 per share, the basis of each share acquired May 20 would be $90. That is, the basis of shares sold ($100) minus the difference between the sale and repurchase prices ($90 – $80). (Reg § 1.1091-2(a))

¶2495 Like-kind exchange or other nontaxable exchanges of properties.

The basis of property received in a like-kind exchange or certain other nontaxable exchanges where no part of the gain is recognized is the adjusted basis of the property traded away. (Code Sec. 1031(d))

If money is received as part of the exchange and some gain is recognized, basis in the property received is decreased by the money received and increased by the gain recognized. (Reg § 1.1031(d)-1(b)) If money is paid, basis is increased by the amount paid. (Reg § 1.1031(d)-1(a))

If other property (boot) is received and some gain is recognized, basis must be allocated (according to fair market value) to all the properties received. (Reg § 1.1031(d)-1(c))

If boot is given as part of the exchange, and gain or loss is recognized on transfer of the boot, the basis of the nonrecognition property received is the total basis of all the properties given, increased by any recognized gain on the boot, or decreased by any recognized loss on the boot. (Reg § 1.1031(d)-1(e))[28]

¶2496 Basis after exchange of multiple properties.

In an exchange of multiple properties qualifying for nonrecognition of gain or loss (see ¶2423), the aggregate basis of properties received in each of the "exchange groups" is determined under regs. (Reg § 1.1031(j)-1(c))[29]

¶2497 Basis of property acquired after involuntary conversion.

If property is involuntarily converted (¶2427 *et seq.*), the basis of qualifying replacement property is its cost less the amount of gain not recognized. If more than one piece of property is bought as replacement, the basis (cost less nonrecognized gain) is allocated to each piece in proportion to its respective cost. (Code Sec. 1033(b))[30]

If property not qualifying as replacement property is acquired in exchange for the involuntarily converted property, then that property's basis is the basis of the involuntarily converted property decreased by any money also received (and not used to buy replacement property) and increased by any gain or decreased by any loss recognized. (Code Sec. 1033(b))[31]

¶2498 Basis of new residence where gain was rolled over from old residence.

When a taxpayer buys a new principal residence and thereby avoids recognition of all or part of the gain on the sale of the old principal residence, the taxpayer's basis in the new residence is the cost of the new residence minus the gain not recognized on sale of the old residence. (Code Sec. 1034(e))[32]

¶2499 Basis of replacement for stock sold to ESOP or EWOC.

If the seller of qualified securities to an ESOP or EWOC reinvests in qualified replacement property and elects nonrecognition of gain (¶2453), the basis in the qualified replacement property is reduced by the amount of gain not recognized. If more than one item of replacement property is purchased, the basis reduction is allocated among the replacement properties (as the cost of that item bears to the cost of all those items). (Code Sec. 1042(d))[33]

---

28. ¶I-3173 *et seq.*; ¶10,314.13.   30. ¶P-1154; ¶10,334.18.   32. ¶I-4649; ¶10,344.05.   33. ¶H-12110; ¶10,424.
29. ¶I-3190; ¶10,314.14.   31. ¶P-1154; ¶10,334.33.

Footnote references beginning with letters are to paragraphs in RIA's Federal Tax Coordinator 2d and RIA's Analysis of Federal Taxes: Income. Footnote references beginning with numbers are to paragraphs in RIA's United States Tax Reporter.

¶ 2500 Basis for specialized small business investment company (SSBIC) rollovers.

Any gain not recognized under the SSBIC rollover rules (¶ 2424 *et seq.*) reduces taxpayer's basis in any SSBIC investment made during the 60-day rollover period. If taxpayer makes more than one SSBIC investment during this period, the bases of those other investments are reduced in the order they were acquired. (Code Sec. 1044(d))[34]

¶ 2501 Property Acquired by Gift, from a Decedent, or Spouse ▬▬▬▬▬▬

Special rules apply to determine the basis of property acquired by gift, from a decedent, or from a spouse.

The basis of property acquired by gift or transfer in trust is its basis in the hands of the donor ("carryover" basis) except:

■ in determining loss, where the property's fair market value on date of gift was less than the donor's basis on that date, see ¶ 2502;

■ where a gift tax was paid, see ¶ 2505;

■ where gain or loss is recognized to a grantor on a transfer in trust;

■ where the property is treated as property acquired from a decedent because it is required to be included in the deceased donor's gross estate, see ¶ 2510, or because it was transferred in trust and the deceased transferor retained certain powers, see ¶ 2513.

For the basis of property acquired from a spouse (or former spouse), see ¶ 2517.

¶ 2502 Property acquired by gift.

A donee's original or unadjusted basis (that is, the basis before adjustments made while the donee owned it) for property the donee acquires by gift is the same as the property's adjusted basis in the hands of the donor, or in the hands of the last preceding owner who did not acquire the property by gift. (Code Sec. 1015(a))[35] But if the property's fair market value at the date of the gift is lower than that adjusted basis, then the property's basis for determining *loss* is its fair market value on that date. (Code Sec. 1015(a))[36] For part sales and part gifts, see ¶ 2503.

¶ 2503 Part purchase, part gift.

Where a transfer of property is in part a purchase and in part a gift, the transferee's basis is the greater of cost or the transferor's adjusted basis for the property at the time of the transfer.[37] However, for determining loss, the basis can't exceed the property's fair market value at the time of transfer. (Reg § 1.1015-4) In either event, basis is increased to the extent of gift tax paid (¶ 2505).

¶ 2504 Basis rules for donees of partial interests.

If more donees receive partial interests in the same property, the basis to each is his or her proportionate part of the donor's basis. To determine the part of total basis allowable to life tenants and remaindermen, apply the rules at ¶ 2516. (Reg § 1.1015-1(b))[38]

¶ 2505 Increase in basis for gift tax.

If the property's fair market value at the date of the gift is greater than the donor's adjusted basis, the donee's basis (donor's adjusted basis) is increased by the portion of the gift tax paid that is attributable to the net appreciation in value of the gift. This portion is determined by multiplying the gift tax paid on the gift by a fraction whose numerator is the net appreciation in value of the gift and whose denominator is the amount of the gift.

---

34. ¶ I-3791.   36. ¶ P-3104; ¶ 10,154.01.   37. ¶ P-1113; ¶ 10,154.   38. ¶ P-3131; ¶ 10,154.06.
35. ¶ P-3103; ¶ 10,154.

Footnote references beginning with letters are to paragraphs in RIA's Federal Tax Coordinator 2d and RIA's Analysis of Federal Taxes: Income. Footnote references beginning with numbers are to paragraphs in RIA's United States Tax Reporter.

(Code Sec. 1015(d)(6))

If a gift consists of more than one item of property, the gift tax paid with respect to each item is computed by allocating to each item a proportionate part of the gift tax paid with respect to the gift. If more than one gift was made during the calendar year (or preceding calendar period), the total tax paid must be apportioned to each gift to determine the amount paid on each gift. (Code Sec. 1015(d)(2))

The amount of gift tax paid on a husband-wife split gift is the sum of the taxes, computed separately, paid with respect to each half of the gift. (Code Sec. 1015(d)(3); Reg § 1.1015-5(b)(3))[39]

For gifts made before '77, (but after Sept. 1, '58) the donee's basis (donor's adjusted basis) was increased by the total gift tax paid on the gift, but not above the fair market value at the date of the gift. (Code Sec. 1015(d)(1))[40]

¶ 2506 Property acquired from a decedent.

The basis of property acquired from a decedent by inheritance, bequest, devise, etc., (see ¶ 2509) that hasn't been sold, exchanged, or otherwise disposed of before the decedent's death, is generally equal to its fair market value at the date of the decedent's death. (Code Sec. 1014(a)(1)) However, if:

(1) the fiduciary elects for estate tax purposes to value the decedent's gross estate at the alternate valuation date (¶ 5027), the basis of the property is its fair market value at that alternate date; (Code Sec. 1014(a)(2))

(2) the fiduciary elects for estate tax purposes the special use valuation method of valuing farm or other closely held business real property included in the decedent's gross estate (¶ 5028), the basis of the real property is its value determined for purposes of the special use valuation election (rather than its fair market value). (Code Sec. 1014(a)(3))[41]

The above rules don't apply to determine the basis of property:

■ included in the decedent's estate but disposed of by the taxpayer before the decedent's death, see ¶ 2510;

■ that is appreciated property reacquired by the donor within one year of transfer to decedent, see ¶ 2508;

■ that is stock in a DISC or former DISC, (Code Sec. 1014(d)) or of certain foreign entities;

■ that is a right to receive income in respect of a decedent, (Code Sec. 1014(c)) see ¶ 3965 *et seq.*.[42]

¶ 2507 When estate tax value is also income tax basis.

The fair market value of property at the decedent's death or at the alternate valuation date as appraised for federal estate tax purposes (or, if no federal estate tax return is required to be filed, the fair market value of the property appraised as of the date of death for purpose of state inheritance taxes) is considered to be also the fair market value for purposes of determining the income tax basis of property acquired from a decedent. (Reg § 1.1014-3(a))[43] But the value for estate tax purposes is only presumptively correct for basis purposes. Except where facts have been misrepresented, neither taxpayer nor IRS is barred from using a value for basis purposes that differs from the value accepted for estate tax purposes.[44]

---

39. ¶ P-3108; ¶ 10,154.01.   41. ¶ P-4001; ¶ 10,144.   43. ¶ P-4022; ¶ 10,144.05.   44. ¶s P-4023, P-4024.
40. ¶ P-3107.   42. ¶ P-4001; ¶ 10,144.

Footnote references beginning with letters are to paragraphs in RIA's Federal Tax Coordinator 2d and RIA's Analysis of Federal Taxes: Income. Footnote references beginning with numbers are to paragraphs in RIA's United States Tax Reporter.

¶ 2508 Appreciated property reacquired by donor.

For a decedent dying after '81, if: (1) appreciated property was acquired by the decedent by gift after Aug. 13, '81 and during the one-year period ending on the date of death, and (2) that property is acquired from the decedent by (or passes from the decedent to) the donor of the property (or the donor's spouse), the basis of the property in the hands of the donor (or spouse) is the adjusted basis of the property in the decedent's hands immediately before his death. (Code Sec. 1014(e)(1))[45]

¶ 2509 When is property considered acquired from a decedent?

Property is acquired from a decedent if it is acquired by bequest, devise, or inheritance, or if it is acquired by the decedent's estate from the decedent. (Code Sec. 1014(b)(1))[46] Property acquired from a decedent also includes certain pre-death transfers and other classes of property, as explained at ¶ 2513 *et seq.*

Qualified terminable interest property (QTIP) that is includible in a surviving spouse's estate, is treated as passing from that surviving spouse for purposes of determining the remaindermen's basis. (Code Sec. 1014(b)(10))[47]

Property acquired from a decedent doesn't include:

■ Property the fiduciary acquires after the decedent's death. Its basis to the fiduciary (or a distributee, if it's distributed) is its cost or other basis with appropriate adjustments. (Reg § 1.1014-3(c))[48]

■ Property bought from a decedent's estate. Its basis to the purchaser is its cost or other basis with appropriate adjustments.[49]

■ Income in respect of a decedent. (Code Sec. 1014(c)) Its basis is equal to the decedent's basis (if any).[50]

■ Property transferred by the executor, administrator or trustee to a beneficiary in discharge of a specific pecuniary bequest. The beneficiary's basis is the fair market value of the property on the date of the transfer. (Reg § 1.1014-4(a)(3))[1]

¶ 2510 Property acquired from decedent and included in decedent's gross estate.

Property is considered to have been acquired from a decedent if it was acquired from a decedent by reason of: death, form of ownership, or other conditions and the property is required to be included in determining the value of decedent's gross estate whether or not an estate tax return is required or an estate tax is payable. Acquisitions covered by this rule include acquisitions as surviving joint tenant or tenant by the entireties (see ¶ 2511), acquisitions through exercise or failure to exercise a power of appointment (¶ 2514), and gifts within three years of death (if includible in gross estate for estate tax purposes, see ¶ 5004). (Reg § 1.1014-2(b))[2]

If property received as a gift (including a gift in trust) is disposed of by the donee before the donor's death, the property isn't treated as acquired from a decedent and the donee's basis is determined under the rules for gifts, see ¶ 2502. But property received in exchange for such gift property, or property acquired through reinvesting proceeds of sale of such gift property (or property acquired in further exchange or reinvestments), is treated as acquired from a decedent if it is includible in the decedent's gross estate. (Reg § 1.1014-3(d))[3]

---

45. ¶ P-4002; ¶ 10,144.   48. ¶ P-4054; ¶ 10,144.09.   50. ¶ P-4003.   2. ¶ P-4103; ¶ 10,144.26.
46. ¶ P-4102; ¶ 10,144.   49. ¶ P-4118.   1. ¶ P-4055.   3. ¶ P-3124.
47. ¶ P-4104; ¶ 10,144.24.

Footnote references beginning with letters are to paragraphs in RIA's Federal Tax Coordinator 2d and RIA's Analysis of Federal Taxes: Income. Footnote references beginning with numbers are to paragraphs in RIA's United States Tax Reporter.

¶ 2511 Tenants by the entirety and joint tenants.

Property that a person acquires as the surviving tenant by the entireties or as a surviving joint tenant is property acquired from a decedent if the property is includible in the decedent's gross estate. The part of the property that is treated as acquired from the decedent gets a stepped-up basis if the surviving tenant can prove that the property was required to be included in the decedent's estate for estate tax purposes.[4]

Where the surviving tenant and the deceased tenant were husband and wife who filed joint returns claiming deductions for depreciation, etc., the deceased tenant's portion of the property gets a stepped-up basis at death, while the surviving tenant's portion keeps its depreciated basis. In calculating the property's basis, the survivor's portion of the property is allocated that proportion of the depreciation, etc., deductions allowed in joint return years which the survivor's income from the property (determined under applicable local law) bears to the total income from the property. (Reg § 1.1014-6(a)(2))[5]

¶ 2512 Community property.

Where a spouse dies owning community property and at least one-half of the entire community interest is includible in the deceased spouse's gross estate (whether or not an estate tax return is required or an estate tax is payable), the surviving spouse's interest is treated as property acquired from a decedent. (Code Sec. 1014(b)(6))[6]

¶ 2513 Inter vivos trust with power to revoke, alter, etc.

Property acquired from a decedent includes property that the decedent during his lifetime transferred in trust to pay the trust income to, or on the order of, the decedent, where the decedent also reserved to himself at all times before his death:

■ the right to revoke the trust, (Code Sec. 1014(b)(2))

■ the right to make any change in the enjoyment of the trust through the exercise of a power to alter, amend, or terminate the trust (whether alone or with the consent of another not having an interest adverse to his). (Code Sec. 1014(b)(3))[7]

¶ 2514 Power to appoint property.

Property acquired from a decedent includes property passing without full and adequate consideration under a general power of appointment exercised by the decedent in his will. (Code Sec. 1014(b)(4)) The property passes from the decedent-holder, rather than from the grantor of the power.[8]

¶ 2515 Basis of postponed or contingent remainder interests.

Taxpayer's basis for property acquired from a decedent is determined on the date of the decedent's death under the rules at ¶ 2506 *et seq.*, whether or not, at the decedent's death, the taxpayer's interest was conditional or contingent, and whether or not the taxpayer can immediately possess and enjoy the property. (Reg § 1.1014-4(a)(2))[9]

¶ 2516 Multiple interests in one property.

Where more than one person has an interest in property acquired from a decedent, the basis in the property is determined and adjusted without regard to the multiple interests. Therefore, a life tenant makes basis adjustments for depreciation as if he were the absolute owner. His basis adjustments constitute an adjustment in the hands of every person who receives an interest by reason of the decedent's death. (Reg § 1.1014-4(b))[10]

---

4. ¶ P-4115; ¶ 10,144.22.
5. ¶ P-4030; ¶ 10,144.22.
6. ¶ P-4112; ¶ 10,144.19.
7. ¶ P-4109; ¶ 10,144.24.
8. ¶ P-4110; ¶ 10,144.26.
9. ¶ P-4015.
10. ¶ P-4026; ¶ 10,144.01.

Footnote references beginning with letters are to paragraphs in RIA's Federal Tax Coordinator 2d and RIA's Analysis of Federal Taxes: Income. Footnote references beginning with numbers are to paragraphs in RIA's United States Tax Reporter.

¶ 2517 **Basis of property transferred between spouses or incident to a divorce.**

The transferee is treated as acquiring the property by gift and the transferee's basis in the property received is the adjusted basis that the transferor had in the property. (Code Sec. 1041(b)) This rule applies even where the transaction is a sale between the spouses or where the transferee-spouse pays a sum of money to the transferor-spouse (as required under the divorce settlement) for the transfer of title to the property to the transferee-spouse. (Reg § 1.1041-1T(a), Q&A-2) This carryover basis rule applies whether the adjusted basis of the transferred property is less than, equal to, or greater than its fair market value at the time of transfer and applies for purposes of determining loss as well as gain, upon later sale by the transferee. (Reg § 1.1041-1T(d), Q&A-11)[11] Exceptions apply to certain transfers in trust (where liabilities assumed by the trust exceed the transferor's adjusted basis) (Code Sec. 1041(e)) and to transfers of installment obligations into a trust (Code Sec. 453B(g)).[12]

The transferor must, at the time of the transfer, give the transferee records sufficient to determine the adjusted basis and holding period of the property at the date of transfer. (Reg § 1.1041-1T(e), Q&A-14)[13]

For transfers made before July 19, '84, the transferee's basis in the property received is its fair market value at the time of transfer (unless certain elections were made to apply post-July 18, '84 rules).[14]

---

11. ¶ P-1146; ¶ 10,144.22.   12. ¶ P-1147; ¶ 10,144.22.   13. ¶ P-1153; ¶ 10,144.22.   14. ¶ P-1151.

Footnote references beginning with letters are to paragraphs in RIA's Federal Tax Coordinator 2d and RIA's Analysis of Federal Taxes: Income. Footnote references beginning with numbers are to paragraphs in RIA's United States Tax Reporter.

Chapter 9 Capital Gains and Losses—Section 1231— MACRS/ACRS/Depreciation Recapture

¶ 2600 Capital Gains and Losses

The tax treatment of capital gains and losses depends on whether the gains and losses are long-term or short-term and on whether the taxpayer is a corporation or not. For noncorporate taxpayers, the maximum tax rate on net long-term capital gains is lower than the top rate on ordinary income. The long-term capital gains of corporations, and the short-term gains of corporations and of noncorporate taxpayers are taxable at the same rates as their ordinary income. The deduction for capital losses is limited, but unused capital losses may be carried over to the next taxable year.

The main features of the income tax treatment of capital gains and losses are:

■ short-term capital gains and losses are netted, long-term capital gains and losses are netted, and then long- and short-term are netted with each other (¶ 2602 *et seq.*);

■ Section 1231 nets gains and losses to arrive at a net of long-term capital gain or ordinary loss (¶ 2667 *et seq.*);

■ recapture provisions restrict the possibility of converting ordinary income into capital gains via cost recovery or depreciation (¶ 2675 *et seq.*).

Capital gains and losses are the gains and losses from sales or exchanges (¶ 2660) of capital assets (¶ 2610). But capital gain or loss treatment also applies to gains in certain transactions involving assets that aren't capital assets (such as depreciable property used in business, ¶ 2669).[1]

observation: Designation of a loss as capital (or ordinary) doesn't make it deductible. An individual may only deduct losses incurred in business, transactions for profit, casualty or theft. Thus, a loss on sale of a personal residence is a nondeductible capital loss.

Report capital gains and losses on Schedule D (Form 1040, 1041, 1065, 1120 or 1120S).

¶ 2601 Tax effect of capital asset sales and exchanges.

If a capital asset is held for not more than the short-term holding period (¶ 2651), the gain or loss from its sale or exchange is short-term. If held for more than the short-term holding period, gain or loss is long-term. (Code Sec. 1222)[2]

Short-term capital gains and losses are netted to get net short-term capital gain or net short-term capital loss. (Code Sec. 1222(5), (6))

Long-term capital gains and losses are netted to get net long-term capital gain or net long-term capital loss. (Code Sec. 1222(7), (8))

There is a further netting if one group shows a loss and the other a gain. *If net long-term capital gains exceed net short-term capital losses*, the excess is net capital gain, taxed under the rules at ¶ 2602 *et seq.* (individuals and other noncorporate taxpayers) or ¶ 2607 *et seq.* (corporate taxpayers). (Code Sec. 1222(11))

If there is a net short-term gain, it is taxable (both for noncorporate and corporate taxpayers) at the same rate as ordinary income.[3]

If capital losses exceed capital gains, see ¶ 2604 *et seq.* (noncorporate) or ¶ 2608 (corporate).

¶ 2602 Capital gain net income for noncorporate taxpayers.

A noncorporate taxpayer who has an excess of capital gains over capital losses (whether long-term or short-term), for the tax year, has "capital gain net income," (Code

1. ¶ I-5100 *et seq.*; ¶ 12,009.   2. ¶s I-5103, I-5104; ¶ 12,014.   3. ¶s I-5111, I-5116; ¶ 12,224.01.

Footnote references beginning with letters are to paragraphs in RIA's Federal Tax Coordinator 2d and RIA's Analysis of Federal Taxes: Income. Footnote references beginning with numbers are to paragraphs in RIA's United States Tax Reporter.

Sec. 1222(9)) which is included in gross income.[4]

¶ 2603 Noncorporate taxpayers' capital gain tax computation.

Noncorporate taxpayers' tax on net capital gains can't exceed:

(1) a tax computed at the taxpayer's regular rates (¶ 1101 *et seq.*) on the greater of (a) taxable income reduced by the amount of net capital gain, or (b) the amount of taxable income that is taxed at a rate below 28%; (Code Sec. 1(h)(1)) plus

(2) a tax of 28% on the amount of taxable income in excess of the amount in (1). (Code Sec. 1(h)(2))[5]

observation: Thus, the maximum tax rate on a noncorporate taxpayer's net capital gain is 28%.

The amount of net capital gain qualifying for the 28% ceiling is reduced to the extent taxpayer elects (see ¶ 1725) to include the gain in investment income. (Code Sec. 1(h))[6]

¶ 2604 Capital losses of noncorporate taxpayers.

A noncorporate taxpayer may deduct capital losses only to the extent of capital gains plus (if the losses exceed the gains) the lower of:

(1) $3,000 ($1,500 for married individuals filing separate returns), or

(2) the excess of the losses over the gains. (Code Sec. 1211(b))[7]

illustration: B's capital gains and losses for the year are as follows:

	Short-term	Long-term
Gains	$ 1,200	$ 600
Losses	(1,300)	(4,200)
Net gain (or loss)	($ 100)	($ 3,600)

The excess of capital losses over capital gains is $3,700 ($100 + $3,600). This excess is deductible from ordinary income up to a maximum of $3,000.

A noncorporate taxpayer's capital losses for the tax year consist of the capital losses sustained during the year plus the total of all capital losses sustained in other years that are carried to the tax year (¶ 2605). (Code Sec. 1212(b); Reg § 1.1211-1(b)(1))[8]

¶ 2605 Noncorporate capital loss carryovers.

If an individual, trust or estate sustains a net capital loss that exceeds the maximum deductible in the current year (¶ 2604), the excess is carried over to later years indefinitely until it is absorbed. (Code Sec. 1212(b))[9] However, a decedent's unused capital loss is lost; it can't be carried over.[10] The capital loss keeps its original character as long- or short-term when carried over. (Code Sec. 1212(b)(1))[11] Thus, a long-term capital loss carried over from an earlier year first offsets long-term capital gains of the current year before it offsets short-term capital gains of the current year.

For purposes of determining the amount of excess long-term or short-term capital loss that is carried over, that excess is reduced by assuming the existence of a short-term capital gain equal in amount to the least of: (1) $3,000 ($1,500 for marrieds filing separately), (2) the excess of losses over gains (¶ 2604), or (3) "adjusted taxable income." Adjusted taxable income is taxable income (a) increased by the lesser of the amounts computed in (1) and (2), above, (b) increased by the personal exemption. For this purpose, any excess of deductions allowed over gross income is taken into account as negative

---

4. ¶ I-5111; ¶ 12,224.03.   6. ¶ I-5110.   8. ¶ I-5113; ¶ 12,124.   10. ¶ I-5133.
5. ¶ I-5110 *et seq.*; ¶ 12,009.3.   7. ¶ I-5112.   9. ¶ I-5122; ¶ 12,124.01.   11. ¶ I-5123; ¶ 12,124.01.

Footnote references beginning with letters are to paragraphs in RIA's Federal Tax Coordinator 2d and RIA's Analysis of Federal Taxes: Income. Footnote references beginning with numbers are to paragraphs in RIA's United States Tax Reporter.

taxable income. (Code Sec. 1212(b)(2))[12]

✏️illustration: For '93, an unmarried taxpayer has negative taxable income of $4,200 (i.e., the taxpayer's deductions exceed the taxpayer's gross income by $4,200). In addition, the taxpayer's capital gains and losses for the year are as follows:

	Short-term	Long-term
Gains	$ 500	$ 1,000
Losses	(900)	(7,300)
Net gain (or loss)	($ 400)	($ 6,300)

Thus, taxpayer's total capital loss is $6,700. Under the above rule, of the $6,700, only $5,550 is carried over to the next year, computed as follows:

Adjusted taxable income treated as short-term capital gain for purposes of determining the carryover (see computation below)	$1,150
Short-term capital gain	500
Total short-term capital gain	1,650
Short-term capital loss	900
Net short-term capital gain	750
Long-term capital loss carryover ($6,300 – $750)	$5,550

"Adjusted taxable income treated as short term capital gain" (above) is the least of: (1) $3,000, (2) the excess of losses over gains, or (3) adjusted taxable income. This taxpayer's adjusted taxable income is taxable income (here, negative taxable income ($4,200)) (a) increased by the lesser of $3,000 or (the excess of losses over gains) $6,700, and (b) increased by the personal exemption (for '93, $2,350).

¶ 2606 Capital gains of corporate taxpayers.

Corporate taxpayers must include capital gains in full in gross income but only to the extent that they exceed capital losses.[13]

¶ 2607 Corporation's alternative tax on capital gains.

A corporation with an excess of net long-term capital gain over net short-term capital loss ("net capital gain") (Code Sec. 1222(11)) pays an alternative tax instead of the regular corporate tax if the alternative tax is smaller. The alternative tax applies a special alternative tax rate to the corporation's net capital gain. But the alternative tax doesn't apply unless the top regular corporate tax rate for the year (see ¶ 1111) is higher than 35% (determined without regard to the additional tax on the corporation's taxable income over $15,000,000). (Code Sec. 1201(a))[14]

✏️observation: Thus, the alternative tax doesn't apply for '93.

¶ 2608 Corporation's capital losses.

Corporations may deduct capital losses only to the extent of their capital gains. The excess capital losses aren't allowed as deductions from a corporate taxpayer's ordinary income. (Code Sec. 1211(a))[15]

A corporation's capital losses in excess of its capital gains for the current year are carried back three years. But this is allowed only to the extent the loss is not attributable to a foreign expropriation capital loss and to the extent that the carryback does not increase or produce a net operating loss for the tax year to which it is carried back. (Code Sec. 1212(a)(1)(A)) A net capital loss cannot be carried back to a tax year in which the

---

12. ¶ I-5123; ¶ 12,124.01.   13. ¶ I-5116; ¶ 12,009.03.   14. ¶ I-5117; ¶ 12,014.   15. ¶ I-5121; ¶ 12,114.

Footnote references beginning with letters are to paragraphs in RIA's Federal Tax Coordinator 2d and RIA's Analysis of Federal Taxes: Income. Footnote references beginning with numbers are to paragraphs in RIA's United States Tax Reporter.

corporation is either a foreign personal holding company, a regulated investment company, a real estate investment trust or a foreign investment company electing to distribute income currently. (Code Sec. 1212(a)(3))

The carryforward period is five years (eight years for regulated investment companies; ten years for foreign expropriation capital losses). (Code Sec. 1212(a)(1)(B), (C))[16]

A capital loss carryback or carryover is treated as a short-term capital loss whether or not it was short-term when sustained. (Code Sec. 1212(a)(1)) However, a short-term capital loss carryover from one year may not be included in computing a new net capital loss for another year. (Code Sec. 1222(10))[17]

¶ 2609 Assets to Which Capital Gain and Loss Rules Apply

The capital gain or loss rules apply to those assets that are capital in nature. The character of an asset depends upon what it is and what use it has in taxpayer's hands.

¶ 2610 Capital assets defined.

Capital assets include all assets held by the taxpayer except:

(1) Stock in trade of the taxpayer or other property of a kind that would properly be included in the inventory of the taxpayer if on hand at the close of the tax year.

(2) Property held by the taxpayer primarily for sale to customers in the ordinary course of his trade or business.

(3) Accounts or notes receivable acquired in the ordinary course of a trade or business for services rendered or from the sale of any properties described in (1) or (2), above.

(4) Depreciable property used in the taxpayer's trade or business.

(5) Real property used in the taxpayer's trade or business.

(6) Certain copyrights, and literary, musical or artistic compositions, see ¶ 2615.

(7) Letters, memorandums or similar property in the hands of the writer, donees of the writer and persons to whom they were sent or for whom they were produced.

(8) U.S. government publications (e.g., the Congressional Record) received from the U.S. government without charge or below the price sold to the public, in the hands of the recipient and carryover-basis transferees. (Code Sec. 1221)[18]

Thus, property held for personal use is a capital asset, as is property used for the production of income (even if depreciable). But inventory, and real estate and depreciable property used in taxpayer's trade or business, are not capital assets. (Reg § 1.1221-1(b)) Examples of capital assets include stock and securities held for investment.[19]

¶ 2611 Hedging transactions.

The term capital asset does not include property that is part of a hedging transaction. (Reg § 1.1221-2T(a))

A hedging transaction is a transaction that taxpayer enters into in the normal course of taxpayer's trade or business, primarily to reduce the risk of price changes or currency fluctuations with respect to ordinary property, or to reduce the risk of interest rate or price changes or currency fluctuations with respect to borrowings or ordinary obligations. (Reg § 1.1221-2T(b)(1)) Property is ordinary property if a sale or exchange of the property by the taxpayer could not produce capital gain or loss regardless of the taxpayer's holding period. An obligation is an ordinary obligation if performance or termination of the obligation by the taxpayer could not produce capital gain or loss. (Reg § 1.1221-2T(b)) Thus, hedging in corn futures (to stabilize the cost of corn inventory) as an integral part of a

---

16. ¶ I-5125; ¶ 12,124.04.   17. ¶ I-5125; ¶ 12,124.04.   18. ¶ I-6001; ¶ 12,214.   19. ¶ I-6003; ¶ 12,214.

Footnote references beginning with letters are to paragraphs in RIA's Federal Tax Coordinator 2d and RIA's Analysis of Federal Taxes: Income. Footnote references beginning with numbers are to paragraphs in RIA's United States Tax Reporter.

taxpayer's inventory-purchase system produces ordinary income and loss.[20]

For transactions entered into after Dec. 31, '93 (or entered into before Jan. 1, '94, if still in existence Mar. 31, '94), a taxpayer must unambiguously identify the transaction as a hedging transaction for tax purposes (on its books and records) before the close of the day the taxpayer enters the transaction (by the close of business Mar. 31, '94 for pre-'94 transactions). (Reg § 1.1221-2T(c))[21]

¶ 2612　Options to buy or sell; stock warrants; certain terminations.

Gain or loss from the sale or exchange of a noncompensatory option (or privilege, e.g., a warrant) to buy or sell property is considered a gain or loss from the sale or exchange of a capital asset if the optioned property is (or would be if acquired) a capital asset in the taxpayer's hands. (Code Sec. 1234(a)(1); Reg § 1.1234-1(a))[22] If the holder of an option incurs a loss because he fails to exercise the option, the option is considered to have been sold or exchanged on the date it expires. (Code Sec. 1234(a)(2); Reg § 1.1234-1(b))[23]

A dealer in options is considered a dealer in the property subject to the option, and any gain or loss received from sale or exchange of the option is ordinary. (Reg § 1.1234-1(d))[24]

¶ 2613　"Put" and "call" options; straddles.

There are no tax consequences to the buyer or writer of an option until the option is exercised, otherwise closed out or lapses. The holder treats the premium paid as a nondeductible capital expenditure at the time of payment. The premium is not included in income of the writer at the time of receipt.[25] The premium received by the writer for granting a "put" or "call" option which is not exercised ("lapses"), so that the writer simply keeps the money, is generally treated as ordinary income, and gain or loss to the writer on repurchase of an option ("closing transaction") is also generally ordinary. (Reg § 1.1234-1(b)) However, gain or loss to a nondealer from a lapse or closing transaction involving options in stocks, securities, commodities or commodity futures is treated as short-term capital gain or loss. (Code Sec. 1234(b); Reg § 1.1234-3)[26]

Where a put is exercised, the premium received by the writer for granting the option is deducted from the option price for the property in determining the net basis to the writer of the property purchased. The holder deducts the premium from the amount received from the writer, in computing the gain or loss realized on the sale. Where a call is exercised, the premium received by the writer (i.e., seller) for granting the option is added to the sale proceeds received. This is included in the holder's (buyer's) basis for the property.[27]

When the put or call is bought from the original holder (or his assignee), the buyer is treated as a holder, and the amount paid by him to the original holder is likewise treated as a premium. However, the original holder is not treated as a writer, and must include that premium in his amount realized upon disposition of the option (see ¶ 2612).[28]

observation: Thus, if a holder (other than a dealer) of a put or call option on publicly traded stock closes out a position by selling the option on an exchange, the gain or loss is a capital gain or loss.

A "straddle" option combines a put and a call. For example, the writer agrees to buy a stated number of shares of stock within a definite period at a specified price (a put) and simultaneously agrees to sell a like number of shares of the same stock, at the same price, within the same time (a call). For this, the buyer of the straddle pays the writer a premium.

The writer must allocate a single premium received between the put and the call

---

20. ¶ I-6218 et seq.
21. ¶ I-6218 et seq.
22. ¶ I-6504; ¶ 12,344.

23. ¶ I-6510; ¶ 12,344.
24. ¶ I-6509.
25. ¶s I-6521, I-6522; ¶ 12,344.03.

26. ¶ I-6515; ¶ 12,344.
27. ¶s I-6530, I-6531; ¶ 12,344.04.

28. ¶ I-6523; ¶s 12,344.03, 12,344.04.

Footnote references beginning with letters are to paragraphs in RIA's Federal Tax Coordinator 2d and RIA's Analysis of Federal Taxes: Income. Footnote references beginning with numbers are to paragraphs in RIA's United States Tax Reporter.

options on the basis of their relative market values at the time the straddle is issued or on any other reasonable and consistently applied basis. (Reg § 1.1234-3(e))[29]

¶ 2614 Patents.

If an individual inventor or his financial backer transfers (other than by gift, inheritance or devise) all substantial rights to a patent, or an undivided interest (e.g., a half, a third) in those rights, the transfer is considered a sale or exchange of a long-term capital asset even though the transferor hasn't held the patent property for the period required for long-term treatment (see ¶ 2651), and even though the payments to the seller are: (1) made periodically during the buyer's use of the property, or (2) contingent on the productivity, use or disposition of the buyer's rights in the property (i.e., are like royalties). (Code Sec. 1235(a))[30]

It's not necessary that the patent or patent application be in existence at the time of that transfer for long-term capital treatment to apply. (Reg § 1.1235-2(e))[31]

This treatment doesn't apply to a transfer by the inventor's employer. (Code Sec. 1235(b)(2)(A))[32] Nor does it apply to transfers made (directly or indirectly) to or by certain persons related to the inventor. (Code Sec. 1235(b)(2)(B); Reg § 1.1235-2(f))[33]

Transferors that don't qualify for this special long-term capital gain treatment nevertheless qualify for capital gain or loss treatment if they can establish that the patent is a capital asset or a Code Sec. 1231 asset. (Reg § 1.1235-1(b))[34]

The long-term capital gain rule doesn't apply unless all substantial rights (or an undivided interest therein) are transferred. (Reg § 1.1235-2(b))[35]

¶ 2615 Copyrights, literary, musical, artistic composition, etc.

Copyrights, literary, musical, artistic composition, etc., are not capital assets or Section 1231 assets if the taxpayer is either:

■ the author or creator of property through his own personal efforts, or

■ the donee of the author or creator, or one who otherwise has a basis for the property determined in whole or in part by reference to the basis in the hands of that donor.

A letter, memorandum or similar property prepared or produced for a taxpayer isn't a capital asset to him (or his donee or other carryover-basis transferee). (Code Sec. 1221(3))[36]

¶ 2616 Real property.

Real property held primarily for sale in the ordinary course of the taxpayer's trade or business doesn't qualify as a capital asset. Whether particular real estate sold is a capital asset is decided on a case by case basis taking into consideration many factors including number and taxpayer's frequency of sales, subdividing and promotional activities.[37]

¶ 2617 Five-year land subdivision rule for noncorporate taxpayers.

An individual, trust or estate won't be considered to be holding land primarily for sale to customers merely because he has subdivided a tract of land into lots or parcels and engaged in advertising, promotion, selling activities or the use of sales agents in selling lots in the subdivision, if:

■ he has not previously held any part of the same land primarily for sale to customers in the ordinary course of business, and, in the year of sale doesn't hold any other real estate for sale to customers;

■ he doesn't (while he holds the land or as part of a contract of sale) make "substantial

29. ¶ I-6528; ¶ 12,344.06.
30. ¶ I-8301; ¶ 12,354.
31. ¶ I-8321.
32. ¶ I-8322; ¶ 12,354.04.
33. ¶ I-8325; ¶ 12,354.06.
34. ¶ I-6700.
35. ¶ I-8301; ¶ 12,354.09.
36. ¶ I-6601 *et seq.*; ¶ 12,214.
37. ¶ I-6300 *et seq.*; ¶ 12,214.

Footnote references beginning with letters are to paragraphs in RIA's Federal Tax Coordinator 2d and RIA's Analysis of Federal Taxes: Income. Footnote references beginning with numbers are to paragraphs in RIA's United States Tax Reporter.

improvements" on the land that substantially increase the value of the lot sold (except, if elected, improvements needed to make marketable land that has been held for ten years or more); and

■ he either has owned the land for five years or more, or acquired it by inheritance or devise. (Code Sec. 1237(a); Reg § 1.1237-1(a)(2), (a)(5), (b)(1))[38]

However, if more than five lots or parcels in the same tract are sold or exchanged, 5% of any gain from the later (sixth, etc.) transactions is ordinary gain. (Code Sec. 1237(b)(1))

The sale or exchange of qualifying subdivided land that is business property can result in an ordinary loss, see ¶ 2667. (Reg § 1.1237-1(f))[39]

¶ 2618 Sale of a sole proprietorship.

When a sole proprietorship is sold, there is not a sale of just one asset (the business). Rather, there is a sale of the individual assets that comprise the business. Thus, gain or loss on some assets will be ordinary while on others it will be capital.[40]

¶ 2619 Allocation of selling price on sale of business.

If assets of a going business are sold, the selling price must be allocated among the assets (including goodwill) for purposes of determining gain or loss (and the type of gain or loss, e.g., capital gain or ordinary income) separately for each. Allocation is made under the rules for determining the buyer's basis in each of them, see ¶ 2468.[41]

¶ 2620 Goodwill and covenants not to compete.

Goodwill is a capital asset. Proceeds from the sale of a business that are allocable (¶ 2619) to goodwill are taxed under the capital gain and loss rules.[42] Payments for a covenant not to compete also can result in capital gain (or loss).[43] But a covenant not to compete that is severable from the sale of goodwill results in ordinary income.[44]

¶ 2621 Investments by dealer in securities.

A securities dealer who buys securities for resale to customers may also hold securities purchased as investments for the dealer's own account. But gain from the sale or exchange of those securities won't be capital gain unless:

(1) the security is clearly identified in the dealer's records as a security held for investment on the day it is acquired, and

(2) the security is not held by the dealer primarily for sale to customers in the ordinary course of a trade or business at any time after the acquisition date. (Code Sec. 1236(a))[45]

A loss is a capital loss if the security has ever been clearly identified in the dealer's records as held for investment, even though held primarily for sale at the time of its disposition. (Code Sec. 1236(b); Reg § 1.1236-1(b))[46]

¶ 2622 Franchise, trademark or trade name transfers.

The transfer of a franchise, trademark or trade name isn't a sale or exchange of a capital asset if the transferor retains any significant power, right or continuing interest (such as the right to terminate at will, prescribe standards of quality or require the transferee to sell only the transferor's products). (Code Sec. 1253(a), (b)(2))[47]

In any case, ordinary income treatment applies to payments received by a transferor that are contingent on production, use, or disposition received by the transferor of a franchise, trademark or trade name. (Code Sec. 1253(c))[48]

---

38. ¶ I-6401 et seq.; ¶ 12,374.01.   41. ¶ I-8508 et seq.; ¶ 12,214.51.   44. ¶ I-8603; ¶ 12,214.56.   47. ¶ I-8401; ¶ 12,534.01.
39. ¶ I-6424.   42. ¶ I-8601; ¶ 12,214.55.   45. ¶ I-6209; ¶ 12,364.01.   48. ¶ I-8412; ¶ 12,534.01.
40. ¶ I-8501; ¶ 12,214.53.   43. ¶ I-8606; ¶ 12,214.56.   46. ¶ I-6215; ¶ 12,364.01.

Footnote references beginning with letters are to paragraphs in RIA's Federal Tax Coordinator 2d and RIA's Analysis of Federal Taxes: Income. Footnote references beginning with numbers are to paragraphs in RIA's United States Tax Reporter.

¶ 2623 Life estate, etc.

A life tenant, a tenant for a term of years or an income beneficiary of a trust is generally entitled to capital gain on sale of that interest.[49]

But where the interest was acquired by gift, from a decedent, by a transfer in trust or by a transfer from a spouse (or a former spouse incident to divorce), that part of the basis which is determined under the Code rules for those types of acquisitions (e.g., fair market value basis where acquired from a decedent, see ¶ 2510) is not taken into account in computing gain or loss on the sale or exchange of the interest, unless the entire interest in the underlying property is transferred in the same transaction. (Code Sec. 1001(e); Reg § 1.1001-1(f))[50]

¶ 2624 Small business investment company (SBIC) stock.

Losses from the sale, exchange or worthlessness of SBIC stock are deductible by a shareholder as an ordinary loss attributable to the shareholder's business. (Code Sec. 1242; Reg § 1.1242-1) Gains on the sale or exchange of SBIC stock are capital gains.[1]

¶ 2625 Regulated investment company stock.

A loss realized on the sale or exchange of stock in a regulated investment company is a long-term capital loss to the extent of any long-term capital gain realized via a distribution made with respect to the stock, if the taxpayer held the stock for six months or less. Rules for periodic liquidations differ.[2]

¶ 2626 Sale or exchange of debt instruments issued with original issue discount.

If a debt instrument is issued with original issue discount (OID) as defined in ¶ 1319, and if at the time of original issue there was an intention to call the debt instrument before maturity, any gain realized on the sale or exchange of the instrument is treated as ordinary income to the extent the gain does not exceed the OID reduced by the part of the OID previously included in the income of any holder. For purposes of this rule, any part of the OID that would have been included in the income of the holder had there been no acquisition premium is treated as if it had been included. (Code Sec. 1271(a)(2)(A))

The above rule does not apply to the following:

■ Any obligation issued by a natural person. (Code Sec. 1271(b)(1))

■ Tax-exempt obligations. (Code Sec. 1271(a)(2)(B)(i))

■ Obligations issued before July 2, '82, by an issuer which is neither a corporation nor a government or political subdivision. (Code Sec. 1271(b)(2))

■ Debt instruments issued before May 28, '69, and after Dec. 31, '54, by a corporation, or before July 2, '82, and after Dec. 31, '54, by a government (or political subdivision), see ¶ 2627. (Code Sec. 1271(c)(2)(B))

■ The sale or exchange by a holder who purchased the debt instrument at a premium. (Code Sec. 1271(a)(2)(B)(ii))[3]

¶ 2627 Ordinary income on sale or exchange of debt instruments issued with OID by a government before July 2, '82, or by a corporation before May 28, '69.

On the sale or exchange of any debt instrument issued by: (1) a government (or political subdivision of a government) before July 2, '82, and after Dec. 31, '54, or (2) by a corporation before May 28, '69, and after Dec. 31, '54, any gain realized by the seller is treated as ordinary income to the extent it does not exceed:

---

49. ¶ I-7014; ¶ 12,214.66. 1. ¶ I-9543; ¶ 12,424.01. 2. ¶ E-6162; ¶ 8524.02. 3. ¶ I-8001; ¶ 12,714.
50. ¶ I-7014.

Footnote references beginning with letters are to paragraphs in RIA's Federal Tax Coordinator 2d and RIA's Analysis of Federal Taxes: Income. Footnote references beginning with numbers are to paragraphs in RIA's United States Tax Reporter.

■ the amount of the OID, or

■ if, at the time of original issue there was no intention to call the debt instrument before maturity, an amount that bears the same ratio to the OID as the number of complete months that the debt instrument was held by the seller bears to the number of complete months from the date of original issue to the date of maturity. (Code Sec. 1271(c)(2)(A))

The rule described above does not apply to:

(1) tax-exempt obligations; (Code Sec. 1271(a)(2)(B)(i))

(2) the sale or exchange by a holder who bought a debt instrument at a premium. (Code Sec. 1271(a)(2)(B)(ii))[4]

¶ 2628 Sale or exchange of short-term government obligations.

On the sale or exchange of any short-term government obligation, any gain realized that does not exceed an amount equal to the ratable share of the acquisition discount is treated as ordinary income. (Code Sec. 1271(a)(3)(A)) This rule doesn't apply to a seller who was required to include the acquisition discount in gross income currently under the rules discussed in ¶ 1332. (Code Sec. 1283(d)(3))[5]

¶ 2629 Sale or exchange of short-term nongovernment obligations.

On the sale or exchange of any short-term nongovernment obligation, any gain realized that does not exceed an amount equal to the ratable share of OID is treated as ordinary income. (Code Sec. 1271(a)(4)(A))[6] This rule doesn't apply to a seller who was required to include the acquisition discount in gross income currently under the rules discussed in ¶ 1332. (Code Sec. 1283(d)(3))[7]

¶ 2630 Sale or exchange of tax-exempt obligations.

The sale or exchange of tax-exempt obligations results in taxable gain or loss. It makes no difference that the interest on the obligations is exempt. The seller has gain (capital, if the obligation is a capital asset) to the extent that the amount realized exceeds his adjusted basis in the bonds, see ¶ 2401. The seller's basis for this purpose means the price he paid, whether or not he purchased the bonds at a discount.[8]

¶ 2631 Short Sales ▉

In a short sale, an investor sells a security for delivery in the future. The short seller may meet his obligation to deliver by buying the security on the delivery ("closing") date. If the security declines in value when he closes or covers the sale, he has a gain equal to the price at which he sold minus his cost; if the value increases, his purchase price is higher than the sale price, and the short seller has a loss. The nature of the gain or loss on a short sale depends upon the nature of the property used to close the short transaction.

If the property used to close the short sale is a capital asset in the hands of the short seller, the gain or loss on the transaction is capital gain or loss. (Code Sec. 1233(a); Reg § 1.1233-1(a)(2))[9] Where the property used to close the short sale is a capital asset, the period the taxpayer held the property determines whether the gain or loss is long or short term, unless the limitations at ¶ 2642 *et seq.* apply. (Reg § 1.1233-1(a)(3))[10]

Illustration: Jan. 2, Year 1: taxpayer buys 100 shares of Corp A stock for $10 per share. Nov. 1, Year 2: he sells short 100 shares of Corp A stock for $16 per share. Nov. 15, Year 2: he closes the short sale by delivering the 100 shares bought on Jan. 2 of Year 1. Result: The taxpayer has a $600 gain that is long term because he covered the

---

4. ¶ I-8002; ¶ 12,714.01.   6. ¶ I-8005; ¶ 12,714.02.   8. ¶ I-4001.   10. ¶ I-7708; ¶ 12,334.01.
5. ¶ I-8004.   7. ¶ I-8005; ¶ 12,714.03.   9. ¶ I-7704; ¶ 12,334.01.

Footnote references beginning with letters are to paragraphs in RIA's Federal Tax Coordinator 2d and RIA's Analysis of Federal Taxes: Income. Footnote references beginning with numbers are to paragraphs in RIA's United States Tax Reporter.

short sale with property which he held for the long-term holding period.

¶ 2632 Capital gain limits on short sales.

The capital gain realized by the seller in a short sale is short-term, regardless of the actual holding period, where the seller either: (1) as of the date of the short sale, has owned for the short-term holding period, property that is "substantially identical" to that which he used to close the sale, or (2) after the short sale and on or before its closing, he acquires substantially identical property. (Code Sec. 1233(b); Reg § 1.1233-1(c)(2)) This doesn't apply to any capital gain on property in excess of the amount of substantially identical property. This prevents the taxpayer from converting what would normally be a short-term capital gain into a long-term capital gain.[11]

Illustration: Taxpayer entered into this transaction: Feb. 1, Year 1: bought 100 shares of Corp A stock at $10 per share. June 1, Year 1: sold short 100 shares of Corp A stock at $16 per share. Dec. 1, Year 2: closed out the short sale by delivering the 100 shares purchased on Feb. 1 of Year 1. Result: The $600 gain is short term because the stock used to cover the short sale was held for the short term period on June 1, the time of the short sale. It is immaterial that the stock was held for more than the short term period as of the closing date. (Reg § 1.1233-1(c)(6))

The above rule applies only to stocks, securities and commodity futures. (Code Sec. 1233(e)(2)(A))[12] For definition of "substantially identical," see ¶ 2456.

¶ 2633 Capital loss limits on short sales.

If property "substantially identical" to that sold short was held by the taxpayer for the long-term holding period (¶ 2651) as of the sale date, any loss on closing of the short sale is long-term capital loss, regardless of how long he held the property used to close the sale. (Code Sec. 1233(d)) This doesn't apply to any capital loss on property used to close the short sale in excess of the amount of substantially identical property. (Code Sec. 1233(e)(1))[13] This rule applies only to stocks, securities and commodity futures. (Code Sec. 1233(e)(2)(A))[14] For definition of "substantially identical," see ¶ 2456.

¶ 2634 When the wash sale rule applies to short sales of stock or securities.

A loss on the closing of such a short sale is disallowed if, within the period from 30 days before the closing date through 30 days after, substantially identical stock or securities are sold or sold short. (Code Sec. 1091(e))[15]

¶ 2635 Commodity futures and hedging transactions.

Commodity transactions are generally subject to the same rules for short sales as stocks and securities. (Reg § 1.1233-1(b)) A commodity future is a contract to purchase some fixed amount of a commodity at a future date at a fixed price. Gain or loss from the short sale of a commodity future is capital gain or loss if the future used to close the short sale is a capital asset to the taxpayer.

However, the short sale rules don't apply where the sale of the commodity future is a bona fide hedging transaction, see ¶ 2649. (Code Sec. 1233(g); Reg § 1.1233-1(b))[16] A transaction is a bona fide hedging transaction if the commodity future purchased is directly related to the taxpayer's business, e.g., flour millers buying and selling wheat futures.[17]

---

11. ¶ I-7710; ¶ 12,334.06.
12. ¶ I-7708; ¶ 12,334.06.
13. ¶ I-7714; ¶ 12,334.03.
14. ¶ I-7708; ¶ 12,334.03.
15. ¶ I-3905; ¶ 10,914.
16. ¶ I-6218 *et seq.*; ¶s 12,334.09, 12,336.
17. ¶s I-6218, I-6222; ¶s 12,336, 12,336.41.

Footnote references beginning with letters are to paragraphs in RIA's Federal Tax Coordinator 2d and RIA's Analysis of Federal Taxes: Income. Footnote references beginning with numbers are to paragraphs in RIA's United States Tax Reporter.

¶ *2636* Section 1244 ("Small Business Corporation") Stock ▬▬▬▬▬▬

Loss on the sale, exchange or worthlessness of Section 1244 stock is deductible, within limits, as an ordinary loss, even though gain on the stock is capital gain.

This ordinary deduction is available only to individuals, and only if the individual (or a partnership) was the original purchaser. Transferees of these original purchasers don't qualify. (Code Sec. 1244(a))[18]

The aggregate amount of the ordinary loss is limited to $50,000 on separate returns and $100,000 on joint returns each year. Spouses may deduct the $100,000 maximum in a joint return even if only one spouse owned the stock. (Code Sec. 1244(b))[19]

A loss on qualifying Section 1244 stock is deductible as an ordinary loss attributable to the shareholder's business. As such, the loss is deductible in full from gross income and may give rise to a net operating loss. Losses exceeding the limitations must be treated as regular capital losses. (Reg § 1.1244(b)-1(a))[20]

¶ *2637* Qualifying for Section 1244 ordinary loss treatment.

To qualify as Section 1244 stock, all of the following requirements must be met: (Code Sec. 1244(c))[21]

■ The stock must be stock (it must be common stock, nonconvertible into other securities, (Reg § 1.1244(c)-1(b)) if issued before July 19, '84),[22] voting or nonvoting, of a domestic corporation.

■ The stock must have been issued for money or other property, other than stock, securities or services. But stock issued for the cancellation of corporate debt (that was not evidenced by a security or issued for services) does qualify. (Reg § 1.1244(c)-1(d)(1))

■ The issuing corporation must have met a test in which it shows that over 50% of its receipts were from business operations. (Code Sec. 1244(c))[23]

■ The stock must have been issued by a domestic "small business" corporation (¶ 2639).

Stock issued before Nov. 7, '78, must have been offered under a *written* plan.[24]

¶ *2638* How to claim the Code Sec. 1247 ordinary loss—Form 4797.

Claim the ordinary loss on Form 4797 (attached to Form 1040). In addition, attach to Form 1040 a statement setting forth: (1) the address of the corporation that issued the stock; (2) the manner in which the stock was acquired and the nature and amount of the consideration paid for the stock and (3) if the stock was acquired in a nontaxable transaction in exchange for property other than money, the type of property, its fair market value on the date of transfer to the corporation, and its adjusted basis on that date. (Reg § 1.1244(e)-1(b)) Strict compliance with these rules is required.[25]

¶ *2639* "Small business corporation" (SBC) defined.

A corporation is an SBC if at the time the stock is issued its capital receipts don't exceed $1,000,000. (Special designation rules must be met for stock issued in a year capital receipts do exceed $1,000,000.)[26] Capital receipts means the aggregate amount of money and other property received by the corporation for stock, as a contribution to capital, and as paid-in surplus. This determination includes amounts received for the Section 1244 stock and for all stock issued previously. (Code Sec. 1244(c)(3)(A))[27]

---

18. ¶ I-9503; ¶ 12,444.07.
19. ¶ I-9505; ¶ 12,444.01.
20. ¶ I-9502; ¶ 12,444.01.

21. ¶ I-9508 *et seq.*; ¶ 12,444.03.
22. ¶ I-9509; ¶ 12,444.03.
23. ¶ I-8524.

24. ¶ I-9508; ¶ 12,444.05.
25. ¶ 9537; ¶ 12,014.

26. ¶ I-9518 *et seq.*; ¶ 12,444.05.
27. ¶ I-9518; ¶ 12,444.05.

Footnote references beginning with letters are to paragraphs in RIA's Federal Tax Coordinator 2d and RIA's Analysis of Federal Taxes: Income. Footnote references beginning with numbers are to paragraphs in RIA's United States Tax Reporter.

¶ 2640 Exclusion of 50% of Gain from Qualified Small Business Stock ▰▰▰▰▰▰

A noncorporate taxpayer may exclude 50% of gain on the disposition of qualified small business stock (QSBS) issued after Aug. 10, '93 and held over five years.

This 50% exclusion is allowed only to taxpayers other than corporations, (Code Sec. 1202(a), (b)(2)) i.e., individuals, trusts and estates.[28]

For each corporation in which taxpayer invests, the total amount of gain eligible for the 50% exclusion for a tax year may not exceed the greater of:

■ $10,000,000 ($5,000,000 for a married individual filing separately), (Code Sec. 1202(b)(1)(A), ((3)(A)) reduced by taxpayer's total gain on dispositions of the corporation's stock that he took into account in earlier years. (Code Sec. 1202(b)(1)(A)) The amount of eligible gain is allocated equally between spouses who file jointly, to apply this limit to later years; (Code Sec. 1202(b)(3)(B)) or

■ ten times the aggregate adjusted bases of any of the corporation's QSBS that taxpayer disposed of during the year. (Code Sec. 1202(b)(1)(B)) For this purpose, the adjusted basis of any stock doesn't include any additions to basis after the date it was originally issued, (Code Sec. 1202(b)) or any reductions for SSBIC rollovers (¶ 2500) (Code Sec. 1044(d))[29]

The taxpayer must hold the QSBS for more than five years before the sale or exchange to exclude 50% of the gain. (Code Sec. 1202(a))[30]

The exclusion is denied for any gain from the sale of QSBS if taxpayer or any related person held an offsetting short position with respect to the stock anytime before the five-year holding period requirement is met. (Code Sec. 1202(j))[31]

The exclusion also is denied where the corporation redeems stock from taxpayer or a related person during certain periods, or buys its own stock in excess of certain amounts during specified periods. (Code Sec. 1202(c)(3))[32]

Special rules apply where pass-thru entities hold the stock. (Code Sec. 1202(g))[33]

For alternative minimum tax treatment of any exclusion claimed, see ¶ 3208.

¶ 2641 Qualified small business stock (QSBS) defined.

Qualified small business stock (QSBS) is any stock in a C corporation which is originally issued after Aug. 10, '93 if:

■ as of the date of issuance, the corporation is a qualified small business. (Code Sec. 1202(c)(1)(A)) This means a domestic C corporation whose total gross assets (treating all members of the same parent-subsidiary controlled group as one corporation) at all times after Aug. 10, '93 and before the issuance, and immediately after the issuance (taking into account amounts received in the issuance), don't exceed $50,000,000, and that meets certain reporting requirements; (Code Sec. 1202(d))

■ the taxpayer claiming the exclusion acquired the stock at its original issuance for money or other property (not stock) or as compensation for services provided to the corporation; (Code Sec. 1202(c)(1)(B)) and

■ during substantially all of taxpayer's holding period for the stock, the corporation is a C corporation (other than certain excluded corporations) and meets this active business test: at least 80% of the corporation's assets must be used in the active conduct of one or more trades or businesses other than banking, insurance, or other business having the reputation or skill of its employees as its principal asset (an SSBIC (¶ 2426) meets this test). (Code Sec. 1202(c)(2), (d)(4), (e))[34]

---

28. ¶ I-9100.1; ¶ 12,024.   30. ¶ I-9100.1; ¶ 12,024.   32. ¶ I-9102; ¶ 12,024.03.   34. ¶ I-9101; ¶ 12,024.02.
29. ¶ I-9112 *et seq.*; ¶ 12,024.01.   31. I-9115; ¶ 12,024.03.   33. ¶ I-9116; ¶ 12,024.03.

Footnote references beginning with letters are to paragraphs in RIA's Federal Tax Coordinator 2d and RIA's Analysis of Federal Taxes: Income. Footnote references beginning with numbers are to paragraphs in RIA's United States Tax Reporter.

¶ 2642 Tax Straddles and Section 1256 Contracts

Losses on certain unregulated straddles are deferred, to the extent taxpayer has an offsetting unrecognized gain. Related interest and carrying charges must be capitalized. Regulated futures contracts are subject to the "mark-to-market" rule which treats the unrealized capital gain (or loss) from the contract for the year as 60% long-term and 40% short-term. Hedging transactions are excepted from these rules.

There are a number of specific rules provided to restrict tax avoidance opportunities in commodity futures straddles and to curb certain tax shelters involving tax straddles.[35]

¶ 2643 "Straddle" defined.

A "straddle" is "offsetting positions" with respect to personal property. (Code Sec. 1092(c)(1)) A "position" is an interest, including a futures or forward contract or option, in personal property. (Code Sec. 1092(d)(2)) A taxpayer holds "offsetting positions" with respect to personal property if he has reduced his risk of loss from holding the property by holding one (or more) other positions, whether or not the items of personal property involved in the different positions are the same kind. (Code Sec. 1092(c)(2)(A))[36]

¶ 2644 Recognition of losses postponed on certain nonregulated futures straddles (loss deferral rule).

Loss deductions on nonregulated straddles, that is, those straddle positions not on the "mark-to-market" system (see ¶ 2645) are limited to the amount by which the losses exceed "unrecognized gains" on any offsetting straddle positions. Losses in excess of the limitation (deferred losses) are carried forward to the next year and are subject to the deferral rules in that year. (Code Sec. 1092(a)(1))[37]

¶ 2645 Regulated futures contracts, etc., (Section 1256 contracts) under "mark-to-market" system.

Taxpayers must report (on Form 6781) gains and losses from regulated futures contracts and other "Section 1256 contracts" (¶ 2646) on an annual basis under the "mark-to-market" rule.

All Section 1256 contracts must be marked to market at year end. Each Section 1256 contract held by a taxpayer is treated as if it were sold for fair market value on the last business day of the year. (Code Sec. 1256(a)(1)) If a taxpayer holds Section 1256 contracts at the beginning of a tax year, any gain or loss later realized on the contracts must be adjusted to reflect any gain or loss taken into account with respect to the contracts in an earlier year. (Code Sec. 1256(a)(2))

Any capital gain or loss on a Section 1256 futures contract that is marked-to-market is treated as if 40% of the gain or loss is short-term capital gain or loss, and as if 60% of the gain or loss is long-term capital gain or loss. (Code Sec. 1256(a)(3))[38]

¶ 2646 Section 1256 contracts defined.

Section 1256 contracts include: regulated futures contracts, foreign currency contracts, nonequity options, and dealer equity options. (Code Sec. 1256(b))[39] For a partnership that is a qualified fund, Section 1256 contracts include post-Oct. 21, '88 bank forward contracts, foreign currency futures contracts, and similar instruments prescribed by IRS regs. (Code Sec. 988(c)(1)(E)(iv)(I))[40]

---

35. ¶ I-7500 *et seq.*; ¶ 10,924.
36. ¶ I-7504; ¶ 10,924.
37. ¶ I-7523; ¶ 10,924.
38. ¶ I-7602; ¶s 12,564.03, 12,564.05.
39. ¶ I-7604; ¶ 12,564.01.
40. ¶ I-7607; ¶ 9884.01.

Footnote references beginning with letters are to paragraphs in RIA's Federal Tax Coordinator 2d and RIA's Analysis of Federal Taxes: Income. Footnote references beginning with numbers are to paragraphs in RIA's United States Tax Reporter.

¶ 2647 Election for mixed straddles.

There is a special election for the taxation of straddles composed of at least one position in a Section 1256 contract (¶ 2646) and one or more positions in interests in property which are not Section 1256 contracts. A taxpayer may elect (use Form 6781) to exclude all positions in the mixed straddle, including Section 1256 contracts, from the mark-to-market rules in which case they will be subject to the loss deferral, wash sale, and short sale rules, and the straddle will not be a mixed straddle. (Code Sec. 1256(d))[41]

If that election is not made, so that the straddle is a mixed straddle, a taxpayer may elect to offset gains and losses in the mixed straddle by either separately identifying the positions of the mixed straddle, or establishing a mixed straddle account. (Reg § 1.1092(b)-4T(f))[42]

¶ 2648 Carryback election for losses from Section 1256 contracts—Form 6781.

Noncorporate taxpayers can elect (on Form 6781) to have net commodity futures capital losses carried back three years and applied against net commodities futures capital gains during that period. (Code Sec. 1212(c)) The carryback applies only if, after netting Section 1256 contracts with capital gains and losses from other sources, there is a net capital loss for the tax year that, but for the election, would be a capital loss carryforward under the normal rules (¶ 2605). The lesser of the net capital loss or the net loss resulting from the application of the mark-to-market rule is a "net Section 1256 contracts loss" which may be carried back. (Code Sec. 1212(c)(4)) Capital losses carried back under the election are to be treated as if 40% of the losses are short-term capital losses and 60% are long-term capital losses. (Code Sec. 1212(c)(1)) The losses must be absorbed in the earliest year to which they may be carried back. Any remainder is then carried forward to the next year.

The losses may be applied in the carryback year against the lesser of "net Section 1256 contracts gain" or capital gain net income for that year. (Code Sec. 1212(c)(5))

Capital losses that are carried forward, to the extent they were determined under the mark-to-market rule, continue to be treated as losses from Section 1256 contracts in the year to which they are carried. (Code Sec. 1212(c)(6))[43]

The above carryback election applies to Section 1256 contracts which are part of a mixed straddle.[44]

¶ 2649 Hedging transactions.

The "mark-to-market" rules do not apply to "hedging transactions" (Code Sec. 1256(e)(1)) (see also ¶ 2635).

A hedging transaction is a transaction:

■ entered into by the taxpayer in the normal course of a trade or business primarily—

(a) to reduce risk of price change or currency fluctuations with respect to property the taxpayer holds or will hold, or

(b) to reduce risk of interest rate or price changes or currency fluctuations with respect to borrowings made, or to be made, or obligations incurred or to be incurred;

■ the gain or loss from which is treated as ordinary income or loss; and

■ that, before the close of the day on which it was entered into, the taxpayer clearly identifies as a hedging transaction. (Code Sec. 1256(e)(2))[45]

---

41. ¶ I-7616; ¶ 12,564.03.
42. ¶ I-7543 *et seq.*; ¶ 12,564.03.
43. ¶ I-7606; ¶ 12,124.02.
44. ¶ I-7606; ¶s 10,924, 12,124.02, 12,564.03.
45. ¶ I-7623; ¶ 12,564.05.

Footnote references beginning with letters are to paragraphs in RIA's Federal Tax Coordinator 2d and RIA's Analysis of Federal Taxes: Income. Footnote references beginning with numbers are to paragraphs in RIA's United States Tax Reporter.

¶ 2650 Conversion transactions—investments that are similar to loans ■■■■■■

Capital gain on the disposition of property that was part of a conversion transaction (i.e., functionally equivalent to a loan) is treated as ordinary income.

Gain recognized on the disposition or other termination of any position held as part of a conversion transaction, that would otherwise be treated as capital gain, is treated as ordinary income, to the extent that it doesn't exceed the applicable imputed income amount. (Code Sec. 1258(a))[46] The applicable imputed income amount equals the excess of (1) taxpayer's net investment in the transaction multiplied by 120% of (a) the applicable federal rate (¶ 1116) (compounded semiannually) for the period covered by the transaction, if the transaction has a definite term, or of (b) the federal short-term rates in effect under Code Sec. 6621(b) for the period of the conversion transaction, if the term of the transaction is indefinite, over (2) the amount already so treated with respect to the same transaction. (Code Sec. 1258(b), (d)(2))[47]

Illustration: On Jan 1 of Year 1, A buys 100 shares of stock for $100 and on the same day agrees to sell the stock to B on Jan. 1 of Year 3 for $115. Assume this is a conversion transaction. On Jan. 1 of Year 3, A delivers the stock to B in exchange for $115. A's gain is $15. Assume the applicable federal rate is 5%. Using 120% of 5%, compounded semiannually, the applicable computed income amount is $12.36, which A must treat as ordinary income.

A conversion transaction is any transaction (entered into after Apr. 30, '93) where substantially all of taxpayer's expected net return is attributable to the time value of his net investment, and which is:

■ the holding of any property (whether or not actively traded) and substantially contemporaneous making of a contract to sell that or substantially identical property at a price determined in accordance with the contract; (Code Sec. 1258(c)(2)(A))

■ a straddle (¶ 2643) of actively traded personal property; (Code Sec. 1258(c)(2)(B))

■ a transaction that was marketed or sold as producing capital gains; (Code Sec. 1258(c)(2)(C))

■ a conversion transaction as specified in regs to be issued. (Code Sec. 1258(c)(2)(D))[48]

Conversion transactions don't include transactions of options dealers and commodities traders in the normal course of their trade or business. (Code Sec. 1258(c)(5)(A))[49]

¶ 2651 Holding Period ■■■■■■■■■■■■■■■■■■■■■■■■■

The length of time that a capital asset is held before its sale or exchange determines whether the proceeds from the sale or exchange are taxable as long-term gain or loss or as short-term gain or loss.

Qualification for Section 1231 (capital gain/ordinary loss) treatment also depends on the holding period, see ¶ 2669.

Holding a capital asset for the short-term holding period (one year or less) results in short-term capital gain or loss on the sale or exchange of that asset. (Code Sec. 1221(1), (2)) Holding a capital asset for the long-term holding period (more than one year) results in long-term gain or loss on the sale or exchange of that asset. (Code Sec. 1221(3), (4))[50]

For commodity futures, the holding period is more than six months. This applies to futures transactions in any commodity subject to the rules of a board of trade or commodity exchange. (Code Sec. 1222)[1]

---

46. ¶ I-8200; ¶ 12,584.   48. ¶ I-8205; ¶ 12,584.   50. ¶ I-8901; ¶ 12,009.04.   1. ¶s I-8901, I-8971; ¶ 12,234.27.
47. ¶ I- 8208; ¶ 12,584.   49. ¶ I-8210 *et seq.*; ¶ 12,584.

Footnote references beginning with letters are to paragraphs in RIA's Federal Tax Coordinator 2d and RIA's Analysis of Federal Taxes: Income. Footnote references beginning with numbers are to paragraphs in RIA's United States Tax Reporter.

¶ 2652 How to measure the holding period.

The holding period is computed in terms of calendar months, not days.[2]

The holding period for an asset begins on the day after the day of acquisition and ends on the day of sale, exchange or other disposition. In other words, the taxpayer excludes the day of acquisition but includes the date of disposition.[3]

Illustration: A capital asset is acquired on Feb. 15. To meet the long-term holding period, it must be held until Feb. 16 of the following year. To meet the six-month long-term holding period for a commodity future (¶ 2651), it must be held until Aug. 16. If the asset were acquired on Jan. 31, it would have to be held until Feb. 1 of the following year to meet the one-year holding period, or until Aug. 1 to meet the six-month period.

¶ 2653 Holding period for stocks and securities.

Holding period for stocks and securities acquired by purchase, whether on a registered securities exchange or in the "over-the-counter" market, is determined by reference to the "trade date" on which the stock or security is acquired and the "trade date" on which it is sold. The "settlement dates" are not considered.[4]

The holding period for stock or securities acquired from a corporation by the exercise of rights begins on and includes the day the rights are exercised. (Code Sec. 1223(6); Reg § 1.1223-1(f))[5]

The holding period for property "substantially identical" to that sold short in a transaction to which the rule at ¶ 2632 applies is considered to begin on the day the short sale is closed or, if earlier, on the date the property is sold, given away or otherwise disposed of. (Code Sec. 1233(b)(2); Reg § 1.1233-1(c)(2))[6]

The holding period for stock, stock rights or other property received as a taxable dividend begins on the date the distribution is actually or constructively received.[7] If the distribution is tax-free, the holding period for the stock, etc., includes the period that the underlying stock was held. (Code Sec. 1223(5); Reg § 1.1223-1(e))[8]

The holding period for restricted stock (or property) begins after it is substantially vested, unless an election (¶ 1217) is made to include the property in income in the year of transfer, in which case the holding period begins just after the transfer. (Code Sec. 83(f); Reg § 1.83-4(a))[9]

Where the loss on sale of stock or securities is disallowed under the "wash sale" rules, see ¶ 2454 *et seq.*, the holding period for the new similar stock includes the holding period for the old stock that was sold. (Code Sec. 1223(4))[10]

¶ 2654 Property acquired through options.

The holding period for property acquired through the exercise of an option begins the day after the option is exercised.[11]

¶ 2655 Inherited property.

The holding period of property acquired from a decedent starts with the date of death.[12]

However, property acquired from a decedent which is sold within the short-term capital gain holding period after the decedent's death is considered to be held for the *long*-term capital gain holding period where:

(1) the person selling the property has a basis that is determined under Code Sec. 1014 (by reference to the property's fair market value on date of death or alternate valuation

---

2. ¶ I-8904; ¶ 12,234.01.
3. ¶s I-8904, I-8906; ¶ 12,234.01.
4. ¶ I-8914 *et seq.*; ¶ 12,234.07.

5. ¶ I-8924; ¶s 12,234.07, 12,344, 12,234.25.
6. ¶ I-7720; ¶ 12,234.07.

7. ¶ I-8918; ¶ 12,234.25.
8. ¶ I-8921; ¶ 12,234.25.
9. ¶ I-8916; ¶ 834 *et seq.*

10. ¶ I-8929; ¶ 12,234.25.
11. ¶ I-8949; ¶ 12,234.10.
12. ¶ I-8944; ¶ 12,234.21.

Footnote references beginning with letters are to paragraphs in RIA's Federal Tax Coordinator 2d and RIA's Analysis of Federal Taxes: Income. Footnote references beginning with numbers are to paragraphs in RIA's United States Tax Reporter.

date), and

(2) the property is sold (or disposed of) within one year after the date of the decedent's death. (Code Sec. 1223(11))[13]

The long-term holding period is also met where special use valuation property (¶ 5028) is acquired, as in satisfaction of a pecuniary bequest or by purchase from the decedent's estate, and is sold within the short-term holding period to another "qualified heir." (Code Sec. 1223(12))[14]

The holding period of the surviving spouse's share of community property that vested at the time of the acquisition by the community (as opposed to the share inherited from the deceased spouse) starts from the date of acquisition.[15]

¶ 2656   Gifts.

The donee's holding period for property acquired by gift includes the donor's holding period if the property has the same basis for gain or loss (see ¶ 2458 *et seq.*) in the hands of the donee as it would have in the donor's hands. (Code Sec. 1223(2); Reg § 1.1223-1(b)) But if the property is sold by the donee at a loss based on its market value on the date of the gift (and not based on the donor's basis), the holding period starts from the date of the gift.[16]

¶ 2657   Tax-free exchange property.

The holding period for property received in a partially or wholly tax-free exchange (¶ 2413 *et seq.*) includes the holding period for the property surrendered. This "tacking on" applies where the new property has the same basis, in whole or in part, as the old property, (Code Sec. 1223(1)) e.g., like-kind exchanges, tax-free stock distributions (¶ 2653), involuntary conversions (¶ 2658), replacement residences (¶ 2659), or incorporations and tax-free corporate reorganizations (¶ 3510 *et seq.*).[17]

¶ 2658   Replacements for property lost or damaged in an involuntary conversion.

The holding period of the original property is tacked on to that of property acquired to replace property lost or damaged in an involuntary conversion, (¶ 2427 *et seq.*) where gain isn't recognized.[18]

¶ 2659   Replacement of residence.

Where gain on the sale of a residence isn't taxed because of the nonrecognition rules on replacement as explained in ¶ 2437 *et seq.*, the holding period of the new residence includes the period the old residence was held. (Code Sec. 1223(7))[19]

¶ 2660   Sales and Exchanges ▬▬▬▬▬▬▬▬▬

Unless a transaction involving a capital asset is treated as a sale or exchange, any resulting gain or loss does not qualify as capital gain or loss.

A sale is a transfer of property for an amount of money or a money equivalent that is fixed or determinable. An exchange is a transfer of property for property other than money or a cash equivalent. (Reg § 1.1002-1(d))[20]

To qualify as a sale or exchange, the transaction must be complete, and bona fide in all respects. If it is real in substance as well as form, it qualifies as a sale or exchange even though it was designed to reduce taxes.[21] Where shareholders deal with their corporation, or family members sell or exchange property among themselves, IRS scrutinizes the deal closely. If a sale or exchange is a sham, IRS can disallow any of the sought-after tax

---

13. ¶ I-8942; ¶ 12,234.21.   16. ¶ I-8966; ¶ 12,234.22.   18. ¶ I-8963; ¶ 12,234.18.   20. ¶ I-1002; ¶ 10,014.
14. ¶ I-8943; ¶ 12,234.21.   17. ¶ I-8960 *et seq.*; ¶ 12,234.18.   19. ¶ I-8941; ¶ 12,234.18.   21. ¶ I-1212 *et seq.*; ¶ 10,014.
15. ¶ I-8945; ¶ 12,234.21.

Footnote references beginning with letters are to paragraphs in RIA's Federal Tax Coordinator 2d and RIA's Analysis of Federal Taxes: Income. Footnote references beginning with numbers are to paragraphs in RIA's United States Tax Reporter.

consequences.[22]

¶ 2661 Creditor collecting or compromising a claim.

The receipt of amounts in full or partial satisfaction of a debt instrument issued by an individual isn't an exchange. (Code Sec. 1271(b)(1))

However, the retirement of corporate or government debt instruments, (Code Sec. 1271(a)(1))[23] and noncorporate or nongovernment (e.g., trust or estate) debt instruments issued after July 1, '82, (Code Sec. 1271(a)(1), (b)(2))[24] are considered exchanges.

¶ 2662 Payment with property as a sale.

A debtor realizes gain or loss when he transfers property to his creditor in complete or partial satisfaction of his debt. The transfer is treated as a sale or exchange of the property by the debtor. Gain or loss is the amount of debt satisfied minus the basis of the property.[25]

¶ 2663 Cancellation of lease or distribution agreement as sale or exchange.

Amounts received by a lessee or tenant for the cancellation of a lease, or by a distributor of goods for the cancellation of a distributorship agreement, are considered amounts received *in exchange* for the lease or agreement. (Code Sec. 1241)[26] Thus, Section 1231 treatment (see ¶ 2667) is available for gain or loss from the cancellation of a business lease or distributorship held long-term. If the lease was for the tenant's home, a gain would be taxed as a capital gain, but any loss would not be deductible.[27]

¶ 2664 Convertible bonds.

No gain or loss is realized upon the conversion of bonds into stock of the *same* corporation under a conversion privilege set forth in the terms of the bond.[28]

¶ 2665 Sale with leaseback, reservations or restrictions.

The fact that a sale of property is accompanied by a leaseback doesn't bar recognizing the sale as closed for tax purposes.[29] But a leaseback of realty (including renewal options) extending for 30 years or more may be considered an exchange of like-kind property in which gain or loss is not recognized.[30] A sale restricting the buyer's use of the property may be recognized as a completed sale, as where stock is sold subject to security-device restrictions,[31] but if the rights retained are significant enough, the seller may be considered as selling only a partial interest or as granting a license to use.[32]

¶ 2666 Part gift, part sale; conditional gifts.

If an owner combines a gift with a sale (e.g., to a family member) gain is realized to the extent the price received exceeds the owner's adjusted basis. (Reg § 1.1001-1(e))[33]

If a donor gives appreciated property to a donee on condition that the donee pay the donor's gift tax, there is a sale by the donor for the amount of the gift tax. To the extent the gift tax paid by the donee exceeds the donor's basis, the donor has income.[34]

¶ 2667 Capital Gain-Ordinary Loss Rule

Under Section 1231, if there is a net gain for the tax year from sales, exchanges, and involuntary or compulsory conversions of certain assets, it is treated as long-term capital gain. A net loss is treated as an ordinary loss.

---

22. ¶ I-1201 *et seq.*; ¶ 10,014.06.　　26. ¶ I-1400; ¶ 12,414 *et seq.*　　29. ¶ I-1122; ¶ 79,006 *et seq.*　　32. ¶ I-1602 *et seq.*
23. ¶ I-1901; ¶ 12,714 *et seq.*　　27. ¶ M-1500; ¶ 12,414.　　30. ¶ I-3077.　　33. ¶ I-1006; ¶ 10,014.06.
24. ¶ I-1801; ¶ 12,174 *et seq.*　　28. ¶ I-1909.　　31. ¶ I-1125 1.　　34. ¶ I-1007.
25. ¶ I-1501 *et seq.*; ¶ 10,014.17.

Footnote references beginning with letters are to paragraphs in RIA's Federal Tax Coordinator 2d and RIA's Analysis of Federal Taxes: Income. Footnote references beginning with numbers are to paragraphs in RIA's United States Tax Reporter.

¶ 2668 **Applying the Section 1231 rules—Form 4797.**

If the recognized gains are greater than the recognized losses on sales, exchanges and involuntary conversions of Section 1231 assets, the net amount is treated as a long-term capital gain, except as discussed below. But, if those losses are greater than those gains, the net amount is treated as an ordinary loss. (Code Sec. 1231(a); Reg § 1.1231-1(b))[35] Section 1231 gains and losses are reported and netted on Form 4797.

A net Section 1231 gain is treated as ordinary income to the extent of nonrecaptured net Section 1231 losses. (Code Sec. 1231(c)(1))

A nonrecaptured net Section 1231 loss is the net Section 1231 loss for the five most recent preceding tax years that has not been offset by a net Section 1231 gain in an intervening tax year. (Code Sec. 1231(c)(2)) Net Section 1231 gain means the excess of the Section 1231 gains over the Section 1231 losses. Net Section 1231 loss means the excess of the Section 1231 losses over the Section 1231 gains. (Code Sec. 1231(c)(3), (4))[36]

Illustration: X Corp, a calendar year taxpayer, had a net Section 1231 loss of $1,000,000 in '89 that was offset against ordinary income. X Corp had no net Section 1231 gain in '90, '91 or '92, but has a net Section 1231 gain of $1,400,000 (consisting of a $2,000,000 gain on condemnation of land, and a $600,000 loss on the sale of machinery) in '93. $1,000,000 of the net Section 1231 gain for '93 is treated as ordinary income, and the remaining $400,000 is treated as long-term capital gain.

If the recognized losses from involuntary conversions arising from fire, storm, shipwreck or other casualty, or from theft exceed the recognized gain, they are not included in the Section 1231 computations. (Code Sec. 1231(a)(4), (c)(5))[37]

Capital gain treatment under Section 1231 is also barred to the extent that the depreciation recapture rules apply, see ¶ 2675 *et seq.*

¶ 2669 **Section 1231 assets defined.**

Section 1231 assets are certain assets used in taxpayer's trade or business, and that were held for the long-term holding period at the time of disposition. Except as explained below, these assets include depreciable tangible and intangible personal property, and real property, whether or not depreciable. They include timber, certain livestock (other than poultry), and unharvested crops that are transferred with land. (Code Sec. 1231(b))

They don't include: (1) inventory, (2) property held primarily for sale to customers in the ordinary course of taxpayer's business, (3) copyrights or similar musical, artistic, etc., creations in the hands of the creator or his donee, etc., (carryover basis transferee) or (4) U.S. government publications obtained without charge or below the price sold to the general public. (Code Sec. 1231(b); Reg § 1.1231-1(c))[38]

Property held for rent usually is treated as property used in business, but IRS (with the support of some, but not all, courts) denies this status where rental activity is slight.[39]

¶ 2670 **Timber cutting treated as sale or exchange.**

A taxpayer may elect to treat the cutting of timber as a sale or exchange qualifying for Section 1231 capital gain-ordinary loss treatment. (Code Sec. 631(a), Code Sec. 1231(b)(2))[40] Taxpayers who elect must file Form T with their returns.[41]

The taxpayer must have owned the timber, or held a contract right to cut it, for more than one year before the timber is cut. (Code Sec. 631(a); Reg § 1.631-1(b)(1)) The timber must be cut for sale or for use in the taxpayer's business. (Reg § 1.631-1)[42]

---

35. ¶ I-9001; ¶ 12,314.
36. ¶ I-9003; ¶ 12,314.15.
37. ¶ I-9004; ¶s 12,314.09, 12,314.15.
38. ¶ I-9007 *et seq.*; ¶ 12,314.
39. ¶ I-9013; ¶s 12,314.02, 12,314.03.
40. ¶ N-6201; ¶ 12,314.
41. ¶ N-6213.
42. ¶ N-6208; ¶ 6314.01.

Footnote references beginning with letters are to paragraphs in RIA's Federal Tax Coordinator 2d and RIA's Analysis of Federal Taxes: Income. Footnote references beginning with numbers are to paragraphs in RIA's United States Tax Reporter.

¶ 2671 **Timber, coal or U.S. iron ore sold with a retained economic interest.**

A disposition of timber, coal or U.S. iron ore with a retained economic interest qualifies for Section 1231 treatment. (Code Sec. 631(b), (c), Code Sec. 1231(b)(2))

When the disposition qualifies for Section 1231 treatment, no cost depletion deduction (¶ 1995) is allowed. (Reg § 1.611-1(b)(2)) And, for dispositions of coal and iron ore, no percentage depletion deduction is allowed if the maximum tax rate for the year on net capital gain is less than the maximum rate for ordinary income. (Code Sec. 631(c); Reg § 1.611-1(b)(2))[43]

The timber, coal or U.S. iron ore must have been:

■ held by taxpayer for more than one year before disposition, and

■ disposed of under a contract in which the taxpayer retains an economic interest in the timber, etc. (Code Sec. 631(b), (c); Reg § 1.631-2(a)(1), Reg § 1.631-3(a)(1))[44]

¶ 2672 **Advance payments for timber, coal or domestic iron ore.**

Advance or minimum royalty payments or other amounts received or accrued before cutting of timber or before the mining of coal or iron ore (disposed of with a retained economic interest) are treated as realized from a sale subject to Section 1231 if the contract of disposal provides that they are to be applied as payment for timber cut later or coal or iron ore mined later. (Reg § 1.631-2(d)(1), Reg § 1.631-3(c)(1)) But if the right to cut or to mine ends or is abandoned before the timber, coal or iron ore which has been paid for is cut or mined, the advance payments for them are ordinary income. (Reg § 1.631-2(d)(2), Reg § 1.631-3(c)(2))

If the taxpayer elects to treat the date of payment as the date of disposal of timber, (Code Sec. 631(b); Reg § 1.631-2(b)(1)) Section 1231 applies only if the timber is held for the required period at the time of the advance payment. (Reg § 1.631-2(c)(2)) If the election is not made, the required holding period is measured as of the time it is cut. (Reg § 1.631-2(d)(1))[45] This election is made by attaching a specified statement to the return (filed not later than the due date, including extensions) for the year payment is received. (Reg § 1.631-2(c))[46]

¶ 2673 **Sale of Depreciable Property to Related Parties** ▮▮▮▮▮▮▮▮▮

Any recognized gain on the sale or exchange of depreciable property is ordinary income if it's made directly or indirectly between related persons.

¶ 2674 **Capital gain bar on sales or exchanges of depreciable property.**

In a direct or indirect sale or exchange of property between related persons, any gain recognized is treated as ordinary income if that property is, in the hands of the transferee, subject to the Code Sec. 167 allowance for depreciation. (Code Sec. 1239(a)) It also applies to property that would be subject to depreciation except that the buyer has elected amortization instead of depreciation, (Reg § 1.1239-1(a)) and to recovery property.[47]

No gain is recognized on transfers between spouses, (Code Sec. 1041(a))[48] see ¶ 2449.

Related persons are:

(1) a person and all entities that are controlled entities with respect to that person (see below); (Code Sec. 1239(b)(1))

(2) a taxpayer and any trust in which the taxpayer or his spouse is a beneficiary

---

43. ¶ N-7021; ¶ 6314.
44. ¶ N-7001.
45. ¶ N-7025 *et seq.*; ¶ 6314 *et seq.*

46. ¶ N-7026; ¶ 6314 *et seq.*
47. ¶ I-8702; ¶s 12,394, 12,394.01.

48. ¶ I-3601; ¶ 10,414.

Footnote references beginning with letters are to paragraphs in RIA's Federal Tax Coordinator 2d and RIA's Analysis of Federal Taxes: Income. Footnote references beginning with numbers are to paragraphs in RIA's United States Tax Reporter.

(unless the interest is a remote contingent interest); (Code Sec. 1239(b)(2))

(3) an employer and any person related to the employer (within the meaning of (1) and (2) above); (Code Sec. 1239(d)(1))

(4) a welfare benefit fund controlled directly or indirectly by anyone in (3), above. (Code Sec. 1239(d)(2))[49]

A controlled entity ((l), above) means, with respect to any person:

■ a corporation more than 50% of the value of the stock of which is owned (directly or indirectly) by or for the person, (Code Sec. 1239(c)(1)(A))

■ a partnership more than 50% of the capital interest or profits interest in which is owned (directly or indirectly) by or for the person, (Code Sec. 1239(c)(1)(B)) or

■ any entity that is a related person to the person under Code Sec. 267(b)(3) (controlled group of corporations), Code Sec. 267(b)(10) (certain related corporations and partnerships), Code Sec. 267(b)(11) (S corporations controlled by the same person) or Code Sec. 267(b)(12) (S corporations and C corporations controlled by the same person). (Code Sec. 1239(c)(1)(C))

And, under Code Sec. 267(c), there is attribution for stock owned by children, grandchildren, ancestors and siblings, as well as for the spouse. (Code Sec. 1239(c)(2))[50]

¶ 2675   MACRS/ACRS and Depreciation Recapture

Two special provisions restrict the possibility of converting ordinary income into capital gains by use of cost recovery or depreciation deductions.

One applies to personal property that is Section 1245 property; the other, to real property that is Section 1250 property. (Code Sec. 1245(a)(3), Code Sec. 1250(c))

Recapture applies only to the extent of gain. (Code Sec. 1245(a)(1), Code Sec. 1250(a))

Compute recapture on Form 4797.

recommendation: To avoid realizing recapture income, consider:

■ trading in the property for replacement property in a tax-free exchange;

■ using depreciable property to exhaustion, instead of selling it, if practical;

■ borrowing against the property instead of selling it (especially applicable to buildings).

¶ 2676   What is Section 1245 property?

Section 1245 property includes:

(1) all MACRS property other than residential real property (27.5-year class) and non-residential real property (39-year class; 31.5-year class before May 13, '93);

(2) all ACRS property other than 19-year, 18-year or 15-year real property: (a) that is residential rental property, (b) that is foreign-held realty, (c) with respect to which an optional (straight-line) cost recovery period was elected, or (d) that includes any one of certain categories of subsidized low-income rental housing;

(3) other property subject to the depreciation rules of Code Sec. 167 that is personal property, certain real property (not including buildings) and real property to the extent of certain amortization deductions taken.[1]

Section 1245 property includes property, other than a building or its structural components, used as an integral part of manufacturing, production or extraction, or for furnishing transportation, communication or other public utility services, and research or storage facilities used in connection with any of these activities. (Code Sec. 1245(a)(3);

49. ¶ I-8703 *et seq.*; ¶ 12,394.01.   50. ¶ I-8704; ¶ 12,394.01.   1. ¶ I-10101 *et seq.*; ¶ 12,454.01.

Footnote references beginning with letters are to paragraphs in RIA's Federal Tax Coordinator 2d and RIA's Analysis of Federal Taxes: Income. Footnote references beginning with numbers are to paragraphs in RIA's United States Tax Reporter.

Reg § 1.1245-3)[2]

¶ 2677 What is Section 1250 property?

All real property subject to depreciation that isn't Section 1245 property is Section 1250 property. (Code Sec. 1250(c)) Thus, Section 1250 property includes:

(1) MACRS residential real property (in the 27.5-year class) and nonresidential real property (in the 39-year class; 31.5-year class before May 13, '93).

(2) The four types of ACRS real property that are not Section 1245 property (see ¶ 2676).

(3) The following real property placed in service before '81: (a) depreciable intangible real property, such as a leasehold interest in land, (b) all depreciable buildings and their structural components, and (c) other depreciable real property excluded from the definition of Section 1245 property (¶ 2676). (Reg § 1.1250-1(e)(3))[3]

¶ 2678 Recapture rules for Section 1245 property.

A gain on the disposition of Section 1245 property is treated as ordinary income to the extent of depreciation allowed or allowable on the property. (Code Sec. 1245(a))[4] The amount of gain treated as ordinary income on the disposition is limited to the lower of:

(1) the recomputed basis of the property minus the adjusted basis of the property. (Code Sec. 1245(a)(1)(A)) Recomputed basis is the adjusted basis of the property increased by the recapturable depreciation and amortization deductions reflected in the adjusted basis; (Code Sec. 1245(a)(2)) or

(2) in the case of a sale, exchange or involuntary conversion, the amount realized minus the adjusted basis of the property; or in the case of any other disposition, the fair market value of the property minus the adjusted basis of the property. (Code Sec. 1245(a)(1)(B)[5]

¶ 2679 Recapture rules for Section 1250 property.

Part or all of the gain on the sale or other disposition of Section 1250 property may be treated as ordinary income. (Code Sec. 1250(a))[6] For Section 1250 property held more than one year, the amount of gain treated as ordinary income is the lower of:

(1) the "applicable percentage" of the portion of the "additional depreciation" (see below) attributable to periods after '75, or

(2) in the case of a sale, exchange or involuntary conversion, the excess of the amount realized over the adjusted basis; or in the case of any other disposition, the fair market value of the property over its adjusted basis. (Code Sec. 1250(a)(1))[7]

For property disposed of after '69, if (2) exceeds (1), above, then the "applicable percentage" of the lower of: (a) the portion of the additional depreciation attributable to periods after '69 and before '76; or (b) the excess of the amount determined under (2) over (1), above, is also treated as gain which is ordinary income. (Code Sec. 1250(a)(2))[8]

For property disposed of after '63, if (2) exceeds the sum of (1) and (a), above, then the "applicable percentage" of the lower of: (i) the portion of the additional depreciation attributable to periods before '70; or (ii) the excess of the amount determined under (2) over the sum of (1) and (a), above, is also treated as gain which is ordinary income. (Code Sec. 1250(a)(3))[9]

Additional depreciation is the excess of actual post-'69 depreciation deductions over the amount that would have resulted during the same period had the straight-line method been used for the entire period the property was held. But if the property is held for one

---

2. ¶ I-10101; ¶ 12,454.01.   4. ¶ I-10200 *et seq.*; ¶ 12,454.05.   6. ¶ I-10400 *et seq.*; ¶ 12,504.06.   8. ¶ I-10402;; ¶ 12,504.06.
3. ¶ I-10112 *et seq.*; ¶ 12,504.01.   5. ¶ I-10201 *et seq.*; ¶ 12,454.05.   7. ¶ I-10400 *et seq.*; ¶ 12,504.06.   9. ¶ I-10402;; ¶ 12,504.06.

Footnote references beginning with letters are to paragraphs in RIA's Federal Tax Coordinator 2d and RIA's Analysis of Federal Taxes: Income. Footnote references beginning with numbers are to paragraphs in RIA's United States Tax Reporter.

year or less, the additional depreciation is the entire amount of the post-'69 depreciation deductions. (Code Sec. 1250(b)(1))[10] For additional amounts for corporations, see ¶ 2680.

The applicable percentage differs depending upon various factors, including whether the property is nonresidential real property, residential real property or low income housing.[11]

¶ 2680 Additional 20% recapture on disposition of realty by corporations.

For sales or other dispositions (of both residential and nonresidential property), 20% of the amount by which the gain recapturable if Section 1245 rules applied exceeds the gain recaptured under Section 1250 is treated as ordinary income (to the extent of gain) to a corporation. (Code Sec. 291(a))[12] This rule applies to an S corporation only if it was formerly a C corporation and only for the first three tax years that it is an S corporation after a C tax year. (Code Sec. 1363(b))[13]

¶ 2681 Recapture of Sec. 179 expensed amounts.

The Section 179 expense election is treated as a MACRS or ACRS deduction for Section 1245 recapture purposes. (Code Sec. 1245(a)(2))[14]

¶ 2682 Treatment of basis reduction for investment credit.

In determining the recapturable amount, the reduction of basis for the investment credit is treated as a deduction allowed for depreciation. (Code Sec. 50(c)(4)(A))[15] However, this basis reduction is disregarded in computing straight-line depreciation for purposes of determining "additional depreciation" subject to recapture in the case of Section 1250 property. (Code Sec. 50(c)(4)(B))[16]

¶ 2683 MACRS, ACRS or depreciation recapture.

Events that may trigger MACRS, ACRS or depreciation recapture include:

■ Sale, including sale and leaseback, generally triggers recapture, but the mere creation of a security interest does not. (Reg § 1.1245-1(a)(3), Reg § 1.1250-1(a)(2)(i))

■ Trade-ins, exchanges and involuntary conversions. Section 1245 depreciation not recaptured except where gain is recognized or non-Section 1245 property is acquired. (Code Sec. 1245(b)(4); Reg § 1.1245-4(b)) Section 1250 depreciation not recaptured except where gain is recognized, stock is purchased to acquire control of a corporation owning replacement property, or non-Section 1250 property is acquired. (Code Sec. 1250(d)(4); Reg § 1.1250-3(d))

■ Conversion to personal use doesn't trigger recapture, but later sale will.

■ Lease termination or disposition where depreciation was taken by lessee (or sublessee). Generally recaptured. (Reg § 1.1245-2(a)(3)(i), (d)(2))

■ Incorporation of a business. Not recaptured except to the extent that gain is otherwise recognized. (Code Sec. 1245(b)(3), Code Sec. 1250(d)(3); Reg § 1.1245-4(c)(4), Ex (1), Reg § 1.1250-3(c))

■ Corporate distributions in kind including liquidating distributions. Generally recaptured except in tax-free complete liquidation of a subsidiary with carryover basis (recaptured on disposition by parent-transferee). (Code Sec. 1245(b)(3), Code Sec. 1250(d)(3); Reg § 1.1245-4(c), Reg § 1.1250-3(c))

■ Corporate split-ups and reorganizations. Generally not recaptured except to extent that gain is otherwise recognized on transfer of the property. (Code Sec. 1245(b)(3), Code

---

10. ¶ I-10403; ¶ 12,504.06.
11. ¶ I-10417 *et seq.*;
     ¶s 12,504.04, 12,504.06.
12. ¶ I-10422 *et seq.*; ¶ 2914.
13. ¶ D-1555; ¶s 2914, 13,634
     et seq.
14. ¶ L-9936; ¶ 12,454.
15. ¶ I-10204; ¶ 12,454 *et seq.*
16. ¶ I-10507; ¶ 12,504 *et seq.*

Footnote references beginning with letters are to paragraphs in RIA's Federal Tax Coordinator 2d and RIA's Analysis of Federal Taxes: Income. Footnote references beginning with numbers are to paragraphs in RIA's United States Tax Reporter.

Sec. 1250(d)(3); Reg § 1.1245-4(c)(4), Ex (1), Reg § 1.1250-3(c))

■ **S corporations.** Not recaptured on election or termination of status.

■ **Partnerships.** Recaptured on sale of partnership interest. Not recaptured on contribution to a partnership but may be if property is subject to a liability. (Code Sec. 1245(a), (b)(6), Code Sec. 1250(a), (d)(6); Reg § 1.1245-1(e), (f), Reg § 1.1250-1(f), Reg § 1.1250-3(f))

■ **Gifts.** Not recaptured, but recapturable depreciation carried over to donee. (Code Sec. 1245(b)(1), Code Sec. 1250(d)(1); Reg § 1.1245-2(a)(4), Reg § 1.1250-3(a))

■ **Death of owner.** Neither recaptured nor carried over. (Code Sec. 1245(b)(2), Code Sec. 1250(d)(2); Reg § 1.1245-4(b), Reg § 1.1250-3(b))[17]

■ Gain realized by an estate or trust from distribution of depreciable property in satisfaction of a fixed dollar bequest or from a distribution in kind where gain or loss is realized by election is recapturable. (Reg § 1.1245-4(b), Reg § 1.1250-3(b))[18]

¶ 2684 Special recapture rules for listed property.

A reduction of business use of listed property (¶ 1959 *et seq.*) from more-than-50% to 50% or less triggers recapture of excess depreciation previously taken. (Code Sec. 280F(b)(2)(A)) "Excess depreciation" means depreciation allowable for years before the first year in which the property was not predominantly used in a qualified business use, over the amount of depreciation which would have been allowable for those years if the property had not been predominantly used in a qualified business use for the year it was acquired and there had been no Section 179 expense election for the property. (Code Sec. 280F(b)(2)(B))[19]

---

17. ¶s I-10002, I-10301 *et seq.*;   18. ¶ C-7151; ¶s 12,454.03,   19. ¶ L-10032; ¶ 280F4.
¶ 12,454.03.   12,504.01.

Footnote references beginning with letters are to paragraphs in RIA's Federal Tax Coordinator 2d and RIA's Analysis of Federal Taxes: Income. Footnote references beginning with numbers are to paragraphs in RIA's United States Tax Reporter.

Chapter 10   Installment and Deferred Payment Sales

¶ *2700* Installment Sales and Other Deferred Payment Sales ▬▬▬▬

Under the installment method, the taxpayer reports gain on a sale as payments are received, instead of reporting all the gain in the year of sale. A nondealer who sells real or personal property must use the installment method to report gain (but not loss) if at least one payment is to be received after the close of the tax year in which the sale occurs, unless the seller elects out of the installment method. The installment method can't be used to report recapture income, gain on the sale of publicly traded property, or gain on the sale of depreciable property to a related person. A dealer, with limited exceptions, may not report income on the installment method. If the selling price is over $150,000, the seller may have to pay interest on the tax that is deferred when the installment method is used and must treat the proceeds of a loan secured by an installment obligation as a payment of the obligation.

🅡/*observation:* A sale qualifies as an installment sale even if only one payment is to be received, if that payment is made after the close of the year of sale.

For unstated interest on installment (and other deferred payment) sales, see ¶ 1311 *et seq.*

For limits on the use of the installment method in alternative minimum tax computations, see ¶ 3207.

¶ *2701* Who uses the installment method.

The installment method must be used to report income from sales or other dispositions by nondealers of real or personal property unless the taxpayer elects (¶ 2704) otherwise.[1]

Dealers in property, real or personal, may not use the installment method (Code Sec. 453(b)(2))[2] except on:

(1) dispositions of any property used in the trade or business of farming; (Code Sec. 453(l)(2)(A)) and

(2) dispositions in the ordinary course of a taxpayer's trade or business of the following but only if interest is paid on the tax deferred when the installment method is used: (Code Sec. 453(l)(2)(B))

. . . a timeshare right to use, or a timeshare right to an ownership interest in, residential real property for not more than six weeks per year, or a right to use specified campgrounds for recreational purposes (timeshare rights or ownership interests held by the spouse, children, grandchildren or parents of an individual are treated as held by the individual), or

. . . any residential lots, but only if the taxpayer (or any related person) is not to make any improvements with respect to the lots.[3]

For nondealers' dispositions of real property for more than $150,000, see ¶ 2709.

¶ *2702* How to report income from installment sales—Form 6252.

Use Form 6252 to report income from casual sales of real or personal property.[4]

¶ *2703* Situations where the installment method is not available.

The installment method can't be used to report sales of stock or securities traded on an established securities market. (Code Sec. 453(k)(2))[5] Nor does it apply to sales at a loss.[6]

If the asset sold is recovery or depreciable property giving rise to depreciation recapture

---

1. ¶ G-6000; ¶ 4534.01.   3. ¶ G-6600 *et seq.*; ¶ 4534.01.   5. ¶ G-6016 *et seq.*; ¶ 4534.01.   6. ¶ G-6011; ¶ 4534.15.
2. ¶ G-6601; ¶ 4534.01.   4. ¶ G-6051.

Footnote references beginning with letters are to paragraphs in RIA's Federal Tax Coordinator 2d and RIA's Analysis of Federal Taxes: Income. Footnote references beginning with numbers are to paragraphs in RIA's United States Tax Reporter.

(ordinary income), the amount of the gain that is recapturable under Code Secs. 1245 or 1250 (including the gain attributable to the Code Sec. 179 expense election (¶ 1956 *et seq.*)), is fully taxed as ordinary income in the year of sale. Only the gain, if any, that isn't recapture income is taken into account under the installment method. (Code Sec. 453(i))[7]

In the case of an installment sale of depreciable property between related persons, the installment method of treating the gain is not available. All payments to be received except for certain contingent payments are considered received in the tax year in which the sale occurs. (Code Sec. 453(g)(1))[8]

A "related person" for this purpose means a related person within the meaning of the Code Sec. 1239(b) rules barring capital gain treatment on sales of depreciable property between related persons (see ¶ 2448 *et seq.*) and the Code Sec. 707(b)(1) rules, (Code Sec. 701(b)(1))[9] which disallow losses on sales between certain commonly-controlled partnerships and on sales between a partnership and a controlling person, see ¶ 3732 *et seq.*.

¶ 2704 Electing out of the installment method.

An election not to have the installment method apply to a particular sale must be made on or before the due date (including extensions) for filing the income tax return for the year in which the sale occurs. (Code Sec. 453(d)(2))[10]

The election may be made by reporting an amount realized equal to the selling price (including the full face amount of any installment obligation) on the tax return filed for the tax year in which the installment sale occurs. (Reg § 15A.453-1(d)(3)(i)) An election out made after the due date is only rarely permitted, when IRS concludes the taxpayer had good cause for the failure to timely elect. (Reg § 15A.453-1(d)(3)(ii))[11] An election out may be revoked only with IRS consent. (Code Sec. 453(d)(3))[12]

¶ 2705 Computing income under the installment method.

Under the installment method, the amount of any payment that is income to the taxpayer is that portion of the installment payments received in the year that the gross profit realized or to be realized bears to the total contract price. This portion is known as the "gross profit ratio." (Code Sec. 453(c); Reg § 15A.453-1(b)(2)(i))[13]

Gross profit means the selling price less the adjusted basis of the property. (Reg § 15A.453-1(b)(2)(v))[14]

The seller's adjusted basis is increased by selling expenses, (Reg § 15A.453-1(b)(2)(v)) recaptured ACRS or depreciation deductions and recaptured Code Sec. 179 expenses.[15]

The "total contract price" is the selling price, reduced by any debt on the property that the buyer assumes (or takes subject to) but only to the extent of the seller's basis in the property. (Reg § 15A.453-1(b)(2)(iii))[16]

The "selling price" is the gross selling price without reduction to reflect any existing mortgage or other encumbrance on the property (whether assumed or taken subject to by the buyer) and without reduction to reflect any selling expenses. Neither interest (whether stated or unstated) nor original issue discount is considered to be a part of the selling price. (Reg § 15A.453-1(b)(2)(ii))

illustration: Taxpayer sells personal-use property at a contract price of $8,000, and there is a gross profit of $2,000. The gross profit ratio is 25% ($2,000 ÷ $8,000). Therefore, 25% of each payment collected on the sale (including the down payment) is gain and must be included in gross income for the tax year in which collected. The ratio remains constant for all installment payments received on the sale.

---

7. ¶ G-6097 *et seq.*; ¶ 4534.05.   10. ¶ G-6351; ¶ 4534.08.   13. ¶ G-6011; ¶ 4534.21.   15. ¶ G-6054.
8. ¶ G-6201; ¶ 4534.17.   11. ¶ G-6359; ¶ 4534.08.   14. ¶ G-6053; ¶ 4534.21.   16. ¶ G-6053; ¶ 4534.21.
9. ¶ G-6208; ¶ 4534.17.   12. ¶ G-6362; ¶ 4534.08.

Footnote references beginning with letters are to paragraphs in RIA's Federal Tax Coordinator 2d and RIA's Analysis of Federal Taxes: Income. Footnote references beginning with numbers are to paragraphs in RIA's United States Tax Reporter.

¶ 2706 What are payments?

Payments include: (a) amounts actually received by the seller,[17] (b) the buyer's payments of the seller's selling expenses,[18] and (c) the amount by which the seller's mortgage exceeds the seller's basis. (Reg § 15A.453-1(b)(2)(iii), Reg § 1.453-4(c))[19]

¶ 2707 Sale, exchange, or satisfaction of installment obligations.

For installment obligations satisfied at face value, gain or loss is computed under the general rules (¶ 2705) for computing income on the installment method.[20]

If an installment obligation is satisfied at other than face value or is sold or exchanged, gain or loss is the difference between the basis of the obligation and the amount realized. If it is distributed, transmitted, or disposed of otherwise than by sale or exchange, gain or loss is the difference between its basis and its fair market value, (Code Sec. 453B(a))[21] except that if it's distributed in a liquidation to which Code Sec. 337(a) applies (¶ 3576) no gain is recognized. (Code Sec. 453B(d))[22]

The basis of an obligation is the excess of its face value over the amount equal to the income that would be returnable if the obligation were fully satisfied. (Code Sec. 453B(b))[23]

✔ *observation:* Since this excess always equals the unrecovered cost, the "basis" is the unrecovered cost.

¶ 2708 Sale to related person who then resells.

If an installment sale (first disposition) is made to a related person (see below) who then makes a second disposition (sale, exchange, gift or cancellation of the installment note), within two years of the first disposition, and before all payments are made on the first disposition, the amount the related person (the buyer in the first disposition) realizes as a result of the second disposition is treated as being received by the original seller at the time of the second disposition. (Code Sec. 453(e)(1), (2)) The amount treated as received by the person making the first disposition because of the second disposition can't be more than:

■ the lesser of the total amount realized on any second disposition of the property occurring before the close of the tax year, or the total contract price for the first disposition; minus

■ the sum of the aggregate amount of payments received with respect to the first disposition before the close of the tax year in which the second disposition occurs, and the aggregate amount treated as received with respect to the first disposition because of earlier dispositions of installment obligations by related persons. (Code Sec. 453(e)(3))[24]

For this purpose, "related person" means:

■ a person whose stock would be attributed to the initial seller under Code Sec. 318(a) (¶ 3533) other than under the option attribution rules; (Code Sec. 453(f)(1)) or

■ a person who bears a relationship to the initial seller under Code Sec. 267(b) (¶ 2450) for purposes of the rules disallowing the deduction of losses on sales between related persons. (Code Sec. 453(f)(1))[25]

✔ *illustration:* F sells his home to his son, S, on the installment basis. If S immediately sells it to a third party for a single payment at the same price (i.e., so S has no gain), then the F-S family unit has received the full purchase price, but could, without the resale rule, continue to spread the gain (F's gain) over the years S is paying off his

---

17. ¶ G-6011; ¶ 4534.22.
18. ¶ G-6151.
19. ¶ G-6060; ¶ 4534.27.

20. ¶ G-6053; ¶ 4534.22.
21. ¶ G-6454 *et seq.*; ¶ 453B4.05.

22. ¶ G-6488; ¶ 453B4.11.
23. ¶ G-6456; ¶ 453B4.05.

24. ¶ G-6401; ¶ 4534.18.
25. ¶ G-6416; ¶ 4534.18.

Footnote references beginning with letters are to paragraphs in RIA's Federal Tax Coordinator 2d and RIA's Analysis of Federal Taxes: Income. Footnote references beginning with numbers are to paragraphs in RIA's United States Tax Reporter.

installment obligation.

There are exceptions for involuntary conversions, deaths, and corporations' reacquisitions of their own stock, (Code Sec. 453(e)(6)) and for situations where IRS is satisfied that tax avoidance is not involved. (Code Sec. 453(e)(7))[26]

The two-year period stops running when puts, options, or short sales, etc., are involved. (Code Sec. 453(e)(3))[27] In the case of marketable securities, there is no two-year time limit. (Code Sec. 453(e)(2)(A))[28]

¶ 2709 Sales of certain property for more than $150,000.

The following rules apply to an installment sale of "any" property (except personal use property or farm property, and the sale by dealers of timeshares or residential lots) where the selling price is over $150,000: (Code Sec. 453A)[29]

(1) If an installment obligation from the sale plus all other installment obligations that arose from dispositions during the tax year and are still outstanding at the close of the tax year total over $5,000,000, the seller must pay interest on the deferred tax attributable to those installment obligations. Interest is based on the underpayment rate (¶ 4862) and is payable as additional tax. (Include interest on the total tax line—Line 53 of Form 1040 for individuals—and write "Section 453A(c) interest" to the left of the amount.)

(2) If an installment obligation from the sale becomes security for any indebtedness, the net proceeds of the indebtedness is treated as a payment of the obligation as of the later of the time the indebtedness becomes secured or the proceeds of the indebtedness are received by the seller.

¶ 2710 Deferred payment (including "open") sales not reported on the installment method.

A taxpayer who elects not to report a deferred-payment sale on the installment method recognizes gain on the sale according to the taxpayer's method of accounting. The receipt of an installment obligation is treated as a receipt of property equal to the fair market value (FMV) of the obligation. (Reg § 15A.453-1(d)(2)(i))[30] For contingent payment obligations, the FMV of the obligation may be ascertained from, and in no event is considered to be less than, the FMV of the property sold (less any other consideration received in the sale). Only in those "rare and extraordinary" cases where the FMV can't reasonably be ascertained will taxpayer be entitled to assert that the transaction is "open." (Reg § 15A.453-1(d)(2)(iii))

26. ¶ G-6411; ¶ 4534.18.   28. ¶ G-6408; ¶ 4534.18.   30. ¶s G-6351, G-6550 et seq.;
27. ¶ G-6408; ¶ 4534.18.   29. ¶ G-6300 et seq.; ¶ 453A4.   ¶ 4534.45 et seq.

Footnote references beginning with letters are to paragraphs in RIA's Federal Tax Coordinator 2d and RIA's Analysis of Federal Taxes: Income. Footnote references beginning with numbers are to paragraphs in RIA's United States Tax Reporter.

Chapter 11 Tax Accounting—Inventories

¶ 2800 Accounting Periods

The law requires each taxpayer to compute taxable income and file a return on the basis of an accounting period called a tax year. An S corporation or personal service corporation generally has to use a calendar year as its tax year unless it specially elects to use a fiscal year. A partnership generally has to use a "majority interest tax year" unless it makes the fiscal year election.

¶ 2801 Tax year.

Taxpayers must compute their taxable income on the basis of their tax year. (Code Sec. 441(a)) "Tax year" is defined as the taxpayer's annual accounting period (the annual period on the basis of which a taxpayer regularly computes his income in keeping his books), (Code Sec. 441(c)) but only if that is the calendar year or a fiscal year. (Code Sec. 441(b)(1))[1]

The calendar year is the 12-month period ending on Dec. 31. (Code Sec. 441(d)) A taxpayer must use the calendar year, if the taxpayer keeps no books, or has no annual accounting period, or has an annual accounting period that does not qualify as a fiscal year, (Code Sec. 441(b)(2), (g)) or if the taxpayer has not established a fiscal year. (Reg § 1.441-1T(g)(3))[2]

A fiscal year is any 12-month period ending on the last day of a month other than December, or the 52-53 week tax year described at ¶ 2802. (Code Sec. 441(e))[3]

If a return is properly made for a period of less than 12 months, the tax year is the short period for which the return is made (a "short tax year," see ¶ 2804). (Code Sec. 441(b)(3))[4]

¶ 2802 Tax year of 52-53 weeks.

A 52-53 week tax year varies from 52 to 53 weeks and always ends on the same day of the week. The day chosen must be either the day of the week that last occurs in a calendar month or the day that falls nearest to the end of the calendar month (in which case the last day of the tax year may fall in the next month). (Code Sec. 441(f)(1))[5]

Wherever the applicability of any provision of the Code, or filing date, is expressed in terms of tax years beginning, including, or ending with reference to a specified date that is the first or last day of the month, the actual opening and closing dates of 52-53 week years are disregarded. The year is considered to begin on the first day of the calendar month beginning nearest to the first day of that tax year, and to end on the last day of the calendar month ending nearest to the last day of that tax year. (Code Sec. 441(f)(2)(A))[6]

¶ 2803 Establishing a tax year.

A new taxpayer must adopt its first tax year on or before the due date, excluding extensions, for filing a return for that tax year. IRS permission is not required to adopt either a calendar or a fiscal tax year. (Reg § 1.441-1T(b)(2))[7]

If taxpayer's "annual accounting period" (¶ 2801), as established by the basis on which taxpayer keeps his books, is the calendar year or a fiscal year, his tax year is that annual accounting period. year. (Code Sec. 441(b)(1), (c)) Otherwise, the taxpayer must use the calendar year as his tax year. (Code Sec. 441(b)(2), (g))[8]

A new taxpayer using a 52-53 week tax year (¶ 2802) must file a statement (specified in the regs) with the return for his first 52-53 week tax year. (Reg § 1.441-2T(c)(1))[9]

---

1. ¶ G-1001 *et seq.*; ¶ 4414.   4. ¶ G-1001; ¶ 4414.   6. ¶ G-1103; ¶ 4414.   8. ¶ G-1051; ¶ 4414.
2. ¶s G-1001, G-1003; ¶ 4414.   5. ¶ G-1101; ¶ 4414.   7. ¶ G-1057; ¶ 4414.   9. ¶s G-1054, G-1753; ¶ 4414.
3. ¶ G-1004; ¶ 4414.

Footnote references beginning with letters are to paragraphs in RIA's Federal Tax Coordinator 2d and RIA's Analysis of Federal Taxes: Income. Footnote references beginning with numbers are to paragraphs in RIA's United States Tax Reporter.

¶ 2804 Short tax years.

Taxpayers must use a tax "year" of less than 12 months if:

■ taxpayer is not in existence for what would otherwise be his full tax year; (Code Sec. 443(a)(2))[10]

■ taxpayer properly changes his annual accounting period. (Code Sec. 443(a)(1))[11]

But if the short year arises because of the taxpayer's death, his last return may be filed and the tax paid as if he had lived to the end of his last tax year. (Reg § 1.443-1(a)(2))[12]

For filing requirements for short years, see ¶ s 4713, 4721.

¶ 2805 Computing tax for a short year.

If the short year results from a change of the taxpayer's annual accounting year, the short period's taxable income must be annualized. (Code Sec. 443(b))

Under the general method of annualization, the gross income for the short period (less allowable deductions for the short period and, for individuals, the ratable amount of personal exemptions) is multiplied by 12 (months) and divided by the number of months in the short period. The result is the annualized taxable income on which the tentative tax is computed. The tax due is arrived at by multiplying the tentative tax by the number of months in the short period and dividing by 12 (months). (Code Sec. 443(b)(1); Reg § 1.443-1(b)(1)(i))[13] Special annualization rules apply to the alternative minimum tax. (Code Sec. 443(d))[14]

There are exceptions to the annualization requirements for self-employment tax, accumulated earnings tax, personal holding company tax, undistributed foreign personal holding company income and income of regulated investment companies.[15]

The net operating loss (NOL) deduction can reduce actual income for the short period before computing short period income on an annual basis. Therefore, if the NOL deduction wipes out short period actual income there would be nothing to annualize and therefore no short period taxable income.[16]

The income is *not* annualized if the short year is caused by the taxpayer not being in existence for a full tax year. (Code Sec. 443(b)) In this case, tax is computed as if the short period were a full year, and individuals need not prorate their personal exemptions.[17]

¶ 2806 Optional look-back method of computing tax for the short period.

The annualizing method at ¶ 2805 may create a tax hardship for taxpayers who have a disproportionately large amount of taxable income in the short period. To avoid this, taxpayers may use an optional method that computes the tax for the full 12 months starting at the beginning of the short year and prorates the tax according to the amount of income earned in the short period. (Code Sec. 443(b)(2))

The optional method is available only on a claim for credit or refund, filed no later than the due date (including extensions) of taxpayer's return for the first tax year that ends on or after the day that is 12 months after the first day of the short period. (Reg § 1.443-1(b)(2)(v)(a))[18]

¶ 2807 Short period on change to or from 52-53 week year.

If a taxpayer changes to or from a 52-53 week year, income for the short period must be annualized, with this exception: if the short period is 359 days or more, it is treated as a full tax year, while if it is six days or less it is added to the following tax year.[19]

10. ¶ G-1153; ¶ 4434.   13. ¶ G-1166; ¶ 4434.   16. ¶ G-1166; ¶ 4434.   18. ¶ G-1170 *et seq.*; ¶ 4434.
11. ¶ G-1155; ¶ 4434.   14. ¶ A-8139; ¶ 4434.   17. ¶ G-1162; ¶ 4434.   19. ¶ G-1108; ¶ 4434.
12. ¶ G-1154; ¶ 4434.   15. ¶ G-1163.

Footnote references beginning with letters are to paragraphs in RIA's Federal Tax Coordinator 2d and RIA's Analysis of Federal Taxes: Income. Footnote references beginning with numbers are to paragraphs in RIA's United States Tax Reporter.

¶ 2808 Tax year of sole proprietorship.

A business that is conducted as a sole proprietorship must use the same tax year as the proprietor. Thus, a calendar year employee who later operates as a sole proprietorship must use the calendar year for the proprietorship unless he gets IRS consent to use a fiscal year.[20]

¶ 2809 Tax years of trusts and estates.

Trusts must use the calendar year, except for trusts exempt from tax under Code Sec. 501(a), wholly charitable trusts described in Code Sec. 4947(a)(1) (Code Sec. 645)[21] and grantor trusts.[22]

Estates may adopt either a calendar year or a fiscal year.[23]

¶ 2810 Tax years of foreign sales corporations and DISCs.

Foreign Sales Corporations (FSCs) and Domestic International Sales Corporations (DISCs) must use the tax year of the shareholder (or group of shareholders with the same 12-month tax year) with the highest percentage of voting power. (Code Sec. 441(h)(1))[24]

¶ 2811 Tax year of S corporation.

An S corporation (unless it makes the election at ¶ 2814) must have a "permitted year," i.e., a calendar year or any other accounting year for which it shows a business purpose satisfactory to IRS. (Code Sec. 1378)[25]

¶ 2812 Tax year of personal service corporation.

The tax year of a personal service corporation (PSC) must be a calendar year unless the corporation makes the election at ¶ 2814 or can satisfy IRS that there is a business purpose for having a different tax year. (Code Sec. 441(i)(1))[26]

A PSC is, as defined under the rules permitting IRS to reallocate PSC income and deductions (¶ 2862), any corporation whose principal activity is the performance of personal services that are substantially performed by employee-owners. But for this purpose, PSC does not include S corporations, and the term "owner-employee" includes all employees with *any* stock ownership in the corporation. In determining ownership, attribution from a corporation (under Code Sec. 318(a)(2)(C)) is applied if *any* stock is owned by the shareholder in that corporation. (Code Sec. 441(i)(2))[27] Certain independent contractors who own stock in the corporation and perform personal services for or on behalf of the corporation are treated as employees. (Reg § 1.441-4T(h)(2))[28]

The performance of personal services is considered the corporation's principal activity if the corporation's compensation cost for a testing period for activities that are considered the performance of personal services exceeds 50% of its total compensation cost for the period. (Reg § 1.441-4T(f)) The testing period is the preceding tax year (or, for a corporation's first tax year, the period beginning the first day of the first tax year and ending the last day of that tax year or, if earlier, the last day of the calendar year in which that tax year began). (Reg § 1.441-4T(d)(2)) Personal services are substantially performed by employee-owners if during the testing period more than 20% of the corporation's compensation cost attributable to the performance of personal services is attributable to personal services performed by employee-owners. (Reg § 1.441-4T(g))[29]

---

20. ¶ G-1061; ¶ 4414.	23. ¶ G-1450; ¶ 4414.	26. ¶ G-1300; ¶ 4414.	28. ¶ G-1306; ¶ 4414.
21. ¶ G-1400; ¶ 6454.	24. ¶ O-1726; ¶ 4414.	27. ¶ G-1302; ¶ 4414.	29. ¶ G-1303; ¶ 4414.
22. ¶ G-1401; ¶ 6454.	25. ¶ G-1250; ¶ 13,784.		

Footnote references beginning with letters are to paragraphs in RIA's Federal Tax Coordinator 2d and RIA's Analysis of Federal Taxes: Income. Footnote references beginning with numbers are to paragraphs in RIA's United States Tax Reporter.

¶ 2813 **Tax year of partnership.**

Unless the partnership makes the election at ¶ 2814, or can satisfy IRS that there is a business purpose for a different tax year, (Code Sec. 706(b)(1)(C))[30] a partnership must adopt:

(1) the "majority interest tax year" (Code Sec. 706(b)(1)(B)(i))—the tax year of one or more of the partners having an aggregate interest in partnership profits and capital of more than 50% on each testing day (the first day of the partnership's tax year as otherwise determined, or days prescribed by IRS); (Code Sec. 706(b)(4)(A))

(2) the tax year of all its principal (5%-or-more) partners, if there is no majority interest tax year; (Code Sec. 706(b)(1)(B)(ii))

(3) the "least-aggregate-deferral" year, if there's no majority interest tax year and the principal partners don't have the same tax year; (Reg § 1.706-1T(a)(1);

(4) the calendar year, if no tax year can be established under (1), (2) or (3).(Code Sec. 706(b)(1)(B)(iii))[31]

A partnership that is required to change to a majority-interest tax year isn't required to change to another tax year for either of the two tax years following the year of change. (Code Sec. 706(b)(4)(B))[32]

A partnership tax year ends as dictated by the accounting period selected or required, except that it closes earlier: (1) with respect to a partner who sells out or whose interest is liquidated, (Code Sec. 706(c)) and (2) with respect to all its partners on the date the partnership terminates for tax purposes. (Reg § 1.708-1(b)(1)(iii))[33]

¶ 2814 **Election of tax year other than required year by S corporations, personal service corporations and partnerships—Section 444 election.**

An S corporation, personal service corporation (PSC, see ¶ 2812), or partnership may elect (on Form 8716) to have a tax year other than the required tax year, (Code Sec. 444(a)) but only if the deferral period (number of months between beginning of elected fiscal tax year and following Dec. 31) for the tax year elected is not longer than three months. (Code Sec. 444(b)(1))[34]

A partnership or S corporation that elects has to make a "required payment" (report on Form 8752) that approximates the tax the partners or S corporation shareholders would have paid on short-period income if the election had not been made. (Code Sec. 7519)[35]

A PSC that elects a fiscal tax year but does not make required minimum distributions to its employee-owners before the end of the calendar year must postpone part or all of its corresponding deduction to its next fiscal tax year. (Code Sec. 280H)[36]

¶ 2815 **How to change accounting periods—Form 1128.**

If a taxpayer wants to change his annual accounting period, he must get prior IRS approval unless the change is one of those listed at ¶ 2816. (Reg § 1.442-1(a)(1))[37]

IRS will approve a request for a change in tax years only if the taxpayer establishes a substantial business purpose for the change (Reg § 1.442-1(b)(1))[38] and only if the taxpayer agrees to any terms, conditions or adjustments required to effect the change, including any that IRS feels are necessary to avoid a substantial distortion of the taxpayer's income as a result of the change. (Reg § 1.442-1(b)(1))[39]

To request IRS approval, file Form 1128 on or before the fifteenth day of the second month following the close of the short period for which a return would be required to effect the change. (Reg § 1.442-1(b)(1))[40]

---

30. ¶ G-1200 *et seq.*; ¶ 7064.01.
31. ¶ G-1200 *et seq.*
32. ¶ G-1201.
33. ¶ G-1225; ¶ 7064.02.
34. ¶ G-1500 *et seq.*
35. ¶s G-1500, G-1550; ¶ 75,194.
36. ¶ G-1600; ¶ 280H4.
37. ¶ G-1800; ¶ 4424.
38. ¶ G-1803 *et seq.*; ¶ 4424.
39. ¶ G-1812 *et seq.*; ¶ 4424.
40. ¶ G-1815; ¶ 4424.

Footnote references beginning with letters are to paragraphs in RIA's Federal Tax Coordinator 2d and RIA's Analysis of Federal Taxes: Income. Footnote references beginning with numbers are to paragraphs in RIA's United States Tax Reporter.

IRS won't approve a request made within ten tax years after a previous change.[41]

¶2816 "No prior approval needed" changes of accounting period.

A taxpayer may change his annual accounting period without IRS approval, or with "automatic" IRS approval, where the taxpayer:

■ changes to a 52-53 week tax year that ends with reference to the same calendar month as the month ending his previous tax year; (Reg § 1.441-2(c)(2))[42]

■ is an individual who marries a person with a different tax year; (Reg § 1.442-1(e)(1))[43]

■ is an individual with a fiscal year tax year who changes to a calendar year tax year;[44]

■ is a partnership changing its tax year to meet the requirements described at ¶ 2813;[45]

■ is a C corporation that meets certain requirements;[46]

■ is an S corporation changing its tax year to meet the requirements described at ¶ 2811;[47]

■ is a tax-exempt organization;[48]

■ is a personal service corporation changing its tax year to meet the requirements described at ¶ 2812, or to a "natural business year."[49]

Notwithstanding these rules, any taxpayer who is a partner in a partnership needs prior IRS approval to change his tax year. (Reg § 1.442-1(b)(2)(ii), Reg § 1.706-1(b)(2))[50]

¶2817 Accounting Methods

Methods of tax accounting are the methods and systems by which taxpayers determine the amount of their income, gains, losses, deductions and credits, as well as the time when those items must be realized and recognized. Various methods of tax accounting are permissible, but each must be used consistently, and each must clearly reflect income.

¶2818 Establishing a method of accounting.

Because a taxpayer's book accounting method determines his accounting method, a taxpayer establishes a tax accounting method by setting up books, keeping accounts and preparing income tax returns under any of the permissible methods. The method first used in accounting for business income and deductions in connection with each trade or business, as evidenced in the taxpayer's income tax return in which the income or deductions are first reported, must be followed consistently after that. (Reg § 1.446-1(d)(1))[1]

A taxpayer whose only income is wages does not have to keep formal books in order to establish an accounting method, but may establish a method of accounting by means of the originals or copies of tax returns or other records. (Reg § 1.446-1(b)(2))[2]

A new taxpayer may adopt a method of accounting in connection with filing the first income tax return. An existing taxpayer entering into a business that is separate and distinct from any trade or business that the taxpayer previously carried on (¶ 2819) may adopt a method of accounting for the separate and distinct business in connection with filing the first tax return reporting income from the business. (Reg § 1.446-1(e)(1))[3]

¶2819 Multiple methods of accounting.

A taxpayer may use one method of accounting to keep his personal books and use another method of accounting to keep the books for his trade or business. But the two

---

41. ¶ G-1802; ¶ 4424.
42. ¶ G-1752; ¶ 4414.
43. ¶ G-1759; ¶ 4424.
44. ¶ G-1754; ¶ 4424.

45. ¶ G-1761; ¶ 4424.
46. ¶ G-1763 *et seq.*; ¶ 4424.
47. ¶ G-1779; ¶ 4424.

48. ¶ G-1785 *et seq.*; ¶ 4424.
49. ¶ G-1780; ¶ 4424.
50. ¶ G-1760; ¶s 4424, 7064.

1. ¶ G-2051.
2. ¶ G-2051.
3. ¶ G-2051; ¶ 4464.01.

Footnote references beginning with letters are to paragraphs in RIA's Federal Tax Coordinator 2d and RIA's Analysis of Federal Taxes: Income. Footnote references beginning with numbers are to paragraphs in RIA's United States Tax Reporter.

must be strictly separated. (Reg § 1.446-1(c)(1)(iv)(b))

A taxpayer who is engaged in more than one trade or business may use a different method of accounting for each trade or business. (Code Sec. 446(d)) This rule applies only if the trades or businesses are truly separate and distinct, and if the method of accounting adopted for each one clearly reflects its income. (Reg § 1.446-1(d)(1))

No business is treated as separate and distinct unless a complete and separate set of books and records is kept for that trade or business. (Reg § 1.446-1(d)(2))

Use of different accounting methods is not permitted if there is a creation or shifting of profits or losses between the taxpayer's various trades or businesses, for example, by means of inventory adjustments, sales, purchases or expenses, and this results in a distortion of the taxpayer's income. (Reg § 1.446-1(d)(3))[4]

¶ 2820 Hybrid methods.

Taxpayers may use any combination of the cash, accrual, and specifically permitted special methods of accounting if the combination clearly reflects income and is consistently used. (Reg § 1.446-1(c)(1)(iv))[5]

¶ 2821 Limits on choice of accounting methods.

The cash method is mandatory where the taxpayer's records reflect only cash transactions, and there are no inventories.[6]

The accrual method is mandatory for purchases and sales (unless IRS consents to a change) where inventories must be used. (Reg § 1.446-1(c)(2)(i)) Inventories must be used where the production, purchase or sale of merchandise is an income-producing factor. (Reg § 1.446-1(a)(4)(i))[7]

C corporations (other than qualified personal service corporations), and partnerships with a C corporation (other than a qualified personal service corporation) as a partner, with average annual gross receipts of $5,000,000 or more for the three prior tax years (or the period of its existence, if less) cannot use the cash method of accounting. Tax shelters are barred from use of the cash method in any event. (Code Sec. 448(a))[8] Farming businesses (except tax shelters) are not subject to this restriction, (Code Sec. 448(b)(1)) but for special farm accounting rules, see ¶ 4501 *et seq.*[9]

For purposes of these restrictions, an accounting method that records some but not all items on the cash method—that is, a hybrid method that incorporates elements of the cash method—is treated as the cash method of accounting. (Reg § 1.448-1T(a)(4))[10]

Tax-exempt trusts are treated as C corporations with respect to unrelated trade or business income. (Code Sec. 448(d)(6))[11]

¶ 2822 The Cash Method of Accounting ◼◼◼◼◼◼◼◼◼◼◼

Under the cash method, gross income includes cash or property actually or constructively received during the tax year. Deductions are generally taken in the year cash or property is actually paid or transferred. It doesn't matter when the income was earned, or when the expense was incurred.

¶ 2823 Cash basis accounting.

Under the cash basis method of accounting, income is reported when cash or property is actually or constructively received (¶ 2825) and deductions are taken in the year cash or property is paid or transferred.[12]

---

4. ¶ G-2052; ¶ 4464.01.
5. ¶ G-2003; ¶ 4464.07.
6. ¶ G-2053; ¶ 4464.05.

7. ¶ G-5000; ¶ 4464.07.
8. ¶ G-2054; ¶ 4484.
9. ¶ G-2057.

10. ¶ G-2054; ¶ 4484.
11. ¶s G-2059, G-2064; ¶ 4484.

12. ¶ G-2350 *et seq.*; ¶s 4464.05, 4514.003.

Footnote references beginning with letters are to paragraphs in RIA's Federal Tax Coordinator 2d and RIA's Analysis of Federal Taxes: Income. Footnote references beginning with numbers are to paragraphs in RIA's United States Tax Reporter.

For income a taxpayer receives under a claim of right, see ¶ 1204.

For restrictions on use of the cash method by certain taxpayers, see ¶ 2821.

¶ 2824 When is a check income?

A check issued by a solvent payor is income when received by a cash basis payee, unless there is a restriction on the payee's right to cash the check.[13]

Receipt of a check by an agent is considered receipt by the principal.[14]

¶ 2825 Constructive receipt of income.

Income not actually received is constructively received and reportable if it is within the taxpayer's control. Cash basis taxpayers must report money unconditionally subject to their demand as income, even if they have not received it.[15]

There is no constructive receipt if the amount is available only on the surrender of a valuable right,[16] or if there are substantial limitations on the right to receive it. (Reg § 1.451-2(a))[17]

¶ 2826 Cash method deductions.

Cash method taxpayers generally take deductions (if otherwise allowable) in the year the items are paid. (Reg § 1.461-1(a)(1))[18] There is no constructive payment doctrine.[19]

Where an expense (e.g., rent or an insurance premium) relates to a period covering more than 12 months, IRS and most courts agree that the deduction must be spread over the period to which the expense applies.[20] For deduction of prepaid taxes, see ¶ 1754.

A check is payment when delivered, not when cashed, if it's honored when it's presented for payment.[21]

¶ 2827 The Accrual Method of Accounting

Under the accrual method, income is reported in the tax year in which the right to the income becomes fixed and the amount of the income can be determined with reasonable accuracy. Deductions are claimed in the period in which all events have occurred that determine the fact of the liability and the amount of the liability can be determined with reasonable accuracy.

¶ 2828 Accrual basis accounting.

Income accrues and must be reported in the year all events have occurred that determine taxpayer's right to receive it, and the amount can be determined with reasonable accuracy, (Reg § 1.451-1(a)) even if it is received in a later year. That is, the right to receive the income must not be contingent on a future event; the amount must be reasonably susceptible of accurate estimate; and there must be a reasonable expectation that it will be received in due course.[22]

Accrual basis taxpayers need not accrue income from the performance of services that, based on their experience, will not be collected. But this rule doesn't apply if the debtor owes interest on the uncollected income or if there is a penalty for late payment. (Code Sec. 448(d)(5))[23]

¶ 2829 Contingent rights to income.

Where the right to income is contingent on a future event, an accrual basis taxpayer doesn't have to recognize the income until that event occurs.[24]

---

13. ¶ G-2355; ¶s 4514.003, 4514.004.
14. ¶ G-2359.
15. ¶ G-2364; ¶ 4514.003.
16. ¶ G-2366; ¶ 4514.006.
17. ¶ G-2365; ¶ 4514.006.
18. ¶ G-2376 et seq.
19. ¶ G-2383.
20. ¶s L-3526, L-6616 et seq.; ¶ 4609.
21. ¶ G-2378; ¶ 4614.02.
22. ¶ G-2451; ¶ 4514.012.
23. ¶ G-2481; ¶ 4484.
24. ¶s G-2464, G-2465; ¶s 4514.011, 4514.012, 4514.013.

Footnote references beginning with letters are to paragraphs in RIA's Federal Tax Coordinator 2d and RIA's Analysis of Federal Taxes: Income. Footnote references beginning with numbers are to paragraphs in RIA's United States Tax Reporter.

Where litigation is involved and liability to the taxpayer is admitted, the income must be recognized if the taxpayer can accurately estimate the amount of recovery.[25] But if liability isn't admitted, the income accrues when the litigation is concluded or settlement reached, whichever is earlier.[26]

An offer in compromise is income when the dispute is settled or the offer is unconditionally accepted.[27]

¶ 2830 Dealers' reserves.

Dealers commonly discount customers' notes with a finance company that retains a portion of the amount due the dealer as security against possible default by the customer. A dealer that uses the accrual method must include the full amount of the discount price, undiminished by the portion retained by the finance company—the "dealer reserve," in income as soon as the notes are sold to the finance company. This is so even if the dealer assigned the notes to the finance company "without recourse."[28]

¶ 2831 Credit balance write-offs.

Accumulated credit balances (accounts payable) that an accrual method taxpayer deducted but never actually paid must be reported as income when, as a practical matter, liability to pay them stops and the credit is transferred to income or surplus.[29]

¶ 2832 Advance payments received for services.

Advance payments received for services to be performed must be reported by an accrual basis taxpayer in the year received[30] with this exception: taxpayer can elect (file Form 3115, see ¶ 2843) to defer advance payments over the period services are performed if they are received under a written or other agreement requiring all the services to be performed by the end of the next year. Deferral isn't allowed if any of the services may be performed beyond the next year or if the agreement doesn't specify when they must be performed.[31]

¶ 2833 Advance payments received for merchandise or construction.

Advance merchandise payments and advance payments under long-term construction contracts are reported by accrual method taxpayers when the income is properly accruable under their method of accounting.[32] But that method must be used for all tax reporting and for credit purposes. (Reg § 1.451-5(b))[33]

An accrual basis taxpayer or a taxpayer using one of the long-term contract methods (¶ 2850 *et seq.*) can defer reporting an advance payment received under an agreement for the sale or other disposition in a future tax year of goods held primarily for sale to customers, or for the building, installing, constructing or manufacturing of items, where the work isn't completed in the year the advance payment is received. (Reg § 1.451-5(a)(1)) Deferral also applies to advance payments for services to be performed under the agreement as an integral part of the above activities, and for gift certificates. (Reg § 1.451-5(a)(2))[34]

Amounts due and payable under the contract are treated as advance payments received. (Reg § 1.451-5(a))[35]

There is a limited deferral for certain inventorial goods. Where a payment for goods is received several years before they are delivered, taxpayer can postpone reporting the advance payments for one year past the year total advance payments first equal or exceed

25. ¶ G-2486; ¶s 4514.021, 4514.055.
26. ¶ G-2486; ¶ 4514.055.
27. ¶s G-2486, G-2487; ¶ 4514.058.
28. ¶ G-2493; ¶ 4514.017.
29. ¶ G-2466.
30. ¶ G-2501; ¶s 4514.011, 4514.190, 4514.197.
31. ¶ G-2508; ¶ 4514.191.
32. ¶ G-2511 *et seq.*; ¶s 4514.121 *et seq.*, 4514.191.
33. ¶ G-2514.
34. ¶s G-2511, G-2513.
35. ¶ G-2518; ¶ 4514.121 *et seq.*

Footnote references beginning with letters are to paragraphs in RIA's Federal Tax Coordinator 2d and RIA's Analysis of Federal Taxes: Income. Footnote references beginning with numbers are to paragraphs in RIA's United States Tax Reporter.

the anticipated cost of the goods. Thereafter, all prepayments received are reported and actual or expected costs deducted. (Reg § 1.451-5(c))[36]

A taxpayer who defers reporting advance payments for merchandise must attach to its tax return for each year an annual information schedule. (Reg § 1.451-5(d))[37]

Use Form 3115 (¶ 2843) to get IRS consent to switch to deferral. (Reg § 1.451-5(e))[38]

¶ 2834 Advance payments or security deposits.

Amounts received as security are not taxable until used. A deposit that guarantees the customer's payment of amounts owed to the creditor is not a deposit but an advance payment includible in income (unless deferred under rules at ¶s 2832, 2833), while a deposit that secures someone's property is a true security deposit and not an advance payment.[39]

¶ 2835 Timing of expense deductions.

Expenses are deductible under the accrual method in the period in which all events (¶ 2836) have occurred that determine the fact of the liability, and the amount of the liability can be determined with reasonable accuracy. (Reg § 1.461-1(a)(2)) A reasonable estimate of the liability must be accrued for the tax year in which it was incurred. If there is a difference between the estimate and the amount finally determined, the difference is to be added to or deducted from income when the final determination is made.[40]

Where the accrual doesn't involve a current expense, but results in the creation of an asset having a useful life extending substantially beyond the end of the tax year, the deduction must be taken as depreciation, amortization or similar deduction (¶ 1900 *et seq.*). (Reg § 1.461-1(a)(2))[41]

An accrual basis taxpayer is entitled to a deduction for a properly accrued expense, regardless of whether he has actually paid that expense.[42]

Where the taxpayer has borrowed on a *nonrecourse* basis (at-risk rules), see ¶ 1791 *et seq.*

For treatment of bonuses paid, see ¶ 1356.

¶ 2836 Economic performance.

Accrual basis taxpayers won't be considered to have met the all events test (¶ 2835) until economic performance has occurred. (Code Sec. 461(h))[43] Economic performance occurs when the property or service to which the accrual relates is actually provided or used. (Code Sec. 461(h)(2)(A))[44]

Certain "recurring" expenditures may be treated as incurred in the year the all events test is otherwise met, even though economic performance doesn't occur until the following year. This applies if:

■ economic performance occurs on or before the date taxpayer files a timely (including extensions) return for the tax year the expense is accrued or, if shorter, 8½ months after the close of that year; and

■ the item is recurring and taxpayer consistently treats items of that kind as incurred in the tax year the all-events test (not including the economic performance test) is met; and

■ the item is either not a material item or its accrual in the year before economic performance results in a more proper match against income than would accruing it in the year of economic performance. (Code Sec. 461(h)(3)(A); Reg § 1.461-5(b))[45]

A taxpayer is permitted to adopt the recurring item exception as part of its method of

---

36. ¶ G-2515.
37. ¶ G-2516.
38. ¶ G-2517.

39. ¶ J-1410 *et seq.*; ¶ 4514.193.
40. ¶ G-2550 *et seq.*; ¶ 4609
41. ¶ G-2550; ¶ 4609.

42. ¶ G-2550; ¶ 4609.
43. ¶ G-2577; ¶ 4614.15.

44. ¶ G-2578; ¶ 4614.15.
45. ¶ G-2611; ¶ 4614.15.

Footnote references beginning with letters are to paragraphs in RIA's Federal Tax Coordinator 2d and RIA's Analysis of Federal Taxes: Income. Footnote references beginning with numbers are to paragraphs in RIA's United States Tax Reporter.

accounting for any type of income for the first tax year in which that type of item is incurred. (Reg § 1.461-5(d)(1))

A tax shelter may not use the above "recurring item" exception. (Code Sec. 461(i)(1); Reg § 1.461-5(c))[46]

¶ 2837 Accruing contested liability.

An otherwise deductible expense is not allowable, as long as the taxpayer denies and contests the liability, until the contest is resolved by agreement or final court decision.[47] However, a deduction is allowed in the year of transfer (payment) where:

(1) the taxpayer contests an asserted liability;

(2) the taxpayer transfers money or other property to satisfy the liability;

(3) the contest with respect to the asserted liability exists after the time of the transfer; and

(4) but for the contest, a deduction would be allowed for the tax year of the transfer (or an earlier year). (Code Sec. 461(f)) The contest need not involve court proceedings.[48]

¶ 2838 Accrual basis taxpayer's payments for tort liabilities.

If the liability of a taxpayer requires a payment to another person that arises out of a tort, "economic performance" (¶ 2836) occurs as the payments are made. (Code Sec. 461(h)(2)(C))[49] A qualified payment to a court-ordered or designated settlement fund which extinguishes a taxpayer's tort liability is economic performance with respect to the liability as the payment is made. The present or future claims against the taxpayer must arise out of personal injury, death or property damage. (Code Sec. 468B)[50]

¶ 2839 Accrual basis taxpayer's payables to related cash basis taxpayer.

An accrual basis taxpayer can deduct expenses and interest owed to a related cash basis person when payment is made and the amount involved is includible in the gross income of the cash basis payee. (Code Sec. 267(a)(2)) In other words, an accrual basis taxpayer is treated as being on the cash method for purposes of deducting amounts owed to a related cash basis person.[1]

The rule applies in general to all deductible expenses (even if the expense is not covered under Code Sec. 162, Code Sec. 163 or Code Sec. 212) if the timing of the deduction depends on the taxpayer's method of accounting or on the making of an election to expense the item. But it doesn't apply to defer the deduction of otherwise deductible original issue discount or below-market loan interest. (Reg § 1.267(a)-2T(b), Q&A-2) Nor does it apply to defer the deduction of otherwise deductible cost recovery depreciation, or amortization, except as to amounts owed to a related person for interest, rent or for the performance or nonperformance of services (which amount the payor capitalized or treated as a deferred expense). (Reg § 1.267(a)-2T(b), Q&A-4)[2]

¶ 2840 Changes of Accounting Methods

Usually, taxpayers may change their methods of accounting only with IRS consent, and only on IRS-imposed terms, conditions and adjustments. However, automatic consent is available in certain circumstances where IRS-prescribed procedures are followed.

---

46. ¶ G-2408; ¶ 4614.15.
47. ¶ G-2568; ¶s 4614.56, 4614.59.
48. ¶ G-2570; ¶s 4614.56, 4614.59.

49. ¶ G-2706; ¶s 4614.56, 4614.59.

50. ¶ G-2759 *et seq.*; ¶ 468B4.
1. ¶ G-2650 *et seq.*

2. ¶ G-2651 *et seq.*; ¶ 2674.

Footnote references beginning with letters are to paragraphs in RIA's Federal Tax Coordinator 2d and RIA's Analysis of Federal Taxes: Income. Footnote references beginning with numbers are to paragraphs in RIA's United States Tax Reporter.

¶ 2841   IRS permission to change method of accounting.

Generally, once a taxpayer has adopted an accounting method, he must continue to use that method until: (1) IRS requires him to change the method, or (2) he requests, and gets, IRS permission to change. (Code Sec. 446(e); Reg § 1.446-1(e)(2)) This applies even if the taxpayer has been using an incorrect method of accounting, or a method that doesn't clearly reflect income.[3]

Taxpayers may not, without IRS consent, retroactively change from an erroneous to a permissible method of accounting by filing amended returns, even if the period for amending the return for the first year in which the erroneous method was used has not expired.[4]

¶ 2842   What is a change in accounting method?

A change in accounting method is a change of the taxpayer's overall method of accounting or a change in the treatment of a material item of income or expense. Changes in overall methods of accounting include changes:

■ from the cash to accrual basis, or vice-versa;

■ from one basis of inventory valuation to another;

■ to or from a specialized basis, e.g., the crop basis used by farmers. (Reg § 1.446-1(e)(2)(ii))[5]

A material item is any item that involves the proper time for the inclusion of the item in income or the taking of a deduction. It doesn't include corrections of mathematical or posting errors, or errors in computing tax liability. (Reg § 1.446-1(e)(2)(ii))[6]

¶ 2843   Applying for a change in accounting method—Form 3115.

An application for change must be filed with IRS on the latest version of Form 3115 within 180 days[7] (nine months on a showing of good cause)[8] after the beginning of the tax year for which the change is desired. The taxpayer must include all information required by the form, and state that he agrees to the conditions set by IRS and will take into account any required adjustments (¶ 2844)[9]

¶ 2844   Adjustments required on change in accounting method—Code Sec. 481(a) adjustments.

In any year in which taxpayer computes taxable income using a different accounting method from the method used in the preceding year, adjustments (Code Sec. 481(a) adjustments) must be made to prevent items of income or expense from being duplicated or entirely omitted. The adjustments must take into account inventories, accounts receivable, accounts payable, and any other items necessary. (Code Sec. 481(a); Reg § 1.481-1(b))[10]

Code Sec. 481(a) adjustments can be "positive" (resulting in an increase in taxable income), or "negative" (resulting in a decrease). (Reg § 1.481-1(c))[11]

¶ 2845   When Code Sec. 481(a) adjustments are taken into account.

Except as noted below or where the Code or another federal statute provides otherwise, the Code Sec. 481(a) adjustment required as a result of an accounting method change (¶ 2844) must be taken into account in the year of change—i.e., the first tax year in which the taxpayer's method of accounting is different from that used in the previous tax year.

---

3. ¶ G-2201; ¶ 4464.
4. ¶ G-2201; ¶s 4464.21, 4464.22.
5. ¶ G-2103; ¶ 4464.21.
6. ¶ G-2104; ¶ 4464.24.
7. ¶ G-2224; ¶ 4464.22.
8. ¶ G-2226; ¶ 4464.22.
9. ¶ G-2220 *et seq.*; ¶ 4464.22.
10. ¶ G-2250 *et seq.*; ¶ 4814.
11. ¶ G-2264; ¶ 4814.

Footnote references beginning with letters are to paragraphs in RIA's Federal Tax Coordinator 2d and RIA's Analysis of Federal Taxes: Income. Footnote references beginning with numbers are to paragraphs in RIA's United States Tax Reporter.

(Code Sec. 481(a); Reg § 1.481-1(a)(1)) This applies to both positive and negative adjustments. (Reg § 1.481-1(c))[12]

Instead of taking the Code Sec. 481(a) adjustment into account in the year of change, taxpayer may take it into account over an "appropriate" period agreed to (in writing) by taxpayer and IRS. (Code Sec. 481(c); Reg § 1.481-5(b)) The adjustment must be taken into account ratably over the tax years included in the adjustment inclusion period (¶ 2846).[13]

¶ 2846 Adjustment inclusion periods prescribed by IRS.

For accounting method changes generally, for taxpayers that IRS hasn't contacted for examination, the appropriate adjustment inclusion period is six years (three years or less, if taxpayer was using an impermissible accounting method). A shorter period may apply under these three exceptions:

(1) If the net adjustment is less than $25,000, taxpayer may elect to use a one-year adjustment period.

(2) If 90% or more of the net amount of an adjustment is attributable to the tax year immediately preceding the year of change, the total net adjustment must be taken into account in computing taxable income for the year of change.

(3) If (1) and (2) don't apply and the present method has been used for less than the otherwise required adjustment period, taxpayer must take the net adjustment into account ratably over the number of tax years the present method has been used.[14]

The terms and conditions for the adjustment inclusion period are less favorable for taxpayers that have been contacted for or are under examination.[15]

Situations with a different "adjustment inclusion period" are explained at the place in this Handbook where the item subject to the accounting rule is discussed.

¶ 2847 Relief for high-impact adjustments.

Where Code Sec. 481(a) adjustments increase taxable income of the change-over year by more than $3,000, the taxpayer can compute his tax for that year using whichever of these two methods produces the lower tax:

(1) *Three-year allocation* —The tax that would have resulted if one-third of the increase had been included in taxable income in each of the two preceding years and in the change-over year. (Code Sec. 481(b)(1); Reg § 1.481-2(a))

(2) *Allocation of specific years under new method of accounting*—Where the taxpayer establishes his taxable income under the new method of accounting for one or more tax years consecutively preceding the year of change (in which the old method was actually used), the tax is reduced to the amount that would have been paid if:

(a) the tax for the preceding years was figured under the new method, and

(b) the then remaining adjustments were allocated to the change-over year. (Code Sec. 481(b)(2); Reg § 1.481-2(b))[16]

In making the above computations, the entire amount of the Code Sec. 481(a) adjustment required as a result of the accounting method change is taken into account. (Reg § 1.481-1(d))[17]

¶ 2848 Reserves for Expenses

Taxpayers often maintain accounting reserves for various future liabilities. Generally, no deduction is allowed for additions to these reserves.

---

12. ¶ G-2268; ¶ 4814. 14. ¶ G-2275.2 *et seq.*; ¶ 4814. 16. ¶ G-2301; ¶ 4814. 17. ¶ G-2301; ¶ 4814.
13. ¶ G-2269; ¶ 4814. 15. ¶ G-2275.2 *et seq.*; ¶ 4814.

Footnote references beginning with letters are to paragraphs in RIA's Federal Tax Coordinator 2d and RIA's Analysis of Federal Taxes: Income. Footnote references beginning with numbers are to paragraphs in RIA's United States Tax Reporter.

¶ 2849 Reserves for estimated expenses and contingent liabilities.

Deduction or exclusion from income isn't allowed for additions to reserves for estimated expenses or contingent liabilities, even if reserves are required by state law or by contract, unless the reserve is expressly authorized by the Code (e.g., depreciation),[18] or is a reserve for trading stamps or coupons (Reg § 1.451-4(a))[19] or for container deposits. However, the use of the reserve method for container deposits applies only when the containers are not sold, but merely leased or loaned. Thus, no reserve is permitted for refundable deposits on empty beverage containers under states' environmental and conservation laws. The deposits are includible in income when received and refunds are deductible when paid.[20]

¶ 2850 Long-Term Contracts

Long-term contracts entered into after July 10, '89, must be accounted for by the percentage-of-completion method.

For how to account for long-term contracts for alternative minimum tax purposes, see ¶ 3207.

¶ 2851 Special accounting methods for long-term contracts.

Taxpayers must account for long-term contracts (except for certain home and other real property construction contracts, see ¶ 2852) under the percentage-of-completion method (¶ 2854), subject to an election to use a modified percentage-of-completion method ("10% method," see 2855). (Code Sec. 460)[21]

A long-term contract is any contract for the manufacture, building, installation or construction of property, if not completed in the tax year in which entered into. (Code Sec. 460(f)(1)) Whether the taxpayer reasonably expected that the contract would be completed within the tax year is irrelevant.[22]

But a manufacturing contract is not long-term unless it involves manufacture of a unique item (of a type not normally included in inventory), or an item that normally requires more than 12 months to complete.[23] (Code Sec. 460(f)(2))

For contracts made before July 11, '89, the percentage-of-completion/capitalized cost method (¶ 2856) is available. (Code Sec. 460)[24]

¶ 2852 Exception for small construction contracts.

Home construction contracts (specially defined) are not limited to the percentage-of-completion method, or the percentage-of-completion/capitalized cost method. Nor are any other real property construction contracts if originally estimated to be completed within two years of the contract commencement date, and if the taxpayer's average annual gross receipts for the three previous tax years do not exceed $10 million (including receipts of certain commonly controlled or related businesses). But home construction contracts that don't meet these requirements must be accounted for under the uniform capitalization rules (¶ 1661). (Code Sec. 460(e))[25]

¶ 2853 Allocation of costs to long-term contracts.

All costs that directly benefit, or are incurred by reason of, a long-term contract (including research and experimental costs) must be allocated to the contract in the same manner as costs were allocated to extended-period long-term contracts entered into before

---

18. ¶s G-2703, G-2707;   20. ¶ G-2710.   22. ¶ G-3103.   24. ¶ G-3237; ¶ 4514.125.
¶ 4514.017.   21. ¶s G-3100, G-3228;   23. ¶s G-3102, G-3106;   25. ¶ G-3208; ¶ 4604.
19. ¶ G-2712; ¶s 4514.161,   ¶ 4514.125.   ¶ 4514.124.
4514.163.

Footnote references beginning with letters are to paragraphs in RIA's Federal Tax Coordinator 2d and RIA's Analysis of Federal Taxes: Income. Footnote references beginning with numbers are to paragraphs in RIA's United States Tax Reporter.

Mar. 1, '86, under Code Sec. 451 and Reg § 1.451-3(d) except that past service pension costs must be allocated to the contract. Also, in the case of a cost-plus contract or a federal long-term contract or subcontract, any other costs (e.g., general and administrative expenses) must be allocated to the contract if identified by the taxpayer (or a related person) as being attributable to it under the contract, or under federal, state, or local law or regulation. (Code Sec. 460(c)(1), (2))[26]

Interest costs are allocated to long-term contracts in a way that is similar to the way interest costs are allocated under the uniform capitalization rules (Code Sec. 263A(f)) (¶ 1661) that apply to property produced by a taxpayer. (Code Sec. 460(c)(3))[27]

The allocation rules don't apply to any expenses for unsuccessful bids and proposals; marketing, selling, and advertising expenses; or independent research and development expenses (IR&D). IR&D expenses don't include expenses directly attributable to a long-term contract in existence when the expenses are incurred, or expenses under an agreement to perform research and development. (Code Sec. 460(c)(4), (5))[28]

In addition, home construction contracts and real property construction contracts not subject to long-term contract accounting restrictions (¶ 2851) are exempt from the above cost allocation rules other than the interest allocation rules. (Code Sec. 460(e)) Those contracts, however, are subject to regulations applicable to pre-Mar. 1, '86 nonextended-period long-term contracts.[29]

¶ 2854 Percentage-of-completion method.

Under this method, a long-term contract's percentage of completion must be determined by comparing costs allocated to the contract and incurred (generally under the "all-events" test (¶ 2835), regardless of the taxpayer's overall method of accounting) before the close of the tax year, with estimated total contract costs. (Code Sec. 460(b)(1)(A)) Events that occur after the end of the tax year that were not reasonably subject to estimate as of the last day of the tax year aren't taken into account.[30]

Gross income recognized in a particular year under the percentage-of-completion method equals total revenue expected from the contract times the cumulative percentage of the contract completed as of the end of the tax year, less the total cumulative amount of contract revenue required to be included in gross income in all preceding tax years. (This can result in a deductible loss for a year if total estimated contract costs increase.)[31]

IRS has provided an elective "simplified cost-to-cost method" for determining the percentage of completion of a contract for this purpose. Under the simplified cost-to-cost method, only the following expected costs (rather than all expected costs) are used to determine the percentage of completion: direct material and direct labor costs; and depreciation, amortization and cost recovery allowances on equipment and facilities directly used to construct or produce the subject matter of the long-term contract.[32]

When the contract is completed (or, with respect to amounts received or accrued after completion, when those amounts are received or accrued), the taxpayer must either pay or is entitled to receive interest computed under the look-back method discussed at ¶ 2857. (Code Sec. 460(b)(1)(B))[33]

¶ 2855 Modified percentage-of-completion method—"the 10% method."

For purposes of the percentage-of-completion method, a taxpayer may elect not to recognize income under the contract and not to take into account any costs allocable to the long-term contract for any tax year if, as of the end of the tax year, less than 10% of the estimated total contract costs have been incurred. (Code Sec. 460(b)(5); Reg § 1.460-6(c)(2)(v)(A))[34]

---

26. ¶ G-3142 *et seq.*
27. ¶ G-3149.
28. ¶ G-3153; ¶ 4604.
29. ¶ G-3208 *et seq.*; ¶ 4604.
30. ¶s G-3122, G-3124.
31. ¶ G-3125 *et seq.*
32. ¶ G-3137.
33. ¶ G-3155; ¶ 4604.
34. ¶ G-3228 *et seq.*; ¶ 4604.

Footnote references beginning with letters are to paragraphs in RIA's Federal Tax Coordinator 2d and RIA's Analysis of Federal Taxes: Income. Footnote references beginning with numbers are to paragraphs in RIA's United States Tax Reporter.

¶ 2856 Percentage-of-completion/capitalized cost method for pre-July 11, '89 contracts.

Under this method, for contracts entered into before July 11, '89, the taxpayer must account for 90% (70% for contracts entered into before June 21, '88; 40% for contracts entered into before Oct. 14, '87) of the long-term contract items under the percentage-of-completion method described in ¶ 2854, including the look-back provisions (¶ 2857). The remaining 10% (30% for pre-June 21, '88 contracts; 60% for pre-Oct. 14, '87 contracts) of the contract items must be taken into account under the taxpayer's normal accounting method.[35]

Residential construction contracts that aren't "home construction contracts" use a 70%/30% split. (Code Sec. 460(e)(5))[36]

¶ 2857 Look-back method for payment (or receipt) of interest on underpaid (overpaid) tax.

In the tax year a long-term contract (with certain exceptions, see below) is completed, the taxpayer must compare the amount of taxes paid in previous years under the percentage method (including the 90% (70% or 40%) method used in the percentage-of-completion/capitalized cost method, see ¶ 2856) with the tax that would have been owed if actual, rather than anticipated, costs and contract price had been used to compute gross income. Interest at the overpayment rate (¶ 4851), compounded daily, is owed by or payable to the taxpayer (use Form 8697) if there is, respectively, an underpayment or overpayment for any tax year. (Code Sec. 460(b)(2), (3))[37] For application to pass-through entities, see ¶ 2858.

The look-back method doesn't apply to any contract whose gross price (as of completion) doesn't exceed the lesser of $1,000,000 or 1% of taxpayer's average annual gross receipts for the three tax years preceding the tax year the contract was completed if the contract is completed within two years of its commencement date. (Code Sec. 460(b)(3)(B))[38] Nor does it apply to home construction contracts or other contracts described at ¶ 2852. (Reg § 1.460-6(b)(2)(i))[39]

¶ 2858 Simplified look-back marginal-impact method for pass-through entities.

For partnerships, S corporations and trusts (which are not 50% or more held by five or fewer persons), a simplified look-back marginal-impact method is applied at the entity level where substantially all the income from the contract is U.S.-source. The amount of taxes treated as overpaid or underpaid under a contract in any year is determined by multiplying the amount of contract income over- or under-reported for the year by the top marginal tax rate applicable for the year. (Code Sec. 460(b)(4))[40] Individuals, C corporations and owners of closely held pass-through entities may elect to use this method. Also, widely held pass-through entities may apply it for foreign contracts. (Reg § 1.460-6(d)(4)(ii)(A))[41]

¶ 2859 Reconstruction of Income by IRS ▄▄▄▄▄▄

Where taxpayer's records are inadequate, IRS can reconstruct taxpayer's income by whatever method will in its opinion most clearly reflect income.

The methods most often used are:

The net worth method. Here, IRS attempts to establish an opening net worth or total value of the taxpayer's assets at the beginning of a given year. It then proves increases in the taxpayer's net worth for each later year during the period under examination and calculates the difference between the adjusted net values of the taxpayer's assets at the

---

35. ¶ G-3237; ¶ 4604.   37. ¶ G-3160 *et seq.*; ¶ 4604.   39. ¶ G-3158; ¶ 4604.   41. ¶ G-3200; ¶ 4604.
36. ¶ G-3223; ¶ 4604.   38. ¶ G-3157; ¶ 4604.   40. ¶ G-3194 *et seq.*; ¶ 4604.

Footnote references beginning with letters are to paragraphs in RIA's Federal Tax Coordinator 2d and RIA's Analysis of Federal Taxes: Income. Footnote references beginning with numbers are to paragraphs in RIA's United States Tax Reporter.

beginning and end of each of the years involved. The taxpayer's nondeductible expenditures, including living expenses, are added to these increases. If the resulting figure for any year is substantially greater than the taxable income reported by the taxpayer for that year, IRS treats the excess as unreported taxable income.[42]

Bank deposit method. The bank deposit method assumes that all deposits represent income unless the taxpayer can show otherwise.[43]

Percentage markup method. IRS determines taxpayer's net income by applying certain percentages, such as gross profit to sales, or net income to gross income, or net income to sales, derived from other taxpayers in the same kind of business.[44]

¶ 2860 IRS's Section 482 Power to Reallocate Income and Deductions—Transfer Pricing Rules

IRS is authorized (under Code Sec. 482) to distribute, apportion or allocate gross income, deductions, credits or allowances among two or more organizations, trades or businesses that are owned or controlled by the same interests in order to prevent tax evasion or to reflect the true taxable income of any of those entities. This prevents the shifting of income and deductions among related taxpayers to minimize taxes.

IRS can reallocate income regardless of the entities' *motives* for shifting it, and can reallocate even if the shifting was unintentional. (Reg § 1.482-1(c))[45]

¶ 2861 What entities are affected.

Any business entities controlled by the same interests are subject to IRS's Code Sec. 482 allocations, including sole proprietorships, partnerships, trusts, estates or corporations. (Reg § 1.482-1(a)(1))[46] Any kind of actual control, direct or indirect, will suffice. (Reg § 1.482-1(a)(3))[47] However, no allocations will be made in the case of certain small taxpayers who elect a specified safe harbor. (Reg § 1.482-1T(f)) For special rules for personal service corporations, see ¶ 2862.

¶ 2862 Personal service corporation.

If a personal service corporation (i.e., whose principal activity is the performance of personal services, substantially all of which are performed by employee-owners for one other corporation, partnership, or entity (including related parties)) is availed of principally to avoid federal income tax by securing for any employee-owner significant tax benefits that would not otherwise be available, then IRS may allocate all income, as well as those deductions, credits, exclusions, etc., as may be allowable, between or among the corporation and employee-owners involved. (Code Sec. 269A(a))[48]

An "employee-owner" is any employee who owns, on any day during the tax year, more than 10% of the outstanding stock of the corporation. The Code Sec. 318 attribution rules apply for purposes of this 10% ownership test, except that for purposes of applying the Code Sec. 318(a)(2)(C) rules for attribution from a corporation to a shareholder, attribution is triggered by 5% rather than 50% stock ownership. (Code Sec. 269A(b)(2))[49]

¶ 2863 Previously Reported Income Repayments

Taxpayers who must repay amounts they previously reported as income may deduct the repayments in the year made. If the amount repaid exceeds $3,000,

---

42. ¶ G-2911; ¶s 4464.41, 4464.42.
43. ¶ G-2940; ¶s 4464.41, 4464.67.
44. ¶ G-2947; ¶s 4464.41, 4464.76.
45. ¶ G-4014; ¶ 4824.
46. ¶ G-4000; ¶ 4824.
47. ¶ G-4009; ¶ 4824.
48. ¶ G-4751; ¶ 2694.
49. ¶ G-4756; ¶ 2694.

Footnote references beginning with letters are to paragraphs in RIA's Federal Tax Coordinator 2d and RIA's Analysis of Federal Taxes: Income. Footnote references beginning with numbers are to paragraphs in RIA's United States Tax Reporter.

the taxpayer may recover the tax paid on that amount in the year he reported it, if that gives him the greater tax benefit.

¶ 2864 Deducting the repayment of previously reported income.

If a taxpayer must repay previously reported income, he is entitled to a deduction for the amount repaid.[50]

For relief where the repayment exceeds $3,000, see ¶ 2865.

For a cash basis taxpayer, the year of the deduction, and accordingly the year that the special compution might be available, is the year the income previously reported was actually repaid. Where the taxpayer reported the income under the constructive receipt theory, the year of deduction is the year he was required to relinquish his claim to the income. (Reg § 1.1341-1(e))[1]

For an accrual basis taxpayer, the year of deduction is the year liability for repayment becomes fixed. Where the taxpayer received the income reported, the year of deduction is the year it is finally established that the taxpayer had no unrestricted right to it. (Reg § 1.1341-1(e))[2]

¶ 2865 Repayments that exceed $3,000.

If the amount of the deduction allowed for a tax year (¶ 2864) with respect to an item reported as income in an earlier tax year is more than $3,000, and:

■ that item was included in gross income in the earlier year because it appeared that the taxpayer had an unrestricted right to it then; and

■ the deduction is allowed because it was shown after the close of the earlier year that taxpayer did *not* have an unrestricted right to all or part of that item, then the tax for the year in which the deduction is allowed is the lesser of:

(1) the tax for that year computed with the deduction,

(2) the tax for that year computed *without the deduction,* minus the decrease in tax for the earlier year that would result solely from excluding the deductible repayment. (Code Sec. 1341(a))

This relief for repayments exceeding $3,000 doesn't apply:

■ where repayment is required because of a liability that arose later, as distinguished from absence of an unrestricted right to the income previously reported;[3]

■ where an item was originally included in gross income by reason of the sale or other disposition of stock-in-trade, or other property includible in inventory if on hand at close of the earlier tax year, or property held primarily for sale to customers in the ordinary course of business—i.e., it does not apply to sales returns and allowances and similar items; (Code Sec. 1341(b)(2); Reg § 1.1341-1(f))

■ to deductions attributable to bad debts or to legal fees and other expenses incurred in contesting the repayment of income previously included. (Reg § 1.1341-1(g), (h))[4]

¶ 2866 Inventories

Inventories are necessary for the determination of the correct cost of goods sold, in every case where the production, purchase or sale of merchandise is an income-producing factor.

Inventories serve to allocate the expense of merchandise purchased to the year in which merchandise is sold.[5]

---

50. ¶ G-3001; ¶ 13,414.   2. ¶ G-3027; ¶ 13,414.   4. ¶ G-3031; ¶ 13,414.01.   5. ¶ G-5000 *et seq.*; ¶ 4714.
1. ¶ G-3026; ¶ 13,414.   3. ¶ G-3019; ¶ 13,414.

Footnote references beginning with letters are to paragraphs in RIA's Federal Tax Coordinator 2d and RIA's Analysis of Federal Taxes: Income. Footnote references beginning with numbers are to paragraphs in RIA's United States Tax Reporter.

Inventories must be used whenever in the opinion of IRS their use is necessary in order to clearly determine the income of any taxpayer. (Code Sec. 471) Generally, this is the case where the "production, purchase or sale of merchandise" is an income-producing factor. (Reg § 1.471-1)[6]

A taxpayer that must use inventories also must use the accrual method of accounting with respect to its purchases and sales. (Reg § 1.446-1)[7]

⚠️*caution:* Under the uniform inventory inclusion and capitalization rules (¶ 1661 *et seq.*), certain direct and indirect costs are either included in inventory or capitalized.

¶ 2867 What goods are included in inventory?

Inventories include all merchandise that is held for sale in the ordinary course of business or that is to become a physical part of merchandise intended for sale. Inventories generally cover finished or partly finished goods as well as raw materials and supplies acquired for sale or that will physically become a part of merchandise intended for sale. For items to be included in inventory, taxpayer must have title. (Reg § 1.471-1)[8]

Merchandise shipped on approval or sold on sample is included in the seller's inventory until its acceptance. Consigned goods or goods in the hands of others for processing (bleaching, dyeing, etc.) and returnable in kind should also be included in the consignor's inventory. A seller's inventory includes goods he has contracted to sell but not yet segregated and applied to the contract, while a purchaser's inventory includes merchandise in transit to him or that for other reasons has not been reduced to possession but to which he has title. The purchaser, however, does *not* include in inventory goods ordered for future delivery.[9]

Containers that are *sold* with the merchandise they contain should be included in the seller's inventory, regardless of whether they are returnable. If the containers are merely leased or loaned with a deposit received to guarantee the return, they aren't included in inventory since they aren't part of the merchandise held for sale. In that case they can be inventoried at cost the same as supplies, considered as fixed assets and depreciated, or, if they have a useful life of less than a year, currently deducted.[10]

¶ 2868 Valuing inventory.

The two most commonly recognized bases of valuing inventories are: (1) cost, and (2) cost or market, whichever is lower. (Reg § 1.471-2(c))[11] Dealers in commodities may also use market value. (Reg § 1.471-5)[12] Farmers may use other valuation methods, see ¶ 4509 *et seq.* For dealers in securities, see ¶ 2883.

Consistency from year to year in whatever inventory procedure is adopted is of first importance. (Reg § 1.471-2(b))[13]

¶ 2869 Valuation of unsalable, slow-moving and traded-in goods.

Any goods in inventory that are unsalable at normal prices or in the normal way because of damage, imperfections, style changes, etc., can at the taxpayer's option be written down—that is, valued at selling prices less direct costs of disposition, whether the cost or the lower of cost or market method is used. If the goods consist of raw materials or partly finished goods held for use or consumption, they must be valued upon a reasonable basis, considering the usability and condition of the goods, but in no case shall they be valued at less than scrap value. (Reg § 1.471-2(c))[14] Selling price means the actual price at which goods are offered for sale during a period ending not later than 30 days after the date of inventory. (Reg § 1.472-2(c))[15]

---

6. ¶ G-5001; ¶ 4714.
7. ¶ G-2085; ¶s 4714, 4714.21.
8. ¶ G-5006 *et seq.*; ¶ 4714.21.
9. ¶ G-5009; ¶ 4714.21.

10. ¶ G-5010; ¶ 4714.21.
11. ¶ G-5101; ¶s 4714.21, 4714.41, 4714.51.

12. ¶ G-5021 *et seq.*; ¶s 4714.51, 4714.67.
13. ¶ G-5002; ¶ 4714.21.

14. ¶ G-5709; ¶ 4714.55.
15. ¶ G-5711; ¶ 4714.35.

Footnote references beginning with letters are to paragraphs in RIA's Federal Tax Coordinator 2d and RIA's Analysis of Federal Taxes: Income. Footnote references beginning with numbers are to paragraphs in RIA's United States Tax Reporter.

Normal but slow-moving inventory (i.e., goods in excess of current demand) can't be written down based on arbitrary cut-off time periods.[16]

¶ 2870 Prohibited valuation methods and practices.

The following are not permitted:

(1) Deducting from inventory a reserve for price changes or an estimated depreciation in the value of inventory.

(2) Valuing work in process, or other parts of the inventory, at a nominal price or at less than its proper value.

(3) Omitting portions of the stock on hand.

(4) Using a constant price or nominal value for so-called normal quantity of material or goods in stock.

(5) Segregating indirect production costs into fixed and variable classifications and allocating only the variable costs to the cost of goods produced while treating fixed costs as currently deductible (the "direct cost" method).

(6) Treating all or substantially all indirect production costs (whether classified as fixed or variable) as currently deductible (the "prime cost" method). (Reg § 1.471-2(f))[17]

¶ 2871 What is cost?

The cost of goods on hand at the beginning of the accounting period is the amount at which they were included in the closing inventory of the preceding year. (Reg § 1.471-3(a))[18]

The cost of the goods purchased ordinarily is the invoice price reduced by trade or other discounts. Strictly cash discounts approximating a fair interest rate may be deducted at the option of the taxpayer if the method is consistently followed. (Reg § 1.471-3(b))[19] To this net invoice price should be added transportation or other necessary charges incurred in acquiring possession of the goods. (Reg § 1.471-3(b))[20]

The costs of goods produced by the taxpayer include, in addition to the opening inventory, cost of raw materials and supplies entering into or consumed in manufacture, regular and overtime direct labor costs, and the indirect costs required to be included under the "full absorption" method. (Reg § 1.471-3(c))[21]

For the uniform capitalization rules for including costs in inventory, see ¶ 1661 et seq.

¶ 2872 Valuing at the lower of cost or market.

Under the lower of cost or market method, market value on the inventory date is compared with the cost of each item. The lower of the two is the inventory value of the particular item. Total inventory is the aggregate of the inventory values so computed for each item in the inventory. It is not the lower of the total cost or total market value of all items. (Reg § 1.471-4(c))[22]

¶ 2873 Market value defined.

Market value normally means the current bid price prevailing at the inventory date for the particular merchandise in the volume usually purchased by the taxpayer. Market price is applied to: (1) goods purchased and on hand, and (2) the basic elements of cost (materials, labor and overhead) of goods in process of manufacture and of finished goods on hand. (Reg § 1.471-4(a))[23]

Market price may not be applied to goods on hand or in process if the merchandise is covered by a firm sales contract at fixed prices (i.e., not legally subject to cancellation by

---

16. ¶ G-5714; ¶ 4714.35.   18. ¶ G-5102; ¶ 4714.41.   20. ¶ G-5103; ¶ 4714.41.   22. ¶ G-5700; ¶ 4714.51.
17. ¶ G-5123; ¶ 4714.   19. ¶ G-5107; ¶ 4714.41.   21. ¶ G-5102 et seq.; ¶ 4714.41.   23. ¶ G-5701; ¶ 4714.51.

Footnote references beginning with letters are to paragraphs in RIA's Federal Tax Coordinator 2d and RIA's Analysis of Federal Taxes: Income. Footnote references beginning with numbers are to paragraphs in RIA's United States Tax Reporter.

either buyer or seller). If, under the contract, the taxpayer is protected against actual loss, the goods must be inventoried at cost with no deduction for inventory decline. (Reg § 1.471-4(a)) Moreover, goods covered by firm sales contracts at the end of the year must be valued at cost even though the contracts are cancelled after the close of the year at the customer's request.[24]

If the contract gives the seller an almost certain loss, IRS states that the seller isn't allowed to write the inventory down but must value it at cost, thus taking the loss when actually realized, (Reg § 1.471-4(a)) but some courts disagree.[25]

A taxpayer may write down his inventory below market where in the regular course of business he has offered for sale such merchandise at prices lower than market. (Reg § 1.471-4(b))

If no market exists, or if quotations are nominal because of an inactive market, the taxpayer must use whatever evidence of a fair market price at the date or dates nearest his inventory date as may be available, such as specific purchases and sales made by the taxpayer or others in reasonable volume and in good faith, or compensation paid for cancellation of contracts for purchase commitments. (Reg § 1.471-4(b))[26]

¶ 2874 Inventory cost identification methods.

Under the specific identification method, goods are matched with their invoices (less appropriate discounts) to find the cost of each item.[27]

Where it is not possible or practicable to identify each item of inventory with its cost, an assumption must be made to determine which items were sold and which remain in inventory. Although only two methods of costing intermingled merchandise are specifically approved, namely the "first-in, first-out" (¶ 2875) and the "last-in, first-out" (¶ 2876) method, any method that comes within the best accounting practice of the particular business and that clearly reflects income will be acceptable. Two permissible cost identification methods are averaging the cost of each type or grade of goods in the inventory (¶ 2880) and mainly relying on the taxpayer's accounting records to arrive at the correct inventory value (¶ 2881). The base stock method (the assumption that a certain portion of inventory will be maintained from year to year and therefore need not be revalued) is not permitted.[28]

¶ 2875 FIFO (first-in, first-out).

The cost of goods that are so intermingled they cannot be identified with specific invoices will be considered to be the cost of goods most recently purchased or produced. (Reg § 1.471-2(d))[29]

¶ 2876 LIFO (last-in, first-out).

The "last-in, first-out" method of inventory valuation assumes that the most recently purchased merchandise is the first sold. (Code Sec. 472(b)(1))[30]

In order to use LIFO for tax purposes, the enterprise must also use LIFO in its reports to partners, stockholders, etc., and for credit purposes. (Code Sec. 472(c))[31]

LIFO may generally be used only where inventory is valued at cost. (Reg § 1.472-2(b))[32] If a taxpayer had written down inventory to a lower market value, the difference between that value and cost must be restored to income ratably over a three-year period (beginning with the year of the election to LIFO). (Code Sec. 472(d))[33]

---

24. ¶ G-5704 *et seq.*; ¶ 4714.51.
25. ¶ G-5704 *et seq.*; ¶ 4714.51.
26. ¶ G-5707; ¶ 4714.51.
27. ¶ G-5120; ¶ 4714.
28. ¶ G-5125 *et seq.*; ¶ 4714.
29. ¶ G-5120; ¶s 4714.21, 4724.
30. ¶ G-5750; ¶ 4724.
31. ¶ G-5815; ¶ 4724.
32. ¶ G-5762; ¶ 4724.
33. ¶ G-5758; ¶ 4724.

Footnote references beginning with letters are to paragraphs in RIA's Federal Tax Coordinator 2d and RIA's Analysis of Federal Taxes: Income. Footnote references beginning with numbers are to paragraphs in RIA's United States Tax Reporter.

¶ 2877   Electing LIFO—Form 970.

File Form 970 (or other acceptable statement) with the return for the tax year as of the close of which LIFO is first to be used. (Reg § 1.472-3)[34] Once made, the election applies to all later years unless IRS grants permission to change. (Reg § 1.472-5)[35]

¶ 2878   Retailers' inventory.

Retailers can value each item of merchandise in stock at the end of the year at its retail selling price but adjusted to approximate cost by eliminating the average percent of markup. (Reg § 1.471-8(a))[36] This retail inventory method may be used in conjunction with FIFO and specific identification methods, as well as LIFO, if the taxpayer adjusts his selling price for both markups and markdowns. (Reg § 1.471-8(g))[37] Price change adjustments are determined by reference to price indexes, generally those provided by the U.S. Bureau of Labor Statistics. (Reg § 1.472-1(k))[38]

¶ 2879   Dollar value LIFO.

Under this method a taxpayer who deals in a large variety of products may value inventory by the use of the dollar value rather than by the use of natural units. The assumption is that the items in the inventory are homogeneous. The taxpayer is therefore required to break up the inventory into a series of "pools"—the natural business unit pool or multiple pools. (Reg § 1.472-8)[39]

¶ 2880   Simplified dollar value LIFO.

An eligible small business may elect to use a simplified dollar-value method of pricing inventories for purposes of the LIFO method. Under the method, the cost of each grade of goods is averaged. (Code Sec. 474(a)) An eligible small business is a taxpayer whose average annual gross receipts do not exceed $5,000,000 for the three-tax-year period ending with the tax year. (Code Sec. 474(c))[40]

¶ 2881   Book (perpetual) inventory method.

Under this method inventory accounts are charged with the actual cost of goods purchased or produced, and credited with the cost of goods used, transferred or sold. The net amount in the accounts is considered to be the cost of the goods on hand, if the balances shown on the books are adjusted at reasonable intervals to conform to physical inventories. (Reg § 1.471-2(d))[41]

¶ 2882   Miners' and manufacturers' inventory.

Miners and manufacturers who use a single process or uniform series of processes, and derive a product of two or more kinds, sizes or grades with a unit cost substantially alike, may allocate a share of total cost to each kind, size or grade as a basis for pricing inventories. (Reg § 1.471-7)[42]

¶ 2883   Securities dealers' inventories—mark-to-market rules.

For tax years ending before Dec. 31, '93, and for certain securities not subject to the rules below, a securities dealer inventories securities at (1) cost, (2) lower of cost or market, or (3) market value.

For later years (including calendar '93), any security that is inventory in the hands of a securities dealer must be included in inventory at its fair market value. (Code Sec. 475(a)(l)) In the case of a non-inventory security that is held at the close of a tax year, the

---

34. ¶ G-5752; ¶ 4724.
35. ¶ G-5751; ¶ 4724.
36. ¶ G-5851; ¶ 4724.06.
37. ¶ G-5856; ¶ 4724.06.
38. ¶ G-5863; ¶ 4724.06.
39. ¶ G-5788 *et seq.*; ¶ 4714.21.
40. ¶ G-5810 *et seq.*; ¶ 4744.
41. ¶ G-5119; ¶ 4714.21.
42. ¶ G-5020; ¶ 4714.85.

Footnote references beginning with letters are to paragraphs in RIA's Federal Tax Coordinator 2d and RIA's Analysis of Federal Taxes: Income. Footnote references beginning with numbers are to paragraphs in RIA's United States Tax Reporter.

dealer must recognize gain or loss as if the security were sold for its fair market value on the last business day of that year, and any gain or loss must be taken into account for that tax year, generally as ordinary income or loss. (Code Sec. 475(a)(2), (d)(3))[43] A "security" doesn't include any security held for investment and certain other securities, but only if the security is clearly identified as covered by an exception in the dealer's records before the close of the business day on which it was accquired, originated or entered into. (Code Sec. 475(b)) (For securities held on Aug. 10, '93, an identification was timely if made by Oct. 31, '93.) A dealer is one who regularly buys and sells securities to customers (or enters into or terminates positions in securities with customers) in the ordinary course of business. (Code Sec. 475(c)(1))[44] (Code Sec. 475(c)(1)) A taxpayer whose sole business consists of trading in securities is not a dealer in securities.

¶ 2884 Refund of taxes attributable to qualified liquidation of LIFO inventories.

If there is a qualified liquidation of LIFO inventories (a decrease attributable to a qualified inventory interruption, as may be specified in a published notice by IRS), the taxpayer can elect to adjust its gross income for the liquidation year where the liquidated goods are replaced within three tax years after the liquidation year or a shorter period specified by IRS. The taxes attributable to the qualified liquidation can be refunded under special procedures. (Code Sec. 473) The inventories here are inventories of petroleum and petroleum by-products.[45]

¶ 2885 Changing inventory method.

Any change in the method of valuing inventory, with the exception of a change to LIFO, requires IRS approval. This includes adoption of either: (1) cost, or (2) cost or market, whichever is lower, where the taxpayer has been on a different basis, and changes to and from the various methods of determining inventory costs. Use Form 3115, under the rules at ¶ 2843. (Reg § 1.446-1(e))[46]

Where a change is made from LIFO, a special automatic consent procedure is available for certain taxpayers.[47]

Automatic changes are permitted only for those changes required as a result of the uniform inventory inclusion rules. Other changes require prior IRS consent.[48]

---

43. ¶ G-5021.
44. ¶ G-5023.
45. ¶ G-5826 *et seq.*; ¶ 4734.

46. ¶s G-2101 *et seq.*, G-5751 *et seq.*; ¶ 4464.21.

47. ¶ G-5767 *et seq.*; ¶s 4464.21, 4724.

48. ¶ G-5612 *et seq.*; ¶ 263A4.

Footnote references beginning with letters are to paragraphs in RIA's Federal Tax Coordinator 2d and RIA's Analysis of Federal Taxes: Income. Footnote references beginning with numbers are to paragraphs in RIA's United States Tax Reporter.

Chapter 12 Withholding Tax on Wages and Other Income Payments

¶ *3000* Withholding on Wages

Employers must withhold income tax from wages paid to employees, but not from amounts paid to independent contractors. "Wages" includes most forms of taxable compensation. Employees are entitled to minimum, and sometimes additional, withholding exemptions or allowances. Withheld tax must be paid through the tax deposit system.

¶ *3001* Withholding by employers.

Employers must withhold. (Code Sec. 3402(a)(1); Reg § 31.3402(a)-1(b))[1]

An employer is any person or organization for whom an individual performs any service as an employee. (Code Sec. 3401(d)) An employer includes any person paying wages to a former employee, (Reg § 31.3401(d)-1(b)) and includes tax-exempt organizations. (Reg § 31.3401(d)-1(d))[2]

If the actual employer doesn't have control over the payment of wages, the person who does have control must withhold. (Code Sec. 3401(d)(1)) A lender, surety or other person who directly pays wages to employees of another becomes personally liable for the employee income tax required to be withheld. (Code Sec. 3505)

If a person pays wages on behalf of a nonresident employer not engaged in trade or business in the U.S., that person must withhold. (Code Sec. 3401(d)(2))[3]

¶ *3002* Employees defined.

Every individual who performs services subject to the will and control of an employer both as to what shall be done and how it shall be done, is an employee for withholding purposes. It doesn't matter that the employee has considerable discretion and freedom of action, so long as the employer has the *legal right* to control both the method and the result of the services. (Reg § 31.3401(c)-1(b)) For factors used to determine whether a worker is an employee or independent contractor, see ¶ 3003.

🔷*observation:* Although many agent-drivers, full-time salesmen and industrial home-workers are treated as employees under social security, the above "control" test applies to determine if the person is an employee for withholding purposes.

It doesn't matter that the employee is designated a partner, agent or independent contractor, or how the payments are measured or paid or what they are called. (Reg § 31.3401(c)-1(e))[4]

No distinction is made between classes of employees. Managers and other supervisory personnel are employees. An officer of a corporation is an employee, (Code Sec. 3401(c)) but a director in his capacity as director isn't an employee. (Reg § 31.3401(c)-1(f))[5]

Persons in business for themselves aren't employees. For example, physicians, lawyers, dentists, veterinarians, construction contractors and others who offer their services to the public aren't employees. (Reg § 31.3401(c)-1(c))[6]

Qualified real estate agents and direct sellers are treated as independent contractors, not employees. (Code Sec. 3508(a))[7]

Crew leaders who pay agricultural laborers that they provide to another person are employers unless a written contract designates them as employees of that person. (Code Sec. 3401(h))[8]

🔷*observation:* A person not treated as an employee for tax purposes can't be covered

---

1. ¶ H-4222; ¶ 34,024.
2. ¶ H-4221; ¶ 34,014.60.
3. ¶s H-4228, H-4232, H-4445; ¶ 34,014.60.

4. ¶ H-4251.
5. ¶ H-4252; ¶s 34,014.39, 34,014.40.

6. ¶ H-4258; ¶s 34,014.47, 34,014.50, 34,014.61.

7. ¶ H-4284; ¶ 34,014.37.
8. ¶ H-4226; ¶ 34,014.18.

Footnote references beginning with letters are to paragraphs in RIA's Federal Tax Coordinator 2d and RIA's Analysis of Federal Taxes: Income. Footnote references beginning with numbers are to paragraphs in RIA's United States Tax Reporter.

under employee plans such as those for medical reimbursement and group-term life insurance.

If payment is made for services rendered and the payor isn't sure whether the payee is an employee or independent contractor, the payor may get an IRS ruling by filing Form SS-8. (Reg § 31.3401(d)-1(d))[9]

¶ 3003 IRS's 20-factor test to determine employee or independent contractor status.

IRS has developed a 20-factor test to use as a *guide* in determining whether a worker is an employee or an independent contractor. These factors help ascertain whether sufficient control is present to establish an employer-employee relationship. The twenty factors are:[10]

(1) A worker required to comply with others' instructions on when, where, and how to work is usually an employee.

(2) Training a worker indicates that services are to be performed in a particular method.

(3) Integration of a worker's services into the business operations indicates control.

(4) Services to be rendered personally indicates control.

(5) The right to hire, supervise, and pay assistants shows control.

(6) A continuing relationship indicates an employment relationship.

(7) Set hours of work for the worker indicates control.

(8) Full time work indicates control. An independent contractor is free to work when and for whom he chooses.

(9) Work performed on a business's premises suggests control.

(10) Requiring work be performed in a set order indicates control.

(11) A requirement that the worker submit regular or written reports indicates control.

(12) Payment by the hour, week, or month indicates an employment relationship.

(13) Payment of business expenses indicates an employment relationship.

(14) Furnishing of tools and equipment indicates an employment relationship.

(15) Investment by the worker in facilities indicates an independent contractor.

(16) The ability to realize a profit or loss from services indicates an independent contractor.

(17) Working for more than one firm at a time indicates an independent contractor.

(18) Services available to the general public on a regular and consistent basis indicates an independent contractor.

(19) The right to discharge a worker indicates an employment relationship.

(20) The worker's right to terminate his relationship without liability indicates an employment relationship.

¶ 3004 Compliance with statutory ("section 530") requirements to avoid employee treatment.

A taxpayer's treatment of an individual as a nonemployee will be upheld for withholding purposes if:[11]

(1) the taxpayer does not treat the individual as an employee, and

(2) all required federal tax returns (e.g., Form 1099-MISC) are filed by the taxpayer on a basis consistent with the taxpayer's treatment of the individual as a nonemployee, and

(3) the taxpayer has a reasonable basis (such as judicial precedent, published rulings, a

---

9. ¶ H-4282; ¶ 34,009.   10. ¶ H-4259.   11. ¶ H-4352; ¶ 34,014.37.

Footnote references beginning with letters are to paragraphs in RIA's Federal Tax Coordinator 2d and RIA's Analysis of Federal Taxes: Income. Footnote references beginning with numbers are to paragraphs in RIA's United States Tax Reporter.

letter ruling from IRS, past IRS audit allowance, long-standing industry practice) for not treating the individual as an employee.

observation: If these requirements are met, a worker who would otherwise be treated as an employee won't be treated as an employee for withholding tax purposes.

However, the above section 530 rules (referring to section 530 of the '78 Revenue Act, not to a Code Section) don't apply (and instead the generally applicable common law "control" standards discussed at ¶ 3002 apply) to determine the employee/independent contractor status of an individual who, under an agreement between the taxpayer (payor, i.e., technical services firm) and another person (e.g., taxpayer's client), provides services to that other person as an engineer, designer, drafter, computer programmer, systems analyst or other similarly skilled worker engaged in a similar line of work. For factors used to determine whether a worker is an employee or independent contractor, see ¶ 3003.[12]

¶ 3005 Wages subject to withholding.

"Wages" cover all types of employee compensation, including salaries, fees, bonuses, commissions and fringe benefits. It's immaterial whether payments are based on the hour, day, week, month, year or on a piecework or percentage plan, or whether they're called wages, salaries, fees, etc. (Code Sec. 3401(a); Reg § 31.3401(a)-1(a)(2), (3))[13]

Noncash wages are the fair market value of the goods, lodging, meals or other consideration given for services. (Reg § 31.3401(a)-1(a)(4))[14]

Vacation allowances[15] and back pay, including retroactive wage increases are wages. (Reg § 31.3401(a)-1(b)(3))[16]

The amount to be withheld is computed on gross wages before any deductions by the employer for social security tax, pensions, union dues, insurance, etc. (Reg § 31.3401(a)-1(b)(5))[17]

¶ 3006 Tips.

Wages includes tips. (Code Sec. 3401(f)) However, withholding isn't required on cash tips of less than $20 a month received by an employee, or for tips paid in any medium other than cash (such as passes, tickets or other goods or commodities). (Code Sec. 3401(a)(16); Reg § 31.3401(a)(16)-1) But if cash tips amount to $20 or more in a month, none of the cash tips are exempt. The $20 test is applied separately with respect to cash tips received by the employee for his services to each employer. (Reg § 31.3401(a)(16)-1)[18]

¶ 3007 Christmas and other gifts.

IRS requires withholding on gift certificates or similar items of readily convertible cash value, given to employees, but not for merchandise, facilities or privileges of relatively small value (such as Christmas turkeys, entertainment, courtesy discounts or medical services) furnished or offered to employees generally, merely to promote their health, good will, contentment or efficiency.[19]

¶ 3008 Exempt "wages."

The following are not wages subject to withholding:

■ Fringe benefits if it's reasonable to believe that the employee will be able to exclude them from income as a qualified scholarship, a no-additional-cost service, a qualified employee discount, a working condition fringe, a de minimis fringe, a qualified transportation fringe, a qualified moving expense reimbursement, an on-premises athletic facility

---

12. ¶ H-4357 et seq.; ¶ 34,014.37.   14. ¶ H-4402; ¶ 34,009.   16. ¶ H-4430; ¶ 34,014.09.   18. ¶ H-4416; ¶ 34,014.31.
13. ¶ H-4401; ¶ 34,009.   15. ¶ H-4435; ¶ 34,014.04.   17. ¶ H-4406.   19. ¶ H-4438; ¶ 34,014.09.

Footnote references beginning with letters are to paragraphs in RIA's Federal Tax Coordinator 2d and RIA's Analysis of Federal Taxes: Income. Footnote references beginning with numbers are to paragraphs in RIA's United States Tax Reporter.

or an employee achievement award. (Code Sec. 3401(a)(19))[20] (For the employer's election not to withhold on a vehicle fringe benefit, see ¶ 3009.)

■ Medical care reimbursements made for the benefit of an employee under a self-insured medical reimbursement plan. (Code Sec. 3401(a)(20))[21]

■ Amounts specifically advanced or reimbursed to employees for traveling or other ordinary and necessary expenses incurred or reasonably expected to be incurred in the employer's business. But they must be paid separately or specifically identified where both wages and expense allowances are combined in a single payment. (Reg § 31.3401(a)-4(a)) If a reimbursement or other expense allowance arrangement meets the requirements of Code Sec. 62(c) (see ¶ 3103) (i.e., an "accountable plan"), payments that don't exceed the substantiated expenses are not wages and aren't subject to withholding. Payments that are not substantiated within a reasonable period of time or are in excess of substantiated expenses are wages and subject to withholding. Per diem or mileage allowances at a rate in excess of the deemed substantiated amount are subject to withholding. If the arrangement doesn't meet the Code Sec. 62(c) requirements (i.e., a "nonaccountable plan"), all amounts paid are wages and subject to withholding. (Reg § 31.3401(a)-4(a), (b), Reg § 1.62-2(h)(1), (2))[22]

■ Moving expense reimbursements, if a corresponding deduction is allowable under the normal Code Sec. 217 rules (see ¶ 1645) (determined without regard to the Code Sec. 274(n) percentage limit on meal expenses). (Code Sec. 3401(a)(15))[23]

■ Salesman's advances or drawings against future commissions if he must repay advances or drawings not covered by commissions earned, but withholding is required if he needn't repay.[24]

■ Tips, under the circumstances at ¶ 3006.

■ Benefits paid by a labor union to workers unemployed because of a strike or lockout.[25]

■ Payments for agricultural labor except if during the year: (1) cash payments to an employee are $150 or more, or (2) the employer pays all such employees $2,500 or more (unless the employee is a hand harvest laborer who is paid on a customary basis, commutes daily to the farm from his permanent residence and was employed in agriculture less than 13 weeks during the prior year). (Code Sec. 3401(a)(2))[26]

■ Payments for domestic service in a private home, local college club or fraternity or sorority chapter. (Code Sec. 3401(a)(3))[27]

■ Payments for services by a minister of a church in the exercise of his ministry or by a member of a religious order in the exercise of the duties of the order. (Code Sec. 3401(a)(9); Reg § 31.3401(a)(9)-1(a))[28]

■ The profits of newspaper and magazine vendors who buy at fixed prices from the publisher and sell to the public. (Code Sec. 3401(a)(10)(B))[29]

■ Payments to newspaper carriers under age 18 delivering to consumers. (Code Sec. 3401(a)(10)(A))[30]

■ Certain payments for services by a U.S. citizen for an employer outside the U.S. (Code Sec. 3401(a)(8)(A)(i))[31]

■ Premiums paid by an employer for group term insurance on an employee's life. (Code Sec. 3401(a)(14))[32]

■ Payments to or on behalf of an employee or his beneficiary to or from a qualified plan (except payments for services rendered by an employee of the plan); (Code Sec. 3401(a)(12)(A)) to or under a qualified annuity plan (Code Sec. 3401(a)(12)(B)) or, if

20. ¶ H-4500 et seq.; ¶s 34,014.09, 34,024.

21. ¶ H-4550 et seq.; ¶ 34,014.34.

22. ¶ H-4415; ¶ 34,014.03.

23. ¶ H-4516; ¶ 34,014.30.

24. ¶ H-4441.

25. ¶ H-4429; ¶ 34,014.10.

26. ¶ H-4551; ¶ 34,014.18.

27. ¶ H-4570 et seq.; ¶ 34,014.19.

28. ¶ H-4577; ¶ 34,014.24.

29. ¶ H-4581; ¶ 34,014.25.

30. ¶ H-4582; ¶ 34,014.25.

31. ¶s H-4567, H-4568; ¶ 34,014.23.

32. ¶ J-8535; ¶ 34,014.29.

Footnote references beginning with letters are to paragraphs in RIA's Federal Tax Coordinator 2d and RIA's Analysis of Federal Taxes: Income. Footnote references beginning with numbers are to paragraphs in RIA's United States Tax Reporter.

it's reasonable to believe the employee will be entitled to exclude the payment, for contributions to a simplified employee pension for an employee. (Code Sec. 3401(a)(12)(C))[33]

■ Payments made under educational assistance or dependent care programs if it's reasonable to believe that the employee can exclude them. (Code Sec. 3401(a)(18))[34]

■ Payment of deceased employee's accrued wages to his estate or beneficiaries.[35]

¶ 3009 Employer's election not to withhold on vehicle fringe benefit.

An employer may elect not to withhold with respect to the use by an employee of a highway motor vehicle provided to the employee by the employer where that use constitutes wages to the employee. The employer must notify the employee of the election and include the amount of the benefit on a timely furnished W-2. (Code Sec. 3402(s))[36]

¶ 3010 Withholding on sick pay.

If the recipient of sick pay that isn't wages requests the payor (on Form W-4S) to withhold a specified amount from each payment, the payor must withhold that amount. (Code Sec. 3402(o); Reg § 31.3402(o)-3(b)) An employee does not have to request withholding if his employer makes the sick payments since employers are required to withhold income tax from sick pay.[37]

¶ 3011 Voluntary withholding agreements—Form W-4.

Household, and other employees who aren't subject to income tax withholding may elect to have tax withheld from their pay, if their employers agree. (Code Sec. 3402(p)) Other employees can also have their withholding increased voluntarily. (Code Sec. 3402(i))

The rules generally applicable to mandatory withholding, including withholding rates and tables, apply to the voluntary withholding. An employee requests voluntary withholding by filing a Form W-4 with his employer—unless he wants the voluntary withholding to apply for a *limited period of time*. In that case, he must also give the employer a statement that includes the date the voluntary withholding is to terminate.

A voluntary withholding agreement may be terminated by employer or employee by giving advance notice to the other in accordance with the regs. (Reg § 31.3402(p)-1)[38]

¶ 3012 Computing the amount withheld.

The amount withheld is taken from a table (wage bracket method) or separately computed (percentage method), see ¶ 3014.

Employers may treat fringe benefits as part of regular wages for the payroll period and compute withholding on the total, or instead withhold 28% (20% before '94) of the value of the benefit from regular wages. (Reg § 31.3501(a)-1T, Q&A-10) Any noncash fringe benefit provided in a calendar quarter may be treated as provided on the last day of that quarter. (Reg § 31.3501(a)-1T, Q&A-1)[39]

For the election to not withhold on the value of a vehicle fringe benefit provided to the employee, see ¶ 3009.

¶ 3013 Supplemental wage payments.

Withholding on bonuses, commissions, overtime pay or other supplemental wages paid:

■ *with regular wages*, should be determined as if the total supplemental and regular wages were a single payment for the regular payroll period; (Reg § 31.3402(g)-1(a))

■ *at a different time*, can be determined by adding the supplemental wages either to the regular wages for the current payroll period or to the last preceding payroll period within

---

33. ¶ J-8535; ¶ 34,014.27.
34. ¶ H-4501; ¶ 34,014.05.
35. ¶ H-4425; ¶ 34,014.07.

36. ¶s H-4511, H-4512; ¶ 34,024.27.

37. ¶ H-4408 et seq.; ¶ 34,024.25.
38. ¶ H-4602 et seq.; ¶ 34,024.19.

39. ¶ H-4720; ¶s 34,024, 34,024.27.

Footnote references beginning with letters are to paragraphs in RIA's Federal Tax Coordinator 2d and RIA's Analysis of Federal Taxes: Income. Footnote references beginning with numbers are to paragraphs in RIA's United States Tax Reporter.

the same calendar year; (Reg § 31.3402(g)-1(a))

■ *where tax has been withheld on regular wages,* can be determined by using a flat rate of not less than 28% (a rate of 20% before '94) without allowance for exemptions and without reference to any regular wage payment. (Reg § 31.3402(g)-1(a))[40]

Where tax isn't withheld from regular wages for employees who receive both regular wages and supplemental wages (e.g., tips), a flat rate not less than 28% (a rate of 20% before '94) can't be used. Add the tips to the current or preceding regular wage payment and compute withholding at the regular graduated rates.[41]

Extra pay for working during a vacation period is treated as a supplemental wage payment. (Reg § 31.3402(g)-1(c))[42]

¶ 3014 Withholding methods.

There are two principal systems of withholding: (1) the percentage or exact method, and (2) the wage bracket method. Whichever method is used, the employer applies the withholding allowances and marital status indicated by the employee, see ¶ 3016 *et seq.* For variations of these two methods, see ¶ 3015.

Under the percentage method, the income tax to be withheld is computed as follows:

(1) Multiply the amount of *one* withholding exemption (from a table provided by IRS) by the number of withholding exemptions claimed.

(2) Subtract the amount claimed in (1) (above) from the employee's wages.

(3) Compute the tax by referring to the appropriate percentage table. There are tables for both single persons (including heads of household) and married persons. For each category, there is a weekly, biweekly, semimonthly, monthly, quarterly, semiannual, annual and a daily (or miscellaneous period) table. (Code Sec. 3402(b))[43]

Wage bracket table method. These tables show the amount to be withheld from various amounts paid to employees with different numbers of withholding exemptions. The tables may be used for weekly, biweekly, semi-monthly, monthly, and daily or miscellaneous payroll periods. (Code Sec. 3402(c))[44]

¶ 3015 Alternative methods.

IRS also authorizes withholding on the basis of: (1) annualized wages, (2) cumulative wages, (3) part-year employment, (4) average estimated wages, and (5) any other method that results in substantially the same amount of withholding as the percentage method. (Methods (2) and (3) are at the employee's request.) (Code Sec. 3402(h))[45]

¶ 3016 Employee's withholding allowance certificate—Form W-4.

Each employer should ask each new employee to fill out a Form W-4 withholding allowance certificate before employment begins. (Code Sec. 3402(f)(2)(A)) Employers must take into account the marital status and exemptions and allowances of each employee on the basis of that Form W-4. A certificate filed by a new employee is effective on the first payment of wage. (Code Sec. 3402(f)(3)) If an employee fails to furnish a certificate, the employer must withhold tax as if the employee is a single person who has no withholding exemptions or allowances. (Code Sec. 3401(e); Reg § 31.3402(f)(2)-1(e))[46]

¶ 3017 Withholding exemptions.

An employee is allowed:

■ a regular exemption for himself, unless he is claimed as the dependent of another

---

40. ¶ H-4723; ¶ 34,024.13.
41. ¶ H-4721.
42. ¶ H-4722; ¶ 34,024.13.

43. ¶ H-4708; ¶ 34,024.04.
44. ¶ H-4709; ¶s 34,024.05, 34,024.06.

45. ¶ H-4707; ¶s 34,024.18, 34,024.22.

46. ¶ H-4735 *et seq.*; ¶ 34,024.09 *et seq.*

Footnote references beginning with letters are to paragraphs in RIA's Federal Tax Coordinator 2d and RIA's Analysis of Federal Taxes: Income. Footnote references beginning with numbers are to paragraphs in RIA's United States Tax Reporter.

person;

■ a regular exemption for his spouse, unless the spouse is employed and claims a regular exemption;

■ an exemption for each dependent he may claim on his tax return; (Code Sec. 3402(f)(1); Reg § 31.3402(f)(1)-1)[47]

■ additional withholding allowances, ¶ 3018.

A taxpayer working for more than one employer must allocate his allowances on separate withholding certificates filed with each employer. (Code Sec. 3402(f)(7); Reg § 31.3402(m)-1(f)(2))[48]

The withholding exemption allowance is the same amount as allowed for a personal exemption (¶ 3113). (Code Sec. 3402(a)(2))[49]

¶ 3018 Additional withholding allowances.

Employees may claim (on Form W-4) additional withholding allowances for: estimated tax credits like those shown on Form 1040, except for any earned income credit if the employee is receiving advance payment of it; and estimated itemized deductions and other deductions including the additional standard deduction for the aged and blind, but only if his spouse doesn't have in effect a Form W-4 claiming the same allowances. (Code Sec. 3402(m); Reg § 31.3402(m)-1)[50]

caution: A taxpayer who has too little withholding taken out because he has claimed too many withholding allowances may have to pay a penalty for underpayment of estimated tax, see ¶ 3155.

An additional withholding allowance (called a "standard deduction allowance") can be claimed by an employee who is single and has only one job; is married and has only one job, if his spouse does not work; or if his wages from a second job or his spouse's wages (or the total of both) are $2,500 or less. (Code Sec. 3402(f)(1)(E); Reg § 31.3402(f)(1)-1(e))[1]

¶ 3019 Employees with no tax liability.

Employees with no tax liability can be exempt from income tax withholding. To qualify, the employee certifies on Form W-4 to his employer that:

■ he expects to have no federal income tax liability for the current year, *and*

■ he had no federal income tax liability in the preceding year. (Code Sec. 3402(n))[2]

An employee usually cannot claim exemption from withholding, however, if he can be claimed as a dependent on someone else's tax return (whether or not actually claimed), has any unearned income such as interest or dividends, and has wages and unearned income totalling more than $600 for '94 (and '93). Special calculations have to be made by an employee who is 65 or older and/or blind.[3]

¶ 3020 Amending withholding certificate.

The employee *must* amend his Form W-4, reducing the number of allowances, within ten days:

■ when the spouse he has been claiming is divorced or legally separated from him, or claims her own allowance on a separate W-4;

■ when he loses the right to exemption for a claimed dependent;

■ when he loses the right to the number of withholding allowances he has claimed.[4] The employer must give effect to an amended W-4 no later than the beginning of the first payroll period ending (or the first payment of wages made without regard to a payroll

47. ¶ H-4724; ¶ 34,024.10.   49. ¶ H-4707; ¶ 34,024.10.   1. ¶ H-4725; ¶ 34,024.10.   3. ¶ H-4738; ¶ 34,024.24.
48. ¶ H-4728; ¶ 34,024.10.   50. ¶ H-4730 *et seq.*; ¶ 34,024.10.   2. ¶ H-4738; ¶ 34,024.24.   4. ¶ H-4743; ¶ 34,024.11.

Footnote references beginning with letters are to paragraphs in RIA's Federal Tax Coordinator 2d and RIA's Analysis of Federal Taxes: Income. Footnote references beginning with numbers are to paragraphs in RIA's United States Tax Reporter.

period) on or after the 30th day after the day the amended W-4 is furnished. (Code Sec. 3402(f)(3)(B)(i))[5]

An amended Form W-4 must be filed by Dec. 1 if the number of allowances is expected to *decrease* for next year. If the change resulting in the decrease occurs in December, the amended Form must be furnished within ten days of the date of the change. The number of allowances drops if a spouse or dependent died during the year or an individual will no longer qualify as a dependent.[6]

If the number of allowances is expected to increase next year, the employee can amend his W-4 by Dec. 1. If the change arises in December, the amended W-4 may be filed on or after the date of the change. (Code Sec. 3402(f)(2)(C); Reg § 31.3402(f)(2)-1(c)) This W-4 doesn't take effect and is not to be made effective with respect to any payment of wages in the calendar year it is furnished. (Code Sec. 3402(f)(3)(B)(iii))[7]

¶ 3021 Employer withholding tax return—Forms 941 and 945.

Every employer must file with IRS a quarterly return on Form 941 covering withheld income taxes for the quarters ending Mar. 31, June 30, Sept. 30 and Dec. 31. (Reg § 31.6011(a)-1, Reg § 31.6011(a)-4) The employer must include with Form 941 copies of all Forms W-4 submitted by each employee who claims more than ten exemptions or who claims exempt status and normally earns over $200 per week at the time the Form W-4 was filed. (Reg § 31.3402(f)(2)-1(g))[8]

In certain cases (e.g., for taxpayers who must separately account, see ¶ 3026) IRS can require monthly wage withholding returns. (Reg § 31.6011(a)-5(a)(1))[9]

Form 941 must be filed by Apr. 30, July 31, Oct. 31 and Jan. 31 for the calendar quarters ending Mar. 31, June 30, Sept. 30 and Dec. 31, respectively, unless monthly filing is required. But the returns may be filed ten days later if timely deposits in full payment of the tax are made. (Reg § 31.6071(a)-1(a))[10]

Beginning in the first quarter of '94, nonpayroll items (backup withholding, withholding for pension, annuities, and gambling winnings, etc.) are reported on Form 945, not Form 941. Beginning Jan. 1, '94 tax withheld on nonpayroll items reported on Form 945 are to be deposited separately.

¶ 3022 Errors in withholding and payment of tax.

Where underwithholding of FICA and income tax is ascertained before the return is filed, the employer must report and pay the correct amount of tax by the due date of the return. (Reg § 31.6151-1, 31.6205-1(b)(1), -1(c)(1); Prop Reg § 31.6205-1(b)(1), -1(c)(1)["Taxpayer may rely," Preamble to Prop Reg 12/10/92])[11]

Where underpayment of FICA and income tax is ascertained after the return is filed, the additional amount due should be reported on a return filed by the due date for the return period in which the error is ascertained (in order to qualify for as a interest-free adjustment). (Reg § 31.6205-1(b)(2); Prop Reg § 31.6205-1(b)(3)["Taxpayer may rely," Preamble to Prop Reg 12/10/92])[12]

If *more* than the correct FICA and income tax is collected from an employee and paid to IRS, the employer should:

(1) repay the overcollection to the employee in any later return period in the same calendar year and and obtain a dated written receipt from the employee, or

(2) reimburse the employee by reducing the tax to be withheld for the balance of the same calendar year. Reg § 31.6413(a)-1(b)(1)); Prop Reg § 31.6205-1(b)(1), -1(c)(1))[13]

An employer should not report or pay to IRS an overage of tax if the employer: (1)

---

5. ¶ H-4745; ¶ 34,024.11.   8. ¶ S-2603; ¶ 34,024.   10. ¶ S-4918.   12. ¶ S-5526.
6. ¶ H-4744; ¶ 34,024.11.   9. ¶ S-2610.   11. ¶ S-5525.   13. ¶ S-5729
7. ¶ H-4744; ¶ 34,024.11.

Footnote references beginning with letters are to paragraphs in RIA's Federal Tax Coordinator 2d and RIA's Analysis of Federal Taxes: Income. Footnote references beginning with numbers are to paragraphs in RIA's United States Tax Reporter.

repays the overwithholding to the employee before the return for the period is filed and before the end of the calendar year in which the overcollection was made and (2) obtains and keeps the written receipt of the employee showing the date and amount of the repayment. Reg § 31.6413(a)-1(a)(1), -1(a)(2))[14]

¶ 3023 Wage and tax statement—Form W-2.

An employer in business must give each employee copies of Form W-2, on or before Jan. 31 of the year after the calendar year for which the wages were paid. If an employee leaves the job before the end of the calendar year and isn't expected to return within the calendar year, Form W-2 must be given to him not later than 30 days after the employer receives a written request for it from the employee, if that 30-day period ends before Jan. 31. (Code Sec. 6051; Reg § 31.6051-1(d))[15]

¶ 3024 Nonreceipt of Form W-2 by employee.

If an employee does not receive a Form W-2, he should ask his employer for it. If the employer does not provide the form, the taxpayer should telephone IRS toll-free at the number listed in the instructions to Forms 1040, 1040A, or 1040EZ to have IRS ask the employer to send a copy or duplicate form. If the employee hasn't received a Form W-2 in time to file his tax return, he should file a return estimating wages and the income tax withheld on Form 4852.[16]

¶ 3025 Earned income credit notice to certain employees with no tax withheld.

An employer must notify any employee who has not had any tax withheld from his wages (other than an employee who certifies (see ¶ 3019) that he has no tax liability) that the employee may be eligible for a refund because of the earned income credit (¶ 2336 *et seq.*). IRS Notice 797 or a written statement containing an exact reproduction of the wording in Notice 797 must be used and must be furnished within one week (before or after) of the date the employee should receive a timely Form W-2 or, if none is required, before Feb. 8th of the following calendar year.(Reg § 31.6051-1(h))[17]

¶ 3026 Separate accounting for employment tax.

IRS can require an employer who fails to collect, account for, deposit, etc., income or related employment taxes or make timely deposits or file returns to make deposits in a special trust account. (Code Sec. 7512; Reg § 301.7512-1(b))[18]

¶ 3027 Deposit of employment taxes.

An employer is either a monthly or semi-weekly depositor, see below. (Reg § 31.6302-1(a))

Monthly depositor. An employer is a monthly depositor for the entire calendar year if the aggregate amount of employment taxes reported for the lookback period (i.e., the 12 month period ended the preceding June 30) is $50,000 or less. (Reg § 31.6302-1(b)(2)(i), (4)) The employer must deposit taxes on or before the 15th day of the following month. (Reg § 31.6302-1(c)(1))

Semi-weekly depositor. An employer is a semi-weekly depositor for the entire calendar year if the aggregate amount of employment taxes reported for the lookback period (i.e., the 12 month period ended the preceding June 30) exceeds $50,000. (Reg § 31.6302-1(b)(3), (4)) The employer must deposit taxes on or before the following dates: (Reg § 31.6302-1(c)(2))

---

14. ¶ S-5530   16. ¶ S-3193.   17. ¶ H-4801; ¶ 60,514.   18. ¶ S-5541 *et seq.*; ¶ 75,124.
15. ¶ S-4930; ¶ 60,514.

Footnote references beginning with letters are to paragraphs in RIA's Federal Tax Coordinator 2d and RIA's Analysis of Federal Taxes: Income. Footnote references beginning with numbers are to paragraphs in RIA's United States Tax Reporter.

Payment Dates/ Semi-weekly Period	Deposit Date
Wednesday, Thursday and/or Friday	On or before the following Wednesday
Saturday, Sunday, Monday and/or Tuesday	On or before the following Friday

Semi-weekly depositors have at least three banking days following the close of the semi-weekly period to deposit taxes. (Reg § 31.6302-1(c)(2)(iii)) If a return period (quarterly or annual) ends during a semi-weekly period, the employer must designate on his deposit coupon the proper return period for which the deposits relates (the period in which the payment is made). If the return period ends during a semi-weekly period during which the employer has two or more payment dates, two deposit obligations may exist. (Reg § 31.6302-1(c)(2)(ii))

One-day rule. Notwithstanding the above rules, if on any day an employer has $100,000 or more of employment taxes accumulated, these taxes must be deposited by the close of the next banking day. In determining whether the $100,000 threshold is met under this "one-day rule":

(1) a monthly depositor takes into account only those employment taxes accumulated in the calendar month in which the day occurs, and

(2) a semi-weekly depositor takes into account only those employment taxes accumulated in the Wednesday-Friday or Saturday-Tuesday semi-weekly periods in which the day occurs. (Reg § 31.6302-1(c)(3))

An employer will no longer be a monthly depositor on the first day after being subject to the one-day rule and will instead become a semi-weekly depositor for the remainder of the calendar year and for the following calendar year. (Reg § 31.6302-1(b)(2)(ii))

Deposits are only required on banking days. For taxes required to be deposited on a day that is not a banking day, the taxes will be timely deposited if deposited on the next day that is a banking day. (Reg § 31.6302-1(c)(4))[19]

Deposits are considered timely if mailed (postmarked) at least two days before the due date if the deposit is actually received by the bank. (Code Sec. 7502(e)) But a deposit of $20,000 or more by a person who is required to make a deposit more than once a month must be actually received by the due date. (Code Sec. 7502(e)(3))[20]

¶ 3028 Deposit safe harbor and de minimis rules.

Under the single deposit safe harbor, an employer will be considered to have satisfied his deposit obligations if:

(1) the amount of any shortfall (the excess of the amount required to be deposited over the amount deposited for the applicable period—monthly, semi-weekly or daily) does not exceed the greater of $100 or 2% of the amount of employment taxes required to be deposited, (Reg § 31.6302-1(f)(1)(i), (2)) and

(2) the employer deposits the shortfall on or before the shortfall make-up date. (Reg § 31.6302-1(f)(1)(ii)) For a monthly depositor this is no later than the due date for the quarterly return. For a semi-weekly and one-day depositor this is on or before the first Wednesday or Friday (whichever is earlier) falling on or after the 15th day of the month following the month in which the deposit was required to be made. (Reg § 31.6302-1(f)(3))

Under the de minimis rule, an employer's obligation is satisfied if the total amount of accumulated employment taxes for the quarter is less than $500 and the amount is fully

---

19. ¶ S-5501 *et seq.*   20. ¶ T-10727; ¶ 63,014.

Footnote references beginning with letters are to paragraphs in RIA's Federal Tax Coordinator 2d and RIA's Analysis of Federal Taxes: Income. Footnote references beginning with numbers are to paragraphs in RIA's United States Tax Reporter.

deposited or paid with a timely filed return for the quarter. (Reg § 31.6302-1(f)(4))[21]

¶ 3029 Withholding on Gambling Winnings

Payors must withhold 28% from certain gambling winnings paid.

Payors must withhold 28% on proceeds of more than $5,000 (Code Sec. 3402(q)(1)) from:

(1) a wagering transaction in a parimutuel pool with respect to horse races, dog races or jai alai if the amount of the proceeds is at least 300 times as large as the amount wagered; (Code Sec. 3402(q)(3)(C)(ii))

(2) a wager placed in a state-conducted lottery; (Code Sec. 3402(q)(3)(B))

(3) a sweepstakes, wagering pool or lottery (other than a state-conducted lottery); (Code Sec. 3402(q)(3)(C)(i))

(4) all other wagering transactions if the amount of the proceeds is at least 300 times as large as the amount wagered. (Code Sec. 3402(q)(3)(A))[22]

"Proceeds" means amount received from the wager reduced by the amount of the wager. (Code Sec. 3402(q)(4)(A))[23] Amounts paid with respect to identical wagers are treated as paid with respect to a single wager. (Reg § 31.3402(q)-1(c)(1)(ii))[24]

The above withholding rules don't apply to slot machines, keno and bingo winnings. (Code Sec. 3402(q)(5)) However, backup withholding (¶ 3039) may apply.[25]

A person who receives gambling winnings subject to withholding must provide certain information on Form W-2G or Form 5754 and give it to the payor. (Code Sec. 3402(q)(6); Reg § 31.3402(q)-1(e))[26]

¶ 3030 Pension, Annuity and Other Withholding

Withholding is required on periodic and lump-sum payments from certain employee plans and certain annuities. However, certain recipients may elect not to have any tax withheld.

¶ 3031 Eligible rollover distributions.

Unless a distributee elects to have the distribution paid directly to an eligible retirement plan under the Code Sec. 401(a)(31)(A) trustee-to-trustee rules, a payor must withhold 20% of any designated distribution that is an "eligible rollover distribution." The Code Sec. 3405(a) and (b) withholding rules (¶ 3033 *et seq.*) don't apply to an eligible rollover distribution. (Code Sec. 3405(c)) An exception to this 20% withholding rule applies to pre-'94 distributions for certain annuities purchased by a state where state law prohibits a direct trustee-to trustee transfer.[27]

An eligible rollover distribution (reported by the payor on Form 1099-R) (Reg § 31.3405(c)-1T, Q&A-12) is any distribution to an employee from a qualified trust *other than* a required distribution under Code Sec. 401(a)(9) or any distribution which is one of a series of substantially equal periodic payments made not less frequently than annually: (1) for the life (or life expectancy) of the employee (or joint lives or expectancies of the employee and his designated beneficiary), or (2) for a specified period of ten years or more. (Code Sec. 3405(c)(3), Code Sec. 402(f)(2)(A), (c)(4); Reg § 1.402(c)-2T, Q&A-5)[28]

No withholding is required if the total distribution paid to the distributee under the plan within one tax year is expected to be less than $200. (Reg § 31.3405(c)-1T, Q&A-10)[29]

21. ¶ S-5513 *et seq.*.	24. ¶ J-8609; ¶ 34,024.26.	26. ¶ J-8613; ¶ 34,024.26.	28. ¶ J-8541.
22. ¶ J-8603; ¶ 34,024.26.	25. ¶ J-8604; ¶ 34,026.26.	27. ¶ J-8540 *et seq.*	29. ¶ J-8542.
23. ¶ J-8606 *et seq.*; ¶ 34,024.26.			

Footnote references beginning with letters are to paragraphs in RIA's Federal Tax Coordinator 2d and RIA's Analysis of Federal Taxes: Income. Footnote references beginning with numbers are to paragraphs in RIA's United States Tax Reporter.

¶ 3032 Required withholding for designated distributions.

Withholding is required for designated distributions. (Code Sec. 3405(d)(1))[30] Designated distributions are periodic as well as nonperiodic (including lump-sum) payments from pension, profit sharing, stock bonus or other employer deferred compensation plans, as well as from IRAs and commercial annuities, whether or not the contract was purchased under an employer's plan for employees. (Code Sec. 3405(e)) Annuity payments and other distributions under a state or local government deferred compensation plan, other than a Code Sec. 457 plan, including the Civil Service Retirement System are subject to income tax withholding as well. (Reg § 35.3405-1, Q&A-22, -23)[31]

The payor of a designated distribution must withhold and is liable for the payment of the tax (unless the payee elects out). But in the case of a qualified pension, profit sharing, stock bonus or annuity plan, the plan administrator has the responsibility, unless he directs the payor to withhold and provides the payor with the information set out in the regs. In that case, the responsibility reverts to the payor. (Code Sec. 3405(d); Reg § 35.3405-1, E-3)[32]

¶ 3033 Withholding from periodic payments.

Tax must be withheld in accordance with a recipient's withholding certificate or, if none, by treating the payee as a married individual claiming three withholding exemptions (Code Sec. 3405(a)(4))[33] even if the payor is aware the payee is single. (Reg § 35.3405-1, B-4) The amount to be withheld is calculated separately from any amounts that actually are wages to the payee for the same period. (Reg § 35.3405-1, B-1)

¶ 3034 Election out of withholding on periodic payments—Form W-4P.

A recipient of periodic payments (except for certain U.S. citizens and expatriates living abroad, see ¶ 3038) may elect not to have any tax withheld. The election remains in effect until revoked. (Code Sec. 3405(a)(2))[34] Elect (or revoke) on Form W-4P.[35]

If the recipient doesn't furnish his taxpayer identification number (TIN) to the payor or if IRS has notified the payor that the TIN furnished is incorrect, an election out of withholding is not effective. (Code Sec. 3405(e)(12))[36]

For 20% mandatory withholding on "eligible rollover distributions," see ¶ 3031.

¶ 3035 Withholding from nonperiodic distributions.

The payor of any nonperiodic distribution must withhold an amount equal to 10% of that distribution. (Code Sec. 3405(b)(1))[37]

¶ 3036 Electing out of withholding on nonperiodic distributions—Form W-4P.

A payee (except for certain U.S. citizens and expatriates living abroad, see ¶ 3038) may elect exemption from withholding for any nonperiodic distribution. The election is made on a distribution-by-distribution basis. (Code Sec. 3405(b)(2)(A), (B))[38] Elect (or revoke) on Form W-4P.[39]

If the recipient doesn't furnish his taxpayer identification number (TIN) to the payor or if IRS has notified the payor that the TIN furnished is incorrect, an election out of withholding is not effective. (Code Sec. 3405(e)(12))[40]

For 20% mandatory withholding on "eligible rollover distributions," see ¶ 3031.

---

30. ¶ J-8501 *et seq.*; ¶ 34,054.
31. ¶ J-8504 *et seq.*; ¶ 34,054.
32. ¶ J-8524 *et seq.*; ¶ 34,054.

33. ¶ J-8521; ¶ 34,054.
34. ¶ J-8522; ¶ 34,054.
35. ¶ J-8524; ¶ 34,054.

36. ¶ J-8512.
37. ¶ J-8526; ¶ 34,054.
38. ¶ J-8533; ¶ 34,054.

39. ¶ J-8533; ¶ 34,054.
40. ¶ J-8512.

Footnote references beginning with letters are to paragraphs in RIA's Federal Tax Coordinator 2d and RIA's Analysis of Federal Taxes: Income. Footnote references beginning with numbers are to paragraphs in RIA's United States Tax Reporter.

¶ 3037 Payor must notify payee of right to elect to have no tax withheld.

For periodic payments, the notice to make, renew, or revoke the election is required no earlier than six months before and no later than the date of the first payment. For nonperiodic payments the notice should be given not earlier than six months before the distribution and not later than the time that will give the payee reasonable time to elect out. (Code Sec. 3405(e)(10)(B); Reg § 35.3405-1, D-9)[41]

The notice must state that withholding will apply unless the payee elects otherwise, and if he elects no withholding, estimated tax may apply. A sample statement is in the regs. (Reg § 35.3405-1, D-21, D-25)[42]

¶ 3038 Electing out of withholding where payment is to be delivered outside the U.S.

An election out of withholding may not be made for any periodic or nonperiodic payment that is to be delivered outside the U.S. and possessions of the U.S. (Code Sec. 3405(e)(13)(A)) *unless* the recipient certifies to the payor that the recipient is neither a U.S. citizen, a resident alien of the U.S., nor a nonresident alien who in the last ten years has lost his U.S. citizenship in order to avoid U.S. taxes and is therefore subject to Code Sec. 877. (Code Sec. 3405(e)(13)(B))[43]

¶ 3039 Backup Withholding

A payor of any reportable payment must deduct and withhold 31% of the payment under various circumstances.

Reportable payments (¶ 3041) are treated as if they were wages. Amounts deducted and withheld are treated as if they were deducted and withheld from wages. (Code Sec. 3406(h)(10))[44]

¶ 3040 When backup withholding is required.

A payor of any reportable payment (¶ 3041) must deduct and withhold 31% of the payment if:

(1) The payee has failed to furnish his taxpayer identification number (TIN) to the payor (Code Sec. 3406(a)(1)(A)) or furnishes an "obviously incorrect number," (Code Sec. 3406(h)(1)) i.e., one without nine digits or which includes letters of the alphabet. (Reg § 35a.9999-3, Q&A-33)

(2) IRS or a broker has notified (the "B-notice") the payor that the TIN furnished by the payee is incorrect. (Code Sec. 3406(a)(1), (d)(2))

(3) There has been a notified payee underreporting with respect to interest and dividends. (Code Sec. 3406(a)(1)(C))

(4) The payee has failed to make the exemption certification (on Form W-9) with respect to interest and dividends. (Code Sec. 3406(a)(1)(D))[45]

Backup withholding doesn't apply to any payment made to an organization exempt from tax under Code Sec. 501(a) (with certain exceptions); the U.S., a state, the District of Columbia, a U.S. possession, or their political subdivisions; a foreign government or its political subdivisions; an international organization; any wholly-owned agency or instrumentality of any of the above political entities; or any other person specified in regs. (Code Sec. 3406(g)(1)) Payments to a fiduciary or nominee account, (Reg § 31.3406(d)-5(b)) and payments of U.S. source portfolio interest to sources outside the U.S. (Reg § 35a.9999-5(a), Q&A-2) are not subject to backup withholding.[46]

---

41. ¶s J-8525, J-8534; ¶ 34,054.   43. ¶ J-8537; ¶ 34,054.   45. ¶ J-9001; ¶ 34,064.   46. ¶ J-9107; ¶ 34,064.
42. ¶ J-8534; ¶ 34,054.   44. ¶ J-9007; ¶ 34,064.

Footnote references beginning with letters are to paragraphs in RIA's Federal Tax Coordinator 2d and RIA's Analysis of Federal Taxes: Income. Footnote references beginning with numbers are to paragraphs in RIA's United States Tax Reporter.

¶ 3041 **Reportable payments.**

Reportable payments include most payments for which information returns are required, such as an interest or dividend payment, (Code Sec. 3406(b)(1))[47] payment of interest to a mortgage escrow account, (Reg § 35a.9999-3, Q&A-5)[48] and certain reinvested stock dividends. (Reg § 35a.9999-3, Q&A-8)[49]

---

47. ¶ J-9101; ¶ 34,064.   48. ¶ J-9109; ¶ 34,064.   49. ¶ J-9111.

Footnote references beginning with letters are to paragraphs in RIA's Federal Tax Coordinator 2d and RIA's Analysis of Federal Taxes: Income. Footnote references beginning with numbers are to paragraphs in RIA's United States Tax Reporter.

Chapter 13   Individual's Tax Computation—Kiddie Tax—Self-Employment Tax—Estimated Tax

¶ *3100* How Income Tax on Individuals is Computed ▬▬▬▬▬▬▬▬

The annual income tax liability of an individual on taxable income is computed by using either the tax rate schedules or (when taxable income is $100,000 or less) the tax tables. The tax liability so determined is increased for some individuals by other taxes, e.g., the self-employment tax and the alternative minimum tax, and is reduced by certain credits.

For taxation of unearned income of children under 14 (kiddie tax), see ¶ 3133 *et seq.*

¶ *3101* Steps in computing taxable income.

An individual taxpayer must first compute gross income. Gross income generally means all income from all sources. (Code Sec. 61)

After determining gross income, taxpayer subtracts certain allowable deductions to reach his adjusted gross income (¶ 3102). (Code Sec. 62)

Finally, taxpayer subtracts other allowable deductions to reach taxable income. Itemizers reduce adjusted gross income by allowable deductions (other than the standard deduction) and personal exemptions, see ¶ 3106 *et seq.* (Code Sec. 63(a)) Nonitemizers reduce adjusted gross income by the standard deduction and personal exemptions. (Code Sec. 63(b))[1]

¶ *3102* Computing adjusted gross income (AGI).

Subtract the following deductions from gross income to arrive at AGI: (Code Sec. 62)[2]

■ Trade or business expenses (other than unreimbursed employee business expenses).

■ Pre-'94 self-employed medical insurance deduction (¶ 1528).

■ Moving expense deduction after '93 (¶ 1645 *et seq.*).

■ 50% of self-employment tax (¶ 1745).

■ Deduction for amortization of reforestation expenditures (¶ 1988).

■ Amounts forfeited to a bank or savings institution for premature withdrawal of funds from a deposit account (¶ 2167).

■ Alimony and separate maintenance payments (¶ 2150 *et seq.*).

■ Employee expenses that are reimbursed by the employer or a third party (¶ 3103).

■ Employee business expenses of certain performing artists (¶ 3104).

■ Deduction for jury duty pay remitted to an employer (¶ 3105).

■ Contributions to a qualified retirement plan for the self-employed.

■ Deductions allowed for contributions to individual retirement accounts (IRAs) (¶ 4352).

■ The "total taxable amount" of a lump-sum distribution from an employee benefit plan (¶ 4351 *et seq.*).

■ Deductions in connection with property held for the production of rents or royalties.

■ Depreciation and depletion deductions of a life tenant or an income beneficiary of a trust, or of an heir, legatee or devisee of an estate.

■ Losses from the sale or exchange of property.

■ Deduction for the repayment of supplemental unemployment compensation benefits.

■ Deduction for certain foreign housing costs by qualified individuals having income earned abroad.

■ Deduction for qualified clean-fuel vehicles and refueling property.

---

1. ¶ A-2500 *et seq.*; ¶ 634.   2. ¶ A-2601; ¶ 624.

Footnote references beginning with letters are to paragraphs in RIA's Federal Tax Coordinator 2d and RIA's Analysis of Federal Taxes: Income. Footnote references beginning with numbers are to paragraphs in RIA's United States Tax Reporter.

¶ 3103 Reimbursed and unreimbursed employee expenses.

An employee can deduct from gross income in computing adjusted gross income employee expenses for which the employee is reimbursed by the employer, its agent, or third party (for whom the employee performs a benefit as an employee of the employer) under an express agreement for reimbursement or other expense allowance arrangement. (Code Sec. 62(a)(2)(A); Reg § 1.62-1T(c)(2))

If the reimbursement is for less than the total expenses paid or incurred by the employee, the unreimbursed expenses are deductible from *adjusted* gross income (not gross income) subject to, for example, the 2%-of-AGI floor (¶ 3107) and the percentage limit on meal and entertainment expenses (¶ 1562). (Reg § 1.62-1T(e)(3))[3]

¶ 3104 Expenses of certain performing artists—Form 2106.

Expenses of certain performing artists are deductible (use Form 2106) in arriving at adjusted gross income despite the general disallowance of unreimbursed employee business expenses as above-the-line deductions. (Code Sec. 62(a)(2)(B)) To qualify, the taxpayer must have earned at least $200 as a performing artist from each of at least two employers during the tax year. (Code Sec. 62(b)(1)(A), (b)(2)) In addition, the allowable expenses must exceed 10% of gross income from the services, and AGI for the year (before deducting these expenses) cannot exceed $16,000. (Code Sec. 62(b)(1)(B), (C)) A married performing artist who lives with his spouse at any time during the year must file a joint return to deduct these expenses in arriving at AGI. (Code Sec. 62(b)(3)(A)) The two-employer requirement and 10%-of-gross-income test are applied separately to each spouse, but the $16,000 test is applied to their combined income. (Code Sec. 62(b)(3)(B))[4]

¶ 3105 Jury duty pay remitted to an employer.

An individual can deduct jury pay from gross income if the employer requires the individual to remit the pay in exchange for a payment by the employer of compensation for the period the individual was performing jury duty. (Code Sec. 62(a)(13))[5]

¶ 3106 Itemized deductions.

Itemized deductions are all allowable deductions except those subtracted from gross income in arriving at adjusted gross income (see ¶ 3102), and except the deductions for personal exemptions. (Code Sec. 63(d))[6]

For treatment of itemized deductions for alternative minimum tax purposes, see ¶ 3208.

¶ 3107 Miscellaneous itemized deductions—2%-of-AGI floor.

Miscellaneous itemized deductions are allowed only to the extent that they, in the aggregate, exceed 2% of adjusted gross income. (Code Sec. 67(a))[7] To the extent any other limit or restriction is placed on a miscellaneous itemized deduction, that other limit applies before the 2% floor. For example, the 2% floor is applied after the percentage limit for business meals and entertainment. (Reg § 1.67-1T(a)(2))[8]

observation: Miscellaneous itemized deductions that don't exceed 2% of AGI are lost. There is no carryover.

Miscellaneous itemized deductions are itemized deductions *other than* deductions for:

- medical expenses;
- taxes;
- interest;

---

3. ¶ A-2605 *et seq.*; ¶ 624.   5. ¶ A-2623; ¶ 624.   7. ¶ A-2707 *et seq.*; ¶ 674.   8. ¶ A-2707; ¶ 674(a).
4. ¶ A-2611; ¶ 624.   6. ¶ A-2700 *et seq.*; ¶ 634.

Footnote references beginning with letters are to paragraphs in RIA's Federal Tax Coordinator 2d and RIA's Analysis of Federal Taxes: Income. Footnote references beginning with numbers are to paragraphs in RIA's United States Tax Reporter.

- charitable contributions;
- casualty losses;
- gambling losses;
- moving expenses before '94;
- impairment-related work expenses;
- estate tax in the case of income in respect of a decedent;
- personal property used in a short sale;
- restored amounts held under a claim of right;
- annuity payments that cease before investment is recovered;
- amortizable bond premium;
- payments by tenant-stockholders in connection with co-op housing corporations. (Code Sec. 67(b))

Miscellaneous itemized deductions include unreimbursed employee business expenses, including union and professional dues and office-at-home expenses to the extent deductible; expenses related to investment income or property, such as investment counsel or advisory fees; tax return preparation costs and related expenses; appraisal fees paid to determine the amount of a casualty loss or a charitable contribution of property; and hobby expenses to the extent of hobby income. (Reg § 1.67-1T(a)(1))[9] For deduction of tax determination costs as business expenses, see ¶ 1610.

If an expense relates to both a trade or business activity (not subject to the 2% floor) and a production of income or tax preparation activity (subject to the 2% floor) the taxpayer must allocate it between the activities on a reasonable basis. (Reg § 1.67-1T(c))[10]

¶ 3108 **Application of 2% floor to partners, S corporation shareholders and other interests in pass-through entities.**

A partner or S corporation shareholder must take into account separately his or her distributive or pro rata share of the partnership's or S corporation's miscellaneous itemized deductions. Similarly, the 2% limit applies to the grantor (or other person treated as the owner) of a grantor trust with respect to items treated as miscellaneous itemized deductions of the grantor (or other owner) under the grantor trust rules. (Reg § 1.67-2T(b)(1))[11] Similar rules apply to affected investors in common trust funds, (Reg § 1.67-2T(d)(1)(ii))[12] nonpublicly offered regulated investment companies (Reg § 1.67-2T(e)(1)(ii))[13] and REMICs. (Reg § 1.67-3T(b)(1))[14]

The above rules don't apply to publicly offered regulated investment companies, (Code Sec. 67(c)(3)) cooperatives, REITs and (except as provided in regs) estates and trusts. (Code Sec. 67(c)(3))[15] For application to estates and trust, see ¶ 3918.

¶ 3109 **Standard deduction.**

The standard deduction is the sum of the basic standard deduction and the additional standard deduction. (Code Sec. 63(c)(1))[16] The basic and additional standard deductions are adjusted each year for inflation. (Code Sec. 63(c)(4))[17]

For '93, the basic standard deduction is $6,200 for joint filers and surviving spouses, $5,450 for heads of household, $3,700 for single people and $3,100 for married people who file separate returns.[18]

For '94, the basic standard deduction is $6,350 for joint filers and surviving spouses, $5,600 for heads of household, $3,800 for single people and $3,175 for married people who

9. ¶ A-2709; ¶ 674(a).
10. ¶ A-2709; ¶ 674.
11. ¶ A-2716; ¶ 674(d).
12. ¶ A-2717; ¶ 674(d).
13. ¶ A-2718; ¶ 674(d).
14. ¶ A-2714; ¶ 674(d).
15. ¶ A-2719; ¶ 674(d).
16. ¶ A-2801; ¶ 634.
17. ¶ A-2801; ¶ 634.
18. ¶ A-2803; ¶ 634.

Footnote references beginning with letters are to paragraphs in RIA's Federal Tax Coordinator 2d and RIA's Analysis of Federal Taxes: Income. Footnote references beginning with numbers are to paragraphs in RIA's United States Tax Reporter.

file separate returns.

Elderly and blind taxpayers get an additional standard deduction. (Code Sec. 63(c)(3)) A taxpayer who is 65 before the close of his tax year is entitled to the additional standard deduction for the elderly. (Code Sec. 63(f)(1))[19] The additional deduction is $700 for '93 ($750 for '94) for a married person or a surviving spouse (Code Sec. 63(f)(1), (2), (c)(4)) (whether or not a joint return is filed), and $900 for '93 ($950 for '94) for a single taxpayer or head of household. (Code Sec. 63(f)(3), (c)(4))[20] One who is both elderly and blind is entitled to each additional standard deduction. (Code Sec. 63(c)(3))[21]

A married individual who files a separate return can claim a spouse's additional standard deduction if the spouse has no gross income and is not the dependent of another taxpayer. (Code Sec. 63(f)(1)(B), (2)(B), Code Sec. 151(b))[22]

The standard deduction is zero for:

- a married individual filing separately whose spouse itemizes deductions;
- a nonresident alien individual;
- an individual filing a short-year return due to a change of accounting period;
- an estate or trust, common trust fund or partnership. (Code Sec. 63(c)(6))[23]

For treatment of the standard deduction for alternative minimum tax purposes, see ¶3208.

¶3110 Limits on basic standard deduction.

For '93 and '94, the basic standard deduction of individuals who can be claimed as dependents by another taxpayer for a tax year beginning in the same calendar year as their own can't exceed the greater of $600 or the individual's earned income. (Code Sec. 63(c)(5))[24]

observation: There's no limit on the *additional* standard deduction, so an elderly and/or blind person who can be claimed as a dependent by another gets this limited basic standard deduction, plus the full elderly and/or blind additional standard deduction(s).

¶3111 Election to itemize deductions in computing taxable income.

No itemized deductions are allowed unless an election to itemize is made on the return. (Code Sec. 63(e)(1), (2)) A taxpayer who elects to itemize and wants to switch to the standard deduction, or vice versa, can do so. But the change cannot be made unless a separately filing spouse makes a consistent change, (Code Sec. 63(e)(3)(A)) and both spouses consent in writing to the assessment of any deficiency resulting from the change. (Code Sec. 63(e)(3)(B))[25]

¶3112 Reduction in itemized deductions.

If an individual's adjusted gross income exceeds the "applicable amount" (see below), otherwise allowable itemized deductions are reduced by the lesser of:

(1) 3% of the excess of adjusted gross income over the applicable amount, or

(2) 80% of the amount of itemized deductions otherwise allowable for the tax year. (Code Sec. 68(a))[26]

The reduction is determined after the application of any other limitations on the allowance of an itemized deduction (Code Sec. 68(d))[27] and it does not apply to the deductions for medical expenses, for investment interest, for nonbusiness casualty and theft losses, and for gambling losses. (Code Sec. 68(c))[28]

---

19. ¶A-2801.
20. ¶A-2809; ¶634.
21. ¶A-2801; ¶634.

22. ¶A-2801.
23. ¶A-2802; ¶634.
24. ¶A-2811 *et seq.*; ¶634.

25. ¶A-2702; ¶634.
26. ¶A-2704; ¶684.01.

27. ¶A-2706; ¶684.01.
28. ¶A-2705; ¶684.01.

Footnote references beginning with letters are to paragraphs in RIA's Federal Tax Coordinator 2d and RIA's Analysis of Federal Taxes: Income. Footnote references beginning with numbers are to paragraphs in RIA's United States Tax Reporter.

For '93, the applicable amount (above) is $108,450 ($54,225 for marrieds filing separately). For '94, the applicable amount is $111,800 ($55,900 for marrieds filing separately). (Code Sec. 68(b)(1))[29]

¶ 3113   Deduction for personal exemptions.

Each taxpayer may be entitled to an exemption for himself and spouse (¶ 3115) and may qualify for an additional exemption for each dependent (¶ 3116 *et seq.*).

The exemption amount for each dependent is $2,350 for '93, $2,450 for '94. (Code Sec. 151(d))[30]

However, an individual (e.g., a child) who can be claimed as a dependent by another (e.g., the child's parent) cannot claim a personal exemption for himself. (Code Sec. 151(d)(2)) The personal exemption phase-out rules (¶ 3114) do not apply in determining whether a deduction for a personal exemption is available to another taxpayer. (Code Sec. 151(d)(3)(D))[31]

caution: The child can't claim a personal exemption even if the parent doesn't take the dependent exemption.

For treatment of personal exemptions for alternative minimum tax purposes, see ¶ 3208.

¶ 3114   Phase-out of personal exemptions.

The personal exemption amount of a taxpayer whose adjusted gross income (AGI) exceeds a specified threshold amount, described below, is reduced by an "applicable percentage." (Code Sec. 151(d)(3)(A)) This applicable percentage is 2% for each $2,500 (or fraction thereof) by which the AGI of a taxpayer (other than a married taxpayer filing separately) exceeds the threshold amount for that taxpayer. For marrieds filing separately, the applicable percentage is 2% for each $1,250 (or fraction of that amount) by which the taxpayer's AGI exceeds the threshold amount. The applicable percentage can't exceed 100%. (Code Sec. 151(d)(3)(B))

The statutory (AGI) threshold amounts (at which the phase-out of personal exemptions begins) that apply for '93 are:

- $162,700 for joint return filers and surviving spouses,
- $135,600 for heads of household,
- $108,450 for unmarried individuals,
- $81,350 for marrieds filing separately.[32]

For '94, the AGI threshold amounts are:

- $167,700 for joint return filers and surviving spouses,
- $139,750 for heads of household,
- $111,800 for unmarried individuals,
- $83,850 for marrieds filing separately.

¶ 3115   Exemptions for spouse.

If a married couple files a joint return, each spouse is allowed one personal exemption. These exemptions are allowed whether or not a spouse has gross income or is a dependent of another taxpayer (though the *other* taxpayer will be denied an exemption, see ¶ 3125). (Reg § 1.151-1(b))[33]

If one spouse dies during the year, the survivor can claim the deceased spouse's exemptions on a joint return, unless the survivor remarries during the same year.[34]

29. ¶ A-2704; ¶ 684.02.   31. ¶ A-3500 *et seq.*; ¶ 1524.   33. ¶ A-3501; ¶ 1514.01.   34. ¶ A-3504; ¶ 1514.01.
30. ¶ A-3500; ¶ 1514.   32. ¶ A-3502; ¶ 1514(a).

Footnote references beginning with letters are to paragraphs in RIA's Federal Tax Coordinator 2d and RIA's Analysis of Federal Taxes: Income. Footnote references beginning with numbers are to paragraphs in RIA's United States Tax Reporter.

On a separate return, the taxpayer may claim an exemption for a spouse only if, for the calendar year in which the taxpayer's taxable year begins, the spouse has *no* gross income, *and* is not the dependent of another. (Code Sec. 151(b))[35]

¶ 3116 Exemption for dependents.

A taxpayer is entitled to a deduction equal to the exemption amount (see ¶ 3113) for each person who qualifies as his "dependent." (Code Sec. 151(c))

A person qualifies as taxpayer's dependent only if *all* of these tests are met:[36]

(1) Relationship (¶ 3117) or member of household (¶ 3118) test.

(2) Gross income test (except for certain children) (¶ 3119).

(3) Support test (¶ 3120 *et seq.*).

(4) Joint return test (¶ 3125).

(5) Citizenship or residence test (¶ 3126).

¶ 3117 Relationship test.

A person meets the relationship test only if he has one of the following relationships to the taxpayer:

- child or descendant of child;

- stepchild;

- brother, sister, by whole or half blood;

- stepbrother, stepsister;

- father, mother or ancestor of either (grandparent, great-grandparent, etc.);

- stepfather, stepmother;

- nephew, niece;

- brother or sister of father or mother (uncle, aunt);

- brother-, sister-, father-, mother-, son-, or daughter-in-law. (Code Sec. 152(a), (b)(1); Reg § 1.151-3(a))[37]

A child born alive qualifies for the full exemption (if other tests are met) even if the child lives only momentarily.[38]

A person is treated as the taxpayer's child if the child is:

- legally adopted by the taxpayer; (Code Sec. 152(b)(2)) or

- a member of a taxpayer's household, and is placed with taxpayer by an authorized placement agency for legal adoption by the taxpayer under a formal application filed with the agency—the agency must be authorized to place children for adoption by a government or governmental subdivision (state, foreign country, etc.); (Code Sec. 152(b)(2); Reg § 1.152-2(c)(2))[39]

- a foster child *if* he meets the member of household test (¶ 3118). (Reg § 1.152-2(c)(4))[40]

Death or divorce doesn't terminate relationships established by marriage. Thus, the relationship of son-in-law and father-in-law survives the spouse's death. (Reg § 1.152-2(d))[41]

If a dependent died during the year, and the dependency tests were met for the part of the year he lived, the taxpayer can claim a full exemption for him.[42]

The relationship must exist with respect to the taxpayer claiming the exemption on his separate return. On a joint return, the relationship need exist with respect to only one

35. ¶ A-3501; ¶ 1514.01.   37. ¶ A-3606 *et seq.*; ¶ 1524.03.   39. ¶ A-3612; ¶ 1524.03.   41. ¶ A-3607; ¶ 1524.03.
36. ¶ A-3600; ¶ 1524.   38. ¶ A-3602; ¶ 1524.03.   40. ¶ A-3613; ¶ 1524.03.   42. ¶ A-3602; ¶ 1524.03.

Footnote references beginning with letters are to paragraphs in RIA's Federal Tax Coordinator 2d and RIA's Analysis of Federal Taxes: Income. Footnote references beginning with numbers are to paragraphs in RIA's United States Tax Reporter.

spouse, and it doesn't matter which spouse furnishes the dependent's support.[43]

These individuals don't meet the relationship test : taxpayer's grandnephew, grandniece, stepchild's descendant, aunt's husband, foster parent.[44]

¶ 3118 Member of household test.

A person (other than taxpayer's spouse) meets this test if, for more than half the taxpayer's tax year, that person has as his principal place of abode the home of the taxpayer and is a member of the taxpayer's household. (Code Sec. 152(a)(9))[45]

¶ 3119 Gross income test.

Except for certain children, see below, a person with gross income equal to or greater than the exemption amount (see ¶ 3113) during the calendar year in which the taxpayer's taxable year begins can't qualify as a dependent. (Code Sec. 151(c)(1))[46]

The gross income test doesn't apply to a child of the taxpayer who *either*:

■ hasn't reached age 19 at the end of the calendar year in which taxpayer's tax year begins, *or*

■ is a student who has not reached age 24 at the close of the calendar year. (Code Sec. 151(c)(1)(B))[47]

To qualify as a student, the child must, during some part of each of at least five calendar months, whether or not consecutive, during the calendar year in which taxpayer's year begins, be a full-time student enrolled at an educational institution, or must pursue a full-time course of institutional on-farm training. (Code Sec. 151(c)(4); Reg § 1.151-3(b))[48] A child who attends school exclusively at night isn't a full-time student. (Reg § 1.151-3(b))[49]

An educational institution doesn't include: correspondence schools; employee training courses; on-the-job training (generally including hospital internship), except on-farm training. (Reg § 1.151-3(c))[50]

¶ 3120 Support test.

Except for a divorced or separated parent claiming his child as a dependent, a taxpayer can claim a person as a dependent only if he furnishes more than half that person's support (or, under a multiple support agreement, more than 10% of that person's support) for the calendar year in which taxpayer's tax year begins. (Code Sec. 152(a))[1]

The source of support funds is immaterial. Funds used for support are counted in total support even though they are tax-free.[2] Where the claimed dependent is in an institution supported by a state, charity, etc., the amount spent by the agency on the claimed dependent is part of support and is treated as furnished by the agency.[3]

Where a husband and wife receive social security benefits in one check in joint names, half of the total is considered used for the support of each unless shown otherwise.[4]

¶ 3121 Multiple support agreement—Form 2120.

A taxpayer who fails to furnish more than half a person's support can claim that person as a dependent if, for the calendar year in which the taxpayer's tax year begins, taxpayer meets these tests:

■ over half the person's support was received from a group of persons (including the taxpayer) who would each have been entitled to claim the person as a dependent for a tax year beginning in the calendar year if each had furnished more than half the claimed dependent's support; *and*

---

43. ¶ A-3607.
44. ¶ A-3607.
45. ¶ A-3608 *et seq.*; ¶ 1524.03.

46. ¶ A-3616; ¶ 1524.01.
47. ¶ A-3617; ¶ 1524.01.
48. ¶ A-3617; ¶ 1524.01.

49. ¶ A-3620; ¶ 1524.01.
50. ¶ A-3619; ¶ 1524.01.
1. ¶ A-3700 *et seq.*; ¶ 1524.05.

2. ¶ A-3711.
3. ¶ A-3711.
4. ¶ A-3712; ¶ 1524.09.

Footnote references beginning with letters are to paragraphs in RIA's Federal Tax Coordinator 2d and RIA's Analysis of Federal Taxes: Income. Footnote references beginning with numbers are to paragraphs in RIA's United States Tax Reporter.

- no one person furnished more than half that support; *and*

- the taxpayer contributed more than 10% of support; *and*

- each person in the group who contributed more than 10% (except the taxpayer) signs a written declaration (Form 2120 can be used) that he will not claim that individual as a dependent for any tax year beginning in the calendar year. (Code Sec. 152(c))

All the declarations must be attached to the return of the taxpayer claiming the dependency deduction. (Reg § 1.152-3(c))[5]

¶ 3122 "Support" defined.

Support includes:[6]

- food, school lunches, toilet articles and haircuts;

- clothing;

- recreation, including toys, summer camp, horseback riding, entertainment and vacation expenses;

- medical and dental care, including premiums on accident and health insurance;

- child care expenses, even though a credit is also allowed for these expenses;

- allowances, gifts;

- son's or daughter's wedding costs;

- lodging—when furnished in kind, it is measured by its fair market value rather than actual cost; (Reg § 1.152-1(a)(2))[7]

- education—these costs include board, uniforms at military schools, and tuition, even where free schooling is available. Scholarship payments received by a dependent are treated as support furnished by someone other than the taxpayer. However, scholarships aren't counted in determining whether the taxpayer furnished more than half the dependent's support if these tests are met:

> . . . the dependent is a child (including stepchild, foster child, or child adopted or placed for adoption) of taxpayer, and

> . . . is a full-time student at an educational institution, (Reg § 1.152-1(c))[8]

- social security benefits received by a child and used for his support are considered provided by the child, (Reg § 1.152-1(a)(2)(ii))[9]

- Armed Forces dependency allotments—the amount contributed by the government *and* the amount withheld from the pay of the member of the Armed Forces are treated as contributed by the member.[10]

¶ 3123 Allocating support of several contributors to several dependents.

Where more than one member of a household contributes towards expenses that are equally applicable to all members of the household, the contributors are presumed (absent contrary evidence) to have pooled their contributions towards the support of all members of the household. The total contributed is divided equally among the members as amounts paid for their support, unless there is proof of how much was actually spent for particular members. Members receiving more than they contribute are treated as receiving support from members receiving less than they contribute, to the extent the amount received exceeds the amount contributed.

Where members of a household contribute to their own support and also receive support from an individual outside the household, the "outsider" is presumed, absent contrary evidence, to be contributing equally to each member.

---

5. ¶ A-3731; ¶ 1524.09. 7. ¶ A-3714 *et seq.*; ¶ 1524.09. 9. ¶ A-3712; ¶ 1524.09. 10. ¶ A-3711; ¶ 1524.09.
6. ¶ A-3711 *et seq.*; ¶ 1524.05. 8. ¶ A-3721; ¶ 1524.07.

Footnote references beginning with letters are to paragraphs in RIA's Federal Tax Coordinator 2d and RIA's Analysis of Federal Taxes: Income. Footnote references beginning with numbers are to paragraphs in RIA's United States Tax Reporter.

These rules can give one contributor the dependency exemptions for the entire household, if he contributes more than half the support of the entire household.[11]

A taxpayer who contributes less than half the support of the entire household can get an exemption for a particular member if the taxpayer shows that his contribution was more than half the support of that member and was clearly spent for *that* member's support.[12]

¶ 3124 Children of divorced or separated parents.

The custodial parent is entitled to the exemption, (Code Sec. 152(e)(1)) unless:

■ a multiple support agreement designates another person to get the exemption; (Code Sec. 152(e)(3)) or

■ the custodial parent releases (on Form 8332) the claim to the noncustodial parent (Code Sec. 152(e)(2)(A)) (release can be for a single year, for a number of specified years, or for all future years; (Reg § 1.152-4T(a), Q&A-4)) or

■ a qualified pre-'85 instrument shifts the exemption to the noncustodial parent. (Code Sec. 152(e)(4))[13]

¶ 3125 Joint return test.

A taxpayer can't take a dependency exemption for a married person who files a joint return with his or her spouse for a tax year beginning in the same calendar year that the taxpayer's tax year begins. (Code Sec. 151(c)(2)) However, an exemption may be claimed for a married dependent if neither the dependent nor his or her spouse is *required* to file a return but they file only to claim a refund of tax withheld.[14]

¶ 3126 Citizenship or residence test.

The claimed dependent must be: a U.S. citizen or U.S. resident; a U.S. national, e.g., an American Samoan; certain legally adopted children of U.S. citizens or nationals; or a resident of Canada or Mexico. (Code Sec. 152(b)(3); Reg § 1.152-2(a))[15]

¶ 3127 Dependents of married couples.

On a joint return, the married couple can claim exemptions for all persons who are dependents of either or both spouses. On a separate return, however, a spouse can claim exemptions only for his or her own dependents.[16]

If a husband and wife in a community property state file separate returns, they may divide the total of their exemptions for dependents between them, but they may not divide up an exemption for any one dependent between them.[17]

¶ 3128 Tax rate schedules.

There are four tax rate schedules. (Code Sec. 1) They are reproduced in ¶ 1100 *et seq.* There is a schedule for:

(1) Single persons (not married at year's end), including certain marrieds living apart (¶ 3131). These rates are more favorable than those for married persons filing separate returns, but less favorable than head of household and (generally) joint return rates.

(2) Married couples filing joint returns and certain widows and, widowers who qualify as "surviving spouses." (¶ 3130) These are often the most favorable rates.

(3) Heads of household. These rates are more favorable than those for single persons.

(4) Married persons filing separate returns—the least favorable rates. (Code Sec. 1)[18]

There are five tax brackets, with rates of 15%, 28%, 31%, 36% and 39.6%. (Code

---

| 11. ¶ A-3708. | 13. ¶ A-3800 *et seq.*; ¶ 1524.10. | 15. ¶ A-3623; ¶ 1524.04. | 17. ¶ A-3615. |
| 12. ¶ A-3709. | 14. ¶ A-3622; ¶ 1524.02. | 16. ¶ A-3607; ¶ 1524.03. | 18. ¶ A-1100; ¶ 14.03. |

Footnote references beginning with letters are to paragraphs in RIA's Federal Tax Coordinator 2d and RIA's Analysis of Federal Taxes: Income. Footnote references beginning with numbers are to paragraphs in RIA's United States Tax Reporter.

Sec. 1)[19]

The tax is computed by applying the tax rate schedules (or tax tables, ¶ 3129) to taxable income.

¶ 3129 Tax tables.

IRS has drawn up tax tables, based on the tax rates. (Code Sec. 3(a)(1))[20] Tax tables, reproduced in ¶ 1110 *et seq.*, are used by those whose taxable income does not exceed $100,000. (Code Sec. 3(a))[21]

However, the tables aren't used by those who file a short period return because they changed their accounting period. (Code Sec. 3(b)(1))[22]

¶ 3130 When surviving spouse (qualifying widow(er)) gets benefit of joint return rates.

A surviving spouse (qualifying widow(er)) whose spouse died during either of the surviving spouse's two tax years immediately preceding the tax year (Code Sec. 2(a)(1)) is taxed at joint return rates (Code Sec. 1(a)(2)) if the surviving spouse:

■ has not remarried at any time before the close of the tax year, (Code Sec. 2(a)(2)(A))

■ "maintains" (pays more than 50% of the costs of) a household as his or her home which is the "principal place of abode" of a son or daughter (including adopted and foster children) or a stepson or stepdaughter,

■ is entitled to a dependency deduction for at least one child, (Code Sec. 2(a)(1)) and

■ was entitled to file a joint return with the deceased spouse for the year of death. (Code Sec. 2(a)(2)(B))[23]

⊘ *observation:* These surviving spouse rules *don't* apply for the year the spouse died. For when a joint return can be filed (and thus joint return rates used) in a year a spouse dies, see ¶ 4707.

¶ 3131 Certain married individuals living apart ("abandoned spouses").

A married taxpayer is considered single for tax purposes if he or she meets all of the following tests:

(1) Files a separate return.

(2) Maintains as his or her home a household that for more than half the tax year is the principal place of abode of a son, daughter, stepson or stepdaughter for whom taxpayer is entitled to a dependency deduction even if the custodial parent allows the other parent to claim the exemption for the child. (Code Sec. 7703(b)(1))

(3) Furnishes more than half the cost of maintaining the household. (Code Sec. 7703(b)(2))

(4) Does not have the other spouse living with him or her during the last six months of the tax year. (Code Sec. 7703(b)(3); Reg § 1.143-1(b))[24]

These individuals can use the tax rates for single persons or, if they qualify, the more favorable head of household rates.[25]

⊘ *observation:* Both spouses, or either spouse, can qualify as an unmarried taxpayer by meeting the tests. If one spouse qualifies and the other does not, the spouse who does not qualify must use married-filing-separately tax rates.

---

19. ¶ A-1100; ¶ 14.
20. ¶ A-1004; ¶ 60,144.
21. ¶ A-1100; ¶s 14.16, 90,650.
22. ¶ A-1100; ¶ 34.02.
23. ¶ A-1700 *et seq.*; ¶ 24.02.
24. ¶ A-1610; ¶ 77,034.01.
25. ¶ A-1403; ¶ 14.04(1).

Footnote references beginning with letters are to paragraphs in RIA's Federal Tax Coordinator 2d and RIA's Analysis of Federal Taxes: Income. Footnote references beginning with numbers are to paragraphs in RIA's United States Tax Reporter.

¶ 3132 Head of household status.

To qualify as a head of household, the taxpayer must be a U.S. citizen or resident throughout the year, unmarried at the close of the year, except that a married individual living apart from his or her spouse ¶ 3131may qualify, and must:

■ maintain as his home a household that for more than one-half of taxable year is the "principal place of abode" for a relative for whom he is entitled to a dependency deduction (even if, for divorced parents, the custodial parent allows the noncustodial parent to claim the dependency exemption), except that if the relative is taxpayer's unmarried child (including adopted or foster child) or grandchild it doesn't matter whether or not the taxpayer is entitled to a dependency deduction, (Code Sec. 2(b)(1)(A)) or

■ maintain a household (not necessarily his own) that for the taxable year is the principal place of abode for either of his parents, if taxpayer is entitled to a dependency deduction for either parent. (Code Sec. 2(b)(1)(B)) Supporting a dependent parent in a rest home or old age home qualifies for this purpose.[26]

Maintaining a home or household requires a contribution of more than 50% of its cost. (Reg § 1.2-2(d))[27]

A person's temporary absences from the household doesn't prevent treating the household as his principal abode. (Reg § 1.2-2(c))[28]

¶ 3133 Tax on Unearned Income of Children Under 14 (Kiddie Tax) ▬▬▬▬▬

A child under age 14 pays tax at his or her parents' highest marginal rate on the child's net unearned income (i.e., unearned income over specified levels) if that tax is higher than what the child would otherwise pay on it. The parents can instead elect to include on their own return the child's gross income in excess of (for '93 or '94) $1,200.

The child pays a tax (computed on Form 8615) equal to the *greater* of:

(1) the sum of (a) the tax that would be imposed if the taxable income of the child for the tax year were reduced by the net unearned income (¶ 3135) of the child, plus (b) the child's share of the allocable parental tax (below), (Code Sec. 1(g)(1)(B)) or

(2) the tax imposed on the child without regard to (1), above, (Code Sec. 1(g)(1)(A)) that is, the tax imposed on the child as a single person.[29]

The "child's share" of the allocable parental tax ((1), above) equals the amount that bears the same ratio to the total allocable parental tax (below) as the child's net unearned income bears to the aggregate net unearned income of all children of the parent to whom this tax applies. (Code Sec. 1(g)(3)(B))[30]

The "allocable parental tax" is the excess of: (1) the tax that would be imposed by these rules on the parent's taxable income if that income included the net unearned income of all children of the parent to whom these rules apply, over (2) the tax imposed on the parent without regard to these rules. (Code Sec. 1(g)(3)(A))[31]

For the child's alternative minimum tax, see ¶ 3203.

¶ 3134 Child defined.

A child is any child for any tax year who hasn't reached age 14 before the close of the tax year, if either parent of the child is alive at the close of the tax year. (Code Sec. 1(g)(2))[32]

---

26. ¶ A-1400 *et seq.*; ¶ 14.04(3). 28. ¶ A-1414; ¶ 14.04(3). 30. ¶ A-1308; ¶ 14.061. 32. ¶ A-1301; ¶ 14.061.
27. ¶ A-1416; ¶ 14.04(2).   29. ¶ A-1300; ¶ 14.061. 31. ¶ A-1305; ¶ 14.063.

Footnote references beginning with letters are to paragraphs in RIA's Federal Tax Coordinator 2d and RIA's Analysis of Federal Taxes: Income. Footnote references beginning with numbers are to paragraphs in RIA's United States Tax Reporter.

¶ 3135 Net unearned income.

"Net unearned income" is adjusted gross unearned income reduced by the sum of the amounts determined under (1), (2) and (3), below. (Code Sec. (1)(g)(4(A); Reg § 1.1(i)-1T, Q&A-6)

These are:

(1) the standard deduction in effect for the tax year which is allowable to a child who can be claimed as a dependent on another person's return; (Code Sec. 1(g)(4)(A)(ii)(I); Reg § 1.1(i)-1T, Q&A-6)

(2) the greater of (a) the standard deduction amount determined in (1), above, or (b) the amount of the itemized deductions which are directly connected with the production of the unearned income if the child itemizes deductions; (Code Sec. 1(g)(4)(A)(ii)(II); Reg § 1.1(i)-1T, Q&A-6)

(3) adjustments to income attributable to the unearned (investment) income, such as the penalty on early withdrawal of savings.[33]

However, net unearned income for any tax year can't exceed the child's taxable income for the year. (Code Sec. 1(g)(4)(B))

As a result of the above rules, the child's first $600 of unearned income in '93 and '94 is not taxed at all, the next $600 of unearned income in '93 and '94 is taxed at the child's tax rate, and the excess of the child's unearned income is taxed at the parent's marginal rate.[34]

Earned income means earned income as defined in Code Sec. 911(d)(2), i.e., income attributable to wages, salaries, or other amounts received as compensation for personal services. (Code Sec. 1(g)(4)(A)(i); Reg § 1.1(i)-1T, Q&A-6) Thus, any social security or pension benefits paid to the child would not be earned income (and would be unearned income). (Reg § 1.1(i)-1T, Q&A-9)[35]

¶ 3136 Parents' election to claim child's unearned income on parent's return—Form 8814.

A parent can elect (on Form 8814) to include in the parent's gross income for the tax year the gross income (in excess of $1,000) of each child for whom the election is made. (Code Sec. 1(g)(7)(B)(i); Reg § 5h.6(a)(1)) The child is then treated as having no gross income for the year and isn't required to file a return. (Code Sec. 1(g)(7)(A))

This election only applies if the child's gross income is only from interest and dividends, is more than $500 and less than $5,000, and the child made no estimated tax payments and backup withholding didn't apply. (Code Sec. 1(g)(7)(A))

The electing parent's tax equals the sum of the tax determined with the child's gross income in excess of $1,000, plus, for each child to whom the election applies, the lesser of $75 or 15% of the excess of the gross income of the child over $500. (Code Sec. 1(g)(7)(B)(ii)) Any interest income that is a tax preference item of the child is treated as a tax preference item of the parent. (Code Sec. 1(g)(7)(B)(iii))[36]

Illustration: S, age six, received $2,200 in interest income in the tax year. He had no other income. S's parents elect to include his income on their tax return. They include $1,200 of S's gross income ($2,200 gross income – $1,000). They also must include $75 (the smaller of $75 or 15% of $1,700 ($2,200 – $500)) tax on their return.

¶ 3137 Self-Employment Tax

Self-employed persons pay social security and Medicare taxes for themselves as part of their income tax. This self-employment tax is based on net earnings from

---

33. ¶ A-1304; ¶ 14.061.   34. ¶ A-1304 *et seq.*; ¶ 14.061.   35. ¶ A-1302.   36. ¶ A-1312; ¶ 14.067.

Footnote references beginning with letters are to paragraphs in RIA's Federal Tax Coordinator 2d and RIA's Analysis of Federal Taxes: Income. Footnote references beginning with numbers are to paragraphs in RIA's United States Tax Reporter.

self-employment, not on taxable income.

Combined social security (OASDI) and Medicare (hospital insurance) taxes are imposed on self-employment income. The applicable contribution base for social security tax is determined for each calendar year under the Social Security Act.[37]

For contribution bases and rates for these taxes, see ¶ 1108.

Compute the tax on Schedule SE, Form 1040.

¶ 3138 Self-employment income subject to self-employment tax.

Self-employment income consists of net earnings from self-employment (¶ 3139). However, in computing the self-employment tax, the maximum amount of self-employment income taxable is the excess of the applicable contribution base (¶ 3137) which is in effect for the calendar year in which the tax year begins *minus* the amount of any wages subject to social security received by the individual in the same tax year. But if net earnings from self-employment are *less* than $400, no self-employment tax is imposed. (Code Sec. 1402(b))[38]

¶ 3139 Net earnings from self-employment.

This is gross income, under the individual's income tax accounting method, from a trade or business carried on by him, less allowable deductions attributable to that business, plus the distributive share of partnership taxable income or loss from any business conducted as a partnership of which he is a member. (Reg § 1.1402(a)-1)[39] Among the deductions allowed is an amount equal to 7.65% times the taxpayer's net earnings from self-employment for the tax year (determined without regard to this deduction). (Code Sec. 1402(a)(12))[40]

If a person is engaged in a part-time business in addition to his regular job as an employee, the income from the part-time business is included in determining net earnings from self-employment.[41]

In computing the gross income and deductions of a trade or business or the distributive share of partnership ordinary income or loss, the following items are excluded:[42]

■ operating loss carrybacks and carryovers;

■ nonbusiness deductions;

■ the pre-'94 limited deduction for a self-employed person's health insurance costs; (Code Sec. 162(l)(4))

■ deduction for personal exemptions;

■ standard deduction;

■ foreign expropriation loss deduction. (Code Sec. 1402(a))

Net earnings from self-employment do not include:

■ certain income received by a retired partner under a written plan of the partnership;[43]

■ dividends or interest on investments; (Code Sec. 1402(a)(2))[44]

■ gains (or deduction for losses) from property that is not inventory or held for sale to customers, (Code Sec. 1402(a)(3))[45] however, gains and losses derived by option and commodity dealers in the normal course of trading in options and regulated futures subject to mark-to-market rules are included in net earnings from self-employment; (Code Sec. 1402(i))[46]

■ rents from real estate held for income or value growth, (Code Sec. 1402(a)(1)) but rent

37. ¶ A-6036; ¶ 14,024.02.   41. ¶ A-6083; ¶ 14,024(c).   43. ¶ A-6157; ¶ 14,024.16.   45. ¶ A-6109; ¶ 14,024.06.
38. ¶ A-6031; ¶ 14,024.02.   42. ¶s A-6105, A-6113;   44. ¶ A-6108; ¶ 14,024.05.   46. ¶ A-6112; ¶ 14,024.06.
39. ¶ A-6100 *et seq.*; ¶ 14,024.07.   ¶ 14,024.03.
40. ¶ A-6114; ¶ 14.024(d).

Footnote references beginning with letters are to paragraphs in RIA's Federal Tax Coordinator 2d and RIA's Analysis of Federal Taxes: Income. Footnote references beginning with numbers are to paragraphs in RIA's United States Tax Reporter.

is self-employment earnings if received by real estate dealers who get rent on property held for sale to customers in the normal course of business (Reg § 1.1402(a)-4(a))[47] or if the rent is for living quarters where *services* (e.g., maid service) are also rendered primarily for the occupant's convenience (Reg § 1.1402(a)-4(c)(2)) such as in hotels, apartment hotels, boarding houses, tourist camps or homes, parking lots, warehouses and storage garages;[48]

■ rents paid in crop shares unless the landowner is a real estate dealer, materially participates in the production of the crop or controls and directs the farming operation and pays the farmer at a fixed rate as his employee; (Reg § 1.1402(a)-4(b))[49]

■ a shareholder's share of the income of an S corporation.[50]

A passive activity loss that is disallowed for income tax purposes is not taken into account in computing net earnings from self-employment. (Reg § 1.469-1T(d)(3), Ex)[1]

¶ 3140 Partner's self-employment tax.

A partner's net earnings from self-employment are, generally, his distributive share of the partnership's income arising out of the trade or business of the partnership plus his guaranteed payments. (Reg § 1.1402(a)-1(a)(2)) Losses from one business offset the income of another. (Reg § 1.1402(a)-2(c))[2]

The distributive share of any item of income or loss of a limited partner is excluded for purposes of the self-employment tax. But this exclusion doesn't apply to guaranteed payments to that partner for services actually rendered to or on behalf of the partnership, to the extent the payments are shown to be remuneration for those services. (Code Sec. 1402(a)(13))[3]

¶ 3141 Husbands and wives.

Tax on self-employment income is computed on the separate self-employment income of each spouse, whether or not they file joint returns. But the spouses are jointly and severally liable for self-employment tax due on a joint return. (Reg § 1.6017-1(b))[4]

¶ 3142 Optional determination of nonfarm self-employment earnings under $1,600.

Under this method, two-thirds of gross nonfarm profits (up to $1,600) can be treated as net self-employment earnings. To claim this option, all these conditions must be met:

■ The nonfarm option can be used no more than five times by any individual. (Code Sec. 1402(a))

■ The individual must have had actual net earnings of $400 or more from self-employment in at least two of the three consecutive taxable years immediately preceding the particular taxable year. (Code Sec. 1402(h))

■ Earnings from nonfarm self-employment must be less than $1,600 and less than 66 ⅔% of gross self-employment income. (Code Sec. 1402(a))[5]

¶ 3143 Who is subject to tax?

The self-employment tax is a tax on self-employed persons.

Income earned as an employee is not subject to self-employment tax,[6] with these exceptions:

■ Members of the clergy, see ¶ 3144.

■ Persons 18 or older employed to sell magazines and newspapers to the public at a fixed price and whose compensation is the excess of the fixed price over their cost. (Code

---

47. ¶ A-6106; ¶ 14,024.04.
48. ¶ A-6107; ¶ 14,024.04.
49. ¶ A-6202 *et seq.*; ¶ 14,024.04.
50. ¶ A-6084.
1. ¶ M-4603; ¶ 4694.47.
2. ¶ A-6150; ¶ 14,024.16.
3. ¶ A-6156 *et seq.*; ¶ 14,024.16.
4. ¶ A-6155; ¶ 14,024.17.
5. ¶ A-6117; ¶ 14,024.20.
6. ¶ A-6092; ¶ 14,024.09.

Footnote references beginning with letters are to paragraphs in RIA's Federal Tax Coordinator 2d and RIA's Analysis of Federal Taxes: Income. Footnote references beginning with numbers are to paragraphs in RIA's United States Tax Reporter.

Sec. 1402(c)(2)(A))[7]

■ U.S. citizens employed by a foreign government, or its wholly owned instrumentality, or an international organization (e.g., the U.N.). (Code Sec. 1402(c)(2)(C))[8]

■ Fishing boat crewmen who work for percentage shares of the catch, receive no fixed wages, and who work on boats with crews of ten or fewer. (Code Sec. 1402(c)(2)(F))[9]

■ Sharecroppers whose earnings depend on production.[10]

■ State or local government official whose remuneration consists *solely* of fees, unless the services are covered by social security under a federal-state agreement. (Code Sec. 1402(c)(1))[11]

Members of religious sects conscientiously opposed to social security benefits may apply (on Form 4029) for exemption from the self-employment tax. The sect must oppose acceptance of benefits of private or public (including social security) insurance providing payments on death, disability, retirement, old age or for medical services and must have been in existence since Dec. 31, '50. (Code Sec. 1402(g))[12]

¶ 3144 Members of the clergy.

Members of the clergy, members of religious orders who have not taken a vow of poverty, and Christian Science practitioners are subject to self-employment tax on services performed in the exercise of their ministry *unless* they irrevocably elect (on Form 4361) *not* to be covered. (Code Sec. 1402(e))[13]

¶ 3145 Farmers.

Farmers who are self-employed must pay the self-employment tax on the income from their farming operations. (Code Sec. 1402(a)) Since a farmer has an optional method of computing the self-employment tax on his farm income (¶ 3146) it may be necessary to distinguish farm income from other self-employment income. Farm income comes from an operation on a farm in which more than half of the time is devoted to farming activities. (Reg § 1.1402(a)-13(a)(1))[14]

¶ 3146 Farmer's optional computation method.

If gross income from farming is $2,400 or less, then the farmer may use two-thirds of his gross income as his net self-employment earnings. The farmer can use this optional method to either raise or lower his tax.

If gross income from farming is more than $2,400 but actual net earnings are less than $1,600, the farmer may treat $1,600 as his net self-employment earnings.[15]

¶ 3147 Using both optional farm method and optional nonfarm method.

If a self-employed individual has both nonfarm and farm income, he may only use the nonfarm option if his actual net earnings from nonfarm self-employment are less than $1,600. In all combined cases, net nonfarm earnings must be less than two-thirds of gross nonfarm profits to use the nonfarm option. If a self-employed individual qualifies to use both options, he may report less than actual total net earnings but not less than actual net earnings from nonfarm self-employment alone.

If both options are used in figuring net earnings from self-employment, the maximum combined total of net earnings from self-employment for any tax year cannot be more than $1,600. (Code Sec. 1402(a); Reg § 1.1402(a)-15)[16]

7. ¶ A-6092; ¶ 14,024.09.   10. ¶ A-6202; ¶ 14,024.04.   13. ¶ A-6321 *et seq.*; ¶ 14,024.10.   15. ¶ A-6118; ¶ 14,024.20.
8. ¶ A-6097; ¶ 14,024.09.   11. ¶ A-6095; ¶ 14,024.13.   14. ¶ A-6201 *et seq.*; ¶ 614.051.   16. ¶ A-6120; ¶ 14,024.20.
9. ¶ A-6090; ¶ 14,024.14.   12. ¶ A-6327 *et seq.*; ¶ 14,024.15.

Footnote references beginning with letters are to paragraphs in RIA's Federal Tax Coordinator 2d and RIA's Analysis of Federal Taxes: Income. Footnote references beginning with numbers are to paragraphs in RIA's United States Tax Reporter.

¶ 3148 Individual Estimated Tax

An individual must generally pay 25% of a "required annual payment" by Apr. 15, June 15, Sept. 15 and Jan. 15, in order to avoid an underpayment penalty. The required annual payment is ordinarily the lower of 90% of the tax shown on the current year's return or 100% of the tax shown on the prior year's return. The required annual payment is higher for taxpayers who have adjusted gross income over certain levels. There's no underpayment penalty if the tax due (after withholding) is less than $500. There's also no penalty if other specified exceptions or waivers apply.

To avoid the underpayment penalty, an individual must either: (1) pay each "required installment" (see ¶ 3149) by the due date of that installment (see ¶ 3152), (2) meet one of more of the exceptions to the penalty (¶ 3156), or (3) get a waiver of the penalty (¶ 3157).[17]

Make estimated tax payments on payment-voucher Form 1040-ES (Form 1040-ES(NR) for nonresident aliens).[18]

¶ 3149 Amount of required installment.

General Rule. Except as provided in ¶ 3150, the amount of each required installment is 25% of the "required annual payment." For most taxpayers, the required annual payment is the lower of: (1) 90% of the tax shown on the current year's return (or, if no return is filed, 90% of the tax for the current year), or (2) 100% of the tax shown on the individual's previous year's return, if the preceding tax year was a tax year of 12 months and the taxpayer filed a return for that year. (Code Sec. 6654(d)(1))[19]

For individuals with adjusted gross income (AGI) shown on the previous year's return exceeding $150,000 ($75,000 for marrieds filing separately), the "required annual payment" is either payment (1), above, or 110% of the prior year's tax. (Code Sec. 6654(d)(1)(C))[20]

For tax years beginning before '94 (i.e., for tax payments applicable to tax years beginning before '94), some taxpayers could not base their required annual payment on 100% of the prior year's tax. This limit applied to taxpayers (other than farmers and fishermen):

■ whose "modified" AGI for the current year exceeded the previous year's AGI (not modified) by more than $40,000 ($20,000 for marrieds filing separately),

■ whose AGI for the current year (not modified) exceeded $75,000 ($37,500 for marrieds filing separately), and

■ who had paid estimated tax for at least one of the three preceding tax years (not counting taxes withheld or prior years' overpayments credited to estimated taxes) or had been assessed a penalty for failing to do so.[21]

For these taxpayers, the required annual payment was the lesser of:

■ 90% of the current year's tax liability, or

■ 100% of the tax shown on the prior year's return *or* 90% of the current year's tax based on "modified" AGI, whichever was *larger.*[22]

A taxpayer's "modified" AGI didn't include any gain reported on the current year's return from an involuntary conversion or from the sale or exchange of a principal residence. Also, for computing "modified" AGI, a special rule applied to "qualified pass-through items." These were items of income, expense, etc., attributable to less-than-10% S corporation and limited partnership interests (not including gain or loss on the sale of an interest in a partnership or S corporation). A taxpayer's "qualified pass-through items" for

---

17. ¶ S-5200; ¶ 66,544.   19. ¶ S-5204; ¶ 66,544.   21. ¶ S-5206.   22. ¶ S-5205.
18. ¶ S-5253; ¶ 66,544(b).   20. ¶ S-5204.1.

Footnote references beginning with letters are to paragraphs in RIA's Federal Tax Coordinator 2d and RIA's Analysis of Federal Taxes: Income. Footnote references beginning with numbers are to paragraphs in RIA's United States Tax Reporter.

the prior year were treated as shown on the taxpayer's return for the current year and his actual partnership and S corporation items for the current year were disregarded.[23]

Taxpayers subject to the limitation could still compute their first estimated tax installment based on the prior year's tax. However, they had to make up any underpayment on the second installment.[24]

Taxpayers who could show that their annualized AGI for the months ending before the installment date didn't satisfy the more-than-$40,000 or more-than-$75,000 threshold could continue using the general rule to compute the amount due on that installment. Any underpayment resulting from this exception had to be made up along with the first payment that was subject to the limitation.[25]

¶ 3150 Annualized income method.

For any installment for which the taxpayer establishes that the "annualized income installment" (below) is less than the required installment determined under the rules at ¶ 3149, the annualized income installment becomes the required installment. (Code Sec. 6654(d)(2)(A)(i)) The annualized income installment is the excess (if any) of:

(1) an amount equal to the "applicable percentage" (below) of the tax computed by placing on an annualized basis the taxable income, alternative minimum taxable income, and adjusted self-employment income as defined below, for the months in the tax year ending before the due date for the installment, over

(2) the sum of any earlier required installments for the taxable year. (Code Sec. 6654(d)(2)(B))

The applicable percentages are 22.5%, 45%, 67.5% and 90%, respectively, for the first, second, third and fourth required installment. (Code Sec. 6654(d)(2)(C)(ii))

Adjusted self-employment income means self-employment income except that wages for the calendar months preceding the installment due date must be annualized in a manner consistent with the method for annualizing taxable income, alternative minimum taxable income and adjusted self-employment income. (Code Sec. 6654(d)(2)(C)(iii))

If for any installment, the required installment is the annualized income installment, then the amount by which the installment determined under the rules at ¶ 3149 exceeds the annualized income installment must be added to the next required installment that is not an annualized income installment. (Code Sec. 6654(d)(2)(A)(ii))[26]

¶ 3151 Withholding as payment of estimated tax.

Any withholding is treated as a payment of estimated tax. An equal part of the withheld tax is considered paid on each installment date unless the individual establishes the dates the amounts were actually withheld. (Code Sec. 6654(g)(1))[27]

recommendation: This means a taxpayer who may otherwise be subject to an underpayment penalty for earlier periods in the year can avoid or reduce the penalty by increasing withholding in later months.

¶ 3152 Time for paying installments.

To avoid penalty, calendar year taxpayers other than farmers and fishermen (see ¶ 3153) and nonresident aliens (¶ 3154) must pay estimated taxes in four installments, due by Apr. 15, June 15, Sept. 15 of the current year, and Jan. 15 of the following tax year. (Code Sec. 6654(c))[28]

The last installment, ordinarily due on Jan. 15, needn't be paid at all if taxpayer files his income tax return and pays the tax shown to be due on it by Jan. 31. (Code

---

23. ¶ S-5214 et seq.   25. ¶ S-5208.   27. ¶ S-5248; ¶ 66,544(c).   28. ¶ S-5241; ¶ 66,544(c).
24. ¶ S-5207.   26. ¶ S-5219; ¶ 66,544(e)(2).

Footnote references beginning with letters are to paragraphs in RIA's Federal Tax Coordinator 2d and RIA's Analysis of Federal Taxes: Income. Footnote references beginning with numbers are to paragraphs in RIA's United States Tax Reporter.

Sec. 6654(h))[29]

¶ 3153 Farmers and fishermen.

A farmer or fisherman (a person for whom 66⅔% of gross income for the current or preceding tax year comes from farming or fishing)[30] does not have to pay estimated tax if he files his return and pays the tax on or before Mar. 1 of the following year. If he doesn't file and pay on or before Mar. 1 he need only make one estimated tax payment for the year, which is due on or before Jan. 15 of the next tax year.[31] Also, he substitutes 66⅔% for 90% each time "90%" appears in the 90%-of-current-year-tax factor that is used in the required installment calculation in ¶ 3149. (Code Sec. 6654(i))[32]

¶ 3154 Nonresident aliens.

Nonresident aliens have three required installments: June 15, Sept. 15, and Jan. 15 of the following year. (Code Sec. 6654(j)(2))[33] The required installments are 50%, 25% and 25%, respectively, of the required annual payment (¶ 3149). (Code Sec. 6654(j)(3)(A)) For purposes of the annualized income method (¶ 3150) the applicable percentages are 45%, 67.5% and 90%, respectively. (Code Sec. 6654(j)(3)(B))[34]

¶ 3155 Penalty for underpayment of estimated tax.

The penalty for underpayment equals the product of the interest rate (using simple interest) (Code Sec. 6622(b)) on deficiencies (¶ 4862) times the amount of the underpayment (below) for the period of the underpayment (below). (Code Sec. 6654(a))[35]

The *amount of the underpayment* is the excess of the "required installment" (see ¶ 3149) over the amount, if any, paid on or before the due date of the installment. (Code Sec. 6654(b)(1))

The *period of underpayment* runs from the due date of the installment to the earlier of: (1) Apr. 15 following the close of the tax year, or (2) the date the underpayment is paid. (Code Sec. 6654(b)(2)) For purposes of (2), above, a payment of estimated tax is credited against unpaid installments in the order in which the installments are required to be paid. (Code Sec. 6654(b)(3))[36]

¶ 3156 Exceptions to underpayment penalty.

The underpayment penalty doesn't apply:

(1) if the tax shown on the return (or the tax due if no return is filed) is less than $500 after reduction for withholding tax paid, (Code Sec. 6654(e)(1)) or

(2) if the individual was a U.S. citizen or resident for the entire preceding tax year, that tax year was 12 months, and the individual had no tax liability for that year, (Code Sec. 6654(e)(2))[37] or

(3) for the fourth required installment, if the individual (who isn't a farmer or fisherman, see ¶ 3153) files his tax return by the end of the first month after the tax year (Jan. 31 for calendar year taxpayers), and pays in full the tax computed on the return, (Code Sec. 6654(h))[38] or

(4) under certain circumstances with respect to a period during which a Title 11 bankruptcy case is pending. (Code Sec. 6658(a))[39]

¶ 3157 Waiver of penalty.

The underpayment penalty may be waived by IRS:

(1) if failure to pay was due to casualty, disaster, or other unusual circumstances

---

29. ¶ S-5268; ¶ 66,544(c).
30. ¶ S-5238; ¶ 66,544(f).
31. ¶ S-5247; ¶ 66,544(f).
32. ¶ S-5237; ¶ 66,544(f).
33. ¶ S-5246; ¶ 66,544(g).
34. ¶ S-5236; ¶ 66,544(g).
35. ¶ S-5260; ¶ 66,544(e).
36. ¶ S-5261 *et seq.*; ¶ 66,544(e).
37. ¶ S-5266 *et seq.*; ¶ 66,544(b).
38. ¶ S-5268; ¶ 66,544(c).
39. ¶ S-5269; ¶ 66,584.

Footnote references beginning with letters are to paragraphs in RIA's Federal Tax Coordinator 2d and RIA's Analysis of Federal Taxes: Income. Footnote references beginning with numbers are to paragraphs in RIA's United States Tax Reporter.

where it would be inequitable or against good conscience to impose the penalty, or

(2) for reasonable cause during the first two years after the taxpayer retires (after reaching age 62) or becomes disabled. (Code Sec. 6654(e)(3))[40]

Also, no underpayment penalty applies for any period before Apr. 16, '94 with respect to any underpayment to the extent it was created or increased by any provision of the '93 Revenue Reconciliation Act.[41]

---

40. ¶s S-5270, S-5272;   41. ¶ S-5272.1.
    ¶ 66,544(i).

Footnote references beginning with letters are to paragraphs in RIA's Federal Tax Coordinator 2d and RIA's Analysis of Federal Taxes: Income. Footnote references beginning with numbers are to paragraphs in RIA's United States Tax Reporter.

Chapter 14   Alternative Minimum Tax

¶ *3200* Alternative Minimum Tax

The alternative minimum tax (AMT) equals the excess (if any) of the tentative minimum tax over the regular tax.

All taxpayers who are subject to the regular tax are subject to the AMT. (Code Sec. 55(a), (b)) Thus, partnerships (Code Sec. 701) and S corporations are not subject. (Code Sec. 1363(a)) Foreign corporations are subject only as to taxable income effectively connected with conduct of a trade or business in the U.S. (Code Sec. 882(a)(1))[1]

For the minimum tax credit available in tax years that follow years in which a taxpayer was liable for the AMT, see ¶ 2356.

¶ *3201* Computing the AMT.

The alternative minimum tax is equal to the excess (if any) of (Code Sec. 55(a)) the tentative minimum tax for the tax year, over (Code Sec. 55(a)(1)) the regular tax for the tax year. (Code Sec. 55(a))

For a noncorporate taxpayer (other than a married person filing a separate return), the tentative minimum tax for the tax year is equal to 26% of the "taxable excess" that doesn't exceed $175,000, plus 28% of the "taxable excess" that does exceed $175,000, reduced by the alternative minimum tax foreign tax credit for the tax year. (Code Sec. 55(b)(1)(A)(i)) "Taxable excess" means the excess of alternative minimum taxable income for the tax year over the "exemption amount" (¶ 3202). (Code Sec. 55(a)(1)(A)(ii)) For marrieds filing separately, $87,500 replaces $175,000 in the above calculation. (Code Sec. 55(b)(1)(A)(iii))

For a corporation, the tentative minimum tax for the tax year is (Code Sec. 55(b)(1)) 20% of so much of the alternative minimum taxable income for the tax year as exceeds the exemption amount, reduced by (Code Sec. 55(b)(1)(B)(i)) the alternative minimum tax foreign tax credit for the tax year. (Code Sec. 55(b)(1)(B)(ii))

Alternative minimum taxable income is taxable income, less possessions source income if the taxpayer is a corporation qualifying for the possessions tax credit (see ¶ 2365), (Code Sec. 59(b)) plus or minus various adjustments, plus tax preferences (¶ 3204 *et seq.*). (Code Sec. 55(b)(2))[2] One of the adjustments is a special net operating loss deduction, the alternative tax net operating loss deduction (ATNOLD), that applies only for purposes of the AMT (¶ 3211). If a taxpayer's regular tax is determined by reference to an amount other than taxable income (such as unrelated business taxable income), that other amount is treated as taxable income in determining alternative minimum taxable income. (Code Sec. 55(b)(2))

Rules are provided for the apportionment of items that are treated differently for AMT purposes among holders of interests in regulated investment companies, real estate investment trusts, and common trust funds. (Code Sec. 59(d))[3]

The regular tax is the regular tax liability used for determining the limitation on various nonrefundable credits (see ¶ 2355), reduced by the regular (as opposed to the AMT) foreign tax credit and the possessions tax credit, and without inclusion of: (1) the five- and ten-year averaging taxes on lump sum distributions from qualified retirement plans; and (2) any investment credit recapture. (Code Sec. 55(c))[4]

Form 6251, Schedule H (Form 1041) and Form 4626 are used to compute the AMT liabilities of individuals, fiduciaries (estates and trusts), and C corporations, respectively.[5]

---

1. ¶ A-8104; ¶ 554.   3. ¶ A-8106; ¶ 594.   4. ¶ A-8119; ¶ 554.01.   5. ¶ A-8115.
2. ¶ A-8115; ¶ 554.01.

Footnote references beginning with letters are to paragraphs in RIA's Federal Tax Coordinator 2d and RIA's Analysis of Federal Taxes: Income. Footnote references beginning with numbers are to paragraphs in RIA's United States Tax Reporter.

¶ 3202 Exemption amount.

The exempt portion of alternative minimum taxable income is:

Corporations: $40,000, less 25% of alternative minimum taxable income exceeding $150,000 (thus, zero exemption when alternative minimum taxable income is $310,000 or more).

Married individuals filing jointly and surviving spouses : $45,000, less 25% of alternative minimum taxable income exceeding $150,000 (zero exemption when alternative minimum taxable income is $330,000).

Unmarried individuals: $33,750, less 25% of alternative minimum taxable income exceeding $112,500 (zero exemption when alternative minimum taxable income is $247,500). (For the limit where a child subject to the kiddie tax is involved, see ¶ 3203.)

Married individuals filing separately, estates and trusts : $22,500, less 25% of alternative minimum taxable income exceeding $75,000. However, alternative minimum taxable income of married individuals filing separately must be increased by the lesser of $22,500 or 25% of the excess of alternative minimum taxable income (before considering this increase) over $165,000.

In no case can the exemption amount be less than zero. (Code Sec. 55(d))[6]

¶ 3203 AMT of a child subject to the kiddie tax.

The child's AMT exemption amount can't exceed the sum of the child's earned income for the year plus the greater of: (1) $1,000, or (2) the child's share of the parent's unused parental minimum tax exemption. (Code Sec. 59(j)(1)) The parent's unused parental minimum tax exemption is the excess (if any) of the parent's exemption amount over the parent's alternative minimum taxable income. (Code Sec. 59(j)(3)(A)) The child's AMT itself can't exceed the child's share of the allocable parental minimum tax, (Code Sec. 59(j)(2)(A)) determined under rules similar to those for kiddie tax purposes, as discussed in ¶ 3133 *et seq.*(Code Sec. 59(j)(2)(C)) The allocable parental minimum tax is the excess of the AMT that would be imposed on the parent if: (1) the parent's tentative minimum tax were increased by the aggregate of the tentative minimum taxes of all children of the parent to which the kiddie tax applies, and (2) the parent's regular tax were increased by the aggregate of the regular taxes of all those children, over the AMT otherwise imposed on the parent. (Code Sec. 59(j)(2)(B))[7]

¶ 3204 Adjustments and tax preferences.

AMT adjustments differ from preferences in that adjustments involve a *substitution* of a special AMT treatment of an item for the regular tax treatment, while a preference involves the *addition* of the difference between the special AMT treatment and the regular tax treatment. Some (but not all) adjustments can be negative amounts, i.e., they may result in alternative minimum taxable income that is less than taxable income; tax preferences cannot be negative amounts.

¶ 3205 Depreciation adjustment.

Except as provided below, the following rules apply to all taxpayers that are subject to the AMT, with respect to depreciable property placed in service after Dec. 31, '86, and property placed in service after July 31, '86, and before Jan. 1, '87, for which the taxpayer elects to have the MACRS rules (see ¶ 1909 *et seq.*) apply:

■ For Code Sec. 1250 property (i.e., most depreciable real property), and property depreciated under the straight-line method for purposes of the regular tax, depreciation for purposes of the AMT (AMT depreciation) is computed under the Alternative Depreciation

6. ¶ A-8122 *et seq.*; ¶ 554.01.   7. ¶ A-8107; ¶ 594.

Footnote references beginning with letters are to paragraphs in RIA's Federal Tax Coordinator 2d and RIA's Analysis of Federal Taxes: Income. Footnote references beginning with numbers are to paragraphs in RIA's United States Tax Reporter.

System (ADS) described in ¶ 1931 *et seq.*

■ For all other property, AMT depreciation is computed under ADS except that the 150% declining balance method (switching to straight-line in the year necessary to maximize the allowance) is substituted for straight-line depreciation. (Code Sec. 56(a)(1)(A), (C)(ii))

The AMT adjustment (i.e., the amount that must be added or subtracted in the calculation of alternative minimum taxable income) that is generated by the above calculations is determined by subtracting the amount of AMT depreciation for all property covered by the above rule from the MACRS depreciation for that property.

The above rules don't apply to certain property to which the MACRS rules don't apply, (Code Sec. 56(a)(1)(B), (C))[8] or to qualified Indian reservation property placed in service after '93. (Code Sec. 168(j)(3))[9]

IRS has issued optional MACRS tables for determining alternative minimum taxable income.[10]

¶ 3206 Depreciation preference—property placed in service before Jan. 1, '87.

The following are tax preferences with respect to any property that *isn't* subject to the depreciation adjustment in ¶ 3205: (Code Sec. 57(a)(6))[11]

(1) *Accelerated cost recovery deduction on real recovery property*: (a) The excess of the accelerated cost recovery deduction taken on each item of 19-, 18- or 15-year real property, or the deduction allowed under the rule allowing 60-month depreciation of expenditures to rehabilitate low income rental housing, over the deduction that would have been allowable had the property been depreciated using a 19-, 18- or 15-year period and the straight line method (without salvage value), and (b) the excess of the accelerated cost recovery deduction taken on each low income housing property, over the deduction that would have been allowable had the property been depreciated using a 15-year period and the straight-line method.

There is no preference for a piece of property for which the recovery period is longer than the applicable (19-, 18- or 15-year) period, if the taxpayer has elected the longer optional recovery period for regular tax purposes or if the property is used predominantly outside the U.S.[12]

(2) *Accelerated depreciation on nonrecovery real property.* The excess depreciation allowable on each item of nonrecovery real property (Code Sec. 1250 property which is not subject to ACRS, see ¶ 1936 *et seq.*) over the amount that would have been allowable under the straight-line method.[13]

(3) *Accelerated cost recovery deduction for noncorporate taxpayers and personal holding companies on leased personal property and certain leased real property*. This tax preference applies to each item of recovery property other than 19-year, 18-year or 15-year real property, for which depreciation is computed under ACRS and which is subject to a lease. It equals the excess of the deduction allowed under ACRS for the taxable year over the deduction that would have been allowable for the taxable year had the property been depreciated using the straight-line method and the following recovery period:[14]

In the case of	Recovery period is
3-year property	5 years
5-year property	8 years
10-year property	15 years
15-year public utility property	22 years

(4) *Accelerated depreciation for noncorporate taxpayers and personal holding companies on nonrecovery personal property subject to a lease.* The excess depreciation allowable on

8. ¶ A-8210; ¶ 564.   10. ¶ A-8209; ¶ 564.   12. ¶ A-8214; ¶ 574.01.   14. ¶ A-8222; ¶ 574.01.
9. ¶ L-8806.   11. ¶ A-8213; ¶ 574.   13. ¶ A-8217; ¶ 574.01.

Footnote references beginning with letters are to paragraphs in RIA's Federal Tax Coordinator 2d and RIA's Analysis of Federal Taxes: Income. Footnote references beginning with numbers are to paragraphs in RIA's United States Tax Reporter.

leased nonrecovery personal property (Code Sec. 1245 property which is not subject to ACRS, see ¶ 1936 *et seq.*) over the amount that would have been allowable as depreciation calculated over the useful life of the property under the straight-line basis.[15]

¶ 3207 Other tax preferences and adjustments applicable to all taxpayers.

(1) *Installment sales.* The installment method of reporting income isn't allowed for AMT purposes with respect to dispositions of the taxpayer's stock in trade or other property which would properly be accounted for as inventory if on hand at year end, except, in certain cases, for timeshares and residential lots. All payments to be received from these dispositions are considered to have been received in the taxable year of the disposition. (Code Sec. 56(a)(6))[16] (For rules regarding when the installment method may be used for regular tax purposes, see Chapter 10.)

(2) *Tax exempt interest.* Tax-exempt interest earned on certain private activity bonds is a preference item. (Code Sec. 57(a)(5))[17]

(3) *Excess of percentage depletion over cost basis.* Except with respect to depletion taken by independent oil and gas producers and royalty owners, the excess of the allowable depletion on each depletable asset over the adjusted basis (before considering the current year's depletion) of the property at the end of the year is a preference item. (Code Sec. 57(a)(1))[18]

(4) *Excess intangible drilling costs.* These are the excess of the allowable expense deduction for the tax year for intangible drilling and development costs in connection with oil, gas and geothermal wells, over the amount that would have been allowable had the costs been capitalized and straight-line recovery of intangibles used with respect to them.[19] For integrated oil companies the preference equals this excess amount reduced by 65% of the net income received from all oil and gas properties. For taxpayers other than integrated oil companies, the preference applies only to the extent that, had it applied fully, it would have increased alternative minimum taxable income by an amount that exceeds 30% (40% for taxable years beginning after '93) of the alternative minimum taxable income for the taxable year determined without the intangible drilling cost preference and without the alternative tax net operating loss deduction.

The net income from oil and gas properties is the gross income received or accrued for the year from all oil and gas properties less deductions (not including excess intangible drilling costs) allocable to those properties. (Code Sec. 57(a)(2))[20]

(5) *Pollution control facilities.* The deduction for amortization of pollution control facilities placed into service after Dec. 31, '86, is the amount allowable under the Alternative Depreciation System (ADS). The Code Sec. 291 20% cutback (see ¶ 1987), which applies for purposes of computing a corporation's pollution control facility amortization deduction for regular tax purposes, doesn't apply for AMT purposes. (Code Sec. 56(a)(5)) For facilities placed into service before '87, any excess of amortization allowable under the 60 month rule for regular tax purposes on any given facility, over the otherwise allowable depreciation, for noncorporate taxpayers, is a preference. In the case of corporations, further adjustments are required. (Code Sec. 57(a)(6))[21]

(6) *Mining exploration and development costs.* The following deduction is allowed: The amount that results from capitalizing mine exploration and development expenditures (¶ 1617 *et seq.*) (without regard to the Code Sec. 291 30% cutback) that are paid or incurred after Dec. 31, '86, and amortizing them on a straight-line basis over ten years. (Code Sec. 56(a)(2)(A))[22]

(7) *Reserve for bad debts of financial institution.* The preference equals the amount allowable as an addition to the reserve for bad debts over the amount that would have

---

15. ¶ A-8223; ¶ 574.01.
16. ¶ A-8242; ¶ 564.
17. ¶ A-8236; ¶ 574.
18. ¶ A-8225; ¶ 574.
19. ¶ A-8232.
20. ¶ A-8234; ¶ 574.
21. ¶ A-8229; ¶ 574.01.
22. ¶ A-8226; ¶ 564.

Footnote references beginning with letters are to paragraphs in RIA's Federal Tax Coordinator 2d and RIA's Analysis of Federal Taxes: Income. Footnote references beginning with numbers are to paragraphs in RIA's United States Tax Reporter.

been allowable had the institution maintained its reserve on the basis of its actual experience. (Code Sec. 57(a)(4))[23]

(8) *Long-term contracts.* For purposes of computing alternative minimum taxable income, taxpayers must use the percentage-of-completion method of accounting for long-term contracts entered into after Feb. 28, '86, except for certain home construction contracts entered into after June 20, '88, and all home construction contracts entered into after Sept. 30, '90. (Code Sec. 56(a)(3))[24] For small construction contracts (under Code Sec. 460(e)(1)) the percentage of the contract completed is determined by using the simplified method for allocating costs in Code Sec. 460(b)(4).[25]

(9) *Alcohol fuel credit amount.* The amount includible in gross income for the alcohol fuel credit is not included in alternative minimum taxable income. (Code Sec. 56(a)(8))[26]

For contributions made after June 30, '92 (after Dec. 31, '92 for contributions of capital gain property that isn't tangible personal property), the former preference for appreciated charitable deduction property (generally, the excess of the fair market value of the donated property over its adjusted basis) has been retroactively repealed. Thus, taxpayers get the same charitable contribution deduction for both alternative minimum tax and regular income tax.[27]

¶ 3208 Preferences and adjustments applicable to noncorporate taxpayers only.

(1) *Itemized deductions.* Itemized deductions for AMT purposes are computed the same as for regular tax purposes, except:

... Medical expenses are deductible only to the extent they exceed 10% of the taxpayer's adjusted gross income. (Code Sec. 56(b)(1)(B))

... Property and income taxes are not deductible unless they are deductible in computing adjusted gross income. (Code Sec. 56(b)(1)(A)(ii))

... Qualified housing interest, rather than qualified residence interest, is deductible. (Code Sec. 56(b)(1)(C))

... Net investment income (the limit on the deduction for investment interest) for AMT purposes, equals the sum of the taxpayer's interest on tax exempt bonds that is includible in alternative minimum taxable income (see ¶ 3207) net of expenses associated with that interest, plus his net investment income for regular tax purposes. (Code Sec. 56(b)(1)(C))

... No deduction is allowed for miscellaneous itemized deductions. (Code Sec. 56(b)(1)(A)(i))

Itemized deductions which are otherwise allowed in computing alternative minimum taxable income are *not* reduced by the 3% reduction (¶ 3112) that applies to itemized deductions for regular tax purposes. (Code Sec. 56(b)(1)(F))

(2) *Standard deduction and personal exemptions.* The standard deduction and the deduction for personal exemptions (including the personal exemptions for trusts and estates) aren't allowed. (Code Sec. 56(b)(1)(E))[28]

(3) *State, etc., tax recoveries.* If an itemized deduction for state, etc., taxes paid is permitted for regular tax purposes but is denied for AMT purposes (above), and any portion of that tax is refunded, the refund is not included in alternative minimum taxable income. (Code Sec. 56(b)(1)(D))[29]

(4) *Research and experimental expenditures.* The deduction allowed is the amount that results from capitalizing research and experimental expenditures (as defined in Code Sec. 174(a), see ¶ 1594) that are paid or incurred after Dec. 31, '86, and amortizing them on a

---

23. ¶ A-8246; ¶ 574.   25. ¶ A-8237 *et seq.*; ¶ 564.   27. ¶ A-8243 *et seq.*   29. ¶ A-8308; ¶ 564.
24. ¶ A-8237; ¶ 564.   26. ¶ A-8247; ¶ 564.   28. ¶ A-8310 *et seq.*; ¶ 564.

Footnote references beginning with letters are to paragraphs in RIA's Federal Tax Coordinator 2d and RIA's Analysis of Federal Taxes: Income. Footnote references beginning with numbers are to paragraphs in RIA's United States Tax Reporter.

straight-line basis over ten years. (Code Sec. 56(b)(2)(A)(ii)) This rule does not apply to expenses incurred after '90 in an activity in which the taxpayer materially participates (as defined in Code Sec. 469(h), see ¶ 1814 *et seq.*). (Code Sec. 56(b)(2)(D))[30]

(5) *Incentive stock options.* The Code Sec. 83 restricted property rules, rather than the Code Sec. 421 stock option rules, apply, unless the stock is disposed of in the same tax year. (Code Sec. 56(b)(3))[31]

(6) *Qualified small business stock exclusion.* One-half of the amount excluded from gross income at the disposition of "qualified small business stock" (¶ 2640 *et seq.*) is an AMT preference. (Code Sec. 57(a)(7))[32]

¶ 3209 Preferences and adjustments applicable to all noncorporate taxpayers and to certain corporations.

(1) *Farm losses.* No loss is permitted from any "tax shelter farm activity" of any noncorporate taxpayer or personal service corporation, except to the extent the taxpayer is insolvent at the close of the tax year. A tax shelter farm activity is either (a) a farming syndicate, or (b) any other activity consisting of farming that is a passive activity, unless the taxpayer materially participates in the activity. (Code Sec. 58(a))[33]

(2) *Passive losses.* The rules limiting the deduction for regular tax purposes of losses from passive activities (see ¶ 1791 *et seq.*) apply for AMT purposes except that:

. . . the amount of losses that otherwise would be disallowed under the regular tax limitation is reduced by the amount, if any, by which the taxpayer is insolvent;

. . . in computing income and losses from passive activities, other AMT adjustments and preferences are taken into consideration. (Code Sec. 58(b))[34]

(3) *Circulation expenditures.* Noncorporate taxpayers and personal holding companies may deduct the amount that results from capitalizing circulation expenditures and amortizing them over three years (see ¶ 1612). (Code Sec. 56(b)(2))[35]

¶ 3210 Preferences and adjustments applicable to corporations only.

(1) *Earnings and profits adjustment.* Alternative minimum taxable income of a corporation is *increased* by 75% of the amount by which adjusted current earnings (as defined below) exceeds alternative minimum taxable income determined without regard to this adjustment or the AMT net operating loss deduction (ATNOLD). (Code Sec. 56(c)(1), (g)(1)) This rule does not apply to S corporations, regulated investment companies, real estate investment trusts and real estate mortgage investment conduits. (Code Sec. 56(g)(6)) If alternative minimum taxable income (before this adjustment and the ATNOLD) exceeds the amount of adjusted current earnings, alternative minimum taxable income is *reduced* by 75% of the difference. This reduction, however, is limited to the aggregate amount of increases in alternative minimum taxable income under this provision in earlier years. (Code Sec. 56(g)(2))[36]

Adjusted current earnings (ACE) is alternative minimum taxable income, plus those items that are included in earnings and profits (E&P) as computed for purposes of Subchapter C but that never enter into the calculation of regular or alternative minimum taxable income (e.g., interest on certain tax-exempt bonds). In addition, there are numerous adjustments: including adjustments requiring a special method for depreciation, including the "inside buildup" on life insurance contracts in ACE, disallowing the dividends received deduction and the use of the installment method, and providing for certain of the statutory adjustments required in calculating earnings and profits. (Code Sec. 56(g)(3), (4))[37]

---

30. ¶ A-8315; ¶ 564.
31. ¶s A-8313, A-8314; ¶ 564.

32. ¶ A-8316.
33. ¶ A-8501; ¶ 584.

34. ¶ A-8503; ¶ 584.
35. ¶ A-8504; ¶ 564.

36. ¶ A-8401; ¶ 564.
37. ¶ A-8403 *et seq.*; ¶ 564.

Footnote references beginning with letters are to paragraphs in RIA's Federal Tax Coordinator 2d and RIA's Analysis of Federal Taxes: Income. Footnote references beginning with numbers are to paragraphs in RIA's United States Tax Reporter.

(2) *Special deduction for Blue Cross/Blue Shield, etc.* The special deduction allowed Blue Cross, Blue Shield and similar organizations is not allowed for AMT purposes. (Code Sec. 56(c)(3))[38]

(3) *Merchant Marine capital construction funds.* For the AMT, amounts deposited in these funds are not deductible, and earnings (including gains and losses) of the funds are not excludable. Special rules are applicable to withdrawals of amounts deposited in these funds in earlier years, when deposits were deductible for purposes of the AMT. (Code Sec. 56(c)(2))[39]

¶ 3211 Alternative tax net operating loss deduction.

There is an adjustment for AMT purposes under which the regular net operating loss deduction (RNOLD, see ¶ 1828 *et seq.*) isn't allowed and instead, an alternative tax net operating deduction (ATNOLD) is allowed.

The ATNOLD is the same as the RNOLD except that: (1) the amount of the ATNOLD is limited to 90% of the alternative minimum taxable income determined without regard to the ATNOLD, and (2) for any loss year beginning after '86, the ATNOLD is determined with each of the AMT adjustments and reduced by each of the items of tax preference (but only to the extent the tax preference item increased the amount of the NOL for the year). (Code Sec. 56(d))

For corporations, regular tax net operating loss carryforwards from tax years beginning before Jan. 1, '87, may be carried forward as alternative tax NOLs to the first tax year for which the AMT applies (Code Sec. 56(d)(2)(B)) and to later years until used up. (Code Sec. 56(d))

An election to forgo the regular net operating loss carryback period (see ¶ 1831) also applies for ATNOLD purposes. (In fact, the election must be made for regular tax purposes in order to get it for AMT purposes.)[40]

¶ 3212 Different adjusted basis for some property.

For purposes of the AMT, the adjusted bases of the following types of property are computed by taking into consideration the AMT preference or adjustment listed below with the property:

(1) Depreciable property subject to the AMT depreciation adjustment, described in ¶ 3205.

(2) Property with respect to which circulation or research and experimental expenditures (described in ¶s 3208 and 3209) were paid or incurred after Dec. 31, '86.

(3) Property with respect to which mine exploration or development expenditures (described in ¶ 3207) were paid or incurred after Dec. 31, '86.

(4) Pollution control facilities (described in ¶ 3207) placed in service after Dec. 31, '86. (Code Sec. 56(a)(7))

(5) Stock acquired under an incentive stock option. Generally, the basis of the stock is determined under the Code Sec. 83 rules rather than the Code Sec. 421 rules (see ¶ 3208). (Code Sec. 56(b)(3))[41]

¶ 3213 Foreign tax credit.

The alternative minimum tax foreign tax credit (AMTFTC) is computed in a manner roughly similar to the computation of the regular foreign tax credit (¶ 2357). (Code Sec. 59(a)(1)) The credit is limited to the excess of:

■ the tentative minimum tax determined without regard to the AMTFTC, over

---

38. ¶ A-8505; ¶ 564.   39. ¶ A-8506; ¶ 564.   40. ¶ A-8200 *et seq.*; ¶ 564.   41. ¶ A-8120; ¶ 564.

Footnote references beginning with letters are to paragraphs in RIA's Federal Tax Coordinator 2d and RIA's Analysis of Federal Taxes: Income. Footnote references beginning with numbers are to paragraphs in RIA's United States Tax Reporter.

■ 10% of the tentative minimum tax determined without regard to the ATNOLD (¶ 3211), the AMTFTC and the exception from the intangible drilling cost preference described at ¶ 3207. (Code Sec. 59(a)(2)(A))[42]

The limit above does not apply to a U.S. corporation if: (1) more than 50% of its stock (by vote or value) is owned by U.S. persons that are not members of its affiliated group, (2) all of its activities are conducted in one foreign country having an income tax treaty providing for an exchange of information, (3) all of its current earnings and profits (other than certain retained amounts) are distributed at least annually, *and* (4) all of its distributions to U.S. persons are used by them in a U.S. trade or business. (Code Sec. 59(a)(2)(C))[43]

If the AMTFTC exceeds the limit above, the excess is treated as an AMTFTC carryover, i.e., it may be absorbed against earlier or later year AMT. (Code Sec. 59(a)(2)(B))[44]

¶ 3214 AMT credit against regular tax.

A special minimum tax credit is available against a taxpayer's regular tax liability for years in which the taxpayer's regular tax liability exceeds its AMT liability. This credit is limited for noncorporate taxpayers to the extent the taxpayer was subject to the AMT because of deferral (rather than exclusion) tax preferences. (Code Sec. 53)[45]

---

42. ¶ A-8127; ¶ 594.   43. ¶ A-8128; ¶ 594.   44. ¶ A-8131; ¶ 594.   45. ¶ A-8132; ¶ 534.

Footnote references beginning with letters are to paragraphs in RIA's Federal Tax Coordinator 2d and RIA's Analysis of Federal Taxes: Income. Footnote references beginning with numbers are to paragraphs in RIA's United States Tax Reporter.

Chapter 15 Corporate Tax Computation—Accumulated Earnings Tax—Personal Holding Companies—Estimated Tax—S Corporations

¶ 3300 Taxation of Corporations

A corporation is an entity distinct from its shareholders. How a corporation is taxed depends on whether it is a C corporation or an S corporation.

¶ 3301 Corporation defined.

Under general corporate law, a corporation is an entity distinct from its shareholders that is formed under federal, state or foreign law. An entity that is treated as a corporation under general corporate law will usually be treated as a corporation for income tax purposes, subject to certain exceptions (¶ 3303). Some organizations are treated as corporations for tax purposes even though they are not corporations under general corporate law (¶ 3304).[1]

¶ 3302 Corporate existence.

A corporation usually comes into existence for tax purposes when it does so under general corporate law, i.e., when its articles of incorporation are filed. However, an entity may be treated as a corporation for tax purposes even though it did not complete all the general corporate law requirements.[2]

A corporation's tax existence generally ends when it is considered dissolved under local law.[3] However, a corporation that continued to do business after its charter expired continued to be taxable as a corporation.[4]

¶ 3303 Corporate entity ignored.

A corporation may not be recognized for tax purposes if it is inactive, is merely to hold title,[5] or serves no business purpose other than tax avoidance.[6]

A corporation organized solely to avoid state usury law limits for individual borrowers is treated as an agent with respect to a particular asset if the agency is set forth in a written agreement at the time the asset is acquired, the corporation functions as agent (and not as principal) with respect to that asset for all purposes, and the corporation is held out as agent in all dealings with third parties relating to that asset.[7]

¶ 3304 Associations taxable as corporations.

An organization (including an unincorporated entity like a partnership, LLC, or trust) will be taxed as a corporation only if it evidences a sufficient preponderance of features characteristic of a corporation. (Reg § 301.7701-2(a)(1)) These features are:

- associates,
- an objective to carry on a business and divide the gain from it,
- continuity of life,
- centralized management,
- liability limited to the organization's assets, and
- free transferability of interests. (Reg § 301.7701-2(a)(1))[8]

If an entity has more corporate than noncorporate characteristics, it is treated as a corporation (association taxable as a corporation). (Reg § 301.7701-2(a)(3))[9]

Since the characteristics listed above are used to determine whether an organization is an association taxable as a corporation, characteristics common to both corporations and the type of organization at issue are not considered. (Reg § 301.7701-2(a)(2)) For example,

---

1. ¶ D-1100 *et seq.*; ¶ 77,014 *et seq.*
2. ¶s D-1102, D-1103; ¶s 77,014.01, 77,014.22.
3. ¶ D-1106; ¶ 77,014.21.
4. ¶ D-1102; ¶ 77,014.23.
5. ¶ D-1216; ¶ 79,006.11.
6. ¶ D-1207; ¶s 79,006.07, 79,006.10.
7. ¶ D-1221; ¶ 79,006.10.
8. ¶ D-1303; ¶ 77,014.04.
9. ¶ D-1302; ¶ 77,014.04.

Footnote references beginning with letters are to paragraphs in RIA's Federal Tax Coordinator 2d and RIA's Analysis of Federal Taxes: Income. Footnote references beginning with numbers are to paragraphs in RIA's United States Tax Reporter.

since both trusts and corporations generally have centralized management, free transferability of interests, continuity of life and limited liability, then in determining whether a trust is taxable as a corporation, consider only the presence of associates and the objective of carrying on a business and dividing the profits. (Reg § 301.7701-2(a)(2))[10]

¶ 3305 Publicly traded partnerships as corporations.

A publicly traded partnership is treated as a corporation. (Code Sec. 7704(a))[11] A partnership is a publicly traded partnership if interests in the partnership either: (1) are traded on an established securities market, or (2) are readily tradable on a secondary market or its substantial equivalent. (Code Sec. 7704(b))[12]

However, a publicly traded partnership won't be treated as a corporation if, for each tax year beginning after '87, at least 90% of its gross income is specified passive-type income, and certain other requirements are met. (Code Sec. 7704(c))[13] Certain existing partnerships that were publicly traded partnerships on Dec. 17, '87, won't be treated as corporations until tax years beginning after '97.[14]

¶ 3306 Limited liability companies.

Limited liability companies (LLCs) are owned (in some cases managed) by members, who are not personally liable for the LLC's debts or obligations. LLCs that are classified as partnerships (¶ 3304) offer the flow-through of tax attributes to the members under the partnership tax rules.[15]

observation: An LLC that is classified as a partnership combines the benefits of a pass-through entity with limited liability.

caution: "Partnership" classification for the LLC also means that the members will be subject to the at-risk as well as the passive loss rules (¶ 1786 *et seq.*).

caution: Not all states have LLC statutes.

¶ 3307 C corporations and S corporations.

For income tax purposes, corporations include C corporations and S corporations.

A C corporation is any corporation that is not an S corporation. (Code Sec. 1361(a)(2))[16] For how C corporations are taxed, see ¶ 3308 *et seq.*

An S corporation is a corporation for which an election to be taxed under Subchapter S of the Code is in effect. (Code Sec. 1361(a)(1))[17] For how S corporations are taxed, see ¶ 3359 *et seq.*

¶ 3308 How C Corporations Are Taxed

C corporations generally are subject to tax at graduated rates on their taxable income. The benefits of the graduated rates phase out after taxable income reaches a specified amount.

For the rates at which a C corporation's income is taxed, and for the amount at which the graduated rates are phased out, see ¶ 1111. For limits on the use of graduated rates and other tax benefits by members of a controlled group of corporations, see ¶ 3347.

C corporations that are personal service corporations are taxed at a flat 35% rate (¶ 1111). (Code Sec. 11(b)(2))[18]

Some C corporations are also subject to an accumulated earnings tax (¶ 3320 *et seq.*), a personal holding company tax (¶ 3330 *et seq.*), an environmental tax (¶ 3358) and an

---

10. ¶ D-1303; ¶s 77,014.04, 77,014.13.
11. ¶ D-1341; ¶ 77,044.
12. ¶ D-1355; ¶ 77,044.03.
13. ¶ D-1375; ¶ 77,044.
14. ¶ D-1380; ¶ 77,044.23.
15. ¶ D-1250 *et seq.*
16. ¶ D-1422; ¶ 13,609.
17. ¶ D-1421; ¶ 13,609.
18. ¶ D-1005; ¶s 114.01, 114.02.

Footnote references beginning with letters are to paragraphs in RIA's Federal Tax Coordinator 2d and RIA's Analysis of Federal Taxes: Income. Footnote references beginning with numbers are to paragraphs in RIA's United States Tax Reporter.

alternative minimum tax (Chapter 14).

For income tax returns to be filed, see (¶ 4722).

¶ 3309 Computing a C corporation's taxable income.

A C corporation's taxable income equals its gross income less the deductions allowed by the Code. (Code Sec. 63)[19]

A C corporation's gross income does not include contributions to its capital. (Code Sec. 118)[20] Special rules also apply to determine the amount and type of gain or loss recognized by a C corporation from distributing property to its shareholders (¶ 3519 *et seq.*).

There are some important differences between deductions allowed to C corporations and those allowed to individuals, in computing taxable income, as described in the following paragraphs.

¶ 3310 Computing a C corporation's tax.

A C corporation's tax is computed by applying the Code Sec. 11 rates in effect for its tax year (¶ 1111) to its taxable income for that year, and then subtracting any available tax credits (¶ 2300 *et seq.*).[21]

¶ 3311 Dividends-Received Deduction

Corporate shareholders are allowed a deduction for dividends received, subject to certain limits.

¶ 3312 Deduction for dividends received from domestic corporations.

Subject to specific disallowances, reductions, and limitations (¶ 3316 *et seq.*), a C corporation may deduct 70% of the dividends received or accrued from domestic corporations. (Code Sec. 243(a)(1))[22] The deduction is 80% for dividends received or accrued from a 20%-owned corporation, (Code Sec. 243(c)(1)) i.e., any corporation at least 20% of whose stock (not counting preferred stock described in Code Sec. 1504(a)(4)), by vote or value, is owned by the corporate shareholder. (Code Sec. 243(c)(2))[23]

The deduction is 100% if the shareholder is a small business investment company (¶ 4205). (Code Sec. 243(a)(2))[24]

Also, members of an affiliated group (as specially defined) which file separate returns may deduct 100% of the dividends received from other group members if certain requirements are met. (Code Sec. 243(a)(3), (b))[25]

The deduction applies to taxable "dividends" (¶ 1288 *et seq.*), "boot" dividends (¶ 3551) consent dividends (¶ 3343),[26] and the "dividend equivalent" portion of high yield OID obligations (¶ 1742). (Code Sec. 243(a))[27]

¶ 3313 Dividends from regulated investment companies (RICs).

A dividend (other than capital gain or exempt-interest dividends) from an RIC (e.g., a mutual fund) may be designated as a dividend eligible for the dividends-received deduction only to the extent of the amounts the RIC received from domestic corporations that it would have been allowed to treat as dividends in computing its *own* dividends-received deduction if it had been a regular corporation. (Code Sec. 854(b)(4))[28]

---

19. ¶ D-1001; ¶ 634.
20. ¶ F-1901; ¶ 1184.
21. ¶ D-1001; ¶ 634.
22. ¶ D-2201; ¶ 2434.01.
23. ¶ D-2204 *et seq.*; ¶ 2434.01.
24. ¶ D-2242; ¶ 2434.01.
25. ¶ D-2222 *et seq.*; ¶ 2434.01.
26. ¶ D-2208 *et seq.*; ¶s 1634.057, 2434.04.
27. ¶ D-2220; ¶ 1634.051.
28. ¶ E-6163; ¶ 8524.02.

¶ 3314 Dividends on certain public utility preferred stock.

Corporate shareholders may deduct dividends *received* from a public utility, but the deduction is reduced if the utility was entitled to a special dividends-paid deduction on those dividends. (Code Sec. 244(a))[29]

¶ 3315 Deduction for dividends received from a foreign corporation.

A U.S. corporation that owns at least 10% (by vote or value) of a foreign corporation's stock may deduct the applicable Code Sec. 243 percentage (70% or 80%, see ¶ 3312) of the U.S.-source portion of the dividends received from that corporation. (Code Sec. 245(a)(1), (2))[30] The U.S.-source portion of any dividend is the amount that bears the same ratio to the dividend that: (1) the payor's post-'86 undistributed U.S. earnings, bears to (2) its total post-'86 undistributed earnings. (Code Sec. 245(a)(3), (4), (5))[31] Special rules apply for dividends paid out of pre-'87 earnings.[32]

A 100% dividends-received deduction is allowed (instead of 70%) if all the foreign corporation's gross income is effectively connected with its U.S. business in the year the earnings and profits arose and all its outstanding stock is owned by the domestic payee both in that year and in the payee's tax year in which the dividends are received. (Code Sec. 245(b))[33]

A domestic corporation is allowed to deduct certain dividends it receives from a FSC (¶ 4629). (Code Sec. 245(c))[34]

¶ 3316 Taxable income limit on dividends-received deduction.

A corporation's percentage dividends-received deduction (but not the 100% deduction) for any tax year can't exceed the applicable percentage of its taxable income (below). (Code Sec. 246(b)(1)) But this limit doesn't apply for any tax year for which the shareholder has a net operating loss (NOL). (Code Sec. 246(b)(2))[35]

A corporate shareholder's dividends-received deduction is generally limited to 70% of its taxable income. But if the dividends are received *only* from 20%-owned corporations (i.e., the deduction is 80%), an 80%-of-taxable-income limit applies. If a corporate shareholder receives dividends from both 20%-owned *and* non-20%-owned corporations, the taxable income limit is applied first to the "20%-owned" dividends so that their deduction can't exceed 80% of taxable income. (Code Sec. 246(b)(3)(A)) If this 80% limit isn't exceeded, a separate limit is then applied to the "non-20%-owned" dividends so that their deduction doesn't exceed 70% of taxable income (as reduced by the total amount of the "20%-owned" dividends). (Code Sec. 246(b)(3)(B))[36]

For this purpose, taxable income is computed without regard to the deductions for capital loss carrybacks, NOLs, or dividends received, and without regard to any basis reduction for extraordinary dividends. (Code Sec. 246(b)(1))[37]

¶ 3317 Holding period requirement.

A corporate shareholder gets no deduction for dividends received on: (1) stock it held for 45 days or less, (Code Sec. 246(c)(1)(A)) or (2) preferred stock it held for 90 days or less where the dividends received are attributable to a period or periods aggregating more than 366 days. (Code Sec. 246(c)(2))[38]

In determining how long the shareholder has held the stock, the day of disposition but not the day of acquisition is taken into account. (Code Sec. 246(c)(3)(A))[39]

Also, the shareholder's holding period for the stock is suspended (reduced) for any period during which, while holding the stock, it:

---

29. ¶ D-2221; ¶ 2434.02.
30. ¶ D-2243; ¶ 2434.03.
31. ¶s D-2243, D-2245; ¶ 2434.03.
32. ¶ D-2243; ¶ 2434.04.
33. ¶ D-2246; ¶ 2434.03.
34. ¶ O-1696 *et seq.*; ¶ 2434.03.
35. ¶s D-2250, D-2251; ¶ 2434.04.
36. ¶ D-2252; ¶ 2434.04.
37. ¶ D-2250; ¶ 2434.04.
38. ¶ D-2262; ¶ 2434.04.
39. ¶ D-2262.

Footnote references beginning with letters are to paragraphs in RIA's Federal Tax Coordinator 2d and RIA's Analysis of Federal Taxes: Income. Footnote references beginning with numbers are to paragraphs in RIA's United States Tax Reporter.

(1) has an option to sell, is under a contractual obligation to sell, or has made (and not closed) a short sale of substantially identical stock or securities, (Code Sec. 246(c)(4)(A))

(2) is the grantor of an option to buy substantially identical stock or securities, (Code Sec. 246(c)(4)(B)) or

(3) has diminished its risk of loss by holding one or more other positions with respect to substantially similar or related property. (Code Sec. 246(c)(4)(C))[40]

¶ 3318 Reduced dividends-received deduction when portfolio stock is debt-financed.

The percentage dividends-received deduction (but not the 100% deduction) is reduced for dividends on debt-financed portfolio stock with a holding period that began after July 18, '84. As reduced, the applicable percentage for deducting these dividends equals: (1) 70% (80% for dividends from 20%-owned corporations), times (2) 100% minus the "average indebtedness percentage." (Code Sec. 246A(a), (b)) But the reduction for any dividend may not exceed the interest deduction (including short sale expense) allocable to that dividend. (Code Sec. 246A(e))[41]

¶ 3319 Dividends from certain corporations are not deductible.

No dividends-received deduction is allowed for:

■ Dividends from a Code Sec. 501 tax-exempt corporation. (Code Sec. 246(a)(1))[42] However, dividends from federal home loan banks qualify to the extent set out in a specific formula. (Code Sec. 246(a)(2)(A)(i))[43]

■ A dividend from a Code Sec. 521 farmer's cooperative. (Code Sec. 246(a)(1))

■ A dividend from a DISC or former DISC to the extent paid out of accumulated DISC income or previously taxed income, or amounts deemed distributed in the year of qualification as a DISC. (Code Sec. 246(d))

■ A dividend received under the Code Sec. 936(h)(4) or Code Sec. 934(c)(3) distribution rules (relating to the possessions tax credit). (Code Sec. 246(e))

■ Any dividend received from a REIT. (Code Sec. 243(d)(3))

■ A capital gains dividend from a RIC (¶ 3313). (Code Sec. 243(d)(2), Code Sec. 854(a))

■ Any amount received from a mutual savings bank, etc., that the bank is allowed to deduct under Code Sec. 591. (Code Sec. 243(d)(1))[44]

¶ 3320 Accumulated Earnings Tax

Every corporation, unless specifically exempt, is subject to the accumulated earnings (penalty) tax if it is formed or availed of for the purpose of avoiding the income tax with respect to its shareholders by permitting earnings and profits to accumulate instead of being distributed.

¶ 3321 Application of the accumulated earnings tax.

The accumulated earnings tax applies to every corporation unless specifically exempt (¶ 3322). (Code Sec. 532(a))[45]

A corporation may accumulate up to a specified amount of undistributed earnings and profits without penalty (¶ 3329), and won't be penalized for accumulating additional amounts if it has a reasonable business need for doing so (¶ 3325).

The accumulated earnings tax applies to foreign corporations on their U.S.-source income if *any* of their shareholders is subject to U.S. income tax on distributions.

---

40. ¶ D-2263 *et seq.*
41. ¶ D-2254; ¶ 2434.05.
42. ¶ D-2212; ¶ 2434.01.

43. ¶ D-2218; ¶s 2434.01, 2434.04.

44. ¶ D-2213 *et seq.*; ¶s 2434.01, 8514.

45. ¶s D-2602, D-2603; ¶ 5324.

Footnote references beginning with letters are to paragraphs in RIA's Federal Tax Coordinator 2d and RIA's Analysis of Federal Taxes: Income. Footnote references beginning with numbers are to paragraphs in RIA's United States Tax Reporter.

(Reg § 1.532-1(c))[46]

¶ 3322 Corporations exempt from the accumulated earnings tax.

The accumulated earnings tax *doesn't apply* to:

- personal holding companies (¶ 3330 *et seq.*); (Code Sec. 532(b)(1))
- foreign personal holding companies (¶ 4644); (Code Sec. 532(b)(2))
- tax-exempt corporations (Code Sec. 532(b)(3))
- passive foreign investment companies (¶ 4641)
- S corporations (¶ 3359 *et seq.*). (Code Sec. 1363(a))[47]

¶ 3323 Accumulated earnings tax rate.

The accumulated earnings tax is 39.6% of accumulated taxable income (¶ 3327). (Code Sec. 531)[48]

¶ 3324 "Purpose" to avoid tax.

The accumulated earnings penalty tax is only imposed on a corporation whose earnings and profits (E&P) were accumulated with the purpose of avoiding income tax on its shareholders. (Code Sec. 532(a))[49] A corporation that accumulates E&P beyond the reasonable needs of its business is considered to have done so to avoid tax on its shareholders *unless* the corporation proves the contrary by the preponderance of the evidence. (Code Sec. 533(a))[50]

recommendation: A build-up of cash and other liquid assets that is large relative to the corporation's working capital needs indicates an unreasonable accumulation unless a reasonable business need for the build-up is shown. Accordingly, keep cash balances as low as possible at year-end. A high cash balance may be a red flag to an agent.

The fact that a corporation is a mere holding or investment company is prima facie evidence of this tax avoidance purpose. (Code Sec. 533(b))[1]

Key factors indicating a purpose to avoid shareholder tax are:

- withdrawals by the shareholders as personal loans, or expenditures out of corporate funds for the shareholder's personal benefit;[2]
- corporation's investment of undistributed earnings in assets having no reasonable connection with its business. (Reg § 1.533-1(a))[3]

A corporation with a history of paying out dividends isn't likely to be hit with the penalty.[4]

¶ 3325 Reasonable needs of the business.

An accumulation is in excess of the reasonable needs of a business if it exceeds the amount that a prudent businessman would consider appropriate for the present purposes of the business and for its reasonably anticipated future needs (below). (Reg § 1.537-1(a))[5]

Accumulations for future needs of a business are justifiable if the needs are *reasonably anticipated.* (Code Sec. 537) This won't be satisfied where the future needs of the business are uncertain or vague, where plans for the future use of an accumulation are not specific, definite or feasible, or where execution of the plan is postponed indefinitely. (Reg § 1.537-1(b)(1))[6]

---

46. ¶ D-2607; ¶ 5324.
47. ¶ D-2602; ¶ 5324.
48. ¶ D-2601; ¶s 5324.01, 5354.

49. ¶ D-2601; ¶ 5324.
50. ¶ D-2704; ¶s 5324.01, 5374.
1. ¶ D-2706; ¶ 5374.

2. ¶ D-2719; ¶ 5374.
3. ¶ D-2713; ¶ 5374.
4. ¶ D-2715; ¶ 5374.

5. ¶s D-2779, D-2792; ¶s 5314, 5374.
6. ¶ D-2783; ¶ 5374.

Footnote references beginning with letters are to paragraphs in RIA's Federal Tax Coordinator 2d and RIA's Analysis of Federal Taxes: Income. Footnote references beginning with numbers are to paragraphs in RIA's United States Tax Reporter.

¶ 3326 Operating cycle formula *(Bardahl).*

Corporations facing an accumulated earnings tax penalty may use a formula to compute the amount reasonably needed for working capital. This eliminates or reduces the accumulation that has to be justified as reasonable for other business purposes, i.e., for future expansion, etc. The Tax Court in *Bardahl Manufacturing Corp* held that necessary working capital should be determined by: (1) calculating a corporation's operating cycle percentage (the period of time, expressed as a percent of a year, needed to convert cash to inventory, inventory to sales and accounts receivable, and accounts receivable to cash), and then (2) multiplying that percentage times the corporation's total operating expenses for the year (cost of goods sold and other expenses). The result of this two-step *Bardahl* formula is the amount of liquid assets necessary to meet the ordinary operating expenses for one complete operating cycle,[7] see below.[8]

Step 1. Determining the operating cycle percentage:

A. *Inventory turnover percentage* (for businesses without inventories, other reasonable methods can be used).
(i) Inventory beginning of year $ _____
(ii) Inventory end of year   _____
(iii) Average inventory ((i) + (ii) + 2) $ _____
(iv) Cost of goods sold   _____
(v) Inventory turnover percentage ((iii) + (iv))   _____ %

B. *Accounts receivable turnover percentage.*
(i) Accounts receivable beginning of year $ _____
(ii) Accounts receivable end of year   _____
(iii) Average accounts receivable ((i) + (ii) + 2) $ _____
(iv) Total sales $ _____
(v) Accounts receivable turnover percentage ((iii) + (iv))   _____ %

C. *Operating cycle percentage.* A(v) plus B(v) (but IRS or courts may insist on "payables" turnover reduction).   _____ %

Step 2. Determining necessary working capital:

D. *Operating expenses for year.*
(i) Cost of goods sold $ _____
(ii) Other operating expenses $ _____
(iii) Federal income taxes   _____
(iv) Add (i) through (iii)   _____
(v) Depreciation   (_____)
(vi) Total operating expenses ((iv) – (v)) $ _____

Necessary working capital (percentage from C times amount in D(vi)): $ _____

The *Bardahl* formula is not a precise rule of law. But it is a well-established rule of administrative convenience that is routinely applied by the courts.[9]

¶ 3327 Accumulated taxable income.

A corporation's accumulated taxable income is its taxable income, adjusted as discussed at ¶ 3328, *minus* the sum of:

■ the dividends-paid deduction (¶ 3339), plus

---

7. ¶ D-2848; ¶ 5374.   8. ¶ D-2880; ¶ 5374.   9. ¶ D-2850.

Footnote references beginning with letters are to paragraphs in RIA's Federal Tax Coordinator 2d and RIA's Analysis of Federal Taxes: Income. Footnote references beginning with numbers are to paragraphs in RIA's United States Tax Reporter.

■ the accumulated earnings credit (¶ 3329). (Code Sec. 535(a))[10]

¶ 3328 Adjustments to corporation's taxable income.

In computing accumulated taxable income (¶ 3327), a corporation's taxable income is *reduced* by:

■ federal income taxes accrued during the tax year (not the accumulated earnings tax or the personal holding company tax); (Code Sec. 535(b)(1))

■ taxes of foreign countries and U.S. possessions accrued or deemed paid by a domestic corporation and included in the foreign tax credit (¶ 2357 *et seq.*); (Code Sec. 535(b)(1))[11]

■ charitable contributions in excess of the corporate deduction ceiling (¶ 2130 *et seq.*); (Code Sec. 535(b)(2))[12]

■ net capital gains (less attributable taxes); (Code Sec. 535(b)(6)(A)) a mere holding or investment company deducts net *short*-term capital gain (less attributable taxes) to the extent the gain doesn't exceed capital loss carryover to the year; (Code Sec. 535(b)(8)(B)) other corporations must reduce their net capital gain deduction by net capital losses from any earlier year; (Code Sec. 535(b)(7)(A), (B))[13]

■ net capital losses; (Code Sec. 535(b)(5)(A)) but a mere holding or investment company gets no net capital loss deduction, (Code Sec. 535(b)(8)(A)) any other corporation must reduce its net capital loss deduction by the lesser of: (1) its nonrecaptured capital gain deduction, or (2) its accumulated earnings and profits as of the close of the preceding tax year. (Code Sec. 535(b)(5))[14]

Taxable income is *increased* by:

■ special corporate deductions for dividends received (¶ 3311 *et seq.*); (Code Sec. 535(b)(3))

■ net operating loss deduction (¶ 1828 *et seq.*); (Code Sec. 535(b)(4))

■ capital loss carryback or carryover (¶ 2608). (Code Sec. 535(b)(7)(B))[15]

¶ 3329 Accumulated earnings credit.

For corporations other than a mere holding or investment company, the accumulated earnings credit equals the *greater* of:

(1) $250,000 ($150,000 for certain service corporations) *plus* dividends paid during the first 2 ½ months of the tax year *minus* accumulated earnings and profits (E&P) at the close of the preceding tax year; (Code Sec. 535(c)(2), (4)) or

(2) an amount equal to that part of the E&P for the tax year as are retained for the reasonable needs of the business *minus* the net capital gain deduction, if any, allowed in adjusting the corporation's taxable income (¶ 3328). (Code Sec. 535(c)(1)) The "retained" E&P for a tax year is the amount by which, for the year, E&P exceed the dividends-paid deduction. (Code Sec. 535(c)(4))[16]

A mere holding or investment company is entitled to an accumulated earnings credit for the amount, if any, by which $250,000 plus dividends paid during the first 2½ months of the tax year exceeds accumulated E&P at the close of the preceding tax year. (Code Sec. 535(c)(3), (4))[17]

✪*observation:* In other words, a mere holding or investment company gets no credit for reasonable needs.

¶ 3330 Personal Holding Company Tax ▬▬▬▬▬▬▬▬▬▬▬

A penalty tax is imposed on a personal holding company (PHC) used to shelter

---

10. ¶ D-2901; ¶ 5354.01.　　　　12. ¶ D-2906; ¶ 5354.01.　　　　14. ¶ D-2911; ¶ 5354.01.　　　　16. ¶ D-2915; ¶ 5354.01.
11. ¶ D-2913; ¶ 5354.01.　　　　13. ¶ D-2908; ¶ 5354.01.　　　　15. ¶ D-2907; ¶ 5354.01.　　　　17. ¶ D-2915; ¶ 5354.01.

Footnote references beginning with letters are to paragraphs in RIA's Federal Tax Coordinator 2d and RIA's Analysis of Federal Taxes: Income. Footnote references beginning with numbers are to paragraphs in RIA's United States Tax Reporter.

high bracket individual shareholders' passive income from stocks, bonds, or other investments, or where the company receives payments for personal services performed by a shareholder.

The tax is reported on Schedule PH (Form 1120).

¶ 3331 Tax on personal holding companies.

For any tax year in which a corporation is a personal holding company (PHC), it is liable for a 39.6% penalty tax on its undistributed PHC income, in addition to "regular" income tax. (Code Sec. 541)[18]

A PHC is any corporation, other than one specifically exempted (¶ 3332) if, for the tax year:

- at least 60% of its adjusted ordinary gross income is PHC income (¶ 3334), *and*

- at any time during the last half of the year more than 50% in value of its outstanding stock is owned, directly or indirectly, by or for not more than five individuals. (Code Sec. 542(a))[19]

An inactive corporation that is in the process of liquidating may be liable for the penalty tax.[20]

¶ 3332 Corporations exempt from PHC classification.

The following cannot be PHCs:

- S corporations (¶ 3359 *et seq.*); (Code Sec. 1363(a))

- tax-exempt corporations; (Code Sec. 542(c)(1))

- a corporation subject to the jurisdiction of a court in a bankruptcy case or in a receivership, foreclosure or similar proceeding in a federal or state court if the proceedings aren't primarily to avoid the PHC tax; (Code Sec. 542(c)(9))

- a bank or a domestic building and loan association; (Code Sec. 542(c)(2))

- a life insurance company; (Code Sec. 542(c)(3))

- a surety company; (Code Sec. 542(c)(4))

- certain active lending or finance companies; (Code Sec. 542(c)(6), (d))

- a small business investment company, if no shareholders own, directly or indirectly, a 5% or more interest in a small business concern to which the investment company provides funds; (Code Sec. 542(c)(8)) and

- these foreign corporations —

  . . . a foreign PHC, (Code Sec. 542(c)(5))

  . . . a passive foreign investment company, (Code Sec. 542(c)(10))

  . . . a foreign corporation if all its outstanding stock during the last half of its tax year is owned by nonresident aliens (directly or through foreign entities). The exemption does not apply if the corporation has PHC income from personal service contracts. (Code Sec. 542(c)(7))[21]

¶ 3333 Determining stock ownership.

An individual is the owner of any stock that he owns directly or indirectly (Code Sec. 542(a)(2)) under the following constructive ownership rules:

(1) Stock owned by or for a corporation, partnership, estate or trust is considered owned proportionately by its shareholders, partners or beneficiaries. (Code

---

18. ¶ D-3202.   19. ¶ D-3203; ¶ 5424.   20. ¶ D-3204.   21. ¶ D-3301; ¶ 5424.02.

Footnote references beginning with letters are to paragraphs in RIA's Federal Tax Coordinator 2d and RIA's Analysis of Federal Taxes: Income. Footnote references beginning with numbers are to paragraphs in RIA's United States Tax Reporter.

Sec. 544(a)(1))[22]

(2) Stock owned by or for an individual's family or partner is considered owned by the individual. An individual's family includes only his brothers and sisters (whether by the whole or half blood), spouse, ancestors and lineal descendants. (Code Sec. 544(a)(2))[23]

(3) If any person has an option to acquire stock, the stock subject to the option is considered owned by that person. Moreover, an option to acquire the option, and each one of a series of these options, is considered an option to acquire the stock. (Code Sec. 544(a)(3))[24]

Stock that may be considered owned by an individual under either rule (2) or rule (3) is considered owned by him under rule (3). (Code Sec. 544(a)(6))[25]

Rules (2) and (3) apply only if the result is to make the corporation a PHC or to make income PHC income (¶ 3334). (Code Sec. 544(a)(4))[26]

Stock *constructively* owned by a person under rule (1) or rule (3) is considered *actually* owned by that person for purposes of again applying rule (1), or applying rule (2), to make *another* person the *constructive* owner of the same stock. (Code Sec. 544(a)(5))[27]

Outstanding securities convertible into stock are considered outstanding stock *but only if* converting these securities has the effect of making the corporation a PHC or of making income PHC income (except where there are differing conversion dates). (Code Sec. 544(b))[28]

¶ 3334 Personal holding company (PHC) income.

Personal holding company (PHC) income is the portion of adjusted ordinary gross income that consists of: dividends; interest; annuities; rents (¶ 3335); mineral, oil and gas royalties; copyright, patent, etc., royalties (but not certain "active business computer software royalties"); produced film rents; compensation for shareholder's use of corporate property (¶ 3336); amounts received under personal service contracts (¶ 3337); and amounts received from estates and trusts. (Code Sec. 543(a))[29]

Ordinary gross income is gross income minus all gains from the sale or other disposition of capital assets (including unstated interest) and of Code Sec. 1231(b) assets. (Code Sec. 543(b)(1))[30]

Adjusted ordinary gross income is ordinary gross income adjusted as follows: for each of the separate categories of rents, mineral, oil and gas royalties, working interests in an oil or gas well and property produced by the taxpayer, gross income from the category is reduced (but not below zero) by certain expenses allocated to each category. Also, certain interest income is excluded. (Code Sec. 543(b)(2))[31]

¶ 3335 Rents.

The adjusted income from rents is PHC income (¶ 3334) unless *both* these tests are met:

(1) adjusted income from rents is 50% or more of adjusted ordinary gross income; *and*

(2) certain other *undistributed* "PHC income" (as specially defined) is 10% or less of ordinary gross income. This "PHC income" *includes* copyright royalties and adjusted income from mineral, oil and gas royalties but *excludes* rents and compensation for a shareholder's use of corporate property. The 10% test is met if the total of (a) dividends paid during the tax year, plus (b) late-paid dividends (¶ 3341), plus (c) consent dividends (¶ 3343) equals or exceeds the amount, if any, by which "PHC income" exceeds 10% of ordinary gross income. (Code Sec. 543(a)(2))[32]

Rents are compensation (however designated) for the use of, or the right to use, property, (Code Sec. 543(a)(1)(A), (b)(3)) *except* for: compensation for a shareholder's use of

---

22. ¶ D-3406; ¶ 5444.01.   25. ¶ D-3411; ¶ 5444.01.   28. ¶ D-3412; ¶ 5444.01.   31. ¶ D-3506; ¶ 5424.02.

23. ¶ D-3408; ¶ 5444.01.   26. ¶s D-3408, D-3410; ¶ 5444.01.   29. ¶ D-3507; ¶ 5434 *et seq.*   32. ¶ D-3522; ¶ 5434.07.

24. ¶ D-3410; ¶ 5444.01.   27. ¶ D-3411; ¶ 5444.01.   30. ¶ D-3505; ¶ 5424.02.

Footnote references beginning with letters are to paragraphs in RIA's Federal Tax Coordinator 2d and RIA's Analysis of Federal Taxes: Income. Footnote references beginning with numbers are to paragraphs in RIA's United States Tax Reporter.

corporate property that is PHC income (¶ 3336), copyright royalties, produced film rents, or compensation for the right to use any tangible personal property manufactured or produced by the corporation, if during the tax year, it is engaged in substantial manufacturing or production of property of the same type. (Code Sec. 543(b)(3))[33]

¶ 3336 Compensation for use of corporate property by a shareholder.

Amounts received by the corporation from a shareholder as compensation for the use of, or right to use, tangible property of the corporation is included in the corporation's PHC income (¶ 3334) if, during the tax year, 25% or more in value of the corporation's outstanding stock is owned by or for an individual entitled to use that property (directly or through a sublease). (Code Sec. 543(a)(6)(A)) But this doesn't apply if the corporation's "PHC income" doesn't exceed 10% of its ordinary gross income. This specially defined "PHC income" is computed by *excluding* adjusted income from rents and compensation for a 25%-or-more shareholder's use of tangible corporate property, and by *including* copyright royalties and adjusted income from mineral, oil and gas royalties. (Code Sec. 543(a)(6))[34]

¶ 3337 Receipts under personal service contract.

PHC income includes amounts received under a contract under which the corporation is to furnish personal services, and amounts received from the sale or other disposition of the contract, if:

(1) some person other than the corporation has the right to designate (by name or description) the individual who is to perform the services, or if the individual who is to perform the services is so designated in the contract, *and*

(2) at some time during the tax year 25% or more in value of the corporation's outstanding stock is owned, directly or indirectly, by or for that individual. (Code Sec. 543(a)(7); Reg § 1.543-1(b)(8)(i))[35]

¶ 3338 What is undistributed personal holding company income?

A PHC's undistributed personal holding company income is its taxable income (Code Sec. 545(a))[36] adjusted as described below.

■ The following amounts are *subtracted* from taxable income:

. . . Federal income tax accrued during the year, and U.S. possession and foreign income taxes not deductible in computing taxable income. (Code Sec. 545(b)(1))[37]

. . . Excess charitable contributions, i.e., amounts over the *corporate* ceiling up to the amount allowed under the *individual* ceiling (¶ 2122 *et seq.*). (Code Sec. 545(b)(2))[38]

. . . Excess of capital gains over capital losses minus income taxes attributable to that excess. (Code Sec. 545(b)(5))[39]

. . . One-year net operating loss (NOL) carryforward, i.e., NOL from the preceding tax year. (Code Sec. 545(b)(4))[40]

. . . Dividends-paid deduction (¶ 3339 *et seq.*). (Code Sec. 545(a))[41]

■ The following amounts are *added* to taxable income:

. . . Special corporate deductions for dividends received (¶ 3311 *et seq.*). (Code Sec. 545(b)(3))[42]

. . . NOL deduction. (Code Sec. 545(b)(4))[43]

. . . Expenses and depreciation exceeding income from property (unless income was

---

33. ¶ D-3524; ¶s 5434.06, 5434.07, 5434.09.
34. ¶ D-3527 *et seq.*; ¶ 5434.06.
35. ¶ D-3531; ¶ 5434.05.
36. ¶ D-3603; ¶ 5454.
37. ¶ D-3606; ¶ 5454.
38. ¶ D-3609; ¶ 5454.
39. ¶ D-3610; ¶ 5454.
40. ¶ D-3614; ¶ 5454.
41. ¶ D-3800; ¶ 5454.
42. ¶ D-3613; ¶ 5454.
43. ¶ D-3614; ¶ 5454.

highest obtainable). (Code Sec. 545(b)(6))[44]

¶ 3339 Dividend Distributions to Cut Special Taxes on Corporations ▬▬▬▬

A deduction for dividends paid is allowed in computing the accumulated earnings and personal holding company penalty taxes, and in determining a corporation's qualification as a regulated investment company (RIC) or real estate investment trust (REIT). (¶ 4201 *et seq.*) Deduction is also allowed in some cases for undistributed amounts shareholders consent to report as dividends.

A corporation's deduction for dividends paid is the sum of:

(1) dividends paid during the tax year (¶ 3340),

(2) "late paid" dividends (¶ 3341),

(3) liquidating dividends (¶ 3342),

(4) consent dividends (¶ 3343),

(5) dividend carryover—only for personal holding companies (PHCs) (¶ 3344), and

(6) deficiency dividends—only for PHCs (¶ 3345). (Code Sec. 561; Reg § 1.561-1)[45]

¶ 3340 Dividends paid during the tax year.

The dividends-paid deduction includes dividends paid during the tax year. (Code Sec. 561(a)(1)) But the dividend must actually be paid,[46] and must be actually received by the shareholder during the tax year for which the deduction is claimed. (Reg § 1.561-2(a)(1))[47]

But no dividends-paid deduction is allowed if the dividend is preferential, i.e., it must be pro rata. (Code Sec. 562(c); Reg § 1.562-2(a))[48]

For this purpose, the amount of "dividends" paid is the amount by which the distribution reduces the corporation's earnings and profits (E&P). (Code Sec. 316(a), Code Sec. 562(a))[49]

For a PHC (¶ 3330 *et seq.*), the amount of the dividends-paid deduction may equal its undistributed PHC income even if this exceeds its E&P. (Code Sec. 316(b)(2), Code Sec. 562(a))[50]

¶ 3341 Deduction for "late paid" dividends.

For purposes of the accumulated earnings (¶ 3320 *et seq.*) and PHC (¶ 3330 *et seq.*) penalty taxes, a corporation may elect to treat dividends paid after the close of the tax year but within the first 2½ months of the following year, as paid on the last day of the earlier year. (Code Sec. 563(a), (b))[1]

¶ 3342 Liquidating distributions.

Corporations other than PHCs may include liquidating distributions in their dividends-paid deduction, to the extent the distribution is properly chargeable to E&P. (Code Sec. 562(b)(1)(A))[2] Where there is a deficit in E&P at the beginning of the tax year of distribution, no dividends-paid deduction is allowed if current E&P for the distribution year don't exceed the deficit. (Reg § 1.562-1(b)(1))[3] A liquidation for this purpose includes a redemption (other than a redemption by a mere investment or holding company) of stock to which Code Sec. 302 applies (¶ 3525 *et seq.*). (Code Sec. 562(b)(1))[4]

If a *complete* liquidation occurs within 24 months after the plan of liquidation is

---

44. ¶ D-3615; ¶ 5454.
45. ¶ D-3800; ¶ 5614.
46. ¶ D-3806; ¶ 5614.01.
47. ¶ D-3810.

48. ¶ D-3819 *et seq.*; ¶ 5624.
49. ¶ D-3806; ¶s 3164 *et seq.*, 5614, 5624.

50. ¶ D-3807; ¶s 3164.03, 5614, 5644.
1. ¶ D-3825 *et seq.*; ¶ 5634.

2. ¶ D-3828; ¶ 5624.02.
3. ¶ D-3835; ¶ 5624.02.
4 ¶ D-3829; ¶s 5624.02, 5624.05.

Footnote references beginning with letters are to paragraphs in RIA's Federal Tax Coordinator 2d and RIA's Analysis of Federal Taxes: Income. Footnote references beginning with numbers are to paragraphs in RIA's United States Tax Reporter.

adopted, any distribution under the plan within the 24-month period is treated as a dividend for purposes of this deduction, to the extent of the corporation's E&P for the tax year of the distribution. E&P for this purpose are computed without regard to capital losses. (Code Sec. 562(b)(1)(B)) Thus, the dividends-paid deduction is allowed for the amount of the distribution up to the amount of current E&P even if there is an E&P deficit at the beginning of the year. (Reg § 1.562-1(b)(1))[5]

For PHCs, only distributions made within 24 months after the plan of liquidation is adopted qualify for the dividends-paid deduction.[6] Distributions to *corporate* shareholders within this 24-month period qualify to the extent that the undistributed PHC income for the tax year of the distribution is allocable to corporate shareholders. (Code Sec. 562(b)(2))[7] Distributions to *noncorporate* shareholders within this 24-month period qualify if the corporation designates the amount distributed as a dividend and notifies the shareholders that it must be reported as a dividend. (Code Sec. 316(b)(2)(B), Code Sec. 562(b)(2))[8]

¶ 3343 Consent dividends.

A corporation may claim a dividends-paid deduction for amounts with respect to "consent" stock (below) that it doesn't actually pay out as dividends, if those who are shareholders on the last day of its tax year consent to report these hypothetical amounts as dividend income on their tax returns. (Code Sec. 565(a); Reg § 1.565-1(a))[9]

This amount is treated for all tax purposes as if it had been distributed in money to the consenting shareholder on the last day of the corporation's tax year, and contributed to the corporation's capital by the shareholder on the same day. (Code Sec. 565(c))[10]

Consent stock includes common stock, and preferred stock with unlimited participation rights. (Code Sec. 565(c); Reg § 1.565-6(a)(1))[11]

A consent is made on Form 972. (Reg § 1.565-1(b)(1)) The corporation must file Forms 972 duly executed by each consenting stockholder, and a return on Form 973, with its income tax return and not later than the due date of the return. (Reg § 1.565-1(b)(3))

¶ 3344 Dividend carryover for PHC.

A PHC may increase its dividends-paid deduction for the tax year by the excess of: (1) dividends paid in the two preceding tax years, over (2) its undistributed PHC income for those years. (Code Sec. 564; Reg § 1.564-1)[12]

¶ 3345 PHC deficiency dividend deduction.

If a corporation is "determined" to be liable for a deficiency in PHC tax (¶ 3330 *et seq.*) for any tax year, it may reduce or eliminate the deficiency (or get a refund of part of all of any deficiency paid) by making a "deficiency dividend" distribution and then claiming a deduction (on Form 976) for it. This deduction is allowed only for purposes of determining the *PHC tax* for that year (but not in determining interest, additional amounts or assessable penalties computed with respect to the PHC tax). (Code Sec. 547(a))[13]

The deduction isn't allowed if the determination contains a finding that any part of the deficiency is due to fraud or willful failure to file a timely income tax return. (Code Sec. 547(g))[14]

A "determination" is a final court decision, a closing agreement, or a signed agreement with IRS relating to PHC tax liability. (Code Sec. 547(c))[15]

---

5. ¶ D-3836; ¶ 5624.02.
6. ¶ D-3837; ¶s 3164.03, 5624.02.
7. ¶ D-3844 *et seq.*; ¶ 5624.02.
8. ¶ D-3838 *et seq.*; ¶s 3164.03, 5624.02.

9. ¶s D-3851, D-3854, D-3861; ¶ 5654.
10. ¶ D-3852; ¶ 5654.

11. ¶s D-3859, D-3861; ¶ 5654.
12. ¶ D-3869; ¶ 5644.
13. ¶s D-3703, D-3716; ¶ 5474.

14. ¶ D-3719; ¶s 5474, 5474.01.
15. ¶ D-3704; ¶s 5474, 5474.03, 71,214.

Footnote references beginning with letters are to paragraphs in RIA's Federal Tax Coordinator 2d and RIA's Analysis of Federal Taxes: Income. Footnote references beginning with numbers are to paragraphs in RIA's United States Tax Reporter.

¶ *3346*   Multiple Corporations, Consolidated Returns ▬▬▬▬▬▬

A "controlled" group of C corporations is subject to limitations on certain tax benefits. An "affiliated" group can elect to file a single consolidated return instead of each group member filing a separate return.

¶ *3347*   Limit on multiple tax benefits for "controlled groups."

A controlled group of corporations is allowed a total of only one amount in each of the corporate rate brackets below the top bracket, only a single accumulated earnings tax credit (¶ 3329), only one alternative minimum tax exemption amount (¶ 3202), and only one $2 million amount for purposes of computing the environmental tax (¶ 3358). (Code Sec. 1561) In addition, many other Code provisions have special rules for controlled groups.[16]

A *parent-subsidiary controlled group* consists of one or more chains of corporations connected through stock ownership with a common parent where:

■ the common parent owns stock having at least 80% of the total combined voting power of all classes of stock entitled to vote or at least 80% of the total value of shares of all classes of stock, of at least one other corporation in the chain; *and*

■ at least 80% of the stock (combined voting power or value) of each corporation in the chain (other than the parent) is owned by one or more of the other corporations in the chain. (Code Sec. 1563(a)(1))[17]

A *brother-sister controlled group* consists of two or more corporations if:

■ at least 80% of the stock (combined voting power or value) of each corporation is owned by five or fewer persons who are individuals, estates or trusts; (Code Sec. 1563(a)(2)(A)) *and*

■ these persons own more than 50% of the stock of each corporation (combined voting power or value). (Code Sec. 1563(a)(2)(B))[18] For purposes of the 50% test, stock of each person is taken into account only to the extent it is owned identically with respect to each corporation. (Reg § 1.1563-1(a)(3)(i)(b))[19]

Special constructive ownership rules apply in determining whether these stock ownership tests are met. (Code Sec. 1563(d))[20]

¶ *3348*   Consolidated returns by affiliated groups.

Any affiliated group of one or more chains of "includible" corporations (¶ 3349) connected through the requisite stock ownership with a common parent may file a consolidated return in place of separate returns by each. (Code Sec. 1501, Code Sec. 1502, Code Sec. 1503, Code Sec. 1504, Code Sec. 1505)[21] But once a group files a consolidated return, it generally must continue to do so. (Reg § 1.1502-75(a)(2))[22]

Tax saving considerations usually determine whether to file a consolidated return. The key advantages of consolidated returns are:

■ Operating losses of one group member offset operating profits of other members.[23]

■ Intercompany profits and losses aren't generally taken into income until they are ultimately realized in transactions with outsiders.[24]

■ Parent increases its basis in the stock of its sub(s) by the subs' earnings and profits (as specially adjusted for consolidated return purposes) every year, so there's less gain when the parent sells the stock.[25] But with certain exceptions, the parent *loses* basis if the sub generates losses that the group uses. If the losses wipe out the parent's basis, an "excess

---

16. ¶ E-10300 *et seq.*; ¶s 15,014, 15,024 *et seq.*
17. ¶ E-10601; ¶ 15,634.
18. ¶ E-10613; ¶ 15,634.
19. ¶ E-10614; ¶ 15,634.
20. ¶ E-10700 *et seq.*; ¶ 15,634.
21. ¶ E-7500 *et seq.*; ¶ 15,014 *et seq.*
22. ¶ E-10000; ¶ 15,024.16.
23. ¶ E-9050 *et seq.*; ¶ 15,024.
24. ¶ E-8250 *et seq.*; ¶ 15,024.
25. ¶ E-8500 *et seq.*; ¶ 15,024.

Footnote references beginning with letters are to paragraphs in RIA's Federal Tax Coordinator 2d and RIA's Analysis of Federal Taxes: Income. Footnote references beginning with numbers are to paragraphs in RIA's United States Tax Reporter.

loss account" is created which will trigger income when the stock is sold or if certain other conditions occur. (Reg § 1.1502-20(a), (b))[26]

■ Tax exemption (100% deduction) for intercompany dividends (¶ 3312).[27]

However, no deduction is allowed for any loss recognized by a group member on disposition of stock of a sub (i.e., another group member other than the common parent), with certain exceptions. (Reg § 1.1502-20)[28]

¶ 3349 "Affiliated group" defined.

In order to qualify as an affiliated group:

(1) the common parent must directly own at least 80% of the total voting power and 80% of the total value of the stock in at least one other "includible" corporation; *and*

(2) one or more of the other includible corporations must directly own at least 80% of the stock (by vote or value) in each of the remaining includible corporations. (Code Sec. 1504(a))[29]

All corporations connected through these stock ownership requirements are "includible" corporations *except*:

■ tax-exempt organizations;

■ life insurance companies, except (under certain conditions) where two or more insurance companies are themselves an affiliated group;

■ RICs and REITs (¶ 4201 *et seq.*);

■ foreign corporations, except certain Mexican or Canadian subs of a U.S. parent can join in its consolidated return;

■ corporations that have a Code Sec. 936 election (possessions tax credit) in effect for the tax year;

■ a DISC or former DISC (¶ 4634). (Code Sec. 1504(b), (c))[30]

¶ 3350 Forms for consolidated reporting.

A consolidated return is made by the common parent on Form 1120 with an attached Form 851 (affiliation schedule). Each sub must also file a consent on Form 1122 unless a consolidated return was filed (or required) for the preceding tax year. (Reg § 1.1502-75(b), (h))[31]

¶ 3351 Estimated Tax ▬▬▬▬▬▬▬▬▬▬▬▬▬▬▬▬▬▬▬▬▬▬▬

Every corporation subject to U.S. income taxes must make estimated tax payments for a tax year for which its tax can reasonably be expected to be $500 or more.

For quick refund where a corporation pays *too much* in estimated tax, see ¶ 4848.

¶ 3352 The required annual payment.

A corporation must make installment payments (¶ 3354) of its "required annual payment," which equals the *lesser* of: (1) 100% of the tax shown on its return for the year (or if no return is filed, 100% of its tax for that year), or (2) 100% of the tax shown on its return for the preceding tax year. (Code Sec. 6655(d)(1)(B))[32]

However, a corporation may not base its required annual payment for a tax year on the preceding year's tax if:

---

26. ¶ E-8600 *et seq.*; ¶ 15,024.
27. ¶ E-7503; ¶s 15,024, 15,024.03.
28. ¶ E-8650 *et seq.*
29. ¶ E-7601; ¶s 15,024.16, 15,024.17.
30. ¶ E-7646; ¶s 15,024, 15,024.17.
31. ¶ E-7754 *et seq.*; ¶ 15,024.16.
32. FTC: S-5327, S-5328; ¶ 66,554.

Footnote references beginning with letters are to paragraphs in RIA's Federal Tax Coordinator 2d and RIA's Analysis of Federal Taxes: Income. Footnote references beginning with numbers are to paragraphs in RIA's United States Tax Reporter.

■ it didn't file a return for the preceding tax year showing a liability for tax (Code Sec. 6655(d)(1)) (a return showing zero tax, e.g., because of a net operating loss, isn't a return showing a liability for tax);

■ the preceding tax year was less than 12 months; (Code Sec. 6655(d)(1)) or

■ it is a "large corporation" (below), (Code Sec. 6655(d)(2)(A)) except that a large corporation may use its last year's tax to determine the amount of its first required installment for any tax year. But it must recapture any resulting reduction in that first installment, by increasing its next required installment by the amount of the reduction. (Code Sec. 6655(d)(2)(B))[33]

A corporation is "large" in any tax year if it (or any predecessor corporation) had taxable income of $1,000,000 or more for any of the three immediately preceding tax years. For this purpose, taxable income doesn't include carryback or carryover of net operating losses or capital losses. Special rules apply to controlled groups. (Code Sec. 6655(g)(2))[34]

For tax years beginning in '93, the required annual payment was based on 97% (not 100%) of current year tax.[35]

¶ 3353 What is "tax" for estimated tax purposes?

A corporation's "tax" for estimated tax purposes is the excess of: (1) the sum of its regular corporate (income) tax, the alternative minimum tax, the environmental tax, and (for foreign corporations) the tax on gross transportation income, over (2) the sum of its tax credits. (Code Sec. 6655(g)(1))[36]

For S corporations, regular corporate taxes also include: built-in gains tax (¶ 3369) or tax on net capital gains for certain S corporations (¶ 3368); tax on excess passive income (¶ 3372); and tax on recapture of pre-S election investment credit. (Code Sec. 6655(g)(4)(A))[37]

Special rules apply for foreign corporations, insurance companies and tax-exempt organizations. (Code Sec. 6655(g)(1), (3))[38]

¶ 3354 Making the required annual payment: required installments.

A corporation must pay its required annual payment (¶ 3352) of estimated tax in four equal installments ("required installments"). (Code Sec. 6655(c)(1), (d)(1)(A)) For a calendar year corporation, the installments are due as follows: first, Apr. 15; second, June 15; third, Sept. 15; fourth, Dec. 15. (Code Sec. 6655(c)(2)) For a fiscal year corporation, they are due on the 15th day of the corresponding months (Code Sec. 6655(i)(1)) (i.e., the fourth, sixth, ninth and 12th months).[39]

For lower installments in certain situations, see ¶s 3355 and 3356.

¶ 3355 Use of lower "annualized income installment" as required installment.

A corporation may use an "annualized income installment" as its estimated tax installment, if that is less than the "required installment" (¶ 3354). (Code Sec. 6655(e)(1)(A))[40]

The annualized income installment is the excess (if any) of:

(1) the applicable percentage (25%, 50%, 75%, and 100% for the first, second, third and fourth installments, respectively) of the full year's tax, computed by placing on an annualized basis (under regs to be issued) the taxable income, alternative minimum taxable income, and modified alternative minimum taxable income for the months to which the installment applies (i.e., the first three months (first and second installments), first six months (third), and first nine months (fourth)), *over*

---

33. ¶ S-5328 *et seq.*; ¶ 66,554.   35. ¶ S-5327; ¶ 66,554.   37. ¶ S-5401; ¶ 66,554.   39. ¶ S-5353; ¶ 66,554.

34. ¶ S-5331 *et seq.*; ¶ 66,554.   36. ¶ S-5322; ¶ 66,554.   38. ¶ S-5321 *et seq.*; ¶ 66,554.   40. ¶ S-5326; ¶ 66,554.

Footnote references beginning with letters are to paragraphs in RIA's Federal Tax Coordinator 2d and RIA's Analysis of Federal Taxes: Income. Footnote references beginning with numbers are to paragraphs in RIA's United States Tax Reporter.

(2) the sum of any earlier required installments for the tax year. (Code Sec. 6655(e)(2)(A), (B))[41]

Alternatively, a corporation may elect (on Form 8842, by the due date of the first installment) to determine its annualized income based on its income for *either:* (1) the first two months (first installment), first four months (second), first seven months (third) and first ten months (fourth); *or* (2) the first three months (first), the first five months (second), first eight months (third), and first 11 months (fourth). (Code Sec. 6655(e)(2)(C))[42]

Any reduction in an installment resulting from using the annualization method must be made up (recaptured). This is done by increasing the amount of the next required installment that is *not* determined under the annualization method, by the amount of the reduction. (Code Sec. 6655(e)(1)(B))[43]

For tax years beginning in '93, the "applicable percentages" were 24.25%, 48.50%, 72.75%, and 97%, and the taxable income was determined as of the first three, first three or five, first six or eight, and first nine or 11 months, for the first, second, third and fourth installments, respectively.[44]

¶ 3356 Use of lower "adjusted seasonal installment" as required installment.

A corporation may use an "adjusted seasonal installment" as its required estimated tax installment if it is less than the required installment (¶ 3354) or the annualized income installment, (Code Sec. 6655(e)(1)(A)) but only if the corporation's base period percentage (below) for any six consecutive months of the tax year is at least 70%. (Code Sec. 6655(e)(3)(B))[45]

A corporation's adjusted seasonal installment is the excess of (a) 100% times an amount (computed below) over (b) the aggregate of all earlier required installments. (Code Sec. 6655(e)(3)(A))

The amount in (a) above is determined by (1) computing the taxable income for all months during the tax year before the filing month (i.e., the month the installment is required to be paid), (2) dividing this amount by the base period percentage for those preceding months, (3) determining the tax on the result, and (4) multiplying that tax by the base period percentage for the filing month and all preceding months in the tax year. (Code Sec. 6655(e)(3)(C), (D)(ii))[46]

The base period percentage for any specific period of months is the average percent that the corporation's taxable income for the corresponding months in each of the three preceding tax years bears to the taxable income for those three preceding years. (Code Sec. 6655(e)(3)(D)(i))[47]

The adjusted seasonal installments are subject to the same "recapture" that applies to the annualized income installment if the corporation doesn't use the adjusted seasonal exception for any later payment. (Code Sec. 6655(e)(1)(B))[48]

For tax years beginning in '93, the step (b) amount was subtracted from 97% (not 100%) of the step (a) amount.[49]

¶ 3357 Penalty for failure to pay estimated tax.

A corporation that underpays its estimated tax must add to its income tax an amount equal to the underpayment interest rate (¶ 4862) times the amount of the underpayment, for the period of the underpayment. (Code Sec. 6655(a)) Compute on Form 2220.[50]

The amount of the underpayment is the excess of the required installment (¶ 3354) over the amount (if any) of the installment paid on or before the due date for the installment.

---

41. ¶ S-5338; ¶ 66,554.
42. ¶ S-5340.1.
43. ¶ S-5347; ¶ 66,554.
44. ¶ S-5339.
45. ¶ S-5344; ¶ 66,554.
46. ¶ S-5345 *et seq.*; ¶ 66,554.
47. ¶ S-5346; ¶ 66,554.
48. ¶ S-5348; ¶ 66,554.
49. ¶ S-5345 *et seq.*; ¶ 66,554.
50. ¶ S-5358; ¶ 66,554.

Footnote references beginning with letters are to paragraphs in RIA's Federal Tax Coordinator 2d and RIA's Analysis of Federal Taxes: Income. Footnote references beginning with numbers are to paragraphs in RIA's United States Tax Reporter.

(Code Sec. 6655(b)(1))[1]

The period of the underpayment runs from the due date for the installment to the earlier of: (1) the 15th day of the third month after the close of the tax year, or (2) with respect to any portion of the underpayment, the date the portion is paid. (Code Sec. 6655(b)(2)) For this purpose, a payment of estimated tax is credited against unpaid required installments in the order those installments are required to be paid. (Code Sec. 6655(b)(3))[2]

No estimated tax penalty is imposed for any tax year if the tax shown on the return for that year (or if no return is filed, the tax liability) is less than $500. (Code Sec. 6655(f))[3] Nor is the penalty imposed for a period in which the corporation's failure to pay the required installment(s) results from a pending Title 11 bankruptcy case. (Code Sec. 6658(a))[4]

Also, no estimated tax penalty applies for any period before Mar. 16, '94 with respect to any underpayment to the extent it was created or increased by the '93 Revenue Reconciliation Act.[5]

¶ 3358 Environmental Tax

A corporation is liable for an environmental tax if its modified alternative minimum taxable income exceeds $2 million.

In addition to any other income tax, a corporation (other than an S corporation, a RIC or REIT) is liable, for tax years beginning before '96, for an environmental tax equal to 0.12% of the excess of: (1) the corporation's modified alternative minimum taxable income for the tax year, over (2) $2 million. (Code Sec. 59A(a), (c), (e)(1))[6] Compute the tax on Form 4626.

"Modified alternative minimum taxable income" means the alternative minimum taxable income for purposes of the alternative minimum tax (Chapter 14) but (for tax years beginning before '93) disregarding the alternative tax net operating loss deduction, the deduction for the generation-skipping transfer tax, (Code Sec. 59(A)(b)) and the alternative tax energy preference deduction.[7]

¶ 3359 S Corporations

An eligible corporation may elect to be taxed as an S corporation. An electing corporation, with limited exceptions, is not taxed at the corporate level. Instead, its items of income, loss, deduction and credit are passed through to, and taken into account by, its shareholders in computing their individual tax liabilities.

¶ 3360 S election eligibility.

Only a small business corporation may elect to be an S corporation. (Code Sec. 1362(a)(1))[8] To be a small business corporation for this purpose, a corporation must meet all of the following requirements:[9]

(1) It must be a domestic corporation (created under the law of the U.S. or of any state). (Code Sec. 1361(b)(1))[10]

(2) It must not be an ineligible corporation. (Code Sec. 1361(b)(1)) A corporation is ineligible if it:

. . . is a member of an affiliated group (taking into account only active subs) even if it can't file a consolidated return with any other group member, (Code

---

1. ¶ S-5359; ¶ 66,554.
2. ¶ S-5360; ¶ 66,554.
3. ¶ S-5363; ¶ 66,554.
4. ¶ S-5364; ¶ 66,554.
5. ¶ S-5364.1.
6. ¶ D-1081; ¶ 66,554.
7. ¶ D-1082; ¶ 66,554.
8. ¶ D-1431; ¶ 13,614.
9. ¶ D-1432 et seq.; ¶ 13,614 et seq.
10. ¶ D-1433; ¶ 13,614.01.

Footnote references beginning with letters are to paragraphs in RIA's Federal Tax Coordinator 2d and RIA's Analysis of Federal Taxes: Income. Footnote references beginning with numbers are to paragraphs in RIA's United States Tax Reporter.

Sec. 1361(b)(2)(A))

. . . is a bank which is allowed a deduction for reasonable reserves (or would be but for the fact that it is a "large" bank), (¶ 4209)

. . . is a domestic building and loan association, mutual savings bank or cooperative bank which keeps reserves for losses on loans under Code Sec. 593, (Code Sec. 1361(b)(2)(B))

. . . is taxable as an insurance company, (Code Sec. 1361(b)(2)(C))

. . . has elected the Code Sec. 936 possessions credit, (Code Sec. 1361(b)(2)(D))

. . . is a DISC or former DISC (¶ 4634). (Code Sec. 1361(b)(2)(E))[11]

(3) It can't have more than 35 shareholders. (Code Sec. 1361(b)(1)(A)) Each tenant-in-common or joint tenant is counted as one shareholder. A husband and wife (and their estates) are treated as one shareholder, no matter how the stock is held (separately, jointly, etc.). (Code Sec. 1361(c))[12]

(4) All shareholders must be individuals, decedents' estates, bankruptcy estates or trusts described at ¶ 3361. (Code Sec. 1362(b)(1)(B))[13]

(5) No shareholder may be a nonresident alien. (Code Sec. 1361(b)(1)(C))[14]

(6) It must have only one class of stock (¶ 3362). (Code Sec. 1361(b)(1)(D))[15]

For additional tests a corporation must meet to remain eligible to be an S corporation after the election is made, see ¶ 3383.

¶ 3361 Trusts as shareholders.

Only the following trusts may be S corporation shareholders:

(1) Domestic trusts that are treated as being owned by an individual ("grantor") who is a U.S. citizen or resident. The grantor, not the trust, is treated as the shareholder. (Code Sec. 1361(c)(2)(A)(i)) But after the grantor dies, the trust may continue as the shareholder for 60 days in any case, or for two years if the entire trust corpus is includible in the grantor's estate. (Code Sec. 1361(c)(2)(A)(ii))[16]

(2) Voting trusts, but each beneficiary is counted as a separate shareholder. (Code Sec. 1361(c)(2)(A)(iv), (B)(iv))[17]

(3) Testamentary trusts, but only for 60 days beginning with the day when stock was transferred to the trust under the testator's will. (Code Sec. 1361(c)(2)(A)(iii))[18]

(4) "Qualified Subchapter S trusts," where the beneficiary elects (on Form 2553, in certain circumstances) to be treated as the owner of the trust so that it is eligible to hold the S stock (as in (1), above), and is treated as the shareholder. (Code Sec. 1361(d)(1))[19]

¶ 3362 One class of stock.

A corporation is treated as having only one class of stock (¶ 3360) if:

■ all outstanding shares of its stock confer identical rights to distribution and liquidation proceeds, based on certain "governing provisions" (i.e., corporate charter, by-laws, state law, etc.); (Reg § 1.1361-1(l)(1), (2)(i)) and

■ it has not issued any instrument or obligation or entered into any arrangement that is treated as a second class of stock. (Reg § 1.1361-1(l)(4))[20]

The one-class-of-stock rule isn't violated *solely* because of differences in voting rights. Thus, voting and nonvoting common can be issued. (Code Sec. 1361(c)(4))[21]

---

11. ¶ D-1434 *et seq.*; ¶ 13,614.01.
12. ¶ D-1447 *et seq.*; ¶ 13,614.02.
13. ¶ D-1451; ¶ 13,614.03.
14. ¶ D-1482; ¶ 13,614.03.

15. ¶ D-1483; ¶ 13,614.04.
16. ¶s D-1459, D-1460; ¶ 13,614.03.

17. ¶ D-1479; ¶ 13,614.03.
18. ¶ D-1478; ¶ 13,614.03.
19. ¶ D-1461 *et seq.*; ¶ 13,614.03.

20. ¶ D-1483.1 *et seq.*
21. ¶ D-1484; ¶s 13,609.03, 13,614.04.

Footnote references beginning with letters are to paragraphs in RIA's Federal Tax Coordinator 2d and RIA's Analysis of Federal Taxes: Income. Footnote references beginning with numbers are to paragraphs in RIA's United States Tax Reporter.

Buy-sell agreements among shareholders, redemption agreements and agreements restricting the transferability of stock generally won't violate the one-class-of-stock rule *unless*: (1) a principal purpose of the agreement is to circumvent the rule, and (2) it establishes a purchase price for the stock that is significantly above or below its fair market value (FMV). (Reg § 1.1361-1(l)(2)(iii))[22]

A call option, warrant or similar instrument is, with certain exceptions, treated as a second class of stock if it is substantially certain to be exercised and has a strike price substantially below the stock's FMV on the date it is issued, transferred to an ineligible shareholder or materially modified. (Reg § 1.1361-1(l)(4)(iii)(A))[23]

Straight debt isn't treated as a second class of stock if specified safe harbor rules are met. (Code Sec. 1361(c)(5)(A), (B))[24] However, any instrument, obligation, or arrangement is, with certain exception, treated as a second class of stock if: (1) it constitutes equity or otherwise results in the holder being treated as the owner of stock under general tax law, and (2) its principal purpose is to circumvent these rules. (Reg § 1.1361-1(l)(4))[25]

¶ *3363* Tax year.

The tax year of an S corporation must be a "permitted year," (Code Sec. 1378(a))[26] unless a special election is made. For discussion of "permitted year" and the special election, see ¶s 2811, 2814.

¶ *3364* How to elect S corporation status.

The election is made by the corporation (Code Sec. 1362(a)(1)) by filing a Form 2553 signed by its authorized officer, together with the required shareholder consents (¶ 3365), with the IRS Service Center designated on Form 2553. (Reg § 1.1362-6(a)(2))[27]

An election for a tax year must be made during the preceding tax year, or by the 15th day of the third month of the tax year for which it is to be effective. (Code Sec. 1362(b)(1)) If this first tax year is less than two months and 15 days, the election will be effective for that year if made no later than two months and 15 days after the first day of that year. (Code Sec. 1362(b)(4))[28]

However, an election will be effective retroactively to the first day of a tax year only if:

■ on all days in the tax year before the day the election is made, the corporation would have been eligible to elect, (Code Sec. 1362(b)(2)(B)(i)) *and*

■ all persons who were shareholders at any time during the tax year before the day of the election, but who are not shareholders on that date, consent (along with persons who *are* shareholders, see ¶ 3365). (Code Sec. 1362(b)(2)(ii))[29]

If either of the above conditions isn't met, the election is treated as made for the next tax year. (Code Sec. 1362(b)(2), (3))[30]

¶ *3365* Shareholder consents.

All shareholders owning stock in the corporation on the day it elects S status must consent to the election. (Code Sec. 1362(a)(2); Reg § 1.1362-6(b)(2)(i))[31]

The consents may be given on Form 2553, or on separate statements attached to the Form 2553. (Reg § 1.1362-6(b))[32]

A shareholder's failure to file a timely consent won't invalidate an otherwise valid timely filed election if consents are filed within an extended period of time as granted by IRS, and IRS is satisfied that: (1) there was reasonable cause for the failure; (2) the

22. ¶ D-1485 *et seq.*
23. ¶ D-1491 *et seq.*; ¶ 13,614.04.
24. ¶ D-1490; ¶ 13,614.04.
25. ¶ D-1488.1 *et seq.*

26. ¶ G-1250; ¶s 13,609.03, 13,624.01.
27. ¶ D-1512; ¶s 13,624, 13,624.01.

28. ¶s D-1525, D-1528; ¶ 13,624.01.
29. ¶ D-1526; ¶ 13,624.01.

30. ¶ D-1526; ¶ 13,624.01.
31. ¶ D-1514; ¶ 13,624.01.
32. ¶ D-1516; ¶ 13,624.01.

Footnote references beginning with letters are to paragraphs in RIA's Federal Tax Coordinator 2d and RIA's Analysis of Federal Taxes: Income. Footnote references beginning with numbers are to paragraphs in RIA's United States Tax Reporter.

extension was requested within a reasonable time; and (3) its interests won't be jeopardized by treating the election as valid. (Reg § 1.1362-6(b)(3)(iii)(A))[33]

¶ 3366 "Taxable income" of an S corporation.

An S corporation's taxable income is computed in the same manner as an individual's taxable income *except that*: (Code Sec. 1363(b))[34]

(1) Items of income (including tax-exempt interest), loss, deduction or credit must be separately stated if their separate treatment by a shareholder could affect his tax liability. (Code Sec. 1363(b)(1))

(2) The corporation may not take the following deductions allowed to individuals—

   . . . personal exemptions;

   . . . foreign taxes;

   . . . charitable contributions;

   . . . net operating loss (NOL) deduction;

   . . . additional itemized deductions;

   . . . oil and gas depletion. (Code Sec. 1363(b)(2))

(3) A deduction is allowed for the amortization of the corporation's organization expenditures under Code Sec. 248 (¶ 3518). (Code Sec. 1363(b)(3))[35]

(4) The Code Sec. 291 rules that reduce certain corporate tax benefits apply to an S corporation but only if it was formerly a C corporation and only for the first three tax years it is an S corporation after a C tax year. (Code Sec. 1363(b)(4))[36]

Except as otherwise provided in the Code, or to the extent inconsistent with the Subchapter S rules, the Subchapter C rules (transfers to related corporations, redemptions, reorganizations, liquidations, etc., see Chapter 16) apply to an S corporation and its shareholders. (Code Sec. 1371(a)(1))[37] But there are these modifications:

■ With respect to liquidating distributions, no gain or loss is recognized on distributions of installment obligations where the shareholders' receipt of them (as part of a 12-month complete liquidation) isn't treated as payment for their stock by reason of Code Sec. 453(h)(1). (Code Sec. 453B(h)(1))[38]

■ In its capacity as a shareholder in another corporation, an S corporation is treated as though it were an individual. (Code Sec. 1371(a)(2))[39]

■ Except for the organization expenditures deduction (above), Code provisions governing the computation of taxable income which apply only to corporations (e.g., dividends-received deduction, ¶ 3311) don't apply to S corporations. (Code Sec. 1363(b))[40]

■ Limitations on the amount allowed for: (1) expensing certain depreciable assets, (Code Sec. 179(d)(8)) and (2) amortizing reforestation expenses (Code Sec. 194(b)(2)(B)) are determined at both the corporate and shareholder level.[41]

■ In computing an S corporation's taxable income, an item (e.g., an NOL) cannot be carried over from a year the corporation was a C corporation (C year) to an S year (except in computing the built-in gains tax, see ¶ 3369). (Code Sec. 1371(b)(1))[42]

¶ 3367 Deductions for fringe benefits.

In applying the Code's fringe benefit rules, an S corporation is treated as a partnership and its more-than-2% shareholders are treated as partners. (Code Sec. 1372)[43]

---

33. ¶ D-1516.
34. ¶ D-1551; ¶ 13,634.01.
35. ¶ D-1554.
36. ¶ D-1555.
37. ¶ D-1570; ¶ 13,714.
38. ¶s D-1559, D-1560; ¶ 453B4.11.
39. ¶ D-1572; ¶ 13,714.
40. ¶ D-1555; ¶ 13,634.01.
41. ¶ D-1556.
42. ¶ D-1571; ¶ 13,714.01.
43. ¶ D-1581; ¶ 13,724.01.

Footnote references beginning with letters are to paragraphs in RIA's Federal Tax Coordinator 2d and RIA's Analysis of Federal Taxes: Income. Footnote references beginning with numbers are to paragraphs in RIA's United States Tax Reporter.

¶ 3368 Taxation of S corporations.

An S corporation is generally exempt from federal income taxes. (Code Sec. 1363(a))[44] Instead, the corporation's income is passed through to, and taxed to, its shareholders (¶ 3374). However, some S corporations may be subject to one or more of the following corporate-level taxes:

■ tax on recognized built-in gains (¶ 3369);

■ tax on excess net passive income (¶ 3372);

■ tax on capital gains attributable to certain substituted basis property, if S election was made before '87;[45]

■ tax on recapture of investment credit.[46]

In addition, an S corporation may have to make estimated tax payments (¶ 3351 *et seq.*).

¶ 3369 Built-in gains tax.

An S corporation is subject to a built-in gains tax in any tax year beginning in the recognition period (below) in which it has a "net recognized built-in gain" (¶ 3370). (Code Sec. 1374(a)) But the tax is imposed only on S corporations that were formerly C corporations, (Code Sec. 1374(c)(1)) and that made the S election after '86.[47]

In computing the tax, net recognized built-in gains are taken into account only to the extent of the excess of the net *unrealized* built-in gain (below) over net recognized built-in gains for earlier tax years in the recognition period. (Code Sec. 1374(c)(2))[48] Net unrealized built-in gain means the excess (if any) of: (1) the fair market value of the S corporation's assets at the beginning of its first S tax year, over (2) the aggregate adjusted basis of the assets at that time. (Code Sec. 1374(d)(1))[49]

The built-in gains tax (computed on Schedule D, Form 1120S) equals the highest corporate rate (¶ 1111) multiplied by the net recognized built-in gain. (Code Sec. 1374(b)(1))[50]

The recognition period is the ten-year period beginning on the first day of the corporation's first tax year as an S corporation ("S tax year"). (Code Sec. 1374(d)(7))[1]

¶ 3370 Net recognized built-in gain defined.

The *net recognized built-in gain* for any tax year is the lesser of: (1) the excess of recognized built-in gains (below) over recognized built-in losses for that year, or (2) the taxable income for that year determined without taking into account NOL carryovers or special corporate deductions, e.g., for dividends received. (Code Sec. 1374(d)(2)(A))[2] However, if (1) is more than (2), the excess is treated as recognized built-in gain in the next tax year, but only if the S election was made after Mar. 31, '88. (Code Sec. 1374(d)(2)(B))[3]

Recognized built-in gain means any gain recognized during the recognition period on the disposition of any asset held on the first day of the corporation's first S tax year, but only to the extent the gain doesn't exceed the excess (if any) of the asset's fair market value over its adjusted basis, on that first day. (Code Sec. 1374(d)(3))[4]

Special rules apply to determine an S corporation's recognized built-in gain on the disposition of transferred-basis and exchanged-basis property acquired after it became an S corporation.[5]

---

44. ¶ D-1601; ¶ 13,634.   47. ¶ D-1603; ¶ 13,744.01.   50. ¶ D-1617; ¶ 13,744.01.   3. ¶ D-1605; ¶ 13,744.01.
45. ¶ D-1627 *et seq.*   48. ¶ D-1617; ¶ 13,744.01.   1. ¶ D-1615; ¶ 13,744.01.   4. ¶ D-1606; ¶ 13,744.01.
46. ¶ D-1649.   49. ¶ D-1618; ¶ 13,744.01.   2. ¶ D-1604.   5. ¶ D-1610 *et seq.*; ¶ 13,744.01.

Footnote references beginning with letters are to paragraphs in RIA's Federal Tax Coordinator 2d and RIA's Analysis of Federal Taxes: Income. Footnote references beginning with numbers are to paragraphs in RIA's United States Tax Reporter.

¶ 3371 LIFO recapture.

A C corporation that used LIFO for its last tax year before the first tax year its S election is effective must include a "LIFO recapture amount" in its income for that last C year. (Code Sec. 1363(d)(1))[6] Any increase in tax because of that inclusion is payable in four equal installments over four tax years. The first installment is payable with the final return as a C corporation. (Code Sec. 1363(d)(2))[7]

The "LIFO recapture amount" is the excess (if any) of the inventory amount under FIFO over the inventory amount under LIFO (as of the close of the last C tax year). (Code Sec. 1363(d)(3))[8]

¶ 3372 Tax on excess net passive income.

A corporate level tax is imposed on an S corporation's "excess net passive income" (below) for any tax year in which it has: (1) Subchapter C earnings and profits (i.e., E&P from a year it was taxed as a C corporation) at the close of the tax year, and (2) passive investment income that exceeds 25% of gross receipts (¶ 3373). This tax is imposed at the highest regular corporate rate. (Code Sec. 1375(a))[9]

IRS can waive the tax if the S corporation shows that its determination of no year-end Subchapter C E&P was made in good faith, and that once it was determined otherwise, the corporation distributed those E&P within a reasonable time. (Code Sec. 1375(d))[10]

Net passive income is passive investment income reduced by deductions directly connected with the production of that income. (Code Sec. 1375(b)(2)) A deduction item that is attributable partly to passive investment income and partly to other income is allocated on a reasonable basis. (Reg § 1.1375-1A(b)(3))[11] But passive investment income may not be reduced by the NOL deduction or any of the special corporate deductions (e.g., for dividends received). (Code Sec. 1375(b)(2))[12]

Excess net passive income means that amount that bears the same ratio to the total net passive income for the year as: (1) the amount by which the passive investment income for the tax year exceeds 25% of gross receipts for the year ("excess passive investment income"), bears to (2) the total passive investment income for the tax year. However, an S corporation's excess net passive income for the year may not exceed its taxable income for the year computed as though it were a C corporation but without any NOL deduction or any of the special corporate deductions described above. (Code Sec. 1375(b)(1))[13]

¶ 3373 Gross receipts defined.

For purposes of the tax on excess net passive income (¶ 3372), gross receipts are the total amount received or accrued under the S corporation's accounting method before reduction for returns, allowances, cost, or deductions. However, gross receipts don't include amounts received in nontaxable sales or exchanges except to the extent that gain is recognized by the corporation. (Code Sec. 1362(d)(3), Code Sec. 1375(b)(3))[14]

Special rules apply to determine gross receipts from the sale of capital assets.[15]

¶ 3374 Taxation of S corporation's shareholders.

The income of an S corporation is taxed directly to its shareholders by allocating the corporation's items of income, loss, deduction, and credit for each day in the corporation's tax year pro rata among the persons who were shareholders on that day. (Code Sec. 1366(a)(1), Code Sec. 1377(a)(1))[16]

However, if a shareholder sells all his stock in the corporation during a tax year, and if all persons who were shareholders at any time during that year consent, the corporation's

6. ¶ D-1541; ¶ 13,634.02.
7. ¶ D-1543; ¶ 13,634.02.
8. ¶ D-1541; ¶ 13,634.02.

9. ¶ D-1640; ¶ 13,754.
10. ¶ D-1646; ¶ 13,754.01.
11. ¶ D-1644; ¶ 13,624.02.

12. ¶ D-1643; ¶ 13,624.02.
13. ¶ D-1645; ¶ 13,754.
14. ¶s D-1652, D-1653; ¶ 13,625.

15. ¶s D-1654, D-1655; ¶ 13,625.
16. ¶ D-1701 *et seq.*; ¶ 13,664.

Footnote references beginning with letters are to paragraphs in RIA's Federal Tax Coordinator 2d and RIA's Analysis of Federal Taxes: Income. Footnote references beginning with numbers are to paragraphs in RIA's United States Tax Reporter.

tax year can be split into two tax years, the first of which ends on the date the selling shareholder's interest in the S corporation is terminated. Items will be allocated between those tax years according to the books. (Code Sec. 1377(a)(2))[17]

Items of income, loss, deduction and credit are separately allocated to each shareholder whenever separate treatment could affect the tax liability of a shareholder. (Code Sec. 1366(a)(1)(A))[18]

A shareholder's share of an S corporation's items is taken into account in the shareholder's tax year that includes the last day of the corporation's tax year. (Code Sec. 1366(a)(1))[19]

The character of any item in the shareholder's hands is determined as if the item had been realized directly from the source from which the corporation realized it, or as if it had been incurred in the same manner as incurred by the corporation. (Code Sec. 1366(b))[20]

¶ 3375   Reduction in amount passed through to shareholders for taxes paid at corporate level.

If a corporate level tax is imposed on an S corporation's recognized built-in gains (¶ 3369), the amount imposed is treated as a loss sustained by the corporation during the tax year. The character of the loss is determined by allocating it proportionately among the recognized built-in gains giving rise to the tax. (Code Sec. 1366(f)(2)) If a corporate level is imposed on an S corporation's excess net passive income (¶ 3372), each item of passive investment income that is passed through to a shareholder is reduced by a pro rata part of that tax. (Code Sec. 1366(f)(3))[21]

¶ 3376   Deductibility of losses by shareholders.

All losses and deductions of an S corporation (e.g., capital losses and NOLs) are passed through to and (except as otherwise limited by the Code) are deductible by shareholders. However, a shareholder may deduct his pro rata share of these passed-through deductions and losses only to the extent of his total adjusted basis (¶ 3378) in his S corporation stock and any debt owed to him by the corporation. (Code Sec. 1366(d)(1))[22]

Any deduction or loss that can't be deducted (for lack of basis) may be carried over (Code Sec. 1366(d)(2)) to be used whenever the shareholder has basis to apply against all or part of the amount carried over.[23] Special rules apply where the S corporation is in bankruptcy or is insolvent. (Code Sec. 108(d)(7)(B))[24]

If an S corporation's stock, or the debt it owes to a shareholder, becomes worthless in any tax year of the corporation or shareholder, the corporate items for that year will be taken into account by the shareholders and the adjustments to basis of stock or debt will be made, before the worthlessness is taken into account. (Code Sec. 1367(b)(3))[25]

¶ 3377   Consistent treatment on shareholder's return and S corporation's return.

A shareholder must on his own return treat a Subchapter S item in a manner that is consistent with the treatment of that item on the corporation's return (Form 1120S). A shareholder that treats a Subchapter S item differently must notify IRS of the inconsistency (Code Sec. 6242) on Form 8082.[26]

¶ 3378   Basis.

A shareholder's basis in the stock of an S corporation is *increased* by his share of the corporation's income items that are passed through to him—i.e., its separately computed income items, tax-exempt income, nonseparately computed income, and the excess of the deduction for depletion over the basis of depletable property. (Code Sec. 1367(a)(1))[27]

---

17. ¶ D-1709; ¶ 13,744.   20. ¶ D-1702.   23. ¶ D-1723.   26. ¶ D-1741 *et seq.*; ¶ 62,414.
18. ¶ D-1705; ¶ 13,664.   21. ¶ D-1707; ¶ 13,664.02.   24. ¶ D-1724; ¶ 1084.03.   27. ¶ D-1803; ¶ 13,674.
19. ¶ D-1704.   22. ¶ D-1712.   25. ¶ D-1727.

Footnote references beginning with letters are to paragraphs in RIA's Federal Tax Coordinator 2d and RIA's Analysis of Federal Taxes: Income. Footnote references beginning with numbers are to paragraphs in RIA's United States Tax Reporter.

Basis in stock is *decreased* (but not below zero) by: the shareholder's share of the corporation's items of deduction, loss, and nondeductible expenses (except those chargeable to capital account); the shareholder's depletion deduction for oil and gas property; and distributions to the shareholder that aren't taxable as dividends. (Code Sec. 1367(a)(2))[28]

In any tax year of an S corporation in which the total of the amount of items (other than distributions) that reduce a shareholder's basis in stock exceeds the amount that would reduce the stock's basis to zero, the balance is applied to reduce the basis (but not below zero) of any indebtedness of the S corporation to the shareholder. (Code Sec. 1367(b)(2)(A))[29]

If the shareholder's basis in S corporation debt in any tax year is reduced below his original basis in it, that basis has to be increased to (but not above) its original amount, before the shareholder's basis in *stock* is increased. (Code Sec. 1367(b)(2)(B)) In other words, to the extent that, in any later year, the total amount of items that increase basis exceed the total amount of items that decrease basis, the net increase is applied first to increase the basis of debt to its original level before it is applied to increase the basis of stock.[30]

¶ 3379 Tax treatment of S corporation distributions.

The amount of a distribution from an S corporation to a shareholder equals the amount of cash distributed plus the fair market value (at distribution) of any other property distributed. (Code Sec. 301(c), Code Sec. 1368(a))[31]

If an S corporation has no accumulated earnings and profits (E&P), the amount distributed reduces the shareholder's basis in his stock (¶ 3378). If the amount exceeds the basis, the excess is treated as payment in exchange for the stock, (Code Sec. 1368(b)(2)) i.e., as capital gain.[32]

If an S corporation has accumulated E&P, distributions are considered made out of the following sources in this order: (Code Sec. 1368(c))[33]

(1) The accumulated adjustments account (¶ 3381). To the extent a distribution is considered made out of this account, it is taxed in the same manner as if the S corporation had no accumulated E&P (above). If more than one distribution is made in a tax year, and the total amount distributed exceeds the amount in the accumulated adjustments account at the end of that year, the balance in that account is allocated among the distributions in proportion to the size of each distribution. (Code Sec. 1368(c)(1))[34]

(2) Previously taxed income from tax years beginning before '83 for which the S corporation election was in effect.[35]

(3) Accumulated E&P. Distributions considered made out of accumulated E&P are taxed as dividends. (Code Sec. 1368(c)(2))

(4) Other sources, e.g., tax-exempt income for tax years beginning after '82 for which the S election is in effect. Distributions considered made out of other sources are also taxed the same as if the S corporation had no accumulated E&P (above). (Code Sec. 1368(c)(3))[36]

An S corporation may elect, with the consent of all affected shareholders (i.e., to whom distributions are made), to treat distributions as made out of accumulated E&P *before* being made out of the accumulated adjustments account. (Code Sec. 1368(e)(3))[37]

---

28. ¶ D-1804; ¶ 13,664.
29. ¶ D-1807.
30. ¶ D-1808; ¶ 13,674.

31. ¶ D-1752; ¶s 13,684, 3014.06.
32. ¶ D-1754; ¶s 13,684, 13,684.07.

33. ¶s D-1756, D-1758.
34. ¶ D-1763.
35. ¶ D-1756.

36. ¶s D-1756, D-1758; ¶ 13,684.01.
37. ¶ D-1764; ¶ 13,684.01.

Footnote references beginning with letters are to paragraphs in RIA's Federal Tax Coordinator 2d and RIA's Analysis of Federal Taxes: Income. Footnote references beginning with numbers are to paragraphs in RIA's United States Tax Reporter.

¶ 3380 S corporation's earnings and profits.

An S corporation has no current E&P for any tax year beginning after '82, for which the S election is in effect.[38] No adjustments are made in the amount of an its accumulated E&P (i.e., from when it was a C corporation, or an S corporation in pre-'83 tax years) except as follows: (Code Sec. 1371(c)(1))

■ E&P are reduced to reflect distributions that are taxable to the shareholders as dividends. (Code Sec. 1371(c)(3))

■ E&P are adjusted (up or down) to reflect the effect of redemptions, liquidations, tax-free reorganizations and corporate divisions. (Code Sec. 1371(c)(2))

■ E&P are reduced to reflect any tax paid by an S corporation because of the recapture of a pre-S election investment credit. (Code Sec. 1371(d)(3))[39]

¶ 3381 Accumulated adjustments account.

An S corporation's accumulated adjustments account (AAA) equals the sum of the items in (1), less the sum of the items in (2).[40]

(1) The following items for the S period, i.e., the most recent continuous period during which the corporation has been an S corporation, but not including tax years beginning before '83:

(a) Separately computed items of income (other than tax-exempt interest).

(b) Nonseparately computed income.

(c) The excess of deductions for depletion over the basis of property subject to depletion.

(2) The following items for the S period:

(a) Distributions to shareholders that were not includible in the shareholders' income.

(b) Items of separately computed loss and deduction.

(c) Nonseparately computed loss.

(d) Nondeductible expenses (other than expenses chargeable to capital account) unless related to tax-exempt income.

(e) The amount of the shareholder's deduction for depletion under Code Sec. 611 with respect to oil and gas wells.

(f) The amount that was treated as paid out of the AAA on redemptions that were treated as payments in exchange for stock under Code Sec. 302(a) or Code Sec. 303(a). That amount is the same percentage of the amount in the account before the redemption, the number of redeemed shares was of the total number of outstanding shares before the redemption. (Code Sec. 1368(e))[41]

The AAA is not to be adjusted (i.e., reduced) for federal taxes attributable to any tax year when the S corporation was a C corporation. (Code Sec. 1368(e)(1))[42]

There can be a negative balance in the AAA at the end of an S corporation's tax year. (Code Sec. 1368(e)(1)(A)) Thus, income in a later year will cause a positive balance only after offsetting the negative amount.[43]

Special rules apply to distributions after the S election is terminated. (Code Sec. 1371(e))[44]

---

38. ¶ D-1591; ¶ 13,684.01 *et seq.*   40. ¶ D-1759; ¶ 13,684.02.   42. ¶ D-1759; ¶ 13,684.02.   44. ¶ D-1769; ¶ 13,714.04.
39. ¶ D-1593; ¶ 13,714.03.   41. ¶ D-1759; ¶ 13,684.02.   43. ¶ D-1761.

Footnote references beginning with letters are to paragraphs in RIA's Federal Tax Coordinator 2d and RIA's Analysis of Federal Taxes: Income. Footnote references beginning with numbers are to paragraphs in RIA's United States Tax Reporter.

¶ 3382 Voluntary revocation of the S election.

A corporation's S election may be revoked with the consent of holders of a majority of the corporation's issued and outstanding stock (including non-voting stock). (Code Sec. 1362(d)(1); Reg § 1.1362-2(a)(1))[45]

A revocation is effective as of the first day of the tax year unless the revocation statement specifies another date. If no effective date is specified, the revocation is effective for the tax year in which made, if made by the 15th day of the third month of that year. Otherwise, it will be effective as of the first day of the next tax year. (Code Sec. 1362(d)(1)(C))[46] However, if the revocation specifies that it is to be effective on a date that is on or after the date it is made, it will be effective on that date even if it causes the corporation's tax year to be split. (Code Sec. 1362(d)(1)(D))[47]

A corporation may *rescind* the revocation at any time before it becomes effective. A rescission may be made only with the consent of each person who consented to the revocation and of each person who became a shareholder of the corporation during the period from the day after the date the revocation was made through the date the rescission is made. (Reg § 1.1362-2(a)(4))[48]

¶ 3383 Involuntary termination of S election.

A corporation's S election is terminated if:

(1) The corporation ceases to meet any of the eligibility requirements for S corporations discussed at ¶ 3360. (Code Sec. 1362(d)(2)(A)) The termination is effective as of the day the eligibility requirement is no longer met. (Code Sec. 1362(d)(2)(B))[49]

(2) The S corporation's passive investment income (¶ 3373) exceeds 25% of its gross receipts for three consecutive tax years *if* at the end of each of those years, the corporation had Subchapter C E&P (¶ 3372). The termination is effective as of the first day of the first tax year beginning after the third of these years. (Code Sec. 1362(d)(3)(A))[50]

IRS can waive inadvertent terminations if certain conditions are met. (Code Sec. 1362(f))[1] IRS has waived termination where, for example, the S corporation temporarily had an ineligible shareholder such as a nonresident alien, an ineligible trust or another corporation, and where the S corporation had an ineligible subsidiary.[2]

¶ 3384 When new S election can be made after termination or revocation.

After a revocation or termination of its S election, a corporation must wait five years before making a new S election unless IRS consents to an earlier election. (Code Sec. 1362(g))[3]

---

45. ¶ D-1851; ¶ 13,624.02.   48. ¶ D-1855.1 *et seq.*   50. ¶ D-1859; ¶ 13,624.02.   2. ¶ D-1873 *et seq.*
46. ¶ D-1853; ¶ 13,624.02.   49. ¶ D-1856; ¶ 13,624.02.   1. ¶ D-1872; ¶ 13,624.02.   3. ¶s D-1901, D-1902.
47. ¶ D-1855.

Footnote references beginning with letters are to paragraphs in RIA's Federal Tax Coordinator 2d and RIA's Analysis of Federal Taxes: Income. Footnote references beginning with numbers are to paragraphs in RIA's United States Tax Reporter.

Chapter 16 Corporations—Organization—Distributions—Reorganization—Acquisitions—Liquidation

¶ 3510 Incorporations and Transfers to Controlled Corporations ▬▬▬▬▬▬

Tax-free treatment is provided for most transfers of property to a corporation for its stock, if the corporation is controlled by the transferors. This is the case both for incorporating (organizing) transfers to new corporations and for transfers to existing corporations.

No gain or loss is recognized if property (¶ 3511) is transferred to a corporation solely in exchange for stock of that corporation, if immediately after the transfer, the transferor or transferors are in control (¶ 3513) of the corporation. (Code Sec. 351(a))[1]

¶ 3511 Property defined.

Property includes cash, intangible personal property (e.g., stock, partnership interests, patent rights and working interests in oil and gas properties) and tangible property.[2]

Property does not include:

■ indebtedness of the transferee corporation not evidenced by a security; (Code Sec. 351(d)(2))[3]

■ interest on indebtedness of the transferee accrued after the beginning of the transferor's holding period for the debt; (Code Sec. 351(d)(3))[4]

■ services by a transferor to the transferee corporation. (Code Sec. 351(d)(1))[5]

¶ 3512 Stock defined.

The term "stock" is not defined in the Code or regulations. However, the regulations do say that stock rights or warrants, or similar options, are not stock. (Reg § 1.351-1(a)) Stock can be owned even if no stock certificate is issued.[6]

¶ 3513 Control defined.

For purposes of these rules, control is defined in Code Sec. 368(c), i.e., 80% voting power and 80% ownership requirements described in ¶ 3550. (Code Sec. 351(a))[7] A transferor will be treated as part of the control group if he owns stock after the transfer even if he does not own any voting stock.[8]

¶ 3514 Tax where transferors get cash or property ("boot").

If "boot"—property other than stock (e.g., cash, debt obligations including securities, tangible personal property)[9] —is received by the transferors but the exchange otherwise qualifies for nonrecognition, the following rules apply:

■ *Loss isn't recognized* to any transferor.

■ *Gain is recognized* to any transferor up to the amount of "boot" he receives, that is, the cash and the fair market value of any other property (except stock of the transferee corporation). (Code Sec. 351(b))[10] Gain from "boot" that is a debt obligation (including a security) may be reported on the installment method if all the requirements for using that method are satisfied (see ¶ 2701 *et seq.*).[11]

¶ 3515 Assumption or transfer of liabilities.

When the corporation assumes or takes property subject to liabilities in connection with an otherwise tax-free transfer to a controlled corporation, the assumption of or taking property subject to the debt is not treated as the payment of boot, so that the transfer is

---

1. ¶ F-1001; ¶ 3514.
2. ¶ F-1101; ¶ 3514.03.
3. ¶ F-1102; ¶ 3514.03.
4. ¶ F-1103; ¶ 3514.03.
5. ¶ F-1104; ¶ 3514.03.
6. ¶ F-1004 *et seq.*; ¶ 3514.05.
7. ¶s F-1200 *et seq.*; F-5501 *et seq.*; ¶ 3514.05.
8. ¶ F-1202; ¶ 3514.05.
9. ¶ F-1503 *et seq.*; ¶ 3514.10.
10. ¶ F-1501; ¶ 3514.10.
11. ¶ F-1404; ¶ 3514.10.

Footnote references beginning with letters are to paragraphs in RIA's Federal Tax Coordinator 2d and RIA's Analysis of Federal Taxes: Income. Footnote references beginning with numbers are to paragraphs in RIA's United States Tax Reporter.

still tax-free, except: (Code Sec. 357(a))[12]

■ If the principal purpose for assuming the liabilities is tax avoidance or is not a bona fide business purpose, the full amount of all assumed liabilities, even those assumed for nontax avoidance or valid business purposes, is treated as boot and is taxed under the rule at ¶ 3514. (Code Sec. 357(b)(1))[13]

■ If the amount of the liabilities exceeds the transferor's basis in the transferred property, gain is recognized to the extent of the excess. (Code Sec. 357(c)(1))[14]

Where both the tax avoidance rule and excess liability rule apply, tax avoidance takes precedence, i.e., all liabilities are treated as boot. (Code Sec. 357(c)(2)(A))[15]

¶ 3516 Swap funds.

If property is transferred to an "investment company" in exchange for its stock, gain or loss is recognized. (Code Sec. 351(e)(1))[16] This applies where the transfer results in diversification of the transferor's interests and the transferee is a regulated investment company (mutual fund), a real estate investment trust (REIT), or a corporation more than 80% of the value of whose assets (excluding cash and nonconvertible debt obligations) are held for investment and are readily marketable securities or interests in other mutual funds or REITs. (Reg § 1.351-1(c)(1))[17] A transfer results in diversification if a significant portion of the assets transferred by two or more transferors are nonidentical assets. (Reg § 1.351-1(c)(5))[18]

¶ 3517 Issuance of stock.

A corporation recognizes no gain or loss when it exchanges its stock for property or money. This is true regardless of whether the issue or subscription price is above or below par or stated value, and regardless of whether the stock is original issue or treasury stock. (Code Sec. 1032(a))[19] (But if stock is issued to a creditor in satisfaction of the corporation's indebtedness, see ¶ 1384 *et seq.*)

¶ 3518 Deductibility of costs of organizing a corporation.

Instead of capitalizing its organizational costs, a newly organized corporation can elect (by a statement attached to its return for the year in which it begins business) to deduct these expenditures (even though capitalized on its books) ratably over a period of not less than 60 months starting with the first month the corporation is actively in business. (Code Sec. 248; Reg § 1.248-1)[20]

Qualifying expenditures include outlays for legal services, incorporation fees and temporary directors' fees and organizational meeting costs. (Code Sec. 248(b); Reg § 1.248-1) However, costs of issuing stock cannot be deducted.[21]

¶ 3519 Corporate Distributions and Earnings and Profits (E&P) ▰▰▰▰▰▰

A distribution from a corporation to its shareholders is taxable to the shareholders as a dividend, but only to the extent it is out of current or accumulated earnings and profits (E&P).

¶ 3520 Treatment of corporate distributions.

Where a corporation distributes money or other property to its shareholders, the recipient shareholders will be taxed on the amount of money or the fair market value of the property, according to the following rules:

(1) The distribution will be taxed as a dividend (Code Sec. 301(c)(1)) to the extent it is

---

12. ¶ F-1509; ¶ 3574.01.
13. ¶ F-1511 *et seq.*; ¶ 3574.02.
14. ¶ F-1515 *et seq.*; ¶ 3574.03.
15. ¶ F-1519; ¶ 3574.02.
16. ¶ F-1301; ¶ 3514.06.
17. ¶ F-1302; ¶ 3514.06.
18. ¶ F-1305; ¶ 3514.06.
19. ¶ I-3201; ¶ 10,324.
20. ¶ L-5202; ¶ 2484.
21. ¶s L-5206, L-5207; ¶ 2484.

Footnote references beginning with letters are to paragraphs in RIA's Federal Tax Coordinator 2d and RIA's Analysis of Federal Taxes: Income. Footnote references beginning with numbers are to paragraphs in RIA's United States Tax Reporter.

either out of (i) the corporation's E&P for the current taxable year, or (ii) the corporation's E&P accumulated (as of the time of the distribution) after Feb. 28, '13 (Code Sec. 316(a)). In determining whether a distribution is out of current-year E&P, all E&P for the taxable year is taken into account (even if it is earned after the distribution is made). If the distributing corporation has adequate E&P for the current taxable year, a distribution will be taxed as a dividend regardless of whether the corporation has accumulated E&P. (Reg § 1.316-1(a))

(2) To the extent the distribution exceeds the amount taxable as a dividend under the rule of (1), above, it will be applied to reduce the shareholder's basis in his stock (but not below zero). (Code Sec. 301(c)(2))

(3) Any amount not taxable as a dividend which exceeds the shareholder's basis in his stock will be treated as gain from the sale or exchange of the stock (Code Sec. 301(c)(3)) (which, in most cases, will give rise to capital gain treatment).[22]

¶ 3521 Earnings and profits.

Retained earnings as determined under accounting concepts are not necessarily the same as E&P determined under tax concepts. Adjustments for specified transactions may have to be made to determine the increase or decrease in E&P for a particular tax year (¶ 3524). Some adjustments are specifically designed to conform E&P to economic income. (Code Sec. 312(n))[23]

For treatment of increases in E&P for purposes of the alternative minimum tax, see ¶ 3210.

¶ 3522 How distributions affect E&P.

With some exceptions (e.g., redemption distributions, see below), distributions of property reduce E&P by the sum of:

(1) The amount of money distributed. (Code Sec. 312(a)(1))[24]

(2) The principal (face) amount of the corporation's obligations (i.e., its own notes, bonds, etc.) distributed without original issue discount (OID) (as determined under the rules discussed at ¶ 1318 *et seq.*). (Code Sec. 312(a)(2))[25]

(3) The aggregate issue price of the corporation's obligations distributed *with* OID. (Code Sec. 312(a)(2))[26]

(4) The higher of the adjusted basis or fair market value (FMV) of other distributed property. (Code Sec. 312(a)(3), (b))[27] Adjusted basis means the adjusted basis as determined for purposes of computing E&P. (Code Sec. 312(b)(1))[28] This may not be the same as the property's basis for regular income tax purposes, since E&P are different from taxable income.[29]

Distributions of appreciated property. On distributions of property (other than the corporation's own obligations) whose FMV exceeds its adjusted basis to the distributing corporation, E&P are increased by the excess. (Code Sec. 312(b)(1))[30]

Liabilities. The amount by which E&P are decreased is reduced by the sum of any liabilities assumed by the distributee and any liabilities to which the distributed property is subject. (Code Sec. 312(c))[31]

Distributions in redemption that are treated as payment for stock (¶ 3525) reduce E&P by an amount not in excess of the ratable share of the distributing corporation's E&P attributable to the redeemed stock. (Code Sec. 312(n)(7))[32]

Reorganization exchanges (if no gain recognized to the distributee) *and other tax-free*

22. ¶ J-2622 *et seq.*
23. ¶ F-10007; ¶ 3124.07.
24. ¶ F-10501; ¶ 3124.02.
25. ¶ F-10503; ¶ 3124.02.
26. ¶ F-10504; ¶ 3124.02.
27. ¶ F-10505; ¶ 3124.02.
28. ¶ F-10505; ¶ 3124.02.
29. ¶ F-10300 *et seq.*
30. ¶ F-10506; ¶ 3124.02.
31. ¶ F-10508; ¶ 3124.02.
32. ¶ F-10701; ¶ 3124.02.

Footnote references beginning with letters are to paragraphs in RIA's Federal Tax Coordinator 2d and RIA's Analysis of Federal Taxes: Income. Footnote references beginning with numbers are to paragraphs in RIA's United States Tax Reporter.

distributions don't reduce E&P. (Code Sec. 312(d); Reg § 1.312-11(b), (c))[33]

Tax-free distributions by a corporation of its stock or rights don't reduce E&P. (Code Sec. 312(d); Reg § 1.312-1(d)) But if the distribution is *taxable* to shareholders, E&P are reduced by the FMV of the taxable portion of the stock or rights. (Reg § 1.312-1(d))[34]

Distribution to 20% corporate shareholders may require special adjustments to E&P calculations solely for purposes of determining the corporate distributee's income and basis. (Code Sec. 301(e))[35]

¶ 3523 Effect of depreciation on E&P.

Deductions allowed for depreciation in computing E&P are often less than those allowed in computing taxable income (¶ 1900 *et seq.*). Here are the key rules that apply in computing the depreciation deduction for E&P purposes:

■ For *MACRS* property (other than expensed property, see below), the deduction must be computed under the alternative depreciation system (ADS) even if a different system is used in computing taxable income. (Code Sec. 312(k)(3)(A))[36]

■ For *ACRS* property placed in service before '87, the deduction is computed by using the straight line method over the regular or alternative ACRS recovery periods, which may be longer than those used in computing taxable income.[37]

■ For *depreciable property* placed in service before '81, the deduction is computed by using the straight-line or a similar method (e.g., units of production) even if an accelerated depreciation method is used in computing taxable income.[38]

■ For *expensed* property (Code Sec. 179 property), the cost is deducted ratably over five tax years. (Code Sec. 312(k)(3)(B))[39]

¶ 3524 Other adjustments to E&P.

Here are other key items that are treated differently in computing E&P than they are in computing taxable income:

Circulation expenses must be capitalized and treated as part of the basis of the asset to which they relate even if they are deducted currently in computing taxable income. (Code Sec. 312(n)(3))[40]

Completed contract method of accounting can't be used for E&P purposes. The percentage of completion method must be used instead. (Code Sec. 312(n)(6))[41]

Construction period carrying charges (interest, property taxes, etc.) must be capitalized as part of the assets to which they are allocable. (Code Sec. 312(n)(1)(A)) The capitalized amounts must be written off for E&P purposes, as is the asset itself.[42]

✐observation: This means that a corporation with heavy construction costs will not be able to wipe out its E&P with current carrying charge deductions. This will make it harder for that corporation to treat a distribution to shareholders as a nontaxable return of capital instead of as a taxable dividend.

Depletion is taken into account on a *cost,* not percentage, basis. (Reg § 1.312-6(c)(1))[43]

Exempt income, e.g., interest on state or local bonds, is included in E&P. (Reg § 1.312-6(b))[44]

Gross income. All items included in gross income under Code Sec. 61 (see Chapter 2) are included in computing E&P. (Reg § 1.312-6(b))

Installment sale principal payments must be treated as received in the year of sale, i.e., as if the corporation didn't use the installment method. (Code Sec. 312(n)(5))[45]

---

33. ¶ F-10801; ¶ 3124.02.
34. ¶ F-10509 *et seq.*; ¶ 3124.02.
35. ¶ F-10601 *et seq.*; ¶s 3014.02, 3014.06.

36. ¶ F-10303; ¶ 3124.04.
37. ¶ F-10307; ¶ 3124.04.
38. ¶ F-10304; ¶ 3124.04.
39. ¶ F-10304; ¶ 3124.04.

40. ¶ F-10206; ¶ 3124.07.
41. ¶ F-10008; ¶ 3124.07.
42. ¶ F-10208; ¶ 3124.07.
43. ¶ F-10314; ¶ 3124.04.

44. ¶ F-10101; ¶s 3124.01, 3124.07.
45. ¶ F-10405; ¶ 3124.07.

Footnote references beginning with letters are to paragraphs in RIA's Federal Tax Coordinator 2d and RIA's Analysis of Federal Taxes: Income. Footnote references beginning with numbers are to paragraphs in RIA's United States Tax Reporter.

Intangible drilling and development costs that are deductible when paid or incurred for taxable income purposes (other than costs incurred in connection with a nonproductive well), must be capitalized and deducted ratably over a 60-month period for E&P purposes. (Code Sec. 312(n)(2)(A))[46]

Income tax liabilities reduce E&P as of the close of the tax year for an accrual basis corporation. According to IRS and some courts, a cash basis corporation reduces E&P only when the tax is *paid*, but other courts allow reduction for *accrued* tax.[47]

Life insurance proceeds increase E&P if the corporation is the beneficiary even if not includible in taxable income.[48]

LIFO recapture amount increases or decreases at the close of each tax year increase or decrease E&P by the same amount. (Code Sec. 312(n)(4))[49]

Losses may be recognized though not allowed as a deduction, but the mere fact that the losses are not allowed does not prevent a decrease in E&P by the disallowed amount.[50]

Mineral exploration and development costs that are deductible for taxable income purposes must be capitalized and deducted ratably over a 120-month period for E&P. (Code Sec. 312(n)(2)(B))[1]

Loss carryovers and carrybacks do not reduce E&P of the year to which they are carried. Nor does a reduction of a loss carryover increase E&P in a later carryover year.[2]

Organization expenses must be capitalized and treated as part of the basis of the asset to which they relate even if they are amortized in computing taxable income. (Code Sec. 312(n)(3))[3]

Premiums paid for insuring lives of corporate officers reduce E&P even if not deductible in computing taxable income.[4]

Trademark and trade name expenditures must be capitalized and treated as part of the basis of the asset to which they relate. (Code Sec. 312(n)(3))[5]

¶ 3525 Stock Redemptions

The acquisition by a corporation of its own stock from a shareholder in exchange for cash or property is treated as a distribution (taxable under the rules described at ¶ 3520) to the shareholder, unless the redemption qualifies as a distribution in payment for the acquired stock (i.e., as a sale or exchange, for which capital gain treatment is allowed if the stock is a capital asset).

Stock is treated as redeemed by a corporation if the corporation acquires its stock from a shareholder in exchange for property, whether or not the stock acquired is cancelled, retired or held as treasury stock. (Code Sec. 317(b))[6]

If a redemption fits within any of the following categories, the distribution of cash or property to the redeeming shareholders is treated as a payment in exchange for stock. (Code Sec. 302(a))[7]

(1) A redemption that is "substantially disproportionate" with respect to the redeeming shareholder, see ¶ 3526.

(2) A complete redemption of all of a shareholder's stock in the corporation, see ¶ 3527.

(3) A redemption that is "not essentially equivalent to a dividend," see ¶ 3529.

(4) A redemption of stock held by a noncorporate shareholder, in partial liquidation of the distributing corporation, see ¶ 3530.

---

46. ¶ F-10221; ¶ 3124.07.
47. ¶ F-10223; ¶ 3124.07.
48. ¶ F-10102; ¶ 3124.07.
49. ¶ F-10212; ¶ 3124.07.

50. ¶ F-10403; ¶ 3124.05.
1. ¶ F-10220; ¶ 3124.07.
2. ¶ F-10012; ¶s 3124.05, 3124.06.

3. ¶ F-10204; ¶ 3124.07.
4. ¶ F-10234; ¶ 3124.07.
5. ¶ F-10205; ¶ 3124.07.

6. ¶ F-11001; ¶ 3174.01.
7. ¶ F-11101 *et seq.*; ¶ 3024.01.

Footnote references beginning with letters are to paragraphs in RIA's Federal Tax Coordinator 2d and RIA's Analysis of Federal Taxes: Income. Footnote references beginning with numbers are to paragraphs in RIA's United States Tax Reporter.

(5) Certain redemptions of stock from a decedent's estate to pay death taxes and administrative expenses, see ¶ 3531.

¶ 3526 Substantially disproportionate redemptions.

A redemption is "substantially disproportionate" if *both* of these tests are satisfied:

(1) Immediately after the redemption, the ratio of the shareholder's voting stock to the corporation's total outstanding voting stock is less than 80% of that ratio immediately before the redemption. The same 80% test must also be satisfied with regard to the corporation's *common stock* , voting and nonvoting. Where there is more than one class of common stock, the different classes are aggregated for the 80% test.

(2) Immediately after the redemption, the shareholder owns less than 50% of the corporation's total voting stock. (Code Sec. 302(b)(2))[8]

For constructive ownership rules which apply to the foregoing tests, see ¶ 3531.

A redemption solely of nonvoting stock does not qualify as substantially disproportionate. However, if voting stock is also redeemed at the same time and in a redemption that qualifies as substantially disproportionate, then the redemption of nonvoting stock (other than Section 306 stock) will also qualify as substantially disproportionate. (Reg § 1.302-3(a))[9]

¶ 3527 Complete redemptions.

To qualify as a complete redemption, all stock owned (including, subject to the rules discussed at ¶ 3526, stock deemed owned under the constructive ownership rules discussed at ¶ 3531) by the shareholder in the corporation must be redeemed. (Code Sec. 302(b)(3)) Thus, if a shareholder owns both common and preferred stock, the redemption of all the shares of only one of the classes doesn't qualify as a complete redemption.[10]

A redemption on the installment basis can qualify as a complete redemption if the corporation and the shareholder are bound by a purchase agreement to complete the redemption by a certain date and for a maximum price.[11]

¶ 3528 Family attribution rules eased on complete redemptions.

Although the constructive ownership rules described at ¶ 3531 apply in determining the tax treatment of a redemption, in applying the complete redemption test described at ¶ 3525 the *family* attribution rules of Code Sec. 318(a)(1) won't apply in certain circumstances. However, the other constructive ownership rules will still apply.

The family attribution rules won't apply to any shareholder whose actually owned stock is completely redeemed, if:

(1) immediately after the redemption he has no personal financial interest in the corporation, other than as a creditor;

(2) he no longer serves as director, officer or employee;

(3) he doesn't acquire any such interest (except by inheritance) or position for a ten-year period running from the date of the redemption;

(4) he didn't acquire any of the redeemed stock from close family members within ten years before the redemption, and didn't transfer any stock to them within that period except for a transfer not principally motivated by tax avoidance; and

(5) he attaches a separate statement (in duplicate) to his income tax return for the year of redemption, in which he states that he hasn't acquired any new interest in the company (except by inheritance) and that he will notify the district director within 30 days after acquiring any new interest. (Code Sec. 302(c)(2); Reg § 1.302-4)[12]

8. ¶ F-11203 *et seq.*; ¶ 3024.04.   10. ¶ F-11301 *et seq.*; ¶ 3024.05.   11. ¶ F-11307; ¶ 3024.05.   12. ¶ F-11313 *et seq.*; ¶ 3024.05.
9. ¶ F-11212; ¶ 3024.04.

Footnote references beginning with letters are to paragraphs in RIA's Federal Tax Coordinator 2d and RIA's Analysis of Federal Taxes: Income. Footnote references beginning with numbers are to paragraphs in RIA's United States Tax Reporter.

The family attribution rule will be waived for a partnership, estate, trust or corporation ("entity waiver rule") if that entity and each related person meet the above requirements and agree further to be jointly and severally liable for any tax deficiency resulting from any acquisition of interest within the ten-year period. (Code Sec. 302(c)(2)(C))[13]

If the termination of a shareholder's interest also qualifies as payment in exchange for stock under a rule other than the complete termination of interest rule (e.g., as a substantially disproportionate redemption (¶ 3526), or as a redemption not essentially equivalent to a dividend (¶ 3529)), waiver of the family attribution rules isn't required to prevent the transaction from being treated as a dividend. (Code Sec. 302(b)(5))[14]

¶ 3529 Redemptions not essentially equivalent to a dividend.

A redemption is not essentially equivalent to a dividend if it results in a meaningful reduction in the redeemed shareholder's proportionate interest in the distributing corporation. A redemption from a sole shareholder and a redemption that is pro rata cannot result in any reduction in the redeemed shareholder's proportionate interest in the distributing corporation.[15]

A redemption from a shareholder with over 50% of the voting power usually results in a meaningful reduction if that shareholder's voting power is reduced to 50% or less.[16]

A redemption of voting stock from a substantial minority shareholder results in a meaningful reduction if, after the redemption, the number of shareholders the redeemed shareholder must act in concert with to control the corporation is increased.[17]

Any redemption of voting stock from a low percentage minority shareholder usually is treated as a meaningful reduction.[18]

Redemptions of nonvoting preferred stock from shareholders who own no common stock and no voting stock of any class always result in a meaningful reduction.[19]

¶ 3530 Partial liquidations.

Redemption distributions are treated as made in partial liquidation if the distribution: (1) is not essentially equivalent to a dividend (as determined by the effect on the distributing corporation), and (2) is made under a plan within the tax year in which the plan is adopted or the next tax year. (Code Sec. 302(e)(1))[20] Partial liquidations are meant to include cases involving the genuine contraction of a corporate business. (Reg § 1.346-1(a))[21]

If a corporation is engaged in two or more active trades or businesses for five years or more, a distribution in partial liquidation won't be essentially equivalent to a dividend if the corporation terminates one of the businesses, distributes all of the assets of the discontinued business (or its sales proceeds), and continues to operate the second business. (Code Sec. 302(e)(2), (3))[22]

¶ 3531 Redemption of decedent's stock.

Distributions in redemption of stock included in a decedent's gross estate for federal estate tax purposes are treated as payment for stock up to the sum of: (1) all death taxes (federal and state), including interest on the taxes, and (2) funeral and administration expenses allowable as federal estate tax deductions (Code Sec. 303(a))[23] but only if these three tests are met:

(1) The value of the redeeming corporation stock included in the estate must exceed 35% of the decedent's adjusted gross estate. (Code Sec. 303(b)(2)(A)) Stock in two or more corporations is treated as stock of a single corporation if 20% or more in value of the

---

13. ¶ F-11314; ¶ 3024.05.   16. ¶ F-11418; ¶ 3024.03.   19. ¶ F-11429; ¶ 3024.03.   22. ¶ F-11516; ¶ 3024.06.
14. ¶ F-11311 et seq.; ¶ 3024.05.   17. ¶ F-11424; ¶ 3024.03.   20. ¶ F-11504; ¶ 3024.06.   23. ¶ F-11601 et seq.; ¶ 3034.01.
15. ¶ F-11401 et seq.; ¶ 3024.03.   18. ¶ F-11425; ¶ 3024.03.   21. ¶ F-11509; ¶ 3024.06.

Footnote references beginning with letters are to paragraphs in RIA's Federal Tax Coordinator 2d and RIA's Analysis of Federal Taxes: Income. Footnote references beginning with numbers are to paragraphs in RIA's United States Tax Reporter.

outstanding stock of each corporation is included in the estate. A surviving spouse's interest in stock held with the decedent as community property, joint tenants, tenants by the entirety or tenants in common is treated as included in the decedent's gross estate for these purposes. (Code Sec. 303(b)(2)(B))[24]

Shares of stock transferred by gift within three years of a decedent's death are included in his gross estate for purposes of determining whether the 35%-of-adjusted gross estate requirement is met for the redeemed stock.[25]

(2) The redemption distribution must take place after the decedent's death and not later than a specified time.) Code Sec. 303(b)(1))[26]

(3) The redeemed shareholder must bear a burden of taxes or expenses; that is, his interest must be reduced (either directly or through a binding obligation to contribute) by any payment of death taxes or funeral and administration expenses. (Code Sec. 303(b)(3))[27]

¶ 3532 Sales between related corporations as redemptions.

If shareholders sell stock they own in one controlled corporation (issuer) to a related controlled corporation (acquirer) in return for cash or other property, the sale is treated: (1) as a redemption by the *acquirer* if the acquirer is a brother corporation to the issuer, (Code Sec. 304(a)(1)), or (2) as a redemption by the *issuer* if the issuer is a parent of the acquirer. (Code Sec. 304(a)(2))[28]

Whether a redemption is treated as payment for stock or as a dividend is determined by applying the tests discussed at ¶ 3525 *et seq.* to the redeemed shareholder's interest in the issuer after the redemption. (Code Sec. 304(a))[29] If, applying those tests, a transaction does give rise to a dividend, the amount of the dividend is determined as if the property were distributed by the acquirer to the extent of its E&P, and then by the issuer to the extent of its E&P. (Code Sec. 304(b)(2))[30]

A brother-sister relationship exists where the same person or persons controls each of two corporations. (Code Sec. 304(a)(1)) For purposes of both the brother-sister test and the parent-subsidiary test, control means ownership of stock possessing at least 50% of the total combined voting power of all classes of the voting stock, or at least 50% of the total value of all classes of stock. (Code Sec. 304(c)(1))[31] Constructive ownership rules similar to those at ¶ 3533, but with certain modifications, apply in determining whether control exists. (Code Sec. 304(c)(3)(A))[32]

The parent-sub redemption rules apply even if, as a result of the constructive ownership rules, a brother-sister relationship also exists.[33]

¶ 3533 Constructive ownership.

For purposes of the stock redemption rules, a person is treated as owning not only his own direct holdings, but also those of certain closely related taxpayers. (Code Sec. 302(c)) These constructive ownership or attribution rules provide:

■ *Family attribution.* An individual is considered as owning stock owned, directly or indirectly, by his spouse (unless divorced or legally separated), children (including adopted children), grandchildren and parents. (Code Sec. 318(a)(1))[34]

■ *Attribution to and from S corporations, partnerships and estates.* Stock owned by or for an S corporation, partnership or estate is considered as owned proportionately by its shareholders, partners, or beneficiaries, (Code Sec. 318(a)(2)(A), (5)(E)) and stock owned by or for an S shareholder, partner or estate beneficiary is attributed in full to the S corporation, partnership or estate. (Code Sec. 318(a)(3)(A), (5)(E))[35]

---

24. ¶ F-11605 *et seq.*; ¶ 3034.01.
25. ¶ F-11604; ¶ 3034.01.
26. ¶ F-11613; ¶ 3034.01.
27. ¶ F-11617; ¶ 3034.01.
28. ¶ F-11704 *et seq.*; ¶ 3044.
29. ¶ F-11704; ¶ 3044.03.
30. ¶ F-11706; ¶ 3044.03.
31. ¶ F-11711; ¶ 3044.01.
32. ¶ F-11720 *et seq.*; ¶ 3044.01.
33. ¶ F-11723; ¶ 3044.04.
34. ¶ F-11803 *et seq.*; ¶ 3184.02.
35. ¶ F-11812 *et seq.*; ¶ 3184.03.

Footnote references beginning with letters are to paragraphs in RIA's Federal Tax Coordinator 2d and RIA's Analysis of Federal Taxes: Income. Footnote references beginning with numbers are to paragraphs in RIA's United States Tax Reporter.

■ *Attribution to and from trusts.* Stock owned by or for a trust (except an exempt employee's trust) is considered owned by its beneficiaries in proportion to their actuarial interest in the trust. (Code Sec. 318(a)(2)(B)(i)) Stock owned by or for a trust beneficiary (other than the beneficiary of an exempt employee's trust) is attributed in full to the trust unless the beneficiary's interest in the trust is a remote contingent interest. (Code Sec. 318(a)(3)(B)(i))[36]

■ *Attribution to and from C corporations.* A 50% or more shareholder in a C corporation is considered as owning his proportionate share of stock in other corporations owned by the C corporation (Code Sec. 318(a)(2)(C)) and a C corporation is considered as owning all the stock (except its own) owned by a 50% or more shareholder. (Code Sec. 318(a)(3)(C))[37]

■ *Option attribution.* The holder of an option to buy stock is treated as the owner of the stock covered by the option. (Code Sec. 318(a)(4)) This includes an option that isn't exercisable until after the lapse of a fixed period of time.[38]

Stock constructively owned by a person is considered as actually owned by him for purposes of further attribution (Code Sec. 318(a)(5)(A)) *except* in the following situations where "double" or "sidewise" attribution is prohibited:

■ Stock constructively owned by a person under the family attribution rules will not be attributed further to make another family member the constructive owner of that stock. (Code Sec. 318(a)(5)(B))[39]

illustration: If father and son each actually own 50 shares in a corporation, each is treated as owning all 100 shares. But the father's *constructive* ownership of the 50 shares actually owned by his son can't be attributed from him to his daughter. She is considered owner of only her father's *actual* 50 shares.

■ Stock constructively owned by a partnership, estate, trust or corporation can't be further attributed from the partnership, etc., to make another (partner, heir, beneficiary or shareholder) the constructive owner of that stock. (Code Sec. 318(a)(5)(C))[40]

¶ 3534 Section 306 Preferred Stock Bail-Outs

Certain stock issued as a stock dividend or in a corporate reorganization is treated as Section 306 stock. Generally, a shareholder will have ordinary income if Section 306 stock is redeemed or sold.

¶ 3535 Stock treated as Section 306 stock.

"Section 306 stock" includes:

(1) Stock received as a stock dividend, *other than common issued with respect to common* , any part of which was nontaxable on receipt. Usually this is preferred distributed on common. (Code Sec. 306(c)(1)(A))[41]

(2) Stock *(other than common)* received in a corporate reorganization, spin-off, split-up or split-off, to the extent the transaction was substantially the same as the receipt of a stock dividend, or the stock was received in exchange for Section 306 stock. (Code Sec. 306(c)(1)(B))[42]

(3) Stock (except stock received in a transaction described in (2), above, that is not treated as Section 306 stock) whose basis is determined by reference to the basis of Section 306 stock. (Code Sec. 306(c)(1)(C))[43]

(4) Preferred stock received in a Code Sec. 351 transfer (except for certain bank transfers) if, had money been distributed instead of the preferred stock, any part of the money

---

36. ¶ F-11827 *et seq.*; ¶ 3184.04.   40. ¶s F-11811, F-11814, F-   41. ¶ F-12122; ¶ 3064.01.   43. ¶ F-12128; ¶ 3064.01.
37. ¶ F-11808 *et seq.*; ¶ 3184.05.   11824, F-11832; ¶s 3184.03,   42. ¶ F-12124 *et seq.*; ¶ 3064.01.
38. ¶ F-11834 *et seq.*; ¶ 3184.06.   3284.04, 3184.05, 3184.07.
39. ¶ F-11805; ¶ 3184.07.

Footnote references beginning with letters are to paragraphs in RIA's Federal Tax Coordinator 2d and RIA's Analysis of Federal Taxes: Income. Footnote references beginning with numbers are to paragraphs in RIA's United States Tax Reporter.

would have been a dividend. In determining whether a money distribution would have resulted in a dividend, the brother-sister and parent-sub related corporation redemption rules (¶ 3530) apply. (Code Sec. 306(c)(3)(A))[44]

Excluded from Section 306 classification is any stock, whatever its class, that at the time of its distribution would not *in any part* have been a dividend if cash had been distributed instead because the corporation had no current or accumulated earnings. (Code Sec. 306(c)(2))[45]

¶ 3536 Dispositions of Section 306 stock.

If Section 306 stock is redeemed by the corporation, the amount paid to the redeeming shareholders is treated as any current distribution of property subject to the normal dividend rules, see ¶ 1288 *et seq..* (Code Sec. 306(a)(2))[46]

If the Section 306 stock is sold (or otherwise disposed of) to an outsider, the entire amount realized is treated as ordinary *nondividend* income, up to the amount that would have been a dividend at the time the stock was distributed if that were a cash distribution of the stock's then fair market value. (Code Sec. 306(a)(1)(A))[47] No loss is recognized. (Code Sec. 306(a)(1)(B))[48]

Ordinary income is not realized on the following dispositions of Section 306 stock:

■ a complete redemption of all the shareholder's stock; (Code Sec. 306(b)(1)(B))

■ a complete termination of a shareholder's stock interest by any other disposition that leaves him without any stock actually or constructively owned; (Code Sec. 306(b)(1)(A))

■ a partial liquidation redemption from a noncorporate shareholder; (Code Sec. 306(b)(1)(B))

■ a redemption in a complete liquidation of the corporation; (Code Sec. 306(b)(2))

■ any nontaxable disposition, such as an exchange of stock in a reorganization or a gift of the tainted stock (though the stock remains tainted in the transferee's hands); (Code Sec. 306(b)(3))

■ any disposition (including a redemption) of Section 306 stock if IRS is satisfied that federal income tax avoidance was not a principal purpose: (1) for the distribution and disposition of the tainted stock, or (2) if the underlying stock is disposed of before or simultaneously with the tainted stock, for the disposition of the tainted stock.)Code Sec. 306(b)(4)) Showing that the corporation which issued the Section 306 is widely held isn't enough to make this exception apply.[49]

¶ 3537 Nonliquidating Distributions

A corporation recognizes gain but not loss when it makes a nonliquidating distribution of property to its shareholders. Neither gain nor loss is recognized on distributions of a corporation's own stock or stock rights.

¶ 3538 Distributions of appreciated property.

A corporation recognizes taxable gain when it makes a nonliquidating distribution (e.g., redemption, dividend) of property (other than its own obligations) to its shareholders if the fair market value (FMV) of the distributed property at the time of distribution is more than its adjusted basis in the hands of the distributing corporation. Gain is recognized as if the corporation sold the property to the distributee for its FMV. (Code Sec. 311(b)(1))[50]

The FMV of the property is considered to be not less than the sum of liabilities assumed by the distributee shareholder plus liabilities to which the distributed property is subject.

---

44. ¶ F-12123; ¶ 3064.01.
45. ¶ F-12132; ¶ 3064.01.
46. ¶ F-12106; ¶ 3064.02(1).

47. ¶s F-12103, F-12101; ¶ 3064.02(1).
48. ¶ F-12103; ¶ 3064.02(2).

49. ¶ F-12108 *et seq.*; ¶ 3064.02(2).

50. ¶ F-14004 *et seq.*; ¶ 3114.01(a).

Footnote references beginning with letters are to paragraphs in RIA's Federal Tax Coordinator 2d and RIA's Analysis of Federal Taxes: Income. Footnote references beginning with numbers are to paragraphs in RIA's United States Tax Reporter.

(Code Sec. 311(b)(2))[1] If the liability is unsecured, it is allocated among all the distributed assets (including any asset that secures another liability) according to their relative FMVs.[2]

¶ 3539 Loss on nonliquidating property distributions.

A corporation doesn't recognize loss on a nonliquidating distribution of property. (Code Sec. 311(a)(2))[3]

¶ 3540 Distributions of stock or stock rights.

A corporation doesn't recognize gain or loss on distributions (not in complete liquidation) of its own stock or of rights to acquire its own stock. (Code Sec. 311(a)(1))[4]

¶ 3541 Corporate Reorganizations

The term "reorganization" in the Code covers a wide variety of transactions, including mergers, recapitalizations, and divisions of corporations. Qualifying reorganizations are generally tax-free.

The Code provisions contemplate that reorganizations are essentially continuations of the investment in another form, so that exchanges in reorganizations *can be* exempt from tax. Typically, reorganization transactions involve stock or securities exchanged for other stock or securities, which would be taxable exchanges absent special exemptions. The reorganizations provisions are used, among other purposes, to provide tax-free treatment for corporate transactions in: acquiring another corporation (including a loss corporation); dividing corporate activities into separate corporations (which can be owned by differing shareholder groups); and recapitalizing, including passing ownership to younger management.[5]

The Code defines the types of reorganization usually in terms of the form of the transaction rather than by economic effect. These are called Type A, B, etc., through Type G (from Code Sec. 368(a)(1)(A)-(G)). Each type is defined below, beginning at ¶ 3543.

¶ 3542 Conditions common to all reorganizations.

The following definitions and requirements apply to all reorganization types (except as noted below). Failure to meet any requirement may disqualify a reorganization and can result in recognized gain and/or dividend treatment.[6]

Plan of reorganization. There must be a "plan" of reorganization. (Code Sec. 354(a)(1))[7]

A party to a reorganization. The stock or securities exchanged must be those of a "party to the reorganization." (Code Sec. 354(a)(1))[8] A "party" includes any corporation resulting from the reorganization, such as the survivor in a merger, the consolidated company, etc., as well as the corporations merged, consolidated, etc. (Code Sec. 368(b)) A "party" also can include a parent corporation, in some cases.[9]

Continuity of interest. After all the exchanges and other changes under the plan, the target shareholders must have retained continuity of interest, (Reg § 1.368-1(b)) i.e., a substantial proprietary stake in the enterprise,[10] except for a recapitalization involving a single corporation (Type E reorganization, see ¶ 3547). In order for this requirement to be satisfied, a substantial portion of the consideration paid to the target corporation's shareholders must be in the form of stock of the acquiring corporation (or, in some cases, of its parent corporation).[11]

Continuity of business enterprise. An acquiring corporation must either: (1) continue the

---

1. ¶s F-14005, F-14402;   4. ¶ F-14002; ¶ 3114.   7. ¶ F-4009; ¶ 3544.01.   10. ¶s F-3501, F-3600 *et seq.*;
   ¶ 3114.01(a).   5. ¶ F-2000 *et seq.*   8. ¶ F-4013 *et seq.*; ¶ 3684.08.   ¶ 3684.11.
2. ¶ F-14010; ¶ 3114.01(a).   6. ¶ F-3500 *et seq.*; ¶ 3684.   9. ¶ F-4013; ¶ 3684.08.   11. ¶ F-3613; ¶ 3684.05.
3. ¶ F-14002; ¶ 3114.01(c).

Footnote references beginning with letters are to paragraphs in RIA's Federal Tax Coordinator 2d and RIA's Analysis of Federal Taxes: Income. Footnote references beginning with numbers are to paragraphs in RIA's United States Tax Reporter.

acquired corporation's "historic business" (in general, its most recent business unless the most recent business was entered under the plan of reorganization), or (2) use in a business a significant portion of the acquired corporation's "historic business assets" (the assets it used in its historic business). (Reg § 1.368-1(d))[12]

Business purpose. Where there is no business purpose, the transaction is not treated as a reorganization.[13]

Investment companies. In some cases, reorganization status is denied where two or more investment companies are involved, one of which owns investments of limited diversity. This rule denies tax-free status only to an *undiversified* company, whether it is the acquired or acquiring corporation, and its shareholders. A Type E reorganization isn't subject to this rule. (Code Sec. 368(a)(2)(F))[14]

¶ 3543 Type A: Merger or consolidation.

A Type A reorganization is a merger or consolidation effected under the laws of a state, a territory, the District of Columbia or the U.S. (Code Sec. 368(a)(1)(A))[15]

Where the acquirer uses its parent's stock to acquire substantially all the target's properties, the transaction is a forward triangular merger. (Code Sec. 368(a)(2)(D))[16] And if the sub (using its parent's voting stock) merges into the target, the transaction is a reverse triangular merger.) Code Sec. 368(a)(2)(E))[17] Forward and reverse triangular mergers are subject to special requirements which must be satisfied in order to qualify as a reorganization.

¶ 3544 Type B: Stock for stock.

A Type B reorganization is the acquisition by one corporation of stock in a second (target) corporation in exchange *solely* for the acquiring corporation's *voting stock* (or voting stock of its parent—a triangular B reorganization), if the acquiring corporation has "control" of the target immediately after the exchange. (Code Sec. 368(a)(1)(B))[18]

¶ 3545 Type C: Acquiring assets for stock.

A Type C reorganization is the acquisition by one corporation of substantially all the properties of a second (target) corporation in exchange for voting stock of the acquiring corporation (or its parent—a triangular C reorganization). For this purpose, except as noted below, liabilities assumed by (or attached to properties received by) the acquiring corporation are disregarded. (Code Sec. 368(a)(1)(C))[19]

Also, the transaction won't qualify as a C reorganization unless, pursuant to the reorganization plan, the target distributes to its shareholders (i.e., liquidates) all the stock, securities and other property so received, as well as its other properties. But IRS may waive this distribution requirement under certain conditions. (Code Sec. 368(a)(2)(G))[20]

If the acquiring corporation pays cash or other property (boot) as part of the deal, then it must receive at least 80% of the value of *all* the target properties in exchange *solely* for its voting stock. In this case, as long as *some* cash or other property is transferred, then liabilities assumed or attached to acquired properties are treated as cash. (Code Sec. 368(a)(2)(B))[21]

¶ 3546 Type D: Transfer of assets to subsidiary.

A Type D reorganization is used to transfer assets to a controlled corporation, either existing or newly incorporated, followed by either a distribution of the subsidiary's stock or a complete liquidation of the transferor. It can be "nondivisive" (acquisitive) or "divisive."[22]

---

12. ¶ F-3701 *et seq.*; ¶ 3684.11.
13. ¶ F-3800 *et seq.*; ¶s 3684.12, 79,006.07.
14. ¶ F-2101 *et seq.*; ¶ 3684.05.
15. ¶ F-2201; ¶ 3684.01.
16. ¶ F-2301 *et seq.*; ¶ 3684.01.
17. ¶ F-2402 *et seq.*; ¶ 3684.01.
18. ¶ F-2500 *et seq.*; ¶ 3684.02.
19. ¶ F-2600 *et seq.*; ¶ 3684.03.
20. ¶ F-2629; ¶ 3684.03.
21. ¶ F-2613; ¶ 3684.03.
22. ¶ F-2004; ¶ 3684.04.

Footnote references beginning with letters are to paragraphs in RIA's Federal Tax Coordinator 2d and RIA's Analysis of Federal Taxes: Income. Footnote references beginning with numbers are to paragraphs in RIA's United States Tax Reporter.

A *nondivisive* D reorganization is a transfer by one corporation of substantially all of its assets to another corporation if, immediately after the transfer, the transferor corporation and/or its shareholders control the transferee corporation and the transferor then distributes all of its assets (including stock and securities of the transferee) under the plan of reorganization.[23]

In a *divisive* D reorganization, one corporation transfers part of its assets to another corporation. Immediately after the transfer, the transferor corporation and/or its shareholders must control the transferee corporation, and the stock or securities of the transferee are distributed under Code Sec. 355 (i.e., in a tax-free spin-off, split-off or split-up, see ¶ 3556 *et seq.*). (Code Sec. 368(a)(1)(D))[24]

¶ 3547 Type E: Recapitalization.

A Type E reorganization is a "recapitalization" or change in the capital structure of a corporation. (Code Sec. 368(a)(1)(E)) Transactions which qualify as recapitalizations include:

■ issuance of preferred stock in discharge of outstanding bonds;

■ exchanging one class of common for another class of common, or preferred for common (but new preferred may be Section 306 stock, see ¶ 3533), or vice-versa; (Reg § 1.368-2(e))

■ exchange of old bonds for new bonds with a different face value or interest rate or the like;

■ changes in stock or securities effected by a change in the corporate charter.[25]

¶ 3548 Type F reorganization.

A Type F reorganization is limited to a change in identity, form or place of organization *of one corporation.* (Code Sec. 368(a)(1)(F))[26]

¶ 3549 Type G reorganization: Bankruptcy.

A Type G reorganization is the transfer by a corporation of all or part of its assets to another corporation under a court-approved reorganization plan in a title 11 or similar case (e.g., bankruptcy, receivership, or foreclosure) but only if stock or securities of the corporation to which the assets are transferred are distributed in a transaction which qualifies under Code Secs. 354, 355 or 356. (Code Sec. 368(a)(1)(G), (3)(A))[27]

¶ 3550 Control defined.

For purposes of the reorganization rules (other than nondivisive Type D reorganizations, see ¶ 3544), as well as the Code Sec. 351 rules for transfers to controlled corporations (¶ 3510), control means the ownership of:

■ stock possessing at least 80% of the total combined voting power of all voting stock, and

■ at least 80% of the total number of shares of each class of nonvoting stock. (Code Sec. 368(c))[28]

¶ 3551 How reorganization exchanges are taxed to shareholders.

If under a plan of reorganization, the holder of stock or securities receives in the exchange *only* stock in a corporation that is a party to the reorganization, the recipient recognizes no gain or loss. Nonrecognition also applies when securities of a corporate party to the reorganization are received in exchange for other securities, if the principal (face) amount of the securities received is not more than the face amount given up. (Code

---

23. ¶s F-2004, F-2700 *et seq.*;   24. ¶s F-2004, F-4500 *et seq.*;   25. ¶ F-3000 *et seq.*; ¶ 3684.05.   27. ¶ F-3200 *et seq.*; ¶ 3684.07.
     ¶ 3684.04.   ¶ 3684.04.   26. ¶ F-3100 *et seq.*; ¶ 3684.06.   28. ¶ F-5500 *et seq.*; ¶ 3684.13.

Footnote references beginning with letters are to paragraphs in RIA's Federal Tax Coordinator 2d and RIA's Analysis of Federal Taxes: Income. Footnote references beginning with numbers are to paragraphs in RIA's United States Tax Reporter.

Sec. 354(a)(1))[29] This nonrecognition rule does not apply to D or G reorganizations unless the transferee corporation receives substantially all of the transferor's assets, and the stock, securities and other property received by the transferor, as well as its remaining assets, are distributed by the transferor under the plan of reorganization. (Code Sec. 354(b))[30]

But if the securities received exceed in face amount the securities given up, (Code Sec. 354(a)(2)) or if *any other property* is received ("boot," see ¶ 3551), then any *gain* realized by the recipient on the exchange is recognized and taxed to him up to the amount of boot. (Code Sec. 356(a)(1)) This amount is taxed as an ordinary dividend to the extent the exchange has the effect of a dividend distribution. (Code Sec. 356(a)(2))[31] In determining whether dividend treatment applies, the transaction is viewed as though the consideration paid in the reorganization were entirely in the form of acquirer stock, and as though, after the reorganization, the boot had been distributed in redemption of a portion of that stock. The redemption tests (¶ 3525 *et seq.*) are then applied to determine whether the deemed distribution is a dividend or payment for stock (capital gain).[32]

¶ 3552 How reorganization exchanges are taxed to corporate parties.

No gain or loss is recognized by a corporation that is a party to a reorganization, that exchanges property solely for stock or securities of another corporation that is also a party to that reorganization. (Code Sec. 361(a))[33] Also, if the corporation receives other property or money (boot) in addition to stock or securities, then:

- If the recipient distributes all the boot, it does not recognize gain on the exchange (but may recognize gain on the distribution of appreciated property, see below).

- If any part of the boot isn't distributed, gain is recognized on the exchange but only to the extent of the undistributed boot. (Code Sec. 361(b))[34]

Gain or loss is not recognized on the distribution of qualified property received under the plan of reorganization. Qualified property is stock (or the right to acquire stock) in the distributing corporation, and stock or obligations of another party to the reorganization that are received in the reorganization exchange. Gain (but not loss) is recognized on the distribution of property that is not qualified property. (Code Sec. 361(c))[35]

¶ 3553 Boot.

Boot is money or the fair market value (FMV) of property other than stock or securities of a party to the reorganization that is received by the target in exchange for its property, or by target shareholders in exchange for their stock, under the plan of reorganization.[36]

Securities in corporations not parties to the reorganization are always "boot" so that any gain on the exchange is taxable to the extent of the securities' FMV. For securities in corporations that are parties to the reorganization, only the excess face amount of securities received over the face amount of securities surrendered is boot (i.e., no excess face amount means no boot). If no securities are surrendered, the FMV of any securities received is boot. (Code Sec. 354(a)(2), Code Sec. 356(d))[37]

¶ 3554 Assumption or transfer of liabilities.

Where a transferor corporation that is a party to a reorganization exchanges property for stock or securities in another corporation, and the latter also assumes liabilities of the transferor (or the property is subject to liabilities), the liabilities assumed (or attached to the property) are not considered boot for the purpose of *recognizing* gain. (Code Sec. 357(a))[38]

But if the principal purpose for the assumption or acquisition of the liabilities is tax

---

29. ¶ F-4001; ¶ 3544.01.
30. ¶s F-2701; F-3205; ¶s 3544.02, 3684.04, 3684.07.
31. ¶ F-4017; ¶ 3564.
32. ¶ F-4026; ¶ 3564.02.
33. ¶ F-4100 *et seq.*; ¶ 3614.03.
34. ¶ F-4106 *et seq.*; ¶ 3614.01.
35. ¶ F-4100 *et seq.*; ¶ 3614.03.
36. ¶ F-4017.
37. ¶ F-4021; ¶ 3564.01.
38. ¶ F-4201; ¶ 3574.

Footnote references beginning with letters are to paragraphs in RIA's Federal Tax Coordinator 2d and RIA's Analysis of Federal Taxes: Income. Footnote references beginning with numbers are to paragraphs in RIA's United States Tax Reporter.

avoidance, or is something other than a bona fide business purpose, *all* the liabilities assumed or acquired are treated as cash for purposes of both computing *and* recognizing gain. That is, all the liabilities assumed become boot. (Code Sec. 357(b))[39]

In a Type D reorganization (¶ 3544), a special rule applies. If the sum of the liabilities assumed, plus the amount of liabilities to which the transferred property is subject, exceeds the total adjusted basis of the property transferred in the exchange, the excess is taxed as a gain from the sale or exchange of property (capital gain or ordinary, depending on the status of the property in the hands of the transferor). (Code Sec. 357(c))[40]

¶ 3555   Deductibility of reorganization costs.

Attorneys' fees and other expenses incurred in connection with a corporate reorganization are not deductible business expenses but are capital expenditures, because they give rise to a benefit to the corporation which extends beyond the year in which they are incurred.[41]

If a proposed reorganization is abandoned, the costs are deductible in the year of abandonment.[42]

¶ 3556   Spin-Offs, Split-Offs and Split-Ups

Spin-offs, split-offs and split-ups may accomplish a tax-free separation of one corporation (P) into two or more corporations with the same group of shareholders owning the separate corporations directly (though not necessarily in the same proportion).

■ *Spin-off.* Corporation P has carried on one or more businesses for five years or more. P transfers part of the business assets to S, a newly created corporation, in exchange for S's stock, and then distributes the S stock to its (P's) shareholders. Or P, previously owning all the stock of S for at least five years, decides to distribute the S stock to its (P's) shareholders, pro rata. P's shareholders don't surrender any of their P stock, so they end up holding the stock of P and S in the same proportion. If certain requirements are met (as explained at ¶ 3557), the transaction is partially or wholly tax-free to P's shareholders (and to P).

■ *Split-off* is the same as a spin-off except that P's shareholders exchange part of their P stock for the S stock they receive from P. The split-off does not have to be pro rata.

■ *Split-up.* In addition to transferring part of one business or a separate business to S for S's stock, P transfers the remainder of its business (or businesses) to X Corp, also newly incorporated, for X's stock. P (left without a business) distributes the S and X stock to its shareholders in exchange for their P stock. P liquidates and disappears.[43]

¶ 3557   Requirements for a tax-free spin-off, split-off or split-up.

(1) The distributing corporation (P) must (a) distribute to its shareholders solely stock or securities in a corporation (S) that it "controls" (¶ 3550) immediately before the distribution, or (b) distribute to its (P's) security holders, in *exchange* for its securities, solely stock or securities in S. (Code Sec. 355(a)(1))[44]

(2) The distribution must not be used principally as a device for distributing earnings and profits (E&P) of either P or S. (Code Sec. 355(a)(1)(B)) The regs specify "device factors" (the presence of which are evidence of a device) and nondevice factors and certain distributions that ordinarily aren't considered to have been used principally as a device even though device factors are present. (Reg § 1.355-2(d))[45]

(3) There must be a "continuity of interest" (¶ 3542). The pre-distribution shareholders

---

39. ¶ F-4202; ¶ 3574.02.   41. ¶ L-5401; ¶ 2484.   43. ¶ F-4600 *et seq.*; ¶ 3554.01(d).   45. ¶ F-4701 *et seq.*; ¶ 3554.01(b).
40. ¶ F-4205; ¶ 3574.03.   42. ¶ L-5415; ¶ 1654.150.   44. ¶ F-4608; ¶ 3554.01(a).

Footnote references beginning with letters are to paragraphs in RIA's Federal Tax Coordinator 2d and RIA's Analysis of Federal Taxes: Income. Footnote references beginning with numbers are to paragraphs in RIA's United States Tax Reporter.

of P must end up with an amount of stock which is sufficient to establish a continuity of interest in both P and S, though not necessarily proportionately, as explained below. (Reg § 1.355-2(c)(1))[46]

(4) Both P and S (or each controlled subsidiary) must be engaged immediately after the distribution in the active conduct of a trade or business, (Code Sec. 355(b)(1)(A)) i.e., each performing active and substantial management and operational functions (not holding investments or owning and operating real or personal property unless the owner performs significant services). (Reg § 1.355-3(b)(2)(iii))[47] However, if immediately before the distribution P has no (or de minimis) assets except stock or securities in its subs, then only the subs must meet the post-distribution active business requirement. (Code Sec. 355(b)(1)(B); Reg § 1.355-3(a)) These trades or businesses must have been actively conducted throughout the five-year period ending on the date the sub's stock is distributed. (Code Sec. 355(b)(2)(B))[48]

(5) The active trade or business must not have been acquired during the above five-year period in a transaction in which gain or loss was recognized. (Code Sec. 355(b)(2)(C))[49]

(6) P must distribute at least an amount of S stock that is treated as "control." But if P retains *any* stock or securities in S, tax avoidance must not be a principal purpose for the retention. (Code Sec. 355(a)(1)(D))[50]

Even if all the above requirements are met, there must be one or more corporate business purposes for the transaction for it to be tax-free. (Reg § 1.355-2(b))[1]

¶ 3558 Boot.

The receipt of boot in a spin-off, etc., may trigger a tax on the shareholders. Boot includes cash and the fair market value of:

■ *any property* (including stock warrants, short-term notes, etc.) *except* (subject to the limitations below) stock or securities in the spun-off corporation (S) ("qualified property," see ¶ 3552); (Code Sec. 356(a))

■ *any excess in the face amount of securities* of S received over the face amount of securities in P which are surrendered; (Code Sec. 355(a)(3)(A), Code Sec. 356(d)(2)(C))

■ *stock in S* that P acquired in a partially or wholly taxable transaction during the five-year period preceding the distribution. (Code Sec. 355(a)(3)(B))[2]

Boot in a spin-off (where no stock is surrendered) is a fully taxable ordinary dividend to the extent of E&P, and any excess is a nontaxable return of capital. (Code Sec. 356(b))[3]

Boot in a split-off or split-up (where stock in P is surrendered) is taxable to the extent of gain, either as a dividend if the distribution has the effect of one, or as capital gain. (Code Sec. 356(a))[4] In determining whether boot has the effect of a dividend, the transaction is treated as though the shareholder had retained the P stock which he actually surrendered in exchange for S stock, and had received the boot in exchange for an amount of P stock with a value equal to the amount of the boot; the redemption rules (¶ 3525 *et seq.*) are then applied to determine whether the boot is treated as a dividend.[5]

No loss is recognized, whether or not boot is received. (Code Sec. 355(a), Code Sec. 356(c))[6]

¶ 3559 How distributing corporation is taxed.

No gain or loss is recognized by a corporation (P) on its distribution of stock or securities of S in a tax-free corporate separation (Code Sec. 355(c)(1) and 361) unless the distribution is "disqualified" (see below). In the case of a disqualified distribution, P

---

46. ¶ F-4613; ¶ 3554.03.
47. ¶ F-4801 *et seq.*; ¶ 3554.02.
48. ¶ F-4819; ¶ 3554.02.

49. ¶ F-4826 *et seq.*; ¶ 3554.02.
50. ¶ F-4608 *et seq.*; ¶ 3544.01(b).
1. ¶ F-4900 *et seq.*; ¶ 3554.01(b).

2. ¶ F-5003 *et seq.*; ¶ 3554.01(b).
3. ¶ F-5000 *et seq.*; ¶ 3564.02.
4. ¶ F-5000 *et seq.*; ¶ 3554.01(d).

5. ¶ F-4026.
6. ¶ F-5000 *et seq.*; ¶ 3564.02(1).

Footnote references beginning with letters are to paragraphs in RIA's Federal Tax Coordinator 2d and RIA's Analysis of Federal Taxes: Income. Footnote references beginning with numbers are to paragraphs in RIA's United States Tax Reporter.

recognizes gain (but not loss) as if the property were sold for its fair market value (but not less than the amount of any liability on it that is assumed in connection with the distribution). (Code Sec. 355(c)(2), 355(d)(1))[7]

A distribution is "disqualified" if: (1) immediately after the distribution any shareholder holds (actually or constructively) at least 50% of the stock of P or of S, and (2) that stock was purchased (or similarly acquired) within the immediately preceding five-year period (but not before Oct. 9, '90), or was received as a distribution on P stock that was purchased, etc., within that period. (Code Sec. 355(c), (d))[8]

¶ 3560 Carryovers of Tax Items

When a corporation acquires the assets of another corporation in any of the tax-free reorganizations or liquidations described below, the acquiring corporation also carries over numerous tax items of the transferor corporation (also often called the "predecessor" corporation).

The predecessor's tax items are carried over to the successor corporation only in a:

■ *Type A, C or F reorganization*;

■ *Type D or G reorganization* , but only if the transferor transfers substantially all its assets to the acquiring corporation and then (in effect) completely liquidates; or

■ *complete liquidation of an 80% subsidiary.* (Code Sec. 381(a))[9]

¶ 3561 Tax items that are carried over.

In those transactions that come within the Code's carryover provisions, the acquiring corporation succeeds to and takes into account the following tax items of the transferor. (Code Sec. 381(c))[10]

■ accounting method;

■ bond discount amortization;

■ capital loss carryovers;

■ charitable contributions carryover;

■ depreciation allowance and method;

■ earnings and profits (E&P);

■ employee benefit plan contributions;

■ general business credit;

■ installment method;

■ inventory method;

■ involuntary conversions;

■ minimum tax credit;

■ mining development and exploration expenses of distributor or transferor;

■ net operating loss carryovers;

■ percentage depletion on extraction of ores or minerals from waste or residue of earlier mining;

■ personal holding company (PHC) deficiency dividend;

■ PHC dividend carryover;

■ real estate investment trust or regulated investment company dividend;

---

7. ¶s F-14201, F-14300 *et seq.*;   8. ¶ F-14300 *et seq.*; ¶ 3554.04.   9. ¶ F-7001 *et seq.*; ¶ 3814.01.   10. ¶ F-7012; ¶ 3814.02.
   ¶ 3554.04.

Footnote references beginning with letters are to paragraphs in RIA's Federal Tax Coordinator 2d and RIA's Analysis of Federal Taxes: Income. Footnote references beginning with numbers are to paragraphs in RIA's United States Tax Reporter.

■ tax benefit items;

■ items under Subchapter U (dealing with enterprise zones), as prescribed by regs.[11]

¶ 3562 Tax Avoidance (Section 269) Acquisition Bar to Tax Benefits ▬▬▬▬

In general, Code Sec. 269 permits IRS to bar the benefits of any deduction, credit or other allowance where control of a corporation (or its assets) is acquired for the principal purpose of avoiding tax through the use of those benefits.

¶ 3563 The Code Sec. 269 rule.

Any deduction, credit or other allowance may be disallowed where, for the principal purpose of tax avoidance:

■ any person or persons acquire, directly or indirectly, stock having at least 50% of the total combined voting power of all classes of a corporation's voting stock, or at least 50% of the total value of all classes of its stock; or

■ any corporation acquires, directly or indirectly, property of another corporation not controlled, directly or indirectly, by the acquirer (or its shareholders) immediately before the acquisition, if the acquirer takes a carryover basis in the property. (Code Sec. 269(a))[12]

IRS may also apply these disallowances where a target that a corporation acquired in a qualified stock purchase *without* making a Code Sec. 338 election (¶ 3578 *et seq.*) is liquidated primarily for tax avoidance or evasion, under a plan of liquidation that was adopted within two years after the acquisition date. (Code Sec. 269(b))[13]

¶ 3564 Limits On Use of Built-in Gains of One Corporation to Offset Losses of Another Corporation ▬▬▬▬▬▬▬▬▬▬▬▬▬▬▬▬▬

If one corporation is acquired by another corporation, limits are placed on the extent to which built-in gains of one of the corporations (gain corporation) can be used to offset the other corporation's pre-acquisition losses.

If a corporation either acquires directly (or through one or more other corporations) control of another corporation, or acquires the assets of another corporation in a Type A, C or D reorganization, and either corporation is a gain corporation, then any recognized built-in gains of either corporation within five years of the acquisition date may not be offset by any preacquisition loss of the other corporation. (Code Sec. 384(a))[14] Control means stock ownership which satisfies the requirements discussed at ¶ 3349. (Code Sec. 384(c)(5))[15]

Similar rules apply to limit the use of any excess credit or net capital loss. (Code Sec. 384(d))[16]

The offset prohibition rules do not apply to any preacquisition loss of any corporation if that corporation and the gain corporation were members of the same controlled group at all times during:

■ the five-year period ending on the acquisition date, or

■ the shorter of the periods either corporation was in existence if that is less than five years. (Code Sec. 384(b))[17]

¶ 3565 Trafficking in Net Operating Losses and Other Carryovers ▬▬▬▬

If an ownership change occurs with respect to a loss corporation, that corporation's taxable income for any post-change year can be offset by pre-change losses

---

11. ¶ F-7012; ¶ 3814.02.   13. ¶ F-7923 *et seq.*; ¶ 2694.   15. ¶ F-7853; ¶ 3844.02.   17. ¶ F-7860 *et seq.*; ¶ 3844.02.
12. ¶ F-7900 *et seq.*; ¶ 2694.01.   14. ¶s F-7851, F-7852; ¶ 3844.02.   16. ¶ F-7875 *et seq.*; ¶ 3844.04.

Footnote references beginning with letters are to paragraphs in RIA's Federal Tax Coordinator 2d and RIA's Analysis of Federal Taxes: Income. Footnote references beginning with numbers are to paragraphs in RIA's United States Tax Reporter.

only to the extent of a certain percent of the value of the corporation at the time of the change. Similar rules apply to limit the use of capital loss carryovers and carryovers of certain credits.

¶ 3566 "Section 382 limitation" on use of net operating loss carryforwards after ownership change.

The taxable income of a loss corporation for any tax year ending after an ownership change (¶ 3569) may be offset by pre-change loss carryforwards only to the extent of the Section 382 limitation for that year. (Code Sec. 382(a))[18]

The Section 382 limitation is equal to the value of the loss corporation immediately before the ownership change multiplied by the long-term tax-exempt rate (¶ 3567). (Code Sec. 382(b)(1)) The limitation for any post-change year is increased, however, for certain built-in gains and Code Sec. 338 gains recognized in that year, see below.[19] Special rules apply to determine the value of the loss corporation. (Code Sec. 382(e)(1), (2), (l)(1)(A), (l)(4))[20]

Recognized built-in gain in any recognition period tax year increases the Section 382 limitation for that tax year if the loss corporation had a net unrealized built-in gain. Recognized built-in gain is gain recognized on the disposition of an asset within the five-year period beginning on the date of the ownership change but only if the asset was held immediately before the change date and only to the extent of the excess of the asset's fair market value on the change date over its adjusted basis on that date. (Code Sec. 382(h)(1))[21]

Special rules apply to determine the amount (and applicability) of the Section 382 limitation for the tax year that includes the date of the ownership change. (Code Sec. 382(b)(3))[22]

¶ 3567 Long-term tax-exempt rate.

Long-term tax-exempt rate means the highest of the adjusted federal long-term rates in effect for any month in the three-calendar month period ending with the calendar month in which the ownership change occurs. (Code Sec. 382(f))[23]

The long-term tax-exempt rate for ownership changes in:

- Nov., '93 is 5.27%.
- Oct., '93 is 5.27%;
- Sept., '93 is 5.47%;
- Aug., '93 is 5.47%;
- July, '93 is 5.49%;
- June, '93 is 5.49%;
- May, '93 is 5.77%;
- Apr., '93 is 5.87%;
- Mar., '93 is 5.90%;
- Feb., '93 is 6.09%;
- Jan., '93 is 6.09%;
- Dec., '92 is 6.09%;[24]

---

18. ¶ F-7201; ¶ 3824.01.
19. ¶ F-7251; ¶ 3824.12.
20. ¶ F-7301 *et seq.*; ¶ 3824.12.
21. ¶ F-7340 *et seq.*; ¶ 3824.25.
22. ¶ F-7255 *et seq.*; ¶ 3824.25.
23. ¶ F-7336; ¶ 3824.12.
24. ¶ F-7336; ¶s 3824.12, 12,884.01.

Footnote references beginning with letters are to paragraphs in RIA's Federal Tax Coordinator 2d and RIA's Analysis of Federal Taxes: Income. Footnote references beginning with numbers are to paragraphs in RIA's United States Tax Reporter.

¶ 3568 Pre-change losses and credits subject to Section 382 limitation.

The losses and credits which are subject to limitation under Code Sec. 382 include: (1) any NOL carryforward of the old loss corporation to the tax year ending with the ownership change or in which the change date occurs, (2) any NOL of the old loss corporation for the tax year in which the ownership change occurs to the extent that the loss is allocable to the period in that year on or before the change date, (3) any recognized built-in loss for any recognition period tax year, (4) any pre-change capital loss, and (5) any pre-change credits. (Code Sec. 382(d)(1); Reg § 1.382-2(a)(2))[25]

¶ 3569 Ownership change defined.

There is an ownership change if, immediately after any owner shift involving a 5% shareholder or an equity structure shift:

■ the percentage of the stock of the loss corporation owned by one or more 5% shareholders has increased by more than 50 percentage points, over

■ the lowest percentage of stock of the loss corporation owned by those shareholders at any time during a three-year testing period. (Code Sec. 382(g)(1))[26]

Special rules apply under which, for purposes of the foregoing test, groups of shareholders may be treated as though they were a single shareholder.[27]

The percentage of stock owned is determined on the basis of value but nonvoting preferred stock is generally not taken into account. (Code Sec. 382(k)(6))[28] However, certain nonstock interests may be treated as stock. (Reg § 1.382-2T(f)(18)(iii))[29]

¶ 3570 Limitations on use of certain credit carryforwards.

If an ownership change occurs with respect to a loss corporation, the amount of any excess credit carryforwards, and foreign tax credit carryforwards is limited to an amount based on the tax liability which is attributable to the taxable income that does not exceed the Section 382 limitation, to the extent available after the application of the limitation of net capital losses. (Code Sec. 383; Reg § 1.383-1(b))[30]

¶ 3571 Order of absorption of Section 382 limitation.

A loss corporation must absorb its Section 382 limitation in the following order for each post-change year: (1) pre-change losses that are built-in capital losses recognized during that year, (2) pre-change losses that are capital loss carryovers, (3) pre-change losses that are built-in ordinary losses recognized during that year, (4) pre-change losses that are NOL carryovers, (5) pre-change credits for excess foreign taxes carried forward under Code Sec. 904(c), (6) pre-change credits that are unused general business credits carried over under Code Sec. 39, and (7) pre-change credits that are unused minimum tax credits under Code Sec. 53. (Reg § 1.383-1(d)(2))[31]

¶ 3572 Corporate Liquidations

Shareholders ordinarily recognize taxable gain or loss on the receipt of liquidating distributions. Corporations, with some exceptions, recognize taxable gain or loss on the distribution or sale of property in liquidation.

---

25. ¶s F-7363, F-7386, F-7408; ¶s 3824.01, 3824.25.
26. ¶ F-7441; ¶s 3824.03, 3824.10.
27. ¶ F-7500 *et seq.*
28. ¶ F-7505 *et seq.*; ¶ 3824.14.
29. ¶ F-7603; ¶ 3824.14.
30. ¶ F-7400 *et seq.*
31. ¶ F-7360.

Footnote references beginning with letters are to paragraphs in RIA's Federal Tax Coordinator 2d and RIA's Analysis of Federal Taxes: Income. Footnote references beginning with numbers are to paragraphs in RIA's United States Tax Reporter.

¶ 3573 Shareholder's tax on liquidating distributions.

Amounts received by a shareholder in a distribution in complete liquidation of a corporation are treated as made in full payment in exchange for the stock. (Code Sec. 331(a))[32]

⊘*observation:* This means that a distribution in complete liquidation usually results in capital gain or loss to the shareholder.

Gain or loss is the total amount distributed less the shareholder's basis for his stock. (Reg § 1.331-1(b)) The amount of the distribution is the sum of the cash plus the fair market value of any other property received by the shareholder in exchange for his stock. (Code Sec. 1001(b))[33]

¶ 3574 How corporation is taxed on liquidations.

A liquidating corporation recognizes taxable gain or loss on distributions of property as if the property had been sold to the distributee for its fair market value (FMV). (Code Sec. 336(a)) If distributed property is subject to a liability, or if any shareholder assumes a liability of the liquidating corporation in connection with the distribution, the property's FMV is treated as not less than the amount of the liability. (Code Sec. 336(b))[34]

There are exceptions to recognition of gain or loss on liquidating distributions for:

■ certain distributions by 80%-owned subsidiaries to the parent corporation, see ¶ 3576;

■ certain liquidating distributions in connection with tax-free reorganizations (¶s 3550, 3557).)Code Sec. 336(c))[35]

¶ 3575 Deductibility of costs of corporate dissolution and liquidation.

If a corporation is completely liquidated and dissolved, filing fees, attorney's and accountant's fees and other expenditures incurred in connection with the liquidation and dissolution, including payment for tax advice, are generally deductible in full by the dissolved corporation.[36]

¶ 3576 Liquidation of 80% subs.

When a parent corporation completely liquidates its 80%-owned sub, the *parent* (as shareholder) doesn't recognize gain or loss on the liquidating distributions if the requirements set out below are met. (Code Sec. 332(a)) The nonrecognition applies to distributions of *cash* as well as other property.[37]

However, minority shareholders who receive liquidating distributions *do* recognize gain or loss. (Reg § 1.332-5)[38]

These are the requirements for nonrecognition:

(1) The parent must own at least 80% of the sub's total voting stock and at least 80% of the total value of all the sub's stock, on the date the plan of liquidation is adopted and until the final liquidating distribution is received. (Code Sec. 332(b)(1))[39]

(2) The distributions must be made under a plan of *complete* liquidation, and in complete redemption of all of the sub's stock. (Code Sec. 332(b)(2), (3))[40]

(3) If the sub distributes all its assets in complete liquidation *in one tax year* , its liquidation plan or resolution needn't specify a completion time. But if complete distribution doesn't occur within one tax year, the plan must specifically provide for all liquidating distributions to be made within three years from the close of the tax year in which the first of the distributions is made. (Code Sec. 332(b); Reg § 1.332-4(a))[41]

---

32. ¶ F-13101; ¶ 3314.04.   35. ¶ F-14401 *et seq.*; ¶ 3364.01.   38. ¶ F-13223; ¶ 3324.01.   40. ¶ F-13207 *et seq.*; ¶ 3324.01.
33. ¶ F-13108; ¶ 3314.01.   36. ¶ L-5501; ¶ 2484.   39. ¶ F-13202 *et seq.*; ¶ 3324.01.   41. ¶ F-13209; ¶ 3324.01.
34. ¶ F-14401 *et seq.*; ¶ 3364.01.   37. ¶ F-13200 *et seq.*; ¶ 3324.

Footnote references beginning with letters are to paragraphs in RIA's Federal Tax Coordinator 2d and RIA's Analysis of Federal Taxes: Income. Footnote references beginning with numbers are to paragraphs in RIA's United States Tax Reporter.

If the nonrecognition rules are met, the parent will *carry over* the sub's basis in the assets distributed (Code Sec. 334(b)(1)).[42] Special rules apply to debt owed to the parent by its sub. (Reg § 1.332-2(b)(7))[43]

¶ 3577 How 80% subsidiary is taxed on liquidating distributions.

A liquidating sub does not recognize any gain or loss on liquidating distributions to its 80% distributee-parent (Code Sec. 336(d)(3), Code Sec. 337(a)).[44]

¶ 3578 Code Sec. 338 Election

A corporation (acquirer) that purchases stock of another corporation (target) may be able to get a stepped-up basis for the target's assets by electing to treat the stock purchase as an asset purchase.

The Code Sec. 338 election may be made only if the acquirer makes a qualified stock purchase of the target (¶ 3579). However, consistency rules will sometimes "deem" the election to be made even though not actually made, while in other situations an acquirer will not be able to make the election even though a qualified stock purchase of the target was made.[45]

If the election is made (or deemed made), the target may have to recognize gain from the "sale" of its assets (¶ 3580), in addition to any gain recognized by the selling shareholders on the sale of their stock.[46]

caution: Because of this, a Code Sec. 338 election (other than an election described in ¶ 3582) is rarely tax-efficient.

For how and when to make the Code Sec. 338 election, see ¶ 3583.

¶ 3579 Qualified stock purchase.

A qualified stock purchase means one corporation's (acquirer's) purchase, in one or more transactions during a 12-month acquisition period, of another (target) corporation's stock, if the shares so purchased have at least 80% of the target's total combined voting power and at least 80% of the value of all the target's stock. (Code Sec. 338(d)(3))[47]

¶ 3580 Consistency as to purchases from target or target affiliate.

If a qualified stock purchase of a target is made, then all stock or asset purchases from the target and from a target affiliate that are made during a "consistency" period (below) must be treated consistently, i.e., all as stock purchases or all as asset purchases (Code Sec. 338(e), (f)).[48]

The consistency period means the period including the one-year period before the beginning of the 12-month acquisition period, that part of the acquisition period up to and including the acquisition date (i.e., the date the last purchase of stock needed to complete a qualified stock purchase is made), and the one-year period beginning on the day after the acquisition date. (Code Sec. 338(h)(4)(A))[49]

■ If the acquirer makes a Code Sec. 338 election for its first qualified stock purchase during the consistency period, it will be deemed to have made the election for each qualified stock purchase of a target affiliate it makes in that consistency period. (Code Sec. 338(f)(1))

■ If a qualified stock purchase is made and the acquirer, during the consistency period, acquires any asset of the target (or a target affiliate), the district director may deem a Code Sec. 338 election to be made. (Code Sec. 338(e)(1); Reg § 1.338-4T(f)(1)) But the acquirer may avoid this deemed election by making a protective carryover basis election

42. ¶ F-13227 *et seq.*; ¶ 3324.01.   44. ¶ F-14500 *et seq.*; ¶ 3374.01.   46. ¶ F-8300 *et seq.*; ¶ 3384.05.   48. ¶s F-8201, F-8207; ¶ 3384.11.
43. ¶·F-13200 *et seq.*   45. ¶ F-8000 *et seq.*; ¶ 3384.05.   47. ¶ F-8101; ¶ 3384.03.   49. ¶ F-8202; ¶ 3384.11.

Footnote references beginning with letters are to paragraphs in RIA's Federal Tax Coordinator 2d and RIA's Analysis of Federal Taxes: Income. Footnote references beginning with numbers are to paragraphs in RIA's United States Tax Reporter.

(in the form of a statement, as provided in Regs, filed by the fifteenth day of the ninth month beginning after the month in which the acquisition date occurs) with respect to its qualified stock purchase. (Reg § 1.338-4T(f)(6))

⊘recommendation: A taxpayer who decides not to make a Code Sec. 338 election with respect to a qualified stock purchase should always make a protective carryover basis election, in order to avoid being forced into a Code Sec. 338 election under the consistency rules.

A deemed Code Sec. 338 election will not result from sales to the acquirer in the ordinary course of business or from acquisitions where the basis is carried over from the target to the acquirer. (Code Sec. 338(e)(2))[50]

Even if a qualified stock purchase of a target is made, the Code Sec. 338 election may not be made for that target if the election was not made with respect to a qualified stock purchase of a target affiliate previously made during the consistency period. (Code Sec. 338(f)(2))[1]

¶ 3581   Effect of Code Sec. 338 election.

If the Code Sec. 338 election is made, the target is treated (for tax purposes only) as two corporations: an "old target," and a "new target."

The old target is treated as though it had sold its assets as of the close of the acquisition date for their fair market value (FMV) in a single transaction. (Code Sec. 338(a)(1))[2]

⊘observation: This means that gain or loss is recognized on the deemed sale to the extent of the difference between the FMV of the old target's assets and its basis in those assets.

The new target is deemed to have purchased all of the assets of the old target as of the beginning of the day after the acquisition date. (Code Sec. 338(a)(2))[3]

¶ 3582   Election to have selling consolidated group recognize gain or loss on deemed sale of target's assets.

If the target whose stock is acquired in the qualified stock purchase is a member of a selling consolidated return group (selling group), the acquirer and the selling group can jointly elect to have the selling group recognize (and report) gain or loss as though the target sold all of its assets in a single taxable transaction while still a member of the selling group. (Code Sec. 338(h)(10); Reg § 1.338(h)(10)-1T(e))[4]

In addition, making the Code Sec. 338(h)(10) election will have these tax effects:

■ No gain or loss will be recognized by the selling group on the actual sale of target stock in a qualified stock purchase.

■ The target is treated as if, at the close of the acquisition date but after the deemed sale, it had distributed all of its assets under the 80% sub liquidation rules (¶ 3576).

■ If the acquirer owns nonrecently purchased target stock, it is deemed to have made a gain recognition election with respect to that stock. (Reg § 1.338(h)(10)-1T(e))[5]

¶ 3583   How and when to make the Code Sec. 338 election.

The acquirer elects on Form 8023.)Reg § 1.338-1T(d)(1)) The election must be made on or before the 15th day of the ninth month beginning after the month in which the acquisition date occurs. (Code Sec. 338(g)(1); Reg § 1.338-1T(c))[6] Once made, the election is irrevocable. (Code Sec. 338(g)(3))[7]

---

50. ¶ F-8227 et seq.; ¶ 3384.11.   2. ¶ F-8301; ¶ 3384.01.   4. ¶ E-8751; ¶ 3384.01.   6. ¶ F-8800 et seq.; ¶ 3384.01.
1. ¶ F-8210; ¶ 3384.01.   3. ¶ F-8601; ¶ 3384.01.   5. ¶ E-8750 et seq.; ¶ 3384.09.   7. ¶ F-8818; ¶ 3384.01.

Footnote references beginning with letters are to paragraphs in RIA's Federal Tax Coordinator 2d and RIA's Analysis of Federal Taxes: Income. Footnote references beginning with numbers are to paragraphs in RIA's United States Tax Reporter.

¶ 3584 Collapsible Corporations

The collapsible corporation rules deny capital gains treatment to certain sales and distributions where the profit is attributable to ordinary income assets of the corporation.

A 5% or more shareholder's recognized capital gain from the following transactions will be treated as ordinary income if his corporation is "collapsible" (¶ 3584): (1) the sale or exchange of his stock in the corporation, (2) a distribution in complete or partial liquidation of the corporation if the distribution is treated as in part or full payment in exchange for the stock, and (3) a nonliquidating distribution where the excess of the distribution over the basis in the stock is treated as gain from the sale or exchange of property. (Code Sec. 341(a))[8]

¶ 3585 Collapsible corporation defined.

A corporation is collapsible if it is *formed or availed of*:

■ *principally*: (1) to manufacture, construct or produce property, *or* (2) to purchase property that it holds for less than three years and that, in its hands, is (a) inventory or stock in trade, (b) property held for sale to customers in the ordinary course of business, (c) depreciable or real property used in a trade or business (except property described in (a) and (b)), or (d) unrealized receivables or fees pertaining to the foregoing properties or services ("Section 341 assets"), *or* (3) to hold stock in a corporation formed or availed of principally for the purposes in (1) or (2); *and*

■ *with a view to* the sale or exchange of its stock (through a liquidation or otherwise) before the corporation has realized the requisite amount of taxable income to be derived from the property. (Code Sec. 341(b)(1))[9]

A corporation is presumed to be collapsible if the fair market value of its "Section 341 assets" is 50% or more of the value of all its assets (excluding cash, government obligations, obligations held as capital assets, and stock in other corporations) *and* 120% or more of the adjusted basis of its "Section 341 assets." (Code Sec. 341(c))[10]

The Code provides for certain exceptions to collapsible corporation treatment. (Code Sec. 341(d), (e), (f)(4))[11]

¶ 3586 Transfers to Foreign Corporations

When a U.S. person transfers property to a foreign corporation in certain exchanges, the foreign corporation won't be considered a corporation for purposes of determining the extent gain is recognized on the transfer.

Exchanges to which this applies are those under: Code Sec. 332 (complete liquidations of a subsidiary); Code Sec. 351 (transfers to a controlled corporation); Code Sec. 354 (various tax-free reorganizations); Code Sec. 356 (reorganizations and spin-offs, etc., with boot); Code Sec. 361 (reorganizations); and Code Sec. 355 (spin-offs, split-offs and split-ups). (Code Sec. 367(a)(1), (c))[12]

When a U.S. person transfers intangibles to a foreign corporation in a Code Sec. 351 or 361 transaction, the transferor is treated as having sold the property for contingent payments, and recognizes income reflecting those payments over the life of the property. (Code Sec. 367(d))[13]

The Code Sec. 367(a) rule doesn't apply to:

---

8. ¶ F-15050; ¶ 3414.01.
9. ¶ F-15101; ¶ 3414.01.
10. ¶ F-15156; ¶ 3414.02.

11. ¶s F-15351 *et seq.*, F-15400 *et seq.*, F-15700 *et seq.*; ¶s 3414.03(a), 3414.03(b), 3414.03(c).

12. ¶ F-6000 *et seq.*; ¶ 3674.01.
13. ¶ F-6501 *et seq.*; ¶ 3674.03.

Footnote references beginning with letters are to paragraphs in RIA's Federal Tax Coordinator 2d and RIA's Analysis of Federal Taxes: Income. Footnote references beginning with numbers are to paragraphs in RIA's United States Tax Reporter.

■ *Transfers of stock or securities of a foreign corporation* which is a party to the exchange or the reorganization. (Code Sec. 367(a)(2)) Nor does it apply if the U.S. transferor agrees to recognize gain on the later disposition of stock by the foreign corporation.)Reg § 1.367(a)-3T(g)) And it does not apply if the U.S. transferor gets a limited interest in the transferee corporation. (Reg § 1.367(a)-3T(f)) Other transfers of both domestic and foreign stock are taxable, with some exceptions. (Reg § 1.367(a)-3T)[14]

■ *Transfers of property* (including stock) that will be used in the active conduct of a trade or business outside the U.S. (Code Sec. 367(a)(3)(A)) However, inventory and certain other types of property may not be transferred free of tax, even if they are used in the active conduct of a trade or business. (Code Sec. 367(a)(3)(B))[15]

The stock or securities of a foreign corporation exception and the active conduct of a foreign business exception only apply to reorganization exchanges subject to the nonrecognition provisions of Code Sec. 361 if five or fewer domestic corporations control the transferor and conditions prescribed in regs are met. (Code Sec. 367(a)(5))[16]

Special rules apply where the assets of a U.S. person's foreign branch are transferred to a foreign corporation. (Code Sec. 367(a)(3)(C))[17]

---

14. ¶ F-6201 *et seq.*; ¶ 3674.04.   16. ¶ F-6209; ¶s 3674.02,   17. ¶ F-6129 *et seq.*; ¶ 3674.02.
15. ¶ F-6101 *et seq.*; ¶ 3674.02.   3674.04.

Footnote references beginning with letters are to paragraphs in RIA's Federal Tax Coordinator 2d and RIA's Analysis of Federal Taxes: Income. Footnote references beginning with numbers are to paragraphs in RIA's United States Tax Reporter.

Chapter 17 Partnerships

¶ 3700 Partnerships

For tax purposes, a partnership is any unincorporated combination of legal persons who agree, formally or informally, to conduct a business jointly for their mutual profit and who actually conduct such a business.

¶ 3701 Partnership defined.

The term partnership includes a syndicate, group, pool, joint venture or other unincorporated organization through, or by means of which, any business, financial operation or venture is carried on if it is not, within the meaning of the Code, a corporation, trust or estate. (Code Sec. 761(a)) A partnership exists when two or more persons join in carrying on a trade or business, with each person contributing either money, property, labor or skill. The partnership agreement doesn't have to be written—it can be oral. (Code Sec. 761(c); Reg § 1.761-1(c))[1]

An organization may be treated as a partnership for tax purposes even though it isn't a partnership under local law, (Reg § 1.761-1(a)) or conversely, it may not be treated as a partnership for tax purposes even though it is one under local law. (Reg § 301.7701-1(b), (c))[2]

For when an entity which is a partnership under local law may be treated as a corporation for tax purposes, see ¶ 3304 *et seq.*

A joint undertaking merely to share expenses isn't a partnership. (Reg § 1.761-1(a))[3]

For tax years of a partnership, see ¶ 2813.

¶ 3702 Limited partnerships.

A limited partnership is a partnership with two classes of partners: general partners, who may participate in the management of the partnership's business and who have unlimited liability for the partnership's obligations; and limited partners, who may not participate in management, and whose liability is limited to the amount of their capital contribution.[4]

For treatment of certain publicly traded partnerships as corporations, see ¶ 3305.

For treatment of limited liability companies, see ¶ 3306.

¶ 3703 Family partnerships.

If capital is a material income-producing factor in the enterprise, a valid family partnership may be created by gift of a capital interest. (Code Sec. 704(e)(1))

The donee-partner's distributive share of partnership income is included in his or her gross income subject to two limitations:

■ The donee's share must be determined after allowance of reasonable compensation for services rendered to the partnership by the donor.

■ The donee's share attributable to donated capital mustn't be proportionately greater than the donor's share attributable to his capital. (Code Sec. 704(e)(2))

A capital interest purchased from a partner by the partner's spouse, ancestor, lineal descendant or any trust for the primary benefit of such persons, is considered to be a gift of the partnership interest by the seller to the buyer. (Code Sec. 704(e)(3))[5]

A donee or purchaser of a capital interest in a family partnership isn't recognized as a partner unless the transfer to him is bona fide. (Reg § 1.704-1(e)(1)(iii))[6]

A minor child generally won't be recognized as a partner unless either: (1) the child is

---

1. ¶ B-1001 *et seq.*; ¶ 7614.01.   3. ¶ B-1016; ¶ 77,014.24.   5. ¶ B-3402 *et seq.*; ¶ 7044.11.   6. ¶ B-3407; ¶ 7044.15.
2. ¶ B-1015; ¶ 77,014.01.   4. ¶ B-1033; ¶ 77,014.26.

Footnote references beginning with letters are to paragraphs in RIA's Federal Tax Coordinator 2d and RIA's Analysis of Federal Taxes: Income. Footnote references beginning with numbers are to paragraphs in RIA's United States Tax Reporter.

shown to be competent (despite legal disability under state law) to manage his or her own property, or (2) control of the child's interest is exercised by a fiduciary for the child's sole benefit, subject to any required judicial supervision. (Reg § 1.704-1(e)(2)(viii))[7]

¶ 3704 Personal service family partnerships.

If capital isn't a material income-producing factor, a family member is recognized as a partner only if he contributes substantial services.[8]

¶ 3705 Election to be excluded from partnership rules.

An election to be excluded from the partnership rules is available only if the income of each separate member of the partnership can be adequately determined without computation of partnership taxable income. (Code Sec. 761(a); Reg § 1.761-2(a)(1))[9] The election is available for:

■ "Investing partnerships" whose members own property as co-owners, reserve the right separately to dispose of their share of property, and aren't engaged in the active conduct of a business. (Reg § 1.761-2(a)(2))[10]

■ "Operating agreement groups" under which a number of co-owners engage in the joint production, extraction or use of property, but not for the purpose of selling services or property produced or extracted. (Reg § 1.761-2(a)(3))[11]

■ Syndications formed for a short period by dealers in securities to underwrite, sell or distribute an issue of securities. (Code Sec. 761(a)(3))[12]

¶ 3706 Partnerships v. other forms of doing business.

Partnerships are "pass-through entities"—that is, their income is subject to tax only once, at the partner level. They share this characteristic with S corporations, but not C corporations (whose income is taxed twice, at the corporate and again at the shareholder level). Partnerships, however, offer the following additional advantages over S corporations:

■ There are no limitations on who may be a partner, or on how many persons may be partners, unlike an S corporation, which is subject to limitations on who may be a shareholder and on how many shareholders the corporation may have (see ¶ 3360).

■ There is far greater flexibility in allocating the enterprise's profits, losses and credits (by means of special allocations, see ¶ 3735 *et seq.*) among partners of a partnership than among shareholders of an S corporation (see ¶ 3374).

■ A partner's basis in his partnership interest, unlike a shareholder's basis in S corporation shares, includes the partner's share of partnership liabilities (see ¶ 3755 *et seq.*)

¶ 3707 Organization and Syndication Fees

Fees paid to organize a partnership are not deductible, but may be amortized under certain circumstances. Fees paid to syndicate interests in a partnership are not deductible and may not be amortized.

No deduction is allowed to a partnership or to any partner for any amounts paid or incurred to organize a partnership or to promote the sale of, or to sell, an interest in that partnership, except as described below. (Code Sec. 709(a))[13]

The organization expenses may, at the partnership's election (use Form 4562, together with election statement as specified in the Regs), be amortized over not less than 60 months, starting the month the partnership begins business. Any unamortized expenses can be deducted as a loss if the partnership is liquidated before the end of the 60-month

---

7. ¶ B-3415; ¶ 7044.15.   9. ¶ B-1200 *et seq.*; ¶ 7614.02.   11. ¶ B-1208; ¶ 7614.02.   13. ¶ B-1301; ¶ 7094.
8. ¶ B-3426; ¶ 7044.13.   10. ¶ B-1207; ¶ 7614.02.   12. ¶ B-1209; ¶ 7614.02.

Footnote references beginning with letters are to paragraphs in RIA's Federal Tax Coordinator 2d and RIA's Analysis of Federal Taxes: Income. Footnote references beginning with numbers are to paragraphs in RIA's United States Tax Reporter.

period. (Code Sec. 709(b)(1))[14]

Syndication expenses are not amortizable and must be capitalized. Syndication expenses are expenses connected with the marketing of interests in the partnership. (Reg § 1.709-2(b)) Syndication expenses can't be deducted as a loss when the partnership is liquidated (Reg § 1.709-1(b)(2)) or the syndication effort is abandoned.[15]

¶ *3708* Treatment of Contributions to a Partnership ▬▬▬▬▬▬

Contributions from a partner to a partnership are generally tax-free.

¶ *3709* Contributions to a partnership.

Whether contributions to a partnership's capital are made on formation of the partnership or later, no gain or loss is ordinarily recognized. (Code Sec. 721; Reg § 1.721-1)[16] Depreciation or cost recovery recapture isn't triggered, (Code Sec. 1245(b)(3), (6), Code Sec. 1250(d)(3))[17] and investment credit isn't recaptured as long as the transfer is a mere change in the form of conducting the business of the contributing partner. (Reg § 1.47-3(f)(6), Ex (5))[18]

¶ *3710* Exchange fund partnerships.

Gain is recognized where a transfer of appreciated stocks, securities or other property is made to a partnership that would be treated as an investment company under Code Sec. 351 were the partnership a corporation. (Code Sec. 721(b)) The partnership is treated as an investment company if, after the exchange, over 80% of the value of its assets (excluding cash and nonconvertible debt) are held for investment and are readily marketable stocks or securities (or interests in REITs or in regulated investment companies).[19]

¶ *3711* Contribution of services.

Where a taxpayer receives a capital interest in a partnership in exchange for services, the interest is taxable compensation income. When the income must be recognized depends on the facts and circumstances, including whether there are any restrictions on taxpayer's right to withdraw from the partnership or otherwise dispose of the partnership interest. (Reg § 1.721-1(b)(1))[20]

Where a taxpayer receives a profits interest in a partnership in exchange for services, IRS will not treat the transaction as giving rise to compensation income, unless

... the profits interest relates to a substantially certain and predictable stream of income from partnership assets;

... the partner disposes of the profits interest within two years; or

... the profits interest is a limited partnership interest in a publicly traded partnership.[21]

¶ *3712* Contributed property that retains its character in partnership's hands.

When a partner contributes what was an unrealized receivable in his hands to a partnership, the partnership's gain or loss on disposition of the item will still be ordinary income or loss. (Code Sec. 724(a)) The same rule applies to contributed inventory, but in this case, ordinary income or loss will result only if the assets are disposed of by the partnership within five years of the contribution. (Code Sec. 724(b))[22]

If a partner contributes a capital asset with a basis higher than its fair market value, and the partnership disposes of it within five years of the contribution, the partnership's loss will be a capital loss to the extent of the basis/value variance upon contribution. (Code Sec. 724(c))[23]

---

14. ¶ B-1302; ¶ 7094.01.   17. ¶s I-10311, I-10503;   19. ¶ B-1409; ¶ 7214.02.   22. ¶ B-1412; ¶ 7244.
15. ¶ B-1308; ¶ 7094.04.   ¶ 7214.01.   20. ¶ B-1406 *et seq.*; ¶ 7214.01.   23. ¶ B-1413; ¶ 7244.
16. ¶ B-1401; ¶ 7214.   18. ¶ L-17418; ¶ 474.03.   21. ¶ B-1407; ¶ 7215.01.

Footnote references beginning with letters are to paragraphs in RIA's Federal Tax Coordinator 2d and RIA's Analysis of Federal Taxes: Income. Footnote references beginning with numbers are to paragraphs in RIA's United States Tax Reporter.

If any of the above property is disposed of by the partnership in a nontaxable disposition, the above rules apply to the substituted basis property that results. (Code Sec. 724(d)(3))[24]

¶ 3713 Partnership's basis in property contributed to it.

Property received by a partnership from a contributing partner takes the same basis in the partnership's hands as it had in the contributing partner's hands at the time of the contribution (increased by any gain recognized if the partnership is an "investment company partnership," see ¶ 3710). (Code Sec. 723; Reg § 1.723-1)[25]

¶ 3714 Partnership's holding period for contributed property.

A partnership's holding period for property contributed to it includes the contributing partner's holding period. (Code Sec. 1223(2); Reg § 1.723-1)[26]

¶ 3715 Income, gain, loss and deduction on contributed property (including sales and distributions).

If the basis of property contributed to a partnership by a partner is different from the property's fair market value at the time of contribution, then, under regs to be issued, the following rules apply:

(1) Income, gain, loss and deduction with respect to property which was contributed to the partnership after Mar. 31, '84 is to be shared among the partners so as to take into account that difference. (Code Sec. 704(c)(1)(A)) With respect to property contributed before Apr. 1, '84, a similar special allocation applies only if the partnership agreement so provides.[27]

(2) In the case of property which was contributed to a partnership after Oct. 3, '89, if the partnership distributes the property either directly or indirectly to a partner or partners other than the contributing partner within five years of the contribution, then the distributed property is treated as sold by the partnership for its fair market value at the time of the distribution, and the contributing partner must recognize any gain or loss from this constructive sale in an amount equal to the amount of gain or loss that would have been allocated to him under the rule in (1), above, if the property had actually been sold. (Code Sec. 704(c)(1)(B))[28]

(3) Where property is distributed to a partner, the partner will recognize as gain the lesser of (a) the excess of the fair market value of the property over the adjusted basis of the partner's interest in the partnership immediately before the distribution (reduced, but not below zero, by any money also received), or (b) the partner's net precontribution gain, i.e., the gain that would have been recognized by the distributee partner under the rules of (2), above, if all property held by the partnership immediately before the distribution that had been contributed to it by the distributee partner within five years of the distribution, was distributed to another partner. (Code Sec. 737(a), (b))[29] Distributions of property previously contributed by the distributee partner aren't taken into account for purposes of determining (a) and (b), above. (Code Sec. 737(d)(1))[30]

(4) Special rules apply if the partnership distributes to the contributing partner property that is of "like kind" to the contributed property (within the meaning of Code Sec. 1031, see ¶ 2417) to limit recognition of gain by the contributing partner. (Code Sec. 704(c)(2))[31]

¶ 3716 Basis of Partnership Interest ▰▰▰▰▰▰▰▰▰▰▰▰▰▰▰▰

A partner's basis for his interest in a partnership depends on how he acquired it.

---

24. ¶ B-1414; ¶ 7244.01.   26. ¶ B-1411; ¶ 7234.01.   28. ¶ B-3110; ¶ 7044.09.   30. ¶ B-3116.2.
25. ¶ B-1410; ¶ 7234.01.   27. ¶ B-3101; ¶ 7044.09.   29. ¶ B-3116.1.   31. ¶ B-3111 *et seq.*; ¶ 7044.09.

Footnote references beginning with letters are to paragraphs in RIA's Federal Tax Coordinator 2d and RIA's Analysis of Federal Taxes: Income. Footnote references beginning with numbers are to paragraphs in RIA's United States Tax Reporter.

It may consist of the amount of cash he contributed to the partnership, the adjusted basis of the property he contributed or the amount he paid to purchase it.

¶ 3717   Initial basis of partnership interest.

A partner's interest acquired by a tax-free contribution of money or property to the partnership has a basis equal to the amount of money plus the partner's adjusted basis for the property when contributed. (Code Sec. 722)[32] If the contributed property is subject to indebtedness or if liabilities of the partner are assumed by the partnership, the basis of the contributing partner's interest is reduced by the portion of the indebtedness assumed by the other partners. (Reg § 1.722-1)[33]

A partner's capital interest acquired for services has a basis equal to the value of the capital interest acquired. (Reg § 1.722-1)[34]

A partner's interest acquired by purchase or inheritance has a basis determined under the general basis rules, see ¶ 2458 *et seq.* (Code Sec. 742; Reg § 1.742-1)[35]

¶ 3718   Adjustments to basis of partner's interest.

The basis of a partner's interest is increased:

■ by further contributions (but not by his own personal note given to the partnership);[36]

■ by the cost of additional interests purchased or inherited, see ¶ 3717; (Code Sec. 742)

■ by any increase in his share of partnership liabilities since the increase is treated as a contribution of money to the partnership, see ¶ 3756;[37]

■ by his distributive share of partnership income, including tax-exempt income and any excess of net long-term capital gains over losses; (Code Sec. 705(a)(1))

■ by his distributive share of the excess of percentage depletion deductions over the basis of the depletable property. (Code Sec. 705(a)(1))[38]

The basis of a partner's interest is reduced (but not below zero) by:

■ the adjusted basis allocable to any part of his interest sold or otherwise transferred;

■ the amount of money and the adjusted basis of partnership property distributed to him in nonliquidating distributions; (Code Sec. 705(a)(2), Code Sec. 733)[39]

■ by any decrease in his share of partnership liabilities since the decrease is treated as a distribution of money by the partnership, see ¶ 3756;

■ his distributive share of partnership losses (including capital losses) *and* nondeductible expenditures not chargeable to the capital account (Code Sec. 705(a); Reg § 1.705-1(a)) (for the partner's distributive share of losses in excess of his adjusted basis, see ¶ 3739);

■ his percentage depletion deduction for partnership oil and gas property to the extent the deduction doesn't exceed his allocated proportionate share of the property's basis. (Code Sec. 705(a)(3))[40]

¶ 3719   Alternative adjusted basis computation.

The adjusted basis of a partner's interest may be determined under a "short-cut" method by reference to what would be his proportionate share of the adjusted basis of the partnership property upon a termination of the partnership (Code Sec. 705(b)) where: (1) it isn't practicable to use the regular rule, or (2) IRS is satisfied the result under the alternative method won't vary substantially from that under the regular rule. (Reg § 1.705-1(b))[41]

---

32. ¶ B-1502; ¶ 7224.01.   35. ¶ B-1501.   38. ¶ B-1507; ¶ 7054.01.   40. ¶ B-1507; ¶ 7054.02.
33. ¶ B-1506; ¶ 7224.01.   36. ¶ B-1504; ¶ 7054.01.   39. ¶ B-1505; ¶ 7334.01.   41. ¶ B-1513; ¶ 7054.04.
34. ¶ B-1502; ¶ 7224.01.   37. ¶ B-1506; ¶ 7524.

Footnote references beginning with letters are to paragraphs in RIA's Federal Tax Coordinator 2d and RIA's Analysis of Federal
Taxes: Income. Footnote references beginning with numbers are to paragraphs in RIA's United States Tax Reporter.

¶ 3720 Partnership Income and Deductions ▬▬▬▬▬▬▬▬▬▬▬▬▬▬▬▬▬▬▬

A partnership is essentially a conduit which passes through to each partner his share of income and deductions generated by the partnership.

¶ 3721 Partners taxed on partnership income.

The partners, not the partnership, are taxed on the partnership's income. (Code Sec. 701) The partnership only files an information return (Form 1065, see ¶ 4730) showing each partner's distributive share of the partnership income, gains, losses, etc. Each partner includes his share of these items on his own return. (Code Sec. 702)[42]

¶ 3722 Partnership taxable income.

Partnership taxable income is computed the same as an individual's except the following deductions aren't allowed:

- standard deduction; (Code Sec. 63(c)(6)(E))
- personal exemptions;
- charitable contributions;
- nonbusiness expenses, medical expenses, alimony, retirement savings under Code Sec. 219 and taxes and interest paid to cooperative housing corporations;
- capital loss carryovers;
- net operating loss deduction;
- taxes paid to a foreign country or U.S. possession that can be taken as a credit or as a deduction (income and similar taxes);
- oil and gas well depletion. (Code Sec. 703(a)(2); Reg § 1.703-1(a)(2))[43]

¶ 3723 "Separately stated" items of income and deductions.

Partnerships are required to "state separately"—that is, to compute as separate items—certain classes of income and deductions. These are then directly "passed through" to the partnership's partners, who take them into account for tax purposes by including their distributive share of each of the classes as separate items on their tax returns. (Code Sec. 702(a))

Key items that must be separately stated are:

- charitable contributions;
- dividends;
- foreign and U.S. possessions taxes eligible for foreign tax credit;
- income, gains and losses from the sale or exchange of unrealized receivables and substantially appreciated inventory;
- income, gain, loss, deduction or credit items that are specially allocated under the partnership agreement;
- intangible drilling and development expenses;
- long-term capital gains and losses;
- mining explorations expenditures;
- nonbusiness production of income expenses;
- recoveries of bad debts, prior taxes and delinquency amounts;
- Code Sec. 1231 gains and losses;

---

42. ¶ B-1900 *et seq.*; ¶ 7014.   43. ¶ B-1901; ¶ 7034.01.

Footnote references beginning with letters are to paragraphs in RIA's Federal Tax Coordinator 2d and RIA's Analysis of Federal Taxes: Income. Footnote references beginning with numbers are to paragraphs in RIA's United States Tax Reporter.

- short-term capital gains and losses;
- soil and water conservation expenses.

Partnerships must also separately state—and partners must separately take into account their distributive share of—any partnership item, if separately stating that item would result in a tax liability for any partner different from that partner's tax liability if the item were not separately stated. (Reg § 1.702-1(a)(8)(ii))[44]

¶ 3724 Items not required to be separately stated.

After determining which of its items of income, gains, losses, deductions and credits must be separately stated, a partnership computes its taxable income or loss based on items that do not have to be separately stated. The partnership's partners, in computing their income tax liabilities, take into account their distributive shares of the partnership's nonseparately stated income or loss, as well as their distributive shares of each separately stated item. (Code Sec. 702(a)(8); Reg § 1.702-1(a)(9))[45]

¶ 3725 Character of partnership income.

Each item passed through to the partners and separately stated on their returns has the same character as if realized or incurred directly by the partnership. (Code Sec. 702(b); Reg § 1.702-1(b))[46]

¶ 3726 Consistent treatment on partner's and partnership's return.

A partner must, on his own return, treat a partnership item in a manner that is consistent with the treatment of that item on the partnership's return. (Code Sec. 6222(a)) A partner that treats a partnership item differently must notify IRS of the inconsistency on Form 8082. (Code Sec. 6222(b))[47]

The above consistency rule doesn't apply to certain small partnerships that aren't covered by the unified audit and review procedures for partnerships (¶ 4838). (Code Sec. 6231(a)(1)(B))[48]

¶ 3727 When partnership income is reported by the partners.

Each partner reports his distributive share of the partnership income, deductions and other items (including guaranteed salary and interest payments) for a partnership tax year on his individual return for his tax year within or with which that partnership tax year (discussed at ¶ 2813) ends. (Code Sec. 706(a); Reg § 1.706-1(a))[49]

▶ *illustration:* B, a calendar year individual, owns a one-third interest in ABC partnership which has a July 1 through June 30 fiscal year. From July 1 of last year to June 30 of this year, ABC has income of $60,000. B reports his $20,000 share on his return for this year, whether or not funds are distributed to him. Had an advance cash distribution of $10,000 been made to him in December of last year, he would still report his full $20,000 share on this year's return.

If two partnership tax years end within a partner's individual tax year, he must report in that year his share of the partnership income for both partnership years.[50]

¶ 3728 Elections.

Elections affecting partnership taxable income must be made by the partnership *except* for any election under the following, which must be made by each partner for himself:

- Code Sec. 108(b)(5) relating to election to apply reduction in basis (when debt discharge income is excluded from gross income) to depreciable property. (Code Sec. 703(b)(1))

---

44. ¶ B-1903; ¶ 7024.02.   46. ¶ B-1905; ¶ 7024.01.   48. ¶ B-1800; ¶ 62,214.   50. ¶ B-1701; ¶ 7064.
45. ¶ B-1904; ¶ 7024.02.   47. ¶ B-1801; ¶ 62,214.   49. ¶ B-1701; ¶ 7024.01.

Footnote references beginning with letters are to paragraphs in RIA's Federal Tax Coordinator 2d and RIA's Analysis of Federal Taxes: Income. Footnote references beginning with numbers are to paragraphs in RIA's United States Tax Reporter.

- Code Sec. 108(c)(3) relating to election to treat discharged indebtedness as qualified real property business indebtedness. (Code Sec. 703(b)(1))

- Code Sec. 901 for claiming a credit instead of a deduction for foreign and U.S. possessions income and similar taxes. (Code Sec. 703(b)(3))

- Code Sec. 617 dealing with mineral exploration expenditures. (Code Sec. 703(b)(2))

- Code Secs. 871(d)(1) and 882(d)(1) allowing nonresident alien individuals and foreign corporations to treat income from U.S. real property as effectively connected with a U.S. trade or business. (Reg § 1.703-1(b)(2))[1]

¶ 3729 Partner's Dealings with Partnership

Partners may deal with their partnerships in other than their capacity as partners. "Guaranteed payments" to partners are generally treated as made to nonpartners. Certain sales between partners and their partnerships establish the character of any gain, and require the deferral of loss.

¶ 3730 "Separate entity" transactions between partner and partnership.

If a partner provides services for or transfers property to his partnership, he may be treated as dealing with the partnership either as a member or as an outsider. If there is a related allocation and distribution of partnership income (direct or indirect), and the transaction on the whole is properly characterized as a sale or exchange between a partnership and an outsider, it will be treated in that way. (Code Sec. 707(a)(2)(A), (B))[2]

¶ 3731 Guaranteed payments.

Guaranteed payments are payments to a partner for services or capital *without regard to partnership income.*[3] Guaranteed payments for a partner's services or capital are treated like salary payments to employees or interest payments to creditors, not like partnership distributions. (Code Sec. 707(c); Reg § 1.707-1(c))[4]

For a guaranteed payment to be deductible as a business expense by the partnership, it must meet the business expense tests as if the payment had been made to a person who was not a member of the partnership. (Code Sec. 707(c))[5] In determining whether a partnership can deduct or must capitalize a guaranteed payment, the regular capital expenditure rules apply. (Code Sec. 707(c))[6]

¶ 3732 Losses on sales and exchanges with controlled partnership.

No deduction is allowed for losses from sales or exchanges between:

- a partnership and a person owning, directly or indirectly, over 50% of the capital interest, or profits interest, in the partnership; or

- two partnerships in which the same persons own over 50% of the capital or profits interests.

When property on which a loss was disallowed under the above rule is later sold by the transferee at a gain, the gain is taxable only to the extent that it exceeds the loss previously disallowed. (Code Sec. 707(b)(1); Reg § 1.707-1(b)(1))[7]

¶ 3733 Gain on sale or exchange with controlled partnership.

The character of the property in the hands of the transferee, immediately after the transfer, determines the character of a *gain to the transferor* on a direct or indirect sale or exchange of property between:

---

1. ¶ B-1907; ¶ 7034.02.   3. ¶ B-2005; ¶ 7074.02.   5. ¶ B-2005; ¶ 7074.02.   7. ¶ B-2016; ¶ 7074.01.
2. ¶ B-2000 *et seq.*; ¶ 7074.01.   4. ¶ B-2006 *et seq.*; ¶ 7074.02.   6. ¶ B-2009; ¶ 7074.02.

Footnote references beginning with letters are to paragraphs in RIA's Federal Tax Coordinator 2d and RIA's Analysis of Federal Taxes: Income. Footnote references beginning with numbers are to paragraphs in RIA's United States Tax Reporter.

■ a partnership and a person owning, directly or indirectly, over 50% of the capital interest, or profits interest, in the partnership; or

■ two partnerships in which the same persons own, directly or indirectly, more than 50% of the capital interest or profits interest in each. (Code Sec. 707(b)(2); Reg § 1.707-1(b)(2))[8]

¶ 3734 Constructive ownership of partnership interests.

In determining the percentage of ownership of partnership interests for purposes of ¶s 3732 and 3733, the constructive ownership rules for stock under Code Sec. 267(c) (see ¶ 2450) apply (substituting "capital or profits interest" for "stock"), except that a partner isn't considered as owning the interest of his partners (unless they are relatives, etc.). (Code Sec. 707(b)(3))[9]

¶ 3735 Partnership Allocations

A partner's distributive share of income, gain, loss, deduction or credit is controlled by the partnership agreement, unless there is no partnership agreement or the allocation in the agreement has no substantial economic effect; then the allocation is made in accordance with the partner's interest in the partnership.

¶ 3736 Allocation rules.

A partnership's allocations (the partners' distributive shares) of partnership income, gains, losses, deductions and credits are normally determined by the partnership agreement. (Code Sec. 704(a)) If, however, the partnership agreement fails to make such allocations, they must be determined in accord with the partners' interests in the partnership. (Code Sec. 704(b)(1)) If the partnership agreement does make allocations of partnership items, these will be respected for tax purposes if:

■ they have substantial economic effect (see ¶ 3737); or

■ they are in accord with the partners' interests in the partnership; or

■ they are treated as being in accord with the partners' interests in the partnership. (Code Sec. 704(b); Reg § 1.704-1(b)(1))[10]

Special rules govern the determination of partners' distributive shares of certain partnership items: tax preferences associated with pre-'87 cost recovery property;[11] income, gains, losses, etc., with respect to property whose book value differs from its adjusted basis;[12] tax credits and credit recapture amounts;[13] "excess percentage depletion";[14] the basis of partnership oil and gas properties;[15] recapture income under Code Secs. 1245 and 1250;[16] and allocations attributable to the partnership's nonrecourse debt.[17]

Retroactive allocations—that is, allocations that give particular partners shares of partnership items of income, expense, etc., that were paid or accrued before these partners joined the partnership—are not permitted. (Code Sec. 706(d)(1))[18]

¶ 3737 Determining whether an allocation has substantial economic effect.

An allocation of partnership income, gain, loss, deduction or credit among partners has substantial economic effect if it passes a two-part test applied as of the end of the partnership year to which the allocation relates.

First, the allocation must have economic effect. (Reg § 1.704-1(b)(2)(i)) This means that it must be consistent with the underlying economic arrangement of the partners. An allocation will be treated as having economic effect only if throughout the full term of the partnership, the partnership agreement states:

8. ¶ B-2017; ¶ 7074.01.
9. ¶ B-2018; ¶ 7074.01.
10. ¶ B-2401; ¶ 7044 *et seq.*
11. ¶ B-2901.
12. ¶ B-2902; ¶ 7044.07.
13. ¶ B-2903; ¶ 7044.07.
14. ¶ B-2904; ¶ 7044.07.
15. ¶ B-2905; ¶ 7044.07.
16. ¶ B-2906 *et seq.*; ¶ 7044.07.
17. ¶ B-3001 *et seq.*; ¶ 7044.08.
18. ¶ B-3200 *et seq.*

Footnote references beginning with letters are to paragraphs in RIA's Federal Tax Coordinator 2d and RIA's Analysis of Federal Taxes: Income. Footnote references beginning with numbers are to paragraphs in RIA's United States Tax Reporter.

(1) the partners' capital accounts are to be determined and maintained according to rules set forth in the regs;

(2) when the partnership liquidates, or a partner's interest is liquidated, liquidating distributions must be made according to the partners' positive capital account balances; and

(3) a partner with a deficit balance in his capital account after the liquidation, of his partnership interest is unconditionally obligated to restore the amount of the deficit to the partnership. (Reg § 1.704-1(b)(2)(ii))[19]

Second, the economic effect of the allocation must be substantial. (Reg § 1.704-1(b)(2)(i)) The economic effect of an allocation is substantial if there is a reasonable possibility that it will affect substantially the dollar amounts to be received by the partners from the partnership, independent of the tax consequences. (Reg § 1.704-1(b)(2)(iii))[20]

✓observation: Generally speaking, the "economic effect" test is designed to ensure that partnership allocations of income and gain ultimately correspond to real distributions of money and property, and that allocations of deductions, losses and credits ultimately correspond to the partners' actual liabilities for partnership expenses and losses. The "substantiality" test is designed to ensure that the economic effects of an allocation do not arise principally from the tax character of the allocated item—for example, from the fact that an income item is tax-exempt or foreign-sourced, or that a loss is from the sale of partnership property used in its trade or business.

¶ 3738 Limitations on a Partner's Deductible Loss

A partner's deduction for partnership losses may not exceed the basis of his interest in the partnership. However, partners (although not partnerships) are allowed loss carrybacks and carryovers.

¶ 3739 Limitation on partner's share of partnership loss.

A partner can deduct his distributive share of partnership *losses* only up to the amount of the adjusted basis of his interest in the partnership (¶ 3716 *et seq.*) at the end of the partnership's loss year. (Code Sec. 704(d))

Where a partnership has more than one class of losses (e.g., capital losses, Code Sec. 1231 losses and operating losses) in the same year and a partner's total share of those losses exceeds the adjusted basis of his partnership interest, the limitation is allocated proportionately to each type of loss. (Reg § 1.704-1(d))

Excess losses disallowed to a partner in any year are carried over, and are deductible by him at the end of the partnership year in which the adjusted basis of the partner's interest at the end of the year exceeds zero (before reduction by that year's loss). (Reg § 1.704-1(d)(4))[21]

¶ 3740 Basis adjustments made before applying loss limitations.

In determining whether a partner's deductible share of partnership loss exceeds (and is thus limited by) his basis in his partnership interest (¶ 3739), the basis adjustments described at ¶ 3718 are made first. (Reg § 1.704-1(d)(2))[22]

¶ 3741 Loss carrybacks and carryovers.

A carryover or carryback of net operating losses is not allowed to a partnership but a partner may carryback or carryover his share of the partnership's net business loss for any year to the extent it can't be used by that partner in the year it is passed through to

---

19. ¶ B-2502; ¶ 7044.03.   20. ¶ B-2700 *et seq.*; ¶ 7044.02.   21. ¶ B-3500 *et seq.*; ¶ 7044.10.   22. ¶ B-3501; ¶ 7044.10.

Footnote references beginning with letters are to paragraphs in RIA's Federal Tax Coordinator 2d and RIA's Analysis of Federal Taxes: Income. Footnote references beginning with numbers are to paragraphs in RIA's United States Tax Reporter.

him. (Code Sec. 702)[23]

¶ 3742 Distributions to a Partner

A partnership generally doesn't recognize gain or loss on a distribution to a partner, but the partner often will recognize gain or loss.

¶ 3743 Partnership's gain or loss on distribution.

No gain or loss is recognized to a partnership on a distribution to a partner of money or other property, except where a disproportionate distribution is treated as a sale by the partnership, see ¶ 3750. (Code Sec. 731(b)) This rule applies generally to both current and liquidating distributions.[24]

¶ 3744 Partner's gain or loss on receipt of distribution.

Gain or loss isn't recognized to a partner on receipt of a current or liquidating distribution from a partnership, except as follows:

■ Gain is recognized to the extent that *money*distributed exceeds the adjusted basis of the partner's interest in the partnership immediately before the distribution. (Code Sec. 731(a))[25] This is treated as a gain from sale or exchange of the partner's interest. (Reg § 1.731-1(a)(3))[26] A reduction in a partner's liabilities (due either to the partnership's assumption of them or a reduction in the partner's share of partnership liabilities) is treated as a money distribution. (Code Sec. 752(b))[27]

■ Loss is recognized to the extent the adjusted basis of the partner's interest exceeds the sum of any money, and the basis to the distributee of any unrealized receivables and inventories received if the distribution is in liquidation of the partner's interest in the partnership *and* no other property is distributed. This is treated as a loss from sale or exchange of the partner's interest in the partnership. (Code Sec. 731(a))[28]

If gain or loss is recognized under one of the above rules, the partnership may elect to, or may have to, adjust the basis of its assets, as explained at ¶ 3764 *et seq.*

recommendation: As noted above, the tax treatment of a money distribution by a partnership to a partner is determined by the basis of the recipient partner in his partnership interest. Consequently, before making such a distribution, the partnership and the partner should determine the partner's basis in his partnership interest as precisely as possible. Where the partner wishes to receive the distribution tax-free, the amount of the distribution should not exceed the partner's basis in his partnership interest. The partner and the partnership should also consider the impact of a current cash distribution on the ability of the partner to deduct losses in the future. Even if the current distribution is received tax-free, the partner's basis in his partnership interest is reduced by the amount of the distribution—and a partner may deduct his share of partnership losses only to the extent of his basis in his partnership interest (see ¶ 3738 *et seq.*). Given these rules, if a partnership anticipates losses in a particular taxable year, it may be prudent to defer making any cash distributions until after the end of that tax year.

The above rules on recognition of a partner's gains and losses don't apply (Code Sec. 731(c); Reg § 1.731-1(c)) to:[29]

■ disproportionate distributions treated as sales or exchanges of property, see ¶ 3750;

■ liquidation payments made to a retiring partner or to a deceased partner's successor in interest treated as a share of income or as guaranteed payments, see ¶ 3771;

■ recognition of precontribution gain under Code Sec. 737, see ¶ 3715.

---

23. ¶ B-3507; ¶ 7024.01.   25. ¶ B-3602; ¶ 7314.01.   27. ¶ B-3605; ¶ 7524.01.   29. ¶ B-3604; ¶ 7314.01.
24. ¶ B-3601; ¶ 7314.01.   26. ¶ B-3610; ¶ 7314.01.   28. ¶ B-3603; ¶ 7314.01.

Footnote references beginning with letters are to paragraphs in RIA's Federal Tax Coordinator 2d and RIA's Analysis of Federal Taxes: Income. Footnote references beginning with numbers are to paragraphs in RIA's United States Tax Reporter.

¶3745 Partner's holding period.

A partner's holding period for property distributed to him in kind includes the period that the partnership held the property. (Code Sec. 735(b)) If it was contributed to the partnership by a partner, the recipient partner's holding period also includes the period that the property was held by the contributing partner before contribution. (Reg § 1.735-1(b))[30]

¶3746 Partner's basis for property received in nonliquidating distributions.

The basis to a partner of property distributed to him, in kind, other than in liquidation of his partnership interest, is the same as the property's adjusted basis to the partnership immediately before the distribution. But the basis of the property to the partner may not exceed the adjusted basis of his interest in the partnership reduced by any money distributed to him in the same transaction. (Code Sec. 732(a); Reg § 1.732-1(a))[31]

¶3747 Partner's basis for property distributed in liquidation.

A partner's basis for property distributed in liquidation of his partnership interest is the same as the adjusted basis for his partnership interest reduced by any money distributed to him in the same transaction. (Code Sec. 732(b); Reg § 1.732-1(b))[32]

¶3748 Allocation of basis to distributed property when limited by basis of partner's interest.

In a liquidating distribution, or in a nonliquidating distribution of property for which the partnership's basis exceeds the basis of the partner's interest in the partnership, the total basis to the partner of the property distributed to him is the same as the adjusted basis of his partnership interest reduced by any cash distributed to him in the same transaction (¶s 3746, 3747). This total basis is allocated as follows:

(1) To any unrealized receivables and inventory items in an amount equal to the partnership's adjusted basis in each such asset. However, if the total basis to be allocated is less than the sum of the partnership's adjusted basis of such assets, the total basis is allocated in proportion to the partnership's adjusted basis for the assets. (Reg § 1.732-1(c))

(2) Any balance of the total basis to be allocated is assigned to any other distributed assets in proportion to their adjusted basis to the partnership. (Code Sec. 732(c))[33]

¶3749 Disproportionate Distributions ▬▬▬▬▬▬▬▬▬▬▬▬▬▬▬▬

Disproportionate distributions of partnership property that includes "unrealized receivables" and "substantially appreciated inventory" may trigger ordinary income, gain or loss to both the partnership and its partners. Unrealized receivables and substantially appreciated inventory are sometimes informally referred to as "hot assets."

¶3750 Disproportionate distributions defined.

A disproportionate distribution of partnership assets to a partner is treated as a sale or exchange that may result in recognition of gain or loss to the partner and the partnership. The rule applies to all distributions, both liquidating and nonliquidating except for:

■ a distribution of contributed property to the same partner who contributed it;

■ liquidation payments to a retiring or deceased partner that are treated as ordinary income under the rules at ¶3771. (Code Sec. 751(b))[34]

---

30. ¶ B-3705; ¶ 7354.02.   32. ¶ B-3702; ¶ 7324.01.   33. ¶ B-3703; ¶ 7324.01.   34. ¶ B-3906; ¶ 7514.01.
31. ¶ B-3701; ¶ 7324.01.

Footnote references beginning with letters are to paragraphs in RIA's Federal Tax Coordinator 2d and RIA's Analysis of Federal Taxes: Income. Footnote references beginning with numbers are to paragraphs in RIA's United States Tax Reporter.

A distribution is "disproportionate" if a partner receives more than his proportionate share of partnership property in the first of the following categories and less than his proportionate share of property in the second category, or vice versa:

■ "hot assets"—that is, unrealized receivables (including recapturable deductions, certain transfers of franchises, trademarks or trade names) and substantially appreciated inventory items, see ¶ 3751 *et seq.*;

■ other property (including money).[35]

In such a case, a partner, in effect, sells or exchanges part or all of his share in property of one category for property of the other category (see ¶ 3753). The general rules on partnership distributions apply to the balance of the distribution not treated as a sale or exchange. (Reg § 1.751-1(b))[36]

The partners may agree as to which particular assets in one category shall be considered to have been sold or exchanged for particular assets in the other category. Absent such an agreement, a proportionate part of each asset relinquished in one category will be considered to have been sold or exchanged for excess assets received in the other category. (Reg § 1.751-1(g))[37]

¶ 3751 "Unrealized receivables."

Unrealized receivables include any contractual or other rights to payment for:

■ goods delivered, or to be delivered, to the extent the proceeds would be treated as amounts received from sale or exchange of noncapital assets;

■ services rendered, or to be rendered.

Such receivables are included only to the extent not previously includible in income under the method of accounting used by the partnership. (Code Sec. 751(c))[38]

Unrealized receivables also include (other than for payments to retiring partners or deceased partners under Code Sec. 736, see ¶ 3771): (Code Sec. 751(c))

■ depreciation recapturable under Code Secs. 1245 and 1250;

■ mine exploration deductions recapturable under Code Sec. 617;

■ soil and water conservation and (pre-'86) land clearing cost deductions recapturable under Code Sec. 1252;

■ recapturable deductions for oil, gas or certain geothermal well intangible costs under Code Sec. 1254;[39]

■ DISC stock;

■ stock in certain foreign corporations as described in Code Sec. 1248 (¶ 4638);[40]

■ market discount bonds, to the extent they would give rise to ordinary income if sold by the partnership (¶ 1329);

■ short term obligations as defined in Code Sec. 1283 acquired after July 18, '84 (¶ 1332);[41]

■ franchises, trademarks or trade names whose transfer is treated as a sale of a noncapital asset under Code Sec. 1253.[42]

¶ 3752 "Inventory items."

Inventory items include property properly includible in inventory and property held primarily for sale to customers in the ordinary course of business, (Code Sec. 751(d)(2)(A)) and also:

■ any other property that would produce ordinary income on sale or exchange by the

---

35. ¶ B-3905; ¶ 7514.02.   37. ¶ B-3901 *et seq.*   39. ¶ B-3916; ¶ 7514.02.   41. ¶ B-3918; ¶ 7514.02.
36. ¶ B-3910 *et seq.*; ¶ 7514.01.   38. ¶ B-3914; ¶ 7514.02.   40. ¶ B-3919; ¶ 7514.02.   42. ¶ B-3920; ¶ 7514.02.

Footnote references beginning with letters are to paragraphs in RIA's Federal Tax Coordinator 2d and RIA's Analysis of Federal Taxes: Income. Footnote references beginning with numbers are to paragraphs in RIA's United States Tax Reporter.

partnership, (Code Sec. 751(d)(2)(B)) including accounts receivable for goods or services and unrealized receivables as described at ¶ 3751; (Reg § 1.751-1(d)(2)(ii))

■ property that would result in a gain under Code Sec. 1246(a), on foreign investment company stock; (Code Sec. 751(d)(2)(C))

■ any other property held by the partnership that would be inventory items, as defined above, if held by the selling or distributee-partner. (Code Sec. 751(d)(2)(D)) However, this rule doesn't apply to property actually distributed to a partner. (Reg § 1.751-1(d)(2)(iii))[43]

Inventory items are "substantially appreciated" in value if the fair market value of *all* such items (including unrealized receivables) exceeds 120% of their adjusted basis to the partnership. (Code Sec. 751(d)(1)(A)) The 120% limit is computed by excluding any item acquired principally to avoid meeting it. (Code Sec. 751(d)(1)(B))

If the substantial appreciation test is met on the basis of all the inventory items, a distribution of any inventory item is a distribution of substantially appreciated inventory even though the particular item may not have appreciated at all. If the test isn't met on the basis of all the inventory items, no distribution of inventory items is a distribution of substantially appreciated inventory items. (Reg § 1.751-1(d)(1))[44]

For sales, exchanges or distributions before May 1, '93, inventory was substantially appreciated only if the fair market value of all such items exceeded (i) 120% of their adjusted basis to the partnership, and (ii) 10% of the fair market value of all of the partnership's noncash property. Also, the rule which disregards items acquired with a principal purpose of avoiding the 120% test did not apply.[45]

¶ 3753 Gain or loss on disproportionate distribution.

If a distributee-partner receives *more* than his share of unrealized receivables and substantially appreciated inventory items and *less* than his share of other property (including money), he is considered to have sold or exchanged the portion of his share of the other property that he relinquished for the excess unrealized receivables and substantially appreciated inventory items he received. (Reg § 1.751-1(b)(2)(i), (iii))

The partnership (as constituted after the distribution) is considered to have sold or exchanged the excess other property distributed to the partner for the unrealized receivables and substantially appreciated inventory items he relinquished. (Reg § 1.751-1(b)(2)(i), (ii))[46]

Rules analogous to those described above apply where the distributee partner receives a disproportionate distribution of *less* than his share of unrealized receivables and substantially appreciated inventory items and *more* than his share of other property (including money). (Reg § 1.751-1(b)(3))[47]

¶ 3754 Disposition of unrealized receivables and inventory by a distributee-partner.

Gain or loss on disposition of unrealized receivables and inventory by a distributee-partner is:

■ in the case of *unrealized receivables*, ordinary gain or loss; (Code Sec. 735(a)(1))

■ in the case of *inventory items* (whether or not substantially appreciated) sold or exchanged within five years from the date of the distribution, ordinary gain or loss. (Code Sec. 735(a)(2)) If disposed of after five years from the date of distribution, the character of the gain or loss depends upon the character of the item in the partner's hands on the date of disposition. (Reg § 1.735-1(a)(2))[48]

---

43. ¶ B-3921; ¶ 7514.02.   45. ¶ B-3922.   47. ¶ B-3911.   48. ¶ B-3704; ¶ 7354.01.
44. ¶ B-3922; ¶ 7514.02.   46. ¶ B-3910; ¶ 7514.01.

Footnote references beginning with letters are to paragraphs in RIA's Federal Tax Coordinator 2d and RIA's Analysis of Federal Taxes: Income. Footnote references beginning with numbers are to paragraphs in RIA's United States Tax Reporter.

¶ 3755 Liabilities of Partnerships and Partners ▰▰▰▰▰▰

Changes in partners' shares of partnership liabilities are treated as contributions to, or distributions by, the partnership. Partners' shares of partnership liabilities depend on whether the liability is recourse or nonrecourse.

¶ 3756 Partnership liabilities.

If a partner's share of the partnership liabilities increases, or if he assumes any partnership liabilities, it is treated as a contribution of money from the partner to the partnership. (Code Sec. 752(a); Reg § 1.752-1(b))[49]

If a partner's share of the partnership liabilities decreases, or if the partnership assumes any of his liabilities, it is treated as a distribution of money to the partner. (Code Sec. 752(b); Reg § 1.752-1(c))[50]

An unassumed liability to which property is subject is considered a liability of the owner of the property (e.g., the partnership) to the extent of its fair market value. (Code Sec. 752(c))[1]

¶ 3757 Share of recourse liabilities.

A partnership debt is a recourse liability to the extent that any partner bears the economic risk of loss for the liability. A partner's share of a recourse liability is the part of the economic risk of loss for the liability the partner bears. (Reg § 1.752-1(a)(1))[2]

Generally, a partner bears the economic risk of loss for a partnership liability to the extent that he (or a related person) would be obligated to pay the creditor or contribute to the partnership (and wouldn't be entitled to reimbursement) in case of a constructive liquidation. (Reg § 1.752-2(b)(1))[3]

¶ 3758 Share of nonrecourse liabilities.

If no partner bears the economic risk of loss for a partnership liability (such as an unassumed mortgage), the liability is nonrecourse. (Reg § 1.752-1(a)(2)) Nonrecourse liabilities of a partnership are first allocated among all the partners to reflect their shares of:

■ "partnership minimum gain" (gain on the disposition of property subject to a nonrecourse liability that exceeds its adjusted basis); and

■ the gain that would be allocated to the partners under Code Sec. 704(c), or under similar principles in connection with a revaluation of partnership property, if, in a taxable transaction, the partnership disposed of all property subject to a nonrecourse liability in satisfaction of those liabilities and for no other consideration.

Any excess is allocated among the partners in proportion to their interests in partnership profits. The partnership agreement may specify the partners' profit interests as long as those interests are reasonably consistent with allocations (which have substantial economic effect) of some significant item of partnership income or gain among the partners. Alternatively, the excess may be allocated in accordance with the manner in which it is expected that the deductions attributable to the nonrecourse debt would be allocated. (Reg § 1.752-3(a))[4]

¶ 3759 Transfer and Liquidation of Partnership Interest ▰▰▰▰▰▰

The transfer or liquidation of a partnership interest, while generally resulting in capital gain or loss, is subject to special rules that may turn part of the gain or

---

49. ¶ B-1601; ¶ 7524.01.   1. ¶ B-1608; ¶ 7524.01.   3. ¶ B-1610 et seq.; ¶ 7524.03.   4. ¶ B-1627; ¶ 7524.03.
50. ¶ B-1602; ¶ 7524.01.   2. ¶ B-1612 et seq.; ¶ 7524.03.

Footnote references beginning with letters are to paragraphs in RIA's Federal Tax Coordinator 2d and RIA's Analysis of Federal Taxes: Income. Footnote references beginning with numbers are to paragraphs in RIA's United States Tax Reporter.

loss from capital to ordinary.

¶ 3760 Sale or exchange of partnership interest.

If a partner sells or exchanges all or a part of his interest in the partnership, gain or loss is capital gain or loss except to the extent attributable to unrealized receivables and substantially appreciated inventory (¶ 3751 *et seq.*). (Code Sec. 741, Code Sec. 751(a), (c))[5]

The capital gain or loss is the difference between:

■ the amount realized *reduced* by the portion attributable to unrealized receivables and substantially appreciated inventory items; *and*

■ the transferor-partner's adjusted basis for the partnership interest transferred *reduced* by the portion attributable to unrealized receivables and substantially appreciated inventory items. (Reg § 1.741-1(a))[6]

¶ 3761 Ordinary gain or loss.

If the partnership has unrealized receivables or substantially appreciated inventory, then the transferor-partner's ordinary gain or loss is the difference between the amount realized for his partnership interest attributable to those items and the portion of the basis of his partnership interest attributable to those items. (Code Sec. 751(a); Reg § 1.751-1(a))[7]

The transferor-partner's basis for unrealized receivables and substantially appreciated inventory equals the basis those items would have if distributed in a current distribution immediately before the sale. (Reg § 1.751-1(a)(2))[8]

¶ 3762 Sale of partnership business v. sale of partnership assets.

Where *all* of the old partners sell out, whether the transaction is a sale of the partnership interests or a sale of the partnership assets generally depends on whether what was actually transferred was a going business or simply assets.[9]

¶ 3763 Liquidation v. sale of partner's interest.

Withdrawal of a partner from a partnership ordinarily may be accomplished either by sale or by liquidation of his interest in the partnership.

Where a retiring partner's interest is liquidated, payments are taxable to that partner as guaranteed payments or income distributions to the extent they exceed the value of his interest in the partnership property.[10]

Where a retiring partner *sells* his interest, payments to him that exceed his basis for his interest are capital gain except to the extent of payments for unrealized receivables and substantially appreciated inventory items. (Code Sec. 741; Reg § 1.741-1)[11]

¶ 3764 Special Basis Adjustments to Partnership Property ▮▮▮▮▮▮▮

A partnership's basis in its assets is unaffected by partnership distributions and transfers of partnership interests unless the partnership makes a special basis election. Under certain circumstances, the transferee of a partnership interest may elect to adjust the basis of property distributed to him as if the partnership had made the special basis election.

---

5. ¶ B-3802 *et seq.*; ¶ 7514.01.   7. ¶ B-3901; ¶ 7414.01.   9. ¶ B-3812 *et seq.*   11. ¶ B-3810; ¶ 7414.01.
6. ¶ B-3801; ¶ 7414.01.   8. ¶ B-3903; ¶ 7514.02.   10. ¶ B-3810; ¶ 7414.01.

Footnote references beginning with letters are to paragraphs in RIA's Federal Tax Coordinator 2d and RIA's Analysis of Federal Taxes: Income. Footnote references beginning with numbers are to paragraphs in RIA's United States Tax Reporter.

¶ 3765   Post-transfer adjustments to basis.

A partnership may *elect* to adjust the basis of the property held by it at the time an interest in the partnership is transferred by sale or exchange or on the death of a partner. This election is available where there is a difference between the basis of the transferee-partner's partnership interest and his proportionate share of the adjusted basis of the partnership's property before the election. It applies with respect to the transferee-partner only. (Code Sec. 743(a), (b)) This adjustment is made by increasing or decreasing the adjusted basis of the partnership property to reflect the amount by which the transferee partner's basis for his interest differs from his proportionate share of the adjusted basis of the partnership property.[12]

Where a partnership terminates due to the sale of a 50% interest (¶ 3778) when a special basis adjustment election is in effect, the adjustment is applied to the partnership's assets immediately before their deemed distribution. The new partner is considered to be a partner in the old partnership for an instant before the considered liquidation distribution.[13]

¶ 3766   Post-distribution adjustments to basis of undistributed property.

Where a partnership elects to adjust the basis of partnership assets, upon a partnership distribution, the partnership's basis in retained property is increased by any gain recognized to the distributee-partner and by the excess of the partnership's adjusted basis for the distributed property over the distributee-partner's basis for it. (Code Sec. 734(b)(1); Reg § 1.734-1(b)(1))

The basis of remaining partnership property is reduced by any loss recognized by the distributee, and by the excess of the distributee-partner's basis for the distributed property over its basis to the partnership immediately before the distribution. (Code Sec. 734(b)(2); Reg § 1.734-1(b)(2))[14]

¶ 3767   Partner's basis adjustments.

Where a partnership interest is transferred and the partnership later distributes property, but has not made the election described at ¶ 3765, the transferee-partner may elect to have the basis of the property distributed to him adjusted as if the partnership had made the election. This adjustment will reflect any difference between the basis of the transferee-partner's partnership interest and his proportionate share of the adjusted basis of the partnership's property at the time he acquired his interest. (Reg § 1.732-1(d)(1))

The transferee-partner may make this election only with respect to property (other than money) distributed to him within two years after he acquired his interest by transfer. (Code Sec. 732(d))[15]

The adjustment is *required* (without regard to the two-year limit) if at the time the transferee-partner acquired the transferred partnership interest all three of the following conditions existed:

(1) The fair market value of all partnership property (other than money) exceeded 110% of its adjusted basis to the partnership.

(2) Allocation of basis under Code Sec. 732(c) (general rule for allocation of basis of distributed properties) upon a liquidation of his interest immediately after the transfer of the interest would have resulted in a shift of basis from property not subject to depreciation, depletion or amortization to property that is so subject.

(3) The post-transfer adjustment would change the basis to the transferee-partner of

---

12. ¶ B-4005 *et seq.*; ¶ 7434.   13. ¶ B-4012; ¶ 7044.04.   14. ¶ B-4002; ¶ 7344.01.   15. ¶ B-4032; ¶ 7324.01.

Footnote references beginning with letters are to paragraphs in RIA's Federal Tax Coordinator 2d and RIA's Analysis of Federal Taxes: Income. Footnote references beginning with numbers are to paragraphs in RIA's United States Tax Reporter.

the property actually distributed. (Code Sec. 732(d); Reg § 1.732-1(d)(4))[16]

¶ 3768 Basis of unrealized receivables and inventory items distributed to a partner.

If unrealized receivables or inventory items are distributed to a *transferee partner* who has a special basis adjustment for those assets under either the post-transfer adjustment rule (¶ 3765) or the distributed property adjustment rule (¶ 3766), the partnership's adjusted basis, immediately before distribution, of any unrealized receivables or inventory items distributed to such a partner takes into account the following portions of the post-transfer or distributed property basis adjustments that the distributee partner has for those assets:

■ The entire amount of the post-transfer or distributed property basis adjustments *if* the distributee-partner receives his entire share of the fair market value of the unrealized receivables or inventory items of the partnership.

■ The same proportion of the post-transfer or distributed property basis adjustments as the value of the unrealized receivables or inventory items distributed to him bears to his entire share of the total value of all those items of the partnership, *if* the distributee-partner gets less than his entire share of those items. (Reg § 1.732-2(c))[17]

¶ 3769 Electing basis adjustments.

The election to adjust the basis of the partnership assets on a distribution or a sale or transfer of a partnership interest (¶s 3765, 3766) is made by the partnership filing a statement of election with the partnership return for the tax year during which the transfer of interest or the distribution of property occurs. (Code Sec. 754; Reg § 1.754-1(b))

Once made, the election applies to all current and future distributions and transfers until revoked. (Code Sec. 754; Reg § 1.754-1(a))[18]

A transferee-partner who wishes to make the distributed property adjustment (¶ 3767) must elect as follows:

■ If the distribution includes any depreciable, depletable, or amortizable property, elect with the return for the distribution year.

■ If it doesn't include any such property, elect not later than the first tax year in which the basis of any of the distributed property is pertinent in determining the transferee-partner's tax. (Reg § 1.732-1(d)(2), (3))[19]

¶ 3770 Payments After Partner's Death or Retirement ▬▬▬▬▬▬▬▬▬▬

When a partner either retires or dies and payments are made in liquidation of his partnership interest, the payments are broken down into several categories, which are treated as ordinary income or capital gains.

¶ 3771 Liquidation payments to retiring or deceased partners.

These payments may be for the partner's interest in the fair market value of the partnership assets, his interest in unrealized receivables or payments under an agreement akin to mutual insurance. These amounts have to be separately considered.[20]

Liquidation payments received by a retiring partner, a partner expelled from a partnership or by a deceased partner's successor in interest are treated as distributions taxable under the rules for regular distributions discussed at ¶ 3744 if they are for the partner's interest in partnership property (see ¶ 3772). (Code Sec. 736(b)(1))[21] Payments for *substantially appreciated* inventory (¶ 3752) may result in ordinary income under the rules governing disproportionate distributions (see ¶ 3753). (Reg § 1.736-1(b)(1))

---

16. ¶ B-4035 *et seq.*; ¶ 7324.01.   18. ¶ B-4027; ¶ 7544.   20. ¶ B-4102 *et seq.*   21. ¶ B-4106.
17. ¶ B-4017.   19. ¶ B-4034; ¶ 7544.

Footnote references beginning with letters are to paragraphs in RIA's Federal Tax Coordinator 2d and RIA's Analysis of Federal Taxes: Income. Footnote references beginning with numbers are to paragraphs in RIA's United States Tax Reporter.

Liquidation payments that aren't in exchange for partnership property are treated either as distributive shares of partnership income (if the amount is determined with regard to partnership income) or as guaranteed payments (if the amount is determined without regard to partnership income). (Code Sec. 736(a); Reg § 1.736-1(a)(3))[22]

¶ 3772 Payment for interest in partnership property.

Payments for partnership property do not include payments to a retiring or deceased general partner in a partnership in which capital is not a material income-producing factor for (i) unrealized receivables (which for this purpose includes only accounts receivable and unbilled amounts) or (ii) goodwill (unless the partnership agreement provides for payment with respect to goodwill). (Code Sec. 736(b)(2); Code Sec. 736(b)(3))[23]

For payments to partners retiring or dying before Jan. 5, '93, and payments to partners retiring after Jan. 4, '93 if a written contract to buy the partner's interest in the partnership was binding on Jan. 4, '93 and at all times afterwards until the purchase,

■ payments for unrealized receivables and goodwill were not treated as in exchange for partnership property (unless, in the case of goodwill, the partnership agreement so provided) regardless of whether the retiring or deceased partner was a general partner, and regardless of whether capital is a material income-producing factor for the partnership, and

■ the definition of unrealized receivables was not restricted to include only accounts receivable and unbilled amounts, but included, in addition, the other items described at ¶ 3751.[24]

¶ 3773 Allocation of payments between income and property.

The allocation problem comes up where payments are made over two or more years. Retirement or death payments must be allocated between the portion received in exchange for partnership property and the balance, received in the form of guaranteed payments or as a distributive share of partnership income. This allocation may be made in any manner in which the remaining partners and the withdrawing partner (or a deceased partner's successor in interest) agree. However, the *total* allocated to property mustn't exceed the fair market value of the property at the date of death or retirement. (Reg § 1.736-1(b)(5)(iii))

In the absence of an allocation agreement, payments will be apportioned between income and property, as follows:

■ Payments that aren't fixed in amount are first treated as made in exchange for the partner's interest in partnership property to the extent of the value of that interest. Additional amounts are ordinary income. (Reg § 1.736-1(b)(5)(ii))

■ Payments fixed in amount and to be received over a fixed number of years are apportioned year by year in accordance with the overall ratio of property payments to total payments. (Reg § 1.736-1(b)(5)(i))[25]

A payment for goodwill is treated as a payment made in exchange for partnership property where payment for goodwill is provided by the partnership agreement. (Reg § 1.736-1(b)(3))[26]

¶ 3774 Withdrawing partner's share of final year's income.

A retiring partner must pick up his distributive share of the partnership income for the partnership year in which he retires. His share of the partnership income for the year is allocable to him only for the portion of the year he was a member of the partnership. (Reg § 1.736-1(a)(4))[27]

---

22. ¶ B-4103; ¶ 7364.03.   24. ¶ B-4106.1.   26. ¶ B-4107; ¶ 7364.02.   27. ¶ B-4101; ¶ 7064.02.
23. ¶ B-4106.1.   25. ¶s B-4108, B-4109; ¶ 7364.01.

Footnote references beginning with letters are to paragraphs in RIA's Federal Tax Coordinator 2d and RIA's Analysis of Federal Taxes: Income. Footnote references beginning with numbers are to paragraphs in RIA's United States Tax Reporter.

¶ 3775 Share of final year's income for successor to deceased partner.

The deceased partner's share of the partnership income for the entire year of death is included in the return of the decedent's successor in interest. (Reg § 1.706-1(c)(3)(ii), (iv)) The successor reports the decedent's full year share even though the decedent may have withdrawn it before he died.[28]

¶ 3776 Partner status continues as long as liquidation payments continue to retiring or deceased partner.

A retiring partner or a deceased partner's successor in interest who receives retirement or death payments is regarded as a partner until his entire interest in the partnership is liquidated. Thus, even in a two-man partnership, the partnership isn't terminated until the retiring or deceased partner's interest is liquidated. (Reg § 1.708-1(b)(1)(i)(a), Reg § 1.736-1(a)(6))[29]

¶ 3777 Terminations

A partnership ordinarily terminates only on discontinuance of operations or on sale or exchange of 50% or more of the total interests in the partnership.

¶ 3778 Termination of partnership.

A partnership terminates for tax purposes (whether or not it has terminated under applicable local law) when:

■ it stops doing business as a partnership, or

■ 50% or more of the total interest in partnership capital and profits changes hands by sale or exchange (or by distribution, unless excepted by regs) within 12 consecutive months. (Code Sec. 708, Code Sec. 761(e); Reg § 1.708-1(b)(1))[30] There has been such a change if a corporation transfers its 50% or more interest in a partnership to a new or different corporation in connection with a tax-free corporate reorganization.[31]

This sale or exchange is treated as a liquidation in which the partnership distributes its assets to the remaining partners (including the purchaser of the retiring partner's interest) and they immediately contribute the properties to a new partnership. (Code Sec. 708(b))[32]

The sale may be made either to an existing partner or an outsider and it may be made by one or more persons. A gift, bequest, or inheritance or liquidation of a partnership interest doesn't count; nor does a contribution of property to a partnership in exchange for a partnership interest, even though this produces a 50% or more change. (Reg § 1.708-1(b)(1)(ii))[33]

¶ 3779 Split-up of partnership.

If a partnership splits up into two or more partnerships, each resulting partnership is considered a continuation of the old partnership as long as the members of the resulting partnership had more than a 50% interest in the capital and profits of the old partnership. A resulting partnership whose members had an interest of only 50% or less in the old partnership is treated as a new partnership.

If the members of none of the resulting partnerships had more than a 50% interest in the old partnership, the old partnership is considered terminated as of the date of the division, and all the resulting partnerships are treated as new partnerships. (Code Sec. 708(b)(2)(B); Reg § 1.708-1(b)(2)(ii))[34]

---

28. ¶ B-4201.
29. ¶ B-4101; ¶ 7084.02.
30. ¶ B-4301; ¶ 7084.
31. ¶ B-4303; ¶ 7084.05.
32. ¶ B-4305.
33. ¶ B-4303; ¶ 7084.02.
34. ¶ B-4307; ¶ 7084.06.

Footnote references beginning with letters are to paragraphs in RIA's Federal Tax Coordinator 2d and RIA's Analysis of Federal Taxes: Income. Footnote references beginning with numbers are to paragraphs in RIA's United States Tax Reporter.

Chapter 18 Trusts—Estates—Decedents

¶ *3900* Trust and Estate Income Tax Rules

Trusts and estates are generally treated as separate taxpayers and, with some important qualifications, are taxed in the same way as individuals.

¶ *3901* Taxation of trusts and estates.

Trust and estate income is normally taxed to the fiduciary (that is, to the trust or estate itself), if retained by the trust, or to the beneficiary, if distributed. Thus, if the fiduciary passes on income to the beneficiary, the trust or estate deducts the distributed income which then becomes taxable to the beneficiary. A special yardstick called "distributable net income" (DNI) is used to limit both the amount deducted by the trust or estate as a distribution and the amount taxed to the beneficiary. (Code Sec. 643, Code Sec. 651, Code Sec. 652, Code Sec. 661, Code Sec. 662)[1]

The income that is passed on to the beneficiary has the same tax attributes in the beneficiary's hands as when received by the fiduciary, see ¶ 3946.

¶ *3902* Computing tax of trusts and estates.

Trusts and estates compute their tax under a separate tax rate schedule. (Code Sec. 1(e))[2] These rates are in ¶ 1106.

Trusts and estates may not figure their tax from tax tables. (Code Sec. 3(b)(2))

For application of the alternative minimum tax to trusts and estates, see ¶ 3200 *et seq.*

For income tax return requirements of trusts and estates, see Chapter 14.

For the tax years of trusts and estates, see ¶ 2809.

¶ *3903* Code Sec. 644 tax on trust's gain from property sold within two years of receipt.

A tax, computed at the transferor's tax rates and reported on the line for "Other taxes" on Schedule G of the Form 1041, is imposed on "includible" gain from sales by a trust of appreciated property transferred to the trust, if the sale occurs within two years after the transfer and before the transferor's death. (Code Sec. 644(a)(1))[3]

This tax doesn't apply where the property is acquired from a decedent, or by a charitable remainder annuity trust, unitrust or pooled income fund. (Code Sec. 644(e))[4]

Includible gain is the lesser of:

■ the gain recognized by the trust on the sale or exchange of the property; or

■ the excess of the fair market value of the property at the time of its initial transfer in trust over its adjusted basis immediately after the transfer. (Code Sec. 644(b))[5]

The includible gain, reduced by allocable deductions, is excluded from the trust's taxable income (Code Sec. 641(c)(1)) and DNI. (Code Sec. 643(a)) Thus, the gain won't be taxed to the beneficiaries if it is currently distributed, and won't be subject to the throwback rules where the gain is accumulated and then distributed in a later year.[6]

¶ *3904* Estimated tax payments by trusts and estates.

All trusts and certain estates must make estimated income tax payments (using Form 1041-ES and vouchers) under rules similar to those that apply to individuals, with certain adjustments. (Code Sec. 6654(l)(1))[7] Trusts and estates generally have 45 days to compute their estimated tax payments under the annualization rules. (Code Sec. 6654(l)(4))[8]

Estates and grantor trusts that receive the residue of a probate estate are exempt from

---

1. ¶s C-1000 *et seq.*, C-7000   3. ¶ C-2000 *et seq.*; ¶ 6444.   6. ¶s C-2606, C-2703, C-4000   7. ¶ S-5300 *et seq.*; ¶ 66,544.
   et seq.; ¶ 6409.   4. ¶ C-2016; ¶ 6444.   *et seq.*; ¶ 6444.   8. ¶ S-5304; ¶ 6434.08
2. ¶s C-1003 *et seq.*, C-7002   5. ¶ C-2005; ¶ 6444.
   et seq.; ¶ 90,675.

Footnote references beginning with letters are to paragraphs in RIA's Federal Tax Coordinator 2d and RIA's Analysis of Federal Taxes: Income. Footnote references beginning with numbers are to paragraphs in RIA's United States Tax Reporter.

making estimated tax payments for their first two tax years after the date of decedent's death. (Code Sec. 6654(l)(2))[9] Charitable trusts subject to tax under Code Sec. 511 are subject to corporate, not individual estimated taxes. (Code Sec. 6654(l)(3), Code Sec. 6655(g)(3))[10]

¶ 3905 Estimated tax payments for trusts and estates with short year.

A trust or estate with a short tax year must pay estimated tax installments on or before the 15th day of the 4th, 6th and 9th month of such tax year, and the 15th day of the first month of the following year. For a short tax year in which the trust or estate terminates, installments due before the last day of the short year must be paid, and a final installment must be paid by the 15th day of the first month following the month the short year ends.[11]

¶ 3906 Trust's and estate's election to treat estimated tax payments as paid by beneficiary.

A trustee may elect (on Form 1041-T) to treat any part of the trust's estimated tax payments as paid by a beneficiary. Any amount so treated is considered paid or credited to the beneficiary on the last day of the trust's tax year and is considered an estimated tax payment made by the beneficiary on Jan. 15, following the trust's tax year. (Code Sec. 643(g)(1))[12]

This election is available to an estate if a tax year is reasonably expected to be its last tax year. (Code Sec. 643(g)(3))

Elect on or before the *65th day* after the tax year. (Code Sec. 643(g)(2)) A copy of Form 1041-T must be filed with the trust or estate's return for that year.)Reg § 301.9100-8(a)(1)) The election is irrevocable. (Reg § 301.9100-8(a)(4))[13]

✪ *observation:* The income tax return of a trust or estate is normally due 3 ½ months after the close of its tax year, see ¶ 2809. Thus the election must be made before the due date of this return.

¶ 3907 Trust's termination.

When a trust terminates, it ends as a separate tax entity and no longer reports gross income or claims the deductions, credits, etc. (Reg § 1.641(b)-3(d))

Though the duration of a trust may depend on the occurrence of a particular event under the trust instrument such as the attainment of a specified age by the life beneficiary, for tax purposes the trust is not terminated by the occurrence of the event. It is considered to continue for a reasonable time for the orderly completion of administration. (Reg § 1.641(b)-3(b))[14]

¶ 3908 Estate's termination.

An estate's status as a separate taxpayer exists only during the period of administration and settlement of the estate. (Code Sec. 641(a)(3)) This period starts with the deceased's death and generally extends for the entire time actually required to perform the ordinary duties of administration, such as collecting assets and paying legacies and debts.[15] If estate administration is unduly prolonged, IRS considers the estate terminated for tax purposes after expiration of a reasonable period (considering the estate's assets) for performance by the executor of all the duties of administration. (Reg § 1.641(b)-3(a))[16]

¶ 3909 Trust or corporation.

A "trust" is taxed as a corporation if it has been created or used during the tax period to carry on a business and it has corporate characteristics such as centralized management,

---

9. ¶s S-5302, S-5203; ¶ 66,544.
10. ¶s S-5301, S-5420; ¶ 66,554.
11. ¶ S-5308; ¶ 6434.08.
12. ¶ S-5309; ¶ 66,544.
13. ¶ S-5310; ¶ 6434.08.
14. ¶ C-1012; ¶ 6414.07.
15. ¶ C-7010; ¶ 6414.03.
16. ¶ C-7011; ¶ 6414.03.

Footnote references beginning with letters are to paragraphs in RIA's Federal Tax Coordinator 2d and RIA's Analysis of Federal Taxes: Income. Footnote references beginning with numbers are to paragraphs in RIA's United States Tax Reporter.

transferability of interests, continuity of existence, limited liability, etc. (Reg § 301.7701-4(b))[17]

¶ 3910 Liquidating Trusts.

Liquidating trusts are ordinary trusts if their primary purpose is to liquidate the assets transferred to them. They are corporations if liquidation is only an incidental or ultimate intention and the primary objective is to continue normal business operations for an indefinite time. (Reg § 301.7701-4(d))[18]

¶ 3911 Multiple trusts.

If a grantor creates several or "multiple" trusts, each trust is treated as a separate taxpayer. Several separate trusts may be created even though there is only one trust instrument and only one trustee.[19]

Two or more trusts are treated as one if: (1) the trusts have substantially the same grantor or grantors and substantially the same primary beneficiary or beneficiaries, and (2) a principal purpose of the trusts is avoidance of federal income tax. (Code Sec. 643(f))

However, if a trust was irrevocable on Mar. 1, '84, this consolidation rule applies only to that portion of the trust attributable to contributions to corpus after Mar. 1, '84.[20]

¶ 3912 Charitable remainder annuity trust and charitable remainder unitrust.

These types of trusts (¶ 2115) created after July 31, '69, are exempt from income tax unless they have unrelated business taxable income in the tax year. (Code Sec. 664(c); Reg § 1.664-1(a)(1))[21]

¶ 3913 Pooled income fund.

A pooled income fund formed to pay income to noncharitable beneficiaries and the remainder to charity (¶ 2116) is taxed under the general trust rules (except for a deduction for capital gains set aside for charity)[22] even if it isn't a trust under local law. (Reg § 1.642(c)-5(a)(2))[23]

¶ 3914 Gross income of trusts and estates.

What would be gross income in the hands of an individual is gross income when received by a trust or estate—dividends, interest, rents, royalties, capital gains, ordinary gains, etc. (Reg § 1.641(a)-2)[24]

Gross income includes income accumulated or held for future distribution under the terms of a will or trust, income that is currently distributable, income received by a deceased's estate during administration or settlement, and income that, in the fiduciary's discretion, may be either accumulated or distributed. (Code Sec. 641(a))[25]

¶ 3915 Distribution of property in kind.

Gain or loss on distribution of property in kind to a beneficiary is recognized (except as specified below) if the estate or trust irrevocably elects (on its tax return) to recognize the gain or loss as if the property had been sold to the beneficiary for its fair market value. If made, the election applies to all distributions made by the estate or trust during the tax year (Code Sec. 643(e))[26] except:

(1) gifts or bequests of a specific sum of money or of specific property that under the terms of the will or trust are paid to the beneficiary in three or fewer installments;

(2) charitable contributions qualifying for deduction as amounts paid or permanently

---

17. ¶ C-5001; ¶ 77,014.13.   20. ¶ C-5154; ¶ 6697.02.   23. ¶ C-5040; ¶ 6424.03.   25. ¶s C-2101, C-7101.
18. ¶ C-5015; ¶ 77,014.17.   21. ¶ C-5039; ¶ 6644.01.   24. ¶s C-2100 et seq., C-7100   26. ¶s C-2152, C-7152; ¶ 6434.05.
19. ¶ C-5151; ¶ 6697.02.   22. ¶ C-2316; ¶ 6424.03.   et seq.; ¶ 6414.

Footnote references beginning with letters are to paragraphs in RIA's Federal Tax Coordinator 2d and RIA's Analysis of Federal Taxes: Income. Footnote references beginning with numbers are to paragraphs in RIA's United States Tax Reporter.

set aside for qualified charities;

(3) amounts distributed in the current tax year for which a distributions deduction was allowed in an earlier tax year. (Code Sec. 643(e)(4), Code Sec. 663(a))[27]

A trust may not deduct a loss on any distribution, because of the rule barring loss deductions on sales between related parties. But this rule doesn't deny a loss to an estate. See ¶ 2450.

¶ 3916 Estate income from community property.

If a married decedent dies leaving community property, the income from one-half of the property is taxable to the estate and the income from the other half is taxable to the surviving spouse.[28]

¶ 3917 Deductions and credits of trusts and estates.

Deductions and credits of trusts and estates are basically those allowed to individuals with exceptions for special deduction rules that are discussed in the following paragraphs. (Code Sec. 641(b); Reg § 1.641(b)-1)[29]

¶ 3918 Two percent floor on miscellaneous itemized deductions.

For purposes of this floor (see ¶ 3107), the adjusted gross income of a trust or estate is computed the same as for an individual, except the deductions for costs paid or incurred in connection with the administration of the trust or estate (¶ 3919) that wouldn't have been incurred if the property were not held in the trust or estate (such as investment counseling fees paid by the trust to aid the trustees in discharging their fiduciary duty to the trust beneficiaries), the trust's or estate's personal exemptions (¶ 3924), and distribution deductions (¶s 3932, 3934) are allowed as deductions in arriving at adjusted gross income. (Code Sec. 67(e)) Thus, these expenses aren't subject to the floor.

Amounts that would not be allowable as miscellaneous itemized deductions if paid directly by an individual may not be indirectly deducted through grantor trusts. (Code Sec. 67(c); Reg § 1.67-2T(g)(1), (2)) For items paid by a grantor trust that are treated as miscellaneous itemized deductions of the grantor under the grantor trust rules (¶ 3956 *et seq.*), the floor applies to the grantor, not the trust itself. (Reg § 1.67-2T(b)(1))[30]

¶ 3919 Administration expenses.

Reasonable amounts paid or incurred by the fiduciary of an estate or trust on account of administration expenses, including fiduciaries' fees and litigation expenses, that are ordinary and necessary in the performance of duties of administration are deductible. (Reg § 1.212-1(i)) See also ¶ 3922. Deductible items include commissions and legal fees, whether allocable to corpus or income.[31]

¶ 3920 Interest deductions.

An estate or trust may deduct interest to the same extent as an individual, see ¶ 1700 *et seq.* Thus, an estate or trust is subject to the bar on the deduction of "personal" interest. But, interest on estate tax payments that are deferred because of a closely held business interest or a reversionary interest (see ¶ 5036) aren't subject to this limit. (Code Sec. 163(h))[32]

¶ 3921 Expenses of exempt income.

No deduction may be taken for *any* expenses allocable to tax-exempt income. (Code Sec. 265; Reg § 1.212-1(i))[33]

---

27. ¶s C-2531 *et seq.*, C-8022 *et seq.*
28. ¶ C-7108.

29. ¶s C-2200 *et seq.*, C-7200 *et seq.*; ¶ 6414.
30. ¶s C-2202, C-7202; ¶ 674.

31. ¶s C-2217, C-7215; ¶s 2124.09, 6424.
32. ¶s C-2209 *et seq.*, C-7210.

33. ¶s C-2217, C-2219, C-7217; ¶ 2654.

Footnote references beginning with letters are to paragraphs in RIA's Federal Tax Coordinator 2d and RIA's Analysis of Federal Taxes: Income. Footnote references beginning with numbers are to paragraphs in RIA's United States Tax Reporter.

¶ 3922   Income tax or estate tax deduction.

Administration expenses, including commissions and other selling expenses, and casualty and theft losses during administration may be taken either: (1) as a deduction (or as an offset against the sales price of property in determining gain or loss) in computing the estate's taxable income for *income tax* purposes, or (2) as a deduction in computing the decedent's taxable estate for *estate tax* purposes, but not both. (Code Sec. 642(g)) To take the income tax deduction, the executor should file in duplicate (a) a statement that the amount involved has not already been allowed as a deduction for federal estate tax purposes, and (b) a waiver of the right to have it allowed as an estate tax deduction. (Reg § 1.642(g)-1)[34]

Some items or portion of an item can be deducted for income tax purposes if the statement and waiver are filed, while a similar item or different portion of the same item can be taken for estate tax purposes. (Reg § 1.642(g)-2)[35]

The rule barring deductions for *both* income tax and estate tax purposes doesn't apply to obligations of the decedent for interest, taxes and expenses that are allowable as deductions in respect of a decedent as explained at ¶ 3970, (Reg § 1.642(g)-2) or items that qualify for deduction on the estate tax return as claims against the estate, such as divorce settlement payments.[36]

Similar rules apply for purposes of the generation-skipping transfer tax. (Code Sec. 642(g))[37]

¶ 3923   Depreciation and depletion.

Depreciation and depletion deductions of trust or estate property must be apportioned as follows:

For a *trust*, these deductions are generally apportioned between the beneficiaries and the trustee on the basis of the trust income allocable to each. (Code Sec. 167(d), Code Sec. 611(b)(3), Code Sec. 642(e))[38] But if the trustee is required or permitted by the trust instrument or local law to maintain a reserve for the deduction, the deduction belongs to the trust to the extent that income is actually set aside for the reserve. Apart from this, the regs bar any deduction by the trust or a beneficiary that exceeds the trust's or beneficiary's allocable share of trust income. (Reg § 1.167(h)-1(b), Reg § 1.611-1(c)(4))[39]

For an *estate*, the deductions are apportioned between the estate and the heirs, legatees and devisees on the basis of the estate income allocable to each, regardless of the terms of the will. (Code Sec. 167(d), Code Sec. 611(b)(4))[40]

¶ 3924   Personal exemption.

An estate is entitled to a deduction for personal exemption of $600. (Code Sec. 642(b))[41]

A trust that is required to distribute all of its income currently has a $300 exemption (even for a year in which it makes a corpus distribution or a charitable contribution). All other trusts deduct $100. (Code Sec. 642(b); Reg § 1.642(b)-1)[42]

No deduction is allowed in the final year of an estate or a trust.[43]

---

34. ¶ C-7226 *et seq.*; ¶ 6424.07.   37. ¶ C-7227; ¶ 6424.07.   40. ¶ C-7220; ¶ 6424.06.   42. ¶ C-2206; ¶ 6424.01.
35. ¶ C-7232; ¶ 6424.07.   38. ¶ C-2222 *et seq.*; ¶ 6240.06. 41. ¶ C-7207; ¶ 6424.01.   43. ¶s C-2206, C-7207; ¶ 6424.01.
36. ¶s C-7234, C-7235; ¶ 6914.04.   39. ¶ C-2214.

Footnote references beginning with letters are to paragraphs in RIA's Federal Tax Coordinator 2d and RIA's Analysis of Federal Taxes: Income. Footnote references beginning with numbers are to paragraphs in RIA's United States Tax Reporter.

¶ 3925 Standard deduction.

The standard deduction of a trust or estate is zero. (Code Sec. 63(c)(6)(E))[44]

¶ 3926 Net operating loss.

Trusts and estates are entitled to the net operating loss deduction. (Code Sec. 642(d)) In computing the net operating loss, the charitable deduction and the deduction for distributions are disregarded. (Reg § 1.642(d)-1)[45]

¶ 3927 Charitable contributions.

An estate or trust may deduct any amount of gross income, without limitation, that, under the terms of the governing instrument is *paid* during the tax year for a charitable purpose. (Code Sec. 642(c)(1); Reg § 1.642(c)-1(a))[46] These deductions aren't subject to the 2% floor on miscellaneous itemized deductions, see ¶ 3107. (Code Sec. 67(b)(4))

A deduction is also allowed to *estates* for any amount of gross income, without limit, which under the terms of the governing instrument is, during the tax year, permanently *set aside* for a charitable purpose. (Code Sec. 642(c)(2); Reg § 1.642(c)-2(a), (b))[47] *Trusts* are denied the set-aside deduction, except for pooled income funds. (Code Sec. 642(c)(2), (3); Reg § 1.642(c)-2(b), (c))[48]

¶ 3928 Charitable contribution of exempt income.

Contributions made out of tax-exempt income, such as state or municipal bond interest, aren't deductible. (Reg § 1.642(c)-3(b), Reg § 1.643(a)-5(b))[49]

¶ 3929 Election to accelerate charitable deduction.

A fiduciary of a trust or estate can elect to treat a contribution actually paid in one tax year as paid in the preceding tax year. (Code Sec. 642(c)(1))[50]

The election to accelerate the deduction must be made not later than the time, including extensions, prescribed for filing the income tax return for the tax year *following the tax year* to which the deductions are pushed back. The election is made by a statement attached to the return or amended return for the year to which the deductions are pushed back. (Reg § 1.642(c)-1(b))[1]

¶ 3930 Deduction for distributions to beneficiaries.

A deduction is allowed for distributions to beneficiaries up to the "distributable net income" (DNI) of the trust or estate for the tax year. (Code Sec. 651(b), Code Sec. 661(a))[2]

¶ 3931 Distribution deduction of a trust.

The distribution deduction of a trust depends upon whether the trust is a simple trust (¶ 3932) or a complex trust (¶ 3934).

A "simple" trust is one that makes no distribution other than of current income and the terms of which require all of its income to be distributed currently and do not provide for charitable or similar contributions. A "complex" trust permits accumulation of income or charitable contributions or distributes principal.

A trust may shift its character from simple to complex and vice versa. (Reg § 1.651(a)-1, Reg § 1.661(a)-1)[3]

---

44. ¶s C-2204, C-7205; ¶ 634.
45. ¶s C-2226, C-7222; ¶ 6424.05.
46. ¶s C-2301 *et seq.*, C-7301 *et seq.*; ¶ 6424.02.

47. ¶ C-7311; ¶ 6424.02.
48. ¶ C-2312 *et seq.*; ¶ 6424.02.
49. ¶s C-2308, C-7308; ¶ 6424.02.
50. ¶s C-2303, C-7304; ¶ 6424.02.

1. ¶s C-2305, C-7305; ¶ 6424.02.
2. ¶s C-2501, C-8001; ¶s 6514, 6609.

3. ¶ C-2501; ¶ 6514.01.

Footnote references beginning with letters are to paragraphs in RIA's Federal Tax Coordinator 2d and RIA's Analysis of Federal Taxes: Income. Footnote references beginning with numbers are to paragraphs in RIA's United States Tax Reporter.

¶ 3932 Distributions deduction of a simple trust.

This deduction for a simple trust is the amount of its income for the tax year that is required to be distributed currently, up to the ceiling of its DNI for the year (¶ 3933). (Code Sec. 651(b)) Tax-exempt income is excluded both from accounting income and DNI in figuring the deduction. (Reg § 1.651(b)-1)[4]

¶ 3933 Computation of distributable net income for simple trust.

The starting point is *taxable* income, i.e., gross income minus deductions. These adjustments are then made to taxable income:

(1) Add back the deduction for personal exemption and any deduction for distributions. (Code Sec. 643(a)(1), (2); Reg § 1.643(a)-1, Reg § 1.643(a)-2)

(2) Subtract any extraordinary dividends (in cash or property) and taxable stock dividends that the trustee doesn't pay or credit because he determines they are allocable to principal. (Code Sec. 643(a)(4); Reg § 1.643(a)-4)

(3) Subtract any capital gains that are allocated to principal and are not paid, credited or required to be distributed during the tax year. Also add back any capital losses, except to the extent they are taken into account in computing capital gains that are paid, credited or required to be distributed during the tax year. (Code Sec. 643(a)(3); Reg § 1.643(a)-3(b))[5]

¶ 3934 Distributions deduction of a complex trust or an estate.

A complex trust or estate deducts, up to the ceiling of its DNI for the year (¶ 3935), the sum of:

(1) any amount of income for the tax year required to be distributed currently (¶ 3936); and

(2) any other amounts, whether income or principal, properly paid or credited or required to be distributed for that tax year (¶ 3937). (Code Sec. 661(a); Reg § 1.661(a)-2(a))[6]

No distributions deduction may be taken for any portion of DNI that represents an item, such as tax-exempt interest, that is not included in the gross income of the trust or estate. (Code Sec. 661(c); Reg § 1.661(c)-1) Unless the instrument or local law requires another allocation, the distribution is considered to contain the same proportion of tax-exempt items entering into DNI as the total tax-exempt income bears to total DNI. (Code Sec. 661(b); Reg § 1.661(b)-1)[7]

¶ 3935 Computation of distributable net income for a complex trust or an estate.

The DNI of a complex trust or an estate is its taxable income with these adjustments:

(1) No deduction for distributions or personal exemption is allowed.

(2) Capital gains are excluded unless: allocated to income; allocated to principal and actually distributed during the year; used in determining the amount distributed or required to be distributed; or allowed as a charitable deduction. Capital losses are excluded except to the extent they enter into a determination of any capital gains paid, credited or required to be distributed to a beneficiary during the tax year.

(3) Tax-exempt interest, reduced by allocable, nondeductible expenses, is *included* except to the extent allocable to the charitable deduction. (Code Sec. 643(a))[8]

---

4. ¶ C-2603 *et seq.*; ¶ 6514.01.   6. ¶s C-2701, C-8101; ¶ 6614.01.   8. ¶s C-2702 *et seq.*, C-8102
5. ¶ C-2606 *et seq.*; ¶ 6434.01.   7. ¶s C-2707, C-8107.   *et seq.*; ¶ 6434.01.

Footnote references beginning with letters are to paragraphs in RIA's Federal Tax Coordinator 2d and RIA's Analysis of Federal Taxes: Income. Footnote references beginning with numbers are to paragraphs in RIA's United States Tax Reporter.

¶ 3936 "Income required to be distributed currently."

Income required to be distributed currently means accounting income of the trust or estate determined under the trust instrument or will and applicable local law. It doesn't include items of gross income that the fiduciary allocates to corpus. (Code Sec. 643(b))

A distribution required to be made out of income or corpus, such as an annuity, is considered to be out of currently distributable income to the extent it is paid out of income for the tax year. (Code Sec. 661(a)(1); Reg § 1.661(a)-2(b))

Currently distributable income is deductible for the tax year of the trust or estate in which it is received even though, as a matter of practical necessity, it is not distributed until after the end of that year. (Reg § 1.651(a)-2(a), Reg § 1.661(a)-2(b))[9]

¶ 3937 "Other amounts properly paid or credited or required to be distributed."

Other amounts properly paid or credited or required to be distributed must be actually distributed or at least made available on demand by the beneficiary. Even though designated by the fiduciary as a payment of *principal* of the trust or estate, a distribution actually paid or made available is deductible by the fiduciary as a distribution of "other amounts." It is not necessary that the distribution actually be made out of income. (Code Sec. 661(a); Reg § 1.661(a)-2(c))[10] An amount that a trust has elected to treat as an estimated tax payment by a beneficiary (¶ 3906) is a deductible distribution. (Code Sec. 643(g))[11]

¶ 3938 Distributions of property in kind.

Distributions of property in kind qualify for deduction as other amounts paid. (Reg § 1.661(a)-2(c)) If the trust or estate elects to recognize gain or loss (¶ 3915), the property distributed is taken into account at its fair market value for purposes of the distribution deduction. If the election isn't made, the property is taken into account only to the extent of the lesser of the basis of the property in the hands of the beneficiary (¶ 3949) or the fair market value of the property. (Code Sec. 643(e)(2), (3))[12]

¶ 3939 Family support allowances.

Family support allowances (for a decedent's widow or dependent) paid by an estate under a court order or decree, or under local law, are treated as estate distributions deductible by the estate, subject to the regular deduction ceiling measured by DNI. (Reg § 1.661(a)-2(e), Reg § 1.662(a)-2(c))[13]

¶ 3940 Nonqualifying distributions.

No *distributions* deduction is allowed for:

■ distributions to charity; (Reg § 1.663(a)-2)[14]

■ the value of any interest in real estate, title to which passes directly from decedent to his heirs and devisees; (Reg § 1.661(a)-2(e))[15]

■ a gift or bequest of specific property or of a specific sum of money that is paid or credited all at once or in not more than three installments—an amount that can be paid only from income is not considered a gift or bequest of a specific sum of money and is therefore includible in the distributions deduction; (Code Sec. 663(a)(1))[16]

■ any amount reported as a distribution in an earlier year's return because it was credited or required to be distributed in the earlier year; (Code Sec. 663(a)(3);

---

9. ¶s C-2504 *et seq.*, C-8003 *et seq.*; ¶ 6514.01.
10. ¶s C-2524 *et seq.*, C-8014 *et seq.*; ¶ 6614.01.
11. ¶ C-2530; ¶ 6434.05.
12. ¶s C-2525, C-8015; ¶ 6434.05.
13. ¶ C-8011.
14. ¶s C-2533, C-8026; ¶ 6614.01.
15. ¶ C-8027.
16. ¶s C-2531 *et seq.*, C-8022 *et seq.*; ¶ 6614.01.

Footnote references beginning with letters are to paragraphs in RIA's Federal Tax Coordinator 2d and RIA's Analysis of Federal Taxes: Income. Footnote references beginning with numbers are to paragraphs in RIA's United States Tax Reporter.

Reg § 1.663(a)-3)[17]

■ any amount paid or credited within the first 65 days of the current year which the fiduciary elected to treat as paid or credited in the preceding year, see ¶ 3941.

¶ 3941   Trust's election to deduct "late paid" distributions—the "65-day rule."

The fiduciary of a complex trust can elect, by checking a box on the Form 1041, to treat an amount properly paid or credited within the first 65 days of any tax year of the trust as paid or credited on the last day of the preceding tax year. (Code Sec. 663(b))[18] This gives the trustee time to determine income earned by the trust for the year, and the opportunity to deduct distributions of that income on the return for the year earned.

The amount to which the election applies can't exceed the greater of: (1) the trust's accounting income for the year for which the election is made, or (2) the trust's DNI for that year, in each case reduced by any amounts paid, credited, or required to be distributed in that year other than amounts considered paid or credited in a preceding tax year by reason of the "65-day" rule. (Reg § 1.663(b)-1(a))[19]

¶ 3942   Amount taxed to beneficiary of a simple trust.

The beneficiary of a simple trust is in general taxed on the *lower* of these two items:

(1) the amount of trust income for the tax year of the trust required to be distributed to the beneficiary currently whether distributed or not; or

(2) the beneficiary's proportionate share of the trust's DNI. (Code Sec. 652(a); Reg § 1.652(a)-1)

DNI is computed as explained at ¶ 3933, except that for this purpose it includes tax-exempt interest minus allocable deductions. (Code Sec. 643(a)(5)) Tax-exempt income items, however, aren't taxable to the beneficiary because of the character rule explained at ¶ 3946. Income from outside U.S. sources is included for foreign trusts. (Code Sec. 643(a)(6))[20]

¶ 3943   Amount taxed to beneficiary of a complex trust or estate.

The beneficiary of a complex trust or of an estate includes in gross income the sum of the following amounts, subject to the DNI ceiling below and the elimination of tax-exempt items under the character rule (¶ 3946):

(1) income required to be distributed to him currently (though not actually distributed), which includes an annuity or other amount required to be paid out of income or corpus, to the extent it is paid out of income for the tax year; and

(2) all other amounts (whether from income or principal) properly paid, credited or required to be distributed to him for the tax year, (Code Sec. 662(a))[21] including income from property distributed in-kind, see ¶ 3949. (Reg § 1.662(a)-3(b))

DNI ceiling. A beneficiary of a complex trust or an estate need not report as income more than his share of DNI, so that the total amount of income reported by all beneficiaries cannot exceed the total DNI of the trust or estate for the tax year. For this purpose, the beneficiaries are divided into two groups or "tiers":

(1) The first tier composed of beneficiaries entitled to income distributions currently, that is "income required to be distributed currently."

(2) The second tier composed of beneficiaries receiving or entitled to receive other "noncurrent" distributions. (Code Sec. 662(a); Reg § 1.662(a)-3(c))[22]

---

17. ¶s C-2534, C-8028; ¶ 6614.01.   19. ¶ C-2713; ¶ 6634.03.   21. ¶s C-3006 *et seq.*, C-9001   22. ¶s C-3010, C-9006; ¶ 6624.
18. ¶ C-2713; ¶ 6634.03.   20. ¶ C-3001; ¶ 6524.   *et seq.*; ¶ 6624.

Footnote references beginning with letters are to paragraphs in RIA's Federal Tax Coordinator 2d and RIA's Analysis of Federal Taxes: Income. Footnote references beginning with numbers are to paragraphs in RIA's United States Tax Reporter.

¶ 3944 Amounts reported by first-tier beneficiary.

The first-tier beneficiaries report, in the aggregate, the amount of their current distributions, up to the amount of DNI for the tax year of the trust or estate, computed as explained at ¶ 3935 without any charitable deduction. Thus, if the total of first-tier distributions is equal to or less than DNI (without charitable deduction), each first-tier beneficiary reports his full share of the distributions. (Code Sec. 662(a)(1))[23]

But if the total of first-tier distributions exceeds DNI (without charitable deduction) each beneficiary reports an amount equal to his pro rata share of DNI (without charitable deduction). (Code Sec. 662(a)(1); Reg § 1.662(a)-2(b))[24]

¶ 3945 Amounts reported by second-tier beneficiary.

The second-tier beneficiaries report, in the aggregate, the amount of their second-tier distributions up to the DNI of the trust or estate as reduced for first-tier distributions of current income. For this purpose, DNI is computed *with* allowance of any charitable deduction.

If the total of second-tier distributions equals or is less than the ceiling (DNI as reduced for first-tier distributions), each second-tier beneficiary reports his or her full share of the second-tier distributions. But, if the total of second-tier distributions exceeds the ceiling, each second-tier beneficiary reports only his pro rata share of the ceiling amount. (Code Sec. 662(a)(2); Reg § 1.662(a)-3(c))[25]

¶ 3946 Character of income in beneficiary's hands.

For simple trusts, complex trusts and estates, the amounts taxable to the beneficiaries have the same character (e.g., as tax-exempt income) in the hands of the beneficiaries as the amounts had when received by the trust or estate. (Code Sec. 652(b), Code Sec. 662(b); Reg § 1.652(b)-1, Reg § 1.662(b)-1)[26]

Unless the instrument specifically allocates different classes of income to different beneficiaries, amounts distributed are treated as consisting of the same proportion of each class of items entering into the computation of DNI as the total of each class bears to the total DNI of the trust or estate. (Code Sec. 652(b), Code Sec. 662(b); Reg § 1.652(b)-1, Reg § 1.662(b)-1)[27]

Allocation of deductions. Deductions that enter into the computation of DNI are allocated among the various classes as follows:

■ Deductions *directly* attributable to a particular class of income (interest, rents, dividends, capital gains, etc.) are allocated to that class.

■ If deductions *directly* attributable to a class of income exceed that class, the excess may be allocated to any other class (including capital gains) included in DNI in the manner shown below for deductions not directly attributable, except that excess deductions directly attributable to tax-exempt income cannot be used to reduce any other class of income.

■ Deductions not directly attributable to a specific class of income can be allocated to any item of income (including capital gains) included in DNI, but a part must be allocated proportionately to tax-exempt income. Examples of these "neutral" deductions are trustees' commissions (both income and corpus), and state income and personal property taxes. (Reg § 1.652(b)-3)[28]

A *charitable deduction* by an estate or complex trust is allocated just before the other deductions. Allocation follows the terms of the instrument or local law, but if these are

23. ¶s C-3011 *et seq.*, C-9007 *et seq.*; ¶ 6624.
24. ¶s C-3013, C-9009; ¶ 6624.
25. ¶s C-3013, C-9009; ¶ 6624.
26. ¶s C-3002, C-3016, C-9012; ¶s 6524.03, 6624.03.
27. ¶s C-3003, C-3016, C-9012; ¶s 6524.02, 6624.02.
28. ¶s C-3004, C-3017, C-9013; ¶ 6524.02.

Footnote references beginning with letters are to paragraphs in RIA's Federal Tax Coordinator 2d and RIA's Analysis of Federal Taxes: Income. Footnote references beginning with numbers are to paragraphs in RIA's United States Tax Reporter.

silent, the charitable deduction is allocated to each class of income items in the proportion the total that each class bears to the total of all classes. (Reg § 1.643(a)-5(b), Reg § 1.662(b)-2)[29]

¶ 3947 Separate shares of trust beneficiaries as separate trusts.

If a complex trust accumulates income for one beneficiary and distributes principal to another beneficiary, the normal tax rules would impose a tax burden on the recipient of principal since he in effect must pay tax on income accumulated for the other beneficiary. To prevent this, the "separate share rule" treats substantially separate and independent shares of different beneficiaries of a single trust as though each share represented a separate trust. This applies *only* in computing DNI as a ceiling on the amount deductible by the trust and taxable to the beneficiaries, (Code Sec. 663(c); Reg § 1.663(c)-1(b)) only to complex trusts, and is mandatory. (Reg § 1.663(c)-1(d))[30]

¶ 3948 When a beneficiary is taxed.

Current distributions (amounts required to be distributed currently) are taxed to the beneficiary when they are required to be distributed even though not actually distributed. Other distributions are taxed to a beneficiary when they are made or credited, or required to be made. (Code Sec. 652(a), Code Sec. 662(a); Reg § 1.662(a)-3(a))[31]

If a beneficiary's tax year is different from that of the estate or trust, the beneficiary includes his share of the trust or estate income in his return for the tax year in which the tax year of the trust or estate ends. (Code Sec. 652(c), Code Sec. 662(c))[32]

Upon termination of an estate, a beneficiary must include in his calendar year return income received from the estate during both the estate's fiscal year and final short year where both years end within his calendar year.[33]

Where the 65-day rule is elected (¶ 3941), the beneficiary is considered as receiving the distribution in his tax year that includes the close of the trust's tax year in which the distribution is considered made. (Reg § 1.663(b)-1(a)(2)(ii))[34]

¶ 3949 Distributions in kind.

For property distributed in kind, the amount includible in the beneficiary's income and his basis in the property depends on whether the estate or trust elected to recognize gain or loss on the distribution, ¶ 3915.

If the estate or trust elects, the property is taken into account at its fair market value. (Code Sec. 643(e)(3))

If the estate or trust doesn't elect, the property is taken into account only to the extent of the lesser of: (1) the fair market value of the property, or (2) its basis in the hands of the beneficiary. (Code Sec. 643(e)(2))[35]

The beneficiary's basis for property distributed in kind is the adjusted basis of the property in the hands of the estate or trust immediately before the distribution, adjusted for any gain or loss recognized by the estate or trust on the distribution. (Code Sec. 643(e)(1))[36]

¶ 3950 Nontaxable gifts and bequests.

A beneficiary isn't taxable on any amount paid or credited as a gift or bequest of specific property or of a specific sum of money, and that is paid or credited all at once or in not more than three installments. But an amount that can be paid only from *income* isn't excludable. (Code Sec. 663(a)(1); Reg § 1.102-1(c))[37]

29. ¶s C-3018, C-9015.
30. ¶ C-2711 *et seq.*; ¶ 6634.01.
31. ¶s C-3025, C-9017; ¶s 6524.01, 6624.01.
32. ¶s C-3026, C-9018; ¶s 6524.04, 6624.04.
33. ¶ C-9018.
34. ¶ C-3028; ¶ 6634.03.
35. ¶s C-3009, C-9004; ¶ 6434.05.
36. ¶s C-3009, C-9004.
37. ¶s C-2531, C-8022; ¶ 6634.02.

Footnote references beginning with letters are to paragraphs in RIA's Federal Tax Coordinator 2d and RIA's Analysis of Federal Taxes: Income. Footnote references beginning with numbers are to paragraphs in RIA's United States Tax Reporter.

¶ 3951 Beneficiaries' deductions on estate or trust termination.

The beneficiaries who succeed to the property of the trust or estate on its termination can deduct on their own returns the unused deductions in excess of gross income for the last tax year of the trust or estate, other than the personal exemption and charitable contributions. The deduction by the beneficiary is allowed only for his tax year in which the trust or estate terminates. (Code Sec. 642(h); Reg § 1.642(h)-2(a))[38]

¶ 3952 Taxation of beneficiaries of charitable remainder trusts.

Amounts paid to an income beneficiary of such a trust retain the character they had in the hands of the trust, with this qualification: each payment is treated as consisting of: (1) ordinary income, to the extent of the trust's ordinary income for that year and undistributed ordinary income for earlier years, (2) capital gain, to the extent of capital gain for that year and undistributed capital gain (determined on a cumulative net basis) for earlier years, (3) other income (e.g., tax-exempt interest), to the extent of that income for that year and undistributed amounts for earlier years, and (4) trust corpus. (Code Sec. 664(a), (b); Reg § 1.664-1(d)(1))[39]

¶ 3953 Distribution of accumulated trust income—"throwback" rules.

The "throwback rules" tax beneficiaries on distributions of income accumulated by the trust before the year of distribution, as though the income had been distributed currently to the beneficiaries in the years received by the trust. (Reg § 1.665(a)-OA(a)(1))[40]

The throwback rules generally apply only to complex trusts. Estates aren't subject to the throwback rules. (Code Sec. 666; Reg § 1.665(a)-OA(d))[41]

The fiduciary of a trust subject to the throwback rules must complete Schedule J (Form 1041) and attach it to the trust's return.[42]

¶ 3954 Distributions exempt from the throwback rules.

These distributions are exempt from the throwback rules:

■ Distributions of income accumulated before birth of beneficiary or before beneficiary reaches age 21. But this exclusion doesn't apply to distributions from a foreign trust or to certain distributions from multiple trusts. (Code Sec. 665(b))[43]

■ Distributions not exceeding accounting income. (Code Sec. 665(b))[44]

¶ 3955 Beneficiary's tax under throwback rules.

The beneficiary includes in his income for the current year:

■ the amount of the accumulation distribution considered distributed; and

■ the trust's income tax considered distributed. (Code Sec. 667(a), Code Sec. 666(b))

The beneficiary's total tax liability for the current year is:

(1) a partial tax on the beneficiary's taxable income *reduced* by the total amounts considered distributed to the beneficiary under the throwback rules; *plus*

(2) a partial tax on the amounts considered distributed under the throwback rules; (Code Sec. 667(a)) *plus*

(3) in the case of a foreign trust, a special nondeductible interest charge. (Code Sec. 667(b))[45]

The beneficiary's partial tax under (2) is computed (on Form 4970) under a special "shortcut" method. This method in effect averages the tax attributable to the amounts

38. ¶s C-3033 *et seq.*, C-9053 *et seq.*
39. ¶ C-3051; ¶ 6644.01.
40. ¶ C-4001; ¶ 6664.
41. ¶ C-4002; ¶ 6649.
42. ¶ C-4001; ¶ 6664.
43. ¶ C-4007; ¶ 6664.
44. ¶ C-4008; ¶ 6664.
45. ¶ C-4101; ¶ 6664.

Footnote references beginning with letters are to paragraphs in RIA's Federal Tax Coordinator 2d and RIA's Analysis of Federal Taxes: Income. Footnote references beginning with numbers are to paragraphs in RIA's United States Tax Reporter.

considered distributed over the number of years the income was earned by the trust. The tax so computed is then reduced or offset by the trust's income taxes considered distributed to the beneficiary. (Code Sec. 667(b)) This partial tax is then reduced by any estate tax or generation-skipping transfer tax attributable to the partial tax. (Code Sec. 667(b)(6))[46]

¶ 3956 Grantor or others taxed as owner of trust.

A trust grantor or another person with power over the trust or its property may (instead of the fiduciary) be taxed on its income as the "owner" of the trust. These grantor trust rules are discussed at ¶ 3957 et seq.[47]

If a grantor or other person is considered to be the owner of the *entire* trust, he computes his own personal income tax by taking into account all trust income, deductions and credits, as though the trust did not exist. (Reg § 1.671-3(a)(1)) But, where a grantor is treated as owner solely because of his interest in trust *income*, he takes into account only his share of trust items that would be reported by a current income beneficiary. (Reg § 1.671-3(c))[48]

These rules may be applicable to the entire trust or, where appropriate, to only a specific portion of a trust. (Reg § 1.671-3(a))[49]

For purposes of taxing the grantor as the owner of a trust, the grantor is treated as holding any power or interest held by any individual who was the spouse of the grantor at the time of the creation of the power or the interest, or who became the spouse of the grantor after the creation, but only for periods after the individual became the spouse. This rule applies only to transfers in trust made after Mar. 1, '86. (Code Sec. 672(e)(1))[50]

These rules don't apply to charitable remainder trusts or pooled income funds. (Reg § 1.671-1(d))[1]

¶ 3957 Power to revoke.

If the grantor of a trust reserves the power to take back title to the trust funds for himself, he is considered the owner of the trust, whether or not he actually exercises that power. (Code Sec. 671, Code Sec. 676) The power to get back the trust funds may be a power to revoke, terminate, alter or amend, or to appoint. (Reg § 1.676(a)-1)

The grantor is taxed if he can exercise the power alone, if it can be exercised only by another who is regarded as a *nonadverse* party, or if it can be exercised by both the grantor and a nonadverse party together. (Code Sec. 676(a))[2] He is not taxed if the power can be exercised only by or with consent of an adverse party. (Code Sec. 672(a), Code Sec. 676(a); Reg § 1.676(a)-1)[3]

A beneficiary is ordinarily an adverse party. (Reg § 1.672(a)-1(b))[4]

¶ 3958 Income for grantor, spouse or dependent.

The grantor of a trust is treated as its owner and taxed on its income, if the trust income is:

■ distributed actually or constructively to the grantor or his spouse;

■ held or accumulated for future distribution to the grantor or his spouse; or

■ applied to pay premiums on life insurance policies taken out on the life of the grantor or his spouse (and not irrevocably payable to charities). (Code Sec. 677(a))

The income is not taxable to the grantor if the application of the income to any of these purposes requires the approval of an adverse party. (Reg § 1.677(a)-1(b))[5]

---

46. ¶s C-4102, C-4105; ¶6664.   49. ¶ C-5209 et seq.; ¶6714.   2. ¶ C-5301; ¶6764.   4. ¶ C-5312; ¶6724.01.
47. ¶ C-5200 et seq.; ¶6714.   50. ¶ C-5204 et seq.; ¶6724.02.   3. ¶ C-5303; ¶6764.   5. ¶ C-5401; ¶6774.01.
48. ¶ C-5208; ¶6714.   1. ¶ C-5216; ¶6714.

Footnote references beginning with letters are to paragraphs in RIA's Federal Tax Coordinator 2d and RIA's Analysis of Federal
Taxes: Income. Footnote references beginning with numbers are to paragraphs in RIA's United States Tax Reporter.

If trust income is *actually* used to support a beneficiary (other than the grantor's spouse) whom the grantor is legally obligated to support, such as his minor children, the grantor is taxable on that income. But the mere fact that trust income *may* be so used does not make him taxable, unless the use is discretionary with the grantor as an *individual* (not trustee). (Reg § 1.677(b)-1(d), (e), (f))[6]

¶ 3959 Post-Mar. 1, '86 reversionary interests.

For transfers in trust made after Mar. 1, '86, the grantor of a trust is generally taxable as the owner on its income if he has a reversionary interest in the corpus or income and, as of the inception of the trust, the value of that interest is more than 5% of the value of the trust. (Code Sec. 673(a)) The value of the reversionary interest must be determined by assuming the maximum exercise of discretion in favor of the grantor. (Code Sec. 673(c)) But the possibility that an interest may return to the grantor solely by intestacy is disregarded in determining whether there is a more than 5% interest.

Any postponement of the date specified for the reacquisition of possession or enjoyment of the reversionary interest is treated as a new transfer in trust starting with the date the postponement is effective and terminating with the date prescribed by the postponement. However, income for any period is not included in income of the grantor by reason of this rule if it would not be includible in the absence of the postponement. (Code Sec. 673(d))

The grantor isn't treated as the owner where the reversionary interest takes effect only upon the death of a beneficiary before the beneficiary reaches age 21, if the beneficiary: (1) is a lineal descendant of the grantor, and (2) holds all present interests in the trust. (Code Sec. 673(b))[7]

¶ 3960 Pre-Mar. 2, '86 reversionary interests or "short-term" trusts.

For transfers in trust made before Mar. 2, '86, the grantor of a trust is generally taxable as the owner on its income if he can get trust funds back through a reversionary interest (in corpus or income) within ten years or less from the date of the transfer in trust.[8]

Where the reversionary interest is subject to a contingent event, the grantor isn't taxed on the income as long as the event may not "reasonably be expected to occur" within the ten-year period. (Reg § 1.673(a)-1(d))

If the period is geared to a person's life, the grantor isn't taxable unless the life is of a person other than the income beneficiary, the trust funds will be returned on that person's death, and that person's life expectancy on the date of transfer was ten years or less. (Reg § 1.673(a)-1(b), (c))[9]

¶ 3961 Power to control beneficial enjoyment.

Trust income is generally taxable to the grantor as the owner of the trust property if the beneficial enjoyment of trust corpus or income is subject to a power of disposition that may be exercised by him personally, or by a nonadverse party, or both, and requires no consent or approval of an adverse party. (Code Sec. 674)[10]

Similarly, the grantor will be taxed if he retains certain administrative powers, such as borrowing powers and dealing with the trust for less than full consideration. (Code Sec. 675)[11]

But certain relatively broad powers to shift benefits may be given to "independent" trustees without causing the grantor to be taxed on the income as owner. These so called "sprinkling" and "spray" powers permit the trustee to distribute, apportion or accumulate income, or to pay out corpus to or among beneficiaries, (Code Sec. 674(c)) but not to add beneficiaries except to include after-born or after-adopted children. These powers vested

---

6. ¶ C-5423; ¶ 6774.04.   8. ¶ C-5501 *et seq.*; ¶ 6734.02.   10. ¶ C-5531; ¶ 6744.   11. ¶ C-5551 *et seq.*; ¶ 6754.
7. ¶ C-5450 *et seq.*; ¶ 6734.01.   9. ¶ C-5503; ¶ 6734.02.

Footnote references beginning with letters are to paragraphs in RIA's Federal Tax Coordinator 2d and RIA's Analysis of Federal Taxes: Income. Footnote references beginning with numbers are to paragraphs in RIA's United States Tax Reporter.

solely in trustees will not cause the grantor to be taxed as the owner of the trust if the grantor is not eligible as a trustee or co-trustee and no more than half the trustees vested with the power are related or subordinate parties subservient to the wishes of the grantor. (Code Sec. 674(c), (d); Reg § 1.674(d)-2(b))

Also, a power to distribute, apportion or accumulate income won't subject the grantor to tax if he and his spouse (living with him) are ineligible to exercise the power as trustee or co-trustee and the power is limited by a reasonably definite external standard set forth in the trust instrument, such as needs for education, sickness, support in an accustomed manner, etc. (Code Sec. 674(d); Reg § 1.674(d)-1)[12]

¶ 3962 Person other than the grantor as owner.

A trustee, beneficiary, or some other person may be taxable on the income as the owner, if that person:

■ has a power exercisable solely by himself to vest the corpus, or income from it, in himself; or

■ has previously modified or released such a power and afterward retains sufficient control which would make the grantor taxable under the rules discussed at ¶ 3956 *et seq.* (Code Sec. 678)[13]

IRS says a beneficiary of a "Crummey" power (noncumulative right to withdraw a specified amount of property transferred to a trust within a specified period) will be treated as owner under the above rule.[14]

¶ 3963 Foreign trust grantors or other transferors.

If a U.S. person (e.g., a grantor) makes a transfer to a foreign trust with a U.S. beneficiary, the income of the trust (including foreign source income) will be taxed currently to the transferor as the owner of the trust. (Code Sec. 679(a)(1))[15] The U.S. person must report the creation of or any transfer to the trust on Form 3520, and must file an annual information return on Form 3520-A. (Code Sec. 6048(c))[16]

The above rules don't apply where: (1) the transfer of property to the trust is by reason of death, (2) the transferor recognizes all of the gain on the transfer, (3) the transfer is to a foreign employee benefit trust, (Code Sec. 679(a)(2)) or (4) the transfer occurred before May 22, '74.[17]

¶ 3964 Beneficiary treated as grantor of trust to the extent of gifts to foreign grantor.

Where: (1) a foreign person would ordinarily be treated as the owner of any portion of a trust, and (2) the trust has a beneficiary who is a U.S. person, the beneficiary is treated as the grantor of that portion to the extent the beneficiary has after Nov. 5, '90, made transfers by gift (directly or indirectly) to the foreign grantor. Gifts which are excluded from the calculation of gift tax under Code Sec. 2503(b) (generally, gifts of present interests of up to $10,000 per calendar year, see ¶ 5048) are not included. (Code Sec. 672(f)(1)) This rule applies even if the beneficiary was not a U.S. person at the time of the transfer.[18]

¶ 3965 Decedent's Income and Deductions ▆▆▆▆▆▆▆

A decedent's last tax year ends on his death. A cash basis decedent's final return includes only the income he actually or constructively received before he died. An accrual basis decedent's return includes income and deductions properly accruable at death (but not solely by reason of death). After-death income and deductions "in respect of a decedent" must be reported by decedent's estate or others

---

12. ¶ C-5542 *et seq.*; ¶ 6744.   14. ¶ C-5574; ¶ 6784.   16. ¶ S-3644 *et seq.*; ¶ 60,484.   18. ¶ C-5608; ¶ 6724.03.
13. ¶ C-5571; ¶ 6784.   15. ¶ C-5600 *et seq.*; ¶ 6794.   17. ¶ C-5600 *et seq.*; ¶ 6794.

Footnote references beginning with letters are to paragraphs in RIA's Federal Tax Coordinator 2d and RIA's Analysis of Federal Taxes: Income. Footnote references beginning with numbers are to paragraphs in RIA's United States Tax Reporter.

who acquire his rights or obligations.

¶ 3966 Income includible on decedent's last return (before-death income).

The last tax year of a decedent ends with the day of his death. (Reg § 1.451-1(b))[19]

For a *cash basis* decedent, include only the income received, actually or constructively, up to the end of the day of death, (Code Sec. 691(a); Reg § 1.451-1(b)(1), Reg § 1.691(a)-1(b)) and deduct expenses only to the extent paid before death (except for the special deduction for the unrecovered investment in an annuity contract, see ¶ 3967, and certain medical expenses paid within one year after death, see ¶ 2146).[20]

For an *accrual basis* decedent, include income and deductions computed on the accrual method (including the deduction for the unrecovered investment in an annuity contract, ¶ 3967). But an amount of income or deduction accrued *solely* by reason of death is not includible on the final return. (Code Sec. 451(b), Code Sec. 461(b))[21]

¶ 3967 Deduction for unrecovered investment in annuity contract.

A decedent's unrecovered investment in an annuity contract is an itemized deduction (*not* subject to the 2%-of-AGI floor) (Code Sec. 67(b)(11)) for the decedent's last tax year, if the annuity payments cease by reason of his death. (Code Sec. 72(b)(3)(A))[22]

¶ 3968 Income in respect of a decedent (after-death income).

Income in respect of a decedent covers income (including capital gain) to which a decedent had a right to receive but that: (1) was not actually or constructively received by a cash basis decedent, or (2) was not accrued by an accrual basis decedent. The income in respect of a decedent includes insurance renewal commissions, a monthly pension paid to deceased employee's widow and taxable distributions from a qualified employee plan.[23]

¶ 3969 Who is taxed on income in respect of a decedent?

A decedent's after-death income not includible on his last return must be reported, for the tax year when received, by:

- the decedent's estate, if it acquired the right to receive the item of income from the decedent;

- the person who, by reason of the decedent's death, acquires the right to the income whenever this right is not acquired by the decedent's estate from the decedent; or

- the person who acquires the right from the decedent by bequest, devise or inheritance, if the amount is received after distribution by the decedent's estate of the right to the income. (Code Sec. 691(a)(1))[24]

¶ 3970 Decedent's after-death deductions, etc., available to estate or beneficiaries.

Deductions for a decedent's Code Sec. 162 business expenses, Code Sec. 212 expenses for the production of income, interest, taxes, depletion and the credit for foreign taxes are available to the decedent's estate if the estate is liable for the obligation giving rise to the deduction or credit and it is not allowable in the decedent's final (or any previous) return. If not available to the estate, the deduction or credit may be taken by the person who acquires an interest in the decedent's property from the decedent by reason of the decedent's death, or by bequest, devise or inheritance, subject to the obligation to which the deduction or credit relates. (Code Sec. 691(b))[25]

---

19. ¶ C-9601.
20. ¶ C-9605; ¶ 6914.01.
21. ¶ C-9606; ¶ 6914.03.
22. ¶ C-9608; ¶ 672.
23. ¶ C-9505 *et seq.*; ¶ 6914.
24. ¶ C-9501; ¶ 6914.
25. ¶ C-9551; ¶ 6914.04.

Footnote references beginning with letters are to paragraphs in RIA's Federal Tax Coordinator 2d and RIA's Analysis of Federal Taxes: Income. Footnote references beginning with numbers are to paragraphs in RIA's United States Tax Reporter.

¶ *3971* **Deduction for estate tax attributable to after-death income.**

The decedent's right to after-death income is frequently included in his gross estate for federal estate and generation-skipping tax purposes although the after-death income is taxed as income to the recipient. As a relief, the recipient of the income can deduct the estate and generation-skipping tax attributable to inclusion of the right to income in the gross estate. (Code Sec. 691(c)(1); Reg § 1.691(c)-1(a)) This relief is available to an individual only if he itemizes his deductions. (The itemized deduction isn't subject to the 2%-of-AGI floor.) (Code Sec. 67(b)(8))[26]

Annuity payments received by the surviving annuitant of a joint and survivor annuity are after-death income of the deceased annuitant to the extent that the payments are includible in gross income of the survivor. The portion of the estate tax attributable to the survivor's annuity is allowable as a deduction to the survivor over his life expectancy (determined under IRS tables). (Code Sec. 691(d); Reg § 1.691(d)-1(c))[27]

¶ *3972* **Bankruptcy Estate for Bankrupt Individual**

The bankruptcy estate of an individual is treated as a separate taxable entity for income tax purposes, subject to special rules.

¶ *3973* **Bankruptcy estate as separate taxable entity.**

The separate entity rules apply if a bankruptcy case involving an *individual* debtor (not a corporation or partnership) is brought under Chapter 7 (relating to liquidations) or Chapter 11 (reorganizations) of Title 11 of the U.S. Code, (Code Sec. 1398(a)) but not Chapter 12 (adjustment of debts of family farmers) or Chapter 13 (adjustment of debts of an individual with regular income).[28]

¶ *3974* **Debtor's election to close tax year.**

An individual debtor can elect to close his tax year as of the day before the date the bankruptcy case commences. (Code Sec. 1398(d)(2)(A), (d)(3)) If the election is made, the debtor's tax year that otherwise would include the commencement date is divided into two "short" tax years. The first year ends on the day before the commencement date; the second begins on the commencement date. (Code Sec. 1398(d)(2)(A))[29]

¶ *3975* **Tax liability of bankruptcy estate.**

The gross income of the bankruptcy estate of an individual consists of: (1) any gross income of the individual debtor (other than any amount received or accrued as income by the debtor before the commencement of the case), that under the substantive law of bankruptcy (Title 11 of the U.S. Code), is property of the bankruptcy estate, and (2) the gross income of the estate beginning on and after the date the case commenced. (Code Sec. 1398(e)(1))[30] No income tax return for the estate need be filed and no income tax is due if the estate's gross income for the year is less than the sum of the exemption amount plus the basic standard deduction for a married individual filing a separate return. (Code Sec. 6012(a)(9))[31]

Except as otherwise provided, the taxable income of the bankruptcy estate is computed the same as in the case of an individual. (Code Sec. 1398(c)(1))[32] The estate is allowed a personal exemption deduction equal to that of an individual[33] and the same standard deduction as married individuals filing separately. (Code Sec. 1398(c)(3)) The tax rate schedule applicable to the estate is the same as for married individuals filing separate

26. ¶ C-9557 *et seq.*; ¶ 674.   28. ¶ C-9701; ¶ 13,984.   30. ¶ C-9711; ¶ 13,984.01.   32. ¶ C-9708; ¶ 13,984.01.
27. ¶ C-9569; ¶ 6914.07.   29. ¶ C-9802 *et seq.*; ¶ 13,984.02.   31. ¶ C-9723; ¶ 60,124.01.   33. ¶ C-9709; ¶ 13,984.01.

Footnote references beginning with letters are to paragraphs in RIA's Federal Tax Coordinator 2d and RIA's Analysis of Federal Taxes: Income. Footnote references beginning with numbers are to paragraphs in RIA's United States Tax Reporter.

returns. (Code Sec. 1398(c)(2))[34]

The estate succeeds to various income tax attributes of the debtor (including certain carryovers). (Code Sec. 1398(g))[35]

¶ 3976 Business and administrative expenses.

An amount paid or incurred by the bankruptcy estate is deductible or creditable by the estate to the same extent that the item would be by the debtor had the debtor remained in the same trades, businesses or activities after the case commenced as before and had the debtor paid or incurred the amount. (Code Sec. 1398(e)(3))[36]

The estate can deduct: (1) any administrative expense allowed under 11 U.S. Sec. 503 (11 USCS 503), and (2) any court fees and costs assessed against the estate under Chapter 123 of Title 28 of the U.S. Code. (Code Sec. 1398(h)(1))[37]

¶ 3977 Carrybacks and carryovers.

Any deduction for administrative and related expenses not used in the current year can be carried back by the estate three years and carried forward seven years, (Code Sec. 1398(h)(2)) but only to a tax year of the *estate,* not of the debtor. (Code Sec. 1398(h)(2)(D))

The administrative expense carrybacks and carryovers that may be carried to a particular taxable year are "stacked" after the net operating loss deductions (allowed by Code Sec. 172) are computed for the particular year. (Code Sec. 1398(h)(2)(C))[38]

If the bankruptcy estate itself incurs a net operating loss (apart from losses passing to the estate from the individual debtor), the bankruptcy estate can carry back its net operating losses not only to earlier tax years of the estate, but also to tax years of the debtor before the year in which the case commenced. (Code Sec. 1398(j)(2)(A))[39]

¶ 3978 Tax attributes on termination of estate.

On termination of the bankruptcy estate, the debtor succeeds to various tax attributes of the estate (including certain carryovers). (Code Sec. 1398(i))[40]

---

34. ¶ C-9707; ¶ 13,984.01.   36. ¶ C-9714; ¶ 13,984.01.   38. ¶ C-9720; ¶ 13,984.01.   40. ¶ C-9812; ¶ 13,984.01.
35. ¶ C-9718; ¶ 13,984.01.   37. ¶ C-9715; ¶ 13,984.01.   39. ¶ C-9721; ¶ 13,984.01.

Footnote references beginning with letters are to paragraphs in RIA's Federal Tax Coordinator 2d and RIA's Analysis of Federal Taxes: Income. Footnote references beginning with numbers are to paragraphs in RIA's United States Tax Reporter.

Chapter 19 Exempt Organizations

¶ 4100 Tax-Exempt Organizations

Certain nonprofit organizations are exempt from federal income taxation, though they may be taxable on income from businesses they conduct. Prohibited transactions are subject to excise taxes.

Exempt organizations include:

■ U.S. corporate instrumentalities organized under Act of Congress; (Code Sec. 501(c)(1))[1]

■ corporations exclusively holding title to property, and collecting and remitting the income from it (less expenses) to an exempt organization; (Code Sec. 501(c)(2))[2]

■ pooled real estate investment funds of exempt organizations, i.e., corporations or trusts having no more than 35 (exempt) shareholders or beneficiaries and one class of stock or beneficial interest, organized exclusively for acquiring, holding title to, and collecting income from, real property, and remitting that income (less expenses) to those shareholders, etc.; (Code Sec. 501(c)(25))[3]

■ religious, charitable, scientific, literary and educational organizations, organizations testing for public safety, and those organized and operated for preventing cruelty to children or animals (¶ 4102); (Code Sec. 501(c)(3))

■ organizations that foster national or international amateur sports competition, if no part of their activities involves providing athletic facilities or equipment; (Code Sec. 501(c)(3))[4]

■ religious and apostolic organizations (¶ 4105);

■ nonprofit civic organizations operated exclusively for social welfare, and local employees' associations whose net earnings are used solely for charitable, educational or recreational purposes; (Code Sec. 501(c)(4))[5]

■ labor, agricultural or horticultural organizations; (Code Sec. 501(c)(5), (g))[6]

■ chambers of commerce, business leagues, real estate boards, boards of trade or professional football leagues not organized for profit or private benefit; (Code Sec. 501(c)(6))[7]

■ social and athletic clubs (¶ 4106); (Code Sec. 501(c)(7))

■ fraternal beneficiary societies, orders or associations operating under the lodge system and providing life, sick, accident or other benefits to members and their dependents; (Code Sec. 501(c)(8))[8]

■ domestic fraternal societies operating under the lodge system that don't provide payment of benefits, if their net earnings are devoted exclusively to religious, charitable, etc., and fraternal purposes; (Code Sec. 501(c)(10))[9]

■ voluntary employees' beneficiary associations (VEBAs) providing for benefit payments to members and their dependents, if no part of the VEBA's earnings (other than the benefit payments) goes to benefit a private shareholder or individual; (Code Sec. 501(c)(9))[10]

■ local teachers' retirement fund associations; (Code Sec. 501(c)(11))[11]

■ local benevolent life insurance associations, mutual ditch or irrigation companies, mutual or cooperative telephone companies or like organizations, but only if 85% or more of the income is collected from members solely to meet losses and expenses; (Code Sec. 501(c)(12))[12]

■ nonprofit cemetery companies and burial corporations; (Code Sec. 501(c)(13))[13]

---

1. ¶ D-6301; ¶ 5014.02.
2. ¶ D-5801; ¶ 5014.03.
3. ¶ D-5850 *et seq.*; ¶ 5014.04.
4. ¶ D-4181; ¶ 5014.07.

5. ¶ D-5100 *et seq.*; ¶ 5014.13.
6. ¶ D-4600 *et seq.*; ¶ 5014.14.
7. ¶ D-4800 *et seq.*; ¶ 5014.15.

8. ¶ D-4300 *et seq.*; ¶ 5014.17.
9. ¶ D-4304; ¶ 5014.19.
10. ¶ D-4400 *et seq.*.

11. ¶ D-5501; ¶ 5014.20.
12. ¶ D-6100 *et seq.*; ¶ 5014.21.
13. ¶ D-6000 *et seq.*; ¶ 5014.22.

Footnote references beginning with letters are to paragraphs in RIA's Federal Tax Coordinator 2d and RIA's Analysis of Federal Taxes: Income. Footnote references beginning with numbers are to paragraphs in RIA's United States Tax Reporter.

■ credit unions without capital stock that are organized and operated for mutual purposes without profit, and certain mutual financial organizations without capital stock organized before Sept. 1, '57, to provide reserve funds and insurance of shares or deposits in building and loan associations, cooperative banks or mutual savings banks; (Code Sec. 501(c)(14))[14]

■ nonlife insurance companies or associations whose net written premiums (or, if greater, direct written premiums) for the tax year do not exceed $350,000; (Code Sec. 501(c)(15))[15]

■ farmers' cooperatives meeting certain qualifications; (Code Sec. 501(c)(16))[16]

■ certain domestic veterans' organizations, if no part of net earnings benefits any private shareholder or individual; (Code Sec. 501(c)(19))[17]

■ any association organized before 1880, if more than 75% of its members are present or past members of the U.S. armed forces, and its principal purpose is to provide insurance and other benefits to veterans or their dependents; (Code Sec. 501(c)(23))[18]

■ qualified employee benefit trusts (Chapter 21);

■ trusts established by the Pension Benefit Guaranty Corporation (PBGC) in connection with a terminated plan; (Code Sec. 501(c)(24))[19]

■ supplemental unemployment benefit plans (SUBs); (Code Sec. 501(c)(17))[20]

■ black lung benefit trusts; (Code Sec. 501(c)(21))[21]

■ certain trusts created before June 25, '59, to pay benefits under a pension plan funded only by employee contributions. (Code Sec. 501(c)(18))[22]

¶ 4101   Feeder organizations.

An organization operated for the primary purpose of carrying on a business for profit is taxable on all its income, even if all its profits are payable to exempt organizations. (Code Sec. 502(a); Reg § 1.502-1(a))[23]

However, a "feeder" organization is exempt if it's controlled by and furnishes its services *solely* to: a single exempt organization, an exempt parent organization and its exempt subs, or exempt subs having a common parent. (Reg § 1.502-1(b))[24]

"Businesses" that make a feeder organization taxable *do not include*:

(1) any business (a) in which substantially all the work is performed for the organization without compensation, or (b) that is the selling of merchandise substantially all of which has been received by the organization as gifts or contributions; or

(2) deriving rents that wouldn't be included as unrelated business income (¶ 4115). (Code Sec. 502(b))[25]

¶ 4102   Special rules for religious, charitable, educational and similar organizations.

Corporations, community chests, funds or foundations and other organizations are exempt if:

■ it is both organized *and* operated exclusively for religious, charitable, scientific, literary or educational (including certain child care) purposes; for public safety testing; for the prevention of cruelty to children or animals; or to foster national or international amateur sports competition (even if it has local or regional membership); (Code Sec. 501(c)(3); Reg § 1.501(c)(3)-1(a))

■ no part of its net earnings goes to any private shareholder or individual; *and*

■ no substantial part of its activities consists of carrying on propaganda or otherwise attempting to influence legislation, i.e., lobbying (subject to the special election, see

---

14. ¶ D-4900 *et seq.*; ¶ 5014.23.   17. ¶ D-5200 *et seq.*; ¶ 5014.28.   20. ¶ D-4501; ¶ 5014.26.   23. ¶ D-7101; ¶ 5024.03.
15. ¶ D-5900 *et seq.*; ¶ 5014.24.   18. ¶ D-5205; ¶ 5014.28.   21. ¶ D-6200 *et seq.*; ¶ 5014.30.   24. ¶ D-7101; ¶ 5024.01.
16. ¶ E-1007 *et seq.*; ¶ 5014.25.   19. ¶ D-5303.   22. ¶ D-5401; ¶ 5014.27.   25. ¶ D-7102; ¶ 5024.02.

Footnote references beginning with letters are to paragraphs in RIA's Federal Tax Coordinator 2d and RIA's Analysis of Federal Taxes: Income. Footnote references beginning with numbers are to paragraphs in RIA's United States Tax Reporter.

¶ 4103), or intervening in any political campaign for or against any candidate. (Code Sec. 501(c)(3))[26] (For excise tax on these expenditures, see 4105.)

For "private foundation" presumption, see ¶ 4118.

¶ 4103 Limited lobbying expenditures allowed for electing Code Sec. 501(c)(3) organizations.

Certain Code Sec. 501(c)(3) organizations (other than church-related organizations or private foundations) may elect (on Form 5768) to make limited lobbying expenditures without losing their tax-exempt status. (Code Sec. 501(h))[27] The election is effective for all tax years that end after it is made, and that begin before it is revoked. (Code Sec. 501(h)(6))[28] The charity must show these expenses on its annual return (¶ 4117). (Code Sec. 6033)[29]

An electing charity's permissible lobbying expenditures for any tax year can't exceed ("general limit") the lesser of: (1) $1,000,000, or (2) the sum of 20% of the first $500,000 it paid or incurred for exempt purposes (including related administrative costs) for the year, plus 15% of the second $500,000, plus 10% of the third $500,000, plus 5% of any additional such expenditures. (Code Sec. 4911(c)(2)) Also, only 25% of this lobbying amount may go to influencing legislation ("grass roots expenditures"). (Code Sec. 4911(c)(4))[30]

In any tax year when an electing charity's lobbying expenditures exceed either the general or the grass roots limit, a 25% excise tax is imposed on that excess. Where both limits are exceeded, the tax is imposed on the greater excess. (Code Sec. 4911(a), (b))[31] Pay the tax on Form 4720.[32]

Also, an electing charity can lose its tax exemption if its lobbying expenditures over a four-year period exceed 150% of either the general or grass roots limits. (Code Sec. 501(h)(1), (2))[33]

¶ 4104 Political and lobbying expenditures taxes on religious, charitable, etc., organizations.

A Code Sec. 501(c)(3) organization is subject to a two-tier excise tax on its *political expenditures.* An initial tax of 10% of the amount of the expenditure is imposed on the organization, and an initial 2 ½% tax is imposed on any organization manager who willfully and without reasonable cause agreed to the expenditure. (Code Sec. 4955(a))[34] Form 4720 is used to report these taxes.[35] Additional taxes are imposed on both the organization (100%) and management (50%) if the expenditure isn't corrected within a reasonable time. (Code Sec. 4955(b))[36]

A Code Sec. 501(c)(3) organization (other than private foundations, church-related organizations and electing Code Sec. 501(h) organizations) whose *lobbying expenditures* for a tax year cause it to lose its tax exemption (¶ 4103) is subject to a 5% tax on those disqualifying amounts. An additional 5% tax is imposed on any organization manager who agreed to the expenditure knowing that disqualification could result. (Code Sec. 4912)[37] Use Form 4720.[38]

¶ 4105 Religious or apostolic associations.

Even if an organization carries on business activities so that it's not organized and operated exclusively for exempt purposes, it still can be exempt as a *religious or apostolic association.* The organization may thus be exempt if it has a common or community treasury, and if its income (whether or not distributed) is taxed pro rata to its members, as a dividend received, for the organization's tax year ending with or within the member's tax year. (Code Sec. 501(d); Reg § 1.501(d)-1)[39]

---

26. ¶ D-4101; ¶ 5014.05.
27. ¶ D-6500 *et seq.*; ¶ 5014.12.
28. ¶ D-6501; ¶ 5014.12.
29. ¶ D-6571; ¶ 60,334.
30. ¶ D-6507 *et seq.*; ¶ 49,114.
31. ¶ D-6532 *et seq.*; ¶ 49,114.
32. ¶ S-2512.
33. ¶ D-6572 *et seq.*; ¶ 5014.12.
34. ¶ D-6421 *et seq.*; ¶ 49,554.
35. ¶ S-2512.
36. ¶ D-6421 *et seq.*; ¶ 49,554.
37. ¶ D-6417 *et seq.*; ¶ 49,124.
38. ¶ S-2512.
39. ¶ D-5601; ¶ 5014.33.

Footnote references beginning with letters are to paragraphs in RIA's Federal Tax Coordinator 2d and RIA's Analysis of Federal Taxes: Income. Footnote references beginning with numbers are to paragraphs in RIA's United States Tax Reporter.

¶ 4106　Social clubs.

For a social club to be exempt, it must be organized and operated substantially for pleasure, recreation or other nonprofit purposes, its governing instruments or written policies can't provide for discrimination based on color, race or religion, and no part of its earnings may benefit any private shareholder. (Code Sec. 501(c)(7))[40]

Social clubs may receive up to 35% of their gross receipts (including investment income) from sources outside of their membership without losing their exemption. Not more than 15% of this 35% may be from the general public's use of the club's facilities or services (i.e., not members or their guests).[41]

If the club fails the 35% or 15% tests (and a facts and circumstances test) in any tax year, all of its income, even amounts (reduced by allocable costs) received from members, are subject to tax in that year. (Code Sec. 277)[42]

¶ 4107　Nondiscrimination requirements for VEBAs and SUBs.

A VEBA or SUB won't be exempt unless it satisfies nondiscrimination rules similar to those applicable to qualified employee benefit plans (¶ 4325). (Code Sec. 501(c)(17)(A), Code Sec. 505(a)(1), (b)(1))[43]

¶ 4108　Application for exemption—advance rulings.

An organization must apply in writing (on Form 1023 for Code Sec. 501(c)(3) organizations, on Form 1024 for most others, with the appropriate user fee) for an IRS ruling or determination that it is exempt from federal income tax. (Reg § 1.501(a)-1(a)(2))[44] Commonly controlled organizations may apply on a group basis.[45]

¶ 4109　Modification or revocation of exemption.

IRS may modify or revoke rulings and determination letters that granted exempt status to an organization (e.g., for failure to comply with exemption requirements, or prohibited transactions, see ¶ 4112). The revocation may be retroactive, in which case deficiencies and penalties may imposed for open years.[46]

¶ 4110　Political organizations.

A political organization is a party, committee, association, fund (including certain newsletter funds) or other organization (whether or not incorporated) that is organized and operated primarily to accept contributions and/or make expenditures for an "exempt function," e.g., influencing or attempting to influence the selection, nomination, election or appointment of any individual to public office. (Code Sec. 527(e)(1), (2), (g))[47] Although generally tax-exempt, (Code Sec. 527(a)) a political organization is taxed, at the *highest* corporate rate, on income (minus expenses connected with it) from assets it invests rather than uses currently in its exempt function (Code Sec. 527(b)(1), (c))[48] Report on Form 1120-POL.[49]

¶ 4111　Homeowners' associations.

Associations for the management of residential real estate and condominiums (but not cooperative housing corporations) may elect (by filing Form 1120-H) to be treated as tax-exempt organizations. (Code Sec. 528(a), (c))[50] Electing associations are taxed at a 30% rate on income other than amounts received as membership dues, fees or assessments

---

40. ¶ D-4201; ¶ 5014.16.
41. ¶ D-4205; ¶ 5014.16.
42. ¶ D-4206; ¶ 5014.16.

43. ¶s D-4418, D-4501, D-6351; ¶ 5054.
44. ¶ T-10471 *et seq.*; ¶ 5014.01.

45. ¶ T-10485.16; ¶ 5014.01.
46. ¶s T-10485.20, T-10485.21.
47. ¶s D-5002, D-5021; ¶ 5274.

48. ¶ D-5008; ¶ 5274.
49. ¶ S-2108.
50. ¶ D-5701 *et seq.*; ¶ 5284.

Footnote references beginning with letters are to paragraphs in RIA's Federal Tax Coordinator 2d and RIA's Analysis of Federal Taxes: Income. Footnote references beginning with numbers are to paragraphs in RIA's United States Tax Reporter.

from members. (Code Sec. 528(b))[1] This taxable income must be reported on Form 1120-H. (Code Sec. 6012(a)(6))[2]

¶ 4112 Loss of exemption for engaging in prohibited transactions.

Some employee trusts (including church and governmental plans) will lose or be denied their exemption from income tax (and are subject to an excise tax, see ¶ 4348) if they engage in "prohibited transactions." (Code Sec. 503(a)(1))[3]

A *prohibited transaction* occurs if a trust engages in an activity with its creator, a substantial contributor or person related to either, in which it:

(1) lends any part of its income or corpus without receiving adequate security and a reasonable rate of interest;

(2) pays any compensation in excess of a reasonable allowance for personal services actually rendered;

(3) makes any part of its services available on a preferential basis;

(4) makes any substantial purchase of securities or any other property for more than adequate consideration;

(5) sells any substantial part of its securities or any other property for less than adequate consideration; or

(6) engages in any other transaction that results in a substantial diversion of its income or corpus. (Code Sec. 503(b))[4]

¶ 4113 Fundraising disclosure requirements.

Certain exempt organizations that aren't eligible to receive deductible contributions must expressly state that fact (in a conspicuous and easily recognizable format) in every fundraising solicitation. (Code Sec. 6113(a))[5]

Certain charities that are eligible to receive deductible contributions must, in connection with soliciting or receiving a quid pro quo contribution after '93 in excess of $75, inform the donor in writing that his charitable deduction is limited to the excess of his contribution over the value of the goods or services provided by the charity (with a good faith estimate of the value of those goods and services). (Code Sec. 6115)[6]

¶ 4114 Unrelated business income tax.

Tax-exempt organizations (other than U.S. corporate instrumentalities and certain other exempt organizations) are subject to a tax on income from any unrelated business (¶ 4115). (Code Sec. 511(a), Code Sec. 512(a), (b)(12); Reg § 1.511-2(a)(1))[7] Imposition of this tax doesn't affect the organization's exempt status. (Code Sec. 501(b), Code Sec. 511)[8]

An *unrelated business* is a trade or business (i.e., carried on for the production of income, whether or not profit results) regularly carried on (including seasonally) by the organization, that isn't substantially related (aside from providing funds) to the exercise or performance of its exempt purpose or function. (Code Sec. 513(a), (c); Reg § 1.513-1)[9]

For exempt SUBs, qualified employee pension, etc., trusts, and nonexempt trusts, *any* business it regularly carries on is "unrelated." (Code Sec. 513(b))[10]

But an unrelated business doesn't include an activity where substantially all the work is performed for the organization without compensation, e.g., by volunteers. (Code Sec. 513(a)(1))[11]

The rules on assessment, collection, and penalties applicable to income tax (including

---

1. ¶ D-5712; ¶ 5284.
2. ¶ S-2109; ¶ 60,124.
3. ¶ D-6701.
4. ¶ D-6702 *et seq.*; ¶ 5034.02.
5. ¶ D-4004 *et seq.*; ¶ 61,134.
6. ¶s K-3099.1, K-3099.2; ¶ 61,150.
7. ¶ D-6800 *et seq.*; ¶ 5109.
8. ¶ D-6800; ¶ 5114.
9. ¶ D-6804 *et seq.*; ¶ 5134.01.
10. ¶ D-6807; ¶ 5134.
11. ¶ D-6836; ¶ 5134.

Footnote references beginning with letters are to paragraphs in RIA's Federal Tax Coordinator 2d and RIA's Analysis of Federal Taxes: Income. Footnote references beginning with numbers are to paragraphs in RIA's United States Tax Reporter.

estimated tax) apply. (Code Sec. 6655(g)(3)(A); Reg § 1.511-3(a)) The corporate tax rates and filing dates apply if the organization is a corporation, and those for trusts if it is a charitable trust. (Code Sec. 511(a), (b))[12] Form 990-T is used to report and pay the tax. (Reg § 1.6012-2(e), -3(a)(5))[13]

¶ 4115 Unrelated business taxable income defined.

Unrelated business taxable income (UBTI) is the gross income derived from any unrelated trade or business (¶ 4114) less directly connected allowable deductions, but with certain exceptions (below), additions and limitations, (Code Sec. 512(a), (b)) including a specific deduction of $1,000. (Code Sec. 512(b)(12))[14] Social clubs, VEBAs, SUBs and veterans organizations are allowed special exclusions. (Code Sec. 512(a)(3))[15]

Dividends, interest, rents, royalties, annuities, payments with respect to securities loans, loan commitment fees (received after '93), and gains or losses from property dispositions are excluded from UBTI, as are gains or losses received after '93 from the lapse or termination of options to buy or sell securities or real property, or from the forfeiture of good-faith deposits to buy, sell, or lease real property in connection with the organization's investment activities. (Code Sec. 512(b)) But to the extent the dividends, etc., are attributable to property acquired through debt financing (¶ 4116), they *are* included. The includible portion (computed separately for each property) equals a percentage (not over 100%) of the dividends, etc., derived from the property during the tax year, based on the ratio of: (1) the average acquisition indebtedness, to (2) the average adjusted basis of debt-financed property, for the year. (Code Sec. 514(a)(1))[16] This same percentage also is used to compute the allowable deductions for that property (other than capital loss carryovers or depreciation). (Code Sec. 514(a)(2), (3))[17]

¶ 4116 What is debt-financed property?

Debt-financed property, with certain exceptions, is any property held to produce income (including gains from its disposition, as well as rents, dividends and other recurring income), (Code Sec. 514(b); Reg § 1.514(b)-1(a)) with respect to which there is an acquisition indebtedness (below) at any time during the tax year.[18]

"Acquisition indebtedness" for any property generally means: (1) the unpaid amount of indebtedness incurred by the organization in acquiring or improving the property; and (2) indebtedness incurred at other times which *but for* the acquisition or improvement would not have been incurred (if incurred after the acquisition, etc., the debt must have been reasonably foreseeable at that time). (Code Sec. 514(c))[19]

The amount of any mortgage or other lien encumbering the acquired property is considered incurred in that acquisition, whether or not it is thus assumed by the organization. (Code Sec. 514(c)(2)(A))[20]

¶ 4117 Filing requirements for exempt organizations.

In general, every organization that is exempt from tax (for private foundations, see ¶ 4122), or whose exemption application is pending, must file an annual information return (Form 990 series) and keep the records and make sworn statements as required by IRS. (Code Sec. 6033; Reg § 1.6033-2)[21]

The return must be for the organization's annual accounting period or if it has none, the calendar year. (Reg § 1.6033-2(b)) It must be filed by the fifteenth day of the fifth full month after this annual period. (Reg § 1.6033-2(e))[22] Use Form 2758 to extend the return.

And, with certain exceptions, an exempt organization must file an information return on liquidation, dissolution, termination or contraction if it was exempt for any of its last

---

12. ¶ D-6928.	15. ¶ D-6929 *et seq.*; ¶ 5124.	18. ¶ D-7012 *et seq.*; ¶ 5144.	21. ¶ S-2801 *et seq.*; ¶ 60,334.
13. ¶ S-2101.	16. ¶ D-7000 *et seq.*; ¶ 5144.	19. ¶ D-7040 *et seq.*; ¶ 5144.	22. ¶ S-4928; ¶ 60,334.
14. ¶ D-6900 *et seq.*; ¶ 5124.	17. ¶s D-7008, D-7010; ¶ 5144.	20. ¶ D-7043; ¶ 5144.	

Footnote references beginning with letters are to paragraphs in RIA's Federal Tax Coordinator 2d and RIA's Analysis of Federal Taxes: Income. Footnote references beginning with numbers are to paragraphs in RIA's United States Tax Reporter.

five years. (Code Sec. 6043(b))[23] For other information return requirements, see ¶ 4745.

¶ 4118 Private foundations.

Private foundations are generally exempt from income tax, but are subject to special excise taxes (¶ 4121), notification requirements and other restrictions.[24]

A private foundation is any domestic or foreign religious, scientific, charitable, etc., organization described in Code Sec. 501(c)(3) (¶ 4102) *other than* organizations that:

(1) are 50% charities (¶ 2123) except operating foundations and membership organizations; (Code Sec. 509(a)(1))[25]

(2) meet detailed public support tests; (Code Sec. 509(a)(2), (d))[26]

(3) operate exclusively for the benefit of one or more of the above organizations, and aren't controlled by disqualified persons (other than foundation managers), see ¶ 4121; (Code Sec. 509(a)(3))[27]

(4) are organized and operated exclusively for testing for public safety. (Code Sec. 509(a)(4))[28]

A Code Sec. 501(c)(3) organization (other than a church or an organization whose annual gross receipts don't exceed $5,000) is presumed to be a private foundation unless it notifies IRS to the contrary (Code Sec. 508(b), (c))[29] on Form 1023 within 15 months from the end of the month it was organized. (Reg § 1.508-1(b)(2))[30]

¶ 4119 Taxable trusts and foreign organizations subject to private foundation rules.

Certain charitable trusts and split interest trusts, and foreign organizations meeting the "private foundation" definition (¶ 4118), may be subject to the private foundation excise taxes (¶ 4121) and rules on prohibited acts, but not the notification requirements. (Code Sec. 4947, Code Sec. 4948)[31]

¶ 4120 Termination of private foundation status.

An organization's status as a private foundation will terminate if it:

(1) notifies IRS of its intent to terminate *and* then (a) distributes all its net assets to one or more public charities, or (b) becomes a public charity; (Code Sec. 507(b)(1))[32] or

(2) is guilty of willful repeated acts or omissions, or of a willful and *flagrant* act or omission, resulting in liability for an excise tax (¶ 4121) *and* IRS notifies the organization that it is liable for a termination tax (below). (Code Sec. 507(a))[33]

The organization must pay a tax on termination of its private foundation status. Unless abated by IRS, the tax equals the lesser of: (1) the aggregate tax benefit (as adequately substantiated by the foundation) resulting from its Code Sec. 501(c)(3) status, or (2) the value of its net assets. (Code Sec. 507(c))[34]

¶ 4121 Excise taxes on private foundations.

Private foundations may be subject to the following *excise taxes*:

Net investment income. An *exempt* private foundation is liable for an excise tax of 2% on its net investment income for the tax year. (Code Sec. 4940(a); Reg § 53.4940-1)[35] The tax is reduced to 1% if the foundation makes certain charitable distributions (Code Sec. 4940(e))[36] and is eliminated altogether for certain operating foundations. (Code Sec. 4940(d))[37] For a *taxable* foundation, the excise tax equals the amount (if any) by which: (1) the sum of 2% of its net investment income (computed as if it were exempt)

---

23. ¶ S-2883; ¶ 60,434.
24. ¶ D-7200 *et seq.*; ¶ 5069.
25. ¶ D-7203; ¶ 5069.
26. ¶s D-7204, D-7207, D-7209; ¶ 5069.
27. ¶ D-7209 5; ¶ 5069.
28. ¶ D-7202; ¶ 5069.
29. ¶s D-7216, D-7217; ¶ 5069.
30. ¶ T-10484; ¶ 5069.
31. ¶s D-7300 *et seq.*, D-7400 *et seq.*; ¶s 49,474, 49,484.
32. ¶s D-7220, D-7221; ¶ 5069.
33. ¶s D-7220, D-7222; ¶ 5069.
34. ¶ D-7228; ¶ 5069.
35. ¶ D-7501; ¶ 49,404.
36. ¶ D-7503; ¶ 49,404.
37. ¶ D-7504; ¶ 49,404.

Footnote references beginning with letters are to paragraphs in RIA's Federal Tax Coordinator 2d and RIA's Analysis of Federal Taxes: Income. Footnote references beginning with numbers are to paragraphs in RIA's United States Tax Reporter.

plus the unrelated business income tax (¶ 4115) that would have been imposed on it had it been exempt, *exceeds* (2) the income tax actually imposed on it for the tax year. (Code Sec. 4940(b))[38] Report the tax on Form 990-PF. (Reg § 53.6011-1(d))[39]

Self-dealing. An excise tax is imposed when a disqualified person (substantial contributors, foundation managers, and specified owners, family members and related entities of these, as well as government officials) (Code Sec. 4946(a)(1)) engages in any of these acts of self-dealing with a private foundation:[40] (1) selling, exchanging or leasing property; (2) lending money or other extension of credit; (3) furnishing goods, services or facilities; (4) paying compensation or reimbursing expenses; (5) transfer of the foundation's income or assets to or for the use of a disqualified person; or (6) agreement by a foundation to pay any money or property to a government official. (Code Sec. 4941(d)(1))[41]

For *each* act of self-dealing, (Code Sec. 4941(a), (b))[42] the disqualified person (except foundation managers) is subject to an initial tax of 5% on the amount involved (Code Sec. 4941(a)(1); Reg § 53.4941(a)-1(a))[43] and an 200% additional tax if the self-dealing isn't timely corrected. (Code Sec. 4941(b)(1))[44] Any foundation manager who knowingly participates in the act is subject to an initial 2½% tax (Code Sec. 4941(a)(2))[45] and, if the manager refuses to agree with all or part of the correction, an additional 50% tax. (Code Sec. 4941(b)(2))[46] Managers may be jointly and severally liable, but their maximum liability for any one act is $10,000 in initial tax and $10,000 in additional tax. (Code Sec. 4941(c))[47] Report the initial taxes on Form 4720. (Reg § 53.6011-1(b))[48]

Failure to distribute income. A foundation (other than an operating foundation) that fails to distribute its income for a tax year by the end of the *next* year is subject to an initial tax equal to 15% of the income (based on a minimum investment return), which IRS may abate for reasonable cause, (Code Sec. 4942(a), Code Sec. 4962(a); Reg § 53.4942(a)-1(a))[49] and a 100% additional tax if the foundation fails to distribute the income by the date the initial tax is assessed or IRS issues a 90-day letter for it. (Code Sec. 4942(b))[50] Report the initial taxes on Form 4720. (Reg § 53.6011-1(b))[1]

Excess business holdings. A foundation that has any excess business holdings is subject to an initial tax (which IRS may abate for reasonable cause) equal to 5% of those excess holdings, based on their value on the day during the tax year when those holdings were the greatest. (Code Sec. 4943(a), Code Sec. 4962)[2] If the foundation fails to timely correct its holdings, an additional 200% tax is imposed. (Code Sec. 4943(b))[3] Report the initial taxes on Form 4720. (Reg § 53.6011-1(b))[4]

Investments that jeopardize a foundation's charitable purpose. An excise tax is imposed if a foundation makes investments that jeopardize its charitable purpose. An initial tax of 5% of the amount invested is imposed on the foundation, *and* on any foundation manager who knowingly participated in the investment. (Code Sec. 4944(a))[5] Additional taxes are imposed on the foundation (25%) if the investment is not timely removed from jeopardy, (Code Sec. 4944(b)(1))[6] and on any manager (5%) who refuses to agree to removing the investment from jeopardy. (Code Sec. 4944(b)(2))[7] Foundation managers may be jointly and severally liable for these taxes, but the initial tax on management with respect to any one investment is limited to $5,000, and the additional tax to $10,000. (Code Sec. 4944(d))[8] Report the initial taxes on Form 4720. (Reg § 53.6011-1(b))[9]

Propaganda, legislative activities and other taxable expenditures. An excise tax is imposed for engaging in propaganda or legislative activities or for making other taxable expenditures. An initial tax equal to 10% of the amount of the taxable expenditure is

---

38. ¶ D-7506; ¶ 49,404.
39. ¶ S-2511; ¶ 60,334.
40. ¶ D-7600 *et seq.*; ¶ 49,464.
41. ¶ D-7609 *et seq.*; ¶ 49,414.01.
42. ¶s D-7606, D-7608; ¶ 49,414.02.
43. ¶ D-7601; ¶ 49,414.02.
44. ¶ D-7602; ¶ 49,414.02.

45. ¶ D-7601; ¶ 49,414.02.
46. ¶ D-7602; ¶ 49,414.02.
47. ¶s D-7603, D-7604; ¶ 49,414.02.
48. ¶ S-2511.
49. ¶s D-7701, D-8201; ¶s 49,424, 49,614.

50. ¶s D-7701, D-7706; ¶ 49,424.01.
1. ¶ S-2511.
2. ¶s D-7800 *et seq.*, D-8201; ¶s 49,434, 49,614.
3. ¶ D-7801; ¶ 49,434.
4. ¶ S-2511.

5. ¶s D-7901, D-7903; ¶s 49,444, 49,614.
6. ¶ D-7905; ¶ 49,444.
7. ¶ D-7906; ¶ 49,444.
8. ¶ D-7907; ¶ 49,444.
9. ¶ S-2511.

Footnote references beginning with letters are to paragraphs in RIA's Federal Tax Coordinator 2d and RIA's Analysis of Federal Taxes: Income. Footnote references beginning with numbers are to paragraphs in RIA's United States Tax Reporter.

imposed on the foundation, and a 2½% initial tax is imposed on any foundation manager who willfully agreed to the expenditure. (Code Sec. 4945(a))[10] An additional tax is imposed on the foundation (100%) if the expenditure isn't timely corrected, and on any foundation manager (50%) who refuses to agree to part or all of the correction. (Code Sec. 4945(b))[11] Foundation managers may be jointly and severally liable, but the maximum tax that may be imposed on them for any one taxable expenditure is $5,000 of initial tax and $10,000 of additional tax. (Code Sec. 4945(c)) These taxes don't apply if the political expenditures tax (¶ 4104) applies. (Code Sec. 4955(e))[12] Report the initial taxes on Form 4720. (Reg § 53.6011-1(b))[13]

¶ 4122 Annual return of private foundations—Form 990-PF.

A private foundation must file an annual information return on Form 990-PF (Reg § 1.6033-2(a)(2)(i)) on or before the fifteenth day of the fifth month following the close of the tax year. (Reg § 1.6033-2(e))[14]

---

10. ¶ D-8001; ¶s 49,454, 46,614.   12. ¶ D-8003; ¶ 49,554.   13. ¶ S-2511; ¶ 60,334.   14. ¶s S-2801, S-4928; ¶ 60,334.
11. ¶ D-8001; ¶ 49,454.02.

Footnote references beginning with letters are to paragraphs in RIA's Federal Tax Coordinator 2d and RIA's Analysis of Federal Taxes: Income. Footnote references beginning with numbers are to paragraphs in RIA's United States Tax Reporter.

Chapter 20 Banks, Regulated Investment Companies, REITs, REMICs and Other Special Corporations

¶ 4200 Special Corporations and Other Entities

Regulated investment companies, real estate investment trusts, real estate mortgage investment conduits and certain other investment entities are granted special tax treatment because of the nature of their business. Cooperatives, banks and insurance companies are also granted special tax treatment.

¶ 4201 Regulated investment companies (RICs).

If it meets certain distribution requirements, a RIC is taxed only on: (1) the undistributed portion of its ordinary net income, at the regular corporate rates; and (2) the undistributed portion of its net long-term capital gains, at the corporate capital gains rate. (Code Sec. 852(b))[1]

The RIC is not taxed on the amounts it distributes to shareholders, effectively allowing it to pass through ordinary income, net capital gains, tax-exempt interest and certain other items to the shareholders without any tax at the RIC level (if the relevant requirements are met). (Code Sec. 852(b))[2]

Undistributed capital gains may also be designated (on Form 2438) and passed through to shareholders. The effects of the designation are that the shareholders: (1) include their shares of the undistributed capital gains in income, (2) receive a credit or refund for their shares of the tax paid by the RIC on the undistributed capital gains, and (3) receive a step up in their basis in their shares equal to 65% of the amount subject to tax. (Code Sec. 852(b)(3)(D))[3]

A RIC is a domestic corporation (or mutual or common trust fund) that at all times during the tax year is registered with the SEC as a management company or unit investment trust, or has an election in effect to be treated as a business development company, under the '40 Investment Company Act. (Code Sec. 851(a))[4]

In addition, it must elect to be taxed as a RIC, (Code Sec. 851(b)(1))[5] meet certain gross income (Code Sec. 851(b)(2), (3))[6] and diversification tests (Code Sec. 851(b)(4))[7] and certain distribution requirements.[8] (Code Sec. 852(a)(1))

¶ 4202 Real estate investment trusts (REITs).

REITs are taxed only on amounts not distributed to their shareholders or beneficiaries, as follows: (1) at *regular* corporate rates on undistributed earnings and profits and net capital gains, and (2) at the *highest* corporate rate on net income from foreclosure property. (Code Sec. 857)[9]

A REIT, a vehicle for investing in real estate, must be a calendar-year (Code Sec. 859) corporation, trust or association that meets certain requirements as to the source of its income, the type of its investments, the nature of its activities, and its relationships with financially interested parties, (Code Sec. 856(a)) as well as certain recordkeeping and distribution requirements. (Code Sec. 857(a)) And it must elect on its return (Form 1120-REIT) to be treated as a REIT. (Code Sec. 856(c)(1); Reg § 1.846-2(b))[10]

¶ 4203 RIC and REIT dividends paid after close of tax year; year-end dividends.

A RIC (¶ 4201) or REIT (¶ 4202) may elect to treat all or part of any dividend paid after the end of a tax year as paid during the year, if the dividend is: (1) declared before the due date of the return (REITs must state a dollar amount), and (2) paid not later than the first regular dividend date after declaration, but in no case later than 12 months after the end of the tax year. (Code Sec. 855(a), Code Sec. 858(a)) The dividends are still deemed to

---

1. ¶ E-6102; ¶ 8524.02.
2. ¶ E-6150.
3. ¶ E-6155.

4. ¶ E-6001 *et seq.*; ¶ 8514.
5. ¶ E-6002.
6. ¶s E-6004, E-6006.

7. ¶s E-6012, E-6015; ¶ 8514.03.
8. ¶ E-6101.

9. ¶ E-6500 *et seq.*; ¶ 8574.01.
10. ¶ E-6501.

Footnote references beginning with letters are to paragraphs in RIA's Federal Tax Coordinator 2d and RIA's Analysis of Federal Taxes: Income. Footnote references beginning with numbers are to paragraphs in RIA's United States Tax Reporter.

be received by the shareholders in the tax year in which they are actually paid. (Code Sec. 855(b), Code Sec. 858(b))[11]

A dividend declared in October, November or December of any calendar year, that is payable to shareholders of record on a specified date in one of those months, is considered to have been paid by the RIC or REIT and received by the shareholders on Dec. 31 if the dividend is actually paid during January of the following calendar year. (Code Sec. 852(b)(7), Code Sec. 857(b)(8))[12]

¶ 4204   Real estate mortgage investment conduits (REMICs).

REMICs are fixed mortgage pools with multiple classes of investment interests, that have elected REMIC status. (Code Sec. 860D; Reg § 1.860D-1T(c))[13] REMICs, which are treated as partnerships for procedural purposes, (Code Sec. 860F(e))[14] are not subject to tax. (Code Sec. 860A(a))[15] The REMIC's income is instead allocated to, and taken into account by, the holders of its interests. (Code Sec. 860A(b)) REMICs report on Form 1066.[16]

Although not subject to federal income tax, a REMIC is subject to certain penalty taxes.[17]

¶ 4205   Small business investment companies (SBICs).

SBICs are licensed and operated under the Small Business Investment Act of '58.[18] The following special tax rules apply to SBICs:

■ Loss (to investor) on stock received through the conversion of convertible debentures originally acquired for long-term equity capital supplied to small business concerns is a fully deductible ordinary loss. (Code Sec. 1243)[19]

■ An SBIC's gain or loss on sale of bonds, debentures, etc., (regardless of issuer) is ordinary gain or loss. (Code Sec. 582(c); Reg § 1.582-1(d))[20]

■ Dividends the SBIC receives from taxable domestic corporations are 100% deductible. (Code Sec. 243(a)(2))[21]

■ An SBIC is exempt from personal holding company tax (¶ 3330 *et seq.*), unless at any time in the tax year any shareholder of the SBIC owns, directly or indirectly, a 5% or more interest in the companies financed by the SBIC. (Code Sec. 542(c)(8))[22]

¶ 4206   Cooperatives (co-ops).

A cooperative is an entity in which the same persons are both owners and customers. All co-ops may deduct patronage dividends (¶ 4207). (Code Sec. 1382(b)) "Exempt" farmers co-ops also may deduct certain nonpatronage distributions. (Code Sec. 1382(c))[23]

¶ 4207   Patronage dividends and per-unit retain allocations.

Both "exempt" farmers' co-ops and nonexempt co-ops exclude (deduct) from their income amounts paid as patronage dividends or per-unit retain allocations. (Code Sec. 1381(a), Code Sec. 1382(b))[24] For how the patrons or shareholders treat these amounts, see ¶ 1306.

A patronage dividend represents distributions of net earnings among the cooperators and other patrons on the basis of each person's patronage. (Code Sec. 1388(a))[25] It may be paid in money, a certificate of indebtedness, or other property, including a qualified written notice of allocation.[26]

---

11. ¶s E-6201, E-6701;   14. ¶ E-6927.   18. ¶ I-9541; ¶ 12,424.01.   23. ¶ E-1100 *et seq.*; ¶ 13,814.01.
     ¶s 8554.01, 8584.   15. ¶ E-6917; ¶ 860A4.04.   19. ¶ I-9544; ¶ 12,424.02.   24. ¶ E-1100 *et seq.*; ¶ 13,814.
12. ¶ E-6202; ¶s 8524.02,   16. ¶ E-7000 *et seq.*; ¶s 860A4.01,   20. ¶ I-9546; ¶ 5824.   25. ¶ E-1104; ¶ 13,814.01.
     8574.02.   860A4.02.   21. ¶ I-9542; ¶ 12,424.02.   26. ¶ E-1120; ¶ 13,814.01.
13. ¶s E-6901, E-6903; ¶ 860A4.   17. ¶ E-6920 *et seq.*   22. ¶ D-3311; ¶ 5424.02.

Footnote references beginning with letters are to paragraphs in RIA's Federal Tax Coordinator 2d and RIA's Analysis of Federal Taxes: Income. Footnote references beginning with numbers are to paragraphs in RIA's United States Tax Reporter.

A per-unit retain allocation is an allocation by a co-op to a patron with respect to products marketed for him. (Code Sec. 1388(f))[27]

A written notice of allocation must disclose the dollar amount allocated to the patron on the co-op's books and the portion that is a patronage dividend. (Code Sec. 1388(b); Reg § 1.1388-1(b))[28]

¶ 4208 Nonpatronage distributions.

An "exempt" farmers co-op may deduct: (1) dividends paid during the tax year on its capital stock and on any other evidence of proprietary interest in the co-op, (Code Sec. 1382(c)(1); Reg § 1.1382-3(b)) (2) distributions to patrons on a patronage basis out of earnings from nonpatronage sources, (Code Sec. 1382(c)(2)(A); Reg § 1.1382-3(c)) and (3) payments in redemption of nonqualified written notices of allocation issued to patrons on a patronage basis with respect to earnings from nonpatronage sources. (Code Sec. 1382(c)(2)(B); Reg § 1.1382-3(d))[29]

¶ 4209 Taxation of banks and other financial institutions.

Banks, trust companies, domestic savings associations, (Reg § 1.581-1) mutual savings banks, building and loan associations and cooperative banks (Reg § 1.581-2) are generally taxed the same as regular corporations (Chapter 15), subject to these special rules:[30]

Gains and losses from sales or exchanges of bonds, debentures, notes or certificates or other evidences of indebtedness (including any regular or residual interest in a REMIC, ¶ 4204) are treated as ordinary gains and losses. (Code Sec. 582(c)(1)) Sales of stock and securities are subject to the regular wash sale provisions (¶ 2454).[31]

Interest paid or credited on deposits or CDs is deductible (special rules apply to frozen deposits).[32] But no deduction is allowed for any portion of interest expense that is allocable (comparing the bank's adjusted bases in taxable and exempt investments) to investment in tax-exempts. (Code Sec. 265(b)(1), (2))[33] However, interest allocable to tax-exempts acquired (or treated as acquired) before Aug. 8, '86, is 80% deductible (100% deductible if acquired before '83). (Code Sec. 291(a)(3), (e)(1)(B))[34]

Bad debt reserves. Commercial banks (other than "large" banks, see below) must use the experience method to figure deductions for bad debt reserves if a reserve method is used.(Code Sec. 585(b)(1))[35] Under this method, the additions to the reserve can't bring it above its loans outstanding at year-end multiplied by a six-year moving average percentage (ratio of total bad debts to total outstanding loans). (Code Sec. 585(b)(2))[36]

Losses that a bank incurs on account of its deposits in other banks must be specifically deducted ("charged-off"), whether or not it uses the reserve method for other bad debts. (Code Sec. 582(a))[37]

Also, "large" banks (with assets over $500,000,000) may not use *any* reserve method, but must instead use the specific charge-off method to deduct bad debts. (Code Sec. 585(c)(1))[38]

Worthless securities. A bad debt deduction is allowed to banks for total or partial worthlessness (¶ 1769) of debts evidenced by securities. (Code Sec. 582(a))[39]

Net operating losses (NOLs) of banks are subject to the same three-year carryback, 15-year carryforward rules that apply to taxpayers generally (¶ 1830).[40] However, a ten-back, five-forward rule is allowed for any part of an NOL occurring in tax years beginning after '86 and before '94, that is attributable to bad debt losses. (Code Sec. 172(b)(1)(D))[41]

---

27. ¶ E-1126; ¶ 13,814.01.
28. ¶ E-1123; ¶ 13,814.01.
29. ¶s E-1140, E-1141, E-1142; ¶ 13,814.14.
30. ¶s E-3000 *et seq.*, E-3300 *et seq.*; ¶ 5809.

31. ¶ E-3022 *et seq.*; ¶ 5824.
32. ¶ E-3105; ¶ 5914.
33. ¶ E-3108; ¶ 2654.
34. ¶s E-3111, E-3124; ¶ 2914.

35. ¶ E-3227; ¶ 5854.
36. ¶ E-3227; ¶ 5854.
37. ¶ E-3201; ¶ 5824.
38. ¶ E-3231; ¶ 5854.

39. ¶ E-3201; ¶ 5824.
40. ¶s M-4300 *et seq.*, M-4330; ¶ 1724.08.
41. ¶ M-4326; ¶ 1724.08.

Footnote references beginning with letters are to paragraphs in RIA's Federal Tax Coordinator 2d and RIA's Analysis of Federal Taxes: Income. Footnote references beginning with numbers are to paragraphs in RIA's United States Tax Reporter.

Mutual savings banks or stock associations, savings and loan associations, building and loan associations, and cooperative banks are subject to special tax rules.[42]

¶ 4210 Insolvent banks and trust companies.

Insolvent banks and trust companies are excused from paying federal taxes where the payments would leave them without sufficient assets to pay their depositors in full. (Code Sec. 7507(a)) But this immunity, which is a *postponement of collection* and not an *exemption,* doesn't apply to any taxes attributable to the receipt of certain federal financial assistance.[43]

¶ 4211 Common trust funds.

A common trust fund isn't subject to tax (Code Sec. 584(b)) but must report (on Form 1065) the amount of income or loss attributable to each participant. (Reg § 1.6032-1)[44]

Common trust funds are funds maintained by a bank or trust company exclusively to collectively invest and reinvest moneys that it, in its capacity as a trustee, executor, administrator, guardian or custodian, contributes to it. (Code Sec. 584(a))[45]

¶ 4212 Taxation of insurance companies.

Life insurance companies are taxed, at the regular corporate rates, on their "life insurance company taxable income" (LICTI). (Code Sec. 801(a)(1))[46] Gain recognized on the redemption at maturity of certain market discount bonds is taxed under a special rule.[47]

A company's LICTI is its: (1) life insurance company gross income, i.e., the sum of (a) premiums, (b) decreases in certain reserves, and (c) all other amounts includable in gross income; minus (2) its (a) general deductions, and (b) if applicable, the small life insurance company deduction. (Code Sec. 803(a), Code Sec. 804)[48]

A corporation (whether stock, mutual, or mutual benefit) is taxed as a life insurance company if: (1) it's an insurance company, (2) it's engaged in the business of issuing life insurance and annuity contracts, and (3) it meets a reserve test. (Code Sec. 816(a))[49]

Nonlife insurance companies (stock and mutual) are taxed like corporations generally (Chapter 15), with certain deductions peculiar to the insurance industry. Gross income includes investment income, underwriting income and gain or loss from property dispositions. (Code Sec. 831, Code Sec. 832)[50] Companies whose net written premiums (or direct written premiums, if greater) for the year exceed $350,000 but do not exceed $1,200,000 may elect to be taxed only on investment income. (Code Sec. 831(b))[1] Companies whose net written premiums (or direct written premiums, if greater) do not exceed $350,000 are eligible for tax-exempt status. (Code Sec. 501(c)(15)(A))[2]

Certain health insurance providers are subject to the rules and rates applicable to nonlife insurance companies generally, as modified. (Code Sec. 833)[3] A special 25% deduction is permitted (only for regular tax purposes) with respect to health insurance items. (Code Sec. 833(b))[4]

---

42. ¶ E-3300 *et seq.*; ¶ 5809.
43. ¶ E-3700 *et seq.*; ¶ 75,074.
44. ¶ E-3610; ¶s 5844, 60,324.
45. ¶ E-3600 *et seq.*; ¶ 5844.

46. ¶ E-4801; ¶ 8014.
47. ¶ E-4801.
48. ¶ E-4801 *et seq.*; ¶s 8034, 8044.

49. ¶ E-5401; ¶ 8164.
50. ¶ E-5500 *et seq.*; ¶ 8324.01.
1. ¶ E-5503; ¶ 8314.

2. ¶ E-5502; ¶ 5014.24.
3. ¶ E-5500 *et seq.*; ¶ 8334.
4. ¶ E-5625; ¶ 8334.

Footnote references beginning with letters are to paragraphs in RIA's Federal Tax Coordinator 2d and RIA's Analysis of Federal Taxes: Income. Footnote references beginning with numbers are to paragraphs in RIA's United States Tax Reporter.

Chapter 21 Pension and Profit-Sharing Plans—Keogh (H.R.10)— Individual Retirement Accounts

¶ 4310 Employee Benefit Plans

Qualified pension, profit-sharing and stock bonus plans offer substantial tax benefits to sponsor-employers and their employees.

The principal tax advantages are:

■ the employer gets an immediate deduction for contributions under the plan (¶ 4333), even though the employee does not receive benefits until some time in the future; (Code Sec. 404)[1]

■ the income earned by funds while held under the plan is tax-exempt; (Code Sec. 401, Code Sec. 501)[2]

■ the employee isn't taxed on his share of the fund until amounts are distributed to him after retirement or at some other time (¶ 4338 *et seq.*); (Code Sec. 402, Code Sec. 403; Reg § 1.402(a)-1)[3]

■ qualifying "lump-sum" distributions can get favorable tax treatment (¶ 4339 *et seq.*); (Code Sec. 402(d))[4]

■ amounts transferred in a direct trustee-to-trustee transfer are excluded from income (¶ 4359) (Code Sec. 402(e)(6)) and eligible rollover distributions can be rolled over tax-free to eligible retirement plans (¶ 4360); (Code Sec. 402(c)(1))[5]

■ payments on death of the employee can qualify for the $5,000 employee death benefit exclusion from gross income (see ¶ 1262); (Code Sec. 101)[6]

■ if qualifying distributions are made in the form of stock of the employer corporation, tax on the appreciation in value of the stock is deferred until the stock is sold, see ¶ 4342. (Code Sec. 402(e)(4))[7]

¶ 4311 Pension plans.

A qualified pension plan provides systematically for the payment of definitely determinable benefits to employees (and their beneficiaries) after retirement over a period of years, usually for life.[8]

Retirement benefits are generally measured by such factors as years of the employee's service and compensation received. (Reg § 1.401-1(b)(1)(i))[9]

Benefits under a defined benefit plan are "definitely determinable" if they are determined actuarially, on a basis that precludes employer discretion. (Code Sec. 401(a)(25))[10]

A "money-purchase" plan, where contributions are geared to a fixed formula (e.g., 10% of compensation), rather than to profits, qualifies as a pension plan, if the plan "designates" its intent to be qualified as a money purchase pension plan. (Code Sec. 401(a)(27)(B); Reg § 1.401-1(b)(1)(i))[11]

¶ 4312 Profit-sharing plans.

A qualified profit-sharing plan must have a definite, predetermined formula for allocating contributions made under the plan among the participants, and for distributing the funds accumulated under the plan only after a fixed number of years, the attainment of a stated age or upon the occurrence of some event (such as disability, retirement, death or severance of employment). (Reg § 1.401-1(b)(1)(ii))[12]

Contributions can be made to a qualified profit-sharing plan whether or not the employer has current or accumulated profits, and whether or not the employer is a tax-exempt organization. (Code Sec. 401(a)(27)(A))[13]

1. ¶ H-10000 *et seq.*; ¶ 4014.	5. ¶ H-8250 *et seq.*	9. ¶ H-5328; ¶ 4014.02.	12. ¶ H-5337 *et seq.*; ¶ 4014.03.
2. ¶ H-10500 *et seq.*; ¶ 4014.	6. ¶ H-11228; ¶ 1014.06.	10. ¶ H-5328; ¶ 4014.10.	13. ¶ H-5337; ¶ 4014.03.
3. ¶ H-11006 *et seq.*; ¶ 4014.	7. ¶ H-11500 *et seq.*; ¶ 4014.	11. ¶s H-5205, H-5337;	
4. ¶ H-11200 *et seq.*; ¶ 4014.	8. ¶ H-5328; ¶ 4014.02.	¶ 4014.02.	

Footnote references beginning with letters are to paragraphs in RIA's Federal Tax Coordinator 2d and RIA's Analysis of Federal Taxes: Income. Footnote references beginning with numbers are to paragraphs in RIA's United States Tax Reporter.

¶ 4313 Age-weighted profit-sharing plans.

These are profit-sharing plans in which each employee is given points based on age, service and compensation. The plan need not grant points for *both* age and service (but must grant points for one of them) or for compensation. Each employee must get the same number of points for each year of age, service, and unit (not more than $200) of compensation. Employer contributions and forfeitures are then allocated in proportion to each employee's total points. Specific nondiscrimination rules must also be met. (Reg § 1.401-1(a)(4)-2(b)(3))[14]

☝ observation: Traditional profit-sharing plans allocate the employer's contribution solely on the basis of compensation, not age or length of service. By considering age, age-weighted plans can provide significantly larger amounts to older employees than to younger employees.

¶ 4314 Stock bonus plans.

A qualified stock bonus plan provides benefits in the form of the employer-corporation's own stock. Stock bonus plans must generally satisfy the qualification requirements that apply to profit sharing plans, plus some additional requirements.[15]

¶ 4315 Employee stock ownership plans (ESOPs).

An ESOP is a qualified defined contribution plan that is either a stock bonus plan, or a combination stock bonus and money purchase plan, that invests primarily in employer securities, (Code Sec. 4975(e)(7)) and is formally designated as an ESOP.[16]

¶ 4316 Annuity plans.

The tax advantages of a qualified plan can be obtained without a trust through the use of a qualified annuity plan under which contributions are used to buy retirement annuities directly from an insurance company. (Code Sec. 403(a)(1), Code Sec. 404(a)(2))[17]

For annuities for employees of tax-exempt organizations and public schools, see ¶ 4370 *et seq.*

¶ 4317 "Thrift" and "savings" plans.

A thrift plan is in the nature of a profit-sharing plan and provides for the contribution by the participants of a specified percentage (the same for all participants) of their salaries. This employee contribution is then matched by the employer, either dollar for dollar or in some other specified manner, out of profits.[18]

A savings plan permits employees to make voluntary employee contributions which are not limited to any specific percentage of compensation.[19]

These plans may allow withdrawal of the voluntary employee contributions (plus earnings) before retirement or termination.[20]

¶ 4318 Cash or deferred arrangements—401(k) plans or CODAs.

Cash or deferred arrangements (CODAs), also known as "401(k)" plans (from Code Sec. 401(k)) allow an employee to choose whether the employer should pay a certain amount directly to the employee in cash, or should instead pay that amount on the employee's behalf to a qualified trust under a profit-sharing plan, a stock bonus plan, a pre-ERISA money purchase plan or a rural cooperative defined contribution pension plan. (Code Sec. 401(k))[21] For arrangements similar to CODAs under SEPs and tax-sheltered annuities, see ¶s 4365 and 4370.

14. ¶ H-6154 *et seq.*
15. ¶ H-5209; ¶ 4014.04.
16. ¶ H-9300 *et seq.*; ¶ 49,754.
17. ¶ H-5212 *et seq.*; ¶ 4044.05.
18. ¶ H-5214.
19. ¶ H-5215.
20. ¶ H-5313.
21. ¶ H-8950 *et seq.*; ¶ 4014.17.

Footnote references beginning with letters are to paragraphs in RIA's Federal Tax Coordinator 2d and RIA's Analysis of Federal Taxes: Income. Footnote references beginning with numbers are to paragraphs in RIA's United States Tax Reporter.

However, an employee may elect to defer no more than $8,994 (effective Jan. 1, '93, as indexed; the '94 amount had not been released by IRS as we went to press) tax-free under a CODA for any tax year. (Code Sec. 402(g)(1),(5)) Excess deferrals must be either corrected (i.e., distributed) by Apr. 15 of the following tax year, (Reg § 1.402(g)-1(e)(2)(ii)) or else included in the employee's gross income. (Reg § 1.402(g)-1(a))[22]

An employee who participates in a CODA under a Code Sec. 403(b) annuity maintained by a tax-exempt employer or public school (see ¶ 4370) may elect to defer no more than $9,500 tax-free for any tax year. Amounts above the limit are included in the employee's gross income. (Code Sec. 402(g)(4); Reg § 1.402(g)-1(a))[23]

A 401(k) plan must meet all the normal tax qualification rules (¶ 4320), including the nondiscrimination rules (¶ 4325) and, in addition, all of the following requirements:

(1) amounts must not be distributable except by reason of (a) retirement, death, disability or other separation from service, (b) hardship (see below) or attainment of age 59½ (for profit-sharing or stock bonus plans), (c) in a lump sum on termination of the plan, or (d) in a lump sum, on the employer's disposition of (i) substantially all of its trade or business assets, or (ii) a subsidiary; (Code Sec. 401(k)(2)(B))[24]

(2) employer contributions made under the employee's election must be nonforfeitable at all times; (Code Sec. 401(k)(2)(C))[25] and

(3) a covered employee must be able to elect to have the employer make plan contributions on the employee's behalf or make the payment directly to the employee in cash; (Code Sec. 401(k)(2)(A))[26] and

(4) elective deferrals under the plan (as aggregated with all other plans, etc., of the employer) must be prohibited from exceeding the above indexed dollar limits;[27] and

(5) special CODA nondiscrimination rules that require the plan to satisfy one of two "actual deferral percentage tests," so that highly compensated employees can't elect to defer a disproportionately higher amount of their salary, must be met. (Code Sec. 401(k)(3)(A))[28]

An in-service distribution on account of hardship may only be made if the employee has "an immediate heavy financial need" and the distribution is "necessary to meet such need." But a distribution may be considered for "hardship" only to the extent that, as shown by the employee, the need can't be relieved by certain alternate sources, e.g., loans, insurance. (Reg § 1.401(k)-1(d)(2))[29]

¶ 4319 Defined contribution and defined benefit plans.

Certain rules governing employee benefit plans specifically apply either to "defined contribution plans" or to "defined benefit plans."

A "defined contribution plan" provides for individual accounts for participants and for benefits based on those accounts. (Code Sec. 414(i)) Included are money purchase pension plans, profit-sharing plans and stock bonus plans.

A "defined benefit plan" is a pension plan other than a defined contribution plan. (Code Sec. 414(j)) It provides for the payments of definitely determinable benefits to the employee over a period of years, usually for life, after retirement. (Reg § 1.401-1(b)(i))[30]

¶ 4320 Qualification requirements for a qualified employee plan.

The chief requirements for tax qualification of an employee benefit plan and tax-exempt trust are:

---

22. ¶ H-9151 *et seq.*; ¶ 4014.17.   25. ¶ H-9007; ¶ 4014.17.   28. ¶ H-9050 *et seq.*; ¶ 4014.17.   30. ¶ H-5200 *et seq.*; ¶s 4014.02,
23. ¶ H-9156; ¶ 4034.04.   26. ¶ H-8951; ¶ 4014.17.   29. ¶ H-9211 *et seq.*; ¶ 4014.17.   4014.03.
24. ¶ H-9201 *et seq.*; ¶ 4014.17.   27. ¶ H-9155; ¶ 4014.17.

Footnote references beginning with letters are to paragraphs in RIA's Federal Tax Coordinator 2d and RIA's Analysis of Federal Taxes: Income. Footnote references beginning with numbers are to paragraphs in RIA's United States Tax Reporter.

(1) The plan must be a definite written program[31] which is communicated to the employees. (Reg § 1.401-1(a)(2))[32]

(2) The plan must be established by the employer for the *exclusive* benefit of the employees or their beneficiaries. (Code Sec. 401(a)(1))[33]

(3) The plan must generally provide that benefits can't be assigned, except for transfers under a qualified domestic relations order. (Code Sec. 401(a)(13))[34]

(4) The plan must meet special tests based on coverage and eligibility of employees to participate. See ¶ 4323.

(5) The plan must not discriminate in favor of highly compensated employees with respect to contributions or benefits. See ¶ 4325.

(6) The plan must be properly funded (¶ 4330) and must meet certain vesting requirements (¶ 4322).

(7) Under a defined benefit plan, forfeitures must not be applied to increase the benefits of the employees. (Code Sec. 401(a)(8))[35]

(8) A pension plan (and certain other plans) must in general pay a married participant's benefits in the form of a qualified joint and survivor annuity, unless the participant elects otherwise (with his spouse's written consent). A qualified pre-retirement survivor annuity must be provided to a surviving spouse of a vested participant who dies before the annuity starts, unless the participant (with his spouse's written consent) elected to waive it. (Code Sec. 401(a)(11), Code Sec. 417)[36]

(9) In the event of a merger or consolidation with, or transfer of assets or liabilities to, any other plan, each participant must be entitled under the plan to a termination benefit after the merger, etc., at least equal to his pre-merger, etc., termination benefit. (Code Sec. 401(a)(12))[37]

(10) The plan may not provide for contributions or benefits that exceed specified overall limitations. (Code Sec. 401(a)(16))[38] See ¶ 4328.

(11) The plan must provide that benefit payments begin (unless otherwise elected) no later than the 60th day after the plan year in which occurs the latest of: (a) the date the participant reaches age 65 (or earlier retirement age), (b) the 10th anniversary of the employee's participation in the plan, or (c) the date the participant terminates service. (Code Sec. 401(a)(14); Reg § 1.401(a)-14(a))[39]

(12) The plan must provide that the employee's entire interest will be distributed, starting Apr. 1 of the calendar year following the year in which he: (a) reaches age 70½ or (b) retires (for government and church plans), no later than over (i) his life, (ii) his life and the life of a designated beneficiary, (iii) a period of not more than his life expectancy, or (iv) a period of not more than his life expectancy and that of a designated beneficiary. (Code Sec. 401(a)(9))[40] Failure to make the required distributions is subject to an excise tax (report on Form 5329) equal to 50% of the minimum amount that should have been distributed over the amount actually distributed. (Code Sec. 4974(a))[41]

(13) A pension plan can't allow withdrawal of employer contributions before termination of employment, or of the plan.[42] But employer contributions accumulated in a profit-sharing plan may be distributed after a fixed number of years (not less than two years). (Reg § 1.401-1(b)(1)(ii))[43] A profit-sharing plan may also permit withdrawal of employer contributions for hardship[44] or by participants with at least 60 months of participation.[45]

(14) Every plan must provide that a distributee of an eligible rollover distribution may elect to have the distribution transferred directly to an eligible retirement plan (¶ 4360).

---

31. ¶ H-5301; ¶ 4014.05.	35. ¶ H-7502; ¶ 4014.11.	39. ¶ H-8301; ¶ 4014.15.	43. ¶ H-5346.
32. ¶ H-5303; ¶ 4014.05.	36. ¶ H-8600 *et seq.*; ¶ 4014.16.	40. ¶ H-8400 *et seq.*; ¶ 4014.15.	44. ¶ H-5348.
33. ¶ H-5304; ¶ 4014.09.	37. ¶ H-8800 *et seq.*; ¶ 4014.07.	41. ¶ H-8500 *et seq.*; ¶ 49,744.	45. ¶ H-5346.
34. ¶ H-8200 *et seq.*; ¶ 4014.14.	38. ¶ H-5901 *et seq.*; ¶ 4154.	42. ¶ H-5310.	

Footnote references beginning with letters are to paragraphs in RIA's Federal Tax Coordinator 2d and RIA's Analysis of Federal Taxes: Income. Footnote references beginning with numbers are to paragraphs in RIA's United States Tax Reporter.

(Code Sec. 401(a)(31)(A)) If the direct rollover is at least $500, a recipient can elect to have a distribution paid partly to an eligible retirement plan in a direct rollover with the remainder paid to the distributee. (Reg § 1.401-(a)(31)-1T, Q&A 9) Distribution among two or more transferee plans need not be be permitted. (Reg § 1.401-(a)(31)-1T, Q&A 10) However, if the total amount expected to be paid to a distributee in any year is less than $200, a direct rollover isn't required to be provided. (Reg § 1.401-(a)(31)-1T, Q&A 11)[46]

(15) The plan may not reduce plan benefits (including death or disability) to account for post-separation social security benefit increases. (Code Sec. 401(a)(15))[47]

(16) A plan may take into account only the first $150,000 for '94 (reduced by legislation from $235,840 for '93), adjusted after '94 for inflation, of each employee's annual compensation. (Code Sec. 401(a)(17))[48]

¶ 4321 Incidental benefits.

If life or accident and health insurance features are "incidental" to the primary benefit of a qualified plan, they may be included in the plan to a limited extent. (Reg § 1.401-1(b)(1)(i), (ii))[49]

¶ 4322 Vesting of benefits.

Plans must provide that a participant's right to his "accrued benefit" vests at certain rates during the years of his employment. Benefits derived from employee contributions must be 100% vested at all times. (Code Sec. 411(a); Reg § 1.411(a)-1(a)(2)) Benefits derived from employer contributions must become nonforfeitable when the employee reaches "normal retirement age." (Code Sec. 411(a)) The plan also must meet one of two alternative minimum vesting standards for vesting in benefits derived from employer contributions before normal retirement age: (1) a five-year cliff schedule requiring full vesting after five years of service, or (2) a three-to-seven year graded schedule requiring 20% vesting after three years of service and 20% additional vesting in each of the following years. (Code Sec. 411(a)(2); Reg § 1.411(a)-3T)[50]

"Accrued benefit" means the participant's annual benefit (or its actuarial equivalent) starting at normal retirement age (defined benefit plans) or the balance in the participant's account (defined contribution plans). (Code Sec. 411(a)(7)(A))[1]

Normal retirement age is the earlier of the time a participant attains normal retirement age under the plan or the later of: (1) the time the participant reaches age 65, or (2) the 5th anniversary of the individual's participation in the plan. (Code Sec. 411(a)(8))[2]

¶ 4323 Coverage and eligibility requirement.

A qualified plan must meet special tests designed to insure adequate coverage of rank and file employees and avoid discrimination.

The plan must, on at least one day in each quarter of its tax year, either: (1) benefit 70% of the employees who are not "highly compensated" (¶ 4326), (2) benefit a percentage of nonhighly compensated employees that is at least 70% of highly compensated benefiting, or (3) meet an average benefits test under which the average benefit for the nonhighly compensated is at least 70% of the average benefit for the highly compensated. (Code Sec. 410(b)(1)) The "average benefits test" also requires that the plan benefit employees under a nondiscriminatory classification. (Code Sec. 410(b)(2))[3] However, a plan maintained by an employer that has no employees other than highly compensated employees for a year is treated as meeting the coverage requirement for the year. (Code Sec. 410(b)(6)(F))[4]

---

46. ¶ H-8250 *et seq.*
47. ¶ H-5311; ¶ 4014.22.
48. ¶ H-5918; ¶ 4014.18.
49. ¶ H-8104 *et seq.*; ¶ 4014.13.

50. ¶ H-7400 *et seq.*; ¶s 4114; 4114.01.
1. ¶ H-7200 *et seq.*; ¶ 4114.06.

2. ¶ H-7404; ¶ 4114.08.
3. ¶ H-5410 *et seq.*; ¶s 4104.11, 4104.12.

4. ¶ H-5410; ¶ 4104.12.

Footnote references beginning with letters are to paragraphs in RIA's Federal Tax Coordinator 2d and RIA's Analysis of Federal Taxes: Income. Footnote references beginning with numbers are to paragraphs in RIA's United States Tax Reporter.

A qualified plan cannot require as a condition of participation that any employee complete a period of service extending beyond the later of the date he: (1) reaches age 21, or (2) completes one year of service (or two years, if the plan provides full and immediate vesting for all participants). (Code Sec. 410(a)(1)(A), (B)(i))[5]

¶ 4324 Minimum participation requirement—the 50-employee/40% test.

A plan won't be qualified unless, on each day of the plan year, the plan benefits the lesser of 50 employees of the employer, or 40% or more of all employees of the employer. (Code Sec. 401(a)(26)(A))[6] Instead of meeting the test on each day of the plan year, compliance on a single representative day during the year is sufficient. (Reg § 1.401(a)(26)-7(b))[7]

¶ 4325 Contributions or benefits must be nondiscriminatory.

Contributions or benefits under a plan must not discriminate in favor of "highly compensated employees" (see ¶ 4326). (Code Sec. 401(a)(4))[8] A plan will meet the nondiscrimination requirements if it is operated according to a reasonable, good faith interpretation of the Code provisions. (For plan years beginning before '96, generally, the nondiscrimination requirements are deemed satisfied for governmental plans.)[9]

For plan years beginning after '93 (after '95 for plans maintained by a tax-exempt organization), a plan must satisfy three requirements: (1) either the contributions or benefits under the plan must be nondiscriminatory in amount, (2) the plan's optional forms of benefit, ancillary benefits (e.g., disability benefits), and other rights and features (e.g., plan loans and investment alternatives) must be made available to employees in a nondiscriminatory manner, and (3) the effect of the plan under certain plan amendments, grants of past service credit, and plan terminations must be nondiscriminatory. (Reg § 1.401(a)(4)-1(b))[10]

¶ 4326 Highly compensated employee.

A highly compensated employee is any employee who, during the tax year or preceding tax year: (1) was at any time a 5% owner, or (2) received compensation from the employer in excess of $96,368 (effective Jan. 1, '93, as indexed; the '94 amount had not been released by IRS as we went to press), or (3) received compensation from the employer in excess of $64,245 (effective Jan. 1, '93, as indexed) and was in the "top-paid group" of employees (top 20%) for the year, or (4) was at any time an officer of the employer and received compensation greater than 50% of the defined benefit annual limitation (¶ 4328) for the year. (Code Sec. 414(q); Reg § 1.414(q)-1T)[11]

¶ 4327 Plans covering self-employed persons (Keogh plans).

A person who is a "self-employed individual," i.e., derives "earned income" from a business or profession that he owns or conducts, or who has earned income from a partnership in which he is a partner, or has other self-employment income, can establish and be covered by a qualified retirement plan (sometimes called a Keogh plan). (Code Sec. 401(c)(1))[12] Earned income consists essentially of earnings attributable to personal services, whether from a sole proprietorship, partnership or other unincorporated venture. (Code Sec. 401(c)(2))[13]

¶ 4328 Overall limitations on plan contributions and benefits.

A plan cannot be qualified if it provides for contributions or benefits that exceed the overall limitations described below.

---

5. ¶s H-5804, H-5807 *et seq.*;
   ¶ 4104.02.
6. ¶ H-5701 *et seq.*; ¶ 4014.25.
7. ¶ H-5704; ¶ 4014.25.

8. ¶ H-6105; ¶ 4014.19.
9. ¶ H-6103.
10. ¶ H-6350 *et seq.*; ¶ 4014.19.

11. ¶ H-6702; ¶ 4144.21.
12. ¶s H-5218, H-9500 *et seq.*;
    ¶ 4014.24.

13. ¶ H-9513 *et seq.*; ¶ 4014.24.

Footnote references beginning with letters are to paragraphs in RIA's Federal Tax Coordinator 2d and RIA's Analysis of Federal Taxes: Income. Footnote references beginning with numbers are to paragraphs in RIA's United States Tax Reporter.

Benefits under a defined benefit plan will disqualify the plan if the "annual benefit" for each participant beginning at age 65 exceeds the lesser of: (1) $115,641 (effective Jan. 1, '93, as indexed; the '94 amount had not been released by IRS as we went to press), or (2) 100% of the participant's average compensation for his three high consecutive years of active plan participation. (Code Sec. 415(b))[14] The maximum dollar benefit is reduced if the employee has rendered less than ten years of plan participation at the time he begins to receive retirement benefits. (Code Sec. 415(b)(5)) This reduction doesn't apply to pro rata benefit increases under a terminating plan if there is no discrimination in favor of highly compensated employees. (Code Sec. 4908(d)(4)(C))[15] Neither the dollar nor the percentage limitation applies if benefits payable under a defined benefit plan don't exceed $10,000 and the employer has never had a defined contribution plan in which the employee participated. (Code Sec. 415(b)(4))[16]

Annual additions under a defined contribution plan may not exceed the lesser of: (1) $30,000, or if greater, ¼ of the dollar limitation for a defined benefit plan, or (2) 25% of the participant's compensation. (Code Sec. 415(c)(1))

🅡🅘🅐 *observation:* In other words, the $30,000 limit won't change until the defined benefit plan limit, above, exceeds $120,000 (because ¼ of $120,000 is $30,000).

Annual addition includes employer contributions, employee contributions and forfeitures by other employees. (Code Sec. 415(c))[17]

If an employee participates in both a defined benefit plan and a defined contribution plan of the same employer, a special limitation is imposed on total contributions and benefits that can be provided under the plans. (Code Sec. 415(e))[18]

Special rules are available for applying the limits to certain ESOPs. (Code Sec. 415(c)(6))[19]

Benefits provided to alternate payees under any qualified domestic relations order (QDROs) relating to a participant's benefits must be aggregated with benefits provided to the participant from all defined benefit and defined contribution plans in applying the Code Sec. 415 limitations.[20]

¶ 4329 Additional qualification requirements for "top-heavy" plans.

A "top-heavy" plan must meet specified additional requirements in the areas of minimum vesting and minimum benefits or contributions for non-key employees, in determining contributions or benefits. (Code Sec. 416(a))[21]

Vesting requirements. For any plan year for which a plan is a top-heavy plan, an employee's rights to accrued benefits must be 100% vested after three years of service or, at the employer's option, 20% vested after two years' service and 20% in each of the following years (100% vested after six years of service). (Code Sec. 416(b))[22]

Minimum benefits or contributions. A defined benefit plan must provide a minimum annual retirement benefit, not integrated with Social Security, for a non-key employee equal to the lesser of: (1) 2% of the participant's average compensation for years in the testing period multiplied by his years of service with the employer, or (2) 20% of his average compensation in the years in the testing period. (Code Sec. 416(c)(1))[23]

In a defined contribution plan, the employer must contribute for each non-key employee not less than 3% of that employee's compensation. But the percentage contributed for non-key employees doesn't have to exceed the percentage at which contributions are made, or required to be made, for the key employee with the highest contribution percentage. (Code Sec. 416(c)(2))[24]

Combined limits for both defined benefit and defined contribution plans if either is top

---

14. ¶ H-5950; ¶ 4154.02.
15. ¶ H-5962; ¶ 4154.02.
16. ¶ H-5965; ¶ 4154.02.

17. ¶ H-6000 *et seq.*; ¶ 4154.06.
18. ¶ H-6050 *et seq.*; ¶ 4154.13.
19. ¶ H-6016; ¶ 4154.09.

20. ¶s H-5950, H-6000, H-8217 *et seq.*; ¶ 4154.02.
21. ¶ H-8000 *et seq.*; ¶ 4164.

22. ¶ H-7423; ¶ 4164.04.
23. ¶ H-8025; ¶ 4164.05.
24. ¶ H-8032; ¶ 4164.06.

Footnote references beginning with letters are to paragraphs in RIA's Federal Tax Coordinator 2d and RIA's Analysis of Federal Taxes: Income. Footnote references beginning with numbers are to paragraphs in RIA's United States Tax Reporter.

heavy. When a key employee participates in both a defined contribution plan and a defined benefit plan, either of which is top-heavy, the combined limit on his benefits and contributions from both plans for any year in which the plan is top-heavy is reduced. (Code Sec. 416(h)(2))[25]

¶ 4330 Minimum funding requirements.

Defined benefit plans and money purchase plans (including target benefit plans) must maintain a "minimum funding standard account," to which credits and charges (including interest) are made, and satisfy a "minimum funding standard" each plan year. (Code Sec. 412(a), (b))[26]

¶ 4331 How to get IRS approval of plan.

Although advance IRS approval is not required, it is desirable and customary to seek it by requesting a determination letter on special forms issued by IRS.[27]

Master and prototype plans. Instead of establishing a plan on its own, an employer can set up a qualified pension or profit-sharing plan by using an IRS-approved master or prototype plan prepared and sponsored by trade or professional associations, banks, insurance companies or regulated investment companies (mutual funds).[28]

¶ 4332 Employee contributions and employer matching contributions.

A plan may require an employee to contribute to the plan, as a condition to participation, or it may permit such contributions, or both, if no discrimination results.[29]

Employee contributions and employer matching contributions under defined contribution plans (and those under a defined benefit plan treated as made under a defined contribution plan) are subject to a special nondiscrimination test. This test restricts the extent to which the actual contribution percentage (ACP) of eligible highly compensated employees can exceed the ACP for all other eligible employees. (Code Sec. 401(m), Code Sec. 414(k)(2))[30]

¶ 4333 Employer deductions.

The employer can deduct its contributions to a qualified plan. (Code Sec. 404(a); Reg § 1.404(a)-1(b))[31] However, the plan to which the contribution is made must be in existence by the end of the year. No deduction is allowed for a contribution to a plan that is merely contemplated and materializes only in a later year.[32] Also, the contribution must be timely paid (¶ 4337).

¶ 4334 Special ceiling on deductions for contributions to pension and annuity plans.

The employer may choose one of three alternative special ceilings on annual deductions for contributions to a pension or annuity plan, to get the largest deduction:[33]

(1) The "level cost" ceiling permits a deduction equal to an amount necessary to provide for all participating employees the remaining unfunded cost of their past and current service credits, distributed as a level amount (or level percentage of compensation) over the entire future remaining service of each employee. If the remaining unfunded cost with respect to any three individuals is more than 50% of the total remaining unfunded cost, the unfunded cost attributable to those three must be distributed over at least five tax years. (Code Sec. 404(a)(1)(A)(ii))

(2) The "normal cost" ceiling permits the employer to deduct contributions equal to (a) the "normal cost" (cost of credits for current services determined as though past service credits had been properly funded), plus (b) an amount necessary to amortize the cost of

25. ¶ H-6054; ¶ 4167.07.
26. ¶ H-7600 *et seq.*; ¶ 4124.01.
27. ¶ T-10500 *et seq.*; ¶ 4014.01.
28. ¶ T-10601; ¶ 4014.01.
29. ¶ H-6510 *et seq.*; ¶ 4014.21.
30. ¶ H-6513; ¶ 4014.21.
31. ¶ H-10001; ¶ 4044.01.
32. ¶ H-10021; ¶ 4044.02.
33. ¶ H-10102 *et seq.*; ¶ 4044.04.

Footnote references beginning with letters are to paragraphs in RIA's Federal Tax Coordinator 2d and RIA's Analysis of Federal Taxes: Income. Footnote references beginning with numbers are to paragraphs in RIA's United States Tax Reporter.

past service or supplementary or annuity credits provided by the plan in equal annual payments (until fully amortized) over ten years. (Code Sec. 404(a)(1)(A)(iii))

(3) If the minimum funding standard (¶ 4330) exceeds the "level cost" or "normal cost" ceiling applicable to the plan, the employer can deduct the amount necessary to satisfy the minimum funding standard. (Code Sec. 404(a)(1)(A)(i))

The maximum annual deduction under the above ceilings, however, cannot exceed the full funding limitation for the year. (Code Sec. 404(a)(1)(A))[34]

Contributions in excess of the amount deductible are subject to a 10% excise tax in certain cases, but may be carried over and deducted in later years, subject to the above limitations. (Code Sec. 404(a)(1)(E))[35]

¶ 4335 Special ceiling on deductions for contributions to profit-sharing and stock bonus plans.

The special ceiling on deductions for contributions under a profit-sharing or stock-bonus plan is 15% of the aggregate compensation (exclusive of qualified plan contributions) paid or accrued during the tax year for all employees participating in the plan. (Code Sec. 404(a)(3)(A); Reg § 1.404(a)-9(c)) Contributions in excess of this limit may be carried over and deducted in a later year to the extent that contributions for that later year are below the 15% limit for that year. (Code Sec. 404(a)(3)(A)(ii))[36]

¶ 4336 Deduction ceiling for combinations of qualified plans.

If there is a mixture of one or more defined contribution plans and one or more defined benefit plans, or any combination of two or more pension trusts, annuity plans, and stock bonus or profit-sharing trusts, an overall limit on deductible contributions applies. Under this limitation, the total amount deductible for *all* plans is the greater of: (1) 25% of the compensation (exclusive of qualified plan contributions) paid or accrued during the tax year to the beneficiaries of the various trusts or plans, or (2) the total contributions to the trusts or plans to the extent those contributions don't exceed the amount necessary to satisfy the minimum funding standards. (Code Sec. 404(a)(7)(A))[37]

¶ 4337 Timely payment requirement.

A contribution must be actually paid to the trust or under the plan to be deductible. (Code Sec. 404(a))[38] However, payments made after the end of a year are considered paid on the last day of the year if paid by the employer no later than the due date of its tax return (including extensions). (Code Sec. 404(a)(6))[39] This applies to both cash and accrual employers, even if other accrual requirements are not met. (Reg § 1.404(a)-1(c))[40]

¶ 4338 How employees are taxed.

Apart from certain "lump-sum" payments (below) qualifying for the preferential tax treatment at ¶ 4339 *et seq.*, and "rollovers" (¶ 4360), distributions from a qualified plan (reported to recipients on Form 1099-R) generally are taxed to the employee under the annuity rules (see ¶ 1357 *et seq.*), in the year distributed or otherwise made available to the employee. (Code Sec. 402(a); Reg § 1.402-1(a)) Thus, the excess of the distribution (cash or fair market value of property) over the amount of any plan contributions made by the employee, is ordinary income to the employee. (Code Sec. 402, Code Sec. 403; Reg § 1.402(a)-1(a)(1)(i))[41]

Deductible pre-'87 qualified voluntary employee contributions are taxable when distributed, and do not qualify for the relief granted lump-sum distributions. (Code Sec. 402(d)(4)(A)) However, such distributions may be rolled over tax-free to an IRA or to

---

34. ¶ H-10105 *et seq.*; ¶ 4044.04.   36. ¶ H-10202; ¶ 4044.06.   38. ¶ H-10010; ¶ 4044.02.   40. ¶ H-10017; ¶ 4044.02.
35. ¶ H-10125 *et seq.*; ¶ 4044.04.   37. ¶ H-10120 *et seq.*; ¶ 4044.09.   39. ¶ H-10016; ¶ 4044.02.   41. ¶ H-11006 *et seq.*; ¶ 4024.

Footnote references beginning with letters are to paragraphs in RIA's Federal Tax Coordinator 2d and RIA's Analysis of Federal Taxes: Income. Footnote references beginning with numbers are to paragraphs in RIA's United States Tax Reporter.

another plan (¶ 4360 *et seq.*). (Code Sec. 403(b)(8))[42]

Certain early (¶ 4345) and excess (¶ 4346) distributions are subject to penalty.

¶ 4339 Preferential treatment for lump sum distributions.

Distributions from a qualified plan to an employee or his beneficiaries, that are lump sum distributions, are taxable as ordinary income, subject to special elections for pre-'74 capital gain amounts or five-year (¶ 4340) or ten-year (¶ 4341) forward averaging.

A lump-sum distribution eligible for preferential tax treatment is a distribution or payment from an exempt trust or annuity within one tax year of the recipient of the balance to the credit of the participant:

(1) on account of his separation from service if he is an employee (other than self-employed), or

(2) after he attains age 59½ (whether or not on account of his separation from service), or

(3) on account of his death, or

(4) on account of disability if he is self-employed. (Code Sec. 402(e)(4)(A))[43]

If the exclusion for eligible rollover distributions applies to the distribution of the balance to an employee's credit in a qualified plan, then five-year averaging for lump sum distributions won't apply to any later distribution under that plan. (Code Sec. 402(c)(10))[44]

¶ 4340 Five-year averaging for lump sum distributions.

A recipient of a lump-sum distribution (as defined at ¶ 4339) with respect to an employee or owner/employee may elect (on Form 4972) to have the taxable portion of the distribution taxed separately from his other income, under a special five-year averaging election, (Code Sec. 402(d)(1)(A))[45] if the employee or owner/employee:

■ is age 59½ or older when the distribution was made[46] or reached age 50 before '86,[47] and

■ was an active participant in the plan making the distribution for at least five years before the year of the distribution. (Code Sec. 402(d)(4)(F))[48]

The separate tax is imposed at the rates applicable to unmarried individuals who aren't either heads of households or surviving spouses (whether or not the recipient is married), and computed as if the recipient had no other income and no deductions. (Code Sec. 402(d)(1)(B))[49]

The five-year averaging tax for any tax year is an amount equal to five times the tax which would be imposed if the taxpayer were an unmarried individual and the taxable income was an amount equal to one-fifth of the excess of:

(1) the total taxable amount of the lump sum distribution for the tax year, over

(2) the minimum distribution allowance. (Code Sec. 402(d)(1)(B))[50]

The minimum distribution allowance is:

(1) the smaller of $10,000, or ½ of the amount of the total taxable amount of the lump sum distribution for the tax year reduced (but not below zero), by

(2) 20% of the excess (if any) of the total taxable amount over $20,000. (Code Sec. 402(d)(1)(C))

A taxpayer may make the election to use five-year averaging only once with respect to any employee. (Code Sec. 402(d)(4)(B))[1]

---

42. ¶ H-11082; ¶ 4024.04.
43. ¶ H-11200 *et seq.*; ¶ 4024.03.
44. ¶ H-11235.
45. ¶ H-11231; ¶ 4024.03.
46. ¶ H-11235; ¶ 4024.03.
47. ¶ H-11229; ¶ 4024.03.
48. ¶ H-11205; ¶ 4024.03.
49. ¶ H-11241; ¶ 4024.03.
50. ¶ H-11242 *et seq.*; ¶ 4024.03.
1. ¶ H-11235; ¶ 4024.03.

Footnote references beginning with letters are to paragraphs in RIA's Federal Tax Coordinator 2d and RIA's Analysis of Federal Taxes: Income. Footnote references beginning with numbers are to paragraphs in RIA's United States Tax Reporter.

¶ 4341 Special lump-sum distribution elections for participants reaching age 50 before '86.

A participant who reached age 50 before '86 (or an individual, estate or trust that receives a distribution with respect to that employee) is permitted:

(1) to elect capital gains treatment without regard to the phase-out of elective capital gains treatment of distributions for pre-'74 plan participation, and

(2) to elect either five-year averaging at current tax rates or ten-year averaging at '86 tax rates with respect to a lump-sum distribution, whether or not he has reached age 59½.

This election can only be made once with respect to an employee and is treated as if it were a one-time five-year averaging election (¶ 4340) made with respect to a distribution after age 59½.[2]

¶ 4342 Lump-sum distributions of securities of employer corporation.

If a lump sum distribution consists in part of securities of the employer, the net unrealized appreciation in value of the securities while held by the trust is not taxed to the recipient at the time of distribution. But the same amount also is excluded from the recipient's basis in the securities, so that it is taken into account for tax purposes if and when the securities are later disposed of in a taxable transaction. The distributee, however, has the right to elect, on the tax return on which a distribution is required to be included, to have this rule not apply, i.e., to include any net unrealized appreciation in income. (Code Sec. 402(e)(4)(B); Reg § 1.402(a)-1(b)(1))[3]

¶ 4343 Tax on current payments for life insurance protection.

The cost of current life insurance protection under a life insurance contract purchased with employer contributions to a qualified plan (or earnings thereon) is income to the insured employee for the tax year of purchase, where the benefits are payable to him or his beneficiaries. (Code Sec. 72(m)(3); Reg § 1.72-16(b)) The taxable amount is generally determined under IRS's "PS-58" table reproduced in ¶ 1119.[4]

¶ 4344 Loans from qualified plans.

A loan by a qualified plan can be made tax-free to plan participants only if the loan is required to be repaid within five years (except for certain home loans) and does not exceed the *lesser* of: (1) $50,000, or (2) the greater of (a) ½ of the present value of the employee's nonforfeitable accrued benefit under the plan, or (b) $10,000. If a plan loan (when added to the employee's outstanding balance of all other plan loans) exceeds these limits, the excess is treated (and taxed) as a plan distribution (¶ 4338). The entire amount of a plan loan that is not required to be repaid within five years (except for certain home loans) is treated as a plan distribution. (Code Sec. 72(p))[5]

The $50,000 limit is reduced by the highest outstanding loan balance during the one-year lookback period before any new loan, unless the loan was made, renewed, renegotiated, modified or extended before '87. (Code Sec. 72(p)(2)(A)(i))[6]

A plan loan must be amortized in substantially level payments, made not less frequently than quarterly, over the term of the loan. (Code Sec. 72(p)(2)(C))[7]

For loans as prohibited transactions, see ¶ 4348.

---

2. ¶ H-11229; ¶ 4024.03.
3. ¶s H-11501, H-11503; ¶ 4024.02.
4. ¶ H-10507 *et seq.*; ¶ 724.24.
5. ¶ H-11067; ¶ 724.23.
6. ¶ H-11068; ¶ 724.23.
7. ¶ H-11069; ¶ 724.23.

Footnote references beginning with letters are to paragraphs in RIA's Federal Tax Coordinator 2d and RIA's Analysis of Federal Taxes: Income. Footnote references beginning with numbers are to paragraphs in RIA's United States Tax Reporter.

¶ 4345 Penalty for premature distributions.

Early withdrawals from a qualified retirement plan result in the addition of a tax (reported on Form 5329) equal to 10% of the amounts withdrawn which are includible in gross income. (Code Sec. 72(t)(1)) Technically, the 10% addition to tax applies to all withdrawals unless specifically excepted. The withdrawals that are excepted include distributions made on or after the date the employee attains age 59½. (Code Sec. 72(t)(2)(A)(i)) The other principal exceptions include distributions on death or disability, on separation from service after age 55, distributions that don't exceed certain medical expenses amounts, and certain distributions that are part of a series of substantially equal periodic payments (not less frequently than annually) made after separation from service for the life (or life expectancy) of the employee or the joint lives (or joint life expectancies) of the employee and his beneficiary. (Code Sec. 72(t)(2), (3))[8]

The tax applies to certain involuntary cash-outs. The tax does not apply to amounts distributed from unfunded deferred compensation plans of tax-exempt employers or state and local government employees, i.e., Code Sec. 457 plans.[9]

¶ 4346 Fifteen percent excise tax on excess distributions.

An individual who receives an excess distribution under any qualified employer plan or individual retirement plan is liable for a 15% nondeductible excise tax on the amount of the excess. The tax imposed (reported on Form 5329) is reduced by the amount of any early distribution tax (¶ 4345) attributable to the excess distributions. (Code Sec. 4980A(a))[10] With certain exceptions, an excess distribution is the excess of an individual's total retirement distributions for a calendar year over the greater of $150,000 or a dollar amount adjusted annually for cost of living increases ($144,551 as of Jan. 1, '93; the '94 amount had not been released by IRS as we went to press). (Code Sec. 4980A(c)(1))[11]

If the retirement distributions for a calendar year include a lump-sum distribution for which an individual has elected special lump sum tax treatment: (1) the determination of whether there is an excess distribution is applied separately for the lump sum, and for any other retirement distributions, and (2) in making the determination of whether the lump sum distribution produces an excess distribution, instead of using the applicable annual ceiling discussed above, a figure equal to five times that amount is used. (Code Sec. 4980A(c)(4)) So, if the annual ceiling is $150,000, the ceiling for lump-sum distributions (where lump-sum tax treatment is elected) is $750,000.[12]

Special rules apply to employees whose accrued benefit as of Aug. 1, '86 exceeded $562,500, and who made a special grandfather election. (Code Sec. 4980A(f); Reg § 54.4981A-1T(b))[13]

For an additional estate tax imposed on excess retirement accumulations, see ¶ 5002.

¶ 4347 Excise tax on employer reversions.

An "employer reversion" from a qualified plan (except for certain exempt employers and government plans) is, in addition to being includible in the employer's gross income, also subject to a 50% excise tax (20% in certain cases). (Code Sec. 4980(a), (b), (c)(1), (d)) A separate quarterly return on Form 5330 must be filed.[14]

¶ 4348 Excise tax on prohibited transactions.

An excise tax is imposed on a disqualified person who takes part in a prohibited transaction with a qualified plan or IRA. The tax (report on Form 5330) is 5% of the amount involved in the prohibited transaction for each tax year (or part of the year) in the taxable period. And if the prohibited transaction isn't timely corrected, the disqualified

---

8. ¶ H-11100 *et seq.*; ¶ 724.22.   10. ¶ H-11300 *et seq.*; ¶ 4980A4.   12. ¶ H-11309; ¶ 4980A4.   14. ¶ H-8900 *et seq.*; ¶ 49,804.
9. ¶ H-11101; ¶ 724.22.   11. ¶ H-11301; ¶ 4980A4.   13. ¶ H-11311; ¶ 4980A4.

Footnote references beginning with letters are to paragraphs in RIA's Federal Tax Coordinator 2d and RIA's Analysis of Federal Taxes: Income. Footnote references beginning with numbers are to paragraphs in RIA's United States Tax Reporter.

person must pay an additional tax of 100% of the amount involved. Neither tax is imposed on a fiduciary acting only as such. (Code Sec. 4975(a), (b))[15]

¶ 4349 Transfers to health benefits accounts.

For tax years beginning before '96, excess pension assets may be transferred to a retiree health benefit account without being treated as either a prohibited transaction or a reversion to the employer. (Code Sec. 420(a))[16]

¶ 4350 Nonqualifying employee benefit plans.

The following rules apply to a plan that fails to qualify or loses its qualified status:

Contributions to the trust by an employer are included in the gross income of the employee. (Code Sec. 402(b)) The employee must report the value of his interest in the employer's contributions the first time his interest is not subject to substantial risk of forfeiture, or is transferable free of such risk, whichever occurs first. (Reg § 1.402(b)-1[17]

An employer's contributions are deductible in the tax year in which an amount attributable to the contribution is includible in the gross income of employees participating in the plan, (Code Sec. 404(a)(5)) even if the employer is an accrual basis taxpayer.[18]

The amount actually distributed or made available to the employee or other distributee (beneficiary, etc.) is taxable in the year distributed or made available under the regular annuity rules (see ¶ 1357 *et seq.*) with a minor exception for distribution of trust income before the annuity is to begin. (Code Sec. 402(b)(2))[19]

Premiums paid by an employer for an annuity contract not purchased under a qualified annuity plan (¶ 4316) are included in the employee's gross income. Amounts actually paid or made available to any employee-beneficiary under the nonqualified annuity contract are taxed under regular annuity rules in the year paid or made available. (Code Sec. 403(c))[20]

¶ 4351 Retirement Savings Plans for Individuals (IRAs) ▬▬▬▬▬

Employees and self-employed individuals who are not active participants in an employer-maintained retirement plan can set aside and deduct up to $2,000 each year for contributions to an individual retirement account (IRA), or for the purchase of individual retirement annuities or endowment contracts. An active participant can make deductible IRA contributions only if his adjusted gross income is below specified levels.

An individual retirement account (IRA) is a trust (or custodial account) created or organized in the U.S. with a written governing instrument.[21] The assets of the account must be invested in a trusteed or custodial account with a bank, savings and loan association, credit union or other qualified person. (Code Sec. 408(a)(2))[22]

IRAs may be set up by employers for employees and by unions for members if these employer- and association-sponsored IRAs separately account for the interest of each participant (or his spouse). (Code Sec. 408(c); Reg § 1.408-2(c))[23]

IRA funds can't be used to buy life insurance contracts. (Code Sec. 408(a)(3))[24] Nor can they be invested in "collectibles," the acquisition of which is treated as an includible distribution (and possibly subject to premature distribution penalties). (Code Sec. 408(m))[25]

Individual retirement annuities are nontransferable flexible premium annuity or endowment contracts issued by an insurance company. (Code Sec. 408(b))[26]

15. ¶ H-12500 *et seq.*; ¶ 49,754.
16. ¶ H-8163; ¶ 4204.
17. ¶ H-3204 *et seq.*; ¶ 4024.01.
18. ¶ H-3673 *et seq.*; ¶ 4044.03.

19. ¶ H-3215; ¶ 4024.01.
20. ¶ H-3219; ¶ 4034.05.
21. ¶ H-12201; ¶ 4084.02.

22. ¶ H-12202 *et seq.*; ¶ 4084.02.
23. ¶s H-12212, H-12213; ¶ 4084.02.

24. ¶ H-12201; ¶ 4084.02.
25. ¶ H-12259; ¶ 4084.03.
26. ¶ H-12208 *et seq.*; ¶ 4084.03.

Footnote references beginning with letters are to paragraphs in RIA's Federal Tax Coordinator 2d and RIA's Analysis of Federal Taxes: Income. Footnote references beginning with numbers are to paragraphs in RIA's United States Tax Reporter.

No tax is paid on income earned on contributions until the retirement savings are distributed or retirement bonds are cashed, at which time the distributions or retirement bond proceeds are generally taxable (Code Sec. 408(d)(1))[27] although they are subject to tax-free "rollover" provisions (¶ 4360). Special rules penalize excess contributions, premature (before age 59½) distributions, and certain distributions deferred beyond age 70½ (¶ 4357).

¶ 4352   Deduction for IRA.

An individual who is not an active participant in certain employer-sponsored retirement plans (and, if the individual is married, whose spouse is not an active participant) can deduct, for a tax year (subject to the limitation below), cash contributions to an IRA for that year, up to the lesser of: (1) $2,000 (or $2,250 for a spousal IRA, see ¶ 4355), or (2) 100% of the compensation that is includible in his gross income for that year. (Code Sec. 219(b)(1))[28]

If the individual or his spouse: (1) is an active plan participant (for any part of a plan year in his tax year), and (2) has adjusted gross income (AGI) that exceeds an "applicable dollar limit," each of the above dollar maximums is reduced (but not below zero) by an amount (rounded to the next lowest multiple of $10) which bears the same ratio to $2,000 (or $2,250) that his AGI (determined without regard to the IRA and with certain other modifications), minus the applicable dollar limit, bears to $10,000. (Code Sec. 219(g)(1), (2)) But the maximum IRA deduction can't be reduced below $200 unless the applicable dollar limit is reduced to zero. (Code Sec. 219(g)(2)(B))[29]

The "applicable dollar limits" that trigger the above reduction are: $40,000 for an individual filing a joint return, $25,000 for an unmarried individual and zero for a married individual filing a separate return. (Code Sec. 219(g)(3)(B))[30]

Thus, the IRA deduction is reduced or eliminated entirely as follows:

Filing Status	IRA deduction reduced in this AGI range:	IRA deduction eliminated if AGI is:
Single or head of Household	$25,000-$34,999	$35,000 or more
Married-Joint return or qualifying widower	$40,000-$49,999	$50,000 or more
Married-separate return	$ 0-$ 9,999	$10,000 or more

Spouses who file separate returns and live apart at all times during the year are not treated as married individuals for purposes of the above IRA deduction phase-out. (Code Sec. 219(g)(4))[31]

"Compensation" means wages, salaries, commissions, tips, bonuses, professional fees and other amounts received for personal services. It doesn't include earnings from property, such as interest, rents and dividends, or pension and annuity payments or other deferred compensation. It does include alimony. Only compensation includible in gross income is used. (Code Sec. 219(f)(1))[32]

IRS will treat as a "safe harbor" for use in calculating an individual's compensation the amount shown on Form W-2 as "Wages, tips, other compensation," less any amount shown as distributions from nonqualified plans.[33]

The "compensation" of a self-employed individual includes net earnings from self-employment reduced by any amount allowable as a deduction for contributions on his behalf to a tax-qualified plan, i.e., a Keogh plan. (Code Sec. 219(f)(1))[34] A self-employed individual's net earnings from self-employment are also reduced by the deduction allowed for one-half of the self-employment tax (see ¶ 1744). (Code Sec. 219(f)(1), Code

---

27. ¶ H-12253; ¶ 4084.03.   29. ¶ H-12217; ¶ 2194.02.   31. ¶ H-12217; ¶ 2194.02.   33. ¶ H-12226.
28. ¶ H-12215; ¶ 2194.   30. ¶ H-12217; ¶ 2194.02.   32. ¶ H-12226; ¶ 2194.01.   34. ¶ H-12226.

Footnote references beginning with letters are to paragraphs in RIA's Federal Tax Coordinator 2d and RIA's Analysis of Federal Taxes: Income. Footnote references beginning with numbers are to paragraphs in RIA's United States Tax Reporter.

Sec. 401(c)(2)(A)(vi))[35] Compensation includes earned income exempt from self-employment tax because the individual is a member of a religious faith opposed to social security benefits. (Code Sec. 219(f)(1))[36]

No deduction is allowed for contributions by an individual for the tax year he attains age 70½ or any later year. (Code Sec. 219(d)(1))[37]

The IRA must be established no later than the due date (*not* including extensions) of the taxpayer's federal income tax return for the year the deduction is claimed. To be deductible, the contribution must be made, *in cash*, by that date. (Code Sec. 219(f)(3))[38]

⚫*observation:* Thus, deductible IRA contributions for '93 must be made no later than April 15, '94.

No part of a premium (under an IRA endowment policy) that is used to buy life insurance is deductible. (Code Sec. 219(d)(3))[39]

No deduction is permitted for rollover contributions (¶ 4360). (Code Sec. 219(d)(2))[40] Nor is a deduction permitted for any contribution to an "inherited" IRA, i.e., one which is acquired by other than the surviving spouse as a result of the death of the employee-participant. (Code Sec. 219(d)(4))[41]

¶ 4353 Active participant defined.

An individual who is an active participant in a qualified pension, profit-sharing, stock bonus or annuity plan, government plan, tax-sheltered annuity plan, SEP, or certain other trusts can't make deductible IRA contributions unless his adjusted gross income falls with the dollar limits described at ¶ 4352. (Code Sec. 219(g))[42]

An individual is an active participant for any tax year in which he makes a contribution to the plan, but not if the income earned on his benefit is merely allocated to him. But he is an "active participant" for a year in which only a single dollar is allocated to his account (defined contribution plan) or accrues to his benefit (defined benefit plan).[43]

¶ 4354 Nondeductible IRA contributions.

An active participant in a qualified plan who may not be eligible to make deductible contributions either in whole or in part to an IRA (see ¶ 4353) can make designated nondeductible contributions (DNCs) to an IRA. A DNC is any contribution to an IRA for a tax year, which is designated as a contribution for which a deduction is not allowable. (Code Sec. 408(o)(2)(C)(i)) A DNC for a tax year can be made up to the due date (without extensions) for the taxpayer's income tax return for that year. (Code Sec. 408(o)(3)) The designation is made on Form 8606, to be attached to that return. (Code Sec. 408(o)(2)(C)(ii))[44]

The amount of any DNCs made in any tax year on behalf of an individual is limited to the excess of: (1) the lesser of $2,000 ($2,250 in the case of a spousal IRA) or 100% of compensation, over (2) the amount allowable as a deduction for IRA contributions by active participants. (Code Sec. 408(o)(2)(B)(i))[45]

A taxpayer can elect to treat an otherwise deductible contribution as a DNC, thereby increasing, to that extent, his DNC limit for that year. (Code Sec. 408(o)(2)(B)(ii))[46]

DNCs and deductible contributions may be made to the same IRA.[47]

¶ 4355 Deductions for married taxpayers.

Married taxpayers can *separately* get the maximum $2,000 IRA deduction ($4,000 total) if each otherwise qualifies under the rules set forth in ¶ 4352. (Code Sec. 219(c)(2))[48] If one

35. ¶s H-9514, H-12228.	39. ¶ H-12236.	43. ¶ H-12219; ¶ 2194.02.	46. ¶ H-12240; ¶ 4084.01.
36. ¶ H-12226.	40. ¶ H-12235.	44. ¶ H-12238; ¶ 4084.01.	47. ¶ H-12238; ¶ 4084.01.
37. ¶ H-12234; ¶ 2194.01.	41. ¶ H-12237.	45. ¶ H-12239; ¶ 4084.01.	48. ¶ H-12229; ¶ 4084.
38. ¶ H-12233; ¶ 2194.01.	42. ¶ H-12219; ¶ 2194.02.		

Footnote references beginning with letters are to paragraphs in RIA's Federal Tax Coordinator 2d and RIA's Analysis of Federal Taxes: Income. Footnote references beginning with numbers are to paragraphs in RIA's United States Tax Reporter.

spouse is unemployed, or has compensation less than $250, the working spouse can deduct up to $2,250 under a special "spousal" provision. (Code Sec. 219(c)(1))[49]

The spousal provision applies where the couple files a joint return, and the unemployed spouse doesn't have *any* compensation for the year, determined without regard to any community property laws or the exclusion for certain foreign source earned income. (Code Sec. 219(c)(1), (f)(2)) However, a spouse with less than $250 in compensation can elect to be treated as having no compensation for this purpose. (Code Sec. 219(c)(1)(B))[50] Taxable alimony is considered compensation for this purpose. (Code Sec. 219(f)(1))[1] Also, even if the working spouse has attained age 70½, the spousal deduction is available if the non-working spouse doesn't reach that age by year-end.[2]

The spousal deduction is available to a married taxpayer who makes contributions to separate IRAs for himself and his unemployed spouse, or to separate subaccounts in a single IRA. The maximum spousal deduction is reduced by any individual IRA contributions made by the working spouse. The "spousal" deduction is limited to the *smaller* of:

(1) 100% of compensation (or earned income) included in the *employed* spouse's gross income, or

(2) $2,250 (not more than $2,000 for either spouse). (Code Sec. 219(c))[3]

Married taxpayers can each make deductible contributions to separate IRAs but must either have joint adjusted gross income (AGI) within the dollar limits described at ¶ 4352 *or* both must not be active participants in a retirement plan. If one spouse is an active participant in a retirement plan, *both* spouses are subject to the dollar limit in determining each spouse's deductible IRA contribution. (Code Sec. 219(g)(1))[4]

¶ 4356 Penalties for excess contribution.

An individual who contributes more to an IRA than he is entitled to deduct must pay (use Form 5329) a 6% excise tax on that excess *every year* until the excess is either: (1) withdrawn from the IRA, or (2) deducted in a later year in which the individual contributes less than he is entitled to deduct. The tax for any particular year, however, can't exceed 6% of the value of the IRA (as of the close of the tax year). (Code Sec. 4973(a))[5]

There's no 6% penalty for the year of the contribution (or any other year) if the taxpayer is allowed no IRA deduction for the excess *and* withdraws the excess (together with any net income earned on it) by the due date for filing his income tax return for the year the excess contribution was made. (Code Sec. 4973(b))[6]

¶ 4357 Distributions from IRAs and individual retirement annuities.

Payouts from an IRA can begin when the participant attains age 59½ (or earlier in the case of death or disability) without penalty. These distributions can be made in a lump-sum or in installments and are taxable as ordinary income under the annuity rules (see ¶ 1357 *et seq.*) when received, except that distributions are tax-free if reinvested ("rolled over") within 60 days in another IRA or the qualified plan of a new employer (see ¶ 4360 *et seq.*). (Code Sec. 408(d)(3)(A)(i), (B))[7] (If not reinvested, the distribution is taxable in the year received, not the year in which the 60-day rollover period ends.)[8]

Distributions from an IRA are reported on Form 1099-R. Distribution recipients who at any time made nondeductible contributions to a IRA (¶ 4354) must file Form 8606.

The transfer of an interest in an IRA to a spouse under a divorce or separation instrument isn't taxable (the transferred IRA is treated as that of the spouse). (Code Sec. 408(d)(6))[9]

In applying the annuity rules, all IRAs are treated as one contract, all distributions

---

49. ¶ H-12230; ¶ 4084.01.
50. ¶ H-12230; ¶ 4084.01.
1. ¶ H-12226; ¶ 4084.01.

2. ¶ H-12230; ¶ 4084.01.
3. ¶ H-12231; ¶ 4084.01.
4. ¶ H-12215; ¶ 4084.02.

5. ¶ H-12246; ¶ 49,734.
6. ¶ H-12248; ¶ 49,734.
7. ¶ H-12265; ¶ 4084.03.

8. ¶ H-12253; ¶ 4084.03.
9. ¶ H-12261; ¶ 4084.03.

Footnote references beginning with letters are to paragraphs in RIA's Federal Tax Coordinator 2d and RIA's Analysis of Federal Taxes: Income. Footnote references beginning with numbers are to paragraphs in RIA's United States Tax Reporter.

made during any tax year are treated as one distribution, and the value of the contract, income on the contract, and investment in it are determined at the end of the calendar year in which the tax year begins. (Code Sec. 408(d)(2))[10]

Early distributions from all qualified plans, including IRAs, are subject to a 10% additional tax, see ¶ 4345.

Distribution of a participant's entire interest in his IRA must be made under rules similar to the Code Sec. 401(a)(9) required distribution rules for qualified plans, see ¶ 4320. (Code Sec. 408(a)(6), (b)(3)) While the required minimum distribution must be separately calculated for each IRA an individual has, the amounts may then be totalled, and the total distribution taken from any one or more of the individual's IRAs. Failure to make the required distributions results in a nondeductible excise tax payable (on Form 5329) by the recipient. The tax is 50% of the excess of the minimum amount that should have been distributed over the amount actually distributed. (Code Sec. 4974(a))[11] IRS can waive the 50% tax if the shortfall in the amount distributed is due to "reasonable error" and reasonable corrective steps are taken. (Code Sec. 4974(c))[12]

¶ 4358 Exemption of IRA from tax.

Income earned by an IRA is tax-exempt until distribution, permitting tax-free buildup of funds in the account. This tax exemption doesn't apply to the unrelated business income tax (see ¶ 4114). Engaging in a "prohibited transaction," see ¶ 4348, causes loss of the exemption. (Code Sec. 408(e))[13]

Certain nominal gifts, free banking services, and free group term life insurance offered by banks for opening and contributing to an IRA are exempted from the prohibited transaction rules.[14]

If the owner of an IRA annuity borrows any money under, or by use of, the annuity contract, the contract stops being an annuity as of the first day of the tax year, and the owner must include in income for that year an amount equal to the fair market value of the contract on the first day of the year. (Code Sec. 408(e)(3)) If the individual for whom an IRA is established uses the account or any portion of it as security for a loan, that portion is treated as distributed to that individual. (Code Sec. 408(e)(4))

¶ 4359 Exclusion for direct trustee-to-trustee transfer of eligible rollover distributions.

Any amount transferred in a direct trustee-to-trustee transfer (under Code Sec. 401(a)(31)) is excludable from income for the tax year of the transfer. (Code Sec. 402(e)(6))[15]

¶ 4360 Tax-free rollovers from qualified plans.

A tax-free rollover from a qualified plan is any portion of the balance of an employee's credit in a qualified trust paid to the employee in an "eligible rollover distribution," any portion of which the employee then transfers to an "eligible retirement plan." (Code Sec. 402(c)(1))[16]

An "eligible rollover distribution," which is excludable from income, is any distribution to an employee of all or any portion of the balance to the credit of the employee in a qualified trust. (Code Sec. 402(c)(4)) An "eligible rollover distribution" does *not* include:

(1) any distribution which is one of a series of substantially equal periodic payments made (not less frequently than annually) for (a) the life (or life expectancy) of the employee, or the joint lives (or joint life expectancies) of the employee and the employee's designated beneficiary, or (b) a specified period of ten years or more; (Code Sec. 402(c)(4)(A)) and

---

10. ¶ H-12253; ¶ 4084.03.   12. ¶ H-8508; ¶ 49,744.   14. ¶ H-12530.   16. ¶ H-11402.
11. ¶ H-12271; ¶ 49,744.   13. ¶ H-12214; ¶ 4084.03.   15. ¶ H-11403.

Footnote references beginning with letters are to paragraphs in RIA's Federal Tax Coordinator 2d and RIA's Analysis of Federal Taxes: Income. Footnote references beginning with numbers are to paragraphs in RIA's United States Tax Reporter.

(2) any distribution to the extent it is a required distribution under Code Sec. 401(a)(9). (Code Sec. 402(c)(4)(B); Reg § 1.402(c)-2T, Q&A 5)[17]

🅡/caution: An eligible rollover distribution is subject to 20% withholding, unless there is a direct trustee-to-trustee transfer, see ¶ 3031.

Certain payments can't be rolled over, e.g., corrective distributions of excess 401(k) contributions and dividends paid on employer securities. (Reg § 1.402(c)-2T, Q&A 4)

An "eligible retirement plan" is: (Code Sec. 402(c)(8)(B))

(1) an individual retirement account,

(2) an individual retirement annuity (other than an endowment contract),

(3) a qualified trust, or

(4) an annuity plan.[18]

The maximum amount of an "eligible rollover distribution" that may be rolled over tax-free can't exceed the portion of the distribution which would be includible in income if there were no income exclusion for rollovers. (Code Sec. 402(c)(2))[19]

A distribution must be rolled over within 60 days after receipt to be tax-free. (Code Sec. 402(c)(3))[20]

If noncash property (e.g., securities) is distributed, the employee can sell the property and roll over the proceeds. There is no gain or loss recognized on the sale if the full proceeds are rolled over. (Code Sec. 402(c)(6)(A))[21]

Plan administrators must inform recipients of potential rollovers in writing ("a section 402(f) notice") of the applicable rollover rules, no less than 30 day, and no more than 60 days before making an eligible rollover distribution (but this 30-day time period may be waived by a participant in certain cases). (Code Sec. 402(f); Reg § 1.402(c)-2T, Q&A 12) IRS has provided a model safe harbor explanation of this notice.[22]

¶ 4361　Types of rollovers.

The permissible types of tax-free rollovers are:

(1) From one type of IRA (individual retirement account or individual retirement annuity) to the same or another type. (Code Sec. 408(d)(3))[23]

(2) Qualified plan to an IRA (or IRA annuity). (Code Sec. 402(c)(5), Code Sec. 403(a)(4))[24]

(3) Qualified plan to qualified plan through the use of a "conduit" IRA (or IRA annuity). (Code Sec. 408(d)(3)(A)(ii))[25]

(4) Qualified plan directly to qualified plan. (Code Sec. 403(a)(4))[26]

(5) Tax-sheltered annuity to an IRA or to another tax-sheltered annuity (either directly or through a "conduit" IRA). (Code Sec. 403(b)(8), Code Sec. 408(d)(3)(A)(iii))[27]

The rollovers described in (1) may be made only at one-year intervals. (Code Sec. 408(d)(3)(B))[28]

¶ 4362　Partial rollovers.

When an employee elects to roll over less than his entire distribution:

(1) the portion not rolled over is taxed under the regular rules for taxing ordinary income. Five-year forward averaging rules (or ten-year forward averaging and/or capital gains treatment, where applicable) for lump-sum distributions do not apply if any part of

---

17. ¶ H-11406.
18. ¶ H-11440.
19. ¶ H-11444.
20. ¶ H-11452.
21. ¶ H-11448.

22. ¶ H-11455 7etseq;.
23. ¶ H-11460 et seq.; ¶ 4084.03.
24. ¶ H-11442; ¶s 4024.04, 4034.03.

25. ¶ H-11464; ¶ 4024.04.
26. ¶ H-11441; ¶s 4024.04, 4034.03.

27. ¶ H-12436 et seq.; ¶ 4034.04.
28. ¶ H-11444 et seq.; ¶s 4024.04, 4084.03.

Footnote references beginning with letters are to paragraphs in RIA's Federal Tax Coordinator 2d and RIA's Analysis of Federal Taxes: Income. Footnote references beginning with numbers are to paragraphs in RIA's United States Tax Reporter.

the lump-sum distribution is rolled over; (Code Sec. 402(d)(4)(K), (c)(10))

(2) the basis recovery rules of Code Sec. 72(e) apply to a distribution that is rolled over under Code Sec. 402(c); and

(3) any net unrealized appreciation in employer securities attributable to nondeductible employee contributions is subject to tax immediately.[29]

¶ 4363 Surviving spouse's rollover of distribution from decedent's IRA.

The spouse of a deceased employee can roll over a distribution attributable to the employee made by a qualified trust, a qualified annuity or a tax-sheltered annuity, as if the spouse were the employee but only to an IRA account or IRA annuity, and not to a qualified trust or annuity plan. (Code Sec. 402(c)(9), Code Sec. 408(d)(3)(C))[30]

¶ 4364 Rollover by beneficiary other than surviving spouse.

A distribution from an IRA to a beneficiary other than a surviving spouse of a deceased IRA participant may not be rolled over to another IRA. (Code Sec. 408(d)(3)(C))[31]

¶ 4365 Simplified Employee Pensions (SEP) ██████████

An employer can make deductible contributions on behalf of its employees to a simplified employee pension (SEP). These deductible employer contributions are excluded from the gross income of the employee.

¶ 4366 Simplified employee pension (SEP) defined.

A SEP is an individual retirement account or individual retirement annuity, (IRA, see ¶ 4351 *et seq.*) established by an employer by filing Form 5305-SEP, in which:

(1) The employer contributions are made only under a definite written allocation formula that specifies (a) the requirements that an employee must satisfy to share in an allocation, and (b) how the allocated amount is computed. (Code Sec. 408(k)(5))[32]

(2) Employer contributions for a year must be made to each SEP of each employee who has reached age 21, performed service for the employer during at least three of the immediately preceding five years and has received at least $385 (effective Jan. 1, '93, as indexed; the '94 amount had not been released by IRS as we went to press) in compensation. (Code Sec. 408(k)(2))[33]

(3) The employer contributions do not discriminate in favor of highly compensated employees. (Code Sec. 408(k)(3)(A))[34]

(4) The employer contributions are not conditional on the retention in the plan of any portion of the amounts contributed. (Code Sec. 408(k)(4))[35]

(5) The employer imposes no prohibition on withdrawals by the employee. (Code Sec. 408(k)(4)(B))[36]

(6) Elective deferrals made by each highly compensated employee under a salary reduction arrangement may not exceed the average of the deferral percentage of all other eligible employees multiplied by 1.25. (Code Sec. 408(k)(6)(A)(iii))[37]

Employer contributions are discriminatory unless they bear a uniform relationship to the first $150,000 for '94 (reduced by legislation from $235,840 for '93) of the compensation, adjusted after '94 for inflation, (including self-employed income) of each employee maintaining the SEP. (Code Sec. 408(k)(3)(C)) This indexed amount can't exceed the limit on the amount of annual compensation taken into account under a qualified plan (see

---

29. ¶ H-11405 *et seq.*
30. ¶ H-11467 *et seq.*; ¶ 4084.03.
31. ¶ H-11469; ¶ 4084.03.
32. ¶ H-12310; ¶ 4084.05.
33. ¶ H-12305; ¶ 4084.05.
34. ¶ H-12306; ¶ 4084.05.
35. ¶ H-12309; ¶ 4084.05.
36. ¶ H-12309; ¶ 4084.05.
37. ¶ H-12321; ¶ 4084.05.

Footnote references beginning with letters are to paragraphs in RIA's Federal Tax Coordinator 2d and RIA's Analysis of Federal Taxes: Income. Footnote references beginning with numbers are to paragraphs in RIA's United States Tax Reporter.

¶ 4320). (Code Sec. 408(k)(8))[38]

Employees covered by a collective bargaining agreement and nonresident aliens may be excluded from participation in the plan and from the discrimination test under certain conditions. (Code Sec. 408(k)(3)(B))[39]

Maximum allowable contributions made by an employer to a SEP on behalf of an employee for any year cannot exceed the lesser of: (1) 15% of the compensation from the employer includible in the employee's gross income for the year (determined without regard to the employer's contributions to the SEP), or (2) the dollar limitation for defined contribution plans (¶ 4328). Where the SEP is integrated with Social Security, the dollar limitation in (2) is reduced by the amount taken into account above the integration level, in the case of a highly compensated employee. (Code Sec. 402(h)(2))[40]

¶ 4367 Employer's deduction for contributions to a SEP.

A contribution by an employer to a SEP is deductible for the employer's tax year with which or within which the calendar year ends.[41] The deduction can't exceed 15% of the compensation paid to the employees during the calendar year, up to the defined contribution plan limit (¶ 4328). Contributions that exceed this limit can be carried over to, and deducted in, succeeding tax years in order of time. (Code Sec. 404(h))[42]

An employer may elect to use either the calendar year or, subject to such terms and conditions as IRS may prescribe, its own tax year as the computation period for purposes of determining contributions to a SEP. (Code Sec. 408(k)(7)) If the calendar year is used, contributions made for a year are deductible for the employer's tax year with which or within which the calendar year ends. If the employer's "regular" tax year is used, contributions are deductible for that tax year. For purposes of deductibility, contributions are treated as if they were made for a tax year if the contributions are made on account of the tax year and are made not later than the time prescribed by law for filing the return for the tax year, plus extensions. (Code Sec. 404(h)(1)(A), (B))[43]

Special rules apply where the employer also contributes to other plans. (Code Sec. 404(h)(2), (3), (4))[44]

¶ 4368 Employee's treatment of contributions to and withdrawal from a SEP.

Contributions made to a SEP by an employer on behalf of an employee are excluded from the employee's gross income, up to the deduction limits at ¶ 4367. (Code Sec. 402(h)(1)) Contributions in excess of those limits are taxed to the employee in the year made. (Code Sec. 402(h)(2))[45]

Payments or withdrawals from the SEP are taxed to the recipient under the IRA rules (¶ 4357). (Code Sec. 402(h)(3))[46]

¶ 4369 Small SEP salary reduction arrangement.

A SEP that is maintained by an employer (except for tax-exempt or governmental employers) with no more than 25 employees at any time during the year before a particular tax year may include a salary reduction arrangement with the SEP for that year. Not less than 50% of the participating employees must be able to elect to have the employer either make contributions to the SEP on his behalf or pay him cash. The amount of the elective deferrals for any year must satisfy the CODA deferral limits (¶ 4318). Also, the SEP must provide for distribution of excess contributions. (Code Sec. 408(k)(6))[47]

---

38. ¶ H-12307; ¶ 4084.05.   41. ¶ H-12312 et seq.   44. ¶ H-12318 et seq.; ¶ 4044.08.   46. ¶ H-12324.
39. ¶ H-12306.   42. ¶ H-12315; ¶ 4044.08.   45. ¶ H-12319; ¶ 4084.05.   47. ¶ H-12321; ¶ 4084.05.
40. ¶s H-12308, H-12311;   43. ¶ H-12317; ¶ 4044.08.
    ¶ 4084.05.

Footnote references beginning with letters are to paragraphs in RIA's Federal Tax Coordinator 2d and RIA's Analysis of Federal
Taxes: Income. Footnote references beginning with numbers are to paragraphs in RIA's United States Tax Reporter.

¶ 4370 Tax-Sheltered Annuities

Employees of tax-exempt educational, charitable, religious, etc., organizations, or public schools, and their beneficiaries get special tax advantages from annuities bought for them by the exempt employers.

Tax-sheltered annuities offer benefits similar to those available under a qualified employee plan. The basic tax advantage is that tax is not imposed when the annuity is bought, but is deferred until payments are received under the annuity contract. (Code Sec. 403(b); Reg § 1.403(b)-1)[48] These annuities may be bought only for common law employees of certain exempt educational, charitable, religious, etc., employers. (Code Sec. 403(b)(1)(A))[49] The annuity must be nonforfeitable (except for failure to pay premiums) and nontransferable. (Code Sec. 403(b)(1)(C); Reg § 1.401-9(b)(3))[50] Certain elective deferral limits must be met if the annuity is part of a salary reduction arrangement (¶ 4372). (Code Sec. 403(b)(1)(E))[1] Also, except for annuities bought by church employers, certain nondiscrimination tests must be met. (Code Sec. 403(b)(1)(D))[2] Tax-sheltered annuities are treated as defined contribution plans for purposes of the contribution limitations, ¶ 4328. (Reg § 1.415-6(e)(1)) Limitations are also imposed on the amount of employer contributions for the purchase of the annuity that may be excluded from the employee's gross income. (Code Sec. 403(b)(2); Reg § 1.415-6(a)(1))[3] But employees of certain schools, hospitals or churches, who have a pattern of low contributions in the early years of their careers, can elect to make "catch-up" contributions in later years that exceed the regular limits. (Code Sec. 415(c)(4))[4]

¶ 4371 How tax-sheltered annuity arrangements work.

Employees of a qualifying exempt employer can receive up to 20% of their taxable compensation, multiplied by their years of service, in the form of a "tax-sheltered" annuity, with these tax effects:

(1) The employee pays no immediate income tax on the amount the employer pays for the annuity, but is taxed when the annuity payments are made, under the regular annuity rules (see ¶ 1357 *et seq.*). (Code Sec. 403(b)(1))

(2) If the employee dies, payments received by his beneficiary can qualify for the $5,000 employee death benefit exclusion (see ¶ 1262). (Code Sec. 101(b)(2)(B)(iii)) But this benefit doesn't apply to annuities bought by state and local governments for employees of public educational organizations.[5]

The above tax deferral is denied for distributions attributable to contributions made under a salary reduction agreement (¶ 4372), unless the annuity provides that payments may be paid only: (1) when the employee attains age 59½, separates from service, dies, or becomes disabled, or (2) in the case of hardship. (Code Sec. 403(b)(11)) (The premature distribution penalty applies (¶ 4345)). (Code Sec. 72(t)) The contract may not provide for the distribution of any income attributable to such contributions in the case of hardship. (Code Sec. 403(b)(11))[6] Tax-sheltered annuities are subject to the loan rules at ¶ 4344. (Code Sec. 72(p)(4)(A))[7]

¶ 4372 Salary reduction agreements.

An employee can agree to reduce his salary or forego an increase. But tax deferment applies only to amounts earned *after* the agreement with the employer becomes effective. The agreement must be legally binding and irrevocable while in effect. An employee can't make more than one agreement a year with the same employer during any tax year. He

---

48. ¶ H-12400 *et seq.*; ¶ 4034.04.   1. ¶ H-12427; ¶ 4034.04.   4. ¶ H-12454 *et seq.*; ¶ 4034.04.   6. ¶ H-12430; ¶ 4034.04.

49. ¶ H-12409; ¶ 4034.04.   2. ¶ H-12420; ¶ 4034.04.   5. ¶ H-12433; ¶ 1014.06.   7. ¶ H-11066; ¶ 724.23.

50. ¶ H-12415; ¶ 4034.04.   3. ¶ H-12439; ¶ 4034.04.

Footnote references beginning with letters are to paragraphs in RIA's Federal Tax Coordinator 2d and RIA's Analysis of Federal Taxes: Income. Footnote references beginning with numbers are to paragraphs in RIA's United States Tax Reporter.

can terminate the entire agreement with respect to amounts not yet earned. Thus, the employee can *choose each year* whether to take his future pay in cash or in a tax-deferred annuity (within allowable limits). (Reg § 1.403(b)-1(b)(3))[8]

All of the employer's employees (except those covered by a CODA or an eligible Code Sec. 457 plan for tax-exempt and governmental employers) must be given the opportunity to elect to have the employer contribute more than $200 under the salary reduction agreement, on a nondiscriminatory basis, if *any* employee may so elect. (Code Sec. 403(b)(12)(A))[9]

The employee's elective deferrals for a tax year can't exceed the CODA limits (¶ 4318). (Code Sec. 403(b)(1)(E))[10]

¶ 4373 Exclusion allowance.

If a qualifying employer buys a tax-sheltered annuity for one of its employees in which the employee's rights are nonforfeitable, all or part of the premium paid is not taxable to the employee at that time, up to the amount of his "exclusion allowance" for that year. (Code Sec. 403(b)(1))[11]

An employee's "exclusion allowance" for any tax year is equal to the excess (if any) of: (1) 20% of his "includible compensation" (¶ 4374), multiplied by the number of his "years of service" with the employer, over (2) the aggregate amounts that his employer contributed for annuity contracts, which were excludable from the employee's gross income in earlier years for any reason. (Code Sec. 403(b)(2)(A))[12]

¶ 4374 "Includible compensation" and "years of service."

"Includible compensation" means the amount of compensation received by the employee from the qualified employer, which is includible in his gross income (without regard to the exclusion for certain foreign source earned income), for the most recent period ending not later than the close of the employee's tax year which can be counted as one "year of service." Amounts contributed by the employer for tax-sheltered annuities are not included, even if any part is taxed to the employee because it exceeds the exclusion allowance. (Code Sec. 403(b)(3); Reg § 1.403(b)-1(b)(2))[13]

"Includible compensation" doesn't include any compensation *earned* during a period when the employer wasn't a qualified employer. However, it's immaterial whether the employer was qualified when the compensation is actually *received* by the employee. (Reg § 1.403(b)-1(e)(4))[14]

The employee's "years of service," which can't be less than one, includes one year for each full year when he was a full-time employee of the organization buying the annuity for him, plus a fraction of each year, as prescribed by regs, for each full year when he was a part-time employee, or for each part of a year when he was a full- or part-time employee. (Code Sec. 403(b)(4))[15]

¶ 4375 Minimum exclusion allowance for certain church employees.

An employee of a church whose adjusted gross income for the year from all sources does not exceed $17,000 (without considering community property laws and without including his spouse's income) is entitled to a minimum exclusion allowance that may be larger than the exclusion allowance discussed at ¶ 4373. This *minimum* exclusion allowance is the *lesser* of: (1) $3,000, or (2) the employee's includible compensation (¶ 4374) (but including contributions for tax-sheltered annuities, for foreign missionaries) for the year. (Code Sec. 403(b)(2)(D))[16]

---

8. ¶ H-12427; ¶ 4034.04.
9. ¶ H-12420; ¶ 4034.04.
10. ¶ H-12428; ¶ 4034.04.

11. ¶ H-12439; ¶ 4034.04.
12. ¶ H-12439; ¶ 4034.04.
13. ¶ H-12443; ¶ 4034.04.

14. ¶ H-12443; ¶ 4034.04.
15. ¶ H-12444 *et seq.*; ¶ 4034.04.

16. ¶s H-12448, H-12449; ¶ 4034.04.

Footnote references beginning with letters are to paragraphs in RIA's Federal Tax Coordinator 2d and RIA's Analysis of Federal Taxes: Income. Footnote references beginning with numbers are to paragraphs in RIA's United States Tax Reporter.

Chapter 22   Farmers

¶ *4500* **Farmers** ▮▮▮▮▮▮▮▮▮▮▮▮▮▮▮▮▮▮▮▮▮▮▮▮▮▮▮▮▮▮▮▮

Farmers get tax breaks not generally available to others: favorable accounting and inventory methods, and the deduction of items normally capitalized.

For limits on farmers' deductions and credits under the passive loss rules, see ¶ 1798 *et seq.*

¶ *4501* **Farmers' accounting methods.**

Farmers (other than those listed at ¶ 4506) may use the cash method, the accrual method, the crop method or a "hybrid" method combining the cash and accrual methods if the hybrid method clearly reflects income (¶ 2817 *et seq.*). (Reg § 1.61-4, Reg § 1.446-1(c), Reg § 1.471-6(a))[1]

While most taxpayers who produce, buy or sell merchandise must use inventories (and thus must use the accrual method, see ¶ 2866), farmers may generally choose not to, except to the extent that they are subject to the uniform capitalization rules (¶ 4514). (Reg § 1.471-6(a))[2] But a farmer who does use inventories must use the accrual method at least for purchases and sales.[3]

¶ *4502* **Cash method farmers.**

Farmers using the cash method report their income in the year it is actually or constructively received (¶ 2822 *et seq.*). The farmer's gross income for the year includes receipts of: (1) proceeds from sales of *raised* livestock or produce; (2) profits from the sale of any *purchased* property, including livestock, (3) breeding fees, (4) fees from rent of teams, machinery or land, (5) taxable subsidy and conservation payments, (6) crop insurance proceeds (¶ 4504), and (7) all other gross income. Expenses (e.g., feed) are ordinarily deductible in the year paid (other than the cost of animals and plants bought for resale (¶ 4503)). (Reg § 1.61-4(a))[4]

¶ *4503* **Cash method farmer's election to deduct costs of purchased animals and plants in year bought or year sold.**

In general, the purchase price of animals or plants bought for resale is deducted by cash basis farmers only in the year the animals or plants are disposed of. (Reg § 1.61-4(a)) But farmers may elect to deduct the costs of the following animals and plants either for the year they are purchased or for the year they are sold, if the method chosen clearly reflects income:

■ baby chicks and pullets bought for raising and resale;

■ hens bought for commercial egg production;

■ seeds and young plants (other than Christmas trees, orchards and timber) bought for further development and cultivation before sale. (Reg § 1.162-12)[5]

The farmer makes the election by deducting the cost for the first year in which he buys the items. Once the farmer elects this option—which is a method of accounting—he must use it consistently until IRS consents to a change (¶ 2841).[6]

¶ *4504* **Special one-year deferral elections for cash method farmers.**

A cash basis farmer can elect to defer reporting certain insurance proceeds and certain federal disaster payments (including payments under Title II (but not Title I) of the '88 Disaster Assistance Act) until the tax year following the tax year of the destruction or damage to the crops, if he establishes that, under his practice, the income from the crops

---

1. ¶ N-1010 *et seq.*; ¶s 614.051,   2. ¶ N-1100 *et seq.*; ¶ 4714.73.   4. ¶ N-1013; ¶ 614.051.   6. ¶ N-1022.
   4464.09.   3. ¶ N-1017.   5. ¶s N-1021, N-1022.

Footnote references beginning with letters are to paragraphs in RIA's Federal Tax Coordinator 2d and RIA's Analysis of Federal Taxes: Income. Footnote references beginning with numbers are to paragraphs in RIA's United States Tax Reporter.

would have been reported in a tax year after the destruction year. Elect on a statement attached to the return (or amended return) for the year the payments are received. (Code Sec. 451(d); Reg § 1.451-6)[7]

One-year deferral also may be elected for income from livestock sold on account of drought if the drought caused the sale to take place in an earlier year than normal. Elect on a statement attached to the return (or amended return). (Code Sec. 451(e); Reg § 1.451-7(g))[8] (For treatment of these sales as involuntary conversions, see ¶ 2427 *et seq.*)

¶ 4505 Accrual method farmers.

Farmers using the accrual method include farm income for the year earned, regardless of when payment is received, and deduct farm expenses for the year when the "all events test" is satisfied (¶ 2827 *et seq.*). Inventories must be used. (Code Sec. 461(h); Reg § 1.61-4(b))[9]

An accrual basis farmer's gross income for a tax year from inventoried livestock or farm products is the sum of: (1) the sales price of all livestock and other products held for sale that are sold during the year, (2) the inventory value (below) of the livestock, etc., (3) miscellaneous farm receipts, e.g., fees from breeding or from renting teams, (4) all subsidy and conservation payments includible that year, plus (5) gross income from all other sources. The inventory value in (2) equals the inventory value of livestock, etc., not sold at the end of the year, reduced by the inventory value of livestock, etc., on hand at the beginning of the year, and by the cost of any livestock, etc., purchased during the year and included in inventory. Crop shares are included in gross income in the year they are reduced to money or its equivalent. (Reg § 1.61-4(b))[10]

¶ 4506 Mandatory accrual accounting for large corporations, certain partnerships and farm syndicates.

Corporations (except as noted below) and any partnership in which a corporation is a partner must use the accrual method of accounting to compute their taxable income from farming (as must tax shelters, which include farm syndicates, see ¶ 4507). Raisers and harvesters of nut and fruit trees are covered by this rule, but nurseries, sod farms and raisers and harvesters of other types of trees are not. (Code Sec. 447(a))[11]

The mandatory accrual rule doesn't apply to:

(1) S corporations. (Code Sec. 447(c)(1))

(2) A "family corporation" (i.e., a corporation in which at least 50% of (a) the total combined voting power of all voting stock, and (b) the total number of shares of all other classes of stock are owned by members of the same family) other than one whose gross receipts exceed $25 million for any tax year after '85. (Code Sec. 447(c)(2), (d)(2))[12] Two- or three-family corporations must meet special stock ownership tests, and must have been engaged in farming since Oct. 4, '76. (Code Sec. 447(h))[13]

(3) A corporation whose gross receipts (or any predecessor's) don't exceed $1 million for any tax year beginning after '75. (Code Sec. 447(c)(2), (d)(1))[14]

(4) Certain corporations (and partnerships in which a corporation is a partner) engaged in growing sugar cane, that used "annual accrual" methods of accounting for that business for a ten-tax year period ending with its first tax year beginning after '75. (Code Sec. 447(g))[15]

---

7. ¶ N-1024 *et seq.*; ¶ 4514.171.   10. ¶ N-1014, N-1017; ¶ 614.051.   12. ¶s N-1037, N-1041; ¶ 4474.   14. ¶ N-1037; ¶ 4474.
8. ¶ N-1032; ¶ 4514.176.   11. ¶ N-1037 *et seq.*; ¶ 4474.   13. ¶ N-1057.   15. ¶ N-1050; ¶ 4474.
9. ¶ N-1017; ¶ 4614.15.

Footnote references beginning with letters are to paragraphs in RIA's Federal Tax Coordinator 2d and RIA's Analysis of Federal Taxes: Income. Footnote references beginning with numbers are to paragraphs in RIA's United States Tax Reporter.

¶ 4507   Rules for tax shelters and farming syndicates.

All tax shelters, including farm syndicates, must:

■ use the accrual method of accounting, (Code Sec. 448(a)(3); Reg § 1.263A-1T(c)(2))[16] and

■ follow uniform capitalization rules without regard to how long the plant's pre-productive period is (¶ 4513), and without being allowed to elect out of the rules (¶ 4516). (Code Sec. 263A(d)(1)(B), (3)(B))[17]

A farming syndicate is any partnership (or other noncorporate enterprise) or an S corporation, engaged in the business of farming if:

■ at any time interests in the partnership or other enterprise have been offered for sale in an offering required to be registered with any federal or state agency having authority to regulate the offering of securities for sale; or

■ more than 35% of the losses during any periods are allocable to limited partners or limited entrepreneurs; (Code Sec. 464(c)) or

■ it is a tax shelter. (Code Sec. 461(i)(3), (4))[18]

For the limitation on losses from tax shelter activities for alternative minimum tax purposes, see ¶ 3209.

¶ 4508   Crop method.

A farmer may, with IRS consent, use the crop method to report income from crops (other than timber) for which the process of planting, harvesting and sale isn't completed within the same tax year. (Reg § 1.61-4(c))[19]

Under the crop method, all expenses of the crop (including expenses of seed or young plants) are charged, and all crop receipts are credited, to a crop account. Profit (or loss) is realized and included in income (or loss deducted) only in the year the crop is harvested and disposed of. The profit (or loss) is all the receipts less all the expenses. (Reg § 1.61-4(c), Reg § 1.162-12(a))[20]

¶ 4509   Farmers' inventories.

A farmer using inventories *must* inventory:

■ all livestock and poultry, raised or purchased, held primarily for sale; (Reg § 1.61-4(b))

■ all harvested and purchased farm products held for sale, feed, or seed, such as grain, hay ensilage, concentrates, cotton, tobacco;

■ supplies, unless only small amounts are on hand;

■ if in the hatchery business, eggs in incubation and growing and pre-market chickens. (Inventories *may* be used for hens primarily held for egg production which are also held for sale after their egg-producing life.)[21]

Livestock acquired for dairy, breeding, sporting or draft purposes by an accrual basis farmer may be inventoried at taxpayer's election. But raised livestock must be inventoried by farmers using the unit-livestock-price method. (Reg § 1.61-4(h), Reg § 1.471-6(f))[22]

¶ 4510   Inventory valuation methods.

Method that farmers use to value inventory include:

■ *Cost method* (¶ 2871). (Reg § 1.471-3)[23]

■ *Lower of cost or market method* (¶ 2872). (Reg § 1.471-4)[24]

---

16. ¶ G-2406; ¶ 4484.   19. ¶ N-1018 *et seq.*; ¶ 614.056.   22. ¶ N-1109; ¶s 614.057,   23. ¶ N-1106; ¶ 4714.41.
17. ¶s N-1080, N-1089.   20. ¶ N-1019; ¶ 614.056.   4714.73.   24. ¶ N-1107; ¶ 4714.51.
18. ¶s N-1037, G-2406 *et seq.*;   21. ¶ N-1102.
     ¶ 4644.

Footnote references beginning with letters are to paragraphs in RIA's Federal Tax Coordinator 2d and RIA's Analysis of Federal Taxes: Income. Footnote references beginning with numbers are to paragraphs in RIA's United States Tax Reporter.

■ *Farm price method.* Each item, raised or purchased, is valued at its market price less estimated direct cost of disposition. If this method is used, taxpayer must use it for the entire inventory, except that livestock may be inventoried on the unit-livestock-price method. (Reg § 1.471-6(d))[25]

■ *Unit-livestock-price method.* Livestock is reasonably classified according to kind and age, and a standard unit price is used for each animal within a class. The unit prices must reflect any costs required to be capitalized under the uniform capitalization rules at ¶ 4514. But no adjustments are made for a decrease in market value because of age. If this method is chosen, all raised livestock must be included in inventory. (Reg § 1.471-6(f))[26]

¶ 4511 Feed.

The cost of feed purchased for livestock is a deductible business expense. (Reg § 1.162-12(a))[27]

A cash basis farmer may deduct in the year paid, the cost of feed his livestock will consume in that year. Payments for feed to be used in the following tax year ("prepaid feed") aren't deductible until the year of consumption. But the farmer may deduct the cost in the payment year if: (1) the payment represents a purchase rather than a deposit, (2) the advance payment is for a business purpose and not merely for tax avoidance, and (3) deduction in the payment year doesn't result in a material distortion of income.[28] For pre-paid farm expenses generally, see ¶ 4512.

¶ 4512 Pre-paid farm expenses—cash basis taxpayer.

A cash basis taxpayer's current deduction for prepaid farm expenses (i.e., payments for feed, seed, fertilizer, and similar farm supplies that won't be used until a later tax year) is limited to one-half of his other deductible farming expenses for the year (subject to a special rule for feed, see ¶ 4511). The "excess" portion (i.e., over that one-half amount) isn't deductible until the year the supplies are used. (Code Sec. 464(a), (f)(1), (f)(2))[29]

But if taxpayer's (or a family member's) principal home is a farm or his principal business is farming, his pre-paid expense deduction for the tax year is exempt from this limit if: (1) for the three preceding tax years, his total pre-paid farm expenses are less than 50% of his total other deductible farm expenses, or (2) for the current year, his pre-paid farm expenses are more than 50% of his other farm expenses because of a change in business operations attributable to extraordinary circumstances. (Code Sec. 464(f))[30]

The pre-paid expenses of tax shelters, including farming syndicates, are deductible only when economic performance occurs, i.e., when the property or services paid for are actually delivered or performed. (Code Sec. 461(i)(4))[31]

¶ 4513 Pre-productive period expenses.

Taxpayer has the option to either deduct or capitalize the costs of developing and operating his farm and crops (e.g., taxes, interest, upkeep) during its pre-productive period. (Reg § 1.162-12(a))[32] (However, for the requirement to capitalize certain pre-productive period costs, see ¶ 4514.) But he can't deduct any capital expenditures.[33]

The pre-productive period begins when the farmer first acquires the seed or plant, and ends when the plant produces marketable quantities or is reasonably expected to be sold or otherwise disposed of. (Code Sec. 263A(e)(3))[34]

---

25. ¶ N-1112; ¶ 4714.73.   28. ¶ N-1312; ¶ 1624.340.   31. ¶ N-1307; ¶ 4614.15.   33. ¶ N-1303; ¶ 1624.349.
26. ¶ N-1113; ¶ 4714.73.   29. ¶ N-1320; ¶ 4644.   32. ¶ N-1302; ¶ 1624.349.   34. ¶ N-1074.
27. ¶ N-1311; ¶ 10,154.   30. ¶ N-1319; ¶ 4644.

Footnote references beginning with letters are to paragraphs in RIA's Federal Tax Coordinator 2d and RIA's Analysis of Federal Taxes: Income. Footnote references beginning with numbers are to paragraphs in RIA's United States Tax Reporter.

¶ 4514 Application of uniform capitalization rules to farmers and ranchers.

Farmers and ranchers are subject to the uniform capitalization rules that apply to taxpayers generally (described at ¶ 1661). The rules apply to the production, growing, or raising of property that:

■ is produced by a farmer required to use the accrual method (i.e., corporations, partnerships with a corporation as a partner, and tax shelters, see ¶ 4506); (Code Sec. 263A(a), (d)(1))[35] or

■ has a pre-productive period of more than two years. (Code Sec. 263A(d)(1)(A)(ii))[36]

For taxpayers not subject to the mandatory accrual method, the uniform capitalization rules *do not apply* to costs related to any animal, or any plant having a pre-productive period of two years or less, which is produced by a taxpayer in a farming business. (Code Sec. 263A(d)(1)(A)) Nor do they apply to costs of replanting certain plants lost by casualty (¶ 4515).[37]

For election out of the uniform capitalization rules, see ¶ 4516.

¶ 4515 Exception for costs of replanting plants lost in casualties.

A taxpayer doesn't include in inventory or capitalize costs incurred to replant plants bearing an edible crop for human consumption that were lost or damaged (while in taxpayer's hands) by freezing temperatures, disease, drought, pests, or casualty. (Code Sec. 263A(d)(2)(A))[38]

This casualty exception generally applies to the costs of the person owning ("owner") the plants at the time of the loss or damage. But costs paid or incurred by another person (payor) in any tax year also may qualify if in that year: (1) the owner has a more-than-50% equity interest in the plants, and (2) the payor owns any of the remaining equity interest in them *and* materially participates in their planting, maintenance, cultivation or development. (Code Sec. 263A(d)(2)(B); Reg § 1.263A-1T(c)(3)(ii))[39]

¶ 4516 Election to have uniform capitalization rules not apply.

Except as described below, a farmer may elect to have the capitalization rules at ¶ 4514 *not* apply to any plant produced in any of his farming businesses. (Code Sec. 263A(d)(3)(A)) That is, he may elect to deduct currently all pre-productive costs.[40]

If taxpayer or any related person (as specially defined) makes the election, he must use the Code Sec. 168(g)(2) alternative (i.e., straight-line) depreciation for all his property used predominantly in the farming business which was placed in service in any tax year during which the election is in effect. (Code Sec. 263A(e)(2)(A))[41]

If the election is made, any plant with respect to which amounts would have been capitalized but for the election is treated as Code Sec. 1245 property (if it's not otherwise Code Sec. 1245 property). (Code Sec. 263A(e)(1)(A)(i)) And deductible amounts that *but for* the election would have been capitalized ("recapture amounts") (Code Sec. 263A(e)(1)(B)) are treated as depreciation deductions for purposes of Code Sec. 1245. (Code Sec. 263A(e)(1)(A)(ii)) This means that those deductions taxpayer otherwise would have had to capitalize are recaptured as ordinary income when the product is disposed of.[42]

The election may not be made by a corporation, partnership, farm syndicate or tax shelter required to use an accrual method of accounting under the rules discussed at ¶ 4506. (Code Sec. 263A(d)(3)(B))[43]

And the election may not be made with respect to any item attributable to the planting,

35. ¶ N-1080; ¶ 263A4.   38. ¶ N-1082.   40. ¶ N-1085; ¶ 263A4.   42. ¶ N-1093; ¶ 263A4.
36. ¶ N-1071; ¶ 263A4.   39. ¶ N-1083; ¶ 263A4.   41. ¶ N-1090; ¶ 263A4.   43. ¶ N-1089; ¶ 263A4.
37. ¶ N-1071; ¶ 263A4.

Footnote references beginning with letters are to paragraphs in RIA's Federal Tax Coordinator 2d and RIA's Analysis of Federal Taxes: Income. Footnote references beginning with numbers are to paragraphs in RIA's United States Tax Reporter.

maintenance or development of any citrus or almond grove (or part of a grove) that is incurred before the close of the fourth tax year beginning with the tax year the trees were planted. For this purpose, the portion of a grove planted in one tax year must be treated separately from the portion planted in another tax year. (Code Sec. 263A(d)(3)(C))[44]

Unless IRS consents, the election may only be made for the taxpayer's first tax year during in which he engages in a farming business or produces property subject to the uniform capitalization rules. Make the election on the Schedule E, F, or other schedule required to be attached to the income tax return for the first tax year for which it is to apply. (Code Sec. 263A(d)(3)(D); Reg § 1.263A-1T(c)(6))[45]

¶ 4517 Fertilizer.

The cost of acquiring fertilizer, lime, marl, and other materials used to enrich, neutralize, or condition farmland, and the costs of applying them, are deductible business expenses. Deduction is allowed in the year the costs are paid or incurred if the benefit doesn't last beyond one year. If the benefit lasts substantially more than a year (so that the costs would have to be capitalized), taxpayer may either capitalize the costs or elect to deduct them in the year paid or incurred, (Code Sec. 180(a))[46] by deducting them on his return for that year. (Code Sec. 180(c); Reg § 1.180-2)[47]

The election to deduct isn't allowable for costs of preparing land not previously used for farming by taxpayer or his tenant. (Code Sec. 180(b); Reg § 1.180-1(b))[48]

If fertilizer expenses are capitalized, taxpayer may deduct a portion of the capitalized amounts for each year the benefits last. The portion deducted each year need not be the same if benefits are clearly greater in the early years.[49]

¶ 4518 Soil and water conservation, erosion prevention, and land clearing costs.

Soil and water conservation, erosion prevention, and land clearing costs incurred with respect to land used in farming may be deducted at taxpayer's election, (Code Sec. 175(a)) even though the costs would ordinarily be capitalized. The election is limited to expenditures that are consistent with a federal or state approved conservation plan. (Code Sec. 175(c)(3))[50]

Expenditures qualifying for the election include costs of: treatment or movement of earth (e.g., leveling, terracing or restoration of fertility); construction and protection of diversion channels, drainage ditches, earthen dams; eradication of brush; planting of windbreaks; producing vegetation primarily for soil or water conservation, or prevention of soil erosion. (Code Sec. 175(c); Reg § 1.175-2(a), (b)(2)) Costs of draining or filling wetlands or for center pivot irrigation systems don't qualify. (Code Sec. 175(c)(3)(B)) Nor does the election apply to depreciable assets. (Reg § 1.175-1)[1]

The amount deducted under this election can't exceed 25% of taxpayer's gross income from farming for the tax year. Any excess is a carryover to future years. (Code Sec. 175(b); Reg § 1.175-5(b))[2]

The election is made by deducting these expenses on the return for the year taxpayer first pays or incurs them, (Reg § 1.175-6(a)) attaching a Form 8645 to establish government certification.[3]

¶ 4519 MACRS or depreciation for farm property.

A farmer is entitled to take cost recovery (MACRS) or depreciation deductions on property used in a farming business, (Code Sec. 168(b)(2)(B)) including:

■ farm buildings (except his dwelling);

---

44. ¶ N-1089; ¶ 263A4.   47. ¶ N-1307.   50. ¶ N-1402; ¶ 1754.01.   2. ¶ N-1415; ¶ 1754.02.
45. ¶ N-1088; ¶ 263A4.   48. ¶ N-1306.   1. ¶ N-1406; ¶ 1754.01.   3. ¶ N-1421; ¶ 1754.01.
46. ¶ N-1306; ¶ 1804.   49. ¶ N-1306.

Footnote references beginning with letters are to paragraphs in RIA's Federal Tax Coordinator 2d and RIA's Analysis of Federal Taxes: Income. Footnote references beginning with numbers are to paragraphs in RIA's United States Tax Reporter.

- farm machinery;

- other physical property (not including land);

- orchards (trees and vines bearing fruits or nuts);

- draft, breeding, sporting or dairy livestock (unless included in inventory, see below). (Reg § 1.167(a)-6(b))[4]

The above farm property is depreciated under MACRS using the 150% declining balance method (switching to straight-line for the first tax year for which that would give a larger allowance). (Code Sec. 168(b)(1)(B), (2)(B))[5]

Livestock. The cost of purchased dairy, etc., livestock may be recovered under MACRS or useful life depreciation (if the livestock is not recovery property). The cost of *raised* livestock may be either deducted (but costs so deducted can't be included in depreciable basis) (Reg § 1.61-4(a), Reg § 1.162-12(a)) or capitalized as taxpayer chooses.[6] But accrual method farmers using inventories may not depreciate any purchased dairy, etc., livestock that is inventoried. (Reg § 1.167(a)-6)[7]

¶ 4520 Unharvested crop sold with land.

Gain or loss on an unharvested crop sold, exchanged, or compulsorily or involuntarily converted with the underlying land qualifies under the capital gain-ordinary loss rule of Code Sec. 1231 (¶ 2667 *et seq.*) if: (1) the land was used in taxpayer's trade or business and was held for the long-term capital gain holding period, *and* (2) the land and crops are sold at the same time and to the same person. (Code Sec. 1231(b)(4)) It doesn't matter how long the *crops* were held, or their state of maturity. (Reg § 1.1231-1(f))[8]

¶ 4521 Breeding, dairy, sporting, draft livestock.

Gains and losses from the sale, exchange, or involuntary conversion of animals held for draft, breeding, dairy, or sporting purposes qualify for capital gain-ordinary loss treatment under Code Sec. 1231 (¶ 2667 *et seq.*) as follows:

- cattle and horses held for 24 months or more from the date of acquisition;

- other livestock (except poultry) held for 12 months or more from the date of acquisition. (Code Sec. 1231(a), (b)(3); Reg § 1.1231-2(a))[9]

The fact that taxpayer includes the livestock in an inventory doesn't prevent Code Sec. 1231 treatment if the animal is held for the required purposes and period and not for sale to customers.[10]

¶ 4522 Like-kind exchange of livestock.

The trading of livestock can under certain circumstances qualify as a tax-free like-kind exchange (¶ 2417 *et seq.*). But the exchanged animals must be of the same sex. (Code Sec. 1031(e); Reg § 1.1031(e)-1)[11]

---

4. ¶ N-1304; ¶ 1674.035.
5. ¶ L-8912; ¶ 1684.01.
6. ¶s N-1020, N-1350 *et seq.*; ¶ 1624.339.

7. ¶ N-1353; ¶ 1674.035.
8. ¶ N-1206; ¶ 12,314.13.

9. ¶s N-1209, N-1223; ¶s 12,314, 12,314.12.

10. ¶ N-1209.
11. ¶ N-1215; ¶ 10,314.04.

Footnote references beginning with letters are to paragraphs in RIA's Federal Tax Coordinator 2d and RIA's Analysis of Federal Taxes: Income. Footnote references beginning with numbers are to paragraphs in RIA's United States Tax Reporter.

Chapter 23　Foreign Income—Foreign Taxpayers— Foreign Currency Transactions

¶ 4610 Foreign Income of US Taxpayers

U.S. taxpayers—U.S. citizens, U.S. residents, U.S. (domestic) corporations and other taxable U.S. entities—ordinarily are fully taxable on their income from outside the U.S., subject to special exemptions and other special treatment for particular taxpayers, and particular kinds and sources of income. Nonresident aliens, foreign corporations and other foreign entities, however, are subject to federal income tax only with respect to their income that is effectively connected with a U.S. trade or business, and with respect to certain passive income derived from U.S. sources.

For the foreign tax credit, see ¶ 2357 *et seq.* For certain transfers of property by U.S. persons to foreign corporations, see ¶ 3586 *et seq.*

¶ 4611 Foreign income of U.S. citizens and resident aliens.

U.S. citizens, whether they reside in the U.S. or abroad, are generally subject to U.S. income tax whether their income is from sources within or outside the U.S., (Reg § 1.1-1(b)) as are resident aliens (¶ 4612). (Reg § 1.871-1) Exemption or partial exemption from U.S. tax is allowed only for foreign earned income (¶ 4614), income from U.S. possessions, and certain allowances for U.S. government employees (¶ 4626).[1] For when a U.S. citizen or resident is taxed on *undistributed* income of a foreign corporation in which he is a shareholder, see ¶s 4635, 4644.

Every person born or naturalized in the U.S. and subject to its jurisdiction is a U.S. citizen. A foreigner who has filed a declaration of intention to become a U.S. citizen but who has not yet been admitted to citizenship by a final order of a naturalization court is an alien. (Reg § 1.1-1(c))[2]

For U.S. tax on nonresident aliens, see ¶ 4649 *et seq.*

¶ 4612 Who are resident aliens?

An alien individual is treated as a U.S. resident for any calendar year in which he meets either: (1) a lawful permanent residence (green card) test, or (2) a "substantial presence" test (below). (Code Sec. 7701(b)(1)(A)(i), (ii))[3]

Subject to certain exceptions, an individual meets the substantial presence test for any calendar year if:

(1) he is present in the U.S. on at least 31 days during the year, *and*

(2) the sum of the number of days he was present during the current year and the two preceding calendar years, when multiplied by the applicable multiplier (1 for the current year, ⅓ for the first preceding year, and ⅙ for the second preceding year), equals or exceeds 183 days. (Code Sec. 7701(b)(3)(A))[4]

illustration: A foreign citizen was present in the U.S. from Jan. 1 through Jan. 31 of Year 3. He was also present in the U.S. for all of Year 2. In Year 1, he was present in the U.S. from July 1 through Dec. 31. Here's how to determine if he meets the substantial presence test (in Year 3):

Year	Multiplier		Days Present		Total
Year 3	1	×	31	=	31
Year 2	⅓	×	365	=	122
Year 1	⅙	×	184	=	31
					184

---

1. ¶ O-1001 *et seq.*; ¶s 14.05, 9109. 2. ¶ O-1003; ¶ 14.05. 3. ¶ O-1051; ¶ 8714. 4. ¶ O-1057; ¶ 8714.

Footnote references beginning with letters are to paragraphs in RIA's Federal Tax Coordinator 2d and RIA's Analysis of Federal Taxes: Income. Footnote references beginning with numbers are to paragraphs in RIA's United States Tax Reporter.

Since the total exceeds 183 days, he meets the test in Year 3.

An individual doesn't meet the "substantial presence" test for any year if: (1) he is present in the U.S. on fewer than 183 days during the year, and (2) it is established that (use Form 8840), for that year, he has a tax home in a foreign country to which he has a closer connection than to the U.S. (Code Sec. 7701(b)(3)(B))[5]

Qualifying aliens may elect (on a statement attached to the income tax return) to be taxed as U.S. residents in a calendar year if they meet the substantial presence test in the following calendar year. (Code Sec. 7701(b)(1)(A)(iii); Reg § 301.9100-7T(a)(3)(ix))[6] For joint return election where one spouse is a nonresident alien, see ¶ 4706.

¶ 4613 Reporting requirements of passport and green card applicants.

Applicants for passports and green cards must give IRS their names (and taxpayer ID numbers if they have them) and any other tax information IRS may require (Code Sec. 6039E) on Form 9003.[7]

¶ 4614 Partial exclusion for foreign earned income.

For any tax year in which an individual "qualifies" (¶ 4618), he may elect (¶ 4619) to exclude from gross income up to $70,000 (¶ 4615) of foreign earned income. (Code Sec. 911(a), (b)(2))[8]

An individual's "foreign earned income" is his earned income from foreign sources attributable to services he performed during the period he is a "qualified individual" (¶ 4618). (Code Sec. 911(b)(1)(A)) Foreign earned income also includes moving expense reimbursements attributable to performing those services. (Reg § 1.911-3(e)(5), (a))[9]

"Foreign earned income" doesn't include certain amounts paid by the U.S. or a federal agency to an employee of the U.S. or of the agency. (Code Sec. 911(b)(1)(B)(ii))[10]

For *separate* exclusion for a portion of foreign housing costs, see ¶ 4616.

¶ 4615 Ceiling on foreign earned income exclusion.

An individual's foreign earned income exclusion for a tax year can't exceed his foreign earned income for the year, as computed on a daily basis at an annual rate of $70,000. (Code Sec. 911(b)(2)(A))[11]

If the individual also elects the foreign housing costs exclusion, his foreign earned income exclusion is the *lesser* of: (a) $70,000, multiplied by the number of days in the tax year on which he "qualified" for the exclusion (¶ 4618), and divided by the number of days in the tax year, or (b) his foreign earned income as reduced by the foreign housing costs exclusion for the tax year. (Reg § 1.911-3(d)(2), Reg § 1.911-4(d))[12]

For married couples, the exclusion (and ceiling) is computed separately for each spouse based on the income attributable to the spouse's services. If the spouses file separate returns, each may exclude the amount of his foreign earned income attributable to his services, subject to the ceilings. If the spouses file a joint return, the sum of those separate amounts may be excluded. (Reg § 1.911-5(a)(2))[13]

¶ 4616 Partial exclusion for foreign housing costs.

A qualified individual (¶ 4618) may elect to exclude from gross income a limited amount based on his housing costs paid or incurred as a result of his foreign employment. (Code Sec. 911(a)(2))[14] This exclusion is in addition to any allowable foreign earned income exclusion (¶ 4614), but the sum of those exclusions for any tax year can't exceed the

---

5. ¶ O-1063; ¶ 8714.
6. ¶ O-1051; ¶ 8714.
7. ¶ S-3699; ¶ 6039E4.
8. ¶ O-1100 *et seq.*; ¶ 9114 *et seq.*

9. ¶s O-1111, O-1140; ¶s 9114.01, 9114.06 *et seq.*
10. ¶ O-1143; ¶ 9114.10.

11. ¶ O-1102.
12. ¶ O-1102 *et seq.*; ¶s 9114.01, 9114.12.

13. ¶ O-1115; ¶ 9114.09.
14. ¶ O-1161 *et seq.*; ¶ 9114.02.

Footnote references beginning with letters are to paragraphs in RIA's Federal Tax Coordinator 2d and RIA's Analysis of Federal Taxes: Income. Footnote references beginning with numbers are to paragraphs in RIA's United States Tax Reporter.

individual's foreign earned income for the year (¶ 4614). (Code Sec. 911(d)(7))[15] For deduction of nonemployer-provided housing expenses, see ¶ 4617.

A qualified individual who elects the housing costs exclusion may not claim less than the full amount of the allowable exclusion. (Reg § 1.911-4(d)(1))[16]

The amount of housing costs eligible for exclusion in a tax year is the excess of: (1) the individual's housing expenses for the year, over (2) 16% of the salary (computed on a daily basis) of a U.S. employee compensated at a rate equal to the annual rate paid for step 1 of grade GS-14 ($54,607 for '93 returns), *multiplied* by the number of days in the tax year within the individual's period of foreign residence or presence. (Code Sec. 911(c)(1))[17]

Where spouses reside together and both claim a foreign housing costs exclusion (or deduction), they may compute their exclusion separately or jointly. Spouses who file separate returns must make separate computations, but they may allocate the housing expenses between them. (Reg § 1.911-5(a)(3)(i)) Where spouses reside apart, they both may exclude (or deduct) their respective housing cost amounts if their tax homes aren't within reasonable commuting distance of each other and neither spouse's residence is within a reasonable commuting distance of the other spouse's tax home. If the spouses' tax homes or residences *are* within reasonable commuting distance, only one spouse may exclude or deduct his housing cost amount. In either case, and whether they file separately or jointly, the amount of the housing costs exclusion (or deduction) is determined separately for each spouse. (Reg § 1.911-5(a)(3)(ii))[18]

¶ 4617 Deduction for foreign housing expenses not provided by employer.

A qualified individual (¶ 4618) who has foreign housing expenses that aren't attributable to employer-provided amounts may deduct those expenses. (Code Sec. 911(c)(3)(A))[19] The deduction is limited to the individual's foreign earned income for the tax year which isn't otherwise excluded from gross income under either the foreign earned income exclusion (¶ 4614) or the foreign housing costs exclusion (¶ 4616). (Code Sec. 911(c)(3)(B)) Any unused housing expenses may be carried over and deducted in the next tax year, subject to that year's limits. (Code Sec. 911(c)(3)(C))[20]

¶ 4618 Who qualifies for the foreign earned income and foreign housing costs exclusions?

To qualify for the foreign earned income and housing costs exclusions for a tax year, an individual must have his "tax home" (below) in a foreign country *and* must be either:

■ a U.S. citizen who meets a *foreign residence test*. To meet this test, the individual must be a bona fide *resident* of one or more foreign countries for an uninterrupted period including an entire tax year. (Code Sec. 911(d)(1)(A))[21] (A resident alien who's a national of a "treaty" country may qualify.)[22] or

■ a U.S. citizen or resident who meets a *foreign presence test*. To meet this test, the individual must, in any period of 12 consecutive months, be *present* in one or more foreign countries during at least 330 full days. (Code Sec. 911(d)(1)(B)) This means *physically* present, including time while on vacation or unemployed.[23]

For married couples, if both spouses "qualify," each may elect the exclusion or deduction. (Reg § 1.911-5(a)(1))[24]

An individual's "tax home" is his home for purposes of deducting travel expenses while away from home (¶ 1536). He has no "tax home" in a foreign country for any period his abode is in the U.S. (Code Sec. 911(d)(3)) But the fact that an individual is temporarily present in the U.S. or maintains a U.S. dwelling (even if used by the individual's spouse or dependents) doesn't necessarily mean his abode is in the U.S. (Reg § 1.911-2(b))[25]

---

15. ¶ O-1168; ¶ 9114.01.
16. ¶ O-1168; ¶ 9114.02.
17. ¶s O-1166, O-1167; ¶ 9114.02.
18. ¶s O-1174, O-1175; ¶ 9114.02.
19. ¶ O-1171; ¶ 9114.02.
20. ¶ O-1173; ¶ 9114.02.
21. ¶ O-1250 *et seq.*; ¶ 9114.04.
22. ¶ O-1271.
23. ¶ O-1300 *et seq.*; ¶ 9114.05.
24. ¶ O-1351; ¶ 9114.09.
25. ¶s O-1202, O-1203, O-1250 *et seq.*

Footnote references beginning with letters are to paragraphs in RIA's Federal Tax Coordinator 2d and RIA's Analysis of Federal Taxes: Income. Footnote references beginning with numbers are to paragraphs in RIA's United States Tax Reporter.

The foreign presence or residence time requirements may be waived by IRS if it determines that local unrest (war, civil disturbance, etc.) precludes the normal conduct of business, but only for taxpayers already present in, or bona fide residents of, the foreign country. (Code Sec. 911(d)(4)) (These countries include Afghanistan, Bosnia and Herzegovina, Haiti, Iran, Lebanon, Libya, Yugoslavia and Zaire.)[26]

¶ 4619 How to elect foreign earned income and foreign housing costs exclusions—Form 2555.

The foreign earned income and housing costs exclusions won't apply unless elected. (Code Sec. 911(a)) Each exclusion must be elected separately, generally on a Form 2555 attached to taxpayer's return. (Reg § 1.911-7(a)(2)(i)) (Form 2555-EZ may be used for the foreign earned income exclusion if none of the individual's income was from self-employment, his total foreign earned income didn't exceed $70,000, *and* he doesn't claim the foreign housing costs exclusion.)[27]

If the taxpayer elects either exclusion for a tax year, the election remains in effect for that year and all later years, unless revoked (Code Sec. 911(e))[28] (or taxpayer claims the foreign tax credit in a later year).[29]

¶ 4620 Income earned in countries in which travel is barred by U.S.

If U.S. law bars travel (or any related transaction) with respect to a foreign country for any period, any earned income attributable to services performed in that country, and any housing costs allocable to that country, during that period, aren't eligible for the foreign earned income or housing costs exclusions. (Code Sec. 911(d)(8)) "Restricted" countries are Cuba, Libya and Iraq.[30]

¶ 4621 Denial of double deduction, exclusion or credit.

No deduction, exclusion or credit, including any credit or deduction for foreign or possessions taxes (¶ 2357 *et seq.*), is allowable to the extent the deduction, etc., is allocable to or chargeable against foreign income excluded from gross income under the foreign earned income or housing costs exclusions. (Code Sec. 911(d)(6))[31]

¶ 4622 Exclusion for meals and lodging furnished to employee at a foreign "camp."

Where an individual is furnished lodging at a "camp" located in a foreign country by or on behalf of his employer, the camp is considered part of the employer's business premises for purposes of the exclusion for employer-provided meals and lodging (¶ 1270 *et seq.*). (Code Sec. 119(c)(1))[32]

¶ 4623 Income from certain U.S. possessions.

An individual who is a bona fide resident of Guam, the Northern Mariana Islands or American Samoa during the entire tax year is exempt from U.S. tax on his income (except for amounts earned as a an employee of the U.S.) from sources within, or effectively connected with his conduct of a trade or business within, *any* of these possessions. (Code Sec. 931(a), (d)(1)) This applies only for the period in which an implementing agreement is in effect between the possession and the U.S. (i.e., for American Samoa).[33]

¶ 4624 Individuals with a bona fide Puerto Rican residence.

Any individual (regardless of citizenship) who is a bona fide resident of Puerto Rico during the entire tax year is exempt from U.S. tax on income from Puerto Rican sources, *except* for amounts received for services performed for the U.S. government. But no

---

26. ¶ O-1273; ¶ 9114.03.
27. ¶ O-1351 *et seq.*; ¶ 9114.13.
28. ¶ O-1351, O-1353.
29. ¶ O-1354.

30. ¶ O-1148; ¶ 9114.06.
31. ¶ O-1112; ¶ 9114.11.
32. ¶ H-1770; ¶ 1194.05.

33. ¶s O-1371, O-1383 *et seq.*, O-1410 *et seq.*, O-1432 *et seq.*; ¶ 9314.01 *et seq.*

Footnote references beginning with letters are to paragraphs in RIA's Federal Tax Coordinator 2d and RIA's Analysis of Federal Taxes: Income. Footnote references beginning with numbers are to paragraphs in RIA's United States Tax Reporter.

deductions or credits, other than the deduction for personal exemptions, are allowed (i.e., from *taxable* non-Puerto Rican source income) for items attributable to these excluded amounts. (Code Sec. 933(1))[34]

A U.S. citizen who gives up Puerto Rican residence after being a bona fide resident there for at least two years may exclude from gross income for the year of change in residence, any income from Puerto Rican sources attributable to the period before the change (including amounts received *after* that year), to the extent allowed above. (Code Sec. 933(2); Reg § 1.933-1(b))[35]

¶ 4625 U.S. and Virgin Islands—taxation of individuals.

A U.S. citizen (or resident) who derives income from the Virgin Islands (VI) but is *not a bona fide resident* there on the last day of his tax year must file two identical returns, one with the U.S. and one with the VI (Form 8689). The individual's VI tax liability is a fraction of his U.S. tax liability, based on the ratio that his adjusted gross income from VI sources bears to his worldwide adjusted gross income. (Code Sec. 932(a), (b)) The VI portion (if paid) is credited against his total U.S. tax liability (¶ 2357 *et seq.*). (Code Sec. 932(b)(3))[36]

An individual who is a *bona fide VI resident* on the last day of his tax year (or files a joint return with a person who is a VI resident on the last day of his tax year) files a VI return and pays VI tax on his worldwide income for that year. As long as the individual files a VI return for that year on which he reports income from all sources, identifying the source of each item shown, *and* fully pays the VI tax liability, he may excludes from U.S. gross income any amount included in gross income on the VI return. Allocable deductions and credits are not taken into account. (Code Sec. 932(c)(4))[37]

For a joint return, the resident status of both spouses is determined by the residence of the spouse who has the greater adjusted gross income for the tax year, without regard to community property laws. (Code Sec. 932(d))[38]

¶ 4626 U.S. government employees.

The following are exempt from U.S. tax:

■ Cost-of-living allowances received by U.S. government civilian officers and employees (including judicial employees) stationed outside the continental U.S. (except Alaska). (Code Sec. 912(2))[39]

■ Amounts received as allowances or otherwise under: Chapter 9 of Title I of the '80 Foreign Service Act; Section 4 of the '49 Central Intelligence Agency Act; Title II of the Overseas Differentials and Allowances Act; or Subsection (e) or (f) of the first section of, or Section 22 of, the '46 Administrative Expenses Act. (Code Sec. 912(1))[40]

■ Allowances to a Peace Corps volunteer or volunteer leader and members of his family under Section 5 or 6 of the Peace Corps Act, *except* : termination payments, leave allowances, allowances to members of the family of a volunteer leader who is training in the U.S. and the portion of the living allowances designated as basic compensation. (Code Sec. 913(3))[41]

The above exemptions don't apply to recruitment incentives given because of station location, foreign post or service differentials, or allowances that are part of a salary.[42]

¶ 4627 U.S. beneficiaries of foreign trusts.

A U.S. beneficiary of a foreign trust is taxed on the trust's foreign- and U.S.-source income, at the time the income becomes distributable. (Code Sec. 643(a)(6), Code

---

34. ¶ O-1450 *et seq.*; ¶ 9314.04. 37. ¶ O-1472; ¶ 9314.05. 39. ¶ H-3134; ¶ 9124.01. 41. ¶ H-3137; ¶ 9124.02.
35. ¶ O-1453; ¶ 9314.04. 38. ¶ O-1473; ¶ 9314.05. 40. ¶ H-3136; ¶ 9124. 42. ¶ H-3135.
36. ¶ O-1471; ¶ 9314.05.

Footnote references beginning with letters are to paragraphs in RIA's Federal Tax Coordinator 2d and RIA's Analysis of Federal Taxes: Income. Footnote references beginning with numbers are to paragraphs in RIA's United States Tax Reporter.

Sec. 652(a))[43] Distributions to the U.S. beneficiary of accumulated trust income are subject to the trust throwback rules (¶ 3953 *et seq.*)[44] and a nondeductible interest charge. (Code Sec. 668)[45]

¶ 4628 Domestic corporations—taxation of U.S. and foreign income.

A corporation incorporated in the U.S. is subject to U.S. tax on its income from both foreign and U.S. sources (except for certain "possessions" corporations, see ¶ 2365). (Code Sec. 63)[46] In addition, a domestic corporation may also be taxed on the *undistributed* income of a controlled foreign corporation (¶ 4635) or foreign personal holding company (¶ 4644) in which it is a shareholder.[47]

¶ 4629 Taxation of foreign sales corporations (FSCs).

A portion of the foreign trade income earned by a foreign sales corporation (FSC, see ¶ 4630) is exempt from U.S. tax. (Code Sec. 921(a))[48] If the amount of income earned by the FSC from a transaction is based on arm's-length pricing between unrelated parties, or between related parties under Code Sec. 482, 32% of the foreign trade income derived from the transaction is exempt (30% for corporate shareholders). (Code Sec. 923(a)(2), Code Sec. 291(a)(4)(A)) If special administrative pricing rules are used, the exempt portion is $16/23$ of the foreign trade income from the transaction ($15/23$ for corporate shareholders). (Code Sec. 291(a)(4)(B), Code Sec. 923(a)(3))[49]

To the extent that an FSC's foreign trade income from a transaction isn't "exempt," it is subject to U.S. tax, based on the pricing method used to determine the exempt portion. (Code Sec. 921(d); Reg § 1.921-3T(a)(2))[50]

An FSC's foreign trade income is its gross income attributable to foreign trading gross receipts, (Code Sec. 923(b)) i.e., its gross receipts (excluding interest and carrying charges) from exporting certain goods and services. (Code Sec. 924(a), (f)(4)) However, an FSC won't have foreign trading gross receipts in a tax year unless it meets foreign management and foreign economic process requirements. (Code Sec. 924(b))[1]

An FSC is required to file Form 1120-FSC.[2]

¶ 4630 FSC requirements.

To qualify as an FSC, a corporation must (in addition to electing FSC status, see ¶ 4632):

■ be created or organized under the laws of a "certified" foreign country or U.S. possession (except Puerto Rico); (Code Sec. 922(a)(1)(A); Code Sec. 927(d)(3))

■ have no more than 25 shareholders (counting joint owners separately) (Code Sec. 922(a)(1)(B); Reg § 1.921-2(a)) at any time during the tax year (up to 25 small to medium exporters may join as shareholders in a single FSC (shared FSC) to share costs and enjoy the FSC tax benefits); (Code Sec. 927(g))

■ have no preferred stock outstanding—however, it may have more than one class of common stock; (Code Sec. 922(a)(1)(C); Reg § 1.922-1(g))

■ maintain an office in a certified foreign country (not necessarily the country or possession of the corporation's incorporation), and keep its permanent books and records there; (Code Sec. 922(a)(1)(D); Reg § 1.922-1(h))

■ hold all shareholders' and directors' meetings outside the U.S. unless local law permits otherwise; (Code Sec. 924(c)(1))

■ have on its board of directors at least one nonresident of the U.S. (who may be a U.S.

43. ¶ C-3001; ¶s 6524, 6431.01.   46. ¶ O-1006; ¶s 9109, 9314.06.   48. ¶ O-1672.   50. ¶ O-1671.
44. ¶ C-4003; ¶s 6664, 6684.   47. ¶s O-2300 *et seq.*, O-8000   49. ¶s O-1752, O-1753; ¶s 9214,   1. ¶ O-1840 *et seq.*
45. ¶ C-4107 *et seq.*; ¶ 6684.   *et seq.*; ¶ 9509 *et seq.*   9214.02.   2. ¶ S-1916.

Footnote references beginning with letters are to paragraphs in RIA's Federal Tax Coordinator 2d and RIA's Analysis of Federal
Taxes: Income. Footnote references beginning with numbers are to paragraphs in RIA's United States Tax Reporter.

622

citizen, or even a nonresident alien who elects to be treated as a U.S. resident for purposes of filing a joint U.S. return); (Code Sec. 922(a)(1)(E); Reg § 1.922-1(j)) *and*

■ not be a member of a controlled group of corporations that includes an IC-DISC (¶ 4634). (Code Sec. 922(a)(1)(F))[3]

¶ 4631 Small FSCs.

A small FSC doesn't have to meet the foreign management and foreign economic process requirements that FSCs must meet to have foreign trading gross receipts. But a small FSC can't take into account more than $5 million of those receipts in determining its exempt foreign trade income for a year (¶ 4629). (Code Sec. 924(b); Reg § 1.924(a)-1T(j))[4]

Treatment as a small FSC must be elected (¶ 4632). It isn't allowed for any year that the FSC is a member of a controlled group with another FSC member (unless that other FSC also makes the election). (Code Sec. 922(b)(2))[5]

¶ 4632 Election to be treated as an FSC or small FSC—Form 8279.

A corporation may elect to be treated as an FSC (or small FSC) for a tax year (using Form 8279) at any time during the 90-day period immediately preceding the beginning of the tax year. The shareholders must consent in writing. (Code Sec. 927(f)(1)(A))[6]

Once made, the remains effective (unless revoked) for later years in which the corporation qualifies as an FSC (or small FSC), except that it terminates automatically if the corporation fails to qualify for five consecutive tax years. (Code Sec. 927(f)(2), (3); Reg § 1.927(f)-1(a))[7]

¶ 4633 Treaty benefits denied.

Any corporation electing to be treated as an FSC may not claim any benefit under any U.S. income tax treaty with any foreign country. (Code Sec. 927(e)(4))[8]

¶ 4634 Interest charge domestic international sales corporation (IC-DISC).

A qualifying corporation that elects (on Form 4876A) to be an IC-DISC can defer income attributable to $10 million or less of qualified export receipts. However, an interest charge is imposed on the DISC's shareholders (report on Form 8404). The amount of the interest is based on the tax otherwise due on the deferred income computed as if it were distributed. The interest rate is tied to the Treasury bill (T-bill) rate. (Code Sec. 995(f)(1))[9]

An IC-DISC must file Form 1120-IC-DISC.[10]

¶ 4635 Tax on U.S. shareholders of controlled foreign corporations (CFCs).

If a foreign corporation is a CFC for an uninterrupted period of 30 days or more during its tax year, every person who is a "U.S. shareholder" of the CFC (¶ 4636) at any time during that year, and who owns stock in the CFC on the last day of its tax year, must report (on Form 5471) his pro rata share of the foreign corporation's undistributed earnings ("Subpart F income," see ¶ 4637) for that year. (Code Sec. 951(a)(1); Reg § 1.951-1(a))[11]

In addition to Subpart F income, a CFC's "U.S. shareholders" are also taxed on their proportionate shares of:

■ the CFC's increase during the tax year in earnings invested in U.S. property (to the extent not included as Subpart F income); (Code Sec. 951(a)(1)(B))[12]

3. ¶ O-1710 *et seq.*; ¶ 9214.01.
4. ¶s O-1752, O-1996 *et seq.*; ¶ 9214.10.
5. ¶ O-1728; ¶ 9214.10.
6. ¶ O-1730 *et seq.*; ¶ 9214.01.
7. ¶s O-1735, O-2014; ¶ 9214.01.
8. ¶ O-1681.
9. ¶ O-2020 *et seq.*; ¶ 9914 *et seq.*
10. ¶ S-1917.
11. ¶s O-2600 *et seq.*, O-2701; ¶s 9514, 9514.01.
12. ¶ O-2546 *et seq.*; ¶ 9564.01.

Footnote references beginning with letters are to paragraphs in RIA's Federal Tax Coordinator 2d and RIA's Analysis of Federal Taxes: Income. Footnote references beginning with numbers are to paragraphs in RIA's United States Tax Reporter.

- the CFC's "excess passive assets," (Code Sec. 951(a)(1)(C)) for tax years of CFCs beginning after Sept. 30, '93;

- the CFC's previously excluded income withdrawn from investment in less developed countries (under the rules in effect before the Tax Reduction Act of '75); (Code Sec. 951(a)(1)(A)(ii))[13]

- the CFC's previously excluded Subpart F income withdrawn from foreign base company shipping operations for that year; (Code Sec. 951(a)(1)(A)(iii))[14] and

- the CFC's decrease in investments in export trade assets. (Code Sec. 970(b))[15]

¶ 4636 Controlled foreign corporation (CFC) defined.

A CFC is a foreign corporation more than 50% (25%, for insurance companies) of whose stock *by vote or value* is, on any day during the corporation's tax year, owned (directly or indirectly) by "U.S. shareholders." (Code Sec. 957(a), (b)) A "U.S. shareholder" is a U.S. citizen or resident (including a corporation, partnership, estate or trust) that owns, directly or indirectly, more than 10% of the corporation's voting stock. (Code Sec. 951(b))[16]

¶ 4637 What is Subpart F income?

A CFC's Subpart F income consists of:

(1) Income derived from insuring (or reinsuring) certain foreign risks. (Code Sec. 953)[17]

(2) Foreign base company income (FBCI), which is (a) foreign personal holding company income (as defined at ¶ 4644 but with modifications), and (b) foreign base company sales, services, shipping and oil-related income. (Code Sec. 954(a))[18]

(3) Income from operations in compliance with an unsanctioned international boycott. (Code Sec. 952(a)(3))[19]

(4) The amount of any nondeductible payment made (directly or indirectly) by or for the CFC to a government official, employee or agent in fact (i.e., payments violating the U.S. Foreign Corrupt Practices Act). (Code Sec. 952(a)(4))[20]

(5) Income (reduced by allocable deductions and taxes) derived from a foreign country that the U.S. doesn't recognize, has severed relations with, or the Secretary of State has designated as a country that repeatedly supports international terrorism. (Code Sec. 952(a)(5))[21]

Also, in any tax year when the sum of the CFC's FBCI and insurance income exceeds 70% of its gross income, *all* of its income for the year is treated as FBCI or insurance income (subject to the "high foreign tax" exception, below). If this sum is less than 5% of the CFC's gross income or $1,000,000 (whichever is smaller), then *none* of the CFC's income is FBCI or insurance income. (Code Sec. 954(b)(3))[22]

Any FBCI or insurance income that is subject to an effective rate of foreign tax which is greater than 90% of the maximum U.S. corporate rate, may, at the CFC's election, be excluded from Subpart F income. (Code Sec. 954(b)(4))[23]

¶ 4638 Disposition of CFC stock.

Gain from the sale, exchange or redemption (under Code Sec. 302, see ¶ 3525 *et seq.*) of stock in, or from the liquidation of, a foreign corporation is taxable as ordinary dividend income *if*:

- the selling or exchanging shareholder is a U.S. citizen or resident, or a domestic partnership, corporation, trust or estate; *and*

---

13. ¶ O-2531; ¶ 9514.01.
14. ¶ O-2531; ¶s 9514.01, 9554.
15. ¶ O-2538 *et seq.*; ¶ 9704.01.
16. ¶ O-2300 *et seq.*; ¶ 9574.01.

17. ¶ O-2404 *et seq.*; ¶ 9534.01.
18. ¶ O-2424 *et seq.*; ¶ 9544 *et seq.*

19. ¶ O-2528; ¶ 9524.02.
20. ¶ O-2529; ¶ 9524.03.
21. ¶ O-2530; ¶ 9524.04.

22. ¶ O-2508 *et seq.*; ¶ 9544.01.
23. ¶ O-2508 *et seq.*; ¶ 9544.01.

Footnote references beginning with letters are to paragraphs in RIA's Federal Tax Coordinator 2d and RIA's Analysis of Federal Taxes: Income. Footnote references beginning with numbers are to paragraphs in RIA's United States Tax Reporter.

■ the shareholder was a "U.S. shareholder" (¶ 4636) of the corporation at some time during the five-year period ending on the date of the sale, etc.; *and*

■ the foreign corporation was a CFC (¶ 4636) at some time during the period the shareholder was a "U.S. shareholder," during that five-year period. (Code Sec. 1248)[24]

This dividend treatment also applies with respect to a *domestic* corporation formed or availed of principally for holding (directly or indirectly) stock of one or more foreign corporations. (Code Sec. 1248(e))[25]

This dividend treatment doesn't apply to Code Sec. 303 redemptions, amounts otherwise treated as dividends, ordinary income, short-term capital gains, or gains from sales made by non-U.S. persons. (Code Sec. 1248(g)) Nor does it apply to gifts or other transfers that don't result in recognized gain.[26]

There is a ceiling on the tax on the "dividend" income for an individual shareholder who held the stock for the long-term holding period (¶ 2651). (Code Sec. 1248(b))[27]

¶ 4639 Sales of patents, etc.

A U.S. citizen or resident, or a domestic partnership, corporation, trust or estate, that sells (or exchanges) a patent, invention, formula or process, or similar property right to a foreign corporation in which the seller owns (directly, indirectly or constructively) stock with over 50% of the combined voting power must treat *as ordinary income* any gain recognized on that sale (exchange). (Code Sec. 1249)[28]

¶ 4640 Foreign investment company (mutual fund) stock.

Gain realized on the sale or exchange of stock in a foreign investment company (FIC) that otherwise would be long-term capital gain is generally treated as ordinary income to the extent of the seller's share of the FIC's post-'62 earnings and profits *unless* the FIC elected, before '63, to distribute its income. (Code Sec. 1246, Code Sec. 1247)[29]

¶ 4641 Passive foreign investment companies (PFICs).

A PFIC is any foreign corporation if: (1) at least 75% of its gross income for its tax year is passive, or (2) at least 50%, by value (or adjusted basis, if elected), of the assets it held during the year produce passive income (i.e., Subpart F foreign personal holding company income, see ¶ 4637). However, if the corporation is also a controlled foreign corporation, the 50% test *must* be made with respect to the adjusted basis, not to the value, of the assets (for tax years of foreign corporations beginning after Sept. 30, '93). (Code Sec. 1296)[30] For how PFIC's shareholders are taxed, see ¶ 4642.

¶ 4642 How U.S. shareholder in passive foreign investment company (PFIC) is taxed.

A U.S. shareholder in a PFIC (¶ 4641) may defer the U.S. tax (with respect to that investment) until the shareholder disposes of the PFIC stock or receives an "excess distribution." At that time, the shareholder must pay U.S. tax, plus interest, based on the value of the tax deferral (unless the PFIC is a qualified electing fund, see ¶ 4643). (Code Sec. 1291(a)(1), (2)) All gain recognized and all distributions are ordinary income, allocated ratably to each day the shareholder held the stock. (Code Sec. 1291(a)(1)(A), (B))[31] Report the distributions and dispositions on Form 8621.[32]

An "excess distribution" is a current year distribution received by a shareholder on PFIC stock, that represents a ratable portion of the average PFIC stock distributions during the year which exceeds 125% of that yearly average for the three preceding years. (Code Sec. 1291(b))[33]

---

24. ¶ O-2801; ¶ 12,484 *et seq.*
25. ¶ O-2805.
26. ¶ O-2803; ¶ 12,484.01.
27. ¶ O-2811; ¶ 12,484.02.

28. ¶ O-2900 *et seq.*; ¶ 12,494.
29. ¶ O-3000 *et seq.*; ¶ 12,464 *et seq.*

30. ¶ O-2202 *et seq.*; ¶ 12,914.01.
31. ¶s O-2201, O-2218, O-2228; ¶ 12,914.02.

32. ¶ O-2228.
33. ¶ O-2005; ¶ 12,914.02.

Footnote references beginning with letters are to paragraphs in RIA's Federal Tax Coordinator 2d and RIA's Analysis of Federal Taxes: Income. Footnote references beginning with numbers are to paragraphs in RIA's United States Tax Reporter.

Portions of distributions that aren't "excess distributions" are taxed in the current (distribution) year under the normal rules for distributions (¶ 1288 *et seq.*). (Code Sec. 1291(a)(1)(B))[34]

A transfer of stock on which gain otherwise wouldn't be recognized under these rules is nevertheless treated as gain on the sale or exchange of that stock. (Code Sec. 1291(f))[35]

A PFIC shareholder may claim both direct and indirect ("deemed") foreign tax credits (¶ 2357 *et seq.*) with respect to these dispositions and distributions. (Code Sec. 1291(g))[36]

¶ 4643 Qualified electing fund (QEF).

A PFIC is treated as a qualified electing fund (QEF) with respect to a particular shareholder if that shareholder so elects, and the PFIC complies with certain notification requirements. (Code Sec. 1295) If the election is made, the shareholder's U.S. tax on disposition of the stock or receipt of an excess distribution will not be increased by any interest charge (that applies to PFICs, see ¶ 4642). (Code Sec. 1291(d)(1))[37]

However, the electing shareholder must currently include in income his share of the PFIC's earnings and profits (with appropriate basis adjustments for amounts not distributed or previously included in income). The fund's ordinary income and net capital gain will be passed through to the shareholder as ordinary income and long-term capital gain. (Code Sec. 1293) A 10% corporate shareholder is allowed a foreign tax credit on its share of the PFIC's earnings. (Code Sec. 1293(f))[38]

A shareholder makes a QEF election by attaching an election statement, PFIC annual information return, and Form 8621 to a timely filed income tax return. (Reg § 1.1291-10T(d))[39]

¶ 4644 Foreign personal holding companies (FPHCs).

U.S. shareholders of a FPHC are taxed on their share of its undistributed FPHC income for the tax year. (Code Sec. 556; Reg § 1.556-1, Reg § 1.556-2)[40] The amount so taxed can be reduced by certain distributions the FPHC makes on or before the 15th day of the third month after the end of its tax year. (Code Sec. 563(c)(2))[41]

A foreign corporation (other than tax-exempt organizations and certain banks) is a FPHC for a tax year if: (1) 60% (50% after the first year) or more of its gross income for the year is FPHC income (below), *and* (2) more than 50% of its total outstanding stock (by vote or value) is owned (directly or indirectly) by fewer than six individual U.S. citizens or residents. (Code Sec. 552)[42]

FPHC income is passive investment income such as interest, dividends, rents (unless they exceed 50% of gross income), annuities and royalties (except active business computer software royalties), and income from the use of corporate property by a 25%-or-more shareholder, or from personal services rendered under contract by a 25%-or-more shareholder. (Code Sec. 553; Reg § 1.553-1)[43]

¶ 4645 Coordination of CFC, FPHC, FIC and PFIC rules.

Any amount that, for a tax year, could be included in gross income under the rules for CFCs (¶ 4635), PFICs (¶ 4642), or FPHCs (¶ 4644) is included only under the CFC rules. (Code Sec. 951(d), (f)) The CFC rules also have priority over the FIC rules (¶ 4640) (unless the pre-'63 election was made). (Code Sec. 951(c))[44]

¶ 4646 Transfer of property to foreign corporation, partnership, trust or estate.

A 35% excise tax is imposed on a U.S. citizen or resident, or a domestic corporation, partnership, estate or trust, that transfers appreciated property to a foreign corporation

---

34. ¶ O-2218.	37. ¶ O-2262 *et seq.*; ¶ 12,914.04.	40. ¶ O-3622; ¶ 5514.	43. ¶ O-3611 *et seq.*; ¶ 5524.
35. ¶ O-2039; ¶ 12,914.02.	38. ¶ O-2262; ¶ 12,914.04.	41. ¶ O-3623; ¶ 5634.	44. ¶ O-2603 *et seq.*; ¶s 9514.02,
36. ¶ O-2253 *et seq.*; ¶ 12,914.02.	39. ¶ O-2268.	42. ¶ O-3600 *et seq.*; ¶ 5524.	9514.03.

Footnote references beginning with letters are to paragraphs in RIA's Federal Tax Coordinator 2d and RIA's Analysis of Federal Taxes: Income. Footnote references beginning with numbers are to paragraphs in RIA's United States Tax Reporter.

as paid-in surplus or as a capital contribution, or to a foreign partnership, trust or estate. The amount subject to tax is the fair market value of the property transferred less the sum of the property's adjusted basis and gain recognized (if any) at the time of the transfer. (Code Sec. 1491)[45] The transferor must report the transfer and pay the tax on the date the transfer is made (on Form 926). (Code Sec. 1494(a); Reg § 1.1494-1(a)(1))[46]

The excise tax does *not* apply if: (1) the transferee is a tax-exempt organization (other than an employee benefit trust); or (2) the transfer is described in Code Sec. 367 (¶ 3585), or is not so described but taxpayer elects (before the transfer) to apply similar principles; or (3) taxpayer elects to recognize the gain, by treating the transfer as a sale or exchange of the property. (Code Sec. 1057, Code Sec. 1492)[47]

¶ 4647 Tax sanctions for international boycott activities.

Participation in or cooperation with an international boycott can result in: (1) reduction of the allowable foreign tax credit (¶ 2357 *et seq.*), (2) reduced deferral under the FSC (¶ 4629) or DISC (¶ 4634) rules, and (3) a CFC's undistributed earnings being currently taxed to its U.S. shareholders (¶ 4637). (Code Sec. 908, Code Sec. 927(e)(2), Code Sec. 952(a)(3)) Taxpayers must report (on Form 5713) boycott operations and requests to participate or cooperate. (Code Sec. 999)[48]

In general, a person participates in or cooperates with a boycott if, as a condition of doing business (directly or indirectly) either within a "boycott country" or with its government, companies or nationals, the person agrees to refrain from doing business with governments or companies that are the object of the boycott, or from employing individuals of particular nationality, race, religion, etc. (Code Sec. 999(b)(3)(A))[49] The following are "boycott countries": Bahrain, Iraq, Jordan, Kuwait, Lebanon, Libya, Oman, Qatar, Saudi Arabia, Syria, United Arab Emirates and Yemen.[50]

¶ 4648 Tax sanctions for bribes of government officials.

If an illegal (by U.S. law) bribe, kickback or other payment, is made, directly or indirectly, by or for an IC-DISC (¶ 4634) to an official, employee or "agent in fact" of a government, the payment is treated as a dividend and must be included in the DISC shareholders' income. (Code Sec. 995(b)(1))[1] For treatment of such payments by or for a CFC, see ¶ 4637.

¶ 4649 Taxation of Nonresident Aliens and Foreign Corporations ▬▬▬▬

A nonresident alien individual or foreign corporation is taxed at a 30% (or lower treaty) rate on certain (usually investment) income from U.S. sources. A nonresident alien or foreign corporation that is engaged in a U.S. trade or business is taxed at regular U.S. rates on income effectively connected with that business.

A foreign corporation also may be subject to other taxes, including the accumulated earnings tax (¶ 3320 *et seq.*), the personal holding company tax (¶ 3330 *et seq.*), (Reg § 1.881-1(e))[2] a branch profits tax (¶ 4655), and the alternative minimum tax (Chapter 14).

A nonresident alien or foreign corporation is exempt from U.S. tax for any tax year in which that person is not engaged in business in the U.S. and does not have income from U.S. sources.[3]

For allowance of deductions and credits, see ¶ 4658.

---

45. ¶ O-3701; ¶ 14,914.
46. ¶s O-3705, O-3706; ¶ 14,944.
47. ¶ O-3700 *et seq.*; ¶ 14,914.
48. ¶ O-3500 *et seq.*; ¶ 9994.01.
49. ¶ O-3503 *et seq.*; ¶ 9994.01.
50. ¶ O-3513; ¶ 9994.03.
1. ¶ O-2125; ¶ 9954.01.
2. ¶ O-10300; ¶ 8824.
3. ¶s O-10101, O-10301; ¶s 8714.01, 8814 *et seq.*

Footnote references beginning with letters are to paragraphs in RIA's Federal Tax Coordinator 2d and RIA's Analysis of Federal Taxes: Income. Footnote references beginning with numbers are to paragraphs in RIA's United States Tax Reporter.

¶ 4650 Foreign corporations and nonresident alien individuals.

A *foreign corporation* is one that is organized outside the U.S. or under any law other than that of the U.S., a state or the District of Columbia. (Code Sec. 7701(a)(3), (4), (9))[4]

A corporation created or organized in or under the law of Guam, American Samoa, the Northern Mariana Islands, or the Virgin Islands won't be treated as a foreign corporation for any tax year if: (1) at all times during the tax year less than 25% (by value) of its stock is owned (directly or indirectly) by foreign persons; (2) at least 65% of its gross income for the preceding three-tax-year period (or shorter period of existence) is shown to IRS's satisfaction to be effectively connected with the conduct of a trade or business in either the possession or the U.S.; *and* (3) no substantial part of its income is used (directly or indirectly) to satisfy obligations to persons who are not bona fide residents of that possession or the U.S. (Code Sec. 881(b)(1))[5]

A *nonresident alien individual* is an individual who is not a U.S. citizen or resident (¶ 4612), (Code Sec. 7701(b)(1)(B)) as well as a nonresident alien fiduciary. (Reg § 1.871-2(a)) Aliens who are residents of Puerto Rico, Guam, American Samoa or the Northern Mariana Islands for the entire tax year are generally taxed the same as resident aliens (Code Sec. 876)[6] (except for their income from within these possessions, see ¶ 4623).

¶ 4651 Tax on income "effectively connected" with a U.S. business.

A foreign corporation or nonresident alien engaged in a U.S. business (¶ 4652) at any time during the tax year is taxed at regular U.S. rates on taxable income "effectively connected" with that business. (Code Sec. 871(b); Code Sec. 882(a))[7] For tax on nonbusiness income, see ¶ 4653.

"Effectively connected" taxable income is the gross income effectively connected with the U.S. business, less allowable deductions (¶ 4658). (Code Sec. 871(b)(2); Code Sec. 882(a)(2))[8]

All *U.S.-source* income, gain, or loss (other than periodical income and capital gains and losses) derived by a nonresident alien or foreign corporation engaged in a U.S. business at any time in the tax year is treated as "effectively connected" income. (Code Sec. 864(c)(3))[9]

The *foreign-source* income treated as "effectively connected" is limited to the items below, and only to the extent the item is attributable to an office or other fixed place of business in the U.S.:

■ Rents, royalties and gains on intangible personal property from active licensing business.

■ Dividends, interest or gain from stock or obligations from active banking, financing or trading business.

■ Income from the sale, exchange or other disposition of real property interests located in the U.S. (Code Sec. 864(c)(4))[10] (or outside the U.S., if taxpayer so elects, see ¶ 4654).

¶ 4652 What is "engaging in a U.S. business"?

A nonresident alien who performs personal services in the U.S. for compensation during the tax year is engaging in business in the U.S. that year, with this exception: An alien isn't taxed on this compensation if it is $3,000 or less, he is in the U.S. for 90 days or less, *and* he works for a foreign person. (Code Sec. 864(b))[11] Special rules apply to foreign students, trainees, etc. (Code Sec. 871(c), Code Sec. 872(c))[12]

---

4. ¶ O-10310; ¶ 8814.01.
5. ¶ O-10310; ¶s 8814.01, 8814.02.
6. ¶ O-1008; ¶s 8714, 8764, 9314 *et seq.*

7. ¶s O-10501, O-10602.
8. ¶s O-10601, O-10602.
9. ¶ O-10604.

10. ¶s O-10622, O-10700 *et seq.*; ¶ 8644.02.
11. ¶ O-10502; ¶ 8644.01.

13. ¶ O-10503; ¶s 8714.03, 8724.03.

Footnote references beginning with letters are to paragraphs in RIA's Federal Tax Coordinator 2d and RIA's Analysis of Federal Taxes: Income. Footnote references beginning with numbers are to paragraphs in RIA's United States Tax Reporter.

An alien isn't subject to U.S. tax on compensation received for services as an employee of a foreign government or international organization, *except* where the services are primarily in connection with the foreign government's commercial activities, or where the alien is an employee of a "controlled commercial entity." (Code Sec. 893)[13]

In the case of a partnership, estate or trust that is engaged in a U.S. business, any of the entity's nonresident alien or foreign corporate partners or beneficiaries are considered so engaged. (Code Sec. 875)[14]

¶ 4653 Tax on U.S.-source income not "effectively connected" with a U.S. business.

Nonresident alien individuals and foreign corporations are taxed at a flat 30% (or lower treaty rate) on the following types of income, if U.S.-source and not "effectively connected" with taxpayer's conduct of a U.S. business:

■ Interest (other than original issue discount (OID) and certain portfolio and bank account interest), dividends, rents, salaries, wages, premiums, annuities, compensations, remunerations, emoluments and other fixed or determinable annual or periodical gains, profits and income. (Code Sec. 871(a)(1)(A), Code Sec. 881(a)(1))

■ Gains from lump-sum distributions from qualified employee benefit plans. (Code Sec. 871(a)(1)(B))

■ Payments on bonds issued with OID, and amounts received on their disposition, that are ordinary income under the OID rules (¶ 1318 *et seq.*). (Code Sec. 871(a)(1)(C), Code Sec. 881(a)(3))

■ Amounts includible in income from holding a residual REMIC interest. (Code Sec. 860G(b)(1))

■ One-half of social security benefits paid to nonresident aliens. (Code Sec. 871(a)(3))

■ Gains on sale or exchange of patents, copyrights, and the like, or of interests in patents, etc., where payments are contingent on productivity, etc. (Code Sec. 871(a)(1)(D), Code Sec. 881(a)(4))

■ Certain types of gambling winnings (but not winnings from blackjack, baccarat, craps, roulette or big six wheel, except to extent provided in regs). (Code Sec. 871(j))

■ Gains from the disposal, with a retained economic interest, of timber, coal or iron ore. (Code Sec. 871(a)(1)(B), Code Sec. 881(a)(2))[15]

No deductions are allowed against this income. The tax is on the *gross* amount. (Code Sec. 873, Code Sec. 882(c))[16] (But if a nonresident alien has a U.S. spouse, the couple can, effectively, elect to be taxed at regular rates (¶ 4706).)

Non-"effectively connected" long- and short-term capital gains (except for patents, timber, etc., noted above) are not taxed to foreign corporations, (Code Sec. 881) and are taxed to nonresident aliens only if they are present in the U.S. for 183 or more days during the tax year. (Code Sec. 871(a)(2))[17]

¶ 4654 Election for income from U.S. real estate.

A nonresident alien or foreign corporation may elect to treat certain income from U.S. real property held for investment as income effectively connected with the conduct of a U.S. business. (Code Sec. 871(d), Code Sec. 882(d)) The foreign taxpayer is thus taxed at regular U.S. rates (rather than 30%) on net rather than gross income, taking advantage of depreciation deductions, etc., see ¶ 4651.[18]

Elect on a statement attached to the income tax return for the election year.

---

13. ¶ O-11829; ¶ 8934.
14. ¶ O-10504; ¶ 8754.
15. ¶ O-10201 *et seq.*; ¶s 8714.02, 8814.02.

16. ¶ O-10641, O-10648; ¶s 8734, 8814.02.

17. ¶ O-10231; ¶s 8714.02, 8814.02.

18. ¶ O-10615 *et seq.*; ¶ 8714.04.

Footnote references beginning with letters are to paragraphs in RIA's Federal Tax Coordinator 2d and RIA's Analysis of Federal Taxes: Income. Footnote references beginning with numbers are to paragraphs in RIA's United States Tax Reporter.

(Reg § 1.871-10(d)(1)(ii))[19]

¶ 4655 Branch profits tax imposed on foreign corporations.

A foreign corporation engaged in a U.S. trade or business through a branch office during the tax year is liable for a branch profits tax (in addition to regular income tax) equal to 30% of the year's "dividend equivalent amount." (Code Sec. 884(a); Reg § 1.884-1(a)) The "dividend equivalent amount" is the corporation's effectively connected earnings and profits (E&P), *reduced* (not below zero) by any increase for the year in its U.S. net equity (i.e., amounts reinvested in the U.S. business), and *increased* (within limits) by any decrease for the year in its U.S. net equity (i.e., amounts remitted to the foreign head office). (Code Sec. 884(b); Reg § 1.884-1(b))[20]

If a foreign corporation is subject to the branch profits tax for any tax year (whether any branch profits tax is actually due), *income* tax withholding is not required on any dividends it pays out of its E&P for that year. (Code Sec. 884(e)(3))[21]

🄡observation: The branch profits tax is the counterpart of the withholding tax, at the shareholder level, on dividends paid by a U.S. sub to its foreign parent (¶ 4653).

The branch profits tax won't generally be imposed on the complete termination of a foreign corporation's U.S. trade or business. But it is imposed, under special rules, where there is a corporate liquidation or reorganization, or a Code Sec. 351 incorporation transfer. (Reg § 1.884-2T)[22]

The branch profits tax doesn't apply if it's inconsistent with existing U.S. income tax treaties, provided the foreign corporation is a qualified resident of the treaty country, except for treaty shopping situations. (Code Sec. 884(e)(1); Reg § 1.884-1(g))[23]

¶ 4656 Branch-level interest tax.

If a foreign corporation is engaged in a U.S. trade or business (or has gross income treated as "effectively connected"), interest (including original issue discount) paid to the corporation by its U.S. trade or business (i.e., U.S. branch) is treated as if it were paid by a U.S. corporation (i.e., the foreign corporation's U.S. branch is treated as a sub). The interest is thus subject to the withholding tax discussed at ¶ 4670. (Code Sec. 884(f)(1)(A); Reg § 1.884-4(a)(1)) To the extent the amount of interest allowable as a deduction in computing the foreign corporation's taxable "effectively connected" income exceeds the amount thus treated as paid by a U.S. corporation, the foreign corporation is liable for the withholding tax on the excess as if it were paid by its wholly-owned U.S. sub. (Code Sec. 884(f)(1)(A), (B), (f)(2); Reg § 1.884-4(a)(2))[24] This treatment doesn't apply where the payor and recipient meet certain residency standards. (Code Sec. 884(f)(3))[25]

¶ 4657 Tax on transportation income.

A 4% tax is imposed on the U.S.-source gross transportation income of foreign corporations and nonresident aliens. (Code Sec. 887(a)) Income subject to this 4% gross-basis tax isn't subject to the 30% tax (¶ 4653) or the regular U.S. tax on "effectively connected" income (¶ 4651). (Code Sec. 887(c))[26]

¶ 4658 Deductions and credits of foreign corporations and nonresident aliens.

Foreign corporations and nonresident aliens generally may take deductions only to the extent related to "effectively connected" income (¶ 4651). (Code Sec. 873(a); Code Sec. 882(c)(1)(A))[27] But some deductions are allowed whether or not related to that income: for charitable contributions; and for nonresident aliens, for casualty and theft

---

19. ¶ O-1619.
20. ¶ O-11301 *et seq.*; ¶ 8844.
21. ¶ O-11427; ¶ 8844.

22. ¶ O-11356 *et seq.*; ¶ 8844.
23. ¶ O-11335; ¶ 8844.
24. ¶s O-11340, O-11341; ¶ 8844.

25. ¶ O-11415; ¶ 8844.
26. ¶ O-11501.

27. ¶ O-10641, O-10648; ¶s 8734, 8824.

Footnote references beginning with letters are to paragraphs in RIA's Federal Tax Coordinator 2d and RIA's Analysis of Federal Taxes: Income. Footnote references beginning with numbers are to paragraphs in RIA's United States Tax Reporter.

losses, and personal exemptions (limited). (Code Sec. 873(b), Code Sec. 882(c)(1)(B))[28]

Credits also generally are allowable only if attributable to "effectively connected" income, except for certain credits (e.g., for taxes withheld at source). (Code Sec. 874(b); Code Sec. 882(c)(2))[29]

Generally, a return must be filed to get the benefit of an otherwise allowable deduction or credit. (Code Sec. 874(a); Code Sec. 882(c)(2))[30]

¶ 4659 Whether income is from U.S. sources.

Specific rules are used to determine the source of the following types of income:

Compensation—generally where the services were performed.[31]

Interest—generally where the debtor is located.[32]

Dividends—generally where the corporation is incorporated. But dividends from a foreign corporation are U.S.-source unless less than 25% of all its income for the last three years is effectively connected with a U.S. business.[33]

Rents and royalties—generally where the property is used.[34]

Sales of personal property—generally where the seller resides. (Code Sec. 865(a)) Special provisions also apply to the sale of depreciable and intangible property, (Code Sec. 865(c), (d)) and to inventory. (Code Sec. 865(b)) Income from the sale of any personal property (other than inventory sold for use or disposition outside the U.S.) that is attributable to a nonresident's U.S. office is U.S.-source income. Sales of certain property by a U.S. resident through a foreign office is foreign-source if at least a 10% foreign tax is paid on it. (Code Sec. 865(g))[35]

Sales of real property or natural resources—where the property or resource is located. (Code Sec. 897)[36]

Transportation income from transportation that either begins or ends in the U.S. (but not both) is half foreign- and half U.S.-source. (Code Sec. 863(c)(2)(A))[37]

International communications income of a U.S. person is half foreign- and half U.S.-source. (Code Sec. 863(e)(1)(A)) A foreign person's international communications income is foreign-source, except where it is attributable to an office or fixed place of business in the U.S. (Code Sec. 863(e)(1)(B))[38]

Space and ocean activity income of a U.S. person is U.S.-source, while that of a foreign person is foreign-source. (Code Sec. 863(d)(1))[39]

Insurance underwriting income from insuring U.S. risks is U.S.-source. (Code Sec. 861(a)(7))[40]

¶ 4660 Foreign-source income treated as U.S.-source for certain purposes.

In applying the foreign tax credit limitation (¶ 2360), certain amounts derived from a U.S.-owned foreign corporation that are included in gross income as Subpart F income (¶ 4637), foreign personal holding company income (¶ 4644), interest, dividends, or income from a QEF (¶ 4643) are treated as U.S.-source income. (Code Sec. 904(g)(1))[41] This rule applies notwithstanding any contrary treaty obligation unless the treaty expressly shows an attempt to override the rule.[42]

---

28. ¶ O-10243, O-10648; ¶s 8734, 8824.
29. ¶s O-10643, O-10675.
30. ¶s O-10644, O-10676.
31. ¶ O-10931.1 *et seq.*; ¶ 8614.15 *et seq.*

32. ¶ O-10906 *et seq.*; ¶ 8614.01.
33. ¶ O-10926 *et seq.*; ¶ 8614.10 *et seq.*
34. ¶ O-10936; ¶ 8614.22.
35. ¶ O-10948 *et seq.*; ¶ 8654 *et seq.*

36. ¶ O-10945; ¶s 8614.24, 8974.
37. ¶ O-10941; ¶ 8634.03.
38. ¶ O-10984; ¶ 8634.04.
39. ¶ O-10976; ¶ 8634.04.

40. ¶ O-10985; ¶ 8614.27.
41. ¶ O-4501 *et seq.*; ¶ 9044.01.
42. ¶ O-4511; ¶ 9044.01.

Footnote references beginning with letters are to paragraphs in RIA's Federal Tax Coordinator 2d and RIA's Analysis of Federal Taxes: Income. Footnote references beginning with numbers are to paragraphs in RIA's United States Tax Reporter.

¶ 4661 Recapture of deducted foreign losses.

A taxpayer's "overall foreign losses" in a separate foreign tax credit limitation category (¶ 2360) are recharacterized as U.S.-source ("recaptured") if foreign operations in later years produce a profit in that category, or if foreign business property in that category is disposed of. One-half (more if taxpayer so elects) of foreign taxable income in any one year is recharacterized as U.S.-source income (but limited to the amount of income in the separate limitation category that offsets the U.S. income), until the amount recharacterized equals the amount of those offsetting losses. Where a foreign loss in one separate limitation category offsets income in a second limitation category, income in a later year in the first category will be recharacterized as income in the second category up to the amount of the original offset. (Code Sec. 904(f)) Schedule G (Form 1118) is used by corporations to keep track of these amounts.[43]

¶ 4662 Disposition of U.S. real property interest.

A gain or loss of a nonresident alien individual or a foreign corporation from the disposition of a U.S. real property interest (USRPI) is treated as effectively connected with a U.S. trade or business. (Code Sec. 897(a)(1))[44]

A USRPI includes: (1) an interest in real property located in the U.S. or the Virgin Islands, and (2) any interest (other than solely as a creditor) in any U.S. corporation unless it's shown *not* to have been a U.S. real property holding corporation (USRPHC) during the five-year period ending on the date of disposition. (Code Sec. 897(c)(1)(A))[45]

Foreign taxpayers that hold USRPIs indirectly (e.g., as shareholders, partners or beneficiaries of a corporation, partnership, or estate or trust that owns the property) are also, when they dispose of their interest in the entity, subject to U.S. tax on any gain attributable to the entity's USRPIs. (Code Sec. 897(g); Reg § 1.897-7T)[46]

Gain is recognized even if the disposition is made as a transfer to paid-in surplus or as a capital contribution to a foreign corporation. (Code Sec. 897(j))[47]

¶ 4663 Election by foreign corporation to be treated as a U.S. corporation.

Any foreign corporation protected by treaty may elect to be treated as a U.S. corporation for purposes of the rules on USRPI dispositions (¶ 4662), including the reporting and withholding provisions (¶ 4674). (Code Sec. 897(i))[48]

To make the election, the foreign corporation must qualify as a U.S. real property holding corporation (¶ 4662), (Reg § 1.897-8T(b)) must hold the USRPI at the time of the election, and must submit an election statement in proper form. (Reg § 1.897-3(b))[49]

¶ 4664 Tax treaties.

Tax treaties typically exempt or reduce U.S. tax on certain business, compensation and investment income. (Code Sec. 894(a))[50]

Treaty partners appoint competent authorities to carry out the various provisions of treaties in force between them. For the U.S., the Assistant Commissioner (International) acts as "competent authority."[1]

The U.S. has income tax treaties with Australia, Austria, Barbados, Belgium, Canada, China, Cyprus, Denmark, Egypt, Finland, France, Germany, Greece, Hungary, Iceland, India, Indonesia, Ireland, Italy, Jamaica, Japan, Korea (South), Luxembourg, Malta, Morocco, Netherlands, New Zealand, Norway, Pakistan, Philippines, Poland, Romania, Spain, Sweden, Switzerland, Trinidad & Tobago, Tunisia, the former U.S.S.R., and the United Kingdom.[2]

---

43. ¶ O-4700 et seq.; ¶ 9044.01.
44. ¶ O-10700 et seq.; ¶ 8974.
45. ¶ O-10735 et seq.
46. ¶ O-10733 et seq.; ¶ 8974.
47. ¶ O-10702; ¶ 8974.
48. ¶ O-10810 et seq.; ¶ 14,454.
49. ¶ O-10812; ¶ 8974.
50. ¶ O-15000 et seq.; ¶ 8944.
1. ¶ O-15100 et seq.; ¶ 8944.
2. ¶ O-16500 et seq.; ¶ 8944.

Footnote references beginning with letters are to paragraphs in RIA's Federal Tax Coordinator 2d and RIA's Analysis of Federal Taxes: Income. Footnote references beginning with numbers are to paragraphs in RIA's United States Tax Reporter.

A taxpayer who takes a return position that a treaty overrules or otherwise modifies the Code and thereby effects (or potentially effects) a reduction of any tax incurred at any time, must disclose that return position on Form 8833 attached to the return. (If a return wouldn't otherwise be required, taxpayer must nevertheless file one, signed, but need only include taxpayer's name, address, TIN and disclosure statement.) Disclosure is waived for certain treaty-based return positions. (Code Sec. 6114(a); Reg § 301.6114-1)[3]

¶ 4665 Return of nonresident alien individual.

A nonresident alien individual must file a U.S. tax return (on Form 1040NR) for any tax year in which he was engaged in business in the U.S. (which includes most employees, see ¶ 4652), whether his income met the minimum (exemption amount); his tax was fully covered by withholding; or he claims tax treaty benefits. (Reg § 1.6012-1(b))[4]

Form 1040NR must be filed by the 15th day of the sixth month after the end of the tax year, or of the fourth month if the alien had wages subject to withholding. (Reg § 1.6072-1(c))[5]

¶ 4666 Departing alien—"sailing permits."

An alien (whether resident or nonresident) leaving the U.S. generally must get a "certificate of [tax] compliance" ("sailing permit"), except for most tourists, students and foreign government personnel. (Code Sec. 6851(d)(1); Reg § 1.6851-2(a)(2)) Form 1040C is used if the alien has income subject to U.S. tax (and Form 1040NR if required, see ¶ 4665). (Reg § 1.6851-2(b))[6]

¶ 4667 Return of foreign corporation.

A foreign corporation must file a U.S. income tax return on Form 1120F if it was engaged in business in the U.S., or its tax was not fully satisfied by withholding, or it claims tax treaty benefits (a statement claiming the benefits must be attached to the return). Otherwise, no return is required. (Reg § 1.6012-2(g))[7]

¶ 4668 Information returns relating to foreign corporations—Form 5471, Form 5472, Form 926.

A U.S. person who controls a foreign corporation for at least 30 consecutive days during the tax year must furnish IRS with certain information concerning the foreign corporation, on Form 5471. (Code Sec. 6038) Taxpayers who control more than one foreign corporation must report the activities between the corporations on Schedule M (Form 5471). (Reg § 1.6038-2(f)(ii))[8] "Control" means more than 50% ownership (by total vote or total value) of the corporation's stock. (Reg § 1.6038-2(b))[9]

The organization or reorganization of a foreign corporation, or an acquisition of a foreign corporation's stock, must be reported on Form 5471 by certain U.S. persons. (Code Sec. 6046A)[10]

If a U.S. corporation, or a foreign corporation engaged in a U.S. trade or business, is controlled by a foreign person at any time during the tax year, it must maintain records and furnish IRS with certain information concerning specified transactions with related parties during the tax year. This information is filed on Form 5472, using a separate form with respect to each related party. (Code Sec. 6038A(a), Code Sec. 6038C; Reg § 1.6038A-1)[11] To be in "control," the foreign person must own: (1) stock with at least 25% of the total combined voting power of all classes of voting stock, or (2) at least 25% of the total value of shares of all classes of stock. (Code Sec. 6038A(c)(1))[12]

Each U.S. person transferring property to a foreign corporation in specified tax-free exchanges or distributing property in complete liquidation to a person who isn't a U.S.

---

3. ¶ O-15010 *et seq.*; ¶ 61,144.   5. ¶ S-4701; ¶ 60,724.   8. ¶ S-3585; ¶ 60,384.   11. ¶ S-3510; ¶ 60,38A4.

4. ¶s S-1750, S-1752, S-1755;   6. ¶ S-1760 *et seq.*; ¶ 68,514.04.   9. ¶ S-3588; ¶ 60,384.   12. ¶ S-3580; ¶ 6038A4.
    ¶ 60,124.02.   7. ¶ S-1910; ¶s 8814, 60,124.03.   10. ¶ S-3552 *et seq.*; ¶ 60,464.

Footnote references beginning with letters are to paragraphs in RIA's Federal Tax Coordinator 2d and RIA's Analysis of Federal Taxes: Income. Footnote references beginning with numbers are to paragraphs in RIA's United States Tax Reporter.

person must report the transfer to IRS (on Form 926) (Code Sec. 6038B)[13]

Foreign investors in U.S. real property must report their direct ownership interests to IRS. (Code Sec. 6039C)[14]

¶ 4669 Tax Withholding on Payments to Foreign Taxpayers

A tax must be withheld at source on certain U.S.-source amounts paid to nonresident aliens and foreign corporations. The rate of tax is 30% unless reduced by treaty.

¶ 4670 Tax withholding on nonresident aliens and foreign corporations.

Ordinarily, the U.S. tax liability of nonresident aliens and foreign corporations for U.S.-source income (unless "effectively connected," below) is satisfied by the income payor's (¶ 4671) withholding the necessary tax at source. Thus, withholding is required on payments of U.S.-source interest (except OID and portfolio and bank account interest, ¶ 4653), taxable dividends, rents, other fixed or determinable annual or periodical income, and the other income items at ¶ 4653. The withholding rate is 30% (or lower treaty rate) of the gross amount. (Code Sec. 1441(b))[15]

Compensation (including pensions from an exempt employees' trust, see Chapter 21) for services performed in the U.S. by a nonresident alien is subject to regular income tax wage withholding (¶ 3000 *et seq.*) unless exempt from tax by law or treaty. The exemption won't apply unless a confirming statement (on Form 8233) is filed with the employer. (Reg § 31.3401(a)(6)-1)[16]

Income (other than compensation for personal services) that is effectively connected with a U.S. business (and taxed at the regular U.S. tax rates, see ¶ 4651) is exempt from withholding. (Code Sec. 1441(c)(1), Code Sec. 1442(a)) Taxpayers get this exemption by filing Form 4224.[17]

¶ 4671 Which payors must withhold tax?

Any person having the control, receipt, custody, disposal or payment of any amounts must deduct and withhold tax from the items to the extent they are gross income from U.S. sources of foreigners, and subject to withholding. (Code Sec. 1441(a))[18]

If dividends are paid to an address in the U.S., the payor can assume no withholding is required. If paid to an address abroad, the payor must withhold. Where the address is in a country with which the U.S. has an income tax treaty (¶ 4664), the treaty withholding rate is used.[19]

A withholding agent who fails to withhold the U.S. tax as required is subject to penalty, even if the tax is paid by the income recipient. (Code Sec. 1463)[20]

¶ 4672 Withholding on foreign partners' share of partnership's "effectively connected" income.

A partnership must pay a withholding tax if it has "effectively connected taxable income" for the tax year (whether or not the income is distributed), if any portion of the income is allocable to a foreign partner. (Code Sec. 1446(a)) The amount of withholding tax is the applicable percentage (highest rate of U.S. tax to which each foreign partner is subject) of its effectively connected taxable income which is allocable to the foreign partners, (Code Sec. 1446(b)) i.e., 35% for foreign corporate partners and 39.6% for foreign noncorporate partners. (Code Sec. 1, Code Sec. 11(b)(1))[21] Pay the withheld amount in installments with Form 8813. Report the partnership's total withholding liability for the

---

13. ¶s S-3560.1, S-3563.1;   15. ¶ O-11900 *et seq.*; ¶ 14,144   17. ¶ O-11908; ¶ 14,414.02.   20. ¶ O-11903; ¶ 14,614.01.
    ¶ 60,38B4.   *et seq.*   18. ¶ O-11905; ¶ 14,414.   21. ¶ O-11949.
14. ¶ S-3517; ¶ 60,39C4.   16. ¶ O-11926; ¶ 14,414.02.   19. ¶s O-11919, O-11921.

Footnote references beginning with letters are to paragraphs in RIA's Federal Tax Coordinator 2d and RIA's Analysis of Federal Taxes: Income. Footnote references beginning with numbers are to paragraphs in RIA's United States Tax Reporter.

partnership year on Form 8804. Prepare information statement Form 8805 for each foreign partner.[22]

¶ 4673 Withholding on partnership distributions not effectively connected with a U.S. business.

A domestic partnership must withhold a 30% tax on taxable items that are not effectively connected with its U.S. trade or business if those items are included in the distributive shares of its nonresident alien or foreign corporate partners. (Reg § 1.1441-3(f))[23]

¶ 4674 Withholding on disposition of foreign investment in U.S. real estate.

U.S. tax must be withheld when a foreign investor disposes of a USRPI (¶ 4662), (Code Sec. 1445(a))[24] including certain interests in a partnership, trust, or estate that directly or indirectly owns a USRPI. (Code Sec. 1445(e)(5); Reg § 1.1445-11T(b))[25]

The amount to be withheld generally is 10% of the amount realized on the disposition. (Code Sec. 1445(a)) The amount realized is the sum of cash received (not including any stated or unstated interest, or any OID), the fair market value of any other property received, and any liability assumed by the transferee (e.g., buyer) or to which the USRPI was subject. (Reg § 1.1445-1(g))[26]

The withholding obligation is generally imposed on the transferee, (Code Sec. 1445) who must report the amounts withheld and pay them over (to IRS) by the 20th day after transfer. (Reg § 1.1445-1(c)) Forms 8288 and 8288-A are used for this purpose.[27]

Withholding isn't required if the transferor gives the transferee a sworn "nonforeign affidavit" showing the transferor's U.S. taxpayer identification number and stating that he isn't a foreign person, (Code Sec. 1445(b)(2); Reg § 1.1445-2(b)) or a sworn "non-USRPHC affidavit" stating that it's not a U.S. real property holding corporation.[28] But in both cases, the transferee won't be excused from withholding if it knows that the affidavit is false. (Code Sec. 1445(b)(7))[29]

Nor does withholding apply if the USRPI is acquired by the transferee as his residence, and the amount realized doesn't exceed $300,000. (Code Sec. 1445(b)(5))[30]

IRS will issue a certificate excusing withholding if the transferor is exempt from U.S. tax, or if either the transferor or transferee agrees to pay the tax and gives security for its payment. (Reg § 1.1445-3(e)) A certificate gotten before a transfer notifies the transferee that no withholding is required or that reduced withholding is required. A certificate gotten after the transfer may authorize a normal or early refund. (Use Form 8288-B to request a certificate.)[31]

¶ 4675 Foreign Currency Rules

Special rules govern the measurement, recording and reporting of transactions involving foreign currency.

¶ 4676 Functional currency.

All U.S. taxpayers are required to make all federal income tax determinations in their "functional currency." (Code Sec. 985(a))[32] This must be done on a transaction-by-transaction basis.[33]

"Functional currency" generally means the U.S. dollar. (Code Sec. 985(b)(1)(A)) However, "qualified business units" (QBUs) that conduct a significant part of their activities in an economic environment with a currency other than the dollar, and that keep their

---

22. ¶ O-11955.	26. ¶ O-12002.	29. ¶ O-12013.	32. ¶ G-6900 *et seq.*; ¶ 9854 *et seq.*
23. ¶ O-11937; ¶ 14,414.	27. ¶ S-5662; ¶ 14,454.	30. ¶ O-12016; ¶ 14,454.	
24. ¶ O-12001.	28. ¶s O-12010, O-12011;	31. ¶s O-12021 *et seq.*, S-5664;	33. ¶ G-6901.
25. ¶ O-12036; ¶ 14,454.	¶ 14,454.	¶ 14,454.	

Footnote references beginning with letters are to paragraphs in RIA's Federal Tax Coordinator 2d and RIA's Analysis of Federal Taxes: Income. Footnote references beginning with numbers are to paragraphs in RIA's United States Tax Reporter.

books and records in that currency, have that currency as their "functional currency." (Code Sec. 985(b)(1)(B))[34]

A QBU is any separate and clearly identified unit of a trade or business of a taxpayer which maintains separate books and records. (Code Sec. 989(a)) A corporation is a QBU. A partnership, trust or estate is a QBU of a partner or beneficiary. An individual is not a QBU. (Reg § 1.989(a)-1(b)(2)(i)) An *activity* of a corporation, partnership, trust, estate or individual is a QBU (separate from the QBU represented by the entity) if the activity is a trade or business for which a complete and separate set of books is maintained. (Reg § 1.989(a)-1(b)(2)(ii))[35]

A taxpayer may elect (on Form 8819) to use the dollar as the functional currency for any eligible QBU. (Code Sec. 985(b)(3); Reg § 1.985-2)[36]

¶ 4677 Section 988 transactions.

Foreign currency gain or loss attributable to a "Section 988 transaction" must generally be computed separately and be treated as interest income or interest expense, as the case may be. (Code Sec. 988(a)(1)(A), (a)(2))[37] However, taxpayer may elect to treat the foreign currency gain or loss attributable to certain of these transactions as capital gain or loss. (Code Sec. 988(a)(1)(B); Reg § 1.988-2(e)(2))[38]

Recognition of foreign currency gain or loss requires a closed and completed transaction, such as the payment of a liability.[39]

A "Section 988 transaction" is any of specified transactions if the amount taxpayer is entitled to receive, or is required to pay, by reason of the transaction is either: (1) denominated in terms of a nonfunctional currency; or (2) determined by reference to the value of one or more nonfunctional currencies. (Code Sec. 988(c)(1)(A))[40]

¶ 4678 Source of foreign currency gains and losses.

The source of foreign currency gains and losses that are treated as ordinary income or loss (or would be but for the election at ¶ 4677) is determined by reference to the residence of the taxpayer or QBU on whose books the relevant asset, liability or item of income or expense is properly reflected. (Code Sec. 988(a)(3); Reg § 1.988-4T)[41] There are special rules for certain related corporations, (Code Sec. 988(a)(3)(C))[42] currency swaps[43] and hedging transactions. (Code Sec. 988(d)(2))[44]

¶ 4679 Personal transactions.

The Code Sec. 988 rules apply to transactions entered into by an individual only to the extent the expenses properly allocable to them satisfy the requirements of Code Sec. 162, Code Sec. 212(1) or Code Sec. 212(2), i.e., they're deductible as expenses of a trade or business or for the production of income. But the Code Sec. 988 rules won't apply to a transaction whose allocable expenses are deductible under Code Sec. 212(3)—i.e., they're in connection with determination, collection, or refund of any tax, but don't also qualify under Code Sec. 162, Code Sec. 212(1) or Code Sec. 212(2). (Code Sec. 988(e)) Whether expenses would be deductible under Code Sec. 212(1) or Code Sec. 212(2) is determined without regard to the 2%-of-AGI floor on certain itemized deductions (¶ 3107).[45]

¶ 4680 Recording and translating the results of foreign currency operations.

Any foreign business entity—whether a branch or a sub—that uses a functional currency other than the dollar is required to use a profit-and-loss method to translate the results of its operations into U.S. dollars, at the "appropriate exchange rate" (as specially

---

34. ¶ G-6901 *et seq.*; ¶ 9854   37. ¶ G-6917 *et seq.*; ¶ 9884   40. ¶ G-6918 *et seq.*; ¶ 9884.01.
    et seq.   *et seq.*   41. ¶ G-6927; ¶ 9884.01.
35. ¶ G-6907.   38. ¶ G-6924 *et seq.*; ¶ 9884.01.   42. ¶ O-4504; ¶ 9884.01.
36. ¶ G-6908 *et seq.*; ¶ 9854.   39. ¶ G-6919.   43. ¶ G-6926; ¶ 9884.01.

44. ¶ G-6925 *et seq.*; ¶s 9884.01, 9884.02.
45. ¶ G-6938; ¶ 9884.01.

Footnote references beginning with letters are to paragraphs in RIA's Federal Tax Coordinator 2d and RIA's Analysis of Federal Taxes: Income. Footnote references beginning with numbers are to paragraphs in RIA's United States Tax Reporter.

defined). (Code Sec. 987; Reg § 1.987-1)[46]

---

46. ¶ G-6910 *et seq.*; ¶ 9874
    et seq.

Footnote references beginning with letters are to paragraphs in RIA's Federal Tax Coordinator 2d and RIA's Analysis of Federal Taxes: Income. Footnote references beginning with numbers are to paragraphs in RIA's United States Tax Reporter.

Chapter 24   Returns and Payment of Tax

¶ 4700 Returns and Payment of Tax

An individual taxpayer must file an income tax return if his gross income equals or exceeds a specified amount. Married taxpayers may file a joint return. Corporations, trusts and estates must also file income tax returns. A partnership files an information return of income. Payors and others must file information returns to report specified payments, sales, etc. Times, places and methods of paying tax are specified.

¶ 4701 Who must file individual income tax returns?

An income tax return must be filed by every individual U.S. citizen and resident alien (including an alien who is a bona fide resident of Puerto Rico during the entire tax year) (Reg § 1.1-1(b), Reg § 1.6012-1(a)(1))[1] who has gross income that equals or exceeds the following amounts:

	'93	'94
(1) Single		
(Code Sec. 6012(a)(1)(A)(i))	$6,050	$6,250
—65-or-over (Code Sec. 6012(a)(1)(B))	6,950	7,200
(2) Married filing joint return		
(Code Sec. 6012(a)(1)(A)(iv))	10,900	11,250
—one 65-or-over (Code Sec. 6012(a)(1)(B))	11,600	12,000
—both 65-or-over (Code Sec. 6012(a)(1)(B)).	12,300	12,750
(3) Married filing separate return		
(Code Sec. 6012(a)(1)(A)).	2,350	2,450
(4) Head of Household		
(Code Sec. 6012(a)(1)(A)(ii))	7,800	8,050
—65-or-over (Code Sec. 6012(a)(1)(B))	8,700	9,000
(5) Surviving spouse		
(Code Sec. 6012(a)(1)(A)(iii))	8,550	8,800
—65-or-over (Code Sec. 6012(a)(1)(B))	9,250	9,550

The above rules don't apply to an individual who can be claimed as a dependent by another. That individual/dependent must file a return if his or her income, other than earned income, is more than $600 (for '93 and '94), plus the additional standard deduction (for aged and blind), if any, or his or her total gross income is more than the standard deduction. (Code Sec. 6012(a)(1)(C)(i))[2] (However, no return is required for a child where the child's parent elects to include the child's income on the parent's return under the "kiddie tax" rules, see ¶ 3133 *et seq.*)

The cut-off in (2), above, applies only if the spouses, at the close of the tax year, had the same household as their home (Code Sec. 6012(a)(1)(A)(iv)) and no other taxpayer could claim either spouse as an exemption. (Code Sec. 6012(a)(1)(A))

An individual who has $400 or more net earnings from self-employment (¶ 3139) must file an income tax return even though his gross income is less than the required amount. (Code Sec. 6017)[3]

Every individual who has received advance payments of his earned income credit (¶ 2342) from his employer must file a return regardless of the amount of his income. (Code Sec. 6012(a)(8))[4]

Persons required to file a short year return because of a change in accounting period

---

1. ¶ S-1701; ¶s 14.07, 60,124.   2. ¶ S-1705; ¶s 14.07, 60,124.   3. ¶ S-1717; ¶s 14.07, 60,174.   4. ¶ S-1710; ¶s 14.07, 60,124.

Footnote references beginning with letters are to paragraphs in RIA's Federal Tax Coordinator 2d and RIA's Analysis of Federal Taxes: Income. Footnote references beginning with numbers are to paragraphs in RIA's United States Tax Reporter.

must file a return if gross income amounts to $2,350 or more in '93 ($2,450 in '94) even if those persons are 65 before year-end. (Code Sec. 6012(a)(1)(C)(ii))[5]

¶ 4702 Individual income tax return forms.

U.S. citizens and residents can use Form 1040, (Reg § 1.6012-1(a)(6)) Form 1040A (Reg § 1.6012-1(a)(7)(i)) or Form 1040EZ.

Form 1040A may be used by a taxpayer in any filing status who has income only from wages, salaries, tips, interest, dividends and unemployment compensation, who has only certain adjustments to gross income, who doesn't itemize, whose taxable income is less than $50,000, and who has only certain tax credits.

A single (filing status) taxpayer under 65 who is not blind can use Form 1040EZ if he claims no dependents, has income only from wages, salaries, tips, taxable scholarships or fellowships, and interest (of $400 or less), no adjustments to gross income, no itemized deductions, taxable income of less than $50,000 and no tax credits.[6]

¶ 4703 Electronic filing.

Tax preparers can electronically file returns (Forms 1040, 1040A and 1040EZ) for individual taxpayers,[7] including returns that show a balance due.[8]

An electronic return consists of data transmitted to IRS electronically and of paper documents (filed later) that can't be electronically transmitted, such as taxpayer signatures, documents prepared by third parties, etc.[9] Any payment is mailed separately to IRS (use Form 9282).[10]

¶ 4704 Form 1040PC optically scanned paper returns.

Return preparers may file plain paper "answer sheets" generated by a personal computer using IRS approved software which are scanned by IRS Optical Character Recognition equipment.[11]

¶ 4705 Husband and wife—joint or separate returns.

Married persons have the choice of filing a joint return (one return reporting their combined incomes and deductions) (Code Sec. 6013(a))[12] or separate returns. (Code Sec. 1(d))[13]

¶ 4706 Qualifying for joint returns.

A husband and wife may file a joint return even if only one has income, (Code Sec. 6013(a))[14] and even if they have different accounting *methods*. But they must be legally married as of the *end* of the tax year. (Code Sec. 6013(d))[15]

If the parties filed a joint return during their "marriage" and later get an annulment, they must refile as separate unmarried persons.[16]

A joint return *can't* be filed:

■ *if either spouse was a nonresident alien* at any time during the tax year, (Code Sec. 6013(a)(1))[17] but where one spouse is a nonresident alien for the entire year (Code Sec. 6013(g)) or where a nonresident alien spouse becomes a U.S. resident during the tax year, (Code Sec. 6013(h)) both spouses can *elect* to file a joint return by agreeing to subject their worldwide income to U.S. taxation;[18]

■ *if the spouses have different tax years*, (Code Sec. 6013(a)(2))[19] except when one spouse dies, see ¶ 4707.

---

5. ¶ S-1707; ¶ 60,124.
6. ¶ S-1715; ¶s 14.10, 60,114.01.
7. ¶ S-1601.
8. ¶ S-1617
9. ¶ S-1601 *et seq.*

10. ¶ S-1617.
11. ¶ S-1619 *et seq.*
12. ¶ S-1801; ¶s 60,134 *et seq.*, 24.01.

13. ¶ A-1502; ¶ 14.03.
14. ¶ S-1801; ¶ 60,134.
15. ¶ S-1803; ¶ 60,134.03.
16. ¶ A-1609; ¶ 60,134.03.

17. ¶ S-1802; ¶ 60,134.
18. ¶ A-1800 *et seq.*; ¶ 60,134.01.
19. ¶ S-1804; ¶ 60,134.

Footnote references beginning with letters are to paragraphs in RIA's Federal Tax Coordinator 2d and RIA's Analysis of Federal Taxes: Income. Footnote references beginning with numbers are to paragraphs in RIA's United States Tax Reporter.

¶ 4707 Joint return for year spouse(s) dies.

A joint return may be filed for a husband and wife where their tax years start the same day and end on different days because of the death of either or both (unless the survivor remarries before the close of his or her tax year). The joint return must be made with respect to the tax year of each. (Code Sec. 6013(a)(2))[20] For when to file, see ¶ 4713.

A surviving spouse may file a joint return for the deceased spouse and herself (or himself) if: the deceased spouse didn't previously file a return for the tax year; an executor/administrator hasn't been appointed by the time the joint return is made; and an executor/administrator hasn't been appointed before the due date for filing the return of the surviving spouse (including extensions). (Code Sec. 6013(a)(3))[21]

If an executor or administrator is appointed on or before the filing due dates, the surviving spouse *can't* file a joint return for the decedent. Only the fiduciary (executor or administrator) can act for the decedent, so both the fiduciary and the surviving spouse must sign the joint return. Even if the surviving spouse properly filed a joint return (because no fiduciary had been appointed by the due date), the fiduciary may disaffirm (revoke) the joint return by filing a *separate* return for the decedent within one year after the due date (including extensions). Any "joint" return improperly filed by the survivor or disaffirmed by the fiduciary is treated as a *separate* return of the survivor. (Code Sec. 6013(a)(3))[22]

For use of joint return *rates* where the survivor has a dependent child, see ¶ 3130.

¶ 4708 Liability for tax, penalties, and interest on spouses' returns.

Joint returns. Except in the case of certain omissions from gross income (¶ 4709) and the civil fraud penalty, each spouse is jointly and severally liable for the full amount of the tax, penalties, and interest arising out of their joint return, regardless of the amount of his or her separate taxable income. (Code Sec. 6013(d)(3))

Only the spouse committing the fraud, of whatever type, can be subjected to *criminal* penalties.[23]

Separate returns. Each spouse is liable only for his or her own tax and penalties.[24]

¶ 4709 Relief of spouse from joint tax liability (innocent spouse rule).

If, under regs to be issued: (1) a joint return is filed, and (2) there is a substantial (i.e., in excess of $500) (Code Sec. 6013(e)(3)) understatement of tax attributable to grossly erroneous items of one spouse, and (3) the other spouse did not know and had no reason to know there was a substantial understatement at the time the return was signed, and (4) it would be inequitable to hold the other spouse liable for the deficiency attributable to the substantial understatement, taking into account all facts and circumstances, then the other (innocent) spouse will be relieved of liability for tax (including interest, penalties, etc.) to the extent the liability is attributable to the substantial understatement. (Code Sec. 6013(e)(1))[25]

The tax liability (other than for an omission from gross income) must also exceed a certain percentage of the innocent spouse's adjusted gross income (AGI). (Code Sec. 6013(e)(4)) If AGI for the preadjustment year is $20,000 or less, innocent spouse relief from the liability will apply only if the liability attributable to the substantial understatement exceeds 10% of AGI. (Code Sec. 6013(e)(4)(A)) If AGI for preadjustment year is over $20,000, the liability attributable to the substantial understatement must exceed 25% of AGI. (Code Sec. 6013(e)(4)(B))

---

20. ¶ S-1805; ¶s 24.01, 60,134.   22. ¶ S-1806; ¶s 24.01, 60,134.   24. ¶ V-8503.   25. ¶ V-8504; ¶ 60,134.05.
21. ¶ S-1806; ¶s 24.01, 60,134.   23. ¶ V-8502.

Footnote references beginning with letters are to paragraphs in RIA's Federal Tax Coordinator 2d and RIA's Analysis of Federal Taxes: Income. Footnote references beginning with numbers are to paragraphs in RIA's United States Tax Reporter.

¶ 4710 Returns for minors and incompetents.

Returns for minors and incompetents and others who are incapable of filing their own returns should be filed for them by their guardians or other fiduciaries. A minor may make his or her own return. (Reg § 1.6012-3(b)(3))[26]

¶ 4711 Self-employment tax returns.

Every individual (except a nonresident alien) who has self-employment income of $400 or more for the tax year must file a self-employment tax Schedule SE (Form 1040) (Code Sec. 6017) unless he had wages (including tips) subject to social security taxes in excess of the yearly tax base. The self-employment tax, which is in addition to the income tax, must also be reported on Form 1040 and paid as part of the income tax.[27]

¶ 4712 Decedent's final return.

A final income tax return must be filed for a deceased person who would be required to file if alive, for the part of the year up to the date of death. A decedent's final return is filed by the person entrusted with his property. Ordinarily, this would be the executor or administrator of his estate, and if such a fiduciary is appointed, he will be responsible for decedent's final return. (Code Sec. 6012(b)(1))[28]

For the surviving spouse filing a decedent's joint return, see ¶ 4707.

¶ 4713 When to file individual returns.

Income tax returns (including self-employment tax returns) of U.S. citizens and resident aliens must be filed on or before the fifteenth day of the fourth month following the close of the tax year (Apr. 15 for calendar year taxpayers). (Code Sec. 6072(a))

A "short period return" must be filed by the fifteenth day of the fourth month following the close of the short period. (Reg § 1.6071-1(b))[29]

A decedent's final return is due on the filing date that would have applied had the taxpayer lived. (Reg § 1.6072-1(b))[30]

¶ 4714 Extensions of time for filing individual returns—Form 4868.

File Form 4868 to get an automatic extension of four months for filing (until Aug. 15 for a calendar year taxpayer). (Reg § 1.6081-4(a)(1))[31] The form must show the full amount properly estimated as tax for the year, (Reg § 1.6081-4(a)(4))[32] but it need not be accompanied by payment of the balance of the tax estimated to be due.[33] For an extension of time to pay, see ¶ 4718; for paying in installments, see ¶s 4719, 4720.

In undue-hardship cases, the taxpayer can skip the automatic four-month procedure and apply on Form 2688 or by letter for a longer period. (Reg § 1.6081-1(b))[34]

Extensions can't exceed six months unless the taxpayer is abroad. (Code Sec. 6081(a))[35]

¶ 4715 Taxpayers abroad—Form 2350.

A U.S. citizen or resident whose tax home and abode is outside the U.S. and Puerto Rico (Reg § 1.6081-4T(a)(5)) and a U.S. citizen or resident in military or naval service on duty outside the U.S. and Puerto Rico, (Reg § 1.6081-4T(a)(6)) get automatic extensions until the fifteenth day of the sixth month after the close of the tax year. A statement should be attached to the return which shows that the taxpayer qualified for this extension. (Reg § 1.6081-4T(b)) However, there is *no* automatic extension for a U.S. citizen or resident *traveling* outside the U.S. and Puerto Rico.[36]

---

26. ¶ S-1712; ¶s 60,124, 60,124.04.
27. ¶ S-1717; ¶s 14,024.01, 60,174.
28. ¶ S-2003; ¶ 60,124.04.
29. ¶ S-4701; ¶ 60,724.
30. ¶ S-4702; ¶ 60,724.
31. ¶ S-5017; ¶ 60,814.03.
32. ¶ S-5019; ¶ 60,814.03.
33. ¶ S-5011; ¶ 60,814.03.
34. ¶ S-5020; ¶ 60,814.04.
35. ¶ S-5003; ¶ 60,814.04.
36. ¶ S-5050; ¶ 60,814.01.

Footnote references beginning with letters are to paragraphs in RIA's Federal Tax Coordinator 2d and RIA's Analysis of Federal Taxes: Income. Footnote references beginning with numbers are to paragraphs in RIA's United States Tax Reporter.

U.S. citizens or U.S. resident aliens who expect to qualify for the foreign earned income exclusion (¶ 4614 *et seq.*) (and owe no tax), but not until more than two months after the regular due date of the return, should file extension request Form 2350 by the due date of Form 1040.[37]

¶ 4716 Place for filing.

File as specified on the return form (or instructions). For individuals, this usually is the service center for the place where the individual lives. For the service center addresses, see ¶ 1117.[38]

¶ 4717 Payment deadline.

The tax is due on the original due date for filing the return despite any extensions of time for *filing* the return. (Code Sec. 6151(a); Reg § 1.6151-1(a))[39] If IRS computes the tax, the tax due date is the later of the thirtieth day after the date IRS mails the tax bill or the tax return due date. (Reg § 1.6151-1(b))[40] The automatic filing extension for taxpayers with a tax home and abode, or in military service, outside the U.S. (see ¶ 4715) also extends the time for payment. (Reg § 1.6081-5(f))[41] For IRS acceptance of individuals' extension requests without full payment, see ¶ 4714.

¶ 4718 Extension of time for paying individual income tax—Form 1127.

Apply on Form 1127 for a reasonable extension of time (not to exceed six months, unless taxpayer is abroad) to pay the tax. (Code Sec. 6161(a)(1)) File on or before the date prescribed for payment of the tax. (Reg § 1.6161-1(c)) IRS grants extensions only on a satisfactory showing that payment on the due date will result in undue hardship (more than an inconvenience), e.g., that taxpayer would have to sell property at a great financial sacrifice (i.e., below fair market value) to pay the tax. (Reg § 1.6161-1(b))[42]

¶ 4719 Installment payments of individual income tax—Form 9465.

To request an agreement to pay installments, attach Form 9465 to the front of the balance-due return. Interest and a late-payment penalty of ½% per month apply. For accounts under $10,000, taxpayers need not complete financial statements. An individual who had an automatic four-month extension of time to file without paying the tax estimated to be due (¶ 4717) but can't pay by the extended due date should use Form 9465 to arrange an installment agreement.[43]

¶ 4720 Electing three-payment installment of '93 tax attributable to '93 Act rate increases—Form 8841.

Individual taxpayers may elect to pay the additional '93 tax attributable to the 35% and 39.6% tax rates added by the '93 Revenue Reconciliation Act in three equal installments. The election doesn't apply to estates and trusts.[44]

The amount eligible for the installment payment election is the excess of the individual's net income tax liability as shown on his tax return, over the amount that would have been his net liability but for the '93 Act's imposition of the 36% and 39.6% tax rates. These amounts are computed after applying any credits (except the credits for wage withholding and special fuel uses) and before crediting any payment of estimated tax. Amounts required to be shown on the return but not actually shown are ineligible for the election.[45]

illustration: X and Y, joint filers, have taxable income of $300,000 for '93. Under the tax rates that were to apply for '93 before the '93 Act, they would have a tax liability of

---

37. ¶ S-5021; ¶ 9114.13.   40. ¶ S-5452; ¶ 61,514.   42. ¶ S-5852; ¶ 61,614.   44. ¶ S-5453.1.
38. ¶ S-5100 *et seq.*; ¶ 60,914.   41. ¶ S-5050; ¶ 60,814.   43. ¶ S-5451.   45. ¶ S-5453.1.
39. ¶ S-5451; ¶ 61,514.

Footnote references beginning with letters are to paragraphs in RIA's Federal Tax Coordinator 2d and RIA's Analysis of Federal Taxes: Income. Footnote references beginning with numbers are to paragraphs in RIA's United States Tax Reporter.

$85,529. Under the Act, their tax liability is $95,329. Therefore, $9,800 of their tax liability is eligible for the election.

⊘*observation:* The extension applies only to additional tax due because of the increase in individual income tax rates, and not to any additional tax that may be due because of other provisions of the '93 Act, such as the increased alternative minimum tax rate.

Under the election, the first installment is due on the due date (without extensions) of the tax return for the tax year that begins in calendar year '93. The second installment is due one year after that date, and the third installment is due two years after that date. No interest is due on the installments.

⊘*observation:* Thus, individuals can elect to pay the additional tax in three equal, interest-free installments due on Apr. 15 of '94, '95, and '96. In essence, this means a one-year, interest-free loan for one-third of the additional tax and a similar two-year, interest-free loan for another third.

Although the first installment of '93 taxes must be paid on or before the unextended due date of the return, the payment doesn't have to be paid with the return. The payment can be made as an additional payment with a Form 4868 extension of time to file.

The election must be made on the individual's original return for the tax year that begins in '93, filed by the due date of the return, determined *with* regard to extensions. To elect, attach a completed Form 8841 to Form 1040 (or Form 1040NR).[46]

IRS must immediately terminate the installment payment election, and the entire unpaid tax must be paid on notice and demand, if either (1) the taxpayer doesn't pay an installment by the required date, or (2) IRS believes that the collection of any amount under the election is in jeopardy.[47]

¶ 4721 Amended income tax returns.

Amended income tax returns (on Form 1040X) (Reg § 301.6402-3(a)(2))[48] may be filed at any time on or before the due date for the original return, and generally will be accepted as the taxpayer's return.[49]

¶ 4722 Corporate returns.

Every corporation that is subject to federal income tax, and that is in existence during any portion of a tax year, must file an income tax return for that year (or portion), regardless of the amount of its gross income or whether it has taxable income. (Code Sec. 6012(a)(2); Reg § 1.6012-2(a))[50]

A corporation which has merely received a charter will be relieved from filing a return if it furnishes a statement that it hasn't perfected its organization, has transacted no business, and has received no income from any source, to the district director. (Reg § 1.6012-2(a)(2))[1]

After a corporation ceases business and dissolves, retaining no assets, it must make a return for that fractional part of the year during which it was in existence. But retention of even a small amount of cash keeps the corporation alive for filing purposes until the cash is distributed or paid. (Reg § 1.6012-2(a)(2)[2] A receiver, trustee in bankruptcy or dissolution, or assignee that has control and custody of all (or substantially all) of a corporation's business or property must make the return in the same manner and form as would the corporation. (Code Sec. 6012(b)(3))[3]

A corporate income tax return, and all related documents requiring a signature on behalf of the corporation, must be signed by the president, vice-president, treasurer,

46. ¶ S-5453.1.
47. ¶ S-5453.1.
48. ¶ S-6704; ¶s 60,114.01, 64,024.15.
49. ¶ S-6701; ¶ 60,114.01.
50. ¶s S-1900, S-1901, S-1908; ¶ 60,124.03.
1. ¶ S-1908; ¶ 60,124.03.
2. ¶ S-1909; ¶ 60,124.04.
3. ¶ S-2014; ¶ 60,124.04.

Footnote references beginning with letters are to paragraphs in RIA's Federal Tax Coordinator 2d and RIA's Analysis of Federal Taxes: Income. Footnote references beginning with numbers are to paragraphs in RIA's United States Tax Reporter.

assistant treasurer, chief accounting officer (controller) or any other officer duly authorized to sign. If a return is made for the corporation by a trustee, receiver or assignee, that fiduciary must sign. (Code Sec. 6062)[4]

¶ 4723 Forms to file—Form 1120.

Most domestic corporations file Form 1120 as their income tax return. (Reg § 1.6012-2(a)) Schedule PH must be attached if the corporation is a personal holding company (¶ 3330 et seq.). (Reg § 1.6012-2(b))[5] (For foreign corporation returns, see ¶ 4667.)

A corporation may use the short Form 1120-A if its gross receipts, total income and total assets are each under $500,000, and it meets certain ownership and other requirements.[6]

Form 1120L is used by life insurance companies, and Form 1120-PC is used by property and casualty insurance companies.[7]

A regulated investment company uses Form 1120-RIC,[8] a real estate investment trust uses Form 1120-REIT,[9] and a designated settlement fund uses Form 1120-DF.[10]

An S corporation files on Form 1120S. (Code Sec. 6037(a); Reg § 1.6012-2(h)) Also, on or before the date the S corporation files the return, it must furnish any information contained on it, to anyone who was a shareholder during the tax year. (Code Sec. 6037(b))[11]

¶ 4724 When to file corporate returns.

Domestic corporations (including RICs, REITs and S corporations) must file their income tax returns on or before the 15th day of the third month following the close of the tax year (Mar. 15 for a calendar year corporation). (Code Sec. 6072(b); Reg § 1.6037-1(b))[12]

"Short period" returns must be filed by the 15th day of the third month following the close of the short period. If a corporation dissolves and distributes all its assets, its final return is due by the 15th day of the third *full* month following the dissolution or liquidation.[13]

¶ 4725 Extensions for filing corporate returns.

Automatic extensions—Form 7004. A corporation (including an S corporation or an affiliated group planning to file a consolidate return, see ¶ 3348) can get an automatic six-month extension by filing a Form 7004 that shows its estimated tax liability by the original due date. (Reg § 1.6031-3)[14]

However, the automatic filing extension won't extend the time for *paying* the tax (¶ 4729). (Reg § 1.6081-3(c))[15]

IRS has discretion to terminate the extension on ten days' notice. (Reg § 1.6081-3(d))[16]

Blanket extensions. A domestic corporation: (1) that transacts its business and keeps its records outside the U.S., or (2) whose principal income is from sources within U.S. possessions, may file its return up to the 15th day of the sixth month following the close of the tax year. A statement that sets forth the qualifying facts must be attached to the return. (Reg § 1.6081-5(a)(2), (a)(4), (b))[17]

¶ 4726 Place for filing corporate returns.

File as directed on the instructions for the returns. (Code Sec. 6091(b)(2)(A); Reg § 1.6091-2(c)) Hand-carried returns may be filed with heads of area, zone and local IRS offices that are permanent posts, or with the director's office in the district where the corporation's principal place of business, etc., is located. (Code Sec. 6091(b)(4);

---

4. ¶ S-4508; ¶ 60,614.

5. ¶s S-1902, S-1903; ¶ 60,124.03.

6. ¶ S-1902; ¶ 60,124.03.

7. ¶ S-1904; ¶ 8009.

8. ¶ S-1920; ¶ 8514.09.

9. ¶ S-1919; ¶ 8564.10.

10. ¶ S-1925; ¶ 60,374.

11. ¶s S-1905, S-1906; ¶ 60,374.

12. ¶ S-4704; ¶s 60,374, 60,724.

13. ¶ S-4710; ¶ 60,724.

14. ¶ S-5022 et seq.; ¶ 60,814.02.

15. ¶ S-5022; ¶ 60,814.02.

16. ¶ S-5009; ¶ 60,814.02.

17. ¶ S-5050; ¶ 60,814.01.

Footnote references beginning with letters are to paragraphs in RIA's Federal Tax Coordinator 2d and RIA's Analysis of Federal Taxes: Income. Footnote references beginning with numbers are to paragraphs in RIA's United States Tax Reporter.

Reg § 1.6091-2(d))[18]

¶4727 When to pay corporate tax.

Pay in full on or before the due date (without extension) for filing the return (¶4724). (Code Sec. 6151(a))[19] For extension of time for paying tax, see ¶4729.

For corporate estimated tax, see ¶3351 *et seq.*

¶4728 Tax deposits—Form 8109.

All corporations must make their income and estimated tax payments by depositing them with a Federal Reserve Bank (or authorized commercial bank) by the due date (¶4727). (Code Sec. 6302; Reg § 1.6302-1(a))[20] The deposits must be accompanied by Form 8109 deposit coupons.[21]

Deposits are timely if mailed (postmarked) at least two days before the due date. (Code Sec. 7502(e)(2))[22]

¶4729 Extension of time for paying corporate tax.

Sixth-month extension for undue hardship—Form 1127. Extension of time (not to exceed six months) for paying corporate tax or any installment of the tax may be granted by the IRS at the taxpayer's request (on Form 1127), on a showing of undue hardship, see ¶4718. (Code Sec. 6161(a); Reg § 1.6161-1)[23]

Loss carryback expected—Form 1138. If a corporation expects a net operating loss in a current year, it can get an extension of the time for paying the *preceding* year's tax based on the expected carryback. (Code Sec. 6164(a)) The time for payment is automatically extended by filing Form 1138. (Reg § 1.6164-1)

The time for payment expires the last day of the month for filing the return for the current loss year or, if an application for a tentative carryback adjustment is filed before that date, on the date IRS sends notice that the application is allowed or disallowed. (Code Sec. 6164(d))[24]

¶4730 Partnership return of income—Form 1065.

Every partnership must file Form 1065 to report its gross income and deductions for its tax year. (Reg § 1.6031-1(a)(1))[25]

A partnership needn't file a partnership return for any period before it receives taxable income or incurs deductible expenses. (Reg § 1.6031-1(a)(1))[26] Nor does it file if it doesn't carry on a business in the U.S. and has no U.S. source income. (Reg § 1.6031-1(d)(1))[27]

A partnership return must be filed by the 15th day of the fourth month after the close of the partnership's tax year (Apr. 15 for a calendar year partnership). (Code Sec. 6072(a))[28]

Every partnership required to file a return must furnish a written statement, Schedule K-1 (Form 1065), containing information from the return to every person who was a partner (or who held an interest in the partnership as a nominee for another person) at any time during the partnership's tax year. (Code Sec. 6031(b); Reg § 1.6031(b)-1T(a))[29] (The nominee must in turn give the information it gets to the other person (Code Sec. 6031(c)(2); Reg § 1.6031(c)-1T(h)) and must furnish the partnership with specified information about that person.) (Code Sec. 6031(c)(1); Reg § 1.6031(c)-1T(a))[30]

---

18. ¶S-5104; ¶60,914.
19. ¶S-5601 *et seq.*; ¶61,514.
20. ¶s S-5601, S-5607; ¶63,014.
21. ¶S-5614.

22. ¶T-10726; ¶s 63,014, 75,024.
23. ¶S-5850 *et seq.*; ¶61,614.
24. ¶S-5865 *et seq.*; ¶61,644.

25. ¶S-2701; ¶60,314.
26. ¶S-2701; ¶60,314.
27. ¶S-3640; ¶60,314.

28. ¶S-4923; ¶60,634.
29. ¶S-2710; ¶60,314.
30. ¶S-2740; ¶60,314.

Footnote references beginning with letters are to paragraphs in RIA's Federal Tax Coordinator 2d and RIA's Analysis of Federal Taxes: Income. Footnote references beginning with numbers are to paragraphs in RIA's United States Tax Reporter.

¶ 4731   Extension for filing partnership return—Forms 8736 and 8800.

For an automatic three-month extension of time for filing a partnership return, use Form 8736. (Reg § 1.6081-2T) Use Form 8800 for further filing extension.[31]

¶ 4732   Returns of trusts and estates—Schedule K-1 (Form 1041), etc.

Trusts and estates must file income tax returns (see ¶s 4733 and 4735, respectively) and a variety of information returns.[32]

If there are *joint* fiduciaries, a return by one will suffice if he states in the return that he has sufficient knowledge of the facts to make the return and that it is true to the best of his knowledge and belief. (Reg § 1.6012-3(c))[33]

The fiduciary who prepares the income tax return filed by the trust or estate must furnish to beneficiaries (or their nominees) receiving distributions or to whom an income item is allocated, a Schedule K-1 (Form 1041) or a substitute that contains the same information. This must be furnished on or before a return is filed with IRS, and a copy must be filed with Form 1041. (Code Sec. 6034A(a)) (If a nominee is given this information, he must furnish it to his beneficiary, and he must furnish to the estate or trust specified information about the beneficiary.) (Code Sec. 6034A(b))[34]

¶ 4733   Income tax returns of trusts—Form 1041.

The trustee must file on Form 1041 if the trust is not tax-exempt and if the trust:

- has any taxable income for the year; or
- has gross income of $600 or more; or
- if any beneficiary is a nonresident alien. (Code Sec. 6012(a)(4), (5))[35]

Trust income taxable to the grantor or other "owner" must be reported on a separate statement attached to Form 1041, unless the grantor is also the trustee (or co-trustee), in which case he just reports the income on his own return and doesn't file a Form 1041. (Reg § 1.671-4(b))[36]

The rules on when income tax returns are filed and the tax paid, including short-year returns, are the same for trusts as they are for individuals, see ¶ 4713 *et seq.* Foreign trusts that do not have an office or place of business in the U.S. must file on or before the 15th day of the sixth month following the end of the tax year. (Reg § 1.6071-1(c))[37]

¶ 4734   Extension for filing trust return—Forms 8736 and 8800.

Trusts get an automatic three-month filing extension by filing Form 8736. (Reg § 1.6081-3T) For further filing extensions by trusts, use Form 8800.[38] *Payment extensions* must be separately applied for under the rules at ¶ 4718.

¶ 4735   Income tax returns of estates—Form 1041.

The executor or administrator must file Form 1041 if gross income for the estate's tax year is $600 or more (Code Sec. 6012(a)(3)) *or* if any beneficiary is a nonresident alien. (Code Sec. 6012(a); Reg § 1.6012-3(a)(1)(iii))[39]

The executor who probates the entire will (in the state the decedent was domiciled) files Form 1041 reporting all the income. Any out-of-state or "ancillary" executor *also* files a Form 1041, but it shows only the gross income received by the ancillary fiduciary and the deductions attributable to that income. (Reg § 1.6012-3(a)(3))[40]

The rules on when income tax returns are filed and the tax paid, including short-year

---

31. ¶ S-5028; ¶ 60,814.
32. ¶s S-2004, S-2007; ¶ 60,124.04.
33. ¶ S-2002; ¶ 60,124.04.
34. ¶s S-2019, S-2020; ¶ 60,34A4.
35. ¶ S-2007; ¶ 60,124.04.
36. ¶ S-2009; ¶ 6714.
37. ¶ S-4707.
38. ¶ S-5029 *et seq.*; ¶ 60,814.06.
39. ¶ S-2004; ¶ 60,124.04.
40. ¶ S-2004.

Footnote references beginning with letters are to paragraphs in RIA's Federal Tax Coordinator 2d and RIA's Analysis of Federal Taxes: Income. Footnote references beginning with numbers are to paragraphs in RIA's United States Tax Reporter.

returns, are the same for estates as they are for individuals, see ¶ 4713 *et seq.* Estates of nonresident aliens that do not have an office in the U.S. must file on the 15th day of the sixth month following the end of the tax year.[41]

¶ 4736 Extension for filing estate return—Form 2758.

Extensions of time for filing returns of an estate are made on Form 2758.[42] *Payment extensions* must be separately applied for under the rules at ¶ 4718.

¶ 4737 Copy of will or trust with Form 1041.

A fiduciary does not have to file a copy of the will or trust instrument for income tax purposes unless IRS *requests* a copy. If IRS does ask for a copy, the fiduciary must file it (including amendments) together with a declaration (under penalties of perjury) that the copy is true and complete and a statement indicating the provisions that determine the extent to which the income is taxable to the estate or trust, the beneficiaries, or the grantor. (Reg § 1.6012-3(a)(2))[43]

¶ 4738 Information returns on interest and dividends.

Every person who pays interest (¶ 4741), dividends (¶ 4740), and patronage dividends of $10 or more to any person (individual or otherwise) during a calendar year must, for each payee, file an information return (on the appropriate Form 1099, or in certain cases use magnetic media, see ¶ 4754) (and furnish a payee statement, see ¶ 4743), setting forth the aggregate amount of the payments and the name and address of the payee. (Code Sec. 6042(a)(1), Code Sec. 6044(a)(1), Code Sec. 6049(a)(1))[44] For nominee reporting, see ¶ 4739.

These forms must be filed (with a Form 1096 transmittal statement) after Sept. 30 of the calendar year of the payment (but not before the payor's final payments for the year) and on or before the following Feb. 28. (Reg § 1.6042-2(c), Reg § 1.6044-2(d), Reg § 1.6049-1(c))[45] For extension of time to file, see ¶ 4747.

¶ 4739 Nominees and middleman returns.

If reportable interest or dividends are paid to any person who, as middleman or nominee, then pays them over to the actual (or beneficial) owner, the original payor (corporation, bank, etc.) must file an information return (Form 1099) with respect to the nominee, and the nominee must file another Form 1099 with respect to the actual or beneficial owner. (Code Sec. 6042(a)(1)(B), Code Sec. 6049(a)(2); Reg § 1.6042-2(a)(1)(iii), Reg § 1.6049-4(b)(3))[46]

A nominee is any payee who isn't the actual owner of the dividend or interest, but who would be required to furnish his taxpayer identification number (¶ 4751) to the payor for inclusion on the *payor's* return. Nominees include banks, trust companies, etc., and, with respect to dividends, dealers and brokers. (Reg § 1.6042-2(a)(2), Reg § 1.6049-1(a)(2))[47]

¶ 4740 Dividend reporting—Form 1099-DIV, Form 5452, Form 1099-PATR.

A payor must file a Form 1099-DIV for each person to whom it pays "reportable" dividends aggregating $10 or more during the calendar year. (Code Sec. 6042(a), Reg § 1.6042-2(a)(1))[48]

Reportable dividends are corporate "dividends" as defined in ¶ 1288 *et seq.*, as well as substitute dividends (e.g., that brokers pay on short sales). (Code Sec. 6042(b)(1))[49]

---

41. ¶ S-4707.
42. ¶ S-5031; ¶ 60,814.06.
43. ¶ S-2004; ¶ 60,124.04.
44. ¶s S-2901, S-2951, S-3001; ¶s 60,424, 60,494.
45. ¶ S-4930; ¶s 60,424, 60,494.
46. ¶ S-2904 *et seq.*; ¶s 60,424, 60,494.
47. ¶s S-2904 *et seq.*, S-3003 *et seq.*; ¶s 60,424, 60,494.
48. ¶ S-4930; ¶ 60,424.
49. ¶ S-2910; ¶ 60,424.

Footnote references beginning with letters are to paragraphs in RIA's Federal Tax Coordinator 2d and RIA's Analysis of Federal Taxes: Income. Footnote references beginning with numbers are to paragraphs in RIA's United States Tax Reporter.

Corporations must file Form 5452 to report nontaxable dividends.[50] For liquidating dividends, see ¶ 4745.

Patronage dividends aggregating $10 or more to any payee in a calendar are reported by the payor cooperative (¶ 4206) on Form 1099-PATR. (Code Sec. 6044(a)(1); Reg § 1.6044-2(b))[1]

¶ 4741 Reporting interest—Form 1099-INT.

Payments of $10 or more of reportable interest to any person in a calendar year must be reported (Code Sec. 6049(a)(1)) on Form 1099-INT.[2]

Reportable interest includes interest on obligations issued publicly or in registered form (other than a short-term obligation held by a corporation), on deposits with banks or brokers, on amounts held by insurance or investment companies. (Code Sec. 6049(b)(1))[3] It also includes OID (¶ 4742), and amounts includible in gross income with respect to regular interests in REMICs (¶ 4204). (Code Sec. 6049(d)(6)(A)(i), (7)(A))[4] But interest on obligations issued by a natural person, or on tax-exempt bonds, isn't "reportable." (Code Sec. 6049(b)(2))[5]

¶ 4742 Reporting original issue discount (OID)—Form 1099-OID, Form 8281.

Original issue discount (OID) of $10 or more on any obligation must be reported by the issuer (or nominee) as a payment of interest. (Code Sec. 6049(d)(6)) Form 1099-OID is used to report the OID, as well as any interest actually paid on the obligation.[6]

In addition, an information return (Form 8281) must be filed by certain issuers of publicly-offered debt instruments having OID, within 30 days after issuance. (Code Sec. 1275(c)(2); Reg § 1.1275-3(c))[7]

🄰*observation:* The one-time reporting requirement on Form 8281 is in addition to the annual information reporting on Form 1099-OID.

¶ 4743 Statements to payees.

Payors of reportable interest (including OID) and dividends must also furnish the payee with a specified written statement of the amount reported to IRS (normally, Copy B of the Form 1099 sent to IRS). This must be done, either in person or in a "statement mailing," on or before Jan. 31 of the year following the calendar year for which the payor's Form 1099 was required. (Reg § 1.6042-4(c)(1), Reg § 1.6044-5(c)(1), Reg § 1.6049-3(c)(1))[8]

¶ 4744 Information returns on business payments of $600 or more—Form 1099-MISC.

With limited exceptions, every person, corporate or otherwise, engaged in a trade or business who, in the course of that business, makes payments aggregating $600 or more to another person in a calendar year must file an information return (Form 1099-MISC) setting forth the name and address of the payee and the amount paid, and furnish a statement to the payee. The payments which must be reported are: rent, salaries, wages, premiums, annuities, compensations, remunerations, emoluments, or other fixed or determinable gains, profits and income. (Code Sec. 6041; Reg § 1.6041-1)[9]

Exceptions to the above rule apply to transactions covered by other information return rules (e.g., for interest and dividends, see 4738 *et seq.*) and with respect to most payments to corporations. (Reg § 1.6041-3)[10]

---

50. ¶ S-2914; ¶ 60,424.
1. ¶ S-2953; ¶ 60,444.
2. ¶ S-3011 *et seq.*; ¶ 60,494.

3. ¶ S-3711 *et seq.*; ¶ 60,494.
4. ¶ S-3073, S-3093; ¶ 60,494.
5. ¶s S-3040, S-3042; ¶ 60,494.

6. ¶s S-3073, S-3074; ¶ 60,494.
7. ¶ S-3082 *et seq.*
8. ¶ S-2927 *et seq.*; ¶ 60,410(d)

9. ¶ S-3655 *et seq.*; ¶s 60,414, 60,414.06.
10. ¶ S-3676; ¶ 60,414.06.

Footnote references beginning with letters are to paragraphs in RIA's Federal Tax Coordinator 2d and RIA's Analysis of Federal Taxes: Income. Footnote references beginning with numbers are to paragraphs in RIA's United States Tax Reporter.

¶ 4745 Other information returns.

Other information returns include:

■ *Abandonment or foreclosure of property held as security* for a business loan must be reported by the lender on Form 1099-A. (Code Sec. 6050J; Reg § 1.6050J-1T)[11]

■ *Barter exchanges* through which at least 100 exchanges of property or services are made during the calendar year must report each exchange on Form 1099-B. (Code Sec. 6045; Reg § 1.6045-1(e))[12]

■ *Brokers* must report on Form 1099-B the gross proceeds of sales of securities and commodities by customers. (Code Sec. 6045)[13] For real estate reporting persons, see below.

■ *Cafeteria plan* information must be reported to IRS on the Form 5500 series by every employer that maintains such a plan. (Code Sec. 6039D)[14]

■ *Cash of more than $10,000*, including certain cash equivalents (e.g., cashier's checks, foreign currency), received in connection with a trade or business must be reported on Form 8300 by the recipient. (Code Sec. 6050I(a); Reg § 1.6050I-1(e)(2)) Special rules apply if the cash is paid in installments (Reg § 1.6050I-1T) Special rules apply to casinos. (Reg § 1.6050I-1(d)(2)) Banks report cash deposits, etc., of $10,000 or more on Form 4789.[15]

■ *Change in control or recapitalization of corporation* must be reported on an information return showing the parties to the transaction, the fees involved, the changes in capital structure and any other information IRS requires. (Code Sec. 6043(c))[16]

■ *Charitable property sale* by donee within two years of contribution must be reported on Form 8282 by the charity, where the deduction claimed for the property exceeds $5,000 (but the sale of items appraised for $500 or less doesn't have to be reported). (Code Sec. 6050L; Reg § 1.6050L-1)[17]

■ *Direct sales of consumer goods* of $5,000 or more to any one buyer must be reported by the seller (Code Sec. 6041A(b)) on Form 1099-MISC.[18]

■ *Discharge of indebtedness by banks and certain other financial entities* (after '93) of $600 or more must be reported (on Form 1099-C) to IRS. (Code Sec. 6050P)[19]

■ *Fishing boat operators* must report on Form 1099-MISC certain payments to their crewmen. (Code Sec. 6050A; Reg § 1.6050A-1)[20]

■ *Foreign bank accounts* must be reported on Form TDF 90-22.1 by any person with an interest in or signature authority over such an account.[21]

■ *IRA contributions and withdrawals* must be reported by the IRA trustees or issuer on Form 5498. (Code Sec. 408(i))[22]

■ *Liquidating corporations* must report the adoption of the plan of liquidation on Form 966. (Code Sec. 6043(a)(1))[23] Liquidating distributions must be reported on Form 1099-DIV. (Code Sec. 6043(a)(2))[24]

■ *Mortgage interest* receipts of $600 or more on any one mortgage must be reported by the recipient on Form 1098. The return must also include any points paid on the mortgage. These rules apply to interest received on a qualified mortgage (a mortgage secured all or in part by real property and the payor of record of which is an individual) in the course of the interest recipient's trade or business (including cooperative housing corporations). (Code Sec. 6050H(a); Reg § 1.6050H-1)[25]

■ *Mortgage credit certificate* (MCC) information return Form 8329 must be filed by each

---

11. ¶ S-4200 *et seq.*; ¶ 60,50J4.

12. ¶ S-3700 *et seq.*; ¶ 60,454.

13. ¶ S-3700 *et seq.*; ¶ 60,454.

14. ¶ S-3412 *et seq.*; ¶ 60,39D4.

15. ¶ S-4000 *et seq.*; ¶s 60,409, 60,50I4 *et seq.*

16. ¶ S-4308; ¶ 60,434.

17. ¶ S-2873; ¶ 60,5024.

18. ¶ S-3677; ¶ 60,41A4.

19. ¶ S-4251; ¶ 60,50P4.

20. ¶ S-3695; ¶ 60,50A4.

21. ¶ S-3650; ¶ 60,114.06.

22. ¶ S-3390; ¶ 4084.04.

23. ¶ S-4314; ¶ 60,434.

24. ¶ S-4315; ¶ 60,434.

25. ¶ S-3901 *et seq.*; ¶ 60,50H4.

Footnote references beginning with letters are to paragraphs in RIA's Federal Tax Coordinator 2d and RIA's Analysis of Federal Taxes: Income. Footnote references beginning with numbers are to paragraphs in RIA's United States Tax Reporter.

person who makes a loan that is a certified indebtedness under an MCC program. (Reg § 1.25-8T(a))[26]

■ *Partnership interests* (attributable to unrealized receivables or substantially appreciated inventory) sold or exchanged must be reported by the partnership on Form 8308. (Code Sec. 6050K; Reg § 1.6050K-1(a)(1))[27] However, the partnership doesn't have to file until it's notified of the exchange. (Code Sec. 6050K(c)(2)) A partnership is notified when either: (1) it receives written notification from the transferor, or (2) it has knowledge of the transfer. (Reg § 1.6050K-1(e))[28]

■ *Pension, profit-sharing plans* file annual return/report forms in the 5500 series (Code Sec. 6058(a))[29] and file Form 5310 to notify IRS of a merger, consolidation or division of the plan. (Code Sec. 6057(b)(4))[30]

■ *Prizes and awards* (taxable) of $600 or more (not paid for services rendered) must be reported by the payor on Form 1099-MISC.[31]

■ *Railroad retirement benefit* payments must be reported on Form RRB-1099 by the appropriate federal official. (Code Sec. 6050G)[32]

■ *Real estate* reporting persons (as specially defined) (Reg § 1.6045-4(e)) must report real estate transactions (Code Sec. 6045(e))[33] on Form 1099-S. (Reg § 1.6045-4(g)) A transaction is a real estate transaction if it consists in whole or in part of the sale or exchange of land (including air space), any inherently permanent structure (whether residential, commercial or industrial, any condominium unit or any stock in a cooperative housing unit. (Reg § 1.6045-4(b)(2))[34] The information to be reported with respect to a transaction involving a residence includes the portion of any real property tax that is treated as imposed on the purchaser. (Code Sec. 6045(e)(4))[35]

■ *Refunds of state and local income tax* of $10 or more must be reported by the state or local tax authority/payor on Form 1099-G. (Code Sec. 6050E; Reg § 1.6050E-1)[36]

■ *Royalty payments* that aggregate $10 or more per year per payee (including nominees) must be reported on Form 1099-MISC unless the payee is a corporation, exempt organization or government. (Code Sec. 6050N)[37]

■ *Sick pay* (nonwage) paid by a third party to an employee must be reported by the third party to the employee's employer. (Code Sec. 6051(f)(1); Reg § 31.6051-3(a))[38]

■ *Simplified employee pension (SEP) contributions* must be reported on Form 5498 by the SEP trustee or issuer of a SEP endowment contract. (Code Sec. 408(l))[39]

■ *Social security* benefit payments must be reported to IRS and the payee on Form SSA-1099 (Form SSA-1042S for nonresident aliens) by the appropriate federal official. (Code Sec. 6050F)[40]

■ *Tips* must be reported by employees to employers on Form 4070. (Code Sec. 6053(a); Reg § 31.6053-1(b)(2))[41] Large food and beverage establishments (with more than ten employees on a typical business day) must report to IRS (on Form 8027) and to employees, tips reported by the employees to the employer plus the excess (as specially allocated) of 8% of the establishment's gross receipts (as specially defined) over the amount reported to the employer by the employees, (Code Sec. 6053(c)(3)(B); Reg § 31.6053-3(d), (e), (f)) subject to a petition to IRS to reduce the 8% to not below 2%. (Code Sec. 6053(c)(3)(C); Reg § 31.6053-3(h))[42]

■ *Unemployment insurance benefit* payments of $10 or more must be reported by the payor on Form 1099-G. (Code Sec. 6050B; Reg § 1.6050B-1)[43]

---

26. ¶ S-4206; ¶ 254.03.
27. ¶ S-2725 *et seq.*; ¶ 60,50K4.
28. ¶ S-2733 *et seq.*; ¶ 60,50K4.
29. ¶ S-3351; ¶s 4014.01, 60,584.
30. ¶s S-3383, S-3384; ¶s 4014.01, 60,574.

31. ¶ S-3656; ¶ 60,409.
32. ¶s S-3688, S-3689; ¶ 60,50G4.
33. ¶ S-3800; ¶ 60,454.04.
34. ¶ S-3812 *et seq.*; ¶ 60,454.04.
35. ¶ S-3819; ¶ 60,454.04.

36. ¶ S-3690; ¶ 60,50E4.
37. ¶ S-3684 *et seq.*; ¶ 60,50N4.
38. ¶ S-3173; ¶ 60,514.
39. ¶ S-3399; ¶ 4084.05.

40. ¶ S-3688; ¶ 60,50F4.
41. ¶ H-4419; ¶ 60,534.
42. ¶ S-3250 *et seq.*; ¶ 60,534.
43. ¶ S-3694; ¶ 60,50B4.

Footnote references beginning with letters are to paragraphs in RIA's Federal Tax Coordinator 2d and RIA's Analysis of Federal Taxes: Income. Footnote references beginning with numbers are to paragraphs in RIA's United States Tax Reporter.

¶ 4746 Tax shelter registration and investor lists.

Registration. Any tax shelter organizer must register the tax shelter on Form 8264 not later than the day when interests in the shelter are first offered for sale, (Code Sec. 6111(a)(1); Reg § 301.6111-1T, Q&A-47)[44] at which time IRS assigns it an ID number. Any person who sells or otherwise transfers an interest in the shelter must give the shelter's ID number to each investor (on Form 8271) in the shelter. (Code Sec. 6111(b))[45] "Projected income investments" don't have to be registered. (Reg § 301.6111-1T, Q&A 57)[46]

Investor lists—potentially abusive tax shelters. Any person who organizes or sells any interest in any potentially abusive tax shelter must maintain a list identifying each person who was sold an interest in it, (Code Sec. 6112(a)) until the later of (1) seven years after the last transfer of an interest or (2) three years after a transfer of which the organizer (or a designated person) has notice. (Reg § 301.6112-1T, Q&A 19) Regs specify the contents of the list. (Reg § 301.6112-1T, Q&A-17) A potentially abusive tax shelter is one that must be registered with IRS (above), as well as any other entity, investment plan or arrangement IRS determines to have the potential for tax avoidance or evasion. (Code Sec. 6112(b))[47]

¶ 4747 Extension of time for filing information returns—Form 8809.

Use Form 8809 to request a 30-day extension to file the following forms: W-2, -2G, -2P, 1098, 1099-A, -B, -DIV, -G, -INT, -MISC, -OID, -PATR, -R, -S, 5498. Filers of paper forms or magnetic media can use the form. Approval is *not* automatic. For an additional 30-day extension, submit a letter and attach a copy of the first approval letter from IRS.[48]

Make a written application (don't use Form 8809) to request an extension of up to 30 days for furnishing the payee statement.[49]

¶ 4748 Returns prepared by income tax return preparers.

An income tax return preparer (defined at ¶ 4749) must:

■ *manually sign the return* (signature stamp is no good); (Reg § 1.6695-1(b)(1))[50] except that: a photocopy of a manually signed completed return can be filed, if the preparer keeps the manually signed copy available on request; (Reg § 1.6695-1(b)(4)(i))[1] a manually signed attestation can be attached to a computer-prepared return; (Reg § 1.6695-1(b)(4)(ii))[2] a facsimile signature can be used for a nonresident alien's return (Reg § 1.6695-1(b)(4)(iii)) and for fiduciary (Form 1041) returns, in certain cases;[3]

■ *enter his (preparer's) ID number* (Code Sec. 6109(a)(4))[4] *and address* (Reg § 1.6109-2(b)(1))[5] on any return he prepares;

■ *furnish the taxpayer with a completed copy of the return* no later than when he presents the return for taxpayer's signature; (Code Sec. 6107(a))[6]

■ *retain for three years a completed copy of each return* or a list of the name and ID number of each taxpayer for whom a return was prepared; (Code Sec. 6107(b))[7]

■ *retain a record of the name, ID number, and principal place of work of each income tax return preparer* employed or engaged by the preparer/employer during each July 1 through June 30 period. (Reg § 1.6060-1(a))[8]

---

44. ¶ S-4400 *et seq.*; ¶ 61,114.
45. ¶ S-4413; ¶ 61,114.
46. ¶s S-4411, S-4412; ¶ 61,114.
47. ¶ S-4414 *et seq.*; ¶ 61,124.

48. ¶ S-5041; ¶ 60,814.07.
49. ¶s S-5041, S-5042; ¶ 60,814.07.
50. ¶ S-4603; ¶ 66,954.

1. ¶ S-4608.
2. ¶ S-4609; ¶ 66,954.
3. ¶ S-4610.
4. ¶ S-1522; ¶ 61,094.

5. ¶ S-1523; ¶ 61,094.
6. ¶ V-2671; ¶ 61,074.
7. ¶ V-2672; ¶ 61,074.
8. ¶ V-2673; ¶ 60,604.

Footnote references beginning with letters are to paragraphs in RIA's Federal Tax Coordinator 2d and RIA's Analysis of Federal Taxes: Income. Footnote references beginning with numbers are to paragraphs in RIA's United States Tax Reporter.

¶ 4749 Income tax return preparer defined.

An income tax return preparer is any person (including a partnership or corporation) who for compensation prepares, or employs another to prepare, all or a substantial portion of an income tax return or refund claim. (Code Sec. 7701(a)(36)(A))[9] For example, a general partner's preparation of a partnership's Schedule K-1 can be preparation of a substantial portion of a limited partner's individual return.[10]

A portion of a return prepared by any one of several persons won't be "substantial" if, aggregating all schedules, etc., he prepared, that portion involves amounts of gross income, deductions, or amounts on which credits are based that are: (1) less than $2,000, or (2) less than $100,000 *and* less than 20% of the gross income (adjusted gross income, for individuals) as shown on the return. (Reg § 301.7701-15(b)(2))[11]

A tax consultant is a return preparer even though he may do no more than review a return already prepared by the taxpayer.[12]

A person isn't a return preparer is he merely furnishes typing, reproducing or other mechanical assistance with respect to preparing a return. (Code Sec. 7701(a)(36)(B)(i)) A person who provides a computerized return preparation service is a preparer if his computer programs provide substantive tax determinations, but not if his services are limited to mechanical calculations and processing.[13]

¶ 4750 Rounding to nearest dollar.

Rounding to the nearest dollar is permitted, to the extent indicated on the specific form. This means that amounts of 1¢ through 49¢ are disregarded, while $1.00 is substituted for any amounts from 50¢ through 99¢. (Code Sec. 6102(a)(2); Reg § 301.6102-1(a))[14]

¶ 4751 Taxpayer identification number (TIN).

Any person who files a return, statement, or other document must include his own TIN (Code Sec. 6109(a)(1))[15] and the TIN of any other person, as required by the form or instructions to the form. (Code Sec. 6109(a)(3); Reg § 301.6109-1(c))[16] Thus, an alimony payor's return must include the payee's TIN. (Use Form W-9 to request another person's TIN.)[17]

A taxpayer must include the TIN of any dependent he claims on his return, if the dependent is at least one year old. (Code Sec. 6109(e))[18]

A child to whom the unearned income rules (¶ 3133 *et seq.*) apply for any tax year must provide his parent's TIN on his (child's) tax return for that year. (Code Sec. 1(g)(6))[19]

If a seller of a residence receives or accrues interest on seller-provided financing for that residence, the seller must include the buyer's name, address and taxpayer identification number on his income tax return. (Code Sec. 6109(h)(1))[20] The buyer must include that same information with respect to the seller if the buyer claims a deduction for qualified residence interest (as discussed in ¶ 1726 *et seq.*). (Code Sec. 6109(h)(2))[21]

Social security numbers are used to identify individuals, sole proprietors and estates. (Code Sec. 6109(d); Reg § 301.6109-1(a))[22] To get a social security number, file Form SS-5 with IRS. (Reg § 301.6109-1(d)(1))[23]

Other entities use the employer identification number (EIN). (Reg § 301.6109-1(a)) To get an EIN, file Form SS-4. (Reg § 301.6109-1(d)) Numbers can be obtained by phone in some circumstances under a "Tele-TIN" program—check with the applicable IRS Service Center. Fiduciaries and others represent ten or more estates or trusts can request a series or block of EINs under a special procedure.[24]

---

9. ¶ S-1107; ¶ 61,074.
10. ¶ S-1116.
11. ¶ S-1116; ¶ 61,075.
12. ¶ S-1109; ¶ 61,075.

13. ¶ S-1110; ¶ 61,075.
14. ¶ S-1006; ¶ 61,014.
15. ¶ S-1502; ¶ 61,094.
16. ¶ S-1531; ¶ 61,094.

17. ¶ S-1532; ¶ 2154.03.
18. ¶ S-1504; ¶ 61,094.
19. ¶ S-1544.
20. ¶ S-1525.

21. ¶ S-1524.
22. ¶ S-1505; ¶ 61,094.
23. ¶ S-1581; ¶ 61,094.
24. ¶ S-1582 *et seq.*; ¶ 61,094.

Footnote references beginning with letters are to paragraphs in RIA's Federal Tax Coordinator 2d and RIA's Analysis of Federal Taxes: Income. Footnote references beginning with numbers are to paragraphs in RIA's United States Tax Reporter.

All employers, whether corporations, partnerships or sole proprietors, must get and use EINs for reporting employment and excise taxes.[25]

A special 15-digit identifying number must be used by large food and beverage establishments for tip reporting. (Reg § 31.6053-3(a)(5))[26]

Buildings that have been or will be allocated a low-income housing credit must be assigned a building identification number (BIN) by the applicable state housing credit agency.[27]

For special rules applicable to tax shelter investors and tax return preparers, see ¶s 4746 and 4748, respectively.

¶ 4752 Getting blank tax forms.

Practitioners may order without charge a tax practitioner kit (major forms without instructions; one per firm), Package X (many forms with instructions; one per practitioner), and unlimited quantities of Forms W-2, W-3, 1096, 1098, 1099-A, 1099-B, 1099-DIV, 1099-G, 1099-INT, 1099-MISC, 1099-OID, 1099-PATR, 1099-R, 1099-S, and 5498. Use Form 3975. The Government Printing Office sells commonly used forms in packages of 100. Use GPO Form 3565.[28]

¶ 4753 Reproduction of tax forms.

Reproductions meeting IRS requirements (set out in periodic revenue procedures) may be filed without IRS approval instead of the official forms. For certain forms, IRS also provides reproduction proofs. However, certain OCR (optically scannable) forms should never be reproduced as photocopies. Among these are Forms W-2, W-3, 1096, 1098, the 1099 series, 2284, 5498, and 8109.[29]

¶ 4754 Magnetic media.

Certain information returns *must* be filed on magnetic media. (Code Sec. 6011(e)(2)(A))[30] There are exceptions for certain low-volume filers (fewer than 250 returns). Hardship waivers (request on Form 8508) are available. (Reg § 301.6011-2)[31] For other returns (e.g., the 5500 series), magnetic media is encouraged but not required.[32]

For electronic filing of income tax returns, see ¶ 4703.

¶ 4755 Timely mailing as timely filing and paying.

A return, claim, statement, document or payment (except a tax deposit) that must be filed or made by a certain date will generally be considered timely filed or made if it has a timely postmark. (Code Sec. 7502(c)(1))[33]

For the timely mailing rule to apply, the return, etc., must be: (1) deposited in the mail in the U.S. in a properly addressed envelope or wrapper with sufficient postage; (Code Sec. 7502(a)(2)(B)) (2) postmarked on or before the prescribed filing or payment date (Code Sec. 7502(a)(2)(A)) (returns postmarked after the due date are considered filed when received by IRS); and (3) actually delivered by U.S. mail to the proper place. (Code Sec. 7502(a)(1))[34]

The postmark stamp date on the mailing envelope overrides the postmark stamp date on a Certificate of Mailing (P.S. Form 3817).[35]

If a private postage meter is used, the postmark is not enough. The document must actually be received by the proper office or officer not later than the time the postmark indicates it ordinarily would be received. If it is actually received later, taxpayer can prove timely mailing only by showing: (1) that the document was deposited in the mail

25. ¶ S-1505; ¶ 61,094. 28. ¶ S-1203. 31. ¶ S-1314; ¶ 60,114.07. 34. ¶ T-10701.
26. ¶ S-3289. 29. ¶ S-1204. 32. ¶ S-1300. 35. ¶ T-10722.
27. ¶ S-1521. 30. ¶ S-1301; ¶ 60,114.07. 33. ¶ T-10701; ¶ 75,024.

Footnote references beginning with letters are to paragraphs in RIA's Federal Tax Coordinator 2d and RIA's Analysis of Federal Taxes: Income. Footnote references beginning with numbers are to paragraphs in RIA's United States Tax Reporter.

before the last collection that was postmarked (by the U.S. Post Office) on the last day for filing; and (2) that the delay in receiving the document was due to delay in transmission of the mail; and (3) the cause of the delay. (Reg § 301.7502-1(c)(1)(iii)(b))[36]

¶ 4756 Effect of registered or certified mail.

The date of registration is considered to be the postmark date, (Code Sec. 7502(c)(1)(B)) and registration is prima facie evidence the return, etc., was delivered to the agency, officer or office to which addressed. (Code Sec. 7502(c)(1)(A))[37] The date of the U.S. postmark on the sender's receipt is treated as the postmark date of a document sent by certified mail, (Reg § 301.7502-1(c)(2)) and proof that a properly postmarked certified mail sender's receipt was properly issued and that the envelope or wrapper was properly addressed will be prima facie evidence that the document was properly delivered. (Reg § 301.7502-1(d)(1))[38]

¶ 4757 Due date on Saturday, Sunday or holiday.

If a due date falls on Saturday, Sunday or legal holiday, there is an automatic extension of time to the next succeeding day that is not a Saturday, Sunday or legal holiday. The rule applies to *all acts* required to be performed under the Code both by the *taxpayer* and IRS. "Legal holiday" includes: (1) the legal holidays throughout the state or possession where the office at which the act to be performed is located even if not a legal holiday in the state or possession where the taxpayer resides, and (2) all legal holidays in the District of Columbia, (Code Sec. 7503) i.e.,: New Year's Day—Jan. 1; Inauguration Day—Jan. 20 (every fourth year); Martin Luther King, Jr.'s birthday—third Monday in January; Washington's birthday—third Monday in February; Memorial Day—last Monday in May; Independence Day—July 4; Labor Day—first Monday in September; Columbus Day—second Monday in October; Veterans Day—Nov. 11; Thanksgiving Day—fourth Thursday in November; Christmas Day—Dec. 25. If a holiday in the District of Columbia falls on Sunday, the next day is a holiday in the District of Columbia. When a legal holiday in the District of Columbia (other than Inauguration Day) falls on a Saturday, it's treated as falling on the preceding Friday. (Reg § 301.7503-1(b)(1))[39]

¶ 4758 How to get a copy of a previously filed tax return—Form 4506.

Use Form 4506.[40] IRS charges a nominal fee. There is no charge for a Form 4506 request for a transcript of individual income tax account information,[41] which includes name and social security number, type of return filed, marital status, adjusted gross income, taxable income, tax shown on the return, self-employment tax and number of exemptions.[42]

---

36. ¶ T-10712.
37. ¶ T-10720; ¶ 75,024.
38. ¶ T-10721.
39. ¶ T-10750 *et seq.*; ¶ 75,034.
40. ¶ S-6407; ¶s 61,034, 61,034.09.
41. ¶ S-6409.
42. ¶ S-6407.

Footnote references beginning with letters are to paragraphs in RIA's Federal Tax Coordinator 2d and RIA's Analysis of Federal Taxes: Income. Footnote references beginning with numbers are to paragraphs in RIA's United States Tax Reporter.

Chapter 25 Deficiencies—Refunds—Penalties

¶ 4800 Tax Audits, Deficiencies and Assessments ▬▬▬▬▬▬▬▬▬▬

IRS makes certain preliminary cursory checks of every return filed; it selects returns for audit based on various criteria. Once IRS finishes an audit, a taxpayer has various alternatives it can pursue to resolve any disputed items.

¶ 4801 Mathematical, etc., check of returns.

IRS checks every return for mathematical errors and computes the tax using the figures on the return. Where taxpayer's computational error results in an underpayment of tax, IRS sends a corrected computation and a notice and demand for payment of any balance due (which doesn't entitle taxpayer to go to Tax Court). (Code Sec. 6213(b)(1)) If correction of the error results in a reduced refund, IRS sends a corrected computation and a reduced refund. If it results in an overstatement of tax paid, IRS will ordinarily refund the excess. (Reg § 601.105(a))[1]

IRS's "Unallowable Items Program" allows certain simple and obvious errors to be informally corrected by correspondence. (Reg § 601.105(a))

¶ 4802 Check against information returns.

IRS compares taxpayers' income tax returns against information returns, such as wage, interest and dividend statements, under a document matching program (Information Returns Program). If there is a mismatch, IRS sends taxpayer a computer-generated notice (CP-2000). The notice must contain both a description of the basis for, and an identification of any amounts of, taxes, additions, interest or penalties claimed to be due. (Code Sec. 7522) The notice, which is not a demand for payment, can be challenged by taxpayer, who has the burden of proof.[2]

¶ 4803 Returns selected for examination.

IRS selects returns for examination under various criteria, e.g., discrepancy with information returns (¶ 4802), history of deficiencies, etc. Returns may also be selected by random sampling (Taxpayer Compliance Measurement Program (TCMP)) or because of questionable refunds (Questionable Refund Program). IRS's computerized "discriminant function" (DIF) technique ranks and selects returns having the greatest audit potential.[3]

¶ 4804 What are the chances of an IRS audit.

The percentage of returns examined varies each year depending on IRS's available manpower. Returns least likely to be audited are those on which all or most of the income was subject to withholding and where taxpayer didn't itemize.[4]

Statistical data from IRS shows that a total of 1,039,355 individual income tax returns were audited during '92 (the latest year for which data were available as we went to press). This works out to an average of 0.91%. For examined returns, the "no-change" rate for individual returns averaged 16% for office audits and 11% for field audits. The overall "no-change" rate on corporate audits was 23% (ranging from 4% to 25%). The actual chances of examination varied sharply depending on geographical location.

¶ 4805 Types of examinations (audits); time and place.

IRS fixes the time and method, which must be reasonable under the circumstances. (Code Sec. 7605(a); Reg § 301.7605-1(a)) Depending on the amounts and sources of income and the nature of taxpayer's business, an examination may take place at: (1) an IRS office, with taxpayer bringing (office audit) or mailing (correspondence audit) his records, (Reg § 601.105(b)(2)(ii)) or (2) at the office of taxpayer (or taxpayer's representative) (field

---

1. ¶ T-1002; ¶s 62,134.02, 76,557.   2. ¶s T-1003, T-1004.   3. ¶s T-1021, T-1061.   4. ¶ T-1065.

Footnote references beginning with letters are to paragraphs in RIA's Federal Tax Coordinator 2d and RIA's Analysis of Federal Taxes: Income. Footnote references beginning with numbers are to paragraphs in RIA's United States Tax Reporter.

audit). (Reg § 601.105(b)(3))[5]

IRS generally won't conduct the audit at taxpayer's place of business if the business is so small that doing so essentially requires the taxpayer to close the business.[6]

¶ 4806 Market Segment Specialization (MSSP) audit guidelines.

These provide revenue agents and tax examiners with a broad and detailed review of the way a particular industry works and the things an agent should be looking for when reviewing a return from within that industry. The guides cover, for example, attorneys, taxicabs, air charters, trucking, bed and breakfasts, and other industries. The guides are available to practitioners and others.

¶ 4807 Taxpayer's rights in an examination.

Before or at an initial in-person interview (other than criminal investigations), IRS must give taxpayer an explanation (written or oral) of the audit process (and assessment and collection) and taxpayer's rights under that process. (Code Sec. 7521(b)(1), (d))[7]

A taxpayer has the right to: be represented by an advisor (¶ 4808); make certain audio recordings of meetings (on advance notice) with the IRS agent (Code Sec. 7521(a)(1)) (but generally not videotape recordings); claim additional deductions not claimed on the return; ask that a particular technical question raised in the examination be referred to IRS's National Office for technical advice; not be subjected to unnecessary examinations (¶ 4810); and claim constitutional rights if questioned about possible criminal violations.[8]

¶ 4808 Who can represent the taxpayer?

Taxpayer may be represented at an IRS audit by any attorney, CPA, enrolled agent, enrolled actuary or any other person permitted to represent taxpayer before IRS, who isn't disbarred or suspended from practice before IRS, and who has a written power of attorney (Form 2848 may be used) executed by taxpayer. In the absence of a summons, IRS may not require taxpayer to accompany the representative. (Code Sec. 7521(c))[9]

If, during an interview, taxpayer clearly states a desire to consult with a representative, IRS must suspend the interview for that purpose. (Code Sec. 7521(b)(2))[10]

¶ 4809 IRS's power to summon persons and records is broad.

IRS may issue a summons for taxpayer's testimony and records (Code Sec. 7602(a), (b)) for a legitimate purpose if IRS doesn't already have the requested materials and doesn't make unreasonable demands.[11] The summons (Form 2039) must describe with reasonable certainty the books and records sought (Code Sec. 7603) and set the time for examination—not less than ten days from the summons date. (Code Sec. 7605(a))[12].

If taxpayer intentionally disregards the summons, IRS can apply to the district court (or U.S. Commissioner) for an order directing compliance. (Code Sec. 7604(b))[13]

IRS may issue a summons ("third-party summons") to a person other than the taxpayer (e.g., his employer, bank, etc.) for testimony and records bearing on its examination of taxpayer. (Certain communications (e.g., attorney-client) are privileged.) Within three days of service, but no later than 23 days before the date fixed for examination, IRS must give notice of the third-party summons to taxpayer, who has 20 days to request noncompliance by the third party until a court decides the issue. (Code Sec. 7609(a))[14]

A summons may not be issued (or enforced) against a person for whom a Justice Department referral is in effect (i.e., criminal tax prosecution is recommended). (Code

---

5. ¶ T-1090 *et seq.*; ¶ 76,054.
6. ¶ T-1094; ¶ 75,214.
7. ¶ T-1112; ¶ 75,214.
8. ¶s T-1110 *et seq.*, T-10052; ¶s 75,214, 76,557, 76,559.
9. ¶ T-1116; ¶ 75,214.
10. ¶ T-1117; ¶ 75,214.
11. ¶s T-1201, T-1212 *et seq.*; ¶ 76,024 *et seq.*
12. ¶ T-1306; ¶s 76,024.04, 76,054.
13. ¶ T-1305.
14. ¶ T-1241 *et seq.*; ¶ 76,024.04.

Footnote references beginning with letters are to paragraphs in RIA's Federal Tax Coordinator 2d and RIA's Analysis of Federal Taxes: Income. Footnote references beginning with numbers are to paragraphs in RIA's United States Tax Reporter.

Sec. 7602(c))[15]

¶ 4810 One examination rule—unnecessary examinations.

Unnecessary examinations are barred. IRS may make only one inspection of a taxpayer's books and records for each tax year unless taxpayer requests otherwise, or IRS notifies taxpayer *in writing* that an additional inspection is necessary, (Code Sec. 7605(b)) or IRS suspects fraud. (Code Sec. 6212(c)) Re-examination also is permitted if taxpayer doesn't file a timely Tax Court petition after receiving a 90-day letter for the year.[16]

¶ 4811 IRS's Problem Resolution Program—Taxpayer Assistance Orders.

A taxpayer who is suffering or about to suffer a significant hardship as a result of IRS's administration of the tax laws may get help through IRS's Problem Resolution Program, by applying (on Form 911 or on a statement specified in the regs) (Reg § 301.7811-1(b)(1)) to the Taxpayer Ombudsman for a Taxpayer Assistance Order (TAO). (Code Sec. 7811(a)) There is an Ombudsman in each IRS district and service center (for addresses and phone numbers, see ¶ 1117). "Significant hardship" means a serious privation—more than a mere economic or personal inconvenience. (Reg § 301.7811-1(a)(4)(ii)) A TAO is generally binding on IRS, and may require IRS to cease (or not start) any action with respect to any provision of law, or to release property of taxpayer IRS has levied on. (Code Sec. 7811(b), (c)) A TAO generally may not be issued with respect to a criminal tax investigation or to enjoin an act of the Office of Chief Counsel (except for appeals). (Reg § 301.7811-1(c)(3))[17]

¶ 4812 Proposed deficiencies.

The IRS examiner may propose adjustments to taxpayer's return before *determining* a deficiency (¶ 4820), which doesn't exist until either IRS issues a statutory notice of deficiency ("90-day letter," see ¶ 4821) or taxpayer enters into an agreement with IRS.[18] The examiner will discuss the proposed adjustments with taxpayer to settle the case informally. Taxpayer may agree to the proposed adjustments or argue that they should be modified ("unagreed" case) before the examiner submits his report proposing the deficiency. After the report is submitted, taxpayer may discuss and settle the case only in an Appeals Division conference (¶ 4814).[19]

In an unagreed field examination case, the examiner will prepare a report explaining the proposed adjustments. After the report is reviewed by the district review staff, it is sent to taxpayer together with a transmittal letter ("30-day letter"). (Reg § 601.105(c)(2)(i))[20] For taxpayer's options on receiving a 30-day letter, see ¶ 4813.

In an office examination, taxpayer will usually be informed of the examiner's findings and given an opportunity to agree at the end of the interview. If he doesn't agree, he may request an immediate meeting with an appeals officer. If taxpayer doesn't request an immediate conference, or it isn't practicable, the examination report (and 30-day letter) will be mailed to him. (Reg § 601.105(c)(1)(ii))[21]

¶ 4813 The 30-day letter.

If taxpayer rejects the examiner's findings after a field or office examination, IRS will send taxpayer the examiner's report along with a transmittal ("30-day letter") showing the basis for and amount of any proposed adjustments. The letter also explains the appeal procedures and requests taxpayer to indicate, within 30 days, whether he will:

■ accept the findings and sign a waiver of restriction on assessment (Form 870), which allows IRS to collect the deficiency without issuing a 90-day letter (¶ 4821) and limits

---

15. ¶s T-1205, T-1206; ¶ 76,024.
16. ¶ T-1360 *et seq.*; ¶ 76,024.10.
17. ¶ T-10200 *et seq.*; ¶ 78,114 *et seq.*

18. ¶ T-1550 *et seq.*; ¶s 62,109 *et seq.*, 76,557.

19. ¶ T-1550 *et seq.*; ¶ 76,557.
20. ¶ T-1601; ¶ 76,557.

21. ¶ T-1604 *et seq.*; ¶ 76,557.

Footnote references beginning with letters are to paragraphs in RIA's Federal Tax Coordinator 2d and RIA's Analysis of Federal Taxes: Income. Footnote references beginning with numbers are to paragraphs in RIA's United States Tax Reporter.

taxpayer's appeal to a claim or suit for refund (no Tax Court petition);

- request an Appeals Division conference (¶ 4814); or
- do nothing and IRS will send a 90-day letter.[22]

¶ 4814 Appeals Office conference.

Taxpayer can get an Appeals Office conference by sending a written request (in response to a 30-day letter) and any required protest (¶ 4815) to the local district director.[23]

The Appeals Office proceedings are informal and testimony is not under oath, although taxpayer may be asked to submit affidavits. (Reg § 601.106(c))[24]

An Appeals Office conference still is available to a taxpayer even after IRS has issued a 90-day letter, e.g., where taxpayer ignored the 30-day letter or where the assessment period was about to expire (or taxpayer requested the 90-day letter). If taxpayer then files a Tax Court petition (income, estate or gift tax cases) or pays the additional tax assessed (other taxes), taxpayer may have an Appeals Office conference. (Reg § 601.106(a)(1))[25]

¶ 4815 Protest.

An oral request is enough to get Appeals consideration in all office interview or correspondence examination cases. In a field examination case, a written protest is: *required* if the total amount of the proposed increase in tax (including penalties), proposed overassessment or claimed refund, or compromise offer, exceeds $10,000 for any tax period; *optional* (but a statement of issues is required) if that total amount is between $2,500 and $10,000; and *not required* if it is less than $2,500. (Reg § 601.106(a)(1)(iii)(a))[26] The 30-day letter contains instructions for the protest, Reg § 601.105(d)(2)) and spells out the required information.[27]

¶ 4816 Appeals Division settlement authority.

The Appeals Office has authority to settle all factual and legal issues raised by the examiner's report or the taxpayer's protest, (Reg § 601.106(f)(2))[28] as long as the case isn't docketed in the Tax Court. (Reg § 601.106(a)(2))[29]

If no settlement is reached, IRS will prepare a 90-day letter (¶ 4821).[30]

¶ 4817 Execution of Appeals Division settlement—Form 870; Form 890.

If taxpayer accepts IRS's position in full, with no concessions, he signs a Form 870 (Form 890, in gift, estate or generation-skipping transfer tax cases), waiving restrictions on assessment (¶ 4826). (Reg § 601.106(d)(2))[31]

¶ 4818 Final closing agreements—Form 866; Form 906.

Taxpayer and IRS may conclusively settle a tax dispute by entering into a final closing agreement (Code Sec. 7121(a)) either to close a tax year (use Form 866) or to close a *specific transaction,* past or future (use Form 906).[32] Once executed, the agreement is irrevocable (except for fraud, malfeasance or misrepresentation of a material fact) and binds *both* parties. (Code Sec. 7121(b))[33]

¶ 4819 Compromise—Form 656; Form 433.

Civil or criminal tax cases can be compromised by IRS, after assessment, before referral to Department of Justice. After referral, cases can be compromised only by the Attorney General. (Code Sec. 7122(a)) A compromise is essentially an accord and satisfaction of

22. ¶ T-1601 *et seq.*; ¶ 76,557.
23. ¶ T-1709; ¶ 76,557.
24. ¶ T-1712.
25. ¶s T-1708, T-1900 *et seq.*; ¶ 76,557.
26. ¶ T-1710; ¶ 76,557.
27. ¶ T-1602 *et seq.*; ¶ 76,557.
28. ¶ T-1713; ¶ 76,557.
29. ¶ T-1715; ¶ 76,557.
30. ¶ T-1721; ¶ 76,557.
31. ¶ T-1720.
32. ¶ T-9501; ¶ 71,214 *et seq.*
33. ¶ T-9507; ¶s 71,214.07, 71,214.08.

Footnote references beginning with letters are to paragraphs in RIA's Federal Tax Coordinator 2d and RIA's Analysis of Federal Taxes: Income. Footnote references beginning with numbers are to paragraphs in RIA's United States Tax Reporter.

taxpayer's tax liability, binding both taxpayer and the government. (Reg § 601.203)[34]

IRS will compromise civil tax liabilities on two grounds only: (1) doubt as to liability (file Form 656) and/or (2) inability to pay (file Form 433). (Reg § 301.7122-1(a))[35] Taxpayer must agree (on Form 656) to a suspension of the limitations period for the tax at issue, while the compromise offer is pending, plus one year. (Reg § 301.7122-1(f))[36]

¶ 4820 Deficiency defined.

A deficiency is the amount by which taxpayer's correct tax liability is more than the excess of: (1) the tax shown on the return (mathematical or clerical errors corrected), plus (2) the amounts previously assessed (or collected without assessment) as a deficiency, over (3) the amount of any rebates (credits, refunds, or other repayments). (Code Sec. 6211(a), Code Sec. 6213(b)) This computation doesn't include any payment of estimated tax. (Reg § 301.6211-1(b)) If no return is filed, or if a return doesn't show any tax, the "tax shown" is considered to be zero. (Reg § 301.6211-1(a)) Additional taxes reported on an amended return filed after its due date are treated as amounts "shown on the return" ((1) above), not deficiencies. (Reg § 301.6211-1(a))[37]

Where a deficiency on a joint return is challenged by only one spouse, the deficiency as to that spouse is reduced by any tax collected from the other spouse.[38]

¶ 4821 Notice of deficiency—"90-day letter."

A statutory notice of deficiency ("90-day letter") tells taxpayer that IRS has determined a deficiency (in income, estate or gift tax, or excise tax on private foundations or pension plans). This is the only notice IRS will issue for that determination.[39] It must describe the basis for and identify the amounts (if any) of tax, interest, additional amounts, additions to tax and assessable penalties (for exceptions, see ¶ 4823). (Code Sec. 7522(a))[40]

After receiving the letter, taxpayer can: pay the deficiency, not pay and seek to rescind it, pay and file a refund claim (¶ 4846), take no action (let tax be assessed) and then file a compromise offer (¶ 4819), or file a Tax Court petition (¶ 4856).[41]

observation: The 90-day letter is taxpayer's "ticket to Tax Court." It is only when (and if) IRS issues the letter that taxpayer can go to Tax Court.

¶ 4822 Time for making assessments.

Unless taxpayer and IRS sign a closing agreement (¶ 4818), or taxpayer voluntarily pays the deficiency or signs a Form 870 (¶ 4813), or IRS determines collection is in jeopardy (¶ 4824), IRS can't assess deficiencies in income, estate, and gift taxes, and the excise taxes on private foundations and qualified pension, etc., plans until after taxpayer has had an opportunity to make a Tax Court appeal. (Code Sec. 6213(a))[42]

¶ 4823 Assessment of interest and penalties.

Interest may be assessed when the underlying tax is collectible. (Code Sec. 6601(g))[43]

In the case of income, estate and gift and certain excise taxes, the negligence and fraud penalties are assessed the same as deficiencies (¶ 4822). The delinquency penalty (¶ 4867) is assessed only if it is attributable to a deficiency and not if it is measured by the tax shown on the return. The penalty for estimated tax underpayments (¶s 3115, 3357) is assessed as a deficiency only if no return is filed. (Code Sec. 6665(b); Reg § 301.6659-1(c))[44]

The normal assessment and collection rules don't apply to the penalties for promoting

34. ¶ T-9600 *et seq.*; ¶ 71,224 *et seq.*
35. ¶ T-9602.
36. ¶ T-9605.
37. ¶ T-1501 *et seq.*; ¶ 62,114 *et seq.*
38. ¶ T-1503.
39. ¶ T-3001; ¶ 62,109 *et seq.*
40. ¶ T-3006; ¶ 75,224.
41. ¶ T-3027; ¶ 76,557.
42. ¶ V-5502; ¶s 62,009, 62,134.
43. ¶ T-3646; ¶ 66,014.01.
44. ¶ V-2753; ¶ 66,654.

Footnote references beginning with letters are to paragraphs in RIA's Federal Tax Coordinator 2d and RIA's Analysis of Federal Taxes: Income. Footnote references beginning with numbers are to paragraphs in RIA's United States Tax Reporter.

an abusive tax shelter (¶ 4881) or for aiding and abetting a tax understatement (¶ 4878). Taxpayer may delay collection of these penalties by paying at least 15% of the penalty and filing a claim for refund of it, within 30 days of notice and demand for payment. If IRS denies the claim, taxpayer has 30 days to sue for refund in a district court (where IRS may counterclaim for the unpaid penalty amount). The normal procedures also don't apply to the penalty for filing a frivolous return (¶ 4885). (Code Sec. 6703(b), (c))[45]

¶ 4824 Jeopardy assessment and termination of a tax year.

If IRS believes assessment or collection of a deficiency will be jeopardized by delay, it can immediately assess the deficiency (plus any interest and penalties) and demand payment ("jeopardy assessment"). (Code Sec. 6861(a); Reg § 301.6861-1(a)) However, within 60 days after making the assessment, IRS must issue taxpayer a 90-day letter if it hasn't already done so. (Code Sec. 6861(b))[46]

IRS can presume the collection of income tax is in jeopardy if an individual who has physical possession of more than $10,000 in cash (or cash equivalents such as coins, precious metals or stones, jewelry, postage stamps), (Code Sec. 6867(d)(1); Reg § 301.6867-1T(b)) denies ownership of it and doesn't claim that it belongs to another identifiable person who acknowledges ownership. (Code Sec. 6867(a)) In that case, the entire amount of the cash is presumed to represent taxable income of the possessor for the year and is taxable at the highest individual tax rate (¶ 1101). (Code Sec. 6867(b))[47]

IRS can also terminate a tax year and demand immediate payment of income taxes for the current and preceding year, if it finds that taxpayer plans to leave (or remove his property from) the U.S. quickly, conceal himself or his property in the U.S., or do any other act that would prejudice the collection of those taxes ("termination assessment"). Within 60 days after the due date (with extensions) of taxpayer's return for the full tax year or, if later, the date the return is actually filed, IRS must issue a 90-day letter to taxpayer for the full year. (Code Sec. 6851(a), Code Sec. 6852(a))[48]

¶ 4825 Immediate assessments in bankruptcy proceedings, etc.

IRS *must* "immediately assess" income, estate and gift taxes (together with any interest and penalties), regardless of whether it issued a 90-day letter, where:

■ taxpayer is adjudicated bankrupt in any liquidation proceeding,

■ taxpayer files a petition, or a petition is filed against taxpayer, in any other bankruptcy proceeding, or

■ a receiver for taxpayer is appointed in a receivership proceeding. (Code Sec. 6871)[49]

¶ 4826 General three-year statute of limitations on assessments.

Generally, all taxes must be assessed:

■ within three years after the date the return was filed (below), or

■ if the tax is payable by stamp, within three years after the date any part of the tax was paid. (Code Sec. 6501(a))[50]

A return filed before the filing deadline is considered filed on the due date. (Code Sec. 6501(b)(1))[1] But a return of tax withheld from wages or withheld at source for any period ending with or within a calendar year, if filed before Apr. 15 of the next calendar year, is considered filed *on* Apr. 15. (Code Sec. 6501(b)(2); Reg § 301.6501(b)-1(b))[2]

Where an S corporation shareholder's return is being examined with respect to Subchapter S items (not subject to the unified audit procedures at ¶ 4842), the filing of the shareholder's return triggers the start of the three-year assessment period, not the filing

45. ¶ T-3500 *et seq.*; ¶ 67,034.   47. ¶ T-3731; ¶ 68,674.   49. ¶ T-3800 *et seq.*; ¶ 68,714.   1. ¶ T-4002; ¶ 65,014.09.
46. ¶ T-3700 *et seq.*; ¶ 68,614   48. ¶ T-3717 *et seq.*; ¶ 68,514.   50. ¶ T-4001; ¶ 65,014.   2. ¶ T-4010; ¶ 65,014.09.
    et seq.

Footnote references beginning with letters are to paragraphs in RIA's Federal Tax Coordinator 2d and RIA's Analysis of Federal Taxes: Income. Footnote references beginning with numbers are to paragraphs in RIA's United States Tax Reporter.

of the S corporation's return.[3]

The assessment period for a late-filed return starts on the day after the actual filing, whether the late filing is due to taxpayer's delinquency, or under a filing extension granted by IRS. (Code Sec. 6501(a))[4]

If within 60 days before the limitations period expires, IRS receives an amended return that shows an increase in tax liability, IRS has 60 days from the receipt to assess the additional tax. (Code Sec. 6501(c)(7))[5]

¶ 4827   Expiration of the limitations period as a bar to assessment.

A taxpayer who claims that the assessment of a tax is barred by the expiration of the limitations period must raise the issue and has the burden of proof.[6]

¶ 4828   Six-year assessment period.

Over-25% omissions. The assessment period is six years for income tax (or estate, gift or excise tax) returns that omit from gross income (or gross estate, total gifts made in the return period, or excise tax) more than 25% of the gross income (or gross estate, total gifts or excise tax) that is reported. But these "omissions" don't include amounts for which adequate information is given on the return or attached statements. (Code Sec. 6501(e))[7]

Personal holding company tax on a personal holding company (PHC) that didn't file a PHC schedule with its income tax return may be assessed within six years after the income tax return was filed. (Code Sec. 6501(f))[8]

¶ 4829   When assessment period remains open.

The assessment period is open indefinitely where taxpayer:

■ fails to file a required return, (Code Sec. 6501(c)(3)) but the assessment period starts to run where a trust or partnership return was filed by a taxpayer later held to be a corporation (Code Sec. 6501(g)(1)) or where an exempt organization return was filed by an organization later held to be taxable; (Code Sec. 6501(g)(2))[9]

■ files a false or fraudulent income, gift or estate tax return with intent to evade tax (Code Sec. 6501(c)(1))[10] (and the filing of a later amended, nonfraudulent return won't starting the normal three-year assessment period running);[11]

■ willfully attempts in any manner to defeat and evade taxes; (Code Sec. 6501(c)(2))[12]

■ fails to pay any part of a tax required to be paid by stamp; (Code Sec. 6501(a); Reg § 301.6501(a)-1)[13]

■ for gift tax, fails to show or adequately disclose any gift of property (or increase in taxable gifts) whose value is determined under the special valuation rules. (Code Sec. 6501(c)(9))[14]

The penalties for promoting abusive tax shelters, or for aiding and abetting an understatement, can be assessed at any time,[15] as can the penalty (but not the tax) imposed on a return preparer for willful tax understatements. (Code Sec. 6696(a)).[16]

¶ 4830   Voluntary extension of the assessment period—Forms 872.

At any time *before* expiration of the assessment period, taxpayer and IRS can agree in writing (usually on one of the Form 872 series) to extend the assessment period (except for estate taxes). They can also enter into successive agreements further extending the limitation period. (Code Sec. 6501(c)(4))[17]

---

3. ¶ T-4021.1; ¶ 65,014.04.
4. ¶ T-4003; ¶s 65,014.01, 65,014.02.
5. ¶ T-4209; ¶ 65,014.28.
6. ¶ T-4029; ¶ 65,014.01.

7. ¶ T-4201 *et seq.*; ¶ 65,014.15.
8. ¶ T-4218.
9. ¶ T-4101 *et seq.*; ¶s 65,014.05, 65,014.06, 65,014.14.
10. ¶ T-4127; ¶ 65,014.13.

11. ¶ T-4209; ¶ 65,014.04.
12. ¶ T-4141; ¶ 65,014.13.
13. ¶ T-4122.
14. ¶ T-4147.

15. ¶s T-4125, T-4126.
16. ¶ T-4145.
17. ¶ T-4400 *et seq.*; ¶ 65,014.17 *et seq.*

Footnote references beginning with letters are to paragraphs in RIA's Federal Tax Coordinator 2d and RIA's Analysis of Federal Taxes: Income. Footnote references beginning with numbers are to paragraphs in RIA's United States Tax Reporter.

Restricted consent. There is also a restricted consent which postpones the close of the tax year with respect to an unsettled issue. It is used where some issues are resolved, but settlement of others must await the establishment of an IRS position through a court decision, etc., or where other equally meritorious circumstances exist.[18]

Indefinite consent. A taxpayer whose case is before the Appeals Office (¶ 4814) may be asked to execute Form 872-A. This is an indefinite extension which expires 90 days after the Appeals office either: (1) notifies taxpayer of its determination, or (2) receives notification from taxpayer (on Form 872-T) of his desire to terminate the extension.[19]

Special rules govern who can execute a consent.[20]

¶ 4831　Suspension of the assessment period.

IRS's issuance of a 90-day letter (¶ 4821) suspends the assessment period. It stops running as of the date of mailing, and doesn't resume until 60 days after: (1) the 90-day period (150-day period if the letter is addressed to a person outside the U.S.) if no petition is filed, or (2) the Tax Court's decision becomes final if a petition is filed. (Code Sec. 6503(a))[21]

Taxpayer's application for a Taxpayer Assistance Order (¶ 4811) also suspends the assessment period, up to the date the Ombudsman makes a decision. (Code Sec. 7811(d))[22]

For corporate returns, the issuance of a summons to determine the amount of tax ("designated summons") also suspends the assessment period, pending final resolution of its enforcement. (Code Sec. 6503(k))[23]

For effect of compromise, see ¶ 4819. For suspension during bankruptcy or receivership proceedings, see ¶ 4896.

¶ 4832　Request for prompt assessment—Form 4810.

The normal three-year assessment period can be cut to 18 months *at taxpayer's request* (use Form 4810) for an income tax return of a decedent or an estate, or for a return of a dissolved or dissolving corporation. (Code Sec. 6501(d))[24]

¶ 4833　Carrybacks to and carryovers from closed years.

A deficiency attributable to taxpayer's carryback of a net operating loss (NOL), capital loss, or business credit may be assessed at any time before expiration of the period applicable to the year the loss was sustained or the credit earned. (Code Sec. 6501(h), (j))[25] A deficiency attributable to a foreign tax credit carryback may be assessed up to one year after the credit year's assessment period expires. (Code Sec. 6501(i))[26]

Where a credit carryback results from the carryback of an NOL, capital loss or other credit carryback from a later year, a deficiency for the carryback year can be assessed at any time before the expiration of the period for the later year. (Code Sec. 6501(j))[27]

¶ 4834　Early discharge of executor's personal liability.

An executor or administrator can be discharged from personal liability for estate tax as early as nine months or less after the estate tax return is due (or filed, if later) if he makes a written request to IRS to determine the estate tax liability, and any tax determined to be due is paid (or a bond is posted if the payment period was extended). (Code Sec. 2204(a))[28] A trustee or other fiduciary can get a similar discharge. (Code Sec. 2204(b))[29]

An executor or administrator can also request (on Form 5495) early discharge from

---

18. ¶ T-4442.
19. ¶ T-4402.
20. ¶ T-4410 *et seq.*; ¶s 65,014.21, 65,014.22.
21. ¶ T-4300 *et seq.*; ¶ 65,034.01.

22. ¶ T-4323; ¶ 78,114.
23. ¶ T-4332; ¶ 65,034.04.
24. ¶ T-4500 *et seq.*; ¶ 65,014.16.
25. ¶ T-4033; ¶ 65,014.28.

26. ¶ T-4041; ¶ 65,014.28.
27. ¶ T-4038; ¶ 65,014.28.
28. ¶s T-4511, T-4512; ¶ 22,044 (Estate & Gift).

29. ¶ T-4513; ¶ 22,044 (Estate & Gift).

Footnote references beginning with letters are to paragraphs in RIA's Federal Tax Coordinator 2d and RIA's Analysis of Federal Taxes: Income. Footnote references beginning with numbers are to paragraphs in RIA's United States Tax Reporter.

personal liability for a decedent's income and gift taxes. (Code Sec. 6905(a))[30]

¶ 4835　Mitigation of statute of limitations.

Generally, after the period for assessment or refund has run, IRS can't make an assessment and taxpayer can't get a refund. But an otherwise closed year may be reopened under the Code's "mitigation" provisions under certain circumstances. (Code Sec. 1311, Code Sec. 1312, Code Sec. 1313)[31]

¶ 4836　Judicial relief from the limitations periods.

Relief from the limitation periods may be available in the district court or Claims Court if the statutory mitigation conditions aren't met, under equitable recoupment (closed year's overpayment or underpayment used to offset open year's deficiency or refund),[32] estoppel[33] or election.[34]

¶ 4837　Unified Audit and Review for Partnerships and S Corporations ▬▬▬

IRS generally can't adjust partnership or S corporation items on a partner's or S corporation shareholder's return except through a unified entity-level proceeding.

¶ 4838　Unified audit and review procedure for partnerships and partners.

If the treatment of a "partnership item" on the partner's return is consistent with its treatment on the partnership return (under the rules described at ¶ 3720 et seq.), IRS generally cannot adjust the partner's treatment (other than to make computational adjustments) except through a partnership-level proceeding. Nor may the partner put partnership items at issue in a proceeding relating to nonpartnership items (on the partner's return). (Code Sec. 6221; Reg § 301.6221-1T(a), Reg § 301.6222(b)-2T(a)) The unified partnership-level determination binds all of the partners (as to partnership items), and permits IRS to make corresponding adjustments on the partners' returns. (Code Sec. 6225)[35]

No assessment of a deficiency attributable to any partnership item may be made before the end of the 150th day after IRS issues a notice of final partnership administrative adjustment (FPAA, see ¶ 4840) to the tax matters partner (TMP, see ¶ 4839) or, if the TMP files a Tax Court petition during that 150-day period, before the Tax Court decision becomes final. (Code Sec. 6225(a))[36] However, IRS can make an earlier assessment in certain abusive tax shelter situations. (Reg § 301.6231(c)-1T)[37]

The above rules apply to any partnership (other than certain small partnerships, see ¶ 4841) required to file a partnership return (Form 1065), and to any entity that, for the year it filed a partnership return, either wasn't a partnership or wasn't in existence for the full year. (Code Sec. 6231(a)(1), Code Sec. 6233)[38] A REMIC (¶ 4204) is treated as a partnership for these purposes. (Code Sec. 860F(e))[39]

The unified proceedings usually begin when IRS notifies the partnership that its return has been selected for audit. Or the TMP may file (use Form 8082) an "administrative adjustment request" (AAR) for the partnership. The AAR is treated as a substituted return (correcting errors) or a claim for refund. (Code Sec. 6227(a)).[40]

¶ 4839　Tax matters partner (TMP).

The partnership's tax matters partner (TMP) acts on behalf of the partners in the unified partnership proceedings. The TMP is the general partner the partnership designates as such on its return (Form 1065) (Form 1066, for a REMIC). (Code

---

30. ¶ T-4518; ¶ 69,054.
31. ¶ T-5000 et seq.; ¶ 13,134.
32. ¶ T-5200 et seq.; ¶ 65,144.

33. ¶ T-5300 et seq.; ¶ 74,338.400 et seq.
34. ¶ T-5400 et seq.; ¶ 74,338.424.

35. ¶ T-2500 et seq.; ¶ 62,214.
36. ¶ T-2593.
37. ¶ T-6517.

38. ¶ T-2501; ¶ 62,214.
39. ¶ E-6927; ¶ 860A4.04.
40. ¶ T-2552.

Footnote references beginning with letters are to paragraphs in RIA's Federal Tax Coordinator 2d and RIA's Analysis of Federal Taxes: Income. Footnote references beginning with numbers are to paragraphs in RIA's United States Tax Reporter.

Sec. 6231(a)(7)(A); Reg § 301.6231(a)(7)-1(c)(1)) If no designation is made, the TMP is the general partner with the largest profits interest in the partnership at the end of the tax year. (Code Sec. 6231(a)(7)(B)) The other partners must receive notice from the TMP of both IRS's and the TMP's actions. (Code Sec. 6223(g); Reg § 301.6223(g)-1T(b)(3))[41]

¶ 4840 Final partnership administrative adjustment (FPAA).

If after auditing the partnership IRS concludes that adjustments to the return are needed, it will issue a "final partnership administrative adjustment" (FPAA), which must be sent to the TMP and to "notice partners" IRS knows are eligible to receive notice. (Code Sec. 6223(a))[42] The TMP has 90 days from when the FPAA was mailed to file a petition for judicial review of the FPAA. (Code Sec. 6226(a)) If the TMP doesn't file within that time, any notice partner can file the partnership petition within the next 60 days. (Code Sec. 6226(b)(1)) Detailed procedures govern the conduct of the partnership-level proceeding, (Code Sec. 6224; Reg § 301.6224(a)-1T, Reg § 301.6224(c)-3T)[43] assessments, (Code Sec. 6225, Code Sec. 6229; Reg § 301.6229(b)-1T) judicial review of FPAAs (Code Sec. 6226, Code Sec. 6228; Reg § 301.6226(a)-1T, Reg § 301.6226(f)-1T) and other matters.[44]

observation: The notice of FPAA has the same effect as a 90-day letter (¶ 4821).

¶ 4841 Exception for certain small partnerships.

The unified partnership rules at ¶ 4838 *et seq.* don't apply to certain partnerships with ten or fewer partners who are natural persons (other than nonresident aliens) or estates at any time during the partnership tax year, but only if each partner's share of each partnership item is the same as his share of every other partnership item. (Code Sec. 6231(a)(1)(B))[45]

However, the partnership may elect to be subject to the rules. (Code Sec. 6231(a)(1)(B); Reg § 301.6231(a)(1)-1T(a)(1))[46] To elect, attach a statement (specified in the regs) to the partnership return for the first tax year for which the election is be effective. (Reg § 301.6231(a)(1)-1T(b))[47]

¶ 4842 Unified audit and review procedure for S corporations.

If the treatment of a Subchapter S item on the S corporation's shareholder's return is consistent with how the item is treated on the S corporation return (under the rules ¶ 3359 *et seq.*), IRS generally can't adjust the shareholder's treatment of that item except through a corporate-level proceeding. Nor may the shareholder put a Subchapter S item in issue in a proceeding relating to non-Subchapter S items. (Code Sec. 6241; Reg § 301.6241-1T(a))[48] IRS may not assess or collect any deficiency attributable to a Subchapter S item until the unified proceeding is completed. (Code Sec. 6244(1)(A))[49]

The partnership audit provisions (¶ 4838 *et seq.*) also apply to the treatment of Subchapter S items, except to the extent modified or made inapplicable by regs. (Code Sec. 6244)[50]

Shareholders of an S corporation are to be notified of and can participate in any administrative or judicial proceedings for the determination at the corporate level of the tax treatment of any Subchapter S item. (Code Sec. 6243)[1]

A "tax matters person," designated by the S corporation on its Form 1120S, acts on the corporation's behalf, in the way the TMP acts for a partnership.[2]

These rules don't apply to small S corporations—those with five or fewer shareholders, each of whom is a natural person or an estate, and none of whom is a pass-through

41. ¶ T-2546.
42. ¶ T-2534 *et seq.*
43. ¶ T-2534 *et seq.*
44. ¶ T-2565 *et seq.*
45. ¶ T-2500 *et seq.*; ¶ 62,214.
46. ¶ T-2505; ¶ 62,214.
47. ¶ T-2505.
48. ¶ T-2600 *et seq.*; ¶ 62,414.
49. ¶ T-2610.
50. ¶ T-2610; ¶ 62,414.
1. ¶ T-2609; ¶ 62,434.
2. ¶ T-2611.

Footnote references beginning with letters are to paragraphs in RIA's Federal Tax Coordinator 2d and RIA's Analysis of Federal Taxes: Income. Footnote references beginning with numbers are to paragraphs in RIA's United States Tax Reporter.

shareholder (trust, nominal or similar pass-through entity)—unless the corporation elects to have them apply. To elect, attach a statement (specified in the regs) to the S corporation's return for the first tax year for which the election is to apply. (Reg § 301.6241-1T(c)(2))[3]

¶ 4843 Refunds; Tax Litigation

A taxpayer who pays more than his correct tax liability can recover the overpayment as a credit or a refund by following the proper procedures for filing a claim or bringing suit. If a 90-day letter has been issued, taxpayer can go to Tax Court without first paying the disputed tax.

¶ 4844 Overpayments.

An overpayment is the excess of the amount paid as tax over taxpayer's correct tax liability. It also includes the part of a correct tax paid after the applicable assessment period has run. (Code Sec. 6401)[4]

An overpayment may be recovered as a refund or credit, generally only by the taxpayer who paid the tax. However, IRS may first credit the overpayment (including interest) against *any* of taxpayer's past due tax liability (including interest, additions, penalties) (Code Sec. 6402(a), Reg § 301.6402-3(a)(5)) and nontax debts (¶ 4845).[5]

Electronic filers may elect (on Form 8453) to have their refunds deposited directly into their bank accounts.[6]

A refund may be claimed on behalf of a deceased taxpayer by attaching Form 1310 (not needed for surviving spouse filing jointly with decedent) to the refund claim (¶ 4846).[7]

¶ 4845 Overpayments applied to child support and other nontax debts.

If a state notifies IRS that taxpayer owes any child support payments, IRS must first apply taxpayer's overpayment (including earned income amounts) to those past-due obligations, before making any refund or credit. (Code Sec. 6402(c))[8] If a federal agency notifies IRS of any past-due, legally enforceable nontax debt taxpayer owes the agency, IRS must apply the balance (i.e., after the child support offset) of taxpayer's overpayment to that nontax debt. IRS must give taxpayer a Notice of Offset (CP47), which gives the agency's address and phone number. (Code Sec. 6402(d); Reg § 301.6402-6)[9]

In the case of a *joint* overpayment, the spouse not liable for the past-due support or nontax debt (the "injured spouse"), can file Form 8379 as an attachment to Form 1040X (amended return) so IRS can allocate the refund properly. (Reg § 301.6402-6(i)(2))[10]

¶ 4846 Refund claim.

A timely (¶ 4852) written claim must be filed for taxpayer to get a refund. For income, gift and federal unemployment taxes, a separate claim must be made for each tax year or period. (Reg § 301.6402-2(a), (d))[11] Official forms are:

■ Form 1040X (amended U.S. individual income tax return). (Use Forms 1040, 1040A, or 1040-EZ *only* for refund of overwithheld taxes or excess estimated taxes.) (Reg § 301.6402-3(a)(2), Reg § 301.6402-4)

■ Form 1120 or Form 1120X (original or amended corporate income tax return). (Reg § 301.6402-3(a)(2))

■ Amended returns for taxpayers who filed a form other than Form 1040, 1040A, 1040-EZ or 1120 (e.g., a fiduciary tax return). (Reg § 301.6402-3(a)(4))

3. ¶s T-2602, T-2603; ¶ 62,414.
4. ¶ T-5500 *et seq.*
5. ¶s T-5600 *et seq.*, T-5700 *et seq.*

6. ¶ T-5610.
7. ¶ T-5710.
8. ¶ T-6012 *et seq.*; ¶ 64,024.26.

9. ¶ T-6023 *et seq.*; ¶ 64,024.23.
10. ¶ T-6041; ¶s 64,024.23, 64,024.26.

11. ¶ T-6702; ¶s 64,024, 64,024.08.

Footnote references beginning with letters are to paragraphs in RIA's Federal Tax Coordinator 2d and RIA's Analysis of Federal Taxes: Income. Footnote references beginning with numbers are to paragraphs in RIA's United States Tax Reporter.

- Form 843 for refunds of taxes other than income taxes. (Reg § 601.105(e)(1))[12]

For use of a form in the 870 or 890 series (waiver of restrictions on assessment) as a refund claim, see ¶s 4813, 4817.

¶ 4847 Quick refund for carrybacks and claim of right—Form 1045; Form 1139.

A taxpayer who reports a carryback of a net operating loss (NOL), business credit or capital loss on his return can quickly recover a refund based on the carryback by filing Form 1045 (individuals) or Form 1139 (corporations) *on or after* the date the return for the loss or credit year is filed, and within 12 months after the end of the tax year *from which* the carryback is made. (Code Sec. 6411(a))[13] This procedure also applies to overpayments attributable to a "claim of right" adjustment (see ¶ 2863 *et seq.*), where the amount of repayment in any one year exceeds $3,000. (Code Sec. 6411(d))[14]

IRS has 90 days from the later of the date the claim is filed or the last day of the month the loss year return is due (with extensions), to make any credit or refund. (Code Sec. 6411(b))[15]

IRS's determination is tentative. If the claim is rejected, taxpayer can't sue but must first file a standard refund claim. (Reg § 1.6411-3(c)) Even if IRS grants the refund, it can later examine the loss year return and the application. IRS may assess any portion of the refund it determines to be excessive, without issuing a 90-day letter. (Code Sec. 6213(b)(3))[16]

¶ 4848 Quick refunds of corporate estimated tax overpayments—Form 4466.

A corporation that has overpaid its estimated tax (¶ 3351 *et seq.*) can get a refund within 45 days after filing an application (on Form 4466). (Code Sec. 6425(b)(1), (2)) The Form must be filed *after* the close of the corporation's tax year and *on or before* the 15th day of the third month after the end of the year (or before the corporation first files its income tax return for that year, if earlier). (Code Sec. 6425(a)(1)) To qualify for the quick refund, the corporation's estimated tax overpayment must be at least 10% of its revised expected annual tax, *and* at least $500. (Code Sec. 6425(b)(3)) If the refund is excessive, an addition to tax equal to the underpayment interest rate (¶ 4862) times the excessive amount is imposed. (Code Sec. 6655(h))[17]

¶ 4849 Refunds resulting from retroactive changes under the '93 Revenue Reconciliation Act.

As we went to press, IRS had issued guidance to assist taxpayers entitled to refunds of taxes paid on returns filed for '92 (or withheld in '93), as a result of the following retroactive changes made by the '93 Revenue Reconciliation Act:

Reinstatement of self-employed health insurance deduction. Taxpayers should file an amended return (Form 1040X) to get a refund of '92 income taxes because of the retroactive reinstatement of the 25% health insurance deduction for self-employed individuals (¶ 1528), which expired as of June 30, '92. To claim this deduction for the second half of '92, use the worksheet in the '92 Form 1040 Instructions, using the full-year payment instead of the half-year payment, and 100% instead of 50%.

Repeal of AMT preference for appreciated charitable gifts. Taxpayers who included the preference for appreciated charitable gifts (¶ 3207) in computing their '92 alternative minimum tax may be entitled to a refund because the '93 Act repealed the preference for gifts of tangible personal property after June 30, '92 and gifts of intangibles and real property after Dec. 31, '92. Taxpayers should refigure their tax and claim any resulting refund by filing Form 1040X.

Extension of exclusion for educational assistance benefits through '94. Employees whose

---

12. ¶ T-6707 *et seq.*; ¶ 64,009 (Estate & Gift), ¶ 64,024 (Excise).
13. ¶ T-6501 *et seq.*; ¶ 64,114.
14. ¶ T-6522; ¶ 64,114.
15. ¶ T-6509; ¶ 64,114.
16. ¶ T-6513; ¶ 62,134.02.
17. ¶ T-6600 *et seq.*; ¶s 64,254, 66,554.

Footnote references beginning with letters are to paragraphs in RIA's Federal Tax Coordinator 2d and RIA's Analysis of Federal Taxes: Income. Footnote references beginning with numbers are to paragraphs in RIA's United States Tax Reporter.

employers withheld federal income, social security and/or medicare taxes on educational assistance benefits (the exclusion for which had expired as of June 30, '92, see ¶ 1258) provided in the second half of '92 or in '93 may get a refund of '92 income taxes on the excludible amount of those benefits by filing a Form 1040X (write "1992 tax year" and "IRC 127" at the top), attaching a Form W-2c which he must get from his employer. An employee whose Form W-2c shows corrected wages of $22,370 or less for '92 and who qualifies for an earned income credit (¶ 2338) should attach a completed '92 schedule EIC to the Form 1040X (unless he has already received the earned income credit for '92 in which case IRS will automatically recalculate the credit and make the appropriate adjustments). Employees whose employers won't refund their overpaid '92 and '93 social security and medicare taxes should file Form 843 with IRS, writing "IRC 127" at the top.

Employers who refund overwithheld social security and medicare taxes to their employees may be able to reduce their federal tax liability and deposits for both the employer and employee portions of these taxes (¶ 1746). Adjustments should be reported on Form 941, and explained on Form 941c. If instead an employer wants to claim a refund, it should file Form 843, writing "IRC 127" in the top margin to speed processing.

¶ 4850 Protective refund claims.

Protective refund claims are regular refund claims (using the regular forms, see ¶ 4846) filed merely to keep a particular claim alive. It's generally used where IRS has a settled view adverse to the taxpayer on an issue being litigated by other taxpayers. A protective refund claim is usually filed just before the refund claim period expires. It will keep the taxpayer's claim alive (i.e., protect his right to sue) for the additional period from the date of filing to the date of rejection plus the refund suit period.[18]

¶ 4851 Interest on overpayments.

Interest on overpayments is allowed. (Code Sec. 6611(a)) The interest (compounded daily) runs from the date of the overpayment (below) to a date not more than 30 days before the refund is made (or to the (unextended) return due date for the amount against which the overpayment is credited). (Code Sec. 6611(b))[19]

But no interest is payable on a refund arising from an original income tax return (income, employment, excise, estate or gift tax return, for returns due, disregarding extensions, after '93) made within 45 days after the later of the due date of the return (disregarding extensions) or the date the return was filed. (Code Sec. 6611(e)(1); Reg § 301.6611-1(g))[20] With respect to returns filed after the due date (with extensions), no interest is payable for the period preceding the actual filing date. (Code Sec. 6611(b)(3))[21] And, no interest is payable on an estate's overpayment unless it shows that the interest (and refund) won't escheat to the state. (Code Sec. 6408)[22] IRS also won't pay interest when it refunds a conditional or advance payment of taxes.[23]

If a refund arising from an amended return or refund claim filed after '94 (regardless of the tax period) is issued within 45 days, no interest is payable for that up-to-45 day period. (Code Sec. 6611(e)(2))[24] If a refund (credit) from an adjustment initiated by IRS is paid after '94 (regardless of the tax period involved), the interest period is reduced by 45 days. (Code Sec. 6611(e)(3))[25]

The overpayment rates are:[26]

- 6% (Oct. 1, '92—Dec. 31, '93)
- 7% (Apr. 1, '92—Sept. 30, '92)
- 8% (Jan. 1, '92—Mar. 31, '92)

---

18. ¶ T-6742; ¶ 64,024.17.   20. ¶ T-8024; ¶ 66,114.   23. ¶ T-8044; ¶ 66,114.   25. ¶ T-8026.3.
19. ¶s T-8008, T-8029, T-8032;   21. ¶ T-8011; ¶ 66,114.   24. ¶ T-8026.1.   26. ¶ T-8003.
   ¶ 66,114.   22. ¶s T-8061, T-8063; ¶ 64,084.

Footnote references beginning with letters are to paragraphs in RIA's Federal Tax Coordinator 2d and RIA's Analysis of Federal Taxes: Income. Footnote references beginning with numbers are to paragraphs in RIA's United States Tax Reporter.

■ 9% (Apr. 1, '91—Dec. 31, '91)

■ 10% (Oct. 1, '89—Mar. 31, '91)

The overpayment date for taxes withheld or paid as estimated taxes is the unextended due date of the return. (Code Sec. 6513(b))[27]

Overpayments resulting from the carryback of an NOL, net capital loss, business credit, or foreign tax credit, are considered not to have been made before the "filing date" for the tax year in which the loss or credit arose or the foreign tax was in fact paid or accrued. (Code Sec. 6611(f)(1), (2), (g))[28] Similarly, where a business credit carryback is attributable to an NOL, etc., carryback from a later year, the overpayment is considered not to have been made before the filing date for that later year. (Code Sec. 6611(f)(2)(A))[29]

¶ 4852 Deadline for refund claims.

A claim for credit or refund of a tax paid by *return* must be filed within the later of: (1) three years from the date the return was filed (or the due date if filed earlier), or (2) two years from the date the tax was paid. If the required return wasn't filed, the claim must be filed within two years from when the tax was paid. Stamp tax claims must be filed within three years from when the tax was paid. (Code Sec. 6511(a))[30]

However, a longer refund claim period applies in these cases:

■ If taxpayer and IRS execute one of the Form 872 series extending the assessment period, the claim can be filed within six months after the expiration of the extended assessment period. (Code Sec. 6511(c)(1))[31]

■ For an overpayment resulting from carryback of an NOL, net capital loss, or business credit, the period expires three years after the time the return is due (including extensions) for the year the loss or credit arose, not the year to which it is carried back. (Code Sec. 6511(d)(2), (4))[32] If the overpayment is attributable to a carryback from a later year, the period expires three years after the time for filing the return (including extensions) for that later year. (Code Sec. 6511(d)(4))[33]

■ For an overpayment resulting from the payment or accrual of foreign taxes for which a foreign tax credit is allowed, the claim period is extended to ten years. (Code Sec. 6511(d)(3))[34]

■ For an overpayment resulting from a bad debt or from worthless securities, the claim period is extended to seven years. (Code Sec. 6511(d)(1))[35]

¶ 4853 Refund suit period.

Taxpayer *must* file a refund claim with IRS before starting a suit for refund (or credit). (Code Sec. 7422(a))[36] The refund suit can't be started *before* six months from filing the claim (unless IRS acts on the claim within that period), or *after* two years from the date IRS mails a notice of disallowance. (Code Sec. 6532(a)(1)) Taxpayer can waive (on Form 2297) issuance of this notice and the two-year period will start on the date the waiver is filed. (Code Sec. 6532(a)(3)) Also, taxpayer and IRS can execute a Form 907 and extend the two-year period. (Code Sec. 6532(a)(2))[37]

A taxpayer who wants to file suit as soon as possible, and whose refund claim is based solely on contested income, estate or gift tax issues considered in previously examined returns, can request in writing that the refund claim be immediately rejected. A notice of claim disallowance will then be promptly sent to the taxpayer.[38]

27. ¶ T-7530; ¶s 66,114, 65,134.
28. ¶ T-8047 *et seq.*; ¶ 66,114.
29. ¶ T-8049; ¶ 66,114.
30. ¶ T-7501; ¶ 65,114,01.

31. ¶ T-7574; ¶ 65,114.09.
32. ¶ T-7554; ¶s 65,114.11, 65,114.13.

33. ¶ T-7563; ¶ 65,114.13.
34. ¶ T-7569; ¶ 65,114.12.
35. ¶ T-7552; ¶ 65,114.10.

36. ¶ T-6701; ¶ 74,224.
37. ¶ T-9034; ¶ 65,324.01.
38. ¶ T-9017.

Footnote references beginning with letters are to paragraphs in RIA's Federal Tax Coordinator 2d and RIA's Analysis of Federal Taxes: Income. Footnote references beginning with numbers are to paragraphs in RIA's United States Tax Reporter.

¶ 4854 Limits on amount of refund.

If a claim is filed within three years from the time the return was filed, the credit or refund is limited to the portion of tax paid during the three years (plus the period of any filing extension) immediately preceding the filing of the claim. (Code Sec. 6511(b)(2)(A))[39]

If the claim was not filed within the three-year period, the refund or credit is limited to the portion of the tax paid during the two years immediately preceding the filing of the claim. (Code Sec. 6511(b)(2)(B)) This two-year limitation also applies if a claim, but no return, was filed. (Reg § 301.6511(b)-1(b)(1)(iii))[40]

Where no claim is filed and a credit or refund is allowed within three years from the time the return was filed, the credit or refund is limited to the portion of the tax paid during the three years immediately before the allowance. If the credit or refund is not allowed within that three-year period, it is limited to the portion of the tax paid during the two years immediately before the allowance. (Code Sec. 6511(b)(2)(C))[41]

¶ 4855 Tax litigation.

A taxpayer may go to:

■ the Tax Court to set aside a deficiency determined by IRS; (Code Sec. 6214(a))[42]

■ a U.S. district court or the U.S. Court of Federal Claims to recover an overpayment of taxes (after filing refund claim); (Code Sec. 6532(a))[43]

■ the Tax Court, the district court for the DC Circuit or the Claims Court for a declaratory judgment on the tax status of a charity or foundation; (Code Sec. 7428(a))[44]

■ the Tax Court for a declaratory judgment on retirement plan qualification; (Code Sec. 7476(a))[45]

■ a district court to enjoin IRS from assessing and collecting a tax in certain cases (¶ 4893), or to get damages for IRS's unauthorized collection activities or failure to release a lien. (Code Sec. 7432, Code Sec. 7433)[46]

Taxpayers who prevail against the U.S. in court (or at the administrative level) may be awarded reasonable litigation and administrative costs (including the costs of getting the award). (Code Sec. 7430)[47]

¶ 4856 The Tax Court.

To get Tax Court review of a deficiency, taxpayer must file a petition with the Tax Court at Washington, D.C., in response to a notice of deficiency (90-day letter, see ¶ 4821) issued by IRS. The petition must be filed within 90 days (150 days if the notice is addressed to a person outside the U.S.) after the notice is mailed (i.e., postmarked). (Code Sec. 6213)[48]

The Tax Court's jurisdiction is limited to the review (without a jury) of deficiencies asserted by IRS. It can order payment of a refund if it determines that taxpayer made an overpayment. (Code Sec. 6512(b)) But it can't grant equitable relief.[49]

¶ 4857 Settlement after Tax Court petition filed.

IRS District Counsel will refer all docketed Tax Court cases to the Appeals Division for consideration of settlement (unless Appeals issued the deficiency notice, in which case there will be no referral if there is little likelihood that all or part of the case can be

39. ¶ T-7537; ¶ 65,114.07.
40. ¶s T-7546, T-7547;
   ¶ 65,114.07.
41. ¶ T-7548; ¶ 65,114.07.
42. ¶ U-2100 et seq.; ¶s 62,144
   et seq., 74,414 et seq.

43. ¶ U-4000 et seq.; ¶ 74,224
   et seq.
44. ¶s U-3800 et seq., U-4115;
   ¶ 74,284.

45. ¶ U-3700 et seq.; ¶ 74,764.
46. ¶s V-5801, V-6113; ¶s 74,209,
   74,324, 74,334.
47. ¶ U-1250 et seq.; ¶ 74,304.

48. ¶ U-2300 et seq.; ¶s 62,134
   et seq., 74,424 et seq.
49. ¶ U-2101; ¶s 65,124, 74,424,
   74,536.

Footnote references beginning with letters are to paragraphs in RIA's Federal Tax Coordinator 2d and RIA's Analysis of Federal Taxes: Income. Footnote references beginning with numbers are to paragraphs in RIA's United States Tax Reporter.

settled in a reasonable period of time). Counsel and Appeals can agree otherwise, work together, or transfer the case back and forth to promote efficient disposition of the case. The taxpayer-petitioner and/or his representative will be notified as to who has the case and the settlement authority.[50]

If taxpayer and IRS agree on a settlement, they enter into a written agreement stipulating the amount of any deficiency or overpayment. This stipulation is filed with the Tax Court which will enter a decision in accordance with it. (Reg § 601.106(d)(3)(i))[1]

¶ 4858 Small tax claims in Tax Court.

Special informal procedures apply, at taxpayer's election and with the Tax Court's concurrence, to any Tax Court case where the amount (including any additions to tax, additional amounts and penalties) of the deficiency disputed or of any claimed overpayment exceeds $10,000. Taxpayer thus gets the court's decision faster and more easily, but gives up the right to appeal. (Code Sec. 7463)[2] Where a deficiency exceeds $10,000, the taxpayer can concede enough to bring it down to that threshold.[3]

¶ 4859 Appeals from Tax Court, district court and U.S. Claims Court.

Decisions of the Tax Court and U.S. district courts are appealable to the U.S. Court of Appeals.[4] The appeal is made generally in the circuit where taxpayer's legal residence (for appeals from Tax Court)[5] or the trial court (for appeals from district courts) is located.[6] U.S. Court of Federal Claims decisions may be appealed to the Court of Appeals for the Federal Circuit.[7]

Appeals from the U.S. Courts of Appeals are heard by the U.S. Supreme Court.[8]

¶ 4860 Interest and Penalties

Interest is charged on underpayments of tax. Various civil and criminal penalties may apply where taxpayer (or taxpayer's return preparer) violates the tax law.

¶ 4861 Interest on underpayments.

Interest is generally payable whenever any tax or civil penalty isn't paid when due, (Code Sec. 6601(a)) even if taxpayer has been granted an extension of time to pay the tax. (Code Sec. 6601(b)(1); Reg § 301.6601-1(a)) There is no interest on late payments of estimated tax (Code Sec. 6601(h)) (but there are comparable penalty computations, see ¶ 3155 (individuals) and ¶ 3357 (corporations)), or of unemployment tax. (Code Sec. 6601(i))[9]

¶ 4862 Interest rate.

Rate of interest on tax underpayments and penalties is keyed to the short-term federal rate for the previous calendar quarter, (Code Sec. 6621(a)(2)) and is compounded daily.[10] The rates (applicable federal rate (AFR) plus three percentage points) are:[11]

7% (Oct. 1, '92—Dec. 31, '93)

8% (Apr. 1, '92—Sept. 30, '92)

9% (Jan. 1, '92—Mar. 31, '92)

10% (Apr. 1, '91—Dec. 31, '91)

11% (Oct. 1, '89—Mar. 31, '91)

12% (Apr. 1, '89—Sept. 30, '89)

---

50. ¶ T-1901 *et seq.*; ¶ 76,557.
1. ¶ T-1909.
2. ¶ U-3600 *et seq.*; ¶ 74,536.1704.
3. ¶ U-3605.
4. ¶ U-5000 *et seq.*; ¶s 74,336.12, 74,824.
5. ¶ U-5202; ¶ 74,824.
6. ¶ V-5401.
7. ¶ U-6001; ¶ 74,336.10.
8. ¶s U-5600 *et seq.*, U-7000 *et seq.*; ¶ 74,336.15.
9. ¶ V-1000 *et seq.*; ¶s 66,014, 66,014.01.
10. ¶s V-1101, V-1104; ¶ 66,214.
11. ¶ V-1102.

Footnote references beginning with letters are to paragraphs in RIA's Federal Tax Coordinator 2d and RIA's Analysis of Federal Taxes: Income. Footnote references beginning with numbers are to paragraphs in RIA's United States Tax Reporter.

11% (Oct. 1, '88—Mar. 31, '89)

If a C corporation's tax underpayment for any tax period exceeds $100,000, a higher interest rate (AFR plus 5 percentage points) applies for the period after the 30th day following a notice (or proposed notice) of deficiency. (Code Sec. 6621(c)(3); Reg § 301.6621-3T)[12]

¶ 4863 Interest accrual period.

Interest on unpaid tax liabilities runs from the last day prescribed by the Code for payment (disregarding extensions or any installment payment agreement), (Code Sec. 6601(b)(1)) to the date paid. (Code Sec. 6601(a)) However, where the tax is paid within ten days after notice and demand, the interest stops on the date of the notice and demand. (Code Sec. 6601(e)(3))[13] (For "payments" that stop interest, see ¶ 4864.)

Also, where taxpayer consents to immediate assessment (by signing one of the Form 870 waiver of assessment series) and pays the tax assessed within ten days after notice and demand, interest stops on the 30th day after the waiver is filed, if that is earlier than the date of notice and demand. (Code Sec. 6601(c))[14]

Interest on civil penalties runs from the date of notice and demand if not paid within ten days after that date. (Code Sec. 6601(e)(2)(A)) However, for the penalties for failure to file, valuation misstatement (income tax) or understatement (estate or gift tax), substantial understatement of tax, negligence, and (except for returns due (without extension) before '89) fraud, the interest period begins on the *return* due date (including extensions). In either case, the interest stops on the date the penalty is paid. (Code Sec. 6601(e)(2)(B))[15]

¶ 4864 "Advance payments" to prepay and/or stop the running of interest.

A taxpayer whose return is being or has been audited by IRS may choose to pay, before receiving a 90-day letter, all or part of the underpayment IRS says is due. This payment will be treated as a payment of tax unless designated as a deposit. In either case, it will stop the interest from running.[16] But the taxpayer cannot go to Tax Court unless the payment is designated as a deposit.[17]

¶ 4865 How other year's tax payments affect interest.

Interest on a deficiency isn't eliminated when the deficiency is eliminated by a net operating loss (NOL), net capital loss or credit carryback. It accrues from its original due date to the filing date for the tax year in which the NOL, net capital loss or credit carryback arose (or, with respect to any portion of a credit carryback attributable to a carryback from a later year, to the filing date for that later year). (Code Sec. 6601(d))[18]

An underpayment of tax in one year may be paid by crediting against it an overpayment of tax in another year. (Code Sec. 6402(a)) No interest accrues on any portion of the underpayment so paid for any period after the return due date (*without* extension) for the overpayment year or, if later, when the offsetting return is filed. (Code Sec. 6601(f))[19]

Where an overpayment on a return is refunded or credited (e.g., against the next year's estimated tax), interest on a later-determined *underpayment* for the return runs from the date of the refund (if the original overpayment was refunded) or as of which the credit was effective.[20]

¶ 4866 Abatement of interest, penalties and additions to tax.

IRS has discretion to abate any interest that was assessed because of a deficiency attributable to any error or delay by an IRS officer or employer acting in his official

---

12. ¶ V-1106 *et seq.*; ¶ 66,214.
13. ¶ V-1200 *et seq.*; ¶ 66,014.02.
14. ¶ V-1307; ¶ 66,014.02.

15. ¶ V-1227; ¶ 66,014.02.
16. ¶ V-1306.

17. ¶ T-1555.
18. ¶ V-1302; ¶ 66,014.03.

19. ¶ V-1301; ¶ 66,014.03.
20. ¶ V-1211.

Footnote references beginning with letters are to paragraphs in RIA's Federal Tax Coordinator 2d and RIA's Analysis of Federal Taxes: Income. Footnote references beginning with numbers are to paragraphs in RIA's United States Tax Reporter.

capacity when performing a ministerial act, or that is due on a notice of deficiency to the extent any error or delay in payment is attributable to an IRS employee or officer being erroneous or dilatory in performing a ministerial act, but only if no significant aspect of the error or delay can be attributed to the taxpayer involved. (Code Sec. 6404(e)(1))[21]

IRS must abate any portion of any penalty or addition to tax attributable to erroneous written advice (as specifically defined) (Reg § 301.6404-3(c)(1)) furnished to a taxpayer by an IRS officer or employee acting in an official capacity in response to a specific written request. The taxpayer must have reasonably relied on the advice, (Code Sec. 6404(f)(1), (f)(2)(A)) and the portion of the penalty or addition to tax must not have resulted from taxpayer's failure to provide adequate or accurate information. (Code Sec. 6404(f)(2)(B))[22]

Make the abatement request on Form 843 (as annotated and with certain attachments as required by the regs). (Reg § 301.6404-3(d))[23]

¶ 4867 Failure to file income, estate or gift tax returns when due.

The penalty is 5% of amount of tax required to be shown on the return (less any earlier payments and credits) for the first month, (Code Sec. 6651(b)(1)) plus an additional 5% for each additional month (or fraction of a month), that the failure continues without reasonable cause, but not more than 25%. (Code Sec. 6651(a)(1))[24]

There's a minimum penalty for failure to file any income tax return within 60 days of the due date (including extensions), except if due to reasonable cause and not willful neglect. This minimum penalty is the lesser of $100 or the amount of tax required to be shown on the return. (Code Sec. 6651(a))[25]

The failure-to-file penalty (5%) is reduced (but not below the above minimum) by the amount of any failure-to-pay penalty (½%) for that month (¶ 4868). (Code Sec. 6651(c)(1)) The 25% ceiling is applied to each penalty before making this reduction.[26]

If the failure to file is fraudulent, the penalty is increased to 15% per month (or fraction of a month), up to a 75% maximum, but only for returns due after '89. (Code Sec. 6651(f))[27]

For failure to file partnership returns or other information returns, see ¶s 4884, 4885.

¶ 4868 Failure to pay tax.

A penalty is imposed on a taxpayer who, without reasonable cause, fails to pay the tax shown on a return or an assessed deficiency of that tax by the prescribed date. The penalty is ½% of tax shown (or assessed) for each month (or fraction of a month) that it isn't paid (but not more than 25%). (Code Sec. 6651(a)(2), (3))[28] The penalty is increased to 1% per month or fraction (up to 25% penalty maximum) if the tax isn't paid within ten days after IRS serves notice of levy. (Code Sec. 6651(d))[29]

An individual who gets an automatic extension of time for *filing* is subject to the penalty (absent reasonable cause) if any additional payment due with the extended return *either*: (1) exceeds 10% of the total shown on Form 1040, or (2) isn't paid by the extended filing date. (Reg § 301.6651-1(c)(3))[30]

For penalty for failure to pay estimated tax, see ¶ 3155 (individuals) and ¶ 3357 (corporations).

¶ 4869 Accuracy-related penalty.

A 20% "accuracy-related" civil penalty applies if any portion of an understatement of tax on a tax return is due (absent reasonable cause) to:

1. ¶s T-3919, T-3920.
2. ¶ T-3908 et seq..
3. ¶s T-3914 et seq., T-3925; ¶ 64,044.

24. ¶ V-1750 et seq.; ¶ 66,514.01.
25. ¶ V-1752; ¶ 66,514.01.
26. ¶ V-1781; ¶ 66,514.01.

27. ¶ V-1753; ¶ 66,514.01.
28. ¶ V-1658 et seq.; ¶ 66,514.01.

29. ¶ V-1666; ¶ 66,514.01.
30. ¶ V-1660.

Footnote references beginning with letters are to paragraphs in RIA's Federal Tax Coordinator 2d and RIA's Analysis of Federal Taxes: Income. Footnote references beginning with numbers are to paragraphs in RIA's United States Tax Reporter.

■ negligence (¶ 4870); or

■ substantial income tax valuation misstatements (¶ 4871), income tax understatements (¶ 4872), estate or gift tax valuation understatements (¶ 4874) or pension liability overstatements (¶ 4875). (Code Sec. 6662(a), (b), Code Sec. 6664(c)(1))[31]

The accuracy-related penalty doesn't apply to any portion of an underpayment for which the fraud penalty (¶ 4876) is imposed. (Code Sec. 6662(b))[32] Also, it only applies if the taxpayer files a return. (Code Sec. 6664(b))[33]

¶ 4870 Negligence.

The "accuracy-related" penalty is imposed if any part of an underpayment of tax is due either to negligence or to disregard of rules or regs but without intent to defraud. The penalty is 20% of the portion of the underpayment attributable to the negligence, etc. (Code Sec. 6662(a), (b)(1)) For rules common to all accuracy-related penalties, see ¶ 4869.

"Negligence" includes any failure to make a reasonable attempt to comply with the law or to exercise ordinary and reasonable care in preparing a tax return, as well as failure to keep adequate books and records or to substantiate items properly. "Disregard" includes any careless, reckless or intentional disregard. (Code Sec. 6662(c); Reg § 1.6662-3(b)(1))[34]

The failure by a taxpayer/payee to report properly on his own return an amount reported as paid to him by a payor on an information return is strong evidence that any portion of an underpayment attributable to that failure is negligent.[35]

¶ 4871 Misstating value or basis of property on income tax return.

The accuracy-related penalty is imposed on any taxpayer who makes any of these "substantial valuation misstatements": (Code Sec. 6662(b)(3))

■ any value (or adjusted basis) claimed on an income tax return that is 200% or more of the correct figure; (Code Sec. 6662(e)(1)(A))

■ Code Sec. 482 transfer price adjustments where the price for any property (or its use) or services on an income tax return is 200% or more, or 50% or less, of the correct figure; (Code Sec. 6662(e)(1)(B)(i))

■ a net increase in taxable income for a tax year (without regard to carryovers) resulting from all Code Sec. 482 adjustments in the transfer price of any property (or its use) or services, that (with certain adjustments) exceeds $10 million (exceeds the lesser of $5 million or 10% of taxpayer's gross receipts for tax years beginning after '93). (Code Sec. 6662(e)(1)(B)(ii), (e)(3))

The penalty equals 20%—40% if the above 200%, 50%, and $10 million ($5 million/10%) figures are, respectively, 400%, 25%, or $20 million ($20 million/20%)—of the portion of any income tax underpayment that results from the misstatement (except to the extent the fraud penalty is imposed). (Code Sec. 6662(a), (b), (h))[36]

The penalty doesn't apply unless the amount of the underpayment for the tax year attributable to all these overstatements for the year exceeds $5,000 ($10,000 for corporations other than S corporations or personal holding companies). (Code Sec. 6662(e)(2))[37]

A reasonable basis on which taxpayer in good faith relied excuses the penalty. (Code Sec. 6662(e)(3)(D); Code Sec. 6664(c)(1))[38] Strict appraisal requirements apply to overvalued charitable gifts. (Code Sec. 6664(c)(2))[39]

For rules common to all accuracy-related penalties, see ¶ 4869.

---

31. ¶ V-2000 et seq.; ¶ 66,624.   34. ¶ V-2106; ¶ 66,624.   36. ¶ V-2201 et seq.; ¶ 66,624.   38. ¶ V-2214; ¶ 66,644.
32. ¶ V-2002; ¶ 66,624.   35. ¶ V-2119; ¶ 66,624.   37. ¶ V-2202; ¶ 66,624.   39. ¶ V-2215; ¶ 66,644.
33. ¶ V-2051; ¶ 66,624.

Footnote references beginning with letters are to paragraphs in RIA's Federal Tax Coordinator 2d and RIA's Analysis of Federal Taxes: Income. Footnote references beginning with numbers are to paragraphs in RIA's United States Tax Reporter.

¶ 4872 Penalty on substantial understatement of income tax.

The 20% accuracy-related penalty is imposed on any portion of an underpayment of tax that (absent reasonable cause) is attributable to any substantial understatement of income tax (Code Sec. 6662(a), (b)(1))[40] or self-employment tax (¶ 3137 *et seq.*). (Reg § 1.6661-2(d)(1))[41] For rules common to all accuracy-related penalties, see ¶ 4869.

An understatement of income tax is "substantial" if it exceeds the greater of: (1) 10% of the tax required to be shown on the return, or (2) $5,000 ($10,000 for corporations other than S corporations and personal holding companies). (Code Sec. 6662(d)(1))[42]

The understatement is reduced to the extent it is attributable to any item (other than tax shelter items which are reduced under special rules) for which:

(1) there is or was substantial authority (¶ 4873) for how taxpayer treated it, (Code Sec. 6662(d)(2)(B)(i)) or

(2) there is (a) adequate disclosure either in the return (IRS each year lists which items in the return qualify) or on a Form 8275 (or Form 8275-R if taxpayer's position is contrary to a regulation) attached to the return (Reg § 1.6662-4(f)) *and* (b) the position is not frivolous (Reg § 1.6662-4(e)(2)(i)) (for returns due without extensions after '93, there instead must be a reasonable basis for taxpayer's treatment of the item). (Code Sec. 6662(d)(2)(B)(ii))[43]

¶ 4873 "Substantial authority."

"Substantial authority" exists for the tax treatment of an item (for purposes of the reduction described at ¶ 4872) only if the weight of the authorities supporting the treatment is substantial in relation to the weight of authorities supporting contrary positions (determined in the light of the pertinent facts and circumstances). (Reg § 1.6661-3(b)(1)) "Authorities" include the Code (and other statutes), temporary, proposed, and final regs, cases, administrative pronouncements (Rev Ruls, Rev Procs, private letter rulings, technical advice memoranda, actions on decisions, General Counsel Memoranda, press releases, Notices, and similar documents), tax treaties (and regs and official explanations), Congressional intent (in reports, etc.) and General Explanations of Tax Laws after enactment (Blue Books).[44]

IRS is to publish (and thereafter issue annually) a (nonexhaustive) list of positions believed to lack substantial authority and to affect a significant number of taxpayers. (Code Sec. 6662(d)(2)(D))[45]

¶ 4874 Penalty for understating value of property on gift or estate tax return.

If the value of any property claimed on any gift or estate tax return is 50% or less of the correct value, the 20% accuracy-related penalty (¶ 4869) is imposed on any underpayment of tax of $1,000 or more that is attributable to that understatement. (Code Sec. 6662(a), (b)(5), (g)(1)) A higher 40% penalty applies if the claimed value is 25% or less of the correct figure. (Code Sec. 6662(h)(1), (2)(C))[46]

The penalty won't apply unless the portion of the underpayment attributable to all these undervaluations for the tax period exceeds $5,000. (Code Sec. 6662(g)(2))[47]

¶ 4875 Overstatement of pension liabilities.

A taxpayer who (absent reasonable cause) substantially overstates pension liabilities for a tax year is subject to the accuracy-related penalty (¶ 4869) if the overstatement results in an income tax underpayment of $1,000 or more. (Code Sec. 6662(a), (b)(4),

---

40. ¶ V-2150 *et seq.*; ¶ 66,624.
41. ¶ V-2155.
42. ¶ V-2159; ¶ 66,624.

43. ¶s V-2154, V-2167 *et seq.*; ¶ 66,624.
44. ¶ V-2162; ¶ 66,624.

45. ¶ V-2166; ¶ 66,624.
46. ¶s V-2219, V-2220; ¶ 66,624 (Estate & Gift).

47. ¶ V-2219; ¶ 66,624 (Estate & Gift).

Footnote references beginning with letters are to paragraphs in RIA's Federal Tax Coordinator 2d and RIA's Analysis of Federal Taxes: Income. Footnote references beginning with numbers are to paragraphs in RIA's United States Tax Reporter.

(f)(2))[48] The penalty equals 20% of the underpayment (40% for "gross" overstatements). (Code Sec. 6662(a), (h)(1))[49]

Pension liabilities are substantially overstated if the actuarial determination of the liabilities taken into account in computing the contribution deduction (¶ 4333) is at least 200% of the correct amount. (Code Sec. 6662(f)(1)) The overstatement is "gross" if it is 400% or more of the correct figure. (Code Sec. 6662(h)(2)(B))[50]

¶ 4876 Fraud.

Fraudulent underpayment of tax required to be shown on a return results in a civil penalty of 75% of the portion of the underpayment attributable to fraud. (Code Sec. 6663(a)) For returns due (without extension) before '89, the fraud penalty also includes 50% of the interest on the portion of the resulting underpayment.[1]

The fraud penalty can be imposed only if a return is filed (not by IRS). (Code Sec. 6664(b))[2] It won't be imposed where taxpayer shows good faith reliance on a reasonable basis for the underpayment. (Code Sec. 6664(c)(1))[3]

Imposition of the fraud penalty on any part of an underpayment precludes any of the accuracy-related penalties (¶ 4869) from being imposed on that same part. (Code Sec. 6662(b))[4]

If IRS establishes that any part of an underpayment is attributable to fraud, the entire underpayment is treated as attributable to fraud, except for any part taxpayer establishes (by a preponderance of the evidence) is not so attributable. (Code Sec. 6663(b))[5]

¶ 4877 Willful failure to collect or account for and pay over a tax—trust fund recovery penalty.

Willful failure to collect or account for and pay over a tax or willful attempt to evade or defeat a tax, by a "responsible person" required to collect, account for, and pay over the tax carries a civil "trust fund recovery penalty" equal to 100% of the total tax evaded or not accounted for and paid over. (Code Sec. 6672)[6]

¶ 4878 Penalty for aiding and abetting understatement of tax liability.

A penalty of $1,000 ($10,000 for a corporation) (Code Sec. 6701(b))[7] is imposed on any person who:

■ aids or assists, procures or advises with respect to the preparation or presentation of any portion of a return, affidavit, claim or other document connected with any matter arising under the internal revenue laws,

■ knows (or has reason to believe) that the portion will be used in connection with any material matter arising under those laws, *and*

■ knows that an understatement of another person's tax would result from that use (Code Sec. 6701(a)) even if there is no actual understatement.[8]

The term "advises" includes the actions of lawyers and accountants who counsel a particular course of action, and of appraisers who falsely or fraudulently overstate the value of property in a qualified appraisal (of property for which a charitable contribution is claimed, see ¶ 2136). (Reg § 1.170A-13(c)(3)(iii))[9]

¶ 4879 Understatements by return preparer—"unrealistic position" and "willful or reckless conduct" penalties.

An income tax return preparer (¶ 4749) is subject to a $250 civil penalty for each tax

48. ¶ V-2250 *et seq.*; ¶ 66,624.
49. ¶ V-2252; ¶ 66,624.
50. ¶ V-2253; ¶ 66,624.
1. ¶s V-2303, V-2300 *et seq.*; ¶s 66,634, 66,534.
2. ¶ V-2051; ¶ 66,634.
3. ¶ V-2060; ¶ 66,644.
4. ¶ V-2002; ¶ 66,624.
5. ¶ V-2302; ¶ 66,634.
6. ¶ V-1700 *et seq.*; ¶ 66,724.
7. ¶ V-2352; ¶ 67,104.
8. ¶ V-2351; ¶ 67,014.
9. ¶ V-2353; ¶ 67,014.

Footnote references beginning with letters are to paragraphs in RIA's Federal Tax Coordinator 2d and RIA's Analysis of Federal Taxes: Income. Footnote references beginning with numbers are to paragraphs in RIA's United States Tax Reporter.

return or refund claim prepared if: (1) any part of any understatement of tax liability for the return or claim is due to a position that has no realistic possibility of being sustained on the merits, (2) the preparer knew (or should have known) of that "unrealistic position," *and* (3) the position wasn't disclosed as required or was frivolous. But the penalty won't apply to a preparer who shows both reasonable cause for the understatement *and* his good faith. (Code Sec. 6694(a); Reg § 1.6694-1(e)(1))[10] Whether an understatement of liability exists for this purpose may be determined in a proceeding unrelated to any proceeding involving the taxpayer. (Reg § 1.6694-1(c))[11]

A position meets the "realistic possibility" standard if a reasonable and well-informed analysis by a person knowledgeable in the tax law would lead him to conclude it has an approximately one in three, or greater, chance of being sustained. (Reg § 1.6694-2(b)(1))[12] This standard generally reflects the professional conduct standards for lawyers and CPAs.[13]

The preparer is not required to examine or review documents or other evidence in order to verify independently the taxpayer's information, but he must make reasonable inquiries if the information appears to be incorrect or incomplete, or to determine the existence of required facts and circumstances incident to a deduction. (Reg § 1.6694-1(e)(1))[14]

A $1,000 penalty is imposed on the preparer for each return or claim prepared if any part of an understatement is due to the preparer's willful attempt to understate that tax or to his reckless or intentional disregard of rules or regs. But the amount of this penalty can be reduced by the amount of any "unrealistic position" penalty (above) the preparer pays for the same return or claim. (Code Sec. 6694(b))[15]

For other preparer penalties, see ¶ 4880.

¶ 4880 Other penalties on income tax return preparers.

An income tax return preparer who fails to perform the duties described at ¶ 4748 is subject to these civil penalties (up to a maximum $25,000 per calendar year for any single type of failure):

■ $50 for each failure to sign a return as required. (Code Sec. 6695(b))[16]

■ $50 for each failure to reflect his taxpayer identification number as required. (Code Sec. 6695(e))[17]

■ $50 for each failure to furnish a completed copy of the return to the taxpayer. (Code Sec. 6695(a))[18]

■ $50 for each failure to retain a copy of a prepared return or to include it on a list of prepared returns. (Code Sec. 6695(d))[19]

■ $50 for each failure to retain and make available a record of the preparers employed or engaged, plus $50 for each failure to include a required item in the record required to be retained and made available. (Code Sec. 6695(e))[20]

■ a $500 penalty (with no annual maximum) for each income tax check issued to a taxpayer that the preparer endorses or otherwise negotiates, except where the preparer is a bank and deposits the check to the taxpayer's account in the bank. (Code Sec. 6695(f))[21]

Improper disclosure or use of information by return preparers is subject to a civil penalty of $250 for each improper disclosure or use ($10,000 maximum per calendar year), (Code Sec. 6713(a))[22] as well as a criminal penalty. (Code Sec. 7216)[23]

---

10. ¶ V-2651.
11. ¶ V-2664; ¶ 66,944.
12. ¶ V-2651; ¶ 66,944.
13. ¶ V-2651 *et seq.*; ¶ 66,944.

14. ¶s V-2661, V-2662; ¶ 66,944.
15. ¶ V-2660; ¶ 66,944.
16. ¶ V-2670; ¶ 66,954.
17. ¶ V-2674; ¶ 66,954.

18. ¶ V-2671; ¶ 66,954.
19. ¶ V-2672; ¶ 66,954.
20. ¶ V-2673; ¶ 66,954.

21. ¶ V-2668; ¶ 66,954.
22. ¶ V-2675; ¶ 67,134.
23. ¶ V-3308.

Footnote references beginning with letters are to paragraphs in RIA's Federal Tax Coordinator 2d and RIA's Analysis of Federal Taxes: Income. Footnote references beginning with numbers are to paragraphs in RIA's United States Tax Reporter.

¶ 4881 Abusive tax shelters.

A person who promotes an abusive tax shelter is subject to a penalty equal to the lesser of $1000 or 100% of the gross income derived or to be derived from the activity. (Code Sec. 6700(a))[24]

IRS may seek to enjoin the promoter from further engaging in acts subject to the penalty. (Code Sec. 7408(a))[25]

¶ 4882 Potentially abusive tax shelters.

Any organizer or seller of a potentially abusive tax shelter who doesn't maintain a list of investors (¶ 4746) is subject to a penalty of $50 for each failure to include a person on a list unless the failure is due to reasonable cause and not willful neglect. The maximum penalty for any calendar year is $100,000. (Code Sec. 6708)[26]

¶ 4883 Failure to register tax shelter promotions or to furnish or report shelter ID numbers.

Any person required to register a tax shelter (as specially defined (Code Sec. 6111(c))) (¶ 4746) who, absent reasonable cause, fails to timely do so or who files false or incomplete information with respect to the registration is subject to a penalty (Code Sec. 6707(a)(1)) equal to the greater of: (1) $500, or (2) 1% of the aggregate amount invested in the shelter. (Code Sec. 6707(a)(2))[27]

Any person who sells or otherwise transfers an interest in a tax shelter who fails to furnish the tax shelter ID number to the investor is subject to a penalty of $100 for each failure. And any investor claiming a deduction, credit, etc., with respect to the shelter is subject to a $250 penalty for failing to include the number on the return, unless the failure is due to reasonable cause. (Code Sec. 6707(b))[28]

¶ 4884 Information return penalties.

A payor who, without reasonable cause, fails to timely file a required information return (¶ 4738 *et seq.*), or fails to include all of the information required to be shown on the return, or includes incorrect information, is subject to a $50 penalty for each return, up to a $250,000 calendar year maximum. (Code Sec. 6721(a), Code Sec. 6724(a)) The penalty and maximum are reduced to $15 per return ($75,000 maximum) if the failure is corrected within 30 days from the required filing date, or (except for returns that are not due on Feb. 28 or Mar. 15) to $30 per return ($150,000 maximum) if corrected on or before Aug. 1 of the calendar year of the required filing date. (Code Sec. 6721(b); Reg § 301.6721-1(b)(6))[29]

A payor who, without reasonable cause, fails to timely furnish a payee statement to the person prescribed, fails to include all of the required information on the statement, or includes incorrect information, is subject to a penalty of $50 for each such statement, up to a $100,000 calendar year maximum. (Code Sec. 6722(a), (b), Code Sec. 6724(a))[30]

However, the above penalties are increased *with no calendar year maximum* if the failure is due to intentional disregard. (Code Sec. 6721(e), Code Sec. 6722(c))[31]

¶ 4885 Other civil penalties.

Other civil penalties are provided for:

■ failure to file actuarial report of pension plan; (Code Sec. 6692)[32]

■ failure to file annual return for a pension plan, (Code Sec. 6652(f))[33] or for an exempt

24. ¶ V-2403; ¶ 67,004.
25. ¶ V-2451; ¶ 74,084.
26. ¶ V-2503; ¶ 67,084.
27. ¶ V-2501; ¶ 67,074.
28. ¶ V-2502; ¶ 67,074.

29. ¶ V-1804 *et seq.*; ¶s 67,214, 67,244.01.
30. ¶ V-1815 *et seq.*; ¶s 67,224, 67,244.01.

31. ¶s V-1812 *et seq.*, V-1817 *et seq.*; ¶s 67,214, 67,224.

32. ¶ V-1937; ¶ 66,924.
33. ¶ V-1937; ¶ 66,524.

Footnote references beginning with letters are to paragraphs in RIA's Federal Tax Coordinator 2d and RIA's Analysis of Federal Taxes: Income. Footnote references beginning with numbers are to paragraphs in RIA's United States Tax Reporter.

organization; (Code Sec. 6652(c)(1), Code Sec. 6685)[34]

■ failure to file fringe benefit plan return; (Code Sec. 6652(e))[35]

■ failure to provide a written explanation to the recipient of a qualified rollover distribution; (Code Sec. 6652(i))[36]

■ failure to file report on deductible employee contributions; (Code Sec. 6652(g))[37]

■ failure to file notification of change of status of pension plan; (Code Sec. 6652(d)(2))[38]

■ failure to keep records necessary for plan administrators to meet reporting requirements; (Code Sec. 6704)[39]

■ failure to file registration statement of pension plan, (Code Sec. 6652(d)(1))[40] or to give a plan participant a statement of the information in the statement; (Code Sec. 6690)[41]

■ failure to file individual retirement account reports; (Code Sec. 6693)[42]

■ overstatement reported on return by IRA participant of the amount of designated nondeductible contributions; (Code Sec. 6693(b))[43]

■ failure to keep records for reporting on pension, annuity, etc., payments subject to withholding; (Code Sec. 6704(a))[44]

■ failure to notify recipients of plan distributions of their option to elect out of withholding. (Code Sec. 6652(i))[45]

■ failure to file certain returns for foreign corporations, partnerships (Code Sec. 6679)[46] and trusts; (Code Sec. 6677)[47]

■ failure of foreign corporations to file PHC tax returns; (Code Sec. 6683)[48]

■ failure to keep records, furnish information, or file DISC (or former DISC) returns; (Code Sec. 6686)[49]

■ failure to keep records, furnish information or file returns for a FSC (or former FSC); (Code Sec. 6686)[50]

■ failure to meet FIRPTA reporting requirements; (Code Sec. 6652(f))[1]

■ failure to file notice of redetermination of certain foreign taxes; (Code Sec. 6689)[2]

■ failure to withhold tax on U.S. income of certain foreign persons; (Code Sec. 1463)[3]

■ failure by green card or passport applicants to furnish required tax information (¶ 4613); (Code Sec. 6039E(c))[4]

■ failure to disclose a treaty-based position taken on a return that overrules or otherwise modifies the tax law; (Code Sec. 6712)[5]

■ failure to file exempt organization returns; (Code Sec. 6652(c))[6]

■ failure by an exempt organization to disclose that information it is offering to sell or soliciting money for is available free from the federal government; (Code Sec. 6711)[7]

■ failure to disclose that fundraising solicitations are nondeductible as charitable contributions by organizations required to so disclose; (Code Sec. 6710)[8]

■ failure by an exempt organization to make the required disclosure for quid pro quo contributions of $75 or more; (Code Sec. 6714)[9]

■ failure to file private foundation returns, (Code Sec. 6652(c)) to make returns available for public inspection, (Code Sec. 6685; Reg § 301.6652-2(c))[10] and for any repeated or willful and flagrant act or failure to act by any person who becomes liable for any excise

34. ¶ V-1906; ¶s 66,524, 66,854.
35. ¶ V-1938; ¶ 66,524.
36. ¶ V-1944; ¶ 66,524.
37. ¶ V-1940; ¶ 66,524.
38. ¶ V-1937; ¶ 66,524.
39. ¶ V-2717; ¶ 67,044.
40. ¶ V-1937; ¶ 66,524.

41. ¶ V-1937; ¶ 66,904.
42. ¶ V-1939; ¶ 66,934.
43. ¶ V-1941; ¶ 66,934.
44. ¶ V-2717; ¶ 67,044.
45. ¶ V-1945; ¶ 66,524.
46. ¶ V-1901; ¶ 66,794.
47. ¶ V-1901; ¶ 66,774.

48. ¶ V-1757; ¶ 66,834.
49. ¶ V-1908; ¶ 66,864.
50. ¶ V-1908; ¶ 66,864.
1. ¶ V-1903; ¶ 66,524.
2. ¶ V-1943; ¶ 66,894.
3. ¶ O-11903; ¶ 14,614.01.
4. ¶ V-1904; ¶ 60,934E4.

5. ¶ V-2720; ¶ 67,124.
6. ¶ V-1905; ¶ 66,524.
7. ¶ V-2703; ¶ 67,114.
8. ¶ V-2701; ¶ 67,104.
9. ¶ V-2720.1.
10. ¶s V-1905, V-2801; ¶s 66,524, 66,854.

Footnote references beginning with letters are to paragraphs in RIA's Federal Tax Coordinator 2d and RIA's Analysis of Federal Taxes: Income. Footnote references beginning with numbers are to paragraphs in RIA's United States Tax Reporter.

tax on a private foundation by reason of the act or failure to act; (Code Sec. 6684)[11]

■ making a negligent or fraudulent misstatement in connection with the issuance of a mortgage credit certificate or failing to file the required report; (Code Sec. 6709)[12]

■ failure to file partnership return, (Code Sec. 6698) but certain domestic partnerships with ten or fewer partners (each of whom is a natural person or estate) are considered to meet the reasonable cause exception to this penalty;[13]

■ failure to file returns with respect to qualified rental housing projects; (Code Sec. 42(l)(2), Code Sec. 6652(j))[14]

■ failure to supply place of residence on returns, etc.; (Code Sec. 6687)[15]

■ failure to deposit taxes; (Code Sec. 6656(a))[16]

■ use of bad checks or money orders to pay taxes; (Code Sec. 6657)[17]

■ failure to pay stamp taxes; (Code Sec. 6653)[18]

■ claiming excessive gasoline tax rebates; (Code Sec. 6675)[19]

■ filing a frivolous income tax return; (Code Sec. 6702)[20]

■ use of Tax Court primarily for delay or where taxpayer's position is frivolous or groundless or where taxpayer hasn't exhausted administrative remedies or where taxpayer has instituted a frivolous or groundless claim for damages against the U.S.; (Code Sec. 6673)[21]

■ failure to supply taxpayer identification numbers; (Reg § 301.6723-1T(a))[22]

■ failure to report tips; (Code Sec. 6652(b))[23]

■ failure by broker to provide back-up withholding notice; (Code Sec. 6705)[24]

■ failure to file information return for change in control or recapitalization of corporation; (Code Sec. 6652(l))[25]

■ making a false statement that results in reduced amounts of withholding, (Code Sec. 6682)[26] or relates to the applicability of backup withholding; (Code Sec. 6682)[27]

¶ 4886 Criminal tax evasion.

Tax evasion is a felony punishable by a fine of not more than $100,000 ($500,000 for a corporation) and/or up to five years' imprisonment, plus costs of prosecution. The elements of the crime are willfulness, an attempt to evade tax and additional tax due. (Code Sec. 7201)[28]

¶ 4887 Criminal penalty for false or fraudulent tax advice.

Any person who willfully aids or assists in, or procures, counsels or advises the preparation or presentation of a materially false or fraudulent return, affidavit, claim or other document, is subject to a criminal penalty of not more than $100,000 ($500,000 for a corporation) and/or up to three years' imprisonment, plus costs of prosecution. (Code Sec. 7206(2))[29]

¶ 4888 Other criminal penalties.

Other criminal penalties (fines and/or imprisonment) are imposed for:

■ willful failure to file a return; (Code Sec. 7203)[30]

■ willful filing of a false or fraudulent return; (Code Sec. 7207)[31]

11. ¶ V-2716; ¶ 66,844.
12. ¶ V-2718; ¶ 67,094.
13. ¶ V-1755; ¶ 66,984.
14. ¶ V-1914; ¶ 66,524.
15. ¶ V-2722; ¶ 66,874.
16. ¶ V-1652; ¶ 66,564.

17. ¶ V-2712; ¶ 66,574.
18. ¶ V-1651; ¶ 66,530.40.
19. ¶ V-2721; ¶ 66,754 (Excise).
20. ¶ V-2551; ¶ 67,024.
21. ¶ V-2601; ¶ 66,734.
22. ¶ V-1822 et seq.; ¶ 67,234.

23. ¶ V-2719; ¶ 66,524.
24. ¶ V-1912; ¶ 67,054.
25. ¶ V-1909; ¶ 66,524.
26. ¶ V-2713; ¶ 66,824.
27. ¶ V-2715; ¶ 66,824.

28. ¶ V-4100 et seq.; ¶ 72,014 et seq.
29. ¶ V-3110.
30. ¶ V-3002; ¶ 72,034.
31. ¶ V-3114; ¶ 72,074.

Footnote references beginning with letters are to paragraphs in RIA's Federal Tax Coordinator 2d and RIA's Analysis of Federal Taxes: Income. Footnote references beginning with numbers are to paragraphs in RIA's United States Tax Reporter.

- willful failure to pay a tax; (Code Sec. 7203)[32]

- willful failure to collect or pay over a tax as required; (Code Sec. 7202)[33]

- willful failure to furnish a W-2 to employees in the manner, at the time or with the information required, or willful filing of a false or fraudulent W-2; (Code Sec. 7204)[34]

- willful failure to keep proper records; (Code Sec. 7203)[35]

- willful failure to supply tax information; (Code Sec. 7203)[36]

- failure to obey a summons; (Code Sec. 7210)[37]

- various other offenses relating to returns, statements, stamp taxes, etc.[38]

¶ 4889 Tax Collection

IRS has broad tax collection powers, including liens and seizure and sale of taxpayer's property.

¶ 4890 Collection procedures.

Within 60 days after a tax has been assessed, IRS must send the taxpayer a notice of the amount assessed and a demand for payment, before it can start administrative collection proceedings. (Code Sec. 6303(a), Code Sec. 6331(a))[39] The taxpayer usually gets at least ten days from a date stated in the notice and demand in which to pay the tax, unless IRS finds that collection is in jeopardy. (Code Sec. 6331(a); Reg § 301.6331-1(a)(3))[40] But taxpayers suffering undue hardship can get an extension of time for paying the assessed taxes.[41]

IRS is authorized to enter into written agreements allowing the taxpayer to satisfy a tax liability in installment payments. (Code Sec. 6159)[42]

If any IRS officer or employee recklessly or intentionally disregards any Code or reg section in connection with any collection of tax, the taxpayer may file an administrative claim for damages, and if the claim is denied, bring a civil suit for damages against the U.S. in a district court. (Code Sec. 7433; Reg § 301.7433-1)[43]

¶ 4891 Seizure and sale of delinquent taxpayer's property.

IRS has power to collect taxes by levy and distraint. This means it may seize any property (except for the principal residence, certain clothing, tools, etc.) of a delinquent taxpayer (whether held by taxpayer or someone else), sell it, and apply the proceeds to pay the unpaid taxes.[44] The property seized may be real, personal, tangible, or intangible, including present and future wages. (Code Sec. 6331; Reg § 301.6331-2(c)) There is a minimum exemption for wages and certain other income and property, and a complete exemption for taxpayer's principal residence (except for jeopardy). (Code Sec. 6334)[45]

IRS must give 30 days' advance written notice to the person in possession of taxpayer's property before making the levy, except where collection is in jeopardy. (Code Sec. 6331(d))[46] A penalty (plus costs and interest) applies if the person fails or refuses to surrender the property. (Code Sec. 6332(d))[47]

If IRS is unable to sell the seized property for the minimum price it establishes, it can return the property to the taxpayer and add the cost of the unsuccessful sale to the unpaid tax liability. (Code Sec. 6335(e)(1)(D))[48]

If IRS wrongfully seizes property of a person other than the taxpayer, the third party

2. ¶ V-3001; ¶ 72,034.
3. ¶ V-3016; ¶ 72,024.
4. ¶ V-3012; ¶ 72,044.
5. ¶ V-3007; ¶ 72,034.
6. ¶ V-3008; ¶ 72,034.
7. ¶ V-3503; ¶ 72,104.

38. ¶ V-3500 *et seq.*; ¶ 72,009 *et seq.*
39. ¶s V-5003, V-5004; ¶s 63,014.03, 63,314.01.
40. ¶ V-5007; ¶ 63,314.01.

41. ¶ V-5008.
42. ¶ V-5009; ¶ 61,594.
43. ¶ V-5800 *et seq.*
44. ¶ V-5100 *et seq.*; ¶ 63,314 *et seq.*

45. ¶ V-5200 *et seq.*; ¶s 63,314.03, 63,314.05.
46. ¶ V-5101; ¶ 63,314.01.
47. ¶ V-5115; ¶ 63,314.04.
48. ¶ V-5413; ¶ 63,354.01.

Footnote references beginning with letters are to paragraphs in RIA's Federal Tax Coordinator 2d and RIA's Analysis of Federal Taxes: Income. Footnote references beginning with numbers are to paragraphs in RIA's United States Tax Reporter.

may sue (in the district court) for its return (or the sale proceeds, if it has been sold), (Code Sec. 7426) as long as the suit is begun within nine months from the date of levy. (Code Sec. 6532(c)(1))[49]

The owner (or his heirs, etc.) of any real estate sold to satisfy a tax liability can redeem the property at any time within 180 days after the sale. (Code Sec. 6337(b)(1))[50]

¶ 4892 Collection period.

IRS must generally start distraint or court proceedings within ten years after assessment (Code Sec. 6502(a)) (within six years for pre-Nov. 6, '90 assessments open as of Nov. 5, '90). But if no return is filed, a collection suit may be brought at any time, without assessment. (Code Sec. 6501(c)(3))[1]

The collection period may be extended by written agreement before the ten-year period expires. (Code Sec. 6502(a); Reg § 301.6502-1)[2]

¶ 4893 Injunctions against tax collection.

Injunctions against collection of taxes are generally barred. But exceptions apply during the period allowed to file a Tax Court petition or, where a petition has been filed, before the Tax Court's decision becomes final, and where an individual other than the taxpayer sues to recover property wrongfully seized. (Code Sec. 7421(a))[3]

¶ 4894 Federal tax liens.

Federal tax liens are claims against a taxpayer's property for payment of delinquent taxes (including any interest, additional amounts, additions to tax, assessable penalties or accrued costs).[4] There are various federal tax liens, including:

- general tax lien, which applies to all property, both real and personal, tangible and intangible; (Code Sec. 6321)[5]
- gift tax lien; (Code Sec. 6324(b))[6]
- estate tax lien; (Code Sec. 6324(a))[7]
- special lien for deferred estate tax attributable to closely held business; (Code Sec. 6324A)[8]
- special estate tax lien on farm or closely held business real property for which special use valuation was elected; (Code Sec. 6324B)[9]
- generation-skipping transfer tax lien. (Code Sec. 2661; Reg § 26.2662-1(f))[10]

¶ 4895 Priority of tax liens.

Priority of tax liens is governed by federal, not state, law.[11] The general rule is that a lien first in time is first in right.[12] But a tax lien is subordinated to certain later liens that arise either before notice of the tax lien is filed, or before the other lienor has actual knowledge of it. This protects purchasers for adequate consideration without actual notice, mortgagees, pledgees and other lienors whose rights arose before notice of the tax lien was filed. (Code Sec. 6323(a))[13] It also protects certain interests arising even after the notice was filed, e.g., attorney's liens and certain security interests. (Code Sec. 6323(b))[14]

The special gift and estate tax liens don't have to be filed to be superior to claims

---

49. ¶s V-5119, V-5120; ¶s 65,324.04, 74,264.
50. ¶ V-5422; ¶ 63,354.03.
1. ¶ V-5600 et seq.; ¶ 65,024 et seq.
2. ¶ V-5603; ¶ 65,024.
3. ¶ V-5701; ¶ 74,214 et seq.
4. ¶ V-6000 et seq.; ¶ 63,209 et seq.

5. ¶ V-6002 et seq.; ¶ 63,214 et seq.
6. ¶ V-6040; ¶ 63,244 (Estate & Gift).
7. ¶ V-6042; ¶ 63,244 (Estate & Gift).

8. ¶ V-6044; ¶ 63,24A4 (Estate & Gift).
9. ¶ V-6049; ¶ 63,24B4 (Estate & Gift).
10. ¶ V-6052; ¶ 26,634 (Estate & Gift).

11. ¶ V-6324; ¶ 63,214.04.
12. ¶ V-6301; ¶ 63,214.04.
13. ¶s V-6400 et seq., V-6426 et seq.; ¶ 63,234 et seq.
14. ¶ V-6401; ¶ 63,234.

Footnote references beginning with letters are to paragraphs in RIA's Federal Tax Coordinator 2d and RIA's Analysis of Federal Taxes: Income. Footnote references beginning with numbers are to paragraphs in RIA's United States Tax Reporter.

arising after the special lien arises. But certain later purchasers and creditors are protected, including holders of a security interest and holders of mechanics', repairmen's and attorney's liens. (Code Sec. 6324)[15]

¶ 4896 Taxes in bankruptcy or receivership proceedings.

A receiver in a receivership proceeding must give IRS written notice (use Form 56) of the receivership. (Code Sec. 6036) But a bankruptcy trustee, debtor-in-possession, or other like fiduciary in a bankruptcy proceeding is not required to give notice, (Reg § 301.6036-1(a)(1)(i)) because notice under the Bankruptcy Rules is sufficient.

The filing of a federal bankruptcy petition (but not the start of a state receivership proceeding) automatically stays any tax proceedings against the taxpayer-debtor.[16] The running of the assessment period is suspended from the date a bankruptcy or receivership proceeding is instituted until 30 days after IRS has received notice of the proceeding, but the suspension may not exceed two years. (Code Sec. 6872; Reg § 301.6872-1)[17]

Any income, estate or gift tax deficiency may be immediately assessed whenever a taxpayer goes into bankruptcy or receivership (¶ 4825). But collection of the tax is stayed while the taxpayer-debtor's assets are under the control of a federal or state court in bankruptcy or receivership proceedings.[18]

With some exceptions, debtor relief proceedings don't discharge the taxpayer's liability for taxes or interest (including certain post-petition interest).[19]

¶ 4897 Transferee's liability for transferor's unpaid taxes.

A transferee is liable for a taxpayer-transferor's unpaid taxes (and interest and penalties) where:

■ the transfer is void or voidable under rules of equity,[20]

■ transferee liability is imposed by statute,[21]

■ transferee liability arises under contract.[22]

Transferees include a donee, heir, legatee, devisee or distributee of a decedent's estate, a shareholder of a dissolved corporation, the assignee or donee of an insolvent person, certain fiduciaries, a successor in a tax-free corporate reorganization, and various other classes of distributees. (Code Sec. 6901(h); Reg § 301.6901-1(b))[23]

IRS must assess the (first) transferee within one year after the limitations period against the transferor has run. (Code Sec. 6901(c)(1))[24]

---

15. ¶s V-6455, V-6456; ¶ 63,244 (Estate & Gift).

16. ¶ U-1220; ¶ 68,714.

17. ¶ T-4322; ¶ 68,724.

18. ¶ V-7301 *et seq.*; ¶ 68,714.

19. ¶ V-7333 *et seq.*; ¶ 68,734.

20. ¶s V-9100 *et seq.*, V-9200 *et seq.*; ¶ 69,014 *et seq.*

21. ¶ V-9300 *et seq.*; ¶ 69,014 *et seq.*

22. ¶ V-9400 *et seq.*; ¶ 69,014.02.

23. ¶ V-9001; ¶ 69,014.01.

24. ¶ V-9801; ¶ 69,014.10.

Footnote references beginning with letters are to paragraphs in RIA's Federal Tax Coordinator 2d and RIA's Analysis of Federal Taxes: Income. Footnote references beginning with numbers are to paragraphs in RIA's United States Tax Reporter.

Chapter 26   Estate, Gift and Generation-Skipping Transfer Taxes

¶ *5000* Estate Tax ▬▬▬▬▬▬▬▬▬▬▬▬▬▬▬▬▬▬▬▬▬▬

The federal estate tax is imposed on the transfer of an individual's property at his death and on certain other transfers considered to be the equivalent of transfers at death. The tax is imposed on the "taxable estate," which is the value of the total property transferred or considered transferred at death (the "gross estate"), reduced by various deductions. The tax is computed under a unified rate schedule under which lifetime taxable gifts and transfers at death are taxed on a cumulative basis.

In determining the tax on estates of decedents who at death were citizens or residents of the U.S., the entire estate is considered. (Code Sec. 2033)[1]

In determining the tax on the estate of a nonresident not a citizen of the U.S., only property situated in the U.S. is considered. (Code Sec. 2103)[2]

¶ *5001* Computation of estate tax.

Computation of estate tax begins with figuring a tentative tax under the unified rate schedule (see ¶ 1112) on the total of: (1) the amount of the taxable estate (¶ 5018), and (2) the total amount of taxable gifts made by the decedent after '76 that are not includible in the decedent's gross estate. (Code Sec. 2001(b)(1)) This tentative tax is increased by an amount equal to 5% of so much of the amount (with respect to which the tentative tax is computed) as exceeds $10,000,000, but does not exceed $21,040,000. (Code Sec. 2001(c)(2))

This amount is then reduced by the amount of gift tax payable on the decedent's post-'76 gifts to get the gross estate tax payable (before credits). (Code Sec. 2001(b)(2))

The net estate tax payable is the gross estate tax minus the unified credit (see ¶ 5029 *et seq.*) and allowable credits for state death taxes, gift taxes on pre-'77 gifts, estate taxes on earlier transfers and foreign death taxes. (Code Sec. 2010, Code Sec. 2011, Code Sec. 2012, Code Sec. 2013, Code Sec. 2014)[3]

¶ *5002* Additional estate tax on excess retirement accumulations.

The estate tax of a decedent is increased by 15% of the excess of:

(1) the value of the decedent's interests in qualified employer plans and IRAs, *minus*

(2) the present value of a hypothetical life annuity. (Code Sec. 4980A(d))[4]

A special grandfather rule concerns elections which were made where the pre-Aug. 1, '86 accrued benefit exceeded $562,500. (Code Sec. 4980A(f))[5]

No credits, deductions, exclusions, etc., that apply for estate tax purposes are allowed to offset the tax. (Reg § 54.4981A-1T, Q&A-8)[6] Certain spouses may elect to have excise tax on distributions (¶ 4346) apply instead of estate tax.[7]

¶ *5003* Property owned by decedent.

The gross estate of a decedent includes the value of all property owned by him at his death (to the extent of the decedent's beneficial interest in the property). (Code Sec. 2033; Reg § 20.2033-1(a))[8]

¶ *5004* Gifts within three years of death.

Gifts within three years of death aren't usually included in a decedent's gross estate. (Code Sec. 2035(d))[9] However, a gift made by a decedent within three years of his death is included in his estate whether or not a gift tax return was required if the gift consists of

---

1. ¶s R-1000 *et seq.*, R-2000   2. ¶ R-8008; ¶s 21,014, 21,014.03.   5. ¶ R-7047; ¶ 20,014.10.   8. ¶ R-2001; ¶ 20,334.
   et seq.; ¶s 20,314 *et seq.*, 20,334   3. ¶ R-7001 *et seq.*; ¶ 20,014.02.   6. ¶ R-7041; ¶ 20,014.10.   9. ¶ R-2200; ¶ 20,354.
   et seq.   4. ¶ R-7041 *et seq.*; ¶ 20,014.10.   7. ¶ R-7048; ¶ 20,014.10.

Footnote references beginning with letters are to paragraphs in RIA's Federal Tax Coordinator 2d. Footnote references beginning with numbers are to paragraphs in RIA's United States Tax Reporter (Estate & Gift Taxes).

interests in property otherwise included in the gross estate under Code Sec. 2036 (transfers with retained life estate, etc., see ¶ 5006), Code Sec. 2037 (transfers taking effect at death, see ¶ 5008), Code Sec. 2038 (revocable transfers, see ¶ 5009), or Code Sec. 2042 (life insurance proceeds, see ¶ 5016). (Code Sec. 2035(d)(2))[10]

If the decedent during his lifetime made any of the transfers listed at ¶s 5006 through 5009, the value of the property transferred is included in his gross estate (except to the extent made for adequate and full consideration).

¶ 5005 Gift tax "gross-up."

Gift tax paid by the decedent, his estate or his donees on gifts made by decedent or his spouse within three years of decedent's death is included in his gross estate. But gift tax paid by the spouse on the spouse's share of decedent's gifts under the gift-splitting rules isn't included. (Code Sec. 2035(c))[11]

¶ 5006 Retained life estate.

A decedent's gross estate includes transfers under which he retained the possession or enjoyment of, or the right to the income from, the transferred property. (Code Sec. 2036(a)(1); Reg § 20.2036-1)[12]

The decedent's gross estate also includes transfers where he retained the right to designate the person(s) to possess or enjoy the transferred property or its income. (Code Sec. 2036(a)(2))[13]

The decedent need not have a legally enforceable right, but there must be an agreement, either expressed or implied, that the decedent will retain the benefit.[14]

The possession, enjoyment or right to income is "retained" to the extent it is to be applied toward the discharge of a legal obligation of the decedent or otherwise for his pecuniary benefit—e.g., the support of a dependent during the decedent's lifetime. (Reg § 20.2036-1(b)(2))[15]

¶ 5007 Retention of voting rights in stock of a controlled corporation.

Retention of voting rights in stock of a controlled corporation is a retention of the enjoyment of the transferred stock. The value of the transferred stock is included in the decedent's gross estate. (Code Sec. 2036(b))[16]

¶ 5008 Transfers taking effect at death.

If a decedent transfers property during his lifetime, but the transferee cannot possess or enjoy the property except by surviving the decedent, and the decedent retained a significant reversionary interest (exceeding 5% of the value of the transferred property immediately before the decedent's death), then the value of the property is includible in decedent's gross estate. (Code Sec. 2037)[17]

Where the value of the reversion does not exceed 5% so that *the value of the property* is not included as a transfer taking effect at death, *the value of the reversion itself* can be included as property owned at death. (Reg § 20.2037-1(c))[18]

¶ 5009 Revocable transfers.

The decedent's gross estate includes his lifetime transfers if the enjoyment of the transferred property was subject at his death to any change through the exercise by him of a power to *alter, amend, revoke or terminate.* This includes any power affecting the time or manner of enjoyment of property or its income. (Code Sec. 2038(a)(1))[19]

10. ¶ R-2201 *et seq.*; ¶ 20,354.
11. ¶ R-2210; ¶ 20,354.
12. ¶ R-2400 *et seq.*; ¶ 20,364.
13. ¶ R-2450; ¶ 20,364.
14. ¶ R-2422.
15. ¶s R-2415, R-2517; ¶ 20,364.
16. ¶ R-2436; ¶ 20,364.
17. ¶ R-2500 *et seq.*; ¶ 20,374.
18. ¶ R-2506; ¶s 20,334.50, 20,334.53.
19. ¶ R-2600 *et seq.*; ¶ 20,384 *et seq.*

Footnote references beginning with letters are to paragraphs in RIA's Federal Tax Coordinator 2d. Footnote references beginning with numbers are to paragraphs in RIA's United States Tax Reporter (Estate & Gift Taxes).

Includible revocable transfers include: savings bank (Totten) trusts that are revocable in form,[20] and custodial accounts where the donor appoints himself or succeeds another as custodian.[21]

¶ 5010 Qualified terminable interest property (QTIP).

Qualified terminable interest property (QTIP) for which the estate tax (¶ 5023) or gift tax (¶ 5049) marital deduction was elected is includible at its then fair market value in the estate of the surviving (donee) spouse at his or her death if he or she has not disposed of any part of the qualifying income interest for life. (Code Sec. 2044) The property is treated as passing from the surviving spouse. (Code Sec. 2044(c))[22]

¶ 5011 Powers of appointment.

If the decedent possessed a general power of appointment (created after Oct. 21, '42) at the time of his death, the property subject to the power is included in his gross estate. (Code Sec. 2041(a))[23] A "general" power is one exercisable in favor of the decedent, his estate, his creditors, or the creditors of his estate. (Code Sec. 2041(b)(1))[24]

¶ 5012 Jointly-held property.

Joint ownership acquired through gift, bequest, devise, or inheritance from another. The decedent's fractional share of the property is included. (Reg § 20.2040-1(a)(1))[25]

Joint ownership created by co-owners. Except for husband-wife tenancies (¶ 5013), the rule is: the *entire* value of the property is included in the co-owner's gross estate except the part, if any, attributable to the consideration in money or money's worth furnished by the other joint owner(s). Consideration furnished by the surviving joint owner(s) doesn't include money or property acquired from the decedent for less than a full and adequate consideration in money or money's worth. (Reg § 20.2040-1(a)(2))[26]

Tenancy in common. Only the value of decedent's undivided share of the property is included in his gross estate.[27]

¶ 5013 Spouses' jointly-held property.

If an interest in property created after '76 is held by a decedent and his spouse as tenants by the entireties or as joint tenants with right of survivorship (if the decedent and his spouse are the only joint tenants), one half of the value of the jointly-owned interest will be included in the estate of the decedent spouse regardless of which spouse furnished the original consideration. (Code Sec. 2040(b)) Where the surviving spouse is not a U.S. citizen, this rule applies only if the property passes in a qualified domestic trust (¶ 5025). (Code Sec. 2056(d)(1)(B), (2))[28]

Thus, the survivor gets a new basis for one-half of the property, see ¶ 2501 *et seq.*

For joint interests in property created by a husband and wife before '77, the "consideration furnished" test (¶ 5012) applies in determining what portion of the property is included in the estate of the first spouse to die.[29]

¶ 5014 Community property.

The value of the interest in community property vested in the decedent by state law—ordinarily, half of the community property—is included in the decedent spouse's estate.[30]

¶ 5015 Annuities.

The value of an annuity or other payment receivable by a beneficiary is included in the decedent's gross estate if under the contract or agreement, either:

---

20. ¶ R-2620.

21. ¶ R-2619; ¶ 20,384.03.

22. ¶ R-2900 *et seq.*; ¶ 20,444.

23. ¶ R-3000 *et seq.*; ¶ 20,414.

24. ¶ R-3006; ¶ 20,414.

25. ¶s R-2705, R-2709; ¶ 20,404.

26. ¶ R-2700 *et seq.*; ¶ 20,404.

27. ¶ R-2707; ¶ 20,334.15.

28. ¶ R-2724 *et seq.*; ¶ 20,404.

29. ¶ R-2705; ¶ 20,404.

30. ¶ R-2800 *et seq.*; ¶s 20,334.16, 20,334.17.

Footnote references beginning with letters are to paragraphs in RIA's Federal Tax Coordinator 2d. Footnote references beginning with numbers are to paragraphs in RIA's United States Tax Reporter (Estate & Gift Taxes).

(1) an annuity or other payment was payable to decedent, either alone or with another person(s), for decedent's life or for any period not ascertainable without reference to his death or for any period that doesn't in fact end before his death, or

(2) the decedent possessed, for one of the periods described in (1), above, the right to receive such an annuity or other payment, either alone or with another person(s). (Code Sec. 2039(a))

The amount included in the gross estate is an amount proportionate to the part of the purchase price contributed by the decedent. Contributions made by an employer or former employer are considered made by the employee if made by reason of his employment. (Code Sec. 2039(b))[31]

For additional estate tax on excess retirement accumulations, see ¶ 5002.

¶ *5016* Life insurance.

Proceeds of insurance on the life of the decedent receivable by the executor or administrator, or payable to the decedent's estate, are includible in decedent's gross estate. (Code Sec. 2042(1)) The estate needn't be specifically named as the beneficiary. (Reg § 20.2042-1(b)(1))[32]

Proceeds of insurance on the life of the decedent not receivable by or for the benefit of the estate are includible if the decedent possessed at his death any of the incidents of ownership in the policy, exercisable either alone or with any other person. (Code Sec. 2042(2)) "Incidents of ownership" includes the power to change the beneficiary, to revoke an assignment, to pledge the policy for a loan, etc., (Reg § 20.2042-1(c)(2)) and certain reversionary interests. (Reg § 20.2042-1(c)(3))[33]

¶ *5017* Group insurance.

An employee can prevent inclusion in his estate (under the insurance provision) of the proceeds of group life insurance furnished by his employer by transferring the insurance before his death, if:

(1) the group policy and applicable state law permit the employee to make an absolute assignment of all his incidents of ownership, and

(2) the employee irrevocably assigns all policy rights.[34]

¶ *5018* Computing the taxable estate.

The decedent's taxable estate is arrived at by deducting from the gross estate the following items:[35]

■ Funeral expenses. (Code Sec. 2053(a)(1))

■ Administration expenses, such as commissions of executors and administrators, attorney's fees, accountant's and appraisers' fees, and court costs. (Code Sec. 2053(a)(2); Reg § 20.2053-3)

■ Claims against the estate, including property taxes accrued before the decedent's death, unpaid income taxes, unpaid gift taxes, and medical expenses of the decedent paid by his estate after his death (to the extent those expenses aren't claimed as an income tax deduction (see ¶ 2146)). (Code Sec. 2053(a)(3); Reg § 20.2053-6)

■ Transfers in satisfaction of certain claims by a decedent's former spouse. (Code Sec. 2043(b)(2))

■ Indebtedness on property if the total value of the property is included in the gross

---

31. ¶ R-4401 *et seq.*; ¶ 20,394.
32. ¶ R-4002 *et seq.*; ¶ 20,424.01.
33. ¶ R-4006 *et seq.*; ¶ 20,424 *et seq.*

34. ¶ R-4033; ¶s 140,059, 140,060.

35. ¶ R-5400 *et seq.*; ¶s 20,514, 20,534, 20,544, 20,554, 20,564.

Footnote references beginning with letters are to paragraphs in RIA's Federal Tax Coordinator 2d. Footnote references beginning with numbers are to paragraphs in RIA's United States Tax Reporter (Estate & Gift Taxes).

estate. (Code Sec. 2053(a)(4))

■ Casualty and theft losses. (Code Sec. 2054)

■ Transfers to charitable and similar organizations, (Code Sec. 2055) see ¶ 5020.

■ Transfers to surviving spouse (marital deduction), (Code Sec. 2056) see ¶ 5021.

■ The additional estate tax on excess retirement accumulations (¶ 5002). (Code Sec. 2053(c)(1)(B))

For an item to be deductible as a debt, claim, or expense it must also be allowable under the law of the jurisdiction under which the estate is being administered. (Code Sec. 2053(a))[36]

If, at the time of filing the estate tax return, the exact amount of a deductible item is not known, an estimated amount may be entered on the return if that amount is ascertainable with reasonable certainty and it can be shown the item will be paid. (Reg § 20.2053-1(b)(3))[37]

¶ 5019 Income v. estate tax deduction.

Many estate administration expenses can qualify as an estate tax deduction on the estate tax return and as an income tax deduction, or an offset against the sales price of property in determining gain or loss, on the estate's income tax return. But the estate is entitled to an income tax deduction or offset only if an estate tax deduction for the item is waived. (Code Sec. 642(g))[38] For estates' income taxes, see ¶ 3900 *et seq.*

¶ 5020 Deductions for charitable bequests.

Deductions are allowed (on Schedule O, Form 706) for the value of property included in the decedent's gross estate and transferred by him during his lifetime or by will to or for the use of the U.S., any state, political subdivision thereof, or the District of Columbia, and to various types of charitable organizations (Code Sec. 2055(a)) including foreign organizations.[39]

Strict requirements apply where the charitable bequest is of an income interest or a remainder interest. (Code Sec. 2055(e))[40]

¶ 5021 Marital deduction.

A marital deduction is allowed (on Schedule M, Form 706) for the value of all property included in the gross estate that passes to the decedent's surviving spouse in a manner qualifying for the deduction. (Code Sec. 2056(a))[41]

¶ 5022 Terminable interests.

With certain exceptions (see, e.g., ¶ 5023), a terminable interest will not qualify for the marital deduction if another interest in the same property passed from the decedent to some other person for less than adequate and full consideration in money or money's worth and by reason of its passing that other person or his heirs may enjoy part of the property after the termination of the surviving spouse's interest. (Code Sec. 2056(b)(1); Reg § 20.2056(b)-1(c)) A terminable interest is one that will terminate or fail after a certain period of time, the happening of some contingency, or the failure of some event to occur. (Reg § 20.2056(b)-1(b))[42]

---

36. ¶ R-5405; ¶ 20,543 *et seq.*
37. ¶ R-5403.
38. ¶ R-5505; ¶ 20,534.

39. ¶ R-5700 *et seq.*; ¶ 20,554 *et seq.*
40. ¶ R-5733 *et seq.*; ¶s 20,554, 20,554.14, 20,554.16.

41. ¶ R-6000 *et seq.*; ¶ 20,564 *et seq.*
42. ¶ R-6300 *et seq.*; ¶ 20,564.

Footnote references beginning with letters are to paragraphs in RIA's Federal Tax Coordinator 2d. Footnote references beginning with numbers are to paragraphs in RIA's United States Tax Reporter (Estate & Gift Taxes).

¶ 5023 Election of marital deduction for qualified terminable interest property (QTIP).

Property in which a spouse is given only a life estate may qualify for the marital deduction as an exception to the terminable interest rule if the executor elects (by listing the property on Form 706, Schedule M and deducting its value) to have all or part of the property so qualify and the surviving spouse has a "qualifying income interest for life." A spouse has such an interest if:

(1) the surviving spouse is entitled for life to all the income from the property (or from a specific fraction or percentage of the property), payable annually or at more frequent intervals, or the spouse has a usufruct interest for life in the property, and

(2) no person (including the spouse) has a power to appoint any part of the property to any person other than the surviving spouse during the surviving spouse's life. Powers over the corpus may be retained or created, if they are exercisable only at or after the spouse's death.[43]

An annuity where only the surviving spouse has the right to receive payments before the death of that surviving spouse qualifies and the QTIP election is treated as made with respect to it unless the executor otherwise elects. (Code Sec. 2056(b)(7))[44]

Certain individual retirement accounts (IRAs) qualify.[45]

If the election is made, the qualified terminable interest property will be included in the surviving spouse's estate at death (Code Sec. 2044) unless that spouse makes a gift of all or part of the income interest during his or her lifetime, in which case that spouse is treated as having made a gift of the qualified terminable interest property. (Code Sec. 2519) To the extent that property is included in a surviving spouse's estate, the surviving spouse's executor may recover the estate taxes caused by that inclusion from the persons to whom the property passes at the surviving spouse's death, unless the surviving spouse directs otherwise by will. (Code Sec. 2207A(a))[46]

¶ 5024 Effect of death taxes on amount of marital deduction.

Federal estate or other death taxes payable out of the marital share reduce the amount of the bequest that qualifies for the marital deduction. (Code Sec. 2056(b)(4)(A))

The spouse's interest can be completely absolved from the burden of the tax by a provision in decedent's will that is effective under local law. In such a case, death taxes won't affect the amount of the deduction.[47]

¶ 5025 Marital deduction where surviving spouse is not a U.S. citizen—qualified domestic trust (QDOT) requirement.

No marital deduction is allowed if the surviving spouse is not a U.S. citizen, (Code Sec. 2056(d)(1)(A)) unless the property passes to the spouse in a QDOT (Code Sec. 2056(d)(2))—a trust that satisfies certain requirements. (Code Sec. 2056A)[48]

An estate tax is imposed on any distribution (other than an income distribution or a hardship distribution) from the trust before the date of the surviving spouse's death and on the value of the property remaining in the trust on the date of death of the surviving spouse (Code Sec. 2056A(b)(1)) (or the date the trust ceases to qualify). (Code Sec. 2056A(b)(3))[49]

Use Form 706-QDT to report the estate tax on distributions from a QDOT and on the value of the trust property at the surviving spouse's death.

---

43. ¶ R-6382; ¶ 20,564.08.
44. ¶ R-6382 *et seq.*; ¶ 20,564.08.
45. ¶ R-6408.

46. ¶ R-6382 *et seq.*; ¶s 20,444, 20,564.08, 22,07A4, 25,194.
47. ¶ R-6609 *et seq.*; ¶ 20,564.17.

48. ¶ R-6012 *et seq.*; ¶s 20,564, 20,56A4.

49. ¶ R-7081 *et seq.*; ¶ 20,56A4.02.

Footnote references beginning with letters are to paragraphs in RIA's Federal Tax Coordinator 2d. Footnote references beginning with numbers are to paragraphs in RIA's United States Tax Reporter (Estate & Gift Taxes).

¶ *5026* **Value of property included in the gross estate.**

The value of property included in the gross estate is the fair market value of the property at the date of the decedent's death (or at the alternate valuation date, ¶ 5027).[50]

¶ *5027* **Alternate valuation date.**

The executor can elect (irrevocably, on Form 706) to use an alternate valuation date rather than the decedent's date of death to value the property included in the gross estate. This alternate date is generally six months after decedent's death or earlier date of sale or distribution. (Code Sec. 2032(a))[1]

Alternate valuation can be elected only if its use decreases both the value of the gross estate and the estate tax liability. (Code Sec. 2032(c))[2]

observation: The executor can't elect in order to step up the basis of assets that increase in value after death (for example, where there would otherwise be no estate tax cost to the increased valuation because the marital deduction eliminates any tax).

¶ *5028* **Special-use valuation of farm or other business real property.**

If certain conditions are met, an executor may elect (irrevocably, on Schedule A-1, Form 706) to value qualified real property used for farming purposes or in a trade or business on the basis of the property's value for its actual use, rather than on its highest and best use. The total decrease in the value of all real property under this election may not exceed $750,000. (Code Sec. 2032A)[3] The resulting estate tax savings may be recaptured under certain conditions. (Code Sec. 2036A(c))[4] Use Form 706-A to report the recapture tax.

¶ *5029* **Unified credit against estate tax.**

The credit is $192,800, (Code Sec. 2010(a)) but not in excess of the estate tax imposed. (Code Sec. 2010(c)) The effect of the credit is to exempt up to $600,000 from estate taxation.[5]

observation: However, the effect of the 5% phase-out of the graduated rates (see ¶ 5001) is also to phase out the unified credit.

The credit is reduced by 20% of the amount of the pre-'77 $30,000 gift tax exemption allowed for gifts made before '77 and after Sept. 8, '76. (Code Sec. 2010(b))[6]

No credit is allowable with respect to the additional estate tax on excess retirement accumulations (¶ 5002). (Code Sec. 4980A(d)(2))[7]

¶ *5030* **Credit for state death taxes.**

A credit against the estate tax is allowed for estate, inheritance, legacy, or succession taxes actually paid to any state or the District of Columbia on account of property included in the gross estate. (Code Sec. 2011(a))

The amount allowed as a credit is limited to an amount based on the decedent's adjusted taxable estate and is computed under the state death tax credit table reproduced in ¶ 1114. The "adjusted taxable estate" is the taxable estate (gross estate minus deductions) reduced by $60,000. (Code Sec. 2011(b))

The state death tax credit as limited under the table cannot exceed the estate tax as reduced by the allowable unified credit. (Code Sec. 2011(f))[8]

---

50. ¶ R-1006; ¶ 20,314.   3. ¶ R-5200 *et seq.*; ¶ 20,32A4.   5. ¶ R-7100 *et seq.*; ¶ 20,104.   7. ¶ R-7107; ¶ 20,014.10.
1. ¶ R-5002; ¶ 20,324.   4. ¶ R-5301; ¶ 20,32A4.   6. ¶ R-7103; ¶ 20,104.   8. ¶ R-7200 *et seq.*; ¶ 20,114.
2. ¶ R-5001; ¶ 20,324.

Footnote references beginning with letters are to paragraphs in RIA's Federal Tax Coordinator 2d. Footnote references beginning with numbers are to paragraphs in RIA's United States Tax Reporter (Estate & Gift Taxes).

¶ 5031 Credit for tax on prior transfers.

Credit is allowed (on Schedule Q, Form 706) against the estate tax for federal estate tax paid by the estate of another decedent (the transferor) on the transfer of property to the present decedent from that transferor where the transferor died within ten years before, or within two years after, the present decedent's death. "Tax paid" for this purpose doesn't include the additional estate tax on excess retirement accumulations (¶ 5002). (Code Sec. 2013)[9]

Where a transferor decedent was denied a marital deduction because the surviving spouse was not a U.S. citizen or where the estate tax on qualified domestic trust distributions applied, under the rules discussed at ¶ 5025, the surviving spouse decedent is allowed a credit for the estate tax paid by the transferor decedent, or by the trust, without regard to when the transferor decedent died. (Code Sec. 2056(d)(3))[10]

¶ 5032 Credit for gift taxes paid on pre-'77 gifts.

Credit for gift taxes paid on pre-'77 gifts is allowed against the estate tax where gifts were made by a decedent before '77 of property included in his gross estate. (Code Sec. 2012(a))[11]

¶ 5033 Credit for foreign death taxes.

Credit is allowed (on Schedule P, Form 706), subject to certain limits, against the estate tax for estate, inheritance, legacy, or succession taxes actually paid to any foreign country or U.S. possession. (Code Sec. 2014)[12]

¶ 5034 Return requirements.

An executor must file an estate tax return (Form 706) if the decedent's gross estate at death exceeds $600,000. This dollar amount is reduced by certain gifts made by the decedent. (Code Sec. 6018(a)(1), (3))[13] A return (on Schedule S, Form 706) must also be made in any case where the additional tax on excess retirement accumulations (¶ 5002) applies.[14]

¶ 5035 When to file estate tax return.

File within nine months after the date of death. (Code Sec. 6075(a))[15]

Extensions of up to six months may be granted on written application (Form 4768) of the fiduciary if good cause is shown. If the executor is abroad, the extension may exceed six months. (Reg § 20.6081-1(a))[16]

¶ 5036 When to pay tax.

The estate tax shown on the return must be paid at the time for filing the return. Filing extensions don't extend the time for payment. (Reg § 20.6151-1)[17] However, extensions of time to pay can be granted (use Form 4768) if there is reasonable cause for deferring payment. (Code Sec. 6161(a)(1))[18]

Special extensions (elected on Form 706) are available where a future interest is included in the estate, (Code Sec. 6163)[19] or where the estate consists largely of a closely held business. (Code Sec. 6166)[20]

The estate tax on distributions made from qualified domestic trusts (¶ 5025) before the surviving spouse's death is due on Apr. 15 of the year following the calendar year in which the taxable event occurs. (Code Sec. 2056A(b)(5))[21]

---

9. ¶ R-7300 *et seq.*; ¶ 20,134.
10. ¶ R-7301; ¶ 20,564.
11. ¶ R-7501; ¶ 20,124.
12. ¶ R-7400 *et seq.*; ¶ 20,144.

13. ¶ S-2300 *et seq.*; ¶ 60,184.
14. ¶ R-7049; ¶ 60,184.
15. ¶ S-4902; ¶ 60,754.
16. ¶ S-5032.1; ¶ 60,814.

17. ¶ S-5851; ¶ 61,514.
18. ¶ S-5900 *et seq.*: ¶ 61,614.
19. ¶ S-5910; ¶ 61,634.

20. ¶ S-6000 *et seq.*; ¶ 61,644 *et seq.*
21. ¶ R-7084; ¶ 20,56A4.02.

Footnote references beginning with letters are to paragraphs in RIA's Federal Tax Coordinator 2d. Footnote references beginning with numbers are to paragraphs in RIA's United States Tax Reporter (Estate & Gift Taxes).

¶ 5037   Paying estate tax with "flower bonds."

Certain Treasury bonds issued before Mar. 4, '71 (so-called "flower" bonds) may be applied at par value in payment of federal estate taxes even though they are selling at a discount.[22]

¶ 5038   Estates of nonresident aliens.

Decedents who were neither U.S. citizens nor U.S. residents are taxed only on the transfer of property situated within the U.S. With this exception the make-up of the gross estate is the same as that for a U.S. citizen or resident. (Code Sec. 2103)

The same rate schedule that applies to the estates of U.S. citizens (¶ 1112) applies to the estates of nonresident aliens. (Code Sec. 2101(b))

A marital deduction is allowed under the principles of the regular marital deduction rules (¶ 5021 *et seq.*) with respect to U.S. property. (Code Sec. 2106(a)(3)) Other deductions are also allowed, within limits. (Code Sec. 2106)

A unified credit of $13,000 is allowed against the estate tax, with an alternative credit computations for estates of certain residents of U.S. possessions, (Code Sec. 2102(c)(1), (2)) and to the extent required under certain treaty obligations of the U.S. (Code Sec. 2102(c)(3)(A)) The $13,000 amount is reduced by any gift tax unified credit allowed. (Code Sec. 2102(c)(3)(B))

Credits are also allowed for state death taxes, estate tax on prior transfers and gift tax on certain pre-'77 gifts. (Code Sec. 2102(c)(5))[23]

An estate tax return on Form 706NA must be filed for the estate of every nonresident not a U.S. citizen if the value of the part of the estate in the U.S. exceeds $60,000, (Code Sec. 6018(a)(2)) reduced by: (1) the amount of adjusted taxable gifts made by the decedent after '76, and (2) the amount of any pre-'77 specific exemption allowed for gifts made by the decedent after Sept. 8, '76. (Code Sec. 6018(a)(3))[24] The time for filing the return is the same as for U.S. citizens or residents, see ¶ 5035.

Provisions of tax treaties may affect the Code provisions for nonresident aliens covered by those treaties. The treaty countries are: Australia, Austria, Denmark, Finland, France, Germany, Greece, Ireland, Italy, Japan, Netherlands, Norway, South Africa, Sweden, Switzerland, and the United Kingdom.[25]

¶ 5039   Gift Tax ▬▬▬▬▬▬▬▬▬▬▬▬▬▬▬▬▬▬▬▬▬▬▬▬▬▬▬▬▬▬▬

The gift tax is imposed on the transfer of money or other property by gift. The gift tax is integrated with the estate tax under a "unified" rate schedule and credit into a single tax on transfers during life and at death.

The tax is imposed on the transfer, not on the property transferred. It applies even though the property transferred may be exempt from income or other taxes. (Code Sec. 2501(a); Reg § 25.2501-1, Reg § 25.2511-1(a), Reg § 25.2511-2)[26]

Gifts made by a person who, in a tax year, makes no gift of a present interest with a value of over $10,000 to any one person, and who makes no gifts of future interests, are not subject to tax in that year, see ¶ 5048 (and no gift tax return need be filed, see ¶ 5056).

The gift tax rates are the same as the estate tax rates under a unified rate schedule, see ¶ 1112.

---

22. ¶ R-2028; ¶ 140.075 *et seq.*   24. ¶ S-2302; ¶ 60,184.   26. ¶ Q-1000 *et seq.*; ¶s 25,009,
23. ¶ R-8000 *et seq.*; ¶ 21,014   25. ¶ R-9100 *et seq.*; ¶ 110,001   25,014.
    et seq.   *et seq.*

Footnote references beginning with letters are to paragraphs in RIA's Federal Tax Coordinator 2d. Footnote references beginning with numbers are to paragraphs in RIA's United States Tax Reporter (Estate & Gift Taxes).

¶ 5040 Who must pay gift tax?

The gift tax must be paid by the person (the donor) who makes the gift. (Code Sec. 2501(a); Reg § 25.2511-2(f)) It applies only to donors who are individuals (Reg § 25.2501-1(b)) but a gift by a corporation may be treated as a gift by the stockholders. (Reg § 25.2511-1(h)(1))[27]

If the donor fails to pay the tax when due, the donee of the gift is also liable for the tax to the extent of the value of his gift. (Code Sec. 6324(b); Reg § 25.2502-2, Reg § 301.6324-1(b))[28]

These rules apply to a U.S. citizen or resident no matter where the gift property (tangible or intangible) is situated. (Code Sec. 2501(a); Reg § 25.2501-1(a), Reg § 25.2511-3(a))[29]

¶ 5041 What is a gift?

All transactions whereby property or property rights are gratuitously bestowed upon another are gifts. (Reg § 25.2511-1(c))

A gift isn't complete (i.e., taxable), until the donor parts with dominion or control over the transferred property or property interest. He must be left without power to change the disposition of the property either for his own benefit or for that of others. (Reg § 25.2511-2(b))[30]

There's no gift tax on a transfer to a political organization. (Code Sec. 2501(a)(5))[31]

¶ 5042 Educational or medical payment exclusion.

The gift tax doesn't apply to amounts paid by one individual:

(1) on behalf of another individual directly to a qualifying educational organization as tuition for that other individual. (Code Sec. 2503(e); Reg § 25.2503-6(b)(2))

(2) on behalf of another individual directly to a provider of medical care as payment for that medical care. (Code Sec. 2503(e); Reg § 25.2503-6(b)(3)) Payments for medical insurance qualify for this exclusion. (Reg § 25.2503-6(b)(3))

These exclusions are available in addition to the annual gift tax exclusion see (¶ 5048). (Reg § 25.2503-6(a))[32] No gift tax return is required. (Code Sec. 6019)[33]

¶ 5043 Below-market loans.

If a below-market (or interest-free) loan is a "gift loan" (that is, a below-market loan where the forgoing of interest is in the nature of a gift), it is treated as: (1) a loan to the borrower/donee in exchange for an interest-paying note, and (2) a gift to the borrower of the funds to pay the interest. The amount of the gift equals:

■ the forgone interest—excess of interest payable at the applicable federal rate (see ¶ 1116) over actual interest payable—if the loan is a demand loan, or

■ the excess of the amount loaned over the present value (using a discount rate equal to the applicable federal rate) of all payments required under the terms of the loan, if the gift loan is a term loan. (Code Sec. 7872)[34]

For demand loans, the gift is treated as made on the last day of the calendar year. (Code Sec. 7872(a)) For term loans, the gift is treated as made on the date the loan was made. (Code Sec. 7872(b))[35]

These rules don't apply to certain gift loans between individuals that don't exceed $10,000. (Code Sec. 7872(c)(2))[36]

---

27. ¶s Q-1000 *et seq.*, Q-2400 *et seq.*; ¶s 25,014, 25,114.
28. ¶ V-9301; ¶s 25,024, 63,244.
29. ¶ Q-1015; ¶s 25,014, 25,114 *et seq.*
30. ¶ Q-3004; ¶ 25,114.01.
31. ¶ Q-3203; ¶ 25,014.
32. ¶ Q-5250 *et seq.*; ¶ 25,034.
33. ¶ S-2201; ¶ 25,014.
34. ¶ Q-2150 *et seq.*; ¶ 78,724.
35. ¶ Q-2152; ¶ 78,724.
36. ¶ Q-2172; ¶ 78,724.

Footnote references beginning with letters are to paragraphs in RIA's Federal Tax Coordinator 2d. Footnote references beginning with numbers are to paragraphs in RIA's United States Tax Reporter (Estate & Gift Taxes).

If the outstanding balance of a gift loan made between individual is $100,000 or less, the amount of interest treated as retransferred by the borrower to the lender each year does not exceed the borrower's net investment income for that year. If the net investment income is $1,000 or less, the amount treated as retransferred is zero. (Code Sec. 7872(d)(1))[37]

¶ 5044   Joint ownership of property.

A gift may result where property (real or personal, including securities) is placed in joint ownership or where joint ownership ends. Whether or not there has been a gift depends upon characteristics determined under the applicable local law.[38]

Since present-interest gifts to *spouses* who are U.S. citizens qualify for the unlimited marital deduction and are exempt from gift tax, the law doesn't tax the creation of a joint interest in property between spouses.[39]

Nonspouses. If an individual with his own funds buys property and has the title conveyed to himself and others as joint tenants, with rights of survivorship, but which rights may be defeated by any joint tenant severing his interest, there is an immediate gift to the other joint tenants of equal shares of the property. (Reg § 25.2511-1(h)(5))[40]

An individual doesn't make a gift when he opens a joint bank account with his own funds for himself and another under the terms of which he can regain the entire fund without the other's consent. A gift is made only when the other person withdraws money for his own benefit. (Reg § 25.2511-1(h)(4)) Similar rules apply for joint brokerage accounts and U.S. savings bonds.[41]

Gift tax may be imposed when jointly owned property is divided up between the co-owners, or is sold, exchanged or given away before death of one of the co-owners.[42] This rule does not apply to property co-owned by spouses.

¶ 5045   Qualified disclaimers.

A qualified disclaimer (an irrevocable and unqualified refusal to accept ownership, made in writing by a specified deadline) with respect to any interest in property has the effect of treating that interest, for gift (and estate and generation-skipping tax) purposes, as if it had never had been transferred to the disclaimant. (Code Sec. 2518) And the disclaimant isn't treated as having made a gift to the person to whom the interest passes by reason of the disclaimer. (Reg § 25.2518-1(b))[43]

¶ 5046   Amount of the gift.

The amount of the gift is the money given or, if property is given, the property's value as of the date of the gift. (Code Sec. 2512(a))[44]

¶ 5047   Taxable gifts.

Taxable gifts are the gifts made during the calendar year after the annual exclusion (¶ 5048) and reduced by allowable deductions (¶s 5049, 5050). (Code Sec. 2503(a), (b))[45]

¶ 5048   Annual exclusion.

The first $10,000 of gifts of a present interest made by a donor *to each donee* in each calendar year is excluded from the amount of the donor's taxable gifts. (Code Sec. 2503(b))[46] The first $100,000 of gifts made by a donor to a spouse who isn't a U.S. citizen is excluded. (Code Sec. 2523(i)(2))[47]

No annual exclusion is allowed for gifts of future interests, (Code Sec. 2503(b);

---

37. ¶ J-3038; ¶ 78,724.
38. ¶ Q-2901; ¶ 25,114.
39. ¶ Q-2900 *et seq.*; ¶ 25,234.

40. ¶ Q-2906; ¶ 25,114.
41. ¶ Q-2921 *et seq.*; ¶ 25,114.
42. ¶ Q-2907.

43. ¶ Q-2350 *et seq.*; ¶ 25,184 *et seq.*
44. ¶ Q-1200; ¶ 25,124.

45. ¶ Q-1000; ¶ 25,034.
46. ¶ Q-5000 *et seq.*; ¶ 25,034.
47. ¶ Q-5002; ¶ 25,034.

Footnote references beginning with letters are to paragraphs in RIA's Federal Tax Coordinator 2d. Footnote references beginning with numbers are to paragraphs in RIA's United States Tax Reporter (Estate & Gift Taxes).

Reg § 25.2503-2) e.g., reversions or remainders. (Reg § 25.2503-3)[48]

A "Crummey" power (in general, a trust beneficiary's noncumulative right to withdraw a specified amount of trust principal within a limited period) makes a transfer to the trust a gift of a present interest.[49]

A transfer for the benefit of a *minor* isn't considered a gift of a future interest if the property and its income:

(1) may be expended by or for the benefit of the minor before he reaches 21, and

(2) any balance not so expended *will pass to the minor* when he reaches 21, or if he dies before 21 will go either to his *estate* or as he may appoint under a general power of appointment. (Code Sec. 2503(c); Reg § 25.2503-4(a))[50]

Gifts to minors made through custodians designated under Uniform Acts for gifts or transfers to minors qualify for the annual exclusion.[1]

¶ 5049 Marital deduction.

A marital deduction is allowed for the value of all qualifying gifts made by one spouse to the other, if the donor is a U.S. citizen or resident when he makes the gift; the donee spouse is a U.S. citizen; and the gift is not a nondeductible "terminable interest." (Code Sec. 2523) There are exceptions from the donee-citizenship requirement. (Code Sec. 2523(a))[2]

Qualified terminable interest property (QTIP) qualifies for the marital deduction if the donee spouse receives income payments for life and no person has a power to appoint any part of the property to anyone other than the donee spouse during the donee spouse's life. (Code Sec. 2523(f))[3]

¶ 5050 Charitable gifts.

Charitable gifts and certain similar gifts are deducted in arriving at taxable gifts for the calendar year. (Code Sec. 2522)[4]

¶ 5051 Split gifts to third parties by married donors.

A husband and wife may consent to have their gifts to others treated as if made one-half by each (Code Sec. 2513(a); Reg § 25.2513-1) if:

■ both spouses are U.S. citizens or residents on the date of the gift; (Code Sec. 2513(a))

■ both spouses signify their consent (on Form 709 or 709-A) to have all gifts made to others in the calendar year treated as split gifts; (Code Sec. 2513(a), (b), (c); Reg § 25.2513-1(b)(5))

■ the consenting spouses are married to each other on the date of the gift and don't remarry during the remainder of the calendar year. (Code Sec. 2513(a))[5]

Each spouse is liable, jointly and severally, for the *entire* gift tax for the period in which he or she consents to split gifts. (Code Sec. 2513(d); Reg § 25.2513-4)[6]

Gifts of community property to a third party are generally considered to have been made one half by each spouse.[7]

¶ 5052 Gift tax on "estate freeze" transfers (Chapter 14 rules).

The law disregards, for gift tax valuation purposes, certain interests retained by the transferor after a transfer to a family member. These rules make up Chapter 14 of the Code.[8]

---

48. ¶ Q-5100 *et seq.*; ¶ 25,034.
49. ¶ Q-5112; ¶ 25,034.
50. ¶ Q-5201 *et seq.*; ¶ 25,034.

1. ¶ Q-5212; ¶ 25,034.
2. ¶ Q-6100 *et seq.*; ¶ 25,234.
3. ¶ Q-6300 *et seq.*; ¶ 25,234.

4. ¶ Q-6000 *et seq.*; ¶ 25,224.
5. ¶ Q-7000 *et seq.*; ¶ 25,134.
6. ¶ Q-7000 *et seq.*; ¶ 25,134.

7. ¶ Q-2929 *et seq.*; ¶ 25,134.01.
8. ¶ Q-3350; ¶ 27,009 *et seq.*

Footnote references beginning with letters are to paragraphs in RIA's Federal Tax Coordinator 2d. Footnote references beginning with numbers are to paragraphs in RIA's United States Tax Reporter (Estate & Gift Taxes).

These rules apply to:[9]

■ transfers of interests in corporations and partnerships;

■ transfers of interests in trusts (except that these rules don't apply to certain trusts known as GRATs, GRUTs, and qualified personal residence trusts) ;

■ buy-sell agreements and options; and

■ lapsing rights.

¶ 5053   Unified credit against gift tax.

A "unified" credit of $192,800 is allowed against gift tax on gifts made by a U.S. citizen or resident. The credit against tax on gifts in a calendar period is reduced by the sum of all amounts allowable as a credit in preceding calendar periods. (Code Sec. 2505)[10]

¶ 5054   How to compute gift tax if no gifts made before current year.

If a person has *not* made any taxable gifts (in excess of annual exclusions and deductions and the pre-'77 specific lifetime exemption) before the calendar year for which the tax is being computed, the gift tax is computed as follows:[11]

(1) Determine the aggregate value of the total gifts made during the calendar year for which the tax is being computed. If the donor is married, and he and his wife have consented to split their gifts to third parties, only half of the gifts he made to third parties plus half of the gifts, if any, she made to third parties are included in computing his total gifts. (A separate gift tax computation is made for the wife, and the other half of the husband's gifts to third parties plus the other half of the wife's gifts to third parties are included in computing the wife's total gifts.)

(2) Deduct from the amount in (1), above, any amounts qualifying for the year's annual exclusion (¶ 5048).

(3) From the excess of (1) over (2), above, deduct the amount of charitable and other deductible gifts made in excess of the annual exclusions deducted on account of such gifts under (2). In addition, if the total gifts includes gifts made by the donor to his spouse, deduct the amount of any allowable marital deduction.

(4) Compute a gift tax on the excess of (1) over the sum of (2) and (3) using the unified rate schedule (¶ 1112).

(5) Subtract from the gift tax computed in (4), the allowable unified credit.

illustration: A husband who made no previous gifts made gifts of $150,000 to his wife and $100,000 to his son in the calendar year. Both gifts qualify for the $10,000 annual exclusion and the spouses elect to split the husband's gift to the child. The husband's gift tax is computed as follows:

(1) Total gifts for year	$250,000
(2) Less: One half of child's gift attributable to wife	50,000
(3) Husband's gifts	200,000
(4) Less amount of exclusion on gift to child	10,000
(5) Gifts reduced by exclusion	190,000
(6) Less marital deduction	150,000
(7) Taxable gifts	40,000
(8) Tax before credit on $40,000	8,200
(9) Less unified credit	8,200
(10) Tax due	$ 0

---

9. ¶ Q-3350; ¶s 27,014, 27,024, 27,034, 27,044.   10. ¶ Q-8005; ¶ 25,054.   11. ¶ Q-8028 *et seq.*; ¶ 25,009 *et seq.*

Footnote references beginning with letters are to paragraphs in RIA's Federal Tax Coordinator 2d. Footnote references beginning with numbers are to paragraphs in RIA's United States Tax Reporter (Estate & Gift Taxes).

¶ 5055 Cumulative computation where gifts were made before current year.

Previous taxable gifts affect the amount of gift tax imposed on gifts made in the current year. These taxable gifts are taken into account whether they were made before '77 or after '76. (Code Sec. 2502)

In general the gift tax (before unified credit) is the excess of: (1) a tentative tax computed under the unified rate schedules on the aggregate sum of taxable gifts for the current calendar year for which the tax is being computed *and* taxable gifts (made after June 6, '32) for all preceding years, over (2) a tentative tax computed under the unified rate schedule on the aggregate sum of the taxable gifts (made after June 6, '32) for all of the years preceding the current calendar year for which the tax is being computed. (Code Sec. 2502(a)) The gift tax payable is the excess of the tentative tax in (1) over the tentative tax in (2) reduced by the unified credit allowable.

Taxable gifts for a calendar year are the total gifts for the year which are subject to gift tax reduced by the annual exclusions and allowable deductions applicable to the particular period and, for preceding years the deduction for the pre-'77 lifetime exemption of up to $30,000. (Code Sec. 2503(a), (b))

¶ 5056 Gift tax returns.

Any individual who makes gifts to any one donee during a calendar year which are not fully excluded under the $10,000 annual exclusion must file a gift tax return (Form 709 or Short Form 709-A). But no return is required to report a qualified transfer for educational or medical costs (¶ 5042) or a transfer that qualifies for the marital deduction (¶ 5049). (Code Sec. 6019(a))[12] The return is due on Apr. 15 of the year following the year the gifts were made. (Code Sec. 6075) A different rule applies if the donor has died.[13] An extension for filing the income tax return automatically extends the time for filing the gift tax return for the same calendar year. (Code Sec. 6075(b)(2)) Or the donor may request (in a letter to IRS--there is no official IRS form for this purpose) a separate extension of time to file the gift tax return. (Code Sec. 6081)[14]

¶ 5057 Generation-Skipping Transfer Tax ▄▄▄▄▄▄▄▄▄▄

A transfer tax is imposed on transfers outright or in trust to beneficiaries who are more than one generation below the transferor's generation. Every individual has a $1,000,000 exemption from this tax. These "generation-skipping" transfers are taxed at a flat rate, equal to the maximum gift and estate tax rate (55%).

¶ 5058 Transfers subject to tax.

The generation-skipping tax is imposed on every generation-skipping transfer. (Code Sec. 2601) A generation-skipping transfer is any one of three taxable events: (1) a *taxable termination* of an interest in a trust if, after the termination, all interests in the trust are held by or for the benefit of persons two or more generations below that of the transferor, (2) a *taxable distribution* of income or principal from a trust to or for the benefit of a person two or more generations below that of the transferor, and (3) a *direct skip,* which is a transfer of an interest in property to or for the benefit of a person two or more generations below that of the transferor. (Code Sec. 2611(a), Code Sec. 2612)[15]

¶ 5059 Exemptions from tax.

Every individual is allowed a $1,000,000 exemption which may be allocated to any property transferred. (Code Sec. 2631) Married couples may treat transfers as made one-

---

12. ¶ S-2200 *et seq.*; ¶s 25,014, 60,194.
13. ¶ S-4901; ¶ 60,754.
14. ¶ S-5032; ¶s 60,754, 60,814.
15. ¶ R-9500 *et seq.*; ¶s 26,014, 26,114, 26,124 *et seq.*

Footnote references beginning with letters are to paragraphs in RIA's Federal Tax Coordinator 2d. Footnote references beginning with numbers are to paragraphs in RIA's United States Tax Reporter (Estate & Gift Taxes).

half by each spouse, in effect giving them a combined $2,000,000 exemption. (Code Sec. 2652(a)(2))[16] Once a transfer is designated as exempt, all later appreciation in the value of the exempt property is also exempt.[17]

The tax does not apply to lifetime transfers (except for certain transfers in trust) that are exempt from gift tax because of the annual exclusion (¶ 5048) or the exclusion for certain tuition and medical expense payments (¶ 5042). (Code Sec. 2642(c)(3))[18]

---

16. ¶ R-9541; ¶s 26,014, 26,314,   17. ¶ R-9544; ¶ 26,324.   18. ¶ R-9540 *et seq.*; ¶ 26,424.
    26,524.

Footnote references beginning with letters are to paragraphs in RIA's Federal Tax Coordinator 2d. Footnote references beginning with numbers are to paragraphs in RIA's United States Tax Reporter (Estate & Gift Taxes).

INDEX

References are to paragraph [¶] numbers.

A

Abandonment
. loss
    generally 1771
  . . deductible loss, defined 1763
  . . fruitless searches 1503
  . . mortgaged property 1778
. reporting of, for secured property 4745
. spouse, abandoned 3131

Abatement of interest, penalties and
    additions to tax 4866

Abortion as medical expense.................... 2140

Abusive tax shelters
    generally .... 4881 *et seq.*
. assessments 4823, 4829
. penalties 4823, 4829,
                               4881 *et seq.*
. potentially abusive 4746, 4882
. registration 4746

Accelerated cost recovery system
    See "Depreciation"

Accelerated depreciation
    See "Depreciation"

Accident and health insurance plans
    See "Health and accident insurance
    plans"

Accountants
. audits by IRS, representing taxpayer at 4808
. expenses of 1628
. fees for.................................... 1597, 2164,
                                     5018

Accounting expenses
. deductibility.................................... 1595, 1597

Accounting methods
    generally .... 2817 *et seq.*
. accrual method
    See "Accrual basis"
. carryover by successor corporation.................... 3561
. cash method
    See "Cash basis"
. changes of 2885
    generally .... 2840 *et seq.*
  . . adjustment inclusion period 2846
  . . adjustments required .... 2844 *et seq.*
  . . allocations, relief for high-impact
    adjustments.. 2847
  . . application for.. 2843
  . . definition 2842
  . . IRS permission to change.......................... 2841
  . . Sec. 481(a) adjustments .... 2844 *et seq.*
. farmers.. 4501 *et seq.*
. hybrid methods 2820, 2821
. installment method .... 2700 *et seq.*
. limits on choice of 2821
. long-term contracts .... 2850 *et seq.*
. multiple methods.. 2819
. personal service corporation 2821
. records to substantiate 2818, 2819

Accounting period
    See also "Taxable year"

Accounting period — Cont'd
    generally .... 2800 *et seq.*
. change of 2807, 2815,
                                        2816

Accounting reserves, deductibility.......... 2848, 2849

Accounts receivable
. amortization 1992
. applicable asset acquisitions 2468
. capital assets.. 2610
. intangible assets.. 2467

Accrual basis
    generally .... 2827 *et seq.*
. advance payments .... 2832 *et seq.*
. all-events test.. 2835
. business expenses
  . . compensation deduction.................... 1531 *et seq.*
. charitable contributions, 2 1/2 month rule 2132
. compensation for personal services.............. 1279
. contested liability 2837
. contingent rights to income 2829
. credit balance write-offs 2831
. dealers' reserves 2830
. discounts on purchases 2871
. economic performance 2836
. expense deductions, timing of 2835
. farmers.................................... 4501, 4505
                                      et seq.
. gain or loss on sale or exchange.................... 2409
. interest, time for deduction 1740
. interest income, time to report 1341
. previously reported income, repayments of
  . . time for deduction of repayment 2864
. recurring item exception 2836
. security deposits 2834
. taxes, accrual of
    generally .... 1755 *et seq.*
  . . contested tax.. 1756
  . . personal property taxes 1761
  . . realty taxes.................................... 1757, 1758
  . . tort liabilities 2838

Accrued market discount .... 1327 *et seq.*

Accumulated adjustments account (S
    corporations).................................... 3379, 3381

Accumulated earnings tax
    generally .... 3320 *et seq.*
. dividends-paid deduction .... 3339 *et seq.*
. *Bardahl* operating cycle formula 3326
. reasonable needs of business .... 3325 *et seq.*

Accumulated taxable income 3327

Accumulation distribution .... 3953 *et seq.*

ACE (Adjusted current earnings).................... 3210

Achievement awards, employee
. compensation, as.. 1253
. deduction of 1584
. withholding on.. 3008

Acquiring corporations
. basis 2480
. carrybacks and carryovers.................... 3560, 3561
. net operating loss 3561

Acquisition indebtedness
. exempt organizations 4116

705

References are to paragraph [¶] numbers.

References are to paragraph [¶] numbers.

References are to paragraph [¶] numbers.

References are to paragraph [¶] numbers.

MARGIN INDEX

To use, bend book in half and follow margin index to page with black edge marker.

The left index column refers to the left bank of markers; the right index column to the right bank of markers.

RESEARCH INSTITUTE OF AMERICA